PROFESSIONAL SHAREPOINT® 2010 ENTERPRISE ARCHITECT'S GUIDEBOOK

Continues

PROFESSIONAL

SharePoint® 2010 Enterprise Architect's Guidebook

PROFESSIONAL

SharePoint® 2010 Enterprise Architect's Guidebook

Brian Wilson
Reza Alirezaei
Bill Baer
Martin Kearn

WILEY

John Wiley & Sons, Inc.

SharePoint® 2010 Enterprise Architect's Guidebook

Published by
John Wiley & Sons, Inc.
10475 Crosspoint Boulevard
Indianapolis, IN 46256
www.wiley.com

Copyright ©2012 by John Wiley & Sons, Inc., Indianapolis, Indiana

Published simultaneously in Canada

ISBN: 978-0-470-64319-8
ISBN: 978-1-118-28424-7 (ebk)
ISBN: 978-1-118-28191-8 (ebk)
ISBN: 978-1-118-28293-9 (ebk)

Manufactured in the United States of America

10 9 8 7 6 5 4 3 2 1

For general information on our other products and services please contact our Customer Care Department within the United States at (877) 762-2974, outside the United States at (317) 572-3993 or fax (317) 572-4002.

Wiley publishes in a variety of print and electronic formats and by print-on-demand. Some material included with standard print versions of this book may not be included in e-books or in print-on-demand. If this book refers to media such as a CD or DVD that is not included in the version you purchased, you may download this material at http://booksupport.wiley.com. For more information about Wiley products, visit www.wiley.com.

Library of Congress Control Number: 2011919195

I would like to dedicate this book to my wife, Hayley. Thank you for understanding and supporting me over the years, especially during the writing of this book. Without your love and support, it would've been impossible to complete this book project. And to my daughter, Katherine: You are totally amazing and awesome! You are both the sunshine in my life. I love you both so much! To my inspirational mentors: Lionel Moyal, John Hooper, Callum Shillan, Mark Horsfield, and Chris Kerr. Thank you each for the unique knowledge, opportunity, support, and belief in me. You have helped me grow immensely over the years. Thank you.

—BRIAN WILSON

I would like to dedicate this book to the memory of my late grandmother, S.Khatoon Soltani, who taught me what real love is about!

—REZA ALIREZAEI

I'd like to dedicate this book to my wife, Jessica, whose support throughout the process of writing this book has been instrumental in keeping me focused and on track—all the while managing the day-to-day activities of keeping a home functional—and my son, William, who may one day pick up this book and understand claims mode authentication inside and out at 9 years old.

—BILL BAER

To Laura, Jamie, and baby number 2, thank you for all the support you gave me while writing this book. I love you all very much! Also, to "Lord B"...a promise is a promise!

—MARTIN KEARN

ABOUT THE AUTHORS

BRIAN WILSON is a SharePoint solution and information architect. With more than 14 years of experience (including 4 years as a Senior Consultant in the SharePoint and Information Worker team in Microsoft Consulting Services in the United Kingdom), Wilson works with Microsoft's largest customers architecting solutions for enterprise environments using SharePoint technologies. Since the first version of SharePoint, he has been involved in a variety of leading-edge SharePoint projects for clients in the United Kingdom, South Africa, Europe, China, and globally across all industries and all areas of SharePoint. Before joining Microsoft, he worked directly for a large multinational media enterprise and for a leading Microsoft Gold Partner, where he was involved in all stages of the technical implementation's life cycle, including technical pre-sales, architecture, system design, consulting, and development, to deliver innovative solutions on time and within budget. More recently, Wilson has set up a SharePoint business, and has been designing and developing SharePoint software for WiredLight, which focuses on providing consultancy, products, and solutions for SharePoint. When he gets the time, he enjoys skiing powder in the winter, as well as scuba diving the Red Sea and southeast coast of South Africa in the summer. For more information about Wilson, see www.wiredlight.net or his LinkedIn profile at http://uk.linkedin.com/in/bkvwilson.

REZA ALIREZAEI is a solution architect focused on designing custom applications with SharePoint, Office, and Microsoft Business Intelligence products and technologies. He has been recognized as a Microsoft Most Valuable Professional (MVP), Microsoft Certified Professional (MCP), Microsoft Certified Professional Developer (MCPD), Microsoft Certified IT Professional (MCITP), and Microsoft Certified Technology Specialist (MCTS) for SharePoint 2010. Alirezaei is the founder and president of Development Horizon, where he has helped many customers architect and build large-scale, mission-critical SharePoint applications. He has also co-authored several books, papers and articles. For more information about Alirezaei, see his blog at http://blogs.devhorizon.com/reza or his LinkedIn profile at www.linkedin.com/in/rezaal.

BILL BAER is a Senior Technical Product Manager and Microsoft Certified Master (MCM) for SharePoint in the SharePoint product group in Redmond, Washington. Previously, he was a Hewlett-Packard Technology Solutions Group Most Valuable Professional (MVP) with a background in infrastructure engineering and enterprise deployments of SharePoint Products and Technologies. Baer has gained deep industry experience while working for Apple Computer Corporation, First Data Corporation, Digital Equipment Corporation, Compaq Computer Corporation, Hewlett-Packard, and Microsoft Corporation.

MARTIN KEARN is a Senior Consultant within the SharePoint team in Microsoft Consulting Services United Kingdom. Kearn has been working for Microsoft since 2005, having previously worked for several Microsoft Partners who specialized in collaboration and Information Worker technologies. He has spent many years working with the various iterations of SharePoint, going as far back as "Tahoe" (for those that remember that far back). During the past decade, Kearn has been involved with several large-scale deployments of SharePoint that involve all aspects, including enterprise infrastructure, migration, custom development, and cloud-based deployment. He has participated in several community initiatives, including speaking at conferences and blogging on the "The SharePoint Guys" team blog (http://blogs.msdn.com/b/uksharepoint/).

ABOUT THE CONTRIBUTORS

ARPAN SHAH (Chapter 1) is the Director of Product Management for Microsoft Projects based in Redmond, Washington, and is a frequent speaker at Microsoft and industry events. Before his current role, Shah led SharePoint Technical Product Management for the SharePoint 2010 and 2007 releases. Before Microsoft, he spent several years in the Internet business industry serving in a variety of product management roles. Shaw holds a bachelor's degree and master's degree from Massachusetts Institute of Technology (MIT).

JIM ADAMS (Chapter 5) is a Senior Program Manager in the Collaboration Services group of Microsoft IT (MSIT), responsible for Microsoft's corporate SharePoint services. Adams joined Microsoft in 2000, and in his 12 years at Microsoft, has worked in many IT roles, including Enterprise Directory Management Program Manager, Infrastructure Engineering General Program Manager, SharePoint Operations Manager, and SharePoint Service Manager. He has worked in the SharePoint space since 2003, deploying and running each version of SharePoint since its first version, SharePoint Team Services, and is currently engaged in development and deployment of MSIT's Office365 cloud services.

NIGEL BRIDPORT (Chapter 32) is a collaboration consultant working for Microsoft Consulting Services in the United Kingdom, where he has been since 1998. His main area of responsibility is enabling customers to realize their business process and requirements on applications from Microsoft. This mainly centers on SharePoint technologies, with which he has been engaged since SharePoint Portal Server (SPS) 2001. He has worked on a number of large-scale architectures for the likes of the Ministry of Defense United Kingdom, as well as building custom solutions for those systems.

HUGO ESPERANCA (Chapter 24) is a hands-on Microsoft solutions architect, specializing in SharePoint 2007/2010 enterprise solutions, with more than 20 years of experience in analysis, design, and development of object-oriented component-based software applications using formal and agile methodologies. Esperanca has been the technical lead in some high-profile SharePoint implementations, including LTSB Shareview, the first SharePoint Internet site for a financial institution in the United Kingdom. Together with LTSB, some of Esperanca's past clients include Microsoft, NHS, Universal Music Group, CLS, and BAE Systems. More recently, he has been designing and developing software for Collaboris, a company that he created in 2007 together with another business partner. His latest creation is DocRead, a Reading Compliance add-on for SharePoint 2007 and 2010.

CHRIS GIDEON (Chapter 19) attended Missouri State University to study pre-medicine. After discovering that medicine was not the right profession for him, Gideon began training in Microsoft technologies. This eventually led to a job at Microsoft in 1998. He has served in numerous roles at Microsoft, including Support Engineer, Escalation Engineer, Solution Integration Engineer, Software Design Engineer, Program Manager, and architect. Gideon started his career in the areas of Windows NT domains and Active Directory, but began working with SharePoint in 2002. The challenges of SharePoint have proven to be enough to keep his attention. Gideon is currently a SharePoint Premier Field Engineer (PFE) based out of Dallas, Texas.

SAM HASSANI (Chapter 5) has worked as a Microsoft Premier Field Engineer (PFE) for five years, specializing in SharePoint, and providing on-site proactive support and consulting services with high-profile EMEA-based customers. One of Hassani's most recent achievements was obtaining the SharePoint 2010 Microsoft Certified Master (MCM) certification in May 2011, the highest level of SharePoint technical training and knowledge validation. During his time as an engineer, he has also written a significant portion of the content used for PFE workshop offerings, and has also been part of the SharePoint Risk Assessment Program (SPRAP) development team. In addition to his day-to-day work, Hassani has presented varying SharePoint sessions at a variety of technical conferences, such as Microsoft TechEd Europe and the Microsoft SharePoint Conference 2011.

NEIL HODGKINSON (Chapter 16) is a Senior Engineering Service Engineer with Microsoft Office Division engaged as a Senior Escalation resource for Office 365. Starting his IT career as a SQL and ASP developer, Hodgkinson transitioned to SharePoint technologies in 2000, when no one realized what an incredible platform it was to become. Primarily, his role is keeping the Microsoft SharePoint Online platform in good shape, and adhering to the best practice guidance for very large-scale deployments. He is an instructor and content owner for SharePoint Enterprise Search and FAST for SharePoint Search on the Microsoft Certified Master (MCM) program. He has spoken at many internal, external, and partner conferences for Microsoft, and is a founding contributor to the Microsoft Field Engineering blog at `http://sharepoint.microsoft.com/blogs/fromthe field`. Hodgkinson hails from Manchester, and outside of work, is a fan of classic rock music and United Kingdom metal bands, but most of all enjoys spending time at home with his wife watching their three young children having fun and living life.

VESA "VESKU" JUVONEN (Chapter 15 and Chapter 18) is a Principal Consultant at Microsoft, focusing on SharePoint technologies. He has been involved in numerous global SharePoint deployments, working as lead architect for infrastructure and customizations. Juvonen has been closely involved in creating global readiness material with SharePoint product groups for field readiness for SharePoint 2010 and for "SharePoint 15" versions. Vesa also works as one of the instructors and content owners in the Microsoft Certified Master (MCM) for SharePoint certification program. He achieved his own Master Certification for SharePoint 2007 and for SharePoint 2010.

SCOTT KLEVEN (Chapter 5) is a Program Manager who has been at Microsoft for three and a half years. Since joining Microsoft, his time has been spent in the SharePoint Online Dedicated business unit, and most recently, in Microsoft IT where he manages the early adoption programs within SharePoint. This includes the planning and coordination for Microsoft's global enterprise platforms from SharePoint 2007 and 2010, the next wave of Office, and SharePoint Online. His responsibilities include managing the upgrade of the enterprise-wide SharePoint utility platforms, release management for the overall pre-release rollout ("Dogfood") cycle, and new service onboarding. Kleven's background includes ten years of experience as an analyst and project manager within the telecommunications industry.

IAN MORRISH (Chapter 4) has been a key SharePoint expert at Microsoft New Zealand for many years. He has worked for Microsoft New Zealand in pre-sales and consulting roles with enterprise customers for more than ten years. Morrish has a reputation for a deep understanding of SharePoint and Microsoft technologies, as well as a knack for being able to communicate this to a wide range of audiences. He is the author of wssdemo.com, a well-known and respected SharePoint resource. Morrish regularly presents at TechEd and other events on a wide range of SharePoint topics.

PAUL OLENICK (Chapter 11) is a Senior Consultant for Arcovis, where he leads SharePoint and Enterprise Search engagements for large organizations across multiple vertical markets, including legal, life sciences, financial, utilities, retail, non-profit, and more. Olenick has been dedicated exclusively to SharePoint since 2006, and FAST Search Server 2010 for SharePoint since its beta release in 2009. He has helped dozens of clients solve business problems by leveraging SharePoint and Enterprise Search, and shares his experiences with the greater community by speaking at events, contributing to books, and blogging at olenicksharepoint.wordpress.com.

MATT RANLETT (Chapter 28), a SharePoint Server Most Valuable Professional (MVP), works as a solution architect and consulting practice lead with Slalom Consulting, and is part of the team committed to helping people succeed by delivering innovative solutions that create business value. Ranlett has been a fixture of the Atlanta .NET developer community for many years. A founding member of the Atlanta Dot Net Regular Guys (www.devcow.com), Ranlett has formed and leads several Atlanta area user groups. Included in his community contributions are organizational efforts around five Atlanta Code Camps, two SharePoint Saturdays, and numerous presentations around the Southeast and Texas. When he's not organizing or presenting at user group-related events, Ranlett writes and edits whitepapers, magazine articles, and books on SharePoint's features and capabilities. He also enjoys spending time with his wife, Kim, son, Parker, and daughter, Darby, all of whom help to keep him sane when not focusing on Microsoft technologies and tools.

NATALYA VOSKRESENSKAYA (Chapter 27) has been working in the field of Information Technology for more than 13 years. With experience in design, architecture, development, and deployment of Web-based applications since early 2000, her main area of concentration had been development of portal solutions. Voskresenskaya delivers enterprise portal applications and business solutions, as well as portal systems architecture, design, implementation, and best practices guidance. She has been involved in SharePoint technologies since the 2003 version. An avid blogger at `http://spforsquirrels.blogspot.com/` and writer, Voskresenskaya strives to share her passion for SharePoint and its community, and is often speaking at SharePoint community events, as well as conferences. Besides SharePoint, her interest had been captured by another enterprise-level search technology, FAST Enterprise Search. In 2009, Voskresenskaya co-founded Arcovis LLC, a business solutions consulting company focused on high-quality SharePoint delivery. She was awarded the Microsoft Most Valuable Professional (MVP) award for the first time in 2008.

SIMON WALKER (Chapter 20) is an enthusiastic SharePoint evangelist and business consultant with more than ten years of experience delivering enterprise architecture solutions based upon Microsoft technologies. He is a Director of Foundation IT, and spends most of his time consulting on strategy, design, information architecture, business alignment, and governance of SharePoint — bridging the gap between the technical and business-related aspects of a SharePoint strategy. Solutions delivered on SharePoint range from 50 to more than 100,000 users on a global basis for a wide range of clients, delivering the business case, benefits, design, information architecture, governance, service models, and business change required to ensure a successful adoption of SharePoint technology. For more information about Walker, see his blog at `www.sharepointsimon.net` or his LinkedIn profile at `http://uk.linkedin.com/in/simonmwalker`.

CHRIS WHITEHEAD (Chapter 21) is a Premier Field Engineer (PFE) at Microsoft, working on site with Microsoft's largest enterprise customers around the United Kingdom and Europe. In his role, he provides proactive support and consulting services for all things SharePoint. He completed his Microsoft Certified Master (MCM) for SharePoint 2010 certification in early 2011, and graduates of this program are recognized by Microsoft as the top SharePoint experts in the world. Aside from working directly with customers, Whitehead has developed an array of content that is delivered globally by other PFEs to Microsoft's customers. This includes workshop training material and the tests, along with associated recommendations that are used in the SharePoint Risk Assessment Program (SPRAP) offering delivered by PFEs. More recently, Whitehead has taken on the additional responsibility of EMEA technical lead for the SharePoint PFE team, and works to drive the technical readiness strategy for other team members, along with the strategy for future customer-deliverable content. He has presented at various conferences, including Microsoft TechEd Europe and the Microsoft SharePoint Conference. He has also contributed to the Data Protection Manager (DPM) product group blog, and is a key contributor to his own team's blog at `http://sharepoint.microsoft.com/blogs/fromthefield`.

ABOUT THE TECHNICAL EDITORS

KAYODE DADA is the Principal at TwistEdge, Inc., a technology consulting company focused on Microsoft technologies. At TwistEdge, he architects and develops solutions leveraging SharePoint 2010 social networking capabilities and the Window Azure platform. He has worked with SharePoint since its first version. Prior to founding TwistEdge, he was responsible for the engineering of a technology platform that integrates SharePoint with enterprise content management platforms, as well as a framework for developing enterprise portal solutions based on SharePoint. He blogs at www.twistedge.com/.

MATT RANLETT is a SharePoint Server Most Valuable Professional (MVP) who works as a solution architect and consulting practice lead with Slalom Consulting. He is part of the team that is committed to helping people succeed by delivering innovative solutions that create business value. Ranlett writes and edits whitepapers, magazine articles, and books on SharePoint's features and capabilities.

RAHUL SONI started his career working with Visual Basic and went on to learn VB.NET when he came to Bengaluru, India. After two years of being a dedicated software developer, he joined the Microsoft support team for ASP.NET. Later, he worked for IIS + ASP.NET team as a technical lead at Microsoft for almost two years. Currently, he is a Senior Premier Field Engineer (PFE) for Microsoft, working on multiple technologies, including ASP.NET, Ajax, Silverlight, C#, VB.NET, ADO.NET, LINQ, SharePoint 2007 administration, SharePoint development, and SharePoint 2010. He blogs at www.dotnetscraps.com.

CREDITS

ACKNOWLEDGMENTS

TO THE UNOFFICIAL PROJECT MANAGER of this book, Hayley Wilson: Thank you for being the "project manager" of this book. Your support for all the authors of this book has been invaluable.

To the authors and contributors of this book: Thank you for participating in such an ambitious project. Your wisdom, technical contribution, and insights are out of this world. You are all truly so special and gifted. We did it!

To Spencer Harbar: Thank you for helping to mold this book into something special. Thank you for spending many Fridays over conference calls discussing the structure and design of this book. Your knowledge and experience is outstanding!

To the BAE Systems SharePoint team: Thank you for your understanding and providing me with the time needed to write this book. The lessons I learned on this and previous projects have been instrumental in many of the real-world learnings in this book. Thank you Gordon Reeves, Dave Meredith, Matthew Hallam, and Simon Wills.

Finally, to all the people who indirectly and directly contributed to this book: Todd Baginski, Luca Bandinelli, Ben Curry, Todd Carter, Eric Charran, Andrew Connell, Dave Stewart, Bill English, Kimmo Forss, Bob Fox, Steve Fox, Scott Jamison, Chris Johnson, Tyler Durham, Joel Oleson, Jie Li, Paul Learning, Steve Ledbury, Daniel McPherson, Michael Noel, Chris O'Brien, Dave Pae, Richard Riley, Ben Robb, Steve Smith, Steve Petska, Tom Rizzo, Nick Swan, Sean Squires, Mike Wise, Andrew Woodward — thank you all for your help, advice, assistance, and guidance in making this book a reality. You are all giants in our SharePoint community! Thank you!

—Brian Wilson

CONTENTS

PART III: ARCHITECTING ENTERPRISE PORTAL SERVICES

CHAPTER 13: GETTING STARTED WITH YOUR PROGRAM AND PROJECTS

FOREWORD

I have had the fortunate opportunity to lead the SharePoint Technical Product Management team from SharePoint 2003 to the SharePoint 2010 launch. Over the years, I've seen SharePoint evolve into a rich collaboration platform that has the capability to transform a company. It can help users work together, share information, find data, and build applications. It's a modern platform that has improved organizational productivity across small, medium, and large businesses worldwide. It's a popular replacement for technologies such as Lotus Notes, Documentum, and Windows file shares. And, although it has a lot of potential, it's really important to carefully plan for a successful deployment and end-user adoption.

One of the most common challenges I saw with early SharePoint adopters a few years ago was "under the desk" deployments. Individuals would deploy SharePoint on a single box under their desks, invite many people and departments, and then run into all kinds of issues pertaining to governance. Many people blamed SharePoint, when the real challenge was a lack of planning. This resulted in performance and governance challenges for customers. In SharePoint 2010, a lot of great IT professional and end-user features are available that help you with governance. But, at the end of the day, features can only help. It's important to carefully plan your deployment.

A SharePoint architect must think across multiple dimensions, including hardware, storage, network capacity, and configuration, as well as information architecture and governance. It takes a deep understanding and planning to do a great job with architecting, deploying, and managing SharePoint, especially in organizations that centrally serve thousands of users. Poor planning can result in long response times, low end-user adoption, and even downtime.

This book does a great job in providing guidance on how to successfully deploy SharePoint. This book covers a number of deep technical subjects such as SharePoint 2010 platform architecture, as well as more governance-oriented topics such as defining your SharePoint 2010 governance model. I have had the pleasure of knowing Brian Wilson and many of the other authors/contributors who bring their real-world experience to this book!

— Arpan Shah
Director, Microsoft Project
http://blogs.msdn.com/arpans

INTRODUCTION

By Brian Wilson

MICROSOFT COLLABORATION and companion development technologies have really come a long way over the past 20 years. Over this time, many different technologies have come and gone in the blink of an eye. Others have built up momentum, improving with each new version, providing valuable new features to meet the ever-increasing digital demands of the age in which we live.

One such technology that has done this brilliantly is SharePoint 2010. SharePoint is a culmination of more than 20 years of continual research and investment by Microsoft. Each new version has improved on the previous version, and provided a plethora of new features to incorporate into deployments of SharePoint. With each new version of SharePoint, the knowledge required to design successful deployments has grown astronomically.

In addition, from a design and architecture perspective, learning SharePoint 2010 is a huge undertaking that touches so many specializations. This makes it really difficult for an aspiring architect to understand what knowledge and skills are required to design solutions for SharePoint 2010. The result has been a tendency by SharePoint specialists to learn and focus on a subset of the capabilities of SharePoint 2010, and even then with a business adoption, design, infrastructure, developer, testing, or governance orientation, but not on the overall SharePoint solution provided to customers.

An increased breadth of architectural knowledge and a better understanding of the medium- to long-term impact of key design decisions are required to design successful SharePoint 2010 portal solutions. This knowledge must be coupled with real-world case studies and solid "in the trenches" expert experiences to help you avoid the common pitfalls faced by many SharePoint 2010 deployments.

Although there may be a number of fantastic development, infrastructure, and feature- or capability-oriented books, no books have been dedicated purely to the core architectural issues faced on a day-to-day basis by SharePoint design professionals and architects. As a result, the idea for this book was born, and the long process began of collating the many years of wisdom and experiences, as well as designing and authoring a book that would address each of the key architectural concerns.

The next sections cover who this book is for, and what this book covers.

WHO THIS BOOK IS FOR

The ideal readers for this book are business professionals, technical architects, developers, and IT professionals wanting to improve their SharePoint design and architecture skillsets, design long-lasting portal deployments, and ensure maximum customer and end-user satisfaction.

Those who serve in technically oriented roles will find all the chapters in this book invaluable. It's very important to realize that, to be a good technical SharePoint architect, understanding the business side of the product is a "must-have" skill. Each part of this book is specifically designed to grow your business and technical knowledge in a structured way. Those who serve in business-oriented roles (such as analysts, strategy and design planners, program and project managers, "business/organizational change" teams, and communication teams) will find several of the chapters in this book useful.

WHAT THIS BOOK COVERS

The book is divided into four parts, each containing a set of related chapters.

Part I of this book sets the scene by providing an overview of the business and technical knowledge requirements for a SharePoint architect. This includes the following chapters:

➤ *Chapter 1, "A Digital Workforce for a Digital Age"* — Written by Arpan Shah, this chapter sets the scene by describing the role Enterprise 2.0 and SharePoint 2010 play in the enterprise environment, and the value proposition SharePoint 2010 provides.

➤ *Chapter 2, "Understanding the Enterprise Landscape"* — Written by Brian Wilson, this chapter focuses on the business knowledge required to design and architect successful SharePoint deployments. This chapter drills into key areas of the enterprise landscape that influence and impact the success of any portal deployment in your enterprise.

➤ *Chapter 3, "Supporting Technology Knowledge Requirements"* — Written by Brian Wilson, this chapter provides an overview of the underlying and supporting technologies used by SharePoint. The sections in this chapter are grouped into infrastructure, development, Office technologies, and complementary third-party technologies to help you based on your skillset orientation. For each of these supporting technologies, the chapter considers the impact, required knowledge, and key decisions that must be made.

➤ *Chapter 4, "Design Principles for Successful Deployments"* — Written by Ian Morrish, this chapter provides design principles for successful deployments. Key design issues affecting SharePoint deployments that cause SharePoint deployments to fail are discussed, along with principles that the SharePoint architect can use to counter these failings in the design of enterprise portal services. For example, these include the importance of designing your information architecture, designing for governance, designing for context, solution characteristics, and SharePoint project management.

➤ *Chapter 5, "Learning How Microsoft Uses SharePoint 2010"* — Written by Sam Hassani, Jim Adams, and Scott Kleven from Microsoft, this chapter provides a great real-world case study of how Microsoft has deployed SharePoint 2010 internally.

Part II of this book is designed to grow your knowledge and understanding of the SharePoint 2010 platform. Chapters in this part include the following:

➤ *Chapter 6, "SharePoint Fundamentals"* — Written by Martin Kearn, this chapter provides a great overview of the fundamental concepts someone new to SharePoint must understand. These include the SharePoint farm, servers, service applications, web applications, databases, site collections, sites, libraries, and list items, along with available SharePoint 2010 licensing models.

➤ *Chapter 7, "Evolution of Sharepoint"* — Written by Brian Wilson, this chapter describes the evolution and early days of SharePoint, from the birthing pool of SharePoint 2001, through the growing pains of SharePoint 2003, to coming of age with the SharePoint 2007 release. This chapter provides a solid grounding on the background and evolutionary growth leading up to SharePoint 2010.

➤ *Chapter 8, "SharePoint 2010 Features and Capabilities"* — Written by Brian Wilson, this chapter provides an answer the question, "Why SharePoint?" by looking at the features, workloads, capabilities, and the rich platform extensibility that SharePoint 2010 provides. It covers publishing, information, collaboration, search, individual and social networking, Business Connectivity Services (BCS), business intelligence (BI), and workflow and forms services.

➤ *Chapter 9, "Understanding SharePoint 2010 Service Applications"* — Written by Reza Alirezaei, this chapter helps you understand services applications in SharePoint 2010. It describes the new service architecture model in SharePoint 2010, and how this architecture is used in the platform to offer new or improved functionality. It then provides architectural principles and guidelines that help you understand topics discussed in other chapters of this book.

➤ *Chapter 10, "SharePoint 2010 Platform Architectures"* — Written by Bill Baer, this chapter provides a detailed overview of the various farm, service application, and search topologies. This includes on-premise single-server deployments; small, medium, and large farms; geo-distributed farms; and hosted-in-the-cloud farm environments. Real-world experiences are cited and shared to help SharePoint architects make the right choices. Finally, solid guidelines are provided to help you design the most scalable architecture.

➤ *Chapter 11, "Working with Internal and External Data in SharePoint 2010"* — Written by Paul Olenick, this chapter looks at SharePoint 2010 from a data perspective. This chapter covers the common options available to work with internal and external data in SharePoint 2010. This includes manipulating internal data, integrating external data, list data platform capabilities, BCS, data integration options, content aggregation, server- and client-side APIs at your disposal, taking business data offline, and, finally, incorporating cloud-hosted data and "compute" services (such as Azure).

Part III of this book describes a well-defined and proven process to help architects design and architect enterprise portal services for their organizations. The chapters in this part include the following:

➤ *Chapter 12, "Defining Your SharePoint 2010 Portal Strategy"* — Written by Brian Wilson, this chapter provides guidance and steps to define your enterprise portal strategy and road map. It defines a solid process to review your business environment, and engage key stakeholders to understand the business drivers that your SharePoint 2010 deployment must support. It describes how to define the required portal capabilities, portal blueprints, enterprise portal strategy, and road map. Lastly, it takes a look at the key stakeholder responsibilities required for a successful deployment of SharePoint 2010.

➤ *Chapter 13, "Getting Started with Your Program and Projects"* — Written by Brian Wilson, this chapter illustrates how to get started with your SharePoint 2010 program and projects. It describes the key activities, tasks, and streams of work that must take place. These include requirements-related activities, early technical design activities, early technical leadership activities, program and project management activities, and, lastly, business change and adoption activities.

➤ *Chapter 14, "Designing Your Information Architecture"* — Written by Brian Wilson, this chapter provides detailed architectural guidance to help you design your SharePoint 2010 information architecture. Starting with a solid definition of "SharePoint information architecture," this chapter provides detailed guidance to help you define the overarching information architecture for a SharePoint deployment. This includes understanding the scope, capabilities, and constraints; assessing business information maturity levels; defining personas and scenarios; defining enterprise metadata; defining a SharePoint 2010 containment model; incorporating governance into the design; and defining search, navigation, people, visual experience, and custom functionality. Lastly, it provides detailed insight into how to approach content "onboarding" and migration.

➤ *Chapter 15, "Designing Your Solution Architecture"* — Written by Brian Wilson and Vesa Juvonen, this chapter provides detailed architectural guidance to help you design your SharePoint 2010 solution architecture. Starting with a solid definition of "SharePoint solution architecture," this chapter focuses on designing your site solution architecture, understanding common solution patterns and design options, designing your custom business solutions, and documenting your SharePoint 2010 design.

➤ *Chapter 16, "Designing Your Infrastructure Architecture"* — Written by Neil Hodgkinson, this chapter provides detailed architectural guidance to help you design your SharePoint 2010 infrastructure architecture. This chapter helps you design the underlying infrastructure to support your SharePoint 2010 deployment. This includes designing your data center services, performing a network impact assessment, estimating your farm's capacity and performance requirements, designing your logical and physical architecture, planning your supporting application infrastructure technologies, configuration management, and operations management.

➤ *Chapter 17, "Designing Your Storage Layer"* — Written by Bill Baer, this chapter continues to look at one of the most important elements of your infrastructure architecture — the storage layer. This includes planning storage configurations, planning storage scalability, planning data protection, and detailed guidance on planning your SQL Server database layer.

➤ *Chapter 18, "Developing, Testing, and Deploying Your SharePoint 2010 Solution"* — Written by Vesa Juvonen, this chapter takes a look at key issues related to developing, testing, and deploying your SharePoint 2010 solution. It continues on from Chapter 15 by providing additional guidance on designing your code architecture and designing reusable frameworks. It takes an in-depth look at managing the required application development and deployment life cycles, understanding the SharePoint environments, the typical flow of your solution between these environments, the various release models, key development phases, and solution package design, as well as patching and upgrading options for your solution packages. Lastly, this chapter looks into key considerations, and provides solid guidance for handling development teams for small to large, as well as offshore and onshore, projects.

➤ *Chapter 19, "Designing Your Authentication and Authorization Model"* — Written by Chris Gideon, this chapter goes into an in-depth discussion to help you design your SharePoint 2010 authentication and authorization model. It includes detailed information and planning guidance for the new claim-based authentication model, and the existing forms and classic-mode authentication models.

➤ *Chapter 20, "Defining Your Governance Model and Approach"* — Written by Simon Walker, this chapter takes a detailed look at defining your governance model and approach for your SharePoint deployment and organization. It looks at why governance is important, common governance models, governance principles and guidelines, and the key business, IT, and governance-specific roles you should consider.

➤ *Chapter 21, "Defining Your Business Continuity Management Plan"* — Written by Chris Whitehead, this chapter provides fantastic advice and guidance for defining your business continuity management plan. SharePoint 2010 is fast becoming a key application (and mission-critical application) in many organizations. To protect your organization, this chapter covers topics vital to defining your business continuity management plan, including analyzing your continuity requirements, determining your Service Level Agreements (SLAs), designing your backup and recovery strategy, designing your availability strategy, and designing your disaster-recovery strategy.

➤ *Chapter 22, "Designing for Cloud-Based Solutions and Multi-Tenancy Services"* — Written by Bill Baer, this chapter takes a detailed look at the hosting options for your SharePoint 2010 deployment. This includes a detailed look at key considerations for leveraging cloud-based hosting options such as SharePoint Online.

➤ *Chapter 23, "Designing Virtualized Deployments"* — Written by Brian Wilson, this chapter provides advice and guidance on utilizing virtualization technologies to host your SharePoint 2010 deployment. This chapter provides a detailed overview of the common virtualization technologies in today's marketplace, as well as further guidance on available cloud-based, virtual-machine hosting technologies. Considerations for each of the SharePoint 2010 roles you can virtualize are discussed, and a recommended deployment approach is provided. Lastly, this chapter describes an example deployment scenario to better illustrate implementing SharePoint 2010 on virtual hardware.

Part IV of this book provides in-depth, real-world enterprise portal service design considerations for each of the common SharePoint 2010 workloads and capabilities. These include dedicated chapters for each of the following workloads and capabilities of SharePoint 2010:

➤ *Chapter 24, "Intranet and Internet Publishing Services"* — Written by Hugo Esperanca, this chapter provides in-depth guidance on designing intranet and Internet publishing services, including a detailed overview of the publishing Features options at your disposal for branding Publishing sites, managing publishing content, planning site navigation, and various mechanisms to help you deploy Publishing sites to your environment.

➤ *Chapter 25, "Corporate Information Services"* — Written by Martin Kearn, this chapter takes a detailed look at the key areas related to designing and deploying corporate information services, working with documents, and managing documents in the enterprise.

➤ *Chapter 26, "Business Collaboration Services"* — Written by Bill Baer, this chapter introduces the key business collaboration services provided by SharePoint 2010. This chapter provides insightful advice and guidance on the key business challenges, business scenarios, and architectural considerations related to deploying business collaboration services in your environment.

➤ *Chapter 27, "Enterprise Search Services"* — Written by Natalya Voskresenskaya, this chapter takes a look at the SharePoint 2010 search features at your disposal, including a look at SharePoint search and FAST for SharePoint, components of the SharePoint 2010 search architecture, and other key areas (such as content sources, federation, user experience, scale and redundancy, search performance, search relevancy, and key business challenges) related to enterprise search.

➤ *Chapter 28, "Individual and Social Networking Features"* — Written by Matt Ranlett, this chapter gets you connected to the features SharePoint 2010 provides to enable individual and social networking. This chapter provides a great overview of these features, followed by advice and guidance on the key business and technical challenges, advanced business scenarios, key architectural considerations, and a recommended approach to deploying these features in your environment.

➤ *Chapter 29, "Business Connectivity Services"* — Written by Reza Alirezaei, this chapter describes the wonderful "business data" integration services provided by SharePoint 2010. It includes detailed guidance on the various options to molding and building your BCS solutions using SharePoint Designer and Visual Studio, planning your security, and administrating the BCS service application.

➤ *Chapter 30, "Business Intelligence Services"* — Written by Reza Alirezaei, this chapter helps you design solutions to harness and distribute business information using the BI features. It includes an introduction of the BI features built into SharePoint 2010, followed by structured guidance for each of the BI options SharePoint provides, including common BI features, Excel Services, PowerPivot for Excel, PowerPivot for SharePoint, PerformancePoint Services, Reporting Services, Visio Services, and Access Services.

➤ *Chapter 31, "Forms Services and Workflow"* — Written by Martin Kearn, this chapter shines a light on the world of workflow and forms in SharePoint 2010. It takes a detailed look at how these two technologies are used (and often combined) in SharePoint 2010. Detailed guidance is provided to help you make the right choices.

➤ *Chapter 32, "Records Management Services"* — Written by Nigel Bridport, this chapter helps you learn more about records management, and how to use SharePoint 2010's records management features, including understanding records management, using a file plan, key challenges faced by your business, key architectural considerations, and common business scenarios.

Each chapter shares the wisdom and expert experiences of the authors with you, helping you to avoid pitfalls and follow recommend approaches that result in great deployments of SharePoint technology.

WHAT YOU NEED TO USE THIS BOOK

This book is dedicated to helping you learn the intricacies of architecting SharePoint 2010 environments. As a result, although not required, it would greatly benefit you to have access to the following hardware and software resources:

➤ *Virtualized hosting environment* — A virtual machine hosting environment (such as Microsoft Hyper-V or VMWare virtualization technology) will enable you set up and test single-server, medium-farm, and large-farm configurations. Virtual hosting environments enable your entire installations to be scripted. This improves the speed at which you can stand up "clean" farm environments to test out various SharePoint configurations.

➤ *MSDN subscription* — An MSDN subscription provides all the Microsoft software and product keys you require to set up SharePoint 2010 in your virtualized environment. It provides access to the Visual Studio suite of development, test, and architectural software development tools, as well as a number of other useful tools.

Your desktop or laptop should have the full suite of Microsoft Office products, including Microsoft Visio 2010 for your architectural diagrams, Balsamiq (or a similar tool) for creating mockups and screen prototypes, SharePoint Designer, and the capability to use a "remote desktop connection" to access remote hosted virtual machines.

Finally, if your physical machine has sufficient hardware resources, it is recommended that you invest in virtualization software such as VMWare WorkStation that supports hosting of x64-bit virtual machines. This option provides the greatest flexibility to learn more about SharePoint 2010. Once Windows 8 operating system is released, it is believed it will finally provide the capability to host x64-bit virtual machines.

CONVENTIONS

To help you get the most from the text and keep track of what's happening, we've used a number of conventions throughout the book.

As for styles in the text:

➤ We *italicize* new terms and important words when we introduce them.

➤ We show keyboard strokes like this: Ctrl+A.

➤ We show filenames, URLs, and code within the text like so: `persistence.properties`.

➤ We present code in two different ways:

```
We use a monofont type with no highlighting for most code examples.
```

We use bold to emphasize code that is particularly important in the present context or to show changes from a previous code snippet.

ERRATA

We make every effort to ensure that there are no errors in the text or in the code. However, no one is perfect, and mistakes do occur. If you find an error in one of our books, like a spelling mistake or faulty piece of code, we would be very grateful for your feedback. By sending in errata, you may save another reader hours of frustration, and at the same time, you will be helping us provide even higher quality information.

To find the errata page for this book, go to www.wrox.com and locate the title using the Search box or one of the title lists. Then, on the book details page, click the Book Errata link. On this page, you can view all errata that has been submitted for this book and posted by Wrox editors. A complete book list, including links to each book's errata, is also available at www.wrox.com/misc-pages/booklist.shtml.

If you don't spot "your" error on the Book Errata page, go to www.wrox.com/contact/techsupport.shtml and complete the form there to send us the error you have found. We'll check the information and, if appropriate, post a message to the book's errata page and fix the problem in subsequent editions of the book.

P2P.WROX.COM

For author and peer discussion, join the P2P forums at p2p.wrox.com. The forums are a web-based system for you to post messages relating to Wrox books and related technologies, and interact with other readers and technology users. The forums offer a subscription feature to e-mail you topics of interest of your choosing when new posts are made to the forums. Wrox authors, editors, other industry experts, and your fellow readers are present on these forums.

At http://p2p.wrox.com, you will find a number of different forums that will help you, not only as you read this book, but also as you develop your own applications. To join the forums, just follow these steps:

1. Go to p2p.wrox.com and click the Register link.

2. Read the terms of use and click Agree.

3. Complete the required information to join, as well as any optional information you wish to provide, and click Submit.

4. You will receive an e-mail with information describing how to verify your account and complete the joining process.

You can read messages in the forums without joining P2P, but in order to post your own messages, you must join.

Once you join, you can post new messages and respond to messages other users post. You can read messages at any time on the web. If you would like to have new messages from a particular forum e-mailed to you, click the Subscribe to This Forum icon by the forum name in the forum listing.

For more information about how to use the Wrox P2P, be sure to read the P2P FAQs for answers to questions about how the forum software works, as well as many common questions specific to P2P and Wrox books. To read the FAQs, click the FAQ link on any P2P page.

PART I
SharePoint Architect Knowledge Requirements

1

A Digital Workforce for a Digital Age

By Arpan Shah

"Generation Z" will be entering the workforce this decade. This generation grew up with PCs, cell phones, and MP3 players, and is one of the largest populations on Facebook. Writing wall messages and texting is their preferred method of communication. E-mail is considered a much more formal medium, and faxing is as ancient as snail mail. It's a generation that blogs, tweets, uses, and breathes technology. They are not scared of technology, and they are all "power users." "Security setting" is a foreign concept to them, and privacy is an afterthought. They are the future of the workforce.

In the business world, it's really important to understand the needs and expectations of Generation Z, while balancing the need for compliance, IP protection, governance, and security. It's also important to keep in mind the co-existence of Generation Z with older generations, who are not as tech savvy, and even at times skeptical about the usefulness of technology. Striking the right balance for your organization is important. SharePoint provides that flexibility and power.

Since its inception in 1999, SharePoint has changed the way people in organizations collaborate. SharePoint's core value proposition has remained consistent over the years — delivering the best productivity experience through the Microsoft Office client, browser, and phone. Over the years, SharePoint has evolved into a platform that goes beyond file sharing by enabling people to work in different ways.

What makes SharePoint 2010 special is that it delivers a business collaboration platform for the enterprise and the Internet. If designed and deployed correctly, it can yield a tremendous return on investment through increased organizational productivity and a reduction in costs.

Instead of IT departments having to manage a myriad of application silos, they can consolidate their platforms and reduce overall licensing, operational, and training costs. In fact, a number of case studies and reports show a positive return on investment in the first few months of a SharePoint 2010 deployment.

 For customer success stories and Microsoft case studies, see http://sharepoint.microsoft.com/en-us/customers/ *and* www.microsoft.com/casestudies.

UNDERSTANDING ENTERPRISE 2.0 AND SHAREPOINT 2010

Wikipedia describes *Enterprise 2.0* as the use of "Web 2.0" technologies within an organization to enable or streamline business processes while enhancing collaboration. In short, Enterprise 2.0 is just rebranding of the catch phrase Web 2.0 that many consumers are aware of. Having consumer technology enter the workforce is a phenomenon that has been around for years. Popular examples of Web 2.0 technologies that have entered the workplace include business instant messaging (Lync), social networking features (such as internal blogs and wikis), video sharing sites, as well as taxonomies, folksonomies, and their associated terms, associated to organizational content and presented to users in tag clouds, search refinements, and content filtering options.

What makes Enterprise 2.0 interesting is that it is generally perceived as a disruptor in organizations. Disruption can be a very good thing, but it generally does shake things up. In this particular case, it's a change that involves technology, impacts work culture, and can improve productivity if it is adopted and governed. The Generation Z workforce will get it right away; older generations will be skeptical, and some may even be opposed to Enterprise 2.0.

However, the reality is that Enterprise 2.0 is inevitable, and is happening today in most companies whether IT departments are aware of it or not. One could argue that the phrase "Enterprise 2.0" is misleading and dated. The term was introduced in 2006 when most technology was still deployed by IT. In today's world, it is not uncommon for departments and even small teams to make decisions based on their needs, regardless of what is deployed within the firewall.

With the emergence of Software as a Service (SaaS) technology, the number of options has multiplied, and reliance on IT departments has been dramatically reduced. The challenge with having different departments provisioning different third-party SaaS applications is generally multifold:

➤ You must manage multiple relationships.

➤ Your total cost is generally higher because of licensing and maintenance.

➤ You don't have control over those environments.

➤ One of those companies could go out of business.

➤ It's difficult to integrate these solutions in an end-to-end way.

This is where SharePoint adds a lot of value. SharePoint effectively gives you an Enterprise 2.0 platform that you can deploy and manage inside your firewall, or use as an SaaS application with SharePoint Online. In fact, SharePoint provides many of the Enterprise 2.0 features integrated into one platform.

Released in the second half of 2006, SharePoint 2007 combined several major workloads that customers were looking to deploy in one single product. Figure 1-1 shows a graphical depiction of the SharePoint 2007 product. When you read the Enterprise 2.0 definition and look at Figure 1-1, it looks like SharePoint 2007 was designed with Enterprise 2.0 in mind. In fact, SharePoint 2007 was ahead of its time, because it was designed before the phrase Enterprise 2.0 was even dubbed.

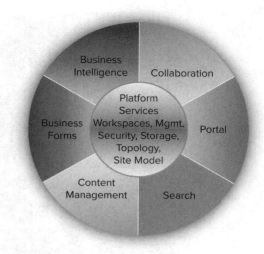

FIGURE 1-1: Microsoft SharePoint 2007 feature areas

SharePoint 2007 was a very well-received product, and helped the SharePoint franchise be one of the fastest growing server products in Microsoft's history. Many IT departments looked to SharePoint to serve their business units in a cost-effective and self-service way.

SharePoint 2010 built on the solid SharePoint 2007 foundation with a focus on end-user, developer, and IT scenarios. Figure 1-2 shows a similar, but slightly different, picture of the SharePoint 2007 feature areas. There are two distinct differences:

➤ *The color is uniform and the lines are blurred* — In SharePoint 2007, the different workload slices were different colors, and the lines between them were distinct. Interestingly enough, many customers interpreted this as decoupled workloads that they must choose from. The reality is that customers can mix these workloads, and choose a mix that's most relevant for them.

In SharePoint 2010, there's even greater integration and flexibility across workloads. Instead of giving the message that customers must choose one workload, this gives a clearer message that SharePoint delivers an integrated set of capabilities.

➤ *The workload names are different* — The first obvious thing is that the "Collaboration" workload is missing. The reality is that the entire product is centered on collaboration and, therefore, collaboration has been elevated into the tagline. In place of Collaboration there is a new workload named "Communities" that centers on social capabilities such as blogging, tagging, and wikis. Other than that, there's a one-to-one mapping between the new workload names and the more familiar industry workload names. The choice of using different names is really centered on simplicity, with the decision to use one word versus multiple words.

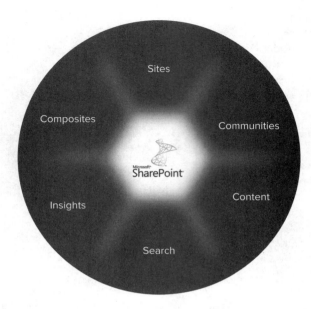

FIGURE 1-2: Alternate view of Microsoft SharePoint 2007 feature areas (SharePoint 2010)

Following is a brief explanation of the various SharePoint 2010 workloads. Keep in mind that the true power is in integrating these features together.

➤ *Sites* — A SharePoint site is where your content lives and where you do your work. A site is a powerful SharePoint feature and concept. A SharePoint site is a rich website that can serve a single purpose or multiple purposes. It is not uncommon to have tens of thousands of SharePoint sites in an organization that span from small team sites to large divisional portals. One way to think about a site is as a web application. Your organization can take advantage of the out-of-the-box SharePoint sites, as well as define custom sites that can easily be provisioned by business users.

➤ *Communities* — Communities allow you to work the way you want. This workload represents the social and collaboration features in SharePoint. This includes features such as easy document sharing, blogs, tagging, and enterprise wikis.

➤ *Content* — Content allows you to manage all your enterprise content with compliance in mind. It is an umbrella category that includes Enterprise Content Management (ECM), Web Content Management (WCM), and Records Management. The scenarios are vast, from large-scale enterprise document libraries, to highly customized and heavily trafficked Internet websites.

➤ *Search* — Search allows you to find information and people. It is vastly improved in SharePoint 2010. Search allows you to index and search everything in SharePoint, on non-SharePoint sites, file shares, Exchange public folders, people, and custom line-of-business (LOB) applications.

➤ *Insights* — Insights surface business intelligence (BI) to be able to make informed decisions. It is the BI capability that offers executive dashboards, key performance indicators (KPIs), PerformancePoint Services, SQL Reporting Services, and Excel Services.

➤ *Composites* — Composites allow your users to rapidly respond to business needs. It represents the capabilities that allow non-developers to create no-code solutions through the browser and with SharePoint Designer (a freely available downloadable tool). Features include Access Services, InfoPath Forms Services, and Business Connectivity Services (BCS), to name just a few. BCS allows you to connect to back-end systems to enable read/write scenarios.

 More detail on these is provided in Chapter 7 and other chapters in Part IV of this book.

To effectively deploy SharePoint, it's important to understand its core value proposition. The discussion in the remainder of this chapter goes through the core value proposition, as well as key things to keep in mind as you look to use SharePoint for your organization.

UNDERSTANDING SHAREPOINT'S VALUE PROPOSITION

The value proposition for SharePoint 2010 can be isolated to three key areas:

➤ Deliver the best productivity experience

➤ Cut costs with a unified infrastructure

➤ Rapidly respond to business needs

Let's take a look at each of these in a bit more detail.

Deliver the Best Productivity Experience

One of the core value propositions of SharePoint 2010 is to deliver the best productivity experience to all users. Users can choose to use a web browser (such as Internet Explorer, Firefox, or Safari), a mobile phone, or the Office suite. Each of these experiences is designed to be intuitive.

New to SharePoint 2010, an array of different browser technologies are supported. Through the use of Ajax (Asynchronous JavaScript and XML), the user interface is fast and responsive. Also new to SharePoint 2010 is the Ribbon that makes it easier for users to find frequently used commands. Similar to the experience in the Office clients, the Ribbon guides the user and exposes different actions in context, and conveniently grays out actions that are not possible. Organizations also have the option to extend the Ribbon to include custom actions.

SharePoint 2010 also delivers a mobile experience that allows users to easily access content from any mobile device. There has also been an ecosystem of rich partner-specialized mobile applications for specific scenarios.

And, of course, users can interact with SharePoint 2010 through Microsoft Office. Office 2010 includes new integration points, including the Backstage that surfaces SharePoint information and commands. SharePoint Workspace (the evolution of the Groove client) delivers a rich SharePoint experience. Some people make the same comparison between Workspace and SharePoint as they do between Outlook and Exchange. SharePoint Workspace allows you to take your document lists and libraries offline — and this includes external lists that might be bringing information from back-end systems.

Along with SharePoint Workspace and core Office integration, Microsoft Lync delivers presence right inside of SharePoint. With the power of Lync, users can connect with other users seamlessly when they are in SharePoint.

Cut Costs with a Unified Infrastructure

Organizations have thousands of applications and terabytes of content. Over time, these applications and content become very difficult and expensive to manage for IT departments. It's also not an ideal user experience to have to jump between different user experiences. Users also can find it difficult to find applications and content that they want to use.

SharePoint delivers a unified platform where terabytes of content can be stored, and thousands of applications can be hosted. Some vendors package and market their functionality as one platform, but, in reality, they have siloed technology that must be glued together. Though the tagline "6 servers in 1" is sometimes used to describe SharePoint, it's misleading. SharePoint is one server that has a set of integrated features. This has multiple benefits, including the following:

➤ A common set of features can be leveraged to create compelling solutions.

➤ Costs can be cut with one platform that end users must be trained on, that developers must develop on, and IT must manage.

It's important for IT departments to plan and think about how SharePoint can help drive real value to an organization. One mental model to use when planning for a SharePoint deployment includes "IT managed applications" and "Unmanaged applications," which are described as follows:

➤ *IT managed applications* — These are applications that are centrally governed, developed, and managed. They are generally considered mission-critical and used by many users. Some examples include a corporate web presence, employee portal, and knowledge management portal.

➤ *Unmanaged applications* — These are the long tail of applications that different users and business units need and want. These can include highly customized applications used by a handful of people. Because IT department resources are limited, it's important to empower individuals and teams to create these applications with a well-thought-out self-service and governance model. By asking teams and individuals what type of applications they want, IT can create reusable templates that can be provisioned and customized.

Figure 1-3 shows the different types of applications that an organization might host with the applications at the head (left-hand side) being the managed applications, and the applications on the tail (right-hand side) being unmanaged.

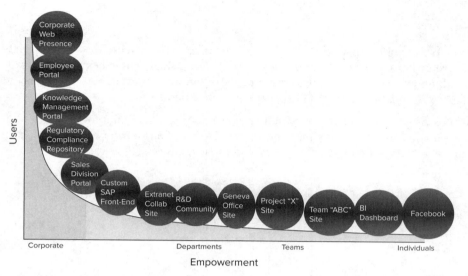

FIGURE 1-3: Applications within an organization

One other way organizations can manage costs is by choosing to use the SharePoint SaaS solution offered by Microsoft — SharePoint Online in Office 365. From a business perspective, this option is interesting for customers who are looking to move to a more operational expense (versus capital expense) model. As for technology, SharePoint Online offers the majority of SharePoint 2010 features with some limitations on the extensibility and management side. It's recommended that organizations explore the scenarios and benefits when looking to move to an SaaS solution.

Rapidly Respond to Business Needs

SharePoint empowers all users to create solutions. With SharePoint, you do not have to write code to develop solutions. SharePoint offers users the capability to create no-code solutions using the browser and SharePoint Designer (which, as mentioned previously, is a free download for SharePoint customers). Solutions can also be reused and provisioned through the use of templates and web parts. Users can easily create custom lists, design workflows, define metadata, integrate with data sources, use Excel and Access to create custom dashboards, and mash up all these different components to create a custom experience.

For professional developers, SharePoint builds on the .NET platform, and offers fantastic tooling with Visual Studio 2010 — features like BCS, RESTful APIs, Silverlight support, a client object model, and much more. On top of all of this, the nice thing with SharePoint 2010 is that many of these things are possible not only with SharePoint on-premises, but with SharePoint Online as well. Of course, with great power comes great responsibility, and investments Microsoft has made with governance and sandboxed solutions help IT allow for secure and safe custom code deployment.

SUMMARY

SharePoint 2010 is a technology that can transform any organization, no matter how big or small. It is feature-rich, versatile, and extensible, allowing IT to deliver a single unified experience to all business units with only one infrastructure to manage. Furthermore, it is available for organizations to deploy inside their firewalls, or as an SaaS application from Microsoft.

The rest of the book provides detailed information on how to design SharePoint for your organization so that you can get the maximum business value based on your business needs. Chapter 2 begins that examination by exploring the enterprise landscape.

2

Understanding the Enterprise Landscape

By Brian Wilson

Described simply, *business information ecology* entails viewing the informational space of your organization as an ecosystem of a number of important dimensions that affect the complete information environment. It is focused on how people create, share, interpret, and use information. More importantly, it sees technology as only one component of a successful business information environment.

The major dimensions of your business information ecology include the following:

> *Business landscape* — The business landscape includes the business drivers, goals, and context in which the business operates, as well as the internal, micro, and macro environment in which the organization operates. Other factors include the sector, business formation and organizational structure, and the model and structure that the IT department uses to support and service business technology requirements.

> *Technology landscape* — The technology landscape involves understanding the SharePoint 2010 ecosystem, your organization's current enterprise architecture and strategy, your existing and planned infrastructure, and your existing portal and collaboration solutions.

> *Legal landscape* — The legal landscape includes understanding and complying with the regulatory and legal requirements under which your organization operates.

> *Information landscape* — This includes content storage locations and volume; common content formats in use; content structure and metadata; content dynamism; control and clearly defined content ownership.

> *End-user landscape* — This looks at patterns across your user base, such as organizational structure, key audiences, number of employees per office location, job roles, age groups, common information-seeking behaviors, and the current and desired user experience.

Gaining a deep understanding of the business dimensions enables you to develop a holistic understanding and snapshot of the organization at a point in time. As a Microsoft Partner or internal business representative, this enables you to define a business case and portal solution that resonates with key stakeholders of the organization.

How long should you spend researching the business information ecology? This largely depends on the size and complexity of the business environment and scope of the project.

Let's take a closer look at these various dimensions of the business information ecology.

REVIEWING THE BUSINESS LANDSCAPE

For new and aspiring SharePoint architects, the focus can sometimes be overly weighted to the technical aspects of SharePoint technology. This often detracts from truly understanding and focusing on the business requirements, as well as the business landscape surrounding the proposed portal solution. A successful SharePoint architect must be cognizant of the internal and external influences operating on a business, and must take these subtle requirements into account when producing a SharePoint portal solution.

This includes understanding key business drivers and the context in which the organization is operating, understanding the impact of various types and sizes of organizations, the typical IT department structures and funding models, and the effect these structures and models have on key decision-making processes.

The SharePoint architect must also be acutely aware of internal and external politics at play, and the key players and influencers that may impact a project. Failing to do this will make it more difficult to propose and design a solution, and even more difficult to get buy-in from key stakeholders across the organization.

Business Drivers, Goals, and Context

On a day-to-day basis, an organization faces all kinds of internal and external operational, tactical, and strategic issues. For the most part, non-unique operational and tactical issues tend to have well-established responses used to handle and resolve them. Naturally, strategic issues focus more on the long term, and deal with key internal and external business drivers (such as improving the corporate culture or responding to the changing market conditions in which the organization operates).

 Chapter 11 provides more detail and information on common business drivers facing most organizations.

Understanding the vision and goals of the organization (and, more importantly, understanding the underlying business drivers that have shaped the vision and goals) will help you understand the context in which your SharePoint solution will contribute to achieving these goals. Context, continued value, and relevance are everything to a successful SharePoint portal deployment.

Factors Influencing the Business Environment

The discussion in this section may remind you of an "Economics 101" class, but it is still an important element when reviewing your business landscape. Proposing and designing solutions entails a detailed understanding of the macro, micro, and internal environment of your business.

Macro Environment

The *macro environment* is made up of the sociocultural, economic, technological, and political/legal forces. These are factors that tend to be out of the direct control of your organization, but influence your organization from the strategy it adopts to respond to the issues it faces in the macro environment. An example that influences most portal strategies and deployments is the regulatory and legal requirements that organizations must implement to ensure that information is held in a compliant fashion.

Micro Environment

Each industry is made up of communities, government, shareholders, creditors, customers, suppliers, competitors, trade associations, and, in some cases, unions. These factors influence your organization and the strategy it adopts to respond to issues faced in the micro environment. Examples of factors that influence your portal strategy and portal deployment may be related to how your organization collaborates and integrates with suppliers, how your organization is able to respond to audit requests, or fierce competition in the market that drives the requirement to collaborate and respond rapidly to changing market conditions.

Internal Environment

The organizational structure, corporate culture, core competencies, and resources at its disposal represent the internal environment of an organization. Examples of factors in the internal environment that influence your portal strategy may be a desire to improve the corporate culture, to improve the retention of knowledge, as well as the retention and growth of intellectual property in your organization.

Industry Sector, Business Formation, and Organizational Structure

A great SharePoint architect has more than just technical knowledge to offer. To recommend the best solution, great SharePoint architects ensure that they understand the industry sector in which the organization operates, the business formation of the organization, the impact of the size of the organization, and the competing and complementary software landscape. Various factors should be considered when proposing and designing portal solutions.

Industry Sector

Each industry sector has its own set of issues and challenges to overcome. Some of these are common across all organizations operating in an industry, and others are unique to a particular organization within an industry. Experienced architects must understand these issues to be able to recommend the most appropriate solution to overcome these challenges.

The organization's industry sector will influence how you position and design a SharePoint solution for your organization or customer. Let's take a look at a few examples of issues from various industry sectors:

➤ *Defense* — Defense organizations place a high priority on the classification and protection of all information, from inception to declaration as a record. Acquisitions of other specialist companies are commonplace. Autonomous business groups and units offer different products and services solutions from air, land, sea, and operational services. These are scaled up in times of increased production, and scaled down in times of peace. The retention of knowledge and the capability to rapidly scale is a high priority for defense organizations. Secure supplier collaboration and integration is imperative to the success of any solution. Redundancy, high availability, multi-device support, and offline working is required.

➤ *Financial services* — Dominating the financial services sector are compliance, risk mitigation, innovation, increasing regulation, dealing with the effect of mergers and acquisitions, and increased competition.

➤ *Government* — Government departments face unique challenges. They often face streamlining, reorganization, and re-engineering activities at irregular intervals in response to initiatives announced by political leaders. Creating difficulties for departments in the public spotlight are cross-government department working, retention and "brain drain" of talent to the private sector, difficulties in agile working, and a constantly changing political landscape. SharePoint provides many solutions across a wide range of areas. Examples include Internet sites such as www.recovery.org. Nimble cross-department collaboration sites incorporating Single Sign-On (SSO) technologies can be created in seconds, and intranet publishing, document management, and enterprise records management solutions can provide a common platform across many government departments to operate from.

➤ *Life sciences* — Most organizations in this sector invest a great deal of time and effort in research and development to produce new medicines and innovations (such as the biotechnology sector). Managing, retaining, and accessing clinical trial information and results in studies that can last over many years are absolutely critical. Measuring profitability, as well as managing and mitigating the risk of litigation from drugs that do not live up to expectations, play a large part in ensuring that processes and procedures are in place, followed, and recorded.

➤ *Legal* — Key issues on which legal firms focus include matter management, employee career management, intellectual property access, retention, management and reuse, and collaborative, secure working environments. Extranet rapid provisioning of collaboration sites enable many parties to work together.

Another aspect related to industry sectors is that, while SharePoint technology can provide solutions to organizations in each sector, competing specialized "best-of-breed" solutions exist to meet the needs of a specific market.

An example in the legal industry might be advanced solutions to help lawyers collaborate on matters. In many cases, SharePoint 2010 makes sense. In other cases, it may not provide out-of-the-box capabilities required to generate legal documents based on pre-completed paragraphs. But it does support multiple authors working on the same document.

Additionally, SharePoint 2010 supports the capability to "roll your own" custom applications and "out-innovate" your competitors. In these cases, deciding whether to build a custom solution or use a specialized application depends on the strategy of the organization and its preferred support model. As a SharePoint architect, be open-minded about what is best for the business. SharePoint is not always the answer.

Business Formation

From a SharePoint perspective, a key goal for analyzing the size and business structure of the organization is to gather information to be able to provide solid recommendations back to the organization. Another key objective is to get a feeling for the magnitude of scope of work and tasks that lie ahead.

There are no hard-and-fast business formation categories. All organizations form and arrange themselves based on a multitude of factors, which are beyond the scope of this book. What is of interest in this discussion are the complexities and challenges that arise from said business formation, and what you can and cannot advise to your customer.

Table 2-1 describes key considerations related to common business formations when designing SharePoint 2010 solutions.

TABLE 2-1: Key Considerations Based on Your Business Formation

BUSINESS FORMATION	CONSIDERATIONS
Small Business — Single or multiple office locations	This is an ideal candidate to use Office 365 Business Productivity online suite. It has a lower cost of ownership and frees up the business to focus on core business activities.
	A business may choose to adopt SharePoint Foundation, or SharePoint Standard License. Be mindful of the capital and operational expenditure required to support your proposed solution.
	A further influencing decision point relates to the functionality required from your SharePoint solution. Office 365 does not provide all the capabilities of an on-premise SharePoint 2010 solution.
Large business — One country head office with regional branch offices	Depending on the geographical location from a Microsoft Online hosting center, this business may be an ideal candidate to use an Office 365 dedicated solution. Alternatively, an on-premise or in-country hosted solution could be used.
	Recommend hardware compression and caching technologies to optimize the experience for users in bandwidth-starved, high-latency regional branch offices. Ensure that a network impact assessment is performed.

continues

TABLE 2-1 *(continued)*

BUSINESS FORMATION	CONSIDERATIONS	
	Much depends on the scope of your project. Are you deploying an enterprise-wide portal solution, or a specific solution for a department within the business? Therefore, consider the use cases, business requirements, department, and employee locations that will use your solution.	
	Consider the requirement to cater to multiple languages. For example, in Canada, law stipulates that both French and English must be supported.	
Large business — Many countries with one head office and satellite country offices (small out-of-country footprint)	Depending on geographical location and network "distance" from a Microsoft Online hosting center, this business may be an ideal candidate to use an Office 365 dedicated solution. Alternatively, an on-premise or in-country hosted solution could be used.	
	Wide-area-network (WAN) performance may be an issue for satellite country offices. In Africa and other third-world countries, keep in mind that some networks run through actual satellites, rather than the traditional fast-wired infrastructure in first-world countries. Therefore, consider implementing hardware-compression and local-caching technologies.	
	Consider the use cases required for satellite country office employees versus the head office employee use cases. It may be that a dedicated extranet solution is all that is required to service satellite country operations.	
	Consider the requirement to cater to multiple languages.	
Large business — Many countries with one head office, regional head offices, in-country head offices (large out-of-country footprint)	The number of hosting and farm design options increase dramatically. A Microsoft Online Office 365 dedicated solution, or an on-premise or in-country hosted solution, are feasible. Additionally, local deployments may be necessary to overcome WAN performance issues from a single centralized deployment. Not all services need to be hosted in each regional area, but collaboration infrastructure should be available in each regional head office.	
	For example, Microsoft provides local hosting of collaboration services in Europe, Middle East, and Africa (EMEA); Americas; and Asia Pacific in separate physical locations, while central solutions (such as the corporate intranet) are hosted in a central farm in the Americas.	

BUSINESS FORMATION	CONSIDERATIONS
	Ensure that hardware-compression and caching technologies are used to optimize the experience for users in bandwidth-starved, high-latency offices. Ensure that a network impact assessment is performed.
	Consider the scope of your project, requirements, and use cases required for different audiences, and where collaboration is required across regions (versus within a region).
	Consider the requirement to cater to multiple languages.

Organizational Structure

Businesses can be structured in many different ways, depending on drivers, operations, and strategy. The organizational structure determines how the business will operate and perform, and is often reflected in the organizational chart of your business. The most common organizational structures can be described as follows:

➤ *Functional structure* — This is the most common structure used in today's business world. In this structure, the business aligns employees based on functional areas. Each department contains employees with similar skills. Examples include an Engineering Department, Sales Department, and Finance Department.

➤ *Divisional or product structure* — This structure is concerned with placing groups of people with similar abilities where they are needed across your organization. For example, marketing personnel or accountants will be found in different divisions of your organization. These individuals are dedicated to separate products and services.

➤ *Matrix structure* — This structure incorporates elements from both functional and divisional structures. From the outside looking in, a functional structure and functional authority exist. What is different is how the resources are utilized in each department. A project authority and project manager uses (or leases) resources from a number of functional departments in the formation of a close-knit team to complete a desired business objective.

➤ *Horizontally linked structure* — This structure groups employees along the value chain. For example, the research and development group passes its output to the engineering group.

➤ *Flat structure* — This structure has few or no levels of management between employees and managers. This structure is typical of smaller businesses, and is not common in larger organizations.

➤ *Multinational structure* — This structure is a complex form of the matrix structure because it coordinates activities across products, services, functions, and geographical areas.

➤ *Team structure* — This is one of the newest structures. It is used within other structures to bring together a set of employee competencies to move rapidly and achieve better results.

➤ *Virtual or "communities of interest" structures* — This structure enables employees in any part of the organization to collaborate, learn, and improve, based on interacting with fellow employees with similar skills, interests, and attributes, virtually by using online and offline technologies. For example, although working as a Senior Consultant for Microsoft Consulting Services UK, this author virtually collaborated across and contributed to a community containing people outside of his direct team. This community consisted of passionate individuals, teams, and product groups all focused on SharePoint technology. This community collaborated via e-mail distribution lists, community and collaboration sites, internal training sessions, and technology conferences.

Table 2-2 describes key considerations for the most common organizational structures when designing SharePoint 2010 solutions.

TABLE 2-2: SharePoint 2010 Considerations Based on Organizational Structure

ORGANIZATIONAL STRUCTURE	CONSIDERATIONS	
Functional structure	Siloing often occurs in functional structures where departments struggle to communicate and work effectively for a joint outcome.	
	Business-wide collaboration is more difficult because employees tend to view the business based on activities occurring within their functions, rather than on the business as a whole.	
	Business requirements for a SharePoint project may be slanted toward a single department, rather than for the benefit of the entire business.	
	In IT department–led projects, there may be a lack of engagement with each business function, and a greater focus on technology and platform provisioning. Lack of engagement may lead to false assumptions, as well as poor user uptake and acceptance of the SharePoint platform provided.	
Divisional or product-based structure	Businesses that use a divisional approach often suffer from the "not invented here" syndrome. In this case, a shared portal platform may not be adopted because the business or IT personnel in the division are protective of the impact of a shared platform.	
	Some of their concerns are reasonable in that they worry about loss of agility for their business, or may have had bad experiences using shared platforms from a poorly perceived central IT team.	
	Other concerns are related to the personnel themselves. They fear losing out on work, gaining valuable SharePoint experience, and ultimately their job security, because a central SharePoint deployment may reduce the value they can offer to the business, and may result in termination of their positions to save on costs.	

ORGANIZATIONAL STRUCTURE	CONSIDERATIONS
	Another important factor to consider is how technology vendors approach divisional or product-based structures. A "divide-and-conquer" approach is more profitable for a technology vendor because it enables the vendor to deploy technologies in each division, rather than once at a reduced rate for the entire business.
	Lastly, as experienced in previous projects, without a strong central architecture strategy, divisional IT departments can get religious about which technology set they use (for example, "that division is an IBM shop," or "that company is a Microsoft house"). This leads to disdain and a poor working relationship between the central team and a divisional team, making it difficult to roll out collaborative technologies that can make a difference across the entire business.
Matrix structure	In businesses that use divisional and matrix-like structures, at some point down the line, the business realizes that it can save money by consolidating certain services into a centralized or shared-service IT department with the authority to bargain with technology vendors on behalf of all the divisional IT departments.
	In some cases, depending on the business's industry sector, specialist infrastructure outsourcers may be used to manage all hardware and certain software systems. Experience with most infrastructure management vendors has shown that they are (understandably) very risk-averse and, as a result, overly process-driven.
	Many of these vendors struggle to cope with the flexibility SharePoint provides because they cannot easily gauge the risk of various actions and the impact it has on their existing service level agreements (SLAs). The recommendation is to implement a governance model detailing various roles and responsibilities to ensure that the benefits and agility SharePoint provides are not lost.
Horizontally linked structure	Horizontally linked structures can benefit greatly from implementing SharePoint technology. Processes across departments can be automated and joined up from start to finish, and this results in better productivity and profitability.
	Additionally, departments can collaborate across these departments. Using portal technologies, members of the originating department that produced the original output can take part and respond to questions from the next department, furthering their original work, saving time, and increasing overall productivity.
Flat structure	Small organizations do not always have the technical expertise required and the training budget to ensure that each end user gets the most from a SharePoint deployment. In non-IT companies, IT operations may not be as structured, disciplined, and mature as larger organizations.

continues

TABLE 2-2 *(continued)*

ORGANIZATIONAL STRUCTURE	CONSIDERATIONS	
	From a partner perspective, this makes it more difficult to complete work, and more difficult to get to a successful result because the IT processes may lack maturity and discipline.	
	Small IT companies often live on the "bleeding edge" of technology. This may cause problems where technologies implemented are not stabilized (for example, they may still be in beta or have no service pack available).	
Multinational structure	Large multinational companies may have different, isolated, or autonomous departments or projects in various countries that don't work in perfect harmony for a joint outcome, but rather in isolation for the users they control in their region.	
	For example, a company may have its headquarters in the U.S. and its central IT team may prefer to implement SharePoint portal technologies. The European division may prefer (or have already implemented) a competing portal technology. Those situations are not typically solved by SharePoint architects, but rather by an enterprise architecture function within the multinational company. Sometimes they don't get solved, because there is no political impetus or underlying business driver to solve the problem.	
Team structure	Teams benefit most from the deployment of SharePoint technologies. It enables them to work collaboratively, and to draw on the experience of previous projects through efficient information-retrieval features that search and portal technologies provide.	
	It enables teams to form, regardless of the location of the individuals. They can be in the same office, in multiple offices in the same country, or even geographically dispersed — all working together to achieve objectives in their respective countries by learning from the experiences of individuals in other countries.	
Virtual and "community of interest" structure	Virtual communities utilize SharePoint technology to share, collaborate, retain, and disseminate best practices across the business, regardless of the title or position of the employee. Individuals with a common interest can join a site and benefit from reuse of proven intellectual property. Additionally, they can then contribute their experiences, leading to increased organizational learning.	

Finally, "organizational change" and the addition (new hires) and removal (resignations and redundancies) of full-time and part-time employees will affect your SharePoint 2010 environment. These changes should be considered and catered for in the structural design and information architecture of your SharePoint 2010 environment.

Important IT Models

SharePoint portal solutions are often designed without considering the impact of the organization's IT department model. This lack of understanding often leads to issues in the governance of the SharePoint platform. Understanding the common IT department models, the roles and responsibilities of the teams, and funding models for IT departments will influence key early design decisions, mitigate risks associated with your project, and help your project successfully navigate a path to success.

IT Organization Model

IT organizations are typically structured to support the ongoing activities of the organization. Employee roles and responsibilities, budgets, and skills are carefully planned and grouped into teams based on your organization's overall enterprise IT strategy. Though common roles exist in most IT departments, the teams and organizational charts differ widely from business to business.

Table 2-3 describes the most common IT organization models.

TABLE 2-3: SharePoint 2010 Considerations Based on an IT Organization Model

IT ORGANIZATION MODEL	CONSIDERATIONS
Centralized model	All or most IT services are consolidated and controlled by a central department. Budget planning and forecasting is controlled by a central IT team.
	In some cases, this model may result in a platform-oriented approach, centered on IT and risk-mitigation concerns.
	Other concerns are the lack of well-developed business relationships necessary to engage and drive out real business requirements.
Federated model	The IT organization maintains a central IT function responsible for coordination of key activities, but additionally devolves various IT functions to corporate IT within a division.
	The more autonomous each division, the more difficult it may be to coordinate activities from a central IT department to the corresponding divisional IT departments. This can lead to rogue SharePoint solutions and duplicated investment.
Outsourced models	The business outsources various aspects of its IT operations to a specialist infrastructure or application vendor. All activities related to the deployment of new hardware, or maintenance and support of new applications, require input and involvement from the outsourcer to implement successfully. In some cases, all stages of your SharePoint project take longer to complete. This is because of a risk-averse and process-driven nature. The internal organizational structure of large infrastructure vendors tends to have many independent specialist teams that must be utilized in a SharePoint project.

Each model has its advantages and disadvantages, all of which will influence your SharePoint portal project.

IT Team Model

A wide variety of skills and roles are required to successfully architect, design, develop, test, deploy, maintain, and optimize. Table 2-4 describes common teams with which various roles in your SharePoint team will interact. Depending on your IT department model, these teams may be an internal team (centralized model), a central team in central IT (federated model), or an external infrastructure or application vendor (outsource model) embedded in your business.

TABLE 2-4: SharePoint 2010 Considerations Based on a Team Model

IT TEAM MODEL	CONSIDERATIONS
Infrastructure team	The infrastructure team is responsible for managing the life cycle of hardware in your data centers. Their responsibilities differ from business to business. In large businesses, many activities are split into dedicated teams. Your SharePoint project will need support from this team to perform a number of activities. The common SharePoint project "touch points" are hardware (physical or virtual), hardware procurement, data center management, network, monitoring, backup and availability, infrastructure optimization, SharePoint configuration, disaster recovery, and hardware or software load balancing.
	To improve agility and ability to respond rapidly to business requirements, businesses may make the infrastructure team responsible for the "boxes and wires," while anything from the operating system layer and above is the responsibility of a dedicated SharePoint team. This is definitely recommended, because SharePoint requires specialist knowledge and focused attention to manage the day-to-day tasks required to manage the SharePoint platform.
Business end user support team	This team is often a central team responsible for all solutions in your business. A first-line support team logs incidents accurately, and responds to issues within its capability to solve. Second-line support handles escalated issues according to severity, and based on the SLAs in place. Third-line support handles escalated issues, and requires specialist SharePoint expertise to resolve. These resources are typically in a dedicated SharePoint support team.
Business solutions team	This varies from business to business, and the activities and makeup of this team are largely driven by the activities and priorities of the business and IT department. This team consists of architects, analysts, developers, testers, and other business-solution specialists.

IT TEAM MODEL	CONSIDERATIONS
	Most SharePoint projects start in the business solutions team. As the business understanding of the impact of SharePoint matures, a dedicated SharePoint team is set up to handle business requirements for custom SharePoint solutions.
IT Portfolio Management Organization (PMO)	This team is responsible for project management, investment decisions, project funding management, and benefits realization from technology investments. This team is closely aligned to the design and strategy authority within the IT department, and to key business partners (internal customers) within the business.
Architecture and strategy team	This team is the technical design-and-strategy authority within the IT department. They work closely with the business to assess strategic business plans and needs with an IT vision. They define the IT requirements and internal practices required to realize the business vision. Key outputs from this team are policies, operational procedures, guidelines, systems life-cycle planning, capital planning and investment control, architecture, future strategy, and realization of benefits.
Business data team	This team is responsible for managing the data of the business. They manage databases, integrate data from internal and external sources, and are often involved in mining of data in business intelligence solutions.
	SharePoint 2010 has a plethora of content, service, and configuration databases. SharePoint database management requires a deep knowledge of how SQL Server functions, how it interacts with the underlying disk and network infrastructure, and how it can be optimized.
	Although it is preferred to have specialist database resources within a dedicated SharePoint support team, the cost and other business responsibilities of these resources often prohibit this. To mitigate the risk of database performance degradation, a close working relationship with the database team is required.
	"Content" databases can contain many terabytes of data. In larger implementations, remote blob storage may be implemented to offload large files from the database to lower cost storage. Third-party solutions exist to improve the experience. Chapter 16 discusses these requirements in more detail.
	SharePoint houses business-critical data, and many options exist to ensure business continuity in the event of failure at the database level. Chapter 21 discusses this in more detail.
Network and security teams	The network and security teams manage the network infrastructure, connectivity, users, and security measures (such as firewalls, threat and vulnerability identification, and resolution).

continues

TABLE 2-4 *(continued)*

IT TEAM MODEL	CONSIDERATIONS	
	This team is involved in the network-impact assessment the SharePoint solution will have on the business. Because SharePoint is a centralized solution, the team may recommend improvements to network links to maintain a solid user experience.	
SharePoint team	The SharePoint team consists of a number of resources, depending on the business. These include analysts, architects, development and testing teams, "IT Pros" responsible for managing required day-to-day activities, project management, and business impact and engagement specialists.	
	It is strongly recommended not to split the resources in this team into disparate teams because this may result in decreased business and technical agility, decreased capability to respond, and increased lack of ownership (which results in "passing the buck" between teams).	
	In federated and outsourced business models (especially in large businesses), it is not always possible to have a single team, because divisions of the business may have many thousands of users under the control of local IT teams. In all models, a clearly defined governance model is required to control and manage the responsibilities of each team, and manage the types of changes that can be made by each team. This avoids paralysis and total lockdown of the SharePoint platform by one team, which results in a decreased capability to respond to business needs and to end users.	

IT Funding Model

"Money makes the world go 'round," and the same statement applies to SharePoint projects. A significant investment is required, not only from a licensing and hardware perspective, but from the perspective of ongoing business solutions, support, and business change. Understanding the funding model in large organizations is important to garnering the financial support needed to make your SharePoint project a success.

Additionally, understanding the funding model enables you to predict how divisions will cater (or not cater) to these costs. This enables you to overcome obstacles related to funding earlier on.

Funding models are largely dependent on the IT organization model and the team model within your IT organization. It must be said that funding models can differ greatly from business to business, and largely depend on the business IT portfolio.

Table 2-5 describes common IT department and project funding models.

TABLE 2-5: SharePoint 2010 Considerations Based on an IT Funding Model

IT FUNDING MODEL	CONSIDERATIONS
No-chargeback (centralized) model	This model relies on a budget as part the central planning-and-approval process for your business to decide on the IT department's budget. This provides a centralized approach to funding for the entire business.
	From a SharePoint perspective, depending on the size of the business, this provides a better position to negotiate better licensing deals from Microsoft, and enables you to get better value from your infrastructure and application partners.
	One of the disadvantages of this model is that users and business divisions may consume IT resources unequally, and may not be aware of the impact of their actions on the IT department.
Metric-based chargeback model	This is similar to the no-chargeback model in that a budget is planned and approved using a central planning-and-approval process. What differs is that IT department funding is split between business divisions based on a non-IT metric (such as percentage of revenue).
Direct chargeback model	This model allocates costs for each service back to the business unit. This approach makes it more difficult to implement business-wide solutions such as SharePoint, and may lead to silos, duplicated hardware, and potentially increased licensing costs for the business.
Federated model	In a federated business model, a central IT team is funded to manage enterprise IT initiatives and core systems (such as e-mail, telephony, and network and hardware infrastructure). Within each of the key business divisions, divisional IT teams are responsible for funding their specific IT requirements.
	Using this model, the central IT team will play a significant part in designing and promoting enterprise-wide solutions.
	In some cases, the central IT team is more used to dealing with infrastructure-related projects, and may feel uneasy about entering the application space using SharePoint technology.
	On the other side, divisional IT teams may feel threatened and resistant to a centrally managed and governed SharePoint solution. Strong leadership and business engagement is required to involve key stakeholders from both central IT and divisional IT teams to ensure that your SharePoint project is a success.

IT Development Model

The IT development model governs how your business will approach each project. This differs from project to project, and depends on a multitude of factors, such as the skills available, as well as the capability and maturity of the internal IT team to architect, develop, and implement the proposed solution. Common IT development models include the following:

➤ *In house* — In this case, the entire project is developed internally using a combination of permanent and contracted personnel. This requires sufficient knowledge of the SharePoint platform.

➤ *Partnership* — The project is developed using a combination of in-house resources, but primed by a deeply knowledgeable Microsoft Partner.

➤ *Outsourced* — The project is developed on behalf of the customer by the infrastructure or application partner. Although the customer is involved in defining the requirements in the early stages, and performing user acceptance testing, little involvement is required during the development, testing, and deployment life cycle.

A key point to make is that no matter the development model, if you do not engage and involve both the IT department and representatives within your organization from the start, you will have issues with winning over the business and gaining their acceptance of your portal solution.

REVIEWING THE TECHNOLOGY LANDSCAPE

The technology landscape involves understanding the SharePoint 2010 ecosystem, your organization's current enterprise architecture and strategy, your infrastructure, and your existing portal and collaboration solutions.

It also provides a number of clues to the associated risks and issues that may affect the outcome of a deployment of a new technology in your organization. Failure to identify risks early on can be fatal, because these become issues that you must overcome to deploy SharePoint successfully.

Understanding the SharePoint 2010 Ecosystem

The SharePoint 2010 ecosystem is a combination of the various Microsoft product and engineering groups, Microsoft Partners adding value to the SharePoint platform, a strong SharePoint community of able like-minded individuals supporting new and existing deployments, and, most importantly, customers and business professionals exploiting these technologies to improve various aspects of their business operations. This section provides more on each of the key groups in the SharePoint 2010 ecosystem.

Microsoft

Microsoft has released four versions of SharePoint. Each release occurs in three- to four-year cycles, with early betas available to provide early insight to the key changes and improvements.

Microsoft has catered to various deployment and licensing models to help businesses of all sizes use these technologies, hosted in the cloud or on-premise in your data center.

Microsoft product, marketing, evangelism, and technical education teams provide detailed information required to train your staff. SharePoint conferences worldwide are supported, online services are available to Partners and customers, and e-learning tools are available on the Microsoft Developer Network (MSDN) and Microsoft TechNet websites.

Microsoft provides certification programs to ensure that technical personnel you employ are suitably qualified to manage your SharePoint environments. The highest level of certification is the Microsoft Certified Master (MCM) program for SharePoint, which involves intense training onsite in Redmond with the best specialists in the field.

Microsoft provides great support for SharePoint technologies through the Microsoft support and incident-management program. Premier Field Engineers (PFEs) are available to assist and resolve a wide variety of issues occurring in your SharePoint environment. Additionally, the Microsoft Services division provides dedicated support engineers (DSEs) to embed in your team.

From an architectural, design, and development perspective, the Microsoft Services division often works together with customers to implement groundbreaking solutions for customers. They also provide technical quality assurance (QA) services to reduce and mitigate risks associated with developing and implementing SharePoint solutions.

Microsoft Partners

Microsoft Partners are independent software vendors (ISVs), and are completely focused on helping customers deploy great solutions using the SharePoint platform.

Microsoft Partners come in many flavors. Examples of the specialist areas provided by Microsoft Partners include infrastructure, development, testing, and niche feature areas. Examples include records management specialists, workflow specialists, and search specialists.

Keep in mind that every project boils down to the individuals doing the work. From a customer perspective, to reduce your risk, ensure that you assess the capabilities of the individuals provided by the Microsoft Partner. Be sure to ask for curriculum vitae (CV) for candidates, and review their SharePoint project history.

Another form of Microsoft Partner is those who provide value-add extensions or third-party add-ons for the Microsoft platform. These partners unleash their creative energy to take SharePoint to the next level. Some of these solutions may be focused on infrastructure management and tooling, while others may drastically improve the workflow and reporting capabilities available to end users in an organization.

SharePoint Community

The SharePoint community is the most amazing community to be a part of. It has grown exponentially over the years, initially through blogging, but more recently through social media technologies such as Twitter, LinkedIn, and Facebook.

Additionally, Microsoft supports a number of community-based sites where business and technical professionals can answer simple and complex questions. Examples include `http://sharepoint .microsoft.com` (business-orientated), `http://social.msdn.microsoft.com/` (for developers), and `http://social.technet.microsoft.com/` (for IT professionals).

Microsoft recognizes and rewards individual contributions to SharePoint using the Most Valued Professional (MVP) program. A number of MVPs exist, and are very valuable members to have on your team. For example, Andrew Connell provides brilliant advice and guidance on building publishing sites, and Spence Harbar contributes fantastic infrastructure knowledge and lessons learned while using and implementing SharePoint 2010.

It is important to distinguish between the MVP award program and the Microsoft Certified Master (MCM). MVP awards go to individuals who contribute significantly to the SharePoint community. Although almost all SharePoint MVPs have exceptional technical talent, keep in mind that this is a community award for contribution to the community. It is not equivalent to the MCM training, where individuals have been rigorously trained, tested, and certified to be competent by Microsoft at its headquarters in Redmond, Washington.

The SharePoint community has reached a crucial milestone and tipping point, in that it is now self-organizing. A ton of community activities occur across the world. Examples include www .sharepointsaturday.org and www.sharepointbestpractices.com conferences, to name a few.

Customers and Business Professionals

Customers and business professionals are the lifeblood of the SharePoint community. They use SharePoint on a day-to-day basis. A number of sites exist to assist them in the exploitation of SharePoint in the day-to-day business activities. A good example is www.endusersharepoint.com.

Understanding Your Enterprise Architecture and Strategy

An up-to-date, overarching IT architecture and strategy provides evidence of a coherent plan for all IT systems of an organization. Though it is not always possible, engage with your enterprise architecture team to ensure that your SharePoint design and architecture is aligned to their vision and requirements.

Microsoft provides an in-depth article of the top four enterprise-architecture methodologies in use today. As a SharePoint architect, you should familiarize yourself with these methodologies, and understand how your SharePoint architecture and strategy supports your enterprise architecture. See the following MSDN article at http://msdn.microsoft.com/en-us/library/bb466232.aspx for more information.

Deploying business-wide solutions requires support and leadership from your enterprise architecture team. They are the design authority that all business teams must follow in the implementation and adoption of new technology.

Understanding Your Existing Infrastructure

The SharePoint 2010 platform relies on infrastructure and software already deployed in your organization. Researching the following areas will help you better understand the infrastructure available in your business:

> ➤ *Data center* — Your data center is used to host the hardware used by your SharePoint solution. Does the data center have sufficient rack space and enough power for a SharePoint farm?

➤ *Network* — Network-related issues severely affect the overall SharePoint end-user experience. Ensure that you evaluate the current network topology, latency between users and your data center, network access to external users through endpoint protection products, concurrent bandwidth usage versus total bandwidth available, and average and peak load for each office location.

➤ *Identity management* — What identity-management software does your business use? Are these technologies managed, maintained, and in a healthy state?

➤ *Monitoring* — Does your IT team use monitoring technologies (for example, Microsoft System Center Suite) to manage and respond to issues with existing hardware and software?

➤ *Communication* — What communications (telephony, e-mail, business instant messaging) technologies are used in the organization? What is the state of these technologies? Are you using a Microsoft technology suite, or a competing vendor's suite?

➤ *Virtualization* — A growing trend in businesses is to use virtualization technologies to reduce costs and get more value out of existing hardware. Does the virtualization team have mature processes, from inception to destruction, in the management of virtual machines? Are there established processes for moving virtual machines between hosts?

➤ *Database* — Do you have a dedicated team to manage your databases? SharePoint 2010 uses a plethora of databases. SQL management and optimization skills are crucial to the continued performance of a SharePoint 2010 environment.

Failure to understand the stability and maturity of underlying supporting infrastructure may cause issues in deploying SharePoint 2010 to your business. Chapter 3 describes these technologies in more detail.

Understanding Your Existing Portal Solutions

A valuable lesson learned during this author's time at Microsoft Consulting Services was to look at the state and adoption levels of existing portal technologies in a business, as well as the maturity, skills, and state of the IT department to handle new portal solution implementations.

For example, in a previous project, the customer was aiming to deploy a "greenfield" SharePoint environment. Numerous issues became evident, some of which related to internal skills, lack of mature IT processes, and maintenance issues with other internal systems. Other issues related to a lack of a clearly defined overall portal solution strategy to govern individual business unit portal solutions.

As you can imagine, all these issues stacked up during the course of the project to present blocking issues in deploying new technology. Therefore, it is important that you take into account the following considerations:

➤ *Understand your existing portal footprint* — What collaboration and portal solutions have been set up? What features do your end users value? Are these technologies centralized, distributed, or geo-distributed? Are existing portal solutions planned and governed? Are there a number of "rogue" deployments? Keep in mind, this point is aimed at understanding your implementation of portal intranet and collaboration platforms.

➤ *Underlying portal technologies* — Has your organization adopted a single portal technology vendor, or are a number of different vendor technologies in use in your organization? What is the state of these portal environments? Is the technology out of date? What are the licensing, support, development, and maintenance costs for each of these environments?

➤ *Content migration* — Is there a requirement to migrate data from one or more legacy portal environments to your new portal solution? Do you require third-party migration tools to migrate this content to your SharePoint 2010 environment?

➤ *Level of customization* — What level of customization has been applied to existing portal solutions? Is there an expectation that custom capabilities will be migrated to your new portal environment?

➤ *Level of politicization* — IT departments consist of people who may have strong opinions and bias toward particular vendor technology suites. Understand the existing portal-related technology investments to make wise decisions in the deployment of new portal technologies. A good deployment of a specific SharePoint 2010 portal feature set will drive adoption and win over the skeptics.

Take time to understand existing portal technology solutions in your organization. New portal technologies will not solve inherent business and portal governance problems. Ignoring previous experience and the lessons learned from these environments can be fatal to a SharePoint 2010 deployment, because similar issues will appear in these new environments.

REVIEWING THE LEGAL LANDSCAPE

Organizations face an ever-increasing and complex legal landscape. Often, technical designers are not aware of the regulatory and compliance obligations they must cater to in the deployment of portal solutions in your organization. Failure to take the legal landscape into consideration increases your exposure to legal risks, financial penalties, and end-user productivity. This section covers the common legal laws and areas you may need to consider.

Disability Discrimination Laws

Disability discrimination laws are civil laws that prohibit discrimination based on disability. These laws make it unlawful to discriminate against people with respect to their disabilities in relation to employment.

From a SharePoint 2010 perspective, this translates to complying with industry standards of the World Wide Web Consortium (W3C). They have published a series of Web Content Accessibility Guidelines (WCAG) 1.0 or 2.0. All requirements are grouped into three priority levels. You can find more information on WCAG at `www.w3.org/TR/WCAG20/`.

Microsoft adopted WCAG 2.0 to make SharePoint 2010 level AA compliant. The article at `http://blogs.msdn.com/b/sharepoint/archive/2010/03/09/accessibility-and-sharepoint-2010.aspx` provides more information on SharePoint 2010 compliance.

Examples of laws in the United States include the Americans with Disabilities Act (1990). In the United Kingdom, the Disability Discrimination Act (1995) and Equality Act (2010) exist.

Freedom of Information Laws

Various countries have provided *freedom of information laws* (also known as *sunshine laws*) to allow for full or partial disclosure of unreleased information from public bodies. Examples include the Freedom of Information Act in the United States and United Kingdom.

Facilitating requests for information can be costly, because it may involve a number of internal requests to different departments. Fortunately, SharePoint provides a number of out-of-the-box capabilities to manage these types of requests.

A site can be set up to manage each case, parallel workflows can be set up to manage and monitor internal parties' responses, search capabilities can be used to surface information required to handle each case, and security and controls can be applied to information returned by each party.

Personal Data Privacy Laws

As described by Wikipedia, *"Information privacy or data privacy is the relationship between collection and dissemination of data, technology, the public expectation of privacy, and the legal and political issues surrounding them."*

Personally Identifiable Information (PII) refers to information that can be used to uniquely identify, contact, or locate a single person. These concerns apply especially where information is stored in an electronic format.

Large organizations usually maintain strict corporate policies that govern what information can be retained, what information can be used, and what information can be shared with third parties.

In some countries, this is strictly governed, and clear laws exist to regulate this area. Examples include the European Union (EU directive 95/46/EC) and the United Kingdom (UK Data Protection Act). Other countries (such as the United States) have a set of laws that indirectly refer and cater to information privacy. Some of these laws only seem to apply within a state. For example, California passed a law called the Online Privacy Protection Act. Although many bills have been proposed, and although the United States Constitution's Fourth Amendment indirectly protects individual's right to privacy, no single law exists to control and regulate the use of PII.

From a SharePoint perspective, if you are architecting any solution that will maintain PII information, you should seek to ensure that your solution complies with the policies set out by the legal department of the organization.

Electronic Records Management Standards and Compliance

Records management refers to the management of records of your organization from the time they are created to the time they are disposed of or deleted in compliance with regulatory and legal requirements of the countries in which your organization operates. Many laws and regulations have been enacted in different countries to govern and regulate the compliance of business activities.

In the United States, Department of Defense (DoD) *5015.2-STD* has become the de facto standard for electronic record management solutions. From a Microsoft perspective, the product team successfully certified SharePoint 2007. As of this writing, one or two Partner solutions that use SharePoint 2010 have passed certification.

In the United Kingdom and Europe, MoReq2 describes model requirements for the management of electronic records. Another internationally recognized standard is ISO 15489.

SharePoint 2010 provides many records management features that can be used to comply with the laws applicable to your country. Chapter 32 provides in-depth detail on records management functionality provided in SharePoint 2010.

Corporate Rules and Regulations

The *Sarbanes Oxley (SOX) Act (2002)* provides civil and criminal penalties to ensure publicly owned companies comply with the regulation of financial practices, such as auditing and finance disclosure, and corporate governance. The act is administered by the Securities and Exchange Commission (SEC).

From a SharePoint perspective, complying with SOX entails ensuring that records are not destroyed, altered, or falsified in any way. It entails ensuring financial records are retained for a period of time before being disposed of, and the types of records that need to be stored.

SEC 17a-3 and 17a4 are rules and regulations that govern exchange member, broker, and dealer organizations. They define the types of records that must be created and retained, and the length of time for which they must be retained.

Many other rules and regulations may affect your SharePoint environment. Two final examples include the *Health Insurance Portability and Accountability Act (HIPAA)* (which guarantees consumers access to their healthcare and protects the privacy of their information) and Federal Drug Administration (FDA) regulation (which governs the use of electronic data and electronic signatures in the pharmaceutical industry). All data modifications must be traceable.

Basel II mandates specific ways of accessing and mitigating operational risks for banks. The regulation establishes rigorous requirements for a bank to hold capital reserves appropriate to the risk they are exposed to.

Finance Standards

Other important financial principles and regulations include International Financial Reporting Standards (IFRS), and the regulation of the financial systems by the Financial Services Authority (FSA) in the United Kingdom.

From a SharePoint perspective, it is the ideal place to surface compliance and risk information as dashboards, support records management activities, and reduce the cost of implementing processes to ensure the compliance of your organization.

Export Control Regulations

Export control regulations are usually found in organizations that work in specialist areas, or in organizations that manufacture and produce military solutions for the government. Export control regulations serve to ensure national security, foreign policy, and economic and technological competitiveness goals are upheld.

Examples in United States are the International Traffic in Military Arms (ITAR) legislation and the Export Administration Regulations (EAR). In the United Kingdom, the Export Control Act and the Official Secrets Act control the dissemination of sensitive information (such as the design of military equipment).

From a SharePoint perspective, developing solutions for defense and government organizations requires much more up-front design work to cater to strong governance, classification, and control of content, compared to other portal solutions.

The cost of legal and regulatory compliance differs widely, depending on the level of compliance required. Keep in mind that compliance requirements affect the productivity of your information workers, and increase the amount of training required. As a SharePoint architect, always attempt to provide simple, productive end-user experiences. This will win over end users and drive support for solutions your team delivers to the organization.

REVIEWING THE INFORMATION LANDSCAPE

We live in an age where organizations use information and corporate knowledge to respond nimbly and adapt quickly to market forces. In today's world, the time available to respond and react has diminished. Survival and continued relevance in today's marketplace requires having access to the right people, knowledge, and information to make informed choices and decisions.

Table 2-6 details key areas to research to understand the information landscape of your organization.

TABLE 2-6: Understanding the Information Landscape of Your Organization

INFORMATION LANDSCAPE	RESEARCH CONSIDERATIONS
Information locations	Review the common file storage locations. Are they distributed in regional office file shares, in central file shares, or portal environments? Build up a picture of the locations of your business-critical information.
	Assess the percentage of content that exists only on employees' workstations and laptops. This percentage is a hidden metric that you can use as a driver for your portal solution. The lower the percentage, the more corporate information is retained in your business. Retained corporate knowledge is a key driver in many organizations.
File formats	What are the common file formats in use in your business? As part of your research, patterns will emerge on the common types of files in use. These will guide you in providing solutions that are best suited to managing these types of information.

continues

TABLE 2-6 *(continued)*

INFORMATION LANDSCAPE	RESEARCH CONSIDERATIONS	
	Not all file formats are suitable to your portal environment. Focus on the file formats you plan to support in your portal environment. Examples of files that may not be suitable are very large CAD drawings.	
Corpus of data statistics	What is the average file size for each file type, and how many files are stored in each of the identified locations? This type of information will enable you to identify which files you might migrate. Large files (such as access databases) may skew your findings for a storage location.	
Structure	How structured is your data? Examples of structured information may be content stored in databases, whereas unstructured information may be a 100-page research Word document, or a very large PowerPoint presentation that mostly contains images. All contain valuable information, but structured data is easier to incorporate in your SharePoint solution.	
	Structure includes the folder structure in place to organize content. This folder structure provides a glimpse of how the business organizes and accesses content. The folder structure hints at common business entities. For example, the folder hierarchy Projects ➪ Client Name ➪ Engagement Name provides clear information on how an organization manages and collaborates for key entities in its business. Chapter 26 provides more detail on how you can design your SharePoint solution to collaborate using these business entities.	
Enterprise taxonomies and structured metadata	*Metadata* is information that further describes and classifies content. A good example is the author property of a file. Is content in your business consistently tagged with meta-information? Is a controlled "top-down" taxonomy or uncontrolled "ground-up" folksonomy used to tag this content? Metadata is useful in that it helps you to understand how information could be organized, assists business professionals with information retrieval, and identifies similar information in your business's information landscape.	
	SharePoint 2010 provides new capabilities to manage and support taxonomies and folksonomies. The most difficult part of introducing this capability is not the technical aspect, but the business aspect. Enterprise-wide classification and labeling hierarchies are difficult to model for a number of reasons. Organizational politics, detailed research, and the constant changing business landscape all are factors that will influence the success of your enterprise taxonomy. Specialist vendors can help you define a good starting point model. However, factor in dedicated resources to continually improve and maintain your enterprise taxonomies.	
Dynamism	*Dynamism* deals with how often the same information or file is updated. Dynamism is important because it shows where information worker activity is occurring in your organization.	

INFORMATION LANDSCAPE	RESEARCH CONSIDERATIONS
"File age" and "last access"	*"File age"* defines how old content is, and *"last access"* determines when it was last used. Documents written five years ago may not be as relevant as documents written in the past three months. Knowing the average age and the last time content was accessed helps you evaluate whether content may be stale and is no longer needed.
Control	What controls are in place for various types of identified content? Are strict retention policies in use? If not, should there be? Are you compliant with the regulatory and legal laws of the market in which your organization operates? Do you require government, security, company markings, or barcodes for specific content?
Content ownership	People move to other departments, leave the organization altogether, or a number of business units or departments are re-organized. What happens to the management and ownership of the information and corporate knowledge?
	This is a really painful issue for any SharePoint team to deal with. Stale content cannot be deleted without owner approval. More importantly, content with no owner is very difficult to migrate to the next version of SharePoint, because no one is available to assess the relevance of the content. A strong recommendation is to tag all content with a business owner at the time of upload. This provides your team with a business, department, or project that can make decisions about the content three to five years down the line. Tagging content using an individual will not work because the individual may have left the business.
	A good SharePoint architect will design a solution that caters for "now" *and* three to five years' worth of business change. A not-so-good SharePoint architect will only cater for today's business structure. The impact is the cost to the organization to fix these issues, the time to address these issues, and the failed opportunity to use this budget in the pursuit of meaningful improvements to your portal environment.

Information and retained corporate knowledge is vital to the long-term success of your organization. Be sure you understand your organization's information landscape.

REVIEWING THE END-USER LANDSCAPE

People are the lifeblood of any organization. They perform the functions and tasks that an organization relies on and requires in the pursuit of a collective outcome. Understanding people and end-users' attributes, their needs, tasks, and desired user experience is important to the success of your portal solution.

Factors Influencing the End-User Environment

Table 2-7 details key areas that are important to understand about the end-user landscape of your business.

TABLE 2-7: Understanding the End-User Landscape of Your Organization

END USER LANDSCAPE	CONSIDERATIONS	
Organizational structure	Your SharePoint design should cater to users who have a great deal of interaction, as well as users who operate only within a team.	
	The organizational chart is a useful tool to help determine the business areas, stakeholders, and hegemonies within the business. In difficult political environments, this helps you make strategic portal decisions. For example, it may be necessary to focus on a particular business group to demonstrate what can be done using SharePoint 2010. This can then be used to encourage and win over other business areas.	
Office locations	The location of users is very important to understand. Are they centralized in a single office building, or decentralized to a number of regional areas? Are users located in a number of countries? Does this introduce the need for multilingual support?	
	As soon as you have more than one office location, you must begin to think about the capability of your underlying network to support a centralized portal solution.	
Audiences	What are the key audiences in your business? Users may work in one area of the business, but could be aligned and contribute to other areas of the business. Start off by identifying the common functions, job roles, and virtual communities that will help your people collaborate across the boundaries of their organizational structure.	
	Recognizing that most employees belong to more than one audience is critical to the design of your SharePoint solution. People want to be a part of something bigger, want to contribute and make a difference. Recognizing these motivations, providing the tools and incentives, as well as rewarding collaborative behavior, is key to cross-pollination of ideas, and removal of redundant tasks and duplication of effort.	
Organizational demographics	Your SharePoint solution must take into account the types of people in your organization today and, more importantly, the type of talent you want to attract. Age groups and different generational cohorts (such as veterans, Baby Boomers, Generation X, Generation Y, and Generation Z) have distinct values and traits. Other demographics include gender, race, income, and disabilities. Focus your design on the people in your business, not on the latest "cool" technology.	

END USER LANDSCAPE	CONSIDERATIONS
	Organizations that contain veterans and Baby Boomers may not respond to new technology as well as an organization containing "Generation X, Y, Z" individuals.
	Organizations that have (on average) extremely long average employee service records may not respond as well to change as organizations where staff turnover is greater and people are comfortable with, accept, and handle change well. Cater to this in your business change and engagement plan.
Information-seeking behaviors	Identifying how people find information in your organization enables you to plan portal services that they recognize and use consistently. This is where SharePoint really excels. It integrates deep scalable search capabilities into your portal environment to provide a seamless experience to your end users. No other enterprise search technology can match the level of integration SharePoint provides out of the box.
Current and desired user experience	Identify how people work today and what improvements will benefit them. Do your users want a formal, rigid experience, or an informal and social interactive experience?
	Do users expect a consistent look and feel, or are they comfortable with a number of different user experiences, each focused on providing a particular solution?
	Most SharePoint deployments adopt a single brand and consistent style across all sites. Other SharePoint sites may be designed to appear completely different. Exceptions to the single brand need to be governed to ensure key elements of your user experience are applied.
	For example, internally, Microsoft provides a corporate intranet that has a different look and feel than the Microsoft consulting services client engagement site. Users recognize and identify the experience based on the internal brand of each of these sites.
	Do users expect a great deal of flexibility to design their own sites, or do they expect these solutions to come from a central team of experts?
	SharePoint 2010 provides a number of options to end users to extend their own sites. These options include user (sandboxed) solutions, SharePoint Designer, and, if configured, the designer role in each site provides access to the master page and page layouts to modify the look and feel of the site.
Level of interaction and personalization	How personal should users' experiences be? Do users expect one-way, top-down information flow, or the capability to comment, respond, interact, and influence?

continues

TABLE 2-7 *(continued)*

END USER LANDSCAPE	CONSIDERATIONS	
	Some organizations prefer a rigid communication structure with little or no feedback loop from end users. Other organizations encourage and provide mechanisms for users to comment and provide feedback on formal communication articles.	
	For example, at a large global insurance firm, most of the board blogged on key aspects of the organization. Employees read and responded regularly. The number of comments on various blog posts was astounding. Having a senior board person read and respond to your comments fosters communication and breaks down the barriers between senior management and information workers.	
	SharePoint 2010 provides the capability for each user to personalize the experience of each page. If enabled, this helps end users tweak their experiences based on their needs and preferences.	
Skills and training	A big part of any SharePoint deployment is about ensuring that end users will be able to take advantage of and exploit the SharePoint platform for the benefit of the business. Failure to provide decent training slows adoption, results in end-user frustration, and can appear to the end user as yet another IT department solution that does not understand the organization.	
	A "help" publishing portal site can be set up relatively easily, and your team can "grow" the content, by using out-of-the-box content editing and publishing features. Alternatively, SharePoint training providers sell prepackaged training content that can be incorporated into your SharePoint environment.	

Tools of the Information Worker

Information workers and end users rely on the tools (namely the hardware, software, and network infrastructure) of your organization. In today's fast-paced business environment outdated hardware, software, and slow networks affect the productivity of your information workers.

The hidden cost of lost productivity is considerable. Common examples include corrupted office files, reboots of computers, long file download times, and unsuccessfully searching for specific files or information. These examples result in small increments of lost time per user, and cumulatively the cost to your business is considerable.

Table 2-8 details the key tools of the information worker.

TABLE 2-8: Understanding the Key Information Worker Tools

INFORMATION WORKER TOOL	CONSIDERATIONS
Hardware	A user relies on existing hardware and software to interact with the rest of the organization. Outdated hardware directly contributes to lost productivity.
	Most organizations provide remote working capabilities to end users. In a permanently connected world, this capability is essential to enable users to complete tasks at home and in other locations. A number of hardware and software solutions exist to enable this capability in your organization.
	Smartphones, slates, and tablet-type devices have become essential tools. Their form factor, great end-user experience, and fantastic "App" ecosystem will result in a slew of new applications that support working with information held in SharePoint 2010.
Browser	The browser is your end user's "window to the world." SharePoint 2010 supports a number of browsers. You can find a full list at `http://technet.microsoft.com/en-us/library/cc263526.aspx`.
	Flash and Silverlight technologies enable rich end-user experiences through the browser. With its new client-side object model, SharePoint 2010 provides significant new support for enabling these types of end-user experiences.
Office technologies	Office technologies (such as Microsoft Word, Excel, PowerPoint, and Outlook) are key tools in any information worker environment. SharePoint 2010 has integrated the Ribbon into all pages of the portal environment. To provide a consistent user experience, ensure that Office 2010 or, at a minimum, Office 2007 is deployed.
	Each version of Microsoft Office provides varying degrees of integration and support for SharePoint portal capabilities. The later the Office version, the more capability and integration provided to your users. More information is provided by Microsoft at `http://go.microsoft.com/fwlink/?LinkId=209803`.
	Be careful when experimenting with non–Microsoft Office technologies. Remember, your aim is to provide a *seamless* office and portal environment to end users of your organization. While your aim may be noble (for example, driving costs down or supporting Open Source software), your end users may suffer, and the hidden cost in supporting a number of patched-together solutions will rise.

continues

TABLE 2-8 *(continued)*

INFORMATION WORKER TOOL	CONSIDERATIONS	
E-mail, calendaring, contacts, task management	Microsoft Outlook is the best e-mail client on the market. It provides a rich client interface, with many capabilities and access points. Key capabilities include "rich" e-mail authoring, advanced calendaring, offline e-mail stores, advanced instant search capabilities, support for records management and compliance tools, information rights management, global and local contacts management, and task management. Key access points include rich client application, browser-based access to support remote working scenarios, and rich device support for a plethora of smartphones on the market.	
	SharePoint 2010 provides support for each of these key workloads. Microsoft Outlook can host and take content offline from a SharePoint 2010 environment. Examples include central calendar synchronization, offline document libraries, tasks lists, contact lists, and the capability to create meeting and document workspace sites from within Outlook. For more information on the deep integration, see `http://office.microsoft.com/en-us/sharepoint-foundation-help/synchronize-sharepoint-2010-content-with-outlook-2010-HA101881295.aspx`.	
	For environments that do not use Microsoft Outlook, and instead opt for other clients (such as Lotus Notes), or alternatively opt for non-Microsoft cloud-based e-mail providers, it becomes your responsibility to understand the key use cases, and maintain a productive experience for your information workers. Plan out what integration your information workers require to work seamlessly between your chosen messaging solution and your chosen portal environment. Failure to do this will result in a poor end-user experience.	
Instant communication	Two key tools that most organizations provide are the capability to host live meetings across a number of locations, and the capability to collaborate using business instant messaging (IM) technologies. Both technologies provide instant communication and collaboration within your business.	
	Microsoft Lync (formerly known as Office Communication Services) can be categorized as a unified communication experience. It caters to IM and presence, audio and video conferencing, and mobile experiences. For more information, see `http://lync.microsoft.com/en-gb/Product/Workloads/Pages/workloads.aspx`.	

INFORMATION WORKER TOOL	CONSIDERATIONS
	SharePoint 2010 supports these technologies by displaying live presence information within the portal experience. For example, you search for a document. In the search results, if presence is enabled, hovering over the author's name will cause a contact card to pop up. A number of communication options are provided to enable you to find out more information about the author, to initiate an e-mail, an IM, as well as an audio or video conversation with the author. If enabled, this experience is pervasive and consistent across all pages in SharePoint.
Note taking	Microsoft OneNote is the often forgotten tool and unsung hero of the Office 2010 suite. Essentially, it manages your rough notes (or a team's rough notes) in a structured way. SharePoint 2010 supports collaborative or team-based notebooks. Once you have uploaded the OneNote file, if you have SharePoint 2010 Office Web Application installed, you can work and annotate the same OneNote file collaboratively with other peers in your organization.
Working offline	Microsoft SharePoint Workspace (formerly known as Microsoft Groove) provides new capabilities to the Microsoft Office 2010 suite. It enables information workers to take SharePoint content offline. It enables real-time synchronization of content on your desktop with SharePoint 2010 document libraries and lists. A key feature that it supports is the capability to edit content offline and synchronize your changes with other users' changes when you are online.
	Microsoft SharePoint Workspace supports rich and secure collaboration environments with suppliers external to your organization. For example, this book uses a peer-to-peer workspace to enable team-based working and to manage individual author contributions. Microsoft SharePoint Workspace is the best choice because it enables peer-to-peer replication of content between authors. Additionally, it is cost-effective because it does not require an expensive server to host the content and authenticate each user.
Business forms	Microsoft InfoPath provides a significant capability to create, manage, and read business or electronic forms. SharePoint 2010 provides deep integration of electronic forms capability. Chapter 31 discusses this in more detail.
	Microsoft supports the saving of InfoPath forms (and all office files) as Adobe PDF read-only files. This technology is a free application provided by Adobe, and is commonly used in the organization to share content in a read-only format.

continues

TABLE 2-8 *(continued)*

INFORMATION WORKER TOOL	CONSIDERATIONS
Information rights management	Information rights management is a persistent file-level technology that uses permissions and authorization to help prevent sensitive information from being printed, forwarded, or copied by unauthorized people. It provides the capability to secure company communication and information. SharePoint 2010 and the Microsoft Office suite deeply integrate information rights capability. For example, e-mail communications can be tagged as "Do Not Forward," thus disabling a recipient's capability to forward the e-mail, and files can be protected to only allow specific individuals access.
Mind mapping	Mindjet MindManager provides a unique capability to structure, organize, and visualize content based on how your brain perceives content. This tool helps overcome "information overload" by enabling information workers to build and retain a visual map or lattice of key ideas and thoughts. MindManager provides a number of collaborative capabilities that integrate into SharePoint and the Microsoft Office suite. For those looking for a more cost-effective mind-mapping tool, XMind currently provides a free and pro version.

All these hardware and software services intimate how forward-thinking an organization is, how well you have adapted to new way of working, and how well you have catered to information workers in your business. Attracting and retaining the best talent involves providing them with the best hardware and software. Today's generation will not accept anything less.

GATHERING ISSUES AND METRICS

Ever hear the phrase, "Fools rush in where angels fear to tread"? This is often the case in the deployment of SharePoint technology. In some cases, businesses deploy SharePoint before truly understanding what problems they are trying to solve. In other cases, the project is overly technology- and feature-centric, resulting in a slew of features the business does not expect or require. Poor adoption and unmet expectations result.

Overcoming issues in your planned deployment requires understanding and quantifying (where possible) issues with existing collaboration and portal technologies. Survey your users, websites, and key stakeholders. Listen to their responses.

Following are some of the questions to ask:

➤ What technologies work in your organization? What areas need improvement, and why?

➤ If current portal technologies have been deployed, what areas of your existing portal site do you use most often, and what areas have become stale or not useful to your job role, and why?

➤ What information can you find easily? What types of information do you struggle to retrieve, and why? How long does it take, on average, to retrieve information when you need it?

➤ Is it easy to find people in your business, or in another area of the business you work for? Is it easy to find people with similar interests and/or job roles to you?

➤ What places do you commonly save your files? How do you share files with other users? Where do you back up files stored on your computer?

Metrics are important to gather on the issues you have ascertained. They provide concrete facts that you can use to develop your business case and portal strategy. For example, if your survey determines that users spend an average of 30 minutes a day searching and finding content, this enables you to quantify what this activity costs your business, and how a particular solution might reduce this cost.

SUMMARY

The enterprise landscape and business information ecology consist of a number of major dimensions that all play a part in the outcome of your SharePoint 2010 design and deployment.

A deep understanding of these business dimensions enables you to design long-lived, well-received solutions. It enables you to make the correct decisions that result in solutions that resonate with key stakeholders of your organization.

Chapter 3 takes a look under the hood at a number of supporting technologies a SharePoint architect must understand.

3

Supporting Technology Knowledge Requirements

By Brian Wilson

In a memorable blog post, Joel Oleson (an ex-Microsoft employee and SharePoint evangelizer) related a story about a question he had been asked by a friend regarding what technologies he worked with in the software industry. Oleson initially responded "SharePoint," but upon reflection, proceeded to explain and describe to his friend all the "hidden" or underlying technologies that must be understood to architect SharePoint solutions successfully. This post highlighted how difficult it must be for new and aspiring SharePoint architects to form a solid understanding and develop the required base level of knowledge to design and architect rock-solid SharePoint solutions.

The SharePoint platform is a cunning and deceptive beast. It shows you the "cheese," draws you in, mesmerizes you, and then starts toying with you, like a cat does with a mouse. It spans and utilizes the breadth and depth of Microsoft (and partner) hardware and software technologies. No other technology is as far-reaching, wide-ranging, or has as many touch points as SharePoint.

What makes it even more interesting is that SharePoint is both an application and a platform. From the application perspective, SharePoint relies on a number of underlying hardware and software technologies (for example, the Windows Server operating system). From the platform perspective, SharePoint supports and encourages custom development on the SharePoint platform, regardless of whether it is developed by an internal development team, or a complex powerful tool developed by a third-party developer or Microsoft Partner.

Because SharePoint 2010 is that big, it is nearly impossible to be an "expert" in every area, and, as a result, many fields of expertise exist. SharePoint user experience design or development experts will differ greatly in their skill sets from a search expert, just as workflow experts will differ greatly from administration and infrastructure-focused experts, and so on.

Furthermore, each area of specialization within SharePoint 2010 requires an understanding and knowledge of the corresponding Microsoft and partner technologies. True experts understand not only the SharePoint 2010 feature, but also the complementary or specialist technologies available, the tradeoffs between them, and which to recommend to the customer.

Each specialty requires "in the field" or "real world" experience to master. The knowledge gained from on-the-job experience in real customer situations separates true experts from the theory-only or product-only based experts. It is all about making the best decision and recommending the best solution that will provide the best result (and hopefully the most value) to the customer. This requires a deep understanding of SharePoint 2010 areas, coupled with a broad and (depending on the area) in-depth knowledge of the complementary and supporting technologies.

This chapter provides an overview of the technologies that support and underpin SharePoint 2010, and the complementary Microsoft and third-party technologies that are commonly used to fill gaps, as well as extend or provide a specific capability or feature to enhance your SharePoint 2010 environment.

This chapter helps you to comprehend what technologies you should understand, actively research, and keep abreast of, based on your area of specialty. The sections in this chapter are grouped as follows:

➤ *Infrastructure technologies* — This section covers the various infrastructure technologies common to most SharePoint 2010 deployments. This includes topics such as the Windows operating system, identity and access, software and hardware load balancing, farm communications and protocols, database, storage, and monitoring technologies, Internet Information Services (IIS), caching, compression and performance, and, finally, virtualization and backup technologies.

➤ *Development technologies* — This section provides an overview of the common development technologies used in most SharePoint 2010 deployments. This includes an overview of the .NET Framework, common development tools, application life cycle management tools, and various code libraries used in SharePoint 2010 development projects.

➤ *Microsoft Office technologies* — This section covers key Office technologies used in large enterprises. This includes the browser, the Microsoft Office 2010 suite, imaging and capture solutions, communications and virtual meeting services, and, finally, offline solutions.

➤ *Complementary third-party technologies* — This section focuses on application extensions, as well as operational and administrative extensions.

 It is extremely important to note that although certain third-party technologies are discussed, the goal isn't to endorse or promote one product over another, but to point out specific use cases and features your business may not realize exist or require in your SharePoint 2010 environment. It is up to you or your business to perform the due diligence and research to determine the suitability of a product before deciding to purchase a particular product.

One last thing to point out about this chapter is that it is written to cover the supporting technology requirements. Though attempts have been made to not discuss overly technical areas, some areas of this chapter get slightly technical to explain key concepts to you. On the whole, the discussion in this chapter has been kept at a fairly high level.

INFRASTRUCTURE TECHNOLOGIES

Let's begin by having a look at the common SharePoint 2010 infrastructure technologies.

Windows Operating System

The Windows Server operating system provides the interface between hardware, virtualized hardware (or virtual machines), and software applications. The Windows operating system provides various features that directly support SharePoint 2010 deployments — for example, the capability to host websites using IIS, or, at a lower level, the capability to support various CPU architectures, drivers, hardware components, and various storage solutions. It automatically provides support for security, management, networking, and administrative features (such as diagnostic tools, as well as event logging and reporting tools).

Windows Server provides other more subtle, yet extremely valuable, capabilities. Most notable is the support for executing unmanaged and managed code, using the .NET Framework, and using the Common Language Runtime (CLR). Other useful features include the capability to host virtual SharePoint deployments using Hyper-V, BranchCache technology for optimization of access to files in regional or geographically dispersed locations.

 For more information on Window Server 2008 (R2) feature sets, see www.microsoft.com/windowsserver2008/en/us/overview.aspx.

SharePoint 2010 requires one of the following operating system versions to host SharePoint 2010 deployments:

➤ 64-bit edition of Windows Server 2008 Standard, Enterprise, Data Center, or Web Server with Service Pack (SP) 2

➤ 64-bit edition of Windows Server 2008 R2 Standard, Enterprise, Data Center, or Web Server, or the 64-bit edition of Windows Server 2008 R2 SP1 Standard, Enterprise, Data Center, or Web Server

The 64-bit operating system and hardware requirements are very important to the scalability of your SharePoint 2010 environment, because this environment can support and use a much larger amount of RAM. Though it may seem simple, the move to 64-bit represents a significant achievement for the SharePoint 2010 product team!

See the TechNet article, "Hardware and software requirements (SharePoint Server 2010)" at http://technet.microsoft.com/en-us/library/cc262485 .aspx *for more information about hardware and software requirements.*

Identity and Access Management Technologies

It is important to understand the "identity flow" in SharePoint 2010, including the following:

➤ The SharePoint 2010 identity architecture

➤ How service accounts and users are authenticated, authorized, and managed

➤ What systems these authentication and authorization systems interface with

➤ The available authentication modes and models

➤ The impact of the chosen authentication model on the development, infrastructure, and end users

"Identity flow" relates to how incoming page requests from users flow from the web front-end (WFE) servers to application servers (or service applications) and the database. It also involves calls to authenticate user accounts with directories (such as Active Directory), calls made within code on behalf of the user to render each web part on the page, and calls made to external systems (such as external databases and web services on different machines).

The SharePoint 2010 identity architecture is based on Windows Identity Foundation (WIF). SharePoint 2010 supports existing identity infrastructure, such as Active Directory, Lightweight Directory Access Protocol (LDAP), SQL, and Web Single Sign-On (SSO), as well as other identity-management systems. It supports multiple authentication methods per SharePoint web application. It enables automatic, secure identity delegation so that both the user identity and service identity that is available in the front end is propagated to the back-end services to use these identities.

It is important to understand the difference between authentication and authorization. *Authentication* is the process that systems use to securely validate a service and user accounts identity. *Authorization* occurs after the user has been securely identified. Authorization assesses the privileges of the service or the user account, and ascertains actions users are authorized to perform.

SharePoint 2010 supports a variety of authentication modes, including the following:

➤ Windows (NTLM, Kerberos, Anonymous, Basic, and Digest)

➤ Forms-based authentication (LDAP, SQL Server database of a custom-developed membership and role provider)

➤ The newly introduced token-based or claims-based authentication mechanism

THE DOUBLE-HOP AUTHENTICATION ISSUE

The *double-hop issue* occurs when a web server is required to impersonate the caller when connecting to resources located on another server. The first hop is from the user's web browser to the web server, and the second hop from the web server to the server containing the resources you are trying to connect. Out-of-the-box examples include Excel Services, RSS feeds, reporting services, and use of external data sources. Implementing claims-based authentication or Kerberos helps to overcome these issues.

There are a number of identity and access areas to research and understand, including the following:

➤ *Plan authentication methods* — A TechNet article at `http://technet.microsoft.com/en-us/library/cc262350.aspx` describes the authentication methods and options in detail.

➤ *Configuring authentication in IIS 7* — To help you understand application pools and how IIS 7 supports authentication, see `http://technet.microsoft.com/en-us/library/cc733010(WS.10).aspx`.

➤ *User Profile and User Profile Synchronization Service* — It is important to understand how the User Profile service and synchronization service interact with source directories such as Active Directory. Check out the article, "User Profile Service Overview," at `http://technet.microsoft.com/en-us/library/ee662538.aspx` and the article, "Plan for Profile Synchronization Service," at `http://technet.microsoft.com/en-us/library/ff182925.aspx`.

➤ *Rational guide to implementing user profile synchronization* — A must-read for this area was written by Spence Harbar and is available at `www.harbar.net/articles/sp2010ups.aspx`.

➤ *Code access security* — To help you understand how the .NET Framework implements and uses code access security to limit the permission set under which managed code in SharePoint 2010 environments run, see `http://msdn.microsoft.com/en-us/library/930b76w0(v=vs.71).aspx`.

➤ *Elevation of privileges* — To help you understand how privileges can be elevated, and the impact of custom code running under elevated privileges, see `http://msdn.microsoft.com/en-us/library/aa543467.aspx`.

➤ *Least privilege* — To help you understand the principle of least privilege and what it means to SharePoint 2010 deployments, read up on Microsoft's trustworthy computing initiative. Also, review and implement your SharePoint 2010 farm using least privileges best practices. See `http://technet.microsoft.com/en-us/library/cc678863.aspx` for a list of accounts used to operate SharePoint 2010.

As with any software system, it is critical that all specialists understand identity and access technologies. Poor implementations make it easier for hackers (both internal and external) to gain access to valuable assets in your SharePoint 2010 environments.

Load-Balancing Technologies

Load-balancing technologies improve the scalability and availability of "mission-critical" services in your business. Load-balancing technologies work by distributing incoming requests over a number of servers to ensure that no individual server is overworked.

This technology is especially suited to "stateless" web applications where each client request made to SharePoint 2010 is a separate transaction. Load-balancing technologies can be grouped into software-based, hardware-based, and "internal" (or built-in) load balancing.

The common software load-balancing technologies include the following:

➤ *Network Load Balancing (NLB)* — NLB is a feature of Windows Server 2008 that enables you to distribute TCP/IP requests over multiple systems to optimize resource utilization, decrease computing time, and ensure system availability. It works by implementing a network load-balancing cluster using Windows Network Load Balancing Manager to configure a "cluster IP" that is represented to users via a specific URL, such as `http://intranet.contoso.com`. One of key issues related to using this technology is the level of intelligence built in to differentiate between servers that are up, and those that are up, but have "hung" or have become incredibly slow.

➤ *DNS Round-Robin* — The DNS Round-Robin option involves utilizing Domain Name System (DNS) to send requests in a "round robin" fashion to enlisted servers. As stated on TechNet, Microsoft did not recommend this technology for SharePoint 2007, and the same applies for SharePoint 2010. One of the reasons why it is not as performant as other technologies is that it requires making changes in DNS whenever a server needs to be taken out of (or put into) rotation. Once the change is made, it isn't immediate. All DNS support, TTL (Time To Live), and the new settings may not have had time to propagate throughout the organization.

Other software technologies are sometimes used in specific scenarios, but not necessarily with the main purpose of load balancing. These include Microsoft Intelligent Application Gateway (IAG) and Microsoft Internet Security and Acceleration Server (ISA) servers. These have been renamed to Microsoft Forefront Unified Access Gateway and Microsoft Forefront Threat Management Gateway, respectively. Both of these products provide load-balancing features.

Hardware load balancing offloads the compute requirements from the WFEs in your farms. It works using hardware (such as a router or a switch box) to direct website traffic between the WFE servers. Hardware load balancing is extremely useful in large farm scenarios, regardless of whether intelligent traffic balancing is required.

Hardware-based devices may provide other features such as caching, compression, and detailed machine up/down detection features to automatically route traffic to responsive servers. Examples of hardware load-balancing technologies include network appliances, switches, and routers from companies such as F5 Networks "BIG-IP" and Cisco.

 Joel Oleson posted a detailed blog discussing various load-balancing options entitled, "Deciding between NLB vs. Hardware Load Balancing," at `www.sharepointjoel.com/Lists/Posts/Post.aspx?ID=209.`

Farm Communications and Protocols

It is important for SharePoint architects to understand what protocols underpin farm communications in SharePoint 2010. It helps you implement SharePoint 2010 farms that are secure and "locked-down" by default. It also helps you troubleshoot issues that may be blocking or preventing SharePoint from working. And, finally, it helps you design optimal, performant, and secure solutions for your customers and business.

Farm communication can be categorized into the following three types:

➤ *Inter-server communication* — This describes traffic that occurs between servers inside a SharePoint 2010 farm, and includes traffic to SQL Server.

➤ *Extra-server communication* — Extra-server communication refers traffic to other servers in your environment. These typically include traffic to Active Directory, domain controllers, DNS, search indexing operations of external content sources, and retrieval of business data from Business Data Connectivity Services. It also includes calls to services hosted outside your environment, such as cloud-based Azure services.

➤ *Client-server communication* — Client-server communication refers to all communication between the SharePoint 2010 farm and clients, such as Office 2010, browsers, SharePoint Designer, and mobile clients.

All SharePoint 2010 farm communication takes place over defined protocols at different layers of the TCIP/IP model. This model specifies groups of protocols at different layers, such as the Link, Internet, Transport, and Application layers.

From a SharePoint perspective, the Application layer is where most of the protocols that are used by SharePoint can be placed. These include common protocols such as Remote Procedure Call (RPC), Simple Message Transport Protocol (SMTP), Server Message Block (SMB), DNS, File Transfer Protocol (FTP), WebDav, LDAP, and HTTP, as well as specific or proprietary protocols developed by Microsoft and used by SharePoint 2010.

 SharePoint 2010 makes use of a number of proprietary protocols. These protocols are thoroughly documented and available to download. Check out MSDN at www.microsoft.com/downloads/en/details .aspx?displaylang=en&FamilyID=5e94ad07-902c-422f-aadd-ff2bba9e540a.

If you are wondering why these protocols are important, they describe SharePoint 2010 processes and mechanisms used to deliver SharePoint 2010 Features. This protocol documentation is invaluable in diagnosing complex environmental issues relating to SharePoint 2010 features.

Database Technologies

As you probably already know, SharePoint 2010 is an application that is heavily reliant on database technologies to host farm configuration and site content. As described on TechNet (in an article at (http://technet.microsoft.com/en-us/library/cc262485.aspx), SharePoint 2010 hardware and software requirements indicate that the following versions of SQL Server are supported:

➤ The 64-bit edition of Microsoft SQL Server 2008 with SP1, plus Cumulative Update 2 (CU2). Microsoft does not recommend CU3 or CU4 for SharePoint 2010, but CU5 and onward are supported and recommended.

➤ The 64-bit edition of Microsoft SQL Server 2005 with SP3, plus CU3.

Following are some of the key databases technologies that you should understand:

➤ *SQL Server core constructs* — SharePoint 2010's application or business logic uses various SQL Server constructs, such as tables, stored procedures, Transact-SQL (T-SQL) language, functions, and indexes, to manage, store, and retrieve SharePoint data. IT professionals are often tasked with improving the performance of your SharePoint 2010 environment. Tuning your database (within the Microsoft support constraints) can really improve overall farm performance. From a development perspective, it is sometimes necessary to look in your development databases to gain a deeper insight into how SharePoint features work under the hood.

➤ *SQL Server auditing* — SQL Server Audit enables businesses to track and log events that occur on the system (for example, detecting changes made to database objects/stored procedures). This feature is often required to meet government or various industry compliance requirements. See http://msdn.microsoft.com/en-us/library/cc280386 .aspx for more information.

➤ *Transparent data encryption* — Transparent data encryption performs real-time I/O encryption and decryption of data and log files of both the communication channel and physical media, without requiring any change to SharePoint. By default, data stored in SQL Server is unencrypted. If someone steals a content backup, your content could be at risk. If enabled, this feature helps protect your important SharePoint content. The beauty of this feature is that it is transparent to applications, including SharePoint 2010. See http:// msdn.microsoft.com/en-us/library/bb934049.aspx for more information.

➤ *Backup compression* — SQL Backup compression reduces the amount of I/O and storage required to write backups to the backup device. The size of your content database will affect the length of time required to successfully back up. Backup compression can help ensure backups are completed within the allotted time available for this maintenance operation. For more information, see http://technet.microsoft.com/en-us/library/bb964719.aspx.

➤ *Remote BLOB storage* — Remote BLOB storage enables administrators to store binary large object (BLOB) data outside of SQL Server, in a way that is transparent to SharePoint. This reduces the amount of disk space and expensive storage required for your SQL Servers. As the growth of content databases reaches into the multi-terabyte range, organizations begin to seek options to reduce the cost of expensive (tier 1) storage by offloading content (stored as BLOBs) within the database to cheaper file storage. See http://technet .microsoft.com/en-us/library/ee748638.aspx for more information.

➤ *SQL Server resource governor* — SQL Server 2008 enables you to specify limits and control the resource consumption of incoming requests. For example, Microsoft recommends that you limit the amount of SQL Server resources used by web servers targeted by the search crawl components. See `http://technet.microsoft.com/en-us/library/cc298801.aspx` for more information.

➤ *SQL database mirroring* — SQL database mirroring provides increased availability to your SharePoint 2010 farm. It enables you to bring a standby copy of your database online. See `http://technet.microsoft.com/en-us/library/ms189852.aspx` for more information.

➤ *Failover clustering* — Failover clustering enables seamless failover between server nodes in your SQL Server cluster in the event of a host failure. See `http://msdn.microsoft.com/en-us/library/ms189134.aspx` for more information.

➤ *SQL log shipping* — Log shipping enables you maintain a separate copy of your databases on a secondary server, thereby providing a standby copy of your data. Log shipping backs up the transaction logs on the primary server, copies them, and restores the log backup on the secondary server. SQL Server log shipping is useful in SharePoint disaster recovery scenarios. See `http://msdn.microsoft.com/en-us/library/ms187103.aspx` for more information.

➤ *Database snapshots* — Database snapshots are read-only, static views of a database. Snapshots are useful especially when combined with content deployment features of SharePoint 2010. See `http://msdn.microsoft.com/en-us/library/ms175158.aspx` for more information.

➤ *SQL Server Reporting Services (SSRS)* — SSRS enables businesses to develop SQL Server reports using data from a variety of sources in your environment. These reports can be displayed in SharePoint 2010. See `http://msdn.microsoft.com/en-us/library/ms159106.aspx` for more information.

➤ *PowerPivot for Excel and SharePoint* — PowerPivot for Excel is a data analysis add-in for Microsoft Excel that enables users to analyze massive quantities of data. PowerPivot for SharePoint enables these users to host these workbooks in SharePoint 2010. See `www.microsoft.com/sqlserver/2008/en/us/powerpivot.aspx` for more information.

➤ *SQL Server Analysis Services (SSAS)* — SharePoint 2010 provides deep support for consuming and mining data held in SSAS in business intelligence (BI) dashboards, scorecards, and key performance indicators (KPIs) in SharePoint 2010. See `http://technet.microsoft.com/en-us/library/ff696762.aspx` for more information.

 For more information, see a Microsoft whitepaper written by one of the authors of this book, Bill Baer, entitled "SQL Server 2008 R2 and SharePoint 2010 Products: Better Together," at `http://go.microsoft.com/fwlink/?LinkID=187264`.

Storage Technologies

Storage technologies require a deep understanding, not only of SharePoint and SQL Server, but also of the underlying hardware infrastructure. The choices made at this level ripple all the way back up to influence overall capacity and performance of your SharePoint 2010 environment.

Chapter 17 provides detailed guidance on planning your storage for your SharePoint 2010 environment. Additionally, TechNet provides a great in-depth article on storage and SQL Server capacity planning at `http://technet.microsoft.com/en-us/library/cc298801.aspx.`

Monitoring Technologies

Monitoring technologies play a very important role in the maintenance and continued performance your SharePoint 2010 environment. They continually evaluate, analyze, and repair problems, and escalate problems for your attention.

Monitoring technologies can be categorized into two major groups — those that are provided by SharePoint, and those provided by specialist products as part of a larger enterprise monitoring solution. SharePoint 2010 provides a number of monitoring features, including the following:

➤ *Unified Logging Service* — The diagnostic logging feature captures information in SharePoint trace logs (located by default in the "14 hive"), Windows event logs, and the SharePoint logging database for each SharePoint Server in your farm. The level of detail captured can be set and controlled in the Central Administration ➪ Monitoring ➪ Configure Diagnostic Logging page. This page enables you to specify exactly what services (and elements within each service) to log.

➤ *Health and Usage Data Collection service* — This service collates data using specific monitoring timer jobs. It pulls together information from a wide range of sources — such as event logs, timer service information, performance counters, site collection and sub-site metrics, search usage, and other sources. This information is written to the unified logging database, and can then be used to create custom reports, web analysis reports, and administrative reports.

➤ *SharePoint Health Analyzer* — The SharePoint Health Analyzer runs checks (by using predefined health rules) on servers in the farm. Any failures are written to the Health Reports list in SharePoint 2010 and to the Windows Events log.

For more information, see the TechNet article, "Monitoring Overview," at `http://technet.microsoft.com/en-us/library/ee748636.aspx.`

Medium to large enterprises primarily use specialized enterprise monitoring solutions. In the Microsoft world, the Microsoft System Center product suite is one of the technologies used. One of its products, System Center Operations Manager (SCOM) 2007 R2, provides support to monitor your SharePoint 2010 environments, as well as providing specific "management packs" that enable service and support teams to manage SharePoint technologies.

For more information about SCOM, see `www.microsoft.com/download/en/details.aspx?displaylang=en&id=4419.`

One of the especially great features is its capability to provide you with an "aerial photograph" or diagram view of your SharePoint 2010 environments, and the capability to "zoom" into specific areas of concern. Figure 3-1 shows a diagram view from TechNet.

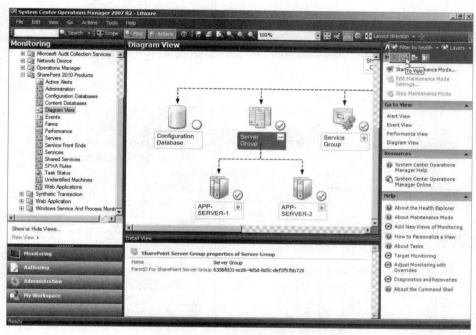

FIGURE 3-1: System Center Operations Manager 2007 R2 — Diagram View

Internet Information Services

IIS can be described as the bedrock of SharePoint Server 2010. Although SharePoint 2010 does a great job of automatically configuring IIS to host web applications and services on various servers in your farm, this doesn't absolve you of your responsibility to understand how SharePoint uses the features of IIS. In fact, it is crucial for you, regardless whether you are a developer or an IT pro, to understand IIS.

First of all, IIS is provided as a feature of the Windows Server operating system. Windows Server 2008 provides IIS 7.0, and Windows Server 2008 R2 provides IIS 7.5. IIS 7.0 and 7.5 use a modular architecture that offers greater flexibility, a much higher level of componentization, increased extensibility, and improved ASP.NET integration.

The components of IIS perform various functions for application and web server roles in IIS 7.0 and IIS 7.5 (for example, listening for requests made to the server). These components include protocol listeners, services, and the Windows Process Activation Service (WAS).

Following are some of key features (as summarized from the IIS Learning website at `learn.iis.net`):

➤ *Protocol listeners* — Protocol listeners listen for protocol-specific requests and route them to IIS for processing. For example, when SharePoint web pages are requested, the HTTP listener picks up the request, processes it, and returns a response.

➤ *HyperText Transfer Protocol Stack* (`HTTP.sys`) — `HTTP.sys` is a protocol listener that processes HTTP and HTTPS requests. `HTTP.sys` is part of the networking subsystem of the operating system, and is implemented as a kernel-mode device driver. This a major improvement from IIS 6.0, which was a user-mode driver.

> Kernel-mode *and* user-mode *are terms used to describe the level of access to execute code on a computer (via the CPU). Code running in kernel-mode is allowed to execute in the unrestricted mode, whereas user mode code must make system calls to request the kernel to perform operations on its behalf. System calls take time, and can degrade performance. This is one of the reasons* `HTTP.sys` *is integrated at such a low level. The* `HTTP.sys` *kernel-mode driver forwards the request directly to the correct worker process (*`w3wp.exe`*).*

➤ *Listener adapters* — Listener adapters allow listeners to connect to WAS. Listener adapters are Windows services that receive messages on specific network protocols, and communicate with WAS to route incoming messages to the correct worker process.

➤ *World Wide Web Publishing Service (WWW Service)* — This process no longer manages worker processes as it did in IIS 6.0. The WWW Service is the listener adapter for the HTTP listener. It is primarily responsible for configuring `HTTP.sys`, updating `HTTP.sys` when a configuration changes, and notifying WAS when a request enters the request queue.

➤ *Windows Process Activation Service (WAS)* — This service manages the protocol listeners configuration (using listening adapters), application pool configuration, and worker processes for both HTTP and non-HTTP requests. When a protocol listener picks up a client request, WAS determines whether or not a worker process is running. If one is available, the request is passed to the worker process. If not, it starts a worker process and then passes the requests. WAS supports the running of applications with different protocols in the same application pool.

➤ *Windows Communication Foundation (WCF)* — WCF, a technology used heavily in SharePoint 2010, can function both as a protocol listener and listener adapter. WCF makes use of the WAS service to host services that do not communicate with HTTP network protocols.

➤ *IIS 7 modules* — IIS 7.0 uses the new IIS architecture to componentize or modularize features of IIS. This enables you to control what modules you want on the server, and to replace existing modules and add new modules. The modules provided by IIS can be grouped into HTTP, security, content, compression, caching, logging and diagnostics, managed, and managed support categories.

➤ *IIS 7 request processing* — IIS 7.0 and ASP.NET request pipelines combine to process requests using an integrated approach. In previous versions of IIS, tasks would go through a process in both the IIS and ASP.NET pipeline. IIS 7.0 eliminates this duplication.

➤ *IIS 7 application pools* — Application pools allow you to provide separate process boundaries. If one application crashes, applications running in other process boundaries will not fail. Two application pool modes are supported: classic and integrated. SharePoint 2010 uses integrated mode.

Figure 3-2 provides a high-level architectural view of an HTTP request, and Figure 3-3 illustrates the worker process (w3wp.exe).

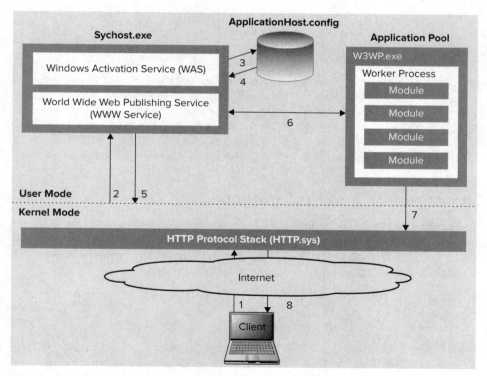

FIGURE 3-2: Overview of an HTTP request

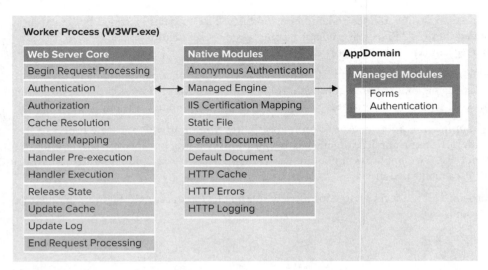

FIGURE 3-3: Overview of a HTTP request inside a worker process

You should review the great, comprehensive learning material provided by the IIS team. Reagan Templin's article, "Introduction to IIS 7 Architecture," provides an in-depth explanation of the IIS 7.0 architecture. To read this article, and many other IIS learning articles, see `http://learn.iis.net/page` `.aspx/101/introduction-to-iis-7-architecture/`.

Caching, Compression, and Performance

SharePoint 2010 supports a number of compression and caching technologies to reduce database and network load, and to improve the end-user experience. These technologies exist as software within SharePoint, IIS, and Windows technologies, and as dedicated hardware and software products from specialist vendors. Key technologies include the following:

➤ *Disk-based BLOB caching (SharePoint 2010)* — Disk-based BLOB caching enables SharePoint to maintain copies of large and frequently used files on the WFE. This reduces load on databases and speeds up performance by serving them directly from each WFE.

➤ *Maximum upload size (SharePoint 2010)* — Limiting the maximum upload size, in effect, limits the impact, duration, and resource usage of large file uploads and downloads.

➤ *Page output caching (SharePoint 2010)* — The page output cache stores the rendered output of a page, as well as different versions of the cached page, based on permissions of the users who are requesting the page. This setting is configurable via cache profiles within the site collection, and requires that publishing Features be turned on.

➤ *Object caching (SharePoint 2010)* — The object cache stores objects in memory on the WFE. This reduces the amount of traffic between the SQL database and each WFE. This increases the rendering of pages (that make use of these cached objects) and speed at which pages are returned to the browser. This setting is configurable within the site collection, and requires that publishing Features be turned on.

➤ *Bit-rate throttling (IIS)* — Bit-rate throttling limits the speed at which types of data (such as audio and video files) are served between WFEs and client computers. This feature helps protect network performance, while still providing a full video and audio end-user experience.

➤ *HTTP compression in IIS 7 (IIS)* — IIS provides features to reduce the consumption of bandwidth available to your network by reducing or compressing responses sent across the wire. A downside to this feature is that it consumes significant CPU time and memory.

Specialist vendors (such as Riverbed, F5 Networks, Cisco, and Juniper) provide hardware and software compression and caching technologies that help reduce the cost of network transport of pages and files across your local area networks (LANs) and wide area networks (WANs), thereby improving the end-user experience and productivity.

These technologies can be broadly grouped into WAN optimization and web acceleration. The cost of these technologies varies greatly. As a result, investment in these technologies typically forms part of a much larger strategy across a number of systems and office locations in your organization.

Virtualization Technologies

In the past couple of years, virtualization technologies have increasingly become the *modus operandi* for IT departments deploying servers into their environments. This is partly as a result of the following:

➤ The maturity of hypervisor, infrastructure, and management technologies

➤ An effort by businesses to reduce operation costs in trying economic times

➤ The increased trust, understanding, and confidence of key business decision makers in virtualization technologies

Virtualization technologies are used heavily by developers and IT professionals to host 64-bit SharePoint environments in an isolated environment. Although SharePoint 2010 now makes it possible to install on a Windows 7 machine, this feature is not recommended. This is because it does not allow you to restore your development environment to a previously known "good" state, and it does not enable you to isolate different customer projects on completely separate development environments.

 Chapter 23 provides detailed guidance on virtualized deployments of your SharePoint 2010 environment.

Backup

Backing up SharePoint 2010 involves careful planning, design, deployment, and operation of backup and recovery solutions. Therefore, this forms a major part of your SharePoint 2010 infrastructure and business continuity management design.

SharePoint 2010 and SQL Server provide tools to assist in the back up of your environment. Microsoft and third-party vendors provide technologies to support your environment (for example,

Microsoft System Center Data Protection Manager). These tools enable you to back up all databases hosted by SQL Server, except the configuration database. At this point, Microsoft only supports backup and restoration of the configuration database using Data Protection Manager (DPM). Specialist infrastructure vendors provide in-depth and wide-scale backup technologies that support various systems in your environment. The big players include specific components to integrate SharePoint into their solutions. Key features include being able to back up server physical or virtual operating systems to tape libraries (thereby requiring tape library management), as well as utilizing advanced granular and consolidated machine backup support. Examples of backup vendors include Symantec NetBackup, AvePoint, and Quest.

 Chapter 21 provides detailed guidance on planning backup, recoverability, and availability of your SharePoint 2010 environment.

A subtle (often forgotten) requirement is the storing of your backups in an offsite and secure location. If your data center is destroyed by fire, would you be able to recover your data to a new server environment from your backups?

DEVELOPMENT TECHNOLOGIES

This section covers the common SharePoint 2010 development technologies.

.NET Framework

The .NET framework is a software development platform and software framework. It consists of the Common Language Runtime (CLR) and an extensive class library. Together, the base class library and the CLR make up the .NET Framework. The CLR provides important services such as security, memory management, and exception handling.

.NET supports several programming languages, including C#, VB.NET, and C++. The .NET base class library is available to all the programming languages supported by .NET.

As you now know, SharePoint 2010 is built on top of Windows Server and IIS. These technologies host and support the .NET Framework, and, in particular, the ASP.NET platform to build and support dynamic websites.

As shown in Figure 3-4, the .NET Framework stack consists of software technologies released as part of the .NET Framework versions over a period of time.

Parallel LINQ	Task Parallel Library			4.0 2010 (Future)
LINQ	ADO.NET Entity Framework			3.5 2007
WPF	WCF	WF	Card Space	3.0 2006
WinForms	ASP.NET	ADO.NET		
Base Class Library				.NET Framework 2.0 2005
Common Language Runtime				

FIGURE 3-4: The.NET Framework stack

Although all technologies in the framework are very important and should be understood, the following technologies should stand out from a SharePoint 2010 perspective:

➤ *Active Server Pages (ASP.NET)* — ASP.NET is a web development framework that includes a number of features to make it easy to build dynamic websites. It enables you to use a language (for example, C# or VB.NET) along with base classes of the .NET Framework to develop your website. SharePoint 2010 is completely built on top of the ASP.NET platform.

➤ *ActiveX Data Object (ADO.NET)* — ADO.NET provides consistent set of base classes to access data stored in various relational database systems. It uses .NET Framework data providers to connect to databases, execute commands, and retrieve results. SharePoint 2010 uses ADO.NET to communicate with databases in the SharePoint 2010 environment.

➤ *Windows Communication Foundation (WCF)* — WCF is a framework for building connected, service-oriented applications. Using WCF, you can send data as asynchronous messages from one service endpoint to another. Endpoints can be hosted in IIS, or can be a service hosted directly in an application. It supports simple to complex messages in XML format. SharePoint 2010 makes extensive use of the support provided by WCF.

➤ *Windows Workflow Foundation (WF)* — WF is a technology that enables you to build workflows within .NET applications. It provides a set of APIs, an in-process workflow engine, and a workflow designer to implement long-running workflows. SharePoint 2010 uses the Visual Studio 2010 Workflow Designer and the WF runtime engine. (For more information, see http://msdn.microsoft.com/en-us/library/ms195750.aspx.)

➤ *ADO.NET Entity Framework (EF)* — The ADO.NET EF is an object relational mapping (ORM) framework for the .NET Framework. It enables developers to write better code by abstracting the relational schema of the data in the database from the business logic represented to the application. In layman's terms, it allows you to write business logic code using concepts natural to the business domain, rather than specific to the underlying database technology. (For more information, see http://msdn.microsoft.com/en-us/data/aa937709.)

➤ *Language Integrated Query (LINQ)* — LINQ is a .NET Framework capability that adds native data-querying capabilities to .NET languages such as C# and VB.NET. SharePoint 2010 provides a LINQ-to-SharePoint provider. This provider translates queries into Collaborative Application Markup Language (CAML) queries. (For more information, see http://msdn.microsoft.com/en-us/library/ee535491.aspx.)

With the exception of SharePoint 2003 (where the SharePoint product team decided to build its own ASPX parser), SharePoint technologies on average tend to lag in their adoption of new features of the .NET platform by one release. This is a good thing, because it provides time to iron out and fix bugs in newly released .NET capabilities, and time for the SharePoint and Office product teams to think about how best (or if) to use these features in future versions of SharePoint 2010. For example, SharePoint 2010 is based on .NET Framework 3.5, and not 4.0.

Development Tools

Microsoft Visual Studio 2010 is a powerful, integrated, and mature development environment that caters to the full development life cycle of customizations produced for your SharePoint 2010 farm. It provides a number of starting-point solution templates to begin development of SharePoint customizations, combined with deployment packaging tools to create Windows solution packages required by SharePoint to deploy fully and partially trusted assemblies and artifacts to your various environments.

Microsoft Visual Studio 2010 provides significant new support for the full application development life cycle. This includes features to plan and track your project, design functionality, code development tools (write, unit test, debug, analyze, and profile), build, testing (manual and automated tests, performance and stress tests), and deployment into virtual environments for further testing.

 MSDN provides detailed articles on the Visual Studio application life cycle management at `http://msdn.microsoft.com/en-us/library/fda2bad5 .aspx`.

SharePoint Designer 2010 is a WYSIWYG (what-you-see-is-what-you-get) tool that enables power users to configure elements of SharePoint sites. Although you could argue that this is not a true development tool, it does provide a deep level of support for customizing sites without requiring any code to be written. It's great for small changes, tweaks, modifications, and extensions to existing site features. Additionally, SharePoint Designer 2010 changes are scoped automatically to a single site collection, and not your entire farm.

Great developers are backed by an even greater set of tools to support their productivity in the production of quality code and business solutions. Table 3-1 provides a list of useful tools to improve the quality and productivity of developers in your business.

TABLE 3-1: Developer Utilities

TOOL	DESCRIPTION	
Code Reflection and .NET Reflector	The .NET Framework supports the capability to "reflect" compiled assemblies to view the contained code and methods. This is an invaluable tool to work out how SharePoint performs certain actions. Think of it as an additional form of documentation that may not be present in MSDN or TechNet. This tool was previously developed by Lutz Roeder, but was sold to Red Gate. See `www.red-gate.com` for more information.	
Fiddler	Fiddler is a web debugging proxy that logs all HTTP(S) traffic between your computer and the Internet. From a SharePoint perspective, it allows you to inspect traffic between your browser and SharePoint server, whether on your development machine or in production. This often helps to identify issues related to authentication, and issues related to caching. Do not install this on production servers. Install only on your client computer. See `www.fiddler2.com` for more information.	

TOOL	DESCRIPTION
Code Performance Profiling and Measurement	Red Gate provides a great tool that is capable of diagnosing code performance bottlenecks and identifying poor-performing code. For more information, see `www.red-gate.com`.
Network Monitor	Network Monitor enables you to detect and troubleshoot problems on LANs. This includes identifying network traffic patterns between client-server applications.
File Monitor and Process Monitor	File Monitor is a tool created by Mark Russinovich and Bryce Cogswell to help you manage, troubleshoot, and diagnose issues occurring on Windows systems and applications. For more information, see `www.sysinternals.com`.
Debug View for Windows	Debug View for Windows is an application that lets you monitor and catch debug output from your SharePoint development environment, without the need of a debugger. It is especially useful in code-development and debugging scenarios when you want to monitor various aspects of your code through output of debug statements. For more information, see `http://download.sysinternals.com/Files/DebugView.zip` and `http://technet.microsoft.com/en-us/sysinternals/bb896647`.
Unit testing and mocking tools	Various tools exist to assist in generating and performing automated testing of code and user interfaces. These include Visual Studio 2010 testing tools, Microsoft Pex and Moles Visual Studio 2010 Power Tools framework, nUnit, as well as external solutions from providers such as TypeMock. For more information, see `http://research.microsoft.com/en-us/projects/pex/` and `www.typemock.com`.
SDKs and community kits	Microsoft typically provides downloadable software development kits (SDKs) that include source code examples and documentation relating to implementation of a particular product. Microsoft provides SDKs for SharePoint 2010 Foundation and SharePoint Server 2010. These are available to download at the Microsoft Download Center. For more information, see `www.microsoft.com/download/en/default.aspx`.
Community Kit	Community Kit for SharePoint: Development Tools Edition provides additional features to assist and improve your productivity in developing solutions for SharePoint 2010. These are available at `http://cksdev.codeplex.com/`.
Microsoft SharePoint Practices Group (SPG)	Microsoft has commissioned the release of a series of SharePoint code patterns and practices that have been reviewed by a number of SharePoint heavyweights within Microsoft and in the community. This information and associated download material is available to view at `http://msdn.microsoft.com/en-us/library/ff770300.aspx`. Additionally, the SharePoint Practices Group provides support and a series of hands-on labs (HOLs) at `http://spg.codeplex.com`.

continues

TABLE 3-1 *(continued)*

TOOL	DESCRIPTION
Windows PowerShell tools and third-party commandlets	Windows PowerShell GUI is a graphical user interface and script editor for Microsoft Windows PowerShell. For more information, see `www.powergui.org`. As described on MSDN, Windows PowerShell *commandlets* (cmdlets) are lightweight commands that can be executed in a Windows PowerShell environment within the context of automation scripts. SharePoint Server 2010 provides many Windows PowerShell commands. See the TechNet article, "Windows PowerShell for SharePoint Server 2010," at `http://technet.microsoft.com/en-us/library/ee662539.aspx` for more information. A number of third-party Windows PowerShell cmdlets are available for SharePoint 2010. The most well-known are available from Gary Lapointe's blog. For more information, see `http://blog.falchionconsulting.com/index.php/stsadmpowershell-commands/`. Ensure that you test and understand what the Windows PowerShell command does before running it in your production environment.
Style and source code analysis	A number of tools are available to analyze and enforce high-quality code. These can be grouped into two categories — those that analyze as the developer enters code, and those that are performed either after the developer compiles code, or as a post-build step. `Jetbrains.com` provides a well-known tool called ReSharper that analyzes code as it is entered. Microsoft provides Visual Studio Code Analysis, FxCop, and StyleCop. Without going into too much detail, these enforce code writing, comment, and style standards based on design guidelines and best practices. They also report on code that does not implement or adhere to good development practices. For more information, see MSDN for design guidelines for class library developers at `http://msdn.microsoft.com/en-us/library/czefa0ke(vs.71).aspx` and "Code Analysis for Managed Code Overview" at `http://msdn.microsoft.com/en-us/library/3z0aeatx.aspx`.
Other useful utilities	So many tools can improve your daily productivity. Tools that you may find useful are NotePad++, ULSViewer and Search Coder, SharePoint Manager 2010, and U2U CAML Builder.

Chapter 17 provides an in-depth look at the use of these in the SharePoint 2010 development and testing process.

Application Life Cycle Management Tools

The phrase *application life cycle* refers to the process of developing software, from inception, design, development, testing, to deployment, and continuing into maintenance and ongoing support activities. It includes the project management activities related to managing and tracking the progress of activities (such as tasks, work items, bugs, and issues) throughout the life cycle of the software development project.

Microsoft Team Foundation Server 2010 is recommended for SharePoint 2010 projects to manage the application life cycle. Team Foundation Server provides the following "must-have" features:

➤ *Methodology or process templates* — Team Foundation Server 2010 supports various agile and waterfall methodologies through the use of process templates. Team Foundation Server provides out-of-the-box process templates, including Microsoft Solutions Framework (MSF) for Agile Software Development and MSF for CMMI Process Improvement. A number of third-party templates can be used. Examples of these include SCRUM and Kanban.

➤ *Source code management* — Team Foundation Server enables development teams to work on the same code project at the same time. It includes features such as check-ins, code branching, merging, shelving, labeling, concurrent check-outs, check-in policies, and the association of check-ins to work items.

➤ *Work item tracking* — Work items consist of requirements, tasks, bugs, issues, and test cases. Team Foundation Server enables flexibility for how these work items are managed via an extensible work item tracking system. This tracking system controls the states a work item can be in, and how the state transitions should occur. This results in better documentation, commenting, visibility of the history of issues, productivity, and discipline for the members of the project team.

➤ *Build automation* — Team Foundation Server provides great build management tools. *Build management* refers to automatic creation and processing of new builds based on updates to code projects. Team Foundation Server supports manual builds, continuous integration, rolling builds, gated check-in, and scheduled builds. For example, it's possible to schedule a nightly build, deploy this build to a virtual machine, and run a series of tests ready to be analyzed in the morning.

➤ *Project management and reporting* — Team Foundation Server 2010 provides reports and dashboards for you to use to assess and report on various aspects of your project's progress. For example, if you have implemented the agile process templates, it is possible to track the progress of the iteration backlog and plan items for the next sprint.

It is important for your project manager and technical lead to be sufficiently skilled in the configuration, optimization, and use of Team Foundation Server 2010. For example, if the customer is demanding an update on your team's progress, can your project manager instantly generate a report to provide an update? If your developers haven't been updating their work items, or your testers haven't been logging and tracking defects, you won't have the data to show your customer. If you don't have the data, you will struggle to report on any part of your team's progress. Team Foundation Server won't solve bad management, bad judgment, and bad developer habits or traits. Therefore, it is up to your project manager and technical lead to instill discipline and structure in your team.

Team Foundation Server can turn invisible progress into visible progress that can be measured and reported on. It reduces inefficiencies, and improves productivity in your application life cycle. Finally, it assists in the improved discipline and maturity of the "software manufacturing process" of your team, resulting in higher quality and time savings.

Code Libraries

SharePoint 2010 takes advantage of a number of code libraries. At a high level, these include the .NET base and Framework class libraries, expansive frameworks such as WCF, Workflow Foundation (WF), Workflow Presentation Foundation (WPF), and Windows CardSpace within the .NET Framework. For more information on these, review the extensive articles available on MSDN.

SharePoint 2010 is a true application development platform. SharePoint 2010 provides extensive server-side and client-side object models and code libraries, impressive integration and support for developing and packaging solutions using Visual Studio 2010, and custom solution deployment management tools for deploying fully trusted solutions across servers in your SharePoint 2010 farm.

 Sandboxed solutions *(user solutions) is a new feature in SharePoint 2010 that enables site collection owners to host custom managed code (partially trusted) solutions within site collections. Under the hood, SharePoint 2010 isolates, manages compute resources, and distributes the load of hosting these to specifically configured servers. Sandboxed solutions only have access to a subset of the APIs, while fully trusted solutions have complete access to the SharePoint object model.*

The SharePoint 2010 server-side object model can be largely grouped into two categories — objects that support SharePoint 2010 Features, and objects that provide site administration via code.

 MSDN provides a great article detailing the server and site architecture from an object model perspective at `http://msdn.microsoft.com/en-us/library/ms473633.aspx`.

SharePoint 2010 supports the development of rich client applications that access SharePoint content without requiring assembly-based code. It is a completely new category of application, not previously supported directly by SharePoint 2010. SharePoint 2010 provides three sets of client object models to support common SharePoint "companion" solutions. These support development of .NET GUI applications, rich client Rich Internet Application (RIA) using Silverlight, and ECMAScript (JavaScript, JScript).

See MSDN at http://msdn.microsoft.com/en-us/library/ee857094.aspx *for a detailed overview of the client-side object model, including examples and use cases.*

One final important technology that has come to the forefront in recent years in SharePoint 2010 UI development is an independent (not developed by Microsoft) framework called jQuery. jQuery is a JavaScript library that provides an array of features that can take your UI development to the next level. Although it is possible for site collection owners to host the JavaScript files in the Style Library, you should implement a wider strategy and set of best practices that your organization should adhere to. Consider packaging and deploying these to the file system of your WFEs to reduce load and improve performance of all consumers of these JavaScript libraries.

For more information, see www.jquery.com.

A number of other important third-party code libraries can improve the productivity and reduce the cost of custom solutions. These range in diversity from independent component vendors (such as Telerik, ComponentOne, DivElements, and Infragistics) that sell fantastic code libraries and components, to "free" solutions developed and released to sites (such as CodePlex, MSDN code gallery projects, and SourceForge).

When deciding whether to use these third-party code libraries, consider these key points:

➤ *Software licensing agreement* — Review and understand under what licensing agreement the code library was released, and what the implications are for using or changing the library to meet your requirements. Consider what environments — developer, testing, user acceptance testing (UAT), pre-production, and production — the license covers. Not understanding software licensing for a particular code library can expose your business to lawsuits and unexpected costs.

➤ *Quality* — Do not (repeat, *do not*) jump on the bandwagon of latest fads. Make mature software design decisions by assessing the quality of a third-party code library. What may appear as a life-saver or amazing UI component can result in sleepless nights, and can actually be a life-killer in terms of debugging, fixing, and supporting third-party code on behalf of your business or customer. Do not make promises to the business unless you are 100 percent certain the third-party code library can deliver what it promised to deliver. Prototype first, then commit.

➤ *Widespread adoption* — Consider and review the level of adoption and recommendations from the SharePoint and development communities. Being one of the first implies you may need to fix the bugs that others will not have encountered in the third-party code library, and lead to frustration and unexpected development and testing costs. A seasoned architect is not the first to eat the food at the table, no matter how good it looks or smells!

➤ *Code Library Maturity (CLM)* — Judge the maturity of the code library. How many versions have been produced? What is the frequency of change? If open source-based, how many contributors support the project? Is it well documented? Are release notes available for each release? Are code examples available to assist your development team?

➤ *Supportability* — If there is bug that breaks your production solution, who will fix it, how long will it take, and how much will it cost your business? Does the third-party code library provide original code, or has it been obfuscated or compiled into a format that requires third-party support? Does your business need a support agreement and contract in place to receive support in acceptable timeframes?

Finally, consider and govern what code libraries are supported in your production environment. Although it may not be possible to completely stop site collection owners from using third-party code libraries, at least ensure that you have a framework in place for managing the introduction and acceptance of third-party code libraries to protect the uptime of key solutions in your production environment, and your business from exposure to lawsuits.

MICROSOFT OFFICE TECHNOLOGIES

This section covers the common Microsoft Office technologies.

Browser

Microsoft SharePoint 2010 supports a variety of browsers in today's marketplace. This includes versions of Internet Explorer (IE), Firefox, and Safari.

See the TechNet article, "Plan Browser Support (SharePoint Server 2010)" at `http://technet.microsoft.com/en-us/library/cc263526.aspx` *for more information.*

Microsoft Office System

Microsoft Office 2010 is the essential companion to SharePoint Foundation and Server 2010. It provides the best experience for users in your organization. Users are still able to work with sites in SharePoint 2010 using previous versions of Office, but some of the new features will not be available using previous versions of Office and SharePoint 2010.

Microsoft has produced a whitepaper detailing the seamless and productive experience of using Office 2010 and SharePoint 2010 together. The whitepaper, "Business Productivity at Its Best," is available at `http://go.microsoft.com/fwlink/?LinkId=209803.`

Imaging and Capture

As an architect, you will often face scenarios and projects that integrate imaging and capture technologies. Understanding this space helps an architect make the right calls when integrating these technologies.

The amount of correspondence a business can receive and send is staggering. Every day, businesses receive and send correspondence from a number of channels. Some of these may be paper-based correspondence either via snail mail or via drop points at retail branches. Others may be electronically submitted via fax, e-mailed to various correspondence e-mail aliases, or directly from a form on the company website.

Electronic imaging and capture solutions enable businesses to capture each piece of correspondence in an electronic format, classify the correspondence, and extract data from scanned documents, e-mails, and faxes — in some cases, automatically. Furthermore, advanced imaging and capture solutions may initiate business processes or workflows, and track the processing of correspondence to completion.

Depending on the volume of your business, these electronic documents may need to be stored in large storage solutions. They may need to be searchable. They may need to be declared as records and held for a period of time to comply with laws in the country of operation.

Large-volume scenarios typically use a combination of workflow, image, and capture solutions. Examples of companies providing these types of solutions include KnowledgeLake, Kofax, RightFax, Fujitsu, and EMC Captiva. In some cases, they provide their own workflow solutions, and, in other cases, they offer the capability to integrate or use your existing enterprise business workflow solution (such as K2, Nintex, Global 360, and others).

Communication and Virtual Meeting Services

Microsoft Lync (formally known as Office Communicator) provides a number of modern enterprise grade communication services. These include the capability to connect via business instant messaging (IM), audio calls, video calls, screen sharing, online presentations (internally and externally), and virtual whiteboards.

These services are designed to work with SharePoint 2010. Presence status of Lync is displayed from Microsoft Outlook, Office SharePoint, and Office applications.

Working Offline

Microsoft Office 2010 provides a new client called SharePoint WorkSpace 2010. SharePoint WorkSpace enables users to work with sites, libraries, and lists while offline. Changes made offline are synchronized with the server when the user is again online.

Although most businesses will use this feature to maintain copies of important project documentation, it does enable a new category of solution — the "mobile-warrior" solution. For example, a sales professional could take orders offline in SharePoint WorkSpace using offline sales order lists. Orders can either be synchronized immediately (via mobile data connection), or at a later time when he or she is back at the office.

For completeness, Microsoft Outlook also provides offline features, such as the capability to maintain copies of document libraries offline. Third-party offline solutions are provided by companies such as Colligo.

COMPLEMENTARY THIRD-PARTY TECHNOLOGIES

There is a rich, diverse ecosystem of supporting complementary SharePoint 2010 technologies. These can be broadly categorized into applications that work with or extend the SharePoint 2010 end-user feature set, and those that improve the administration and operation of your SharePoint 2010 environment.

Literally thousands of solutions are available to extend and manage your SharePoint 2010 environment. These range from simple web parts to advanced in-depth tailor-made business solutions. Unfortunately, it is not possible to cover each individual extension or business solution in this section.

From an application perspective, examples include the following:

➤ *Workflow solutions* — These are dedicated workflow products that provide advanced reporting, people and group management, extremely high volume (thousands to tens of thousands of simultaneous workflows), and enterprise-wide human-to-human and human-to-system workflows. Companies that provide these solutions include K2, Nintex, PNMSoft, and Global 360.

➤ *Replication and offline solutions* — These include dedicated replication of content, libraries and lists, sites, and site collections to remote server farms either one-way or bi-directionally. Remote server farms could exist in the same office location, different office locations, branch offices in the same country, multiple countries, and to bandwidth-starved locations that rely on satellite time to connect and synchronize. Example scenarios include oil and gas, maritime, military, and other advanced file replication requirements. Companies that provide these types of solutions include Infonic, Repliweb, and Syntergy.

➤ *Content aggregation solutions* — Content aggregation can occur within the same site collection, across a set of site collections, across an entire farm, or across multiple farms. SharePoint 2010 provides features to display aggregated views using CQWPs, and across site collections using Search Center. Additionally, it is possible to develop custom solutions to perform full-text SQL Query searches to return results. Companies that provide third-party solutions include Kwizcom and Bamboo Solutions.

➤ *Search solutions* — A number of third-party search enhancements are available to extend the reach of your SharePoint 2010 search environment. Indexing Connectors exist for Documentum, Hummingbird DM, Interwoven, Exchange, and a number of other third-party content sources.

➤ *Business solutions* — Literally hundreds or thousands of great web parts, custom lists and libraries, and extensions to enhance your SharePoint 2010 environment are available. Some of the main vendors in this space include Bamboo Solutions and Kwizcom.

From an administration and operations perspective, examples include the following:

➤ *Administration solutions* — Administration solutions provide additional tooling to support the management, maintenance, and optimization of your SharePoint 2010 environment. A number of solutions are available to help you better administer your SharePoint 2010 environments. Companies offering solutions include Quest and AvePoint.

➤ *Migration solutions* — Migration solutions provide the capability to move legacy content from your previous enterprise content management solution to SharePoint 2010. Migration solutions tend to vary greatly in feature sets provided, and legacy solution supported. A key capability for any migration solution is to write custom conversion extensions (using .NET code) to manipulate and massage content into a suitable SharePoint 2010 format. However, migrations are almost never out-of-the-box solutions. Also, you most likely don't want to add "legacy junk" to your new environment because that perpetuates the same problem of your original environment. For example, legacy intranet pages may require data massaging, and look-and-feel manipulation before they can be converted into SharePoint 2010 publishing pages. Companies offering solutions include MetaLogix, Tzunami, Quest, AvePoint, Idera, and Metavis.

➤ *Compliance solutions* — Compliance solutions vary greatly, depending on the type of compliance required. This category covers auditing, accessibility, and adherence to government and industry regulations. Companies offering solutions include HiSoftware, AvePoint, Syntergy, and Quest.

➤ *Reporting solutions* — SharePoint 2010 provides a fantastic improvement to the out-of-the-box traffic, inventory, and search reports. Third-party solutions extend the level and types of reports users and administrators can view. These include storage trending or report snapshots taken over time to track trends and reporting across site collections. Companies offering solutions include Nintex, AvePoint, and Quest.

➤ *Backup solutions* — Backup and recovery solutions vary greatly in the types of features they provide, their resource utilization, the impact to servers operating in your SharePoint 2010 farm, and the level of available granularity that is offered. There are two types of backup vendors — those that are dedicated SharePoint backup vendors, and those that provide backup as part as much larger backup solution for many solutions in your enterprise. Both have their merits and pitfalls, and each offering should be investigated thoroughly. For better backup performance, ensure that any offering provides a 64-bit agent. Companies offering solutions include Symantec, IBM, CommVault, Quest, and AvePoint.

➤ *Storage optimization and archive solutions* — SharePoint 2010 requires (if not demands) expensive tier 1 storage for your SQL databases. As your farm grows, so does the cost associated with hosting content. Storage optimization and archive solutions address the cost of using high-end storage. Companies offering solutions include Metalogix, AvePoint, Symantec, and Quest.

➤ *De-duplication solutions* — De-duplication solutions help organizations eliminate duplicate or redundant information. These help customers understand their unstructured information stores, determine unnecessary information, organize, derive, and apply metadata, and migrate this to new structures in SharePoint 2010 site collections. Companies offering solutions include Active Navigation, CommVault, NetApp, and Symantec.

You can find more information about each of the technologies and companies on their respective websites. Product listings, along with reviews and comments, are available on the listings at the community-based SharePoint Reviews website at www.sharepointreviews.com. *Microsoft has released a new Microsoft Office 365 Marketplace at* http://office365.pinpoint.microsoft.com/. *This marketplace provides the capability to review and comment on the quality of products. You should participate with commenting and feedback because this helps ensure companies maintain high-quality products.*

Additionally, following are a number of guidelines to improve your third-party product purchasing decision-making process:

➤ *Repeat the mantra, "Out-of-the-box, third-party, then custom development"* — Always attempt to use the out-of-the-box features. If this feature does not exist or does not fully meet your needs, look at what third-party solutions are available. Consider custom development last. Economies of scale dictate that a third-party solution will typically be cheaper than a custom-developed solution. Invest wisely according to your budget, schedule, and available resources.

➤ *Insist on case studies and real-world references* — Don't purchase a product based on the label, packaging, or promises on the tin. Ask for references, chat with other customers who have deployed the product, and ensure that you get independent (non-sales channel-based) advice before you purchase a large application or administration solution.

➤ *Understand your use cases first* — This may seem obvious, but there have been many examples of customers purchasing expensive solutions that they end up rarely using. Understand the key use cases a third-party solution will solve. Quantify this in terms of cost. Purchase when you have a solid requirement that must be solved right away, rather than at some point in the future.

➤ *Involve the right people* — Involve the right stakeholders in the purchase decision-making process, such as people administrating and managing your environment, or the end user who will be forced to use the feature every day, or the architect who has a deep understanding of your SharePoint deployment.

➤ *Be wary of late release-cycle purchases* — Watch out for solutions purchased at the end of SharePoint 2010 life cycle. If you know the next version of SharePoint 2010 will be released 6 to 12 months later, think carefully about large third-party solution investments because this may lock you into the current version for longer than you want.

➤ *Understand available training options* — A third-party product is only as good as the people who understand how to use it. This may require training for administrators, developers, power users, and end users.

➤ *Supportability* — What support options does the third-party solution provide? How often are hot fixes and updates released? What Quality Assurance (QA) processes does the third-party solution use to ensure that hot fixes and patches of their product will not destroy your farm? Does the third-party provider have a good track record for support?

➤ *"Learnability"* — This describes the frustration encountered with some third-party products that do not make it easy for administrators and developers to install and learn in development or test administration environments. Sometimes, this may be because of the prohibitive and restrictive licensing conditions levied by third-party providers for development, test, and pre-production environments. If administrators cannot verify an action of a third-party product in a non-production environment, they will struggle to develop confidence in the product. If developers cannot prototype features, it is likely they will look for an alternative solution.

SUMMARY

There are many infrastructure, development, Microsoft Office, and third-party technologies you, as a design professional or SharePoint architect, should understand.

When acquiring any technology, focus on purchasing a solution that delivers against your previously defined business requirements and core use cases. Ensure that you understand your core use cases before deciding on a particular technology or vendor solution.

Finally, making good, informed decisions at key decision points during the design, development, testing, deployment, and maintenance life cycle will result in a great deployment and experience using SharePoint 2010 and related technologies. This, however, requires an in-depth understanding of the supporting SharePoint 2010 technologies.

Chapter 4 discusses key design principles for successful SharePoint 2010 deployments.

Design Principles for Successful Deployments

By Ian Morrish

As the title of this chapter suggests, design principles are key to delivering a successful SharePoint project. The role of a SharePoint solution architect is critical not only to creating the solution architecture and how it is implemented, but to ensuring that the design principles used are appropriate for the desired solution. A one-size-fits-all approach cannot be used for many aspects of the design.

A SharePoint solutions architect must have a good understanding of the project requirements, and be able to map these requirements to the SharePoint platform. This chapter highlights some of the design principles and requirements for a solution. In particular, you learn about the following:

- ➤ Determining the desired solution
- ➤ Determining solution characteristics
- ➤ Understanding SharePoint management
- ➤ Designing for storage
- ➤ Designing for governance
- ➤ Designing for IT
- ➤ Designing for users
- ➤ Designing for information workers
- ➤ Designing the information architecture
- ➤ Involving key users in the design process

DETERMINING THE DESIRED SOLUTION

Many factors determine the most appropriate design for a project that relies on SharePoint as the foundation and, depending on the type of solution, will require different approaches and skills. Microsoft describes SharePoint's capabilities based on the tenants of sites, communities, content, search, insights, and composites. However, businesses usually want to deploy SharePoint based on business requirements that are often described as one or more of the following:

➤ Document Management System (DMS)

➤ Records Management System (RMS)

➤ Electronic Document and Records Management System (EDRMS)

➤ Knowledge management

➤ Web 2.0 or social media site

➤ Collaboration portal

➤ Internet site

➤ Intranet portal

➤ Extranet portal

➤ Business Intelligence (BI) portal

➤ Line-of-business (LOB) application portal (for example, a Business Portal for Microsoft Dynamics GP 2010)

SharePoint might also be a prerequisite for a solution that has already been selected (such as Microsoft Project Server, Microsoft Dynamics Business Portal, Microsoft Team Foundation Server, or a third-party solution such as a Learning Management solution), with additional capabilities of SharePoint to be incorporated into the solution.

Another driver might be the foundation for consolidating existing SharePoint and other vendor products onto a centralized platform to reduce cost and provide a consistent user experience.

The word "enterprise" can also be added to many of the requirements just described, thus implying that the solution is to be used by all parts of the business, as opposed to a departmental or niche solution not relevant to other parts of the business.

The skills required to design and deploy a SharePoint solution will depend on the business requirements and components of the SharePoint platform that will be required in building the solution.

DETERMINING SOLUTION CHARACTERISTICS

Traditionally, different types of solutions have been deployed in silos used to manage specific content types and use cases. These have been managed by products that were designed with the specific characteristics required for that type of content. Table 4-1 shows some of the characteristics that are typical of these solutions.

TABLE 4-1: Solution Characteristics

CHARACTERISTIC	COLLABORATION WEB 2.0	WEB CONTENT MANAGEMENT	DOCUMENT MANAGEMENT	RECORDS MANAGEMENT
Primary focus	Idea-centric	Author-centric	Information-centric	Policy-centric
Role of content	Context	Information	Production	Evidence
Design	Facilitate	Delegate	Manage	Control
Mantra	"Create anything"	"Publish something"	"Keep everything"	"Destroy everything"

SharePoint is a unique platform in that it can cater to these diverse solution characteristics by using common services all the way from a core infrastructure to the user interface, including integration with client applications.

Following are some of the key principles introduced by the SharePoint platform:

➤ Content owners take on the responsibility of managing content access and life cycle.

➤ Content dynamically changes to suit the audience.

➤ A consistent user experience simplifies how people interact with content, processes, people, and business data.

➤ Content is created in production environment, not in staging.

➤ Rapid solution development in production can be attained by non-developers using out-of-the-box Features.

➤ An enterprise information management strategy is needed.

➤ A flexible platform requires more governance than rigid point solutions.

➤ Additional services can be added by using the service application framework.

UNDERSTANDING SHAREPOINT PROJECT MANAGEMENT

The project manager will depend on a lot of advice from the SharePoint solution architect, along with subject matter experts for specific disciplines required in the solution. A high-level project plan such as the one shown in Figure 4-1 may be required before more detailed project plans can be developed.

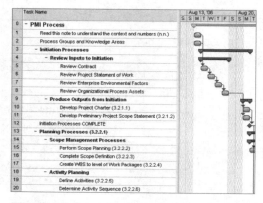

FIGURE 4-1: Example of a project plan framework

Chapter 13 discusses how to develop a detailed SharePoint project plan.

Let's take a look at some key areas of emphasis for solid SharePoint project management.

Defining Success

The success criteria for your project should be defined from several perspectives. The traditional definition of what constitutes successful project management is based on meeting the following three primary goals for any project:

➤ Delivering on time

➤ Providing required functionality

➤ Coming in, on, or under budget

These three goals are really constraints that are the prime focus of most project managers. A more holistic approach also includes additional business, user, and IT criteria for success, which should be identified early in the project to ensure the following outcomes will be achieved:

➤ *Business requirements* — The business success criterion is usually based on return on investment (ROI), which, for commercial organizations, is defined as increased profit, or, for governmental organizations, might be defined as increased services.

➤ *User requirements* — "User adoption" is the new catch phrase for SharePoint success or failure. A key success criterion for users is that the solution makes their lives easier and raises their senses of achievement, either individually or as a team.

➤ *IT requirements* — IT requirements for success can be defined at an implementation and operation level (which includes help desk support). However, overall, it is defined as the reliability of the SharePoint platform, which is also a key underlying requirement for the business and users.

Table 4-2 shows how IT can define the reliability requirement.

TABLE 4-2: Defining Reliability

ASPECT	DEFINITION	
Appropriate use	Policies should spell out how equipment and computing services may be used, as well as the appropriate security measures the staff must take to protect the organization's resources and proprietary information.	
Availability	This is the process of managing a service or application so that it is accessible when users need it. Availability is typically measured in percentage of uptime. *Downtime* refers to periods of system unavailability.	

ASPECT	DEFINITION
Capacity	For IT, this encompasses the processing or performance capability of a service or system. Capacity management is the process used to ensure that current and future business IT needs are met in a cost-effective manner.
Confidentiality	This is the protection of sensitive information from unauthorized disclosure.
Configuration	This includes the settings and software version required for a service. Configuration management is the management of security features and assurances through control of changes made to hardware, software, firmware, documentation, test, test fixtures, and test documentation throughout the life of an information system.
Continuity	This includes disaster-recovery and business processes required to allow an organization to continue functioning after (and ideally during) an incident.
Integrity	This includes the accuracy, completeness, and validity of information. Integrity must be maintained across the data life cycle — no unauthorized changes should occur from input of data into systems, to the processing of data, transfer, and storage.
Performance	This includes the responsiveness of the service or application — how long it takes to complete a requested action.
Privacy	This includes the rights and responsibilities of an individual or organization with respect to the collection, use, retention, and disclosure of personal data.
Security	This includes the discipline, techniques, and tools that protect the confidentiality, integrity, and availability of data and systems.

IT can successfully integrate SharePoint into an operational framework such as the Microsoft Operations Framework (MOF). You learn more about this later in this chapter in the section, "Designing for IT."

Project Scope

Defining a SharePoint project scope should include the capability to provide a Work Breakdown Structure (WBS) for the following main design and implementation areas:

➤ IT platform

➤ Solution and information architecture

➤ Application development

➤ Testing

➤ Training

The primary responsibility of the solution architect is to translate a business process to an information system. In this case, SharePoint is the platform for the information system, but there may also be additional development or use of third-party components to complete the solution.

Application development should be the smallest component of the solution. Unfortunately, this is often the area of a project that causes the most problems because of pitfalls such as the following:

➤ The development and testing environments don't match production.

➤ Code has dependencies outside of SharePoint and the .NET 3.5 Framework.

➤ Deployment complexities are not achievable in a solution package (WSP) or Windows PowerShell script.

There are many configuration options in SharePoint that can be changed to determine how some of the product features behave. The product can also be considered as a platform, which means it can be heavily customized. Many products provide functionality first, followed by limited APIs, which results in customizations that often break the support and upgradability of a product. But SharePoint is different in that most of the functionality provided out of the box is built on APIs that are publicly documented and intended to be used by developers to extend the platform capabilities.

The SharePoint feature and solution framework provides a way to extend and enhance the product to meet business requirements fully without breaking supportability or the possibility of future product upgrades. With this flexibility to access such a rich API comes greater responsibility to use it wisely.

Independent software vendors (ISVs) have extended and built new capabilities for SharePoint, which often means that custom development can be avoided. Low or no custom development usually results in a less complex and more successful project, which is a good driver for the solution architect to evaluate ISV solutions before committing to a large development project on SharePoint.

Project scope can be aligned to a risk matrix, as shown in Figure 4-2. Items that are above the risk profile line should either be removed from the current project scope, or additional risk mitigation steps should be planned to deal with budget or time impacts these items might have on the project.

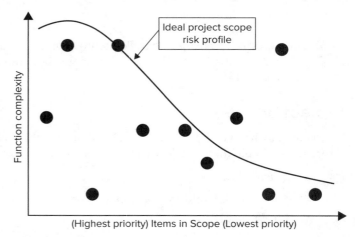

FIGURE 4-2: Project scope risk profile

Function complexity can be broken down into the categories shown in Table 4-3.

TABLE 4-3: Categories for Function Complexity

CATEGORY	CONSIDERATIONS
Low Risk	Out-of-the-box Features
	Sandboxed solutions
Medium Risk	External lists
	Custom workflow activity
	Web part not supported by sandboxed solution, but using the standard SharePoint API
	Solution that deploys the standard SharePoint Features and configuration to out-of-the-box site templates or Web Templates
High Risk	Custom site, list, or field definitions
	Custom code using non-SharePoint APIs
	Dependency on another platform for integration

If you place the scoped items in order of priority, you will quickly see if the majority of effort and potential risk are going into the most important part of the solution. If too many high-risk functions are required to support lower-priority items, the project is likely to run into problems.

Mapping Requirements

When mapping the solution requirements to SharePoint capabilities, the solution architect must have a good understanding of all the functionality that can be leveraged, and whether third-party or custom development is required. Table 4-4 shows some of the features relevant to content management.

TABLE 4-4: SharePoint Product and Platform Features

USER CONFIGURABLE	DEVELOPER IMPLEMENTED
Columns	Custom field types
Content types	Custom content types
Document sets	Custom actions
Document ID service	Event receivers
Document routing	Custom workflow activities
Publishing and approval workflows	Custom workflows

Even though there is a rich collection of user-configurable functionality, you should use custom code to automate the provisioning and configuration of these features to provide a consistent implementation across a large number of sites, and to reduce human effort.

Project Team Members

Qualifications and experience should be sought for key roles on the project team. Ensuring that adequately certified and experienced people are on the project team will reduce the risk that key tasks are not accounted for in the project plan.

Microsoft certifications are often discounted as not a good indicator of a person's capability. However, self-taught people often don't know what they don't know, especially with a complex platform like SharePoint, which also has a critical dependency on other infrastructure such as Active Directory and SQL Server. Table 4-5 shows some of the relevant Microsoft certifications.

TABLE 4-5: Available Microsoft Certifications

ROLE	CERTIFICATION	
Developers	MCTS: Microsoft SharePoint 2010, Application Development (Exam 70-573)	
	MCPD: Microsoft SharePoint Developer 2010 (Exam 70-576)	
SharePoint infrastructure design and administration	MCTS: Microsoft SharePoint 2010, Configuring (Exam 70-667)	
	MCITP: Microsoft SharePoint Administrator 2010 (Exam 70-668)	
Database Administrator	MCTS: Microsoft SQL Server 2008, Installation and Maintenance (Exam 70-432)	
	MCITP: Database Administrator 2008 (Exam 70-450)	
Business Analyst	Delivering Business Value Planning Services (Exam 074-674)	
Trainer	Microsoft Office Specialist (MOS): SharePoint 2010 (Exam 77-886)	

Other industry qualifications and certifications can also be evaluated for non-technical roles, such as the following:

➤ *SharePoint architect* — Microsoft Certified Architect (MCA) for SharePoint

➤ *Project manager* — Project Management Institute (PMI) Project Management Professional (PMP)

➤ *Electronic document or record manager* — Association for Information and Image Management (AIIM) certificate programs

The solution architect should work with the project manager early on to quantify items that should be in the project plan, and to confirm the WBS for each of the teams. This will help the solution architect oversee the various design aspects that different teams are responsible for.

Working with the Infrastructure Team

Regardless of the type of solution being built, a large number of activities are required that are related to building the infrastructure and overseeing the operational aspects. The solution architect should ensure that IT is committed to following best practices such as defined in the MOF. Following are some of the key work item areas:

➤ *Develop a scripted installation procedure* — Because build documentation based on screen shots of a wizard-based installation is usually a sign of poor planning, and is a barrier to rapid provisioning of development, testing, production, and disaster recovery environments.

➤ *Monitor the functioning of the infrastructure* — This is particularly important because SharePoint is a service that has many dependencies (for example, Active Directory and SQL Server).

➤ *Soak-test and load-test a new production environment* — It is important to ensure that any new platform (especially when deployed on new hardware) has been soak-tested for reliability, and a baseline performance measurement recorded, before any customizations are made or production content is deployed. This can help prevent unexpected issues that often delay launches.

➤ *Test the deployment of patches and solutions* — The one thing you can be certain about with a SharePoint project is that, during the life of the project, there will be critical Windows updates and SharePoint cumulative updates that will probably be required before the project is live. Use the time between when the platform is first built through deployment to refine the operations documentation, as well as apply these updates.

➤ *Service desk decision tree and FAQ* — Knowing how to identify an incident type is important in assigning the correct resource to resolve issues as quickly as possible. End-user issues that are not system errors can often be resolved through self-service FAQ resources. A knowledge base with appropriate keywords can help end users and support staff to resolve issues quickly.

➤ *Monitoring* — Treating SharePoint as a service and providing proactive monitoring so that SLAs can be maintained requires additional effort over and above just checking that servers respond to a ping test. Products like Microsoft System Center suite should be considered, and appropriate management packs configured.

➤ *Disaster recovery process* — Relying on existing technology and practices for backup or replication may not be supported by SharePoint. The complexity of the disaster recovery solution will depend on what part SharePoint (or, more importantly, the content and process stored in it) plays in the business continuity plan and the volume of content in SharePoint.

Working with the Development Team

The development team must have strict guidance on the software development life cycle of a SharePoint project, which is different from practices followed during traditional web or .NET development.

Content and code must be treated differently. SharePoint provides a well-defined solution packaging and deployment process. Before placing content in these solutions, you must take into account future requirements to update the solution without overwriting the original content that may have since been modified in the production environment. There is also a danger that content created in development or testing environments is expected to be deployed by copying the content database to production. This approach is discouraged, because it can lead to an inconsistent production environment. Instead, the content deployment should be scripted so that it can be deployed to any environment as required.

The development, functional testing, packaging, and deployment process should be formalized, and then tested end to end using a "Hello World" application before any solution code is developed. This should also include testing a version upgrade of the solution.

Understanding the SharePoint 2010 Containment Model

Understanding the logical and physical containment model of SharePoint 2010 is critical to determining how the solution should be architected.

SharePoint has its own hierarchical taxonomy that is split between back-end services and user functionality. Figure 4-3 shows the back-end architecture, where the primary containment for any solution is the web application. This is where the content starts, and is the primary method of code, authentication, and content isolation between solutions.

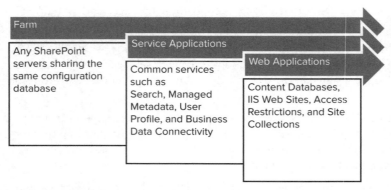

FIGURE 4-3: SharePoint farm architecture

 Chapter 6 provides more detailed information on these back-end farm components.

A SharePoint site collection is the primary method used to deliver end-user functionality and services. As shown in Figure 4-4, a site collection can contain many sites, each with many libraries and lists. A site collection also provides common capabilities that can be shared by all subsites in the site collection, and are controlled by the top-level site (that is, the root site) in the site collection.

These capabilities include the following:

➤ Global navigation provider

➤ Access roles (that is, groups can be reused in subsites)

➤ Metadata (that is, content types and columns that can be used by all subsites, lists, and libraries)

➤ Workflows

➤ Web publishing page templates

➤ Content rollup across lists, libraries, and sites

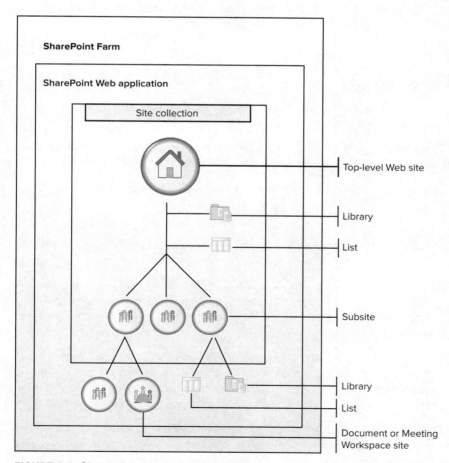

FIGURE 4-4: Sites collection containment model

These capabilities provide a lot of value to developers and solution designers. However, they can be misused, and reliance on these capabilities for large solutions can cause spectacular project failure. Following are the three primary constraints of the site collection:

➤ *Features do not span site collections* — If you must split a site collection because of its size by exporting subsites and importing them into a new site collection, they will be isolated from Features being used in the original site collection (such as the navigation).

➤ *Storage constraints* — A site collection cannot span databases, and all subsites are bound to the same site collection content database.

➤ *Item query limits* — SharePoint enforces query throttling on large lists and libraries to guarantee performance. Although the thresholds can be changed, performance may be unacceptable. Issues can also appear in the navigation provider and Content Query web parts when the site collection has a large number of sites, libraries, lists, and list items.

The template used to create the first site collection in a SharePoint web application determines the default Features that will be available. Out-of-the-box site templates are designed as a starting point to facilitate a particular scenario. Table 4-6 lists some of the more common site collection templates.

TABLE 4-6: SharePoint Site Collection Templates

TEMPLATE	DESCRIPTION	
Blank Site	This template provides a blank site for you to customize based on your requirements.	
Blog	This template provides a site for a person or team to post ideas, observations, and expertise that site visitors can comment on.	
Business Intelligence Center	This template provides a site for presenting Business Intelligence Center.	
Document Center	This template provides a site to centrally manage documents in your enterprise.	
Document Workspace	This template provides a site for colleagues to work together on a document. It provides a document library for storing the primary document and supporting files, a tasks list for assigning to-do items, and a links list for resources related to the document.	
Enterprise Wiki	This template provides a site for publishing knowledge that you capture and want to share across the enterprise. It provides an easy content editing experience in a single location for co-authoring content, discussions, and project management. (This is not to be confused with a wiki or SitePages library.)	
Group Work Site	This template provides a groupware solution that enables teams to create, organize, and share information quickly and easily. It includes Group Calendar, Circulation, Phone-Call Memo, the Document Library, and the other basic lists.	

TEMPLATE	DESCRIPTION
My Site Host	This template provides a site used for hosting personal sites (My Sites) and the public People Profile page. This template must be provisioned only once per User Profile service application.
Publishing Portal	This template provides a starter site hierarchy for an Internet-facing site, or a large intranet portal. This site can be customized easily with distinctive branding. It includes a home page, a sample press releases subsite, a Search Center, and a login page. Typically, this site has many more readers than contributors, and it is used to publish web pages with approval workflows.
Records Center	This template creates a site designed for records management. Records managers can configure the routing table to direct incoming files to specific locations. The site also lets you manage whether records can be deleted or modified after they are added to the repository.
Team Site	This template provides a site for teams to quickly organize, author, and share information. It provides a document library, and lists for managing announcements, calendar items, tasks, and discussions. The home page can be edited like a wiki page.

Each of these site templates can have additional features added, and can include subsites that use the same or other templates. Site collections can share a database, but a single site collection can't span content databases. This requires careful planning of the solution so that performance will not be compromised, and so that solution dependencies on the use of out-of-the-box capabilities of site collection features don't constrain the potential storage requirements of the solution.

DESIGNING FOR STORAGE

For most solution designs, you must plan for the storage requirements over time to take into account the recommendations and limits of SharePoint. Table 4-7 shows the key requirements. Supported vales are not hard limits and are based on maintaining acceptable response times based on recommended hardware requirements.

TABLE 4-7: Site Collection Limits

Content database size	200 GB to 4 TB	Supported
Site collection size	100 GB per site collection	Supported
Site collections per web application	250,000	Supported
Site collections per content database	2,000 recommended; 5,000 maximum	Supported

continues

TABLE 4-7 *(continued)*

File size	2 GB per file	Boundary
Documents	30,000,000 per library	Supported
Major versions	400,000	Supported
Items	30,000,000 per list	Supported

The limits are not cumulative. For example, a site collection that holds 200 GB of collaborative content that is changing all the time should not have any other site collections in the same content database.

Internet-facing web content-management solutions are a common scenario where the content is not expected to exceed 200 GB. In this case, the solution design can incorporate all of the Features scoped to a site collection. These Features are primarily the navigation providers and the Content Query web part, both of which provide aggregation information from all web sites, and content repositories within the site collection.

It is better to break a solution down into multiple site collections to support function or activity instances (such as project sites) if any of the instances are likely to exceed the storage guidelines. This would require custom navigation and aggregation solutions (such as a site collection directory), something that was provided in SharePoint 2007, but has been removed from 2010.

The supported limits are set to ensure acceptable performance for normal usage patterns. A site collection that is dedicated to the archiving of content, and that has very few users accessing it, could be stored in a dedicated content database, and may exceed the recommendations without noticeable performance impacts. However, you must still factor in backup and recovery times.

More details about the software boundaries and limits are published on the Microsoft website at http://technet.microsoft.com/en-us/library/cc262787.aspx.

DESIGNING FOR GOVERNANCE

The purpose of *governance* is to define the policies and enforcement authority for all aspects of a business to ensure consistency and compliance. Several forms of governance should already exist in an organization, including the following:

➤ Business governance

➤ Project governance

➤ IT governance

SharePoint governance overlaps these three areas, and introduces both IT and business policies specific to SharePoint.

SharePoint governance has been recognized as very important to the success of a deployment. Many articles and best practices have been published on SharePoint governance. As with any portal solution, without the right governance plan in place, SharePoint can get "out of control" and become difficult to manage. A key outcome of successful SharePoint governance is to enable access, agility, adaptability, and innovation, while maintaining centralized management, risk mitigation, and cost control.

Self-service site creation is a primary feature in SharePoint that empowers users, but can also lead to a form of controlled chaos. Figure 4-5 illustrates this concept.

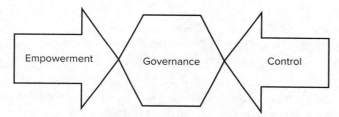

FIGURE 4-5: Empowerment versus control

Aspects of self-service site creation might include the following:

➤ Creating subsites

➤ Creating SharePoint lists and libraries

➤ Creating wiki or web publishing pages

➤ Authoring reports

Other operations will be beyond the capability of self-service, and will require clear guidelines as to how the requests will be auctioned, and by whom. The following list is an example of how more complex requests might be categorized:

➤ Help Desk service requests:

   ➤ Restoring deleted sites

   ➤ Help with access and security requests

   ➤ Enabling enterprise features in site collections

   ➤ Requesting site storage quota increases

➤ Minor IT development request:

   ➤ New site collection requests

   ➤ No-code site creation for a business process that requires specific information architecture to support extensive use of out-of-the-box features such as workflows, views, content types, and Office templates

➤ New personalization requirements requiring Audience or Search configuration

➤ SharePoint Designer–based customizations

➤ Verification, installation, and configuration of third-party party sandbox solutions

➤ Major IT request:

  ➤ Service pack and hot fix deployment

  ➤ Third-party farm or web application solution deployment

  ➤ Code development for back-end integration or front-end automated feature provisioning

  ➤ Configuring enterprise features such as PerformancePoint and data sources to provide dashboards and scorecards

Governance involves defining specific roles, responsibilities, and rules across the life cycle of your SharePoint deployment, and throughout its ongoing use. Because governance involves many different roles, a governance plan should be agreed upon by a group of stakeholders, and communicated out to the larger community.

The aspects of business governance that apply to a SharePoint solution will be specific to the type of solution. This usually relates to regulatory and standards requirements that apply to the content.

Most organizations operate in a regulated environment. The risk of non-compliance drives many projects from a risk-mitigation perspective.

Following are some areas of risk for information disclosure:

➤ European Union (EU) Data Protection Directive (DPD)

➤ Payment Card Industry (PCI) Data Security Standard (DSS)

➤ Trade secrets

Following are some areas of risk for industry-specific compliance requirements:

➤ *Government* — Public records

➤ *Health* — Health Insurance Portability and Accessibility Act (HIPAA) privacy and security rules

➤ *Manufacturing* — ISO compliance

➤ *Business* — Sarbanes-Oxley (SOX) Act Compliance

Not only must content comply with these requirements, the actions of people must also be in compliance. It is important that the design identify the processes involved in the content life cycle, and provide auditing capability for evidential purposes, if required.

 A good place to start is the SharePoint Governance TechNet Resource Center. Chapter 20 also provides additional details about governance.

DESIGNING FOR IT

The MOF provides a framework for managing the life cycle of an IT service, which is illustrated in Figure 4-6. For organizations that adopt an IT Infrastructure Library (ITIL), MOF provides the practical guidance that relates specifically to Microsoft products. MOF 4.0 is provided (with permission) by Microsoft under the Creative Commons Attribution License.

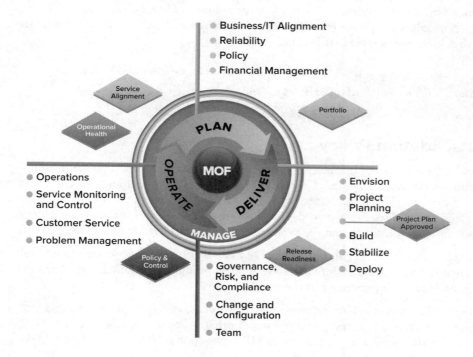

FIGURE 4-6: Life cycle of an IT service

Apart from SharePoint itself, key Microsoft infrastructure components include Windows Server, Active Directory, Internet Information Server (IIS), and SQL Server. MOF provides Service Management Functions (SMF) that describe the basic manual tasks that should be performed to operate these systems. Microsoft System Center Operations Manager (SCOM) uses management packs for each of these infrastructure components to automate these tasks.

See the "SharePoint Server 2010: Operations Framework and Checklists"
(www.microsoft.com/downloads/en/details.aspx?FamilyID=3cd07201-7420-4c12-9639-81da513e728d) *for SharePoint 2010 checklists to find daily, weekly, and monthly tasks that are related to the operations management of a SharePoint Server environment, along with guidance for using Microsoft SCOM.*

Several aspects of an existing IT policy can affect the design considerations for SharePoint. Most of these design requirements should be defined in the project's non-functional requirements. The following are examples of the IT policies that may impact the physical design of the SharePoint solution.

Virtualization Policy

Scaling a SharePoint solution either vertically or horizontally in a virtualized environment is not as predictable as in a physical environment. There is a finite amount of I/O, memory, and CPU available, and if the virtualization platform for SharePoint is shared with other applications, it can be more difficult to achieve predictable performance results.

 See Chapter 23 for more detail on design guidance.

Database Consolidation Policy

The database workload for a SharePoint solution is not the traditional transaction model that database administrators (DBAs) are used to. Sharing a SQL Server instance with other LOB applications is likely to impact the performance of all applications. Adding an additional instance of SQL Server to the same hardware may provide better results, but there will still be I/O, memory, and CPU overhead of the new instance that the existing hardware must be able to provide.

Lots of databases are created by SharePoint, and many of them require special consideration for an enterprise deployment to be successful. More than one SQL Server may be required, depending on the content storage and search requirements of the solution.

To explain to DBAs the importance of SharePoint's specific database design requirements and potential exemptions to standard policies, you can point out that, when a user saves a 10 MB PowerPoint presentation to SharePoint, it creates a 10 MB transaction in SQL Server (even if SQL remote BLOB storage is used).

Storage Policy

Many organizations have invested heavily in Storage Area Network (SAN) technology to eliminate the wasted space of Direct Attached Storage (DAS) for individual servers. These solutions also provide centralized backup solutions, de-duplication, and geographic replication of data. SANs were often sold on the premise of being a high-performance "black box" that negated the need for detailed physical disk design. Many organizations are now finding that SANs must be partitioned for specific workloads if they are to meet the storage demands of applications like SharePoint.

 Chapter 17 provides more guidance on storage design considerations.

Security Policy

Security architects often insist on having firewalls between each of the logical layers of an n-tier application. When taken to the extreme, this can be an impractical environment for SharePoint to operate in.

Trying to isolate Active Directory, SQL Server, SharePoint application servers, content sources for indexing, Web Front-End (WFE) servers, and users will add a lot of complexity to the project. Internet-facing solutions may require this level of isolation, but for internal solutions (such as a document-management solution), try to host all components of the SharePoint solution in a single zone just as if it were a file server.

Disaster Recovery

Understand the existing geographic redundancy, high-availability, and backup/recovery solutions already provided in the data center, and whether these support SharePoint. Most backup solutions provide SharePoint-specific agents to ensure the successful restoration of all the components in a SharePoint farm.

 Chapter 21 provides more guidance on disaster-recovery design considerations.

DESIGNING FOR USERS

It is hard to visualize a SharePoint solution that doesn't incorporate the familiar user interface of the Microsoft Office and SharePoint platform. This often leads to the request, "I want SharePoint, but I don't want it to look like SharePoint." Assuming that the site objectives and business requirements are already defined, it is important to differentiate between user wants and needs. Traditional web content management has evolved into two streams.

Personal or consumer publishing is based on what-you-see-is-what-you-get (WYSIWYG) authoring, with the capability to tag content. The hosting platform provides the visual theme and content storage capability. Creating content on these platforms often involves a cut-and-paste action from authoritative content sources into the WYSIWYG authoring environment, and the author spends a lot of time formatting the content to look acceptable.

Dynamic and data-driven publishing provides the infrastructure to deal with large volumes of information that must be published in a consistent and discoverable way. Users can create content items guided by a template that identifies and provides structure to the elements of the content. Some elements of the content may still allow WYSIWYG authoring, but this is usually constrained to certain fonts and styles. Content can also be created that is an aggregation of content items that are user-created or extracted from external systems. Adding user perception to the solution characteristics table (as shown in Table 4-8) can help focus the solution designer on the challenges of meeting the user requirements, while at the same time, addressing the business requirements and technology constraints.

TABLE 4-8: User Perception

CHARACTERISTIC	COLLABORATION WEB 2.0	WEB CONTENT MANAGEMENT	DOCUMENT MANAGEMENT	RECORDS MANAGEMENT
Primary Focus	Idea-centric	Author-centric	Information-centric	Policy-centric
Role of content	Context	Information	Production	Evidence
Design	Facilitate	Delegate	Manage	Control
Mantra	"Create anything"	"Publish something"	"Keep everything"	"Destroy everything"
User Perception	Freedom	Flexible	Burdensome	Inflexible

Users want the freedom of consumer-style WYSIWYG solutions, but you will often see them incorporating the benefits of content from more formal sources. A classic example of this is a user who authors a wiki page on a topic, but adds links in the page to relevant documents he or she has found in the DMS, or a user who authors content in Word, saves the file somewhere, and then copies and pastes the document content into the wiki page editor. This creates a maintenance burden that prevents a large-scale content solution from being successful.

A well-designed SharePoint solution that focuses on user needs can provide the right balance between flexibility and control across the broad spectrum of content that can be managed by the SharePoint platform.

User Experience

When selecting SharePoint as the basis for a solution, a degree of standardization of the user experience is implied. This user experience provides commonality between the Microsoft Office applications and SharePoint, primarily through the Ribbon interface. Other aspects of the user experience can be expressed using system or user terminology, as shown in Table 4-9.

TABLE 4-9: User Experience

SHAREPOINT	USER
Function specification	Usability
Site hierarchy	Navigation
Library and list interface	Interaction
Theme	Branding

For collaboration and document-management scenarios, the standard navigation and interaction capability of SharePoint should provide adequate usability with minimal user training required. Simple branding can be applied to incorporate corporate standards without dramatically altering the way SharePoint functionality is presented to the user.

Corporate intranet and Internet web content management is the case where there may be a dramatic difference in the required interface from that provided out-of-the-box. SharePoint provides the Page Layout content type that uses field controls, rather than normal list views, to provide total control over the HTML rendering of page layouts. There are thousands of Internet-facing websites built on SharePoint that use the publishing Features to provide content that would normally have to be created by web developers.

Role-Based Design

User needs should be classified by the user roles, as shown in Figure 4-7. A user's role determines how he or she will interact with the content, and any formal part of the content life cycle the user plays a part in. SharePoint provides specific Features to help users.

For content creators, there will always be some traditional page authoring that requires appropriate writing skills and content flexibility (such as the "About us" page). But most content will come from information providers who are responsible for semi-structured content (such as job vacancies or product details). Identifying the specific information requirements for each type of content, how it will be entered, business rules or policies that must be enforced, and how the content will be consumed, is the basis for a user-centered design.

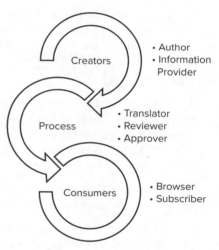

FIGURE 4-7: User role in content life cycle

 Accessibility requirements should also be considered for all roles, not just the consumer.

Visual Design

As with any solution design (whether it is an information system or a physical building), everyone wants to see conceptual visuals before they buy into a project. The importance of visual design and its dominance of the overall project effort will vary depending on the nature of the project. For an Internet-facing site, this might be considered one of the most important design aspects. On the other hand, a DMS might only inherit some corporate colors and logo in the site header, but apart from that, rely on the out-of-the-box SharePoint user interface.

Traditional wireframe design methods are usable only to a point with SharePoint. Developers will have to translate the wireframe into the relevant SharePoint technologies that deal with branding, navigation, and content.

SharePoint provides out-of-the-box components to support the visual design, but these will often have to be extended or replaced to meet the requirements. Components of the design can be divided into the following areas:

➤ *Chrome* — This includes common page elements that are consistent across pages. Custom master page and Cascading Style Sheet (CSS) development is required.

➤ *Navigation components* — This includes global and local navigation concepts, or a "mega menu" approach. You must modify CSS for SharePoint navigation providers, or develop new providers.

➤ *Content* — This includes traditional HTML or rich user interface components such as jQuery, Flash, or Silverlight. Page layout templates are developed to source the structured content from libraries and lists, and rendered as required.

Personalized

To help users deal with the overwhelming amount of information available, consider using audience targeting. This can be used to filter information based on different user categories (such as skill, interests, geographic location, language, or policy-determined membership, like Active Directory groups). Targeting content to users in this way implies a recommendation that the content shown is relevant to the user.

Two aspects exist related to the personalization design requirements: defining the audience properties, and displaying information based on audience membership.

Membership in an audience can be determined by users, or based on business rules. SharePoint provides a mechanism for self-selected properties in the My Site User Profile. Target audiences can be derived from these user profile field values, along with business-specific rules based on Active Directory security and distribution group membership.

Content can be filtered for an audience at the item level in a library view, or by using the Content Query web part. Web part visibility on a page can also be determined by the current user audience membership, which can completely change the appearance of a page.

DESIGNING FOR INFORMATION WORKERS

The goal of this design approach is to help information workers use structured and unstructured content in the context of a business process.

Organizations have a large investment in productivity tools such Microsoft Office, and an even larger investment in their staff, but little is usually invested in assisting staff to get the most out of these tools to improve productivity. E-mail and network shares are often the only tools available to support information workers who collaborate.

Microsoft identified this need to enhance the information worker experience and provides this capability in the SharePoint platform to facilitate people and information-centric business processes to be more efficient.

Effective use of SharePoint as a platform to support information workers requires a strategic approach to provide productivity advice to business process owners, and to back this up with analysis, implementation, and training resources. The problem with deploying SharePoint out-of-the-box is that users will continue to work the same way they always have, and use SharePoint as if it were a network share.

Microsoft developed a programmatic approach to identify and unlock the business value of using the Office and SharePoint solutions for customers. Business Value Planning Services (BVPS) was designed for partners to deliver this consulting service to customers, but it can equally be adopted by an internal IT or business analyst team using a dedicated solution advisor role.

The solution advisor should follow a process similar to the BVPS deliverable guidance, which includes the following:

➤ *Current state analysis* — Review, documentation, and analysis of the way a process is currently performed.

➤ *Future state analysis* — Develop a revised and improved business process utilizing information worker technologies.

➤ *Business case* — Develop a cost/benefit analysis and case for proposed process change, including key performance indicator (KPI) improvement and multi-year cash flow analysis (for large processes that require significant investment).

➤ *Adoption and implementation plan* — Guidance on resources required, solution owners, risk mitigation, task sequencing, change management, and communication required to implement the proposed solution.

➤ *Deliverable/proposal* — Proposal to implement a developed solution, including summary of current state, future state, and business case analyses.

➤ *Implementation* — Using out-of-the-box features where possible to implement the solution and hand over training.

Depending on the complexity of a business process, this could require anything from two or three days to several weeks. It is easy to prioritize the implementation of these solutions based on the value identified in the business cases versus the capacity to implement the solution. Another benefit of this approach is that the actual return on investment (ROI) of both the SharePoint platform and the internal resources required to provide this service is highly visible to the business, and is ongoing.

It might be tempting to jump straight to the implementation phase after reviewing the current state. However, this often leads to ad-hoc design decisions being made, and the final outcome falling short of business expectations.

The current and future state analysis is not intended to be a process re-engineering exercise, but rather an opportunity to facilitate the process to gain efficiency (which might be measured in reduced elapsed time, higher quality output, or reduced risk).

Process Mapping

Process mapping is a key component of BVPS used in the current state and future state analysis. It helps identify the metadata that will be required to automate the decision process, and also to provide a relevant view of information to each stakeholder, as shown in Figure 4-8.

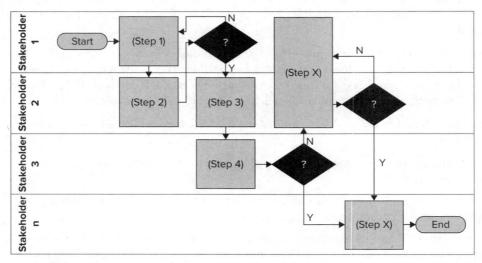

FIGURE 4-8: Process map

This is not an exercise in process re-engineering, although it should highlight how SharePoint can help facilitate and improve the process. Recording the elapsed time and human effort at each step in the current state, and the improvements that the future state solution can deliver, provides a clear indication in the potential benefits to the business.

Focusing on the stakeholders and the use cases for each of the participants or groups engaged in the process helps identify the metadata required to facilitate components of the solution (such as workflow and filtered views). Limiting the metadata requirements to only meet these needs helps to remove any burden being placed on users to provide unnecessary information.

The BVPS website (`https://iwsolve.partners.extranet.microsoft.com/`
`bvps/Resources.aspx`*) provides a number of example scenarios to help identify the types of scenarios that are appropriate for this process. Note that some of the solutions proposed include additional Microsoft products such as Project Server. You can find out more about BVPS from the Microsoft website at* `www.microsoftbvps.com`*.*

SharePoint Solution Center

If SharePoint has been deployed as a central service to support business processes and information workers, a plan will be required to deal with the requests to provision the types of requests that will come from the business. Providing this service may be a function of IT or a business group in its own right (often the case when an organization places high value on business process improvement, and has a large team of business analysts). This could be called a SharePoint Solution Center, and has the advantage of separating traditional IT operations support of the SharePoint infrastructure from the business application.

A Solution Center such as this provides a process for the business to engage with the resources required to deliver solutions that take into account the SharePoint governance plan, as shown in Figure 4-9. It could also have a relationship with the SharePoint steering committee, reporting on progress of projects, and raising any issues or activities other than "business as usual" that might require change requests or budgetary consideration.

Providing a service catalog that describes what the Solution Center can provide, along with examples of the solutions already delivered, will help set the expectations for the business.

To provide transparency to the process, it is important that the capture and evaluate steps are well-defined.

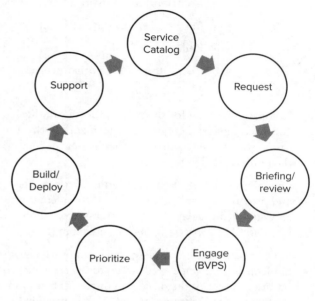

FIGURE 4-9: Solution Center process

➤ *Capture requests* — Collect basic information about the request, including general information that will be required for the evaluation process. Details include the following:

➤ Business process name

➤ Description

➤ Process owner/sponsor

➤ Volume (number of documents per day, and so on)

➤ Number of users

➤ Current issues with process

➤ Improvements that are sought

➤ *Evaluate requests* — Provide an objective view of the suitability of the request based on business drivers and alignment with platform capability. (These should be captured during the briefing/review process.) The evaluation criteria is a bit more detailed than the business request data, but not as extensive as the ROI that can be provided in the BVPS report. Example criteria that might be rated as low, medium, or strong include the following:

> ➤ Productivity improvement
>
> ➤ Quality improvement resulting in increased customer satisfaction
>
> ➤ Contribution to institutional knowledge
>
> ➤ Improvement to staff satisfaction
>
> ➤ Reduction of risk
>
> ➤ Cost offset from another project
>
> ➤ Overall ROI

Resource planning for the BVPS process can then be applied to the currently outstanding list of approved requests. For a large organization, the number of requests each week or month could easily exceed the resources available, but the SharePoint governance steering group could manage the political lobbying.

Engaging in the BVPS process requires commitment from the business to participate in workshops, and provides the relevant experts to complete the current state and validate the future state design. Any significant delays by the business group in meeting its commitments in this process should result in BVPS process being suspended in favor of the next approved request in the queue.

On completion of the BVPS process, another review should be performed that decides if the implementation stage needs to go to the steering group. This should be agreed upon criteria based on the size/cost of the project to implement, resources available, and if any significant investment is required for functionality not already provided by the platform (such as third-party software or custom code development).

The solution implementation will be achieved in one of two ways:

➤ Directly on the production server using self-service Features that can be activated and configured in the browser (and possibly SharePoint Designer, depending on the governance plan)

➤ In a development environment that will follow the application development life cycle, including packaging, testing, and final deployment to production, according to the governance plan

Once the solution is in place, it should be added to the Service Center as a reference, including a "sound bite"–style quote from the business sponsor summarizing the benefits achieved with the new solution.

The information management requirements of the SharePoint Solution Center can be met with a SharePoint site, which makes a nice showcase of how a process like this can be facilitated by SharePoint.

DESIGNING THE INFORMATION ARCHITECTURE

Information architecture is critical to the effective management of information, and should support an information governance strategy. This is primarily to address information management issues, which can be very difficult for an organization that is decentralized, or has business units that have unique requirements. The specific requirements for information architecture will depend on the solution requirements (that is, web content management versus document management), although there are some common dependencies on information architecture such as usability, search, and navigation.

Terminology

Following are some of the terms often used by information architects:

➤ *Terminology* — Has no structure and is open to human interpretation.

➤ *Classification* — Broad organizing or grouping of information.

➤ *Ontology* — Describes things and their meanings.

➤ *Taxonomy* — Hierarchy and relationships.

➤ *Metadata* — Describes an element of an item or container.

➤ *Thesaurus* — Authority for meaning.

➤ *Vocabulary* — The language and terms specific to a domain.

➤ *Folksonomy* — Informal keywords created by users.

The skill of an information architect comes into play when defining taxonomy and metadata requirements for an information system like SharePoint.

Content

One of the main requirements of information architecture (specifically for SharePoint) is that which is used to manage the content stored within SharePoint libraries and lists.

The Microsoft Productivity Hub site template is a good example of how the information architecture, applied to the content, leads to a good user experience. As shown in Figure 4-10, in the Productivity Hub, there is a document library that contains more than a thousand Word documents, PowerPoint presentations, and videos of task-based guidance on using Microsoft products.

Type	Title	Name	Product	ProductVersion	Abstract	IsFeaturedContent	Difficulty
	Customize the Ribbon	customize-the-ribbon-HA010355697	Ribbon	2010	Learn how to customize the Ribbon to fit your needs for better usability.	No	Advanced
	Personalize your e-mail messages	customize-your-e-mail-message-HA010359094	Outlook	2010	Add color and graphics to your e-mail messages for greater impact	No	Beginning
	Customizing charts	Customizing charts	Excel		Find out how to customize your charts, including formatting titles and individual columns.	No	Intermediate

FIGURE 4-10   Productivity Hub document library

The library contains sufficient metadata columns to allow several methods for interacting with the content. The default SharePoint library interface is hidden from the user by default, and the home page of the site (shown in Figure 4-11) is the primary user interface to the content. This allows access to the content through the Quick Launch menu, product icon slider, featured content, or search.

FIGURE 4-11: Productivity Hub home page

When deciding on the metadata requirements of a solution, consider the purpose of the metadata, as shown in the example in Table 4-10.

TABLE 4-10: Metadata by Purpose

IDENTIFICATION	SEARCH	WORKFLOW	COMPLIANCE	KNOWLEDGE MANAGEMENT
Created By; Modified By; Date	Topic	Approver	Classification	Industry-specific

The metadata for an item is always stored in a SharePoint column. The primary methods of defining metadata in columns are as follows:

➤ Single-value column (text, number, person, date/time, and so on)

➤ Choice column

➤ List content used as a column lookup

➤ Term set from the Term Store

➤ External data

The metadata can be managed at several levels:

➤ Local to the library or list (columns)

➤ Local to the site (lookup list)

➤ Site collection-wide (site columns)

➤ Farm-wide (Content Type Hub and Term Store)

➤ External System (Business Connectivity Services)

The Term Store provides a controlled vocabulary that supports hierarchy and synonyms. This is a new capability delivered in SharePoint Server 2010. It might be tempting to use the Term Store for managing all metadata requirements. However, some limitations and constraints exist when taking this approach. Known limitations include the following:

➤ Lack of support in the Document Information panel for previous versions of Office applications

➤ No mechanism for moving the Term Store and tagged content between farms (for example, between development and production)

 Business Connectivity Services (BCS) functionality is covered in Chapter 11.

SharePoint provides the content type object to group metadata that is relevant for an item of content (list item, document, web page, blog post). Content types can be managed at the same levels as the metadata.

Content types encapsulate the settings and metadata requirements that must be assigned to a type of content. SharePoint content types have the following capabilities:

➤ Contain site collection columns (metadata)

➤ Can also contain existing columns from the list or library that the content type is activated in

➤ Workflows

➤ Office template on which new items using this content type will be based

➤ Associated page layouts for publishing site Page libraries

➤ Custom forms (ASP.NET or InfoPath) for New, Edit, and Display of items using this content type

➤ Information policy requirements, including activity recording, retention, barcodes, and document labels

SharePoint also supports a Content Type Hub, which is a dedicated site (one per Term Store Service) that holds master content types with associated metadata, and terms that can be replicated to site collections in web applications that consume the same Term Store Service application. The Content Type Hub is a new Feature in SharePoint 2010 that was created to solve the problem experienced in previous versions of SharePoint when a solution required multiple site collections because of the database constraints described earlier in this chapter, but required consistent metadata.

Deciding which SharePoint Feature should be used to accommodate the metadata requirements will depend on several factors. The first is if metadata is specific to an individual site or process, versus metadata common to a department or the entire organization. The second is based on the nature of the metadata from a hierarchical requirement point of view.

Examples of metadata include the following:

➤ *Regions and countries* — A hierarchy

➤ *Business activity* — Hierarchy or flat, depending on level of detail

➤ *Process* — Hierarchy or flat, depending on level of detail

➤ *Project* — Flat (external data source of project names or codes)

➤ *Status* — Flat (values that reflect phase of life cycle)

➤ *Topic* — Hierarchy derived from a taxonomy (may allow multiple selections)

A metadata column bound to the Term Store is the only mechanism provided by SharePoint to allow for both tagging content and filtering it based on a hierarchical value.

When analyzing the overall metadata requirements for the various content types, a pattern will emerge that indicates the reusability of the metadata, as shown in Figure 4-12.

Metadata	Content Type					
	Contract (Hub)	Change Request	RFI	RFP	Response	
Recorded	✓	✓	✓	✓	✓	Y/N Indicates that physical copy has been filed in Project office
Vendor	✓		✓	✓	✓	External lookup field to approved vendor list
Project	✓	✓				Lookup to project register list
Expiry	✓					Date
Evaluators					✓	Person Lookup - multi select
Vendor Version					✓	Number
Approver	✓	✓	✓	✓		Person Lookup - single
Survey					✓	URL - link to survey for this response

FIGURE 4-12: Example content type and metadata matrix

Columns and content types play a pivotal role in how content is organized and managed in SharePoint. Search is additional area of the design that can make extensive use of metadata through Features such as the refinement panel, and requires appropriate consideration in the information architecture design.

 Chapter 27 provides more information on how indexed metadata can be configured through managed properties and refiners.

INVOLVING KEY USERS

Analysts may use tools and methodologies such as a Swim Lane diagram and Decomposition Matrix, but users don't understand these when it comes time to acknowledge that the requirements have been understood. This is a critical time in the project, because it is often the point at which users disengage from the project because they don't have the confidence that their needs have been addressed. Users have a physiologically based information-processing pattern that isn't fully replicated by a software-based information system.

Following are some processes and tools that can engage the users more effectively:

➤ Focus groups during requirements gathering phase

➤ Card sorting during information architecture design

➤ Prototype and pilot sites for user feedback and testing

Focus Groups

Focus groups help with understanding the "what and why" of a process. They help to collect a list of all the tasks performed, as well as the information inputs and outputs of the process.

Effective focus group facilitation requires clear goals for the outcomes, and carefully designed questions with the capability to record the answers in an unbiased way. Following are key requirements of the focus group:

➤ Intent (goals and objectives of workshop/interview)

➤ Questions (process life cycle, roles and responsibilities) that are not leading questions

➤ Discussion (often will reveal usability and communication requirements)

➤ Outcome (target individual activities, but note dependencies on other activities)

Care must be taken not to allow influential users to drive the discussion toward feature requirements, especially features based on prior experience with specific products.

Some processes may span organizational groups. But a process might be called the same thing in different parts of the organization, yet be completely different. Similar processes may also be variations of the same process based on geographic or industry vertical requirements. Ensure that the focus group members provide the representation to overcome these issues.

Card Sorting

Card sorting is useful for affinity diagramming, which can be used both for user experience and business processes. It helps in organizing observations that are captured during brainstorming, or from the input obtained by capturing existing information that must be restructured (such as the names of subdirectories and files in a network share, or page titles in a large website).

Card sorting is often performed on a whiteboard with a combination of sticky notes and whiteboard marking. This has the disadvantage that all participants must be present in the same room, and that the process must be captured and re-entered into an electronic format. Software products can facilitate the direct capture and manipulation of the process. Various mind mapping and card sorting applications are available to facilitate this process. One such application is Microsoft Office Labs Sticky Sorter, which is freely available from `http://officelabs.com/projects/stickysorter`.

Sticky Sorter (as shown in Figure 4-13) allows cards to be assigned to a group. Additional fields can be added to cards, which can be viewed and edited by flipping the card over from the right-click menu option.

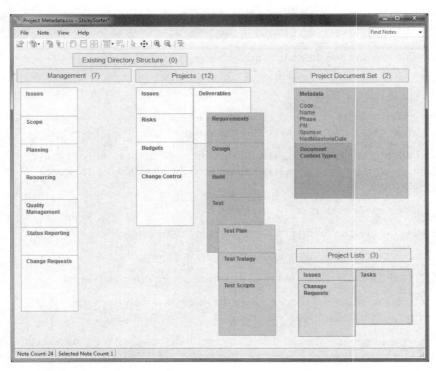

FIGURE 4-13: Sticky Sorter

A comma-separated value (CSV) file format is used by Sticky Sorter to import and export card information. Sticky Sorter can also be used by a virtual team using application-sharing software such as Microsoft Lync to collaborate on the exercise.

To be successful, the facilitator should have seed cards to get the process started, or to fill in when users draw a blank and start to lose interest in the exercise.

Prototypes and Pilots

SharePoint's self-service model makes it easy to prototype a no-code solution for users to pilot. Several issues should be considered if using this approach.

The following should be considered if a production platform is used:

➤ Should pilot data be discoverable in enterprise search?

➤ Scope creep is exasperated because detailed requirements have been replaced by second guessing user needs based on available platform features.

The following should be considered if a non-production platform is used:

➤ A successful pilot may generate content that must be moved to production.

➤ The availability of a platform may be affected by technical needs that may upset users.

➤ Content may be lost or slow to recover in the event of a failure or user error.

In the early stages of a design, artifacts such as branding may not be complete, but parallel streams of work such as training for content creation or usability testing may need to start using a SharePoint platform before the production solution is ready.

The worst way to prototype a solution is to start with a Team Site template, because this sets expectations about the artifacts that are available (Shared Documents, Tasks, Events). Start with a Blank Site template, activate the Features as determined by the requirements, and then create the site artifacts, naming them in a way that is consistent with the desired user experience.

Figure 4-14 shows an example of a prototype site using library and list names that match the process, along with content that indicates purpose.

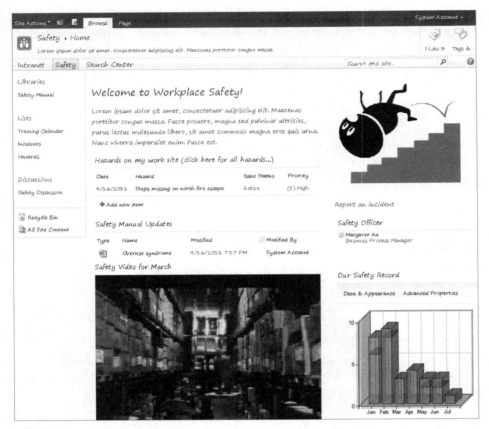

FIGURE 4-14: Prototype site

By using a black-and-white theme with a comic font, you can focus users on the process and content, rather than having them worrying about it being too late in the process to change the visual design.

SUMMARY

The key focus of this chapter has been to raise awareness of business, user, and content requirements in a SharePoint-based solution design, and some of the principles that apply. It is by no means an exhaustive guide to the analysis or design requirements.

Understanding why certain decisions must be made based on the solution requirements will help you select the relevant "how-to" information presented in Chapter 5, which provides some insight as to how Microsoft uses SharePoint.

5

Learning How Microsoft Uses SharePoint 2010

By Sam Hassani, Jim Adams, and Scott Kleven

The Microsoft ecosystem encompasses a globally distributed workforce comprised of 180,000 full-time employees and vendors, which can be further broken down into four classes of users as follows:

- ➤ Office Dweller (40 percent full-time employees)
- ➤ Campus Nomad (40 percent full-time employees)
- ➤ Remote Users (20 percent of full-time employees)
- ➤ Business Partners (approximately 100,000 in total)

Microsoft's worldwide SharePoint deployment consists of approximately 35 TB of content distributed between three data centers located in Seattle, Dublin, and Singapore. This content is made up from a number of different farms containing just under 200,000 site collections and more than 485,000 subsites.

This chapter takes a look at how the vastness of this SharePoint deployment not only allows the dynamic workforce to collaborate and work more efficiently, but provides the breadth and depth of testing for the product group to incorporate feedback from early adopters into final product releases. This discussion focuses on how an internal process known as *dogfooding* allows Microsoft to achieve this. This chapter also looks at some of the best practices and lessons learned internally at Microsoft when considering Business Continuity Management, virtualization, and governance at this scale.

KEY SITES AND SERVICES

Microsoft IT (MSIT) provides a full range of SharePoint hosting services (intranet and extranet) for all internal-facing SharePoint sites at Microsoft. Furthermore, there are numerous portals hosting intranet content, knowledge management solutions, and smaller silos of departmental content. Here are some of key platforms and hosting options for new sites:

➤ *Office 365* — Standard utility environment with an engagement model to man.

➤ *Microsoft Web (MSW)* — This is Microsoft's corporate intranet portal.

➤ *InfoPedia* — This is a knowledge-delivery platform for the sales, marketing, and services fields, enabling topic-based content discovery and field contribution.

➤ *SharePoint Utility* — This is the standard team collaboration SharePoint platform available to all Microsoft users. Self-site creation is enabled. However, server-side deployments are not allowed, and client-side solutions are not supported by IT.

➤ *My Sites* — All corporate users automatically have a My Site, which is a personal server-side workspace.

➤ *Team* — This is a team collaboration service offering with free hosting that enables users to use and test the latest SharePoint features, and to test proof-of-concept solutions. Team sites are subject to continual MSIT SharePoint upgrades and solution deployments. Because of this, the environment has lower support Service Level Agreements (SLAs), and is not intended to be a highly available service. Code that must be installed on the SharePoint server is not allowed, and custom client-side code is not supported by the Helpdesk.

➤ *Portals* — This is a utility platform with an engagement model. It includes a library of free platform solutions and additional fee-based features/integrations. There is limited customization support.

➤ *Custom Portals* — Each custom portal is deployed to a dedicated farm, fully customizable, and has a dedicated support model.

➤ *Shared Services* — This is a federated services farm consisting of user profiles, managed metadata, and Business Connectivity Services (BCS) consumed by other farms.

➤ *Fast Search* — Based on FAST Search for SharePoint 2010, this is an enterprise-wide search farm, indexing a global corpus of approximately 80 million items.

Let's take a closer look at MSW, InfoPedia, and SharePoint Utility in a little more detail.

Microsoft Web (MSW)

MSW is Microsoft's corporate portal, and the place to start internally for information about the company — from news and current events to important information about the business, everyday services, and more, MSW can help employees navigate the ever-expanding Microsoft intranet.

MSW is designed to be the most convenient place to search for everything an employee needs on the intranet, regardless of whether it's hosted on MSW. The home page of MSW provides timely information about what is happening today at Microsoft, and the latest updates about the company, its industry, and related world events.

As you drill into the home page on MSW, some of the following key elements emerge:

➤ The *Top Sites* list on the MSW home page provides one-click access to the most frequently visited sites across the intranet.

➤ *What's Happening* promotions on the home page call readers to take action, from signing up for an event, to participating in a contest, to learning more about an internal resource or new product.

➤ The *Events Calendar* is a listing of upcoming events with links to more information. Employees are invited to submit ideas for an event.

➤ The *Snapshot* feature on MSW provides a slice of life outside the office, by selecting photos taken by Microsoft employees, and featuring Microsoft employees.

➤ The featured *Inside Track* articles are stories and video coverage of Microsoft products, features, and people. The most compelling stories submitted by employees are selected to champion the successes of its products and people. The aim is to tell how and why events have taken place, and, more importantly, why they are important to the readers.

Following are some of the core navigational elements on MSW:

➤ The *Campus* section provides building information, campus maps, commuter options, and cafe menus. This section includes information to help employees get to and around campus.

➤ The *Employee Matters* section provides Human Resources and benefits information, career development tools, volunteer opportunities, and social communities, as well as research and reference information.

➤ The *Workplace Services* section provides employees with information they need to fulfill job responsibilities, including business travel sites, IT, and security.

MSW Search consumes from the FAST Search farm, which has been configured with a full index of Microsoft's intranet content and employees in Active Directory, indexing approximately 90 million items.

The Search box at the top of any MSW page can be used to search throughout the intranet for content across team sites, portals, and My Sites. The scopes within the drop-down menu next to the Search box include the following:

➤ *Intranet* — This includes a variety of content sets and file types from around the corporate network.

➤ *People* — This includes profiles from each employee's public My Sites, as well as Distribution List (DL) memberships.

"Best Bets" are used on search results pages for sites that are editorially selected as the most relevant results on the intranet. Refiners with counts appear down the left-hand side of the page. Thumbnail previews of Office documents, related search suggestions, a glossary of searched terms, people matches, and federated results appear on the right-hand side of the page.

InfoPedia

InfoPedia was created in response to users' requests for one site, optimized for search, to find information being sought as quickly as possible. InfoPedia consolidates into one place all content field–based employees' engagement with customers and partners.

InfoPedia has only one user experience, compared to the hundreds you would typically find in enterprise SharePoint deployments. It's about Search, and it's about finding topics through topic pages. The pages provide a wiki-like functionality so that you can read the wiki article and contribute to the story, view the featured content or must-reads easily, and explore the related documents relevant for the topic. Additionally, you can navigate InfoPedia hierarchically through domain home pages within core areas (such as enterprise, licensing, industry, product, and so on).

InfoPedia also leverages FAST Search for SharePoint 2010. A field-relevant taxonomy is in place with search refiners (such as industries, partners, products, and marketing). Search Relevancy has been configured to present the most relevant topic pages first, followed by the documents. Additionally, a gadget has been created to provide users access to InfoPedia search right from a desktop.

InfoPedia encourages publishers to collaborate, which results in more pages with current and connected content. Pages exist where product, licensing, campaign, and services experts all collaborate to provide a deep, rich story that connects the dots, instead of building their own sites and pages in silos.

SharePoint Utility

The *SharePoint Utility* platforms are shared utility environments and are available on both the Microsoft corporate intranet (North America, EMEA, or Asia regional instances) and the extranet. This standard, highly available team-collaboration SharePoint service offering is limited to SharePoint and SharePoint Designer out-of-the-box functionality. Code that must be installed on the SharePoint server is not allowed. Dedicated SharePoint environments can be requested and paid for by business units that have been approved to deploy custom code to the servers (referred to as Custom Portals, as described earlier in this chapter).

If a business unit requires collaboration between Microsoft and a Partner company, an extranet site is an excellent way to do this. Sites in the extranet are for a one-to-one or one-to-many collaboration between a Partner company (or companies) and a Microsoft sponsor (or group of sponsors). The extranet platform resides in the North America domain.

Following are some of the features and services enabled within the SharePoint Utility environment:

- ➤ Office Web Access
- ➤ Visio Services
- ➤ PerformancePoint Services
- ➤ Web Analytics
- ➤ InfoPath Services
- ➤ FAST Search

➤ Excel Services

➤ Information Rights Management

➤ Managed Metadata

THE MICROSOFT IT SHAREPOINT "DOGFOODING" EXPERIENCE

The MSIT department strives to be "Microsoft's first and best customer." This is achieved via a practice internally called "dogfooding."

Dogfooding is the process of deploying software that is not ready to release, but far enough along for internal Microsoft employees and vendors to use and provide valuable feedback on bugs and the overall user experience. MSIT partners with the product groups (in particular, the Office Product Group), and deploys their builds to production services for user consumption. By deploying and obliging users to utilize the code at such an early state, Microsoft is able to leverage the breadth and depth of the enterprise to drive improvements back into the product prior to customer consumption.

Dogfood cycles can vary from weeks to months, and, in some cases, a year or more. In the case of the SharePoint 2010 upgrade, it lasted nine months across eight different platforms.

The end goal is not necessarily to force users to use early cycles of the product for their daily needs, but instead to build the experience and knowledge to pass on to Microsoft's enterprise customers. Where else can you find a product that has 180,000 users accessing and utilizing it before reaching the customers' hands, even in a pre-release state? By the time SharePoint 2010 launched, the IT Operations and Engineering team completed more than 66 upgrades through the dogfooding cycle, and had nine months of experience to pass on to enterprise customers.

Driving enhancements back into the product through user feedback, or learning how to support the product, aren't the only reasons why Microsoft takes on the dogfooding effort. There are many beneficiaries of the dogfooding efforts. Before diving into the "what" and "how," let's take a look at some of the stakeholders for whom dogfooding is performed.

Customers

Customers are the ultimate benefactor of Microsoft's dogfooding efforts, and the primary reason for going through the exercise. The Product Group (PG) just completed multiple years of design, coding, and feedback to get a product into your hands. MSIT just completed multiple upgrades and patches to continue to drive feedback into the PG on support, scalability, and service usage. Microsoft users just spent months and months utilizing the product to provide feedback, execute just about every possible scenario imagined, and develop real-world solutions on the new product. The end result is a product ready for customer adoption.

The formal release of the product is just another milestone for MSIT. Post-deployment activities are the reward for all of the work put in during the previous dogfood cycle. During the last phases of dogfooding, MSIT works closely with an internal marketing team to develop best practices, white papers, videos, and presentations for customer adoption. For many customers, papers and videos are insufficient, and they require more information on what to specifically expect, as well as how to plan for their own companies' upgrade or deployment. What better way to achieve this than talking directly to the team that just completed the upgrades for Microsoft itself?

Product Group

Whereas customers are the ultimate benefactor of feedback, the PG is the primary recipient of the results of the dogfood cycles. Through weekly triage meetings, documented bugs, and direct user feedback, the PG evaluates the information and plans accordingly. In some cases, the product is performing as designed; in other cases, a design change is in order, and, depending on the severity, the fix may be postponed to a later build to focus on higher priority issues. Those design changes resulting from the feedback and bugs are incorporated in new builds, and the platforms are again upgraded.

Microsoft IT

The teams responsible for the planning, upgrading, and support of dogfooding cycles are the IT departments at Microsoft. As described earlier in this chapter, the motto and vision within MSIT is to be "Microsoft's first and best customer." The meaning behind this is easy: be the first to deploy the product and be the best at it. While the goal of the internal Microsoft user is to provide feedback to IT and the PG on the user experience, the IT mandate is to provide feedback on how to support and scale the product, identify and develop solutions, and suggest best practices to Microsoft's customers.

MSIT provides a production environment that offers breadth and depth that is unable to be replicated in a laboratory instance. There are not many places a PG can find to reach 180,000 people to validate a product than through the MSIT team. For SharePoint, the MSIT team is responsible for running eight different platforms ranging from fully customized environments, standard utility environments, to services.

Microsoft Users

The internal Microsoft user community represents more than 180,000 employees, vendors, and contractors that use SharePoint on a daily basis. When MSIT makes the commitment to deploy an early version of the SharePoint platform, it jumps in feet first and upgrades one or more production farms at a single time. Microsoft users have no choice but to use the newest build to run their daily SharePoint activities.

Dogfooding is a responsibility accepted by every person when they sign on to work at Microsoft. At any given point, a computer an employee or vendor uses is going be running pre-release bits, and they will experience some sort of work-impacting issue. It is a time of frustration and excitement from the end-user's perspective. The headaches and challenges imposed on the users are part of the sacrifice they sign up for when hired. The capability to leverage the new features and services in their everyday tasks, before anyone in the world gets to use it, makes it worthwhile.

The Challenges of Dogfooding

Meeting the expectations of the PG, internal Microsoft users, and Microsoft's own IT commitments does not come without its own challenges. To provide the dogfooding experience to stakeholders,

MSIT must plan for and develop plans to mitigate known challenges. The following topics are typical issues that IT must account for during each and every dogfood cycle.

Service Level Agreements

If you took a step back, and looked at the mission statement of the SharePoint IT team, it would be to provide an enterprise SharePoint offering for Microsoft's employees, vendors, contractors, and partners. Each of these individuals and teams put a critical dependency on the uptime, performance, and accessibility of his or her SharePoint instance that must be upheld. The commitment to the customers is laid out in the SLAs, which include (but are not limited to) the following:

➤ Uptime (availability)

➤ Problem ticket priority

➤ Disaster recovery objectives

➤ Problem escalation paths

➤ Service descriptions

➤ Performance guarantees

As the SharePoint MSIT teams enter dogfooding cycles, plans must take this into consideration because any service degradation will result in upset users, partners, and loss of productivity. The question is: How do the MSIT teams maintain uptime and performance when running pre-release bits?

Understanding the goals and scenarios of the products is vital to contributing to the successful adherence to the SLAs. For customers upgrading or deploying SharePoint 2010 for the first time, this could be equated to understanding the needs of your users, the types of platforms your company plans to deploy and support, and the acceptable performance of your SharePoint instance.

Microsoft's methodology to help mitigate risks includes the creation of the following:

➤ *Shared goals* — Shared goals include the outcomes that both the PG and SharePoint MSIT teams anticipate achieving during the dogfood cycle. Goals could include the scenarios each team wishes to validate, the properties that are candidates to be upgraded, and at which stage each platform could be upgraded. This is typically the first output of the dogfooding process.

➤ *Release criteria* — The release criteria is the second output for each milestone. Each team identifies and agrees upon the minimal level of quality for items such as performance, availability, functionality, and tasks that are to be completed prior to progressing to the next milestone.

➤ *Dogfooding plan* — The dogfooding plan is final output. This captures the "how to" portion of the process. In this, MSIT identifies stakeholders; collects project plans, roles, and responsibilities; reports feedback plans, communication, and escalation plans; and so on. This becomes the touch point for ensuring that the plan is successful and expectations are met.

Communication

Think of how many times something wasn't communicated correctly to your significant other, your kids, or a friend. They didn't get a message or notice, they misinterpreted the message, or they simply ignored it. In the end, when action is actually taken, someone is usually upset because, for one reason or another, the message never got through. Now, multiply that by 180,000 and you can appreciate the importance of effective communication in the dogfooding process.

With few exceptions, each internal Microsoft user accesses a SharePoint page at least once a day. This could be to complete a query through the Search portal, access the company intranet, or collaborate on a project on SharePoint (which sees upward of 60,000 unique visitors a day).

Developing a communication plan to reach each person at Microsoft is a top priority in defining the dogfooding plan. For the SharePoint 2010 upgrades, MSIT adopted a plan that mass-produced e-mails to each individual in Microsoft, alerting them of the upgrade, and setting expectations 45 days, 30 days, and 15 days prior to, week of, and day of the upgrade. In addition to these e-mails, MSIT also worked with executive leadership to compose a communication and published it on the company's intranet site, setting expectations and reaffirming the users' responsibility to dogfooding.

This was fairly effective. However, at least once per upgrade, MSIT would receive an escalation at the eleventh hour from a user saying, "I have to get something out to Steve Ballmer and you can't upgrade this weekend. Can you push it back?" No matter how badly you want to reply with a smile to the user that you will simply delay the entire upgrade of the enterprise SharePoint platform simply for his one site, you can't. MSIT must continue to evaluate the communication process to ensure that this person absorbs the communications next time around.

Communication doesn't end at the point of upgrade. In fact, it is just beginning for an IT team. Yes, the tone changes from awareness notifications to status updates and alerts. Channels and means must be established to post updates on FAQs around the product, known bugs impacting users, downtime, future releases, as well as educational material to empower the users to manage and build their own instances.

Microsoft did this through a (believe it or not) SharePoint portal. It would point users to this portal in any published communications, and educate the Helpdesk staff to reference this portal to any user escalating an issue; support team owners would also reference this site. The goal was to create a one-stop shop for users to understand the service offering, thereby reducing expensive and time-consuming calls to the Helpdesk.

Communication can make a great upgrade appear seamless, and make a difficult upgrade manageable from a user perspective. Setting expectations with the user around expected downtime, mitigation plans, escalation paths, knowledge centers, and the benefits the user will see will make your life much easier. Just remember, when you think you have communicated it enough, continue doing so.

Early Adoption

SharePoint 2010 saw the initiation of the dogfooding process before the final 2007 upgrades were even completed, with actual deployment occurring over a year in advance of market release. The first 6 to 12 months focused on the planning aspects of the dogfooding. This included the scenario definition, shared goals, release criteria, and dogfooding plans. The second phase was the actual deployment or upgrade.

By the time Alpha bits were available for SharePoint 2010, the PG and MSIT already defined whether or not a production platform would be upgraded. At this stage, it is extremely difficult to deploy to an actual production platform because of the functionality parity, as well as the MSIT SLA commitment. For SharePoint 2010, the agreement was that MSIT would not deploy Alpha to any production platform. However, there was a strong desire to get early feedback from users on the build. Instead of production, IT established a lab of virtual machines, and deployed the Alpha bits on these instances for the team and partners.

By deploying the Alpha bits to lab instances, IT was able to focus on the installation process, scenario validation, and start on proof-of-concept projects. IT resources were assigned to specific pillars, or areas of functionality, and were provided a virtual environment with an operating system already in place. Users would then be required to provision and configure SharePoint sites, allowing them to start navigating the environment and running through everyday scenarios, or start building out their concepts.

This proved to be extremely valuable in the feedback generated for the PG. The PG wasn't getting the breadth and depth that an actual production environment could provide to them. However, they were getting targeted feedback from the deployment of the platform, upgrading a SharePoint 2007 to 2010 instance, user experience, targeted scenario validation, and proof of concepts that reflected real-world usage.

Where and how to deploy the bits is just one angle that makes early adoption a challenging period. Because the product is still in a design-and-development stage, the majority of actual deployment and support documentation has not been published. Also, the early deployments were accomplished manually while MSIT worked on automating and scripting the deployments. When you combine the manual aspect of deployment with the need to support multiple platforms, you come up with a recipe for inconsistency.

In the end, this became a positive, because it ensured that tools were created to validate deployment success, including configurations and settings, and deployment automation. By the time SharePoint 2010 was available to the public, Microsoft had developed and documented best practices around automating, scripting, and validating your SharePoint upgrade or deployment.

Early adoption isn't limited to MSIT and the dogfooding process. Each and every company that opts-in to upgrade its existing platform or deploy for the first time can adopt this same approach. No matter how you plan to utilize SharePoint, understanding what the product can do and how it is marketed to your users will set the stage for a successful launch.

Deploy to lab instances and/or pre-production instances to understand the experience. Experiment and familiarize yourself with the features and services, and/or upgrade multiple times in a pre-production instance to ensure that you fully understand your production scenario. All of these tasks that are done in early stages of any product will result in a much smoother production launch, minimizing impact and problems for users.

Platforms

Microsoft has the luxury of investing in the creation of multiple farms for SharePoint users, from standard utility, social, enterprise search, to fully customized, dedicated farms. (Microsoft's current SharePoint offerings were detailed earlier in this chapter.)

Each of these properties represents different scenarios for the SharePoint team and critical feedback areas. With the exception of a handful of environments, MSIT upgraded all properties multiple times during the dogfooding cycle. The impact of this was augmented by two additional outside factors: build dependencies and short timelines.

In concurrence with early adoption, another impact of the immature code was that consuming farms required build parity. In short, if a farm consumed services from another farm, they each were required to be on the same build. Examples of this would be the SharePoint Utility platform consuming from the enterprise search farm.

The problem wasn't that two farms had to be upgraded at once, but that Microsoft had multiple farms consuming from the search farm or shared services. Like most companies, MSIT is bound by available resources. Not only was MSIT not able to upgrade all farms during a single weekend maintenance window, but the potential post-deployment support volumes or troubleshooting issues for such an event would overwhelm the staff on hand.

The mitigation was that MSIT paired upgrades each weekend so that when a property was upgraded, an enterprise service farm (search or services) was also upgraded if there was a critical dependency. The other farms on contrasting builds would be unable to consume the services until the next upgrade window. This meant that farms would have stale profile data, or new content would not be indexed, or the term store was unavailable.

To add the cherry on the sundae, through the first half of the dogfooding cycle, not only did MSIT have a build dependency, but each farm was required to be stripped down to the operating system and have SharePoint redeployed and configured for each upgrade. This was required for the first couple months of dogfooding, as well as each milestone build until market release. Luckily, this is where the early efforts of a skilled engineering team came into play. Based on lessons learned from early builds, the team completely automated and scripted rebuilds and upgrades.

In the end, between October 2009 and April 2010, MSIT performed a total of 66 upgrades spread across multiple platforms. Though not ideal by any means, it was a necessary evil brought upon by numerous SharePoint deployments. It is also a state that can be managed with a good communication plan, and by setting expectations with users early and often.

Dogfooding Multiple Products at a Single Time

The last dogfooding challenge that should be mentioned is that MSIT does not only dogfood for the SharePoint PG. Areas like Windows, SQL, and all the SharePoint services have interest in ensuring their platforms can integrate successfully prior to public launch. Add to that those products that want to take advantage of the massive market growth of SharePoint by developing integration points like Windows Phone 7 and Visual Studio, and the dogfooding opportunities continue to grow.

At any given time, one of the hosted SharePoint platforms could be running one or more dogfood products. Although exciting, it adds additional complexity to an already chaotic environment. Upgrades and troubleshooting take on new angles. MSIT must now collaborate with multiple PGs to ensure that they have validated the scenarios in their own labs to verify compatibility. Automation scripts must be updated, dependencies must be understood, and failure points and workarounds must documented and communicated.

By taking this approach, MSIT is able to extend the scope of feedback and drive quality into other Microsoft products. Internal Microsoft users truly get to be the earliest users, and MSIT can step up and showcase their first and best experience.

Blueprint for Success

One of the first things that should be addressed by any company looking to deploy or upgrade to SharePoint 2010 is to understand the business needs. Microsoft's SharePoint 2010 upgrades were completed during the shared goal mappings, when scenarios were laid out and the appropriate platform was to be validated.

Companies should look to answer at least a few key questions, which include the following:

➤ What is the corporate hierarchy going to look like?

➤ Will you open self-site creation, or manage a few key site collections?

➤ What services are going to be enabled?

➤ Do you need to order new hardware?

➤ If you are upgrading, what is your contingency plan during the upgrade windows?

If your organization is already on MOSS 2007 and you are planning to upgrade to SharePoint 2010, the hierarchy most likely has already been defined. In this scenario, it is critical to understand what your company's use cases and business needs are, because the feature richness of SharePoint 2010 can come with a cost.

In the planning stages leading up to Microsoft's first upgrades to SharePoint 2010, MSIT first took count of the health of the servers and their end-of-life status. Knowing that SharePoint 2010 required 64-bit machines, and that the hardware was reaching end-of-life, Microsoft invested in entirely new hardware.

The second stage of understanding the SharePoint 2010 topology was to review the hardware needs to meet the defined scenarios. In SharePoint 2010, the Shared Service Provider model in MOSS 2007 was disbanded, and the notion of an "a la carte" Service Application model was introduced. Because the code was at such an early state, each of the service pillars communicated that they required their own dedicated Application server to run successfully. Although Microsoft aims to push the boundaries, deploying a dedicated application server for each and every service was not feasible. Instead, part of the early feedback provided was that the services had to co-exist on application servers before MSIT would deploy and showcase them.

A third key factor that went into the topology definition was forecasted growth. Microsoft was already in the process of adding a second SQL instance for the growth, but at a growth rate of 1.5 TB per quarter, it had to plan for the future. Not only was the farm growing at 1.5 TB per quarter, historically, Microsoft experiences a sharp increase in adoption with every dogfood cycle.

It is important to note that as part of the planning, MSIT did not simply focus on running the service. MSIT tried to push the boundaries of the product to help uncover more scenarios and identify those issues the largest of companies may face. Because of this, Microsoft tended to procure servers that far exceeded the minimum requirements.

Table 5-1 provides a reference point for the hardware deployed in the production farm.

TABLE 5-1: Microsoft SharePoint 2010 Farm Production Hardware Specification

SERVER ROLE	CONFIGURATION	
Web Front End (WFE)	Hewlett-Packard SE326M1	
	(2) Intel quad-core Xeon L5520 2.26GHz/8MB	
	32 GB memory	
	136 GB total HD capacity	
	86 GB user capacity	
	Application Software Platform	
Application node	Hewlett-Packard DL580-G5	
	24 processors, (4) Intel Xeon/2.4 GHz 12 cache 6-core	
	32 GB RAM	
	137.6 GB total hard drive capacity	
	86 GB user capacity	
	iLO Advance Pack	
	Redundant power supplies	
	Redundant fans	
Database node	Hewlett-Packard DL580-G5	
	24 processors, (4) Intel Xeon, 2.4 GHz 12MB cache 6-core	
	64 GB RAM	
	137.6 GB total hard drive capacity	
	86 GB user capacity	
	iLO Advance Pack	
	Redundant power supplies	
	Redundant fans	

SharePoint Topology: Moving from 2007 to 2010

At this stage, you have learned about the dogfooding scenarios, how it is mapped to the appropriate platforms, the hardware ordered for each, and how the dogfooding plans started to come together. Besides looking to add a couple of servers to account for service deployments and natural growth, the topologies were not looking much different.

For discussion purposes, let's take Microsoft's largest SharePoint platform as an example. The SharePoint Utility platform is the largest farm with 73 databases, 8 TB of content, and more than 32,000 site collections (at the time of upgrade). To handle this load, Microsoft was running a farm that consisted of two Web Front End (WFE) servers, one Application server, and two SQL instances, as shown in Figure 5-1.

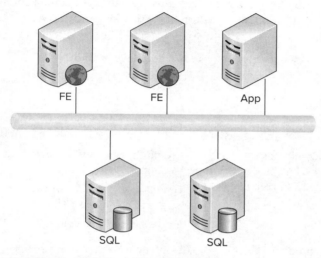

FIGURE 5-1: MSIT SharePoint 2007 farm

To account for the growth, service deployment, and traffic, Microsoft added one WFE server to help with traffic and one Application server for service redundancy. A third SQL server instance was also deployed to account for a forecasted growth model based on usage and adoption, as shown in Figure 5-2.

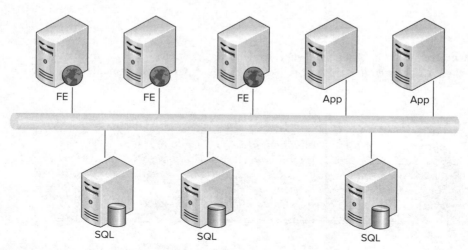

FIGURE 5-2: First SharePoint 2010 dogfood farm

If you are planning ongoing .NET/.NET feature functionality with SharePoint 2007, you are not going to see much need to expand your farm. Microsoft observed that the upgrade itself increased the size of the farm by approximately 10 percent.

However, if you are planning to add any of the new features of the SharePoint 2010 product, additional resources will be required. Microsoft accounted for this by adding a single Application server to deploy services and incorporate redundancy for failover. To mitigate risks caused by introducing new features and functionality at the point of upgrade, Microsoft agreed that no new services would be deployed until the production farm was stabilized after upgrade. The stabilization took approximately eight weeks before the team was truly comfortable with adding new services and features.

Post upgrade, Microsoft experienced three key issues to look out for, as shown in Table 5-2.

TABLE 5-2: Major Post-Upgrade Issues

ISSUES	DESCRIPTION	ACTION ITEM
Large Lists and Data View lookups	SharePoint 2010 enforces a maximum list view of 5,000 and a maximum data view lookup of 6.	Create "happy hour" for usage or cleanup. Grant site exceptions for two weeks to clean up sites. Enforce out-of-box values.
Throttling	Throttling was introduced to ensure that no single action or user could bring down a farm.	Disabled for first month because of an aggressive algorithm. Redefined health score configuration and reintroduced.
Customizations	Upgrading server-side or client-side customizations are always difficult.	Upgrade, validate, fix, recompile, repeat. In preparation stages, this was the routine followed.

Upgrade experience versus actual usage and support definitely generate different feedback. The three key issues highlighted in Table 5-2 reflect the issues experienced immediately following the upgrade.

 On a side note (and to instill a bit of confidence), it is nice to report that MSIT had a war room established the week following upgrade with the PG counterparts, developers, and testers at the ready to address escalations. By midway through the third day, the room was disbanded because escalations had dropped dramatically and were limited to single-site issues, instead of farm-wide issues.

As expected, MSIT started to see a sharp increase in usage and adoption as they continued to roll out the services. While they continued to funnel feedback to the PG, they were starting to see some areas for improvement from the support side of the house. Again, note that Microsoft pushes the boundaries of the product, much more than 99 percent of the customers would ever think of doing. Table 5-3 shows some of the support issues that were starting to emerge.

TABLE 5-3: Post-Upgrade Support Issues

ISSUE	DESCRIPTION	ACTION ITEM
Usage database grew rapidly	SQL performance experienced slowdown because of the heavy usage database write.	Added a new SQL server solely for the usage database. Helped increase performance dramatically.
Crawl freshness	Index was limited to a portion of North America only. No global search index.	Deployed a resource governor on the SQL machines and added two WFE index targets as crawl targets. Resource governor feeds off the SharePoint Health score, and will increase thread counts during low-traffic periods and reduce during high-traffic times. This allows for continuous indexing and the first global search index.
Storage	SharePoint content stored on a shared storage area network (SAN), resulting in performance issues and downtime because of overload.	The shared SAN was configured for a file share and not a collaboration storage solution (heavy read/write). Storage was separated out to a dedicated SAN, and then actually moved to direct attached storage (DAS) system. No more major storage issues experienced since.
Service consumption	As the services were deployed, some proved more expensive to run than others. Office Web Applications is a good example. The read/write of the program to request the content (present in the browser), and the continuous synchronization for co-authoring proved to hit the service harder than others.	Added two new Application servers to the farm to spread the connections. This has helped increase performance and service optimization.

As shown in Figure 5-3, by the end of dogfooding, the farm had more than doubled in size, with a completely new storage system in place. In Figure 5-3, note that the SQL servers are shown as individual entities and not instances (primary/secondary).

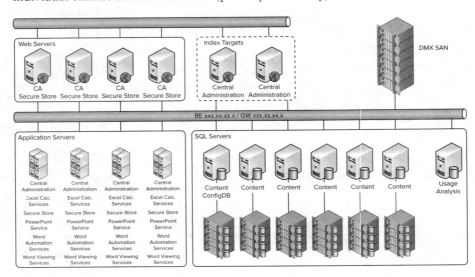

FIGURE 5-3: Final SharePoint 2010 production farm

The service instances deployed and the usage database will be the primary factors for increasing the size of your farm. To reiterate, going from SharePoint 2007 to SharePoint 2010 and keeping the same service offering will not result in much growth at all, outside of the usage database.

From the management perspective, it is important to not deploy all services simply because they are available. That will come with a price. Understand the user and business needs, and only deploy the services required. If you have multiple properties (SharePoint 2010 farms), as Microsoft does, you can deploy a high percentage of the service offerings by enabling a few service applications per farm. For perspective, Table 5-4 shows the service offerings that are currently provided.

TABLE 5-4: Deployed Service Offerings

SERVICES	TEAM	SHAREPOINT	MSW	MY	PORTALS
Usage/Health	X	X	X	X	X
Web Analytics	X	X	X	TBD	X
WAC	X	X	N/A	X	Post RTM
Excel	X	X	N/A	X	N/A
SSRS	X	TBD	N/A	N/A	TBD
Access	X	TBD	N/A	N/A	TBD
Workspace	X		TBD		TBD

SERVICES	TEAM	SHAREPOINT	MSW	MY	PORTALS
BCS	TBD	TBD	TBD	TBD	TBD
PPT Broadcast	X	N/A	N/A	N/A	
PTC	X	TBD	N/A	TBD	TBD
Visio	X	17-Mar	N/A	N/A	TBD
PerformancePoint	X	tbd	N/A	N/A	TBD
Gemini	X	N/A	N/A	N/A	TBD
Project (Pilot)	X	N/A	N/A	N/A	TBD
VSTF	TBD	N/A	N/A	N/A	TBD

The only farm to which the vast majority of services are deployed is the Team farm, which is the perpetual dogfood farm. MSIT uses the farm to deploy the latest and greatest bits, as well as all services, to evaluate before deploying to the other production farms. Those services that are on Team, but no other farm, have been determined to not be necessary on those farms for their business needs, or the adoption was minimal and not worth the investment.

BUSINESS CONTINUITY MANAGEMENT

Historically, MSIT has relied on its backup regimen to protect its digital assets. In the event of a data center disaster, spare servers would be quickly deployed, and content would be restored to those replacement servers in a matter of a few hours (or, in a worst case, a day). At the time, obtaining a couple of WFE and SQL servers in short order to duplicate the SharePoint farm was not an issue. Likewise, restoring less than a terabyte of content from tape was feasible in the expected timeframe. This slowly changed as the popularity and adoption of SharePoint mushroomed to double-digit annual growth.

Not only did the amount of content swell, the infrastructure required for the delivery of that content increased as well. The time required to replace the servers and storage comprising this infrastructure in the event of a data center disaster was no longer measured in hours, but days and weeks. MSIT's ability to respond to a data center disaster in a timely manner was diminishing, and the popularity of SharePoint made it a de facto mission-critical application. A rethinking of the disaster recovery strategy was in order.

The problem needed to be scoped and a solution executed within an established timeframe and within a set budget. It was clear that a solution covering the whole enterprise was not feasible given these constraints, so a phased approach was adopted. An assessment of the SharePoint environment exposed several dozen site collections or "critical applications" that were deemed mission-critical. These sites spanned business units from Human Resources and Finance to MSIT and Marketing and Sales sites, and became the manifest for Phase 1 of the Enterprise Business Continuity Management (EBCM) project — a multi-year disaster preparedness initiative mandated by the Board of Directors.

Another element of the project's scope was the disaster scenario to be covered. The possibilities spanned from a server rack succumbing to a localized electrical fire to a regional natural disaster such as a catastrophic earthquake or eruption of a volcano (several of which were located within a couple hours' drive). In the end, a moderate disaster scenario was adopted that represented a significant impact to services: the loss of our primary Rainier data center in Seattle caused by an electrical fire that renders the data center in its entirety a total loss.

The main corporate campus in Redmond, as well as all satellite offices and global campuses, are assumed to be unaffected by the event, other than loss of all network and data services operating from the Rainier data center. This encompassed not only SharePoint, but Exchange, Live Communications, DNS, Active Directory, and just about everything else MSIT provides to the corporation. All of these services and required infrastructure would need to be activated in the event of the disaster scenario. A target recovery time objective (RTO) of four hours and recovery point objective (RPO) of one hour were set for the SharePoint service.

The following is the hypothetical scenario written into the project specification:

> *At 1:30 AM PST, a fire on the first floor of the Rainier data center causes evacuation of the entire facility and damages inbound and outbound network egress for all floors. There is no physical or network access to any SharePoint servers in the damaged data center.*
>
> *Within 30 minutes of notification of the event, management declares a disaster has occurred and executes a failover authorization. Key enterprise business continuity management (EBCM) personnel (identified by a pre-established calling tree protocol) are notified to execute failover procedures.*
>
> *One member of that team is Sam, a member of the MSIT Collaboration Services SharePoint team, who is on call. Sam acknowledges the failover order and, from his home, remotely logs into SharePoint servers in the Columbia secondary data center in central Washington. He runs a PowerShell script that flips the secondary SharePoint server farms located there from read-only stand-by to read/write active mode. Since there will be no new transaction logs coming from the damaged Rainier data center in the immediate future, the scripts also suspend further local transaction log playback.*
>
> *As Sam executes the Disaster Recovery Procedure, he issues a request to the MSIT network team for a DNS change to remap the server namespaces from the Rainier to the Columbia data center servers to route SharePoint traffic to the secondary servers.*
>
> *By the time the SharePoint servers are brought into Read/Write mode by the failover script, access to the disaster recovery-protected SharePoint "critical apps" has been restored and is being serviced from the Columbia secondary data center.*

The failover scripts used in the hypothetical scenario are written in Windows PowerShell, and are listed in the addendum of the Disaster Recovery Procedure (DRP) manual, and as saved as files on servers in the secondary data center, as well as in multiple network locations and laptops of MSIT operations personnel.

The final part of the planning strategy was to determine where to locate the disaster recovery (or "secondary") data center. Building a new data center was not feasible because of time and budget. Availability of space in an existing Microsoft data center narrowed the candidates to locations in the Midwest and one in central Washington. The location in central Washington was selected, and while only 120 miles from the Rainier facility, it benefited from low operating costs, available space, and ample WAN bandwidth. Its close proximity was mitigated by the fact that a mountain range separates the two data centers, and even the regional natural disaster scenario affecting the Seattle area had a very low probability of significantly impacting central Washington.

With the *what*, *when*, and *where* resolved, MSIT tackled the *how* aspect of the project. Calculations determined that the minimum acceptable throughput required to be able to support a target corpus size of 5 TB was 4.25 MB/sec based on a maximum 4 percent daily change rate.

WAN latency between the primary and secondary data center was measured at 7 milliseconds (ms) and maximum throughput at 2,560 MB/sec (20 Gb/sec). This provided the capability to employ a simple SQL log-shipping solution using Windows Server 2008 synchronous file transfers. If the secondary were located farther away (say, on the East Coast at the Blueridge data center, 2,300 miles away), WAN latency and narrower bandwidth would have reduced throughput significantly. MSIT would have had to use a slightly more complex log-shipping method, such as asynchronous DFS-R to provide sufficient throughput.

The frequency of t-log creation was set to five-minute intervals with log shipping set to every 15 minutes. For the initial project phase, a total of five SharePoint farms plus a services farm were configured for log shipping. Each farm had a similar log-shipping process, as shown in Figure 5-4.

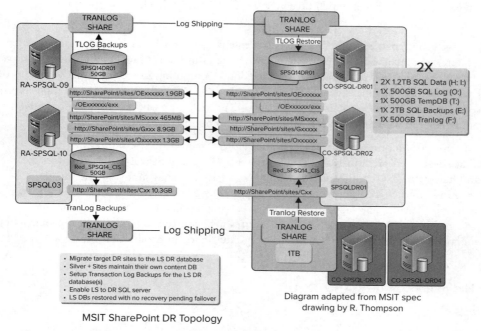

MSIT SharePoint DR Topology

Diagram adapted from MSIT spec drawing by R. Thompson

FIGURE 5-4: MSIT SharePoint disaster recovery topology

While the RTO and RPO were officially published as four and one hour, respectively, in verification and validation testing, the RTO times were 5 to 10 minutes, with an RPO of five minutes or less.

This implementation describes at a high level the first phase of a multi-year plan to protect a majority (if not all) of the Microsoft SharePoint properties managed by MSIT. As of this writing, the entire Microsoft SharePoint corpus contains approximately 30 TB of content in three regions.

To keep that much content synchronized between three pairs of data centers presents a significant challenge to the operations team. Database maintenance tasks must be orchestrated to avoid log-shipping backlogs, to execute server maintenance and patching by taking single servers out of rotation one at a time, and to take advantage of pre-production testing and scripting automation to maximize efficiency and minimize downtime. The penalty for failure is to have to re-seed the secondary (re-starting from scratch) — a time-consuming process that leaves the enterprise temporarily vulnerable to data loss and, potentially, very unhappy customers.

VIRTUALIZATION

The universal IT mantra of "deliver more with less" seems to run counter to the ever-expanding infrastructure requirements of new services, and SharePoint is no exception. Even if new services required no additional hardware, the growing demand for SharePoint requires the addition of hardware to keep up with demand. Combined with the need to maintain development labs, pre-production, user-acceptance, production, and disaster-recovery environments, hardware and data center hosting costs make up a huge chunk of the IT operational budget.

Policies at Microsoft preclude the MSIT group from independently setting up its own Hyper-V farm in a production data center. To virtualize SharePoint farms, MSIT is required to utilize the MSIT corporate Cloud Computing Service, which provides the Tier-1 through Tier-4 support systems every production service must offer.

As of this writing, the group managing this service has been engaged, and MSIT has begun to virtualize North America SharePoint farms and has plans in place to widen this effort to regional farms in Europe and Asia. The extent of virtualization is governed by the Cloud Computing Service offering, which (as of this writing) provides virtual machines (VMs) that are capable of handling the IIS front-end, application, and indexing server roles. The more robust SQL server role is not yet an option, but requirements for virtualizing them have been forwarded to the MSIT Cloud Computing Service Manager.

However, the lab, pre-production, and user-acceptance environments are not bound by the production policies described previously, so MSIT has set up Hyper-V Server 2008 R2 farms for each of these and has utilized Virtual Machine Manager (VMM) to snapshot baseline images of each server role in N and N-1 configurations. So, duplicating any particular environment is as simple as executing a script. The biggest challenge is keeping updated copies of the content databases in sync with the server images. Strict procedures are required to ensure that the snapshots also reflect cumulative and operating system/security updates made in production.

Following are the production Hyper-V SKUs:

➤ Blade Platform

➤ 4-Processor

➤ 16 GB RAM

➤ Windows Server 2008 R2

➤ 2 Gig-E NICs

➤ Static IP

➤ 400 GB SAN storage:

➤ C:\OS 50 GB

➤ D:\50 GB

➤ E:\300 GB

Ultimately, the ideal environment for both production and test would provide the capability to dynamically scale up and down, based on an automated demand-based system. For periods of increased demand (whether they be known ahead of time, or detected through monitoring), VMs could be automatically placed into rotation for the duration of the high demand, and automatically scaled down afterward. Microsoft is not at this stage of integration of services yet, but a project is funded and underway to develop the tools and processes required.

GOVERNANCE AND LIFE-CYCLE MANAGEMENT

When outside customers discuss the topic of SharePoint governance, companies often express how adoption of SharePoint by their users was met with ambivalence and with the perception that SharePoint was yet another file share — only more complicated. These organizations generally had no governance policies in place for their file shares, and the same lack of policy was carried forward to their SharePoint environments.

While Microsoft always had policies in place that addressed the handling and storage of documents, personally identifiable information (PII), and intellectual property, it wasn't until a more comprehensive governance policy was broadly mandated and communicated that Microsoft was able to effectively manage the huge volume of content held within its SharePoint services. This huge volume of data comprising current and legitimate collaborative content is intermixed with old, outdated content of no further utility. Not only does this present additional storage management and backup/recovery costs, but contributes to long lists of irrelevant and outdated search results.

Governance encompasses more than just occasionally cleaning house and setting quota limits on storage. It covers areas such as content classification, security and access, life-cycle management, communication and education of the user community, and business continuity (disaster recovery), to name a few. At the most basic level, policies must be created that establish the following:

➤ Who can create sites

➤ How site membership is controlled

➤ Whether sites expire or can be renewed

➤ How large sites can get (content quotas)

➤ What kind of content is permitted

Site Asset and Content Stewardship

The proper handling of business information requires classifying the information, and then protecting it appropriately. The asset owner must determine which classification fits the information.

Based on the classification, the asset owner determines the right protection to use when transmitting, sharing, storing, and disposing of the information. Highly sensitive information should not be shared on a SharePoint site open to a wide audience, and, likewise, public documents generally should not be sequestered in a site available to an "eyes-only" membership. Clear, unambiguous classification and labeling policies established by Microsoft's Legal and Corporate Affairs staff and MSIT communicate how assets are to be handled. A four-tiered taxonomy was developed, as shown in Figure 5-5.

FIGURE 5-5: Site asset and content stewardship

High Business Impact (HBI)

This classification category must be assigned to information assets where unauthorized disclosure could cause severe or catastrophic material loss to the company, the information asset owner, or relying parties. Access to HBI assets *must* be strictly controlled and limited for use on a "need to know" basis only. An example of an HBI document could be an unannounced financial report. HBI also includes Highly-Sensitive PII, which is also subject to the corporate privacy policy.

Highly-Sensitive PII can include (without limitation) government identification (such as Social Security numbers and driver's license numbers), credit information, or medical information (such as medical record numbers or biometric identifiers).

Moderate Business Impact (MBI)

This classification category must be assigned to information assets where unauthorized disclosure could cause serious material loss to the company, the information asset owner, or relying parties. Access to MBI assets *must* be limited for use by only those who have a legitimate company business need for access. An example of an MBI document could be a team status report.

Low Business Impact (LBI)

This classification category must be assigned to information assets where unauthorized disclosure could result in limited to no material loss to the company, the information asset owner, or relying parties. Examples of documents containing LBI content could be newsletter articles and employee productivity "How-To" guides.

Classification Examples

Table 5-5 provides some examples of common classifications.

TABLE 5-5: Post Common Classification Examples

COMMON CLASSIFICATION EXAMPLES	HBI	MBI	LBI
Audio conferencing LEADERSHIP code	X		
Contact information (business or personal)		X	
Criminal background information		X	
Customer data with Highly-Sensitive PII	X		
Credit card number with name and expiration date	X		
Internal website or file share (based on sensitivity)	X	X	X
Medical information	X		
Personal identification number (PIN)	X		
Public website			X
Published press release			X
Name and Social Security number (SSN)	X		
Unannounced financial data	X		
Credit card number alone (no name or expiration date)			X
Username and password	X		

Provisioning a Classification

MSIT allows individuals with corporate network credentials to self-provision as many SharePoint sites as they feel is necessary. There is no fee or inter-departmental charge for this service. Sites will expire one year from their creation date, unless the site owner or a site collection administrator renews the site for another year.

A custom solution called *Autosites* was created to replace the out-of-box Self-Service Site Creation page to gather additional Microsoft-specific metadata about the site being requested. This metadata is used to determine the new site's content classification, which will, in turn, govern the type and number of members allowed to access the site collection. In addition, the requesting user is asked to read and acknowledge understanding of the site use policies prior to clicking the Create button.

Custom Site Branding

Upon site collection creation, one of three site classifications is affixed to the title banner of each page, based on the metadata gathered during the request process, and is a component of the Autosites custom solution.

The brand reminds each visitor of the site's classification, and reinforces awareness of Microsoft corporate asset management policies. Figures 5-6 and 5-7 provide examples of site branding.

FIGURE 5-6: Site classifications branding

FIGURE 5-7: Site classifications branding example

Compliance and Life-Cycle Management of SharePoint Sites

Any policy set forth without enforcement will eventually be ignored. To maintain adherence to policy, periodic auditing of sites is performed that search sites and document metadata for keywords that may indicate a mismatch between content and site classification. A friendly reminder is automatically sent to site owners and administrators to alert them of the discrepancy, and to re-affirm their site's classification, or reclassify if appropriate. If multiple violations are recorded over consecutive audits, the site owners and administrators receive an e-mail warning them of impending site lockdown and subsequent deletion, as shown in Figure 5-8.

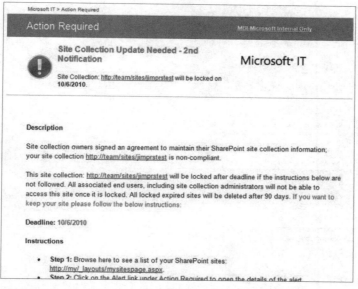

FIGURE 5-8: Site lockdown warning e-mail

 Caution must be used when performing audits of this nature to prevent excessive server and network load. Selective target properties can be scanned during evenings and weekends to minimize impact to the service.

Communication and Education

An important aspect of governance is often overlooked — the need for effective user education and buy-in. When MSIT rolled out its governance campaign, posters, video webcasts, and town-hall style events were orchestrated. Content explaining governance awareness and policies was made available on the company intranet portal, Human Resources and Security portals, and in mandatory training programs. To reinforce compliance with these policies, these governance topics are included in Microsoft's mandatory annual training programs, as shown in Figure 5-9.

FIGURE 5-9: Microsoft Governance Training

SUMMARY

This chapter covered some of the key experiences gained by Microsoft when deploying SharePoint 2010 at true enterprise scale. Significant challenges have been highlighted when deploying a new product at vast scale, particularly when multiple iterations are required, and some of the best practices to minimize the negative impact this may have on a workforce.

This chapter also looked at the approach taken by MSIT to design highly scalable business continuity management plans, some of the challenges faced with when considering virtualization, and some custom solutions to tackle governance at this scale.

Chapter 6 provides an overview of some of the fundamental concepts and terminology used by SharePoint Server 2010.

PART II
The SharePoint 2010 Platform

SharePoint Fundamentals

By Martin Kearn

This chapter provides an overview of some of the fundamental concepts and terminology used by SharePoint Server 2010. You learn about some of the physical architecture components that are used in SharePoint, such as the concept of a farm and the various server roles. You also learn about sites, site collections, lists, and related technologies that are new to SharePoint 2010 (such as sandboxed solutions).

Finally, you learn about the various licensing models that apply to SharePoint 2010, as well as hosting options.

INTRODUCING THE SHAREPOINT FARM

This section discusses the SharePoint farm and the different components that reside in the farm (such as web applications, servers, service applications, and more).

The SharePoint Farm

The term *farm* is used to describe a collection of servers that are combined to provide SharePoint services or workloads.

Farms can range in size from just a single SharePoint server to highly scaled, resilient architectures where each individual server role is hosting on a dedicated set of servers.

Some organizations will have only a single farm that hosts all SharePoint services. Large enterprises or organizations with specific requirements may have multiple farms. Fortunately, SharePoint 2010 has been engineered to make integration of multiple farms much simpler than it has been in the past. You learn more about this later in this chapter.

There are several reasons for needing multiple farms. Let's take a look at some of the most common.

Varying Service Level Agreements

Different SharePoint workloads may have varying levels of importance to the business, and, therefore, have different Service Level Agreements (SLAs).

Hosting multiple farms allows critical workloads to be protected by high-level availability design, and "less important" workloads to have a more cost-effective server architecture.

As an example, if the organization is an Internet-based business, SharePoint may be used to host a customer-facing website, which may be the main source of revenue for the organization. The workload is obviously very important to the organization, and it may well invest significant time and effort to ensure that the website remains operational as close to 24 × 7 as possible.

Conversely, the same company may also use SharePoint to host its social discussion boards. Though important, the internal discussion board may not be a business-critical workload, and, therefore, it may not make sense for the organization to apply the same level of support and investment into its discussion boards as its public-facing website.

If your organization does carry different SLAs for different SharePoint-based workloads, it makes good sense for the organization to host two separate farms.

Customizations and Other Software Products

Some workloads within an organization may require third-party software or customizations to complement the default SharePoint capabilities. Deploying any kind of modification on top of SharePoint carries a particular level of risk. Some organizations may not want to carry that risk across all SharePoint workloads, which they generally would have to do if they had a single farm.

In a similar scenario, specific SharePoint workloads may integrate with other technologies that are on different release cycles to SharePoint. Therefore, there may be upgrade and maintenance disruption involved in maintaining the workload.

Using multiple farms allows customizations, add-on products, and maintenance to be more closely managed and deployed, thus minimizing disruption to the overall user base. Using a separate farm in this scenario may seem unwarranted. However, if your test and deployment processes are lengthy and complex, separate farms may help to expedite the process and, therefore, be justified.

Geography

Out-of-the-box, SharePoint farms cannot span multiple geographic locations apart from in very specific, high-speed, localized scenarios.

If an organization has offices in two or more locations, and slow-speed connections between those offices, it would not be practical for users to access SharePoint services via a single data center. Therefore, multiple farms may be required to disperse the SharePoint workloads around the various geographic offices, and to provide collaboration and My Sites closer to the user.

Licensing

As you will learn later in this chapter, SharePoint has various licensing models that provide users with additional functionality at a cost.

Some parts of the user community may have different requirements than others, meaning that a single license across the entire user base may not be cost-effective. The license level that is used is a farm-scoped configuration, and you are not permitted to mix license types within the same farm.

An example might be that most users require only the Standard Client Access License (CAL). However, a small subset of users may need electronic forms, which requires the more expensive Enterprise CAL. In this situation, the choices are as follows:

➤ Buy an Enterprise CAL for all users. (This is an expensive option, but provides a more feature-rich deployment.)

➤ Do not use InfoPath Form Services and leave all users on the Standard CAL.

➤ Use a separate form for the Enterprise CAL users.

 Note that forms may need to be modified to be "Web browser forms" if the Enterprise CAL was later deployed, and Forms Services was required.

Web Applications

Web applications are comprised of an Internet Information Services (IIS) website that acts as a logical unit for the site collections that you create. For example if a site's URL is: `http://myportal/sites/hr`, then `http://myportal` would be the web application.

All web applications must run within the context of an *application pool*. An application pool defines the actual worker process in Windows that does the work for the web application. Application pools can be shared across multiple web applications, or dedicated to a single web application.

Figure 6-1 shows the relationship between IIS, application pools, and web applications.

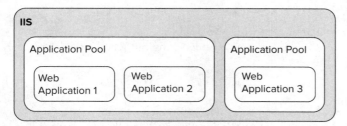

FIGURE 6-1: Relationships between IIS, application pools, and web applications

Sites and site collections reside inside a single web application, and the web application governs the following aspects of the site collections within it:

➤ The root URL, port, and protocol

➤ The way users authenticate (referred to as *authentication providers*)

➤ User permission policy (which includes "deny" permissions)

➤ Default quotas assigned to sites

➤ Various other settings (including RSS, Alerts, Recycle Bin, and more)

Web applications have a one-to-one mapping with websites in IIS. Web applications usually have a dedicated application pool, too. However, this does not have to be the case, and multiple web applications can share a single application pool. This approach can be beneficial when you must simplify administration of the farm and gain small performance improvements. Web applications also have a direct mapping to content databases. Administrators can create up to 300 content databases in a single web application. The web application itself manages which site collection goes into which database.

 The way content databases are designed and sized is a separate topic, which is covered next in the "Databases" section.

Working out the web application design is a key part of SharePoint architecture design.

The first task is to define how many web applications are required, and what their roles will be. As with any aspect of SharePoint, the starting point is the simplest available option — having a single web application for all site collections in the farm. The advantage of this approach is that it requires the minimum level of administration, and users have a single URL, authentication mechanisms, and so on, for all SharePoint workloads.

Although a single web application is the simplest approach, it is not the most common. Typically, organizations will have a web application for most standard sites, and a separate web application that is used to host the organization's My Site infrastructure.

My Sites usually carry a different SLA, quota, and usage policy than other parts of SharePoint, and also are created via self-service. All of these factors mean that it often makes sense to separate My Site into its own web application.

However, there really is no right or wrong approach with web applications. Rather, it is a case of understanding the needs of your users and administrators, and working out what is the best fit for your organization.

Databases

Nearly all of the data that SharePoint uses is stored in SQL databases. When users upload a file into SharePoint, it is actually stored as a Binary Large Object (BLOB) inside the SQL databases. The only data that SharePoint uses that is not stored inside SQL is the search index data, which is stored on the filesystem of the Query servers.

Generally speaking, SharePoint creates two main types of databases:

➤ Content databases

➤ Configuration databases

Content databases are bound to a web application, and are used to store site collections and all the data that is contained within them. In terms of size on disk, content databases are generally responsible for the majority of the overall storage requirements.

The published paper, "SharePoint Server 2010 Capacity Management: Software Boundaries and Limits" (http://technet.microsoft.com/en-us/library/cc262787.aspx), recommends that a "general usage" content database does not exceed 200 GB in size. Therefore, if you have more than 200 GB of data and a design that mandates a single web application, then you must plan for multiple content databases.

There are various types of configuration databases, the most important being the SharePoint Config database, which could also be thought of as the farm configuration database. This database keeps a record of all the farm-level settings, including which servers have which roles. The servers in the farm are in continual communication with this database to check for farm-level changes that must be applied.

By default, a single SharePoint farm with all available service applications and two web applications could start with up to 21 databases!

Service Applications

Service applications are a new concept in SharePoint 2010 and replace what used to be called the Shared Service Provider (SSP) from SharePoint 2007.

SharePoint has always had central services that provide a specific set of functionality. A typical example is the Search service, which provides the capability to index enterprise content and allow users to search against it. In SharePoint 2010, these services are called service applications.

The idea of service applications is to provide administrators with a method to separate the processing, administration, and, in some cases, the farms that are used to provide centralized services that web applications can consume.

The main change in SharePoint 2010 is that service applications can be grouped into different logical groups that are consumed by certain parts of the organization (via service application proxies).

Not all service applications are available in all license editions of SharePoint.

The service application infrastructure is flexible and can support additional service applications that will become available if certain additional software is installed (such as FAST Search for SharePoint or Office web applications).

Using Service Applications in Multiple Farms

Within a single farm, the service application design is normally simple. Usually, all required service applications are grouped into a default group, and consumed by all web applications in the farm.

For organizations with multiple farms, the new flexibility in service applications provides an opportunity to design farms that are dedicated to hosting only service applications that are consumed by other farms. These types of farms are generally referred to as an *enterprise services farm*.

Figure 6-2 shows a typical enterprise services farm sharing services to other farms.

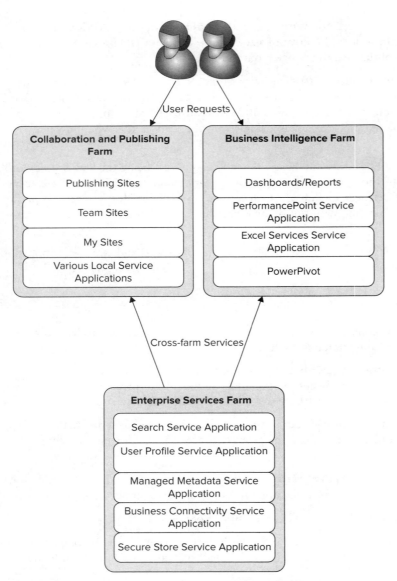

FIGURE 6-2: An enterprise services farm sharing services to other farms

Use of enterprise services farms is ideal if your organization requires multiple farms for any of the reasons listed in the section, "The SharePoint Farm," earlier in this chapter. Using a centrally managed services farm allows the consuming farms to only concern themselves with the content and sites they need to host and rely on the enterprise services farm for provision of central services.

It is worth noting that farms can also consume locally defined services, and can mix and match which services are consumed locally, and which are consumed from an enterprise services farm.

Though this is a great approach for large organizations, not all service applications are suitable for cross-farm sharing, especially across wide area networks (WANs). Later in this chapter, you'll learn about which service application can be used in cross-farm solutions, and whether or not the network connection is relevant.

Servers

This section examines the various server roles that are available with SharePoint, and how you can scale out the server farms based on your requirements.

Service Machine Instances

When a SharePoint server is joined to a farm, it is effectively a "blank" server that has the capability to run any service for which the farm is enabled.

Using Central Administration, it is possible to start or stop certain services that define the work that the server is responsible for. In Central Administration, this interface is called "Manage services on server." However, the services themselves are formally referred to as *service machine instances*, though more commonly they are simply referred to as *services*.

It is important to differentiate between service machine instances and service applications described earlier in this chapter. Service machine instances are processes that run on a physical server. They may or may not support a service application that is a logical entity made up from databases, web services, and potentially one or more service machine instances.

Your service application design could be identical on any farm size, but the placement of service machine instances will vary depending on the size, scale, and intention of your farm.

Web Servers

Web servers are the servers that respond to user requests, and render the SharePoint web pages themselves.

Technically speaking, a web server (also called *Web Front End server*, or *WFE*) is a server that runs the SharePoint Foundation Web Application service machine instance. However, this service machine instance is rarely run in isolation, and is often combined with other "front-end" services such as Search Query. On this basis, the web server should be thought of more as a general front-end server responsible for servicing end-user requests.

Most servers in the farm require some level of automated fault tolerance so that if a single server fails for some reason, the service remains operational — in many cases, in a limited capacity. This is also true with web servers.

The WFE servers do this by using network load balancing (NLB). NLB can be run as part of Windows itself, or as a feature in your firewall, router, or even on dedicated NLB hardware devices (for example, F5 Big IP). NLB distributes network requests for a specific end point (or URL) across any servers that are in the NLB cluster. This has the advantage of spreading the load (thus enabling better performance), but also means that if a server fails, all requests will go to the remaining server and, therefore, the service will remain operational.

Some farms will consist only of web servers and database servers. This is common if the farm uses only SharePoint Foundation, or if there is an enterprise services farm providing services.

Application Servers

The term *application server* is generally used to describe any server that runs back-end application services, as opposed to handling the front-end user requests that web servers handle.

Within SharePoint, many different applications (service machine instances) can be combined or separated onto different servers to suit the needs of the client.

Most SharePoint service machine instances offer built-in redundancy, which means that multiple servers can have the same role. This enables increased performance and fault tolerance, just like NLB does with web servers. The main difference is that application servers do this internally, but web servers require an external NLB solution.

 Microsoft has published some typical topologies on TechNet that outline common architectures, with the primary online resource being the "Topologies for SharePoint Server 2010 Technical Diagram" (http://technet.microsoft.com/en-us/library/cc263199.aspx). *However, these should be considered as examples or starting points, and are open to change and fine tuning, rather than mandated topologies.*

Database

The Database tier is without a doubt the heart of any SharePoint farm because all data and configuration is stored here. If there are problems in the database layer, the entire farm will suffer.

SharePoint supports only SQL server for the database tier (version 2005 upward, though 2008 R2 Enterprise Edition is the recommended version).

As far as SQL is concerned, SharePoint is just another application (albeit a rather busy one) that requires database storage. SharePoint has no specific requirements in terms of SQL in order to facilitate a well-architected farm. Most SharePoint server farms will work well on a single SQL instance, whether that is just a single server, a cluster, or a mirror.

However, in large deployments, SQL instances may be split out to different server groups to distribute the load. That said, SQL is really where your hardware budget should be spent in terms of a SharePoint farm. Typically, the SQL servers are more powerful machines than the SharePoint servers. In fact, the minimum hardware requirements for SharePoint mandate that SQL server should have double the RAM and processing power of SharePoint server for "medium" sized deployments. Refer to "Storage and SQL Server capacity planning and configuration" (http://technet.microsoft.com/en-us/library/cc298801.aspx) for more detail.

 For more information, see the "Hardware and software requirements (SharePoint Server 2010)" article on TechNet at http://technet.microsoft.com/en-us/library/cc262485.aspx.

SharePoint can work with both SQL clusters and mirrors, each of which has pros and cons. The right approach will depend on your availability requirements, physical topology, and existing practices.

That said, SQL mirroring is becoming more common because there are fewer dependencies on the physical location of the nodes, and SharePoint 2010 is now mirror-aware (which previous versions were not). On this basis, mirroring should be carefully considered as an option for SQL fault tolerance.

INTRODUCING SITE COLLECTIONS AND SITES

Let's now take a look at sites and site collections. These are two of the main objects within the overall SharePoint object hierarchy, and it is important to understand the differences between them.

Site Collections Versus Sites

Site collections are an administrative boundary that defines a group of sites. Site collections always contain at least one top-level site, and potentially a large number of structured sub-sites beneath it.

A site collection defines many common settings that apply to all sites contained within the collection, including the following:

➤ Security settings, including ownership

➤ Features

➤ Navigation structure

➤ Visual styling

Site collections directly reside within web applications and, therefore, in the associated content databases.

 Though a web application can have many content databases, site collections cannot span databases, and can only reside in a single database.

A *site* is the object with which users most directly interact. A site is a collection of lists, libraries, and pages that contain content and web parts. Sites will always have a unique URL, which is typically easy to remember and hierarchical in nature, based on the hierarchy of the site collection that contains the site.

Figure 6-3 shows the hierarchy of objects within a web application.

A key architectural decision is how to structure site collections, as well as manage the relationship between site collections and the sites within them.

One approach is to have a larger number of site collections with only a root site, or a small structure of sites beneath it. This is referred to as the *flat* approach. An alternative approach would be to have a fewer number of larger site collections with deeper structures, referred to as the *deep* approach. Each approach has pros and cons.

FIGURE 6-3: Hierarchy of objects within a web application

The first consideration when deciding on flat versus deep is what the sites are actually used for. In a broad sense, there are four main classifications of sites within SharePoint:

➤ *Collaborative sites* — Sometimes referred to as *team sites* or *department sites*, these sites will normally have a relatively small number of users who need to work closely with each other, and collaborate around documents and content. These sites usually have a large ratio of contributing users compared to read-only users.

➤ *Publishing sites* — These sites are mainly used to host web content that is intended to be consumed, rather than collaborated upon. Publishing sites are usually Internet websites, intranet sites, and portals. Publishing sites generally have a much larger number of read-only users than contributing users.

➤ *Application sites* — These sites are heavily customized and are a platform for hosting a specific application or set of features.

➤ *One-off enterprise sites* — These are sites that generally exist in very small numbers, and provide a specific service to the entire enterprise. Examples include Record Center, Document Center, and Search Center.

Each of these main site types has different usage patterns, and it is important to understand these patterns when deciding on the most suitable approach for your organization.

When collaborating, people naturally gravitate to the lowest-level working group to perform their collaboration activities. It is very rare that entire departments need to continually perform internal collaborative activities. Although a department might have a specific home site, teams and projects tend to have specific sites set up for collaboration. Therefore, it is more likely that the department will be split (formally or informally) into small working teams where the users have a natural affinity and naturally collaborate with each other. On this basis, collaborative sites tend to favor the flat approach because of the agility it provides. However, it does entirely depend on how the users within your organization work together.

Publishing sites tend to rely more on branding, navigation, and overall presentation. On this basis, having a single, large, or deep site collection is often the best choice for publishing sites because the presentation, navigation, and overall user experience can be controlled in a single place.

Application sites will generally be a single site within a single site collection because users' interactions are usually through the application itself, rather than through SharePoint's own user interfaces.

One-off enterprise sites will also normally be a single site collection, because the whole point is usually that these sites provide a single entry point or interface to the content and Feature that site provides.

Another important consideration is the size of the site collections. As discussed previously in this chapter, the maximum recommended content database size is 200 GB. A site collection cannot span multiple databases. This makes the maximum recommended site collection size no more than 200 GB for the majority of sites (one-off enterprise sites being a notable exception).

If your organization creates a lot of data, then a flat structure may be more appropriate, because a larger number of site collections mean that the site will generally be smaller, and this will give more flexibility in terms of how content databases are managed.

Site Templates

When a new site is created, the user must choose from a list of site templates. A *site template* (in the broadest sense of the term) defines the default lists, libraries, pages, and features that are included in the newly created site.

 SharePoint includes a wide range of default site templates that can be seen at the "Sites and Site collections overview (SharePoint Server 2010)" article on TechNet (http://technet.microsoft.com/en-us/library/cc262410.aspx).

Though SharePoint's default site templates are a great starting point, most organizations find a need to either complement or replace the default templates with customized ones that meet the organization's needs.

There are two main techniques for creating site templates in SharePoint 2010:

> *Web templates* — A web template is created by creating a site based on one of the default options, configuring it to meet the needs of the organization, and then saving it as a web template. Web templates are very quick to create. However, web templates present some complications in certain areas, such as web part configuration or the use of web templates for root sites.

> *Site definitions* — Site definitions are much more powerful and flexible than web templates, and, therefore, also much more complex. Site definitions are a collection of XML, .ASPX, and other files stored on the filesystem of every SharePoint web server. Site definitions require development skills to create, and have limitations on how they can be changed after sites are "live" based on them.

There is a very good online resource that explores this topic in more detail called "Site Types: Web Templates and Site Definitions," which you can find on TechNet at http://msdn.microsoft.com/en-us/library/ms434313.aspx.

A third, lesser-documented approach is to use Features to make changes to sites created based on out-of-the-box site templates. This approach uses XML features where possible, but may also involve Feature receivers that run custom code upon activation. This is discussed in more detail later in this chapter in the section, "Features and Solutions."

Pages, Web Parts, and Page Content

Pages are the primary interface that users use when interacting with SharePoint. The content displayed on a page can be managed using various approaches. The right approach will depend on the nature of the page — primarily whether it is collaborative in nature, or intended more as a publishing page (refer to earlier section, "Sites Collections Versus Sites," for a definition of these terms).

A page itself is an .ASPX file either stored on the filesystem of SharePoint as part of the site's site definition, or stored in a library called Pages if the Publishing Feature set is activated on the site.

Pages can contain three main components that allow management and presentation of content:

➤ *Web parts* — These are functional components that often display data from the lists and libraries in the site, but may also provide isolated functionality (such as displaying an image or navigation interface).

➤ *Publishing controls* — If Publishing is enabled, pages can be based on page layouts that enable specific pieces of content to be written directly into the page by page authors. Publishing controls are predefined controls that mandate certain types of content within the page. Publishing controls are provided out-of-the-box for all of the main types of publishing content.

➤ *Wiki mark-up* — New in SharePoint 2010, it is now possible for users to directly add content to pages using wiki mark-up.

How users will use pages to post and manage web content is a critical architectural decision. If you give users complete flexibility to add content to a page via wiki mark-up or the Content Editor web part, they may appreciate the flexibility. However, the overall look and feel of your sites may become disjointed and inconsistent as users add their own personal style.

At the other end of the spectrum, it is possible to ensure that all pages are based on a page layout that defines exactly what type of content will appear on the page, where it will appear, and how much control users have over managing the content.

The right approach will depend on the type of site (refer to the "Site Collections Versus Sites" section in this chapter) and your organizational policy toward managing web content.

Permissions and Access Control

SharePoint uses a relatively complex model for applying and managing a user's access to a resource (that is, a site, a library, a document within a library, and so on). Let's take a look at some of the key concepts and terminology, as well as best practices. Figure 6-4 shows the key concepts that will be explained in this examination.

Security in SharePoint is applied to individual user or group objects. The repository that manages these objects will depend on the authentication provider that is being used. For the purposes of this example, let's assume that Active Directory is being used to manage users and groups, and that Windows authentication is the chosen authentication provider.

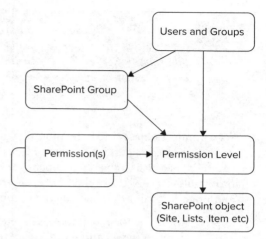

FIGURE 6-4: Permissions and access control concepts

 See Chapter 19 for a more detailed description of security authentication repositories, and the differences between authentication and authorization.

Several different concepts comprise the SharePoint security model. This section explains these concepts and how they interact.

Permission Levels

Permission levels are at the heart of SharePoint's security model. Permission levels are defined groups of individual permissions that can be used to grant user access to a SharePoint resource.

Individual permissions define a specific action that users can take on a site, list, or personal data. Examples of individual permissions include Edit Items, Delete Items, and View Pages.

SharePoint includes various permission levels by default:

- ➤ *Full Control* — Allows full control of the scope.

- ➤ *Design* — View, add, update, delete, approve, and customize items or pages in the website.

- ➤ *Contribute* — View, add, update, and delete items in the existing lists and document libraries.

- ➤ *Read* — View pages, list items, and download documents.

- ➤ *Limited Access* — Allows access to shared resources in the website so that the users can access an item within the site. Designed to be combined with fine-grained permissions to give users access to a specific list, document library, folder, list item, or document, without giving them access to the entire site. Cannot be customized or deleted.

You can find a full description of the default permission levels and associated permissions and dependencies in the "User permissions and permission levels (SharePoint Server 2010)" TechNet article at http://technet.microsoft.com/en-us/library/cc721640.aspx.

As with most objects in SharePoint, it is possible to modify the default permission levels and create your own. Although this is a powerful feature, it is something that should be considered very carefully, because changes may open up security holes in your system, and potentially cause upgrade or migration problems in the future. Several reasons for not modifying the default permissions level and/or adding your own include the following:

➤ All of the documentation will refer to the out-of-the-box permission levels. If you have changed the meaning of these permission levels (that is, added more or fewer permissions), then the standard documentation online could be misleading and drive users to apply permissions incorrectly.

➤ Historically, permission levels have changed slightly between versions of SharePoint, and many upgrade techniques or tools may not account for custom permission levels.

SharePoint Groups

It is possible to take users and groups from Active Directory (or your chosen authentication provider) and directly assign them to permission levels against a given object such as a list or document.

It is also possible to take users and groups and make them members of a *SharePoint group*. SharePoint groups exist within the context of a site collection, and have predefined sets of permission levels. By default, SharePoint creates three SharePoint groups in all new sites:

➤ Owners

➤ Members

➤ Visitors

It is also possible to add your own SharePoint groups, as well as modify the out-of-the-box groups.

The benefit of using SharePoint groups is that a whole group's access level can be changed in one procedure. If users and groups are directly assigned to resources, then they must be individually managed.

The correct approach for your organization will depend on any precedents that already exist regarding user access management.

If other systems within your environment use Active Directory groups to assign permissions rather than directly adding users to resources, then this may be a good model to follow with SharePoint.

However, if the Active Directory group management is minimal or non-existent in your organization, SharePoint groups offer a great opportunity to consolidate the administrative overhead of managing user access.

Site Collection Administrators

Site collection administrators are a collection of user accounts that have overall administrative rights on a site collection. The administrators site collection overrides any permission that is assigned to the site via groups and permission levels, and retains full administrative access to the site collection. Only user accounts can be placed in the administrators site collection.

Features and Solutions

The concepts of *Features* and *solutions* were introduced in SharePoint 2007, and were a great step forward in enabling smooth packaging and deployment of SharePoint customizations. Features and solutions remain largely the same in SharePoint 2010, with a few notable differences.

Features

A *Feature* is a functional component that is activated on a site, site collection, web application, or farm. When activated, the functionality included in the Feature is added to the site, and when the Feature is deactivated, the functionality is taken away.

Features come in lots of different shapes and sizes, and range from very simple functions (such as content types or site columns) to advanced Features that execute custom code on activation (called a *Feature receiver*).

SharePoint itself is built using Features, and the difference between any of the out-of-the-box site templates is a simple case of which Features are activated by default. Following are just a few standard SharePoint Features that you may be familiar with:

> *Document Library* — Provides the capability to create document libraries within a site.

> *Search Server Web Parts* — Enables a series of web parts that can be used to enable advanced search capabilities.

> *Survey* — Enables the capability to create survey lists.

Features support a dependency model whereby certain Features will be marked as dependent on others, meaning they cannot be activated until the dependent Features are also activated. Dependencies can be used to group Features into logical collections that site administrators can activate or deactivate as one.

Out-of-the-box Features such as SharePoint Server Enterprise Site Collection Features are an example of dependencies. This Feature does nothing itself, but has several dependencies that are activated or deactivated in line with the main "parent" Feature.

Customizations should be packaged and deployed as Features. Visual Studio 2010 does a great job of abstracting Feature production from the developer, such that developers may not even realize that they are using Features (a job that was complex in SharePoint 2007 and Visual Studio 2008). Almost any customization can and should be packaged as a Feature or series of Features.

As mentioned earlier in this chapter, the use of Features offers an alternative way of re-creating sites with a specific configuration. Rather than defining custom web templates or site definitions, many architects tend to prefer using standard team site templates, and rely only on Feature activation to many configuration changes to the site. This approach is sometimes referred to as the "100 percent Feature" approach.

The 100 percent Feature approach will normally include one or more feature receivers to make programmatic changes to the site, but, where possible, should use non-code features.

The benefit of the 100 percent Feature approach is that the sites are effectively based on the default site templates, which means that migration, upgrade, and maintenance will be simpler. This approach also offers more granular control of what Features are available on a specific site.

 See Chapter 15 for more details on how Features are scoped, and how Feature receivers can be used to add custom code to Feature events such as activation or deactivation.

Farm Solutions

A *solution* is a deployment package — a Web Site Project (WSP) file — that encapsulates one or more Features with data link layers (DLLs) and other supporting files.

Solutions can either be farm-scoped or sandboxed solutions. You will learn more about sandboxed solutions shortly.

Farm solutions are installed across the entire farm by farm administrators. Typically, the content of a farm solution will be available throughout the farm, and generally involve fairly complex and broad customizations.

Sandboxed Solutions

One of the age-old problems with customizations in the previous versions of SharePoint is the global nature of any customizations that are deployed, and how broadly that may impact the server farm.

Before SharePoint 2010, all customizations had to be deployed as farm-wide solutions, and this had several implications:

➤ Customizations were theoretically available for use across the entire farm, not just the specific site collections that needed them, although an appropriately permissioned user would have to manually activate the Features.

➤ If customizations were unstable or performed badly, they could affect the entire farm, not just the site where they resided.

➤ The impact of customizations had to be much more broadly tested because of the deployment scope. Typically, this meant that it took IT departments a very long time to test and deploy custom solutions.

➤ It was very difficult to use customizations in "cloud" services such as Microsoft Business Productivity Online Suite (BPOS).

To address these issues, SharePoint 2010 has a great new feature called *sandboxed solutions*. A sandboxed solution is like a normal SharePoint solution package, and may contain Features, DLLs, and other files. However, the difference is that sandboxed solutions can be ring-fenced and executed only within the context of a site collection.

Sandboxed solutions are also assigned daily performance quotas. If they exceed the performance quota, they will cease to execute.

The isolated nature of sandboxed solutions means that they address all of the issues with farm-wide SharePoint solutions that were mandated in SharePoint 2007. However, sandboxed solutions are nowhere near as flexible as full farm solutions. Any code that is written in a sandboxed solution can only access a subset of the overall SharePoint API, which essentially limits them to working with the data that exists within the site collection where they reside.

Despite the limitations, sandboxed solutions should be the starting point for any SharePoint customization. However, you should be familiar with the limitations and be sure they will not affect your desired outcome before starting any development projects that involve sandboxed solutions.

For more details on sandboxed solutions, refer to the "Sandboxed solutions overview (SharePoint Server 2010)" article on TechNet at `http://technet.microsoft.com/en-us/library/ee721992.aspx.`

Software Boundaries

SharePoint is a highly scalable product that can be architected to meet the needs of most enterprise organizations. However, as with most software systems, SharePoint does have software boundaries relating to how many objects of a given type can be used in a given context.

If you are designing an architecture for large, enterprise deployments, it is well worth being familiar with the main software boundaries, because, in some cases, they will affect how you design the system.

The software boundaries are documented in detail in the "SharePoint Server 2010 capacity management: Software boundaries and limits" article on TechNet (`http://technet.microsoft.com/en-us/library/cc262787.aspx`).

Table 6-1 provides a summary of some of the key areas of software boundaries.

TABLE 6-1: Key Software Boundaries

LIMIT	MAXIMUM VALUE	OFFICIAL MICROSOFT NOTES		IMPLICATIONS/ WORK-AROUNDS
Content database	300 per web application	With 300 content databases per web application, end user operations such as opening the site or site collections are not affected. But administrative operations such as creating a new site collection will experience a decrease in performance. You should use Windows PowerShell to manage the web application when a large number of content databases is present, because the management interface becomes slow and difficult to navigate.		When joined with the limit of 200 GB database sizes, this puts the theoretical maximum size for all databases in a web application at 60,000 GB (58.59 TB).
Application pools	10 per web server	The maximum number is determined by hardware capabilities. This limit is dependent largely upon the amount of RAM allocated to the web servers, and the workload that the farm is serving — that is, the user base and the usage characteristics. (A single, highly active application pool can reach 10 GB or more.)		If you have a large number of web applications, consider sharing application pools across multiple web applications to keep the overall number of application pools low.
Content database size	200 GB per content database	You should limit the size of content databases to 200 GB to help ensure system performance. Content database sizes up to 1 terabyte are supported only for large, single-site repositories and archives with non-collaborative I/O and usage patterns (such as Records Centers). Larger database sizes are supported for these scenarios because their I/O patterns and typical data structure formats have been designed for, and tested at, larger scales. For more information about large-scale document repositories, see "Estimate Performance and Capacity Requirements for Large Scale Document Repositories," available from "Performance and capacity test results and recommendations (SharePoint Server 2010)" at http://technet.microsoft.com/en-us/library/ff608068.aspx, and "Typical large-scale content management		This boundary is one of the main reasons for going for a flat site structure approach, which will mean smaller site collections that can be distributed across a larger number of smaller databases.

LIMIT	MAXIMUM VALUE	OFFICIAL MICROSOFT NOTES	IMPLICATIONS/ WORK-AROUNDS
		scenarios" at `http://technet .microsoft.com/en-us/library/ 9994b57f-fef8-44e7-9bf9-ca620ce20 734(Office.14)#plan_ent_typlarge`, available from "Enterprise content storage planning (SharePoint Server 2010)" at `http://technet.microsoft .com/en-us/library/cc263028.aspx`.	
Site collection size	100 GB per site collection	A site collection should not exceed 100 GB unless it is the only site collection in the database.	As mentioned, this boundary is a good reason to opt for flat structures with a large number of smaller site collections. For large publishing sites, consider placing them in a dedicated content database.
Documents and Items	30,000,000 per library/list	You can create very large document libraries/lists by nesting folders, or using standard views and site hierarchy. This value may vary, depending on how documents/items and folders are organized, and by the type and size of documents stored.	This value is significantly higher than previous versions of SharePoint.
Major versions	400,000	If you exceed this limit, basic file operations (such as file open or save, delete, and viewing the version history) may not succeed.	Disable version control on libraries with very large numbers of documents. Or, use content organization Features to move documents to other libraries.
Web parts	25 per wiki or web part page	This number is an estimate based on simple web parts. The complexity of the web parts dictates how many web parts can be used on a page before performance is affected.	Use multiple pages in the same site collection to spread out the use of web parts.

continues

TABLE 6-1 *(continued)*

LIMIT	MAXIMUM VALUE	OFFICIAL MICROSOFT NOTES	IMPLICATIONS/ WORK-AROUNDS
Indexed items	100 million per search service application; 10 million per index partition (see Chapter 27 for more information on Search)	SharePoint Search supports index partitions, each of which contains a subset of the search index. The recommended maximum is 10 million items in any partition. The overall recommended maximum number of items (for example, people, list items, documents, web pages) is 100 million.	Consider use of FAST for SharePoint if you must index more than 100 million items. FAST also introduces many performance and functionality benefits, as well as dealing with extreme scale.
Maximum number of levels of nested terms in a term store	7	Terms in a term set can be represented hierarchically. A term set can have up to seven levels of terms (a parent term, and six levels of nesting below it).	Break term sets into smaller, more focused term sets if this limit is reached.

You should now understand sites and site collections, and how they interact with each other. In the next section, you learn more about lists, libraries, and list items, which are some of the main items that exist within sites.

INTRODUCING LIBRARIES, LISTS, AND LIST ITEMS

All sites contain, at the very least, a few basic lists and libraries, and some list items. These objects represent the core make-up of data that users use SharePoint to manage and store.

Lists are the basic repositories that store data within a SharePoint site. Lists come in many shapes and sizes designed to suit different types of data. Following are some examples of popular lists that get created with the default team site:

➤ Announcements List

➤ Calendar List

➤ Tasks List

A list contains *list items*. When a new list item is added to a list, the user may need to fill out the columns that are associated with that type of list item.

Libraries are effectively the same as lists, with one key difference — libraries enable attachments to the list items. For example, a document library enables users to create or upload a document (file) that is associated with the list item.

The core functionality is the same between lists and libraries. However, certain lists or libraries may have additional functionality that is tailored toward the specific type of content it stores. For example, Picture libraries have some special views that allow users to browse through pictures in a more intuitive format than standard lists.

 In documentation, you may see the terms "list" and "library" used interchangeably.

Lists and Library Types

SharePoint contains many different types of lists and libraries by default. Each one is tailored toward serving a specific function. Table 6-2 highlights the lists and libraries that are available with the standard team site (with Enterprise CAL). However, additional lists may become available upon activation of certain Features.

TABLE 6-2: Default Lists and Libraries for Team Site

LIST	DESCRIPTION
Asset Library	A place to share, browse, and manage rich media assets.
Data Connection Library	A place for storing files that contain information about external data connections.
Document Library	A place for storing documents or other files that must be shared.
Form Library	A place to manage business forms like status reports or purchase orders. Requires a compatible XML editor such as Microsoft InfoPath (unless Forms Services is available).
Picture Library	A place to upload and share pictures.
Report Library	A place where you can easily create and manage web pages and documents to track metrics, goals, and business intelligence (BI) information.
Slide Library	Used to create a slide library when you want to share slides from Microsoft PowerPoint, or a compatible application.
Wiki Page Library	An interconnected set of easily editable web pages, which can contain text, images, and web parts.
Announcements List	A list of news items, statuses, and other short pieces of information.
Calendar List	A calendar of meetings and events.
Contacts List	A list of people your team works with, such as customers or partners.

continues

TABLE 6-2 *(continued)*

LIST	DESCRIPTION
Custom List	A blank list that allows you to add your own columns.
Custom List in Datasheet View	A blank list that is displayed in a spreadsheet to allow easy data entry.
Discussion Board	A place to have news group–style discussions.
External List	Used to create an external list to view the data in an external content type.
Import Spreadsheet List	Used to create a list that duplicates the columns and data of an existing spreadsheet.
Issue Tracking List	A list of issues or problems associated with a project or item. You can assign, prioritize, and track issue status.
Links List	A list of web pages of other resources.
Project Tasks List	A place for team or personal tasks. Project tasks lists provide a Gantt Chart view, and can be opened with Microsoft Project or other compatible programs.
Status List	A place to track and display a set of goals. Colored icons display the degree to which the goals have been achieved.
Survey List	A list of questions that you would like to have people answer. Surveys allow you to quickly create questions and view graphical summaries of the responses.
Tasks List	A place for team or personal tasks.

Content Types

Although content types are explained in detail in Chapter 25, they are such an important concept to understanding lists and libraries that this section provides a brief overview.

Content types define a specific type of content inside SharePoint, and govern many aspects of that content, including the following:

➤ The underlying document file template that is used to create documents

➤ Workflows that are associated with any items created from the content type

➤ Custom document information panels that will appear in Microsoft Office for a document created from the content type

 See Chapter 25 for more information on document information panels.

➤ Information management policies that are applied to items created from the document type

➤ Metadata columns that are applied to the content type

Every list item or document in SharePoint is based on a content type of some description. Many content types are provided by default. However, it is possible to create your own content types that define the types of files that are used within your organization.

As is the case with most content-management features, it is possible to create content types directly via the site settings interface of a given site. However, in order for a content type to be transportable and easily supported, it is best practice to use Features to define the content type.

The Managed Metadata Service application contains a Feature called the Content Type Hub that is used to replicate content types around the farm. See Chapter 25 for more information on this.

Columns

Columns are used to capture metadata relating to the list item or document that they are associated with. Columns can be formatted for lots of different data types, such as "Single Line of Text" or "Currency."

When planning how to use columns, it is important to consider where the columns will be created, and how they get associated with list items.

First, it is important to consider how columns become associated with lists. The quick-and-easy way is to create a column directly on the list via "list settings." Though this approach is very quick and easy, the column is then isolated and will exist only within the context of that list. This means that if content is moved to another list that does not contain a column with the same name, the data stored in the column may get lost.

A better alternative is to ensure that content types are always used when users create list items. The content types would include the right columns for that piece of content, and automatically transpose them to the list. The added benefit of this approach is that a single list can host multiple types of content, each with its own columns.

 Use of content types is best practice for several reasons. See Chapter 25 for more detail on content types and their usage.

Once you have decided to advocate the use of lists or content types to host columns, the next decision is where the columns will be initially created. Site collections have the capability to store site-wide columns that can be used by any list or content type in the site. Site columns can be created very easily through the site settings interface, or via SharePoint Designer 2010.

Although site collection columns seem like a good approach, their usage is limited to the context of the site collection, regardless of whether they are used in content types or lists. On this basis, it is best practice to avoid using the user interface to create columns, and use Features instead.

Use of Features will ensure that all sites that use the Feature will include site columns of a consistent name and ID. This means that when items get moved around sites, it is much simpler to move the metadata with the item. It is worth noting that Feature creation is an advanced technique that requires technical skills.

List Views

One of the most powerful features of lists is the capability to define views that can be used to filter, sort, aggregate, and display the list items within the list based on parameters that you define.

Views can be used to modify the following aspects of how list data is displayed to users:

➤ Columns that are shown in the view, and the order in which they are shown

➤ Multiple columns that are used to sort the view

➤ Multiple columns that are used to filter the view

➤ Inline editing capabilities

➤ Capability to select multiple item using check boxes

➤ Columns that are used to group the items in the view

➤ Item totals for columns in the view

➤ The presentation style of the view

➤ Whether or not folders are shown in the view

➤ The maximum number of items that can be shown in the view, and whether the view is mobile-compatible

Each list will include a small number of default views that will always contain "all items" and possibly additional views, depending on the type of content stored in the list.

It is possible to customize the default views, as well as adding custom views directly through the user interface. However, as with many other list-based customizations, use of the user interface to make modifications will mean that the list effectively becomes unique, and the customization will only be valid within the context of that specific list, unless the list has been stored as a template for re-deployment.

If you need your list views to be enabled across a wide range of lists of the same type, it is worth considering the creation of a list definition Feature that includes your custom views. This is a lot of work up front. However, it does give a more flexible solution if you need custom views to be used in more than one list.

LICENSING AND SOFTWARE VERSIONS

As with most Microsoft technologies, SharePoint has various licensing models. The correct model will depend on what you intend to use SharePoint for, and which features you require.

Online or On-premises

Deciding whether to host your SharePoint service in "the cloud" or on your own premises has become a critical architectural decision that dictates many of the other design decisions you will make.

 For the purposes of this discussion, Microsoft's Office 365 service will be used as the online service of choice. However, other online SharePoint services may be available.

Office 365 is a broad subscription-based service offering that includes SharePoint, Exchange, Lync, and, in some plans, Office 2010 client software.

A range of plans define the available features. Naturally, the more features that are included, the more expensive the subscription will be. The exact software will depend on which plan you opt for.

Office 365 allows customers to pay a monthly subscription fee per user. This subscription fee replaces many traditional on-premise costs, which are as follows:

➤ All license costs, including server licenses and CALs throughout the stack

➤ Operational maintenance and support of the overall SharePoint service

➤ Data center costs, including power and other utilities

➤ Future upgrades to service packs and even new versions of the software

The Office 365 service takes care of the physical architecture of your solution, and presents you with a very simple administration interface where basic configuration changes can be made. End users are given a simple Internet URL that they go to in order to access the service.

As part of the service agreement, Office 365 also offers a financially backed uptime guarantee with levels of uptime that it would be hard to achieve in most on-premise infrastructures.

The Total Cost of Ownership (TCO) for a cloud-hosted solution will generally be lower than an equivalent on-premises solution with similar levels of scalability, uptime, and functionality.

With all these clear benefits, you would be forgiven for wondering why everyone does not use Office 365 without giving it too much thought or consideration. For all the clear benefits, many limitations exist when using a hosted solution like Office 365, and some organizations are simply not ready (and may never be ready) to make the jump for various reasons, including the following:

➤ *Limited functionality* — Office 365 is not simply "SharePoint in the cloud." Several notable Feature areas of SharePoint 2010 are not yet available in Office 365, including Record Management and much of the BI Features.

➤ *Limited customization or configuration capability* — Office 365 is a service, not a product. This means that your capability to customize and configure is nowhere near the capabilities of an on-premise deployment. Customization is limited to a sandboxed solution, and what you can do in SharePoint Designer 2010.

➤ *Infrastructural integration* — Office 365 requires a fair amount of infrastructural integration if you want your users to log in effectively using corporate Active Directory accounts.

➤ *General security concerns* — Office 365 is an Internet-hosted service, which means all communication between your client and the service goes via the public Internet. Of course, Office 365 is secure, but some IT professionals will be uneasy about the fact that all interactions are web-based.

➤ *Geographic location of Office 365 servers* — Right now, Office 365 is hosted only in certain countries around the world. This presents an issue for some corporations and government bodies because they may require data to be stored in the same country that the organization is registered in.

If you are considering Office 365, it would be well worth familiarizing yourself with the "Office 365 Beta Service Descriptions" at www.microsoft.com/downloads/en/details.aspx?FamilyID=6c6ecc6c-64f5-490a-bca3-8835c9a4a2ea.

The use of a cloud-based solution like Office 365 is a major decision that must be made in a comprehensive and well-informed way. Cloud services bring great benefits, but are also limited compared to on-premise solutions. As an architect, it is important to understand and accept the limitations if you are entering into a cloud-based deployment.

Comparing On-Premise Editions

The phrase "on premise" is generally used to describe infrastructure that is hosted and managed on the organization's premises, as opposed to being managed by a hosting service such as Office 365.

If you elect to go for an on-premise deployment of SharePoint, the next licensing decision to make is which SharePoint product is required, and what level of CAL is required.

The SharePoint family as a whole is made up from three distinct levels of functionality, each of which carries additional features and costs compared to the previous level.

You can find the exact details of what is included in which version on the "Compare SharePoint Editions" page on the official SharePoint 2010 site at http://sharepoint.microsoft.com/en-us/buy/Pages/Editions-Comparison.aspx.

SharePoint Foundation 2010

Microsoft SharePoint Foundation (SPF) used to be called Microsoft Windows SharePoint Services (WSS). It provides the underlying technology that supports many of SharePoint's features. As such, SPF is a mandatory prerequisite for SharePoint Server.

If you need basic team collaboration functionality, then SPF alone may be a good choice.

SPF carries no license itself, and is a free download that anyone with Windows Server licenses (CAL and server) can use and exploit.

SharePoint Server 2010 plus Standard Client Access License

SharePoint Server builds on top of SPF and adds additional capabilities that many organizations need.

SharePoint Server carries a server license and two different types of CALs. The Standard CAL is the cheaper of the two, and includes all of the SharePoint Foundation features, plus many others. Following are some of the main features:

➤ Social networking

➤ Enterprise search

➤ Records management

➤ Document sets

➤ Managed metadata

➤ Web analytics

➤ Workflow templates

➤ Business Connectivity Services (core services)

➤ Web content management

SharePoint Server 2010 Plus Enterprise CAL (and Standard CAL)

The SharePoint Server Enterprise CAL (ECAL) is the premium offering, and will give you the most feature-rich SharePoint experience available on-premise or online.

The ECAL includes all of the standard features, in addition to some notable extras such as the following:

➤ Access services

➤ Business data integration with the Office client and other enterprise features

➤ Business intelligence

➤ Excel services

➤ Advanced search features

➤ InfoPath Forms Services

➤ Visio Services

SharePoint Server 2010 for Internet Sites

One of SharePoint's core features is web content management, and SharePoint is ideally suited to hosting anonymous websites designed for public consumption.

Clearly, in this kind of deployment, the CAL model does not work, because it is impossible to determine how many clients are accessing SharePoint Server.

To address this situation, it is possible to buy "SharePoint Server 2010 for Internet Sites," which is a server-based license that covers usage for any number of anonymous web users.

 It is worth noting that the "SharePoint Server 2010 for Internet Sites" license is relatively expensive, and customers should carefully evaluate it on a fiscal basis before choosing to go ahead with it.

Companion Technologies

SharePoint has a wide range of other Microsoft products that are required for SharePoint to run, or to exploit the SharePoint capabilities. This section provides a brief summary of some of the more popular companion products.

Windows Server

Regardless of the server role, SharePoint runs on Windows Server2008, or 2008 R2. However, 2008 R2 is naturally the best-practice option. Windows Server is usually licensed via a server and CAL model, and Windows Server licenses are required for users accessing SharePoint.

Whichever edition of Windows Server is used, it must be x64.

SQL Server

SharePoint uses SQL Server for the majority of its data storage. SharePoint is supported on the following SQL Server versions (all x64 editions):

➤ SQL Server 2008 R2

➤ SQL Server 2008 with Service Pack 1 and Cumulative Update 2 for Service Pack 1

➤ SQL Server 2005 with Service Pack 3

As with Windows Server, SQL Server must also be fully licensed if being used to support SharePoint deployments.

FAST for SharePoint

FAST for SharePoint is highly scalable search product that builds on top of the search capabilities found in SharePoint Server.

FAST for SharePoint requires the Enterprise licenses for SharePoint, but also carries its own server license for each server that runs FAST software.

Office Web Applications

Office Web Apps (OWA) is a web-based companion product for Office Word, Excel, PowerPoint, and OneNote, which is built on top of SharePoint. OWA provides browser-based, cut-down versions of these popular Office products, but enables you to perform many of the basic Office functions.

OWA is a server installation that, in itself, carries no license. To use OWA, users must have an Office 2010 license.

SUMMARY

This chapter has provided an overview of SharePoint by highlighting features and architectural best practices across a wide range of topics. This chapter has examined the following:

- ➤ SharePoint Server farms
- ➤ Web applications and service applications
- ➤ Sites and site collections
- ➤ Lists and libraries
- ➤ Licensing and software editions

Many of the topics covered in this chapter will have a more detailed chapter elsewhere in the book, should you wish to delve deeper into specific areas.

In Chapter 7, you will learn about the history of SharePoint and how it has evolved from the initial product (SharePoint Portal Server 2001).

7

Evolution of SharePoint

By Brian Wilson

It all started in the Dot Com boom days, from the mid-1990s to the late 1990s. Organizations were starting to realize the potential of the Web, and use of Internet sites was exploding. Organizations were starting to use internal websites to communicate and share information with employees.

Microsoft picked up on this trend early in the 1990s and delivered a number of products to support businesses, both on the Web and internally. Version 3.0 of Microsoft Site Server (first released in 1996) was released in 1998, which provided a number of features to support websites, such as indexing and search, content management, product management, order processing, site personalization, and, believe it or not, an Ad Server!

From a tooling perspective, Microsoft provided support for intermediate to advanced developers in Visual Studio and Visual Interdev. To support power users and end users, Microsoft FrontPage was purchased from Vermeer Technologies, Inc., to enable users to create and edit web pages on a server configured with Office Server Extensions, and later on servers using FrontPage Server Extensions.

 VTI was the acronym of Vermeer Technologies, Inc., which was acquired by Microsoft in 1996, along with the product known today as FrontPage. The name of /_vti_/ in SharePoint evolved from this acquisition.

In 1998, Microsoft was in the process of developing the next version of Microsoft Exchange, codenamed *Platinum*. A new information store, called the Web Storage System, would combine the features and functionality of the filesystem, the Web, and a collaboration server, all in one location. At the same time, a new product, codenamed *Tahoe*, was being developed to target the growing portal market providing web-based document management.

In April 1999, the Digital Dashboard Starter Kit was released, and was Microsoft's first incarnation of web parts and web part zones (then called "nuggets"), along with support for a web part gallery (then called a "nugget repository"). The "nuggets" would work in a browser or directly in Outlook. The starter kit was Microsoft's first Portal User Interface (UI) framework.

Additionally, a number of internal incubation projects were underway at Microsoft to better understand web-based office tools. One such project, Team Pages, enabled users to create and edit simple web-based lists.

In 2000, Microsoft released a number of enabling technologies, including Windows Server 2000 (which introduced Active Directory), SQL Server 2000 (vastly improved from SQL Server 6.5 and 7.0), and Exchange Server 2000 (which introduced the information store, and catered to documents, web content, and Office workflows). All information was URL-addressable through HTTP and enhanced through the WebDAV specification to support an additional set of commands. (For those unfamiliar with WebDAV, it is a set of methods that helps users access, edit, and work with files through HTTP, thus enabling users to work on files located on web servers.) The stage was set and ready for the introduction of SharePoint Team Services (STS) and SharePoint Portal Server (SPS) 2001. This chapter discusses the evolution of SharePoint through SharePoint 2007.

SHAREPOINT 2001 — FROM THE BIRTHING POOL

Stephen Sinofsky, senior vice president of the Microsoft Office product line in 2001, summed up the vision of SharePoint 2001 in a press article:

"SharePoint Team Services enables any team, whether they reside in a small company, inside a corporation, or are located around the world, to easily share information to increase their productivity and efficiency."

 For more information, see www.microsoft.com/presspass/press/2001/may01/05-02sharepointpr.mspx.

The year 2001 was a busy one for Microsoft, and, in particular, the Microsoft Office and SharePoint teams.

On January 8, 2001, Microsoft announced the availability of the RC1 candidate of the *Tahoe* Server, and officially christened it SharePoint Portal Server 2001. SharePoint Portal Server was released to manufacturing later that year.

On May 1, 2001, Microsoft announced the Digital Dashboard Resource Kit (DDRK), a free developer toolkit designed to support organizations extending SPS 2001. More than 100 web parts were included for use in connecting enterprise content in the kit. On May 31, STS became broadly available in retail stores as part of the Office XP and FrontPage 2002 products. It was also made available as a *hosted* offering from leading website hosting providers. Figure 7-1 shows the look and feel of the box SPS 2001 was delivered in.

FIGURE 7-1: SPS 2001 box

STS enabled users to create and contribute to team- and project-focused websites from their web browsers or Office XP applications, while SPS 2001 enabled a "dashboard" site to display different types of aggregated content, including search results from sites created using STS — all within one extensible portal interface. Using "enhanced folders" and WebDAV, document-management features enabled a rich document-management experience from the filesystem, website, and Office XP. Whereas STS was focused at the individual to team level, SPS was focused at the enterprise, business unit, and function level.

DID "CONTENT TYPES" EXIST IN SHAREPOINT 2001?

Most people believe content types were introduced for the first time in SharePoint 2007. However, they existed (albeit in an earlier incarnation) in SharePoint 2001 as "document profiles." Enhanced Web Folders were special folders, made available by the Exchange Storage System, and accessible via WebDAV using Windows Explorer. Enhanced Folders could be configured to support one or more document profiles.

As shown in Figure 7-2, from an architectural perspective, both products were very different, but nonetheless complementary. SharePoint used Internet Information Services (IIS) 5.0 to host websites, supported by a set of Distributed Authoring and Version (DAV) and custom HTTP extensions (which made heavy use of the INVOKE verb to perform actions against SharePoint). Whereas SPS 2001 used the Exchange-based Web Storage System, STS started using Microsoft SQL Server Desktop Engine (MSDE), SQL Server 7.0, or later versions.

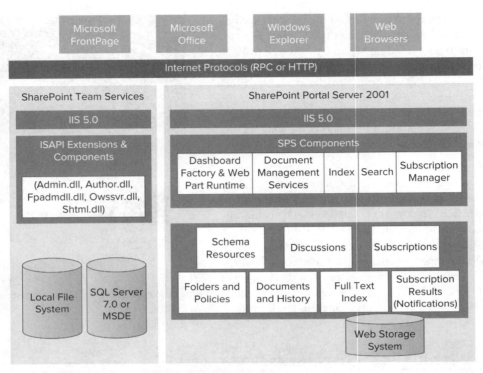

FIGURE 7-2: High-level architecture of STS/SPS 2001

Barring minor exceptions, SharePoint 2001 supported both Internet Explorer (IE) 5.0.1 or later (best results with IE 5.5) on Windows, IE 5.2 or later for the Macintosh, Netscape Navigator 6.2 or later, and Mozilla 1.4 or later. Although Microsoft preferred customers to use its operating system and browser, it provided support for competitor browsers and operating systems, right from the start.

From a development perspective, Microsoft invested heavily in supporting custom business applications. Rich object models included ActiveX Data Objects (ADO), Collaboration Data Objects (CDO), and Publishing and Knowledge Management Collaboration Data Objects (PKMCDO), as well as support for Extensible Markup Language (XML), Extensible Stylesheet Language Transformation (XSLT), HTTP, and WebDAV Internet protocols. Developers could use FrontPage or Visual Studio to customize SharePoint.

WHY DO SOME WEB PARTS END IN .DWP?

SharePoint web parts were originally called Dashboard Web Parts supported by the underlying Digital Dashboard framework implemented in SharePoint 2001.

During the same time period, Microsoft acquired nCompass Labs to improve its publishing and content management features. The product was rebranded as Content Management Server (CMS) 2001. It was subsequently upgraded to use ASP.NET in CMS 2002, and began to compete with SPS 2001 for market share.

SHAREPOINT 2003 — GROWING PAINS

Microsoft released SharePoint Product and Technologies 2003 Beta 2 in March 2003, followed by the RTM (release to manufacturing) version in October 2003. It was one of the biggest betas of the time, and entrenched the rich tradition of providing early technical previews to customers and partners that the Microsoft Office product group has maintained to the current release. Figure 7-3 provides an example of the look and feel of SharePoint in 2003.

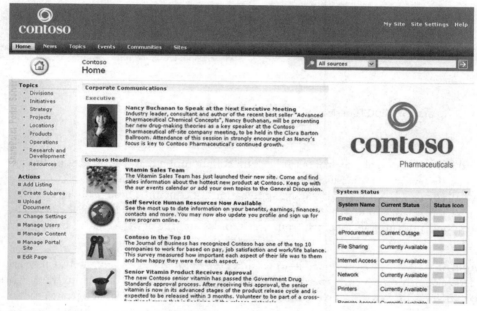

FIGURE 7-3: SharePoint 2003 look and feel

SharePoint 2003 was a significant release for a number of reasons. Two separate product teams had merged into the Office Product Group to release SPS 2003, Windows SharePoint Services (WSS) 2.0, and Office 2003 simultaneously, a massive scheduling and logistical achievement.

As shown in Figure 7-4, WSS 2.0 and SPS 2003 aimed to provide services from the individual, team, business unit, enterprise and beyond, to the extranet and Internet.

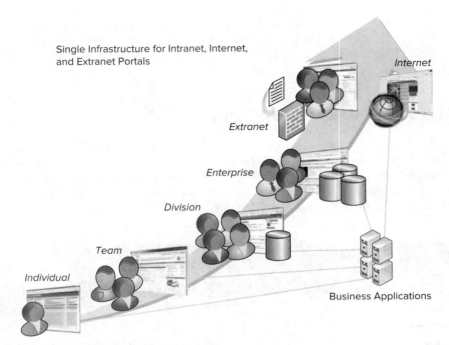

Single Infrastructure for Intranet, Internet, and Extranet Portals

Internet

Extranet

Enterprise

Division

Team

Individual

Business Applications

FIGURE 7-4: WSS 2.0 and SPS 2003 services

WSS 2.0 provided significant enhancements to the team collaboration features of STS, including new sites, lists, and services. And it was free! SPS 2003 was completely revamped to sit on top of WSS 2.0, but still focused heavily on displaying aggregations of content. These included search results from a wide array of supported content sources, lists of collaboration sites in the new site directory, and people information collected from user profiles and the new "My Site" business social networking feature.

Categories (from SPS 2001) were revamped as *areas* and *area templates*. Unfortunately, this feature occasionally led to confusion over whether to use portal areas or team sites. Interestingly, categories (in SPS 2001) and areas (in SPS 2003) were the first attempts by the Office product groups to structure content according into a hierarchal classification structure.

As shown in Figure 7-5, from an architectural perspective, both WSS 2.0 and SPS 2003 used a scalable architecture that enabled deployment from a single server to a server farm, with multiple front-end web servers and back-end database servers.

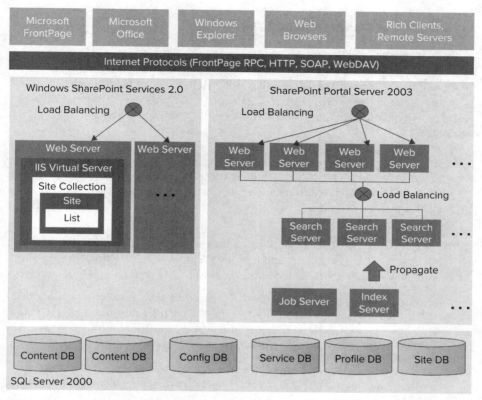

FIGURE 7-5: WSS 2.0 and SPS 2003 architecture

SharePoint 2003 products and technologies ran on Windows Server 2003 or later. IIS 6.0 was used together with ASP.NET 1.1 to host websites. This release provided stateless web servers, enabling large organizations to use load-balancing technologies to distribute load over multiple web servers.

Content storage was moved away from the Exchange-based Web Storage System, and was unified in SQL Server 2000, taking advantage of a new Binary Large Object (BLOB) data type, in one of many content databases. This included all content, not just the metadata of content. This innovation improved reliability by ensuring transactional integrity of the data, and resulted in greater flexibility, maintainability, availability, and scalability at the storage tier.

SPS 2003 introduced additional databases to maintain the service database, the user profile database, and the portal site content database. Both WSS 2.0 and SPS 2003 used a server configuration database to maintain farm settings and configuration information.

At the time, hosting files in the database represented a major paradigm shift, and customers and architects were initially apprehensive in using SQL Server 2000 to move large numbers of Office files from file shares to relational databases.

VIRTUAL SERVERS IN SHAREPOINT 2003?

Web applications were first called *virtual servers* in SharePoint 2003. Virtual servers provided finer control over settings for groups of websites. This feature allowed you to host one or more virtual servers on the same Web Front-End (WFE). Another feature was the capability to provide different authentication methods for the same content, dependent on whether you were internal or external to the organization.

The SharePoint product team had tough choices to make regarding which technologies to use and leave out. These included decisions related to technologies that are rock-solid today, but at the time, were in their infancy and in a state of flux, such as the .NET Framework, XML, and Simple Object Access Protocol (SOAP).

Underpinned by ASP.NET, the new UI framework provided the first true implementation of the SharePoint page model used today. Developers could now develop web parts using Visual Studio and the ASP.NET Framework, and add these web parts into web part zones on a SharePoint page.

While developing the web part framework, a key challenge faced by the SharePoint product team was that they were far ahead of the ASP.NET product team. As a result, a custom ASP.NET handler and ASPX SafeMode Parser was required to retrieve and render pages stored in the database. The ASP.NET 1.1 ASPX Parser only worked with files located on the filesystem.

Figure 7-6 shows how it worked. The ISAPI Filter looked at the requested URL to determine if the request was for a SharePoint-managed path. (In this release, managed paths could be included and excluded.) The ISAPI Filter then passed the request either to the ASP.NET handler, or handled the request through an ISAPI Extension call. For uncustomized/ghosted pages, the ASP.NET Page Parser was used, whereas customized/un-ghosted pages used the SafeMode Page Parser. This led to a number of issues and differences, depending on which parser was invoked. Some pages were not properly initialized with ASP.NET context, causing unexpected failures in pages that had been "un-ghosted" to the database.

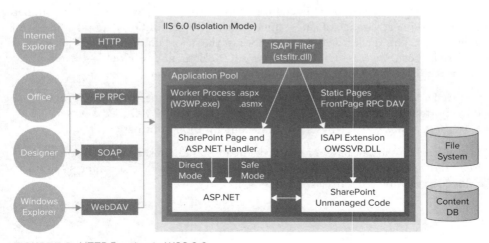

FIGURE 7-6: HTTP Routing in WSS 2.0

An unsung hero of SharePoint 2003 was the release of the powerful *lists* functionality. Lists are generic functionality that underpin a number of different types of lists. For example, document and image libraries provide universal features (such as check-in and check-out). More importantly, a rich object model underpinned lists, and enabled developers to write uniform code against most types of lists.

However, there were "casualties of war," where much-loved features (such as item level security, lists events, "document profiles," and support for workflows) did not make it into this release. The main reason for this was the shift away from the Web Storage System to the new SQL Storage model provided by WSS 2.0. There simply was not enough time to develop these important features.

Jeff Teper, Corporate Vice President of the SharePoint Group, summarized the product team effort beautifully in a blog post on the SharePoint team blog:

"While this was a long release, we could not have gotten the integrated experience and platform without the lots of different skunk works efforts. It really needed teams to research, plan, develop and test together."

SHAREPOINT 2007 — COMING OF AGE

A number of important milestones occurred in the run up to the release of SharePoint 2007 Products and Technologies, including the following:

➤ In 2004, the Content Management Server product team merged into the SharePoint product team, signaling a merging of the two products in SPS 2007.

➤ In 2005, Microsoft released Microsoft Business Scorecard Manager 2005, which integrated a number of business intelligence (BI) features into SharePoint. These included score carding, key performance indicators (KPIs), and strategy maps, using Microsoft Visio. Additionally, Microsoft began working on a dedicated BI product called PerformancePoint 2007.

➤ In 2005, Version 2.0 of the .NET Framework (and specifically, ASP.Net 2.0) was launched, enabling the SharePoint product team to take advantage of the native ASP.NET 2.0 "plumbing."

➤ In late 2006, Microsoft released .NET 3.0, which included Windows Workflow Foundation (WF) for building workflow-enabled applications. It included a workflow runtime engine, design tools in Visual Studio 2005, and a rich base object model to enable developers to build workflow-enabled solutions.

➤ Microsoft Office SharePoint Server (MOSS) 2007, WSS 3.0, and Office 2007 were made available on the November 30, 2006, with full support for 32-bit and 64-bit environments.

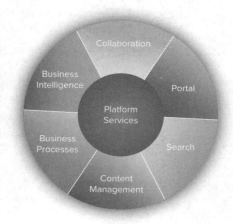

SharePoint 2007 Products and Technologies is best known as the *Pie Release*, because of the wagon wheel presentation slide the marketing team used to communicate the core capabilities of this release. Figure 7-7 shows the Pie Release.

FIGURE 7-7: SharePoint 2007 "Pie Release"

WSS 3.0 provided the platform services that enabled businesses to host thousands of websites, and make them available to tens of thousands of users using a scalable architecture of stateless web front-end (WFE) servers. Core platform services included the following features:

➤ *Management* — Administration tasks could be performed from a central location using a specialized site called Central Administration. Command-line utilities (STSADM and PSConfig) could perform the common administration tasks required to manage your SharePoint 2007 farm. Examples included provisioning site collections and configuring, managing, and maintaining servers (and the services hosted on each server) in your SharePoint 2007 topology.

➤ *Authentication and authorization* — Security features were greatly enhanced in WSS 3.0. A new pluggable authentication provider model enabled support for alternative authentication sources to Active Directory (for example, forms-based authentication). Other security features included item-level security, and rights-trimmed interfaces that ensured users only view content they have permission to see. SharePoint 2007 provided improvements for configuring farms using the principle of least privilege. SharePoint 2007 features could be configured to run under specific service accounts. For example, IT administrators could secure and isolate web applications within security boundaries using IIS application pools.

➤ *Site containment model* — SharePoint 2007 provided a flexible site containment model, starting at the web application or website level in IIS. Web applications hosted site collections, which in turn could support many sites. Web applications used multiple content databases to store site collections.

➤ *Storage* — SQL Server was used to store and manage all content and site-related information in content databases in SQL Server. Thousands of site collections were supported per content database, and up to 100 content databases were supported per web application. If required, these content databases could be distributed over multiple SQL instances to enable scale-out at the Data tier.

➤ *Topology* — SharePoint 2007 supported the capability to scale out the topology of your farm over multiple servers, by enabling servers to run as specific roles. Examples included the WFE, Query, and Index Role. Scale-out at each tier improved the fault tolerance, availability, and load your farm can cater for.

➤ *Application programming interface (API)* — WSS 3.0 provided a number of methods to develop custom solutions that extended SharePoint 2007 sites and services. These features included a rich object model to work with sites, webs, lists, and an in-depth list-eventing model to respond to user actions.

➤ *Content and information governance* — Some consider content types to be the most powerful feature of the SharePoint 2007 release. Content types enable the easy (and uniform) configuration of a library or list based on the type of content. Content types enforce metadata standards by ensuring that users fill in the required information when adding content to a list. They also support and enable a wide range of "downstream" features, such as information policies, workflows, search relevance, accuracy (as a result of better metadata), and content aggregation using either the out-of-the-box Content Query web part or custom queries using Collaborative Application Markup Language (CAML) or the FullTextSQLQuery Search API.

Microsoft Office SharePoint Server (MOSS) 2007 sat on top of WSS 3.0 to provide a number of portal capabilities, including the following:

- ➤ *Collaboration* — The collaboration features included new and improved site templates and lists (for example blogs, wikis, calendars, discussion, and project-management related lists). Deeper integration with Office 2007 clients and the introduction of people "presence" status were provided. Additionally, a new Office client, Groove, was introduced to support new ways of collaboration, such as peer to peer (P2P) and disconnected experiences.

- ➤ *Content management* — New features catered for web content management, as well as document and records management scenarios. Rich authoring and approval experiences enabled and controlled web page publishing. Information Policies could be applied and changes to content could be audited. Other key content management features included the capability to set retention policies, create multi-lingual sites, and deploy content between farms using content deployment features.

- ➤ *Portal* — Rich portal features provided the capability to aggregate and target content in a central site(s) to users based on the audience and personalization settings. Other enhanced features included the Site Directory and My Site templates.

- ➤ *Search* — Search scalability and search result relevance was greatly improved, along with new support for indexing, searching, and surfacing "business data." People search features were enhanced to include expertise searching based on User Profile properties gathered from Active Directory or the My Site profile page.

- ➤ *Business intelligence* — Various BI features made their debuts as part of the SharePoint 2007 release. Excel Services enabled hosting of Excel spreadsheets on the server. KPI lists supported the integration of data from a variety of sources. The reporting site template provided a dedicated site to host reports and BI dashboards.

- ➤ *Business process* — Support for the hosting of business processes was provided using a combination of workflow and browser-based forms technologies. A number of common Office processes (such as approval processes) were available for use. Simple to intermediate processes could be designed and deployed using SharePoint Designer, and advanced processes could be developed using SharePoint sequence or state workflows in Visual Studio. Web-based electronic forms services often "drive" workflows in SharePoint by presenting online forms, or pages for users to complete at various stages of the workflow.

As shown in Figure 7-8, from an architectural perspective, SharePoint 2007 Products and Technologies were underpinned by Windows Server operating services, SQL Server database services, SharePoint search, ASP.NET 2.0, and .NET 3.0 WF services.

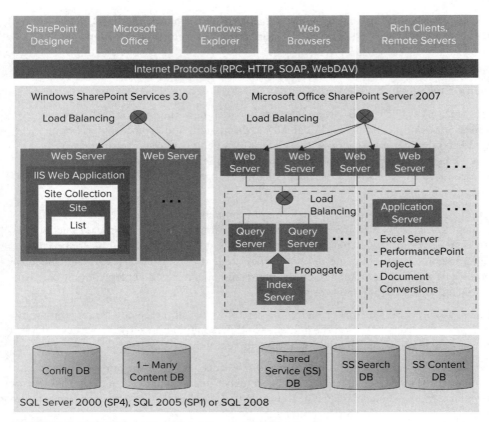

FIGURE 7-8: WSS 3.0 and SharePoint Server 2007 Topology

SharePoint 2007 improved on the "shared services" model first introduced in SharePoint Portal Server 2003, called the *Shared Service Provider* (*SSP*). SSPs managed and controlled a set of services that could be consumed by web applications and sites in a SharePoint farm. SharePoint 2007 services consisted of personalization services, including User Profiles and My Sites, the Business Data Catalog, Excel Services, SharePoint search, and usage reporting features. A key tenet of this feature was the capability to host or consume services from multiple SSPs.

"Shared services" and the SSP model, in SharePoint 2007 were the forerunners to delivering service applications in SharePoint 2010. Figure 7-9 shows the home page of the SSP Administration page in Central Administration.

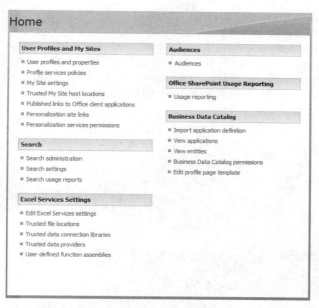

FIGURE 7-9: SharePoint 2007 SSP Administration page

One of key updates to the SharePoint 2007 architecture was the adoption of ASP.NET 2.0. ASP.NET introduced a new mechanism, called a *virtual path provider*, to serve content and files for compilation. The SharePoint product team created a virtual path provider called the SPVirtualPathProvider to fetch pages either from the database or the filesystem that hands off pages to ASP.NET to conduct the required parsing and compilation. As shown in Figure 7-10, this update fixed the problems in WSS 2.0, because all HTTP requests could be fully initialized with ASP.NET context before being forwarded to WSS 3.0.

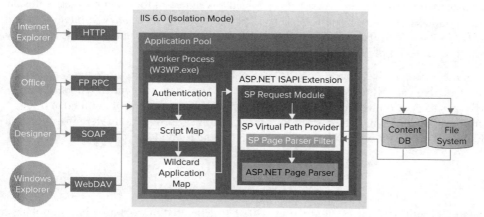

FIGURE 7-10: SharePoint 2007 — Routing in WSS 3.0

A new feature called the Business Data Catalog (BDC) enabled customers to use a common framework for integrating line-of-business (LOB) data from external databases and web services. The BDC enabled developers to define a data model (consisting of entities and methods), and publish it to the BDC metadata database, as shown in Figure 7-11. Solutions could then be developed to use exposed business data in a variety of ways (such as using business data web parts, creating "business data" list columns, indexing via SharePoint search, business data-based User Profile properties, and custom business applications).

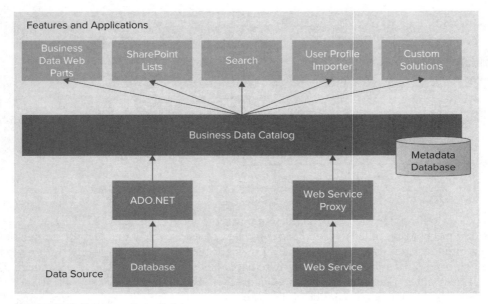

FIGURE 7-11: Business Data Catalog

A key benefit provided by this feature was that it enabled customers to focus on business solution development, as opposed to writing framework and "plumbing" code necessary to integrate external sources of data. SharePoint 2007 did have a limitation, however, in that it was read-only, and not read-write. SharePoint 2010 addresses this feature.

From a development perspective, SharePoint 2007 provided a number of enhancements to the development of custom capabilities targeting SharePoint 2007. A new concept called *Features* enabled developers to develop features scoped at the web, site, web application, and farm levels. The automation of the deployment of custom Features and any customizations were installed to all servers in the SharePoint farm using Windows Solution Packages (WSPs).

SUMMARY

With more than 100 million licenses, SharePoint 2007 has generated more than a billion dollars in revenue for Microsoft. Obviously, it has been a wildly successful product that has evolved from its humble beginnings a decade ago.

The history of SharePoint demonstrates the Office and SharePoint product team's commitment and dedication to innovation and continued evolution of the SharePoint platform. With each new version, Microsoft has learned lessons from the previous release, and made the right technology bets and decisions for the next release.

This consistent approach has made it easy for partners to recommend SharePoint technologies to customers, and easy for customers to benefit from collaboration, publishing, and so many other great SharePoint features.

Chapter 8 describes the capabilities and feature set provided by the latest version of SharePoint, SharePoint 2010.

8

SharePoint 2010 Features and Capabilities

By Brian Wilson

SharePoint 2010 is packed with features and capabilities to help your organization implement intranet, extranet, and Internet-focused solutions. It contains a smorgasbord of features and capabilities to cater to your organization's specific requirements. Without a doubt, it is the most complete information management and versatile business solutions platform on the market today.

SharePoint 2010 is a product resulting from continuous improvement, learning, evolution, and innovation, starting all the way back in the Site Server days, and, officially, with SharePoint 2001, culminating in the release of SharePoint 2010.

 If you have not already, read Chapter 6 (which explains the concept of SharePoint) and Chapter 7 (which describes SharePoint's journey to today, and explains how various features came about).

This chapter has taken up the challenge of providing a succinct overview of the arsenal of features and capabilities available in the SharePoint architect's "tool belt." The key features and capabilities include the following:

- ➤ Publishing services
- ➤ Information services

➤ Collaboration services

➤ Search services

➤ Individual and social networking services

➤ Business connectivity services

➤ Business intelligence services

➤ Workflow and Forms services

Part IV of this book includes chapters that provide detailed design and architecture guidance for each of these services. This chapter does not cover the administration and development capabilities of SharePoint 2010. Both of these subjects are entire books (or even multiple books) in their own right. However, these subjects are discussed from an architectural perspective in later chapters.

PUBLISHING SERVICES

SharePoint 2010 provides a rich set of Web Content Management (WCM) features that enable organizations to rapidly build, deploy, and manage fantastic-looking sites that are dynamic, "standards compliant," and "pixel perfect" user experiences targeting intranet, extranet, and Internet-facing scenarios.

This section provides a summary of the key publishing services features of SharePoint 2010.

Publishing Sites Templates

Although a number of site templates are available to use in SharePoint 2010, the Enterprise Wiki and Publishing Site templates are most suited to catering for unstructured and structured publishing scenarios. One of the reasons is that they are preconfigured with SharePoint publishing features turned on.

The Enterprise Wiki Site templates enable multiple authors to publish content with little or no control as to the structure of the content they submit, similar to the Wikipedia experience. The Publishing Site template enables authors to create web pages using predefined, finely tuned web page layouts and content (data) structures that result in a consistent look and feel across various pages in your site.

Web Page Publishing Life Cycle

Web-based content-authoring tools are provided to facilitate easy authoring and submission of web page content. Figure 8-1 shows the Fluent UI (server-side Ribbon) in action, demonstrating the Browse, Page, and Publish Ribbon menus. Editing Tool contextual actions are currently available as the author is editing content.

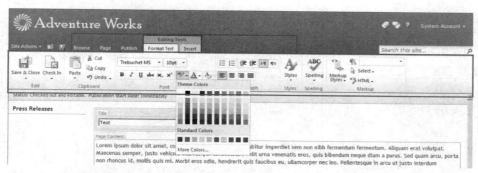

FIGURE 8-1: Browser-based Ribbon-editing experience

Once authors have completed authoring, the web page can be saved (or checked in), submitted to an approver for review and/or approval, and then published to "go live" either immediately, or based on a schedule.

TechNet provides an in-depth article on web page authoring at http://technet.microsoft.com/en-us/library/cc263367.aspx.

A big improvement from SharePoint 2007 is the support for folders in page libraries. Authors can now use folders to group similar pages together. There are two benefits to this enhancement. One is that authors are not forced to always use subsite "structures" to categorize similar pages together. Secondly, by using folders, the Pages Library can support a much larger number of pages in a single library.

Branding

Branding is the process of designing, developing, and deploying a set of user interface (UI) artifacts to SharePoint 2010 site collections or subsites within a site collection. Branding can range from simple tasks that take no time and require little skill, to completion tasks (such as applying a SharePoint 2010 theme), to advanced tasks that require in-depth design and development skill, and time to provide a fully customized user experience.

Figure 8-2 shows an example of a SharePoint website that leverages all of the SharePoint "plumbing," but looks nothing at all like SharePoint.

FIGURE 8-2: Branded SharePoint website

Multi-lingual, Multi-channel, Multi-device, and Multi-farm Support

SharePoint provides great support for developing solutions that target multiple languages, channels, devices, and even SharePoint farms using a combination of SharePoint Language Packs, the Multi-lingual User Interface (MUI), Variations, and content deployment.

SharePoint Language Packs support showing different chrome elements (for example, Site Actions) in a different language. Once Language Packs have been installed and configured on a farm, users will be able to display SharePoint chrome in alternate languages. Content will not change using this feature, only the SharePoint chrome.

To support multi-lingual content, the Variations Feature is required. With Variations, designers create a source language, and a number of target languages, as shown in Figure 8-3.

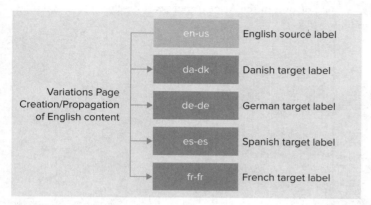

FIGURE 8-3: Variations propagation

Essentially, what happens behind the scenes is that source and target root sites are created, as shown in Figure 8-4. As designers and authors create sites and pages on the source site, these sites and pages are replicated to each of the target sites. Replicated pages are not visible to users until they have been made ready (in this case, translated), checked-in, and published.

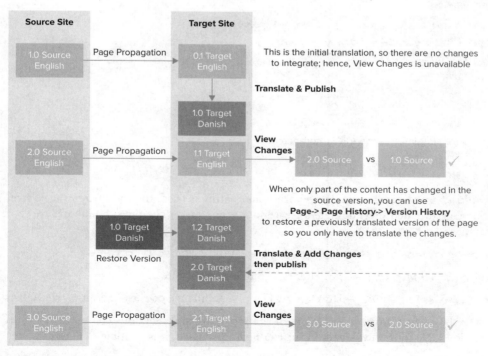

FIGURE 8-4: Target Variation page-publishing process

Users browse to the home page and are redirected to their language-based site. The automatic redirection is based on their browser locale. By default, the browser locale is set based on the language of your operating system. To view or change your default locale settings in Internet Explorer, open the General tab in Internet Options. At the bottom, in the Appearance section, click the Languages button to reveal the dialog shown in Figure 8-5.

FIGURE 8-5: Internet Explorer Language Preference dialog

To support *multi-channel* content, the same Variations Feature is used. Instead of creating source and target language-oriented sites, designers create source and target channels. Following are some common examples:

➤ *Device-based targeting* — Phone Type 1, Phone Type 2, Phone Type 3.

➤ *Country-based targeting* — U.S. Site, U.K. Site, Australia Site.

➤ *Audience-based targeting* — Developers, IT pros, architects, end-user adoption specialists.

To send users to the correct browser Variations, a site providing multi-channel content will require custom redirection logic to be developed. In the examples discussed, it is possible to determine the device based on user agent information submitted as part of the HTTP request. For country and audience, this information may form part of the User Profile in SharePoint 2010.

In SharePoint 2010, Variations have been significantly enhanced from SharePoint 2007. Notable improvements include moving all operations to background timer jobs for pause-and-resume support, more control on the creation of hierarchies, UI and MUI improvements, and, finally, better support for right-to-left languages such as Arabic, Japanese, and Chinese.

 For more information, TechNet provides an overview of Variations at `http://technet.microsoft.com/en-us/library/ff628966.aspx.`

Content deployment enables content to be deployed or copied from one or more locations to one or more target locations, either in the same SharePoint farm, or in separate farms. This feature is useful when content is authored in an authoring environment, deployed to a staging environment for testing, and finally deployed to a production environment for end users to consume.

Content deployment in SharePoint 2010 is more reliable and stable than its predecessor in SharePoint 2007. Notable enhancements include a better capability to handle concurrency, incremental deployment reliability, and the capability to diagnose issues from improved logging support. Content deployment now supports SQL Enterprise database "point-in-time" snapshot technology as the basis from which to create the export packages, as opposed to the ever-changing "live" content database.

 For more information, see the TechNet article "Content Deployment Overview" at `http://technet.microsoft.com/en-us/library/ee721058.aspx.`

Standards and Compliance Support

The SharePoint product teams have invested heavily in improving the accessibility, interoperability, and compliance of sites in SharePoint 2010 in accordance with internationally recognized standards from the Web Accessibility Initiative (WAI), which is part of the World Wide Web Consortium (W3C).

Accessibility is a term used to indicate how many users are able to successfully access, navigate, and consume content from a site. This includes the capability to support users with disabilities or special needs that may require assistive technologies such as screen readers.

SharePoint 2010 adopted the Web Content Accessibility Guidelines 2.0 and set a goal for "AA" compliance. SharePoint leverages Accessible Rich Internet Applications (ARIA) in areas such as the Ribbon, dialogs, and text editor.

For more information, see the SharePoint Team blog post on accessibility and SharePoint 2010 at `http://sharepoint.microsoft.com/blog/Pages/BlogPost.aspx?pID=431.`

SharePoint 2010 uses XHTML 1.0–compliant code to support better accessibility across a number of "user agents," including browsers, screen readers, and mobile devices. Many of the publishing features in SharePoint adhere to the XHTML Strict specification. Adoption and adherence has resulted in faster browser rendering, and allows for better Search Engine Optimization (SEO).

For more information, see the MSDN article, "XHTML Compliance and HTML simplification in SharePoint Server 2010" at `http://msdn.microsoft.com/en-us/library/ff521594.aspx.`

Interoperability is a term used to indicate to what level independent systems are capable of working together. SharePoint 2010 supports the Content Management Interoperability Standard (CMIS), which specifies the interoperability between enterprise content management repositories and applications.

It is worth noting that SharePoint provides a number of web services and an extremely rich object model. This makes it easy for any vendor to integrate a solution with SharePoint via XML/REST-based web services.

Web Analytics and Reporting

One of the biggest features missing from SharePoint 2007 was the capability to understand user interactions with your site over different time periods. SharePoint 2010 rectifies this by incorporating a well-thought-out set of traffic, search, and inventory reports. Following are some examples of traffic reports:

➤ *Number of Page Views* — How much traffic does your site get?

➤ *Top Destinations* — What are your top pages?

➤ *Top Visitors* — Who are your top visitors?

➤ *Top Referrers* — How do visitors arrive at your site?

Figure 8-6 shows an example of a traffic report.

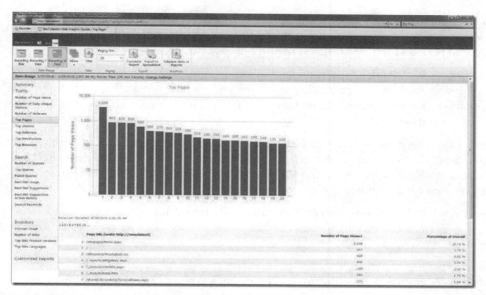

FIGURE 8-6: Traffic report

It is possible to customize results, such as scheduling alerts and reports based on conditions occurring on your site (for example, an unexpected extreme number of users). This feature also helps provide concrete feedback to stakeholders as to the return on investment (ROI) and usefulness of various sites and solutions hosted in your SharePoint 2010 environment.

Chapter 24 provides detailed information on designing publishing sites. TechNet also provides a detailed series of articles, "Plan Web Content Management," at `http://technet.microsoft.com/en-us/library/ee476993.aspx`.

INFORMATION SERVICES

SharePoint provides both broad and in-depth document management (DM) and records management (RM) features that enable organizations to perform simple tasks (such as uploading a document) to advanced tasks (such as applying an information policy to manage documents of a certain type for all document libraries in an entire site collection). This section provides a summary of the key information services features of SharePoint 2010.

Information Management

The following features form the foundation of the information management features in SharePoint 2010:

➤ *Full document life cycle support* — Users use document libraries to upload or create new documents, edit and modify documents, and delete documents.

➤ *Two-stage Recycle Bin* — Deleted documents are moved to a Recycle Bin. If a document is deleted from the Recycle Bin, this is moved to a site collection Recycle Bin. After a configured period of time, SharePoint removes deleted items.

➤ *Versioning* — SharePoint supports major and minor versioning of items in a document library. Each version is maintained in the version history and, if required, users can restore a previous version of an item. The major and minor version, along with how many versions to store, are configurable.

➤ *Check in and check out* — Users can check in and check out documents. Check-out grants the user an exclusive use of the document until check-in. Users can discard their checked-out items, or, alternatively, override another user. Depending on your versioning settings, minor versions (drafts) and major versions (published) can be created.

➤ *Permissions* — All access to content in document libraries can be controlled by individual and group permission sets. Permission can be applied to individual items, to folders, or to the entire library.

➤ *Content types* — Document libraries support the use and application of content types. Content types govern items in document libraries of a certain "type" (for example, Sales Document or Contract Document). The content type specifies what meta-information must be stored with the document, what process the document should follow, and other information policies that should be adhered to. Content types can be applied to many document libraries, enabling your organization to consistently govern types of content. Content types can be created in a central location (Content Type Hub) and pushed out to each site collection's content type gallery. This requires the Managed Metadata Service (MMS) application.

➤ *Workflows* — Workflows can be configured against a site, a list, a document library, a selection of content within a document library of a particular content type, or manually for an individual item. Examples of out-of-the-box workflows include approval, disposition, feedback collection, signature collection, and three-state workflows.

➤ *Information policies* — Information management policies can be applied to all content or content based on a content type in a document library. Examples include retention, auditing, barcodes, and labeling policies. Custom policies can be developed if required.

➤ *Offline document libraries* — Microsoft Outlook 2007 makes it possible to take document libraries offline.

➤ *Location-based and folder-based metadata defaults* — SharePoint enables site administrators to specify different default column values for each folder in a document library. SharePoint ensures that these default metadata properties are applied to items in a document library based on a conditions and precedence rule set.

➤ *Metadata navigation and filtering* — Users can navigate items using indexed columns (based on metadata fields) of the document library to display filtered lists of items to users.

➤ *Document sets* — Document sets enable multiple items to be packaged (and grouped) together into a "single" item. Although each item is separate, the set of items can be acted on as a group. For example, workflows can be used to manage a document set. Other features include support for custom document set templates, and versioning that captures the state of the document set at different points in its life cycle.

➤ *Document IDs* — New support is provided for applying unique Document IDs to items throughout a site collection using either a random prefix or manual prefix. A Document ID can be used with static URLs to retrieve documents by Document ID, regardless of their current or future location.

➤ *Views and throttling* — Views are a feature of libraries and lists in SharePoint 2010. They provide preconfigured "view" of all items in a list or document library. SharePoint 2010 has built-in features to protect and stop bad-performing list views from running. Where large list operations are required, specific time periods can be set to allow these types of queries or views.

Information Service Site Templates

All sites in SharePoint 2010 provide document and records management features, but some site templates are more suited than others. Examples of these include collaboration-focused sites such as a team site, document workspaces, and group work site templates. Enterprise-focused site templates include the "Document and Records Center" site template.

In reality, the differences between various site templates are the default configuration of the site and the Features that have been activated and preconfigured. It is these Features and configuration that make specific document and records management capabilities (from simple to advanced) available to users of a site template.

Large-Scale and Extremely Large-Scale Content Repositories

Given the correct planning, design, and configuration, SharePoint 2010 supports extremely large document libraries that can contain up to tens of millions of items or documents, up to 150 GB in heavy authoring scenarios, and up to 1 TB in large-scale content archiving scenarios, and up to 4 TB in extremely large-scale scenarios.

 TechNet provides extremely detailed information and guidance on designing large-scale authoring environment and content archive solutions at http://technet.microsoft.com/en-us/library/cc263028.aspx.

Enterprise Terms, Metadata, and Content Type Hubs

SharePoint 2010 provides a new service, the Managed Metadata Service (MMS), to manage a hierarchical collection of terms in a centrally managed term store. Terms (which are essentially words or phrases) can be grouped in a hierarchical fashion into a relationship of parent and child terms, called *term sets*.

The MMS supports the following three key approaches:

➤ *Closed (top-down) term set* — The Managed Metadata column is used to connect to the closed term set, and users can only choose from existing terms. Top-down term sets are generally referred to as *taxonomies*.

➤ *Open (bottom-up) term set* — The Managed Metadata column is used to connect to the open term set, and users can contribute terms to the term set. Open term sets are usually referred to *folksonomies*.

➤ *Enterprise Keyword column* — This column has its uses, especially when closed term sets are often used by a business. First, it provides an informal avenue for users to tag content based on terms that do not exist or belong in any of your predefined Managed Metadata (closed term set) columns. Second, it provides a powerful lookup-as-you-type against all terms in your term store. Finally, if required, terms entered in the Enterprise Keyword column can later be moved into formal open or closed term sets.

Content Type Hubs enable you to define content types in one or more Content Type Hub, and push them down to multiple site collections in one or many farms. This reduces (and, in some cases, eliminates) the need for custom code or third-party software to deploy and maintain a consistent set of "base" content types in each of your site collections.

Finally, a number of useful tools are provided to enable term stewards to support multi-lingual terms, provide useful synonyms, and organize and maintain term sets. These also provide the capability to disambiguate, reuse, merge, and deprecate terms.

Content Organizer

The *Content Organizer* (as the Feature name implies) organizes and routes content based on metadata associated with items. This Feature ensures content uploaded by users is saved in the correct library and folder. To do this, the Content Organizer routing engine uses a list of configurable rules to route content to the correct location.

The Content Organizer enables you to control whether users can upload directly to a library or folder. If "Redirect users to the drop off library" is enabled, all users of a site collection (regardless of which library or folder they are in) will be redirected to the "Drop Off Library" to upload content. This Feature also includes automatic folder partitioning to ensure that no one folder grows past SharePoint's software (or your) boundaries. It caters for duplicate submissions to ensure no files are mistakenly overwritten. It also enables you to "preserve context" (which enables you to keep information with the file, such as audit logs and properties, after the file has been routed to a different library).

In-place Records Management

In SharePoint 2007, users could declare a record using the "send to record center" command. This created a copy of the item, and placed the item in the Record Center. In effect, the Record Center site collection became a large archive, and files lived their lives according the retention schedules applied within the Record Center.

SharePoint 2010 provides a new feature that enables users to declare "in-place" records within the site collection or site. Once declared as a record, the user may not be able to edit or delete it. Records managers are able to discover and hold records based on searches within the site collection. Other key features include the capability to use the Content Organizer to control where records are stored, and to generate file plan and auditing reports.

Digital and Rich Media Asset Support

One of the great features of SharePoint 2010 is the support for digital and rich media assets such as audio, video, and image content in a new library template optimized for digital assets. The Asset Library provides a number of features, such as image ingestion and automatic extraction of metadata, thumbnail-centric viewing, and podcasting (including RSS) support.

On the presentation side, SharePoint Media Player (built on Silverlight 3.0) is provided as a rich media web part and as publishing field controls to surface rich media on web pages in SharePoint sites, as shown in Figure 8-7.

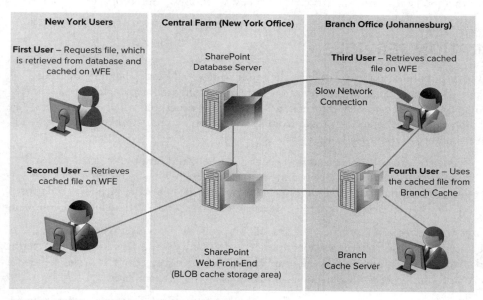

FIGURE 8-7: SharePoint as a Rich Media Server

Under the hood, a number of infrastructure enhancements reduce the impact of streaming large files across your business network. These include a smarter file transfer between the database and the Web Front-Ends (WFEs) in your SharePoint environment, and improved BLOB caching on each WFE.

SharePoint supports the use of an Internet Information Services (IIS) feature in called *bit rate throttling* to minimize the bandwidth consumed during streaming of large rich media files. IIS bit rate throttling ensures that rich media files are only transferred at the speed required to play, rather than at the maximum speed the network can handle. For multi-region deployments, the use of Windows branch cache servers to store and cache files locally is supported.

As with network file shares, not all content is suitable or best placed in SharePoint. Examples include a live event stream that requires multicasting, copy protection, and preventing downloads via digital rights, as well as scenarios where rich media files are larger than 2 GB. In these scenarios, the recommended approach would be to use SharePoint 2010 as the presentation layer to a dedicated or specialist back-end rich media product.

As with all libraries in SharePoint, the Asset Library is still a document library, and, therefore, supports all of the library features (such as content types, workflows, and information policies).

COLLABORATION SERVICES

Business and team collaboration features form the foundation of all sites in SharePoint 2010. SharePoint supports a wide range of collaboration scenarios, from highly formal, planned, and structured collaboration sites, to very informal, ad-hoc, and unstructured collaboration sites. The scope of collaboration and interaction ranges from an individual or small number of users, to an extremely large number of users working together.

Collaboration scenarios can be categorized into general, ad-hoc, and random scenarios, as well as specific core business scenarios that occur all the time. Although you should cater for both scenarios, providing preconfigured collaboration site templates for your core business scenarios is really important. The key collaboration services features of SharePoint 2010 include the following:

➤ *Collaborative sites and workspace* — SharePoint provides many useful collaboration site collections and subsite templates. Examples include Blank, Team, Document and Meeting Workspace, Blog, Enterprise Wiki, Group Work, Project, Issue, Contacts, Visio Repository, Assets Web Database, and Charitable Contributions Web site templates.

➤ *Lists and libraries* — SharePoint provides a number of lists and libraries to meet your collaboration requirements. Chapter 6 provides more information on the types of lists and libraries available in SharePoint.

➤ *Web parts* — Web parts are units or pieces of functionality that can be used to present information on one or more pages in SharePoint. These include web parts that provide a specific Feature, web parts that are directly related to individual lists and libraries that have been created in your site, web parts that require SharePoint Designer to configure (custom XSLT List View and Data View web parts), web parts with the capability to host Silverlight and, finally, custom-developed web parts.

➤ *Pages and personalization* — SharePoint provides different types of web parts for you to add and configure on your site.

➤ *Integrated communication tools* — SharePoint makes it possible to view the availability ("presence") of people on your site. This feature enables you to communicate via instant messaging (IM), along with audio, visual, and web conferencing communication tools (such Office Communicator or Microsoft Lync).

➤ *Seamless Office 2010 working experience* — SharePoint sites and the Office 2010 suite of applications have been designed to provide a seamless working experience between Office and SharePoint, and vice versa.

➤ *Search and "findability"* — SharePoint enables users to search for people and information within a list, a site, and across all sites in your farm, and search external content sources (for example, network shares) in your organization's intranet.

➤ *Capability to respond* — Notifications and e-mail alerts enable users to respond to events occurring within sites.

➤ *Workflows and business process support* — SharePoint provides flexible out-of-the-box workflows, as well as the capability for power users to design and create custom workflows using Microsoft Visio and SharePoint Designer. Advanced workflows can be developed, packaged, and deployed to SharePoint using the Visual Studio toolset.

➤ *Information Rights Management (IRM)* — Using IRM, SharePoint makes it possible to secure the use of files that users already have access to. IRM embeds a persistent set of access controls with the content.

➤ *Site Extensibility* — SharePoint Designer can be used by power users to extend your SharePoint site in a variety of ways. If the user has the required site permissions, SharePoint Designer can be launched directly from the browser.

➤ *Permissions, permission levels, and security* — SharePoint 2010 includes 33 permissions that allow users to perform various tasks. These 33 permissions are grouped into permissions sets (called *permission levels*) and applied to SharePoint users and groups. Chapter 6 and Chapter 19 provide more information.

SharePoint supports different site-provisioning methods within your environment. Depending on your configuration, users are able to provision site collections or sites within a single site collection.

 It is common practice in large collaboration deployments to create a custom site collection provisioning wizard. This empowers users to create and start using sites immediately. This process takes seconds to minutes to complete, rather than the hours-to-days manual request-and-approval process to a central service and support team takes.

Collaboration services can be enhanced by researching, learning about, and understanding your user base's collaboration requirements. Custom, specific business collaboration site templates can be developed to meet your users' requirements, saving them time, and helping them be more efficient and productive. Targeted collaboration site templates drastically improve the consistency and user contribution to knowledge management, adoption and adherence to business processes, knowledge sharing, and access to information.

One other (often forgotten) benefit is that SharePoint enables your organization to collaborate and pivot on key business entities. For example, a financial services business may engage regularly with clients on projects, (such as audits) or bespoke projects (such as developing financial models and forecasts). SharePoint can model these entities as site collections, and subsites in many different ways, with each way influencing your ability to govern, grow, and scale the performance, extensibility, and overall longevity of your solution.

 For more information on designing collaboration services for your organization, see Chapter 26.

SEARCH SERVICES

SharePoint 2010 Search and FAST Search provide the best enterprise search solution on the market today, enabling users to search structured and unstructured content and people information in SharePoint, file shares, websites, Exchange public folders, databases, external line of business (LOB) systems, and other sources of information.

SharePoint 2010 Search scale and performance has dramatically improved, with support of up to 100 million and more items, while FAST Search for SharePoint 2010 can support billions of documents and thousands of queries per second.

Although this chapter mentions FAST Search features, its focus and priority is on SharePoint Search features. Unless specified, the search feature pertains to SharePoint 2010 Search.

Figure 8-8 provides an overview of the search user experience, the content gathering and processing pipeline, and the query processing pipeline of SharePoint 2010.

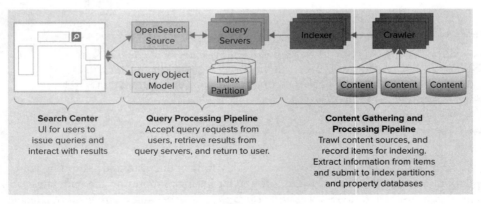

FIGURE 8-8: SharePoint 2010 Search pipelines

User Experience

Following is a high-level summary of the Search and FAST Search user experience features in SharePoint 2010:

- *Search Center site templates* — SharePoint provides a basic, enterprise and FAST Search Center site template to enable you to provision the search user experience in your SharePoint environment.

- *Search pages* — Search pages and tabs can be added and configured in the Search Center. Corresponding search result pages can be configured to display results.

- *Search web parts* — The Search Center encapsulates search features in web parts that you can add to the Search Center. Examples include the search box, results, and related searches web parts.

- *Search results* — The search results web part makes it easy to customize the way search results are presented to the user. All results are security-trimmed, which means that users are not shown results for content they have no access to.

- *Search result item preview* — Using Office Web Applications (OWA), it is possible to preview supported files directly in the browser without having to download them. FAST Search enables users to quickly recognize content by previewing search results using thumbnails and additional preview options.

- *Metadata-based refiners* — Refiners enable users to narrow their search results. The Search Center does this by displaying mini lists, based on key metadata properties, alongside search results. Users select items from the "mini lists" to further refine their results.

- *Best Bets and Visual Best Bets* — Administrators can display Best Bets and Visual Best Bets (FAST) based on specific search keywords.

- *Scopes and scoped queries* — Administrators can group content sources into scopes (logical content groupings) that users select to limit the scope of their searches. For example, users may only be interested in results from the engagement portal sites, or only from the corporate intranet. In these examples, users would not expect to see results from a user's My Sites or network file shares.

- *Social and people search queries* — SharePoint mines people and people-related information from a number of locations to build up a rich index. New SharePoint 2010 features make it possible to incorporate phonetic spelling and nicknames, social tags, and expertise and interests in your search queries.

- *Search result federation* — SharePoint can display search results from external sources of content not indexed by your search environment. The query can be submitted to the external repositories search engine, and returned (using the OpenSearch standard) to be displayed to users.

- *Advanced search queries* — The Search Center provides two mechanisms for performing advanced search queries. The first is the advanced search page that simplifies the creation of an advanced search query. The second is support for new query syntax directly in the search box. Users can use Boolean operators to enter freetext and property-based queries. For example, (`"Alsatian" OR "German Shepherd"`) `AND "animal:dog"` will return results for Alsatian dogs found in the search index. (German Shepherd is another name for an Alsatian.)

➤ *Search analytics* — SharePoint improves on the reporting experience provided in SharePoint 2007. Visual/graphical reports display the number of queries, top queries, failed queries, and no search result queries. Other reports include Best Bet suggestions, Best Bet usage, and action history.

➤ *Other* — Other features include search suggestions as you type, query suggestions, "did you mean?", and the capability to show related searches based on user click-through on existing search results.

FAST Search for SharePoint 2010 provides additional user experience features. These include more search result item preview options, Visual Best Bets, the capability to show deep refiners with precise counts, the capability to take advantage of User Profile information to calculate better user context to better rank and return results, the capability to sort on any property, much broader and better language support, and a richer query language.

Content Gathering and Processing Pipeline

SharePoint supports various content sources including SharePoint, file shares, websites, Exchange Public folders, LOB data, and custom repositories (for example, Lotus Notes or Documentum) using protocol handers and indexing connectors that understand how to extract or pull content from each source.

SharePoint 2010 provides a much improved and enhanced content gathering and processing pipeline. Using either Windows PowerShell or search administration in Central Administration, IT administrators configure a search topology consisting of the following:

➤ *Crawl database* — The crawl database provides a place to manage crawl operations and crawl history. One or more crawl components can use one crawl database, and one or more crawl databases can be created to increase performance and to scale out load.

➤ *Crawl component* — Crawl components are used by SharePoint search to crawl content. One or more crawl components can be configured and deployed. Multiple crawl components will partition crawl activities and speed up crawling activities. Each crawl component can only be associated with one crawl database.

➤ *Crawl or index server* — Crawl components can be scaled out over one or more application servers. These are typically known as *indexing* or *crawl servers*.

➤ *Index propagation* — Crawl components produce portions of the index and propagate them to servers running the query component associated with that crawl components index.

➤ *Index and index partitions* — Crawl components produce portions of the index and propagate them to the servers that are running the query components associated with the index or index partition.

➤ *Property database* — The property database provides a place to store metadata and security descriptors for items in the index. Crawl components store information in the property database.

➤ *Administration component* — The search administration component runs on the configured server. Only one administration component exists per Search service instance.

This component or process listens for incoming user actions, such as a changing crawl rule, pausing a crawl, and, based on the action updates, the administration database so that the changes are processed by the crawler components.

➤ *Administration database* — The administration database hosts the search application configuration and the access control list (ACL) for content crawls.

The gatherer pipeline (inside mssearch.exe) invokes a search component (called a *filter daemon*) to load up the protocol handler (or *indexing connector*) and in a separate process (mssdmn.exe) to connect, fetch, parse, and enumerate content. Unique items are placed in the MSSCrawlQueue table in the crawl database. These items then get picked up in batches by crawl components for fetching and content processing.

The returned items go through a process of extraction and refinement. IFilters open items in their native formats, and filter these into chunks of text and properties. This information is further refined through a set of stages, such as mapping crawled properties to managed properties, file format disambiguation, linguistic processing (using word breakers and stemming), and property extraction. Once items have been "refined," they are handed to the indexing engine for indexing, and submission to the query servers and property databases.

One final important point to make about crawlers in SharePoint 2010 is that they are stateless. This means that they do not store a physical complete copy of the index (or index partition) they are responsible for. Although they do use a temporary location in building up batches to submit, if the server fails, this crawl job is assigned to another crawl server to complete by the Central Search Administration component.

Query Processing Pipeline

The query processing pipeline's purpose and goal is to return the most precise and relevant results based on the user's intent, in the shortest possible time, for small to extremely large concurrent query processing scenarios.

At a high level, the query processing pipeline consists of the following components:

➤ *Query servers* — These serve query results to web servers. The query processor forwards requests to index partitions, and then merges results to display to users.

➤ *Index partitions* — Index partitions are a portion of the entire index. These are typically spread across multiple query servers to create a faster query architecture, allowing the processing power of multiple query servers to respond to queries. Index partitions can be mirrored across query servers to achieve greater redundancy.

Various factors determine which search results the user will see first. These include inferred information about the end user making the search query (for example, a user's search language detection), out of browser (OOB) or custom ranking models, and individual item rankings in the index. Following are some of the key factors that determine an item's ranking:

➤ *Inferred metadata* — SharePoint 2010 uses more than just the Office file properties to ascertain various pieces of information. A common example is the calculation of a real author of a document based on text within the document, rather than solely on the Office author property. This is especially useful when a document has been repeatedly copied and used as a template.

➤ *Social tags* — Social tags for documents and items boost the item's relevancy and ranking.

➤ *Results click-through* — SharePoint 2010 tracks user click-through on search results. This has the effect of boosting an item's relevancy and ranking.

➤ *Term proximity* — Users prefer search results in which most or all of the query terms appear close to each other, because this is evidence that the search result has text focused on their query intent. SharePoint 2010 provides the capability to rank these results higher, thus ensuring users view these results before results with query terms spaced farther out.

➤ *Implicit phrase matching* — Implicit phrase matching ranks search results keywords higher where the user keywords have a good proximity score.

➤ *Search configuration settings* — Search administration pages enable you to configure authoritative pages at different levels of authority. These instruct SharePoint to boost the ranking of items in these locations.

➤ *Automatic document language detection* — Search automatically detects the language of many document types and "parts of documents." This information helps to select the appropriate language-specific dictionaries and algorithms during item processing.

➤ *Improved ranking of documents in multi-lingual site collections* — SharePoint 2010 provides improved support for site collections to index content in multiple languages.

➤ *Compound word handling* — SharePoint 2010 provides improved support to break up compound words into separate terms in the search index. For example, "flowerpetal" provides the terms "flower" and "petal."

➤ *Other* — Other features that influence the item's rank include contextual relevance, metadata extraction, file-type biasing, click distance, anchor text, URL depth, and URL matching.

 For more information on designing and implementing Search services for your business, see Chapter 27.

INDIVIDUAL AND SOCIAL NETWORKING SERVICES

SharePoint 2010 empowers individuals with the best tools to be their most productive and effective. SharePoint provides each user with a personal site to manage their User Profile, store private and public information, and connect to other users through formal and informal social networks and communities. Figure 8-9 shows an example of a My Site home page.

FIGURE 8-9: My Site home page

At the heart and soul of SharePoint is the User Profile. The User Profile contains detailed information about each individual, such as User Profile properties (including properties based on managed metadata terms), social tags, files, and items related to the user. Supporting the User Profile, the User Profile service application provides a central location to store, manage, and consume User Profiles, and User Profile related services.

Following are some key individual and social networking features:

➤ *My Site Hosts* — My Site Hosts is a special site template that enables users to browse User Profile and social networking–related information in the User Profile service application.

➤ *Organization profiles* — Organization profiles is a new concept in SharePoint 2010. It enables you to link user profiles to hierarchical organizational structure defined (or imported) into SharePoint 2010. Organization profiles include the capability to associate leaders and members to an organization profile.

➤ *Profile synchronization* — Profile synchronization enables your organization to synchronize User Profile and group profile information between the User Profile service application store and information stored in directory services (for example, Active Directory) and other external systems.

➤ *Audiences* — Dynamic collections of users can be compiled to target content. The specific membership of the audience can be restricted using existing information in SharePoint, such as information in User Profile properties.

➤ *Content ratings* — Users can rate content, making it easier for others to see what the average "opinion" of a content item is. Ratings are first stored in the social database before they are moved and synchronized into the content database housing the content.

➤ *Social tagging* — Words or phrases can be used to "tag" items in SharePoint 2010. Social tags are surfaced in each user's activity feed, in Tag Cloud web parts (which display an aggregate view of the tags), and via the Search service.

➤ *Social bookmarking* — External and internal sites can be bookmarked and tagged. If the bookmark is public, users will benefit from each other's bookmark.

➤ *Organization chart* — SharePoint provides a great Silverlight organization browser that enables users to navigate colleagues, managers, and direct reports in the organization.

➤ *Colleagues* — SharePoint enables users to maintain a list of colleagues. Users benefit from being able to view colleagues' activities in their activity feed, similar to a Facebook-style activity feed.

➤ *Memberships* — Memberships display lists and sites that you belong to.

➤ *Activity feeds* — The activity aggregates content you track (your own content and your colleagues' content) and activities you publish into a dynamic listing of activities. It is possible to extend activity feeds to support custom activity feeds.

Other trending and behavioral web parts are available to help users find common information. Tag Cloud and Web Analytics web parts enable you to display most-searched (or popular) content, or most frequently used terms to search for in the site collection or in the entire farm.

One of the more subtle and often underused features in SharePoint 2010 is the advanced page personalization features available on every site. For sites and pages that have personalization enabled, users can personalize the page within parameters defined by the shared view page owner. This may include moving web parts, or configuring specific web part settings. Page designers can target content and web parts to specific audiences.

 For more information on incorporating individual and social networking services, see Chapter 28.

BUSINESS CONNECTIVITY SERVICES

SharePoint 2007 introduced a feature called the Business Data Catalog (BDC) to integrate data from external systems and use the "business data" to produce meaningful user experiences in SharePoint sites. The BDC also made it possible to index and search on business data.

In SharePoint 2010, the BDC is now called Business Data *Connectivity* (BDC) Service, and belongs to group of services called Business Connectivity Services (BCS). Figure 8-10 provides a high-level overview of the BCS architecture.

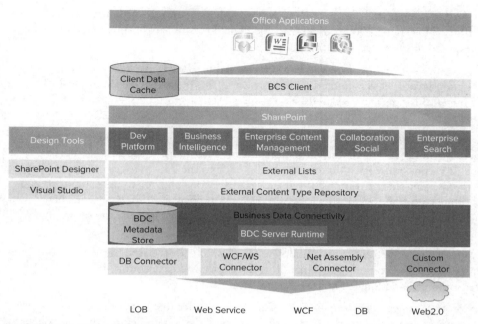

FIGURE 8-10: BCS architecture

BCS provides the following key features:

➤ *Business Data Column* — Business Data Columns enable you to incorporate and use external data in SharePoint lists.

➤ *External lists/External Content Types (ECTs)* — External lists support the presentation of external data as a SharePoint list. These lists provide full CRUD (create, read, update, and delete) support, a familiar UI and navigation, sorting, filtering and grouping, and programmatic access via the standard list object model.

➤ *Office client integration* — Users can view and interact with external lists and business data in Office applications, such as Microsoft Outlook, Microsoft Word, and SharePoint Workspace. External lists can be taken offline in SharePoint Workspace.

➤ *Search integration* — External data can be crawled and surfaced as search results in SharePoint Search. Business data refiners can be configured to further refine searches.

➤ *Search indexing connectors* — Protocol handlers are difficult to write. Indexing connectors provide a method for C# developers to develop custom indexing connectors to enable the crawling and indexing of custom repositories and external systems. Additionally, indexing connectors support reading blogs, incremental crawl, and item-level security.

➤ *Multiple target connection types* — BCS supports connecting to relational databases, web services, Windows communication services, .NET connectivity assemblies, and custom data connectors to connect to external systems.

➤ *Batch and bulk operation support* — BCS now provides support for batch and bulk operations. This enables you to read multiple items in a single call, thus reducing round trips required to the external data source.

➤ *BCS web parts* — A number of web parts are available to surface external data in your presentation layer. These include the Business Data List, Business Data Item, Business Data Item Builder, Business Data Related List, Business Data Connectivity Filter, and Chart web parts.

➤ *Symmetrical client and server run time* — BCS provides a similar/symmetrical client and server run time. In layman's terms, this means that many of the actions on the client side can be run with a direct connection back to the data source, rather than via the server. Client-side operations provide a cached mode behavior to take solutions and lists offline. Under the hood, this uses SQL Server Compact Edition (CE) as a client-side external data cache. Changes made offline can be pushed back to the server in a consistent manner.

➤ *Authentication* — BCS supports Windows, forms, and claims-based authentication. The available authentication modes include RevertToSelf (process account), Pass-Through (logged-on user), and Single Sign-On (secure store).

➤ *Secure Store Service integration* — The Secure Store Service (SSS) provides a way for users to authenticate users and groups on external systems. It stores credential sets for external systems, and associates those credential sets with identities of individuals or with group identities.

➤ *Design and development tools* — The Microsoft Office and SharePoint product groups have produced great a toolset for both power users (no-code solutions) and developers (code solutions) who want to leverage BCS. SharePoint Designer makes it easy to define ECTs and external lists, and to define InfoPath forms to surface data. Visual Studio 2010 provides developers with features to extend those capabilities to create advanced solutions.

 For more information on incorporating BCS, see Chapter 29.

BUSINESS INTELLIGENCE SERVICES

SharePoint 2010 business intelligence (BI) services help users and managers make better, more informed decisions. BI features enable businesses to understand what has happened in the past (and why it happened), what is happening now, and predict what will happen in the future.

SharePoint 2010 provides BI features both out-of-the-box, and as add-ons to your SharePoint 2010 environment. These range from simple scenarios that can be implemented in no time, to really advanced scenarios that may require time (along with specialist development and data warehousing skills).

This section provides a high-level summary of the BI services provided in SharePoint 2010.

Business Intelligence Center Site Template

As shown in Figure 8-11, SharePoint 2010 provides an updated Business Intelligence Center (site template) to help businesses get started with the BI features of SharePoint 2010.

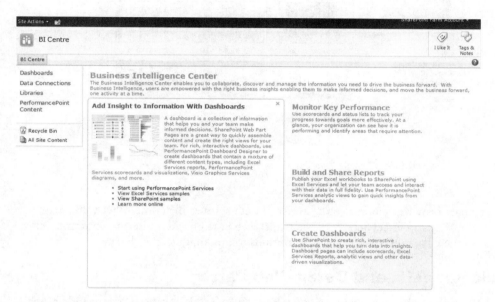

FIGURE 8-11: Business Intelligence Center

The Business Intelligence Center supports and hosts scorecards, dashboards, data connections, status indicator lists, Excel Services–based solutions (such as PivotTables and charts), and PerformancePoint Services features.

Charting Web Part

SharePoint 2010 provides a new charting web part. As shown in Figure 8-12, the Chart Customization Wizard provides a number of different chart types to present content. These include bar, area, line, bubble, pie, radar, polar, Gantt, range, error bar, box plot, funnel, and pyramid.

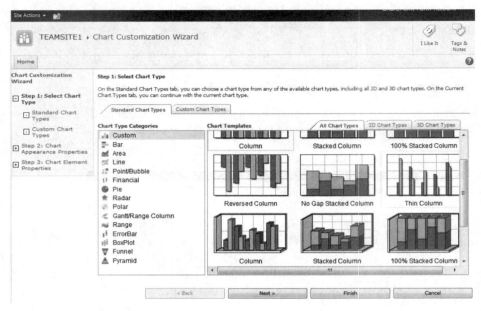

FIGURE 8-12: Chart Customization Wizard

The Chart web part provides support for a variety of data sources including other web parts, SharePoint lists, BDC, and Excel Services. The Chart web part provides filtering options to filter data returned to the Chart web part, as well as options to bind data to the chart.

Status Indicators/List and Detail Web Part

SharePoint 2010 renames key performance indicators (KPIs) and KPI lists to "status indicators" and "status lists," respectively. This is most likely because of a name conflict with KPIs in PerformancePoint. As in SharePoint 2007, status indicators are stored in status lists, and individual status indicators can be displayed separately using the Status Indicator Details web part.

Excel Services

As shown in Figure 8-13, Excel Services enables businesses to load, calculate, and display Microsoft Excel workbooks in SharePoint sites and dashboards. Users who only require the capability to view Excel data can view Excel workbooks on the server.

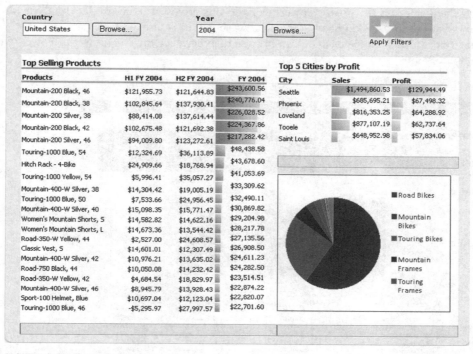

FIGURE 8-13: Excel Services

Excel Services provides an Excel Web Access web part to view and interact with workbooks in the browser. Workbook data can be sorted, filtered, and expanded or collapsed in PivotTables.

Under the hood, Excel provides the Excel Calculation Services (ECS) engine that calculates in full fidelity with Microsoft Office Excel 2007.

PowerPivot for Excel and SharePoint

PowerPivot for Excel is a client-side add-on to Excel 2010 that provides tools for adding and integrating large amounts of data in Excel workbooks.

Data can be consumed from a variety of sources. These include SQL Server, SQL Server Analysis Services Cubes, SQL Server Reporting Services, web data feeds (XML, Atom, WCF, Azure), and other databases and warehouses such as Oracle, DB2, Sybase, and Teradata. Data can also be sourced via Open Database Connectivity (ODBC) and text files.

In order to support Excel workbooks and use the PowerPivot client-side add-on, PowerPivot for SharePoint must be deployed to your topology. Once deployed, PowerPivot for SharePoint extends Excel Services to add server-side processing, collaboration, and document management support for PowerPivot workbooks.

Together, both client-side and server-side PowerPivot add-ons provide further BI data analysis for Excel users on their desktops and on SharePoint sites. As shown in Figure 8-14, www.PowerPivot.com provides great live examples and demos you can browse to experience the true power of PowerPivot for Excel and SharePoint.

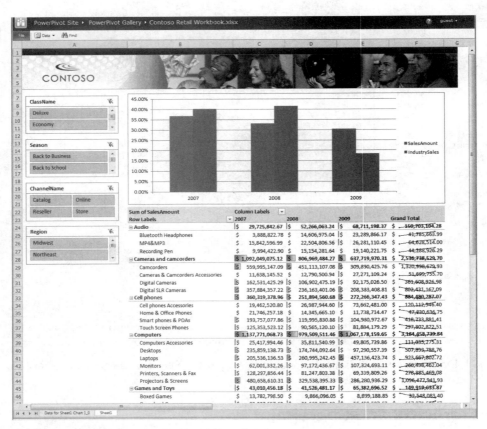

FIGURE 8-14: PowerPivot for Excel and SharePoint

Visio Services

As shown in Figure 8-15, Visio Services enables users to share and view Microsoft Visio web drawings, either in the browser using the Visio Web Access web part, or by downloading the full drawing and viewing it in Microsoft Visio. If items are published using Visio Professional or Premium edition, users will be able to render the .vdw format file natively in their web browsers.

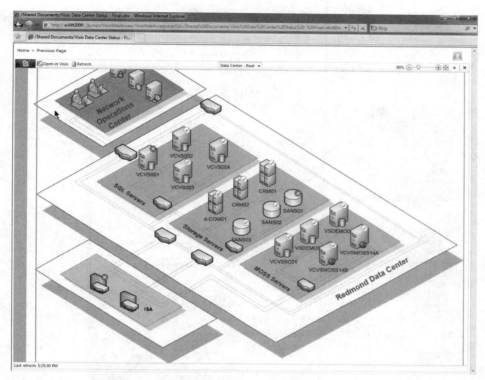

FIGURE 8-15: Visio Services

Visio Services supports data-connected drawings to be refreshed and updated from various data sources (such as SQL Server, Excel workbooks, SharePoint lists, OLE DB, or a custom data provider implemented using a custom .NET assembly).

Access Services

As shown in Figure 8-16, Access 2010 supports integration with SharePoint 2010 via Access Services. It is now possible to publish Access 2010 databases to SharePoint to enable multiple users to interact with the database application from any standards-compliant web browser.

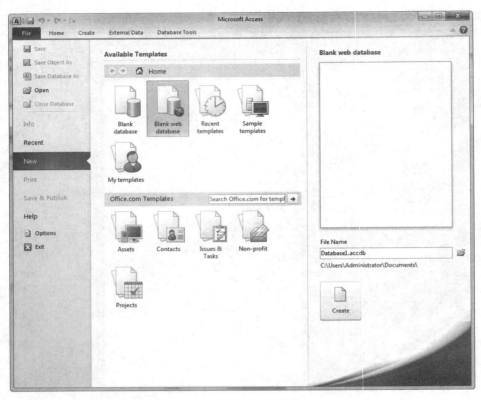

FIGURE 8-16: Access Services

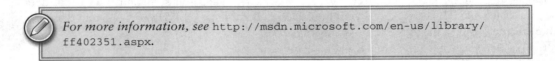

For more information, see `http://msdn.microsoft.com/en-us/library/ff402351.aspx`.

Business Connectivity Services

As discussed previously, BCS supports the capability to read from and write to external data sources. This information can be displayed and integrated into the SharePoint presentation layer and as external lists.

PerformancePoint Service Application

The PerformancePoint Service Application provides the capability to design and publish dashboards to PerformancePoint-enabled sites in SharePoint using a custom dashboard designer launched from a BI site.

A PerformancePoint dashboard supports many types of "reports." These include analytic charts, grids, Excel Services, SQL Services Reporting Service reports, ProClarity Server reports, web page reports, scorecards, strategy maps, and KPI details reports.

PerformancePoint Service Application provides the capability to implement the Kaplan and Norton balanced scorecard framework for measuring corporate enterprise performance. At the core of the balanced scorecard approach are strategy maps and scorecards.

Strategy maps enable senior stakeholders to monitor the performance metrics of the key areas of the organization. Strategy maps can be created using Microsoft Visio, and linked to display underlying performance measures (KPIs) for each strategy area. Current performance can be visualized using color.

Scorecards are a great visual medium to convey current versus target performance metrics. Figure 8-17 shows how scorecards are represented as a table using graphical indicators to reflect current performance against target performance.

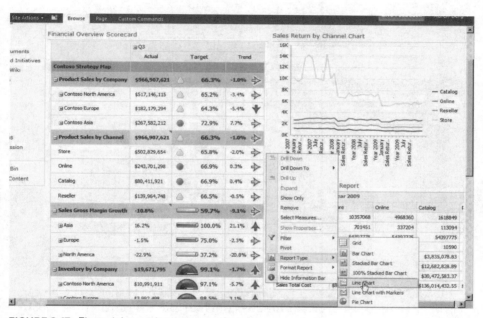

FIGURE 8-17: Financial overview scorecard

Scorecards combine the use of a number of features, including trend indicators, complex KPIs, time intelligence, expandable or collapsible rows or columns, KPI selection filters on other reports, and decomposition trees describing how individual members contribute to the currently displayed value.

Scorecards can consume data from SQL Server Analysis Services (cubes and MDX query supported), SharePoint lists, Excel Services files, tables in SQL Server, and manual information created by the scorecard author.

For more information, see: http://office.microsoft.com/en-us/ sharepoint-server-help/getting-acquainted-with-performancepoint- dashboards-and-web-parts-HA010370245.aspx.

Reporting Services

As shown in Figure 8-18, SQL Server Reporting Services (as provided by SQL Server 2008 R2) provides a robust, complete server-based platform to support a wide variety of reports independent of SharePoint via a Reporting Services website.

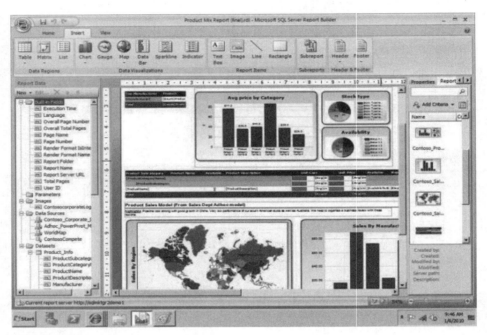

FIGURE 8-18: Reporting Services website

The SQL Server 2008 R2 Reporting Services for SharePoint 2010 add-on enables you to integrate your reporting environment into SharePoint 2010. Users can integrate and surface these reports using the Report View web part (web application pages).

The SQL Server Report Builder enables you to design and format reports, providing an intuitive design interface and wizards to help you build reporting solutions. Various reporting formats are supported, as well as a rich set of data visualizations.

Data sources can be from SQL Server, Oracle, DB2, SQL Azure, PowerPoint Workbooks, SAP NetWeaver BI, Hyperion Essbase, and others.

 For more information on incorporating BI services, see Chapter 30.

WORKFLOW AND FORMS SERVICES

SharePoint 2010 provides deep collaboration and enterprise content-management capabilities that enable end users to be more productive and work better together. Workflow and business forms service capabilities play a vital part in supporting the office and team productivity ecosystem. They entrench structure and precision in the manner people and teams collaborate, in a way that can be tracked, analyzed, and optimized, resulting in greater team efficiency.

Workflow

SharePoint 2010 workflow features enable your organization to host business logic and Office processes in SharePoint sites. SharePoint 2010 supports for the full spectrum of workflows, from simple out-of-the-box workflows, to customization of new or out-of-the-box workflows in SharePoint Designer, to advanced custom developed workflows in Visual Studio. Figure 8-19 shows how it is possible to configure a workflow in SharePoint Designer.

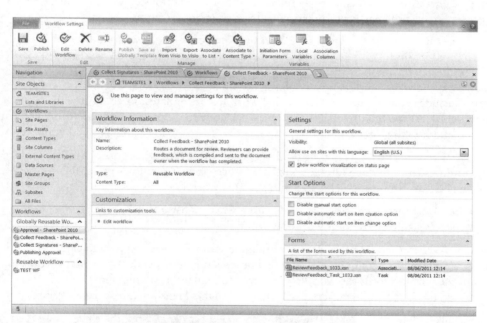

FIGURE 8-19: SharePoint 2010 Designer – Workflow Designer

The full spectrum includes the following:

➤ *Out-of-the-box workflows* — A number of ready-to-use workflows are provided in SharePoint 2010. These include document approval and feedback, collection of signatures, three-state, disposition approval, and translation management workflows.

➤ *Customized out-of-the-box workflows* — Out-of-the-box workflows can be customized. Workflows can be associated with lists, libraries, or content types, and initiation (starting point) settings can be customized based on your specific requirements. Additionally, the logic of these workflows can be enhanced or changed by opening the workflow in the workflow designer in SharePoint Designer. The forms associated with the workflow can be improved and changed using InfoPath Forms.

➤ *Custom declarative workflows* — SharePoint Designer enables you to configure workflows from scratch using the workflow designer in SharePoint Designer. Steps of the workflow can be added, and workflow logic, such as *conditions* (if value equals value) and *actions* (for example, send an e-mail), can be added. Tasks can be raised and assigned to users to complete steps of the workflow. As with out-of-the-box workflows, custom declarative workflows created in SharePoint Designer can be attached to lists, libraries, and content types in your SharePoint site collection. Other key features include the capability to support nested logic, impersonation, enhanced data binding, many conditions and actions to choose from, User Profile lookups, read and write to external lists, export to Visio, and packaging into a solution for portability.

➤ *Custom activities* — Custom or new actions can be developed and deployed either as a fully trusted or partially trusted (sandboxed) solution. Existing actions can be extended and customized to suit the needs and requirements of your organization.

➤ *Custom non-declarative workflows* — Workflows conceptualized and modeled in Visio, or configured in SharePoint Designer, can be imported into Microsoft Visual Studio 2010. Visual Studio 2010 supports the creation of new workflows from scratch. Features (not available via the visual designers) can be used to implement bespoke workflows. These features include sequence and state machine workflows templates, interaction with the rich SharePoint object model, use of .NET Framework code to do pretty much anything you can envision, and hooking up to, handling, and responding to various site, list, and item events.

➤ *Third-party workflows* — Many third-party workflow products support SharePoint. Third-party products can interface into and kick off Office-based workflows in SharePoint, as well as host workflows in dedicated and scalable workflow engines.

You have a number of factors to consider when deciding when to use a third-party product versus a workflow hosted solely using SharePoint workflow technologies.

An important consideration should be made concerning the scenarios that you plan to cater for in your organization. Is the workflow a common Office-based process used independently by many teams in different parts of the business, or is the workflow required to manage a specific important process in your organization (such as handling every call center call that is logged in a bespoke system)?

Other considerations include the volume of workflows you expect per second, the capability to understand and calculate the performance of hundreds to thousands of users to determine their efficiency and productivity levels, monitoring tools to calculate weak points and determine bottlenecks in your business processes, making quick changes to "in-situ" workflows, what system you want to host and store your workflow, and the tools, systems, and licensing costs of third-party products.

Business Forms

Business forms help users to standardize, customize, and validate data collection through a combination of the InfoPath 2010 Office clients (InfoPath Designer and InfoPath Filler) and SharePoint 2010 InfoPath Form Service technologies to render forms either in a rich client or directly in the browser. Figure 8-20 shows an example of an out-of-the-box business form used to collect signatures as part of the collect signatures workflow.

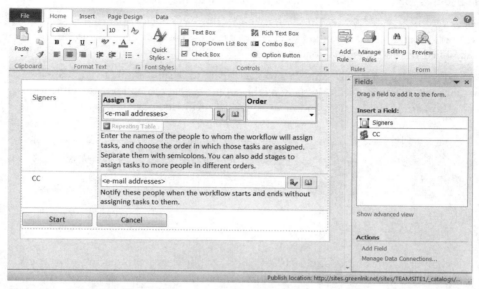

FIGURE 8-20: Signature collection business form

Many people think of forms as a physical or electronic form that can be filled out and saved to a forms library in SharePoint 2010. Though this is a valid (and important) scenario, forms technology has a much greater scope and purpose. A common metaphor used to understand the role of forms technology in SharePoint 2010 is to think of business forms as either the supporting cast of the main act, or the main act supported by a great cast.

Available SharePoint forms include the following:

➤ *SharePoint list forms* — List entry and editing can be replaced with custom "New" and "Edit" forms. Customizations include modification of the form layout, adding pictures, updating formatting, custom data validation, additional views, and rules. For example, a "Contact Us" or "Provide Feedback" list with a rich data entry form can easily be created and deployed using InfoPath forms.

➤ *Offline list forms* — The Microsoft SharePoint Workspace client supports the capability to store lists and libraries offline in a client-based workspace. Offline lists and libraries support the capability to view and edit data offline. This uses forms technology to display content to the user.

➤ *SharePoint workflow forms* — As described earlier, InfoPath forms are commonly used to manage different stages of the life cycle of a workflow, including associating the workflow with list, library, or content type; initiating a workflow against an item that requires initiation data; presenting task forms or user action forms to drive stages of the workflow; and, lastly, modification, to change settings of a running workflow. For example, a holiday request booking workflow could use InfoPath forms to enter and submit the holiday booking, as well as the capability for the manager to approve or reject the booking.

➤ *Browser-based forms web part* — Forms can now be displayed on pages in SharePoint.

➤ *External list forms* — BCS uses InfoPath forms to support CRUD operations, such as to create, read, update, and delete data in external systems. Custom display and business logic can be applied to these business forms.

InfoPath 2010 makes it easy for business users and developers to design simple to sophisticated forms, deploy them to SharePoint, and use them as the supporting act in composite applications, or as the star of the show in forms libraries and browser-based form web parts.

 For more information on incorporating workflow and forms in your solutions, see Chapter 31.

SUMMARY

As shown in this chapter, while SharePoint 2010 provides seriously in-depth feature sets for each core workload or service category, it is both the depth *and* breadth of SharePoint 2010 and Office 2010 (and related products) that make it the best solution and choice for your organization.

No other solution can match the vision, reach, and seamless integration of the SharePoint 2010 and Office 2010 products. No other solution can match the quality of choice provided to businesses, no matter the business size, business sector, or business formation. No other solution can offer you the bewildering amount of control in how you deploy, implement, manage, and govern these technologies and Office systems. Whether you deploy on-premise or to the cloud, SharePoint 2010 and Office 2010 cater to and support your organization, both through browser-based experiences and rich client experiences and Internet applications.

The Office and SharePoint Product Groups *within* Microsoft have done a fantastic job over the past ten years, and rightfully own this space. They have out-innovated their competitors, made sound technology bets along the way, introduced new technologies in a non-disruptive way (for example, the Ribbon over two releases), and executed well to deliver the most complete office productivity and business collaboration platform in the market today.

Chapter 9 discusses how these features are delivered via a service applications framework.

Understanding SharePoint 2010 Service Applications

By Reza Alirezaei

This chapter is focused on helping you understand services in SharePoint 2010. The objective is to make you familiar with the new services architecture in SharePoint 2010, and how this architecture is used in the platform to offer new or improved functionality. The chapter then covers some of the architectural principals and guidelines that help you understand the topics discussed in the other chapters of this book.

The content presented in this chapter targets architects and administrators planning their SharePoint 2010 farm topologies, but the chapter will also be useful for anyone working with the product.

SERVICE APPLICATION MODEL

SharePoint 2010 presents a significant improvement over previous versions in the manner that its services are deployed and consumed. Simply put, a new model has been designed to improve the scalability of the platform, and to offer tremendously exciting opportunities for the customers and third-party companies to take the core capabilities of the platform to the next level.

Bye-Bye Shared Service Provider

In SharePoint 2010, services are no longer available via Shared Services Provider (SSP). Instead, the infrastructure of hosting services moves into SharePoint Foundation 2010, and all services follow a new model known as *service applications*.

By itself, the term "service application" has no special meaning, other than being a logical way of referring to a new deployment model for shared services in SharePoint 2010. The new model provides a framework for adding, administrating, and configuring various features in SharePoint 2010.

One caveat with SSP in Microsoft Office SharePoint Server (MOSS) 2007 was that it was an all-or-nothing proposition. You either consumed all of the services that it provided, or none. With SharePoint 2010, you can select the service applications that are needed.

Figure 9-1 shows the new service application model in SharePoint 2010, and compares it with the previous model (SSP) in MOSS 2007.

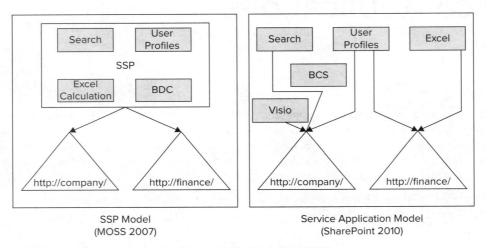

FIGURE 9-1: New service application model in SharePoint 2010

With that cleared up, let's now take a look at what this new model has to offer, and the rationale behind bringing about such a fundamental change in the platform.

Hello Service Applications

The idea with the new service model in SharePoint 2010 is simple. If you don't need a particular service application, you don't deploy it to your farm — period! Additionally, you can deploy multiple instances of the services. In fact, you can create as many instances of a given service application as you like.

The second layer of granular configuration with the new service model comes at the web application level. Unlike the lockdown model in SSP, in SharePoint 2010, web applications can pick and choose which service applications they want to consume, and in which combination.

Once you have an instance of a service application deployed to your farm, it can be shared across multiple web applications in the same farm, or even across different farms. Regardless of the sharing model, you can always modify the association between a web application and service applications at a later time.

Service applications can be deployed to different application pools to support process isolation. You can pick and choose which service applications should be within the same process, or within separate processes.

 One possible reason to think about process isolation from performance or security perspectives is when sharing service data across multiple applications.

Figure 9-2 shows how various services are distributed in two application pools.

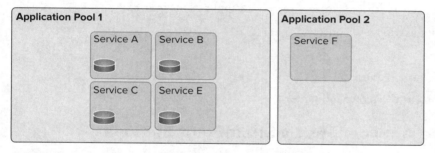

FIGURE 9-2: Distribution of services in two application pools

Although in most implementations, the performance of your farm is best optimized if services exist in one application pool, in some scenarios the highest physical isolation of services is required. Thankfully, the new service application model enables you to create separate instances of service applications, and place them in different application pools.

Another difference between SSP and service applications is a better scalability model. You can select on which servers in the farm a particular service application service will be running by using the "Services on Server" page in Central Administration.

It's worth mentioning that a Search service application is a bit different in terms of how its topology is defined. The Search service application has several underlying components that can run on different servers, which, in turn, offers an extra layer of scale. Figure 9-3 shows the topology page of the Search service application where you can manage its different components, and on which servers those components operate.

FIGURE 9-3: Topology page of Search service application

To wrap this up, following are the advantages of service applications over SSP:

➤ Granular configuration and control

➤ Scalable architecture

➤ Robust logical architecture

➤ Flexible sharing and deployment model

Available Service Applications by SharePoint Editions

As an architect, it's imperative to know the architectural trade-offs and the service applications each edition of SharePoint offers. Table 9-1 provides quick rundown of all the service applications that ship out-of-the-box with different editions of SharePoint 2010, excluding service applications provided by other Microsoft products such Project Server, PowerPivot service, and so on.

TABLE 9-1: Service Applications Available by SharePoint Editions

SERVICE APPLICATIONS	STORAGE TYPE	SHAREPOINT FOUNDATION	SHAREPOINT STANDARD	SHAREPOINT ENTERPRISE
Access Services	Cache	No	No	Yes
Business Data Connectivity Service	Database	Yes	Yes	Yes
Excel Services	Cache	No	Yes	Yes
Managed Metadata Service	Database	No	Yes	Yes
PerformancePoint	Cache	No	No	Yes

SERVICE APPLICATIONS	STORAGE TYPE	SHAREPOINT FOUNDATION	SHAREPOINT STANDARD	SHAREPOINT ENTERPRISE
Search	Database	No	Yes	Yes
Secure Store Service	Database	No	Yes	Yes
State Service	Database	No	Yes	Yes
Usage and Health Data Collection	Database	Yes	Yes	Yes
User Profile	Database	No	Yes	Yes
Visio Graphics Service	BLOB Cache	No	No	Yes
Web Analytics Service	Database	No	Yes	Yes
Word Automation Services	Database	No	Yes	Yes

Following are descriptions of each service application:

➤ *Access Services* — This service application allows for viewing, editing, and interacting with Access databases in a browser.

➤ *Business Data Connectivity Service* — The Business Data Connectivity Service (BCS) allows you to upload BDC models that define interfaces of other enterprise line-of-business (LOB) systems, and enables connectivity to those systems. The Application Registry service application is another service application that is a backward-compatible service to support the BDC API from SharePoint 2007.

➤ *Excel Services* — This service application allows viewing and interacting with Excel files from within the browser.

➤ *Managed Metadata Service* — This service application allows you to manage taxonomy hierarchies, keywords, and social tagging features of SharePoint 2010. This service application also handles content-type publishing across site collections.

➤ *PerformancePoint* — This service application supports configuration and monitoring of PerformancePoint as a business intelligence (BI) product integrated with the Enterprise edition of SharePoint 2010.

➤ *Search* — As its name implies, this service application (which comes with its own topology management configuration) is used to index content, and serves search queries performed by users or custom code.

➤ *Secure Store Service* — This is a credential mapping service to access other enterprise-level service applications or back-end enterprise systems.

➤ *State Service* — The State Service is a temporary storage of any data that deals with a user session.

➤ *Usage and Health Data Collection* — This service application provides storage usage and health information at the farm level, and provides various reporting functionalities on such data.

➤ *User Profile* — As yet another social feature in SharePoint 2010, this service application supports features such as My Sites, My Links, Colleague tracker, profile pages, personal tags and notes, and other social features.

➤ *Visio Graphics Service* — This service application enables viewing, interacting, and refreshing of Visio diagrams within a browser.

➤ *Web Analytics Service* — This service application provides an overarching solution to collecting and reporting on various analytical metrics at the farm, web application, site collection, and site levels.

➤ *Word Automation Services* — This service application allows you to view and edit Word documents in a web browser. It can also be used for document conversions.

Now that you are familiar with service applications in different editions of SharePoint, let's discuss the life cycle of a service application.

SERVICE APPLICATIONS LIFE CYCLE

A typical life cycle for a service application consists of several stages. When you plan your service application, consider each stage of this cycle. For example, you should understand when you must use the Configuration Wizard to provision your service applications or use Windows PowerShell, and when you must create a custom proxy group for your service applications.

Figure 9-4 shows the stages in a life cycle for a service application.

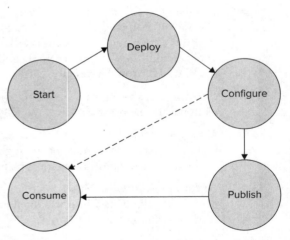

FIGURE 9-4: Life cycle for a service application

Starting Services

Although service applications are different from services, they still confuse many people working with SharePoint 2010.

If you browse to the "Services on Server" page in SharePoint Central Administration, that page lists all services that can be started and stopped on specific servers of the farm, as shown in Figure 9-5.

FIGURE 9-5: SharePoint "Services on Server" page in Central Administration

These services are mostly SharePoint wrappers around Windows services, and may or may not have an associated service application. For example, Central Administration is just a service that can be started on a server of the farm to turn it into a server that can host the Central Administration site — there is no service application associated with it.

As mentioned earlier in this chapter, a service application refers to a new deployment model for shared services. A service application represents a specific instance of a given service that can be configured and shared in a particular way. Service applications are comprised of Windows services, timer jobs, caching, SQL databases, and other stuff. They are just a broader concept than Windows services.

Deploying Service Applications

You can deploy service applications within a farm by using the following methods:

➤ Selecting the service applications in the Initial Configuration Wizard of your farm

➤ Adding new service applications or new instances of the existing service application in the Central Administration site

➤ Using Windows PowerShell

Table 9-2 describes the Windows PowerShell commands that you can use to manage service applications.

TABLE 9-2: Service Application Windows PowerShell Commands

COMMAND	DESCRIPTION
Install-SPService	Installs the services in the farm. It runs once per farm.
Get-SPServiceInstance Start-SPServiceInstance Stop-SPServiceInstance	Operations related to managing the services instance for a specific server or the entire farm.
Get-SPServiceApplication Publish-SPServiceApplication Remove-SPServiceApplication Set-SPServiceApplication Unpublish-SPServiceApplication	Operations related to managing service applications deployed to a farm (such as sharing the specified local service application outside the farm).
Get-SPServiceApplicationProxy Remove-SPServiceApplicationProxy Add-SPServiceApplicationProxyGroupMember	Operations related to managing service application proxies.
Get-SPServiceApplicationPool New-SPServiceApplicationPool Remove-SPServiceApplicationPool Set-SPServiceApplicationPool	Operations related to managing the logical architecture of service applications.

Regardless of your deployment approach, service applications can be isolated. To do so, during the provisioning process, you can either specify to use an existing application pool, or create a new application pool and have the service application run in its own worker process.

Configuring Service Applications

Once the service applications are configured at the farm level, they can all be managed in the Central Administration site. When you click "Manage service applications," you are taken to the "Manage service applications" page, as shown in Figure 9-6.

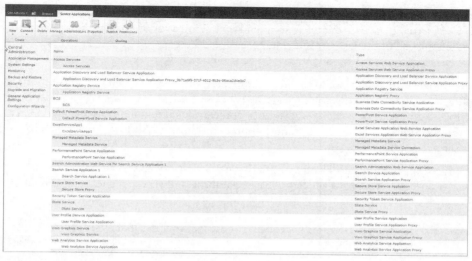

FIGURE 9-6: "Manage service applications" page

In the "Manage service applications" page, you should note three things:

➤ All deployed service applications are listed.

➤ All service application connections are listed. (Service application connections are discussed in more detail later in this chapter.)

➤ You can add new service applications by clicking the New button in the Ribbon.

Once service applications are provisioned, if you open up the Internet Information Services (IIS) manager, you'll see that there is a web application called SharePoint Web Services, and underneath that web application are a bunch of virtual directories. Each of those virtual directories is seen by a globally unique identifier (GUID), or its identifier for the service application, as shown in Figure 9-7.

At a service database level, most of the service applications use their own set of databases.

FIGURE 9-7: Identifier for service application

An important point to remember is that a service application may have one or more databases. For example, the User Profile service application has profile, synchronization, and social tagging databases. Another example is the Search service application with crawl, property, and administration databases. The number of databases can quickly add up, and be difficult to manage if you do not properly plan capacity.

One issue with configuring service applications using the Configuration Wizard is that the associated virtual directory databases will end up having a lot of GUIDs. For example, the name for one of the User Profile databases could be `User Profile Service Application_ProfileDB_899fd696a54a4cbe965dc8b30560dd07`.

Though this might be acceptable in some cases, generally, a more intuitive naming convention makes a lot more sense. One way to resolve this issue is to use the "Manage service applications" page in the Central Administration site to add service applications individually, and then specify meaningful database names. The other alternative approach is to use Windows PowerShell to provision your service applications.

The following code snippet shows how you can provision a State Service service application using Windows PowerShell. Note how the SQL Server database and server name are specified in the code.

```
New-SPStateServiceDatabase -Name "StateServiceDatabase" -DatabaseServer
    "dhsqlsrv" | New-SPStateServiceApplication -Name "State Service Application"
    | New-SPStateServiceApplicationProxy -Name " State Service Application Proxy"
    -DefaultProxyGroup > $null
```

As mentioned previously, you can create and deploy your own service application. In that case, you can override the previous Windows PowerShell commands and add your own parameters.

Configuring Service Application Proxies

If you deploy your service applications using either the Configuration Wizard or via Central Administration, service application proxies are automatically created for you. If you use Windows PowerShell, then you must also manually create the proxy that goes along with that service application.

So, what's the service application proxy, anyway?

Essentially, the *service application proxy* is a virtual link that connects web applications to a particular service application. So, when you create your web application, you'll specify your association to a service application proxy, and it's the proxy that will actually manage the communication back and forth.

In addition to linking web applications to service applications, some proxies also include settings that can be modified independently from the service applications. For example, the proxy for the Managed Metadata Service application indicates whether or not the associated service application is the default storage location for corporate taxonomy store (such as keywords and column-specific term sets), as shown in Figure 9-8.

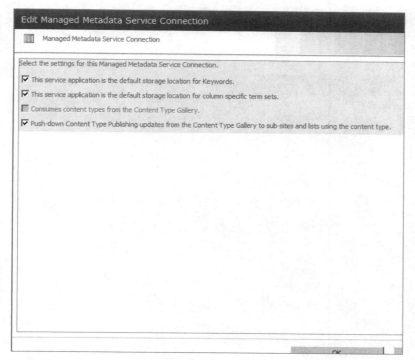

FIGURE 9-8: Managed Metadata Service application

 If there are multiple instances of the Managed Metadata Service application, (and, hence, multiple proxies), one of the instances must be specified as the primary, which hosts the corporate taxonomy store. All other instances are then secondary, providing additional data to the primary data. As an exception, the web parts that work with Managed Metadata Service applications work with data from all instances.

Configuring Proxy Groups

As its name implies, a *service application proxy group* is a grouping for service application proxies that are selected for a web application. A single service application proxy can be included in multiple proxy groups, or a proxy group may choose not to include a service application proxy based on the requirements of the target web applications.

When you set up your farm, by default, a default proxy group is created that includes all service application proxies. During the creation of a web application, you can select the default proxy group, or create a custom proxy group. Figure 9-9 shows a custom proxy group that includes only five of the existing service application proxies.

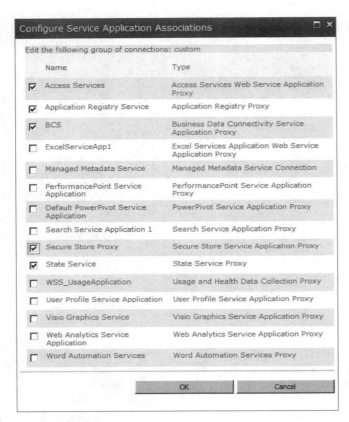

FIGURE 9-9: Custom proxy group

 A custom service application proxy group created for one web application cannot be associated with other web applications.

From Windows PowerShell you can run the Get-SPServiceApplicationProxy cmdlet as shown in Figure 9-10, and that will list the service application proxy IDs. You can then use Remove-SPServiceApplicationProxy (which takes the ID as a parameter) and Add-SPServiceApplicationProxyGroupMember to remove a service application proxy, or to add a member to the service application proxy group.

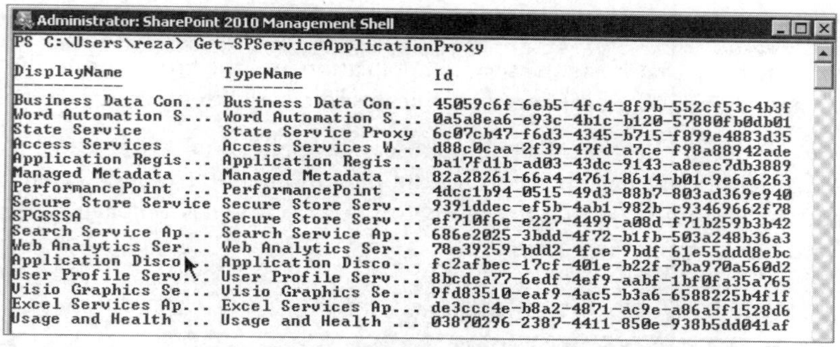

FIGURE 9-10: Service application proxy from Windows PowerShell

Consuming Service Applications

As mentioned previously, by default, all web applications in the local farm are associated with the default proxy group. This means that consuming the services in the local farm is not something that you must worry about, and it's automatically set up for you. If you ever decide to create a custom proxy group, you must decide how you want a specific web application to consume service applications.

To change the default proxy group for a web application, you must select Application Management in the Central Administration site, and click "Configure service application associations." In the Service Application Association page, you'll see the default text under the "Application Proxy Group" heading. If you click it, you will be taken to a page where you can manage the members of that default proxy group. Additionally, if there were any custom proxy groups for each web application, they would be listed in the same page.

Again, it's worth mentioning that some connections might include settings that can be modified. For example, if a web application is connected to multiple instances of the Managed Metadata Service, you must indicate which service application hosts the corporate taxonomy.

Publishing Service Applications

A service application can be consumed with one or more web applications within the local farm, or it can be consumed by web applications in a remote farm.

Before going into more detail, let's clear up some terminology to ensure that you have a clear understanding:

➤ *Publishing a service application* — This means making a service application available for consumption across farms.

➤ *Cross-farm service application* — This is a service application that is made available to be consumed by remote farms.

At a high level, three things must happen to deploy service applications across farms:

1. You must ensure that the farm that hosts the service application and the farm that needs to consume the service application have exchanged certificates to trust each other.

2. You must publish the service application. To publish a service application, you must go to the "Manage service applications" page in Central Administration, and, from the Ribbon, click the Publish button. This will take you to the Publish Service Application page, where you specify a few settings, as shown in Figure 9-11.

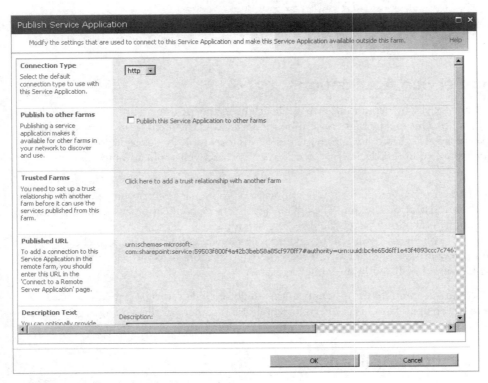

FIGURE 9-11: Publishing a service application

 One thing in Figure 9-11 that must be highlighted is the Published URL. This is the URL that will be used in the remote farm to locate the service application.

3. To consume a published service, go to the "Manage service applications" page in the remote farm and click the Connect button in the Ribbon. Next, choose which type of service you are connecting to, which, in turn, prompts you to enter the URL of the published service, as shown in Figure 9-12. Assuming that the trust has been already set up and properly working, just a service application proxy on the local farm is created to connect to the service application on the remote farm. Once the proxy is there, any web application in the local farm can consume the service application from the remote farm.

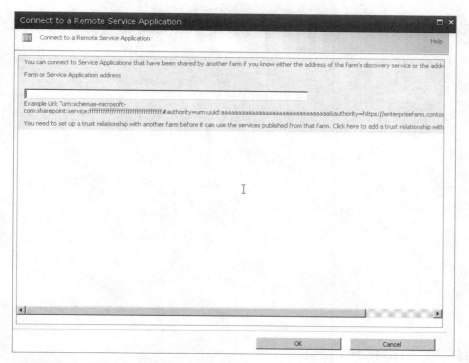

FIGURE 9-12: URL of the published service

One thing that is important to note, however, is that not all service applications can be shared between farms. For example, BCS is a cross-farm service application, whereas other service applications are not designed to be shared between farms. Some cross-farm service applications are not recommended for use in wide area network (WAN) environments. Simply put, those cross-farm service applications that use Windows Communication Foundation (WCF) endpoints are; the ones that use ASMX web service are not.

Table 9-3 lists current recommendations for deploying service applications across farms or over a WAN.

TABLE 9-3: Recommendations for Deploying Service Applications

SERVICE APPLICATIONS	CROSS FARM	WAN FRIENDLY
Access Services	No	N/A
Business Data Connectivity Service	Yes	With limitations
Excel Services	No	N/A
Managed Metadata Service	Yes	Yes
PerformancePoint	No	N/A
Search	Yes	Yes
Secure Store Service	Yes	No
State Service	No	N/A
Usage and Health Data Collection	No	N/A
User Profile	Yes	No
Visio Graphics Service	No	N/A
Web Analytics Service	Yes	No
Word Automation Services	No	N/A

ARCHITECTURAL PRINCIPLES

SharePoint and its architecture have grown in evolutionary fashion over the years. While this process of evolution is one of the main reasons for the technology's success, it seems that one of the long-standing challenges in the SharePoint space is still an agreement on what "architecture" is specifically appropriate for a farm, or the applications that are built on the top of this technology. Do you need to start from modest beginnings and let it grow, or should you have a grand plan from the beginning?

As business goals and emphasis change, business requirements change. When the business requirements change, it has an impact on your overall architecture. So, the question is, how do you make your architecture future-proof? The answer is quite easy: you can't! However, with proper analysis and planning, and by following best practices, you can minimize the impact and narrow down possible flaws in your design in the future.

Well, service application architecture is no exception. This section provides general guidance for SharePoint architects working with SharePoint 2010. This section covers a few different implementations of service applications, and several common types of scenarios and technologies that you need to know upfront.

Architecture Examples

Although it's important to know what Microsoft recommends as possible implementations of service applications, keep in mind that each project has different requirements that should be considered carefully when you are doing your design.

With that being said, let's start with the simplest service application implementation, as shown in Figure 9-13. In this implementation, all service applications are deployed and consumed in a single local farm. They're all using the same application pool (no process isolation), and they're all part of the default proxy group. That means all web applications in the local farm are consuming all of the service applications that are available in this farm as well.

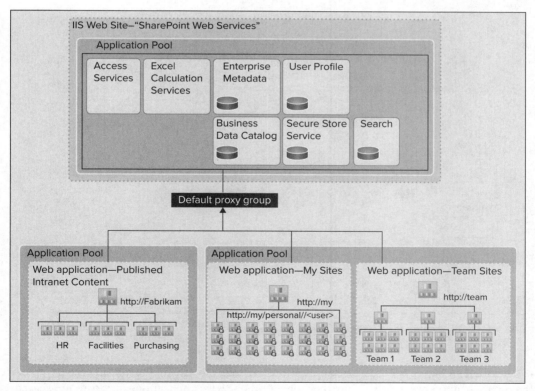

FIGURE 9-13: Implementation of a service application

If you require a simple architecture and most efficient use of farm resources to host a large number of sites, the architecture shown in Figure 9-13 is recommended.

Now, let's look at an architecture for multiple service applications, as shown in Figure 9-14. In this implementation, there are two proxy groups:

➤ *Default proxy group* — This is a subset of all of service applications, and it is associated with the Company Web and My Sites web applications.

➤ *Custom proxy group* — This is a particular web application (such as `http://finance`) that isn't associated with all of the service applications. It's using only a small subset of those. Hence, it's using a custom proxy group.

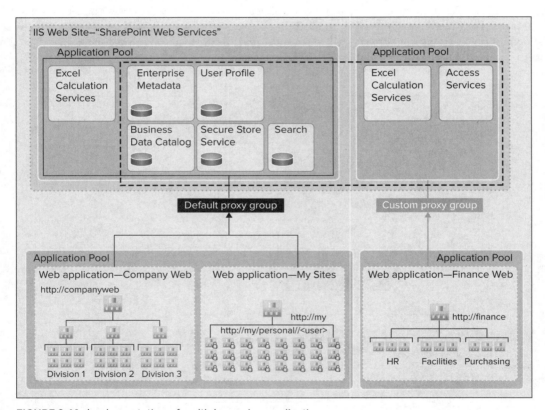

FIGURE 9-14: Implementation of multiple service applications

As you can see in Figure 9-14, service applications are logically isolated by placing them into two different application pools. Also, note that some of the service applications instances are shared between default and custom proxy groups, whereas some are dedicated to a particular web application.

In this architecture, the Finance department is getting its own Excel Calculation Service and Access Services instances to optimize performance for a targeted group, and to isolate sensitive finance data.

Obviously, the architecture shown in Figure 9-14 is more complex to configure, and requires far more resources to support multiple instances of some services. However, it's a flexible model that allows isolation of service data, and more granular configuration and control over service applications associated with different web applications.

Figure 9-15 shows an architecture where a farm (Farm A) is built to include a number of service applications to serve multiple farms across the enterprise. It offers centrally managed resources, and contains no web applications that serve content to end users. Hosted service applications are only meant to be consumed by other farms remotely.

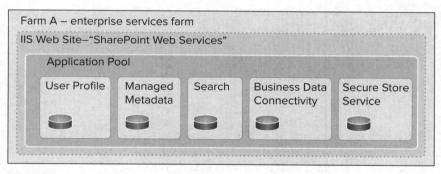

FIGURE 9-15: Enterprise services farm

This architecture is recommended when you want to optimize the resources within a farm for running services, rather than hosting content.

Now, take a look at the content-only farm in Farm B in Figure 9-16. This farm has two characteristics:

➤ No local service applications

➤ All service applications are consumed remotely from Farm A

Unlike Farm A, Farm B contains absolutely no service applications. It just contains web applications.

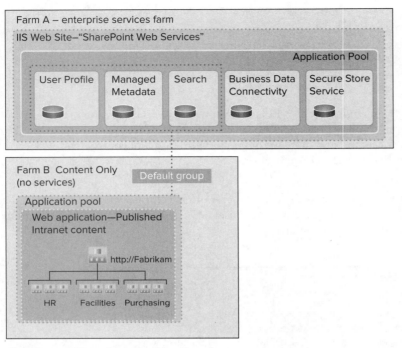

FIGURE 9-16: Farm A versus Farm B

From an implementation perspective, when configuring the web applications in Farm B, there will be a list of service application proxies, and they'll look exactly the same as if those service applications were installed in the local farm (that is, local to Farm B).

This configuration works well if you want to optimize the resources within your farm to host published content, rather than running service applications while consuming organization-wide data and other centrally managed resources from another farm.

Now, look at the combination of local service applications and remote service application consumption, an architecture known as hybrid, as shown in Figure 9-17.

In this architecture, there are two participating farms:

➤ *Farm C* — This farm contains a set of service applications locally for its own use. It's also consuming all enterprise service applications from Farm A remotely. The default proxy group contains proxies for the service applications from Farm A, as well as local proxies.

➤ *Farm D* — Just like farm C, this farm contains local and remote service applications, but it contains a deployment of services for a specialized department farm.

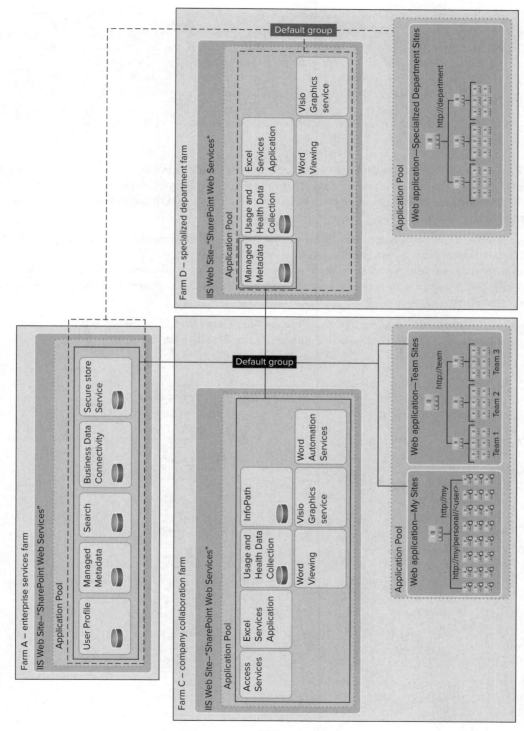

FIGURE 9-17: A hybrid

Note a difference between Farm C and Farm D. Farm C consumes the Managed Metadata Service from Farm D. In this implementation, the department self-governs the taxonomy, and other social features of the Managed Metadata Service application, which is then shared with Farm C. Because this implementation contains two Managed Metadata Service applications, one must be designated as the primary, and the other one as secondary.

The hybrid architecture is recommended if you must host multiple farms across your organization to meet your organizational business needs. This model also works well if you must optimize resources and administrative efforts based on each farm's characteristics and the roles they play in the overall enterprise architecture.

For example, a specialized department farm may not follow the same change-management life cycle that a farm containing a custom-built application follows. Obviously, in this case, process isolation absolutely makes sense. Another example is a published content-only farm that has different capacity and resource requirements from a department farm that comes with a ton of collaboration and less content.

If you decide not to use a dedicated enterprise services farm (Farm A), you can consider using *cross-organization farms*, as shown in Figure 9-18 and Figure 9-19.

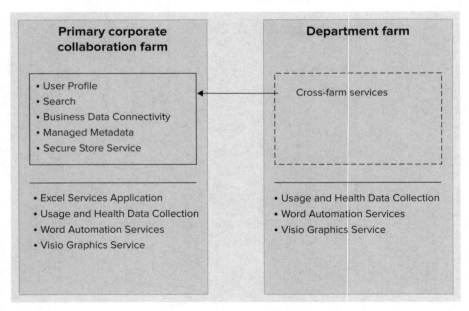

FIGURE 9-18: Cross-organization farms

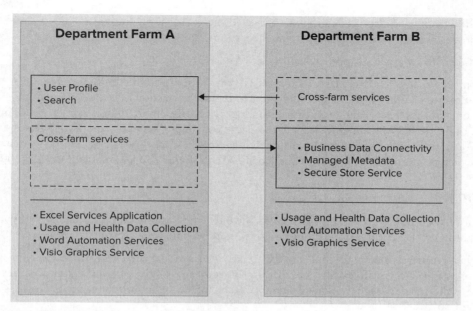

FIGURE 9-19: Cross-organization farms (Farms A and B)

In this architecture, try to share as many services as you can to avoid having a dedicated farm for services. For example, a department farm may choose to consume a subset of services from a primary corporate collaboration farm. Another example is when department Farm A and department Farm B exchange shared services to avoid duplication of services.

Inter-farm SSPs Versus Cross-farm Service Applications

The enterprise services implementation shown in the previous section is most analogous to the inter-farm shared services model in MOSS 2007. This model was used to enable web applications from one farm to use shared services from another farm using a parent/child model.

 Inter-farm *and* intra-farm *shared services are not interchangeable terms. Intra-farm shared services mean that a MOSS 2007 farm uses the shared services of an SSP hosted within the farm.*

There were three primary issues with inter-farm shared service, which have been addressed by cross-farm service applications:

➤ You could configure one SSP to provide shared services to all the other farms, and you could configure one SSP to consume all its services from a parent farm. However, you couldn't go both ways to publish and consume service applications from within a single farm.

➤ Child farms could use services only from one parent SSP.

➤ The child farm level also needed to have access to the parent farm databases, which could be a potential security issue in some implementations.

➤ Inter-farm SSPs were not supported across a WAN.

With cross-farm service applications in SharePoint 2010, any farm can both publish and consume service applications from other farms. More importantly, remote farms don't need permissions to the parent farm databases. Also, each farm can consume services from more than a parent farm. For example, look at Figure 9-17 again. Note how Farm C was consuming services from both Farm A and Farm D. Also, web applications can also use both local service applications and remote service applications, which is another improvement over the inter-farm shared services model in MOSS 2007.

Multi-tenancy

In implementations where you have multiple clients, one of the first architectural decisions that you may need to make is whether the design should follow a multi-tenant architecture.

Multi-tenancy is a relatively new principle in software architecture that revolves around the concept of the Software as a Service (SaaS) business model. In this model, a single software instance serves multiple client organizations, each known as a *tenant*. Remember, the multi-tenant architecture is based on a single software instance.

Multi-instance Architecture

A multi-tenant architecture is often contrasted with the *multi-instance architecture*, where separate software instances (or hardware systems) are implemented to serve multiple client organizations. A typical example of a multi-instance architecture is a hosting model where an authority (person or company) packages software and sells it. The authority provides services and deals with resources, cost, and subscriptions.

Figure 9-20 shows the difference between multi-tenant and multi-instance architectures at a high level. A multi-tenant architecture represents a single logical instance of software shared by many clients. In contrast, a multi-instance architecture follows a separate, logical software instance for each client.

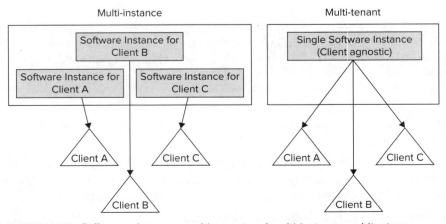

FIGURE 9-20: Difference between multi-tenant and multi-instance architecture

Think of multi-instance architecture in SharePoint 2010 as the traditional model of deploying multiple farms (or a mega parent farm) and smaller child farms (inter-farm services), as explained earlier in this chapter.

It's important to note that the single-instance concept in a multi-tenant architecture does not mean that views of the application's data are shared between clients. For example, in Figure 9-20, Client B must not be able to see or modify Client A's application's data. However, whoever owns the application as a whole will have full access to all the data stored in the application for all clients.

Multi-tenant Architecture in SharePoint 2010

In SharePoint 2010, multi-tenancy is not as straightforward as what is demonstrated in Figure 9-20, because a SharePoint farm can be made up of multiple components, each of which should be considered separately in a multi-tenant architecture.

At a high level, multi-tenancy in SharePoint 2010 refers to a specific type of deployment that has the following two characteristics:

➤ It's on a shared set of resources within a single farm.

➤ It uniquely separates each tenant in the way they use the product's features (that is, it's on a per-tenant basis).

Customers choose a multi-tenant architecture because it creates a true hosting environment, wherein server farm resources are maximized, and IT and licensing costs are dramatically reduced.

Figure 9-21 shows a practical implementation of multi-tenancy in SharePoint 2010. This implementation has one web application with two tenants, each owning a few site collections within the same web application. The web application consumes service applications that are multi-tenant aware, and service data for each tenant is partitioned in the back-end database (that is, data isolation). Although both tenants are using the same service application, they have no visibility to the other tenant's data, because the service data is partitioned.

Two things about Figure 9-21 should be highlighted here.

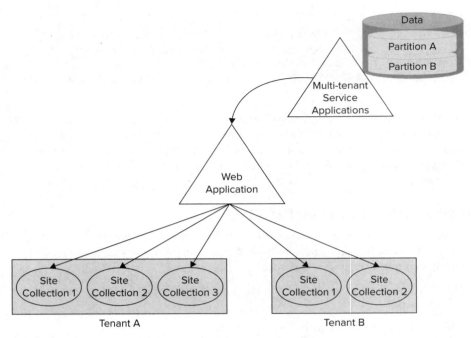

FIGURE 9-21: Implementation of multi-tenancy in SharePoint 2010

First, not all service applications can be partitioned. That's because some services do not need to store tenant data, so they can be shared across multiple tenants without risk of exposing tenant-specific data. Table 9-4 lists the service applications that don't include the capability to be partitioned. A service application that cannot be partitioned is not a multi-tenant aware service application.

TABLE 9-4: Service Applications that Cannot be Partitioned

SERVICE APPLICATIONS	MULTI-TENANT AWARE
Subscription Settings	Yes
Access Services	No
Business Data Connectivity Service	Yes
Excel Services	No
Managed Metadata Service	Yes
PerformancePoint	No
Search	Yes

SERVICE APPLICATIONS	MULTI-TENANT AWARE
Secure Store Service	Yes
State Service	No
Usage and Health Data Collection	No
User Profile	Yes
Visio Graphics Services	No
Web Analytics Service	No
Word Automation Services	Yes

Second, this implementation uses one web application for all tenants. Although it's very common for tenants to have one or more site collections within the same web application, in a few scenarios each tenant may need its own web application, including the following:

➤ A tenant needs to deploy customizations that affect shared resources (such as the `web.config` file).

➤ A tenant requires a dedicated application pool (that is, process isolation) for performance or security reasons.

➤ All authenticated content for each tenant is hosted in one web application, while the other web application contains all publicly available content for each tenant.

If you decide to keep all your tenants in one web application using different site collections, several new or improved site collection features will be at your disposal:

➤ Additional support is provided for vanity domains using host header site collections (that is, multiple root-level site collections within a web application).

➤ Host header site collections support managed paths (for example, site collections `http://foo.com` and `http://foo.com/sites/foo` for tenant A and `http://bar.com` and `http://bar.com/sites/bar` for tenant B can co-exist in the same web application).

➤ Load balancer Single Sockets Layer (SSL) termination support is included.

➤ The Windows PowerShell cmdlet `New-SPSite` accepts a parameter that allows you to target a site collection to reside in a specific content database.

➤ Pluggable custom code (Site Creation Provider) allows you to enforce database organization across all your tenants. This is basically to ensure that, if a tenant creates a new site collection, that site collection ends up in the database you want, not just following the out-of-the-box round-robin algorithm.

➤ Sandboxed solutions allow each tenant to deploy custom code to their own site collection(s).

Although partitioned service applications and new features of site collections in SharePoint 2010 play an important role in the overall multi-tenant architecture, in reality, many more features enable multi-tenancy in SharePoint 2010. Following are some of these features:

➤ Microsoft SharePoint Foundation Subscription Settings Service adds multi-tenant functionality for service applications (available in all editions of SharePoint).

➤ Feature sets are groups of product Features that are enabled by farm administrators for tenants to activate and use.

➤ Site subscriptions are a logical group of site collections that can share settings, Features, and service data. Each site subscription has a subscription ID that is used to map Features, services, and sites to tenants, as well as partitioning their service data.

➤ Centralized and delegated administration allows the delegation of certain Central Administration tasks to tenant administrators using their own administration user interface, while the main Central Administration site is used to administer the entire SharePoint installation.

Many of the multi-tenant features are deployed and managed using Windows PowerShell.

Architecture Example

The new multi-tenant architecture in SharePoint 2010 provides more flexibility in the way you architect your services. You can mix multi-tenancy with previous architecture examples to come up with really optimal service application architectures.

For example, you can share some service data across the organization while other service data can be partitioned. Figure 9-22 shows a practical architecture where a combination of shared and partitioned service applications is employed.

In this architecture, all services are offered through the default group. However, three types of service applications exist:

➤ Service applications that are only shared in the local farm (such as Excel Calculation Services, Access Services, and so on).

➤ Service applications that can be shared cross-farm (such as User Profiles, Search, and BCS).

➤ Cross-farm service applications that can also support multi-tenancy. (For example, the Managed Metadata Service is shared cross-farm, which allows a central corporate taxonomy across the organization, while providing each tenant the capability to manage their own taxonomy. This removes the need for each tenant to have their own specialized farms.)

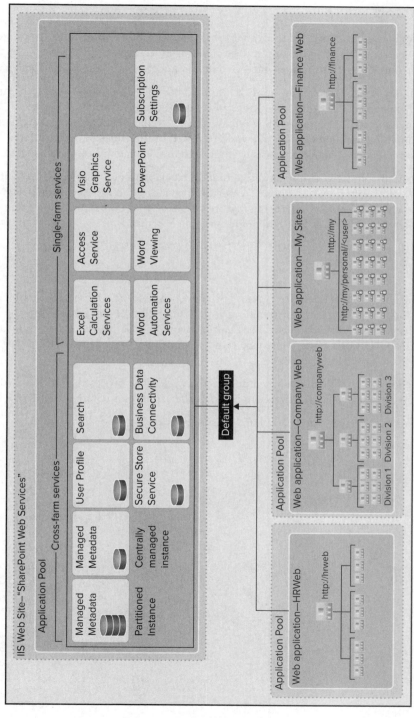

FIGURE 9-22: A combination of shared and partitioned service applications is employed

Load Balancing

SharePoint provides a basic load balancer that uses a round-robin algorithm to send requests to service applications. When a web application requests an endpoint for an associated service application (through proxy), the out-of-the-box load balancer returns the first available endpoint.

The underlying services of the service applications also use the out-of-the-box load balancer. If you click on the "Manage Services on server" page in Central Administration and go to the "Services on Server" page, you will see a list of all services in the current farm. On the top-right corner of the page is drop-down menu allowing you to switch to different machines in the farm, and choose to stop or start services on them. This means that more than one machine can run a particular service.

By default, a round-robin algorithm is used to load-balance SharePoint services, and you do not need to opt to use an external load balancer. Certain services (such as Excel Calculation Services) provide their own software load-balancing feature to ensure that no instance of a given service is overloaded at any time. Obviously, there might be some exceptions.

SUMMARY

Service applications in SharePoint 2010 are a powerful, scalable, and incredibly flexible architecture. They provide lots of new options for designing your farm in SharePoint 2010. Web applications can consume service applications a la carte. They can pick and choose which service applications in the farm or service applications being consumed remotely that they want to use within that particular web application.

Many design choices could be made based on usage, availability, process isolation, hardware, security, and so on. Service applications are really at the center of all SharePoint deployments.

Chapter 10 examines SharePoint 2010 platform architectures.

10

SharePoint 2010 Platform Architectures

By Bill Baer

A properly planned SharePoint topology is of primary importance to delivering a stable, scalable, available, and high-performing SharePoint environment. The process of planning a server farm environment includes many factors — including workload/scenario, business continuity management requirements, demand, and overall business requirements — both for today and in the future. Designing the right server farm environment for your scenario will go a long way toward ensuring that the environment meets the demands of your organization today, and will seamlessly scale in the future.

This chapter discusses the various components associated with a SharePoint 2010 Products topology, their characteristics, and how these components can be implemented to ensure meaningful deployment suitable for meeting existing and future demand.

SERVER FARM TOPOLOGIES

Server farms represent the topology that delivers SharePoint services to end users. A *server farm* is a collection of server machines acting together to provide a single solution or service.

SharePoint 2010 provides a high degree of flexibility when it comes to planning your topology. The core principle behind implementing a server farm is to enable elastic scale in the event the environment is required to support additional workloads, scenarios, or load. Server farms in SharePoint 2010 are implemented by establishing a base topology.

The core components of a server farm environment include the following:

➤ Front-end web servers with which users directly interact.

➤ One or more SQL Server database servers that store both configuration and content.

➤ Optional application servers that provide services tailored to your scenario (for example, servers that host the Search crawl and query components, or a dedicated server that hosts the SharePoint 2010 Central Administration website from where the server farm is centrally managed).

SharePoint 2010 can be deployed in a number of topology configurations. The basic topologies include small, medium, and large — otherwise known as single-tier, two-tier, and three-tier deployments — that define the placement and purpose of individual server machines that comprise the topology.

Each tier in a topology represents the purpose of the server machines hosted within it, or the services dedicated to those server machines. As shown in Figure 10-1 the three tiers in a SharePoint topology are classified as the Web, Application, and Database tiers.

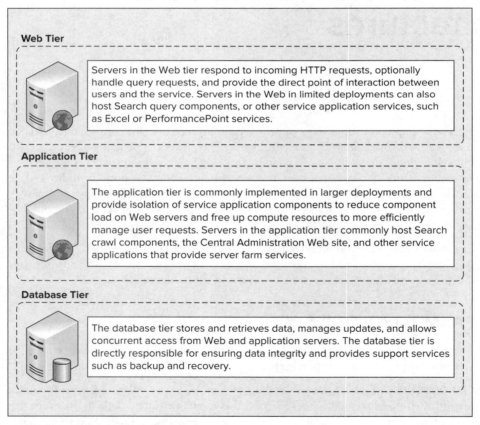

Web Tier

Servers in the Web tier respond to incoming HTTP requests, optionally handle query requests, and provide the direct point of interaction between users and the service. Servers in the Web in limited deployments can also host Search query components, or other service application services, such as Excel or PerformancePoint services.

Application Tier

The application tier is commonly implemented in larger deployments and provide isolation of service application components to reduce component load on Web servers and free up compute resources to more efficiently manage user requests. Servers in the application tier commonly host Search crawl components, the Central Administration Web site, and other service applications that provide server farm services.

Database Tier

The database tier stores and retrieves data, manages updates, and allows concurrent access from Web and application servers. The database tier is directly responsible for ensuring data integrity and provides support services such as backup and recovery.

FIGURE 10-1: SharePoint 2010 tiers

Web Tier

The Web tier is comprised of web servers or other servers that receive and respond to HTTP requests. Web servers host SharePoint web applications in Internet Information Services (IIS). They can support additional services such as the Search query component sending requests to database servers in the Database tier, or communicating with application servers in Application tier to consume services hosted on those servers. Servers in the Web tier are exposed directly to end users, and should be secured behind a firewall or within a perimeter network.

Application Tier

The Application tier is an optional tier comprised of servers that are dedicated to the hosting of service applications associated with SharePoint 2010. Examples of servers in the Application tier include dedicated server machines that host the Search service, administration, and/or query components, in addition to services such as PerformancePoint or Excel Services.

The Application tier is most commonly associated with large server farm environments, where dedicated compute resources are required to support high search query volumes, large index corpuses, or to isolate service applications to free up resources on the Web tier to support high concurrency rates.

Database Tier

The Database tier is comprised of servers hosting SQL Server. Database servers in the Database tier respond to requests initiated by web and application servers, and update the underlying databases that support SharePoint 2010. The Database tier can be scaled both vertically (to improve performance) and horizontally (to improve performance and provide additional server farm resiliency).

In Office SharePoint Server 2007, server machines were often referred to as server roles. In SharePoint Server 2010, roles are provided as components to provide the highest degree of flexibility, whereby a server's role is defined by which components are deployed to it. As a result, the terms "role" and "component" are interchangeable.

Small or Single-Tier Topology

A small or single-tier topology commonly consists of a single server deployment in which all components required to instantiate a SharePoint environment are installed on one machine including the database server — either through a dedicated SQL Server installation, or standalone installation using SQL Server Express edition.

Figure 10-2 shows an example of a single-tier topology, which is designed to support development or small businesses where scale and redundancy are not concerns.

A single-tier topology does not provide any level of redundancy. Therefore, it requires an aggressive backup-and-restore strategy to be implemented, because this is the extent of data protection that can be provided in this deployment topology.

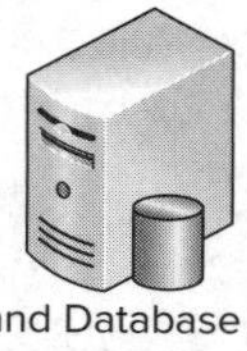

Web and Database Server

FIGURE 10-2: Single-tier topology

Because all components are installed on a single server, single-tier topologies are the least flexible, and do not support seamless scale. Scaling a single-tier topology requires backup of all content and components, as well as redeployment on a more flexible topology (at minimum, a medium or two-tier topology).

Medium or Two-Tier Topology

A medium or two-tier topology consists of two or more servers that support separation of SharePoint and SQL Server components. This includes one or more web servers installed with SharePoint 2010, and one or more database servers installed with SQL Server. Medium or two-tier topologies benefit from their flexibility in that they can seamlessly scale to meet the changing business needs or the demands of the organization.

Figure 10-3 shows a minimal two-tier topology comprised of one web server running SharePoint Server 2010 in the Web tier, and one database server running SQL Server 2005 or SQL Server 2008 in the Database tier.

Figure 10-4 shows a scaled two-tier topology that includes two load-balanced web servers running SharePoint Server 2010 in the Web tier, and two database servers running SQL Server 2005 or 2008 in the Database tier that can be clustered or mirrored to provide high availability and redundancy.

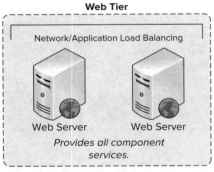

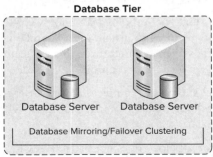

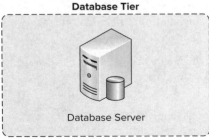

FIGURE 10-3: Two-tier topology

FIGURE 10-4: Two-tier highly available topology

The two-tier topology provides the most flexible deployment type, and is recommended for organizations of all sizes as a base topology. This topology can be both expanded and contracted through the introduction of additional server machines. As such, it is one of the most common deployments of a server farm, providing a flexible and scalable solution. A two-tier server farm enables an organization to seamlessly implement hardware or software load balancing such as Windows NT Load Balancing Service (WLBS) to distribute incoming HTTP requests evenly between web servers. This provides a means to handle an increase in demand as the number of requests submitted to it rise (for example, as the result of a merger or acquisition).

A two-tier server farm can also seamlessly scale at the Database tier through the introduction of additional database servers in a mirrored or clustered configuration. This provides additional resiliency and distribution of load within a server farm environment.

Large or Three-Tier Topology

A large or three-tier topology is designed for large organizations that require performance, scale, and adherence to strict business continuity management objectives.

Figure 10-5 shows a three-tier topology that consists of two or more web servers installed with SharePoint 2010, one or more application servers installed with SharePoint 2010, and two or more database servers installed with SQL Server.

The physical topology selected for SharePoint 2010 will drive the layout of the service application topology. In many cases, it may be easier to map the service application topology to a physical topology to help ensure that sufficient resources exist to support the overall deployment.

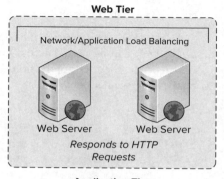

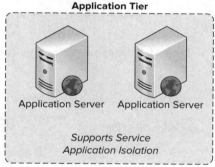

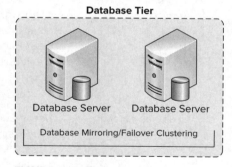

FIGURE 10-5: Three-tier topology

SERVICE APPLICATION TOPOLOGIES

In Office SharePoint Server 2007, services were contained within a Shared Services Provider (SSP). The SSP-provided services such as Search, personalization, business intelligence (BI), and portal usage reporting were self-contained within a separate web application. Although the SSP model provided a valuable function (in that resource-intensive services such as Search could be isolated within and shared across multiple web applications), deployment and flexibility were challenging, and did not provide third-party extensibility.

In SharePoint Server 2010, the SSP model has been retired in favor of a more flexible and á-la-carte consumption model provided through a new Shared Services architecture. In SharePoint Server 2010, services can be distributed as individual service applications, provisioned on demand at run time, or later in the deployment cycle, as business needs change and evolve.

Service applications provide the core capabilities to support the varying workloads in SharePoint 2010. They can be shared across farms, and accessed by users through the web applications hosting them. Service applications are associated with web applications through service application connections.

 Service application connections are also referred to as application proxies, and associate the service application with a web application through membership in a service application connection group, which is described later in this chapter.

Table 10-1 lists the service applications that are available in SharePoint 2010.

TABLE 10-1: Service Applications in SharePoint 2010

SERVICE APPLICATION	DESCRIPTION	EDITION
Business Connectivity Services	Business Connectivity Services (BCS) provides read/write access to external data from line-of-business (LOB) systems, web services, databases, and other external systems within Microsoft SharePoint 2010. For additional information about Business Connectivity Services, see `http://technet.microsoft.com/en-us/library/ee661740.aspx`.	SharePoint Foundation 2010
Usage and Health Data Collection	Usage and Health Data Collection collects farm-wide usage and health data, and provides the capability to view various usage and health reports. For additional information about the Usage and Health Data Collection service, see `http://technet.microsoft.com/en-us/library/ee748636.aspx`.	SharePoint Foundation 2010
Subscription Settings Service	This service provides multi-tenant functionality for service applications. It tracks subscription IDs and settings for services that are deployed in partitioned mode.	SharePoint Foundation 2010

SERVICE APPLICATION	DESCRIPTION	EDITION
User Profile	The User Profile service application stores information about users in a central location, and reuses that information for social computing features (such as My Sites, social tagging, and newsfeeds). For additional information about the User Profile Service Application, see `http://technet.microsoft.com/en-us/library/ee662538.aspx`.	SharePoint Server 2010 Standard Edition
Managed Metadata Service	The Managed Metadata Service (MMS) publishes a term store and, optionally, content types. For additional information about MMSA, see `http://technet.microsoft.com/en-us/library/ee424403.aspx`.	SharePoint Server 2010 Standard Edition
Search	The Search service application crawls content, produces index partitions, and serves search queries. For additional information about the Search service application, see `http://technet.microsoft.com/en-us/library/ff631149.aspx`.	SharePoint Server 2010 Standard Edition
Secure Store Service	This provides Single Sign-On (SSO) authentication to access multiple applications or services. For additional information about the Secure Store Service application, see `http://technet.microsoft.com/en-us/library/ee806889.aspx`.	SharePoint Server 2010 Standard Edition
State	This provides temporary storage of user session data for SharePoint components. For additional information about the State Service Application, see `http://technet.microsoft.com/en-us/library/ee704548.aspx`.	SharePoint Server 2010 Standard
Web Analytics	The Web Analytics Service Application collects and reports on usage information such as page views, unique visitors, search queries issued, and so on. For additional information about the Web Analytics Service Application, see `http://technet.microsoft.com/en-us/library/gg266382.aspx#S1`.	SharePoint Server 2010 Standard
Word Automation Services	The Word Automation Services application enables unattended, server-side conversion of documents supported by Microsoft Word. For additional information about the Word Automation Services Application, see `http://technet.microsoft.com/en-us/library/ee558278.aspx`.	SharePoint Server 2010 Standard

continues

TABLE 10-1 *(continued)*

SERVICE APPLICATION	DESCRIPTION	EDITION
Access Services	Access Services enables users to edit, update, and create linked Microsoft Access 2010 databases that can be viewed and manipulated through the browser, the Access client, or a linked HTML page. For additional information about Access Services, see `http://technet.microsoft.com/en-us/library/ee748634.aspx`.	SharePoint Server 2010 Enterprise
Excel Services Application	This enables simple use, sharing, securing, and management of Excel workbooks as interactive reports and dashboards through Excel Services Web parts. For additional information about Excel Services Application, see `http://technet.microsoft.com/en-us/library/ee424405.aspx`.	SharePoint Server 2010 Enterprise
PerformancePoint Service Application	PerformancePoint Service Application provides a performance-management service that can be used to monitor and analyze your business. For additional information about PerformancePoint Service Application, see `http://technet.microsoft.com/en-us/library/ee661741.aspx`.	SharePoint Server 2010 Enterprise
Visio Graphics Service	Visio Graphics Service enables users to share and view Visio web drawings using Visio Services. For additional information about Visio Graphics Service, see `http://technet.microsoft.com/en-us/library/ee663485.aspx`.	SharePoint Server 2010 Enterprise

Service applications are deployed through three primary entry points:

➤ Windows PowerShell

➤ Farm Configuration Wizard

➤ SharePoint 2010 Central Administration

 Some service applications can be deployed only through Windows PowerShell (such as the Subscription Settings Service Application). To learn more about deploying service applications, see `http://technet.microsoft.com/en-us/library/ee704544.aspx`.

Service Application Groups and Associations

Service applications can be grouped and contained within a service application group, as shown in Figure 10-6. The service application group can be assigned to individual web applications, which allows you to expose only the necessary services needed to support the context of one or more web applications.

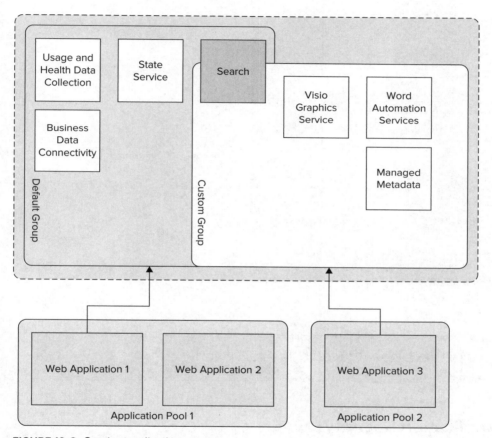

FIGURE 10-6: Service application groups

For example, a web application supporting finance operations within an organization may require PerformancePoint Services and Business Data Connectivity services, whereas a web application supporting document and records management may require the Managed Metadata Services (MMS). In this scenario, custom groups can be defined to support the unique requirements of each scenario, whereas the default group can be used to provide other essential services to facilitate collaboration and discovery (such as the Search services).

Figure 10-7 shows the Configure Service Application Associations dialog in SharePoint 2010 Central Administration.

FIGURE 10-7: Configure Service Application Associations dialog

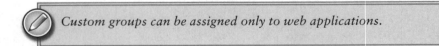

Custom groups can be assigned only to web applications.

Service Application Security

In environments where security is the primary factor in determining the appropriate topology, the flexibility provided through the service application architecture in SharePoint 2010 can be implemented to support those security requirements through concepts such as process isolation. *Process isolation* simply refers to protecting one process from other processes — for example, preventing Process 1 from writing into Process 2.

To utilize process isolation, a separate application pool is assigned to each service application to provide a process boundary. However, there is a tradeoff between security and performance, depending on the number of service applications and the extent of process isolation. Figure 10-8 shows service applications that are assigned to separate application pools.

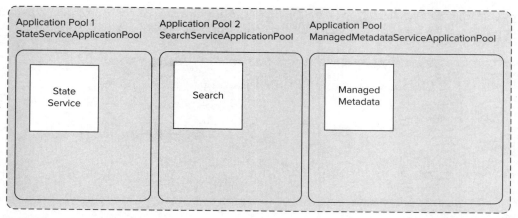

FIGURE 10-8: Process isolation

Multiple application pools should be used when you want to ensure that web applications are secure. For example, an organization can use multiple application pools to separate Human Resources and general open intranet collaboration websites hosted within the same environment, though separated through the assignment of unique application pools. By implementing multiple, dedicated application pools, you can prevent one organization from accessing, changing, or using confidential information from another organization's website.

Each web application within an application pool shares the same worker process, which operates as a separate instance of the worker process executable (w3wp.exe). Figure 10-9 shows the w3wp.exe file as displayed in Windows Task Manager.

Each separate worker process provides a process boundary. Therefore, when an application is assigned to an application pool, problems within it or another application pool do not affect one another. For example, if a worker process fails, it does not affect the applications running in other application pools.

When considering process isolation, you should carefully evaluate the impact on performance that multiple worker processes will have on the resources available to each server in the topology.

A number of methods for monitoring w3wp.exe resource utilization can be employed when evaluating the impact of multiple worker processes, or when attempting to diagnose issues related to worker processes.

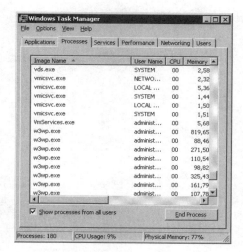

FIGURE 10-9: w3wp.exe in Windows Task Manager

Performance and Resource Monitor

Performance Monitor (shown in Figure 10-10) and *Resource Monitor* (shown in Figure 10-11) are utilities included in Windows Server that enable you to examine how programs you run affect your server's performance by collecting log data for later or real-time analysis. For example, to monitor worker processes, you can use the .NET CLR Exceptions performance object.

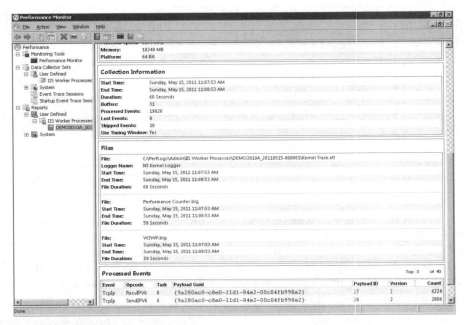

FIGURE 10-10: Performance Monitor

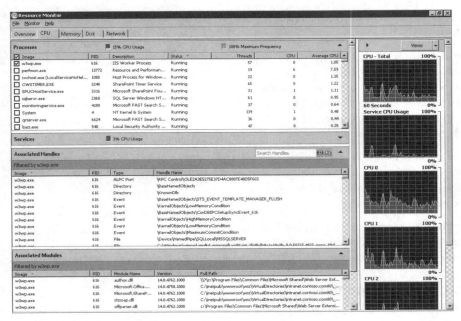

FIGURE 10-11: w3wp.exe in Resource Monitor

Worker processes are exposed with a unique identifier represented as an incremental int, *in order to surface the Process ID (PID) associated with a worker processes, as opposed to* int. *For more information, see* http://support.microsoft.com/kb/281884.

Process Monitor

Process Monitor is a Sysinternals command-line utility that supports the monitoring of filesystem, registry, and process/thread activity. Using Process Monitor, you can surface the PID associated with a specific worker process, and subsequently narrow the monitoring scope to that PID.

For additional information about Process Monitor, see http://technet.microsoft.com/en-us/sysinternals/bb896645.aspx.

ProcDump

ProcDump is a Sysinternals command-line utility that supports the monitoring of worker processes for CPU spikes, in addition to facilitating the generation of crash dumps in the event a suspect worker process requires further evaluation to isolate problems.

For additional information about ProcDump, see http://technet.microsoft.com/en-us/sysinternals/dd996900.aspx.

Planning Service Application Topologies

Planning the service application architecture should include the following considerations.

➤ Business requirements

➤ Federation scenarios

➤ Dedicated services scenario

Business requirements surrounding the deployment of service applications are commonly centered on the problem (or problems) the deployment of SharePoint Server 2010 is intended to solve — such as social networking within an organization, or rich search for quickly surfacing and working with information. Service applications should be carefully evaluated prior to deployment to ensure that they will facilitate meeting your organization's scenarios. Deploying those required service applications may help to satisfy business objectives.

Federated and dedicated services scenarios refer to whether service applications will be published to other deployments of SharePoint 2010, or provided through a dedicated services server farm. SharePoint 2010 refers to the federation of service applications as *publishing*. Publishing service applications enables a distributed organization to work together under a unified experience, and can reduce operational expenditures that accompany the maintenance and operations of multiple server farm environments.

Publishing service applications enables remote and secondary server farms to consume the services of a primary server farm environment. A dedicated services server farm, however, is designed to isolate services, and does not directly serve end-user requests.

Publishing Service Applications

Several service applications in SharePoint 2010 support federation (that is, they can be published and further consumed by another instance of SharePoint 2010). Figure 10-12 shows an example of an organization with a centralized deployment of SharePoint 2010 that supports the majority of end users, and a separate regional deployment that supports a satellite office. In this scenario, the Search service application can be published and consumed by the regional deployment, enabling a unified search experience, where the centralized deployment crawls the content of the regional deployment.

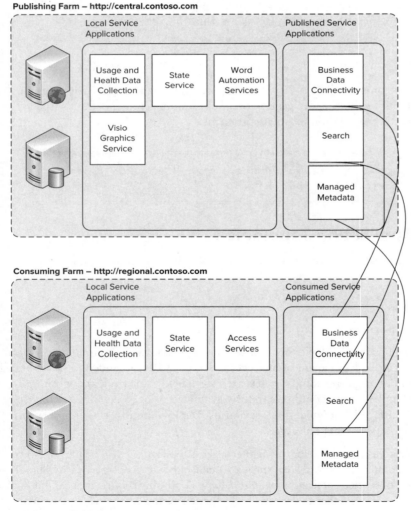

FIGURE 10-12: Published service applications

SharePoint 2010 supports publication of the following service applications:

- ➤ Business Data Connectivity
- ➤ Managed Metadata Service (MMS)
- ➤ User Profile
- ➤ Search
- ➤ Secure Store Service (SSS)
- ➤ Web Analytics

Publishing service applications requires that both the publishing and consuming farms are hosted within domains that share a trust — that is, the publishing farm domain must trust the domain of the consuming farm. To provide the broadest security boundary, one-way transitive (external) trusts can be established between the two domains.

Using external trusts provides access to resources that are located on a Windows NT 4.0 domain, or a domain that is located in a separate forest that is not joined by a forest trust, as shown in Figure 10-13.

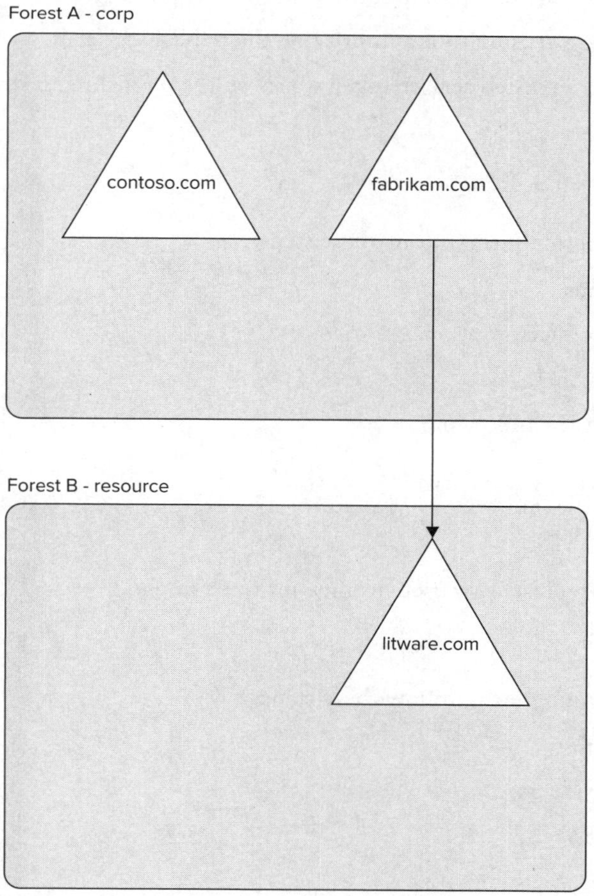

FIGURE 10-13: External trusts

Domain trust relationships are required to support the Business Data Connectivity service application and the Secure Store Service application. The User Profile service application requires a two-way trust.

Once the infrastructure requirements have been met, publishing service applications requires exchanging trust certificates between the farms. These trust certificates include one root and one Security Token Service (STS) certificate. Exchanging trust certificates ensures that each farm acknowledges that the other farm can be trusted.

To exchange trust certificates between farms, the following steps are required:

1. Export the root certificate from the consuming farm.

2. Export the STS certificate from the consuming farm.

3. Export the root certificate from the publishing farm.

4. Import the root certificate and create a trusted root authority on the consuming farm.

5. Import the root certificate and create a trusted root authority on the publishing farm.

6. Import the STS certificate and create a trusted service token issuer on the publishing farm.

Let's take a look at each step in a bit more detail.

Step 1

To export the root certificate from the consuming farm, follow these steps:

1. On the Start menu, click All Programs.

2. Click Microsoft SharePoint 2010 Products.

3. Click SharePoint 2010 Management Shell.

4. At the command prompt (PS>), enter the following:

```
$certificate=(Get-SPCertificateAuthority) .RootCertificate
$certificate.Export("Cert") | Set-Content <drive>:\<path>
    \Root-Consuming.cer -Encoding byte
```

Replace the values for *<drive>:\<path>* to represent your environment (for example, C:\Temp\).

Step 2

To export the STS certificate from the consuming farm, follow these steps:

1. On the Start menu, click All Programs.

2. Click Microsoft SharePoint 2010 Products.

3. Click SharePoint 2010 Management Shell.

4. At the command prompt (PS>), enter the following:

```
$certificate = (Get-SPSecurityTokenServiceConfig).LocalLoginProvider
    .SigningCertificate
$certificate.Export("Cert") | Set-Content <drive>:\<path>
    STS-Consuming.cer> -Encoding byte
```

Replace the values for *<drive>:\<path>* to represent your environment (for example, C:\Temp\).

Step 3

To export the root certificate from the publishing farm, follow these steps:

1. On the Start menu, click All Programs.

2. Click Microsoft SharePoint 2010 Products.

3. Click SharePoint 2010 Management Shell.

4. At the command prompt (PS>), enter the following:

```
$certificate=(Get-SPCertificateAuthority) .RootCertificate
$certificate.Export("Cert") | Set-Content <drive>:\<path>\
    Root-Publishing.cer -Encoding byte
```

Replace the values for *<drive>:\<path>* to represent your environment, for example C:\Temp\.

 The STS certificate does not need to be exported on the publishing farm.

Once the appropriate certificates have been exported on both the publishing and consuming farms, they must be copied across each other, and subsequently imported and installed to establish the needed trust relationship.

Step 4

To import the root certificate and create a trusted root authority on the consuming farm, follow these steps:

1. On the Start menu, click All Programs.

2. Click Microsoft SharePoint 2010 Products.

3. Click SharePoint 2010 Management Shell.

4. At the command prompt (PS>), enter the following:

```
$certificate = Get-PfxCertificate <drive>:\<path>\Root-Publishing.cer
New-SPTrustedRootAuthority <Publishing Farm Identifier>
    -Certificate $certificate
```

Replace the values for *<drive>:\<path>* to represent your environment, for example C:\Temp\.

Trusted root authorities must be uniquely named. `<Publishing Farm Identifier>` *should represent a unique name that represents the name of the consuming farm (for example,* `ContosoCentral`*).*

Step 5

To import the root certificate and create a trusted root authority on the publishing farm, follow these steps:

1. On the Start menu, click All Programs.

2. Click Microsoft SharePoint 2010 Products.

3. Click SharePoint 2010 Management Shell.

4. At the command prompt (`PS>`), enter the following:

```
$certificate = Get-PfxCertificate <drive>:\<path>\Root-Consuming.cer
New-SPTrustedRootAuthority <Consuming Farm Indentifier>
    -Certificate $certificate
```

Replace the values for `<drive>:\<path>` to represent your environment, for example `C:\Temp\`.

 Trusted root authorities must be uniquely named. `<Consuming Farm Identifier>` *should represent a unique name that represents the name of the consuming farm (for example,* `ContosoRegional`*).*

Step 6

To import the STS certificate and create a trusted service token issuer on the publishing farm, follow these steps:

1. On the Start menu, click All Programs.

2. Click Microsoft SharePoint 2010 Products.

3. Click SharePoint 2010 Management Shell.

4. At the command prompt (`PS>`), enter the following:

```
$certificate = Get-PfxCertificate <drive>:\<path>\STS-Consuming.cer
New-SPTrustedServiceTokenIssuer <Consuming Farm Identifier>
    -Certificate $certificate
```

Replace the values for `<drive>:\<path>` to represent your environment, for example `C:\Temp\`.

 Trusted root authorities must be uniquely named. `<Consuming Farm Identifier>` *should represent a unique name that represents the name of the consuming farm (for example,* `ContosoRegional`*).*

Completing the Process

When the required steps are completed to establish the publishing and consuming farm trust relationship, the selected service application can be published.

To set the permission to the application discovery and load-balancing service application on the consuming farm, follow these steps:

On the consuming farm:

1. On the Start menu, click All Programs.

2. Click Microsoft SharePoint 2010 Products.

3. Click SharePoint 2010 Management Shell.

4. At the command prompt (PS>), enter the following:

```
Get-SPFarm | Select Id
```

Note the consuming farm Id returned from the previous cmdlet, as shown in Figure 10-14.

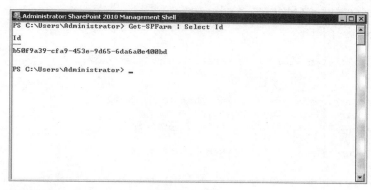

FIGURE 10-14: Farm Id

On the publishing farm, follow these steps:

1. On the Start menu, click All Programs.

2. Click Microsoft SharePoint 2010 Products.

3. Click SharePoint 2010 Management Shell.

4. At the command prompt (PS>), enter the following:

```
$security=Get-SPTopologyServiceApplication | Get-SPServiceApplicationSecurity
$provider=(Get-SPClaimProvider System).ClaimProvider
$principal=New-SPClaimsPrincipal -ClaimType
    "http://schemas.microsoft.com/sharepoint/2009/08/claims/farmid"
    -ClaimProvider $provider -ClaimValue <Consuming Farm Id>
Grant-SPObjectSecurity -Identity $security -Principal $principal
    -Rights "Full Control"
Get-SPTopologyServiceApplication | Set-SPServiceApplicationSecurity
    -ObjectSecurity $security
```

Replace the values for `<Consuming Farm Id>` to represent the value returned in the previous step.

Publishing a service application requires establishing permission to the Application Discovery and Load Balancing service application on the publishing farm for the consuming farm. This is a prerequisite to providing the consuming farm permission to the published service application.

Business Data Connectivity

To publish the Business Data Connectivity service application, complete the prerequisite steps outlined at the beginning of the "Publishing Service Applications" section earlier in this chapter.

On the publishing farm, follow these steps:

1. On the Start menu, click All Programs.

2. Click Microsoft SharePoint 2010 Products.

3. Click SharePoint 2010 Management Shell.

4. At the command prompt (PS>) enter:

```
$security=Get-SPServiceApplication <GUID>| Get-SPServiceApplicationSecurity
$provider=(Get-SPClaimProvider System).ClaimProvider
$principal=New-SPClaimsPrincipal -ClaimType
     "http://schemas.microsoft.com/sharepoint/2009/08/claims/farmid"
     -ClaimProvider $provider -ClaimValue <Consuming Farm Id>
Grant-SPObjectSecurity -Identity $security -Principal $principal
     -Rights <NamedAccessRights>
Set-SPServiceApplicationSecurity <GUID> -ObjectSecurity $security
```

Replace the values for `<GUID>`, `<Consuming Farm Id>`, and `<NamedAccessRights>` with the values returned from the previous steps. Optionally, to return the consuming farm `Id`, run `Get-SPFarm | Select Id` in the SharePoint 2010 Management Shell on the consuming farm to return its `Id`, and then run `Get-SPServiceApplicationSecurity.<GUID>.NamedRights` to return the name of the access rights on the publishing farm. To determine the Service Application GUID for the service application to be published, run `Get-SPServiceApplication` on the publishing farm, and locate the GUID associated with the service application to be published.

To publish a service application, on the publishing farm, follow these steps:

1. On the Start menu, click All Programs.

2. Click Microsoft SharePoint 2010 Products.

3. Click SharePoint 2010 Management Shell.

4. At the command prompt (PS>) enter:

```
Get-SPServiceApplication
```

Locate the desired service application and note the GUID associated with it, as shown in Figure 10-15.

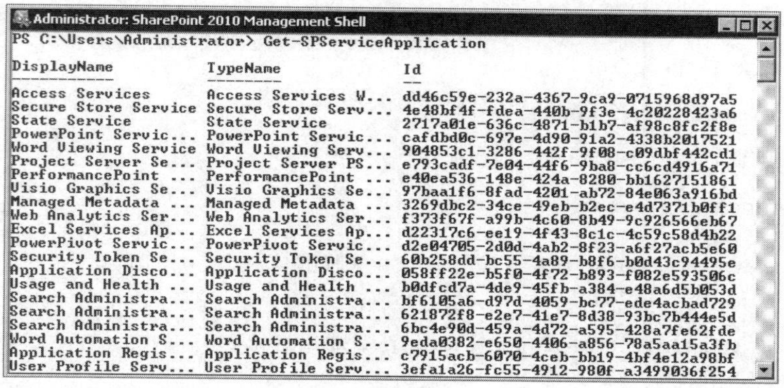

FIGURE 10-15: Service application GUID

At the command prompt (PS>), enter the following:

```
Publish-SPServiceApplication -Identity <Service Application GUID>
```

At the command prompt (PS>), enter the following:

```
Get-SPTopologyServiceApplication
```

Note the information returned from the previous cmdlet. This information will be used when configuring the consuming farm.

On the consuming farm, follow these steps:

1. On the Start menu, click All Programs.

2. Click Microsoft SharePoint 2010 Products.

3. Click SharePoint 2010 Management Shell.

4. At the command prompt (PS>), enter the following:

```
Receive-SPServiceApplicationConnectionInfo -FarmUrl
     <Publishing Farm Topology URL>
New-SPBusinessDataCatalogServiceApplicationProxy
     -Name " <Service Application Proxy Name>"
     -Url "<Publishing Farm Topology URL>"
```

Replace <Service Application Proxy Name> with a unique identifier that represents the service application that will be consumed (for example, Business Data Connectivity service application).

Replace <Publishing Farm Topology URL> with the information returned by the Get-SPTopologyServiceApplication cmdlet on the publishing farm.

Managed Metadata

To publish the MMS, complete the prerequisite steps outlined at the beginning of the "Publishing Service Applications" section earlier in this chapter.

On the publishing farm, follow these steps:

1. On the Start menu, click All Programs.

2. Click Microsoft SharePoint 2010 Products.

3. Click SharePoint 2010 Management Shell.

4. At the command prompt (PS>), enter the following:

```
$security=Get-SPServiceApplication <GUID>| Get-SPServiceApplicationSecurity
$provider=(Get-SPClaimProvider System).ClaimProvider
$principal=New-SPClaimsPrincipal
    -ClaimType "http://schemas.microsoft.com/sharepoint/2009/08/
    claims/farmid" -ClaimProvider $provider
    -ClaimValue <Consuming Farm Id>
Grant-SPObjectSecurity -Identity $security
    -Principal $principal -Rights <NamedAccessRights>
Set-SPServiceApplicationSecurity <GUID> -ObjectSecurity $security
```

Replace the values for *<GUID>*, *<Consuming Farm Id>*, and *<NamedAccessRights>* with the values returned from the previous steps. Optionally, to return the consuming farm Id, run `Get-SPFarm | Select Id` in the SharePoint 2010 Management Shell on the consuming farm to return its Id, and then run `Get-SPServiceApplicationSecurity.<GUID>.NamedRights` to return the name of the access rights on the publishing farm. To determine the service application GUID for the service application to be published, run `Get-SPServiceApplication` on the publishing farm, and locate the GUID associated with the service application to be published.

To publish a service application, on the publishing farm, follow these steps:

1. On the Start menu, click All Programs.

2. Click Microsoft SharePoint 2010 Products.

3. Click SharePoint 2010 Management Shell.

4. At the command prompt (PS>), enter the following:

```
Get-SPServiceApplication
```

Locate the desired service application and note the GUID associated with it, as shown earlier in Figure 10-15.

At the command prompt (PS>), enter the following:

```
Publish-SPServiceApplication -Identity <Service Application GUID>
```

At the command prompt (PS>), enter the following:

```
Get-SPTopologyServiceApplication
```

Note the information returned from the previous cmdlet. This information will be used when configuring the consuming farm, as shown earlier in Figure 10-14.

On the consuming farm, follow these steps:

1. On the Start menu, click All Programs.

2. Click Microsoft SharePoint 2010 Products.

3. Click SharePoint 2010 Management Shell.

4. At the command prompt (PS>), enter the following:

```
Receive-SPServiceApplicationConnectionInfo
    -FarmUrl <Publishing Farm Topology URL>
New-SPMetadataServiceApplicationProxy
    -Name " <Service Application Proxy Name>"
    -Url "<Publishing Farm Topology URL>"
```

Replace *<Service Application Proxy Name>* with a unique identifier that represents the service application that will be consumed (for example, Managed Metadata Service).

Replace *<Publishing Farm Topology URL>* with the information returned by the Get-SPTopologyServiceApplication cmdlet on the publishing farm.

User Profile Service

To publish the User Profile Service Application, complete the prerequisite steps outlined at the beginning of the "Publishing Service Applications" section earlier in this chapter.

On the publishing farm, follow these steps:

1. On the Start menu, click All Programs.

2. Click Microsoft SharePoint 2010 Products.

3. Click SharePoint 2010 Management Shell.

4. At the command prompt (PS>), enter the following:

```
$security=Get-SPServiceApplication <GUID>| Get-SPServiceApplicationSecurity
$provider=(Get-SPClaimProvider System).ClaimProvider
$principal=New-SPClaimsPrincipal
    -ClaimType "http://schemas.microsoft.com/sharepoint/2009/08/
    claims/farmid" -ClaimProvider $provider
    -ClaimValue <Consuming Farm Id>
Grant-SPObjectSecurity -Identity $security
    -Principal $principal -Rights <NamedAccessRights>
Set-SPServiceApplicationSecurity <GUID> -ObjectSecurity $security
```

Replace the values for *<GUID>*, *<Consuming Farm Id>*, and *<NamedAccessRights>* with the values returned from the previous steps. Optionally, to return the consuming farm Id, run Get-SPFarm | Select Id in the SharePoint 2010 Management Shell on the consuming farm to return its Id, and then run Get-SPServiceApplicationSecurity.<GUID>.NamedRights to return the name of the access rights on the publishing farm. To determine the service application GUID for the service application to be published, run Get-SPServiceApplication on the publishing farm and locate the GUID associated with the service application to be published.

To publish a service application, on the publishing farm, follow these steps:

1. On the Start menu, click All Programs.

2. Click Microsoft SharePoint 2010 Products.

3. Click SharePoint 2010 Management Shell.

4. At the command prompt (PS>), enter the following:

```
Get-SPServiceApplication
```

Locate the desired service application and note the GUID associated with it, as shown earlier in Figure 10-15.

At the command prompt (PS>), enter the following:

```
Publish-SPServiceApplication -Identity <Service Application GUID>
```

At the command prompt (PS>), enter the following:

```
Get-SPTopologyServiceApplication
```

Note the information returned from the previous cmdlet. This information will be used when configuring the consuming farm, as shown earlier in Figure 10-14.

On the consuming farm, follow these steps:

1. On the Start menu, click All Programs.

2. Click Microsoft SharePoint 2010 Products.

3. Click SharePoint 2010 Management Shell.

4. At the command prompt (PS>), enter the following:

```
Receive-SPServiceApplicationConnectionInfo
    -FarmUrl <Publishing Farm Topology URL>
New-SPUserProfileServiceApplicationProxy
    -Name " <Service Application Proxy Name>"
    -Url "<Publishing Farm Topology URL>"
```

Replace `<Service Application Proxy Name>` with a unique identifier that represents the service application that will be consumed (for example, Business Data Connectivity service application).

Replace `<Publishing Farm Topology URL>` with the information returned by the `Get-SPTopologyServiceApplication` cmdlet on the publishing farm.

Search

To publish the Search service application, complete the prerequisite steps outlined at the beginning of the "Publishing Service Applications" section earlier in this chapter.

On the publishing farm, follow these steps:

1. On the Start menu, click All Programs.

2. Click Microsoft SharePoint 2010 Products.

3. Click SharePoint 2010 Management Shell.

4. At the command prompt (PS>), enter the following:

```
$security=Get-SPServiceApplication <GUID>| Get-SPServiceApplicationSecurity
$provider=(Get-SPClaimProvider System).ClaimProvider
$principal=New-SPClaimsPrincipal
    -ClaimType "http://schemas.microsoft.com/sharepoint/2009/08/
    claims/farmid" -ClaimProvider $provider
    -ClaimValue <Consuming Farm Id>
Grant-SPObjectSecurity -Identity $security
    -Principal $principal -Rights <NamedAccessRights>
Set-SPServiceApplicationSecurity <GUID> -ObjectSecurity $security
```

Replace the values for *<GUID>*, *<Consuming Farm Id>*, and *<NamedAccessRights>* with the values returned from the previous steps. Optionally, to return the consuming farm Id, run Get-SPFarm | Select Id in the SharePoint 2010 Management Shell on the consuming farm to return its Id, and then run Get-SPServiceApplicationSecurity.<GUID>.NamedRights to return the name of the access rights on the publishing farm. To determine the service application GUID for the service application to be published, run Get-SPServiceApplication on the publishing farm, and locate the GUID associated with the service application to be published.

To publish a service application, on the publishing farm, follow these steps:

1. On the Start menu, click All Programs.

2. Click Microsoft SharePoint 2010 Products.

3. Click SharePoint 2010 Management Shell.

4. At the command prompt (PS>), enter the following:

```
Get-SPServiceApplication
```

Locate the desired service application and note the GUID associated with it, as shown earlier in Figure 10-15.

At the command prompt (PS>), enter the following:

```
Publish-SPServiceApplication -Identity <Service Application GUID>
```

At the command prompt (PS>), enter the following:

```
Get-SPTopologyServiceApplication
```

Note the information returned from the previous cmdlet. This information will be used when configuring the consuming farm, as shown earlier in Figure 10-14.

On the consuming farm, follow these steps:

1. On the Start menu, click All Programs.

2. Click Microsoft SharePoint 2010 Products.

3. Click SharePoint 2010 Management Shell.

4. At the command prompt (PS>), enter the following:

```
Receive-SPServiceApplicationConnectionInfo
    -FarmUrl <Publishing Farm Topology URL>
New-SPEnterpriseSearchServiceApplicationProxy
    -Name " <Service Application Proxy Name>"
    -Url "<Publishing Farm Topology URL>"
```

Replace <Service Application Proxy Name> with a unique identifier that represents the service application that will be consumed (for example, Search service application).

Replace <Publishing Farm Topology URL> with the information returned by the Get-SPTopologyServiceApplication cmdlet on the publishing farm.

Secure Store

To publish the Secure Store Service application, complete the prerequisite steps outlined at the beginning of the "Publishing Service Applications" section earlier in this chapter.

On the publishing farm, follow these steps:

1. On the Start menu, click All Programs.

2. Click Microsoft SharePoint 2010 Products.

3. Click SharePoint 2010 Management Shell.

4. At the command prompt (PS>), enter the following:

```
$security=Get-SPServiceApplication <GUID>| Get-SPServiceApplicationSecurity
$provider=(Get-SPClaimProvider System).ClaimProvider
$principal=New-SPClaimsPrincipal
    -ClaimType "http://schemas.microsoft.com/sharepoint/2009/08/
    claims/farmid" -ClaimProvider $provider
    -ClaimValue <Consuming Farm Id>
Grant-SPObjectSecurity -Identity $security
    -Principal $principal -Rights <NamedAccessRights>
Set-SPServiceApplicationSecurity <GUID> -ObjectSecurity $security
```

Replace the values for <GUID>, <Consuming Farm Id>, and <NamedAccessRights> with the values returned from the previous steps. Optionally, to return the consuming farm Id, run Get-SPFarm | Select Id in the SharePoint 2010 Management Shell on the consuming farm to return its Id, and then run Get-SPServiceApplicationSecurity.<GUID>.NamedRights to return the name of the access rights on the publishing farm. To determine the service application GUID for the service application to be published, run Get-SPServiceApplication on the publishing farm, and locate the GUID associated with the service application to be published.

To publish a service application, on the publishing farm, follow these steps:

1. On the Start menu, click All Programs.
2. Click Microsoft SharePoint 2010 Products.
3. Click SharePoint 2010 Management Shell.
4. At the command prompt (PS>), enter the following:

```
Get-SPServiceApplication
```

Locate the desired service application and note the GUID associated with it, as shown earlier in Figure 10-15.

At the command prompt (PS>), enter the following:

```
Publish-SPServiceApplication -Identity <Service Application GUID>
```

At the command prompt (PS>), enter the following:

```
Get-SPTopologyServiceApplication
```

Note the information returned from the previous cmdlet. This information will be used when configuring the consuming farm, as shown earlier in Figure 10-14.

On the consuming farm, follow these steps:

1. On the Start menu, click All Programs.
2. Click Microsoft SharePoint 2010 Products.
3. Click SharePoint 2010 Management Shell.
4. At the command prompt (PS>), enter the following:

```
Receive-SPServiceApplicationConnectionInfo
    -FarmUrl <Publishing Farm Topology URL>
New-SPSecureStoreServiceApplicationProxy
    -Name " <Service Application Proxy Name>"
    -Url "<Publishing Farm Topology URL>"
```

Replace `<Service Application Proxy Name>` with a unique identifier that represents the service application that will be consumed (for example, Secure Store Service application).

Replace `<Publishing Farm Topology URL>` with the information returned by the `Get-SPTopologyServiceApplication` cmdlet on the publishing farm.

Web Analytics

To publish the Web Analytics service application, complete the prerequisite steps outlined at the beginning of the "Publishing Service Applications" section earlier in this chapter.

On the publishing farm, follow these steps:

1. On the Start menu, click All Programs.

2. Click Microsoft SharePoint 2010 Products.

3. Click SharePoint 2010 Management Shell.

4. At the command prompt (PS>), enter the following:

```
$security=Get-SPServiceApplication <GUID>| Get-SPServiceApplicationSecurity
$provider=(Get-SPClaimProvider System).ClaimProvider
$principal=New-SPClaimsPrincipal
     -ClaimType "http://schemas.microsoft.com/sharepoint/2009/08/
     claims/farmid" -ClaimProvider $provider -ClaimValue <Consuming Farm Id>
Grant-SPObjectSecurity -Identity $security
     -Principal $principal -Rights <NamedAccessRights>
Set-SPServiceApplicationSecurity <GUID> -ObjectSecurity $security
```

Replace the values for *<GUID>*, *<Consuming Farm Id>*, and *<NamedAccessRights>* with the values returned from the previous steps. Optionally, to return the consuming farm Id, run Get-SPFarm | Select Id in the SharePoint 2010 Management Shell on the consuming farm to return its Id, and then run Get-SPServiceApplicationSecurity.<GUID>.NamedRights to return the name of the access rights on the publishing farm. To determine the service application GUID for the service application to be published run Get-SPServiceApplication on the publishing farm, and locate the GUID associated with the service application to be published.

To publish a service application, on the publishing farm, follow these steps:

1. On the Start menu, click All Programs.

2. Click Microsoft SharePoint 2010 Products.

3. Click SharePoint 2010 Management Shell.

4. At the command prompt (PS>), enter the following:

```
Get-SPServiceApplication
```

Locate the desired service application and note the GUID associated with it, as shown earlier in Figure 10-15.

At the command prompt (PS>), enter the following:

```
Publish-SPServiceApplication -Identity <Service Application GUID>
```

At the command prompt (PS>), enter the following:

```
Get-SPTopologyServiceApplication
```

Note the information returned from the previous cmdlet. This information will be used when configuring the consuming farm, as shown in Figure 10-14.

On the consuming farm, follow these steps:

1. On the Start menu, click All Programs.

2. Click Microsoft SharePoint 2010 Products.

3. Click SharePoint 2010 Management Shell.

4. At the command prompt (PS>), enter the following:

```
Receive-SPServiceApplicationConnectionInfo
     -FarmUrl <Publishing Farm Topology URL>
New-SPWebAnalyticsServiceApplicationProxy
     -Name " <Service Application Proxy Name>"
     -Url "<Publishing Farm Topology URL>"
```

Replace <Service Application Proxy Name> with a unique identifier that represents the service application that will be consumed, for example Web Analytics service application.

Replace <Publishing Farm Topology URL> with the information returned by the Get-SPTopologyServiceApplication cmdlet on the publishing farm.

Wide Area Networks

Some service applications in SharePoint 2010 can be published over wide area networks (WANs). This topology is useful when users are geographically distributed across multiple regions or localities.

For example, an organization may have a centralized data center with users from a corporate headquarters clustered around that data center. However, regional users comprise the manufacturing operations, and are distributed across the continent. To accommodate such a distribution, the organization could establish a primary intranet deployment in the primary data center, and extend or publish individual service applications over the WAN to support deployments in the regional locations.

In SharePoint 2010, service applications provide several improvements that enable support for latent links or limited throughput. These improvements include the following:

➤ Communication is over HTTP as opposed to direct database access (as in Office SharePoint Server 2007).

➤ Service applications are built on Windows Communications Foundation (WCF), which provides an optimized protocol that utilizes binary streams as opposed to XML.

SharePoint 2010 supports publishing the following service applications over WANs:

➤ Search

➤ MMS

➤ BBCS

Figure 10-16 shows a web application with a custom proxy group that is using both local service applications and consuming remote service applications from an enterprise services farm. It also shows two MMSs being consumed by a single web app. The MMS permits this, so you end up getting your corporate taxonomy from the enterprise services MMS, and it is merged (in the form of a union) with the MMS created just for this specialized web app.

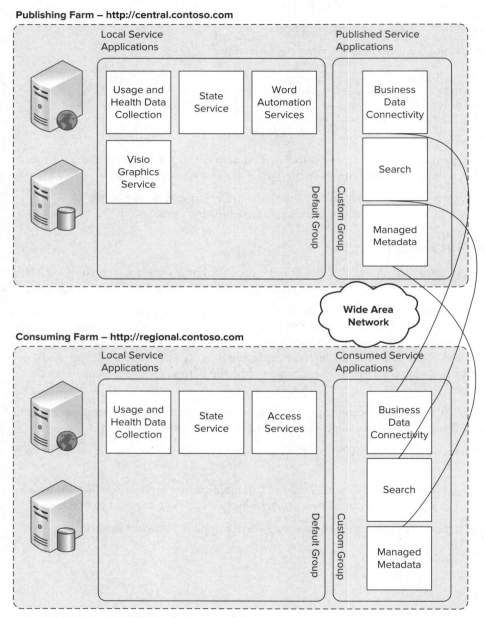

Publishing Farm – http://central.contoso.com

Local Service Applications

Published Service Applications

Usage and Health Data Collection

State Service

Word Automation Services

Business Data Connectivity

Visio Graphics Service

Search

Managed Metadata

Default Group

Custom Group

Wide Area Network

Consuming Farm – http://regional.contoso.com

Local Service Applications

Consumed Service Applications

Usage and Health Data Collection

State Service

Access Services

Business Data Connectivity

Search

Managed Metadata

Default Group

Custom Group

FIGURE 10-16: Service applications over WANs

Putting It All Together

Federation or publishing of service applications is beneficial in a number of deployment scenarios. For example, entire farms can be dedicated to service hosting, enabling centralized shared computing investments for very intense services such as Web Analytics or Search.

With SharePoint 2010, you can configure each web application to use service applications from different server farms. For example, you can share the Search service application across web applications in several server farms, while limiting PerformancePoint Services use to the local environment. This flexibility enables both the distribution of load through the isolation of compute-intensive applications, and improved end-user adoption. This enables the simplicity of providing only the services required to support the needs of the users.

SEARCH TOPOLOGIES

Deciding on the appropriate Search topology should take into consideration the same factors used when planning the server farm topology.

As shown in Figure 10-17, Search in Office SharePoint Server 2007 was provided through a single SSP. Its assets (that is, crawl history and metadata tables) were contained within a single database. Both query and index servers maintained a single copy of the flat-file index.

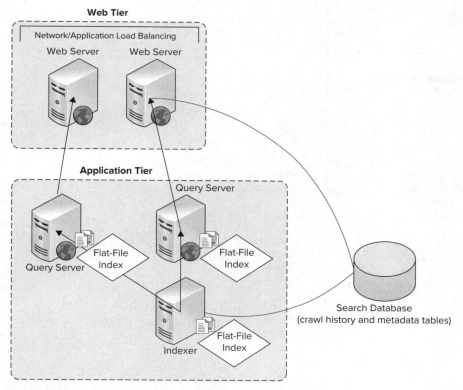

FIGURE 10-17: Office SharePoint Server 2007 Search architecture

Index servers could be associated with a single SSP, thus limiting scale, flexibility, and resiliency. Search in Office SharePoint Server 2007 was capable of scaling up to 50 million items, at which point the system was limited as a result of sharing the database across crawling and querying, and a single homogenous flat-file index. These constraints were exacerbated beyond 50 million items, and resulted in decreases in crawl performance, as well as query latencies and throughput.

As shown in Figure 10-18, SharePoint Server 2010 addresses these constraints and limitations by splitting the system into multiple, independently scalable components that include crawl components (indexer), crawl history and metadata databases, index partitions (query), and an administration component that includes an associated search administration database to store configuration information.

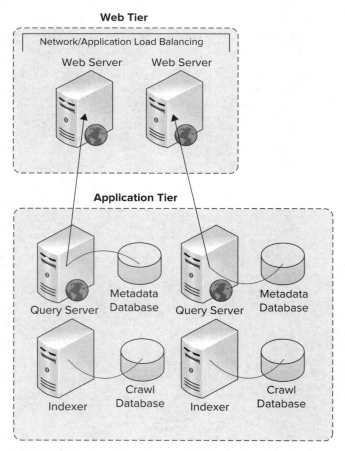

FIGURE 10-18: SharePoint Server 2010 Search architecture

The Search components in SharePoint Server 2010 are distributed across two primary elements, the query and crawl architectures, as shown in Figure 10-19.

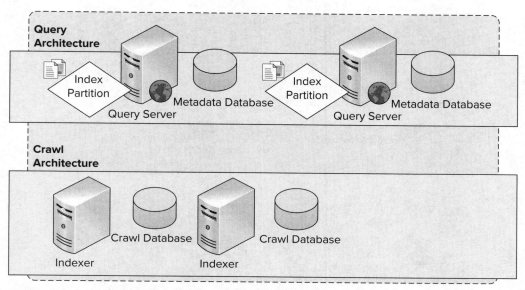

FIGURE 10-19: SharePoint Server 2010 Search architecture elements

Query Architecture

In SharePoint Server 2010 Search, the query architecture consists of query components, index partitions, and property or metadata databases.

➤ The query component returns search results to the query originator or end user. Each query component is part of an index partition, which is associated with a specific property database that contains metadata associated with a specific set of crawled content.

➤ An index partition represents a logical portion of the cumulative index, and is associated with the query component.

Figure 10-20 shows an example where the topology includes three index partitions and a single query component, with each query component hosting a third of the index. This scenario maximizes throughput by enabling parallelism when handling and responding to query requests submitted by end users.

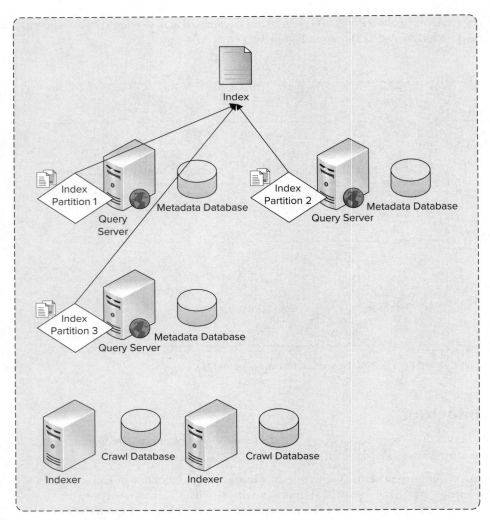

FIGURE 10-20: Index partitions

As shown in Figure 10-21, index partitions can be associated with one or more query components. Deploying multiple query components for a given index partition is useful where a high level of redundancy is required. The recommended initial Search topology should be instantiated with two query components configured for each index partition residing on separate server machines. This configuration will effectively provide a mirror of the index partition, and, in the event a server is lost or becomes inaccessible, the remaining server can continue to respond to queries submitted by end users.

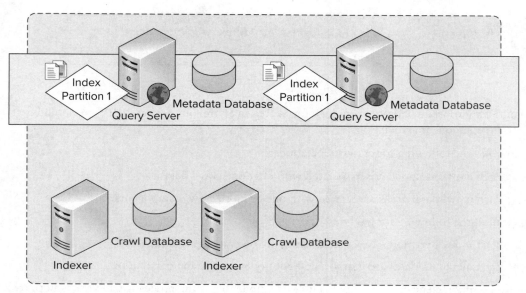

FIGURE 10-21: Mirrored index partitions

Crawl Architecture

In SharePoint Server 2010, the crawl architecture consists of crawl components, crawl databases, and property or metadata databases.

➤ The crawl component produces portions of the index (per index partition) and propagates them to the server machines hosting the query components associated with the specific index partition.

➤ The crawl database manages crawl operations and stores the crawl history. Each crawl database can be associated with multiple crawl components to provide redundancy where each crawl component crawls a separate portion of content during indexing.

➤ The property or metadata database stores properties of the crawled content. Scaling out the property database depends on the volume of content crawled (also known as the *corpus*) and the amount of metadata associated with each item in the scope of the crawl.

The flexibility afforded through Search in SharePoint Server 2010 enables you to address and mitigate system bottlenecks. For example, if you determine the SQL Server database is the bottleneck, you can add additional databases and scale out. Or, if the crawl process is the bottleneck, you can seamlessly add additional crawler machines to the topology.

The topics of scaling up and scaling out are addressed in more detail later in this chapter.

To plan the appropriate scale-out topology for Search in SharePoint Server 2010, you should first understand component associations.

Keep in mind the following for crawl associations:

➤ Each crawl component is associated with only one crawl database.

➤ Each crawl database is associated with one or more crawl components.

Keep in mind the following for query associations:

➤ Each index partition is associated with only one metadata database.

➤ Each metadata database is associated with one or more index partitions.

The most common element to scale out is indexing. Indexing is the process that extracts both text and property information from files stored in content databases and/or on remote, networked hosts such as file shares. Indexing extracts the content by using filter components that understand a file's format (known as *IFilters*). Indexing then merges the extracted information into catalogs of indexes for efficient searches, combining both databases and flat-file indexes.

In short, indexing is the overall process of filtering, creating index entries, and merging them into catalogs to enable efficient lookup of information in a server farm. As a result, indexing can be a resource-intensive operation, depending on the size of the overall search corpus or content sources that are crawled.

You have two options when considering scaling out the indexing process:

➤ Separate the indexing process across machines

➤ Distribute crawler history across databases

In SharePoint Server 2010 Search, the appropriate topology is defined not only by performance and resiliency, but should also consider scale. In SharePoint Server 2010, each crawl component is capable of crawling or indexing up to 10 million items, at which point an additional crawl component should be instantiated in the topology, whether on the same machine hosting the initial crawl component where sufficient resources exist, or through instantiating a new crawl component on a new machine.

Figure 10-22 provides a planning base when considering the most appropriate Search topology, and describes each of the Search services component characteristics.

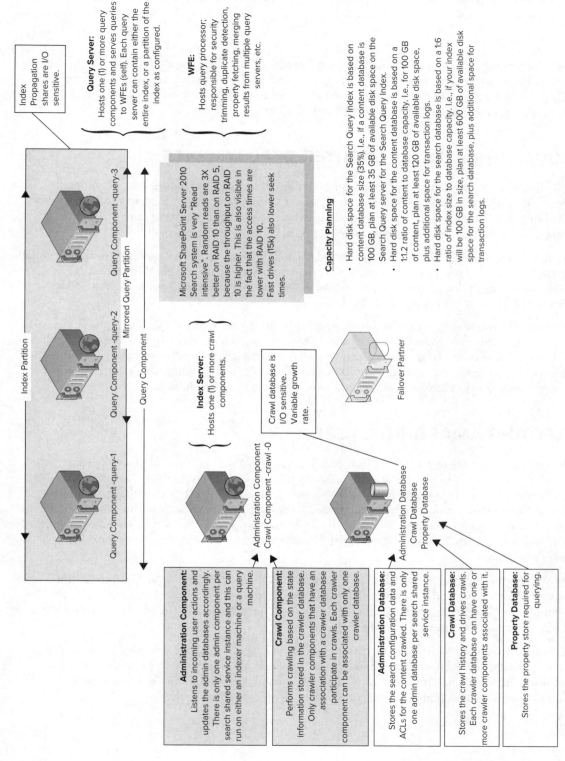

FIGURE 10-22: Search planning guide

When planning your Search architecture, it is important to understand both the impact of these components on server machine resources (where bottlenecks can occur) and what components bottlenecks are associated with. You should also consider the resiliency of both the physical and logical components associated with the SharePoint 2010 Search service.

GEOGRAPHICALLY DISTRIBUTED DEPLOYMENTS

Geographically distributed deployments refer to distributing SharePoint resources to support regional or global users. For example, an organization may have its headquarters in Seattle, Washington. However, many users may be distributed globally to support various corporate functions, or to respond to opportunities in specific geographic locations.

In this scenario, it can be costly to deploy a dedicated instance of SharePoint 2010 to support small pockets of users. Therefore, the organization may opt to introduce WAN optimization devices, whether symmetric or asymmetric, to accommodate latency or leverage technologies such as BranchCache in Windows Server 2008 R2.

In scenarios where the geographically dispersed user base is substantial enough to justify the cost of a localized, dedicated SharePoint 2010 deployment, an organization can opt to federate or publish service applications from the centralized server farm to the distributed server farms. This provides a unified experience to the remote user base. You could optionally isolate these server farms to support regulatory compliance related to those specific geographic locations.

SELECTING AN ARCHITECTURE

In many cases, selecting the appropriate architecture for your SharePoint 2010 deployment is the result of business and financial drivers. Selecting the appropriate architecture for SharePoint 2010 is the most important decision in topology planning, because the selected architecture will dictate its future capability to scale as demand grows. As documented previously in this chapter, a medium server farm provides the most flexible initial deployment topology that can be scaled both vertically and horizontally, and can seamlessly expand its scope to support both disaster recovery and high availability.

When considering your SharePoint 2010 architecture, it is important to consider extensibility, scalability, security, and how your architecture will map to those concerns and requirements. You should also consider how the logical architecture will be bound to the foundation provided through the physical architecture of your environment.

Consider not only how your design choices will impact capabilities, but also how well it will align to your business objectives. For example, what problems are you trying to solve with your deployment — reducing total cost of ownership, indexing large quantities of information, implementing high availability, or a combination of all of these objectives?

Once your objectives are clearly defined, you can move on to the next steps in the planning process, which include the following:

➤ Determining your administrative model

➤ Identifying costs

➤ Determining Service Level Agreements (SLAs) to include Recovery Point Objectives (RPOs) and Recovery Time Objectives (RTOs)

Determining an Administrative Model

Within its hierarchy, SharePoint 2010 provides management services at a number of levels, including the farm level, service application level, and site collection/site level.

The farm-level administrator manages the overall server farm environment through SharePoint 2010 Central Administration, or, optionally, through the SharePoint 2010 Management Shell using Windows PowerShell. More than one individual can be a farm administrator to manage the server farm through SharePoint 2010 Central Administration, or through the SharePoint 2010 Management Shell. Permissions for farm administrators can be assigned through SharePoint 2010 Central Administration, or through Local Users and Groups in the event the delegated administrator requires interactive logon access to machines that comprise the deployment.

New in SharePoint 2010 is the capability to delegate the administration of individual service applications by assigning permissions to individuals or groups of individuals to manage services (such as Search or the MMS). By delegating the administration of service applications, the service application administrator is able to perform all of the administrative tasks related to that service application. However, this administrator cannot manage other service applications or settings contained in Central Administration.

Site collection and site administrators manage the aspects of site collections and sites, such as creation of subsites, adding and removing users, and other administrative tasks associated with that scope.

Identifying Costs

When selecting a SharePoint 2010 architecture, is it important to ensure that the architecture will be within any cost boundaries or constraints that are associated with the service. These factors include the procurement of hardware and software necessary to deploy SharePoint 2010.

For example, you should determine whether existing hardware can be used or repurposed to support your deployment, or whether new hardware will be required — particularly where demand is expected to increase over time. Modeling software costs includes determining the cost of both server and client access licenses.

Determining Service Level Agreements

SLAs define agreements between the organization and service owners. SLAs can include communication protocols, performance requirements, and uptime guarantees (such as the availability expectations associated with the service). An aggressive availability expectation (such as the capability to support 99.99 percent availability) can require additional hardware in order to meet those expectations.

In short, a properly planned architecture will provide the flexibility to continuously scale or contract as business requirements dictate. Ensuring this flexibility should take many factors into account, such as those documented here, as well as unique requirements associated with your organization.

SCALING YOUR ARCHITECTURE

When selecting a topology, it is important to consider both your current and future needs to ensure that the environment provides the best possible flexibility to meet future demand, and offers both performance and high availability. SharePoint 2010 can be scaled both vertically and horizontally, depending on your individual needs. Assessing these needs is an important step in planning your scale strategy.

As demand or business requirements change over time, you must consider whether to scale up (vertically) or scale out (horizontally) to accommodate that demand or change in business requirements. The decision to scale up or scale out is commonly the result of performance monitoring used to identify physical bottlenecks and determine which resources are overused or nearing capacity. In some scenarios, these decisions may be based on whether redundant components are needed to provide high availability.

Factors Affecting Scaling

The most important factors influencing a scale-up or scale-out decision can be categorized as follows:

➤ Processor (compute)

➤ Memory

➤ Disk

Processor

Web and application servers are most commonly constrained by their processing capabilities because of factors that include a large number of worker processes, Secure Sockets Layer (SSL) encryption, and/or performance optimizations such as HTTP compression. Addressing processor bottlenecks most commonly requires scaling up by adding compute capacity through additional physical or logical processors.

Memory

Memory bottlenecks can occur across a server farm as the result of a large number of worker processes, query execution, or search indexing. In many cases, isolated increases in memory utilization can be addressed through increasing the physical memory associated with the constrained server machine. However, sustained high levels of memory utilization should be approached from a scale-out perspective, introducing additional server machines to share the load.

Disk

Disk bottlenecks are most often isolated to the Database tier. Disk bottlenecks can result in increased processing time, delaying the response to end users for such things as page requests. Disk bottlenecks are most commonly addressed by increasing the number of disks allocated to a Logical Unit Number (LUN), increasing the overall I/O available to that LUN, and the databases that reside on it. As a best practice, write optimized Redundant Array of Inexpensive Disks (RAID) sets (such as RAID 1+0 or RAID 0+1) to address the broadest range of I/O and provide the highest level of redundancy.

Deciding to Scale Up

When you scale up a topology, you employ a vertical scale, or, upgrade the hardware components within a server farm to address a specific bottleneck (such as processors, memory, and/or disk I/O). Scaling up defines the addressing of the resources assigned directly to one or more servers in the server farm (such as increasing available memory).

For example, a scale-up decision may be considered where it is determined insufficient memory exists on web and application servers to manage the running worker processes assigned to individual application pools. In this example, if you scale out the Web and/or Application tier using similar hardware, you will be constrained by the same challenges as worker processes associated with web applications, and service applications will be deployed to each node introduced in the topology.

Deciding to Scale Out

When you scale out a topology, you employ horizontal scale, which means the addition of compute units to support an increase in overall demand.

For example, an organization may elect to add web servers to a topology to increase performance, more efficiently distribute load, and, as a result, improve the user experience and performance of the server farm and its operations. Conversely, an organization may elect to add additional database servers to distribute load within a server farm between the Web and Application tiers, or to provide redundancy to support high availability within the server farm.

In a typical scale-out server deployment, multiple web servers share a single database server on a remote SQL Server instance. Figure 10-23 shows an example of a typical scale-out server deployment configuration with a remote SQL Server instance. Deploying SharePoint 2010 in a scale-out deployment provides a highly available and scalable topology.

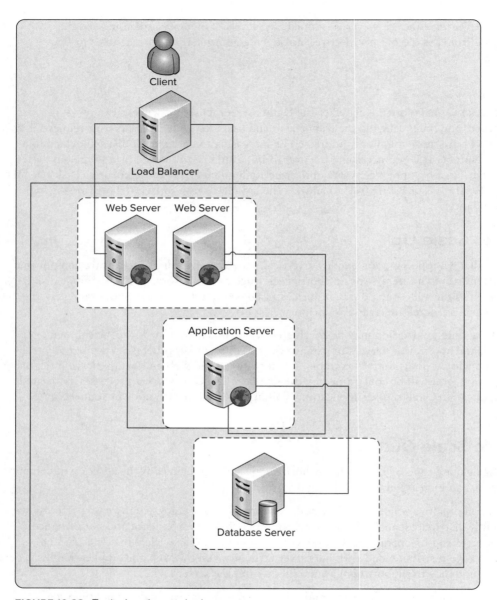

FIGURE 10-23: Typical scale-out deployment

A scale-out server deployment is recommended in the following circumstances and scenarios:

➤ High-collaboration environments where concurrent users or frequency of content updates is the measured value, resulting in decreased processing or rendering times

➤ High-availability scenarios where unplanned downtime is sought to be prevented

➤ To improve the performance of operations and service delivery to end users

Depending on the elected database server configuration in a scale-out deployment, you may be limited to specific versions of SQL Server and the hardware on which it operates — such as failover clustering, or optionally, for a higher degree of hardware flexibility, database mirroring may be considered.

Figure 10-24 shows an example of a scale-out server deployment configuration where SharePoint is deployed on an instance that is part of a failover cluster. By implementing a failover cluster, you can enhance the fault tolerance of SharePoint 2010.

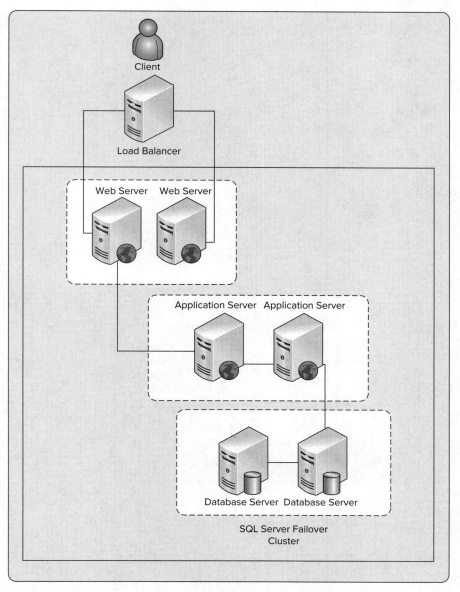

FIGURE 10-24: Scale-out server deployment with failover clustering

In addition to the typical scale-out deployment, it may become necessary to implement an advanced scale-out deployment to support additional performance and resiliency. For example, load-balancing servers can be used to distribute load more evenly and provide high availability within the Web and/or Application tiers. Figure 10-25 shows an example of an advanced scale-out server deployment.

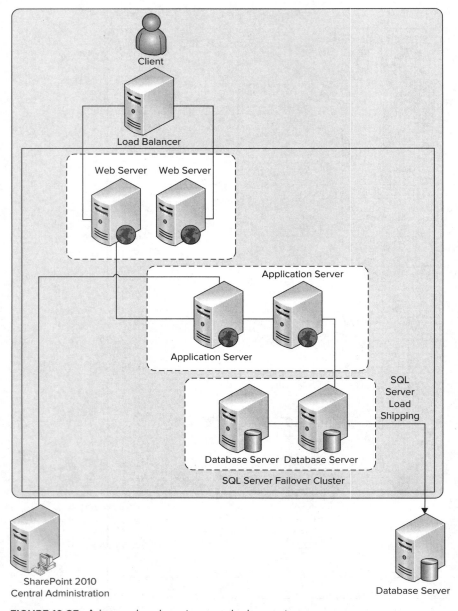

FIGURE 10-25: Advanced scale-out server deployment

The advanced scale-out deployment benefits from many of the same advantages associated with standard scale-out deployments. However, this deployment is optimized for performance through the separation of load-balanced web servers to distribute user requests, multiple application servers to distribute service application services (such as Search processing), and clustered database servers in an Active Directory configuration to provide load distribution within the server farm.

In summary, the following conditions are most commonly considered when planning a scale-out deployment configuration:

> The web, application, and/or database server(s) become a bottleneck attributed to the following conditions:

> > Compute resources are limited or are becoming over-extended, resulting in little to no headroom for growth.

> > Memory and/or I/O capacity is limited or has reached peak utilization, and additional servers are the only possibility for providing more resources.

> The costs associated with scaling up (vertical) are barriers to addressing resourcing within the server farm. For example, high processor utilization can be addressed by increasing the available physical processors, which is often more costly both in procurement and operations than the inclusion of a separate server instance.

> Scale-up does not sufficiently address the bottlenecks within the server farm (such as those associated with I/O or memory-constrained systems).

Considering the Trade-offs

Trade-offs are associated with scale-up and scale-out topologies:

> Scale-out topologies introduce a large number of server machines, thus increasing the operational complexity related to day-to-day management (such as the application of public and cumulative updates, as well as Service Packs).

> Scale-up topologies will generally result in increased capital expenditures because additive hardware is typically more costly than the addition of server hardware. This requires careful planning both to accommodate the required downtime, and development of mitigation plans in the event problems occur as the existing hardware is scaled.

Considering Network Performance

Communication across a network is critical to the performance of both SharePoint 2010 and the clients interacting with it. Often overlooked is network performance. However, it should be considered in the same category as other bottlenecks (such as processors or disk). The performance of your network has an impact on the performance of operations executed by end users. When optimizing SharePoint 2010 performance, you should also consider analyzing network performance, including the monitoring of traffic and resource utilization.

SharePoint 2010 requires that each machine within a server farm environment respond to each other within 1 ms (round-trip time, or RTT) to ensure intra-farm communication is efficient. Also, the storage subsystem should return the first byte of a request (time to first byte, or TTFB) in 20 ms.

There are two primary utilities for monitoring network performance — System Monitor and Network Monitor.

System Monitor

System Monitor periodically captures snapshots of system performance characteristics and displays that information in a visual and structured way through graphs. These can help to quickly identify issues and develop an action plan for future resource requirements.

Using System Monitor, you can create a new Network Interface Data Collector Set to capture information about resource utilization, and to monitor resources for potential spikes in activity, thus enabling you to trace issues back to their origins.

For additional information on how to create a log in System Monitor, see `http://support.microsoft.com/kb/248345`.

Network Monitor

Similar to System Monitor, Network Monitor can track network throughput as captured network traffic both locally and remotely (such as remote frames from other server machines on the network).

To learn more about Network Monitor, see `http://technet.microsoft.com/en-us/library/cc723623.aspx`.

Dealing with Network Bottlenecks

The most common network bottlenecks are related to overloaded servers or network components. Resolving network performance issues can be instrumented through several possible solutions, including the following:

➤ Using network cards with the highest available bandwidth

➤ Using adapters that support checksum offloading, IP Security (IPSEC) offloading, and large send offloading

➤ Placing different protocols on different adapters

➤ Using network adapters that support interrupt moderation

Considering Active Directory

Many SharePoint 2010 deployments continue to use Classic Mode, or Integrated Windows Authentication, which can increase the overall load on domain controllers because of the process through which clients are authenticated. When using Integrated Windows Authentication, the user is not initially prompted for credentials. This initial request is made anonymously, unless the current Windows user information can be used.

If the exchange fails, the user is prompted for credentials, which are processed using Integrated Windows Authentication. Users can be prompted up to three times for credentials, though, in the case where the user has logged on to the local computer as a domain user, then no authentication is required for computers on that domain.

Despite improvements in the management of authentication over time, it is important to weigh the impact of a SharePoint 2010 deployment on your domain controllers, particularly as business dynamics change through scenarios such as mergers and acquisitions, or making the service more broadly available to users (resulting in increased authentication load). Monitoring authentication is one method through which you can determine the impact on domain controllers — or, otherwise, following the guidance of one domain controller per every five web servers.

 For additional information on browser authentication see http://support.microsoft.com/default.aspx?scid=kb;EN-US;264921.

When monitoring authentication load on domain controllers, there are many approaches that cannot be covered here to include compute resource monitoring. A primary instance where monitoring should be considered is on the NETLOGON service. The NETLOGON service is a Local Security Authority Subsystem Service (LSASS) process that runs on each domain controller in a forest, and is responsible for verifying NTLM logon requests, in addition to registering, authenticating, and locating domain controllers. When monitoring or troubleshooting authentication problems, the NETLOGON service log files can be extremely useful for isolating potential issues, or planning future scale.

 For additional information on enabling debug logging for the NETLOGON service, see http://support.microsoft.com/kb/109626 *and* http://support.microsoft.com/default.aspx?scid=kb;EN-US;906736.

Local Security Authority Subsystem Service (LSASS)

The LSASS is a process responsible for enforcing the security policy on the system. LSASS verifies users logging on to a computer or server machine, manages password changes, and creates access tokens.

Monitoring the LSASS is an important step toward understanding the impact of increased authentication load on domain controllers. By using the Active Directory (AD) Data Collector Set in Performance Monitor on each domain controller, you can compile reports using performance counters and tracing to provide insight into potential problems that should be evaluated when troubleshooting issues related to authentication.

To use the AD Data Collector Set, open Server Manager on one or more domain controllers, and expand the `Diagnostics` node. Under the `Diagnostics` node, select Reliability and Performance ➪ Data Collector Sets ➪ System. Right-click Active Directory Diagnostics, and select Start from the list of available options.

Data collection will initiate and gather data for 5 minutes prior to compiling the report. Once the report is available, you should focus on issues where LSASS is causing high CPU utilization, in addition to looking at the specific Lightweight Directory Access Protocol (LDAP) queries that may be impacting server performance.

Domain controllers are often most affected by remote queries from computers in the environment. Using the network information in the report will help determine which remote clients are communicating most with the domain controller. In many cases, operations such as an AD import will result in application and/or web servers appearing in this section of the report. If a domain controller is found to be compute-starved and the problem cannot be attributed to problems on that server machine, consider adding additional domain controllers to accommodate the load.

ADTest.exe

When planning your SharePoint 2010 deployment, you may elect to proactively determine the load that could be generated as a result of authentication. `ADTest.exe` is a load-generation tool you can use that simulates client transactions on a host server to assess the performance of the domain controllers.

 To learn more about `ADTest.exe`, *see* www.microsoft.com/downloads/en/details.aspx?displaylang=en&FamilyID=4814fe3f-92ce-4871-b8a4-99f98b3f4338.

Using Service Farms

Service farms are intended to isolate service applications that would otherwise limit the scale and performance of environments where users are actively using the service (SharePoint 2010). Implementing service farms to isolate service applications enables the scale-out of server farms and scale-up of components to meet the demand and optimize performance of specific service applications.

For example, consider an organization that requires the indexing of a large search corpus and expects a high volume of user transactions to be related to search queries. The organization may consider deploying the Search service application to dedicated hardware components that comprise an isolated server farm. This enables the resources within the server farm where users actively collaborate to be optimized for that specific scenario, while providing the capability to leverage the services provided through the service farm.

Service farms are generally implemented when a specific service is expected to impact the resources available to the primary server farm, or when providing services to multiple server farm environments within an organization.

Figure 10-26 shows two server farms, with a services farm optimized for Search, and a second server farm that hosts any other service applications supported for that server farm's scenario or characteristics.

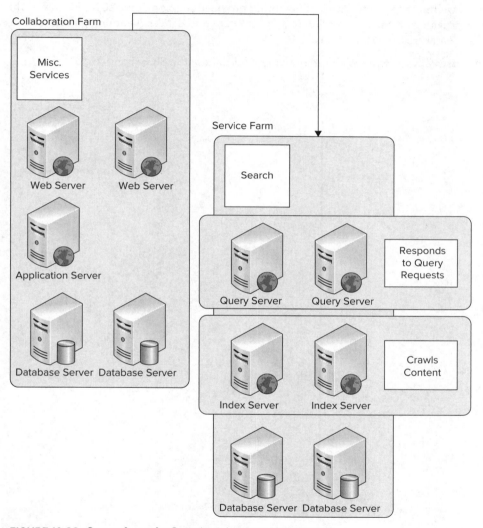

FIGURE 10-26: Server farms for Search and service applications

SUMMARY

Selecting the appropriate topology is essential to ensuring the delivery of a scalable deployment that meets both the current and future performance of your organization, as well as redundancy requirements. Topology planning should consider the business requirements today, and the potential needs of the future to ensure the deployment can scale seamlessly and evolve to support ever-changing business needs and scenarios.

This chapter provided the basic concepts and information to help you start thinking about these requirements, as well as the various levels of flexibility provided in SharePoint 2010. However, this chapter has not provided all the information required to plan and deliver the topologies needed for a variety of unique enterprise considerations.

Chapter 11 discusses how to work with internal and external data in SharePoint 2010.

11

Working with Internal and External Data in SharePoint 2010

By Paul Olenick

At its highest level, SharePoint data falls into one of two categories: *internal* or *external*. This chapter covers tools, options, and considerations for accessing, surfacing, and manipulating data in various scenarios.

Although many core concepts remain the same, the story around working with data has improved significantly in SharePoint 2010. Lists have been enhanced in the areas of relationships and validation, and managing large lists (a known pain point in previous versions) has become easier with query throttling. The Business Data Catalog (BDC) has been overhauled, and introduces new concepts such as the external list, which allows end users to interact with external data as if it was internal (including the capability to write back to the data source).

SharePoint developers will be pleased to learn about amazing new features in SharePoint 2010 such as multiple APIs to accommodate just about any programming scenario, additional events to hook in to for firing their custom code, and support for LINQ. SharePoint 2010 (and supporting technologies) allow architects to plan for special considerations as well, such as working with data in the cloud, and working with SharePoint data while offline.

These enhancements (along with many others) represent a massive improvement in the experience of working with SharePoint data. They provide the architect with an even more robust set of tools to continue creating valuable, manageable, and responsible business solutions.

This chapter provides an introduction to core concepts, important improvements, and guidance on key design decisions related to working with data.

MANIPULATING INTERNAL DATA

With a few exceptions, internal SharePoint data is stored in lists and libraries. Indeed, the SharePoint list is one of the most fundamental constructs within SharePoint, but it is also one of the most powerful.

Out of the box, there is a capability to create complex views of list data, including grouping, filtering, totals, and more. Powerful field types (such as calculated columns, lookups, and managed metadata columns) can be employed to create dynamic and robust solutions. No-code workflows (either prebuilt, or those a user creates with SharePoint Designer) can be bound to lists to manipulate data, or kick off other processes. It is also now possible to enforce unique values for a column, which, in the past, required custom development to accomplish.

If requirements cannot be met with out-of-the-box list functionality, custom list definitions, custom field types, event handlers, and more can be developed to extend SharePoint lists to meet most any need.

INTEGRATING EXTERNAL DATA

Those who have worked with SharePoint in different business scenarios know that it is a platform offering many things to different organizations. It is a document repository, a content management system, a web authoring tool, a website, an intranet portal, an extranet, a collaboration tool, a solutions platform, and so on. As companies have realized the power and flexibility of SharePoint, some now view SharePoint as an information "hub."

Enterprises typically have a myriad of separate systems with disparate data stores throughout their environments. SharePoint can be employed to sit in the middle, and connect to the various systems and data stores to surface, relate, contextualize, write to, and search this information. Even the most basic modern SharePoint deployment usually connects to Active Directory (AD), crawls various systems, file shares, Microsoft Exchange, and data stores with the Enterprise Search functionality, and interacts with line-of-business (LOB) applications through the Business Connectivity Services (BCS) — all without writing code.

SharePoint 2010 offers a rich set of new tools and features that allow integration and interaction with external data — in some cases, delivering the capability to work with the data as if it is native to SharePoint.

The following section explores new features and capabilities of SharePoint's workhorse — the SharePoint list.

LIST DATA PLATFORM CAPABILITIES

The updates to (and investment in) lists in SharePoint 2010 will undoubtedly have significant impact on architects and end users alike. Because lists represent one of SharePoint's fundamental building blocks, those who are using SharePoint are probably interacting with a list whether they know it or not. Improvements to lists in SharePoint 2010 include relationships and lookups, joins and projections, field validation, and tools for managing large lists.

Lists Relationships and Lookups

One of the pain points in previous versions of SharePoint was the limitation around working with lists as relational. By design, SharePoint lists are "flat," and attempts to treat the data relationally often led to frustration. It was possible to create relationships between lists. However, there was no referential integrity. In SharePoint 2010, investment has been made in this regard, resulting in new features that allow more robust relationships between SharePoint lists.

Relationships between SharePoint lists are created using lookup columns. This concept is not new to SharePoint. However, the lookup column has undergone an overhaul in SharePoint 2010, making it a more robust solution for defining relationships.

Two major improvements for the lookup column are:

➤ *The capability to display additional fields* — In past versions of SharePoint, only one field from a lookup list could be displayed in the destination list views. There is now the capability to display additional fields from the lookup list.

➤ *Referential Integrity* — Lookup columns in SharePoint 2010 have an additional relationship setting where it is possible to define the desired behavior when a value is deleted from a lookup list.

 Referential integrity is not enforced on lookups configured to allow multiple values.

For example, Figure 11-1 shows a musical instrument manufacturer called Notable Instruments that has created two lists in its SharePoint site. The "Instrument Name" list contains a list of all the instruments it currently sells. The "Inst Family" list contains categories of instruments and their descriptions.

		Instrument Name	Inst Family	Inst Family:Inst Family Description
☐	@	Saxophone	Woodwind	produces sound when the player blows air against a sharp
		Trombone	Brass	is produced by sympathetic vibration of air in a tubular res the player's lips
		Piano	Percussion	instruments that vibrate when struck, shook, plucked, or s
		Bass	String	produces sound by means of vibrating strings
		Drums	Percussion	instruments that vibrate when struck, shook, plucked, or s

✛ Add new item | Lookup Column | Additional Field from Lookup List

FIGURE 11-1 Lookup column with additional (projected) field

To create a relationship between these two lists, the manufacturer has added a lookup column in the "Instruments" list called "Inst Family" that looks up values from the "Instrument Family" list. This is shown in Figure 11-2.

Notice that an additional field called "Inst Family Description" has been selected in the column configuration. This field becomes available for display in the views for the "Instruments" list (see

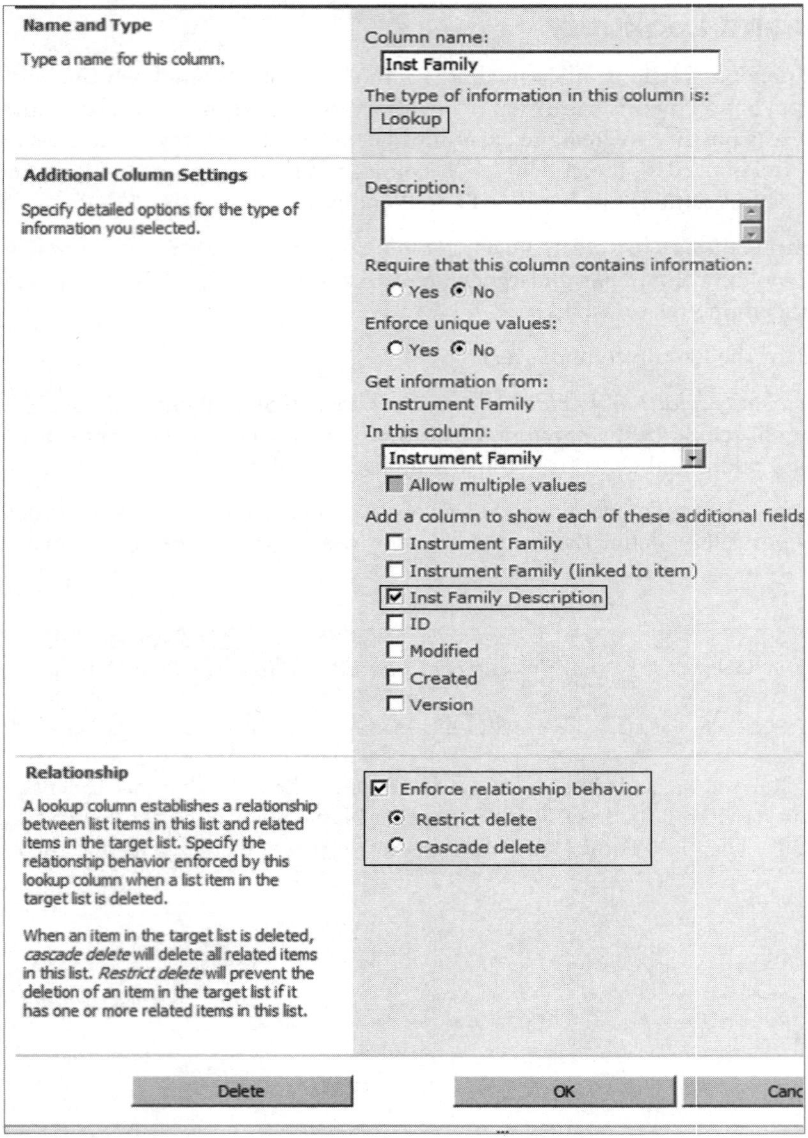

FIGURE 11-2: Lookup column configuration

Figure 11-1). If you were creating this relationship via the API, this would be called a *projected field* (more on this later in this chapter).

Notice also that in "Relationship settings" in the lookup column, the "Enforce relationship behavior" checkbox is selected, and "Restrict delete" has been chosen. With this configuration, if an attempt is made to delete a value from the "Instrument Family" list, and that value has a related item in the "Instruments" list, the user will be presented with an error message, as shown in Figure 11-3.

If instead, the "Cascade delete" option were selected, users would see a warning message indicating that all related items in the "Instruments" list would be deleted, as shown in Figure 11-4.

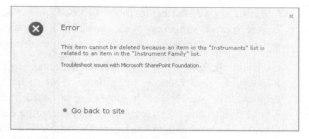

FIGURE 11-3: "Restrict delete" message

List Joins and Projections

Another valuable new functionality in SharePoint 2010 is the capability to create list joins for views and queries. Both the SPView and SPQuery objects have Joins and ProjectedFields properties that developers may use to define joins via the API.

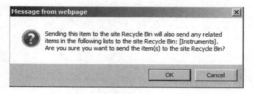

FIGURE 11-4: "Cascade delete" message

It is outside the scope of this book to provide detailed examples. However, the book Professional SharePoint 2010 Development *(Indianapolis: Wiley, 2010) has an excellent section on this subject, including code samples.*

Following are some important notes and limitations to keep in mind:

➤ Options for joins are limited to left and inner joins (no right joins).

➤ When creating a join, the field in the primary list must be a lookup column, and point to the field that is being joined on in the foreign list. This dictates that all joins will be performed on lists that already have a relationship by means of a lookup column.

Because of such limitations, more complex joins or requirements for a true relational database should still be accomplished using SQL Server, and can be integrated into SharePoint via the BCS.

List Validation

In prior versions of SharePoint, there were virtually no out-of-the-box options for validating user input within a list form. Instead, developers were tasked with developing client-side script (which sometimes meant unghosting list form pages), a custom form, an event handler, or an InfoPath form to handle validation requirements.

SharePoint 2010 now includes list validation. It is now possible to configure field validation out of the box at either the list level or site-column level. The aforementioned custom solutions are all still viable options, and should be evaluated if the out-of-the-box list validation proves insufficient for a given requirement.

Creating the validation formula will be familiar to those who have experience with formulas in Excel, or with SharePoint calculated columns. When a user submits the form, if the conditions are not met, users are presented with a configurable message.

Consider the following example, as illustrated in Figure 11-5 and Figure 11-6. The Human Resources department at a company creates a list called "PTO Request" from which employees can request days off. One of the fields users must fill out is "Desired Day Off." The creator of this list would like to ensure that the user has entered a date in the future before the request is submitted. To do this, the creator has configured validation on the "Desired Day Off" column.

FIGURE 11-5: List validation configuration

Let's take a quick look at the simple logic of the validation. If the value in the "Desired Day Off" field is less than today's date, do not submit the request, and present the user with a message that reads "You can only request days off in the future."

This same validation configuration could be implemented via the API instead of the graphical user interface (GUI).

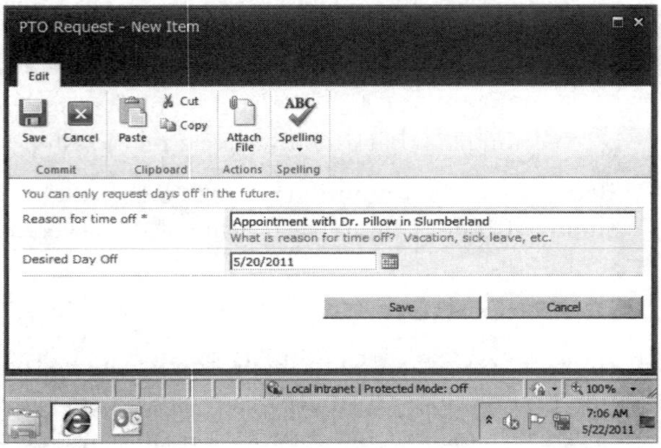

Large Query Throttling

Best practices and performance considerations regarding large SharePoint lists have always been hot topics in the SharePoint community.

FIGURE 11-6: List validation message

A statistic you are likely to hear regarding this subject is that performance will tend to degrade with more than 2,000 items. This number really refers to the number of items that Microsoft recommends retrieving in a view — the list itself can contain millions of items. To address this, SharePoint only allows views of 2,000 items or less. However, in other scenarios (such as accessing data via the API), governance via a list view will not suffice.

New to SharePoint 2010 is an administrative feature called *query throttling*. Query throttling enables SharePoint administrators to head off performance degradation by governing the number of items that can be returned when a query is executed. If a query returns a number of items in excess of this "list view threshold," an error is thrown, and no results are returned.

Administrators configure query throttling via Central Administration at the application level by clicking Central Administration ⇨ Manage Web Applications ⇨ Resource Throttling, as shown in Figure 11-7.

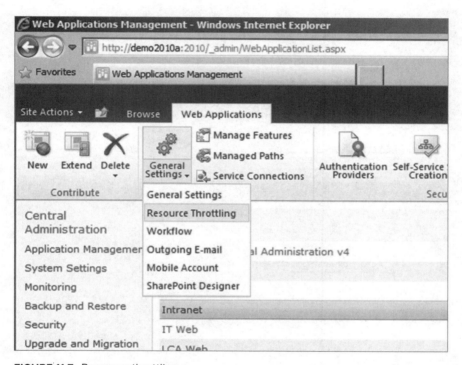

FIGURE 11-7: Resource throttling

As shown in Figure 11-8, a number of settings can be configured here, including the following:

➤ The maximum number of items that can be returned from a database operation (list view threshold). A separate threshold can be set for administrators.

➤ Whether to allow particular users to override the list view threshold when accessing lists via the object model.

➤ The maximum number of lookup, person/group, or workflow status fields that can be contained in a database request.

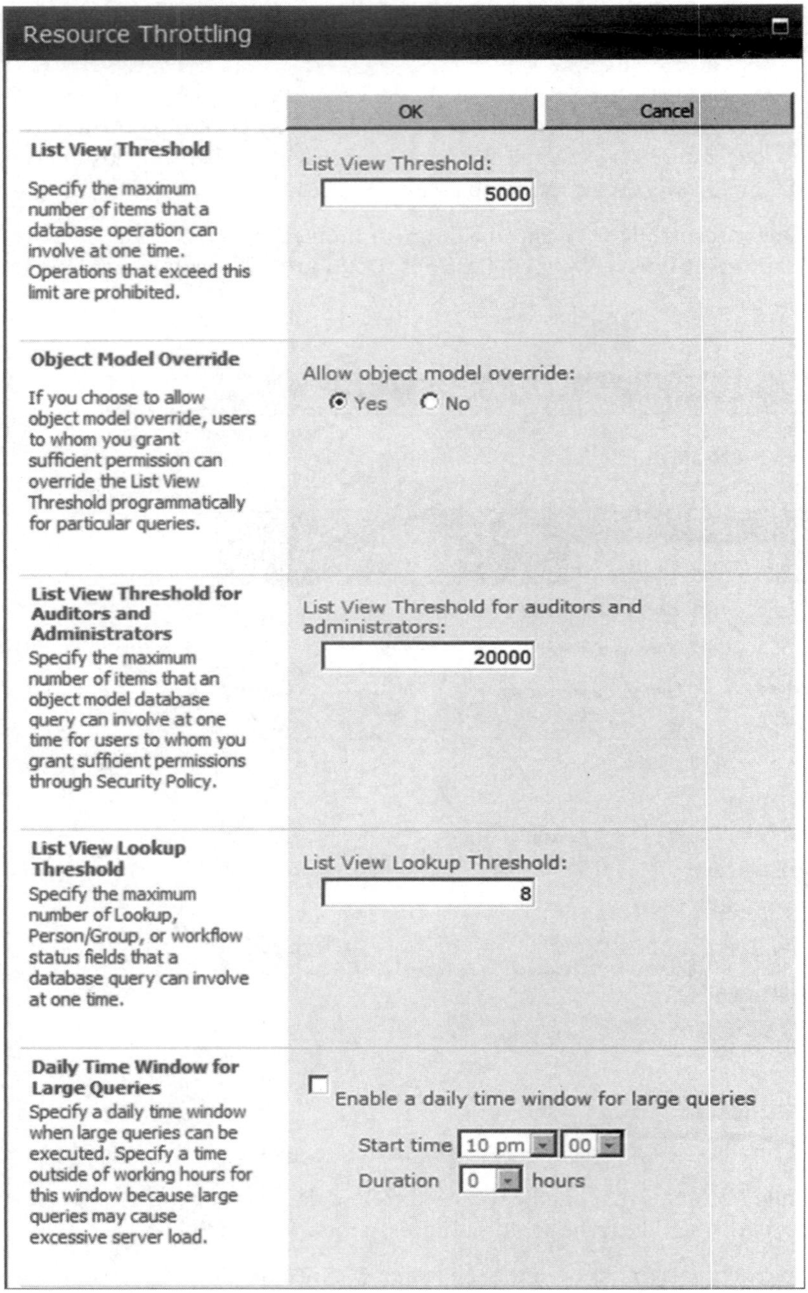

Resource Throttling

| OK | Cancel |

List View Threshold

Specify the maximum number of items that a database operation can involve at one time. Operations that exceed this limit are prohibited.

List View Threshold:

5000

Object Model Override

If you choose to allow object model override, users to whom you grant sufficient permission can override the List View Threshold programmatically for particular queries.

Allow object model override:

◉ Yes   ○ No

List View Threshold for Auditors and Administrators

Specify the maximum number of items that an object model database query can involve at one time for users to whom you grant sufficient permissions through Security Policy.

List View Threshold for auditors and administrators:

20000

List View Lookup Threshold

Specify the maximum number of Lookup, Person/Group, or workflow status fields that a database query can involve at one time.

List View Lookup Threshold:

8

Daily Time Window for Large Queries

Specify a daily time window when large queries can be executed. Specify a time outside of working hours for this window because large queries may cause excessive server load.

☐ Enable a daily time window for large queries

Start time 10 pm ▾ 00 ▾
Duration 0 ▾ hours

FIGURE 11-8: Resource throttling settings

➤ A daily time window reflecting a period during which queries that surpass the list view threshold can be completed. (This allows for scheduling of maintenance operations during off-peak hours.)

This section has described new features and functionalities of the SharePoint list, which is the principal object for storing data within SharePoint. The following section takes you on a tour of the BCS, which is the new feature set that allows easy integration of data that resides outside of SharePoint.

BUSINESS CONNECTIVITY SERVICES

One of the things that makes SharePoint such a powerful platform is its capability to integrate and surface data from disparate systems throughout the enterprise. The key mechanism for accomplishing this is the BCS. This section describes key upgrades to the features set, delves into a few of the underlying constructs, and addresses security and authentication considerations.

Integrating External Data

The BDC was one of the most powerful feature sets in SharePoint 2007. It allowed administrators and developers to integrate LOB applications and other external data sources into their SharePoint 2007 applications. As powerful as the BDC was, there were major limitations. For example, the BDC was not available in the free version of SharePoint 2007, Windows SharePoint Services (WSS). Creating the application definitions required the authoring of complex XML files (or use of third-party tools to create them), and, out of the box, it did not support writing back to external data sources.

In SharePoint 2010, the BDC has been upgraded and renamed Business Connectivity Services (BCS). The BCS is a group of Features and services that allow the integration of external data. The enhancements to this Feature set are many, but a few of the major improvements are inclusion of BCS in SharePoint Foundation (the free version of SharePoint 2010), wizard-based configuration of BCS applications, and, most notably, BCS connections are read/write.

 See Chapter 29 for a deeper dive into the BCS.

External Content Types

The External Content Type (ECT) is a new concept to SharePoint. It is similar to a List Content Type in that it is a reusable set of metadata that can be used to drive lists that end users interact with. However, ECTs also contain information about authentication, connectivity to, and the desired behaviors (that is, CRUD operations) associated with their external data sources.

There are a few methods for adding ECTs to the BCS, including the following:

➤ Microsoft SharePoint Designer 2010 offers a wizard experience for defining and adding new ECTs.

➤ Microsoft Visual Studio 2010 ships with the Business Connectivity Services Model Designer that developers can use to define and package ECTs for deployment via the Solution Framework.

➤ Administrators can import application models as XML files into the BCS service application from Central Administration.

Once added, administrators can modify permissions, or add more Features such as actions and profile pages.

External Lists

External lists are the centerpiece of BCS from the perspective of the user experience. They allow end users to interact with external data as if it is a native SharePoint list. As such, users can create views of (including sorting, filtering, grouping, and so on), edit, add columns to, and otherwise manipulate external data as if it were any other SharePoint list.

As an example, let's say that an online fitness retailer uses SharePoint 2010 to host its intranet where it stores information about its various products. It has a separate custom Customer Relationship Management (CRM) application that is built on .NET with a SQL back end.

In the past, if employees were in the intranet and wanted to access customer information, they had to leave the intranet and open the CRM application. Using the BCS, an administrator could create an ECT defining a connection to the Customers table of the CRM application, create an external list based on the ECT, and end users would be able to view, add, edit, and delete customers from the database without ever leaving the portal.

This is obviously a simple example, but with some creativity and planning, this capability has vast potential for improving the way users work.

Security and Authentication Models

When allowing users to interact with external data in the real world, administrators must address security and authentication. Within the BCS service application, administrators assign permissions for the BCS objects. If users do not have permissions to the BCS object, they will not be able to view the external data, even if they have explicit access at the external system level. These permissions are assigned via Central Administration within the BCS service application.

BCS connections support three authentication models: Pass-Through, Single Sign-On, and RevertToSelf.

Pass-Through Authentication

Pass-Through authentication refers to a model in which the logged-on user's credentials are "passed through" to the back-end system for authentication. It is important to note that, in most cases, if a SharePoint environment is configured for NT LAN Manager (NTLM) authentication, and your external data source requires authentication, the request will fail.

This is because the request results in a double-hop scenario, as shown in Figure 11-9. The first "hop" is from the client computer to the SharePoint server, and the second "hop" is from SharePoint

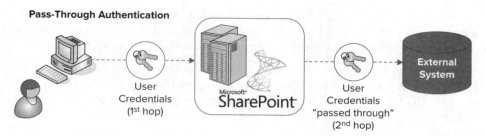

FIGURE 11-9: Pass-Through authentication

to the external system. This type of "delegation" is not supported by NTLM. Therefore, in most configurations, if Pass-Through is the desired authentication model, claims-based authentication or Kerberos must be used.

 For more information on claims-based authentication and Kerberos, see Chapter 19.

Single Sign-On

Single Sign-On (SSO) is an ideal option for authenticating users to external systems for a number of reasons.

First of all, it avoids the double-hop problem by storing and mapping credentials within the SharePoint Secure Store Service (SSS) application. Technically, there are still two hops, but they are broken up into two discrete requests, as shown in Figure 11-10. The first is from the client computer to SharePoint. Then SharePoint makes a separate request to the external system using whichever account the administrator has mapped to the current user for this particular BCS application.

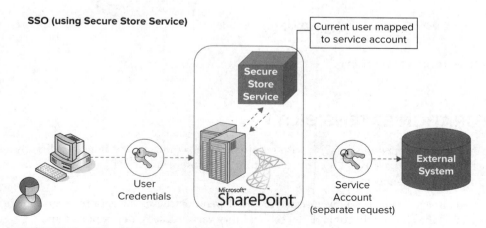

FIGURE 11-10: SSO with Secure Store Service

Another positive for using SSO is that users do not need permissions to the external data source at all. The administrator will assign a service account for this purpose with the minimum permissions necessary. The administrator can then map any number of users to this same service account.

There are performance gains with this model based on how connections from a single logon are handled versus multiple accounts. There is a downside to this approach, though. The external system will not know who has accessed it, because all requests will be made using a single service account. It is possible to work around this issue by using the `UserContextFilter` within BCS application models.

RevertToSelf

RevertToSelf is a holdover from SharePoint 2007. This model uses the identity of the IIS application pool for the given context to make the request. This will vary depending on from where or from what process the request is being made.

In the case of an external list, it would be the identity of the application pool for the application that is serving the page. This can pose real security risks, and, for this reason, in most scenarios, using RevertToSelf in a production environment is not considered a best practice. RevertToSelf is disabled by default, and administrators must enable it using the SharePoint 2010 management shell. Figure 11-11 shows this process.

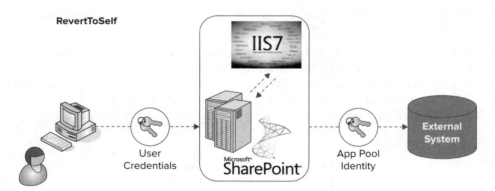

FIGURE 11-11: RevertToSelf authentication

DATA INTEGRATION EXTENSIBILITY

A connector must be developed in scenarios with requirements to connect to systems not directly supported by the BCS. You have two types of connectors to choose from: .NET Assembly Connectors and Custom Connectors.

The appropriate connector type for a given scenario will depend on the specifics of the requirement. In general, however, the choice will come down to flexibility versus ease of development and deployment.

.NET Assembly Connectors

The ease of developing and deploying .NET Assembly Connectors makes them an attractive option. SharePoint Designer and Visual Studio 2010 each have tooling to support development of connectors, and deployment to the BDC store is very simple using the ClickOnce mechanism. Also .NET Connector DLLs are stored in the BDC store, instead of the Global Assembly Cache (GAC), which, in some organizations, is desired (if not required).

.NET Assembly Connectors do, however, have two major limitations:

➤ .NET Assembly Connectors require one-to-one mapping of an ECT to a .NET Framework class.

➤ If changes are made to the back-end interface, the assembly must be recompiled and redeployed.

Custom Connectors

The Custom Connector is the more flexible approach when developing connectors. Unlike the .NET Assembly Connector, it is not necessary to map entities to .NET Framework classes. And, if changes are made to the back-end interface, it is only necessary to update the BDC model (XML configuration file), not the actual assembly.

The downsides to this approach are that the deployment process is more involved, there is no tooling to support development in Visual Studio or SharePoint Designer, and any DLLs must be deployed to the GAC.

This section described the framework and tooling available for developers to integrate data sources that are not supported out of the box. The next section covers a frequent business requirement found in SharePoint projects — data aggregation.

AGGREGATION

Part of why SharePoint is such a compelling repository to store an organization's data is the flexible options for surfacing it. When data residing in disparate locations is surfaced and displayed in a single list, this is called a *roll-up* or *aggregation*. This has always been a core concept in SharePoint. Consider the following scenarios:

➤ A law firm has an intranet with subsites for each practice area (litigation, real estate, and so on). Each of these sites has an "Announcements" section. Users have requested that all announcements from these separate sites automatically appear in one list on the home page of the portal.

➤ A non-profit organization has a partner extranet comprised of many site collections (one for each partner). It requires an easy way to view all of its partner agreements across these site collections.

➤ An electronics manufacturer wants to display a slideshow of only its newest products on the home page of its Internet site.

➤ A large pharmaceutical company is developing a new drug, and has created a team site specifically for this purpose. The team would like to display any content (regardless of format, source system, location, and so on) on this page if the project name appears anywhere in the title, body text, or metadata.

What all of these examples have in common is a requirement to surface information that does not necessarily reside in the same list or location. The methods for accomplishing the task of aggregating data can be roughly lumped into two groups: real-time aggregation and search-based aggregation.

Real-time Aggregation

Real-time aggregation refers to a roll-up that is based on a query against live data. Examples of this are utilizing the Content Query Web Part (CQWP), creating a custom web part that submits a Collaborative Abstract Machine Language (CAML) query, or configuring a Data View Web Part (DVWP) via SharePoint Designer.

Content Query Web Part

In SharePoint 2010, the CQWP remains one of the most powerful and useful out-of-the-box web parts developers and power users have in their arsenal. It is used to aggregate relevant information on a page by allowing users to create queries via a user-friendly user interface (UI). Because results are rendered using Extensible Stylesheet Language Transformations (XSLT), the display is completely flexible, and rich, interesting interfaces can be developed.

The biggest limitation in using the CQWP is that it is designed to be used only within a single site collection. That means that, out of the box, it is not possible to aggregate content from lists in different site collections.

Because it is such a useful and highly leveraged tool, there is a wealth of information on how to best utilize and configure the web part, which makes it an even more attractive option.

Data View Web Part

The DVWP has often been called the Swiss Army Knife of SharePoint. You can configure the DVWP to aggregate SharePoint data, customize the presentation of a list, display a list from another site collection, connect to RSS feeds or external applications, and more.

The main downside in using the DVWP is that it must be created using SharePoint Designer. For this reason, it is usually reserved for developers or highly technical power users. One other limitation (when using it for a roll-up) is that new lists will not appear in roll-ups automatically. Therefore, it is most useful when the data set is somewhat static.

Custom and Third-Party Web Parts

When requirements cannot be met with the out-of-the-box roll-up tools, there is always the option to create a custom web part. Typically a custom SharePoint web part used to aggregate content will utilize a CAML query or LINQ-to-SharePoint (see the section, "Working with Data," later in this chapter for more on LINQ-to-SharePoint). Writing a custom web part offers the greatest flexibility and (unlike the DVWP or CQWP) does not necessitate knowledge of XSLT to format the display.

Many third-party products are similar to the CQWP in that end users are able to configure queries via a user-friendly UI. These web parts usually do not have the same limitations regarding multiple site collections, and the display can be formatted more easily than the CQWP. As with all third-party products, they should be evaluated while keeping in mind manageability, support, cost, and the overall development strategy for the SharePoint platform.

Search-Based Aggregation

Search-based aggregation involves creating a query to surface information from the search index. The easiest way to accomplish this is by configuring an out-of-the-box Search Core Results web part with a predefined (or "canned") query. Search Core Results is the web part that appears on search results pages to render search results, but this web part can be added to any page and configured easily to surface data based on any search criteria.

The obvious limitation with this method is that the query does not return up-to-the-second results. The "freshness" of results will be determined by when the last crawl was completed.

Other than that limitation, search-based aggregation can be a fantastic alternative to other aggregation methods. Among the benefits are ease of configuration that would otherwise be complex (such as queries against unstructured data), along with the fact that it is the only of the out-of-the-box method that allows roll-ups to include items not stored in SharePoint (such as documents in file shares).

The next section covers the many methods now available to developers for accessing and working with SharePoint data.

WORKING WITH DATA

Most custom solutions that are built on or connect to SharePoint involve accessing, adding, updating, deleting, manipulating, or surfacing SharePoint data. To meet various business requirements, developers may find themselves accessing SharePoint data from any number of application types, including browser-based applications, Silverlight applications, Office applications, applications on a SharePoint server, and applications running on remote servers. To give developers the richest set of tools to cover different scenarios, SharePoint 2010 now has many data access technologies to choose from, depending on the situation. These include the server-side object model (OM), client OM, LINQ, and REST.

Server APIs

SharePoint has always offered an incredibly rich experience for developers writing code that runs on SharePoint servers. In SharePoint 2010, the story gets even better with an improved object model and support for LINQ.

Server-Side Object Model

The SharePoint *server-side object model* enables developers to write programs that access SharePoint objects such as lists, libraries, site collections, sites, and just about any SharePoint construct you can think of. The object model is quite large. However, it is rich and user-friendly. Most experienced .NET developers who are new to SharePoint are pleasantly surprised by how easy it is to complete programming tasks using the SharePoint Server OM.

LINQ-to-SharePoint

One of the improvements in SharePoint 2010 that developers have been eagerly awaiting is *LINQ-to-SharePoint*, which is a LINQ provider that translates LINQ queries into CAML queries. Developers no longer have to write CAML queries that many find to have an unfriendly, esoteric syntax. Now they can use the more universal and friendly LINQ to query SharePoint data.

Client APIs

Designing solutions that access SharePoint from external applications has become much easier in SharePoint 2010 thanks to the Client Object Model and REST.

Client Object Model

New to SharePoint 2010 is the *client object model*, which allows developers to program against SharePoint from .NET-managed applications, Silverlight applications, or from ECMAScripts (JavaScript, JScript) run from a browser using many of the types and members present in the server-side object model.

REST

Another new feature in SharePoint 2010 is the capability to access list data using *Representational State Transfer (REST)* style web services. Just like the legacy SharePoint 2007 Simple Object Access Protocol (SOAP) web services, REST provides data access functionality via remote URLs. Indeed, any application that can send REST URLs to SharePoint can access its list data. This data access mechanism has some major limitations, though — it can only be used to access list data and Excel Services data.

 SharePoint SOAP web services are still available. However, Microsoft recommends that working with SharePoint data remotely should be done using the new client object model whenever possible.

Choosing a Data Access Technology

Table 11-1 and Table 11-2 serve as guides for choosing which data access technology to use for various scenarios.

TABLE 11-1: Data Access Technologies Decision Matrix (Part 1)

	CLIENT OM	SERVER OM	REST	LINQ-TO-SHAREPOINT
On SharePoint Server		X		X
On remote computer	X		X	
Site/list objects	X	X		
Traverse relationships		X	X	X
Calling pattern (direct)		X		X
Calling pattern (callback)	X		X	
Strongly typed (columns as properties)			X	X

TABLE 11-2: Data Access Technologies Decision Matrix (Part 2)

MANAGED CLIENT OMs	JAVASCRIPT CLIENT OM
Full URL context	Server-relative context only
`StringCollection`	String array
Null, Infinity	Nan, positive/negative infinity
Explicit FBA support	Context FBA support
Create, update, commit	Create, update, commit
No `FormDigest` required	Needs `<SharePoint:FormDigest>`
Standard server OM identity	No `RoleDefinitionBindingCollection` identity
`SPWeb` locale for comparisons	Invariant culture for comparisons

Table 11-3 also lists the pros and cons of data access technologies for various scenarios.

TABLE 11-3: Pros and Cons of Data Access Technologies

NAME	PROS	CONS
LINQ	Entity-based programming Strongly typed Supports joins and projections Good tool support and IntelliSense	Server-side only New API, so new skills required Pre-processing of list structure required, so changing list could break application

continues

TABLE 11-3 *(continued)*

NAME	PROS	CONS
Server OM	Familiar API Works with more than just list data	Server-side only Strongly typed
Client OM	Works off the server Easier than web services API Works in Silverlight, JavaScript, and .NET More than just list data	New API Weakly typed
REST	Standards-based URL-based commands Strongly typed	Only works with lists and Excel

Source: Professional SharePoint 2010 Development (Indianapolis: Wiley, 2010)

Event Model

SharePoint 2010 improves upon the Microsoft Office SharePoint Server (MOSS) events model by adding receivers for new events. To name a few, there are now add and delete events on lists, and add events on websites. Additionally, there are new "synchronous after" events that provide a way to perform actions on a list after it has been submitted, but prior to rendering.

Further improvements to the event model include event binding at the site collection level, binding of XML event receivers at the site level, and a new class called `SPWorkflowEventProperties` specifically created to improve support for workflows.

This section outlined the various options developers now have for working with SharePoint data. The next section discusses various considerations for designing SharePoint solutions in the cloud.

INCORPORATING CLOUD DATA AND COMPUTE SERVICES

Many organizations are looking to the cloud to host their enterprise applications for ease of deployment, uptime, cost savings, and more. As you will read about in more depth in Chapter 22, Microsoft now has a Software as a Service (SaaS) offering called Office 365 that includes SharePoint Online. Though opting for SharePoint Online over an on-premises solution certainly has its advantages, it also presents various challenges — most notably regarding custom applications. To work around this limitation, some are architecting solutions that combine SharePoint 2010 with another of Microsoft's cloud offerings — the Windows Azure platform.

Developing Cloud-Based Data and Compute Services

Because custom development options are limited in SharePoint Online, and custom databases are not allowed, a common solution is to develop .NET services, deploy them to the Azure platform, and then consume those services from within SharePoint. A how-to on creating services and deploying them to Azure is outside of the scope of this chapter, but many resources are available online on how to do just that.

Incorporating Services into Your SharePoint Solution

A number of potential integration points exist between SharePoint and custom applications in Azure, some of which are described in Table 11-4.

TABLE 11-4: Points of Integration

AZURE INTEGRATION	HOW IT'S DONE
SharePoint client object model	Interact with Windows Azure data in a list
Business Connectivity Services (BCS)	Model data from Windows Azure or build external list to SQL Azure
Silverlight	Create UI against Windows Azure services or data
Sandboxed solutions/SharePoint Online	Silverlight application leveraging Windows Azure deployed to site collection
Office custom client	Consume data directly from Windows Azure or BCS list exposing data
Standard/Visual web parts	Leverage services and data from Windows Azure
Open XML	Manage Windows Azure data in a document
REST	Use REST to interact with Windows Azure data to integrate with SharePoint
Office server services	Combine with Open XML to auto-generate docs (such as PDFs) on a server
Workflow/event receivers	State or events that tie into Windows Azure services, workflows, or data
LINQ	Use for querying Windows Azure data objects
Search	Federate search to include Windows Azure data

Source: "Connecting SharePoint to Windows Azure with Silverlight Web Parts" by Steve Fox (http://msdn.microsoft .com/en-us/magazine/gg309179.aspx)

For the purposes of this discussion, consider the following example. Notable Instruments, a musical instrument manufacturer, has created an e-commerce site that is hosted on SharePoint Online. As part of its solution, its system architect wants to store encrypted customer information in a custom database, and create a custom service to access and edit this data.

This is not an option in SharePoint Online, so a decision is made to host the custom service and data in Windows Azure, and host the back-end in SQL Azure. SharePoint will simply be the consumer of this service, and can surface and interact with the data in any number of ways, as shown in Figure 11-12.

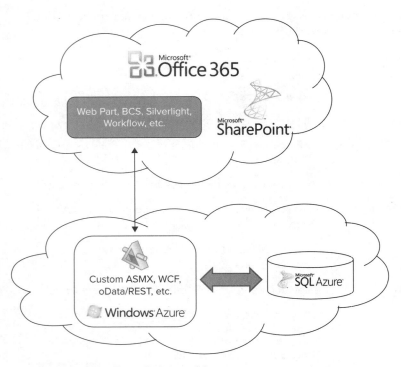

FIGURE 11-12: SharePoint Online and Azure

 For more information on integrating SharePoint 2010 and Azure solutions, seek out Senior Evangelism Manager for Microsoft, Steve Fox, at `http://blogs` `.msdn.com/b/steve_fox/.`

TAKING BUSINESS DATA OFFLINE

With the rollout of SharePoint 2010 and Microsoft Office 2010, users are no longer slaves to an Internet connection. There are now tools for users to work with SharePoint data (and data integrated into SharePoint) even when offline.

Using SharePoint Workspace

SharePoint Workspace 2010 is a client application that provides access to SharePoint 2010 content even when offline. For those familiar with the previous technology, it is the updated version of Microsoft Office Groove 2007. In addition to providing a client for interacting with SharePoint content, SharePoint Workspace 2010 can be used to create Groove collaboration workspaces and synchronized shared folders.

By using SharePoint Workspace 2010, users can view, edit, and add content in SharePoint 2010 lists and libraries while offline. When their PCs are back online, the content is automatically synchronized bi-directionally. This synchronization is optimized by sending only "update packets" (changes), as opposed to entire files over the network.

One of the most exciting features of SharePoint Workspace 2010 is the capability to interact with external lists (that is, SharePoint lists containing external data via the BCS). This functionality allows users to work with back-end data from their PCs, even when offline.

The desktop integration story for SharePoint Workspace 2010 is an impressive one. Workspace recognizes Windows credentials so that authentication and authorization to SharePoint content is seamless. Microsoft Lync is integrated, giving users the capability to view the presence information of others who have access to shared content, and instantly interact with them via instant messaging (IM), e-mail, video chat, or other methods, as shown in Figure 11-13.

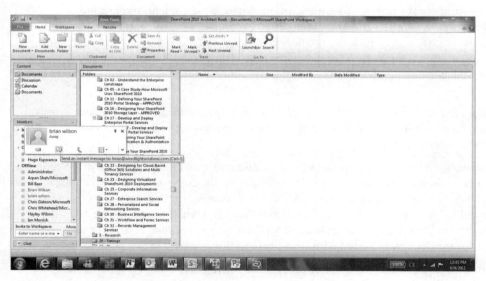

FIGURE 11-13: Workspace Lync integration

Being part of the Office suite (it is part of Microsoft Office Professional Plus 2010), SharePoint Workspace 2010 shares the familiar interface of the other Office products. Lastly, SharePoint Workspace data is searchable from Windows Desktop Search 4.0, as shown in Figure 11-14.

Microsoft has also released SharePoint Workspace Mobile. It is part of Office Mobile on Windows Phone 7 devices. Using the mobile application, users can view libraries and lists; view, add, and edit documents from mobile devices; synchronize documents to a mobile device; and more.

SharePoint Workspace 2010 is a powerful tool that has obvious applications for

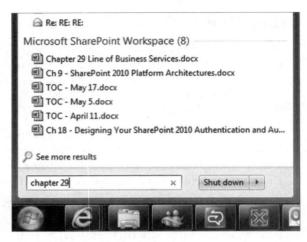

FIGURE 11-14: Workspace Search

any business whose employees operate outside of the office (think oil rig workers, traveling sales representatives, and so on).

Using Microsoft Office

Although Workspace is the premier tool for working with offline content, integration between Microsoft Office 2010 and SharePoint 2010 provides a limited (but useful) offline editing experience as well. Office 2010 includes the Backstage view. This is the area where users can manage documents and their metadata from within the Office client. Creating, sending, and editing metadata, as well as managing document versions, are some of the tasks you can complete from this area.

The Backstage view is located under the File tab in Office applications. When the need arises to work on a document offline — and Workspace is not an option — the Backstage view provides a subset of online functionality.

Consider a scenario in which a user is working on a document and must leave the office to catch a train. The user will not have access to the Internet during the commute, but final changes must be made to the document. That user can check out the document (to prevent others from making changes), download a local copy, make edits while offline, and when the user is back online, upload the document to the library as a new version. Where this gets interesting is that the user is able to make changes to the document metadata in this offline state as well.

Within the Backstage view, there is a list of properties, which include SharePoint metadata fields that are editable offline (Figure 11-15). It is important to note that, if it is a field type that supports auto-complete (such as a managed metadata field), the auto-complete will not be functional in this offline state. However, changes can still be made.

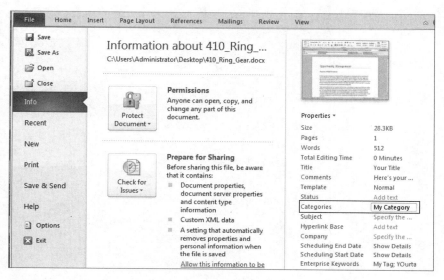

FIGURE 11-15: Word properties

SUMMARY

SharePoint 2010 provides the architect with a truly impressive set of tools for working with data — both internal and external. New events allow custom reactions to list and site creation, and new APIs make it simple to access SharePoint data from various types of applications, including Silverlight and browser-based remote applications. The BCS and connector framework enable easy integration of data from almost any source, and external lists provide the capability to work with this data in native SharePoint lists. SharePoint 2010 also provides functionality to address special considerations, such as cloud solutions and the capability to work with data while offline.

These features and more represent a huge leap forward in working with data in SharePoint, thus allowing architects to design better, more integrated, and sophisticated solutions for their users.

As exciting as all the new tools described in this chapter are, successful SharePoint solutions start with a lot of good planning. Chapter 12 covers the non-technical aspects of creating SharePoint solutions, such as requirements gathering, working with stakeholders, navigating politics, and more.

PART III
Architecting Enterprise Portal Services

12

Defining Your SharePoint 2010 Portal Strategy

By Brian Wilson

The phrase that I hear most often when helping organizations implement collaboration and portal technologies is, "SharePoint is the answer, but what is the question?" Although most organizations identify the need to exploit collaboration and portal technologies, they often fail to clearly research, define, and articulate the business drivers these technologies must support.

This may occur for a number of reasons, which could include the following:

➤ In some organizations, the strategy stage of an IT project tends to focus more on driving funding and project approval, rather than on than developing a clear understanding of the issues occurring in the business domain. Only after project and funding approval, the project team may then shift to the detailed requirements-gathering stage.

➤ The project starts in the IT department and remains in the IT department. There may be no clear engagement, involvement, and research by senior leaders and business stakeholders in the strategy stage.

➤ Focus may be centered largely on a set of capabilities and services, rather than on a more balanced approach that defines the business improvements the technology must support.

➤ A technology-, feature-, and platform-centric orientation is undertaken, rather than a business- and user-centric approach. This may be because of the challenge of a large, complex, and dispersed business environment with many stakeholders and differing requirements. Generic portal capabilities may be provided to get "something" out.

➤ Skills of the team developing the portal strategy are weighted to the technology and IT perspective, rather than the business perspective.

As shown in Figure 12-1, defining your portal strategy involves a number of sequential steps outlined in this chapter, which are as follows:

1. Review your business environment
2. Engage your key stakeholders
3. Define your business drivers
4. Define your portal capabilities
5. Define your supporting capabilities
6. Define your portal blueprint
7. Build your enterprise portal strategy
8. Define your road map
9. Agree on stakeholder responsibilities

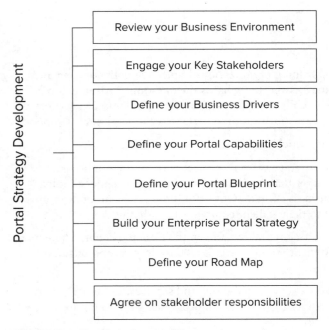

FIGURE 12-1: Portal strategy development process

The information in this chapter will help you develop your organization's portal strategy. Through engaging with your key stakeholders and defining your business drivers, you will be able to define the portal capabilities, blueprint, strategy, and road map. This will help you deliver real value to your business.

THE EXAMPLE SCENARIO

The scenario that is used in this chapter and subsequent chapters entails Global Mega Finance Corporation. This is a large multinational finance organization that has acquired a number of finance-related businesses in many markets and countries.

These businesses have become Strategic Business Units (SBU) of Global Mega Finance Corporation. They provide a combination of products and services to their market segments, either in a specific country or globally. They currently have an existing corporate identity, and are large enough and homogeneous enough to exercise control over most strategic factors affecting their performances.

This example scenario takes into account the following considerations:

➤ Each SBU is largely autonomous, and many have duplicated functions.

➤ Most of the SBUs provide common products and services in their respective markets.

➤ Most have existing deployments of collaboration and intranet technologies.

➤ Numerous business IT departments, fiefdoms, and technologies exist.

As this discussion progresses, you will learn about the various requirements of this finance organization.

REVIEW THE BUSINESS ENVIRONMENT

Gaining a deep understanding of the business environment enables you to develop a holistic understanding and snapshot of the organization at a point in time. As a Microsoft Partner or internal business representative, this enables you to define a portal strategy that resonates with key stakeholders of the business.

In Chapter 2 you learned how you can ensure that you have a good understanding of the major dimensions of your business information ecology. To recap, these dimensions include the following:

➤ *Business landscape* — This includes internal and external issues affecting the business. Internal examples include culture, employee processes and behaviors, and politics. External examples may be new regulatory and legal requirements, or increased competition in the marketplace.

➤ *Technology landscape* — This includes the existence, adherence, and execution against the current enterprise architecture and strategy, current infrastructure and network, existing portal and collaboration technologies, and current maturity and skill set of the IT department.

➤ *Legal landscape* — This includes laws with which your business and portal solution must comply. These laws range from strict export control data protection, to how financial information is retained and disposed of, to ensuring your solution is accessible to people with disabilities.

➤ *Information landscape* — This includes the content storage locations and volume, common content formats in use, content structure and metadata, content dynamism, control, and clearly defined content ownership.

➤ *People and user profile* — This analyzes patterns across your user base, such as the organizational structure, key audience demographics, number of employees per office location, common information-seeking behaviors, as well as the current and desired user experience.

➤ *Metrics and issues* — Gathering and collecting metrics and issues enable you to assess, quantify, and prioritize user and business issues.

How long should you spend assessing the business environment and business information ecology? This largely depends on the size and complexity of the business environment and the scope of the project.

ENGAGE KEY STAKEHOLDERS

An interesting analogy can be made between the evolution of marketing and of collaboration and portal technologies, how they both started on the basics, and how they evolved to a consumer-oriented approach.

In marketing, organizations up to the 1960s were primarily focused on the "basics," such as production techniques and quality of the product. This has transitioned to the marketing-oriented approach in focus today. Product research and development will rarely commence today without detailed market research confirming that the product would satisfy the needs and wants of the target audience.

The same can be said for the evolution of collaboration and portal technologies in the workplace. In the early days, users had basic tools with limited Internet connectivity, storage, and processing power. Over time, storage, processing power, network connectivity, and speed have improved drastically. In the 1990s to the early 2000s, messaging, file shares, and Internet browsers improved at a phenomenal rate, and new ways of working digitally began to emerge.

In today's digital world, using a plethora of technologies, you have so many options to choose from. Your organization can host these technologies and business services in the "cloud" (outsourced hosting) or on premises, in one country, or worldwide. Just as in the marketing-oriented approach, detailed research into user and business requirements of your key stakeholders is required. Understanding these requirements will enable you to define a portal strategy most suited and aligned to the objectives of your users and organization.

Identifying Key Stakeholders

As a Microsoft Partner or business professional, identifying business objectives and requirements from the right people (at the different levels in your organization related to the scope of your project) is vital to the success of your project.

How do you work out who your key stakeholders are? Usually, the scope of your project determines at what levels of the business you should engage. Are you defining a portal strategy for the entire organization, or for a particular department, business unit, or function? Always try to ensure that you collate requirements from strategic, tactical, and operational managers, and end users that exemplify common roles found in your business. Depending on the type of project, Figure 12-2 describes the key stakeholder groups to engage.

FIGURE 12-2: Overview of key stakeholders

A good source to determine your key stakeholders is your organizational chart. Determine the most senior leaders related to the scope of your project, analyze the structure beneath them, and identify the key management roles and end users that you would like to interview.

Internal Stakeholders

Typical engagement begins at the top with the senior and strategic stakeholders, and progresses downward to the end user. The top-to-bottom approach works best because senior stakeholders point you in the direction of quality people beneath them, and ensure that their time is made available to you. Starting from the top allows you to understand the business strategy, and expands your knowledge and understanding of the organization as you traverse down. Finally, issues picked up at ground level give you a chance to provide insight back to the organization at the strategic level.

For each level, you should plan your approach, research common feedback points, and "message" your portal strategy in the language your target audience will understand. For example, strategic management will most likely not be interested in the technical detail of your portal strategy. Therefore, focus and align your strategy to their business strategy, drivers, and business pain points.

Strategic Management

At the highest level, you must engage with strategic leaders of the organization. They are responsible for formulating and determining corporate goals, policies, business objectives, and deciding on the long-term direction of the organization. Your portal strategy must be aligned to their business strategy and what they are trying to achieve.

Common feedback points from strategic management include how they will comply with external regulations enforced on their business, how they can drive culture change and improvement, and how they can harness synergy and increased collaboration across the business.

It is vital to get strategic management support for your portal strategy for two key reasons. The strategic level is responsible for approving funding to execute your portal strategy. They also provide leadership, and can help overcome "resistant to change" issues within lower levels of your organization.

Tactical Management

At the tactical level of the organization, management straddles the strategic and operational activities. These managers tend to be responsible for a division, department, business unit, or function. They are focused on the direction and continued success of their business areas, and they advise and report back to the executive and strategic level.

Many insights can be found at this level, because they have a good understanding of how directives and strategy from the top are aligned to operational execution. Interviewing tactical managers will help you clearly understand the issues an organization faces, and the areas they have identified for improvement.

Operational Management

The operational level is the lowest level within the management layers. These business managers are at the front line of the organization and have a singular focus on the execution of their business processes, their performance metrics, and risks and issues they are facing.

Teams, Information Workers, and End Users

These groups are the most likely to be impacted by your portal strategy. Their daily way of working will be directly influenced by the tools you provide them. Pick out key areas of the business and interview as many people as possible. This can be done via online surveys, e-mail communication, and through direct interviews. Get them involved and inspired, and you will get invaluable feedback on how best to satisfy their needs.

Key Business Departments

Other key stakeholders that may influence your portal strategy include the following departments.

Corporate Communications Department

This department is the voice of the company. They disseminate messages to internal and external audiences, with the aim of maintaining and improving the light in which the organization is viewed. Among other things, they focus on maintaining a strong corporate culture, identity, and philosophy. They play an important part in defining the requirements for internal and external publishing portals, such as corporate intranets and public-facing sites. They are responsible for the organization's brand, and may insist on vetting and signing off on your planned visual experience and portal brand. Be sure to engage and align your vision early on to avoid political and territorial issues.

IT Department

The IT department provides a set of systems and services that support the organization in the execution of its day-to-day operations. Mature IT functions tend to have an enterprise architecture team responsible for ensuring that the overall enterprise IT strategy is aligned to the business objectives. This team is a key source of information in understanding the overall enterprise architecture, the long-term vision, and any dependencies and constraints that may apply to your planned SharePoint deployment. They will play a large role in agreeing to and implementing your portal strategy.

There is a tendency by IT professionals to focus more on technology, risk, and IT department-related requirements than on business requirements. Ensure that your portal strategy is business-centric. The portal strategy depends on your business accepting, adopting, and using your solution. Without this, your business will not realize the benefits of its investment in your portal strategy.

Security Team

Most large organizations today recognize the risks associated with operating in a digital environment, and the need to defend their IT operations from both internal and external attack vectors. Some organizations also have governmental and legal obligations on how they protect, store, and classify their data. Engaging with the security team will ensure your portal strategy complies with the security policies of the business.

Human Resources

The human resources staff are key agents in business change and transformation, human performance management, and organizational design and development. Unfortunately, they are often the forgotten stakeholders in most portal projects. As a key stakeholder, they are a fountain of useful information on your organization's workforce demographics. Additionally, they set out policies and procedures to which all employees must adhere. Always ensure that you engage with the human resources staff to comply with the policies and procedures the organization must adhere to.

Legal Department

The legal department deals with internal issues, (such as patent applications or employee disputes), as well as external issues (such as customer complaints, lawsuits, and business acquisitions). This department advises the senior stakeholders, and works to reduce the risks faced by the organization in the course of its operations. Engaging with the legal team will help ensure that your portal strategy and future deployment is compliant with the regulatory landscape in which your organization operates.

External Stakeholders

Finally, collaborating with suppliers, or publishing information to your customers, requires engaging with these groups to understand how their requirements may influence your portal strategy.

Be careful of the potential political minefield when engaging with external stakeholders. Your organization's client relationships may be sensitive in nature. Your organization may not want suppliers to have insights into your internal company workings.

Suppliers

Suppliers provide products and services to your organization. The most common supplier portal scenarios relate to developing closer working relationships, and sharing information to achieve mutual business objectives. The stakeholders will vary, depending on the type of project, as well as the level and duration of integration required between the businesses. Key stakeholders to engage with include the respective business's executive teams, IT departments, and end users that will use the extranet solution.

Customers

SharePoint 2010 can host public-facing Internet sites. As described earlier in this chapter, using the marketing orientation analogy, numerous qualitative and quantitative research methods are available to define the profile of your target audience, as well their desires, needs, and expectations of your planned Internet site.

At this stage, you may be thinking, "That is a lot of stakeholders to engage with. Do I really need to do all this? Can't I just deploy the technology, grow, and evolve slowly?" The truth is that many organizations do just that, except the "evolve slowly" part takes on a frantic and unexpected pace, resulting in all sorts of issues and unintended results that could have been avoided with more thinking, planning, and research from the outset.

In some cases, the IT department requirements-led approach can work when the IT department works very closely or is embedded in parts of the business. In most cases, though, the "deploy the platform and worry about business onboarding later" approach tends to lead to technological and feature-centric solutions that, even with the best intentions, does not meet the requirements of the end user.

Define the Business Drivers

A *business driver* is a combination of the people, information, and tasks that support the fulfillment of a business objective. In SharePoint projects, you are interested in the business drivers that influence the success of your portal strategy and SharePoint project.

> *A business driver is different from the requirements you will gather in future stages of the project. Here you are totally focused on understanding themes and areas your senior stakeholders want to improve. Future stages will focus on the detailed gathering of personas, scenarios, and use cases.*

What are your key stakeholders' needs and expectations? What have you derived from your initial assessment, surveys, and interviews? Have clear business drivers emerged from your senior stakeholders? Table 12-1 shows some common business drivers that apply to most businesses.

TABLE 12-1: Business Drivers in Your Organization

BUSINESS DRIVERS	EXPECTED BENEFITS FOR ACHIEVING THIS BUSINESS DRIVER
Improve workforce productivity	Improved toolset, collaboration within teams, projects, and across the business.
	Enable access to people, experts, and specialists.
	Improve team access to project information and problem solving tools.
	Enable individuals to participate, network, and share best practices in communities of interest.
	Reduce redundant work caused by duplication of effort in different teams in the business.
	Reduce unnecessary work related to working in an isolated offline, non-connected fashion. Leverage online collaboration tools to help individuals work better with teams. Eliminate the problem of team members working on different versions of the document inadvertently, in which case, one team member's changes could be easily overwritten and lost.
	Provide capabilities to ensure individuals have one place to find authoritative information.
Improve corporate culture	Share knowledge and expertise, and enable collaboration across your business.
	Facilitate working and development of networks outside the traditional organizational boundaries such as a business unit, function, or team.
	Support greater standardization across jobs, roles, processes, and ways of working.
	Support improved communication across your business through the use of synchronous tools such as business instant messaging (IM).
	Provide individuals with the capabilities to build up business networks to assist in the achievement of business objectives.
	Improve "time to talent." Reducing time taken onboarding new employees helps individuals realize their potential in your business.
	Support the cultural integration of mergers and acquisitions by providing a common set of tools and portals.
Legal and regulatory compliance	Support processes and procedures required to comply with legal and regulatory requirements.
	Support the management, retention, retrieval, and disposal of information as required by law.

continues

TABLE 12-1 *(continued)*

BUSINESS DRIVERS	EXPECTED BENEFITS FOR ACHIEVING THIS BUSINESS DRIVER
Corporate knowledge management and retention	Retain and grow corporate knowledge strategic assets.
	Distribute insights and experiences embodied in individuals or embedded in business processes.
	Enable the "emergence" of new insights based on existing knowledge in your business.
	Provide tools to enable the participation of all people in your business to capture, share knowledge, and support the emergence of new and improved insights.
	Improve performance, competitive advantage, innovation, lessons learned, and continuous improvement. Reduce redundant work, reduce training time, and adapt quicker to changing environments and markets.
	Retain intellectual capital when employees leave your business.
	Global content and knowledge management.
	Improve organizational learning through the use of a common platform.
Corporate and leadership communication	Provide a channel for senior leadership to communicate and engage clearly and consistently with all people in your business.
	Provide channels for leaders within businesses and functions to communicate with their business people.
	Provide tools for individuals to receive key messages from the business.
Improve business performance	Improve "speed to performance" by supporting the capability of the individual and teams to execute quickly and successfully.
	Support corporate performance measurement tools to enable management to respond to internal and external conditions (for example, scorecards and dashboards).
	Provide timely access to information.
	Drive synergy across your business through the use of tools that enable your business to connect and work closer together.
Lowering costs	Reduce time to educate, inform, and equip staff, to be productive, learn new skills, and solve problems.
	Help individuals and teams reduce re-work and duplication of effort.
	Remove duplicate investment through use of a common platform.

BUSINESS DRIVERS	EXPECTED BENEFITS FOR ACHIEVING THIS BUSINESS DRIVER
Improve information retrieval	Reduce time spent (and wasted) searching for information necessary to complete a task, process, or objective.
	Improve the capability to problem solve. Enable individuals to find experts who can assist them with a problem, and help them find relevant information.
	Provide access to client and project information background information, to key project documents, and to information based on individual expertise.
	Improve the access to information using a clearly defined business classification system (taxonomy).
Improve business processes	Improve people-driven processes using a common platform and toolset.
	Enable the use of workflow tools on a common platform to facilitate the rigorous execution of work activities of individuals, teams, and business units in your business. Additionally, use these tools to monitor, assess, and improve process performance.
Increase revenue and profit margins	Enable innovation and collaboration, and access to the right information, at the right time to make informed decisions.
	Improve "time to market," from the inception of an idea through to execution.

In summary, business drivers define the way in which you provide capabilities and services to your business. These underpin and align your portal strategy to the business strategy, and guide your decision-making and priority setting in future stages of the project.

DEFINE PORTAL CAPABILITIES AND BLUEPRINT

Incorporating high-level business drivers into a set of portal capabilities for your organization can be difficult to get right. In theory, it is about the application of SharePoint technologies to deliver a solution that meets the needs of your organization. In practice, a number of factors play a part in influencing the portal capabilities you deploy. Organizational politics, existing investments, and embedded business solutions that utilize alternative technology all play a part in influencing or enforcing what capabilities can or cannot be deployed. Examples of these could include a deployed enterprise search technology, or a specialized legal document management solution.

Selecting and deciding on a set of portal capabilities is not just about what the technology provides, but the manner and order in which you introduce them into your organization. For example, consider your portal capabilities you would recommend at a conservative bank, a progressive retailer, or a funky music label representing artists in the music industry. Each business scenario calls for a slightly different approach. Use your SharePoint knowledge, previous experiences, sound judgment, and business acumen to ensure that they survive, grow, and flourish in your business.

Defining the features and capabilities that will form the foundation of your SharePoint 2010 environment from high-level business drivers is difficult to get right. As shown in Figure 12-3, following are a set of steps to derive a high-level set of business features that will form part of your business drivers, such as improving workforce productivity or change to the corporate culture:

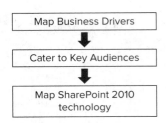

FIGURE 12-3: Steps for deriving high-level features

1. Map features that support your business drivers.

2. Expand your features to ensure key audiences are catered to.

3. Map SharePoint 2010 technology and capabilities to the required features.

These steps require a broad and deep understanding of the workloads and features provided by the SharePoint 2010 platform. This is needed to ascertain what workloads and features are available to exploit, and which should be avoided.

Another important point is to understand the SharePoint ecosystem of complementary and specialized technologies. As much as it pains me to say it, SharePoint is not the answer for every solution. Therefore, it's important you know where SharePoint stops, and another technology starts.

Lastly, utilize and leverage the skills, experience, and lessons learned in the trenches of seasoned SharePoint professionals. This will prove invaluable in defining a mature portal strategy.

Support Business Drivers

Think about what high-level features and solutions will support the business drivers. Map these to the business drivers to begin to determine what capabilities are required.

Continuing with the Global Mega Finance Corporation scenario, Table 12-2 maps features required to support the business drivers of the senior stakeholders.

TABLE 12-2: Business Drivers in Your Organization

BUSINESS DRIVERS	DESCRIPTION	
Merge these businesses into one strong global business.	Provide a single common integrated office and business platform for all employees.	
	Implement a common portal user experience and brand that all sites must implement.	
	Implement site structure and navigation based on well-defined information architecture.	
Ensure senior leaders can communicate with all employees.	Create a global corporate intranet and home page that all employees can use and access to publish global communications content.	
	Provide leaders of regional, function, business, and business units with the capability to publish content to their respective business areas.	

BUSINESS DRIVERS	DESCRIPTION
Improve corporate culture, cross-business working, and best practices.	Provide regional, function, business, and business unit sites to enable each area to collaborate with other businesses and business units.
	Enable employees, from different businesses, to collaborate on a common task, role, or process in a team site accessible to authorized people, or open to all.
Consolidate, grow, share, and retain corporate knowledge.	Enable users to collaborate using team, wikis, community, and other predefined site templates.
	Enable large-scale storage and management of documents using Document Centers.
	Incorporate well-defined global taxonomy to enhance the capability to find content using well-known business terms.
Improve ability to retrieve corporate knowledge.	Enable all users to search for people and information.
	Enable users to refine their search using search scopes, refinements, best bets, and specialized search pages.
Lower costs.	Shut down legacy intranets to eliminate duplicated platform support.
	Reduce training required for different systems in various businesses to one collaboration and portal system across all businesses. Implement a help and training center to support self-help.
	Save on licensing costs by using one rather than multiple platforms.
	Enable strong governance and management of the common platform. Provide a governance center to enable businesses to learn what features they can use and exploit. Provide recommendations and policies to enforce consistency.
	Free up hardware, resources, and data center space for other important business systems.

Support Key Audiences

In the next stage, you must look at the business drivers from the perspective of key audiences in your organization. What features will each audience need to support the business drivers of the senior stakeholders? In this stage, you expand on the features defined in the previous section. Ensure that you validate these features against the business drivers.

Continuing with the Global Mega Finance Corporation scenario, Table 12-3 shows you how to map features to the following key audiences of the organization.

TABLE 12-3 Features to Support Key Audience

FEATURES	DESCRIPTION
Global	Create a global corporate intranet and home page that all employees can use and access to publish global communications content.
	Create a global search center to enable users to find people, expertise, and information.
	Create a Governance and Portal Management Center to enable management and growth of the collaboration and portal platform.
	Create a global taxonomy and base set of content types, containing metadata that must be applied to content in your portal platform.
	Create an End User Help and Training Center to enable users to get answers to frequently asked questions, improve their proficiency, and help them better exploit features available to them.
Regional	Create regional home pages for employees in geographically defined business regions. Roll up key content to regional home pages.
Businesses and business units	Create business sites and empower businesses to use and extend these home pages within the bounds of global information architecture.
	Use employee- and business-focused content.
	Provide Document Centers for businesses to migrate content from file shares or legacy document management systems.
	Provide the capability to comply with legal requirements — either through in-place records management or dedicated record centers.
	Create business unit sites in the business site to share information with the rest of the business.
Functions	Create function sites, to publish content to the organization. For example, policies and procedures or new employee getting-started information can be published from human resources.
Teams	Create a team site home page and aggregate the latest content from key lists in each site.
	Enable collaboration sites to be provisioned as required by users in the organization.
	Enable and automate the provisioning of sites based on predefined governance rules.
	Provide specialized predefined custom site templates aimed at common business collaboration scenarios and processes (for example, Project, Marketing war chest, and research collaboration site templates).
Communities	Create a community home page and aggregate the latest content from key lists in each community site.
	Create "community of interest" or wiki site templates to empower individuals to set up sites based on a common role, task, or interest.

FEATURES	DESCRIPTION
Individuals	Provide a home for each user in the organization.
	Enable private working areas to host important files and documents.
	Enable public profiles.
	Provide end-user help to help users learn how to leverage features available to them.
	Provide business social networking features.
	Enable business IM to ensure presence information is displayed to individuals.

Portal and Supporting Capabilities

Some of the key portal workloads, platform, and supporting capabilities will become evident as you define the enabling features required by your organization.

Portal Capabilities

Let's continue with the example Global Mega Finance Corporation scenario. Table 12-4 shows how to derive the capabilities that will be required to realize the features and key stakeholder's requirements and business drivers.

TABLE 12-4: Deriving Technical Capabilities and SharePoint Features from Required Business Features

BUSINESS FEATURE	KEY SHAREPOINT ENABLING FEATURES	REQUIRED TECHNICAL CAPABILITIES
Corporate intranet, regional sites, business and business unit sites, function sites, Help and Training Center, Governance Center, collaboration site, directory, community site directory	Publishing Site Definition	Web content management
	Variations and multilingual features	
	Web page authoring	
	Content approval and scheduling	
	Master pages for common look and feel	
	Page layouts to display content	
	Content types, information policies, and approval workflows	
	Content Query web part	
	Audiences and content targeting	

continues

TABLE 12-4 *(continued)*

BUSINESS FEATURE	KEY SHAREPOINT ENABLING FEATURES	REQUIRED TECHNICAL CAPABILITIES
Search Center sites	Search Center site definition	Search
	Search scopes	
	Content sources	
	Refinements	
	SharePoint search-based API to display content aggregations across site collections based on content types, managed metadata properties, and search scopes	
Records Center sites	Records Center site definition	Records management
	In-place records management	
	Document routing, content organizer, and rule-based submission	
	Enterprise content types	
	Information policies	
	Declare a document as a record	
Document centers	Document Center site definition	Document management
	Enterprise content types	
	Metadata and metadata-based navigation	
	Unique document identifiers	
	Document sets	
	Information policies	
	Workflows	
	Remote Blob Storage (RBS) API or third-party storage solutions	
	Content organizer	
	Major, minor versioning; check in/out	
	Folder- and item-level permissions	
	Recycle Bin	

BUSINESS FEATURE	KEY SHAREPOINT ENABLING FEATURES	REQUIRED TECHNICAL CAPABILITIES
Business collaboration sites, "Community of Interest" sites	Team and wiki sites	Business collaboration
	Custom site focused on business-specific collaboration scenarios	
	Enterprise and local content types applied to important libraries to enforce consistent application of metadata	
	Incorporation of managed metadata from the global taxonomy enablement of local tagging	
	Custom "Community of Interest" site template consisting of a predefined home page, document libraries, and other lists	
Employee sites, profile information, business networking, employee feedback mechanisms	Blog and "My" Sites	Individual
	Profile pages	
	Tagging	
	Ratings	
	I like it	
	Activity feeds	
	User profile service	
	Personalization features	

Supporting Capabilities

Other capabilities are more subtle and difficult to detect because they only materialize as issues in later stages of your portal deployment. Previous portal deployment experience becomes essential to defining these "expert" requirements.

Ensure that your portal strategy caters to the following non-portal specific capabilities:

➤ *Strategy and governance* — Strategy and governance plays a key part in defining how the portal is managed, planned, and aligned to overall enterprise IT strategy and business objectives.

➤ *Organization change, onboarding, and data/content migration services* — The most difficult aspect of any portal deployment is helping the organization change in a manner that supports (rather than disrupts) core business activities. This requires careful planning, business engagement, and communication of key portal features as they are rolled out, and end-user training and education services. Often, data and content migration will be requested. Support for the onboarding of large content and data sets onto the portal platform may be required.

➤ *Information architecture services* — Various parts of the organization will want to leverage the features of your portal platform. They have existing ways of working, or previous sites and portals, as well as how they structure information. Engage with organizations early on to ensure planned and intentional information architecture is applied to new sites in your portal.

➤ *Infrastructure services* — Infrastructure services are required to operate, maintain, optimize, and extend the infrastructure hosting of your production portal platform. These services relate to all activities required to manage the physical infrastructure and configuration, defining processes that manage ongoing changes to your physical infrastructure, and lastly, providing environments that support the development and improvement of your portal platform. Examples include development, user acceptance testing, and pre-production.

➤ *End-user support services* — These services are set up to support employees using the portal environment. They interface, prioritize, and escalate issues to relevant teams for resolution.

➤ *Business analysis, design, and development services* — Once your portal solution has been deployed, the organization will most likely want to implement specific solutions. Depending on your business and portal strategy, either the core portal team, or individual development teams within the organization, will need to analyze and define custom business solutions. Ensure that you plan for ongoing business development on the portal platform. If you allow for independent developed business solutions, make it clear from the start the types of features your core team will and will not support.

Define Your Portal Blueprint

A golden rule to remember is, "The business and senior stakeholders will only understand what you are deploying when they can visualize and conceptualize it in their own minds." Defining a portal blueprint enables you to communicate your vision of the portal strategy and capabilities to the business. It serves as a useful mechanism to generate discussion and feedback from the senior stakeholders.

Take a look at the Global Mega Finance Corporation portal blueprint shown in Figure 12-4.

Corporate Intranet
Root of navigation
1st stop for corporate news

Possible content
- Global navigation
- Corporate news
- Company information
- Content based on global IA
- Regional sites
- Key business, communities and team
- sites pages

Features: Publishing site
- Content approval and workflow
- Various web parts
- Content query web parts
- Content rollup and aggregation

Multiple pages of content

Content Owner:
Corporate Communications Team

Document Centers
Structured persistent information sharing

Possible content
- Office files, such as word, excel, powerpoint.
- Structured metadata for common office formats using global taxonomy
- Document libraries and lists
- Knowledge retention and IP rating tools

Features: Document center site definition
- Enterprise Metadata
- Enterprise Content Types
- Document Management tools

Multiple folders and files

Content Owner:
Business or Function

Records Centers
Management, retention and disposal of information

Possible content
- Records stored based on a file plan
- Folders and files
- Document libraries and lists

Features: Record center site definition
- Content organizer
- Information policies
- Enterprise content types
- Disposal workflows

Search, advanced search and search result pages

Content Owner:
Legal Team

Businesses & Functions
Flexible home to host business and employee content

Possible content
- News
- Business unit sites
- Core competencies
- Reporting dashboards and scorecards
- Internal employee content
- Best practices, processes, methodologies, operational frameworks

Features: Publishing site
- Content approval and workflow
- Various web parts
- Content query web parts
- Content rollup and aggregation

Multiple pages of content, files and other improtant information

Content Owner:
Business/Function

Help and Training
Help manuals and guides

Possible content
- End user content
- FAQ type material
- Getting started and step by step guides
- Other IT system related guides
- Training videos

Features: Publishing site
- Content approval and workflow
- Various web parts
- Content query web parts
- Content rollup and aggregation

Multiple pages of content, videos and related files

Content Owner:
Web Content Manager

My Site
Public profile and private working area

Possible content
- A central location for you to view and manage your documents, tasks, tags, notes, calendar, colleagues, and other personal information.
- A way for other users to learn about you and your areas of expertise, current projects, and colleague relationships.

Features: "My Site" site definition
- My Site private libraries and lists
- Business networking features
- Facebook style activity feeds, notes, tags and blogging capabilities

Various types of content

Content Owner:
Web Content Manager

Governance Center
Site for governing the site provision and hosting portal service offerings

Possible content
- Portal business deployment resources
- Key service announcements
- Solution development lifecycle guidance
- Managed Services details
- Site lifecycle management processes, reports
- Governance policies and procedures

Features: Publishing site
- Content approval and workflow
- Various web parts
- Contact us
- Report a Security Issue

Multiple pages of content

Content Owner:
Web Content Manager

Business Collaboration
Structured business collaboration sites Individual team sites

Possible content
- Team and Wiki Sites
- Custom developed business collaboration site templates, e.g. Project Site or "community of interest" sites
- Structured metadata incorporate global taxonomy

Features: Team, Wiki site definitions
- Lists and libraries
- Workflows
- Web Parts
- Social networking features

Various types of content

Content Owner:
Web Content Manager

Search Center
Global enterprise search center

Possible content
- SharePoint 2010 content
- Legacy SharePoint 2007 content
- Indexed internal or external Web Sites
- Global File Shares
- Line of Business Information

Features: Search Centre Site Definition
- Search
- Advanced Search
- Refinements
- Scopes

Search, advanced search and search result pages

Content Owner:
Web Content Manager

FIGURE 12-4: Portal blueprint

Each section describes the feature, along with possible content and features that will be provided to the organization. Diagrams such as that shown Figure 12-4 help to convey key portal features in a visual format to technical and business stakeholders. In subsequent chapters, you will see these diagrams fleshed out further as you progress in the analysis and design activities.

BUILD YOUR ENTERPRISE PORTAL STRATEGY

By this stage, you have reviewed the business environment, engaged your key stakeholders, and determined their business requirements and drivers. You have mapped out the key portal and supporting capabilities that will support your business drivers, and have defined an overarching portal blueprint that communicates what features your portal strategy will deliver to the organization.

The final step involves defining the strategy and road map, and agreeing on ongoing responsibilities for the stakeholders.

Define Your Strategy

The strategy mapped out here details how you will meet the business drivers of the senior stakeholders. Be sure to follow and align your strategy to the methodology, enterprise architecture components, or business architecture framework used by your organization. The enterprise architecture team or enterprise architect is a key stakeholder to engage with in the definition of your strategy.

Table 12-5 identifies the strategy for Global Mega Finance Corporation.

TABLE 12-5: Defining Your Strategy

CONSIDERATIONS	DESCRIPTION	
Strategy	Provide Global Mega Finance Corporation with a unified business-collaboration platform that enables people to collaborate across geographically dispersed businesses.	
	Provide world-class search capabilities to enable users to find information from across all businesses.	
	Provide a unified business collaboration platform that differentiates Global Mega Finance Corporation from its competitors.	
Culture	Global Mega Finance Corporation will stimulate employees to share information, by recognizing and awarding people that contribute to the unified business platform.	
	Senior stakeholders to use and champion collaboration and publishing tools.	
	Embed the use of collaboration tools in each employee's performance objectives and appraisal.	
	Ensure a unified business platform is used to communicate key messages to the business at all levels of the business.	

CONSIDERATIONS	DESCRIPTION
Organization	Create a global knowledge management and business change team to roll out key capabilities to the business.
	Assign senior executive sponsors and a working project sponsor.
	Form a steering committee to assist in the piloting and rollout.
	Involve key functions (such Corp Communications, Legal, and Human Resources) from analysis through to launch stage.
	Assign a program manager who will oversee the development and deployment of the portal capability.
Competencies	Skills to analyze and interpret business requirements into a portal solution that is most appropriate for the business.
	Skills to operate and maintain the unified portal platform.
	Skills to design, develop, and deploy the portal platform.
	Skills to measure the success of the portal platform.
	Skills to ensure end users are able to take advantage of the features of the portal platform, through the implementation of an end-user training strategy.
Success metrics or performance measures	Surveying employee base on usage of key capabilities returns a "good" or "improving" score.
	Analysis of communities and collaboration sites demonstrates an increasing number of users are adopting and using the portal platform.
	Users report that collaboration tools are improving their productivity.
	Users report they can find information when they need it.
	Users complete and update their user profile on a regular basis.
	Users develop business networks using SharePoint's social networking capability.
Processes	Provide business analysis and design processes to define what features are required for each audience of the business.
	Provide world-class onboarding processes that provide support to onboard each of the businesses onto the unified platform.
	Set up measurement and feedback processes to monitor and improve the platform.

continues

TABLE 12-5 *(continued)*

CONSIDERATIONS	DESCRIPTION	
Technology	Provide key portal capabilities using SharePoint 2010 either hosted in the cloud or on-premise.	
	Provide a seamless, integrated user experience using SharePoint 2010 and Office 2010.	
	Ensure that a business IM platform (using Office Communications or Microsoft Lync Server) is in place and all users have the client installed.	
	Ensure that all users have at least Internet Explorer 8.0 installed.	
	Provide search capabilities using either SharePoint 2010 embedded search or dedicated FAST For SharePoint search capabilities.	
	Provide predefined site templates to provide key audiences in the business with the tools they require.	
	Surface business data from internal business systems in SharePoint 2010 sites.	
	Surface user profile data from multiple systems in one place.	

DEFINE YOUR ROAD MAP

Your road map defines when each capability will be available to your business. The formation of the road map is based on the following factors:

➤ Foremost, it reflects the business priorities of your senior stakeholders.

➤ It reflects the maturity of your end users and business. For example, you cannot expect users to use advanced collaboration techniques when they are not familiar with the basic portal collaboration concepts.

➤ It reflects the budget, schedule, and resource constraints imposed on your project team.

➤ It reflects the alignment to the deployment of other enabling technologies, such as business IM tools (for example, Microsoft Lync).

➤ It should reflect that portal development is iterative and incremental (versus one "big-bang") in nature.

A key lesson learned from previous projects is that bundling too many capabilities into one release is risky for a number of reasons:

➤ It results in too much business change work to do in one go.

➤ Organizations tend to judge all of your project team's work, rather than each capability provided.

➤ Having to wait for updates can be frustrating to the organizations.

Following is a common approach to laying out what capabilities to deploy:

1. Start off with capabilities that form the foundation of collaboration and portal technologies.

2. After the initial deployment has stabilized, and issues are ironed out, additional capabilities are provided. These expansive capabilities extend and enhance foundational capabilities.

3. As the portal deployment matures, advanced capabilities are requested.

4. Specific capabilities depend on the business scenario. These may be isolated and specific in nature, or added to a number of key business and function sites.

 After each step, it is vital that you plan for, communicate, and market the capabilities of your release to the business. It is crucial that you provide both business transformation (business onboarding) guidance and assistance, and ensure that training is available for end users.

Using the Global Mega Finance Corporation scenario, Figure 12-5 shows a road map that defines a plan for the onboarding of portal services into their environment.

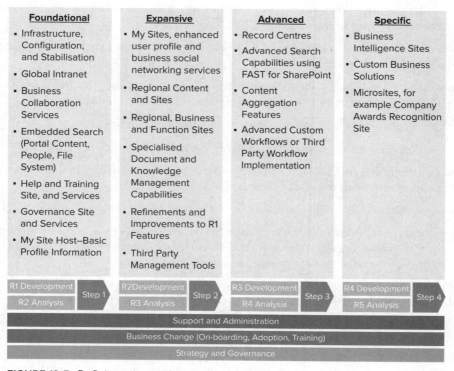

FIGURE 12-5: Defining your road map

As you can see, you start off by focusing on the foundational set of features required by the business. Following are some examples of foundational capabilities:

➤ *Collaboration technologies* — This includes the capability to create and use various team site templates and features. This is often where most users will learn how to leverage SharePoint 2010 business collaboration features.

➤ *Publishing technologies* — This includes the capability to provide a global intranet containing well-defined site structure, global navigation, strong portal brand, and content pertinent to various audiences in the organization.

➤ *Search technologies* — This includes the capability to find people and information in your business collaboration and portal sites. Deploying search capabilities can really help you determine more detailed requirements to expand and drive out the quality of your search results in future releases.

➤ *End-user help and training center* — This includes the capability to find self-help information related to a features set provided by the SharePoint 2010 platform. End users require advice and guidance on how to perform common tasks on a portal platform. Support the business as users begin using your new platform.

➤ *Basic user profile information* — This includes the capability to maintain and search on basic user profile information. Detailed user profile information requires each user to have a My Site to enable users to edit their profile information. In new deployments, it often makes sense to stabilize the infrastructure and teams supporting these environments before adding a large number of My Sites to the mix.

➤ *Simple workflows* — Common out-of-the-box workflows (such as the capability to approve a document) can be made available.

➤ *Governance site* — This is a key site to deploy early on. The governance site will host key business onboarding information, key sites and services, and service announcements.

Following are expansive capabilities that enhance these foundational capabilities:

➤ *"My Site"* — This includes the migration of a user's home drive to his or her "My Site."

➤ *Enhanced user profile* — Additional user profile properties are provided to enable users to share more information with the rest of the business.

➤ *Business social networking* — This includes the enablement of social networking features.

➤ *Business intranets* — This includes the capability for businesses first to leverage publishing portal features to enable them to communicate their core competencies and services, and secondly, to provide targeted tools to employees in their organization.

➤ *Function intranets* — This includes the capability for functions within the organization to provide a one-stop shop for services related to their function. For example, a human resources site might provide policies, tools, procedures, and forms to employees of the entire business.

➤ *Specialized document management capabilities* — Specialized document center and records management features are common features that require a good understanding of the basic collaboration toolset that SharePoint provides.

➤ *Expansive search capabilities* — This may involve configuring refiners of your search criteria, or improving the scopes to enable users to target a search to a subset of your business data.

➤ *Third-party management tools* — Third-party management tools will help your operation team manage the large array of sites in your environment.

Advanced capabilities require a good understanding of basic SharePoint 2010 sites and list concepts. Advanced features tend to rely on and leverage foundational and expansive capabilities. Examples of these include the following:

➤ *Tailored workflows* — Workflows are more advanced in nature. They are custom in nature, and may automate the fulfillment of a specific business process.

➤ *Advanced search capabilities* — Your organization may require more advanced search capabilities (such as FAST for SharePoint 2010). These technologies and the supporting infrastructure require specialist skills and resources to deploy.

➤ *Specialist third-party complementary technologies* — An example is workflow technologies. Although SharePoint provides fantastic workflow capabilities, complementary third-party tools take business process management to a whole new level in SharePoint 2010.

➤ *Content aggregation* — SharePoint stores content in site collections. Often, organizations require aggregated views of content from multiple site collections. These types of requirements need either custom development, or third-party aggregation tools.

➤ *Record centers* — Often, legal and regulatory requirements require detailed data analysis and information repository design. Third-party data cleansing, analysis, and migration tools are used to onboard content.

Finally, specific capabilities provide solutions focused on a narrow set of requirements or business problems. Business priorities govern when these solutions are deployed. Examples of these are as follows:

➤ *Business Intelligence Sites* — These use a plethora of performance management technologies to surface data related to the state of various aspects of your organization in a number of scorecards in real-time dashboards.

➤ *Custom business solutions* — These include custom developed business solutions that integrate and surface line of business (LOB) data in various SharePoint Portals.

➤ *Micro-sites* — These include internally focused publishing sites such as a company recognition and awards program, or an internal product awareness site.

AGREE ON STAKEHOLDER RESPONSIBILITIES

There is a direct relation between the involvement of key and senior stakeholders, and the success and adoption of collaboration and portal strategies.

To provide an example, in a previous project, a large global business was in the process of rebranding and merging a number of individual and largely autonomous businesses under one single global brand. This was a big challenge internally and externally, a truly monumental task!

What made it work? The CEO, CIO, board, and business project team were visionary in their approach. Right from the start, the senior leaders led "from the front," got involved early on, appointed the right people, and, when it was deployed, used the technology to inspire the entire business to get involved. Each stakeholder knew what was required of him or her.

 A very useful tool to help you represent the responsibilities of each stakeholder is called an RACI matrix. This tool is especially useful in clarifying roles and responsibilities relating to your implementation of your portal strategy. RACI is an acronym for four key responsibilities generally used: Responsible, Accountable, Consulted, and Informed. For more information, see: `www.projectsmart.co.uk/raci-matrix.html`.

What key stakeholder inputs do you require to achieve your portal strategy?

Executive Sponsorship

The *executive sponsor* is the leader with overall responsibility for the project in your business. The executive sponsor provides the strategic context and direction, and ensures the project initiative receives the proper level of investment.

The executive sponsor will champion the project internally and externally, communicate throughout the business, and encourage business management to support and resource the project. It is important that the executive sponsor takes the time to understand what will be delivered, and educates himself or herself on the portal strategy, the planned implementation, and how it aligns with the overall business objectives.

The executive sponsor owns the business benefits, signs off on the business case, portal strategy and road map, scope of work, budget, and plan. He or she will monitor progress and direction of the project, and exert influence to keep the project aligned with business objectives. The executive sponsor is accountable for delivering the project's expected business benefits.

Finally, the executive sponsor should accept responsibility for problems escalated from the program and project manager, and resolve these problems in a timely manner.

Steering Committee or Board

The *steering committee/project governance board* consists of a set of individuals from across the business that have a vested interest in realizing the business objectives associated with your portal strategy. They drive the decision making, and serve as the overall decision-maker and governing body of the project.

The steering committee attends regular meetings with the project team to ensure that the project stays on track, and is aligned with the business objectives and strategy. Other key responsibilities include resolving issues escalated by the project team, managing the scope of the project, authorizing changes to the scope of the project, and signing off on the project.

Project Sponsorship

The *project sponsor* is a senior business manager from the IT department, or a business department that is closely aligned and involved in the project. The project sponsor works with the steering committee and executive sponsor, as well as directing the operational execution of the project's program and project management team.

The project sponsor assists the business in planning the required business transformation to adopt the technology to ensure ongoing realization of the business benefits. This includes directing activities such as training, internal communication, championing, implementation, and maintenance.

The project sponsor resolves issues escalated by the project team, monitors progress and direction of the project, communicates regularly with the program manager, project manager, executive sponsor, and the steering committee, manages the scope of the project, and authorizes changes to the scope of the project.

Program Manager

The *program manager* is responsible for operational execution, support, and oversight of the project. This involves working with the project and technical leads to ensure a high-quality product is delivered, and managing the various streams of work. In SharePoint projects, these streams may include the following teams:

- Analysis
- Architecture and Design
- Development
- Quality Assurance
- Implementation
- Infrastructure
- Maintenance
- Business Change and Adoption
- Service and Support

The program manager identifies and mitigates risks, and, when required, escalates these to the project sponsor and steering committee for resolution.

A key activity of the program manager is to educate the project sponsor, executive sponsor, and steering committee on the details related to your project. This will enable them to make better decisions, provide better support, and overcome hurdles and obstacles.

Project Manager

The *project manager's* job is to deliver on time, on budget, and to specification to ensure that the project succeeds. This includes planning, organizing, securing, and managing of resources to create the best possible outcome.

Project Team

The *project team* includes all who are involved in the project, including the project manager. In SharePoint projects, typical members and roles include analysts, architects, developers, testers, infrastructure and configuration specialists, business change specialists, and consultants.

End Users

End users are the people in your business who will provide end-user requirements and benefit from the deployment of SharePoint. End users are involved in various stages of your project, including defining detailed requirements, personas and use cases, validation of the business-oriented feature specifications, and user acceptance testing.

BEST PRACTICES

The following are best practices to follow when defining your portal strategy:

➤ *Don't let "the tail wag the dog"* — Derive your features and portal capabilities based on business drivers and objectives of your key stakeholders, not on the latest "cool" technology.

➤ *Don't deploy all your capabilities in one release* — Form the foundation, review, improve, and expand through a number of iterative releases. Aim to deploy your first release within three to five months of getting started, followed by subsequent updates and releases every six to ten weeks.

➤ *Don't overload users with too much change, too fast* — Take the business on the journey, and educate users in the process of releasing each new capability.

➤ *Set "business change" expectation early on* — Portal technology will not change a business on its own. Portal software is only a facilitator of change. Real change requires a business change plan, engagement, and resources to help your business exploit the capabilities defined in your portal strategy.

➤ *Think about how you will communicate your portal strategy* — Not all business stakeholders have a mature understanding of collaboration and portal technologies. They are business experts and not necessarily IT experts. Your portal strategy must be able to communicate the vision, strategy, and benefits in terms they will understand, buy into, support, and champion.

➤ *Define return on investment, but don't go overboard* — Return on investment (ROI) is difficult to calculate in the early stages of the project because portal capabilities do not always directly link to business processes that may be improved by the introduction of portal software. In the early stages, focus on common end-user activities that will benefit from your portal strategy, and map the ROI back to the business drivers of the senior stakeholders. As your deployment matures, frequently measure against your ROI goals to ensure that you're trending in the right direction as required by the business drivers of the senior stakeholders.

➤ *Galvanize political support* — Senior business leaders have influence and the capability to make strategic decisions. It is not up to you to fight battles, but it is up to you to get the support of senior leaders to overcome roadblocks along the way.

SUMMARY

Defining your SharePoint 2010 portal strategy involves a good understanding of various dimensions of your business information ecology. Engage your key stakeholders to understand their requirements and business drivers. This will help you define the portal and supporting capabilities, and create a blueprint of your portal services.

Develop the strategy you will employ to meet the business drivers and deliver the solution. Ensure that your strategy is aligned with senior stakeholders and the overall enterprise architecture of your business. Define a road map to communicate when the business will be able to benefit from each capability. Finally, set up the correct governance structures and resource responsibilities to support and guide your portal deployment to success.

In Chapter 13, you learn about getting started with your SharePoint 2010 project.

13

Getting Started with Your Program and Projects

By Brian Wilson

In Chapter 12, you learned about the business drivers of your key stakeholders. You learned how to map the business drivers to a set of portal and supporting capabilities that would achieve senior stakeholder objectives. You learned more about each capability by looking at the requirements of each audience affected, and produced a high-level portal blueprint. Finally, you learned how to produce an enterprise portal strategy and a high-level road map for introducing these capabilities into your business.

This chapter uses the previously defined SharePoint 2010 portal strategy to get started with your SharePoint 2010 program and projects.

Getting started with your SharePoint 2010 program and projects can be a bewildering and daunting phase. A number of activities, tasks, and streams of work must take place. This chapter discusses the key activities, work streams, tasks, skills, and outputs required to get started with the inception and early elaboration phases of your projects.

"Rome wasn't built in a day," and neither are SharePoint 2010 portal deployments. In the real world, SharePoint 2010 deployments consist of a number of related projects and streams of work. The grouping of these related projects is what is referred to as a *program*.

In a SharePoint 2010 program of work, the types of projects vary significantly, depending on the stage of your program, the size and reach of your deployment, the feature set you require, and the maturity of your existing portal deployment.

It is important to understand that some of the work streams will continue throughout the life cycle of the program; other work streams will apply chiefly to the "getting started" phases of your program. Furthermore, a number of work streams will evolve into mini projects, each with a clearly defined scope, cost, and schedule for delivery.

Following are some common "getting started" work streams:

➤ Requirements activities

➤ Technical design activities

➤ Early technical leadership activities

➤ Program and project management activities

➤ Business change and adoption activities

Future work streams continue the previously mentioned streams and add the following areas:

➤ Information architecture, solution/application architecture, and infrastructure architecture activities

➤ Development, testing, and deployment activities

➤ Operations and governance activities

Although all topics covered in this chapter are important, this chapter has been designed to enable you to read the sections you are interested in. Additionally, subsequent chapters elaborate in more detail on activities and work streams introduced in this chapter.

REQUIREMENTS ACTIVITIES

There is a great quote that defines requirements:

> *Requirements are the what; design is the how.*

Put simply, requirements define what your business system will do and not do; what capabilities it will provide; how it will perform; and what it will accomplish.

SharePoint 2010 projects vary greatly in scope, size, and complexity, depending on the stage you are at in the portal life cycle. This influences the amount of work and level of detail required in your requirements-capture process.

To illustrate this further, consider the types of requirements you would elicit at the start of a new SharePoint 2010 deployment, versus the requirements for a new team site on an existing SharePoint 2010 platform.

From a SharePoint perspective, although requirements can be grouped in many categories, broadly speaking, requirements can be broken down into functional and non-functional requirements:

➤ *Functional requirements* — These specify what a system should do. An example of a functional requirement is the requirement to be able to upload a document to a document library.

➤ *Non-functional requirements* — These specify how the system should behave. This type of requirement specifies the system's quality characteristics or quality attributes. An example of a non-functional requirement is the requirement that all users must be able to complete a 1 MB document upload to a library within 30 seconds. The requirement relates to performance of your farm and network.

A number of great books, methodologies, and best practices already defined are available on how best to gather functional and non-functional requirements. This section does not aim to redefine the wheel, but instead draw out key issues related to SharePoint 2010 projects.

The first step in any SharePoint 2010 project is to understand and review the body of knowledge developed thus far. The amount of information will vary from non-existent/still to be defined, to detailed and thoughtful.

The following high-level points should be considered when embarking on a requirements-gathering exercise for a SharePoint 2010 project:

> *Focus on the end user* — New and "upgrade" portal projects tend to focus more on delivering various core and support capabilities, or platform-related requirements. Beware of the pitfall of over-focusing on platform capabilities as opposed to end-user benefits and requirements.

> *Do not over-engineer the platform* — The real value derived from a SharePoint 2010 platform comes from the business solutions it hosts and supports. Prefer to focus more time on requirements that deliver business value.

> *Do not write* War and Peace — Microsoft owns the out-of-the-box product and the requirements documentation related to it. Try to focus your energy and limited resources on specifics related to the significant use cases of your project and deployment. It sounds obvious, but teams often attempt to produce exhaustive documentation sets.

> *Gather requirements with delivery in mind* — Always keep at the back of your mind that the requirements will be grouped into buckets of functionality that will be released in successive iterations and deployments to the business. The pace of innovation and new IT releases essentially forces you to work and deliver your project in smaller iterations. Do not gather so many requirements that it will take a full year of development before end users will be able to start benefiting from your SharePoint 2010 deployment.

> *Consider what you can achieve* — Gather requirements that you can achieve, and guard your scope to ensure that you can deliver on time, within budget to a level that excites and exceeds stakeholder expectations.

This section covers the *requirements analysis* activities. This is defined as the process of gathering and eliciting business requirements to understand what the organization requires. It involves refining, validating, and recording those requirements to enable the organization to understand what it will be getting (and signing off on), designing, and developing.

Eliciting Requirements

Eliciting requirements is the structured and organized process that involves a number of techniques to identify all the user and business requirements within a reasonable time span that does not result in a state of "analysis paralysis." Common techniques used today include conducting meetings, interviews, workshops, surveys and questionnaires, use cases and scenarios, mockups, role playing, and prototyping.

Of all the techniques, mockups and prototypes are probably the most useful. There is an old saying that comes to mind: "The business only knows what they want when they can visualize or see it."

The quality of requirements can be improved by demoing features, showing live-site examples, or using tools like Balsamiq and Microsoft Visio to demonstrate how a feature or screen could look. PowerPoint can also be used to demonstrate how a feature or site would function through a series of screens presented as slides.

Often, requirements practitioners advocate a best practice of eliciting requirements in a product-agnostic fashion — in other words, not biasing the requirement to a particular technology such as SharePoint 2010. Though this is helpful for some projects, it does not take into account that the organization may have already accepted and chosen SharePoint 2010 as the platform.

Rigidly applying platform agnosticism, where there is a predefined platform, can sometimes feel like "tugging on Superman's cape." If you are not careful, it can result in a high degree of customization to meet a requirement that may not be suited to SharePoint 2010. Therefore, in some cases, although you should always strive to capture product-agnostic requirements, it helps to limit or scope your requirement gathering to within the bounds and capabilities of the SharePoint 2010 platform, or to interpret requirements that the organization expresses according to what you know SharePoint 2010 can do.

A common type of requirement that is often forgotten is tacit, implied, and non-functional requirements. For example, search must return results to users within 5 seconds, or the page must display within 7 seconds of the user requesting it. These requirements imply performance, which, in turn, constrain designers, developers, and testers to ensure that they meet and adhere to these non-functional requirements. Finally, non-functional requirements influence the infrastructure and solution design decisions.

Mutual understanding is important when eliciting requirements from the organization. Be wary of taking for granted the lack of knowledge a business stakeholder may have in terms of the SharePoint 2010 feature set, information architecture, and the specialism (for example, records management) your solution relates to. Using even simple terms such as "document library," "site collection navigation," or "quick launch" can lose non-technical stakeholders, and degrade the quality of requirements gathered.

Differentiate between "expert" and end-user requirements. An "expert," in this case, may be a member of your team responsible for the implementation of the SharePoint 2010 solution, whereas an end user will be someone stuck with your solution on a day-to-day basis.

Always attempt to capture and win over these users and business champions by including them in the requirements-gathering process. The hardest lesson for any SharePoint specialist and expert is learning that what you think is best may not be what the organization is looking or asking for, and that the product and "field" theory you are prepared to stake your reputation on may not be the right solution for a particular organization.

Workshops are a crucial element for discussing areas of the new portal solution. Be different in these workshops. Make them interesting, entertaining, and fun. The quality of requirements captured from a group of people losing the "will to live" will not be as good as an engaged, empowered, stimulated, and "awake" group of individuals exercising and contributing their ideas.

Another key point about workshops is not to attempt to put too much into a single workshop, but rather to split them out over a number of smaller workshops. People need time to formulate a considered opinion, and one workshop does not give them a chance to do this.

Analyzing Requirements

Planning a SharePoint deployment is similar to architecting the house of your dreams with your spouse or partner. Once you have settled on a floor plan, built the house, and moved in your furniture, it can sometimes be very difficult to change the structure of the house without requiring extensive renovation and work. To make matters worse, your wife or partner is used to the current layout, and may be prepared to mud-wrestle you before changing it! Similarly, if you make a mistake in your SharePoint design, you will have to live with it for the next three to five years, or be prepared to pay for renovations.

New SharePoint deployment projects (especially in large organizations) are often prefaced by a product-selection phase where the business has gathered thousands of generic requirements to impartially judge a number of collaboration tools. Once an organization chooses SharePoint 2010, it may have an expectation that any resulting solution will meet this long list of carefully crafted requirements on Day One.

This in itself is a daunting expectation that can be mitigated by setting expectations using the previously defined road map developed as part of your portal strategy. Depending on the size of the projects and budget available, do not try to meet all of them on Day One. The organization will not appreciate it, and will not be able to take on so many "business change" elements required to use all the features delivered.

New platform deployments of SharePoint 2010 benefit greatly from grouping requirements into "chunks" that the organization can assimilate, consume, and appreciate. The requirements should be grouped into foundational, expansive, advanced, business solutions, and specific issues. This approach dictates small releases with frequent iterations.

Existing SharePoint 2010 deployments benefit greatly from a change-management process that controls and validates new business requirements. This also determines which changes are suitable and in line with the goals and aims of the SharePoint 2010 platform. An ungoverned change process is one of the worst places to be in terms of your SharePoint 2010 deployment. It is critical that you set up a change process to handle, prioritize, deny, and control chargeback for changes required to your SharePoint 2010 platform.

An important tool in the SharePoint designer and architect's tool belt is the *MoSCoW method*. This is a prioritization technique that can be used to determine the importance the business places on the delivery of each requirement. It labels each requirement in the following four buckets:

➤ *M (Must)* — The requirement must be delivered in the current delivery in order for the project to be a success.

➤ *S (Should)* — The requirement is critical to the success of the project, but does not need to be delivered in the current delivery.

➤ *C (Could)* — The requirement is less critical to the success of the project, and includes features that are "nice to have."

➤ *W (Won't)* — The requirement is not critical to the success of the project and won't make a difference to the project. This includes features that the business *would* want in the future.

Other criteria that should influence the MoSCoW rating of each requirement are the balancing of cost (budget and resources at your disposal), schedule (what time frame you have to deliver within), and quality (features you can expect to deliver, given the cost and schedule). Prioritizing everything as a *must* defeats the point of a prioritization exercise, and could result in a lengthy project to deliver the first or next release to the business.

Validating Requirements

Vision demonstrators are a visual representation of the UI and planned user experience. Vision demonstrators are high-level application mockups that describe the functionality, design, structure, and characteristics of a key part of your SharePoint portal solution. They range from a simple web page mockup or set of PowerPoint slides displaying a sequence of screens, to a complex Flash-powered click-through, or even an early SharePoint UI prototype to bring a key use case to life.

Functional storyboards help model business processes, and describe the UI and flow of your SharePoint solution. Whereas vision demonstrators are most commonly used to "sell" a concept, functional storyboards are more commonly used to drive out the detail and flows for individual use cases. They highlight select elements of the UI to help users visualize how they would work with the proposed solution.

Vision demonstrators and functional storyboards are typically mocked up by user experience design specialists on your team using tools ranging from common ones such as PowerPoint, Visio, and Balsamiq, to the more advanced and widely recognized tools such as Expression Blend (SketchFlow) and Photoshop.

These tools should not be underestimated in terms of the value they provide in the early conceptual stages of a SharePoint 2010 project. They are extremely useful for gathering consensus, driving decisions on requirements, and engaging and exciting business stakeholders. Vision demonstrators provide valuable early "quality" feedback and validation to your understanding of the business requirements.

> *What makes a good requirement? The Texas Project Delivery Framework defines the characteristics of a good requirement as "cohesive; complete; consistent; correct; feasible; necessary and prioritized; measurable, testable and verifiable; traceable and unambiguous." You can view more information on this at* http://www.ultimatesdlc.com/are-your-requirements-good/.

All requirements and use cases should be verified, reviewed, and signed-off on by the key business stakeholders. Requirements and use case documents should also be validated for completeness and accuracy. These documents will be passed to the onshore or offshore technical team, and mistakes will lead to additional cost to rework.

One particularly subtle issue relates to the use of the correct terminology across use cases to save on rework and redevelopment later when testers find UI screens that use inconsistent terminology. Although developers will always strive to use .NET "resource" files to make these sorts of changes easier, it still takes time to rework these files and update the solution deployment.

Recording Requirements

The *recording requirements* for SharePoint projects vary greatly, depending on the software development methodology in use, as well as the skills and the knowledge of the analysis team. Common approaches include the following:

➤ *Requirements lists approach* — The traditional (but out of date) way of documenting requirements is to create long lists of requirements. The strengths of this approach include creating a checklist of requirements to tick off, and forming a contract between customer and supplier. Its key weakness is that these requirements are often too generic and not specific enough to be useful or valuable to the business. Recording requirements using this approach does not make it easy to develop a coherent understanding of the intended SharePoint solution. Lastly, these may not be written with the actors or end users of the system in mind. Requirements lists are often seen during the product evaluation and selection process.

➤ *System and user stories approach* — This is the preferred approach to documenting requirements for SharePoint 2010 projects. User stories capture what the user wants to achieve in the language of the business or end user. For example, "As a user, I want to be able to search for documents modified between two dates." User stories typically follow a "as a <role>, I want <goal/desire>" pattern.

➤ *Use cases approach* — Use cases describe a real scenario in detail, along with a set of steps (the primary flow) the users will take using the system to complete their objectives. The use case will also describe the alternative flows that may occur, depending on conditions that occur during the primary flow. This is the method that should always be used to capture business requirements. Use cases enable both business and technical stakeholders to understand what the proposed solution will do and achieve. They simplify the writing of test cases, and make user acceptance testing easier, because the use case can be used to evaluate the developed and deployed solution. Finally, they leave less room for ambiguity, which helps with getting the development right the first time around, reducing the number of bugs, and, therefore, improving the overall quality of the solution.

Before you start writing large volumes of documentation, it is important to understand your purpose, intended usage, and requirements for these documents, because this will determine the level of detail required for this documentation. Key areas of focus include the following:

➤ *Business sign-off* — Will the business use these documents to sign off on its agreement for the captured requirements?

➤ *Design and development team* — Will these documents be used to provide the necessary detail to the design and development team?

➤ *Requirements traceability* — Will these documents provide the source of a requirement, or be the formal "trace" documents to assist in requirements traceability?

➤ *Testability* — Formal mature test teams insist on well-documented, clearly defined requirements to enable them to test and sign off on work from your development team. Will these documents be used by your testing team?

> ➤ *User acceptance testing and sign-off* — Will these documents be used during user acceptance testing to validate correct development and deployment of a solution that meets the requirements?

> ➤ *Business communication* — Will these documents be used as a means to communicate a feature set to your business stakeholders?

Other factors that influence the recording of requirements are the methodology used, and whether you are using an offshore or onshore team.

Waterfall-based methodologies tend to be more prescriptive and require more work up front to ensure that the requirements are accurately captured, whereas Agile-based methodologies tend to favor working software over documentation, and using different methods and documents to capture requirements.

Offshore development teams require very detailed and very prescriptive documentation to ensure that a high-quality product is delivered, whereas onshore teams have the luxury and ease of communication with the business at their side to validate requirements whenever required.

These factors determine the degree of completeness of the documentation, and dictate the level and number of resources required to capture and document the requirements.

Following are reasons to insist on a complete set of up-to-date documentation as part of the delivery of a successful release to the business:

> ➤ *People turnover* — Analysts, designers, architects, developers, testers, and partner development teams may not be available or used in the next phase of the project. How can future development occur with an understanding of previous design decisions without an up-to-date set of documentation?

> ➤ *Service and support team* — How can your support team manage a SharePoint 2010 service/solution/platform that has not been documented?

> ➤ *It's unprofessional* — Releasing a solution that has an incomplete set of accompanying business and technical documentation shows a lack of professionalism.

If you do not insist on this, you will never be able to maintain a complete and consistent documentation set, and your ability to govern and support the SharePoint solution will be reduced.

TECHNICAL DESIGN ACTIVITIES

The early design stage is one of the most demanding stages for a SharePoint architect. It includes activities such as reviewing and understanding existing work, undertaking early design activities, conceptualizing the high-level information, solution and infrastructure design, taking the lead in a number of technical areas, estimating the cost and resources required to enable program and project management to resource up the project, and producing a set of outputs or artifacts that will contribute to the next stage of detailed elaboration and future development phases.

The early design stage involves identifying the key technical decisions that must be made, driving these to successful resolution, mocking up screens, prototyping concepts, solidifying requirements and use cases, and driving down the risk profile of the project.

A key attribute of a design or SharePoint architect is the capability to deal with ambiguity that often characterizes the early stages of a project. It is the SharePoint architect's responsibility to provide structure and methods to drive out key technical decisions. A subtle (but important) hidden requirement is the capability to communicate how this will be done to a non-technical program and project management team. This will help them develop an increasing confidence in your ability to lead the technical aspects of the solution, and help to promote consensus on the proposed solution.

This section discusses a set of steps and activities that technical members should perform during the early stages of a project.

Forming an Understanding of the Project and Customer Requirements

The first step for a technical SharePoint architect involves forming an understanding of the project and customer requirements. This involves analyzing what will be required to achieve the business vision and deliver the capabilities set out in the portal strategy constrained by the scope and road map of the program and immediate project. Table 13-1 lists key areas that should be reviewed and understood.

TABLE 13-1: Forming an Understanding of the Project and Customer Requirements

AREA	CONSIDERATIONS
Portal strategy and business case documentation	The portal strategy documentation describes the business drivers provided by the key stakeholders, the core and supporting capabilities required of the portal deployment, (hopefully) a high-level portal blueprint, and a road map that sets out and prioritizes how the capabilities should be delivered to the business. The business case defines the strategic goals and objectives, the likely outcomes and benefits, and risks and assumptions made.
Functional requirements	Requirements documentation consists of a combination of product list evaluation criteria, as well as functional requirements in the form of requirements lists, user stories, and use cases.
	How far has the analysis team progressed in the gathering, analyzing, validating, and documenting of the requirements? How mature are these requirements? Immature requirements present a risk to your project in the following ways. They often result in late changes and present themselves as an ever-increasing scope. To suppliers delivering this solution on a fixed cost (rather than on time and materials), they present a danger to the profitability and commercial viability of the project.

continues

TABLE 13-1 *(continued)*

AREA	CONSIDERATIONS
Non-functional requirements	Non-functional requirements include a number of factors. The first factor is the geography of the solution — that is, the regions, countries, office locations — and number of end users in each location the solution must support.
	The second factor is the physical network that the portal solution will leverage to enable end users to interact with the portal deployment. This network should be assessed as part of any solution deployment to ascertain whether it will constrain any proposed portal solution.
	Other key factors include key roles, audiences, security and compliance requirements, volumetrics of the proposed solution, and scale required to support the business portal deployment.
Types of content	The range of content dynamism is important to understand. Will content mostly consist of static (hardly changing) content placed on SharePoint pages? Will web pages be highly dynamic with content pulled and aggregated from various locations across a number of site collections? Finally, will pages require a high degree of multimedia assets, such as videos, Flash, or Silverlight media?
Migration requirements	Most businesses today have developed and use a business intranet, extranet, or Internet site. The migration of content from existing legacy SharePoint or legacy solutions can be difficult to achieve, and can significantly impact the design of a new SharePoint 2010 portal solution.
Operating system	The operating system and Microsoft Office version used by the business tells you a lot about where its IT department is today, and its approach to software.
	Are a large portion of the end users still stuck with Windows XP? While this, in itself, will not hamper the capability to deploy SharePoint 2010, it indicates that the business tends to stick with software investments for a long period of time before upgrading. This indicates that your solution and design will need to cope with much longer life cycles.
	Users stuck on operating systems older than Windows Vista may require more education than end users using newer operating systems.
	Is your business using a non-Microsoft operating system (such as Apple or Linux) as the common operating system for all end users? There may be a higher level of resistance to the deployment of any proposed Microsoft technology. Sufficient operational skills may not be available to support the suite of Microsoft server operating systems, and supporting software technologies.
Enterprise e-mail solution	Is the Exchange server and messaging solution in use at the business? Is an alternative solution (such as Lotus Notes) in place? This may indicate that the business is an "IBM shop" and you may struggle (especially without senior executive involvement) to deploy Microsoft technologies that compete with IBM technologies that complement Lotus Notes.

AREA	CONSIDERATIONS
Office Suite version	Which version of Microsoft Office is in place today? Are upgrades planned in the near future? Microsoft Office 2007 introduced the concept of the "Ribbon" to end users in the business. Therefore, businesses using previous versions will require a greater level of education to help them use the SharePoint 2010 Ribbon-based solution.
	The Office version also indicates the level of seamless integration that is provided between SharePoint 2010 and Microsoft Office. The older the Office client, the less integration SharePoint 2010 will provide it.
Browser version	Although Microsoft supports a large number of browsers and browser versions, the amount of support differs greatly. Ensure that your browser is supported by the SharePoint product team. See "Plan browser support" at `http://technet.microsoft.com/en-us/library/cc263526.aspx` for more information.
	Recently, Firefox indicated it no longer provided support for previous versions of Firefox once a new version is released. This greatly affects the supportability and security of existing business deployments, and this subsequently affects the supportability of SharePoint 2010 deployments using the Firefox browser. The SharePoint product team has only tested certain versions of Firefox, and understandably, will not be able to keep pace with the Firefox release schedule because the choice of browsers supported is made early on in SharePoint development life cycle.

As you gather an understanding, and gain a better insight and context, the scope of the project should become clearer. This will help you identify project risks and raise them up to program and project management to manage and resolve.

The next step discusses the early design activities that you will embark on while getting started or in the early elaboration phases of your project.

Beginning Early Design Activities

It is important to point out that, at the "getting started" stage of the project, much of the early and detailed elaboration may not have taken place. Requirements workshops may have just begun, the program and project may still be spinning up, the business change team may not have been recruited, and the technical and requirements team may not yet be fully resourced.

The early technical design activities can be broadly classed into two categories:

➤ Those that relate to strategic, operational, and non-functional business and technical requirements

➤ Those that relate directly to output of the requirements-gathering activities

Strategic, Operational, and Non-Functional Business and Technical Requirements Design Activities

At this stage of the project, these types of requirements refer to fluid or yet-to-be-defined requirements that must be assessed, validated, and closed off. After these have been assessed, a documented recommendation is provided to the program and project management team. Let's take a look at examples of this type of design activity.

The first example describes an increasingly common strategic requirement where the business wishes to leverage cloud-based services (such as Office 365) to host the future portal solutions. From this requirement, the technical SharePoint architect needs to deduce what technical activities are required to assess and validate the suitability of a cloud-based solution. This may include the realization that this requires the help of network architecture and infrastructure team, as well as the Active Directory teams, to understand how to link the business network and enable users to authenticate using their existing credentials to any cloud-based portal solution.

The second example relates to the selection of the SharePoint 2010 licensing model, which may be constrained by the budget or enterprise agreement already in place between Microsoft and the business. In cases where the business does not already have the licenses, the SharePoint architect may be required to assist in understanding what license will be required to support the business drivers, portal strategy, and road map. This decision will impact the immediate project, as well as future projects planned for the SharePoint 2010 platform.

Following are some other examples:

➤ Should the business use FAST Search for SharePoint or SharePoint 2010 search?

➤ Should physical or virtual hardware be used?

➤ Does the business have an archiving strategy that must be integrated into SharePoint 2010 solution?

➤ Does the business have any legal hold and compliance requirements?

➤ What enterprise disk storage solution and infrastructure configuration is required to support the SharePoint 2010 environment?

➤ Does the business anticipate storing a large amount of content, and require the use of a Remote BLOB Storage (RBS) solution to reduce the cost of Tier 1 storage? How does this impact archiving and legal hold requirements?

➤ What design is required for the SQL Server data layer of SharePoint 2010? Does it require clustering, and does the database require a mirroring of databases?

➤ What antivirus solution will be employed to protect the physical machines and the content within the SharePoint 2010 farm?

➤ What authentication model will be used, and what is the impact of using the chosen authentication model (for example, NTLM, Kerberos, or claims-based)?

➤ What design is required to limit the impact on the network of a centrally deployed portal solution?

➤ Will the portal solution be made available to internal users over the Internet? Will the platform be hosted in a DMZ and need to traverse edge firewall software and hardware? Will the portal solution be made available via a gateway product, such as the Citrix Access Gateway?

➤ What is the governance model for the type of customizations that can be developed by a central team versus business department-led development? Do they require sandboxed solutions, or SharePoint Designer access? How will the central team support solutions developed in this manner?

➤ What are the business requirements in terms of backup, availability, and disaster recovery? What backup solutions does the business use today, and does this support SharePoint 2010? Does the program have the budget to support the level of availability and disaster-recovery requirements?

➤ Are there any requirements related to data migration from legacy solutions?

➤ Does the business require an offline solution (such as SharePoint Workspace) to meet its requirements? Are there any additional security policies of the business that must be complied with to store business files in offline workspaces? For example, must BitLocker be deployed on the desktop or laptop to protect the data in the event of theft?

➤ What type of load-balancing solution is available, or is required to meet the requirements of the business?

As you can see, some of these requirements may not relate directly to a functional requirement, but more to an architectural requirement. These architectural decisions are important to resolve as early on as possible to avoid the cost of fixing it later in the portal's development life cycle.

Requirements/Use Case-Related Design Activities

As you progress through the early stages of the project, the analysis of the requirements will start to yield key scenarios and use cases that you can evaluate from a technical perspective. These key scenarios and associated use cases enable you to begin identifying architecturally significant use cases.

Architecturally significant use cases are key scenarios that are the most important to the success of your portal deployment. Architecturally significant use cases are use cases that intersect quality attributes with functionality, or cut across a number of use cases and functionality. They are important because they define areas that your SharePoint 2010 application and infrastructure design must address.

The "Agile Architecture Method Explained Wiki" (from www.guidanceshare.com) defines these as key hot spots that should be evaluated using architecture frame analysis and quality attribute analysis:

➤ *Architecture frame analysis* — The architecture frame represents cross-cutting concerns that will impact your design across layers and tiers, where design mistakes can result in cost and impact in later phases. Architecturally significant use cases should be evaluated against several cross-cutting concerns. These concerns include authentication and authorization; caching and state; communication; composition; concurrency and transactions; configuration management; coupling and cohesion; data access; exception management; logging and instrumentation; user experience; and validation and workflow.

➤ *Quality attribute frame analysis* — Quality attributes refer to cross-cutting concerns that affect performance, system design, and user experience. They refer to *system qualities* (such as supportability and testability), *runtime qualities* (such as availability, interoperability, performance, reliability, scalability, and security), *design qualities* (such as conceptual integrity, flexibility, maintainability, and reusability), and *user qualities* (such as user experience and usability). Architecturally significant use cases should be evaluated against the cross-cutting concerns described here.

 It should be emphasized that these concepts should be credited to the website at `http://www.guidanceshare.com/wiki/Agile_Architecture_Method_Explained`, *which provides a lot more detail on each of these important architectural concepts.*

From a SharePoint perspective, many of these architecture and quality attribute frames are taken care of by the SharePoint 2010 platform. However, that does not absolve you of the requirement to ensure that your solution, application, and infrastructure technical design meets the required quality bar for your business. Make sure any planned customizations achieve and pass the architecture and quality frame analysis requirements.

The next step is to identify the high-level components and modules of the system. Identify the high-level entities, as well as the process and data characteristics of each of these entities. Continue to gather information on each of the entities and processes required for your solution as you progress from the early elaboration stages to the detailed elaboration stages of your project.

Identify high-risk use cases, and, as early as possible in the project, plan and develop proofs of concept to nail down risk associated with these use cases. Do not commit to these use cases until you are confident you can successfully deliver them. Be careful about how you communicate and set expectations with the business related to higher risk/ harder-to-achieve use cases.

Another important point is not to over-analyze the technical solution at this stage of the project, but rather focus your efforts on areas that will yield the best results. The early stages of the project should be focused on developing an understanding of high-level components and modules that will form part of your solution. Later, detailed elaboration and design phases will drive out and solidify your technical design based on detailed requirements and use case analysis.

Conceptualizing the Logical and Physical SharePoint 2010 Solution

Once you have an initial understanding of the requirements of the proposed portal solution, the next step is to start conceptualizing your SharePoint 2010 portal deployment. This involves producing a high-level architecture, diagram, and vision that describes your "starting point" logical and physical architecture.

It is important to define your starting-point SharePoint 2010 architectural vision as soon as it is feasibly possible. This architectural vision acts both as lighthouse casting light on your SharePoint

2010 architecture, and as a lightning rod attracting both positive and negative attention to aspects of your initial design. The earlier you receive feedback, the more chance you have of being able to respond to it. Late-stage design and development feedback has a much higher cost to change (along with higher level of resistance to change) because of the amount of re-work activities required.

You may still be wondering what the point is of doing this activity this early on. The main reason is to establish a "base camp" that will drive key design decisions and improvements to the initially proposed design. Not doing this activity may result in the design living in one or two technical people's heads that is only communicated at a much later stage in the project. This may result in less time to gather feedback, develop consensus, and "buy-in" from technical members of the team. Finally, late-stage feedback often leads to unanticipated schedule and cost impacts.

In SharePoint 2010 projects, the logical and physical architecture involves (among a number of topics) designing your authentication mechanism, server farms, service applications, application pools, web applications, zones, policies, content databases, site collections, and sites. At the "getting started" stage of the project, this activity should not be overly onerous, because validation of this starting-point design will be reviewed and improved through a number of iterations in the detailed elaboration phases of the project.

 Microsoft TechNet provides detailed guidance, design sample, and great Visio templates and diagrams to help you. The Corporate deployment design sample is available at `http://technet.microsoft.com/en-us/library/cc261995.aspx.`

THE VALUE OF A TECHNICAL BLUEPRINT

Addressing the secret of writing a good architecture document, a mentor once said, "Start with the pictures, as they are each worth a 1000 words." This especially applies to SharePoint 2010 architecture diagrams.

Blueprints and site maps serve a very practical purpose. They map out key areas of the architecture to help the customer, key stakeholders, the design team, and development team visualize the intended portal solution. This reduces ambiguity, and helps to drive out a better design, structure, and deployment.

In the discussion presented in Chapter 12, a portal strategy and blueprint of the various portal capabilities was defined. Figure 12-4 shows the blueprint, which provides the basis for the discussion that follows.

Figure 12-4 describes a logical starting point for an internal-facing SharePoint 2010 deployment in the Global Mega Finance scenario introduced in Chapter 12. It is critical that you realize that this diagram may not be the final architecture that is deployed into production.

Have a look at the logical architecture in Figure 13-1, and note as many objections and questions you have with the logical architecture. After doing this, proceed to the next paragraph to assess how many issues you picked up.

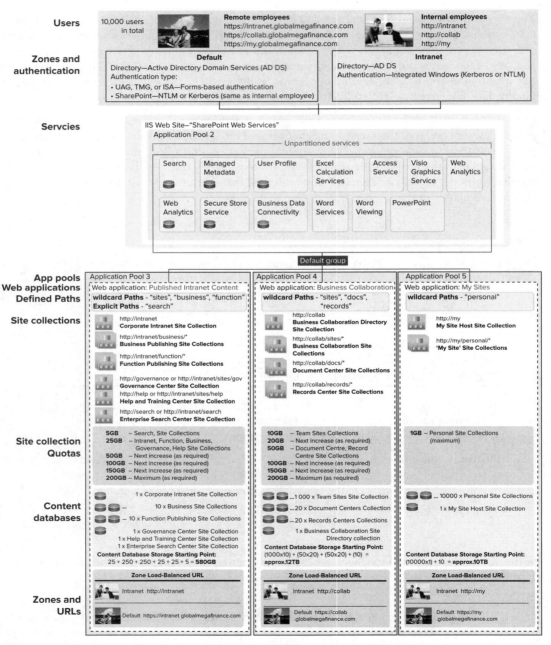

FIGURE 13-1: Global Mega Finance logical SharePoint 2010 architecture Starting Point

Table 13-2 discusses issues and questions related to the initial SharePoint 2010 logical architecture for the Global Mega Finance scenario.

TABLE 13-2: Potential Issues with the Global Mega Finance Logical Architecture

AREA	ISSUES
Users	How many of the 10,000 users will use the portal or have a My Site? A common mistake made by SharePoint architects is that they ask for the total number of employees, rather than the actual number of users who will use the portal.
Zones and authentication	What is the design decision behind *not* using claims-based authentication? Always attempt to at least use Kerberos in your environment. This fixes a number of double-hop issues related to executing custom code or applications that require user impersonation to work.
Service applications	Did you pick up that some of the service applications mentioned require the Enterprise license of SharePoint 2010, which has a cost implication? Does your project have sufficient budget, or is there a Microsoft Enterprise Agreement (EA) in place?
	Have you selected to enable sandboxed solutions? How will you govern the exploitation of this service application? Many SharePoint architects are passionate about technical features, especially new features. Sandboxed solutions may present a significant challenge to your service and support/operational team. If you enable this feature, special Service Level Agreements (SLAs) will be required to handle issues raised by end users related to site collections using sandboxed solutions. This is not to say that you should disallow sandbox solutions, but rather you should think carefully about the types of solutions, the management of code and supporting artifacts in a central repository, and the business development teams that you will support using this feature.
	Office Web Applications (OWA) place additional compute load on your Web Front-Ends (WFEs). How will you cater for this in physical design?
Application pools	Each application pool places greater RAM requirements on your WFE servers. Do you definitely need dedicated application pools for each of the web applications specified?
	Typical reasons for dedicated application pools are dedicated performance, higher resistance to failure, and isolation of "black box" sites (that is, sites that contain highly sensitive data). Using a dedicated application isolates these sites from other web applications, thereby providing a higher level of security.
	In physical environments, memory is "cheap." However, in virtual environments, it can result in a high charge cost from your virtualization host team. Therefore, understand that the number of applications indirectly drives the cost of the amount of RAM required for each WFE server in your pre-production and production environments.

continues

TABLE 13-2 *(continued)*

AREA	ISSUES
Web applications	How many web applications is the "right" number? This question is part information architecture and part technical design. Web applications (essentially IIS websites) provide a URL namespace for your SharePoint 2010 solution.
	The number of web applications differs greatly from deployment to deployment. Some SharePoint architects prefer as few web applications as possible, whereas others use a greater number of web applications. Let a combination of the information architecture requirements, the site provisioning method (do you deploy site collections or subsites?), maximum number of site collections per web application limit, and the compartmentalization of the solution into manageable areas drive the overall number of web applications.
	One of the unwritten limitations of cloud-hosted services is that they usually only provide two web applications to large dedicated deployments — one for everything, and one for My Sites. Based on previous experience, it is really difficult to get the cloud host providers (such as BPOS or Office 365) to make an exception to the technical model they feel comfortable with. This especially applies to hosting providers that back their SLAs with financial guarantees.
	The business collaboration web application caters to team collaboration, large documents centers, and Record Centers. Do any of these workloads belong in an isolated web application? Has the business decided to use in-place records management, or only send to the Record Center?
	A number of settings are applied at the web application level. Will your design limit functionality within a web application because of web application settings? Examples include SharePoint Designer access, resource throttling, maximum file sizes, and alerts and RSS settings. Will any of the web application settings impact sites and features hosted within the web application?
Defined paths	Wildcard and explicit defined paths help structure the URL namespace and navigation to common site collections. Using them requires CPU resources to process incoming requests. Use them sparingly, and stay within the prescribed SharePoint Software boundaries and limits.
Site collections	What site provisioning method will your deployment implement? A gap in SharePoint 2010 is the lack of an end-user site collection provisioning wizard. Large enterprises generally either create site collections manually, or develop a site provisioning wizard to automate the new site request, approval, and creation process.
	Why use site collections over one site collection with many subsites? SharePoint 2010 manages quotas at the site collection level. Site collections provide an easy-to-calculate "chargeback" model to business departments based on the allotted site collection quota.

AREA	ISSUES
	Large numbers of subsites within a single site collection make it more difficult to manage security, because you end up disconnecting from the parent groups to provide additional security to an individual site.
	Another issue with the subsites model is that it is not possible to police subsites storage quota usage. However, out-of-the-box, it is possible to police storage usage through site collection quotas.
Site collection quotas	Site collection quotas are often an underutilized simple feature. It controls the maximum size of a site collection, which, therefore, controls the maximum size of a content database. Site owners are alerted when a warning percentage threshold is passed, allowing them time to request more storage from the operational team. This gives the operational team time to increase the quota and underlying storage. Not using this out-of-the-box feature results in an out-of-disk-space error when no more space is available to the content database, as well as disgruntled, inconvenienced end users.
Content databases	Did you notice that common types of site collections have been grouped into a separate content database? The reason for this is that this improves the performance and caching profile of the underlying SQL content database. For example, compare a publishing site where 90 percent of the end users are readers and 10 percent have contributor permissions to a team site where 100 percent are contributors. From a SQL perspective, this results in a different optimal profile. Therefore, grouping similar site types together can contribute to improved performance.
	Did you notice the size of tier 1 storage required for the business collaboration and My Site web applications? Respectively, this is 12 TB and 10 TB. Methods to mitigate the amount of storage include using lower starting-point site collection quotas and forcing site owners to explicitly request more storage, lowering the estimated number of site collections that will be created over your estimation period, and the realization that on day one of your new portal deployment, you will not require that storage immediately.
	Other key factors include the flexibility of your underlying disk infrastructure to support a "thin provisioning" model, rather than upfront allocation, and the decision as to whether to implement RBS solution to enable you to leverage cheaper storage.

Microsoft has provided a detailed list of SharePoint 2010 software boundaries and limits that your logical and physical solution should adhere to. Ensure that you future-proof your logical design by staying within the boundaries set out by Microsoft. See "SharePoint 2010 Capacity Management: Software boundaries and limits" at http://technet.microsoft.com/en-us/library/cc262787.aspx.

As shown in Figure 13-2, the next diagram provides a highly simplified view of a starting-point physical design for the Global Mega Finance SharePoint 2010 deployment.

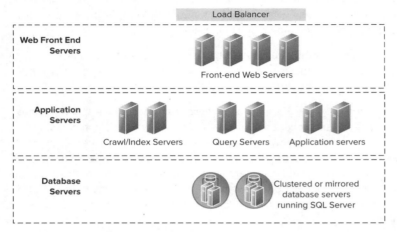

FIGURE 13-2: Global Mega Finance physical SharePoint 2010 architectural starting point

Table 13-3 discusses potential issues and questions related to this initial SharePoint 2010 physical architecture.

TABLE 13-3: Issues with the Global Mega Finance Physical Architecture

AREA	ISSUES	
General	Figure 13-2 does not mention the physical or virtual compute resources required for each server (such as RAM, CPU, disk, and network).	
Virtualization	Figure 13-2 does not specify whether virtualization technologies will be used. It does not provide a set of recommendations as to the placement of virtual machines on virtualized infrastructure. For example, both query servers should not be on the same physical host machine, because if either fails, you lose the capability to respond to query requests. How would a virtualization colleague understand where to place each virtual machine?	
Load balancer	Will you recommend a software-based or hardware-based load-balancing solution?	
WFE Servers	How did you come up with four WFE servers? Why not three or five? Determining the number of WFE servers requires developing a model to estimate the throughput required for each WFE. It also requires developing an understanding of the average number of concurrent users during peak and normal loads that you plan to support.	
	Microsoft provides detailed guidance to estimate, develop, and test your assumptions to help you define the correct number of front-end servers required for your farm. See "Estimate performance and capacity requirements" at http://technet.microsoft.com/en-us/library/cc261716(office.12).aspx.	
	Will you combine the query role on each WFE server, or use dedicated query servers?	

AREA	ISSUES
Application servers	Each service application has a different compute resource usage profile, and each should be assessed and understood before you deploy and enable them in your production environment. Microsoft provides detailed guidance for each service application on the compute resource usage profile on TechNet.
Database servers	The design of your Data tier of a SharePoint 2010 environment is critical to the success of your SharePoint 2010 project. Bad performance at this layer will contribute to even worse performance "up-stream" in the Application and WFE server tiers.
	The initial design does not mention a warm or hot failover disaster-recovery farm. What are your disaster-recovery requirements?
	The initial design does not specify whether to use clustered or mirrored SQL server instances.
	The design does not mention if any databases must be mirrored. Mirroring implies storage costs to maintain two physically separate copies of each database you plan to mirror.
	Do you plan to use content deployment using SQL snapshots? The design does not specify what version and license of SQL server will be implemented.

Hopefully, this exercise has demonstrated the value of creating of the initial logical and physical SharePoint 2010 architecture. As you can see, there are many questions related to the Global Mega Finance scenario. These designs and the questions they raise will feed into future information, solution, and infrastructure architecture streams and activities. These are covered in later chapters in this part of this book, including information architecture, solution architecture, infrastructure architecture, and storage architecture. Additionally, a number of chapters relate to specific topics, including authentication and authorization, business continuity design, specific cloud-based solution design, and virtualized deployments.

 TechNet provides detailed guidance to architect your SharePoint 2010 platform and solutions. See "Planning and Architecture" at http://technet.microsoft.com/en-us/library/cc261834.aspx.

EARLY TECHNICAL LEADERSHIP ACTIVITIES

The SharePoint architect initiates and is involved in the early detailed elaboration activities and streams required to draw out the high-level and detailed information, solution, and infrastructure architecture. The SharePoint architect helps to set the quality bar for any solution by setting the quality standard to which technical resources should adhere.

This section covers important areas the SharePoint or technical architect will need to consider to ensure that a successful SharePoint 2010 solution is delivered.

Selecting a Software Development Methodology

The selection of a software development methodology depends on a number of factors, such as whether the project is in-house, offshore, or a partner-led delivery.

In-house or partner-led deliveries will more than likely use a methodology the team has already adopted and can understand. Common methodologies relating to Microsoft SharePoint projects are SCRUM- or Agile-based methodologies.

Although offshore development and test teams may use an Agile or SCRUM approach, they benefit greatly from an onshore waterfall process that requires rock-solid requirements, technical specifications, and has little ambiguity to ensure that the business or supplier receives the level of quality the first time around. Using the incorrect methodology with an offshore team may decrease the commercial viability of using an offshore team.

The software development methodology must include activities and processes that ensure and maintain the highest level of security. Retrofitting security into existing solutions is more costly to introduce, it increases the cost of ongoing maintenance, and it increases the likelihood of vulnerabilities being introduced when subsequent changes are made.

SharePoint solutions do not often start out as business-critical solutions, but they always invariably end up as business-critical. As a rule, never accept a portal deployment or custom development into a production environment that cannot show it has strived for and adheres to security best practices. This includes ensuring that your team members have the training and support to produce code that is secure and is not vulnerable to standard attacks. Examples of attacks include SQL injection, cross-site scripting (XSS), buffer overflow, and code injection.

Managing, Tracking, and Recording Key Design Decisions

Each key design decision should be tracked in a SharePoint list or Excel spreadsheet. The same applies to key software and infrastructure design decisions. Without a formal process, the same decision tends to get rehashed over and over again. When a key decision is made, it must be documented. This ensures traceability back to the original decision. When future projects occur and people ask why the architect designed the solution in a certain way, often the information and clear-headed reasoning is lost in the shifting sands of foggy memory.

Setting Up Development Standards and Best Practices

It is vital that the SharePoint architect, technical architect, or development lead plan, document, and share a set of development team standards and best practices. If you are a Microsoft Gold Partner or supplier, always attempt to understand if the customer has existing policy documentation related to acceptable development standards, and ensure that your team adheres to these standards.

Development standards include the following areas:

➤ Plan a consistent set of development environments for your development team.

➤ Develop a code project solution organization and management of the code project structure.

➤ Plan and set up your application life cycle management tools such as Team Foundation Services. This includes configuration of the source code control system to set up versioning (numbering), branching policies, and any add-on packs required to support your development methodology (for example, SCRUM or Agile add-on packs).

➤ Plan your build process for development and integration builds on the build server.

➤ Configure Team Foundation Server to kick off builds on a build server upon check-in of any source code. Additionally, ensure that developers are alerted to any failed builds so that they can fix issues as quickly as possible.

➤ Decide on level of automation required for your project. For example, mature development teams deploy nightly builds to a snapshotted SharePoint 2010 environment, and kick off a batch of tests for developers and testers to review in the morning.

➤ Plan and ensure the quality of source code commenting and code style using source and style analysis tools available for Visual Studio and Team Foundation Server.

➤ Set out a consistent set of patterns you want developers to follow relating to the development of common SharePoint 2010 customizations. Consistent code patterns drive higher quality and reduce your bug count.

➤ Think about the level of code layering you require for your project. Do you plan to interface directly with the SharePoint object model, or abstract some of the direct interaction to manager and entity classes?

➤ Set out the types of unit tests, "mocks," or "Coded UI" tests you expect the development team to create.

➤ Plan upfront what type of documentation is required by the customer so that the deployment team can support, deploy, and maintain any code solutions in the production environment. This may include use cases, use case realizations or technical specifications, component maps, application architecture documents, "readme" files, and deployment configuration guides.

➤ Set out what coding standards should be adhered to. Examples include namespaces, exception handling (no empty `try/catch` instances), and UI logic. Ensure the build process performs `SPDisposeCheck`!

Setting Up a Testing Strategy

Set out a test strategy, or plan for your test manager to produce a test strategy that describes the approach that will be used to test the solution and the areas that will be tested. The test strategy should cover the following areas:

➤ *Human resources* — How many resources are required to test the solution?

➤ *Hardware requirements and environments* — This covers the hardware requirements and environments required to adequately test your SharePoint 2010 platform and solution.

➤ *Software requirements and specialist testing tools* — This covers what software is required for the hardware, and the software testing tools needed to adequately test the solution.

➤ *Test case creation process* — This covers what test cases will be written, and the steps required for each test.

➤ *Types of functional and non-functional tests* — This covers how common SharePoint 2010 customizations will be tested, as well as how the non-functional tests will be performed. For example, this may include tests related to accessibility, localization, security, compatibility, performance, maintainability, and data migration.

➤ *Automated Testing* — This covers what testing will be automated, and what testing will be completed manually. Visual Studio 2010 and other products provide valuable test tools such as "coded UI" tests. It must be said, based on previous experiences, the writing of these tests can detract from a dedicated follow-a-test-script manual process. Maintain a healthy balance between manual and automated testing strategies to ensure complete code and product coverage is maintained.

➤ *Testing stages* — This should cover unit, component, integration tests, system, regression, and user acceptance tests.

➤ *Defect tracking* — Defect tracking specifies what tool will be used to track defects. In Microsoft-oriented projects, Team Foundation Server is often used as the tool to track defects.

➤ *Defect classification strategy* — The defect classification strategy ensures that each defect is uniformly categorized and prioritized based on an agreed set of severity definitions. Examples include 1-Critical, 2-Major, 3-Minor, and 4-Trivial. This is really important because, in the commercial contract, customers often stipulate test exit criteria that specify the maximum number of defects allowed for each severity definition.

➤ *Triage strategy and triage process* — This process is used to classify and prioritize defects. This meeting occurs regularly during the development stages of the project, and daily during the stabilization phase near the end of a milestone.

One final area to plan is the test team roles and responsibilities, as well as the responsibilities of the test lead and the test team members.

Planning for Regular Code Reviews

Your development lead or SharePoint technical architect must plan time in the schedule to perform regular (weekly or sprint) code reviews to ensure that produced code adheres to SharePoint 2010 development best practice. Code reviews include the following:

➤ Code has been packaged for deployment so that it can be deployed to various development, testing, user acceptance testing, pre-production, and production environments.

➤ Code revisions have a revision history and appropriate comments in Team Foundation Server.

➤ Code revisions have associated tasks, and the developer has not overridden your check-in requirements.

➤ Code has an appropriate level of logging and instrumentation.

➤ `using` statements have been appropriately applied to release resources as early as possible.

➤ Code will perform in runtime conditions when a component is hit (for example, a thousand times a second). Does the code hit a shared component that will not cope under the load?

➤ Code-profiling tools (such as ANTS Performance Profile) are great at picking up badly performing code and code-related bottlenecks.

➤ Exception handling is present and appropriate. No empty `try/catch` blocks, and preferably `try/catch finally` code blocks exist.

➤ Security-related checks (including any code that runs with elevated privileges, that require special code access security policies, and that require sufficient defense and checks) have been put in place to reduce the attack surface.

➤ Code is written once, and reused as much as possible.

➤ Code is not overly complex. It should not require a genius to decipher and maintain. The ACID test for any code is when someone will else be able to maintain the code after the individual is no longer on the project.

➤ HTML code complies with validation tools, and meets the accessibility requirements of the customer.

MORT, ELVIS, AND EINSTEIN AND SHAREPOINT 2010 DEVELOPMENT!

Microsoft Developer division used three personas or stereotypes to categorize types of developers in the past. Mort was an opportunistic developer, liked to create quick-working solutions for immediate problems, focused on productivity, and learned as needed. Elvis was the pragmatic programmer, liked to create long-lasting solutions addressing the problem domain, and learned while working on the solution. Einstein was the paranoid programmer, liked to create the most efficient solution to a given problem, and typically learned in advance before working on the solution.

In many projects, the Einstein programmer develops a solution, gets bored, and leaves or moves on to the next big challenge. Elvis ends up rewriting some of the solution, partly because he is not at the "Einstein" level. The result is pattern loss, code fragmentation, and bloat. Mort is left to maintain the solution, and is scared of touching any code because he does not want to be responsible for breaking the solution. The result is code that is not maintainable, or requires the customer to hire an expensive Einstein to address the problem.

The moral of the story is to beware of overly complex code that makes it impossible for mid- and maintenance-level coders to maintain.

(For more information, see `http://www.codinghorror.com/blog/2007/11/mort-elvis-einstein-and-you.html`.)

All code must be peer reviewed, and final code should be signed off by your development or team lead.

Planning the Deployment Life Cycle

Portal deployment life cycle planning covers the deployment from development, build, and integration servers, through testing (user acceptance testing) in pre-production and production environments.

A key reason for including this activity at this stage is that if these environments do not exist, they must be purchased and set up, which has an impact on cost and schedule. Also, promotion of code from a development environment must follow a documented process so that your production environment is not affected.

A key point to keep in mind when testing upgrades of SharePoint 2007 environments to SharePoint 2010, or testing code against sites in your test environment based on copies of production sites, is that data derived from production environments should not contain personally identifiable information. If this is not possible, always attempt to make personally identifiable information anonymous.

 Deployment life cycle planning is discussed in greater detail in Chapter 18.

Developing a Quote and Schedule

During the early stages, the program and project management place a number of demands on the technical lead. The demands may occur at the supplier selection stage, and the technical lead needs an idea of the scope and type of development that needs to be delivered. Alternatively, the technical lead may be faced with the challenge of a detailed and sometimes lengthy internal business funding process, and need your help to estimate as accurately as possible the cost of this stage of the project to ensure that funding is allocated for the next stages of the project.

This results in the classic "which comes first — the chicken or the egg" problem. It is not possible to provide estimates that you can stand behind without certain amount of high-level design activity, and it is not possible to perform the high-level design activity until funding is supplied. This can be quite tricky, especially because most funding processes demand a sufficient level of detail before cash is allocated!

Furthermore, funding decisions tend to lock the project into a certain mode of operation and set of financial constraints until the end of the phase, leading to difficult choices and trade-offs between schedule, cost, and feature set. A recommendation to overcome this is to push for an initial stage and period where an accurate quote (rather than an estimate) can be produced.

This involves a 6- to 12-week period where three or four technical resources work together to develop an understanding of the high-level solution, refine the requirements, create a prototype to give to stakeholders, and work out the costs of infrastructure and custom development for the project. The output of this phase is a document and prototype detailing the solution, the quote and cost, resources required, and a recommended schedule of work. This approach gives the project a much higher potential of success.

Be wary of agreeing to a fixed price until a quote has been produced. Some Microsoft Gold Partners have used the approach of time and materials for the inception and elaboration stages, and fixed cost on the development, test, and deployment stages. Microsoft Gold Partners should be at a level and maturity to develop an exact understanding of the cost to develop, once the detailed elaboration phase has completed. This approach largely satisfies the customer's desire to get a fixed price, and the Microsoft Gold Partners' desire to protect themselves.

Another important activity is the planning and prioritizing of development activities. This requires the following steps:

1. Prioritize the use cases into groups of use cases using the MoSCoW method. Defer low-priority features depicted as "Could" or "Would."

2. For the "Must" and "Should" use cases that your team has agreed are required for this phase of the project, provide two scores for each use case. The first score depicts the perceived value to the business, and the second score relates to the risk to development. Assess both requirements, from one to five, and sum the two scores.

3. Use cases with the highest scores should be developed first, because they either present the highest risk and/or highest value to the business. Always attempt to nail down risk elements early on in your project to give them time to stabilize in successive sprints.

In the early stages of a project, a development team may not be available to participate in "planning poker." "Planning poker" is an activity where each development team member provides an estimate as to how long an activity should take to develop. Therefore, ensure that you request help from other colleagues to review your quote before you communicate it to the business or customer. This will reduce the risk of a single person's perspective. This validation of your estimates will help improve the quality of the quote, and the capability for your team to deliver on time, within schedule, to a high level of quality.

Planning and Kicking-off Detailed Elaboration Phases

The start of the detailed elaboration phases are largely guided by your methodology. Most methodologies start with detailed design activities, where there is consensus on the scope, schedule, and features, and the requirements have been documented and agreed on with the organization.

The activities in the detailed elaboration phases often vary from project to project, depending on the stage of the life cycle of the SharePoint 2010 deployment. New SharePoint deployments require significant information architecture, solution architecture, and infrastructure architecture design activities. Existing deployments tend to focus on a business solution development that requires solution and information architecture design activities.

Another factor is that the size of your portal deployment will often dictate the number of resources you have at your disposal. This will guide what can be achieved, given a fixed schedule and cost.

For your project, identify what streams of activities are required. Plan and agree on a schedule with your project manager, and assign responsibilities to your technical and business resources available. Subsequent chapters in this book provide more guidance relating to the detailed elaboration activities involved in the design of your information architecture, solution architecture, and infrastructure architecture.

PROGRAM AND PROJECT MANAGEMENT ACTIVITIES

Although this book is mainly focused on architecture and design of your SharePoint solution, a number of non-technical activities are important and critical to the success of your SharePoint 2010 project. These activities fall mainly under the purview of the program and project management team. The program and project management team is responsible for the overall delivery of a successful SharePoint 2010 deployment and program.

Program management is the process of managing several related projects in a coordinated way, with the aim of obtaining a set of benefits and responding to the business drivers defined by senior stakeholders of the business or customer.

Project management is the process of balancing (work) scope and the quality of features, given the resources (cost) available, and within an acceptable or predetermined delivery timeframe. It also includes managing the activities and resources required to achieve the desired outcome, within the budget and timeframe, and to a level of quality that is acceptable to the business or customer.

Figure 13-3 shows a well-known and generally accepted project management trade-off matrix. It provides a simple strategy for controlling the outcome with regard to the budget, required delivery date, and feature set. The trade-off matrix is used to manage the project so as to optimize, constrain, or accept the outcome.

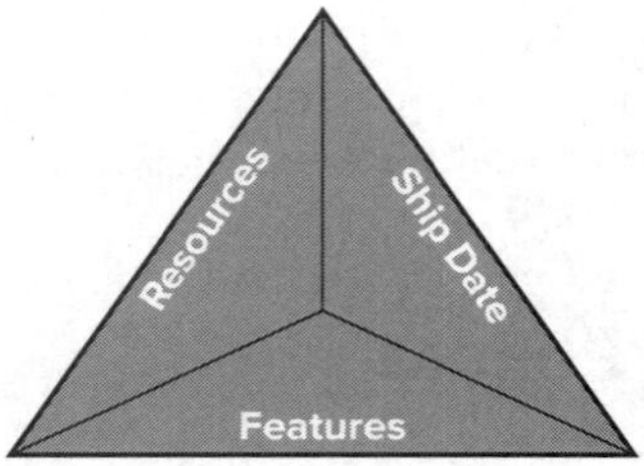

	Optimize	Constrain	Accept
Resources		✓	
Ship Date	✓		
Features			✓

FIGURE 13-3: Project management trade-off matrix

In Figure 13-3, the customer elects to "constrain" the resources (and cost) available, and requires an "optimized" delivery date. In this example, the customer must "accept" that some features will not be available. This matrix is often used to set expectations with the customer based on the feature set required, and the delivery date expected, depending on the given resources available.

Program and project management involve managing the following key areas:

➤ *Project control* — This involves generic project management and control.

➤ *Business alignment* — This involves ensuring that projects support the overall business strategy, and that value is delivered.

➤ *Requirements* — This involves ensuring that business needs are translated into implementable and relevant requirements, and that these requirements are delivered to maximize overall business benefits.

➤ *Information security and continuity* — This involves ensuring that the organization's information assets are adequately secured against likely threats.

➤ *Business change* — This involves addressing business organization and process change issues so that both IT and business systems work well together.

➤ *Architecture and design* — This involves ensuring that IT applications and services are implemented to fit and work well with overall enterprise business and IT systems, and specifying how to realize these business requirements.

➤ *Commercial* — This involves managing acquisition of IT components and use of external services.

➤ *Development and implementation* — This involves producing and transitioning into new (or updated) IT applications and services.

➤ *Service Delivery* — This involves preparing for and managing the operational support and enhancement of IT applications and services.

Like any software projects, SharePoint 2010 projects require strong project management and leadership to drive the projects to success and completion, as well as to manage and guard against "scope creep." Strong project management and leadership is also required to keep track of the costs and expenditure. In some cases, it involves making tough choices — for example, to cut features, or to identify and remove non-performing resources early on in the project.

SharePoint program and project managers must be politically adept and astute at handling the sometimes intricate pathways that must be navigated to achieve and deliver a successful project.

The capability to set expectations, track, and record the resulting expectation is crucial in large software deployments. In large projects, the business may forget an earlier agreement or expectation. E-mail follow-through is a must in order to track and record previously set expectations.

On technical projects, watch out for resource bottlenecks (that is, one person who has taken on too much). Be wary and identify any over-customization of your SharePoint 2010 platform early on.

Train all members of your team to estimate their work and deliver to their estimated delivery date. This is useful to identify how individuals think and approach the planning of their individual tasks, and sets up good habits, which results in better schedule planning. One final good habit to encourage is submission of weekly reports or e-mails detailing "what I did this week, and what I plan to do next week." That forces each individual to think about what he or she accomplished, and what he or she plans to accomplish, as well as allowing the manager to ensure that efforts are coordinated across the team. Therefore, this encourages a more goal-orientated approach.

With any project, program and project managers *must* be great managers of people, both business and technical. This involves understanding the motivations and "drivers" of individuals, and subtly changing communication styles to get the best out of resources in your team. Keep in mind that great technical resources may not always be great managers of people.

Setting Up Your SharePoint 2010 Program and Projects

This involves the definition of the program scope, namely, the set of application, infrastructure, and business capabilities and services that will be provided. This involves planning a number of projects to deliver the required application, infrastructure capabilities, and supporting business services.

Defining Your Program Management Plan (PMP)

The *Program Management Plan (PMP)* establishes the management approach used in the SharePoint project, and ensures that it is consistent with approaches used by the business or customer.

The PMP describes the overall program structure, what deliverables are required, related management plans and procedures, and the methods used to plan, monitor, control, and improve the project development efforts. It should also include lessons learned from early phases in the project, and improvements to the methodologies used to deliver the set of projects related to the program.

It is important that this document be kept as a "living" or dynamic document. It should be kept up to date throughout the life cycle of the program.

Defining Your Project Plan

According to the *Project Management Body of Knowledge (PMBOK)*, the project plan guides both project execution and project control. It documents planning assumptions and decisions, facilitates communication among stakeholders, and describes the approved scope, cost, and schedule baselines.

Understanding Resourcing and Roles in Your SharePoint 2010 Team

The resources required for your SharePoint 2010 program will vary from project to project, because this largely depends on the scope and features required. Small teams usually consist of at least one business and technical resource, and a project manager that may be responsible for one or more projects.

Larger SharePoint 2010 projects tend to consist of a number of business analysts, project managers, SharePoint architects, developers, testers, business change specialists, and operations folk.

SharePoint architect(s) or consultant(s) come in many flavors, and their quality should be judged on previous real-world customer references and experience. Some are dedicated to a specialty within SharePoint, others on the solution or application design and development, whereas others are heavily focused on infrastructure architecture, configuration, and operational aspects. Another group may focus more on the governance and business change and adoption aspects with regard to SharePoint 2010 deployments.

Developers vary from junior to senior, depending on the amount of experience. One of the senior developers will take on the role of development lead, and will be responsible for key coding approaches and ensuring overall code and solution quality.

Test teams involve a test manager, and a number of testers. They are responsible for various testing activities as set in the testing strategy. It really helps to have developers and testers proficient in

SharePoint 2007 and SharePoint 2010. Resources that are pure ASP.NET developers or pure testers will have the additional challenge of learning best practices for SharePoint 2010 development and testing.

Operations resources are focused on deployment, configuration, and maintenance of the platform. In large projects, it is bad practice to have your development team deploy customizations directly to non-development and test environments. Operational resources should be responsible for the operation of your user acceptance test, as well as pre-production and production environment deployments.

Defining Your Business Case and Benefits Realization Plan

The *business case* is a document detailing the basis or "case" for the investment or business improvement. Business cases show how the value or return on investment (ROI) will be delivered. This is achieved by identifying specific benefits that will be gained by making the investment of business improvement.

The business case should describe the strategic goals and objectives, the likely outcomes and benefits, and the risks involved. Lastly, it should call out any assumptions made.

The *benefits realization plan* is used to track realization of benefits across your SharePoint 2010 program. It defines how your SharePoint 2010 project will actually realize the benefits set out in the business case. The plan describes each benefit, and how it will be measured, where and when the benefits will occur, key action points, and who is responsible for the delivery.

Appointing a Governance Board and Technical Design Authority

As mentioned in Chapter 12, the *steering committee or governance board* consists of a set of individuals across the organization that have a vested interest in realizing the business objectives associated with your portal strategy. The governance board should have clear terms of reference (that is, purpose and structure), delegated authority to make decisions and take necessary action when required, and should be composed of stakeholders from across the business, rather than only the IT department.

Complex and highly technical projects will benefit greatly from a *technical design authority* (TDA). The TDA may not necessarily be one person, but a team of experts with responsibility for key technical decisions related to your SharePoint 2010 project. All key software and infrastructure decisions should be validated with the TDA, which is responsible and accountable for the technical quality and strategy aspects of your SharePoint 2010 project.

The TDA role (or team) may either be part of your program and projects, or may be part of the team that reports into or supports the enterprise architecture function of your organization.

Planning Your Operational and Governance Model

There is no way around it. Poorly planned and executed SharePoint 2010 deployments result in chaos. This makes it really important to define a *governance and "service and support" model* and approach. This consists of defining a set of processes, policies, and governance plans that will result in a structured, well-managed environment.

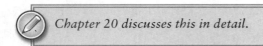
Chapter 20 discusses this in detail.

Deciding on an In-house, Hybrid, or Outsource Model

Selecting the correct model for your project is a difficult and sometimes complicated business decision to make. The model options are as follows:

➤ *In-house model* — An in-house model involves staffing and maintaining a team of suitably qualified infrastructure and application specialists to maintain and grow your SharePoint 2010 environment.

➤ *Hybrid model* — A hybrid model uses a combination of in-house skills along with specialist contractors or a business solution partner.

➤ *Outsource model* — An outsourced model uses an external team and business to deliver the project. This project may be more expensive, but accountability and assurance is built in to protect the business, and to ensure that the outsourcer delivers the required solution.

A number of contributing factors may influence your decision, including the following:

➤ *Business model* — The business model may dictate a common approach to how non-core functions and processes are managed and delivered.

➤ *IT enterprise outsourcing strategy* — This strategy may dictate a common approach or policy as to how IT projects and business solutions are delivered. It may range from simple solutions that require specialist skills, to large partners responsible for handling all IT functions on behalf of the organization. Common examples of outsourcing include dedicated infrastructure partners or dedicated business solution partners.

➤ *Project risk profile* — The organization, program, or IT management team may assess a particular type of project to be of higher risk, and may want to mitigate the risk associated with the project by using specialist solution partners.

➤ *Amount of control required* — Insourcing enables organizations to maintain better control over the work. The amount of control required may dictate whether an organization insources or outsources a piece of work to a third-party supplier.

➤ *Reputational damage* — A key question that is often asked is, "Could outsourcing cause reputational damage to your business?" If yes, then it is recommended to keep the project in-house.

➤ *Timescale* — This may dictate the need to hire an already proven team of experts to deliver your project. Your organization may not have the time to hire and train a team of experts to deliver your project within the timescale required. For example, the organization may require a dedicated Internet-facing site in a very short space of time to take advantage of a marketplace condition.

➤ *Cost savings* — This factor swings many ways. Key business and technical decision makers may identify potential cost savings by using cheaper offshore resources. Alternatively, they may perceive a cost saving in hiring a dedicated onshore solution partner using a fixed price model. They may also perceive it as cheaper to do the project in-house. In short, the pendulum tends to swing in relation to which choice results in the greatest cost savings. This may be based on previous good and bad experiences related to outsourcing and insourcing.

➤ *Individual career path protection* — All politically astute business and technical decision makers seek to ensure that programs under their control succeed, and that their reputation for delivering complex programs and projects is maintained, enhanced, and not tarnished. For example, in large IT projects, it is common for the IT program management team to elect to involve key partners and resources from companies such as Microsoft to mitigate risks in key stages of your SharePoint 2010 project. This may result in a much higher cost, but it increases the confidence of your organization and IT leadership in the program management's ability to deliver a successful solution.

➤ *What to outsource* — The initial stages of your SharePoint 2010 program will require different a set of expertise than future stages of your project. Initial stages may require specialist skills to get things right. Once "live," your SharePoint 2010 platform may require an in-house or outsourced infrastructure partner to perform the "run and maintain" operations. Business platform exploitation-type projects will require specialist skills. Each of these phases and types of projects result in distinct choices on whether to insource or outsource.

➤ *Maturity* — The in-house team may not have the exact skillset required to deliver the project successfully. It may require hiring additional specialist skills or contractors, or using a specialist business solution partner to complete the initial stages of the project, with the long-term intention of knowledge transfer and training to build a competent internal team.

➤ *Ethos, corporate culture, and accountability* — The internal IT department or business may have a history of poor service delivery. Senior management may decide to use an external team to circumvent institutional, company culture, and ethos-based issues to get things done quickly, bring in fresh ideas, and deliver successfully.

The next steps in an *in-house model* are to recruit and staff a competent, multi-disciplined, high-caliber team of experts to deliver your SharePoint project. Previous proven SharePoint architecture, solution development, or infrastructure experience is a "must."

The next steps in a *hybrid or outsource model* involve thinking about what aspects and phases of your project will require third-party or outsource teams. Next, document and submit a "Request for Information" or "Request for Proposal" to carefully chosen SharePoint 2010 industry solution vendors. Finally, evaluate outsource partner proposals, select a partner, and finalize commercial details with the partner.

Deciding on an Onshore, Near-shore, or Offshore Model

The second key decision relates to whether you should leverage onshore, near-shore, or offshore skills and resources. While the first decision relates to a partner model, the second decision is an option that may present itself in each of the first decision options.

These models are each described as follows:

➤ *Onshore* — Onshore describes projects occurring and hosted in the home country of the business or IT team.

➤ *Near-shore* — Near-shore refers to projects occurring in a different country, but with similar time zone, languages, skills, and culture.

➤ *Offshore* — Offshore describes projects occurring using a team in a distant country, with a vastly different time zone, languages, skill, and culture.

Common criteria for deciding between onshore, near-shore, and offshore options include potential cost savings, speed, ability to deliver, expertise and quality available in each location, and, finally, the execution risk related to managing a project over multiple locations.

 You can find a fairly balanced article discussing the merits and perils of each option at http://www.sourcingline.com/resources/pros-and-cons-of-onshore-nearshore-and-offshore-models.

Based on past experience with a number of large SharePoint projects using offshore resources, the following observations may be offered:

➤ *Select the appropriate onshore methodology* — Agile methodology does not always work between an onshore and offshore team. To ensure offshore skills get it right the first time, use cases and technical specifications need to be airtight.

➤ *Use an onshore quality assurance team* — Onshore quality assurance is required to vet quality of the work before it is handed to the customer.

➤ *Constant communication is required* — Dedicated onshore project and technical resources are required to keep track of the offshore team progress. Constant communication is vital.

➤ *Interview all offshore development members* — Offshore development team resources should be vetted and tested for quality. Resumes can be "fudged" to look amazing. As with any onshore team, all offshore development team members should be technically interviewed to assess their understanding of coding language, .NET, and SharePoint technologies.

➤ *Locate an onshore member offshore* — Offshore teams benefit greatly from having an onshore team member on location at the offshore site.

➤ *Proficient offshore language skills are required* — The offshore team must have proficient language skills to communicate, ask questions, and interpret requirements.

➤ *Incentivize offshore team* — Offshore teams are often worked hard, with little reward. This can affect their motivation and desire to deliver at the speed and quality of an onshore "in-front-of-the-customer" team. Mitigations should be put in place to ensure that the offshore team is incentivized to deliver on time to the level of quality expected.

➤ *Be aware of, research, and understand subtle culture differences* — In some cases, Eastern cultures do not like to say "no," and are not as direct or confrontational as Western cultures. This may lead to unexpected delays and frustration on both sides.

Your mileage with offshore teams will vary from awful to a fantastic experience. A conservative estimate often used is to multiply by a factor between 1.8 and 3 the estimated time for work to be completed (by a *new* offshore team) in comparison to an onshore team. Once you have worked with the offshore team for a period of time, only then should you reduce your estimates.

The decision to execute your SharePoint 2010 project offshore should not be taken lightly. It is a complex decision.

BUSINESS CHANGE AND ADOPTION ACTIVITIES

Business change and *adoption* are activities required to help the business realize the benefits of your portal solution. This involves including resources in your SharePoint 2010 team to plan out a business change strategy, and a plan to take the organization from the "current state" to the intended "future state." These resources are involved in the following key areas:

➤ "Future state" vision design

➤ Business engagement

➤ Requirements management

➤ Marketing and communication

➤ Education and training

➤ Business on-boarding and exploitation

➤ Defining and measuring success

➤ Learning lessons about the project and business

Designing Your "Future State" Business Design

A *"future state" business design* provides the organization's leaders with an idea of what the future will entail using your solution. This helps them understand what needs to be done to achieve the "future state."

The "future state" business design should describe the following key areas:

➤ *Define today versus a future way of working* — The design should provide a view of how the organization is likely to leverage your portal solution capabilities, such as personal My Site, business collaboration, document and records management, search, business social networking, and intranet and Internet publishing capabilities.

➤ *Define key affected processes* — The design should highlight key organization processes that are likely to be affected, and how they will work using your SharePoint 2010 portal deployment.

➤ *Define key business roles and responsibilities* — The design should ensure that the organization understands the roles and responsibilities required once the solution is "live." These are the business-as-usual operational roles within each business or business department.

➤ *Define information worker skills and competencies* — The design should ensure that the organization understands what skills and competencies are required to "exploit" and use your new SharePoint 2010 solution.

➤ *Define the operation and support model* — The design should describe the operation and support model, and the services available from your SharePoint 2010 team.

It is important to remember that this design should not be "set in stone." It will evolve as your understanding of the SharePoint 2010 solution improves. Regular updates to this design should be scheduled and planned throughout the full life cycle of your SharePoint 2010 project. This will ensure that this document reflects business feedback on the design, and the SharePoint 2010 solution that is taking shape.

Establishing a Business Engagement Strategy

Deploying your SharePoint 2010 capabilities and platform is the simple part. The complex part requires engaging your organization to help drive the success of adoption among your workforce. To have a chance of success, this requires a *business engagement strategy*.

This strategy involves analyzing your key business stakeholders and deployment leads, defining their onboarding requirements, and working with them to help them undertake their onboarding in a structured and controlled manner.

Effectively Managing Requirements

Managing requirements can be difficult in fast-paced SharePoint 2010 projects. It is important for requirements to be managed to ensure that the agreed business benefits, in fact, are delivered to the business.

You should guard against one of the biggest challenges faced by every SharePoint 2010 project — scope creep! *Scope creep* is the continual changing of the initially identified requirements, which results in unplanned work and, therefore, increased cost or a delayed release date.

To protect against this, once requirements are agreed on and signed off on, all new requirements should go through a change-control procedure so as to force a conscious commercial decision for changes to schedule, cost, and quality.

As a supplier or partner, the onus is on you to set up this procedure and expectation at the beginning of the project. Doing this in the middle of the project results in a difficult and emotional conversation.

Failing to institute a requirements change process decreases the commercial viability of a project, and increases the frustration of the customer. This ultimately may degrade your long-term relationship with the customer.

Defining Your Marketing and Communication Plan

You may wonder what marketing and communication have to do with your SharePoint 2010 project. Well, the reason for addressing this is that the success of your deployment is judged by user adoption, user acceptance, and user satisfaction with the solution you have worked feverishly to deploy. If the employees do not know about it, the chances of a successful SharePoint 2010 implementation will diminish.

An important principle is not to start marketing and communication once you have finished the project and the portal is "live." This is too late. Anticipation and build-up is key.

Consider, for a moment, the *diffusion of innovation theory*. As shown in Figure 13-4, this theory seeks to explain how, why, and at what rate new ideas and technology spread. It groups users into a set of buckets that define the stage they adopt the new idea or technology. These are as follows:

➤ *Innovators* — Innovators are the first individuals to adopt an innovation. They have a higher risk tolerance to ideas or technologies that may fail.

➤ *Early adopters* — This is the second-fastest category of adoption. These individuals have the highest degree of opinion leadership among the other adopter categories.

➤ *Early majority* — Individuals in this category adopt an innovation after a varying degree of time. The time of adoption is significantly longer than the innovators and early adopters.

➤ *Late majority* — Individuals in this category will adopt an innovation after the average member of society. These individuals approach an innovation with a high degree of skepticism, and only after the majority of society members has adopted the innovation.

➤ *Laggards* — Individuals in this category are the last to adopt an innovation. Individuals in this category have little or no opinion leadership, and tend to have an aversion to "change-agents."

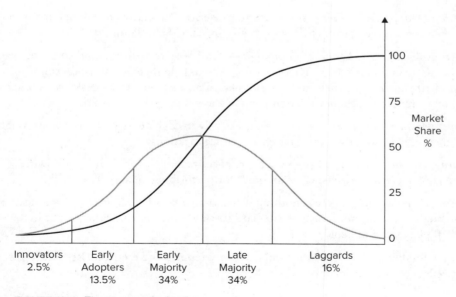

FIGURE 13-4: The stages of adoption

According to the diffusion of innovation theory, each individual in your "society" follows a five-step process, which is as follows:

1. *Knowledge* — In this stage, the individual is first exposed to the innovation, but lacks information about the innovation.

2. *Persuasion* — In this stage, the individual is interested in the innovation, and actively seeks information.

3. *Decision* — In this stage, the individual considers the concept of the innovation, weighs the advantages and disadvantages of using the innovation, and decides whether to adopt or reject the innovation.

4. *Implementation* — In this stage, the individual employs the innovation to a varying degree, depending on the innovation.

5. *Confirmation* — In this stage, the individual makes a conscious or subconscious decision to continue or stop using the innovation.

Applied to your SharePoint 2010 project, the diffusion of innovations theory describes the rate of adoption and the implicit decision-making process each end user in your "society" or business will go through. This theory emphasizes the need to begin education, awareness, and "excitement generation" as early as possible. Throwing the solution or platform "over the fence" at the end of a development and deployment life cycle may not lead to a successful deployment. Therefore, ensure that your project plans include a defined internal marketing and communication plan.

Experience has shown that internal marketing campaigns typically involve a combination of the following techniques:

➤ *Internal e-mail campaign* — This involves sending a series of visually appealing e-mails educating the users on the benefits they will receive by using SharePoint 2010.

➤ *Wall poster, desk leaflet, or "goodie" campaign* — Wall posters are a fun and engaging way of reminding users of a particular URL or training site to help them get started using your SharePoint 2010 platform. Leaflets and goodies placed on each end user's desk are another method to reinforce a key benefit or action you are encouraging the user to do.

➤ *Lunchtime awareness and demos* — This is a great way to educate early innovators through informal lunchtime demos at various branch and office locations.

➤ *Competitions, incentives, and prizes* — Users are encouraged to participate by knowing that they may win a small prize (such as an iPod) for performing an activity or task.

Try to be unique, fun, and engaging. There is nothing worse than a poorly imagined communication and marketing campaign that does not reflect all the hard work your technical team has put in to your SharePoint 2010 platform and deployment.

SharePoint provides a number of search, traffic, and inventory reports and metrics. Use these tools to assess the effectiveness of your campaign.

You should not conduct an internal marketing campaign without getting the appropriate involvement and sign-off from the relevant departments in your organization. This may involve areas such as corporate communications, Human Resources, and senior business leaders.

Defining an Education and Training Plan

Your *education and training plan* should reflect the scope and size of your SharePoint 2010 deployment. It should reflect the skills and competencies of the end users of your organization, and it should reflect the various training options available to the business associates based on the roles and responsibilities they will perform.

It is not sufficient to rely solely on the out-of-the-box SharePoint help. Your organization has a distinct set of benefits it is aiming to realize, and your education and training plan should be aligned to achieving these benefits. This makes it vital to identify your target training groups and analyze what training they require.

A number of education and training options are available in the market today. These range from business and technical classroom training, to e-learning kits (with help and training content) that can be deployed to your SharePoint environment.

Business Onboarding and Exploitation

Business onboarding is a term used to describe the method employed to help key stakeholders and end users adopt and exploit the SharePoint 2010 capabilities your solution provides.

Business onboarding involves providing guidance to support the businesses in the onboarding and exploitation of your SharePoint 2010 portal solution. Guidance provided to the business should include the steps described in the following sections.

Step 1: Engaging with the Central Portal Team

The organization should engage with the SharePoint 2010 business team to understand the capabilities and benefits provided by your SharePoint 2010 solution. This may include one or more of the following activities:

➤ Workshops

➤ Awareness training

➤ Assessing complexity versus business value

➤ Identifying skills requirements

➤ Identifying quick wins

➤ Identifying costs and resource plans

➤ Identifying and agreeing on portal team involvement

➤ Establishing an internal business team

Step 2: Planning to Adopt the New Portal Capabilities and Solution

The organization should plan how it will use the SharePoint 2010 capabilities and portal solution. This may include one of more of the following activities:

➤ Defining current state versus "future state" for your organization, department, or team

➤ Defining your communication plan

➤ Understanding the central portal deployment team's release schedule, and planning a rollout of features based on the release schedule

➤ Assessing the impact to your business

➤ Defining your training plan

➤ Developing your own business change plan

➤ Planning any further customizations you require

➤ Planning any further configuration you require

Step 3: Preparing for the New Portal Capabilities and Solution

The organization, department, or team should prepare to begin using the new capabilities and portal solution. This may include one of more of the following activities:

➤ Analyzing and understanding your data

➤ Piloting the central solution in your organization, department, or team

➤ Defining and implementing your information architecture

➤ Defining your taxonomy and classification hierarchy and term sets

➤ Defining how you will administrate your deployment

➤ Defining what data cleansing is required

 Do not simply move all your data into SharePoint. This is an ideal opportunity to conduct a "data cleanse" of your information.

➤ Developing and testing any customizations planned in Step 2

➤ Educating and training your site administrators and end users

➤ Setting up a retirement plan for legacy services no longer required

Step 4: Implementing and Exploiting the New Portal Capabilities and Solution

The business should begin using the capabilities and portal solution, and maximizing the benefits received from leveraging the portal solution. This may include one of more of the following activities:

➤ Migrating your data to SharePoint 2010

➤ Implementing "lighthouse" sites that demonstrate the new capability

➤ Implementing quick wins (such as collaboration, team sites, and My Sites)

➤ Implementing configuration and deploying any customizations

➤ Retiring the legacy services

➤ Reviewing your deployment

➤ Continually optimizing and improving your deployment

As you can see, a significant amount of work is required (post "go-live") to onboard business organizations, departments, functions, and teams. Therefore, any guidance you provide will be invaluable to external business and technical stakeholders. Make sure the guidance is targeted and appropriate for the "level" of the receiving business and technical stakeholders, and that it is timely.

Defining and Measuring Success

Regardless of whether the SharePoint 2010 portal solution is a small "point" solution or a large full-platform deployment, a key part of any SharePoint 2010 portal solution is the capability to define and measure success. This involves a combination of activities.

The first is to work with your program management team to accurately define the benefits realization plan. This involves mapping key operational and functional benefits to the strategic goals laid out during the definition of your portal strategy. For example, the benefit of improving content security may be mapped to a strategic goal of ensuring information items are appropriately managed and appropriately security-tagged.

The second part of measuring success is to define and agree on a set of measures (metrics) to ascertain the success of the benefits provided. Using the previous example, associated metrics may be the number of security incidents, or the number of secured sites, or the number of "in strict confidence" documents correctly classified and tagged as "in strict confidence."

It is vital that you associate measures with each of the functional and operational benefits associated with your SharePoint 2010 deployment. If you can't define and measure success, you won't be able to assess the ROI, and may not be able to justify further funding.

Capturing Lessons Learned

Learning from your mistakes is vital to the success of any SharePoint 2010 program and project, because it provides your team with a chance to improve how you respond to future tasks, activities, risks, and issues.

This activity usually occurs at the end of a phase or release milestone. It consists of two feedback workshops, consisting of a session focused on external or business stakeholders, and a slightly more informal workshop involving the internal leads and key resources in your team.

The external or business workshop is a chance for business stakeholders to provide *constructive* feedback on areas and approaches of your team. Note the emphasis on the word "constructive," because stress levels may be running high, and important lessons may be missed. The internal workshop is a chance to "air dirty laundry" to find out what worked well and what didn't work that well, and to field suggestions for improvement and optimizations in your team's approach to the next phase or release.

> *Do not combine the business and internal workshops. Feedback from both workshops may be "raw," emotionally charged, potentially unqualified, and not appropriate for business stakeholders. And, vice versa, business stakeholder feedback may discourage and de-motivate your team, decreasing your ability to respond constructively to business feedback.*

At both workshops, attempt to listen, capture, and understand, rather than speak and be heard. This is your internal or business team's chance to be heard, not yours. Ensure that you have a specific person available to record and document key points.

Everyone should have a chance to voice their opinions, and steps should be taken to ensure that the workshop is not railroaded by one or two individuals. A common approach to ensuring everyone's feedback is captured is to provide individuals in the meeting with sticky notes that they can use to capture an issue and attach the paper to a wall topic area. The chairperson of the meeting then groups and discusses each point.

Personal experience has shown that these sessions are highly cathartic because they give you a chance to voice opinions, be heard, and let go of issues experienced with the current release.

SUMMARY

This chapter examined a number of "getting started" work streams relating to requirements activities, technical design activities, early technical leaderships activities, program and project management activities, and business change and adoption activities. Each of these work streams is important to the overall success of your SharePoint 2010 project.

Most SharePoint 2010 projects focus mostly on the requirements, technical, and program and project activities, but fail to sufficiently grasp the importance of business change and adoption activities. Do not make the same mistake! Your project will not succeed without a solid business engagement strategy that supports key activities, including end-user education and training, internal marketing and communication, and business onboarding and exploitation support.

Chapters 14–18 provide detailed guidance to help progress your SharePoint 2010 project and solution. Chapter 14 kicks off that discussion with an examination of how to design your SharePoint 2010 information architecture.

14

Designing Your Information Architecture

By Brian Wilson

In the fantastic book, *Information Architecture for the World Wide Web* (Sebastopol, CA: O'Reilly Media, 2007), Peter Morville and Louis Rosenfeld highlighted a great quote from Winston Churchill: "We shape our buildings; thereafter they shape us." This is profoundly true for SharePoint 2010 information architecture and your business.

The term "information architecture" has reached "buzzword" status in the SharePoint world. Unfortunately, the term has come to mean different things to different people, based on their roles, project experience, and skill sets. This contributes to a lack of clarity for the activities required to diligently define your SharePoint 2010 information architecture.

So, what then is "information architecture"? Let's go back to the non-SharePoint and "pure" definition. The Information Architecture Institute defines information architecture as follows:

➤ The structural design of shared information environments

➤ The art and science of organizing and labeling websites, intranets, online communities, and software to support findability and usability

➤ An emerging "community of practice" focused on bringing principles of design and architecture to the digital landscape

 For more information, see http://iainstitute.org/documents/learn/ What_is_IA.pdf.

What is "SharePoint information architecture"? SharePoint information architecture can be defined as follows:

➤ The structural design of your SharePoint 2010 portal solutions, sites, and content

➤ The maximization of end-user productivity, "utility," "usability," and "findability" provided by your SharePoint 2010 platform and portal solution

➤ The analysis, interpretation, and successful delivery of site, content, and service application requirements that will meet the business drivers, and achieve the benefits expected by the business

➤ The successful incorporation of the key scenarios, and stakeholder, business information management, governance, navigation, people, security, and content migration requirements in your SharePoint 2010 information architecture

➤ The design of an efficient and performant SharePoint 2010 site and content containment model that supports site, content, and usage growth in the short, medium, and long term

➤ The successful consideration and inclusion of infrastructure and technical solution constraints in the design of your SharePoint information architecture

➤ The visual design that reflects the corporate identity and culture of the business that meets the needs, expectations, and user experience required by key stakeholders and end users

➤ The successful contribution of your information architecture requirements relating to any custom functionality required by your SharePoint 2010 portal solutions, sites, and content

➤ The output of a design that documents your "SharePoint information architecture" that both business and technical representatives can take as input to understand, communicate, develop, and deploy

 Have you noticed how, in some cases, the line "blurs" between what is solution, infrastructure, or information architecture? The reality of SharePoint 2010 is that these areas often overlap, seeking to influence and constrain each other. Therefore, your SharePoint information architecture should be designed in conjunction with your solution and infrastructure architecture.

In the real world, depending on the size and scope of your project, you will most likely be "running" the information architecture stream slightly behind your requirements-gathering streams, but slightly ahead of or in parallel with the infrastructure and solution architecture streams. Each of these streams works to influence and constrain each other. In the previous chapters, you learned how to define your portal strategy, and how to kick off key streams of work in your SharePoint 2010 project. The requirements stream started eliciting, analyzing, validating, and recording requirements, while the technical stream began interpreting these requirements to conceptualize a high-level logical and physical SharePoint 2010 solution. This chapter uses these inputs to design a solid information architecture that can be applied to your SharePoint 2010 solution.

Designing your SharePoint 2010 information architecture involves a number of steps outlined in this chapter, which are as follows:

1. Understanding your scope, capabilities, and constraints
2. Assessing your business information maturity level
3. Defining your personas and scenarios
4. Defining your enterprise metadata requirements
5. Defining your SharePoint 2010 containment model
6. Designing for governance
7. Defining your search experience
8. Defining your navigation experience
9. Defining your people experience
10. Defining your visual experience
11. Defining your custom functionality
12. Planning for content migration
13. Refining your design

Each section in this chapter builds on the previous section. Feel free to skip to specific topics that interest you.

Let's begin by looking at your project scope, the capabilities you require, and the constraints that may apply to your project and solution.

UNDERSTANDING YOUR SCOPE, CAPABILITIES, AND CONSTRAINTS

You should review the scope of your solution, define the capabilities required by your SharePoint solution, and understand the constraints that apply.

Scope

The *scope* of your project defines the vision of what your project will achieve, and provides a set of parameters that define the rough boundaries of what will (and won't) be undertaken.

The scope of your information architecture should reflect the size and scale of your project. It should consider information such as the number of affected users and audiences, the required scale of change, the set of capabilities that will be used, the business impact, and the potential impact to your SharePoint 2010 environment.

A key factor influencing the scope and magnitude of your information architecture activity relates to the stage of your SharePoint 2010 portal deployment. Deploying a new SharePoint 2010 platform and portal solution often requires a significant amount of upfront design work, regardless of the approach in the deployment and rollout of capabilities. Upgrading existing environments to the next SharePoint version requires developing an understanding of how the new features will impact your current information architecture, and what needs to change to move to the next version of SharePoint.

Another factor influencing the scope of your information architecture activity relates to business onboarding activities (and resultant information architecture activities required) after you have deployed your SharePoint 2010 environment. The scope varies based on the amount of business onboarding activities required. These business onboarding activities can be classed into the following broad categories:

➤ *Business-wide strategic adoption of all the SharePoint 2010 capabilities provided by your team* — This is a large-scale deployment, and requires a great deal of planning to design the information architecture.

➤ *Business-wide adoption of specific capabilities provided by your SharePoint 2010 deployment* — The scope in terms of audience will be wide, but the range of capabilities will be limited. For example, deploy the collaboration capability across your entire business. Although the capability is for your entire business, it is focused purely on providing a collaboration capability.

➤ *Deployment to support a specific functional area of your business* — Examples might include the finance department, a program, or team in your business. This reduces the size of the audience, but the range of capabilities is likely to be wider and, therefore, the impact on the users higher.

➤ *Deployment to deliver a specific business solution* — This deployment is most likely based on a set of identified key "use cases." For example, an employee induction site may be required to help new employee get started. More often than not, these types of deployments have very specific requirements, and this influences the amount of customization required.

Each "onboarding" exercise will depend on a well-thought-out SharePoint information architecture.

Capabilities

Capabilities define the key portal workloads, platform, and supporting capabilities that are required by your organization. These include portal capabilities provided the SharePoint 2010 platform, as well as ongoing supporting capabilities and services provided by your central SharePoint team.

What portal capabilities and supporting services will your project require? Are you part of a central platform team that looks after the SharePoint 2010 implementation, and maintains the overall SharePoint 2010 information architecture? Or, are you a part of the business department's information technology (IT) team using a centralized portal solution? If so, consider what services you need from the central team, and the type of engagement you will require to implement your portal solution on the centralized platform.

Will your existing platform need to be upgraded or extended to provide the capabilities required by your project? Will the features you require have an impact on existing functionality? Will they be developed for the benefit of your business department or team only, or be rolled out as a generic, reusable capability that other areas of your business can leverage? Will your project output comply with the information architecture design of your existing SharePoint 2010 environment?

For your project, is there a way to better leverage your existing portal capabilities more effectively by slightly modifying and negotiating your requirements with your customer? This will enable you to ensure that the best value approach is taken by aligning to available functionality. This point especially applies to "shared service" SharePoint 2010 platforms that have been designed to host common and specific business solutions across the business.

For existing platforms, will your project depart heavily from your existing overall information architecture? In other words, is the information architecture planned for your SharePoint 2010 environment radically different from your existing information architecture? Will it pass your change control process and be accepted into production? A solution that departs heavily from accepted business best practice may struggle to pass change control on the basis of the risk to other solutions hosted on your platform. Furthermore, it may require extensive performance, capacity, and security testing to mitigate this risk. Aligning your information architecture to the overall information architecture reduces the chance of your project getting rejected by your change control board.

 By the way, if you don't have a change control board and process, you should institute one to protect your investment and SharePoint 2010 platform.

Constraints

Various constraints can affect your information architecture. The key constraints include the following:

➤ *Program and project constraints* — These constraints mostly center on schedule, cost, and feature tradeoffs. Your information architecture may be constrained in that you will not have oodles of time to deliver all features required by your stakeholders.

➤ *SharePoint 2010 hardware and software constraints* — Your information architecture is affected by the hardware you have at your disposal, and the software boundaries of SharePoint 2010. It doesn't matter if you design a Ferrari when you only have a lawn mower engine to use as your hardware. The point is to ensure that your hardware can handle your information architecture design. If you are constrained by available hardware, this should constrain your information architecture. For example, maximum RAM on each Web Front-End (WFE) dictates how many application pools and web applications you can comfortably host. In turn, this influences your URL namespace design. You can find many examples in SharePoint 2010 of how hardware and software boundaries can influence your SharePoint information architecture.

➤ *Organizational constraints* — Your business (or customer) has a number of processes, policies, and procedures that must be adhered to. Your corporate communications team may enforce brand guidelines on the visual design of your site. Your organization may be heavily resistant to culture change. Your organization's business formation may lend itself to a looser, more independent site collection structure.

➤ *Information and regulatory compliance constraints* — Your information architecture may be constrained by the regulatory regime within which your business operates. These regulations must be considered and factored into your SharePoint 2010 solution. Failure to do so could harm the reputation of your organization. For example, your legal team may require that the business retain types of documents using a retention-and-disposal schedule.

➤ *Security constraints* — In today's world, the security of business-critical information is vital. Your SharePoint 2010 content and platform may be subjected to direct internal and external attacks. It may be subjected to indirect attacks where malicious users exploit a vulnerability in your information architecture's security planning, thus enabling attackers to view privileged information. This may occur when a site is hidden through URL namespace obscurity, but not secured through a well-planned permission structure for all sites in your SharePoint 2010 environment.

 Chapter 2 provides detailed information to help you fully understand the subtle requirements emanating from the enterprise landscape.

ASSESSING YOUR BUSINESS INFORMATION MATURITY LEVEL

The first step in defining your SharePoint 2010 information architecture has nothing to do with the design of SharePoint 2010, but everything to do with how your business values and manages its intellectual property.

Gartner provides a great information maturity model and toolkit to help you understand and improve on the maturity of your business information, document, and record management maturity levels. Table 14-1 defines the possible maturity levels.

TABLE 14-1: The Information Management Maturity Levels

	LEVEL	CHARACTERISTICS
0	Unaware	Senior management is unaware that they need information, document, and records management.
1	Opportunistic	Pockets of best practice exist, but it is ad-hoc. There is no overriding policy, and most employees are unaware of the need for document and records management.
2	Fragmented	Senior management commitment emerges, driving the increased use of standards and policies to improve document and records management. No overarching policy exists for the entire business.

	LEVEL	CHARACTERISTICS
3	Standardized	Common policy, standards, and processes across the business. Individuals have greater awareness of the policy and how it relates to their work.
4	Managed	Proactive management of documents in all forms, including legacy data and documents. The value of document and records management as company assets is understood.
5	Optimized	Document and records management supports the business in achieving and maintaining a competitive advantage.

Source: Gartner

It is recommended that organizations assess the information management maturity levels of the areas of the business affected by the scope of the project. A number of valuable toolkits are provided by Gartner to help you develop your information management maturity assessment. You should leverage Gartner's research and toolkits to perform an accurate assessment of your business.

 The open source methodology Method for Integrated Knowledge (MIKE) 2.0 provides more information on this information maturity model at `http://mike2.openmethodology.org/wiki/Information_Maturity_Model`.

From a SharePoint information architecture perspective, your business information management maturity level is a kind of foretelling of what lies in store for your project, program, and business. It is generally accepted that businesses take evolutionary steps to move up the levels toward increasing maturity, progressing through the levels one at a time. People and organizations cannot cope with the concepts and requirements of later stages of maturity without time to adjust to the less drastic changes introduced in the intermediate stages.

This should influence how you approach your SharePoint design and information architecture. SharePoint 2010 is only part of the answer. The rest depends on the maturity of the business and end users, and their approach to document, records, and web content management. Therefore, think carefully as to the set of capabilities provided on Day One. Users need time to learn. Business departments need time to onboard, educate, and train their users.

Think about the steps and road map in the portal strategy created in Chapter 13 (that is, foundational, expansive, advanced, and specific). Align and grow your information design and architecture as part of your release cycle.

DEFINING YOUR PERSONAS AND SCENARIOS

Chapter 13 discussed activities related to gathering, analyzing, validating, and recording requirements. As your team drills into the detail of each requirement, you capture these requirements, either as user stories or as use cases (or both).

Analyzing your personas and scenarios involves reviewing your user stories and/or use cases from the perspective of information architecture. This involves looking more deeply into the key actors and personas to gain a deeper understanding of the users of your business. It involves reviewing the key user stories and use cases to ascertain how they will fit in your SharePoint 2010 information architecture and design. These steps are discussed next.

Defining Your Actors and Personas

This analysis requires a common understanding of the following terms:

- ➤ *Actor* — An actor is a role, category, or group of people played by the user or system that interacts with your SharePoint 2010 solution.

- ➤ *Personas* — Personas are individualized instances of an actor. Personas bring a role to life. This may include further information such as a fictional name, role, professional background, goals and aspirations, a quotation, personal background, and wants and needs.

Personas require more interaction with the business to identify individualized instances of identified actors/roles in your business. For each persona, research the following information:

- ➤ *User* — This is the name of the persona, job role, or description of the user group.

- ➤ *Characteristics* — Describe the general qualities of the users dictated by their job roles.

- ➤ *Goals* — Describe the main objectives of the role.

- ➤ *User context* — Describe the physical, social, and cultural environment in which the work takes place.

- ➤ *Tasks* — Describe the methods by which users accomplish their job goals.

- ➤ *Requirements* — Describe information, tools, and skills necessary to perform the user's role.

- ➤ *Training* — Describe training that enables users to do their jobs.

- ➤ *Current IT systems* — Describe the computers and software a person uses to accomplish his or her job.

- ➤ *Inefficiencies* — Describe aspects of workflow, documents, tools, and so on, that negatively impact the user's job.

Figure 14-1 shows how you visually depict personas and scenarios.

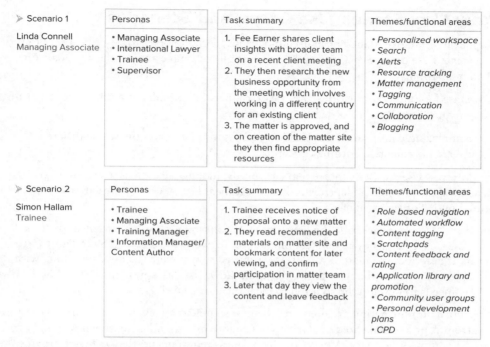

⪢ Scenario 1	Personas	Task summary	Themes/functional areas
Linda Connell Managing Associate	• Managing Associate • International Lawyer • Trainee • Supervisor	1. Fee Earner shares client insights with broader team on a recent client meeting 2. They then research the new business opportunity from the meeting which involves working in a different country for an existing client 3. The matter is approved, and on creation of the matter site they then find appropriate resources	• *Personalized workspace* • *Search* • *Alerts* • *Resource tracking* • *Matter management* • *Tagging* • *Communication* • *Collaboration* • *Blogging*

⪢ Scenario 2	Personas	Task summary	Themes/functional areas
Simon Hallam Trainee	• Trainee • Managing Associate • Training Manager • Information Manager/ Content Author	1. Trainee receives notice of proposal onto a new matter 2. They read recommended materials on matter site and bookmark content for later viewing, and confirm participation in matter team 3. Later that day they view the content and leave feedback	• *Role based navigation* • *Automated workflow* • *Content tagging* • *Scratchpads* • *Content feedback and rating* • *Application library and promotion* • *Community user groups* • *Personal development plans* • *CPD*

FIGURE 14-1: Personas and scenarios

The danger with going only to the actor level is that it stereotypes a set of people into a "black-and-white" class, and does not test any of the assumptions your team has made about them. As a result, it may not reflect their personality attributes and their needs, wants, goals, and aspirations. It is this level of detail that will help you drive out requirements and associated user interactions to improve the usability of your SharePoint 2010 solution.

Why should you care about personas? Isn't this too much detail? Can you get away with defining only actors? Realistically speaking, the answer is that it depends on a number of factors, including the following:

➤ The size and scope of your project, and the budget at your disposal

➤ The number of users, audiences, and level of personalization expected and required

➤ Determining whether your goal is to deliver a capability that will be molded by the business as and when it sees fit, or a specifically tailored solution that needs to hit the spot on Day One

If you are delivering a set of capabilities to a large business, your onboarding processes should have a SharePoint information architecture step where key personas and scenarios are researched.

It may be the case that you invest in researching personas that touch scenarios only with the greatest or broadest impact (for example, authoring and publishing a news article to a corporate intranet home page).

Defining Your User Stories, Use Cases, and Scenarios

The word "scenario" is an overloaded term used in various methodologies to describe a set of user stories and associated use cases. Scenarios outline the user flows, and establish the key goals for each area of your solution.

In this case, you are looking at user stories and use cases that will significantly affect the structure and formation of your SharePoint information architecture.

The first step to analyzing your user stories and use cases is to understand the subtle difference between these two requirements-recording concepts:

➤ *User stories* — User stories capture real user needs, in language the user will understand, and, as much as possible, independent of any technical terms. User stories are usually captured in one or two sentences.

➤ *Use cases* — Use cases describe the behavior your solution will provide to meet the user needs. A use case describes a complete interaction between the user and SharePoint 2010 solution. It describes the main flow of steps required to complete the use case, along with alternate flows that may happen during the main flow. Use cases provide the level of detail a developer needs to develop the solution to meet the user's need.

From the perspective of information architecture, the first step is to review the user stories that have been captured from your key stakeholders during your requirements-gathering stage. As you have probably realized, although user stories describe the business requirement, they may not provide the detail you require. This means that you should review the related use cases to ensure that they have been successfully "interpreted" into a single (or multiple) set of use cases.

Once you are confident your use cases are representative of your business requirements, the next step involves looking at the cross-cutting concerns that affect your information architecture. This involves identifying key use cases that are business-critical, or have the broadest or highest impact, and analyzing these use cases against the following elements:

➤ Business information elements

➤ Enterprise metadata elements

➤ Visual design elements

➤ Governance elements

➤ Search elements

➤ Personalization elements

➤ Navigation elements

➤ SharePoint container elements

➤ Security structures

➤ Individual functionalities

➤ Content migration requirements

Each of these elements is discussed in subsequent sections in this chapter. As your review the use cases, these may result in changes to the use case to enable it to comply with your SharePoint 2010 information architecture.

DEFINING YOUR ENTERPRISE METADATA MANAGEMENT REQUIREMENTS

Enterprise metadata management (EMM) is the practice of effectively managing your digital assets in SharePoint 2010, thus providing your organization and end users with benefits such as increased productivity, improved "findability," better manageability, and an easier, more cost-effective road to achieving compliance against an ever-increasing number of external regulatory requirements.

In the "olden" days, large organizations used dedicated librarians to manage the classification, storage, retrieval, archival, and eventual destruction of paper-based assets. In SharePoint 2010, EMM is commonly practiced by information architects, taxonomists, librarians, records managers, site owners, and content owners. These roles use SharePoint 2010 features to ensure that the information held in sites, libraries, and lists meet your organization's information management requirements.

EMM is especially important in deriving additional value from unstructured information (for example, a document) stored in SharePoint 2010. It does this by applying "structured data" in the form of additional "descriptors" that further classify the unstructured content held in your SharePoint 2010 sites, libraries, and lists.

From an information architecture perspective, this requires an understanding of key influencing factors, and analyzing your business information before you will be able to define your EMM requirements. These topics are covered in this section.

 Don't forget that information analysis and design requires business engagement, and this depends on key stakeholders providing you with their time and the business domain knowledge. Therefore, set clear expectations up front with your key stakeholders to avoid disputes later on. Communicate what input you expect, what your business information design will define, and the (impact of) resultant activities your key stakeholders will need to undertake.

Understanding Your Influencing Factors

Working out the set of activities required to successfully analyze your business information and define your enterprise metadata requirements depends on a number of factors, including the following:

➤ *What is the scope of your SharePoint 2010 project?* — The scope of the SharePoint 2010 project determines the level of detail you will be able to get to in defining your enterprise metadata requirements. A greater scope indicates the enterprise metadata requirements will most likely be defined at a fairly "generic" or "base" level. The smaller the scope, the greater the detail and preciseness of your enterprise metadata requirements. For example, if your project is to deliver a new enterprise-wide platform to a large user base across many business departments, functions, and teams, you will struggle to define enterprise content types that meet the *exacting* requirements of each area of the business, function, department, and team.

➤ *What type of SharePoint solution are you building?* — SharePoint 2010 caters to many types of solutions. Each type of solution requires a set of information analysis activities to be performed. For example, a publishing portal has a vastly different set of activities compared to a collaboration portal.

➤ *What is the purpose and vision of your project?* — Your project may have resulted from an important initiative in your business. This will influence the level of analysis and information design required. For example, your SharePoint 2010 solution may need to support a new business policy that defines a greater need to manage information in accordance with the external regulatory environment.

➤ *What is your team's level of authority?* — Your team may not have the necessary authority to dictate a highly refined SharePoint information architecture to specific businesses in your organization. This should influence the approach you take. In cases where your influence is limited to the SharePoint 2010 platform only (and not over the business), it makes sense to focus your efforts on understanding the base types of information, base types of site and content structures that will be required, and to provide these base-level site and content controls required by the business, along with training required to enable the business IT champions to complete their refined SharePoint information architecture.

➤ *What are your team's responsibilities?* — A specific business or IT strategy department may be responsible for defining the enterprise metadata requirements. Don't take on responsibilities related to IT strategy without a clear brief and mandate from your executive or business sponsor.

➤ *Are you part of SharePoint 2010 platform team or an embedded IT resource within a business department?* — As part of the SharePoint 2010 platform team, you may be responsible for interpreting the business information architecture and implementing base metadata requirements. As an embedded IT resource in a business department, your responsibilities may be to define your business department's SharePoint information architecture within the parameters of the already defined platform information architectures and containment model. This will, most likely, involve following guidelines or toolkits provided by your SharePoint 2010 platform team.

➤ *What is your scope of work for this and future releases?* — Your scope of work may be focused on defining the base SharePoint information architecture, with the further refinements to be fleshed out later during the business onboarding and information architecture definition stages.

➤ *What is expected from your role?* — Understand what is realistically expected from your role as SharePoint information architect. This will help you decide what level of SharePoint information architecture you can achieve in the timeframes expected by the business.

This may sound like a tip from "Captain Obvious," but it is important that you think about the answers to these questions up front, rather than in the later stages of your project. Failure to fully understand the influencing factors may result in wasted effort in producing an enterprise metadata model that is not adopted and incorporated in your SharePoint 2010 environment.

Analyzing Your Business Information

This activity involves researching the characteristics of your business information to gain insight into what will be required to host this information in SharePoint 2010.

 The level and depth of the analysis required should be scoped by the decisions you made at the beginning of this section.

This activity is focused on building up an understanding of your business information, and requires input from stakeholders with the necessary business domain knowledge. It involves identifying the content sources hosting your business information, analyzing business information from these content sources, and developing a thorough understanding of the business information characteristics.

 Advanced tools are available in the market today that will automate this for you. For example, have a look at the Active Navigation website at `www.activenav.com/` *for a well-known tool. These tools provide a number of additional benefits, such as content de-duplication.*

Table 14-2 defines key assessment areas of your current business information content sources.

TABLE 14-2: Assessing Your Business Information

AREA	DESCRIPTION
Identify information characteristics and attributes	It is important to identify key information characteristics and attributes. This entails discovering as much as information as possible about the types of information, average and maximum file sizes, and languages used, as well as the purpose and priority of business information types.
Identify actors	For each type of business information, discover what actors will interact with this data. Consider authors, contributors, information and records managers, consumers (view only), and other actors that use the business information. For example, a view-only role may not need to view previous versions of business information.
Identify location-related information	Identify location-related information, including the physical location of the content, and the type of storage system used to host the content. Are any special requirements, or gaps, needed to ensure that users can manage this information in SharePoint 2010? Will users be negatively impacted by moving this content in a physical location to a centralized portal location?

continues

TABLE 14-2 *(continued)*

AREA	DESCRIPTION
Identify business processes	Identify key business processes that apply to your business information. Are these processes manual or automated? Do you require workflows to act against each information item? For example, each page may require approval by your intranet administrator before it can be published and viewed by other users of your site.
Identify key metadata	Identify key metadata that is associated with your business information. Consider the usage of specific sets of terms that have been applied to your information. Are there inconsistencies in the application of terms applied to similar types of business information? For each type of information, document the additional metadata you require. Document terms, synonyms of terms, specific business vocabulary, and acronyms. These will be useful when defining term sets in the Managed Metadata Service.
Identify "hierarchical content organizing" structures	Identify hierarchical content organizing structures that are being used to manage content in your business information. A good example is your network file shares that host and categorize content using a hierarchical folder structure. For example, information stored at `\\mybusiness\clients\clientname\engagements\engagement` tells you much information as to familiar hierarchical structures used in your business. Other examples include the use of site (and subsite) structures in other legacy websites that structure and present content in logical groupings to users.
	Understanding content organizing structures is vital in the planning and design of your SharePoint 2010 containment model because they present clues as to how users currently categorize and find content. It's worth keeping in mind that just because a content organizing structure exists doesn't make it the best option for your stakeholders. Therefore, endeavor to verify that the structure is still valid, and the most appropriate organizing structure. The "open and closed" card-sorting technique is a valuable tool that will help you verify and select the most appropriate content organizing structures.
Identify entity relationships	Record potential entities and entity relationships that you discover. As an example, it may be that your business stores each client engagement in your client folder. The resulting entity relationship found is Business → Clients → Client → Engagements.
	This structure is extremely useful in planning out site collections and subsite requirements. For example, in the creation of a client engagement portal, you may have to decide to create a site collection per engagement or per client. In its `MSEngage` portal, Microsoft provisioned a site collection per engagement, and surfaced the correct information to enable the easy location of these provisioned engagement sites via custom site listing web parts on the root site collection of the engagement portal.

AREA	DESCRIPTION
Identify rules and policies	Identify the information policies and procedures of the business that may affect or apply to this business information. For example, it may be that you need to comply with a corporate information policy.
Identify trends	It's not often that business information is analyzed in its entirety. This presents an opportunity to feed back key findings and "learnings" to your stakeholders. For example, the average content growth rate over a period of time is useful to stakeholders because it helps them estimate their future storage requirements and plan for future storage costs.

The output produced from this stage will feed into the definition of your enterprise metadata requirements, and the structural design of your SharePoint 2010 containment model.

Understanding SharePoint 2010 Enterprise Metadata Features

Defining your EMM requirements requires understanding the common use cases and features to manage your enterprise metadata in SharePoint 2010. The key use cases include the following:

➤ *Content enrichment* — Rich metadata increases the "findability" and usage of your organization's intellectual property.

➤ *Content compliance* — Rich metadata makes it easier for organizations to comply with external regulatory requirements.

➤ *Metadata navigation* — Rich metadata makes it possible to navigate large content repositories in SharePoint 2010 using common metadata to filter the items shown to the user.

➤ *Content organization* — Rich metadata helps organize disparate types of data effectively through the association of metadata.

➤ *Social tagging and annotation* — Users are able to tag and annotate any content in SharePoint 2010.

➤ *Search refinement* — Users are able to refine search results using metadata refiners to further limit the scope of their search query.

➤ *Consistent vocabulary* — Consistent vocabulary improves the capability to classify and categorize resources in your SharePoint 2010 environment, thus improving the precision of the application of metadata to content.

These use cases are valuable in that they help describe the result of the successful application of managed metadata to your environment.

SharePoint 2010 has evolved the set of features available to manage your enterprise metadata. These include the Managed Metadata Service, term management tool, enterprise content type hub, and business metadata information controls (such as information policies, content types, and site columns that can be applied to manage content in sites, libraries, and lists). The key metadata controls are shown in Figure 14-2.

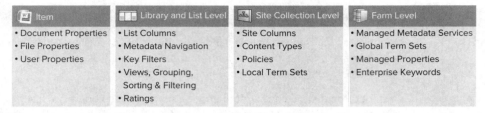

FIGURE 14-2: SharePoint 2010 Managed Metadata Functionality

 For more information on managing metadata in SharePoint 2010, see the in-depth articles by Pat Miller at `http://blogs.msdn.com/b/ecm/archive/2010/06/22/introducing-enterprise-metadata-management.aspx`, *and the MSDN article on managing metadata in SharePoint 2010 at* `http://msdn.microsoft.com/en-us/library/ee559337.aspx`.

Lastly, the Managed Metadata service application has a set of software constraints that it is important to take heed of, including the following:

➤ Maximum number of levels for nested terms in term store: 7

➤ Maximum number of term sets in a term store: 1,000

➤ Maximum number of terms in a term set: 30,000

➤ Total number of terms in a term store: 1,000,000

Defining Your SharePoint 2010 Enterprise Metadata

Now that you have successfully analyzed your business information, and reviewed the key managed metadata use cases and functionality in SharePoint 2010, the next step involves defining your enterprise metadata using the SharePoint 2010 enterprise metadata functionality. This includes the following:

➤ *Defining your Managed Metadata services instance (term store) and content type hub* — An instance of the Managed Metadata service is usually referred to as a *term store*. The term store provides key pieces of functionality, including taxonomies, folksonomies, term organization and management, and a single centralized content type hub for publishing centralized content types to subscribed site collections.

➤ *Considering whether single or multiple term stores are required* — A single term store may be all that is needed in your business. This will provide consistency in the controlled vocabulary. Larger businesses may require that separate, highly sensitive or proprietary information be placed in a dedicated term store.

➤ *Considering your language requirements* — Each term store can have only one default language and multiple working languages. These require the language pack to be installed for each language. Each term can have multiple labels defined for each working language, but only one default label per language.

➤ *Defining your term store groups* — Groups are used to organize term sets. They can contain one or more term sets. Groups provide a security boundary for administration of a term set (that is, who is able to administer the term sets in a group, and who is able to contribute to term sets in a group).

➤ *Differentiating between global groups versus domain-specific groups* — Global groups will contain term sets available to all web applications and site collections, or domain-specific groups that are available, for example, to a specific business department function or team. In these cases, consider whether the global groups require their own term store and content type hub, or whether they will fit into your overarching content type hub.

➤ *Defining your term sets* — Term sets are containers used to organize terms. Terms can either exist in global term sets or in local term sets. Global term sets are available to all site collections, while local term sets are only available to a specific site collection.

➤ *Defining your terms* — Terms are predefined values that represent taxonomy objects in a term set. They include term-related information, including the term itself, the description, and translations of the term. Terms can be nested in a hierarchical structure up to seven levels deep. Additionally, "organizing only" terms can be defined purely to organize other terms. These management terms are not available to use in a data selection. Lastly, terms can be associated with other terms as synonyms.

➤ *Incorporating terms in your content types* — Terms can be associated with content types via a managed metadata column field type. These managed metadata-based columns can then be consistently deployed via a centralized content type hub to your subscribed site collections automatically or manually when creating content types in your site collection, or alternatively via a site-scoped Feature that deploys the site columns and content types to your site collection.

➤ *Defining your additional configuration requirements for your subscribed site collections* — Subscribed site collections, (which receive content types from a central content type hub) will not receive configurations related to, for example, workflows attached to the central content type. These must be configured in each site collection.

 Beware of the implication of creating local term sets. This occurs, for example, when you choose the managed metadata column, and customize a term set within a site collection. At the time of writing, backup and restoring this site collection would sever the connection with the customized term store group, and the currently assigned values would become orphaned. It is possible to re-associate the term set, but this requires additional effort to complete.

It is important not to underestimate how long it takes to mature your taxonomy and enterprise metadata strategy. For new deployments, it is recommended to start off with one term store, keep terms simple, clear, and precise, and ensure term "nesting" structures are a minimum of three levels deep.

Start small and grow with your SharePoint 2010 environment and business requirements. Don't forget to establish a change procedure to govern changes to your enterprise metadata, and ensure you have factored in ongoing maintenance to implement the agreed upon changes in your SharePoint 2010 environment.

DEFINING YOUR SHAREPOINT 2010 CONTAINMENT MODEL

The SharePoint 2010 *containment model* is the logical structuring of how your SharePoint 2010 platform will host and manage your business information in web applications, site collections, sites, and content structures.

The design of the SharePoint 2010 containment model can be compared to the design of a SQL Server database. If you create a bad database design, don't blame SQL Server when it performs poorly. The same applies to a SharePoint 2010 containment model. If you implement a poor design, don't blame SharePoint 2010!

The SharePoint 2010 containment model is important because it helps ensure that your solution will grow in a manageable fashion. It helps ensure that sites are created within the correct web application and site collection, using the most appropriate site template, and following the governance model for the type of site template.

 SharePoint 2010 containment model design activity does not rest solely in the hands of the SharePoint information architect. It is a joint architectural design activity requiring the input of your SharePoint 2010 infrastructure and solution-focused architect(s). Their technical input will constrain and influence your SharePoint information architecture and desired containment model.

Defining your SharePoint 2010 containment model requires a good understanding of the business information that you plan to manage in your SharePoint 2010 environment, and your resulting enterprise metadata requirements defined in the previous section. Without this analysis, your team will struggle to define the appropriate SharePoint 2010 containment model.

This section covers the following topics:

➤ Defining your web application requirements

➤ Defining your site collection and subsite requirements

➤ Defining your content library requirements

Defining Your Web Application Requirements

First off, the design of your web applications is a joint activity between your information, solution, and infrastructure architects. The information architect contributes business domain knowledge, use cases and scenarios, and enterprise metadata requirements that must be delivered. The solution (and infrastructure) architect contributes the logical web application structure that will be able to host the site collections and services required by the information architect. Finally, the infrastructure architect contributes the underlying physical platform that will host the logical web application structure.

To recap from Chapter 6, a SharePoint 2010 web application is composed of an Internet Information Services (IIS) site hosted in a unique or shared application pool. The IIS site can be hosted on one or more WFE servers. User requests can be load-balanced over these servers using either software or hardware-based load-balancing technology. The following list highlights other key aspects of a web application:

➤ It can be configured with a unique domain name.

➤ It can be isolated and executed in a specific process using a unique application pool, running under a specific security account.

➤ It supports various authentication modes (such as claims, classic, and other custom authentication methods).

➤ It supports different logical paths (and authentication methods) to content within a web application.

➤ Web applications host content (site collections) within one or more content databases. Each site collection can only be hosted within a single content database, but a content database can host multiple site collections.

➤ It hosts only one root-level site collection, but supports a number of site collections deployed below it. This is enabled via the use of specific or wildcard managed paths.

➤ Given its underlying hardware, network, and storage topology, a web application is subject to a set of software boundaries and limits that act to constrain the resulting configuration.

 For more information, see the TechNet article at `http://technet.microsoft` `.com/en-us/library/cc262787.aspx`.

Generally speaking, it is recommended that you deploy new site collections to existing web applications, unless one of the following considerations applies:

➤ *Workload/capability grouping* — It is common practice to group and host key workloads in specific web applications. For example, your team may elect to deploy collaboration team sites to `http://sites.yourcompany.com/sites/*`. This makes it easier for IT administrators to manage incidents occurring within a web application.

➤ *URL namespace design* — This includes the site naming structure within a URL, from the root site collection to site collections deployed under managed paths. With the introduction of host header named site collections, this is less of an issue, but it may still be a factor. Additionally, it is important not to overuse managed paths functionality to protect performance. Microsoft recommends a maximum of 20 managed paths per web application. Managed paths are cached on each WFE server, and CPU resources are used to process incoming requests against a managed path list. Exceeding 20 managed paths per web application adds more load to the web server for each request.

 For more information, see the TechNet article at `http://technet.microsoft` `.com/en-us/library/cc262787.aspx.`

➤ *Customization isolation* — Web applications may have specific application customizations applied that are not desired for all site collections in your SharePoint 2010 environment.

➤ *Configuration isolation* — A web application may have a specific configuration (either underlying infrastructure or web application configuration settings) applied to a web application that is not desired for all site collections in your SharePoint 2010 environment.

➤ *Application/solution isolation* — Say that your business would like to host "black box" content in one or more site collections. In other words, you want a site with extremely confidential information that is isolated by URL, by application pool (security and process boundary isolation), by IIS site, by content database, and potentially by authentication method.

➤ *Performance optimization* — Hosting all site collections within a single web application implies using the same application pool for all site collections. Splitting the deployment of site collections into key hosting web applications groups types of site collections into separate web applications. This enables the option to use separate application pools.

➤ *Storage optimization* — Microsoft recommends a maximum size per content database, and supports a maximum number of content databases per web application. In large SharePoint 2010 deployments, more web applications are required to support more content.

➤ *Manageability optimization* — Web applications provide an opportunity to associate site collections within a web application to Service Level Agreements (SLAs), with appropriate response times. For example, My Sites may not be deemed as "mission critical" as more important business intranets or client project sites.

The example scenario in Chapter 13 defined the following "starting-point" web applications:

➤ *Published Intranet Content web application (*`http://intranet/`*)* — You grouped publishing sites, help and training sites, and enterprise search center site workloads into this web application.

➤ *Business Collaboration web application (*`http://collab/`*)* — You grouped team collaboration sites, document center sites, and record center sites in this web application.

➤ *My Sites web application (*`http://my/`*)* — You set this web application aside for the exclusive use of personal My Site site hosting.

Using the scenario from Chapter 13, if your business requirements dictated that you isolate record centers from other areas of your platform, the information architect would inform the solution and infrastructure architect of this requirement. Once the appropriate design has been agreed upon, you would be able to host record center sites in a dedicated web application isolated from other areas of your SharePoint 2010 platform.

As you can see from this example, your web application design determines the site collection hosting areas you are able to recommend to the business.

Defining Your Site Collection and Subsite Requirements

To recap from Chapter 6, a SharePoint 2010 site collection is a hierarchical collection of sites that is made up of one root-level site and a number of sites below it. Only one site collection can exist at the root of a web application, but many can be created within a web application under individual or wildcard-managed paths. The following list highlights other key aspects of a site collection:

➤ Site collections are provisioned from an out-of-the-box or custom site definition. The site definition enables consistent provisioning of different types of site collections and associated functionality.

➤ Content storage quotas can be applied and managed at the site collection level.

➤ Each site collection maintains its own security privileges, using default SharePoint groups. Each SharePoint group has a set of permissions applied, granting access to different Features in the site collection. All subsites and content can have individual security privileges.

➤ Site collections can be stored in only one content database. They cannot be stored over multiple content databases. For especially large site collections (such as large-scale document archives), how you split (or don't split) content over multiple site collections impacts the amount of long-term maintenance work required to maintain the site collection(s).

➤ Site collections deploy additional functionality through site- and web-scoped Features. On activation, site collection Features apply their functionality to the entire site collection, whereas web-scoped Features are applied to an individual site within the site collection.

➤ Site collections support provisioning of new sites, libraries, and lists automatically and on-demand.

The following should be considered in the design of your site collections:

➤ *URL namespace design* — The site structure within a site collection should be carefully planned to ensure users and site owners get the best experience. Each subsite URL name contributes to the overall URL namespace. For example, `http://intranet.contoso.com/sites/marketresearch/countries/china/` informs the users that they are browsing the China site of the market research portal site collection.

➤ *Type of site definition* — Consider which starting site definition you use to provision a site collection. Each site definition provisions a site collection with a specific functionality.

➤ *Security* — Consider your site collection security requirements. Permissions are covered in more detail in the section, "Defining Your People Experience," later in this chapter.

➤ *Functionality* — Consider what functionality your site collection requires, and what Features these map to in SharePoint 2010.

➤ *Site and web Features* — Consider what site-scoped and web-scoped Features should be activated for your site collection.

➤ *Human workflows* — Consider the key business processes that members of your site collection will participate in. Common out-of-the-box examples include approval workflows of web pages and documents.

➤ *Visual design* — Consider the visual design and "brand" you require for your site collection. Visual Design is covered in the section, "Defining Your Visual Experience," later in this chapter.

➤ *Information management and compliance* — Consider what information management controls you want to apply to content in your site collection. These include Features (such as content types), enterprise managed metadata, information policies, and so forth.

➤ *Navigation* — Do not overlook your navigation experience as discussed later in this chapter. "On the hoof" navigation configuration for your *key* site collections should be avoided as much as possible. Navigation design is discussed later in this chapter in the section, "Defining Your Navigation Experience."

➤ *Use case and requirements mapping* — Ensure that you map your use cases, scenarios, and requirements to the appropriate SharePoint functionality you require.

For key site collections, it is important to model the site structure and organization of objects within a site collection. These include objects such as the top-level site, any significant pages in that site, the structure and organization of any child sites, and the structure and planned size of the related content database. Figure 14-3 defines the subsite structure of the "work and office" area of a company intranet.

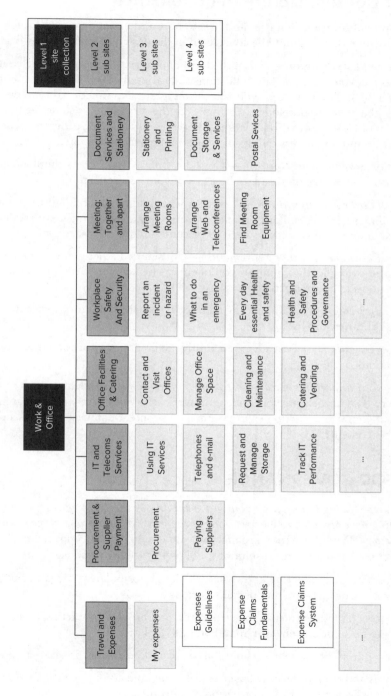

FIGURE 14-3: "Work and office" section of company intranet

Defining Your Content Library Requirements

SharePoint 2010 provides various libraries and lists to host and maintain content, each with specific Features. The following aspects should be considered in the design of your content libraries:

➤ *Libraries and lists selection* — Select the most appropriate libraries for the content you plan to host in your sites and site collections. Libraries and lists are similar, but different. Libraries in SharePoint 2010 provide significant additional functionality to end users, and under the hood, to developers. Examples of the differences include the underlying mechanism of how information is stored, subtle search indexing differences, as well as folder, major and minor versioning, and check-out check-in support.

➤ *Information management controls* — Consider what content types should be applied to enforce consistent entry of metadata by users of your site collection.

➤ *Additional library configuration* — Consider what additional configuration you require for your libraries and lists. For example, do your views, versioning settings, document templates, or approval workflows need to be configured?

➤ *Consider additional feature requirements* — Consider whether you will enable various Features (for example, the configuration of enterprise keywords, item ratings, and publishing tags to a user's activity feed).

➤ *Security requirements* — Plan out any additional security configuration requirements for individual libraries and lists.

➤ *Content aggregations* — Consider your future "aggregations" of content in your sites and site collections.

➤ *Consider your underlying database storage requirements* — Calculate how much content you plan to host in each site collection, and work with your infrastructure architect to ensure that your site collection is provisioned in a content database that has sufficient space to host this content.

DESIGNING FOR GOVERNANCE

You may be thinking, *"Why do we care about governability at the stage of design and architecture? Isn't this something we only need to worry about in the 'run and maintain' stage of our platform and portal life cycle?"* The information architecture you design directly impacts the "governability" of your SharePoint platform and portal solutions. Following are the reasons for this:

➤ Your information architecture and structural design formulates how your business will interact with your platform and portal solutions.

➤ It formulates common elements and structures, and provides a starting point for new business portal solutions on your SharePoint 2010 platform.

➤ It impacts your ability to manage solutions in accordance with the original design intent.

➤ It influences and constrains how businesses develop and configure new solutions in accordance with your overall information architecture.

➤ A well-thought-out information architecture makes it easier for your governance team to pick up and respond to non-compliant business solutions.

Now that you understand why it is important to design your information architecture with governance in mind, the next step is to think about what aspects of your information architecture will contribute to the governability of your environment.

Chapter 20 provides more detail on planning out the business aspects of defining your governance model. This chapter provides guidance related to key areas that may influence the design of your information architecture.

The remainder of this section focuses on governance aspects that will influence your SharePoint 2010 information architecture.

Business Governance

Designing for business governance entails thinking about how your information architecture design will support your management team's future capability to manage your SharePoint 2010 platform.

It entails thinking about what type of engagement model will be required to onboard new business teams and their associated solutions, and who will develop, configure, test, deploy, and maintain these production solutions, along with a service and support model.

You should also consider what business situations you would like to avoid to ensure that a consistent overall information architecture is maintained. For example, rogue SharePoint 2010 deployments drain resources and dilute return on investment (ROI). This may result in independent silos of information, based on different information architectures. Another good example may be the inconsistent application of enterprise metadata to content in different libraries in the same or multiple sites.

This all requires forethought about how you will manage and attribute cost back to the business. How will you charge and fairly allocate cost to businesses, functions, and teams leveraging and consuming resources provided by the SharePoint 2010 platform? For example, this may influence your decision as to whether you allocate site collections (and leverage site storage quotas and additional compute resources), or whether you allocate subsites within a single site collection.

Chapter 2 provides more insight into the common charging models used in organizations today.

Platform Governance

Your information architecture affects the capability to govern and manage your SharePoint 2010 platform.

A common issue that affects many SharePoint environments is where the information architecture has been designed to handle short-term growth, but fails to adequately design and cater for medium- to long-term growth.

An example that brings this to life is the decision to use a single site collection rather than multiple site collections. Depending on how you planned and structured your sites and data, it may be the case that a single site collection grows really, really large over a couple of years. Following are some of the problems this introduces:

➤ The operation team experiences longer and longer backup times for the SQL content database.

➤ The operations team is concerned that, in the event of hardware failure, it may take a long time to restore this site collection.

➤ The original site owners no longer work for the business, and cannot be called upon to cleanse or move their data.

➤ No business area "owns" the site collection. As a result, it becomes an IT department problem.

The operations team will want to split content in the site collection over multiple site collections (to reduce the size of the content database), each with its own content database. This will improve performance and speed of backup and restore, as well as, for example, potentially taking advantage of a new SQL Server instance that may have recently come online.

A seemingly innocent information architecture decision may result in creating a project down the line to split the site collection to improve the operational manageability and improve performance of your environment. This then requires a data analysis and cleansing effort to ascertain what content is still required. The medium- to long-term view illustrates the potential impact of an information architecture decision on the future management and operational activities of your SharePoint 2010 platform.

A number of other operational areas are important to the continued operation of your SharePoint 2010 platform. These should be factored into your information architecture.

Site Collection Life Cycle Governance

Site governance entails designing the governance structures for managing the life cycle of site collections and sites on your SharePoint 2010 platform. This includes the following key stages:

➤ Provisioning the site collection and sites within a site collection

➤ Preparing the site collection by the administrator and site owners

➤ Managing site collection growth and increased usage

➤ Managing site collection "run and maintain" tasks

➤ Managing site collection decline, and eventual archival and deletion

All site collections follow the same life cycle in a SharePoint 2010 environment. The site collection life cycle (along with patterns) is discussed in more detail in Chapter 15.

User Governance

Your information architecture affects the capability to control the types of actions users can execute in sites in your SharePoint 2010 environment. These actions can be detrimental to the health, consistency, and maintainability of individual site collections, thereby making your sites more difficult to support.

By default, SharePoint 2010 (on creation of a site collection) sets up the SharePoint groups and permission sets associated with each group. It is possible to further customize these permissions by updating the configuration of either the permission set or the SharePoint groups the permission set is attached to.

SharePoint user groups and permissions sets control and dictate the actions of roles within your site collection. For example, readers can only view content, whereas site contributors have additional rights to update and delete content.

In advanced customization scenarios (for example, where you have developed a custom site definition), it is possible to automate the configuration of your SharePoint groups and permissions to meet your requirements. A site-scoped feature can be added to your custom site definition. This will automatically prepare the permission structures for your site on creation of the site collection.

Information Governance

Your information architecture affects the capability to manage different types of information in sites within your SharePoint 2010 environment. It specifies how information will be secured, how it will comply with internal business standards and policies (and external regulation), and how it will be stored and managed through inception to destruction.

SharePoint 2010 provides functionality to manage all aspects of the life cycle of information in your site collections and SharePoint 2010 platform. Examples of functionality (to name a few) include versioning, information policies, workflows, event-based triggers, enterprise classification system, enterprise content types, and metadata enforcement.

Customization Governance

Your information architecture affects what customizations should be allowed in your SharePoint 2010 environment, and by whom. In large corporate deployments, these are performed by the following teams and users:

➤ *The central/platform development team* — The central/platform development team is responsible for the majority of development and customization in the early phases of a SharePoint 2010 deployment. In later stages, they enhance functionality, or focus on specific business solutions, while supporting existing functionality in the production environment.

➤ *The multiple "business-embedded" development teams* — SharePoint 2010 supports the capability to develop and host solutions within site collections. Business-embedded teams should subscribe to and adhere to the development, testing, and deployment best practices of the core development team (or work with the core team to agree on a common approach).

➤ *The power user* — Power users are users with a high level of permissions within individual site collections. They have the capability to perform various actions for the benefit of users of the site collection. Power users should adhere to the governance guidelines set out by the central platform governance team to ensure that their site collection is supported into the future.

You may be surprised to learn how much development and configuration can be performed by power users and business development teams after your site collection is live. This includes the following:

➤ *Site configuration* — Users are able to configure almost all elements of a site collection via the user interface.

➤ *SharePoint Designer* — You can use SharePoint Designer (SPD) to create, configure, enhance, and extend a vast array of SharePoint 2010 Features within a site collection.

➤ *Client-side code* — SharePoint 2010 supports the capability to upload and host client-side code (such as JavaScript and jQuery libraries) that may use new SharePoint 2010 client-side object models.

➤ *Sandboxed solutions* — If enabled, sandboxed solutions enable a user to upload code that will execute on the server using a restricted permission set.

Each of these examples serve to remind you to think about what level of site collection customization the central/platform development team is capable of supporting, to think about the impact of this customization on your overall information architecture, and to appropriately turn off/on customization elements you deem to be unsuitable to your environment.

DEFINING YOUR SEARCH EXPERIENCE

Defining your information architecture with search in mind improves the relevance of search results returned by your SharePoint 2010 environment. This contributes to a great search experience.

Entire books have been written on the subject of search, which makes it impossible to adequately cover the entire topic in this section. However, search and "findability" are vital to a great information architecture. Though this section focuses on search aspects, it is important to understand that all the sections in this chapter contribute to a great search experience.

 Chapter 27 provides more detail on enterprise search services.

One of the most important concepts relating to all search technologies in the marketplace is the tradeoff between recall and precision. A search environment that is broad is one with high *recall*, whereas a search environment that is very narrow is one with high *precision*. The greater the recall (search results returned), the higher the chance that the results will be less precise. Conversely, the greater the precision (accuracy of results), the greater the chance that valid results may not be shown.

Therefore, designing any search environment requires understanding the tradeoff between high recall and precision. Applied to defining your search experience, it is imperative for your team to understand the "levers" in SharePoint 2010 that manage this tradeoff. Finding the needle is always better than finding the haystack containing the needle!

You should consider a number of factors when defining your approach to designing your SharePoint 2010 search experience:

➤ *Stage of platform life cycle* — In a brand new portal deployment, it will be more difficult to gather mature search requirements compared to businesses that have previously had a search capability.

➤ *Scope of your search experience* — Is this search experience for the entire business, or for a specific department, function, or team? For example, designing an enterprise-wide search experience is very different from designing a specific search solution for your legal department.

➤ *Internal/public facing* — Is the search experience internal or public facing? Public-facing sites require more attention to detail than internal-facing sites, because the impact could result in customers moving to alternative sites that provide a better experience.

➤ *SharePoint 2010 scenarios* — The scenarios that require a search experience will influence and constrain your planning and design. For example, Web Content Management (WCM) sites structure data using content types, whereas collaboration sites have greater breadth of data and content formats.

➤ *Content sources and formats* — Content sources and data formats within these sources affect SharePoint 2010's capability to infer and, therefore, derive metadata.

Unfortunately, there have been many cases where architects of SharePoint 2010 projects deploy the default SharePoint 2010 or FAST Search capability without spending much time analyzing what their users really need. The impact is that users may not be able to fully benefit and exploit the search capability your SharePoint 2010 platform is providing to your business.

The following steps are discussed in this section:

1. Gathering requirements

2. Planning search

3. Designing your search experience

 If there is anything you should take away from this section, it is the following: Never deploy an out-of-the-box search center or SharePoint business solution without first gathering real business requirements and planning, configuring, and optimizing your search center to meet these business requirements.

Gathering Requirements

Defining your search experience requires the development of a refined understanding of what information your users require, how they search and browse for information, and then applying SharePoint technology to help users find information efficiently.

You must understand how actors and key personas search for information. This entails researching and understanding the key information sources, terminology, vocabulary, and business acronyms, as well as processes, policies, and procedure names. Your user stories, use cases, and scenarios are another valuable source for gathering detailed requirements. This information will be used in later stages to configure SharePoint 2010 content sources, index inside data formats (IFilter deployment), and provide search Best Bets to users.

You must understand what drives actors and key personas to search, rather than browse for information. For example, are they trying to answer a question, find a customer, find a colleague, or retrieve intellectual property (such as document template)? Analyze each type of search and document these as search user stories. These user stories provide a method to check that your search platform is configured to meet the requirements of your users.

As mentioned earlier in this section, your SharePoint 2010 scenarios will dictate your approach to gathering search requirements. In common portal scenarios, data is found in various formats across a number of sites, site collections, and web applications. This breadth and volume of data can be difficult to analyze to produce an efficient search configuration that results in highly relevant results to all end users. In WCM scenarios, the data is mostly well-structured, using content types with their associated page layouts. The breadth and depth of data is usually smaller than common portal scenarios. This provides the capability to highly customize the search experience to meet the needs of consumers of information published via WCM scenarios.

Previous search environments contain a treasure trove of keywords and search phrases, as well as non-functional characteristics that can be used to glean required performance characteristics for your search experience. It is important (and prudent) to learn the lessons from the previous solution to understand what worked, what didn't work, who found it useful, and what users didn't like about it. There is nothing worse or more frustrating to end users than solutions that repeat the mistakes of the previous search solution. Harvest the treasure trove.

Surveys, interviews, and workshops are methods that you can use to gather valuable feedback. Couple this with incentives for feedback and participation, and your return rate will be much higher. Normalize your feedback by ignoring extreme responses, to ensure you hit the sweet spot.

Planning Search

TechNet provides detailed guidance on planning the configuration of your SharePoint 2010 or FAST Search environment. This section does not repeat any of the content, but highlights a few key points.

In large environments, index freshness can be a problem. It is important to ensure that fast-paced sites (such as collaboration and Publishing sites) are indexed as soon as possible. It is possible to provide specific full and incremental crawl schedules for each content source.

Consider the impact on crawling sites and external systems in your organization. It may be that legacy websites may not have sufficient hardware to cope with the load of both indexing operations and end-user operations.

Consider the impact of indexing across your corporate wide area network (WAN). It may be that crawling a regional or branch network file share may starve the shared pipe that end users rely on for their e-mail and daily operations.

Consider the impact of indexing external content types (via Business Connectivity Services, or BCS) from production or "live" databases. You should always attempt to use a decision support copy of the live database to alleviate the burden on a live production system.

Consider what scopes you require. Scopes can be grouped into the following categories:

➤ *Central administration scopes* — Scopes required for all users, and available to all site collections, configured in Central Administration.

➤ *Site collection search scopes* — Scopes configured within a specific site collection to meet a specific requirement.

➤ *Custom search aggregation search scopes* — SharePoint provides a full object model to execute search queries. A common usage scenario is the aggregation of information of a common type, based on a content type. This may use a custom search scope in Central Administration.

Managed properties are vital to efficient searching in your SharePoint platform because they enable you to write queries against common list columns in your environment. For example, company classification may be added to your document content type to force users to add a company classification. Once defined as a managed property, users can query for documents that are "in strict confidence."

When planning your crawl schedules, ensure that your crawls do not overlap each other's content. Overlapping crawls will use up valuable crawling resources, and eat into your crawling schedule.

Designing Your Search Experience

The SharePoint 2010 Search Center and FAST Search Center site definitions provide a number of user experience Features for you to plan and configure.

This includes a slew of rich search web parts, including the refinement panel, search box, search statistics, search action links, search Best Bets, top federated results, search core results, search paging, and related queries. Each of these web parts can be configured and tailored to the specific requirements of your business. Two web parts that stand out are the core results and refinement panel web parts.

There is so much you can do to improve the user experience of the core results web part. The sky is the limit. It gives you a result set, with the capability to customize the rendering of the results. For example, it is possible to customize the XSLT that renders the list of results to include the following enhancements:

➤ *Additional links to improve user productivity* — "Go To Site," "Go to Library," and "Report Restricted Content" are examples.

➤ *Hit highlighting* — It is possible to highlight search terms used by the user to enable the user to instantly identify results that match most of the terms used in the query.

➤ *Displaying additional metadata* — It is possible to display additional metadata underneath specific types of search results (for example, a previous project required additional metadata to be displayed).

➤ *Hover details/dialog details* — It is possible to provide the capability to hover over specific links to display a mini window with more information, or click a link that provides a dialog displaying more detail.

The refinement panel web part is a key feature that you should further configure to improve your user's capability to narrow broad searches (or searches with high recall) to make them more precise. It does this by listing refinements you can make to narrow your search.

Despite the fact that SharePoint 2010 suggests Best Bets for administrators, you should ensure that end users have the capability to suggest search Best Bets to administrators, using a custom add a Search Best Bet web part, suggestion list, and workflow. The approach leverages user's knowledge of the business to enrich the search center, and harnesses collective intelligence to surface important content to users.

Your search experience should be seamless and integrated into your user's desktop experience. A simple enhancement to your master page will allow users to integrate your search provider into their browser search. Have you added it as a search option in Windows 7? Stickiness is important!

With these recommendations, you may be thinking that search experience relates only to planning enterprise-wide search. This couldn't be further from the truth. For individual site collections in your environment, there is much you can do within a site collection, including the following:

➤ *Library/list indexing options* — Specify libraries and lists that should be indexed, and those that should not be.

➤ *Search center* — Specify whether to use the enterprise search center, or a specific search center. Will you configure individual site collections to point to a broad, overarching search center, or will you let them return results within a site collection?

➤ *Custom site search pages* — It is possible to enhance your search within a site.

At Microsoft, custom search solutions have been created for specific business solutions. For example, MSEngage (used by Microsoft Consulting Services globally) provides a tailored search engine to help consultants search across client engagements. MSLibrary (used by all Microsoft employees) provides a tailored solution to help employees find books, courses, and available research information.

The point is that, in some cases, do not assume that only one search center is required. It all depends on your business search requirements.

DEFINING YOUR NAVIGATION EXPERIENCE

Put simply, *navigation* controls how users interpret your design and interact with your SharePoint 2010 portal solution. It allows users to achieve their goals without being encumbered by software, helping users navigate to the content and functionality they seek. Therefore, this design activity is one of most important tasks the SharePoint information architect will influence and contribute to because it controls how users navigate your entire solution.

Defining your navigation involves (and requires) developing an in-depth understanding of the various out-of-the-box SharePoint 2010 navigation methods, complementary and alternative approaches, common navigation approaches, and an appreciation for the use and implementation of each type of navigation system.

This understanding will enable you to design a great navigation system for the end users of your platform and business solution.

Introducing Key SharePoint 2010 Navigation Methods

SharePoint 2010 provides an abundance of primary, secondary, and contextual navigation methods. Figure 14-4 provides an overview of a custom branded publishing site. Various navigation elements of this page are discussed in subsequent sections.

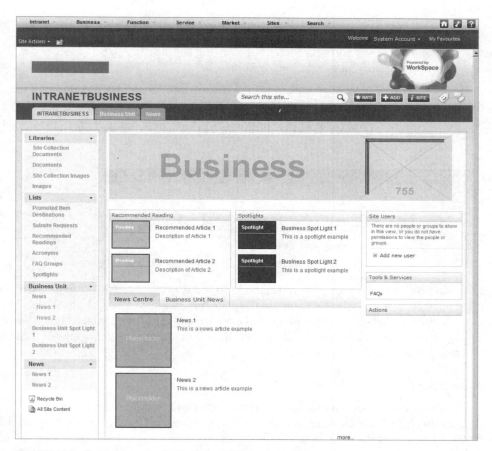

FIGURE 14-4: Publishing site (branded) navigation overview

Primary Navigation

Primary navigation provides links to the most important sites and pages in your site collection. In SharePoint 2010, your primary navigation method depends on whether you have the SharePoint Server Standard or Enterprise Site Collection Features activated.

In Standard sites (for example, team sites), the primary navigation method is the "Top Link Bar." The Top Link Bar provides simple functionality to manage, order, and display navigation elements.

In Enterprise sites (for example, publishing sites), the primary navigation method provides more functionality to display navigation elements, as shown in Figure 14-5. These include the following:

➤ Navigation elements are configurable and customizable, orderable, "styleable," and sortable.

➤ The navigation method enables linking to sites, as well as internal and external web pages and sites.

➤ The navigation method supports organizing links under headings.

➤ The navigation method supports automatically showing subsites and pages in either the global navigation, the current navigation, or both.

➤ The navigation method is security-sensitive, in that users who do not have permission to access an internal SharePoint resource will not see the link.

➤ Headings and links are targetable, in that links can be targeted to "SharePoint audiences."

FIGURE 14-5: Publishing site (branded) navigation bar

The type of site collection will determine what navigation method is available to use. You may wonder why two primary navigation methods exist. Each site template targets a specific set of use cases, scenarios, and workloads. Collaboration sites do not necessarily need the more advanced publishing infrastructure navigation functionality. Conversely, publishing sites require a greater degree of control over how navigation is configured and presented.

Secondary Navigation

Secondary navigation provides links to important content in the *current* site, such as lists and libraries, and pages. In SharePoint 2010, secondary navigation manifests itself on the left (or on the right, for right-to-left pages) of the page, underneath the site collection navigation bar. Figure 14-6 shows the position of the secondary navigation.

It is important to differentiate between sites that have the Standard or Enterprise infrastructure Features enabled. There are noticeable and subtle differences in behavior between the two types of secondary navigation.

Enterprise-enabled sites combine *global* and *current* navigation into one navigation method. For example, a publishing site may display a list of headings and links on the site collection navigation bar (primary), and display a list of links to pages in the current site on the left of the page (secondary navigation).

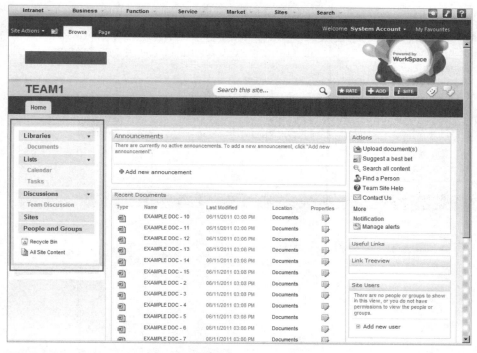

FIGURE 14-6: Team site (branded) Quick Launch Bar

A subtle difference is the lack of the Quick Launch Bar on default (and on pages in publishing sites). This doesn't mean it is not used or available, just that, in WCM sites, they are used only when working with the underlying libraries and lists. On publishing site pages presented to users, the WCM navigation system is used.

Standard-enabled sites split the global and current navigation methods into separate components. These are split into the Top Link Bar and Quick Launch Bar functionality.

The Quick Launch Bar area enables you to configure a "Quick Launch" area using headings to group links to common libraries, lists, pages, and any links you wish to display. The Quick Launch Bar also enables you display a physical representation of the library content in the form of a tree view.

The Quick Launch Bar supports hosting metadata navigation functionality of SharePoint 2010. Users can filter library and list content based on specified fields that have been configured in the Metadata Navigation Settings page for a list or library. For more information, see the later section, "Metadata Refinement Navigation."

Breadcrumb navigation displays a dynamically generated set of links at the top of the page, to show users their current position in the site hierarchy. This enables users to browse "up" or "back" to the top-level sites in the site collection — in essence, using the trail of breadcrumbs they left behind.

Other examples of secondary navigation in SharePoint 2010 include "Summary Links" and the "Table Of Contents" navigation controls in publishing sites.

Contextual Navigation

Contextual navigation displays navigation links based on the current focus of your user, or links to content relating to content the user is currently viewing. Figure 14-7 shows an example of contextual navigation elements.

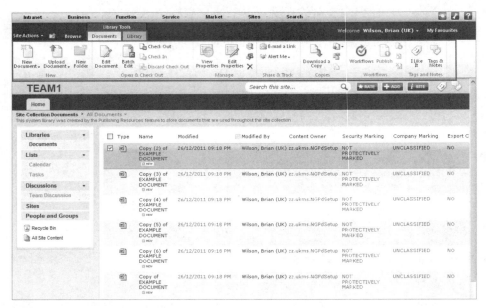

FIGURE 14-7: SharePoint 2010 Ribbon (branded)

Common contextual navigation features include the following:

➤ *SharePoint 2010 Ribbon* — The SharePoint 2010 Ribbon provides contextual navigation and actions on the page based on the focus and actions of the user. For example, if you select an item in a document library, contextual Ribbons appear to users to navigate to and access functionality relating to the item in the document library. It is possible to develop custom contextual "Ribbons" and "Ribbon actions" for users.

➤ *Item-level detail navigation* — SharePoint 2010 libraries and lists often provide a list of items presented as rows. Contextual navigation options are provided to enable users to perform actions or find additional information about the library/list item or the item itself. SharePoint 2010 supports the development of additional custom actions to display to users for specific types of content.

Contextual navigation is an important element in the design of a successful navigation system, and should not be overlooked. It is the last chance you have to help users find information or perform the action required to achieve their desired outcome before they resort to another navigation method.

Complementary/Alternative SharePoint 2010 Navigation Methods

Although primary, secondary, and contextual navigation methods are really useful to users, they are not the only methods available to users in SharePoint 2010. A number of complementary and alternative navigation methods are available that can be implemented in SharePoint 2010.

Search-Based Navigation

The most well-known method of navigation is the use of search functionality, scoped against a library or list, across a site, site collection, or all content in your SharePoint 2010 environment to navigate to digital content required by the user.

The necessity and importance of designing a great search experience starts with the understanding and *acceptance* that not all users start with a primary, secondary, or contextual navigation method. They go straight to search to navigate to digital content. This makes it vital that you consider the key navigation search use cases when designing your navigation system. For example, have you specified a set of search Best Bets to add to your search site? Have you ensured that the refinement panel has the correct set of refinement options? Have you made search-based "navigators" aware of key "managed search metadata properties" they can use to refine their search?

 Chapter 8 provides a detailed discussion of search Features available to provide to users. Chapter 27 provides a detailed discussion of the implementation of these search Features.

Metadata Refinement Navigation

Metadata refinement navigation allows users to filter content based on previously defined metadata options in a library or list. When coupled with well-defined content types and enterprise metadata, it is an extremely powerful list navigation tool.

 For more information on metadata navigation, see "Metadata navigation overview" at `http://technet.microsoft.com/en-us/library/ff608067.aspx`*.*

Social-Based/User-Driven Navigation

Within the SharePoint 2010 environment, the surfacing of content through *collaborative emergent intelligence* is an important addition to the SharePoint 2010 Feature set. Collaborative emergent intelligence occurs when users perform the following types of actions:

➤ *Rate pages and content* — Pages and content support the "I like it" Feature. Additionally, libraries and lists support the capability to rate items. This has the effect of increasing the chance of users finding and using the page content, either through search, or through the fact that users can interpret that a "human" rating has been applied to it. This results in an increased capability to find and, therefore, navigate to rated pages and content.

➤ *Tag content* — Tagging content (using keywords and well-defined enterprise metadata) helps users to find and navigate to information because it improves the "findability" and relevance of the content for that tag. Additionally, "Enterprise terms" support the use of synonyms. This increases the chance of finding of content, given the keywords used to find the content.

From a navigation perspective, the tool used for social classification of content is extremely valuable in helping users navigate to content based on the digital associations peers have noted relating to the content.

 For more information about these Features, see Chapter 8 and Chapter 28.

Aggregation-Based Navigation

Aggregation-based navigation is the surfacing and visualization of content "aggregated" (retrieved) from one or more content sources available to query.

Aggregation is made up of two key steps. The first is the querying and retrieving of data, and the second is the rendering and visualization of the returned data set in a format that the user will to be able to benefit from.

In SharePoint 2010, content aggregations can be categorized into the following queries:

➤ "Live" queries are executed against source content within SharePoint, or content that is exposed to SharePoint 2010 via BCS. Especially when working with large data sets, it's important to realize that live queries can degrade the performance of SharePoint 2010 and the underlying "connected" data sources. "Live" queries can be executed in many ways. Examples include the content query web part, or, alternatively, a custom web part executing a Collaborative Application Markup Language (CAML) query.

➤ "Near-live" queries are executed against a pre-aggregated data source. In the case of SharePoint 2010, this is typically against pre-built search indexes. These are known as "near-live" because the search result will only be as accurate as the freshness of the underlying search index. These are performed using search web parts, or, alternatively, through custom code against the `FullTextSQLQuery` APIs. This option is especially powerful when combined with consistent application of content types (and enforcement of metadata) across all sites in your environment.

Content aggregations are an extremely valuable means to create the sense of dynamism, freshness, and richness of new and unique content, that would otherwise go unnoticed and unappreciated. Figure 14-8 shows how you can visualize the latest blogs in your business using a "near-live" query (combined with XSLT) to render the results to users.

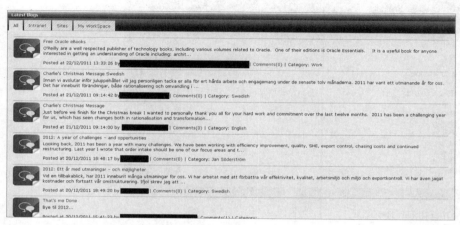

FIGURE 14-8: Blog "near-live" query (branded)

As you can see in Figure 14-8, all users are able to benefit from a blogging home page that aggregates the newest posts. Everyone is now able to navigate to the latest internal posts and hot-button topics of your business. Add-in summary links for each post include information such as number of comments and hyperlinks to add a comment. This allows you to create a two-way blogging interaction tool for your business.

Other Navigation Options

A number of other navigation methods are available for your design team to take advantage of, although it must be said that some of the options presented involve some development. These include the following:

➤ *Site map* — This includes the capability to provide a dynamically generated site map of the sites, libraries, and lists in a site collection, as shown in Figure 14-9.

➤ *Common actions* — As shown in Figure 14-10, you can provide a common actions web part (either using a links or custom web part) that supports a list of configurable common actions for a site collection. These actions often help users be more productive, in that they can shortcut a set of steps to open the relevant site, library, or list.

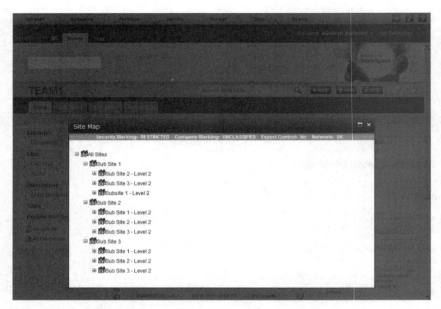

FIGURE 14-9: Site map (branded)

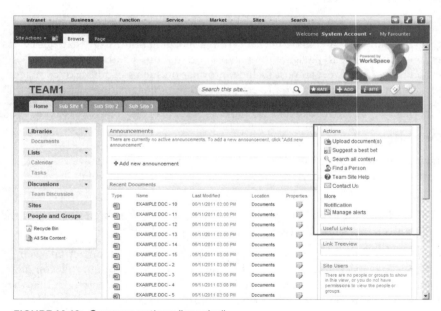

FIGURE 14-10: Common actions (branded)

Be sure you understand each navigation method to ensure that you choose the most appropriate tool for the job. You have so many different ways to surface primary, secondary, contextual, complementary, and alternative navigation to users of your platform and portal solutions.

Implementing a "Truly Global" Global Navigation Method

SharePoint 2010 has a small limitation in that a "truly global" navigation (that is, cross-site collection/cross-farm navigation) feature does not exist. The problem is that, although it is possible to define site collection–based navigation, it is not easy to define navigation that spans across a number of site collections in one or many SharePoint 2010 farms.

In many business scenarios, this isn't an issue. However, medium to large organizations tend to have many independent site collections, each with its own navigation, site template, brand, and purpose. The result is that it is difficult to navigate between all the individual site collections that are affiliated with specific businesses, functions, departments, and teams, hosted on the same or many SharePoint 2010 platforms.

It must be said that this challenge is not new to Microsoft. It attempted to solve this problem by providing the Site Directory template in earlier versions of SharePoint. However, the template was deprecated in SharePoint 2010.

Microsoft IT (the internal IT implementation arm of Microsoft) developed a fantastic solution to overcome this problem. They developed and implemented a SharePoint solution, called Information Web (InfoWeb), that enabled the easy listing and navigation to various site collections across many business divisions, functions, and teams in Redmond, Washington, and across the world.

Microsoft used this model as the basis for a more advanced model to successfully develop and implement a truly global navigation for a large global organization in the United Kingdom, United States, and a number of other countries. Essentially it relies on the following components:

> *Master site collection list (MSCL)* — The MSCL contains a complete list of all site collections that have been created. It contains all the metadata required to enable easy filtering, sorting, and grouping of site collections across the business. The MSCL is hosted in a central governance site collection in the portal.

> *Site collection information panel* — The site collection information panel enables the display and configuration of governance site information within a site collection. (Behind the scenes, this is stored in the site property bag.) The MSCL maintains a copy of the site information, and, if necessary, can synchronize changes from the MSCL to update a site collection's meta information. Figure 14-11 shows how the site information panel is opened and displayed within any site collection.

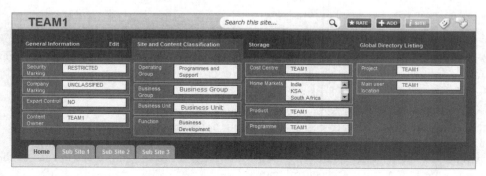

FIGURE 14-11: Site information panel (branded)

➤ *Master site collection metadata timer job* — The timer job picks up new site collections that aren't stored in the master site collection list. It picks up properties stored in the site collection property bag. It is responsible for ensuring that all site collections exist in the master site collection list.

➤ *Global navigation control* — A global navigation control is added to the customized and branded master page that is applied and enforced on all site collections. The global navigation displays a visual "mega menu," enabling users to browse to key areas of the business. As shown in Figure 14-12 and Figure 14-13, these are intranets, businesses, functions, services, markets, sites, and search. Each navigation element links to a summary home page.

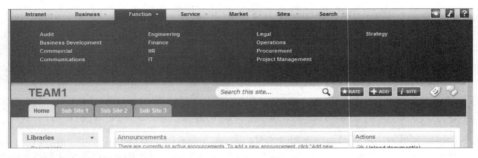

FIGURE 14-12: Mega navigation (branded) — Functions

FIGURE 14-13: Mega navigation (branded) — Search centers

➤ *Global navigation configuration* — The global navigation is configurable through a custom Central Administration page. The underlying configuration of the global navigation is stored in the farm property bag.

➤ *Directory site collection* — A single directory site collection, based on the publishing site template, exists in each farm to host business, function, market, site, sites, and search home pages. These home pages are accessible via the global navigation control on the top of each page. Each page is visually appealing, and is controlled by champions in each of the business, function, market, and central teams.

➤ *Site listings and site filter web parts* — A site listings web part is provided to display listings of sites (based on either preconfigured or dynamic queries) to the master site collection list. When connected to the site listings web part, as shown in Figure 14-14, the site filter web part provides users with the capability to dynamically filter the lists of sites to navigate to a specific site.

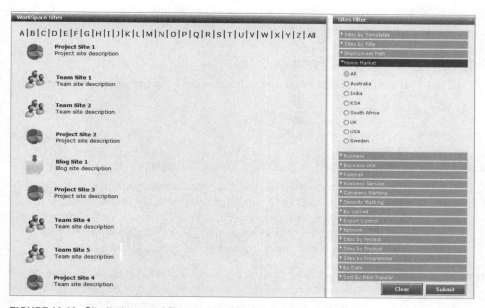

FIGURE 14-14: Site listings and filter web parts

➤ *Site replication timer job* — A timer job exists to pull items of other SharePoint 2010 farm's global site collection list. This lets you provide a consistent global navigation, as well as listings of sites across a number of independent SharePoint 2010 farms.

In summary, it is conceivable (and actually quite easy) to develop and implement a global navigation menu that uses a directory (or "yellow pages") solution of all sites in your organization. The implemented solution provides users with an overarching navigation solution across disparate and unique site collections, no matter what site collection they are currently working in, or the farm it is located in.

Defining Your Navigation Structure

Navigation is easy to implement, hard to get right, and extremely hard to do brilliantly. It requires understanding the influencing design factors, researching the best navigation taxonomic structure, and applying it to your SharePoint 2010 portal solution deployment.

This section takes a look at the following:

➤ Taking into account influential design factors before you design your navigation system

➤ Understanding the different types of navigation models that are commonly used by organizations in the implementation of a navigation system

➤ Designing your navigation model

Navigation design combines creativity, thorough analysis, business and solution domain knowledge, foresight into solution, as well as business and people growth. It is difficult to do brilliantly!

Understanding Influential Design Factors

As shown in Table 14-3, a number of design factors will influence how you design your navigation system.

TABLE 14-3: Design Factors Influencing Navigation

FACTOR	DESCRIPTION
Scope	Are you designing navigation for a single site, site collection, web application, or the entire SharePoint 2010 farm? Put differently, are you responsible for designing navigation for your team, department, business group, or entire organization? The scope of the navigation you are designing will heavily influence the amount of effort required to design a suitable navigation.
Solution type	The type of solution will influence the amount of effort required to develop a suitable navigation. For example, it is often the case that collaboration team sites allow site owners to configure their own site collection navigation as per their requirements. On the other hand, a central portal intranet (or global intranet) requires detailed research, analysis, and design before a navigation system can be implemented to meet the needs of the entire business.
Size of audience	The greater the size of the audience consuming or using the navigation, the greater the emphasis that should be placed on designing a navigation system. For example, a site collection with 1,000 users will rely on an accurate and precise navigation system more than a site collection that has 10 users.
Business purpose	The business purpose of the site and business drivers of the underlying stakeholders will often influence the structure of the site, and, therefore, the navigation.
	Earlier in this chapter, you learned about a shared services business group that wanted common navigation to reflect two key stakeholders — internal and external stakeholders. Users external to the shared services sites would see slightly different navigation than internal users. For example, external users would see links to services offered by one of the shared service departments, whereas internal users would see navigation to internal tools (such as business information systems).

FACTOR	DESCRIPTION
URL name spacing	SharePoint Server 2010 bases its navigation model on the hierarchical structure of the site collection and containment hierarchy design of your SharePoint 2010 environment — that is, web applications, site collections, subsites within a site collection, and so forth.
	If you are designing navigation for a new solution, you have the opportunity to ensure that the correct site structure is applied to complement your intended navigation design.
	If the site collection and subsites have already been deployed, a "hard-coded" structure will be present. For example, `http://intranet` (site collection) may have four level-1 subsites, called `ourbusiness`, `ourservices`, `workandcareer`, and `ourcustomers`.
	These level 1 subsites, in turn, will each have n number of level 2 subsites, level 3 subsites, and so forth. The result is a URL namespace that represents the URL location to a specific site, such as `http://intranet/workandcareer/career/benefits/`. This resultant structure is a form of navigation that users learn when using your website and navigation design. Often, they won't use your navigation, but rely directly on typing the URL into the browser address bar.
Level of organizational change	Organizational change occurs in all organizations to a lesser or greater extent. In organizations that are impacted frequently, it makes sense to factor this into the design of a navigation that will not be frequently invalidated.
Level of control	Have you identified the various levels of control required to set and alter navigation for each key stakeholder? For example, your navigation design may dictate a consistent global navigation, but allow site owners to alter their own site collection navigation bar (Top Link Bar). If site owners have little capability to present specific navigation related to their sites, it may limit their capability to provide navigation to users of their site collections.
Up-front design work versus growth over time	The amount of up-front navigation design work depends on how you plan to grow your solution over time, and the importance, audience, and type of solution you are deploying to the business.

Your design team should consider these factors in the design of your navigation system.

Understanding Navigation Models

It is vital that you understand the different types of navigation models commonly used by organizations in the implementation of a navigation system. These include the following:

> *Alphabetical model* — This model provides navigation options by displaying topics or pages alphabetically.

➤ *Audience-based model* — This model provides navigation options for different audiences. For example, a residential property site often splits the audience into renters and house buyers.

➤ *Category, topic, and subject models* — These models provide navigation options for key categories, topics, and subjects. Good examples include the amazon.com and Wikipedia.com websites.

➤ *Chronological or by-date model* — These models display content according the date it was created, last modified, or published. A news website is a great example of news content ordered by date.

➤ *Geographical/spatial models* — These models provide navigation options using visual representations to help users access information they are seeking (such as a hot-clickable map of the locations your business operates in).

➤ *Hierarchical topic classification model* — This model provides navigation options using a hierarchical structure of topics.

➤ *Organization structure model* — This model provides navigation options according to the structure of the organization. Users navigate to business groups and departments, functions, and teams.

➤ *Social/user driven models* — These models provide navigation options based on user interaction and input. Users drive (and promote) navigation elements, in essence, by participation. Examples of the type of participation include viewing, rating, or tagging an item.

➤ *User/task-centered models* — These models provide navigation options based on key tasks performed by key audiences of your business. For example, PayPal.com provides task-based navigation for each key audience.

As you have probably guessed, depending on your portal scenario, selecting the right model can be a really difficult task. In most cases, your navigation design will use a combination of these models to implement a navigation design that is adopted successfully by your users.

Designing Your Navigation Model

Now that you understand the factors influencing your navigation design, and common navigation models that you can apply to SharePoint 2010 environments, the next step is to design your navigation system. This includes researching, prototyping, and testing the navigational model with your key stakeholders.

 Donna Spencer provides an in-depth article describing a user-centric process (using card sorting) to increase a system's "findability," and, thereby, increase the value that the navigation system provides to end users. See www.boxesandarrows.com/view/card_sorting_a_definitive_guide for more information.

One final point to make regarding the design of your primary and secondary navigation relates to your design team's "frame of reference." This pertains to the perceptions, understanding of terms, labels, and desired hierarchical navigational structure discovered based on research and testing of key stakeholders and users in your organization. Be sure to consider this when formulating your design.

No matter how good or precise you believe your primary, secondary, and contextual navigation methods are, there will always be users who do not interpret content in the same way. Be cognizant of this, and use crystal-clear labeling to ensure as many users interpret your navigation design as you intend them to.

DEFINING YOUR PEOPLE EXPERIENCE

Your information architecture affects and controls the capability of your end users to interact with other users, and what they can and cannot do on your SharePoint 2010 platform.

Defining a Unified, Convergent Experience

A growing trend over the past decade of information technology is the convergence of various technologies to deliver unified experiences. SharePoint 2010 fully supports the trend of convergent collaboration and communications using content, regardless of its format, as its currency.

➤ *Communication* — SharePoint 2010 supports synchronous communication channels. Presence functionality supports the capability to start Voice over IP (VOIP) phone calls, instant messaging (IM) conversations, host live meetings, as well as share desktops and whiteboards. SharePoint supports asynchronous communication channels, such as messaging and e-mail technology integration, RSS feeds, and social networking–based communication.

➤ *Collaboration* — SharePoint 2010 supports people working together toward the collective achievement of goals and desired outcomes. It provides various sites and workspaces containing tools such as document libraries, image libraries, lists, workflows, dashboards, discussions, and tasks. SharePoint 2010 supports both synchronous and asynchronous collaboration technologies. For example, SharePoint 2010 supports the capability for multiple authors to synchronously work on (co-author) the same document, at the same time. SharePoint 2010 supports the capability for users to work asynchronously. For example, users can take libraries and content offline using SharePoint WorkSpace, sign up for and receive alerts and notifications when changes occur, and contribute to wikis.

➤ *Content* — Content, in this case, refers to e-mail, IM, text, alerts and notifications, documents, files, voicemail recordings, page images, audio and video multimedia, VOIP calls, blogs, and wikis. SharePoint 2010 caters to all sorts of content.

Communication, collaboration, and content are the lifeblood of your people experience. Communication is essential to collaboration. Collaboration, in turn, often results in communication. Content is used as a medium by both communication and collaboration. Your portal solution needs all three to complement each other to succeed!

SharePoint 2010 provides the capability for users to personalize various web parts on key shared pages in your environment. Different areas of your portal may have different levels of personalization. Think about the level of personalization required for each area of your solution.

SharePoint 2010 builds social experiences into the heart of the platform. Consider and plan the social experiences you would like to encourage. A good example is the capability to comment on or rate sites and content within a site, as well as tag items so that they appear in people's My Sites.

Attached to social computing is a hidden responsibility to set policies and expectations about acceptable end-user behavior. For example, social computing aspects can be used to bully and intimidate individuals. This type of behavior should be governed in your acceptable usage policy, and all users should be made aware of the terms they need to abide by.

Defining Your Roles, Groups, and Permissions

SharePoint 2010 requires a secure environment that enables site owners and other participants to have enough control over their sites and information without compromising the necessary control required to manage a large-scale SharePoint farm.

Regarding your information architecture, a number of permissions layers need consideration. Your information architecture should map out the roles, SharePoint groups, and permissions of users of your SharePoint 2010 solution. Table 14-4 describes the SharePoint 2010 permissions layers.

TABLE 14-4: SharePoint 2010 Permissions Layers

LAYER	DESCRIPTION
Farm administrators	Farm administrators have permissions to control the entire farm. These user accounts are highly restricted.
Web application permission policy	You can create a web application policy that provides blanket permissions to users to all sites in the web application. Users can be granted (or revoked) read, or read and write, permissions.
	This permission is recommended only in exceptional circumstances, such as to grant an auditor temporary access to information in your SharePoint environment.
Web application permissions	Each web application that is created can have these permissions made available or removed. By removing a specific permission, that permission level will not be made available to any site collection or site that is created.
Site collection permission levels	Site collection permission levels allow different permission levels against particular functionality of SharePoint 2010 for the site collection. These can be customized to meet the needs of the site.
SharePoint site groups and people	SharePoint site collection groups are mapped to site collection permission levels. It is this mapping (or permission levels) that assigns individual permissions to users in the SharePoint group.
	This group is a container for users and Active Directory (AD) groups. Although AD groups and users can have permissions assigned directly, it is not desirable, because this makes it more difficult to manage roles of users and AD groups within your site collection.

LAYER	DESCRIPTION
Site collection, site level	To start with, SharePoint site collection user groups control the root-level permissions of users in a site collection. By default, subsites within a site collection inherit the top-level site collection permission.
	When customized permissions are required, permission inheritance is broken. In essence, this creates a copy of the top-level permissions, which security administrators can modify.
Library/list level security	The second-lowest level of permissions is at the library and list level. It is possible to customize permissions for a library and/or list to allow, restrict, or modify a user's capability to interact with the library or list. Generally, it is recommended to avoid overly customizing library and list permissions.
Item level security	The lowest level of permissions is the direct application of security permissions against an individual item.

Each level allows for the increasingly refined application of security, and an assessment of the permission set required should be conducted for key areas of your solution.

 For more information on the individual permissions available, see the TechNet article, "User permissions and permission levels," at http://technet.microsoft .com/en-us/library/cc721640.aspx.

Audiences

Audiences are created at the farm level, within the User Profile service application. Audiences are a dynamically generated membership based upon one or more rules.

Seasoned veterans will know this tip well. The audience functionality in SharePoint 2010 is not used to set security, but rather to target information and web parts to dynamically created groups of users based on your audience compilation rules.

Remember, just because you have not displayed data to a particular group doesn't mean they won't be able to access it. Hiding items and information through obscurity is not the same as explicitly setting security to control and revoke access.

Following are the criteria that can be applied to the rules for an audience:

➤ *User* — This is used to create a rule based on a Windows Security Group, distribution list, or organizational hierarchy (Reports Under).

➤ *Property* — This is used to create a rule based on a User Profile property.

Various operators are available (for example, Member Of, Contains, and so on) to specify the rule. Multiple rules have an implied AND operator and, therefore, restrictions exist in the flexibility of the definition of rules.

The precise list of audiences required depends largely on your information architecture design. However, the following are likely:

➤ Audiences based on User Profile properties such as Role, Function, and so on

➤ Audiences based on Windows Security Groups that already exist in AD

The User Profile properties must be finalized, and a review of the AD groups available is necessary to design the rules for each of your required audiences.

DEFINING YOUR VISUAL EXPERIENCE

The visual experience you apply is critical to the success of your SharePoint 2010 deployment. We live in a world where employees, suppliers, and customers have come to expect (and demand) exceptional visual digital experiences.

Your visual experience directly contributes to increased adoption and uptake in your platform and solutions, and, therefore, increases the usage (and application) of the information architecture you have applied to your SharePoint 2010 environment.

Although SharePoint 2010 provides a great out-of-the-box user experience, it has become common practice to imprint a visual design or "brand" on SharePoint deployments to create a sense of identity for your organization's SharePoint platform and sites.

It should be emphasized that many great full-length books are dedicated to this subject. However, given the constraints of this book, this section focuses only on specific elements related to the design of your visual experience. This section covers the following topics:

➤ Understanding the resources and skills required

➤ Involving your communication and digital media team

➤ Researching company brand guidelines

➤ Understanding your visual design drivers

➤ Documenting your visual design

➤ Getting feedback

A bad, "over-cooked," or poorly implemented custom visual design can really destroy the good out-of-box experience provided by SharePoint 2010. A good custom visual design applied to SharePoint 2010 can make all the difference in users liking and adopting your SharePoint 2010 platform.

You may be thinking, "Where do I start? How do I imprint a brand and identity to my SharePoint 2010 platform and portals?" This section will help to answer those questions.

Understanding the Resourcing and Skills Required

Finding the right skills and resources needed to design and implement the visual design for your SharePoint 2010 implementation is fundamental to the success of any custom SharePoint 2010 user experience. Similar to cooking *the* perfect meal, it requires the right blend, with just the right amount of the following ingredients:

➤   A creative flair, sense of artistic style, and attention to detail.

➤   A "dash" of perfectionism, a double "dash" of realism, grounded in a triple "dash" of SharePoint implementation practicality.

➤   A good eye for page balance and design married to the "skeletal" structure and page flow of a SharePoint 2010 solution.

➤   The forethought to consider everyday usability that looks great with *real* content (as opposed to "looks perfect" in a mock-up or without real content).

➤   An in-depth knowledge of the visual widgets available to readily exploit. For example, jQuery libraries provide delightful visual elements that, when combined with your SharePoint pages, can provide great digital experiences.

➤   An in-depth knowledge of the appropriate toolset required to create SharePoint visual designs, from envisioning and design, to development and deployment.

➤   The capability to marry and balance both creative and technical innovation.

➤   A thorough knowledge of the SharePoint 2010 feature set and underlying page rendering and ASP.NET platform.

➤   The capability to provide a visual design that considers, incorporates, complements, and promotes the "holistic" information architecture and structure of information in your SharePoint design.

It is rare to find resources with both graphic design skill and deep SharePoint 2010 design and development skill. Graphic design resources tend to have deep skills using tools such as Adobe Photoshop, coupled with experience garnered across a broader range of digital experiences. SharePoint design and development resources tend to have a deep knowledge of Visual Studio and ASP.NET, combined with knowledge (and "bumps and bruises") of implementing visual designs using the SharePoint platform.

Although graphic designers have an excellent eye for design, they may be limited in their knowledge of SharePoint. Conversely, SharePoint designers and developers will have ability to apply a custom visual design to SharePoint 2010, but may have slightly less ability to *envision* a great visual design. Therefore, unless you find the resource of exceptional talent, it is common to hire both resources to work together (and alongside your information and SharePoint architect(s)) in the design and implementation of your custom visual design.

Business users will judge your digital experience provided by the platform features and visual design. They will communicate their like of features and experiences they enjoy to their colleagues. At the same time, they will communicate their dislike of features and digital experiences that annoy and frustrate them.

The resultant groundswell of "hive" opinion of your visual design can make or break the uptake and adoption of your entire platform and portal solutions.

Involving Your Communication and Digital Media Team

It is critical (especially in large organizations) that you involve your communications or corporate brand team in your SharePoint 2010 brand design. Failure to do this may result in resistance from these teams every step of the way, which can be avoided by a more inclusive approach.

In some cases, it may be that your SharePoint design team does not want to take on what they may believe as overly onerous, restrictive, oppressive, and harsh conditions and control imposed by a central communications function of your organization. This is exactly the reason why you *must engage and negotiate* the visual design requirements with these teams.

As SharePoint designers, it is easy to forget that your team does not own the internal and external corporate brands presented to employees, suppliers, and customers. Therefore, always seek to design a corporate brand that includes input and feedback from your key business stakeholders. Failure to do this may result in wasted time and effort developing a visual design that is off-brand and not in line with the guidelines and policies of your corporate communications and digital media teams.

Researching Company Brand Guidelines

It is important to be cognizant of your organization's "company brand" guidelines. These elements are typically captured in the form of a brand standards/guidelines document. The company brand guidelines will typically provide sections with advice and guidance on the following:

➤ *Supported IT browsers* — The supported list of browsers (that is, versions of browsers) will indicate which browsers must be supported by your portal solution.

➤ *Average laptop/desktop screen size and resolution* — The importance of determining the screen size and resolutions you must support cannot be over-emphasized. With the implementation of the Ribbon, SharePoint 2010 takes up more screen real estate than previous versions of SharePoint. Therefore, careful consideration should be applied to your page design for desktop and laptop estates with low average screen sizes and resolutions. It is recommended to agree on a screen resolution up front, design with this in mind, communicate what the end solution will look like as soon as possible to the customer, and negotiate any deviations through constructive, up-front dialogue with the customer.

➤ *Accessibility* — Providing universal access to content is really important to designing an inclusive experience for all users of your solution. Accessibility requirements usually specify, select, and measure conformance standards against the well-known accessibility requirements defined by the World Wide Web Consortium (W3C). An example is the capability to meet the "double-A" requirement.

➤ *Page meta tags* — Public-facing sites may require additional metadata to be injected into pages to enhance the capability of search engines to index content and provide results to users based on keywords relating to your company.

➤ *Compulsory and optional elements* — Your portal's online identity is comprised of compulsory and optional elements. For example, it may be compulsory to display your company logo in a set position at the top of the page. Optional elements may include the additional use of imagery, or the necessity of a footer bar providing links to copyright information.

➤ *Navigation* — Your company brand guidelines may dictate common navigation elements, and the styling of these elements, for your portal. For example, it may instruct you to include a custom global navigation bar at the top of any portal site to provide a unified internal experience, or it may instruct you to provide "related information" contextual navigation links on the right of a news release page.

➤ *Thumbnails and imagery* — Your company brand guidelines may dictate common sizing, required resolutions, and standards for thumbnails, spotlight images, news list images, and other images used on your key intranet pages. It may discuss where images can be sourced from, the type of license that must be purchased, and the approval process that must be followed before they can be used on public- or internal-facing sites.

➤ *Imagery aesthetics* — Your company brand guidelines may also provide aesthetic guidelines on the types of images to use. For example, an organization may want its product images to convey size, power, attention to micro-detail, and operational readiness.

➤ *Logo usage* — Most organizations are very specific about how a corporate or product logo can be displayed. It is vital for you to adhere to (or negotiate, if necessary) these guidelines.

➤ *Typeface and typography* — Your company brand guidelines may specify what typeface and typography should be implemented by your portal solution. When deviating from the standard, you may be required to clear this with the corporate communications and digital media teams.

➤ *Color palette* — Each organization uses a predefined color palette to ensure a consistent brand is applied across internal and external sites. This includes common colors, background colors, "link" colors, and other specific cases. Therefore, ensure that all deviations from your organization's color palette are agreed upon with your corporate communications and digital media teams.

➤ *Header graphics* — Header graphics are key images on the page, and often situated underneath the site collection navigation bar. Your company brand guidelines may provide instructions on the standard width and height, as well as consistent location on your intranet page.

➤ *Iconographic elements* — Your company brand guidelines may specify the type of buttons and icons to use on your portal site. A common example may be specific look and feel applied to a search button on your public- or internal-facing site.

➤ *Flash, Silverlight, and animation* — Your company brand guidelines may shed light on the use of HTML 5 in place of Flash, Silverlight, or other rich interactive and animation tools. It may specify the necessity of providing alternative options to meet accessibility requirements of your business.

➤ *Site and page templates* — Your company brand guidelines may specify a particular page structure. This may include advice on number of columns (for example, a three-column page layout), margins, and gutters, including the structural appearance of the key pages (such as the home page).

After researching the company brand guidelines, you may feel like someone's thrown you in jail, thrown away the key, and taken all the oxygen out of the room. This is where it is important to realize that it doesn't mean that your site needs to look exactly like all the other sites in your business, but it does mean retaining certain elements to give a coherent appearance and "sense of identity" to the internal and external portal communication channels.

Understanding Your Visual Design Drivers

As shown in Figure 14-15, iconic brands such as Coca-Cola, Nike, and the McDonalds "arch" set themselves apart from the crowd. They represent something more than a product or service. A brand with powerful visual cues, functional benefits, and emotions evoked has an advantage over other products and services. Your public- or internal-facing corporate intranet website is an opportunity to represent your company brand to users or customers.

FIGURE 14-15: Iconic brands that are easy to recognize

As a result, you should aim to provide more than just a beautiful website. You should provide a website that captures the essence, ethos, mood, style, drivers of your key stakeholders, and goals and purpose of your site for your business, one that will enable your desired user experience.

For example, your organization may seek a fun, engaging, and lighthearted corporate intranet that encourages and helps users to work better together. Alternatively, your business may have merged a number of corporate brands into one global brand, and may be seeking to unify and promote a single brand across all the merged organizations through a new corporate intranet. In all cases, your visual design drivers provide subtle requirements that will make an "okay" site great!

Defining Your Visual Design

Entire books have been written about defining your brand and user interface design. You should read these books to further your knowledge on this important topic. This section highlights key points and lessons learned from previous experiences.

In the early design and ramp-up stages of your visual design activities, focus on understanding and defining the scope of visual design work required before progressing into the detailed visual design activities. This additional clarity will help you avoid the bottomless pit of "minor tweaks to the visual design" and resulting scope-creep to your tight timelines imposed by your ruthless project manager.

Once the scope of your visual design work is agreed on, this should be followed by research activities and creative design sessions with key stakeholders and end users to drive out the requirements, visual design drivers, and user experience required by your organization.

It is important to be able to rapidly iterate to achieve your final design that can be handed to your SharePoint development team to implement. This includes the capability to rapidly generate wireframes, mockups, and prototypes, and to discuss, get feedback, and respond quickly while you have the attention of your key stakeholders.

To avoid design paralysis, it is necessary to set the expectation of what you require from your stakeholders — that is, their input in a timely fashion, and their sign-off to proceed once agreed upon. The constant changing or reworking of the design is one of the biggest challenges faced by any SharePoint visual design and development team.

Documenting Your Visual Design

You may wonder what artifacts are required to be signed off on for a visual design. Well, it depends in part on your methodology and on your team's unique recipe and process for designing fantastic looking sites. For most projects, wireframes and mockups are the basic artifacts required.

For more mature design agencies and development teams, a visual design specification document will be written to describe the following elements:

➤ *Key site and page visual designs* — These include complete example visual designs and page layout regions with accompanying wireframes detailing expected content and functionality required for each region within a page layout. This will also detail the page margins, page measurements, and page fonts.

➤ *Common visual design elements* — This includes the chosen colors and color scheme; selected colors for common elements of your site and page design; background colors; font face, size, weight, and color for text placed on common elements; and so forth.

➤ *Specific visual design elements* — Custom-built Features may have a specific look and feel, content, and functionality. These may be called out in the visual design document. However, the detail of these will most likely be captured in a specific use case.

Getting Feedback

After development has started, it is important that you are able to handle design refinements required by your key stakeholders. The age-old saying, "a customer will only know what they want when they see it," really applies to SharePoint 2010 visual design customization projects. Therefore, plan for and factor this into your schedule up front, to include time to cater to requests for change to your visual design.

Once you have an initial or updated version of your visual design ready to demo, set it up on a test server and make it available for members of your team to demo to key stakeholders and end users.

Set up feedback sessions for interested stakeholders and users to attend. Provide user acceptance test scripts that cover common actions or tasks of key roles in your portal. Provide enough time for them to record feedback after completing each script. Ask both open questions, and specific metric-oriented questions, to gauge their satisfaction of your visual design.

It is really important to demonstrate you have taken in and listened to feedback from end users. There is nothing worse than going to the effort of logging an issue, and receiving no feedback as to why it wasn't considered in the final design.

Finally, don't wait to let deployment to your production servers be the first time end users get a chance to evaluate your look and feel. At this point, it is too late.

DEFINING YOUR CUSTOM FUNCTIONALITY

Custom functionality is an interesting topic that spans information architecture, solution architecture, and infrastructure architecture and configuration.

➤ *Information architecture elements* focus more on the *what*, *why*, and *when*, and aim to provide a complete picture of the functionality and features your SharePoint 2010 platform and solutions will provide.

➤ *Solution architecture* focuses on *how* and *how best* it will be architected and developed. Solution architecture is discussed in Chapter 15.

➤ *Infrastructure architecture and configuration* focuses on how your custom functionality will be hosted, managed, and maintained in your production environments.

Rather than splitting the content in this section over three separate discussions (information, solution, and infrastructure architecture), a complete discussion appears in Chapter 15. This chapter discusses the key architectural areas relating to each piece of custom functionality you plan to develop.

PLANNING FOR CONTENT MIGRATION

A colleague (who was the governance and application manager of a very large SharePoint 2010 environment) related a common frustration he experienced regarding SharePoint books. He mentioned that they often do a great job of covering product and field theory, as well as related technical implementation best practices, but, in some cases, fail to provide solid approaches to common SharePoint 2010 business onboarding challenges.

The issue that colleague faced is how best to approach onboarding of business departments, functions, and teams. He provided the following example of a question he often received:

> "*I am* [insert department name]. *I want to move my business information from my* [insert legacy environment(s)] *to the new SharePoint 2010 shared platform. I have approximately* [insert number of Terabytes] *TB of data that I need to move. What approach should I follow?*"

He was searching for a thorough explanation and "best practice" approach to provide to business group deployment leads, but was unable to find one.

Let's take his example and use it to produce a "real-world" content migration scenario:

➤ You work in a business department (2,500 employees) in a large business of roughly 40,000 employees. You have been informed that a new portal platform will be used for future business collaboration, and have been instructed by the head of your department to look into how your department will be able leverage this technology.

➤ Your 2,500 users are dispersed in regional offices in the United Kingdom, United States, Australia, India, Saudi Arabia, and South Africa, with each office employing local IT resources to handle and manage common IT solutions.

➤ You estimate that you have 10 TB of "office" files stored on network file shares, gathered over a period of five years.

➤ You have an existing legacy intranet for your department, using a non-SharePoint technology. In this case, let's pretend it's a Documentum intranet. More than 2,000 web pages exist in your legacy business management system (BMS) and a number of "mini" solutions have been built into the legacy intranet.

➤ Based on your previous experience, some of the data stored in your file shares relates to core business operations, while other data relates to project and administration operations. Your preliminary investigation has revealed that the network file structure is out of date, inconsistent, not based on how users currently work in your business department, and, therefore, needs to be revisited.

➤ You notice different "taxonomic" structures in each file share. You notice that a number of folders lie dormant, and some were imported at the time new companies were acquired and merged with your department.

➤ You recently learned that 250 users in the South Africa office commissioned and deployed a "rogue" solution using their own SharePoint 2010 farm, because they could not wait for the central team solution to get their act together. Although this environment has been deemed a "pilot" environment, the reality is that a number of their processes are now being managed on this platform. Other South African-based departments have started requesting access to this rogue, unmanaged, "single box" SharePoint 2010 farm.

Any of these points sound familiar? This is the type of "content migration" challenge faced by many businesses migrating to SharePoint technologies. Let's discuss some of the key issues related to real-world content migration business challenges.

Have you noticed that what may have started off as a "simple" challenge of moving content into SharePoint is more complex and broader than you first imagined it to be? The more you delve into the detail of the content, processes, and business solutions that must be migrated, the more you realize what must be completed to successfully move your business operations from the legacy environments into the central SharePoint 2010 farm.

Have you noticed that the key challenges of content migrations are mostly *not* related to the actual migrating of content? For example, it requires having, understanding, and following a portal strategy; analyzing and defining your business and technical requirements; understanding, planning, and catering to the business change and adoption elements.

 Advice and guidance on these topics is provided in Chapter 12 and Chapter 13.

Finally, have you identified that the key and biggest challenge is defining your SharePoint information architecture — that is, performing the activities covered in the various sections in this chapter?

Only when you have a solid SharePoint information architecture should you consider the content migration steps covered in this section. The content migration steps are defined in Figure 14-16.

FIGURE 14-16: Content migration steps

Content Discovery

In the digital age, businesses, departments, and teams have built up tremendous reservoirs and silos of business information. It is this information that you need to discover, inventory, analyze, and understand. The key elements of content discovery include the following:

➤ *Assess scope* — It is important to define the scope of your content migration. This requires inventorying the content you wish to migrate, and making decisions as to which content sources your team will migrate to SharePoint 2010.

➤ *Consider your tooling* — A number of advanced content migration tools in today's marketplace are specifically designed to help you discover, analyze, and migrate content. For more information, see Chapter 3, which provides more information on common content analysis and migration tools available.

➤ *Assess content formats* — Analyze the types of content that exist in each content source. Gather statistics on the types of content and the number of items that exist for each type of content. For each type of content, assess the average intricacy. Is the content simple office files, or more advanced such as XML, or a large number of different web pages that must be scraped and massaged before they can be migrated into SharePoint? Against each file format found, add a priority and complexity judgment to each file format that can be used in later stages to decide on which formats to focus your efforts.

➤ *Assess source systems* — Gone are the days when content migration meant migrating data from file shares into SharePoint. Most businesses these days have a number of legacy intranet, document, and records management systems. Each of these systems should be analyzed to gather information on what content (and their associated business processes) will need to be migrated. As part of your assessment, it is important to get a feeling for the complexity involved in migrating content from these environments.

➤ *Assess storage size* — As part of your discovery and inventory process, calculate the physical storage size of the content you plan to migrate. This will become important in later stages to determine the sizing and types of site collections you will require to host this content in SharePoint.

➤ *Assess content structure* — For each content source, content format, and source system, learn about what users currently like and dislike about the structure of how content is hosted and made accessible. Assess what metadata is applied to content by the source system to improve "findability" and improve information retrieval. Discover common classification criteria. Have you noticed that this point starts to infer the need for an assessment of your existing information architecture, based on the content you plan to migrate? This is another reason why content migration is more than simply migration of content.

➤ *Assess storage locations* — Discover the locations of systems that house the content. Assess the impact of migrating content to your new platform for users in each of the storage locations. It may be that all your users are in one head office, or, alternatively, as in the example scenario, they are distributed over regional offices in the United States, United Kingdom, and South Africa. This implies developing an understanding of the supporting WAN infrastructure to understand if a user's productivity will be impeded by migrating content to a central location.

➤ *Assess cost choices* — Although not many people realize this, the decision to migrate content is often heavily influenced by cost and ROI for migrating content to the new platform. It may be that your business seeks to save on paying for licenses of two similar systems. This type of information is useful to drive requests for budget decisions because you may be able demonstrate that your content migration project may pay for itself, and potentially provide a short- to long-term net saving and benefit for your business. Alternatively, you may find it is more cost effective for your business to keep the content in its current location.

A final point to note is that, contrary to popular belief, not all content belongs in SharePoint. Some file formats are more suited to the filesystem, or in best-of-breed specialized business solutions. Make the right technology choice that works best for your users and business, rather than a blanket ruling of "chuck it all in SharePoint." Each business is different!

Content Cleansing and Preparation

Once you have completed the content discovery, the next stage involves cleansing and preparing the content you have selected to migrate into your SharePoint 2010 environment. Following are the key elements to consider in this stage:

➤ *Content de-duplication* — Content de-duplication is the process of reducing the number of copies (and versions) of the same file to one version and source location. De-duplication can result in massive storage cost savings because less needs to be migrated into SharePoint 2010. An additional hidden benefit is that fewer versions of a file will improve the precision of searches that match keywords within the file, thereby helping users find information more quickly.

➤ *Content sanitization* — "Sanitization" is a word used commonly at Microsoft to denote that a file has had the appropriate confidential information removed or replaced. Consider the content you are moving, and determine who will have access to it once it has been added to SharePoint 2010. You may find that particular files have snippets of confidential customer information that is not appropriate for a large audience.

➤ *Content format conversion* — In some cases, you may determine that a file needs to be converted to a different file format. For example, you may determine that your business would like to change all documents from Open Document format to OpenXML (or vice versa), or that you would like to convert all files in a particular location into PDF documents. This requires selecting the correct migration tool that will assist you in this endeavor.

➤ *Content scraping and conversion* — Once you have been involved in a number of legacy intranet migration projects, you will understand the importance of selecting the right partner migration tool. Migrating legacy intranet pages from legacy/competitor systems requires a detailed knowledge of both the source and the target system. In most cases, depending on the level of customization, it requires the capability to write custom code procedures that will be executed during the cleansing and conversion process.

➤ *Content permissions conversion* — The source system may have a particular method of applying permissions to individual items. This will need to be analyzed, cleansed, and improved to enable easy migration of these permissions to migrated content in SharePoint 2010.

➤ *Content metadata improvements* — A major problem with migrating content from source systems is the lack of accurate metadata for each content item. Tools exist today to infer metadata from the source content, and update the file metadata directly, or, alternatively, save this inferred metadata during the migration process. For example, authors often forget to update the author fields when writing a document based on a template. This impacts the "findability" of documents when searching using the author managed property in SharePoint 2010. Improving the quality and accuracy of metadata is vital to the value provided by your content migration.

➤ *Interpret content storage structure* — Earlier in this chapter, in "Defining Your Enterprise Metadata Requirements," you learned about processes for assessing your business information. That discussion includes guidance related to the structural design of your site collections, sites, and content libraries. Ensure that you perform the key analysis and design tasks examined in that section during the development of an appropriate target site and content library storage structure.

➤ *Update content size storage estimate* — Update your content size storage requirements as you continue through the content cleansing and preparation stage. Before you migrate, you must have a solid understanding of the storage you will require, as well as ensuring that you have additional space to handle short- and medium-term growth.

Finally, take advantage of this opportunity to fix problems that have built up over time. It is not often that you get an opportunity to apply a wholesale fix to content quality issues in your environment.

Target Environment Validation

A key assumption is that you have followed your SharePoint portal strategy, gathered the relevant business and technical requirements, and have produced and implemented a SharePoint information architecture in your target environment that your content migration will be able to leverage.

Your content migration may require various elements to exist and be correctly configured. These include elements such as web applications, site collections, sites, branding, page layouts, content types, site columns, and so forth. It is vital that you validate that the structures you require exist in your target environment before you start your migration process.

Content Mapping

After preparing your source content for migration, the next stage involves validating the mapping of content to containers that will host the content in your SharePoint 2010 environment.

This involves mapping content to the target containers. For example, these may relate to site collections, sites, libraries, and lists. It may also relate to mapping and associating service applications to sites depending on the content being migrated to a particular site.

Content mapping depends on how you elect to migrate content. If your content happens to be 1,000 team sites from a competing intranet, you may decide to use a migration tool to dynamically create the site using a specially developed site template or definition, and configure the site using custom migration code your team has written. Examples of possible dynamic configuration may include the following elements:

➤ Site- and web-scoped Feature activations

➤ Permission levels, SharePoint groups, and the addition of AD groups and/or users to these groups

➤ Creation and configuration of various types of libraries — for example, adding content types, configuring versioning, association of managed metadata services fields, metadata refinement options, folder structures, and so forth

A final issue related to content mapping is to select the appropriate site template, library, or list — for example, using an asset library versus a document library, or using a style library versus a document library. Be consistent in your mapping of content, and follow existing content storage patterns used on the platform to make it easy for users to learn one way of doing things. This will, in turn, make it easy for administrators of the portal platform to run and maintain.

Content Migration

The reality with cleansing and preparing your content for migration is that it will take a number of trial runs before you are ready to perform the actual migration. In most content migrations (especially those related to old web pages with "screwy" HTML, JavaScript, and custom style sheets), you may opt to perform a two-stage migration of this content using a "staging post-SharePoint environment" as an intermediary step before massaging and migrating again into your production environment.

In all cases, never migrate directly to your production environment, without at least performing a sample migration to an environment (test or pre-production) that reflects your current production environment. The reality is that all migration will have to deal with minor (and major) issues relating to specific nuances of your data and legacy environments. A second point is that it is likely that key stakeholders will require changes once they see the results of the migrated content, and will want to view the results of your trial migration and conversion process.

Selecting the Most Appropriate Migration Tool

Ensure that any tool you select is capable of handling multiple target environments so that you can point to a test server instead of only your production servers. Also, remember to carefully analyze your choice of a SharePoint migration tool, because it will make all the difference when it comes to your actual migration.

Don't rely on website marketing. Always get direct references from customers who have actually used the tool, not through a documented case study, but through a conference call with their technical personnel, without any sales folk on the call! That is the best method to evaluate and validate your investment in expensive migration tools.

During the call, validate that the reference customer has similar requirements to your migration. For example, if your project entails migrating content from Documentum websites to SharePoint 2010, then be sure the reference customer also had to migrate website content from Documentum to SharePoint 2010.

Compare Source Storage Estimate to Available Storage

It is recommended that you compare your updated storage size estimate against the total unused storage quotas available in the site collections you plan to migrate into. Do not migrate into an almost full site collection. This will result in you hitting your site collection quota limit, which may equate to another content migration project to further split your content out.

Discuss and negotiate the required site collection quota up front with your central deployment team before you begin any content migration. (This is especially important if rigid restrictions are being enforced in your SharePoint 2010 farm.)

Executing Your Content Migration

It is important that you follow a well-thought-out plan when migrating large amounts of data in the short allotted windows of time available to perform actions against your production environment.

Figure 14-17 shows the common steps taken in content migrations. These content steps can be described in more detail as follows:

- ➤ *Test, test, test* — Test your migration with a sample or all (if you have the space) of your content and against an environment that reflects your production environment configuration.

- ➤ *Validate your production environment* — Validate any assumptions you may have related to your production environment configuration, and ensure that there is sufficient underlying disk space and storage quota available to sites you plan to migrate into.

- ➤ *Preview with business stakeholders* — Provide access for key stakeholders in your business to look at the fruits of a trial run against a test environment. Set aside time in your schedule to be able to take in and respond to feedback that they deem as critical. This is a vital step in your content migration.

- ➤ *Review internally* — Review the results of additional feedback, decide on priorities, and make tradeoffs between additional requirements from business stakeholders and your schedule and budget. Ensure that all defects found are fixed before performing migration.

- ➤ *Communicate* — Don't forget to work with your business change team to send out appropriate communications to key stakeholders in the time leading up to, before, and after your migration has completed.

- ➤ *Execute your migration* — Once your team and the business are satisfied, schedule and execute your content migration as per your content migration plan.

FIGURE 14-17: Executing your content migration

Consider what to do with the source environments. A common strategy is to make them read-only for a period of time, and communicate to your business stakeholders how much time they have before the source environment will be decommissioned.

Content Navigation, Aggregation, and Visualization

At the beginning of this discussion, you learned about a real-world "content migration" challenge faced by many businesses migrating to SharePoint technologies. Part of this scenario included the requirement to migrate roughly 10 TB of content. Up to this point in the discussion, you have learned about the steps required move this content to SharePoint 2010. There is one final area that your design will need to cater to that has not been covered.

How will your SharePoint information architecture be affected by and cater to large/extremely large content sets?

When migrating content sets greater than 50 GB to 100 GB (especially content sets that are sized in the multiple terabyte range), you must consider and plan for the following issues:

➤ Decide how your migration process will split content into multiple site collections.

➤ Liaise with your solution architect on the visualizations, common navigation elements, and content/data aggregations required across your target site collections.

➤ Liaise with your solution architect on the structural design and number of site collections, sites, and content libraries, and the impact of large data sets on any out-of-the-box/custom functionality in these site collections.

➤ Liaise with your SharePoint infrastructure and storage architect to ensure that your SharePoint 2010 platform will be able to host the amount of data you plan to migrate.

➤ Provide content growth and increased usage estimates to enable your infrastructure and storage architect to provide sufficient storage capacity for short- to medium-term growth, and ensure that overall platform responsiveness is not impeded because of the increased demand by users in your organization.

SharePoint 2010 has hardware and software constraints on how much content can be safely stored and managed in a single site collection, in a single content database, and across an entire farm. These constraints, along with detailed guidance, are provided on the following pages by Microsoft in TechNet:

➤ "SharePoint 2010 Capacity Management" at http://technet.microsoft.com/en-us/library/cc262787.aspx

➤ "Enterprise Content Storage Planning" at `http://technet.microsoft.com/en-us/library/cc263028.aspx`

➤ "Data Storage Changes on SharePoint 2010" at `http://sharepoint.microsoft.com/blog/Pages/BlogPost.aspx?pID=988`

REFINING YOUR DESIGN

As you can see from this chapter, much work goes into defining your SharePoint information architecture. Some of this relates to work that precedes your information architecture (such as requirements activities and technical activities).

From an architectural perspective, it is important to refine your information architecture based on work occurring in other architectural streams. For example, solution architecture, infrastructure, and storage architecture design work may significantly influence your information architecture, and vice versa.

On smaller projects, one architect will be responsible for all tasks related to the three architecture streams, whereas in larger projects, this work will be divided up into the streams defined in this book. For example, the information architecture lead will work with the application lead (or lead developer) and the infrastructure architect to define and design the SharePoint 2010 platform and solutions.

Another key area that should be reviewed is the SharePoint 2010 "Hardware and Software Boundaries" listed on TechNet. These boundaries could significantly impact the scalability of the design you are proposing. Be sure you understand them, and build and document your mitigations and recommendations directly into your design documentation.

Review your non-functional requirements to ensure that they are met/exceeded. Although the solution and infrastructure architects have key responsibilities related to meeting the customer's non-functional requirements, the information architect is equally responsible for ensuring that they have a chance of meeting these non-functional requirements. Your SharePoint information architecture will hurt non-functional requirements in the medium to long term. Apart from throwing more hardware at the problem, solution and infrastructure architects have little power to change issues related to your information architecture.

Review your service application architecture to ensure that it is scalable, available, performant, and secure by default, and designed to work with your proposed information architecture.

Finally, architecture is as much about design as it is about making the right set of tradeoffs against your architectural constraints. Therefore, it is vital to work in conjunction with your solution and infrastructure architecture streams to build a great SharePoint 2010 platform and portal solution.

SUMMARY

Following are three key issues related to a badly designed SharePoint information architecture:

➤ *Too much time spent on fixing the past, rather than focusing on the future* — Your SharePoint 2010 business and technical teams may struggle to focus budget, resources, and schedule on new activities (such as new business solutions) because your environment may be in "fire-fighting" and troubleshooting mode. This leads to dissatisfaction on the part of your program management and executive sponsors, business stakeholders, and, ultimately, the end users. Nothing ever seems to change. Your environment becomes stale.

➤ *Difficult to educate and train your business* — With no overall information architecture, your portal solutions may differ greatly. The result is inconsistency and reduction in the "commonality" a well-thought-out SharePoint platform can provide. This leads to difficulty in educating and training users on how to use the services hosted by your SharePoint 2010 platform.

➤ *Difficult "run and maintain" operational model* — Onerous or faulty information architecture and site collection structure results in more maintenance- and platform-related tasks required by your operational team.

One final point when defining your information architecture that many seasoned veterans have learned from the "hard knocks" in the trenches of real-world experience relates to *"pursuing the rainbow of absolute perfection."*

The reality is that most projects have budget, resource, and delivery date constraints. This implies that the commercial viability of your project may be impacted trying to deliver an out-of-control and perfectionist SharePoint information architecture. The point is not that you should design a compromised solution, but just this: Think carefully (and critically) of the *true value* of the functionality you plan to deliver to the business.

As a SharePoint information architect, this type of restraint really helps businesses that are being advised by and have placed trust in you to keep costs down and deliver their solution in reasonable timeframes.

Chapter 15 examines how to design your SharePoint 2010 solution architecture.

15

Designing Your Solution Architecture

By Brian Wilson and Vesa Juvonen

Authoring a single chapter that tackles the broad and deep topic of SharePoint solution architecture is a significant challenge. To meet that challenge, this chapter focuses on areas critical to your solution architecture, including the following:

➤   Defining the roles and responsibilities of a solution architect

➤   Designing your site solution architecture

➤   Understanding common solution patterns and design options

➤   Designing your custom business solutions

➤   Documenting your SharePoint 2010 design

A number of valuable resources are available to further improve your knowledge of SharePoint solution architecture and technical design, including the Microsoft Developer Network (MSDN), SharePoint community sites, and a number of great design and development-oriented books. Therefore, where content already exists on MSDN or TechNet, links have been provided to these resources, because these provide the primary resources of technical domain knowledge relating to SharePoint solution architecture and technical design.

DEFINING THE ROLES AND RESPONSIBILITIES OF A SOLUTION ARCHITECT

Martin Fowler, author of the acclaimed book, *Patterns of Enterprise Application Architecture* (Reading, MA: Addison-Wesley Professional, 2002), is one of the all-time software design heroes. In his book and subsequent articles, he described feeling uncomfortable about using the term "architecture." He felt it had become fuzzy and overloaded, but at the same time, understood the necessity of using the word.

Extensive research for this chapter seeking a common *agreed-upon* understanding of the terms "architecture," "solution architecture," and "SharePoint solution architecture" revealed many different definitions on influential websites and in well-respected architecture books.

Fowler's eloquently distilled definition was the most impressive. He said, "Architecture consists of two key elements: One is the highest-level breakdown of a system into its parts; the other, decisions that are hard to change." Another notable revelation was the definition of "solution architecture" provided by John Critchley at `solutionarchitecture.org`. He describes solution architecture as, "The discipline of generating a creative and communicable technical design that aligns a feasible business solution with stakeholder expectation within the bounds of mandated delivery parameters."

Nailing down the definition of "SharePoint solution architecture" is a challenge in itself, and by its very nature, is subjective to your set of experiences and history in the "solution architecture space." This makes it important to define the key activities and responsibilities relating to the "SharePoint solution architect" as follows:

➤ Designing applications, business solutions, and services provided by your SharePoint 2010 platform

➤ Working closely with the organization's enterprise architect to align (both conforming to, and helping to define) the SharePoint 2010 solution architecture to the enterprise architect's long-term strategic vision

➤ Helping the information architect formulate the detailed requirements and use cases that have been captured from the high-level business requirements during the early stages of feasibility study

➤ Working closely with the information and infrastructure architect to ensure that the SharePoint 2010 platform and business solution will satisfy both functional and non-functional requirements for the organization

➤ Working closely with the infrastructure architect to ensure that the physical and logical infrastructure will meet the information and solution architecture requirements

➤ Formulating the overall technical architecture and design, providing guidance, frameworks, software development methodology leadership, and documentation requirements

➤ Working closely with the program and project management team, the enterprise architect, the information architect, and the development team to prioritize and "chunk" the deliverables into a set of releases, along with an estimated delivery schedule and cost (in terms of time and resources required) for each release

➤ Designing the "architecturally significant" software patterns, system components, the responsibilities of these elements, and interactions that both constrain and direct how engineers/developers implement any custom software on the SharePoint 2010 platform

➤ Working closely with the development team to ensure that the requirements of the business and key stakeholders are met

➤ Verifying the delivered SharePoint 2010 platform and solution is consistent with the agreed-upon information, solution, and infrastructure architecture

➤ Facilitating, capturing, and recording key technical design decisions along with agreed-upon consensus of the relevant parties

➤ Communicating the technical architecture and design to ensure that key business and technical stakeholders understand the architecture (including both business and technical audiences)

A critical aspect of the role of the SharePoint solution architect is the capability to accurately judge the technical risk and complexity of any proposed solution. An organization is completely reliant on the solution architect's ability to foresee issues stemming from business and technical decisions that could impact the SharePoint 2010 program, project, platform, and key business solutions in the short, medium, and long term.

The skill sets of the SharePoint solution architect vary greatly in the real world, depending on experience and background. However, most solution architects share the following skills, knowledge, and experience:

➤ *Development background* — A solution architect is a competent practitioner of the design and development of solutions using Microsoft technologies and platforms. These include tailor-made .NET applications using ASP.NET, Internet Information Services (IIS), and SQL Server. Additionally, the solution architect is familiar with Visual Studio and team-based development using Team Foundation Server (TFS).

➤ *Understands software design concepts and principles* — The solution architect has a competent knowledge and related working experiences with designing software solutions using pattern-based, object-oriented design techniques, and software design concepts.

➤ *Understands available software development technologies* — The solution architect has an in-depth understanding of the available software technologies that can be leveraged in the design of any custom software for the SharePoint 2010 platform. This knowledge is coupled with real-world experience on which technology is suited for the organization and scenario(s). Examples of software technologies include the .NET Framework, SharePoint Object Models, Representational State Transfer (REST) coupled with ADO.NET data services, Windows Communication Foundation (WCF), Atom, JavaScript Object Notation (JSON), jQuery, Ajax, Collaborative Application Markup Language (CAML), cascading style sheets (CSS), Extensible Markup Language (XML), and Extensible Stylesheet Transformation (XSLT).

➤ *Understands how to design standards-compliant solutions* — The solution architect should be able to design solutions for the SharePoint 2010 platform that comply with the accessibility and other standards enforced in the organization. For example, how will the solution architect design solutions that comply with the Web Content Accessibility Guidelines (WCAG) 2.0 "Double AA" accessibility standard?

➤ *Understands the building blocks of SharePoint 2010 platform and portal solutions* — The solution architect will have in-depth knowledge of the key technical building blocks that make up a SharePoint 2010 portal solution. Examples include service applications, object libraries, site definitions, list definitions, web parts, event handlers, caching technologies, the effect of a chosen authentication model on the software, and so on.

These descriptions may lead you to believe that the "bar of prerequisite knowledge and experience" has been set too high. However, experience has shown that a SharePoint solution architect will struggle without this prerequisite knowledge.

DESIGNING YOUR SITE SOLUTION ARCHITECTURE

One of the most important elements of your solution architecture is how you design sites and site collections for your SharePoint 2010 environment. It is one of those areas where decisions, once made, are expensive to change later on.

This makes it really important for the solution architect to fully appreciate the implications of deciding between site templates, web templates, out-of-the-box site definitions, or custom site definitions, along with the site-provisioning model that will be used to deploy sites and site collections to your SharePoint 2010 environment.

Site Templates

Site templates are site-provisioning definitions that are created by end users of the SharePoint 2010 deployments. Site templates can be created from the Site Settings page of the sites by using the "Save site as a template" functionality. This functionality will convert the current site to a solution package, and store the solution package in a solution gallery of the particular site collection.

In SharePoint 2010, the site template format has been changed to the solution package, which contains all the different definitions required to re-create the site. Because you can import solution packages using the Visual Studio 2010 SharePoint tool, you can also use site templates as your starting point for further customizations. It's important to be aware that when a site template is created from the user interface, all list instances are stored as part of the package using the CustomSchema element.

SITE TEMPLATES AND PUBLISHING FEATURES

Site templates can be used to create generic templates, as long as the publishing Features are not enabled on the site. You cannot create a site template from a Publishing site that has the publishing Features enabled. This is because, in certain scenarios, these kinds of templates will cause issues, especially in future phases of the portal life cycle. There are also dependencies of the site-scoped Features to site collection–scoped Features, and because the site template only contains web-scoped Features, provisioning of the site template can fail.

The CustomSchema element is an option in SharePoint 2010 used to define an alternative schema file for the list instance, which is used during the provisioning time of the list. In this way, you can create alternative list instances without providing new list templates. The "Save site as a template" option will create this alternative schema for each existing list instance on the site. So, if content editors have extended any of the out-of-the-box lists, they will also be created properly when the site template is used for new site instances.

Web Templates

Web templates are a new capability in SharePoint 2010 that provide site-provisioning definitions from Features. Their primary purpose is to provide more flexibility, maintainability, and upgradability compared to site definitions. Web templates can be created using new `WebTemplate` element, which is available in the Feature Framework XML elements. Figure 15-1 shows the process SharePoint 2010 uses to provision a site based on a web template:

➤ Step 1 illustrates that whenever a site collection-scoped or farm-scoped Feature has been activated on an individual site with web templates, these web templates are available from the Create Site functionality.

➤ Step 2 shows that when a web template is selected, the new site is created using the `onet.xml` file definition located in the same Feature folder as the `element.xml` file added in Step 1.

➤ Step 3 shows that web templates work similarly to site definitions. Each feature referenced in the Feature's `onet.xml` file is activated in the order listed. If subsites are being created within a site collection, only the web-scoped Features will activated. If the root site of the site collection is being created, site collection Features will activate, as well as web-scoped Features.

➤ Step 4 shows that the site created from the web template is associated with an existing site definition. This association is defined in the web template element file, or in the `WebTemplate` element.

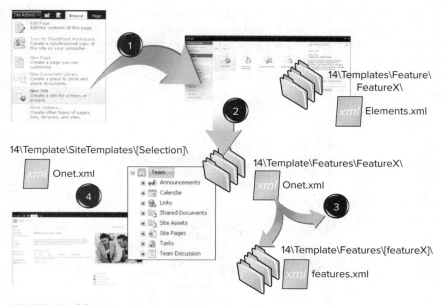

FIGURE 15-1: Web template provisioning process

The `WebTemplate` element is used to define what kind of template is available, and what values are shown in the user interface. Web templates also have their own `onet.xml` file, which is deployed as part of the Feature responsible of the `WebTemplate` definition. Certain limitations exist on what's supported for the `onet.xml` file of the `WebTemplate` element, but these limitations are not commonly encountered, and, if required, they can be replaced with Feature receiver-based code. Similar to site definitions, you can associate Features directly to the `onet.xml` file and configure them in a similar way.

Web templates use a similar provisioning order as the site definition, except that you cannot staple Features to web templates. This can sound like a nasty limitation, but because of the upgradability of the `onet.xml` file, there's no reason for actual Feature stapling for the web templates. It's also important to note that even though publishing Features are not supported in the site template approach, they are supported in web templates, and, therefore, you can create similar site-provisioning definitions as with a site definition.

As mentioned, web templates support easier upgrade of the provisioning rules. This is possible because the `WebTemplate` element defines which site definition the created site will be associated with after the `onet.xml` file of the web template has been executed. In this way, the `WebTemplate` element and configuration properties of the `SPWeb` object (that is, the server-side object for the site) are not dependent on the existence of the `onet.xml` file deployed within the Feature. This means that you can retract the whole web template from the farm, and all sites will continue work as they were created. You can also provide an updated `onet.xml` file for the web template in a new Feature version, and it will not cause any issues with the existing sites.

Web templates are great, because they provide the capability to use an alternative site definition during provisioning time. This means that the `onet.xml` file in the web template is completely replacing the associated site definition from the site.

When designing your site definitions, you should design the Feature associations for your web template carefully to provide even more flexibility with your web templates. Just as you would do for your site definitions, you should provision the site Welcome page and any site structures your web template requires using Features so that you can easily manipulate the site-creation process by updating the Feature code and definitions. Figure 15-2 describes the structure of the web template and its related Features and Feature receivers.

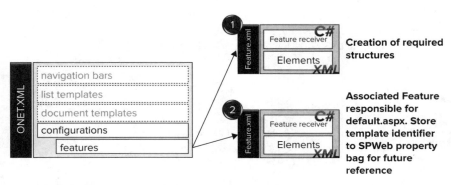

FIGURE 15-2: Web templates, Features, and Feature receivers

Because the site is created based on a web template, it will be associated with an existing site definition. Therefore, you should store the details concerning the web template used in your site's property bag. This could be, for example, done in a Feature receiver of the Feature, which is responsible for provisioning the Welcome page for the site.

Web templates can be deployed as full-trust or as sandboxed solutions, and you can use Feature scopes as a site collection and farm. Feature scope will directly affect the availability of the template to the end users. If you deploy a web template using a farm-scoped Feature, the web template will be available for all web applications and sites in the SharePoint farm. If you deploy the web template using the site collection–scoped Feature, the web template will be available in those site collections where the particular Feature is activated. You can also deploy site collection–scoped Features as farm solutions, but you cannot deploy farm-scoped Features if the sandboxed solution approach is taken.

If you deploy the web template using farm-scoped Feature, it will be available in Central Administration when new site collections are created.

You cannot scope a web template as a web application–scoped Feature, so if you want to limit the visibility of the template for end users, you must model the deployment of the Features more carefully. Here are few options for limiting the visibility of the web template:

➤ If publishing Features are enabled in your web templates, you can filter the listed web templates shown in the Create Site functionality in ways similar to the site definition.

➤ Just as with using the custom site definition option, you can use custom code to solve the visibility of your site.

➤ You can design your deployment model in such a way that you also deploy your root site's definition for the site collection using a site collection–scoped Feature. Because the web template is not scoped as a farm-scoped Feature, it won't be available from Central Administration. You can then script or manually create a new empty site collection, and activate the Feature responsible for the web template deployment to it.

Just as for site definitions, each web template has its own unique identifier, which consists of the Feature globally unique identifier (GUID) responsible for the deployment, and the name defined for the `WebTemplate` element. When the Feature responsible for the web template deployment has been activated, this format can be used to programmatically provision sites or access the web template details using the server-side object model. The same identifier can be also used, for example, in the publishing Feature associations, if you must configure the filtering of visible site templates for the end users.

STORING THE WEB TEMPLATE IDENTIFIER

The actual identifier of the web template that is used for creating the site is not stored anywhere on the site's properties (`SPWeb`), so it can be difficult to figure out which template was used to create the site afterward. Therefore, it's important to store the identifier in the property bag of the particular site. You can do this by using a Feature receiver, which will store the Feature ID and the web template name in the property bag. Remember to use the same key for storing this information in all of your projects, so that you can always pick up the web template used.

An example of the information to store would be following key value pair:

➤ Key: `WebTemplateId`

➤ Value: `[FeatureGUID]#WebTemplateName`

However, with web templates, there is one big disadvantage or case where they cannot be used. This is when you are developing a multilingual solution using the *Variation* publishing functionality. Variations can be used to provide a multilingual solution for your solution when site hierarchies between the different languages are identical (or almost identical). Variations work in a way that you select one language or hierarchy to be your primary language, and other site hierarchies are created based on this primary language.

In SharePoint 2010, the Variation functionality was changed to be timer job–based. The timer job ensures that the sites are copied between different Variations, based on changes in the root language. Because you don't have any out-of-the-box indication in sites that they have been created using a web template, the timer job is unaware of the fact that template information in the `SPWeb` object is not valid because it refers only to some base site definition.

Unfortunately, there's currently no workaround for this limitation concerning web templates, but the Variation functionality may soon be fixed to be aware of some indication of the used web template, hopefully in a future service pack. However, this does not mean that you can't do multilingual sites with web templates; it only means that you can't use Variations with web templates.

Site Definitions

Site definitions are XML-based definitions, which define what will happen when a new site is created. Site definitions live in the `%ProgramFiles%\Common Files\Microsoft Shared\web server extensions\14\TEMPLATE\SiteTemplates` folder. Site definitions consist of two main files: `WebTemp .xml` and `onet.xml`. The `WebTemp.xml` file defines what kinds of site definitions are available, and how they are presented for the end users in the Create Site functionality. The `WebTemp.xml` file contains a *reference* to the site definition folder that contains the `onet.xml` (site definition build instruction set) file.

Many of the out-of-the-box site definitions include site assets that are included in the site definition folder. Despite the fact that an out-of-the-box definition often does this, it's more flexible and maintainable (and definitely recommended) to provision all elements from Features, so that `onet.xml` only references Features and is not responsible for the creation or provisioning of any structures by itself. Figure 15-3 describes the "under the hood" site provisioning process used by SharePoint 2010 to provision a site based on a site definition.

➤ Step 1 shows how sites shown in the Create Site user interface are based on the `WebTemp*.xml` files. Each `WebTemp*.xml` file contains an itemization of the site definition configurations available for users to select.

➤ Step 2 shows that when a site definition is selected, the new site is created using the `onet.xml` file definition located in the specific `Site Template` folder.

➤ Step 3 shows how each Feature referenced in the Feature's `onet.xml` file is activated in the order listed. If subsites are being created within a site collection, only the web-scoped Features will be activated. If the root site of the site collection is being created, site collection Features will activate as well as web-scoped features.

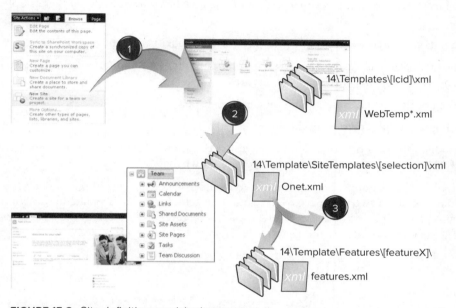

FIGURE 15-3: Site definition provisioning process

Just as with Features, unique naming of the site definition is extremely important to avoid a naming collision in the filesystem. This is related to the naming of the `WebTemp.xml` file and the naming of the site definition folder. A good naming convention would be to have a company and project name included as a filename prefix. For example, you could use `WebTemp.Contoso.Intranet.xml` for the filename and `Contoso.Intranet` as the folder name for site definition files.

Some of the most important things to consider concerning the site definition and Feature design is the provisioning order of the different elements, and the differences in the provisioning logic, if, for example, the site definition is used to create root site or a subsite *within* the site collection. Following is the provisioning order of the different elements:

➤ Creation of the target URL in the database.

➤ Provisioning of the global `onet.xml` file.

➤ Activation of the associated site collection–scoped Features in the order defined in the `onet.xml` file. The associated site collection–scoped Features are activated only when you create the root site of the site collection. This can have a huge impact on your site provisioning design. (You learn about a workaround for this little bit later.)

➤ Activation of site collection–scoped stapled Features in "random order." The same rules apply for the directly associated site collection Features. The site collection–scoped stapled Features are activated only when you create a root site of the site collection. The "random order" implies that you cannot have two different Features that are dependent on each other as stapled Features, unless you've created Feature dependencies between these stapled Features.

➤ Activation of associated web-scoped Features in the order defined in the `onet.xml` file.

➤ Activation of stapled web-scoped Features in "random order." "Random order" here refers to the same as for site collection–scoped Features.

➤ Provisioning of list instances defined in the `onet.xml` file.

➤ Provisioning of modules defined in the `onet.xml` file.

If you have defined list instances or modules (as in pages) in the `onet.xml` file, you should not have any code or XML definitions in your Features that would modify these.

To explain, let's look at the example of a requirement to create a Welcome page in the site that has web part connections between two web parts. This cannot be achieved from associated Features if the Welcome page is provisioned from the `onet.xml` modules. Figure 15-4 describes the structure of a site definition and its related Features and Feature receivers.

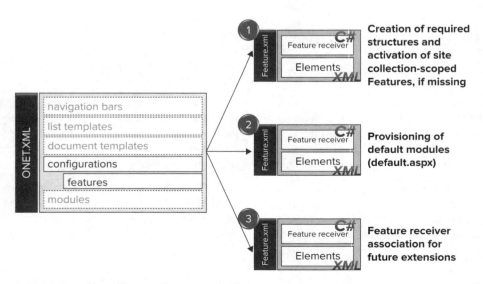

FIGURE 15-4: Site definition, Features, and Feature receivers

To tackle the provisioning order and make the definition as flexible as possible, it is not recommended to use list instance or module elements in `onet.xml`. Rather, you should provision these structures from associated or stapled Features. In this way, you have full control of the provisioning order, and you gain the flexibility to maintain the site definition (using a Feature upgrade in this case).

As already noted in the site definition provisioning order list, the site collection–scoped associated or stapled Features are not activated when subsites are created. This can cause difficulties when designing sites that have dependencies on site collection–scoped elements. The easiest workaround for this kind of requirement is to have the required Feature be activated programmatically from the site-scoped Feature. This can be relatively easily achieved by using Feature receivers.

Because updating of the site definitions is not supported after initial deployment, it's important to set up these additional possibilities for possible future updates, even though you would not need them during first release. Even though you cannot update site definitions, you can update Features, which are exactly the reason you should place all your provisioning logic in Feature files, and not within the site definition file. You'll need to ensure that, when sites are created using a specific site definition, those sites are dependent on the existence of the `onet.xml` file in the filesystem.

Remember that site definitions are available only for full-trust solutions, and, by default, they are always farm-wide. This can cause issues if multiple applications are hosted in a single SharePoint 2010 farm, because end users can, by default, see all the site definitions available at the farm level in each of the web applications.

You have ways to filter the visibility of the site definitions in the web application, or even in the site level, depending on the application design. Following are the main options for filtering the list of visible sites:

➤ If publishing Features are enabled, you can filter the visible web templates that are available for a particular site. You can do this from the user interface. However, it can be done more efficiently directly in the `onet.xml` level, so that there's no need to define these settings from the user interface after the site has been created. This is not security filtering, however, meaning that end users can update these settings manually through the relevant Site Settings pages.

➤ Available templates can be filtered using the `VisibilityFeatureDependency` attribute in the `WebTemp.xml` file. This attribute can be used to define that a particular template is available only when a specific Feature is enabled. For example, you could create an empty web application–scoped Feature that can be activated in a specific web application to provide only the templates you want to make available. However, this does not provide the capability to filter away the out-of-the-box site definitions from the user interface. Because this option is configured in the server-side XML file, it cannot be overwritten by end users.

➤ Develop a custom "Provision a Site" wizard functionality to replace the out-of-the-box user interface. It's relatively simple to hide the existing links to replace the out-of-the-box Create Site functionality with your own custom Create Site page. If you choose this path, you will be forced to write your own provisioning mechanism, which can be a difficult task to do. However, using this kind of approach, you'd have the full flexibility to control what kind of information is requested from the end users concerning the sites to be created.

Another important aspect of site definitions is that one site definition can contain many site configurations. A good out-of-the-box example is the Basic or Team Site (STS#0) site definition. A number of configurations exist in a single site definition to create a wide variety of sites. It is important to understand when you need multiple site definitions, versus when you need one site definition with many configurations.

To answer this simplistically, if your custom site definitions should all be the same, you should create a single site definition with many configurations within it. If your custom site definitions are very different, it makes sense to create these as separate site definitions.

For further information and fantastic advice, see the MSDN article, "Deciding between multiple definitions or multiple configurations," at http://msdn .microsoft.com/en-us/library/ff407262.aspx. *For more information on the out-of-the-box site definitions and configurations, see the MSDN article, "Site Definitions and Configurations," at* http://msdn.microsoft.com/en-us/ library/aa978512.aspx. *For more information from Microsoft on the creation and configuration of a custom site definition for SharePoint 2010, see the MSDN article at* http://msdn.microsoft.com/en-us/library/ms454677.aspx.

Understanding the Common Site Provisioning Models

One of the key advantages of the SharePoint platform is the support for flexible site-provisioning models. Out of the box, you have multiple site definitions and web templates available, which can be extended, for example, using Feature stapling techniques. This is definitely the most efficient model to provide customized site provisioning based on business requirements.

Unfortunately, two massive limitations exist with this approach:

➤ When using the Feature stapling process, there is no way for you to provide new selections to be available in the Create Site functionality.

➤ There is not enough granularity in the application of Feature staples.

For example, say that you want to create a client engagement team site template. Using Feature stapling, you could attach the Feature staple to a team site in your collaboration web application, and it will apply your set of Feature staples faithfully whenever a team site is created.

Now, say your customer also wants to create a supplier management site template and host it in the same web application. It isn't possible to use the team site definition because it will get the Feature staples of the client engagement team site. It is cases like these that unfortunately force you down the web template route, custom site definition route, or "Provision a Site" wizard route that uses workflows under the hood to activate the required set of site and web Features needed for the type of site requested by the user.

In many larger projects, requirements exist, for example, to provide separate collaboration sites for projects and organizational teams. You could definitely extend out-of-the-box empty and team sites for these requirements, but the end-user experience would not be optimal. Also, if, in future phases of portal uses there will be requirements for additional site templates, the Feature staple model would not be that flexible.

Another common example is corporate communication intranets that utilize WCM Features (Publishing Features). In many cases, customer requirements require separate templates for divisional or business group front sites, market intranets, function intranets, content sites, and news sites. Out of the box, only two generic publishing sites are available, and, as you can see, this would be difficult to configure for each intranet requirement.

Based on this type of requirement, it would mean that, based on their particular interest and requirements, your content editors or site users would be forced to activate Features manually after the site has been created. This would enormously increase the amount of time spent for additional configuration of the site before your business could start to get value from it. In smaller deployments, this is not so much of an issue, but in larger deployments, the overall costs of the required training and time spent on non-productive work would result in a much greater cost to your business.

Therefore, planning your site-provisioning model efficiently is a *huge time-saver* for the actual content editing experience. When the publishing Features have been enabled, you can configure most of the initial settings by setting parameters of the publishing Features from the XML files. Using this approach, you can, for example, limit the available site types for a particular SharePoint site to ensure that content editors won't create hierarchies that are not allowed. Another example is creating multiple enterprise Search Centers to multiple places in the portal hierarchy.

Let's take a look at the common site-provisioning models available to you.

Out-of-the-Box Site Definition with Customization after Deployment

In many small SharePoint 2010 deployments, SharePoint Designer is used by your site owners or site developer to configure and create the necessary customizations for end users. SharePoint Designer 2010 is an excellent and extremely powerful tool for configuring and maintaining site structures, but it's mainly targeted for end-user configuration, and should not to be used as the *main* deployment and configuration tool in larger portal deployments.

The main reasons for this are quality and consistency. If you think back over the required portal life-cycle development process, using SharePoint Designer as the deployment tool for the customizations would be extremely time-consuming, and you would be required to configure each site manually in every environment. This increases the possibilities of missing some steps, even though tasks would be documented step-by-step. The level of documentation to reproduce the same configuration in the case of a disaster-recovery situation would have to be really detailed.

However, SharePoint Designer 2010 should not be completely disabled, because it definitely has its purpose, and provides a ton of business value to power users of your organization. All customizations developed and deployed using solution packages should be considered as building blocks for your portal.

SharePoint 2010 provides configuration options to enable and disable SharePoint Designer usage at the web application level or within each site collection. These settings should be considered and configured carefully. The following options are available:

➤ *Enable or disable SharePoint Designer 2010 use for an entire application or site collection* — This completely enables or disables SharePoint Designer 2010 usage from the web application or site collection level.

➤ *Enable or disable the ability to detach pages from the site definition* — This option enables or disables the capability to customize web part pages, which are deployed from the site definitions. Good examples include the default web part pages in the MySite host site definition.

➤ *Enable or disable master pages and page layouts in SharePoint Designer 2010* — This enables or disables master pages and page layout navigations from SharePoint Designer 2010 and, therefore, disables the customization of them.

➤ *Enable or disable the site URL structure and its contents* — This controls visibility of the All Files option in SharePoint Designer 2010. The All Files option can be used to provide a detailed view of the content of the site.

For example, for your company intranet, it would be worthwhile to disable the "Enable or disable master pages and page layouts in SharePoint Designer 2010" option, especially if the page layouts are maintained and created outside of the production environment. This would enable an easier versioning model, because all changes for the page layouts would be immediately available for all of the sites, when a new version of the solution package is deployed. On the other hand, if the content editors of the intranet are experienced enough, it would definitely be the most cost-efficient option to maintain page layouts directly in the production environment. As you can see, this is completely project and deployment dependent, and should be evaluated case by case.

Custom Code Models

For experienced SharePoint developers, writing site-provisioning code completely as custom code is a trivial task, because server APIs are relatively straightforward to utilize, and they provide rich interfaces for this kind of solution.

Using a custom code model, you must do the initial provisioning of the site structures either using a custom site definition or blank site definition. The key difference between using a custom site definition or blank site definition is whether you would like to automatically activate the Features via the custom site definition, or whether you want to activate the required Features on an empty site definition after it has been created.

Although the Microsoft SharePoint product team fully supports custom site definitions, it is recommended to only use them as a last resort. The reasons for this stem from the difficulty of maintaining and supporting sites created off of custom site definitions, and concerns about the future upgradeability to the next version of SharePoint.

Provider-Based Approach

Using portal provisioning providers is a technique where you completely replace the `onet.xml` file using code, except that you usually still use an out-of-the-box site definition as the starting point. This means that you only use a `WebTemp*.xml` file and assign your custom provisioning class to be used, when a particular template is selected. As long as you have implemented your custom provisioning provider by inheriting the out-of-the-box `SPWebProvisioningProvider` class (`Microsoft.SharePoint.SPWebProvisioningProvider`) and the associations in `WebTemp*.xml` are correct, you would have full control on the actions to be performed.

The common implementation uses the `SPWeb.ApplyWebTemplate` method to provision the starting point based on the chosen out-of-the-box site definition, and then manipulates the created site using code. This is an extremely flexible model, because you can easily update the code by deploying a new version of the used assembly. But isn't this almost the same model as for the web templates?

One out-of-the-box implementation of the provisioning providers is the `PortalProvisioning Provider` (`Microsoft.SharePoint.Publishing.PortalProvisioningProvider`) that is available in SharePoint Server, but not in SharePoint Foundation. This provides the capability to create portal site templates (meaning hierarchy files).

Because provisioning providers require that they are introduced using the `WebTemp*.xml` file, which has to be placed in the filesystem, these are not usually supported for the cloud-based services (such as MS Online). This is because the provisioning engine would not be standard, and if all projects could implement their own provisioning engine, the required quality assurance would increase enormously.

SharePoint Server 2010 supports defining portal site template files, which can define the hierarchy of sites to provision immediately when the Create Site functionality is used. This capability is based on the `SPWebProvisioningProvider` *approach.*

Based on the future plans of SharePoint, this model is not recommended. The interface has not yet been deprecated, but you should not bet your business on this one, even though it might sound really compelling.

Deciding between Custom Web Templates, Custom Site Definitions, and Out-of-the-Box Site Definitions and Web Templates

Microsoft recommends that you construct your solutions using a Feature-based approach as much as possible — specifically, whenever possible — instead of creating custom site or custom web templates.

See the MSDN article, "Deciding between custom web templates and custom site definitions" at `http://msdn.microsoft.com/en-us/library/aa979683 .aspx`. *The article does acknowledge that there are cases when it makes sense to build custom site definitions or custom web templates. The article goes on to advise on using web templates over custom site definitions whenever possible to ensure compatibility with future versions of SharePoint.*

In some scenarios it may make sense to use custom site definitions, including the following:

➤ *Feature staple firing in random order* — The order in which stapled Features are fired during the site-provisioning process in SharePoint is not always predictable. Feature activations can "fire" in an order or timeframe not expected.

➤ *Site definition unique name* — A unique name may be required for each site definition. These may be used in your custom Create Site provisioning code to create site collections in your environment. If a unique name is required for a site definition, a custom site definition is required.

➤ *Web template versus site definition performance* — There is a concern that content stored in the database may take longer to render than content on the filesystem of the Web Front-End (WFE) server. In most cases, this is negligible, and can be overlooked. But in a limited number of cases, this may result in slower performance if your WFE must retrieve all the site and page artifacts from the content database.

➤ *Site and web Features that must run only for specific types of sites* — SharePoint doesn't support site and web Features scoped to a particular site path or site instance. SharePoint does support creating custom site definitions that give you complete control of what site and web Features must be automatically activated to configure the site for use.

It is very important that you understand that custom site definitions should be used only as a last resort. As much as possible, try to use out-of-the-box site definitions with Feature activations or web templates with the Feature activations built in.

Features and Feature Receivers

Features are one of the key building blocks for any solution in SharePoint 2010. This makes it especially important to understand the common design patterns relating to implementation of custom Features in your sites.

The Feature framework is used to deploy modular functionalities to SharePoint deployment. Customizations are declared using XML files, and can be activated at different scopes to provide new functionality.

A Feature contains your defined extensions for your SharePoint 2010 environment. It is composed of a set of XML files that are deployed to WFE servers and application servers. Features are deployed via a Windows Solution Package (WSP). Following are the key highlights of using Features:

➤ Features can be scoped at the web, site collection, web application, and farm level.

➤ Features support a wide range of custom solution deployment functionality (for example, provisioning content, making web parts available in the web part gallery, and creating lists instances, as well as creating site columns and content types, among many other great features).

➤ When you use the SPFeatureReceiver class, Features support the capability to execute code on activation and deactivation.

➤ Feature activations can be included in your custom site definition and web templates to be activated on creation of the site definition or web template. Alternatively, they can either be activated manually using Windows PowerShell commands, or via the user interface after a site has been created.

 For more information on Features, see the TechNet Feature introduction article at http://technet.microsoft.com/en-us/library/ff607680.aspx.

Feature dependencies are a useful component that can be leveraged to group Features together, as well as to guarantee dependent functionality is available.

 To better understand how Feature dependencies work, see http://msdn.microsoft .com/en-us/library/aa543162.aspx.

Another significant advantage is the capability to upgrade a Feature in SharePoint 2010 through versioning and declarative upgrade actions. This enables you to perform the following types of upgrades to Features:

➤ Defining upgrade definitions

➤ Provisioning list instances

➤ Creating separate upgrade action sets based on the Feature version that remove different sets of files

➤ Applying settings to site collections where a particular Feature is activated

 TechNet provides detailed information on upgrading Features at http:// go.microsoft.com/fwlink/p/?LinkId=188458&clcid=0x409.

In the context of solution architecture planning, it is important to design the Feature framework model efficiently so that individual functionalities can be activated at the proper scopes on your sites. The Feature framework model is also important to consider when your site-provisioning model is designed, so that you can automate the site-provisioning model efficiently, and end users can concentrate on actual content management, rather than continually having to manually configure sites after initial creation.

All Features deployed as part of the customizations should be named uniquely. This is because, in the case of a full-trust solution, each Feature will be deployed to a dedicated folder under the

SharePoint root folder (that is, so-called *14 root* folders). If two Features are named in the same way, they will overwrite each other, and the functionalities will not work.

Visual Studio 2010 automatically uses the project name as the prefix for the individual Features, which helps to create distinct individual Features and helps to avoid overlapping Feature folders.

The Feature framework also supports customizations to be deployed using code. Each Feature can have a Feature receiver associated with it, which will be executed during the life cycle of the individual Feature. These Feature receivers are defined by assigning Feature receiver class information to Feature XML file, and inheriting the actual implementation from the `SPFeatureReceiver` base class.

When you develop Feature receivers, you should place the actual business logic to execute during the life cycle event of the Feature in separate business logic classes. Figure 15-5 shows how to separate business logic from your Feature receiver classes.

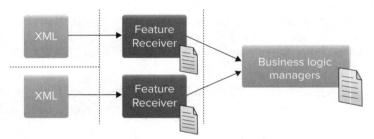

FIGURE 15-5: Separating business logic from your Feature receivers

More often than not, developers add actual business logic to be executed, for example, during Feature activation, directly in the Feature receiver class. The disadvantage of this approach is simply testability of the code. There's no way to execute the business logic without deploying the code to SharePoint and activating it either manually or using scripts. If the business logic code is placed in separate business logic classes, it can be individually tested and executed, even as part of the unit tests. Also, by layering the code efficiently, you promote the reuse of the code, which will decrease the overall costs of the development in the long term.

UNDERSTANDING COMMON SOLUTION PATTERNS AND DESIGN OPTIONS

For the uninitiated, software patterns have been around for a while in software engineering. Christopher Alexander, a pioneer in the use of patterns to solve problems related to building towns and buildings, is quoted as saying the following:

> *"Each pattern describes a problem which occurs over and over again in our environment, and then describes the core of the solution to that problem, in such a way that you use this solution a million times over, without ever doing it the same way twice."*

The "Gang of Four" (which consists of Erich Gamma, Richard Helm, Ralph Johnson, and John Vlissides) is widely recognized as the pioneers of introducing the pattern-oriented design to software design. They wrote the now-famous book, *Design Patterns: Elements of Reusable Object-Orientated Software* (Reading, MA: Addison-Wesley, 1995). In the Introduction, they recognized that software solutions are expressed in terms of objects and interfaces, instead of walls and doors. But at the core of both kinds of patterns is a solution to a problem in a context.

Subsequently, a number of fantastic software pattern-oriented books have been released, with each author(s) contributing innovation and intelligence to help the software community learn better approaches and techniques to software and solution design.

 Other key books that may be tremendously valuable include Patterns of Enterprise Application Architecture *by Martin Fowler, et al. (Reading, MA: Addison-Wesley Professional, 2002),* Pattern-Orientated Software Architecture, Volume 1 *by Frank Buschmann, et al. (New York: John Wiley Publishing, 1996),* Design Patterns in C# *by Steven John Metsker (Reading, MA: Addison-Wesley Professional, 2011), and Rockford Lhotka's "Business Object" series of books*

You may be wondering what this has to do with designing solutions for SharePoint 2010. Or, you may be wondering why you should think about software patterns when designing solutions for the SharePoint 2010 platform. Software patterns, distilled to their essence, provide proven methods to enable you to make the right decision before it is too late to change. They offer a number of important benefits, including the following:

➤ *Improved and consistent design* — Rather than each developer adopting a unique approach, an intentional design encourages consistency in the approach development engineers use to develop code to solve common problems.

➤ *Well-structured code base* — Software patterns result in an improved structure to the customizations developed for your organization's SharePoint deployment. Structure helps your current and future development engineers develop solutions using approaches that are already tested and proven for your organization.

➤ *Improved maintainability* — Software patterns make code easier to understand, especially in large customization code bases. This has the effect of reducing the time to fix issues and produce new solutions by reducing the learning curve to understand and maintain each customization.

➤ *Improved extensibility* — It is easier to extend customizations that follow a consistent structure. Conversely, it may be more difficult to extend customizations that follow a unique approach.

➤ *Improved upgradeability* — It is easier to upgrade your customizations when consistent software patterns have been implemented because less work is required to solve each software customization upgrade challenge.

> ➤ *Improved quality* — An important benefit to implementing consistent software patterns is the reduced number of defects during development and maintenance cycles. An issue is solved once, and applied to all existing and future customizations. This contributes to the overall effect of improving the quality of the customizations in your production environment.

The Microsoft SharePoint Product Group, in conjunction with the Microsoft Pattern and Practices Group, recognized the importance of providing solid software pattern-oriented guidance. As a result, two fantastic pieces of work were delivered and released to the SharePoint community.

 For more information, download "Developing Applications for SharePoint 2007" and "Developing Applications for 2010" at www.microsoft.com/spg.

As you continue to read about the various software patterns, you may pick up (in the context of this book) that the "patterns" discussed here are really "SharePoint 2010 software design options." Patterns, in their essence, tend to be abstract in nature. The reason for continuing to use the term "pattern" is two-fold. First, some are software design patterns. Second, this encourages you to think and design in a pattern-oriented manner. The remainder of this section describes a number of the well-known software design patterns and options for your SharePoint 2010 solutions.

User-Interface Software Patterns

Following are two key architectural patterns that are commonly used and recommended when designing and developing SharePoint 2010 user interfaces and solutions:

➤ Model-View-Presenter (MVP) pattern

➤ Model-View-ViewModel (MVVM) pattern

Both of these patterns are derivatives on the original Model-View-Controller (MVC) pattern. Both patterns solve similar problems in that they work to separate the behavior of the presentation layer from domain logic. They improve the "separation of concerns" in presentation logic, and improve the modularity, reliability, and testability of your code.

Let's take a look at these patterns in more detail.

Model-View-Presenter (MVP) Pattern

The MVP pattern is made up of the *Model* that hosts your business logic. The *View* is the user interface and routes commands (events) to the Presenter to act upon that data. The *Presenter* is the glue between the Model and the View. It retrieves the data from repositories (the Model), and formats it for display in the View. Figure 15-6 provides an overview of interaction in the MVP pattern.

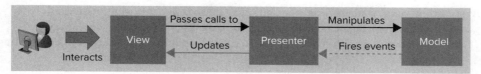

FIGURE 15-6: Model-View-Presenter (MVP) pattern

The Microsoft Patterns and Practices Group has provided detailed guidance and examples using the MVP pattern as part of the freely downloadable guidance at www.microsoft.com/spg. *See page 61 of "Developing Applications for Microsoft SharePoint 2010" for a great example and further guidance on using the MVP pattern in your SharePoint applications.*

Model-View-ViewModel (MVVM) Pattern

In the MVVM pattern, the *Model* is the business component that hosts your business logic. The *View* is the user interface, and the *ViewModel* is the glue between the Model and View. Figure 15-7 provides an overview of interaction in the MVVM pattern.

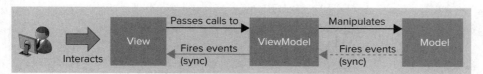

FIGURE 15-7: Model-View-ViewModel (MVVM) pattern

Andrew Connell provides a great series of blog articles to help you learn how to leverage the MVVM pattern to develop better SharePoint solutions. See www.andrewconnell.com/blog/archive/2011/10/28/silverlight-mvvm-sharepoint-about-this-series.aspx *for more information.*

Content Query, Aggregation, and Visualization Solution Options

When using SharePoint 2010, there will be many scenarios where you are required to present "aggregated" content to end users on a page.

For the SharePoint uninitiated, the term "aggregated" may be slightly confusing. Essentially, the terms "aggregated" and "content aggregation" refer to the capability to *dynamically* query and retrieve data from various sources within SharePoint 2010 at the point in time the user is requesting the page.

Content aggregation is not just about how you query and retrieve data, but also about how you present this summarized (aggregated) data to end users in a visually appealing manner. Therefore, to summarize, successful content aggregation can be defined as the capability to define and execute a query in a precise, efficient, and expedient manner, and render the returned data set in the manner required by end users of your site.

Table 15-1 describes the SharePoint 2010 content aggregation features that are available to support you, from simple configuration options, intermediate options that require tools such as SharePoint Designer, to advanced options that require a detailed understanding of custom development for the SharePoint 2010 platform.

TABLE 15-1: Simple, Intermediate, and Advanced Content Aggregation Options

SIMPLE OPTIONS	INTERMEDIATE OPTIONS	ADVANCED OPTIONS
Relevant Documents web parts	Data View web parts	Live query custom web parts
Calendar overlays	XSLT List View web parts	Near-live custom web parts
RSS Feeds web parts	Content Query web parts	Silverlight web parts
Tag Clouds web parts	Core Results Search web parts	Business Connectivity Service suite of web parts
Web Analytics web parts		

The rest of this section provides an overview of these options.

Simple Content Aggregation Options

Simple content aggregation options are Features that are available to add to your site that do not require any major configuration or development effort. SharePoint 2010 provides the following out-of-the-box options:

➤ *Relevant Documents web part* — This web part is a relatively simple web part that doesn't require much configuration. You can show the last document modified or created for individual users, thereby helping find documents they have most recently worked with on a site. It is limited to returning documents within the current web application, rather than the entire site collection.

➤ *Calendar overlays* — SharePoint 2010 provides the capability to overlay calendar entries from multiple calendars on one calendar. In effect, content is aggregated from multiple calendars on one calendar. This is enabled using the Calendar Overlays button on the Ribbon.

➤ *RSS Feeds web part* — This web part is capable of consuming an RSS feed from an internal SharePoint list or external site's RSS feed. This web part requires Kerberos to be configured on your farm. From an end-user's perspective, it is simple to add and configure on your site. It must be noted that more advanced options are available to customize the rendering of the returned data set.

➤ *Tag Cloud web part* — The Tag Cloud web part displays a tag cloud of tags found on the current site. Tag Cloud webparts provide an aggregated view of the tags that a group of users have applied information to in your site. A common example is the aggregation of all tags applied to individual blog entries in a blog site.

➤ *Web Analytics web part* — This web part displays the most viewed content, most popular search queries, or most popular clicked search results as reported by Web Analytics for the site or site collection.

It is relatively straightforward to use these forms of content aggregation and simple visualization options on your site or site collection.

Intermediate Content Aggregation Options

Intermediate content aggregation options are Features that are available to add to your site, but require configuration or development skill, primarily using SharePoint Designer. These include the following options:

➤ *Data View web part (DVWP)* — This web part is configured and added to your site using SharePoint Designer. The web part enables you to query and render data from data sources, including web services, databases, and XML available via the SharePoint Designer interface.

➤ *XSLT List View (XLV) web part* — The XLV web part is a new web part in SharePoint 2010 that helps you create custom library and list views with SharePoint Designer 2010.

➤ *Content Query web part (CQWP)* — The CQWP web part is available if you have enabled the publishing infrastructure Feature on your site. It enables you to aggregate content from libraries and lists in your site collection. It provides neat what-you-see-is-what-you-get (WSIWYG) features to set up your query, and filter, sort, and group content returned by your query. Additionally, it provides a set of preconfigured styles, using XSL under the hood, and the capability to create your own custom XSL styles to render content in the format required by your end users.

➤ *Search Core Results web part* — This web part is great when you want to aggregate content across multiple site collections in your farm. It works by using a preconfigured query that executes against a predefined search scope. Writing the query requires knowledge of underlying predefined managed properties set up in Search Administration in Central Administration. As with the CQWP web part, this web part provides the capability to mark up/render the returned search result set using custom XSL.

As you can see from these features, each requires an additional degree of technical knowledge to master. This includes understanding the underlying querying concepts and methods, understanding how SharePoint uses caching under the hood, and the query languages used in SharePoint 2010. It requires understanding how libraries and lists are structured, and the different methods by which they can be queried, depending on their configuration (for example, using content types) and differences between "live" (CAML-based) queries and "near-live" (search-based) queries in SharePoint 2010.

On the visualization front, SharePoint Designer (and XSL) provides significant additional power to improve the visualization of content. However, this requires increased knowledge of how to leverage SharePoint Designer, XSL, HTML, and CSS to mark up content in a visually appealing way.

Advanced Content Aggregation Options

Advanced content aggregation options are Features that are available to add to your site, but require major development skill/effort, primarily using Visual Studio. These include the following options:

➤ *"Live" (query-based) custom web parts* — A "live" (query-based) web part is a web part that enables the display of real-time results aggregated from one or many site collections. The query (typically using CAML) is performed against the *actual* underlying data in the current site collection, and against one or many site collections, in the same web application, or across different web applications. Because of the "live" nature of this query, even with throttling, if developed incorrectly and executed poorly, it could impact the performance of libraries and lists, and potentially affect the underlying performance of your farm.

➤ *"Near-live" (search-based) custom web parts* — A "near-live" (search-based) web part enables the display of near real time, but *instant* results from all content on the SharePoint 2010 platform. The web part leverages the search index and SharePoint Search APIs, typically using the `FullTextSQLQuery` class to achieve this. The beauty of "near-live" custom web parts is that they do not impact the performance of your farm, because results are returned to the search index, and not directly from sites and site collections in your environment. In most cases, as long as your indexing schedules maintain the freshness of your search indexes, end users will not notice the difference.

➤ *Silverlight web part* — The Silverlight web part is another method for developing graphically rich visualizations against content that has been aggregated either using "live" or "near-live" techniques. This requires an advanced knowledge of Silverlight APIs to develop the visualizations required by your end users.

 Even though it is a fabulous technology, Microsoft has created uncertainty in investing in this technology. As of this writing, it is not clear whether Silverlight will be reaching an unexpected end of life soon, to be replaced by an HTML5-oriented technology.

➤ *Business Connectivity Service suite of web parts* — Microsoft has provided a great suite of "business data" web parts that enable you connect to, present, and display content from predefined content sources. This requires advanced knowledge of the underlying content source, as well as how to define the data model to connect it to enable SharePoint to incorporate this data. Once the data model is defined, it is relatively straightforward to incorporate in your sites.

When developing custom web parts that perform long-running operations, consider the following options:

➤ *Implement the asynchronous web part pattern* — This will ensure pages hosting your custom web part load at the same speed, regardless of the time taken to return a result set.

➤ *Test using simulated real-world loads* — When querying underlying sources using either "live" or "near-live" queries, consider and test the user experience by estimating and generating one to three years' worth of content.

➤ *Think about the user experience* — Consider using jQuery components to show a spinning wheel while content is loading, and update the web part once the query result set has been retrieved. There is nothing worse for an end user than having to go make a cup of coffee while waiting for a long-running web part to return the page.

➤ *Consider REST* — Consider taking advantage of the new capabilities of the SharePoint Foundation data store and REST. Using ADO.NET Data Services under the hood, REST queries provide access to libraries and lists as a relational data store. REST provides a flexible mechanism for working with list data in XML format, and any application that can send REST URLs to SharePoint can retrieve its list data. A number of services are available.

For more information on the SharePoint Foundation REST interface, see http://msdn.microsoft.com/en-us/library/ff521587.aspx. *For more information on querying SharePoint with ADO.NET Data Services, see* http://msdn.microsoft.com/en-us/library/ee535480.aspx.

➤ *Consider JSONP to query across different domains* — For scenarios where you query and return result sets from servers in different domains (such as cross-web application and cross-farm queries), consider using JSON with Padding (JSONP) combined with a custom web service. If you haven't heard of JSONP, it is a hack in HTML to enable sites to call different domains.

Jonathan Roussel has a great blog post explaining how to use this technique in SharePoint. See http://blog.jonathanroussel.com/2010/01/jsonp-your-aspnet-web-service-direction.html.

In all of these cases, once you have retrieved your data, you will need to render it to display it. You have many ways to achieve this.

The first consideration depends on whether you plan to render this using server-side or client-side code. Both have an associated set of pros and cons that must be taken into account, including the following:

➤ Do you want to consume precious server-side compute capacity, or would you prefer to utilize the client-side browsers and underlying compute facilities?

➤ What techniques and classes exist to help you complete your task of rendering on the server side versus client side?

➤ What browsers do you have to support?

➤ Does your render logic require a ton of business logic behind it?

➤ Do you plan to leverage the client-side object model that SharePoint 2010 provides?

Once you have decided, only then can you discern the best course of action in terms of rendering the visualization of the data returned from your query.

Often, based on previous projects, you may rely on the pattern of returning the result set in an XML structure, and leveraging either server-side or client-side XSL transforms to render the content to the end user.

As you can see, all of these considerations demand an in-depth level of technical knowledge of the .NET Framework and object models, the SharePoint server- and client-side object models, the visualization technologies, and the expertise to develop, test, deploy, and maintain in your SharePoint farm. These are exciting, but not for the faint-hearted!

Background Services Patterns

There will be many scenarios where your custom solution will need to process information in the background, on a continuous basis, according to a schedule.

The recommended solution for implementing "background services" in SharePoint 2010 is to take advantage of the SharePoint timer job framework. SharePoint timer jobs run in a specific Windows service, the SharePoint 2010 Timer service (SPTimerv4), for SharePoint 2010.

A SharePoint timer job consists of a definition of the service to execute, and specifies how frequently the timer job is executed. It is possible to develop custom timer jobs that execute custom code according to the schedule and frequency you require.

For operations related purely to content in or related to SharePoint 2010, it is recommended to use timer jobs within SharePoint 2010. For background services that reach out to work with/pull data from other environments, the design options expand, and become slightly more complex. The reason for this is that it all depends partly on what your background service is doing, and your larger strategy for managing background jobs in your organization's IT department.

For example, it may be that you have a dedicated business solution responsible for data processing or crunching. It may be that your business prefers to use Biztalk and its orchestration engine to manipulate content into the preferred format. In these cases, where you reach out into other IT solutions, the choice between using a SharePoint timer job or another solution to push content into SharePoint depends largely on your IT environment.

For more information on SharePoint 2010 timer jobs, see `http://technet`
`.microsoft.com/en-us/library/cc678870.aspx.`

Data Software Patterns

SharePoint 2010 provides a plethora of solutions to integrate and work with data in your custom
business solutions. Chapter 10 provides a detailed review of the design options available to incorporate
internal SharePoint data or external line-of-business (LOB) data into your SharePoint 2010 solutions.

Configuration Software Patterns

Many options are available in SharePoint 2010 to maintain the configuration of your SharePoint
2010 customizations. The type of configuration differs based on the type of customization required.
Table 15-2 describes the common configuration options.

TABLE 15-2: Common Custom SharePoint Software Configuration Options

OPTION	DESCRIPTION
For the entire farm	The Hierarchical Object Store allows user-defined objects to be persisted in a hierarchical nature within the SharePoint configuration database. It uses the `SPPersistedObject` (which is derived from `SPAutoSerializingObject`) to serialize information (such as your configuration) to XML.
	This is useful when your solution requires access to configuration in all web applications in your SharePoint 2010 farm. Typically, custom solutions will require a custom Central Administration page to administer the configuration stored in your farm property bag (Hierarchical Object Store).
For an entire web application	The most common option is to use the out-of-the-box web configuration modification engine SharePoint 2010 provides to deploy custom entries in your `web.config` file for a web application. This requires code to be written to use the `SPWebConfigModification` class to add this configuration, typically via a web application–scoped Feature activation.
	Although possible, it is recommended not to directly update the `web.config` file. The reason for this relates to how SharePoint 2010 supports the addition and removal of WFEs. If using the `SPWebConfigModification` class, your web configuration will be automatically provisioned when a new WFE is added to your farm. See TechNet (`http://msdn.microsoft.com/en-us/library/bb861909(v=office.14).aspx`) for more information.

continues

TABLE 15-2 *(continued)*

OPTION	DESCRIPTION
	Examples include configuration elements for HTTP modules, resource managers, redirects, and Ajax configuration.
For an entire site collection or web	A number of options are available at the site collection level. The choice you make depends largely on the type of custom solution. In almost all cases, a site collection- or web-scoped Feature will be used to apply the configuration to your site collection (or web application within the site collection).
	The site collection property bag, `SPPropertyBag`, stores key/value pairs that contain custom property settings. Properties can be accessed from custom code for all users of the site. While it is possible to read properties from a sandboxed solution, it is not possible to update custom properties.
	Another option is a custom list that can be hidden or shown to users of the site. For example, you may want to enable users to manage configuration for a custom web part. The custom web part is able to read a configuration from the custom list.
	A custom administration page can be used to provide a configuration page to administrators of a site via the Site Settings area of each site. If the page is a custom page, it would need to be a `_layouts` page. The page would be made available via a Feature that adds the relevant heading and link to the page in the Site Settings page.
For a custom SharePoint Feature	SharePoint Features provide mechanisms to store configuration of the Feature in the `elements.xml` file of the Feature, or alternatively read from the `app.settings` file on activation of the Feature. The key difference here is that it is static configuration that is included during compilation of your solution in Visual Studio. If you require the capability to update configuration in production, another option is required.
For a page or web part	Using the underlying ASP.NET engine, SharePoint 2010 supports shared and personalized configuration of pages and web parts. Pages and web parts can be configured for all users, and, if enabled, personalized for individual users. Simple-to-advanced configuration elements can be exposed via the "edit your web part" view of a web part.
For language-specific resources	SharePoint 2010 itself uses, and supports the use of, language-specific resource files (`*.resx`) for custom solutions that need to support multiple languages. TechNet provides detailed guidance on encoding and localization using resource files at `http://msdn.microsoft.com/EN-US/library/ms228208(v=VS.85)`.

As you can see, you have many configuration options to choose from when designing SharePoint 2010 solutions. The key elements to keep in mind are the scope of your configuration, and whether the configuration needs to change after deployment. Keep this in mind when planning the configuration of solutions for SharePoint 2010.

Security Software Patterns

The Delegation, Elevation, and Secure Security patterns describe a pattern for attainment of privileges to execute operations against secure resources that users cannot execute directly using their own security context, and to overcome the "double hop" issue when Kerberos has not been enabled in your farm.

A typical SharePoint 2010 farm contains a number of web applications. Each web application is hosted by IIS, and may be hosted in a separate memory address space, called an *application pool*. Each application pool runs within the security context of a service account. SharePoint hosts sites and services within web applications. Additionally, SharePoint has farm-wide accounts that can perform operations across all servers and web applications in your farm. Your custom solutions may require privileges to perform required actions in the context of the web application's application pool service account, or at the farm level.

For example, a common requirement is the capability to provision a site collection using a custom site collection provisioning wizard in the same or different web application. Although the user is issuing the request, a custom workflow may be required to do the "work" on behalf of the user. This workflow lives in one of your sites within the security context of the web application's application pool service account. In a least-privilege environment, this service account may not have privileges to create site collections in an alternate site collection. As a result, the workflow may need to call out (under elevated application pool–level privileges) to a custom locked-down administration service, running under farm administrator privileges, to provision a site collection to the relevant web application.

Delegation of Security Pattern

Delegation enables the middle-tier servers to pass on credentials to another remote server. These credentials enable access to resources on the remote server that otherwise would not be possible. The Delegation pattern is useful in the following scenarios:

➤ Delegating credentials to a database server

➤ Delegating permissions between web servers

Delegation of Permissions to Database Server

Delegation of credentials enables custom code to read and write information to custom SQL Server Workspace databases on remote machines. Figure 15-8 illustrates how security context is passed from the WFE server to the database server.

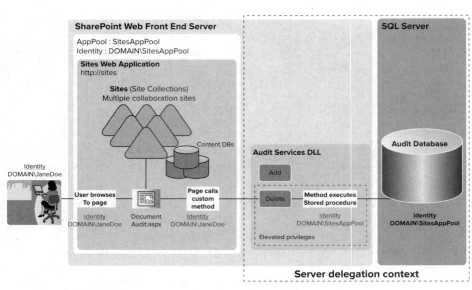

FIGURE 15-8: Delegation of Permission to Database Server

To access the databases, the hosting web application's application pool account must have appropriate permissions to run in the context of an account that SQL Server is configured to provide access. Delegation between servers is configured via Group Policy in Active Directory, whereas permission to access to the databases is set in SQL Server.

Delegation of Permissions between Web Servers

In scenarios where a single web server exists, no delegation of permissions is required because all activities occur on a single machine. Where two or more WFE servers exist in a load-balanced configuration, and custom code calls web services within the farm, delegation of permissions is required to execute code under the caller's elevated permissions. Without delegation of permissions, impersonation of accounts on one machine will not succeed on the second server.

Using the custom site collection provisioning wizard as an example, the "Provision a Site" code submits a new site request to the WCF Administration Service, running under farm privileges. Web Server 1 responds and returns the "Provisions a Site" page. On completion, the user submits the request to the server. The web server executes code to handle the request. Part of the custom code includes a call to the WCF administration web service, which has the appropriate permissions to perform a restricted action. This request is rerouted through the load balancer and may land on another web server in the load-balanced farm. With no delegation of permissions, this call will fail.

One solution is to use the "hosts" file (located at `%Windows%\%System%\Drivers\etc\`) on each server to point the machine to call itself. This results in the call completing on the same machine. An alternative solution is to configure IIS to trust the server for delegation between each of the web servers.

Elevation of Security Pattern

SharePoint provides an extensive object model that enables developers to create custom solutions hosted and managed by SharePoint. The custom solutions leverage the .NET platform and the ASP.NET framework.

Custom solutions are hosted in the web application and application pool of the site that hosts the solution. By default, custom code executes in the context of the user's Active Directory account, and does not use the application pool account. Certain cases exist where custom code requires elevated privileges to execute a permitted operation. In this case, the SharePoint object model provides a method to elevate privileges, which temporarily "boosts" the permissions of custom code to the application pool account hosting the web application.

Restricted Services Security Pattern

Restricted services running under "god-like" farm privileges (such as the WCF administration service example discussed previously) must be locked down to ensure that only restricted accounts can execute operations.

The WCF administrative service can be locked down to deny all users by default, but allow the following application pool accounts contained in an Active Directory group.

Additionally, a double layer of defense can be built in. The first is a setting in the `web.config` `<identity impersonate="false"/>` that forces the service to ignore the caller's security context and run in the security context of its own application pool.

The second is based on a security fix in Service Pack 2 (`http://support.microsoft.com/kb/909455`) that forces the developer to explicitly impersonate (as opposed to implicitly picking up the context) using the following lines of code:

```
using (impersonationContext = WindowsIdentity.GetCurrent().Impersonate())
{
… code here..
}
```

This code forces the execution to run under the security context of the current thread, which, in this case, is the application pool. The caller's context is used only to authorize the call. The actual work is performed under the WCF administration application pool's account that has greater privileges.

Custom Service Application Software Pattern

SharePoint 2010 provides a new concept called the *service application framework* that provides the capability to develop custom service applications.

Custom service applications enable the development of custom services that can be consumed by sites on your SharePoint 2010 platform. Custom services are especially useful in offloading the load of intensive business processes and logic, as well as software components, to specific machines within your SharePoint 2010 farm.

For more information on developing custom service applications, see the TechNet article at `http://msdn.microsoft.com/en-us/library/gg193964.aspx`.

Site Collection Life-Cycle Governance Pattern

Site collection governance entails designing the governance structures for managing the life cycle of site collections on your SharePoint 2010 platform — that is, from creation to archival/deletion. All site collections follow the same life cycle in a SharePoint 2010 environment.

Site Collection Provisioning Solution Options

How will you govern the request and creation of new site collections in SharePoint 2010? Will you automate it? Will you rigorously apply site collection quotas? Will you tag each site collection with custom metadata to associate key site information details? Will users be able to select a preconfigured site definition from a list or site-provisioning wizard?

Your chosen design will depend largely on the size and scope of your project, as well as the resources available for your project. Figure 15-9 shows an example of what is possible, strongly recommended (especially in medium to large SharePoint 2010 farms), and what has been designed and developed for large platform deployments.

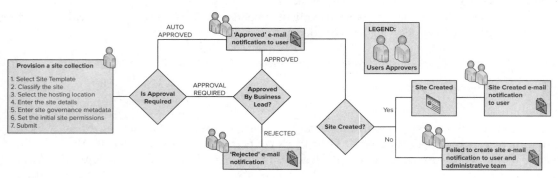

FIGURE 15-9: Provision a site collection flow diagram

Here is how it works in the real world:

1. Provide a custom site collection provisioning wizard (user interface). Any user can request a site by filling out the required information.

2. The new site request is submitted to a central "governance center" site and "new site request" list.

3. The new site request list is associated with a custom new site request workflow that evaluates a set of rules (stored in other lists), and is either automatically approved, or waits for manual approval by either a business deployment lead, or the central portal operations team.

4. Once the site is approved by the appropriate business deployment lead, the workflow submits the request to a locked-down WCF administration service executing under farm-level privileges. This enables it to create the site collection (based on the specified site definition selected in the site-provisioning wizard) in any of the available web applications and application pools you have configured.

5. An initial site quota is applied to the site collection during the creation of the site.

6. On creation of the site, properties are inserted into the site collection property bag, detailing key site information, which is surfaced to users and site owners of the site via a custom site information web part.

7. Upon successful creation, the final step is to add the site collection into a list called the "global site collection list." This list is used in many places. For example, it drives a powerful "Yellow Pages" styled site directory that enables users to look up sites based on the metadata captured during the site provisioning process.

8. At all stages of the process, users, business deployment leads, and central portal team receive e-mails advising on the progress of the user's request.

9. To protect the integrity of the "global site collection list," a background timer job continuously monitors and checks all created site collections that exist in the global site collection list.

Site Collection Automated Configuration Options

Once your site collection has been deployed, how will you configure it? How will you ensure site collections follow a consistent configuration? Will you manually activate site-scoped and web-scoped Features to configure your new site collection, staple your configuration Features to specific site definitions, or will you develop custom site definitions that automatically configure and prepare the site collection?

In SharePoint 2010, it is possible to staple custom-developed Features to existing site definitions. Alternatively, it is possible to create custom site definitions that automatically activate the site-scoped and web-scoped features on creation of your site collection. This enables your business to use consistently preconfigured sites that result in greater value to your business, and lower maintenance to support.

In the preceding "Provision a Site Collection" wizard example, you saw how a number of sites were provided that users could choose from. Based on the type of site the user requested, custom site definitions were specifically configured to create the site requested by the end user.

If you prefer not to use custom site definitions, an alternative option would be to automate the activation of site and web Features after your workflow has provisioned the site collection, based on a site and web Feature rules list in your governance center. In case you're wondering why you might develop some sites as custom site definitions, one reason (among many) is that you need unique site definition names for different types of sites, and you may have some hefty lockdown and control requirements.

Examples of common sites include "war chest" (marketing) sites, advanced project sites, research sites, "client practice" sites, "communities of practice" sites, steering committee sites, operations dashboard sites, and so on.

Site Collection Automated Growth Management Options

The growth of various site collections will manifest itself in a number of ways. The most common growth indicator is when a site owner requests a site quota storage increase. What site quotas will you initially provide, and what is the maximum site storage quota you are prepared to support? In past real-world projects, the site quota increase process has been automated by using the following steps:

1. Site owners are able to request increases to their storage quota via a custom site settings link and administration page in their sites.

2. The site quota change request is submitted to a central governance center site and site quota request list.

3. The site quota request list is associated with a site quota request workflow, which evaluates a set of rules (stored in other lists) and automatically increases to the next level, or waits for manual approval by the central portal operations team. For example, increasing a team site from 5 GB to 10 GB is a small issue, whereas requesting a 100 GB increase to a document center is a big deal to your central portal team in terms of underlying physical content database management.

4. The site owner receives notification on approval or rejection, and upon completion of the request.

5. Once the site quota has been manually or automatically approved, the workflow submits the request to a WCF administration service executing under farm-level privileges. This enables the update of the site quota of any site collection in any web applications and application pools.

Site Archival and Deletion Automation Options

SharePoint 2010 sites decline in usage at different rates. This often has nothing to do with SharePoint 2010, but more to do with the fact that the business purpose for the site has been exhausted. What you're left with is a site that has content, but may no longer be up to date.

As time progresses, the intellectual property (IP) may degrade or become less relevant to your business. Will your information architecture dictate what site owners should do with sites they no longer need? For example, key documents could be harvested and stored in longer-lived document centers.

A site that is no longer actively used can still be of immense value, as long as this content is indexed and searchable. Sites that adopt a "closed security" model where only specific users have access to the site lose value faster than sites with an open security model, because other users will not be able to surface valuable information in these sites in search results. Where feasible, an "open security" model should be encouraged for new site collection requests to ensure that all users have a minimum of read access to the site.

In some past real-world projects, the requirement for a business content owner was always enforced in both a central global site collection list and in the site itself. This provided the central portal team with an agreed-upon business owner of the data and information in the site.

It is the business content owner's responsibility (and cost) to maintain the site and information. If a business department merged with another department, it was possible for them to easily update the site metadata associations using the following governance process:

1. Site owners were able to update their site information through the site information web part. An "edit" link was available to site owners.

2. Site owners were shown an administration page detailing the list of metadata properties associated with their sites.

3. The change was submitted to a custom managed business content owner approval workflow. After approval by the central team, the new business content owner was reflected in the global site collection list, and in the site information web part.

How will you archive sites that you no longer need? It is possible that your IT department may want to make sites that have not been used for a period of time "read-only." After a certain amount of time in read-only mode, your IT department may determine it wishes to archive the site collection.

SharePoint provides a number of options to manage site collections that are no longer needed. These include an automated site collection deletion warning and site collection deletion process, as well as a capability to manually change the permissions of the site collection to site read-only.

Alternatively, you may want to institute a custom process where sites are automatically set to read-only (via code) after a period of time has elapsed from when the site was last accessed. Site owners can still request the site to be unlocked. This would, in effect, refresh the time the site has to live. Sites that aren't refreshed, and that are not subject to retention and disposal schedules, would then be available to be archived, backed up, and deleted.

What's important to realize is that once you have instituted this model, you have, in effect, instituted a site collection lease model. If the business does not maintain or refresh its lease, and the lease expires, the site will be archived and removed from SharePoint 2010.

Once again, the key to making this work relates to whether you provision site collections or subsites. If you cram tons of team subsites into one big site collection, you will have to archive subsites manually, most likely through permissions, and with growth over time, you will have lengthy back-up times and storage issues. Sorting out these types of issues is a heavily onerous and costly IT department task that entails splitting site collections, rather than provisioning and managing site collections using out-of-the-box site collection storage quotas.

In past real-world projects, a site archival process was provided to automate making a site read-only. Rarely do IT departments institute the out-of-the-box automatic site collection deletion process, because they worry about the impact of deleting business sites and content.

Determining what sites to archive and delete is a difficult challenge! It is especially difficult when the original owners of the site have left the business or moved to a different team in the business. Deciding and communicating a lease model up front helps to instill the correct mindset and responsibility that the business must maintain and *own* its content, lest it be archived and deleted.

Execution Model Options

SharePoint 2010 has three key execution models for custom solutions: farm solutions, sandboxed solutions, and hybrid sandboxed solution approaches. The Microsoft Patterns and Practice Group provides detailed guidance to help you learn more about the execution models available to you.

> *Read from page 13 onward of the "Developing Applications for Microsoft SharePoint 2010" document available at* www.microsoft.com/spg.

Solution Deployment Patterns

If there is any advice that you take from this entire chapter, based on hard-learned lessons in large customer deployments, it is that you should split out your solutions into multiple solution packages.

Developers often fail to sufficiently break their solutions into multiple solution packages. In the initial stages and early releases, this doesn't present too much of an issue. But after many releases and staff turnover, it becomes difficult to sufficiently regression-test code that sits in one or two large solution packages.

> *For medium to large custom solutions, do not place your entire custom solution in one solution package!*

Think critically about the how you split your framework, common "shared" library code, and business solution code into framework, shared library, and individual solution packages.

In case you are wondering why it is important to split solutions into multiple solution packages, it is all about being able respond quickly to business requests for updates, being able to update your production environment with the least amount of risk, and reducing the cost and impact of regression-testing single solution packages that have your entire solution and the kitchen sink thrown in.

If you're only developing a few small custom web parts that will be packaged into a single solution package, this issue is not as important, but it's absolutely critical for large projects. It's all about providing cost-efficient maintainability and upgradability of customizations in your production environment.

In a nutshell, the mark of a great solution package design is the ease in which it can be maintained, tested, and upgraded at the lowest level of development, testing cost, and risk to your production environment!

Chapter 18 provides detailed guidance on designing your solution packages for your production environment.

DESIGNING YOUR CUSTOM BUSINESS SOLUTIONS

This section focuses on functionality you require that is not provided out-of-the-box by SharePoint 2010. Custom functionality is an interesting topic that spans information architecture, solution architecture, user experience, and technical design.

Information architecture elements focus more on the *what*, *why*, and *when*, and aim to provide a complete picture of the functionality and features your SharePoint 2010 platform and solutions will provide. Solution architecture focuses on *how* and *how best* it will be architected and developed. User experience focuses on providing a great experience for your end users. Technical design activity drives out the detailed design of the components required to develop the use cases, while satisfying the information architecture, solution architecture, and user experience requirements.

Designing custom functionality for SharePoint 2010 is, without a doubt, one of the most exciting parts of working in the SharePoint industry and community. Being the fantastic platform it is, SharePoint 2010 caters to and fully supports hosting custom developed functionality. It enables you to utilize your creative energy to solve real problems faced by users of your organization using Microsoft SharePoint and related technology toolsets.

SharePoint "Custom Functionality" Rules

As in the movie *Fight Club*, a few unwritten (but well-known) rules apply to designing and developing new custom SharePoint functionality for businesses.

The first rule is as follows: *"Always attempt to use out-of-the-box functionality. If the functionality does not exist, seek a great affordable third-party solution. If no third-party functionality exists, consider well-known free web parts available to you from places such as CodePlex. If none of these options is available, consider negotiating the requirement with the customer to enable one of these options. If all these options have failed, only then should you consider developing custom functionality."*

The reasons for this first rule are based on supportability, "economies of scale" offered by a third-party solution partner, stability, maintainability, and cost effectiveness. It is more advantageous for a customer to purchase an existing solution because it enables the customer to focus efforts on the detail and customizations *specific* to the business.

A second rule is as follows: *"Keep it as simple, stable, scalable, maintainable, and performant as possible."*

For more information and details on this rule, refer to the architectural and quality attribute frames that were discussed in Chapter 12.

A third rule is as follows: *"Consider the return on investment for the cost incurred in developing this solution for the customer. Does the customer really need this feature? Does the customer need it in this release, or can it wait until a future release? Are you providing the customer with the correct guidance as a trusted advisor?"*

This rule asks you to think critically as the customer's trusted advisor and SharePoint partner, rather than as a passionate developer, consultant, or architect. This rule exists to protect you from over-customizing the SharePoint platform, to the detriment of the customer, and ultimately to the detriment of yourself. All customers grow and learn, and they will soon understand the true value versus cost of the functionality you develop. This will feed into their understanding and value of the services you provide to their businesses. This affects your medium- to long-term customer relationship.

The following elements should be considered for each piece of custom functionality you plan to develop:

➤ Vision, concept, and scope

➤ Personas and scenarios

➤ User experience

➤ Pages, web parts, and configuration

➤ Processes, workflows, and structures

➤ Security planning and user permissions

➤ Governance and maintenance requirements

Let's take a look at each of these in a bit more detail.

Vision, Concept, and Scope

Consider the vision, concept, and scope of the custom functionality:

➤ How often will the functionality be used?

➤ Will it be used for a short period, or do you believe it will be a Feature that will be invaluable to the business over the medium to long term?

➤ Is the Feature really required in the first release?

➤ Will the Feature be developed over a number of releases?

➤ For new platforms and newly formed development teams, will the Feature possibly delay the launch of the platform because of the time required to design, develop, and test?

➤ Is this Feature complex and difficult to put together?

➤ Does the Feature complement SharePoint 2010?

These questions help you think objectively and critically when reviewing the vision, the concept, and scope of the intended custom functionality.

Personas and Scenarios

Ensure that you capture the actors and key personas that will interact with and use the custom functionality on a daily basis. Also, capture the user stories and use cases of the custom functionality. Actors, key personas, user stories, and use cases should be documented, communicated, and signed off by your customer *before* you start development.

 This should include high-level screen mockups or visual demonstrators to help the customer visualize the intended solution.

User Experience

There is nothing worse or more sinful than building a great Feature-rich solution that looks awful and/or results in a bad user experience. Users don't care about back-end components. They care about their daily experience using the custom Feature. Following are some examples:

➤ It looks awful — period.

➤ It requires ten clicks to do something when it could be done in two.

➤ It requires you to delete all the sample content before you can start using it.

➤ Performing an action refreshes the page and forces the user to scroll down to the same place they were before the refresh.

➤ Screen real estate and end user average desktop screen resolution is not considered or used properly.

➤ Common browsers used in the organization do not work as expected.

➤ Within the context of the custom functionality, the navigation experience requires increased mouse cursor journey time that could be mitigated with a better user interface.

By capturing personas and use cases, you can really focus on the intended user experience because you think in terms of real people in the organization, and not just actors. Remember, a bad user experience is a recipe for disaster because it starts the ball of end-user negativity rolling!

 A number of great resources are available on the Web that provide detailed guidance, tips, and tricks to help you build better user experiences.

Pages, Web Parts, and Configuration

Consider what pages, web parts, and configuration elements are required for your custom functionality. Be sure to think about the following:

> ➤ Consider the required positioning of web part zones for your custom functionality.

> ➤ Consider whether you require custom application pages to maintain the configuration within the site, in a central site, or at the Central Administration level.

> ➤ Does your custom functionality require configuration through a service request to a central team, or can it be added immediately onto your site? Keep in mind that not all site owners have the access required to activate site collection Features. Therefore, if your custom solution requires a site collection Feature activation, this would result in a service request to the central team.

For advanced web parts, consider using tool parts to make it really easy for site owners to configure your custom web part.

Processes, Workflows, and Structures

Consider the business process that end users follow when using your solution. Does your functionality work with them, or against them?

What underlying processes within SharePoint 2010 used by central administrators or by power users exist to support your custom functionality? Is it intuitive and easy to manage your custom functionality?

What supporting structures does your custom functionality require to work correctly? What assumptions does your custom functionality rely on to function normally? What happens if an underlying list is changed or deleted? How does your custom functionality respond?

Past experience has shown that standout solutions are those solutions that handle unexpected failure well. This is because the architect and developer have thought carefully about the types of issues that could occur, and have written code to handle specific exceptions and to present helpful error messages back to the user.

Security Planning and User Permissions

It is vital that you plan for security in the design of any custom functionality. The custom functionality should not provide unintentional access to users who have not been given permission to view the content.

Another common issue relates to development engineers using "god-like" permissions during development. Once deployed, users with visitor or read-only permissions experience issues relating to use of a low-level permission. Therefore, it is important for developers and testers to test any custom functionality using the lowest permission level your custom functionality supports.

Consider the permission roles your custom functionality requires. Will you automatically configure these permissions when deploying your custom functionality to a site collection? Do you require manual configuration of permissions, and, if so, have you accurately documented the manual configuration steps?

Governance and Maintenance Requirements

It is important to think about how the custom functionality will be managed (governed) in your production environment. What are the roles that are required to manage this solution?

What are the common business and technical maintenance activities you will require to maintain the solution in a production environment? Have you documented and communicated these expectations to your stakeholders to plan in their budget for ongoing maintenance and support?

From a code perspective, how will you maintain the code? Has it been "labeled" and versioned in your source code control environment? If defects are picked up that need resolution, how you will your resolve these issues and regression-test any fixes to enable a smooth update to your production environment? Chapter 18 provides detailed guidance on managing software development from development to production environments.

You should always seek to design solutions where planned updates can be released within two to three months. In today's fast-paced digital world, if end users wait longer than this, they will grow impatient and lose faith in your custom solution.

Keep in mind that most end users are not technical. As a result, they may not appreciate the underlying complexity, cost, and effort that may have been put into your six months' worth of development. All they will see is that it took six months and all they got was "XYX."

Therefore, it is recommended that you structure your maintenance updates so that updates (with exciting new Features) can be deployed and communicated to your key stakeholders on a regular basis.

DOCUMENTING YOUR SOLUTION ARCHITECTURE AND DESIGN

One of the hallmarks of a great solution architect is the ability to capture your solution architecture and technical designs in written format. For technically oriented folk, this can sometimes be quite a challenge for a number of reasons, including the following:

➤ *Demanding delivery schedule* — A demanding schedule, coupled with delivery of the Features required by the business, may provide less time to perform what is deemed to be non-essential tasks (such as documentation).

➤ *Skillset and focus* — Not all technical architects are great technical authors, which is a specialist skill in itself. The solution architect may prefer to focus on non-documentation-oriented tasks.

➤ *Chosen methodology* — The chosen methodology may call for less or more documentation during the course of the project.

If someone were designing your dream home or skyscraper, would you be okay with them doing it from memory? If no blueprint of the skyscraper were available during the construction phase of a large building, would the designers of the building appear "professional" in your eyes? The same applies to the solution architecture and technical design. You will surely agree that, based on previous project experiences, this is an area in which everyone can improve.

How much documentation is enough, how much is overkill, and how little will simply appear unprofessional? The answer depends on a number of factors, including the following:

➤ *Solution complexity* — The amount of documentation required for a small solution (such as a web part) differs greatly from an entire program of work standardizing an enterprise SharePoint 2010 platform and developing the customizations required.

➤ *Chosen development methodology* — The chosen development methodology may prescribe what documentation is required, when it should be written, and what it should cover.

➤ *Customer* — Your customer will most likely have internal software, architecture, development, and deployment documentation standards. Regardless of whether you work directly with a customer, or are a supplier of specialist SharePoint skills, you must not fall short of the customer's expectations. Doing so, unless agreed upon, could jeopardize future business opportunities.

➤ *Microsoft Partner standards* — Microsoft and Microsoft SharePoint Partners seek to maintain high standards of quality. This includes standards related to project documentation.

➤ *Commercial agreement* — Your commercial agreement with the customer may set expectations on the level of quality expected from a supplier of SharePoint skills. Make sure you meet those expectations.

The typical types of documentation that are delivered as part of an enterprise SharePoint solution include the following:

➤ Requirements and use case documentation

➤ User experience designs, prototypes, and vision demonstrators

➤ Solution, information, and infrastructure architecture documentation

➤ A record of key design decisions, who participated, why a particular path was chosen, and so forth

➤ A risk log to manage risks and issues emanating from the software development life cycle

➤ Individual technical designs and use case realizations

➤ Quality assurance evidence of functional and non-functional testing, code reviews, unit testing, and performance testing reports

➤ Deployment documentation, including releases notes, deployment step-by-step guides, and ongoing maintenance actions required

Without documentation, the following may occur:

➤ Your development/engineering team may struggle to understand your blueprint.

➤ Your test team may not understand what to test.

➤ Your project manager may not understand and factor in technical risk.

➤ Your customer or organization may struggle to maintain your solution after you have moved on to the next project.

➤ Your subsequent solution architect may wonder what on earth possessed you during the design phase of your project.

There is always a balance to be maintained relating to documentation. Keep in mind that documentation is not the end deliverable. Rather, it is the supporting act to the main performance. Great supporting documentation separates the amateurs from the professionals.

SUMMARY

It is important to understand the responsibilities of the SharePoint solution architect and the relationships with other key architectural activities occurring in your project.

In large projects, the role of the SharePoint architect tends to be split into information, infrastructure, and solution architecture. More often than not (especially in small- to medium-sized projects), one person fulfills all three roles. Regardless of whether you are responsible for one or all three SharePoint architecture roles, ensure that you understand what is required of your role, and deliver and execute well.

Make the right decisions early on to avoid pain down the line. To do this, there is excellent advice available in this book, and from very experienced members of the SharePoint community on the Web. Finally, Microsoft really has improved the level of content and guidance available to you. This advice and guidance is available from MSDN, TechNet, and through the Microsoft SharePoint Patterns and Practices Group.

Chapter 16 provides a detailed look at the various elements to consider relating to the design of your SharePoint 2010 infrastructure.

16

Designing Your Infrastructure Architecture

By Neil Hodgkinson

A significant part of the process you follow as the architect of a SharePoint Server 2010 platform involves studying the options that are available to meet the needs of the business into which the farm is going to be deployed. This process has several stages, and this chapter helps you draw some of these together into one place where you can make those selections and decide on the best possible option for your circumstance.

In this chapter, you learn about the key pieces of the project documentation needed to gather those key parameters and requirements that will help you design the infrastructure. Earlier chapters of this book covered these topics in much more detail. However, this chapter also looks at the key issues. Following are the topics for review:

- ➤ Project requirements
- ➤ Information architecture
- ➤ Solution architecture
- ➤ SharePoint software boundaries
- ➤ Non-functional requirements of the project

After reviewing what you need and what the business needs, you learn about how and where you can house or locate the platform, including choices for data center services and how they can impact what you design. You also learn about the importance of understanding the impact a deployment of Microsoft SharePoint Server 2010 will have on the network infrastructure, and how it may affect the choices you make for ensuring that the end user has as good an experience as possible.

This chapter concentrates on designing the infrastructure required for your SharePoint 2010 deployment. This involves determining the size and power of your deployed platform in relation to your required capacity and performance requirements. Following this, the actual process of designing the farm topology and dependent technology infrastructure is examined. Technologies included here are SQL Server, Active Directory (AD), and Windows Server, plus other non-essential (but important) products, such as operations manager, antivirus, and backup tools.

The chapter concludes with an examination of operations management, as well as Service Level Agreement (SLA) and Operating Level Agreement (OLA) management, backup and restore operations (including disaster recovery and high-availability choices), plus security.

DESIGNING YOUR DATA CENTER SERVICES

The very concept of a data center often sets the imagination stirring when you think of huge rooms containing thousands of computers and their ancillary supporting equipment (such as tape silos and power supply units). Because it was born from the days of large computer rooms and dedicated engineering requirements and support teams, this view of a data center is a natural projection. Nowadays, the concept of the data center has changed and, gladly, for the better. Computers are now deployed to anything from small departmental locations all the way up to the enterprise Tier 4 extreme-scale computing facilities. Many of the largest corporations in the world must satisfy the demands of their businesses' thirst for compute power.

Probably something that won't need to be given too much thought for the SharePoint architect is planning the data center locations, but what will be important is considering the placement of services within data centers already owned by the corporation. When you think of SharePoint and its many workloads, the question of where to most effectively locate your infrastructure often comes up. Typically, the questions surrounding this consideration are similar to the following:

➤ Should it be closer to the main body of end users?

➤ Do you need to account for usage patterns? Is collaborative use more demanding on the network infrastructure than portal/read-only access?

➤ Do you need multiple locations with some form of replication technology between them?

Traditionally, SharePoint Server architects have opted for one of two models: the single global farm or the distributed farm architecture. Each approach has many pros and cons. However, more recently with the advent of faster, cheaper networking, the single global farm has been the more popular choice for performance-based decisions. The use of a second data center is, however, a preferred choice when it comes to disaster recovery for critical services.

A dual data center provides the ultimate in data redundancy. But setting up an exact duplicate of your existing data center can be expensive, both initially and on an ongoing basis. So, the first question you should ask yourself is, "Does a dual data center make sense for my business?"

The answer to this question really depends on the nature of your business. If your business absolutely depends on 24/7, year-round availability, a dual data center is probably a must. But you have other reasons to maintain a dual location. Knowing that you have a standby location that is outfitted and ready to be used on a few hours of notice certainly provides peace of mind and makes a lot of sense.

Building a secondary data center location for such an eventuality is no mean feat, and from a networking standpoint, requires low latency and high bandwidth to achieve instant synchronization of data. Making use of asynchronous techniques and using storage area network (SAN)—based or storage over IP technologies leads to significant savings in this area. A secondary benefit of asynchronous-based technologies is that they have little or no limitations on the distance between the data centers, which allows you to now support true geographical separation. Geographically separating the two data centers improves your organization's odds of recovering from an environmental disaster that strikes one of your data center locations.

The SharePoint Server architect must have a very good appreciation of cloud-based locations (whether you are referring to the private cloud or a true public cloud). The end game of a new SharePoint deployment is to provide a service that meets the needs of the business, offering it the tools and workloads to succeed. It may not always be necessary to look to deploy a SharePoint Server 2010 farm to achieve that objective. Hosting companies have been around for a long time, offering point solutions of SharePoint Server, but often with little or no integration with other services. Recently, the drive has been to build the holistic platform that integrates SharePoint workloads with Microsoft Office clients, e-mail, and presence capabilities.

For several years, Microsoft has had a hosted platform called Business Productivity Online Suite (BPOS), which comes in a shared and dedicated offering. More recently, Microsoft launched its Office 365 (O365) platform, which is a true scalable, multi-tenant service that offers SharePoint Server 2010, Exchange Server 2010, and Lync 2010 as a combined package. The competition in this space is huge, and Microsoft's competitors are gaining momentum, with Google and SalesForce offering niche capabilities (albeit as a much more fragmented offering).

Many factors are involved when it comes to looking at the data center design. As already mentioned, many years ago, the data center was typically a huge room packed with different equipment from different manufacturers, and was only understood by a few technical staff members. The evolution of the data center is mainstream in the so-called *generation three phase*, where you have high-density computing capabilities in purpose-built facilities, and *generation four* is well on the way to becoming the new mainstream providing ultra-high-density modular computing infrastructure.

Data centers need different types of service infrastructure to not only support the deployment of large-scale computing services, but also to support these deployments reliably and economically. The following sections detail (or reference) the prime considerations for the data center architect.

Power/Electrical Services

Without question, the number one highest cost associated with running a data center is the power required to maintain it. Newer equipment can offer improvements in performance and space, but these improvements typically come with greater requirements for operational and cooling power. In recent times (and with the advent of the mega data center, such as those built by Microsoft in Chicago and Dublin), power for cooling has been a major concern.

Power usage effectiveness (PUE) is a metric used to determine the energy efficiency of a data center. PUE is determined by dividing the amount of power entering a data center by the power used to run the computer infrastructure within it. Therefore, PUE is expressed as a ratio, with overall efficiency improving as the quotient decreases toward 1.

Data center efficiency (DCE) is the reciprocal of PUE, and is expressed as a percentage that improves as it approaches 100 percent. Getting to the Utopian 100 percent DCE is not something that will happen quickly, but with the increasing cost of power all over the world, it is certainly a driver that all data center companies take very seriously.

> *Microsoft has published a number of operational guides explaining how it approaches some of the challenges of building, maintaining, and operating a modern data center. You can find these guides at* www .globalfoundationservices.com/infrastructure/index.html. *To understand the implications of what even a new server farm can add to the resources consumption within the data center, you should review these before considering any data center deployment.*

Network and Connectivity

When deploying to a data center, there is a general assumption that all networking services will be in place, and the servers will be hooked up and ready to run. Although for a properly planned implementation this is probably true, you have a number of things to consider before reaching this point.

Most notably is whether the service being deployed should use different networks for the various services being consumed or offered. For example, in a typical SharePoint farm deployment, the biggest concern might be ensuring that a high-performance connection exists between the SharePoint servers and the end user. Certainly, this is a high priority, but other considerations should also be given attention.

At least three other networks could be required, in addition to the end-user connectivity, when deploying any form of service. These include the following:

➤ Inter-server communications

➤ Management network

➤ Backup network

Each of these networks must be considered as a part of the deployment. Inter-server communications are expected to comply with the planning guidance for SharePoint farms, which broadly states a requirement for sub-millisecond latency, and a minimum of 1 GB bandwidth between servers. Network impact assessment is examined later in this chapter, and it is the outcome of this work that will determine the requirement for the management and backup networks.

Impact assessment aside, the use of separate physical or virtual local-area networks (LANs) for management and backup can be a good practice, and can reduce the load on the user-facing interfaces. In practice, implementing a SharePoint server farm with all these interfaces can be difficult — each server requires multiple network cards, and, to be allocated, multiple IP addresses are required to maintain the network separation. The SharePoint architect should always consider these aspects when designing the deployment. The SharePoint architect should engage the services of a network architect to help develop and design the required infrastructure based on the output from the network impact assessment.

Data and Application Storage

Data storage is covered extensively in Chapter 17, where different types of storage are considered, as well as how to effectively plan that storage based on the business requirements.

Virtualization

Virtualization is having a massive impact on data center operations and management. Being able to run multiple server platforms on hardware that would previously have supported only one server has huge implications for cost and flexibility.

 Chapter 23 covers virtualization exhaustively by looking at different technologies and strategies for virtualization.

Management

When it comes down to determining what management features are required in the data center, you can never really have enough. Physical management of the assets in the server rooms, along with management of the power supply capacity and backup power facilities, are all critically important in any data center management strategy.

In addition to the local resources, there is a huge need for remote-management capability, for clients to manage their own systems, and for the hosting company support teams to be able to access the servers 24 hours a day, 7 days a week. This access should include not only traditional remote desktop access to running servers, but also access to the virtual hosts they run on when the environment is virtualized. With the aid of "lights out" boards, it is possible to access even the BIOS level or a server as it is rebooted, thus further reducing the need for physical presence in the server rooms.

You should manage assets using an effective Configuration Management Database (CMDB), but this is only as good as the people using it. A CMDB is a library of relevant information related to all the components of an information system. It contains the details of the configuration items (CI) in the IT infrastructure. The CMDB is used by an organization to understand and control the relationships between all of the authorized assets within the infrastructure, and how those assets are configured. The CMDB is a fundamental component of the ITIL framework's Configuration Management process.

Configuration managers usually describe CIs using three configurable attributes:

➤ Technical

➤ Ownership

➤ Relationship

A key success factor in implementing a CMDB is the capability to automatically discover information about the CIs (auto-discovery) and track changes as they happen. All modifications and exceptions must be added to the database to make it valuable and relevant to the organization.

Protection

Chapter 21 covers how to protect your SharePoint platform from the perspective of data protection. Realistically, that's what companies want to protect, and an effective business continuity plan is as valuable as any other part of the farm design.

So, what about the other side of the security and protection story — physical protection? You must consider physical protection of the environment from multiple angles, as shown in Table 16-1.

TABLE 16-1: Protection of the Environment

PROTECTION	CONSIDERATIONS
Data center architecture	Consider local environment for flood and other possible physical damage.
Access controls	Strict control over access to the server rooms should be in place at all times. All access and egress should be monitored, captured, and retained for audit purposes.
	Physical unauthorized access to the machines should be impossible. Solid slab-to-slab walls and high-security doors are always preferred.
	Do not broadcast the data center location. If you need to know where it is, you will know. Otherwise, the data center could look like an ordinary warehouse or storage facility from the outside.
	Motion detectors, closed circuit TV, and all lighting cameras are the minimum requirements to assist the security guards in physical protection.
Fire prevention	It's better to invest in fire prevention than firefighting. Take guidance from the local fire brigade on good practice.
	Use professionally installed fire-protection systems, alarms, heat detectors, and smoke detectors.
	Keep server rooms free from clutter, especially packaging and printouts.
	Watch the power loading to ensure no over-loading is done.

The majority of these activities seems to be common sense, and should be second nature to anyone in the industry. Consider treating the data center as a highly secure version of your home (and the contents within it), as if the data center included your personal articles and details. Then consider the fact that the contents of the data center could be millions of records for people or confidential details of company research or activities. The value of this data is incalculable not only to the people who own it or the company that developed and researched it, but to the potential identity or data thief who wants to steal or destroy it.

The highest order of security and safety is an absolute must for these installations, and should local laws allow it, it should not be known that armed guards are employed at these installations.

PERFORMING A NETWORK IMPACT ASSESSMENT

The *network impact assessment* addresses the current network bandwidth compared to planned application moves and changes. It identifies the locations and applications, and any other specific information required to ascertain the impact of application additions and moves between locations.

It is all too easy to overlook this stage of the planning by assuming the network resources will be adequate to handle new loads or changes in load. Imagine a scenario in which a company decides to centralize and consolidate a number of file shares by migrating the required data into SharePoint. Prior to the migration, users may have accessed the data from a much closer location than where it has been moved to, especially if the company is adopting a central farm deployment and some users are in a far-flung location.

Identifying Current WAN Utilization

One of the first things that you must understand is the baseline for the existing network infrastructure. Only when this baseline is established will you be able to predict what the impact from additional SharePoint Server 2010 traffic is likely to be.

The most problematic scenarios are likely to arise when the wide-area network (WAN) bandwidth or latency is sufficiently poor that it cannot take any additional load. As a rule of thumb, you can generally assume network bandwidth or latency within the same LAN is not going to be the cause of bottlenecks, should they arise.

The simplest way to determine the baseline model of the network is to measure incoming and outgoing bytes on the network interface. This can be a daily, weekly, and even monthly roll-up to report on the saturation of the existing network links. Comparing the measured values with what should be known about the WAN link, you can predict whether your expected user load will exceed your circuit limits.

Identifying Bandwidth Demands for Proposed Application Architecture

When you look at the typical user interaction with SharePoint Server 2010, you can see many different workloads and many different types of user activity and requirements within each of the workloads. The task here is to come up with a plan that encompasses all eventualities. In practice, it is better to select only a few scenarios and generalize them based on the type of content you know matches the business needs. This can also be added to the network footprint that is transferred each time a client accesses SharePoint for the first time.

As an example, consider two scenarios — users accessing SharePoint content for the purpose of browsing pages (perhaps a corporate intranet deployment), and users interacting with a document management system also deployed on SharePoint. The first scenario would generally be limited to only a handful of pages per hour, with each page being of web-like content, so it would be relatively lightweight. The latter is quite a different scenario because the users will be working with actual written documentation and content, and will need to download this for editing. Predicting the type and frequency of load on a per-workload/per-user basis will provide values you can use in determining the additional load on the WAN.

Consider a user who is working within the document management facility in a large enterprise. It would not be unrealistic so assume something along the lines of the following:

> 5 requests per hour @ 1 MB per document = 11.11 Kbps

In addition, you could assume the following:

> 3 requests per hour @ 4 MB per document = 26.67 Kbps

This results in a user load of 37.78 Kbps.

If you know how many of these users exist, you can begin to predict the total utilization required on the network. This piece of work is fraught with the possibility of under- and/or over-exaggeration, so it is important (where possible) to use measured data to predict the user load.

Now, SharePoint Server 2010 has far more workloads than the ones discussed so far. The impact these different workloads have on the network will vary, and so it is important to understand each one whenever possible. A number of non-user base interactions, too, such as search crawling, can introduce significant load on the Web Front-End (WFE) and database servers.

Identifying Bottlenecks Likely to Impact Your Enterprise WAN Performance

When all the data is in, and predictions of usage have been made, the data can be compared added to see if it exceeds the planned threshold. A typical acceptable threshold would be 70 percent utilization. A threshold greater than that might result in a propensity for networks to become saturated, and lead to connectivity issues. Network links may be dependent. For example, the link between Country A and Country C might have to traverse Country A to Country B, and then Country B to Country C to reach its destination. When this is the case, be sure to factor in the overall circuit impact for a user in Country C accessing data in Country A.

If a potential bottleneck is discovered, it can be addressed in different ways. A recommended increase in the bandwidth can be an expensive and time-consuming operation, and so can following a suggestion for a network accelerator device to be placed at the slowest links. Short of those choices, though, very limited options are available, and, generally, many projects will go ahead regardless.

To understand the footprint going forward, it is important to ensure that new servers for the farm are added to any management/monitoring for network utilization.

ESTIMATING YOUR FARM'S CAPACITY AND PERFORMANCE REQUIREMENTS

Planning a design to meet the performance characteristics requested by the business is an almost impossible task to get right the first time around. As a result, many deployments will be built around fairly simple server farm topologies that offer fault tolerance and resilience at all tiers.

In these deployments, rules of thumb are used to estimate whether the hardware specifications and the number of machines being deployed will actually meet the design requirements. This approach does not make for bad designs and failed projects. In fact, using rules of thumb and best practices will often lead to designs that have been well-planned with respect to growth. How the architect chooses to approach the performance planning will depend on factors such as amount of data and number of users.

More importantly, the choice depends on the activity that these users will be undertaking, and considerations such as heavy customizations can dramatically alter the design proposal.

You learn about user load, customizations, and performance testing aspects of this design work later in this book. However, here you concentrate on the hardware and software planning guidelines for the different farm tiers, as well as look at ways to manage the farm for future updates and manageability requirements.

Performance Planning Concepts

When planning for performance, you really must understand what it means to examine the characteristics of the farm, and how the design choices affect those characteristics. Microsoft defines the following four fundamentals of performance:

- ➤ *Latency* — This is the time taken from an end user selecting a link on a page to the final byte being returned to the end-user browser after the request has been processed.

- ➤ *Throughput* — This is the total number of concurrent requests that a server or server farm can process. As a best practice, designers should strive to accommodate a peak throughput, even when the average may be much lower.

- ➤ *Data scale* — This includes considerations for total size and shape of the data that will always come into play during scale discussions. How much data there actually is, and how it needs to be stored, will affect database size and requirements for storage design.

- ➤ *Reliability* — This includes the long-term stability of the farm, and its capability to deliver the performance objectives defined at the outset.

The main purpose of performance planning is to design a system that meets the requirements of the organization across all four of the fundamentals. What should be immediately clear is that each of these base performance-defining characteristics is dependent on at least one other. For example, there is no possible way of achieving good end-to-end latency if the throughput or data storage design introduces performance bottlenecks.

Because the performance fundamentals are inextricably linked, each of them must be considered when designing the farm. Concentrating on any one of them at the expense of the others will lead to a less than optimized experience for the end user. Some key considerations (in generic terms) are highlighted here and throughout the book for scenarios in which you have defined specific optimizations for individual components or services.

You can make many optimizations to lessen the impact on the end-user experience, including the following:

- ➤ Architectural components should be procured, developed, and configured to deliver the maximum possible performance. This includes not only the physical servers, their storage, and other hardware or appliances (such as network routers, switches, and firewalls), but also the software-based server applications. SharePoint, IIS, SQL, antivirus software, and everything else defined in the design should also be configured properly.

➤ Web page development and other customizations (including applications and branding) must follow best practice guidelines to ensure that the code isn't a source of processing bottlenecks leading to significant latency impact. Optimizations of this type include making good use of the caching options offered by SharePoint and ASP.NET, while, at the same time, ensuring these options are properly configured. The client-side configuration must also be included in this optimization. Avoid adding custom code to pages that are likely to be accessed frequently (such as a standard corporate landing page). Instead, host the custom code on pages where the users expect to make use of the custom functionality. Use SharePoint Server list column indexes when you are retrieving a filtered amount of data. Page payload optimizations (such as reducing the sizes of image files, as well as making use of ASP.NET sprite controls and framework to decrease page render time) are vitally important to the end user having a good experience.

➤ It is important to think about the placement of content and the number of server round trips with regard to the impact on latency. If possible, locate images and static resources in folders that do not require multiple clients/servers, or web servers, to access SQL Server. Additionally, reduce SQL round trips by requesting only the amount of data you need per request, and limit the number of requests. A simple way to think about this when considering the type of content your pages will display and where that content is being delivered from is not to take a dependency on something you cannot afford. Use asynchronous processing where possible to ensure that the end user can begin to interact with the site pages at the earliest available opportunity. This is especially important with JavaScript, which, if poorly optimized or used inline (as opposed to calling scripts), can lead to poor client-side rendering.

To meet the throughput demands on the system, it is important to design for peak loads so that even when under high load and maximum demand, the system can deliver the required performance to the end users. When planning to meet these required performance levels, you need an understanding of the resource costs for farm operations. This is especially important when planning the type of web and load testing that will be done to measure the maximum throughput of the proposed design. (You learn more about this in Chapter 20.)

In many deployments, inadequate hardware can be a source of bottlenecks, leading to request queuing and long request execution times. Both of these issues can be monitored for and alerted against when using System Center Operations Manager (SCOM) to monitor the farm. Optimizing the farm throughput is a non-trivial task, and will require iteratively measuring, tuning, and re-measuring to get it right. Following are some key points to watch for:

➤ Consider CPU usage when under load. Sustained levels in excess of 80 percent are considered too high, and will result in lengthening ASP.NET queues on the web servers. Mitigate this by adding additional web servers to the farm, or by moving services to less-utilized servers.

➤ Database performance is a key factor in the overall performance of the farm. As you have already learned earlier in this chapter, following the best practice guidelines is essential to making this work. The disk system is often the vital ingredient to a well-performing

SQL server, and redistributing the databases appropriately is important to delivering the optimum throughout.

➤ Consider the role of the Application server in the farm, and the resources required for the enabled services. For example, servers hosting the SharePoint Server 2010 Search Query and Site Settings Service (Query Processor) should have sufficient RAM available to cache as many records as possible from the security descriptors table of the Search Service Administrator database. This reduces database round trips for security trimming of search results.

Data scale encompasses a number of concepts, such as data distribution, data size, and server hardware capabilities. Thus, the data scale of the farm is the amount of data that can be stored on the farm while still meeting the required performance metrics. SharePoint is capable of utilizing multiple SQL Server platforms for holding its data and services databases. Therefore, the main requirement is to ensure that the data hosted by those SQL servers is distributed efficiently across disks that deliver high numbers of Input-Output Operations Per Second (IOPS) with low seek time.

Some of the SharePoint Server 2010 Services are heavy users of disk I/O. Search Crawl, logging, and Web Analytics are good examples of these, and distributing their databases across dedicated spindles to maximize performance is a requirement in larger enterprise deployments.

Finally, *reliability* refers to the capability of the farm to deliver services to end users for the duration of its lifetime in accordance with the required performance levels. A reliable farm is also one where maintenance operations and daily service jobs do not impact the overall end-user experience. Careful consideration of when and where these activities take place is essential planning. To maintain the reliability of the farm, consider the following:

➤ Ensure that operations on the SQL servers are performed outside of core business hours. This includes backup operations and database index-maintenance tasks. Typically, good database administrators will work with the SharePoint administrators to configure appropriate maintenance operations, and this is a great opportunity to build an effective maintenance suite for subsequent deployments.

➤ Modify the more resource-intensive timer jobs on the SharePoint farm to run at periods of low demand, or use the preferred server function of the timer job to run it on a dedicated server.

Run multiple instances of services across several servers to ensure that enough resources are always available to deliver a response to end users within the required latency period. If necessary, scale up or scale out to meet the demand.

Estimating Required Throughput

Now that you know how to plan the ongoing capacity management of your farm, you must determine where to start. That is to say, what is the capacity of the farm you need to deploy for Day One? Understanding the methodology to determine the throughput is essential to this process, and has several stages to it.

Properly sizing a SharePoint Server 2010 implementation requires an understanding of not only the demands that will be placed on it by end users, but also by the farm administrators and any SharePoint functionality that will impact a specific load (such as the timer jobs that affect content databases). These latter two aspects are often overlooked, and, yet, they can have a potentially large contribution to the overall demand.

To be able to approach an accurate model of the desired throughput required for the farm, it is essential that data is available to define the following metrics:

➤ *Workload* — Put simply, this is the user base and the different characteristics of those users for how they interact with the farm.

➤ *Concurrent users* — This is probably the most misinterpreted and misrepresented aspect of capacity planning, and especially usage pattern modeling. Architects must be very wary of this.

➤ *Requests per second (RPS)* — This describes the demand on the server farm expressed in the number of requests processed by the farm per second. This value does not take into account the different user bases and workloads.

➤ *Total daily requests* — This is defined as the total number of requests served by the farm that involve content. Authentication handshakes are not included in this, so be wary of counting requests from an IIS log, because that will undoubtedly result in an overestimate unless the handshake is filtered out.

➤ *Total daily users* — For this, you are looking for unique users per day, and this does not represent the total user population of the organization. It is worth bearing in mind how this value aligns with the total potential number of users as a means to predict future growth as adoption accelerates.

Let's look at some of these parameters and expand on the key points.

Workload Distribution

Before you can predict the workload, you must understand the user activities in terms that can be grouped together. For those who are familiar with Microsoft Office SharePoint Server 2007 (MOSS 2007), the groups were generally described in accordance with workloads based on Shared Service Providers (SSPs), and, in particular, Search, Excel Calculation Services, Business Data Catalog, and the User Profile service. This model will not work for Microsoft SharePoint Server 2010, because the sheer number of workloads has increased to encompass both much-improved and completely new capabilities.

Each SharePoint service application must be considered on its own, and, with a wider range of client applications capable of directly interfacing with the farm, the model becomes more complex and challenging. New client features such as Outlook Social Connector and the co-authoring platforms will be especially demanding, not to mention the expected high adoption of Office Web Applications (OWA) for the rich Office document interaction.

You must place the all projected occurrences of a specific workload type together and express that as a percentage of the overall usage pattern. Microsoft has provided a checklist for this at `http://technet.microsoft.com/en-us/library/ff758645.aspx`.

The checklist includes user activities through the browser interface, through Microsoft Office client interactions (including Outlook RSS), and through SharePoint workspaces. It also accounts for custom web services and activities. The worksheet should be completed as fully as possible with the estimated values. Remember that, until you actually measure the numbers, all you can do is provide estimates.

These values constitute the business and technical demand that form the basis of the business drivers, which, in turn, allow the architect to map to technical drivers. These technical drivers take the form of resources such as CPU, memory, and disk usage that are the basic building blocks for assessing resource supply, as in the number of servers, amount of memory, and number of disks that are needed to satisfy the original demand.

Following the style presented in the Microsoft article mentioned earlier, Figure 16-1 shows data represented as a factor of the percentage of requests per workload and requests per user for each workload.

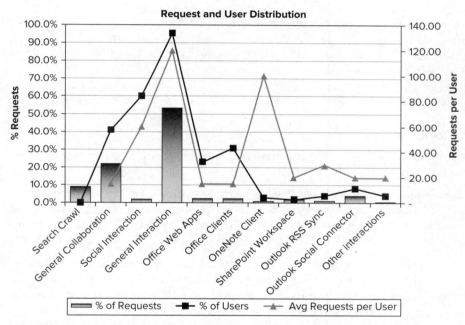

FIGURE 16-1: Chart from using the Microsoft checklist for measuring workload distribution

As already mentioned, the initial pass of defining the workload is based on estimates gathered from business analysis and expected usage. The most important things to understand are the transactions that will impart the biggest impact on the farm in terms of requests per user and the estimated load per transaction.

To estimate your expected workload, collect the following information:

➤ Identify user interactions based on the checklist described earlier. You should be especially focused on identifying the unique interactions for your users and the use of specialized service applications (such as Excel Services, Business Data Catalog, and InfoPath, to name just a few).

➤ Identify system-wide operations, including those scheduled for Search crawls, SQL backups, and SQL maintenance. Profile sync timer jobs. Web Analytics and logging timer jobs can also play a significant part in the overall farm load. Specifically, having crawling overlapping with database index rebuild/reorganization can impart an unacceptable load on SQL Server.

➤ Focus on the peak hours to begin to estimate the total number of users utilizing each product capability, and from there, derive the estimated concurrency and requests per second. You always focus on the peak periods of usage to be sure the farm can comfortably sustain the highest observed load.

If this deployment is a replacement of an earlier build out, analysis of the IIS logs can assist in more accurately tracking the metrics you need.

 For detailed information about how to analyze SharePoint Server 2010 usage using Log Parser, read "Analyzing Microsoft SharePoint Products and Technologies Usage" at `http://www.microsoft.com/downloads/details .aspx?familyid=f159af68-c3a3-413c-a3f7-2e0be6d5532e&displaylang=en&tm.`

Requests per Second

Requests per second (RPS) is almost universally used to define the size of farm that is needed to accommodate the load generated by the user base.

As an example calculation, let's say you have 100,000 users accessing SharePoint 10 times a day, which will generate 27 user transactions per second (that is, users multiplied by transactions, and that number divided by 36,000, which is 10-hour day in seconds). If you take this one step further and assume 10 requests are made to SharePoint per transaction, you get 27*10 or 270 overall RPS.

When using an existing IIS log or the new SharePoint 2010 Logging Database to estimate new farm requirements, or, indeed, to measure the details after going live, it is important to filter out the requests that can bias the results. Authentication handshakes are relatively inexpensive transactions, so it makes sense to remove all 401 responses from the calculation.

Content/Data Set

When you look at the content or the data set for the farm, you should provide a description of the total volume being stored and the characteristics of that content. Bear in mind that while describing these characteristics, it can be difficult to provide parameters that are not generalized and yet still remain useful for your calculations.

➤ *Content size* — Knowing how much content will be stored in SharePoint will help to plan the required number and sizes of databases. From a workload perspective, the biggest impact is on Search. The Search solution will need to be sized to accommodate the indexing of all the content in the farm.

➤ *Number of documents* — The importance of this metric becomes apparent when looking at the overall shape of the data. A simple example would be comparing a farm that has 100 video files that are 1 GB each stored in a document library with another farm that has 20,000 text files that are 5 KB each. The behavior of the SharePoint server farm will be quite different not only with respect to the location of the objects, but also with respect to how a service application such as Search will handle such content.

➤ *Maximum site collections size* — Reviewing the logical architecture, you should be able to predict which will be the largest site collection. Overall, the total number and size of the site collections will help you to plan the data architecture for the farm.

➤ *Service applications* — From a dataset perspective, the service applications have different characteristics. As an example, Search stores its data both on disk and in at least three databases. Other databases such as the Logging database and Web Analytics databases can be very large, too.

Farm Reliability

The last of your four concepts for performance planning is reliability, and this metric should always be included in the requirements-gathering phase of the project. The type of targets here are goals such as page delivery time, or how long it takes for a page to load once the user clicks a link, and the most important metric for the overall availability of the farm, which is usually linked quite closely to the SLA. Tracking unexpected downtime is important to understanding the external influences within the environment that can cause an outage in SharePoint Server 2010.

A well-maintained SharePoint Server 2010 farm should be able to achieve four nines (that is, 99.99 percent) availability, which equates to around 43 minutes per month of unplanned outage. Given the dependency on SQL Server and AD, it is vital to be sure those components are operating optimally, as well as the SharePoint servers. Monitoring the server availability, responsiveness (especially when under load), and the level of resource usage can help you manage and predict when a farm is either at or approaching a stress point.

DESIGNING YOUR LOGICAL AND PHYSICAL ARCHITECTURE

When it comes to designing the required topology of the farm, you have many different opportunities for providing an infrastructure design to offer very high levels of flexibility for collaboration, or for isolating content to ensure data security and privacy. Throughout the process, it is important to ensure that the requirements for the level of collaboration or isolation are known and understood, as well as the consequences of the choices made to satisfy those requirements.

The purpose of logical and physical infrastructure architecture is to provide a SharePoint 2010 platform to host your information and solution architecture.

This section discusses the logical and physical considerations to review when designing the underlying physical infrastructure. The first step will be to look at the logical architecture and the impact those decisions make on what you may deploy. This is followed by a look at the physical deployment needed to support the logical architecture.

Understanding Your SharePoint 2010 Logical Components

Within this book, many sections (and, indeed, whole chapters) are dedicated to the logical farm components. This section looks at those logical components that have a physical manifestation.

For example, here you learn about content databases and site collections, but not zones or web application policies. Following are the aspects of the architecture you learn about here:

➤ *Server farm* — This is the highest least-granular view of a logical architecture design for SharePoint Server.

➤ *Service applications* — These are SharePoint capabilities that can be (and may) run on one or more web servers enabled in the farm, such as Business Connectivity Services (BCS) or User Profile service.

➤ *Web applications* — These are essentially IIS websites that are used by SharePoint Server 2010.

➤ *Content databases* — These provide the web applications with content storage. Content databases can store many different site collections.

➤ *Site collections* — These include one or more related sites that have the same owner and share administration settings.

➤ *Sites* — These include one or more web pages and other items (such as lists, libraries, and documents) that are hosted inside a site collection.

Server Farm

The concept of the server farm has been around for many years. From a SharePoint perspective, a server farm is all of the SharePoint servers that have been joined to the same configuration database, and generally includes the SQL servers hosting all the databases. Unlike SharePoint servers, however, SQL servers may service more than one SharePoint farm at the same time, so they do not truly represent a farm member in that sense.

When planning the deployment, it is important to determine as soon as possible whether one or multiple farms will be required. A number of reasons exist to support the argument for multiple farms. Generally, however, the architect may choose this route to support just one reason: isolation. Though isolation of data, people, and processes can be a major decision factor in deciding on the need for one or more farms, this level of isolation can be obtained with even a single farm.

Prudent design of the IIS application pools can achieve the process-level separation needed in many cases. However, it is just as likely that heavy usage of, for example, Search services or User Profile services, might dictate that a services farm is needed. The requirement to reach performance or scalability goals, or to make use of content deployment publishing between author and consumer farms, can be valid reasons for a multiple farm deployment. Other reasons such as geographic restrictions, operational aspects, or funding concerns can also drive the requirement for multiple farms.

Service Applications

The concept of a SharePoint service being encapsulated into a discrete services application is the next logical step after the SSP approach that was available in the MOSS 2007 product. The entire infrastructure for hosting the shared service applications is now included with SharePoint Foundation Server 2010, and is much more flexible than ever before. The farm administrator can pick and choose the required services, and enable only those that are needed to meet established requirements. Service applications are associated with web applications.

Breaking the service applications into isolated resources that can be enabled or disabled as needed has given the SharePoint architect much more control over the purpose of the farm and the services it offers to its end users. The shared service applications can be consumed by one or many web applications on the same farm (or, in some cases, remote farms), and an individual farm can host more than one version of the same shared service application, each having a different configuration than the others.

Service applications can be deployed and used in different ways. For example, a service application can be deployed in the default configuration where the service application and the data are shared across all web applications that consume from that service application. The classic example is Search, where all users can potentially see results from the same core index. If the service application is deployed in partitioned mode, users of the server farm are constrained by a subscription ID for their site that is added as a query restrictor for every request made, thereby limiting the end users to see data only within their explicitly granted sites.

When planning the level of isolation needed, you should take the following configurable items into consideration:

➤ *Connection group or proxy* — Each service application has a connection that can be added to the default group or a custom connection group. The connection is a virtual entity, and is used to connect web applications to a specific group of service applications. A connection may exist in more than one custom group of connections, and connections for multiple service applications of the same type may also exist within the same connection group. In the scenario where multiple service application connections are in the same connection group, the administrator must designate one of them as the default connection.

➤ *Permissions* — Granting permissions to manage the service applications can ease the burden on the farm administrator, and also ensure that the right people are modifying the service application capabilities. Permissions can also be used to further restrict the Features that are exposed to end users. In the User Profile service application, for example, the capability to create My Sites, user social capabilities, and so on, can be limited to all or a limited group of end users.

Service application administration can benefit from the delegation of tasks to specific corporate experts who specialize in, for example, Search or User Profiles. Another great example here is the delegation of the Managed Metadata Service to the corporation information architecture team.

When taking the next step toward the multi-tenant environment, a number of the service applications expose a management interface on the tenant admin site. The User Profile service is one such service application that allows the tenant admin control over the user profiles of the users within the site subscription.

When creating or planning service applications, you have a number of recommended guidelines to follow:

➤ For effective collaboration in environments where enterprise-wide standardization is a requirement, consider sharing the service applications in the default proxy group. This can provide effective isolation of web applications, while maintaining the shared access to personalization, taxonomy, published content types, and other enterprise Features without multiple service application deployments.

➤ A separate set of service applications can be deployed to provide services to partners or other external agencies. Creating a custom proxy group containing these service application connections provides controlled isolation to only the resources needed by the partners.

Finally, when designing the service application strategy, always consider the capabilities of the services themselves. Providing a shared or isolated service doesn't necessarily complete the final picture, and by carefully configuring the services within the connection groups, a better end-user experience may be delivered.

Web Applications

In web server terms, a SharePoint *web application* is an IIS website that is used to host SharePoint 2010 content. The web application itself may be further extended to multiple zones (maximum of five), each hosted on a different IIS site, but considered part of the same web application. Each zone may have a different domain name and/or a different authentication mechanism.

In a typical SharePoint Server 2010 deployment, the web applications may consist of the following:

➤ *Intranet* — This would be a web application devoted to company information and sharing, which is predominantly read-only for all users except a small community of authors.

➤ *Collaboration* — This is usually associated with team or project-based collaboration and sharing. The make-up of this web application typically consists of many site collections and many authors.

➤ *My Site/Social* — This web application consists of a My Site host and a number of site collections (one per person) containing the person profile pages and personal content for each user.

➤ *Extranet* — This is less frequently deployed, and may well be for internal/partner collaboration with federated authentication and a custom service application group.

You have a number of architectural touch points to consider when configuring service applications.

Choosing to use the default proxy group or to create a custom group is an important decision, and is influenced by the needs of the web application users to share their data and services. If the web application is an internal intranet, for example, there is a good chance it will consume from the default group containing the original set of deployed service applications. If the web application is an extranet or partner-access portal, the likelihood is that it will consume from a separate connection group containing only the minimal services applications needed, with each being configured to support the needs of the users in that environment.

Going hand-in-hand with the type of web application is an appreciation of the zone it resides in, and the security policies applied to that zone. In an extranet/partner collaboration scenario, for example, the default zone may be used by internal users via one URL, whereas the external partners may use a different URL with a wholly different authentication mechanism and different user-access policies.

Following are several recommended guidelines to be aware of when planning web applications:

➤ *Isolation* — This entails managing the number and type of web applications to ensure that the content is provided only to the right people. Examples include keeping anonymously available content restricted to a separate web application, and the same or similar approach for partner access sites.

➤ *Security* — By maintaining effective policies on the web application zones, the administrator can ensure that access to the environment cannot be accidentally granted at a lower level in the hierarchy. If a user or group is denied access via policy, they will never be able to access a site on that web application zone, regardless of the permissions granted at a lower level.

➤ *Performance* — By deploying web applications in accordance with usage type and pattern, the architect can ensure that the databases supporting the web applications are accessed for read/write in a similar way. A dedicated web application for portal or intranet content is likely to support heavy read and low write activity, meaning all the databases on that web application can be optimized with respect to disk placement and maintenance to support that activity pattern.

Content Databases

The *content databases* on a SharePoint farm are the repository for all of the end-user data, including metadata and files. All web applications must have a minimum of one content database to host the root site collection and any other site collections added to the web application.

As recently as July 2011, the Microsoft SharePoint product group made a number of capacity planning guideline changes that significantly broadened the support boundaries for content databases. Following is a summary of the guidelines, but you should see `http://technet.microsoft.com/en-us/library/cc262787.aspx#ContentDB` for the most comprehensive updates:

➤ The supported content database size limit remains at 200 GB for general-use scenarios, but has been increased to 4 TB when optimized disk subsystems and carefully planned disaster-recovery capabilities have been implemented. Even within the support of this new 4 TB limit, it is not recommended that individual site collections exceed 100 GB in size. For document archive scenarios, there is no specified upper limit for content database size.

➤ When considering how many items can be stored in an individual database, the largest supported number is 60 million, and includes both documents and list items. Multiple content databases should be deployed if more than 60 million items are being stored on a single web application. In practice, the architect would choose to add more content databases to a web application a long time before the 60-million limit is reached.

Effective content database management allows for very good control over the density of sites per database. Support is offered for scenarios for high isolation with one site per database, and for high density where there may be many hundreds (even thousands) of site collections in a single database. Some simple math can ensure good content distribution of large and small sites to ensure that the most optimal performance is met for the scale of the environment. This can be especially important where high density rather than isolation is the key requirement.

When data isolation is the main requirement, limiting a content database to a single site collection reduces the dependency between projects, and allows for individual backup/restore operations and different SLAs on a per-site basis. It also allows for a unique opportunity to archive the entire database when the project life cycle is complete.

When configuring the content databases, you have very few options to consider. However, you should consider primary location and the location of the failover server, plus the capacity considerations of how many site collections can be stored in the database itself. Once those parameters are set, the only other task is to ensure that an effective database maintenance strategy is implemented.

Administration of databases includes the following:

➤ Creating new databases for new team sites or site collections that require dedicated databases

➤ Monitoring database sizes and creating new databases when target sizes are approached

➤ Backing up and restoring databases

When it comes to planning for content databases, generally two accepted approaches exist: automated site collection distribution, or the manual creation of new databases per site collection. The former requires the administrator to monitor and control the maximum warning and database-full thresholds, allowing a degree of control over where the sites get created.

Site Collections

A *site collection* entails one or many SharePoint sites residing under the same root web. It is an administrative boundary for security, and a navigational boundary for the navigational web parts in SharePoint.

From a capacity-planning perspective, it is recommended that you not exceed 2,000 site collections in a single database, although the upper support limit is 5,000. The main reason for this limit is to avoid significant delays during an upgrade, thereby reducing the anticipated outage time while an upgrade completes. Site collections can be scaled out across multiple database servers to provide additional capacity and throughout.

As already stated, the use of site collections introduces a number of sharing and isolation opportunities that affect permissions, navigation, and Feature deployment. Master pages, page layouts, local images, and site templates are all consumable from within the same site collection. However, they cannot be shared across a site collection boundary.

Other things to be aware of are the fact that within the site collections and the lists, security inheritance is enabled by default, and can be reset if needed to fix a broken permission set. The root site (root web) cannot inherit permissions from other site collections, and the navigation structure doesn't allow the built-in navigation to cross the site boundary.

From a configuration perspective, the two keys things to be aware of are:

➤ *Ensuring that the correct site template is chosen when creating the site* — It is critical to choose the correct site template the first time around, because it determines which lists and Features will be available on the site, and cannot be changed once the site is created. The site can be customized, but the template cannot be changed.

➤ *Storage quota* — This is effectively a means of selecting the maximum size to which the site is allowed to grow before the end users are blocked from adding more content.

You have several recommended guidelines to be aware of when planning website collections.

Review the information architecture for the farm. The information architecture will reveal the requirements for site naming conventions and, thus, URL naming conventions. This is typically seen when the planning for teams, groups, or divisions with a company where the implementation of explicit and or wildcard-managed paths may be required.

In addition to the provided sites and wildcard-managed paths, SharePoint allows the administrator to create the following additional types of sites:

➤ A *wildcard managed path* is defined with a rule similar to /sites/*, where the * represents the root of a new site collection. In this scenario, there can be many site collections with different names residing under the site's wildcard-managed path.

➤ An *explicit managed path* is generally used to denote a site collection of significant importance, and can host only one site collection. An example would be /finance/, where finance denotes the root of the site collection, and any extension to the URL (such as /finance/team1) represents a site within the site collection, not a site collection in its own right.

There is a special mode called *host-named site collections* that can be used for creating site collections. These are site collections that have a separate DNS domain from the main web application. These are typically implemented to support large-scale hosting scenarios, or to support vanity URLs within a company. Up to 100,000 host-named site collections can be added to a single web application, but they can only be associated to the default web application zone. Host-named site collections are discoverable automatically by the SharePoint Server 2010 Search service application via a change to the site data web service. MOSS 2007 required that each individual URL be added to the search content sources to ensure that the sites were crawled properly.

Sites

A *site* (sometimes referred to as a *web*, or, in object model terms, an *SPWeb*) is a container for the actual end-user content of the SharePoint web application. A site consists of one or more related web pages and other items (such as lists, libraries, and documents) that are hosted inside a site collection. The built-in navigational elements work between sites within a single site collection.

Guidelines for acceptable performance allow up to 250,000 sites per site collection. However, this could very quickly become unwieldy and introduce administrative complexities for managing such a deep and/or side hierarchy of sites. Upgrade and activities such as site creation and deletion are heavily impacted when the site numbers are very large.

Designing Your Logical Architecture

Components in a SharePoint Server 2010 platform can be logically layered following the layered application pattern. These layered components could be packaged and deployed following multitier deployment patterns (for example, a four-tiered distribution model).

 For more details on tiered distribution, see http://msdn.microsoft.com/en-us/library/ms978701(v=MSDN.10).aspx.

The major tiers of the deployment pattern are client applications, web server, application server, and database. All servers in a SharePoint farm are essentially web servers, but their exact role in the farm is determined by the subset of Features and services enabled on each. The logical server deployment roles available in SharePoint normally map to the corresponding deployment tier.

Physical servers are included in a farm by role. In SharePoint deployment scenarios, web server, application server, and database server roles are defined. Each role has some specific characteristics.

Web Server Role

The web server is the user-facing edge of the server farm, and services requests from browser and office client sessions. It hosts the SharePoint application, plus any custom Features, and is responsible for directing requests to the back-end application servers for servicing if required.

Application Server Role

The application server role provides the shared SharePoint service applications. Each service represents a separate application service that can potentially reside on a dedicated application server. Services with similar usage and performance characteristics can be grouped on a server and scaled out onto multiple servers together. A good example of this would be grouping application servers that are participating in the Search crawl or query topology, and having another group that is running OWA and Managed Metadata Services. After deployment, look for services that consume a disproportionate amount of resources, and consider placing these services on dedicated hardware.

Database Server Role

The database server role provides the SQL Server infrastructure for storing SharePoint Server 2010 configuration information and content. In a small or medium farm environment, all databases can be deployed to a single server. In larger environments, consider multiple SQL Server instances, and balancing the databases across these instances based on load and size.

Consider the following databases:

➤ SharePoint configuration and Central Administration content databases

➤ Services application–related databases (including BDC, Search Admin, Search Crawl, Search Property, StateService, Subscription Settings, Managed MetaData, Profile_DB, Social_DB, Sync_DB, LoggingDB(usage), Web Analytics Staging, and reporting databases)

➤ Content databases

Each of these databases may require specific resource allocation to perform in an optimum way. The SharePoint configuration and Central Administration content database must reside on the same instance for supportability reasons, and will be best deployed sharing a SQL instance with regular content databases.

The databases that generate the most concern from a load perspective are the Search Crawl database, Logging database, and the Web Analytics database. Good practice would be to deploy these as a separate SQL instance from the remaining service application databases, and ensure that sufficient disk I/O is available to service their demands.

Microsoft data centers use synchronous database mirroring with witness and automatic failover for high-availability scenarios. Database Transaction log shipping is used for disaster-recovery protection, with the logs being shipped via a distributed filesystem replication (DFSR) share to a secondary data center in a different geographical region.

Applying Your Logical Architecture to Your Physical Infrastructure

Server farms are generally referred to as small, medium, or large. However, a number of variations exist within each classification, and what may be described by some as large could be described as medium by someone else. By logically arranging the servers based on their roles, the farm may be deployed in a single tier, two tiers, and three tiers. The three tiers usually refer to WFE (or a user-facing role), service applications layer, and database layer.

For production environments, topologies vary depending on the solution and performance characteristics that were validated in the pre-production environments. Figure 16-2 shows three levels of scale in appropriate topologies.

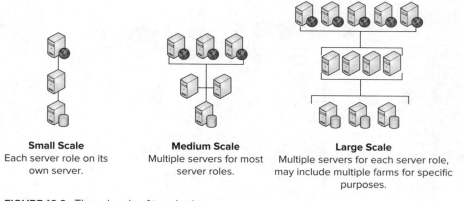

Small Scale	**Medium Scale**	**Large Scale**
Each server role on its own server.	Multiple servers for most server roles.	Multiple servers for each server role, may include multiple farms for specific purposes.

FIGURE 16-2: Three levels of topologies

As shown in Figure 16-3, the following characteristics should be considered when selecting a topology and scale-out mechanism:

➤ *Web and application server roles* — This is affected by the number of users, and, specifically, the RPS. Additional load from workflow processes and timer jobs should be factored into the planning phases. Additional web servers may be added based on an increase in the RPS. Monitor constantly for usage, and add additional servers if required.

➤ *Search role (crawl)* — To maintain optimal index freshness, add crawl components as the number of items to be crawled increases. If the corpus remains relatively static in size and the number of items, you can also add additional crawl components to decrease the amount of time for crawling the content. The optimum number of crawl components per server is two, so additional servers may be needed once that threshold is reached.

➤ *Search role (Query)* — The number of query components is dependent on the query response time and the number of items in the index. If the number of items in the index increases, new index partitions may be required. If the query response time is getting longer, additional index partition mirrors may be needed to service the requests.

➤ *Database* — Distribute the databases across multiple SQL server instances based on anticipated usage of the various service applications. As already discussed, Search Crawl, usage logging, and Web Analytics databases are very I/O hungry, and may require an instance of their own. Generally, multiple content databases can be grouped on the same instance, and some service application databases may reside with those.

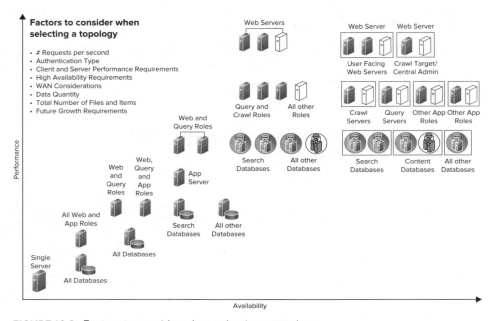

FIGURE 16-3: Factors to consider when selecting a topology

Planning Your Resource Grouping

The principle of *resource grouping* is to allow scalable deployment and growth of logical and physical resources, and, when used for multiple projects, to also bring standardization to deployments, making management and maintainability easier. When projects are standardized, the subsequent support processes can also be standardized and, therefore, the overall total cost of ownership is lowered.

A resource group is the smallest scale unit of resources (machines and other physical resources) that can be deployed and managed. A typical resource group might be a set of two web servers hosting the WFE services for a SharePoint farm. Adding one or more of these groups to the farm would scale up the achievable RPS of the farm without making supportability or management any more complex.

In more complex deployments (for example, those used in Microsoft internal data centers), resources would be categorized into three groups, based on the role the group represents:

➤ *Content resource group* — This provides a set of machines that host the WFE, user-facing services, and non-federated services. Non-federated services are generally computation-based services that act directly on user content stored in the context of a site collection, rather than compiling service-specific data in a separate service database. Examples of such services are Project Server and Excel Services.

➤ *Services application resource group* — This provides a set of machines that host service applications. Each of these service applications has its own set of databases to hold service data. Such resource groups would serve applications such as Search, User Profile service, or Managed Metadata Services. Local and remote content farms will connect to the published service applications. A federated services resource group may service multiple content resource groups.

➤ *The SQL resource group* — This is a set of mirrored SQL pairs. These could be deployed on physical hardware or virtual instances. Until recently, the number of SQL mirrored pairs was constrained within the published boundary of no more than 5 TB of content per instance. This limitation has been lifted now, but the recommendation still stands to monitor and test the deployment for the occurrence of scaling bottlenecks caused by capacity or mirroring threads.

Resource grouping helps organizations determine the hosting capacity needs based on the scale characteristics. For small- to medium-scale deployments, the granularity of resource groups may be identically configured physical or virtual machines with dedicated server roles. As the deployments scale upward, these groups can become four or even eight machines designed to serve a single or multiple purposes. A specific group for Search Services would not be uncommon, perhaps with each resource group being scaled to support 20 million items with crawl component and query component resilience, and associated database roles to support the Search service application database layer.

Organizing Your Logical Topology

When it comes to organizing the farm-level topology you can take the lead from the previous section, "Planning Your Resource Grouping," and build a deployment model based on these scalable units. This provides significant flexibility without the loss of a standard package-based growth.

Looking at a content-derived resource group containing related services for the user-facing servers, this group contains everything needed to perform as a farm, including web servers, application servers, content databases, and Central Administration. At the same time, the web servers and application servers within this resource group could be expanded with more web server–only resources or application server–only resources.

The service applications to be deployed in this farm are Access Services, Reporting Services, Project Server, Excel Web Application, InfoPath, OneNote Web Application, PowerPoint Web Application, Secure Store (un-partitioned), State Service, Subscription Settings Service, Word Web Application, Usage reporting, and Visio Web Application. Criteria in selecting the server roles for this farm include the total number of users, number of tenants, number of site collections, and average site collection size.

To illustrate, you could organize the deployment as a set of the following farms:

➤ *Content farm resource group* — This would include the basic SharePoint Server 2010 farms that handle incoming customer requests, as shown in Figure 16-4.

➤ *Services application farm resource group* — This would contain SharePoint Server 2010 services that can operate across farms, such as Search, the profile store, and shared services, as shown in Figure 16-5.

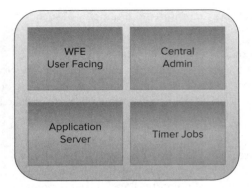

FIGURE 16-4: Content farm resource group

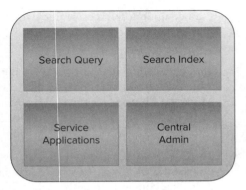

FIGURE 16-5: Services application farm resource group

The services application farm includes server roles such as service applications, Search Query and Index, and Central Administration. Some criteria in selecting the server roles for this farm include number of requests, number of service applications in the farm, and service-specific capacity requirements. Service applications deployed to this farm include BCS, Search, Taxonomy, Topology, User Profile Application, and Web Analytics.

Each of these farms has different scale characteristics and different configurations. This architecture model has been validated for some Microsoft internal deployments. In these farms, it is possible (and recommended) to configure some specialized server roles. For example, set up servers according these roles:

➤   Content farm:

➤   Central Administration

➤   Web Front Ends, Load balanced

➤   User Code execution/sandboxed solutions

➤   SharePoint search crawler target

➤   Timer Jobs

➤   Application server for non-federated services

➤   Federated farm:

➤   Central Administration

➤   Application server

➤   Query

➤   Index

The server roles described here are just an example of what is possible given the flexible nature of the product. This has been proven to work based on this approach, and, as such, is a worthwhile initial design to look at for any greenfield deployment.

Planning Your Hosting Locations

When it comes to planning where to locate sites or locate the SharePoint farm, several factors influence the decision. Chapter 12 provides insight into designing your portal strategy. Chapter 13 provides detailed guidance on requirements-gathering activities and key early technical design activities. Chapter 14 further elaborates on the design of your information architecture and Chapter 15 defines the solution architecture for the portal solutions envisaged for your SharePoint 2010 environment. These chapters are invaluable in that together they define requirements that will help flesh out your infrastructure design.

 Microsoft provides great guidance and samples on TechNet. See `http://technet.microsoft.com/en-us/library/cc261995.aspx` *for a full and proper review of the design process and decisions needed before embarking on your SharePoint 2010 deployment.*

Designing Your Physical Infrastructure

Each of the environments you plan to deploy should be built to reflect the purpose of the role that environment will play in delivering the service. Rather than cover material presented elsewhere in this book, see Chapter 10 for an in-depth treatment of SharePoint platform architectures, and Chapter 18 for a look at the development life cycle and effective use of developer, quality assurance (QA), and testing farms.

Designing Your Network Infrastructure

As SharePoint farms become larger and companies are forced to make decisions about single-farm versus multiple-farm deployments, the network infrastructure begins to play a bigger role in the design and implementation phases, instead of just the operational aspects.

Placement of the SharePoint servers on the network with respect to the end users can vary depending on the design choices made. With the advent of cloud-based services and the gradual trend toward utilizing managed services such as the Microsoft O365 cloud-based service, more and more network infrastructure has been placed between the end user and the servers. Each network device has the potential to add latency to the end-user experience, so the choice of manufacturer and model (as well as the number of devices, and whether hardware devices or software-based solutions are used) becomes vitally important to the end-user experience, as well as the operations side of the farm.

Plan the network connections within and between farms. You should use a network that has low latency.

The following list provides some best practices and recommendations:

➤ All servers in the farm should have LAN bandwidth and latency to the server that is running SQL Server. Latency should be no greater than 1 millisecond (ms).

➤ Do not use a WAN topology in which a server that is running SQL Server is deployed remotely from other components of the farm over a network that has latency greater than 1 ms. This topology has not been tested.

➤ Plan for an adequate WAN network if you are planning to use SQL Server mirroring or log shipping to keep a remote site up to date.

➤ Web servers and application servers should have two network adapters — one network adapter to handle end-user traffic, and the other to handle communication with the servers running SQL Server.

When considering all the factors involved, the key pieces of this puzzle are routers, firewalls, and load balancers from a connectivity perspective, but WAN accelerators, proxies, and other caching devices all have their parts to play. It is beyond the scope of this chapter to detail all the considerations, but it is important to understand that once the deployment steps outside of the small department-level SharePoint farm, factors other than just server configuration come into play and make the overall design significantly more complex.

Following are just three of the network devices that must be considered when deploying larger enterprise-class farms:

➤ *Firewall* — The traditional role of a firewall as a device that blocks or allows network traffic based on simple rules is a long way from the modern capabilities of such a device. Consider Microsoft Forefront Unified Access Gateway (UAG) and Threat Management Gateway (TMG). Both offer publishing and content caching capabilities specifically targeted to SharePoint applications. Both can deliver network load-balancing services and rich client authentication capabilities in addition to their regular role of screening network traffic.

➤ *Router* — Probably the simplest of the network devices being discussed, a router is used to segment a network, and contains routing tables about where to send packets toward their ultimate destinations. Routers are suggested for use to separate parts of an extranet SharePoint deployment — for example, separating the user-facing web servers from the SQL servers, and again from any domain infrastructure such as AD or Domain Name Service (DNS) services.

➤ *Load balancer* — As already mentioned, Forefront TMG and UAG offer load-balancer capabilities, but more commonly hardware appliances are used, especially for enterprise-class deployments where high performance and granular control is needed. Load-balancer devices such as the F5 appliances can be configured to check the health of the content-serving servers, and remove underperforming or unresponsive servers from the pool for maintenance. Windows Server ships with its own software-based network load balancer, which is fully supported for use in both production and test scenarios. From a matter of pure performance and manageability, the use of hardware appliances is recommended if budget allows.

When deploying globally, the discussion of what hardware is needed frequently turns to the benefits of utilizing a *network accelerator* device. A network accelerator can be anything from a caching device to a device capable of compressing the network traffic before transmission, thus requiring decompression on the receiving end. A new type of accelerator called an *XML accelerator* is becoming more popular with web content because it is capable of processing XML and XSLT on behalf of the client, thus speeding up the rendering time in the browser.

From a purely "good practice" point of view, the importance of using the right devices for your specific implementation is key to a good overall user experience and, thus, adoption. Choosing the right hardware should not be taken lightly, and careful testing should be done in the final network location before making a final decision.

PLANNING YOUR APPLICATION INFRASTRUCTURE TECHNOLOGIES

Anyone who has installed even the most basic SharePoint Server 2010 deployment will have come across the dependencies and necessary configuration changes or choices to make with a number of other Microsoft technologies. There is simply no getting away from the fact that a successful rollout of a fully functional SharePoint implementation project will need more than SharePoint skills. This stretches from server deployment and AD configuration and design, to Exchange or other e-mail services configurations, and last (but by no means least) to the SQL servers used to support the services and host the end-user data.

All of these technologies have some required configurations, and some have optional configurations. This section examines a number of these to give the architect a flavor of what is required.

When you consider the server platforms needed to support a successful SharePoint deployment, several choices are available to the architect for each required component of the overall platform. In addition to deciding which edition of the software is required, other factors such as the functional level of AD and IIS configuration must be considered. SharePoint has strong dependencies on each of the following technologies:

- ➤ Active Directory
- ➤ Windows Server 2008 or Windows Server 2008 R2
- ➤ IIS
- ➤ SQL Server 2005, SQL Server 2008, or SQL Server 2008 R2
- ➤ Exchange Server or an alternative SMTP server platform

Active Directory

Active Directory (AD) plays a significant role in any SharePoint deployment, from the management of service accounts with the new managed accounts Feature to the authentication of end users accessing the platform. The introduction of Forefront Identity Manager (FIM) as the user profile synchronization engine also places additional constraints on AD domain implementation, requiring a minimum of Windows Server 2003 AD functional level to operate correctly. The performance of the domain controllers (DCs) plays a significant role in the overall responsiveness of the user experience.

Authentication delays are frequently the root cause of many SharePoint performance issues, and several tried-and-tested approaches to minimizing these potential problems exist:

- ➤ Ensure that all the SharePoint server machines are located in the same AD site, and that at least one Global Catalog (GC) server for each user domain in the forest is added to that site.

➤   The physical location of the DC and GC servers should be as close as possible to the SharePoint farm to avoid unnecessary network latency during the authentication or profile import process. This is especially important if you are auto-discovering a DC for the profile import process, because this selection might direct SharePoint to a remote DC, instead of a DC that is located physically close to the SharePoint farm. This scenario should be avoided where possible.

➤   Always use 64-bit DCs for faster performance. Be aware that if you're running Windows Server 2008 R2 for the DCs, this is a minimum requirement.

There is a registry setting on the SharePoint servers and the DCs that can improve the authentication performance for users. This works by increasing the number of concurrent requests sent from the SharePoint server, while also increasing the number of concurrent requests the DCs can process. The setting is called `MaxConcurrentApi`, and it can be modified by adding or changing the following registry key and restarting the NETLOGON service:

➤   `HKEY_LOCAL_MACHINE\SYSTEM\CurrentControlSet\Services\Netlogon\Parameters`

➤   Value Name: `MaxConcurrentApi`

➤   Data Type: `REG_DWORD`

➤   Value: Between `0` and `10`

The default Value is `2`, with a value of `10` representing the heaviest load. If values in excess of `5` are used, it is vitally important to check the Local Security Authority Subsystem Service (LSASS) performance counters to ensure that the process is not saturated and, thus, a cause of bottlenecks. The bottleneck could be SharePoint waiting on too many requests being returned from the DC, or the DC trying to process too many requests at once. The preferred approach is to make small changes and assess the impact of those before making further adjustments. Use Perfmon or the Windows Server Performance Analyzer to monitor the authentication throughput to assess the impact of making this change. Typically, an average or sustained CPU level of more than 80 percent is considered too high, and will introduce slowdowns and performance bottlenecks in the authentication process.

Kerberos authentication for SharePoint web applications is discussed in Chapter 19. To some degree, this negates the need to tune the `MaxConcurrentAPI` settings, because the number of network round trips required between SharePoint servers and the DCs is significantly reduced with this approach.

Windows Server 2008 or Windows Server 2008 R2

The minimum supported operating system for SharePoint Server 2010 is Windows Server 2008 Service Pack (SP) 1, which makes the deployment of a server farm possible on most of today's entry-level server platforms. This also makes for a convenient deployment approach that reuses existing hardware, which can reduce the overall licensing costs.

Since the release of SharePoint 2010, Microsoft has also released Windows Server 2008 R2, which has many advantages over Windows Server 2008. The vast majority of these advantages and improvements are only realized when looking at the large-scale enterprise use of servers.

As the architect choosing whether to deploy onto Windows Server 2008 or Windows Server 2008 R2, it is important that you understand the features that matter to your business requirements. Large-scale, highly available virtualization is not likely to be a key decision factor for a departmental deployment of less than a thousand users, but could be critical to a large financial institution with tens of thousands of users, and where downtime equals lost revenue.

Larger enterprises such as a financial institution with tens of thousands of end users should consider all factors. SharePoint Server 2010 will perform and function perfectly well on Windows Server 2008, and so for the smaller deployment or more financially constrained organizations, there may well be no benefit in upgrading or deploying on the latest and greatest operating system simply because the cost of doing so outweighs the gains.

Table 16-2 highlights some of the advantages of Windows Server 2008 R2 over Windows Server 2008.

TABLE 16-2: Advantages of Windows Server 2008 R2 Over Windows Server 2008

ADVANTAGE	COMMENT
Improved hardware support	Expands CPU support to run with up to 256 logical processors, and also supports Second Level Translation (SLAT), enabling it to take advantage of CPU improvement to significantly improve memory management.
	Hyper-V in Windows Server 2008 R2 can now access up to 64 logical CPUs on host computers, versus 32 logical CPUs in Windows Server 2008. This leads to high-density capabilities for server consolidation.
	Windows Server 2008 R2 can also support core parking to reduce power consumption based on the workload of the server. Core parking is the capability for the server to determine how many CPU cores are needed to maintain its current workload. Some cores will be switched into an extreme low power mode (or "parked") until such a time as the load on the server increases. At this time, the cores will be re-activated to service demand.
Hyper-V improvements	Quick Migration in Windows Server 2008 has been replaced by Live Migration in Windows Server 2008 R2, reducing downtime from seconds to milliseconds. Live migration is the movement of a virtual machine (VM) from one physical host to another while continuously powered up. When properly carried out, this process takes place without any noticeable effect from the point of view of the end user.
	System Center Virtual Machine Manager (SCVMM) has been integrated for enhanced cluster management.
	Support has been included for 64 logical processors per VM, including the same SLAT capabilities as the host. SLAT allows the virtual operating system to make use of hardware for tracking the mapping of memory between the host and guest systems.
	VMs can add and remove storage without rebooting.

continues

TABLE 16-2 *(continued)*

ADVANTAGE	COMMENT
Branch office performance and management	Windows Server 2008 R2 has a new a feature called `BranchCache`, which is designed to improve the performance of network applications and reduce WAN traffic. With `BranchCache`, essentially a cache of previously requested files is stored on a dedicated server or Windows 7 client in the local network. These files are then available to clients for subsequent requests.
Web server enhancements	Windows Server 2008 R2 has many application server–related updates, the most significant of which is the updated IIS 7.5. It is these improvements that would most likely be of benefit to all deployment designs, regardless of size.
	Significant improvements here include support for custom tracing in the configuration system for improved troubleshooting, which includes auditing for configuration changes, multiple Common Language Runtime (CLR) support for ASP.NET (which allows version switching), improved CLR control and performance monitoring at the application pool level, and custom error control without requiring high privileges on the server.
	To add custom error pages or redirects in IIS 7.0 and earlier required administrator privilege to at least IIS. With IIS 7.5, the developer can add a `<customerror>` node to the `web.config` file and control the error handling on the site without any privileges at all.
	Support has been added for Negotiate Version 2 authentication (Nego2), which is the next generation of negotiation authentication for supporting broader capabilities such as direct live ID integration with IIS and more granular Kerberos/NTLM opportunities.
	Application Pool Warm-Up support has been added to avoid initial request delays.

 For more information on the differences between Windows Server 2008 and Windows Server 2008 R2, see www.microsoft.com/windowsserver2008/en/ us/r2-compare-features.aspx.

IIS Configuration

SharePoint support teams generally recommend not to do IIS configuration, and to allow SharePoint to configure it during installation and configuration of the product.

The following suggestions are based on product experience and reflect on some known best guidelines for IIS running SharePoint Server 2010:

➤ Ensure that the application pool is configured to use the integrated pipeline. This is a requirement, rather than a best practice. This allows ASP.NET modules to participate in IIS request processing, regardless of the type of resource requested. Using this mode makes features of the ASP.NET 2.0 request pipeline available to requests for static content. By default, IIS 7 and IIS 7.5 application pools run in this mode.

➤ On SharePoint, you should configure the application pool to auto-start using the new IIS 7.5 feature available in Windows 2008 R2 only. This provides a well-defined approach that allows you to perform expensive application startup and pre-cache logic that can run before any end users hit your application, and ensures that you have your application "warmed up" and ready from the very beginning, and deliver a consistent high-performance experience.

➤ Tuning the application pool queue length based on number of users indicates to HTTP.sys how many requests to queue for an application pool before rejecting future requests. When the value set for this property is exceeded, IIS rejects subsequent requests with a 503 error. This is, however, similar to SharePoint resource throttling, and might be overkill in the environment, seeing as how it would need to be carefully tuned to match the usage patterns of the farm.

➤ Move the IIS Logs/Compression folder to a separate spindle. This is good practice following the general best practice guidelines of locating all logging activity away from the system drive.

➤ Tune the ASP.NET concurrency settings to optimum for your needs. This is not a simple task, and requires investment in testing and continual monitoring and adjustment to stay optimally configured.

 To learn more about tuning the ASP.NET concurrency settings, see http://blogs.msdn.com/tmarq/archive/2007/07/21/asp-net-thread-usage-on-iis-7-0-and-6-0.aspx.

Other configuration aspects for IIS are taken care of by SharePoint during application deployment and the configuration phase of the farm.

SQL Server 2005, SQL Server 2008, or SQL Server 2008 R2

The minimum supported versions of SQL Server for SharePoint Server 2010 are as follows:

➤ The 64-bit edition of Microsoft SQL Server 2008 R2

➤ The 64-bit edition of Microsoft SQL Server 2008 with SP1 and Cumulative Update 2

➤ The 64-bit edition of Microsoft SQL Server 2005 with SP3 and Cumulative Update 3

Several possible reasons exist as to why you should choose any of these SQL Server versions, and, indeed, the actual edition of the version.

The reasons can be economical in that cost of new software and licenses is simply too great for a company to consider upgrading. Sometimes it is simply convenient to deploy onto an existing in-house platform, thereby avoiding the need to go through the deployment phases for new or upgraded database platforms.

There is a good chance that, in a reasonably mature, predominantly Microsoft technology IT department, there will be SQL Server versions already deployed. Repurposing these platforms either as dedicated or shared environments is a common way to save money. Unfortunately, this approach can lead to performance and/or capacity problems. The SharePoint Server 2010 architecture — especially at the database level — has matured to the degree that the best practice for your SQL implementation for SharePoint is to install a new, fresh instance on dedicated hardware.

That does not mean you can't do it. However, that approach should be limited to very small implementations and generally for testing or development environments. Where production farms are being deployed to support multiple workloads, important or even critical business applications, or information publishing, the choice is simple: Go for the latest and greatest by choosing a SQL Server platform that can be both dedicated to the SharePoint Server farm and offer the feature set to support the demands for high availability, performance, and capacity required by the business. By opting to deploy the latest version of SQL Server, you are also future-proofing the farm by providing an extended support life cycle for the database platform.

The edition of SQL Server may be chosen to reflect the specific requirements of the individual company that may or may not require the highest level of performance or high availability.

Which edition is right for you depends on what you are trying to achieve, and how valuable your data is. It is often just a single feature that only exists in one edition of SQL Server that can drive the choice. Table 16-3 provides a comparison of features for the editions of SQL Server 2008 R2 supported by SharePoint 2010 in production farms.

TABLE 16-3: SQL Server 2008 R2 Editions

FEATURE	DATA CENTER EDITION	ENTERPRISE EDITION	STANDARD EDITION
Number of CPUs (unlimited cores)	OS Maximum	8	4
Maximum memory	OS Maximum	2 TB	64 GB
Maximum database size	524 petabytes (PB)	524 PB	524 PB
Log shipping	Yes	Yes	Yes
Database mirroring	Yes	Yes	Yes (single threaded synchronous only)
Backup compression	Yes	Yes	Yes
Database snapshots	Yes	Yes	No
Online indexing	Yes	Yes	No
Hypervisor support	Yes	Yes	Yes

For more information on detailed specifications of all editions of SQL Server 2008 R2, see http://msdn.microsoft.com/en-us/library/cc645993 (SQL.105).aspx.

Table 16-3 shows that only a few differences exist between the different editions that could be relevant while designing a SQL Server infrastructure to support a SharePoint Server 2010 farm. Some of these differences may not seem that important, but they could actually play a major factor in your decision.

Looking at some of the examples in the table, you can see that SQL Server 2008 R2 Standard supports only single-threaded, synchronous (full safety) mirroring. This means that there will be a lack of multi-threaded support for mirroring, and that will have a performance impact on mirroring throughput. In turn, this means that each transaction will be delayed slightly while waiting for the mirror server to commit its transaction first. This delay could range from an imperceptible period to a noticeable system slowdown, depending on the network latency and speed between the principle and mirror database servers.

It is thus is a best practice for SQL Server deployments supporting SharePoint Server 2010 to deploy the Enterprise Edition of SQL Server 2008 R2 when the following is required in your deployment:

➤ You need to support eight CPUs with unlimited cores, and up to 2 TB of memory for high-demand workloads.

➤ Hot-add hardware capabilities allow the addition of CPUs and memory when needed without interrupting database operations. Backup compression can significantly reduce the capacity required for online backup storage. This allows for more backups to be stored on the same storage capacity, which can also aid lower recovery time and ensure SLAs can be met.

➤ Support for database snapshots has a huge impact on backup/restore of site collections by reducing the performance impact on the database during these operations. SharePoint Server 2010 content deployment jobs can utilize snapshots for improved efficiency in creating the content deployment package. Site- and list-level backup operations can also optionally use snapshots for improved efficiency.

➤ Indexing operations are so vital to the performance characteristics of a SharePoint farm that being able to update them while the databases are online is critical. This is especially important where there is a lot of data change resulting in heavily fragmented indexes.

These are just some of the reasons to choose SQL Server 2008 R2 Enterprise Edition as the database platform for your farm. To review the editions in more detail, see the Microsoft article at http://msdn.microsoft.com/en-us/library/cc645993(SQL.105).asp.

PLANNING YOUR CONFIGURATION MANAGEMENT

Configuration management is the process of recording and tracking hardware and software assets and system configuration information. The end result of a configuration management exercise is the generation of a Configuration Management Database (CMDB). The most common information found in a CMDB is data used to track software licenses, maintain a standard hardware and software build for client computers and servers, and define naming standards for new computers. Configuration management generally covers the following categories:

➤ *Hardware* — This category tracks the pieces of equipment that the IT organization owns, where equipment is located, and who uses the equipment. This information enables an organization to plan and budget for upgrades, maintain standard builds, report on the value of assets for accounting purposes, and help prevent theft.

➤ *Software* — This category tracks software that is installed on each computer, the version numbers, and where the licenses are held. This information helps plan upgrades, ensure that software is licensed, and detect the existence of unauthorized (and unlicensed) software.

➤ *Standard Builds* — This category tracks the current standard build for the client computers and servers, and whether the client computers and servers meet this standard. The existence and enforcement of standard builds helps support staff who need to maintain only a limited number of versions of each piece of software.

➤ *Service Packs and Hotfixes* — This category tracks which service packs are tested and approved for use, and which computers are up-to-date. This information is important to minimize the risk of computers being compromised, and to detect users who have installed unapproved updates.

➤ *System Configuration Information* — This category tracks the function of a system, the interaction between system elements, and the processes that depend on the system running smoothly. For example, a connector to a third-party e-mail system may be configured on a single server. The e-mail system's dependence on this server should be understood, and contingency plans may be required if there is a failure. If a second connector is installed on another server, dependencies and contingency plans will probably change.

➤ *Exceptions* — This category tracks any known exception information for any computer, appliance, or software package in the CMDB. An exception could be because of a known incompatibility or a dependency on a non-current software build.

Implementing Configuration Management

Once the purpose of your configuration management exercise has been determined, and you have decided what items need managing, the data must be collected for reporting. The simplest approach is to collect data manually (number and model of client computers, operating system, software installed) and store it in a Microsoft Office Word or Excel document. For larger, more complex, and constantly changing systems, the discovery of assets and collection of detailed information must be automated. Decide what information is relevant to your organization, and record it in a database.

The CMDB is a useful tool for support staff and management in the following areas:

➤ *Security audits* — The database enables you to identify servers running SharePoint Server, as well as client computer systems that must have hotfixes applied, or that have missed the installation of a service pack or the latest antivirus updates.

➤ *Software installation* — If you identify client computers that already have Microsoft Office installed, this will save time if you are manually deploying Office.

➤ *Configuration information* — If you maintain an up-to-date list of all settings that have been modified from their defaults, you will be able to troubleshoot issues quickly and more effectively.

➤ *Planning upgrades* — If a capacity review reveals that additional storage space is required on your SharePoint database servers, the CMDB will indicate the type of disk that can be installed, the number, and the upgrade path in each case.

Tools Used for Configuration Management

The importance of accurate configuration management cannot be stressed enough. Configuration management is not just about keeping a simple list of assets and changes. The scope of configuration management is also assumed to include (at a minimum) all configuration items used in the provision of live, operational services.

Computer hardware configuration management provides direct control over IT assets, and improves the capability of the service provider to deliver quality IT services in an economical and effective manner. Configuration management should work closely with change management to maintain the CMDB as a living, evolving, and, above all, accurate representation of the state of the infrastructure.

Automated Scripts

You only have to look at the investment in the TechNet script repository to see how important scripting (and especially Windows PowerShell) is to discovering and automating tasks in the environment.

 You can find more than 6,000 scripts (many of which can be used to help discover and deploy platforms in a repeatable consistent manner) at http:// gallery.technet.microsoft.com/scriptcenter/site/search. *Integrating these scripts with a backed CMDB will provide a powerful tool for capturing and maintaining a stable infrastructure.*

Automated Tools

If the business needs dictate an off-the-shelf package for configuration management, then tools such as Microsoft System Center Configuration Manager (SCCM) come into scope of the project.

Microsoft SCCM incorporates standard report templates (such as service pack level), and also enables you to create customized reports (for example, for a custom application). Microsoft Systems Center Operations Manager (SCOM) can also be used to report on hardware and software configurations.

SharePoint Server can be used to record configuration data and make it accessible to the appropriate IT personnel.

Relationship with Change Management

Configuration management is closely related to change management. Configuration management identifies the need for change, and identifies and records that a change has occurred. For example, the CMDB can be used to identify servers that require a hotfix. Change management then defines the process for applying the hotfix.

PLANNING YOUR OPERATIONS MANAGEMENT

The connection between sound operational practices, sound procedures, and a healthy SharePoint Server 2010 infrastructure goes without saying. Well-documented, thorough operational processes and procedures ensure that all the components on which SharePoint Server relies in an organization's environment are managed efficiently and effectively through all the design, deployment, and supporting phases.

Changes to the components of an organization's infrastructure on which SharePoint Server relies can result in unexpected outages. Firmware updates to routers, firewall rule changes, and DC reconfiguration are all areas where changes can happen without the involvement of the organization's SharePoint team, and this is where Microsoft Operations Framework (MOF) or Infrastructure Technology Information Library (ITIL) come into their own. By using MOF/ITIL-based processes to help make sure that there is documentation of these service interdependencies, an organization can help minimize the chances of preventable outages, and reduce the impact of scheduled changes.

The ultimate longevity of the farm to continue to service the demands of end users from both performance and functional perspectives is directly proportional to the investment in ensuring the farm can be (and is) properly maintained. Following are two key areas that require operational investment:

➤ Patching/building to build upgrades.

➤ Daily, weekly, monthly operational maintenance or housekeeping, including password changes.

Each has its own preferred approaches, and some of them are analyzed here.

Patching

Patching server farms can sometimes be looped in with an upgrade because, in essence, each time you patch a SharePoint farm, you are in effect upgrading it. This is a build-to-build upgrade, however, and is not as intense or risky as a version-to-version upgrade (which requires significant planning and testing before executing).

Version-to-version upgrade is not covered here. However, you can learn more from the Microsoft TechNet articles in effective upgrade planning at http://technet.microsoft.com/en-us/library/cc303429.aspx.

With SharePoint Server 2007, the farm administrator had no flexibility around patching. As soon as a patch was required, the appropriate change request would be raised, and, at the point of update, it was an all-or-nothing scenario. This was seen as a significant enough problem that investment was made to make life much easier, and include more options and flexibility around the process. Of course, more options means chances to make mistakes, so best practice guidance around the implementation of patching is vitally important to avoid a disaster scenario.

The first and most notable improvement was the introduction of a compatibility window to the updates themselves. This allows the binary files and some SQL changes to be made, while ensuring that the farm can remain operational during the update.

The second improvement was to introduce some intelligence into the upgrade of database-locking routines, enabling multiple database upgrades to be run either from the same server in a farm, or from multiple servers.

The final improvement was to integrate SharePoint updates with the Windows Software Update Service, although from a best practices standpoint, these updates should always be thoroughly tested before deployment to a production farm.

Patching Strategy

So, as a result of these improvements, the farm administrator now has choices to make as to the best approach to patching. Bear in mind that not all patches are equal, and, in some cases, urgent security-related hotfixes may require emergency implementation procedures, regardless of the uptime impact on the farm. When choosing a patching strategy, the considerations are always based on the acceptable amount of downtime for the business, and how much effort is required to install the update.

In terms of downtime reduction, the following options are available:

➤ Complete end-to-end update consisting of patch installs plus upgrade phase.

➤ Partial update consisting of just installing the patch, but postponing the upgrade phase. It is not considered sensible to run in this mode for longer than a few days, however, so this should not be considered a true production state until the upgrade phase is complete.

When the right strategy for the business has been chosen, the administrator must be sure that a number of steps have been taken to ensure that the patch process flows smoothly, and that the farm is protected in the event of a procedural or operational breakdown. The following steps can be considered best practices for patching:

1. Always ensure that you have a full and (most importantly) tested backup of the current farm. This could be complete SQL backups of content databases, service application backups, or a combination of SQL and server images. Be sure that you have explored whatever backup choices are required to be able to rebuild the farm in the event of a disaster.

2. Document the farm properly to ensure any unusual or unique farm items can be reconfigured. Usually, this data should be available in the build guide and in the change record for the farm, but occasionally these items may have arisen during the normal use of the farm, and so require some additional recording.

3. Ensure that any dependent software can also be upgraded to a version that is compatible with the newly deployed patch — for example, OWA versions or FAST for SharePoint 2010, if it is used.

4. Probably most importantly, test the update process in a suitable environment. This allows you to confirm successful patch deployment, and that the functionality of the farm remains intact. In addition to this, the test phase is important for gathering metrics regarding the time it takes to deploy and upgrade the farm.

5. Implement the patching in production in accordance with the preferred strategy.

6. Confirm functionality is as expected.

7. Back up the farm in the new upgraded state before releasing it back to the users.

Following these simple steps will ensure that you have a planned, tested, and stable platform ready for the next round of required updates.

This leads nicely to the question of how frequently a SharePoint Server 2010 farm should be patched. Microsoft has a bi-monthly cumulative update schedule that provides a single update package for SharePoint Server containing all the updates since the last service pack. So, when should you update? Generally, the answer depends on a number of things for a number of reasons.

➤ If the currently deployed version of SharePoint Server 2010 is a supported build, performs within the acceptable boundaries defined by the business, and has the required functionality, there is no real driving reason to patch the servers.

➤ If the update contains a critical security update or a fix to functionality or performance required by the business, that is a good reason to install the update.

➤ Applying patches may be restricted within the business to core, pre-agreed upon periods of time, perhaps as frequently as each weekend, or as infrequently as once a quarter. These periods are generally pre-arranged and are not considered down time for the purpose of calculating the service level impact.

➤ Although the updates delivered by Microsoft are well-tested, occasionally a new bug or a regression of an old bug is found in the update packages. For administrators who deploy patches on the day they are released, this can be a major problem, especially because patches cannot be uninstalled. You should make sure that the best practice of ensuring a good farm backup has been taken prior to deploying the patch.

 It is very common in large enterprises to find an N-1 *patching strategy, meaning that the business will only accept the deployment of the previous version of a patch, rather than the currently available version. This is often applied to service packs, too. As an example, a company adopting an N-1 service pack strategy will not deploy SharePoint Server at all until SP2 has been released. Only then will it deploy an SP1 version.*

So, in fact, no real concrete best practices define the patching frequency. The choice is a business-driven decision, and as long as adequate and thorough testing is carried out, the farm could be patched as frequently or infrequently as required.

Operational Maintenance or Housekeeping

One of the most annoying situations that can arise is when your SharePoint farm simply runs out of space or horsepower because no one noticed the trend in increasing demand placed on it. Operational maintenance (call it *housekeeping*) is a simple process that provides the farm administrators with a set of checklists or guides to be completed daily, weekly, or monthly. These checklists allow tracking of farm metrics to hopefully prevent any surprises in increased demand or capacity.

Each business will develop its own checklists following appropriate ITIL or MOF guidelines for operational management. To give the administrator a starting point, Microsoft has published a MOF-based guide that contains some best practice approaches to maintenance management, plus a set of pre-created checklists. In addition, the guide discusses the use of SCOM 2007 to automate much of the process.

> *For more information, you can find the guide at* `http://technet.microsoft` `.com/en-us/library/gg277248.aspx.`

Password Changes

During the life of the SharePoint farm, there should be a need for periodic password changes for service accounts. Planning should always include an appropriate strategy for managing these password changes, and ensuring that when they are made, the service interruption is kept to an absolute minimum.

> *The TechNet article at* `http://technet.microsoft.com/en-us/library/` `ee428296.aspx` *provides good insight into the use of the automatic and manual password change processes, as well as the process of how SharePoint implements a password change across multiple services and servers.*

Antivirus

The implementation of an effective antivirus solution has a number of considerations to be aware of:

➤ Choice of antivirus product

➤ Antivirus exclusions and configuration

➤ Definition and Engine maintenance

When it comes to choosing an effective antivirus solution, it is important to ensure that the choice can meet all the required workloads. You want to choose a product that is capable of protecting both the server operating system and meet the specific needs of a SharePoint and SQL deployment. Microsoft Forefront is one such product frequently recommended. However, others are just as effective. One of the key benefits of using Forefront for SharePoint is that the platform is capable of hosting multiple antivirus engines, and using one or all of them to scan for malicious content.

One of the key factors to consider during implementation of the chosen antivirus product is what to include and exclude from scanning. By default, all products will scan all areas of the filesystem, and for a SharePoint or SQL Server deployment, this is not a sensible option. With SQL Server, for example, you certainly want to exclude the database file and log file locations from scanning. With SharePoint, frequently updated locations such as log file locations and, on some servers, search index files should not be scanned.

 Microsoft has a couple of good resources on what to scan and not to scan at `http://support.microsoft.com/kb/943556` *and* `http://support.microsoft.com/kb/952167`.

With SharePoint antivirus products, the platforms allows a number of configuration options:

➤ *Scan on Upload* — This instructs the antivirus engine to check each uploaded document at the time of upload. There is a performance penalty in doing this. However, it is considered the preferred configuration to prevent infected documents from reaching the storage layer.

➤ *Scan on Download* — Just as with the Scan on Upload option, this choice instructs the antivirus engine to check each document as it is downloaded by the client. Once again, there is a performance penalty for enabling this, but it, too, is preferred, because it can also prevent a client from being infected if its own antivirus protection is not robust or up to date.

➤ *Allow the Download of Infected Documents* — By default, any document that is detected as infected cannot be downloaded. The administrator has the option of allowing the download to be available, but generally, this is an option that is not selected unless a specific operational reason requires it.

➤ *Attempt to Clean Infected Documents* — Like all other antivirus engines, a SharePoint-specific scanner can try to remove the virus payload from the document. If the document cannot be disinfected, the previous three rules come into play to determine the course of action taken.

With SharePoint specifically, there is a choice to make on what mode to enable for the scanning engine. When looking at antivirus products and their operational activities, probably the one key aspect is that of maintaining the virus definitions and the engine itself. Generally, these can be automated when the servers have Internet access or can pull the update from a known location within the network. This latter process requires an administrator to periodically drop the latest updates at a shared location. Operationally, an alert should be raised if the update process fails, because failure to apply an update to the virus definitions exposes the whole platform to the chance of infection.

Operational Security

During the operational lifetime of a SharePoint farm, from initial build-out to runtime maintenance and troubleshooting, there will be the need for multiple people (or teams of people) to access the platform for a variety of reasons.

➤ *Deployment phase* — During build-out of the farm, a team will be responsible for installing the operating system and configuring the domain membership, as well as installing the application layers (including SQL Server and SharePoint). These activities require local administrative privileges to the servers, and for some individuals, elevated domain-level privileges will be needed.

➤ *Operation changes* — Throughout the lifetime of the farm, there will be a need to update the environment through operating system patches and upgrades, as well as application-level patches and upgrades. These activities require local administrative privileges to the servers, and probably farm administrator-level access to SharePoint and/or `sysadmin` rights to SQL Server.

➤ *Escalation engineering/troubleshooting* — This team will require high-privilege access to both the SharePoint and SQL servers almost continually. When the farm is in run state, there will always be a need to investigate problems with bugs and configuration.

Of the three teams, the only one needing permanently available access to the environments is the escalation team. If the service operates a strict SLA on availability, this team will need to gain access to the farms and remediate problems as quickly as possible, and so the team cannot waste time requesting access.

The operational change teams will usually operate on a fixed change window, and so access to the environments can be strictly controlled and scheduled.

The build teams will usually never need to access the environments after service acceptance, and so their access can be revoked.

Typically, controlling access to the servers will be implemented via Group Policy, although in very large multi-domain hosting environments, this can become very complex to manage.

The exception to controlling server access based on role can be when certain individuals are members of multiple teams. This makes access control more difficult because access will need to be based on the highest level needed for just one of the roles, even if that is the least-frequently used role.

Another aspect of controlling access to the servers and services is to strictly control the access to the service accounts. Keeping the service accounts in a document of some kind and storing it on a location where administrators can access it might seem like a good idea, but this can often lead to people taking their own copies and eventually leaking the information. Using a password repository tool where a central database and a client tool requiring encrypted credentials or passphrases to access the account details is the preferred option, because access can be quickly blocked if necessary.

SUMMARY

In this chapter, you learned about many of the building blocks that must be researched, investigated, and planned before even beginning to deploy any SharePoint servers. This starts from the initial stages of deciding the right physical location for the farm with respect to the services infrastructure available, and the need for a data center with sufficient power, connectivity, and technical support staff and equipment.

To support the investigation of how much network bandwidth is needed and what latencies can be supported, the process for carrying out a network impact assessment was discussed. You also learned about performance planning concepts, and the determination of the required level of throughput for the farm.

You learned a bit about the architectural aspects of the farm, both logically and physically, including a comprehensive look into the supporting infrastructure. This included which version of Windows Server, Active Directory aspects, and IIS configuration options, as well as the various pros and cons of the SQL Server back-end, can be chosen to support the SharePoint farm.

Finally, you learned about a number of operational management activities, including managing the farm configuration and tracking change requests and deployment. You learned about the preferred approaches to patching a production farm environment, and how to manage password changes and operational security.

The key takeaway from this chapter is to understand that you must undertake a significant amount of groundwork before beginning to design your SharePoint deployment. All too often, the question is asked, "What SharePoint infrastructure is needed to support x number of users?" Quite clearly, any sensible answer to this question will be in the form of a question, because far too many unknowns exist in any deployment to give an answer with so little information. So, as an architect, do your homework first, and answer the questions later. Of course, a number of rules of thumb and key guidance can be used to put a stake in the ground, but only after you perform the due diligence can you create a real design.

Chapter 17 provides detailed guidance on designing your storage layer for your SharePoint 2010 environment.

17

Designing Your Storage Layer

By Bill Baer

In the world of business, data is your most important asset. Data loss results in lost productivity, and, more importantly, substantial losses in revenue. To help protect your data, you must ensure adequate, available, and secure storage. Managing and securing data is possible through a variety of technologies with SharePoint 2010, such as direct attached storage (DAS), network attached storage (NAS), and storage area networks (SANs), in addition to availability solutions such as failover clustering.

Storage planning for SharePoint 2010 is the fundamental step to ensuring reliable and consistent delivery of its benefits and capabilities. Careful consideration and planning of SharePoint's storage architecture is necessary to meeting your organizational need for sufficient scalability, fault tolerance, and recovery. When planning the storage architecture for SharePoint 2010, it is important that you address both the business needs and the specific methods for achieving these requirements.

Storage planning involves a number of sequential steps outlined in this chapter, which include the following:

1. Determining business and application requirements

2. Planning storage configurations

3. Planning storage scalability

4. Planning data protection

5. Planning redundancy

Figure 17-1 illustrates the storage planning process.

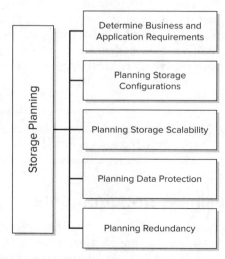

FIGURE 17-1: Storage planning process

Organizations have seen substantial growth in the need for both online and offline storage requirements, whether they are driven by increases in capacity requirements, increased need for fault tolerance, or by the declining costs of storage overall. However, despite these requirements and costs, proper planning cannot be ignored so that you can ensure that your plan addresses the underlying storage requirements.

The information in this chapter will help you address your organization's specific storage needs, and identify what storage technologies and solutions are available to meet those needs. If you understand the fundamentals of the storage planning process, you will be able to develop a storage plan that encompasses scalability, security, availability, and performance.

DETERMINING BUSINESS AND APPLICATION REQUIREMENTS

In SharePoint 2010, the indirect method through which end users access data, as well as the manner by which data is stored, define how you will approach determining the business and application requirements when designing your storage layer.

With SharePoint, end users indirectly access data through the SharePoint user interface (UI). The data those end users access is defined as data within rows in a SQL Server table, or, in some scenarios, large binary objects stored on the filesystem. However, for the purposes of the most common deployments, these items are collectively stored within one or more SQL Server user databases (content databases).

Understanding these data storage fundamentals will help to simplify storage planning. Understanding how user data is stored requires that you carefully optimize not only the web servers that manage the requests, but also the database servers responsible for the hosting of the data, and the unique databases associated with other aspects of the product and its functionality (such as search or Managed Metadata).

It is equally important to understand that, in many cases, business requirements will transcend performance and capacity, and may require satisfying redundancy and replication requirements — or, on occasion, both. For example, business requirements may dictate one or more warm standby locations to meet the requirements of disaster recovery. In this scenario, it is important to ensure that each receiving site has the resources and capacity to sustain the same volume of depth of content offered in the primary site.

 For the purposes of this chapter, the term "replication" is used to define one or more technologies used to mirror data on a remote site.

Business Requirements

Business requirements often comprise a number of scenarios. In many cases, the underlying driver is budget, along with its relationship to business goals and the expected return on investment. This section provides an overview of the factors that influence business requirements and their relationship to determining how a storage architecture should be planned for SharePoint 2010.

To understand the overall business requirements, several areas must be addressed satisfactorily, including the following:

➤ *Prioritization* — Determining priority will help you understand where resources and budget should be aligned. For example, a SharePoint 2010 deployment used by legal and finance, or a deployment that contains critical high business impact information, might require a greater level of service and attention than a utility, social computing deployment used in the business.

➤ *Projected growth* — An often-repeated mistake is planning the storage capacity based on existing conditions, or a previous version of the project. It is important to understand both the characteristics of the new application and the potential for greater adoption as the result of new features (such as those provided by SharePoint 2010).

➤ *Budget* — Budget is the foremost limiting constraint when considering the storage architecture. Budget (or a lack of budget) can limit the features available to the storage solution, and, in turn, change the dynamic of the conversation as related to recovery objectives and the architecture of the overall solution. In many cases, budgetary questions should be asked immediately in the planning process.

➤ *Fault-tolerant requirements, including disaster recovery* — The capability to rapidly recover from a storage failure with minimal impact to end users is critical in many cases where sensitive business-critical information is stored. Not only should high availability be considered when recovering from localized outages, but also disaster recovery in the event of a widespread infrastructure failure (such as that affecting the Fibre Channel, or fabric). For example, multi-pathing provides the capability to mitigate failures occurring on a Small Computer System Interface (SCSI) disk's Fibre Channel (FC) port by seamlessly routing I/O through the other I/O port with minimal disruption (with perhaps the exception of incremental I/O).

➤ *Backup schedule and retention period* — Backup scheduling and retention are critical factors when considering the overall capacity of the storage architecture. For example, if the business requires a 21-day disk-retention schedule, sufficient storage is required to maintain not only 18 differential copies of the data, but also 3 referenced full copies, which (depending on the rate of data change) can be a significant increase in capacity.

➤ *RPO and RTO* — Recovery Point Objectives (RPOs) and Recovery Time Objectives (RTOs) refer to the amount of data that the business is willing to accept the loss of (RPO), and the amount of time the business is willing to accept the application being offline (RTO). These measurements can have the tendency to drive upward the total cost of the solution, and should not be ignored. However, in many cases, these can be negotiated to support budgetary constraints.

Application Requirements

Following the identification of the business requirements associated with storage planning, you should begin considering the application requirements, which additionally will require understanding the problem that the solution (Microsoft SharePoint 2010) is intended to resolve.

For example, if you are deploying to support an Enterprise search scenario, it is important to understand the content sources, their locations, the amount, average size, and type of content hosted on those systems. This will help determine the capacity and performance required to support the solution. Or, if you are considering a traditional collaborative-type solution, it is important to understand the potential number of web applications, how many site collections will be hosted within each, and the quota established for those site collections, including the allotment of sufficient capacity to support sustained growth and exceptions to the rule.

In either scenario, you may decide that the deployment requires 500 gigabytes (GB) of total storage, but you also need fault tolerance. To configure a 500 GB RAID 0+1 disk array to provide fault tolerance, you would need 1 terabyte (TB) of physical disk storage. You would also need to allocate drives for the transaction log files associated with the content databases, system, and other databases required to support the deployment.

 You learn more about Redundant Arrays of Independent Disks (RAID) architectures later in this chapter in the section, "Planning Data Protection."

This approach should be applied on a server-by-server basis to help determine both the number of disks and total storage required. While planning your storage architecture, you should also consider your backup requirements in your estimates. For example, business requirements may require maintaining localized backups either to the same or different storage array for short-term retention, and then later copy the data to offsite storage for long-term retention.

A single full backup of Microsoft SharePoint 2010 will require doubling the storage estimate, which will increase to support any associated differential backup copies. It is important to not only consider the immediate backup needs, but to also ensure that the estimate accounts for future growth of the databases.

```
USE [<databasename>]
GO
SELECT *
FROM sysfiles
WHERE name LIKE '%LOG%'
GO
```

The operating system is another component of the solution that should be properly planned and considered. For example, you should note which servers require disk mirroring to protect their boot and system volumes, and note the number of required disks, along with the amount of required storage for each.

PLANNING STORAGE CONFIGURATIONS

Planning the proper storage configuration is important to reducing both capital expenditures and ensuring a resilient and reliable storage architecture that provides the needed performance while reducing overall operating costs over time. Storage is the fundamental component to ensuring a deployment meets performance expectations, and supports the organization's business continuity management strategy. This section introduces the basic concepts to help plan a storage configuration that meets or exceeds these objectives.

Planning Disk Storage

The principal aspects associated with selecting a storage technology are performance, capacity, reliability, manageability, and, most importantly, cost. Microsoft SharePoint 2010 supports a vast array of options when selecting the appropriate storage technology to include serial Advanced Technology Attachment (ATA), serial attached SCSI, Internet SCSI, and Fibre Channel (FC). Careful selection of disk storage can reduce disk subsystem bottlenecks, which are the most common performance problem in many SharePoint deployments, and often result in more noticeable degradation than processor and/or memory deficiencies.

Disk subsystems that are improperly planned and implemented (or insufficient) result in performance degradation that surfaces throughout the SharePoint technology stack, and can severely impact the capability of end users to adequately leverage the solution.

As a general rule of thumb, a poorly performing disk subsystem can be characterized as follows:

➤ Having read and write latencies exceeding 20 milliseconds (ms)

➤ Having recurring latency spikes exceeding 50 ms with an extended duration

Disk latency is the most common problem resulting in slow performance, whether users are executing queries against the Search Service Application or simply uploading, editing, or downloading content.

To ensure adequate performance, disk storage planning should focus on the following:

➤ *Performance* — High-performance disks should be the primary metric for storage planning, followed by capacity. Large disks and RAID 5 arrays maximize the cost per gigabyte spent on the storage solution. However, these often result in disk subsystem bottlenecks because of disk selection and the RAID level applied to those disks. A general rule of thumb for required Input/Output Operations per Second (IOPS) is as follows:

   ➤ The number of RPS × 5

   ➤ The amount of GB × 2

The greater of these two measurements will provide suitable performance in most cases. However, do not replace the need for proper planning and measurement that should precede production deployments of SharePoint 2010.

 For additional information on performance testing for SharePoint 2010, see `http://technet.microsoft.com/en-us/library/ff758659.aspx`.

➤ *Capacity* — Smaller disks can improve performance by providing more spindles to achieve the same capacity as fewer larger disks.

➤ *Alignment* — Proper disk track sector alignment can increase performance by as much as 20 percent. Disk alignment is achieved through setting the starting offset in the Master Boot Record. For example, with a disk that maintains 64 sectors per track, Windows will create the partition on the 64th sector, which results in misalignment between the partition and its physical disk. Proper alignment can be achieved by using `DiskPart.exe`.

Improper partition alignment is one of the leading performance issues that can impact a SharePoint 2010 Products deployment, and is often one of the most difficult to diagnose. Problems related to improper partition alignment will often only surface as apparent technology issues (such as latent requests issues by end users whether uploading documents or crawling a content source) and do not regularly report themselves through the most common troubleshooting facilities such as the ULS logs. In addition to being difficult to isolate, improper disk alignment is more difficult to resolve once data resides on a misaligned partition. In the discussions that follow, you will learn more about how to validate a partition's alignment and ensure that it is correct.

Validating proper alignment in Windows Server systems can be accomplished using the `Diskpart.exe` *utility, installed on Windows Server 2003 systems, or as a downloadable solution at* www.microsoft.com/download/en/details .aspx?displaylang=en&id=23711.

SharePoint 2010 Products supports a multitude of workloads, each carrying its own unique characteristics when associated with disk utilization. In many cases, it is best to establish a generic baseline to support the evolving and ever-changing scenarios that SharePoint 2010 Products comprise. The most effective method of ensuring adequate performance for a SharePoint-centric disk storage subsystem is to establish a starting offset of 2,048 sectors, or 1 MB, because a starting offset of 2,048 sectors covers most stripe unit size scenarios.

To determine whether an existing partition is configured with a starting offset of 2,048 sectors, the following Windows Management Instrumentation (WMI) query can be executed at the command prompt.

```
wmic partition get BlockSize, StartingOffset, Name, Index
```

The result of the previous WMI query will provide information to include the `BlockSize`, `StartingOffset`, `Name`, and `Index` in tabular format, as shown here:

```
BlockSize  Index  Name                   StartingOffset
512        0      Disk #0, Partition #0  1048576
```

In this example, `Disk #0, Partition #0` is properly aligned because the result of `StartingOffset` divided by `BlockSize` is 2,048.

Windows Server 2008 will align new partitions by default. On disks larger than 4 GB, the default alignment is 1 MB. However, this can be configured through the Registry by modifying the value for the following key:

```
HKEY_LOCAL_MACHINE\SYSTEM\CurrentControlSet\services\vds\Alignment
```

For example, if pre-existing partitions were misaligned on previous operating systems, and they become associated with Windows Server 2008, they will maintain the properties under which they were created.

You should always confirm proper alignment before the introduction of data to your disk subsystem.

Windows Server 2008 partition alignment defaults to 1,048,576 bytes, or (1,024 KB). This provides a durable solution that correlates well with common stripe unit sizes such as 64 KB, 128 KB, and 256 KB, in addition to (though less frequently used) values of 512 KB and 1,024 KB.

Improperly aligned partitions can be corrected. However, these corrections will result in data loss because alignment must occur prior to formatting the partition. Therefore, any data residing on the partition to be realigned must be migrated to another disk while the original partition is aligned, and then subsequently migrated back to this partition. Depending on the amount of data that resided on the partition to be realigned, this can be a time-consuming operation, and, where databases such as Search Crawl and Query resided, can impact the function of SharePoint 2010 Products components such as Search. This is because the relationship or transactional consistency between the Search databases and flat-file indexes will be irreparably damaged, and, in this example, would require re-indexing all content sources.

There are a number of considerations when establishing proper partition alignment; because hardware, disk, and other factors each bring their own unique characteristics, it is impossible to provide guidance targeted at every scenario. However, using the general guidance provided here, you will place yourself in a position to ensure adequate performance for the many workloads provided with SharePoint 2010 products. Later in this chapter, you will learn about the varying hardware options associated with the disk storage subsystem and their characteristics.

There are a number of possible disk architectures available to storage subsystems. Let's take a look at an overview of the most common disk solutions available to those subsystems, their characteristics, and their benefits.

Serial ATA (SATA)

Serial ATA (SATA) is a serial interface for ATA and IDE drives, most often installed in traditional personal computers. Although slower than SCSI or FC disks, SATA drives provide a benefit in the large capacities they are available in. SATA use with SharePoint 2010 should be limited to backup or non–mission-critical data sets.

To ensure adequate performance with SATA and SharePoint 2010, and to maximize transactional throughput, you should ensure that the controller associated with the disks or array is a write-caching array controller. SATA is most appropriate when implemented on solutions designed to support low user impact scenarios such as the disk-based retention of backup sets.

Serial Attached SCSI (SAS)

Serial Attached SCSI (SAS) has become increasingly popular in recent years because of increased density through smaller overall form factors. SAS disks are built on enterprise-class, high-performance disks with rotational speeds up to 15,000 RPM. The increased throughput provided by SAS arrays (which can be measured up to 3 GB per second) provides a solution to meet the most demanding workloads. The drawback to SAS is that, in most cases, the disk capacity is smaller than comparable solutions.

SAS-based solutions are acceptable for all SharePoint 2010 workloads. However, when used in scenarios where write performance is inconsequential (such as those associated with Document Archiving or Records Management), the cost can outweigh the overall benefit of a SAS-based solution.

Internet SCSI

Internet SCSI (iSCSI) connects to a storage server over Ethernet. As such, to avoid contention and performance degradation, the iSCSI storage network should be completely isolated from any other network traffic.

A critical consideration when implementing iSCSI is to make sure that the iSCSI initiator is configured to ensure the automatic reconnection of drives when the server is restarted using persistent logon and persistent volumes.

Multi-path I/O (MPIO) is supported with the Microsoft iSCSI Initiator 2.0, which can significantly increase throughput by providing multiple paths to the storage device providing component redundancy between the storage server and the storage subsystem.

 To learn more about MPIO, see http://technet.microsoft.com/en-us/library/cc725907.aspx.

iSCSI is recommended in document archive and/or records management scenarios when coupled with the SQL Server Remote FILESTREAM Provider. This scenario enables the use of more cost-effective storage solutions such as NAS and/or Content Addressable Storage (CAS). However, it must be implemented within SharePoint 2010 support boundaries that require the Time to First Byte

(TTFB) to be returned by a request from the storage subsystem to the storage server within 20 ms. Because of its relatively unpredictable I/O capacity, iSCSI, should not be considered for write-bound workloads to include core collaboration, Search, and so on, bound by the requirements of 2 IOPs per gigabyte of content.

Fibre Channel (FC)

FC is a network technology that, in most applications, uses fiber-optic cables in SANs. FC provides a gigabit network suitable for supporting high performance, storage consolidation, and federated management. FC configuration varies by storage vendor, and is beyond the scope of this chapter.

Planning Storage Architectures

Whether planning a new configuration or re-engineering an existing configuration for Microsoft SharePoint 2010, you must make decisions about which storage architecture is most appropriate to satisfy your business requirements. As mentioned, Microsoft SharePoint 2010 can make use of DAS, NAS, and SANs.

 NAS is not recommended for use with SharePoint because of the inability to ensure sufficient latency. If networked storage is required, use iSCSI on an iSCSI-dedicated gigabit Ethernet local area network (LAN).

Storage architectures should not be considered isolated entities that operate independently, but rather as complementary with one another and working together to support a single solution. For example, a single Microsoft SharePoint 2010 deployment might use NAS to support a Remote Blob Storage (RBS) implementation, whereas the service applications and other content databases are stored on the SAN.

Direct Attached Storage (DAS)

DAS refers to a storage device that is directly attached to a single server through a number of connections, such as FC, SCSI, SAS, SATA, and Enhanced Integrated Drive Electronics (EIDE). In most cases, it is not separated by switches or routers.

Figure 17-2 illustrates a common DAS implementation.

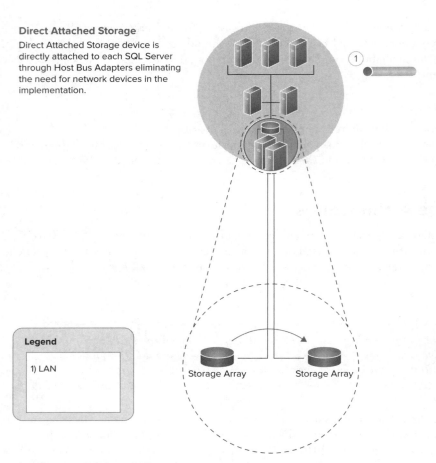

Direct Attached Storage

Direct Attached Storage device is directly attached to each SQL Server through Host Bus Adapters eliminating the need for network devices in the implementation.

Legend

1) LAN

Storage Array   Storage Array

FIGURE 17-2: Common DAS implementation

DAS has been traditionally deployed in small to medium business environments because of its low entry costs and deployment simplicity. However, in recent years, it has made its way into enterprises because of improvements in bus support such as SAS. As organizations seek to reduce capital and operating expenditures related to storage, DAS has become a popular architecture where increased performance, storage isolation, and relative scalability are required.

Cost

Although DAS traditionally offers a lower cost entry point, when measured over time, the costs associated with DAS can exceed those of a SAN. This is demonstrated by the fact that the unused storage associated with DAS cannot be redeployed. For example, an organization may purchase 1 TB of storage and over time leverage only 500 GB of that storage, which results in 500 GB of unused storage that cannot be re-allocated or provided to other services.

Management

Management can also contribute to increased operating costs associated with DAS deployments. This is because of the learning curve required to manage a DAS solution, and the availability of management tools to support a DAS-based solution. Unlike SAN, DAS does not provide the complex and federated management tools often provided with SAN. Therefore, a DAS approach may require more granular monitoring and changes to an organization's storage management practices.

When considering DAS, it is important to understand that DAS provides a solution to your storage needs. However, its capabilities are generally limited to providing storage, and it does not provide the advanced management capabilities that are offered by SAN, such as the following:

➤ Data mirroring

➤ Snapshot technologies

➤ Federated management tools

➤ Seamless and flexible scalability

Fault Tolerance

When compared to NAS or SAN, DAS can have a higher overall probability of cable failure because it requires more cabling than a comparable NAS- or SAN-based solution. However, DAS is beneficial in that it requires significantly less operational expertise and less complex hardware than a NAS- or SAN-based solution. When you are thinking about a DAS-based solution, you should consider connectivity redundancy to reduce the risk of component failure.

Backup and recovery is another area of planning that must be carefully considered when evaluating DAS. In a DAS architecture, two solutions are available to support backup and recovery: local attached backup devices, or (optionally) performing backup and recovery operations over the LAN to a remote device. Each option comes with unique considerations that must be planned accordingly, such as management overhead and available network bandwidth to ensure these operations can be accomplished within the Service Level Agreement (SLA) and both Recovery Point Objective (RPO) and Recovery Time Objective (RTO).

The implementation of DAS should be reserved for scenarios where the following conditions exist:

➤ A high number of disks are required.

➤ A storage network does not exist, or storage isolation is required.

➤ You are addressing a targeted scenario such as search, where limited scalability is required.

➤ Budget constraints prevent a SAN implementation.

Network Attached Storage (NAS)

A NAS unit is essentially a self-contained computer connected to a network, with the sole purpose of supplying file-based data storage services to other devices on the network. The operating system of the storage unit provides the storage-management software.

Figure 17-3 illustrates a common NAS architecture.

Network Attached Storage

Network Attached Storage is data storage connected to a network that provides broad access to a number of clients.

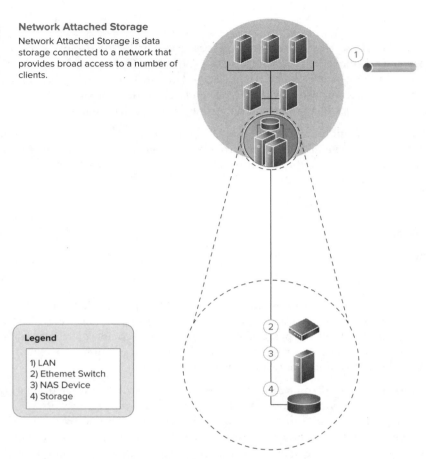

Legend

1) LAN
2) Ethernet Switch
3) NAS Device
4) Storage

FIGURE 17-3: Common NAS architecture

Cost

Similar to DAS, the cost entry point for NAS is generally low because of its simplicity and ease of implementation.

Management

NAS can be used to consolidate storage platforms, enabling an administrator to manage an array of disks in a heterogeneous environment over the network. Because the storage is consolidated and managed through a single server, isolating and resolving issues removes the complexities associated with isolated storage such as DAS.

Fault Tolerance

Although it provides simple deployment and management because of a single point of interaction, NAS also results in a single point of failure, increasing the costs associated with backup and restore processes.

NAS is beneficial to organizations seeking to immediately address storage needs and consolidate projects. However, support with Microsoft SharePoint 2010 products is limited.

The implementation of NAS should be reserved for scenarios where the following conditions exist:

➤ Small to medium business where cost barriers prevent SAN and storage isolation is not required

➤ Light RBS scenarios

Storage Area Networks (SANs)

SANs are among the most robust and capability-rich storage architectures. However, they require careful planning prior to implementation. SANs are similar to NAS in that SANs provide a single view of the underlying storage to its consumers. However, they differ in that SANs access and store data at the block level, whereas NAS accesses the storage store's data at the file level.

Figure 17-4 illustrates a common SAN architecture.

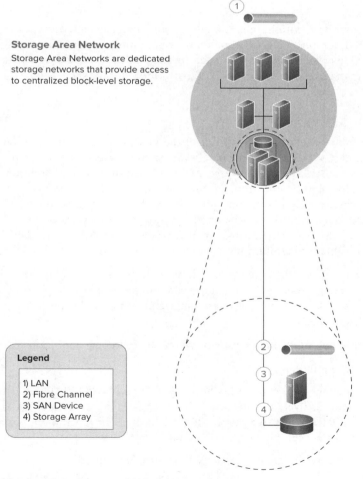

Storage Area Network
Storage Area Networks are dedicated storage networks that provide access to centralized block-level storage.

Legend

1) LAN
2) Fibre Channel
3) SAN Device
4) Storage Array

FIGURE 17-4: Common SAN architecture

File-level access provides benefits to those requiring direct access to a particular file or object. This scenario can be indicative of RBS scenarios with SharePoint 2010. However, the method by which data is accessed on a SAN provides fast and efficient access at the block level.

Cost

SAN offers more efficient disk utilization when compared to both DAS and NAS. It provides the benefit of managing a central pool of storage resources at the network level, and the capability to assign that storage more seamlessly to the servers that require it. In addition to a more centralized and flexible storage management model, SAN provides a method by which to scale storage incrementally, making the most efficient use of disks it hosts.

The entry point costs of SANs tend to be greater than DAS or NAS. This is because of the specialized skills required for their implementation. Additionally, because they are dedicated storage networks, they use their own network protocols and components.

Management

SAN benefits from its dynamic scalability, both in operational cost and management. Storage can be introduced to a SAN as required, permitting a proactive management model to growing storage needs. While SANs typically provide large volumes of storage, the singular model enables ease of management when compared to managing similar amounts of distributed storage such as DAS, which can be spread over many locations.

Fault Tolerance

Fault tolerance is the most appreciable benefit to SAN. Its out-of-the-box capabilities often cannot be met using traditional storage and separate management software without substantial overrun in implementation and management costs. Most SANs offer integrated disaster recovery solutions through intelligent snapshotting, block-level replication, de-duplication, and other solutions integrated into the device. They provide a single view both into the storage and in addition a single point through which it is managed in both run-state and in disaster-recovery scenarios. These features and capabilities can help reduce operating expenditures and simplify day-to-day management tasks for those responsible for maintaining the storage architecture.

Though SAN is occasionally referred to as a single point of failure, multiple host bus adapters (HBAs) and storage processors can reduce the impact of components that most frequently fail. However, it should be noted that SAN is generally a very resilient architecture that is not prone to failure, if managed and maintained properly.

The implementation of SANs should be reserved for scenarios where the following conditions exist:

➤ A high number of disks are required.

➤ Strict business continuity management constraints have low RTO and RPO. RTO refers to Recovery Time Objective, or effectively the mean time between failure and restoration of service on one or more sites. RPO refers to Recovery Point Objective, or the amount of data (measured by time) that can be acceptably lost (for example, 5 minutes).

➤ High rates of data change exist where greater capacity flexibility is required.

➤ Storage will be partitioned and served to other applications.

➤ A high volume of backups is required.

PLANNING STORAGE SCALABILITY

Properly planning storage architectures should not only satisfy immediate requirements, but also should scale to meet future demands. A critical step in understanding scale is to understand the limitations of both the current and planned storage architecture, in addition to understanding how to mitigate those limitations.

Physical Storage Limits

Storage bus is the primary limiting factor when planning your storage architecture and its respective physical limits associated with scalability. In this context, *storage bus* refers to the transmission path on which signals are sent or received at each device attached to the line. To understand the physical storage limits, you might consider a comparison between SCSI and FC.

The SCSI bus will determine the maximum amount of allowable storage devices on each bus, most commonly between 8 and 16 devices. Storage based on FC or SCSI protocol over TCP/IP (iSCSI) provides far greater flexibility and scale as a result. In contrast to the previous example, older architectures such as IDE can support up to four storage devices. Larger bus bandwidth is crucial to maximizing performance and scale.

SAN and NAS systems do not have limits on bus bandwidth capacity. However, it is important to understand that, with DAS systems, bus bandwidth is limited by the number of slots.

In addition to physical storage limitations, it is equally important to understand the various volume types available to Windows Server 2003 and Windows Server 2008. Both operating systems provide improved volume-management capabilities, such as basic disks and volumes, or dynamic disks and volumes.

The *basic disk architecture* is based on a Windows NT 4.0 and Windows Server 2000 design. It allows up to four primary partitions per physical disk, or three primary partitions in addition to one extended partition that can contain multiple logical drives. These primary partitions and logical drives on a basic disk are referred to as *basic volumes*. Basic volumes are limited to a maximum storage allocation of 2 TB, which extends to multiple volumes on a single logical unit. To support larger volumes, dynamic spanned, striped, or RAID 5 volumes are required.

The *dynamic disk architecture* is based on Windows Server 2000 design and can support a variety of volumes. The volumes include simple volumes, spanned volumes, striped volumes, mirrored volumes, and RAID 5 volumes. As such, they provide greater flexibility for volume management through a transparent database, as opposed to a disk partition table (which is used to track information about dynamic volumes on the disk and other dynamic disks in the server). The flexibility provided by dynamic disks support the creation of spanned, striped (RAID 0), and RAID 5 volumes that exceed the 2-TB size limit of basic volumes.

 Simple and mirrored volumes cannot exceed 2 TB.

Although cost effective, basic disks should be considered legacy architecture, and dynamic disks should be implemented in their place where possible.

Dynamic disks should be considered in the following situations:

➤ Creating RAID 0 volumes or fault-tolerant volumes (RAID 1 or RAID 5) and the server does not contain hardware RAID

➤ Combining logical units (LUNs) in a RAID array to create a volume larger than 2 TB

➤ Extending a volume, but the underlying hardware cannot dynamically increase the size of LUNs, or the hardware has reached its maximum LUN size

Disk Performance

The performance of individual disks is perhaps one of the most important considerations when planning your storage architecture. Poorly performing disks can result in excessive paging, excessive queue length, and I/O contention that will surface on the front-end web servers, and result in end-user dissatisfaction with the overall solution.

The performance of disks transcends their rotational speed or bus, but includes the RAID set on which the disks participate. For example, despite the rotational speed of the underlying disks, a search-driven solution implemented on a RAID 5 set will provide inadequate performance to sustain the crawling activity of the search service application (which is a write-bound workload). In this case, using the same essential disks that were in the RAID 5 set, a RAID 1+0 set would provide significantly greater performance to sustain this workload.

 You learn more about Redundant Arrays of Independent Disks (RAID) architectures later in this chapter in the section, "Planning Data Protection."

In many cases, RAID 1+0 will suffice the overall workloads offered by SharePoint 2010. However, where budget constraints apply, or other environmental limitations exist, RAID 5 can be implemented to support some basic workloads.

Determining Application Workloads

Your disk subsystem will be responsible for supporting the I/O requirements of SharePoint 2010. To analyze your requirements, you should begin by classifying the I/O characteristics for each type of workload. This analysis should include the following:

➤ Number of random disk I/O to data files

➤ Number of sequential disk I/O to data files

➤ Number of transaction logs generated

➤ Rate of operation execution by end users

The number of disk I/Os will help you determine the number of disks required. Establishing good performance throughput requires determining the appropriate number of disks required. A general estimation to help with the planning process is that enterprise-class disks can sustain 100–150 random I/O per second and 30–50 MB per second of sequential I/O. In today's market, many enterprise-class disks can support far more than these values. However, lower estimations provide greater opportunity to support long-term growth and future needs.

As an example scenario, let's say that Contoso Financial is a financial services company using SharePoint 2010 for in-place records management requiring up to 10 MB per second of random disk I/O to manage the rate at which records will be introduced and subsequently managed. SQL Server provides an 8 KB transfer size for random I/O operations. Therefore, the disk subsystem must support 1,000 random I/O reads per second. Using the values referenced here, a single drive providing 150 random I/O reads per second would require at least 7 drives, keeping in mind that the select RAID type will impact this capacity.

To calculate the number of disks required to support your workload use the following equation:

$$\text{Number of disks} = ((\text{bandwidth}) / (\text{transfer size})) / (\text{IOPS})$$

A variety of tools can help you to surface the data required to sustain your SharePoint deployment, and should be implemented as part of the overall planning process. These tools include the following:

➤ *SQLIOSim* — SQLIOSim can be used to simulate the I/O patterns of Microsoft SQL Server. It is available as a free download from `http://support.microsoft.com/kb/231619`.

➤ *IOMeter* — IOMeter is an I/O subsystem measurement and characterization tool. It is available as a free download from `www.iometer.org/`.

Monitoring and Measuring Disk Performance

Benchmarking the disk subsystem I/O is crucial to planning so that you can be sure you have the performance necessary to meet the current and future demands of your SharePoint deployment. As mentioned, SQLIOSim and IOMeter are useful software applications you can utilize as an initial component of your planning. However, you must understand what system counters should be used, both to support future demands and when isolating I/O subsystem bottlenecks.

Table 17-1 shows some counters that are useful in determining and measuring your capacity once SharePoint has been deployed.

TABLE 17-1: Counters to Measure Capacity after SharePoint Deployment

COUNTER	DESCRIPTION
Logical Disk: Disk Transfers/sec.	This Logical Disk counter provides the overall throughput on the specific disk measured, and should be used to monitor growth trends to help you plan for future demand.
Logical Disk: Disk Read Bytes/sec & Disk Write Bytes/sec.	This Logical Disk counter provides a measure of the total bandwidth for the measured disk. Using this counter, you can determine whether to introduce additional disks to support demand.

continues

TABLE 17-1 *(continued)*

COUNTER	DESCRIPTION
Logical Disk: Average Disk sec/Read	This Logical Disk counter indicates the time it takes the disk to retrieve or "read" data. The result of this counter should fall between 1 and 5 ms for logs, and between 4 and 10 ms for data.
Logical Disk: Average Disk sec/Write	This Logical Disk counter indicates the time it takes the disk to write data. The result of this counter should fall between 1 and 5 ms for logs, and 4 and 10 ms for data.
Logical Disk: Average Disk Byte/Read	This Logical Disk counter indicates the average size of the I/O SQL Server is issuing. It indicates the overall size of I/Os being read. This value may affect disk latency, and larger I/Os may result in slightly higher latency. When used to monitor SQL Server, this tells you the average size of the I/Os SQL Server is issuing.
Logical Disk: Average Disk Byte/Write	This Logical Disk counter indicates the size of I/Os being written. This value may affect disk latency, and larger I/Os may result in slightly higher latency. When used to monitor SQL Server, this will tell you the average size of the I/Os SQL Server is issuing.
Physical Disk: % Disk Time: DataDrive	Monitor this counter to ensure that it remains below two times the number of disks.
Logical Disk: Current Disk Queue Length	This Logical Disk counter can be used to determine the disk queue length for the specified disk. The optimal range is 20 or below. Ranges exceeding this value are indicative of bottlenecks. Bottlenecks will surface in the deployment, and result in end users experiencing longer than normal wait times for operations to complete. Proper database distribution, added array capacity, or a change in disk architecture may resolve this issue.
Logical Disk: Average Disk Queue Length	This Logical Disk counter can be used to determine the average number of outstanding I/O requests. The optimal range is two or less outstanding I/Os per spindle in the array. To determine whether or not a storage array cache is over-utilized, compare this result set to average disk queue lengths. Higher values on each of these measurements may indicate contention.
Logical Disk: Average Disk Reads/Sec and Logical Disk: Average Disk Write/Sec.	This Logical Disk counter can be used to determine the rate of read and write operations on the specified disk. The optimal range is below 85 percent of the overall disk capacity. In the event the range exceeds 85 percent, you may experience increases in disk access time.

PLANNING DATA PROTECTION

SharePoint has become increasingly adopted across organizations as a mission-critical application supporting a variety of workloads from Internet sites to enterprise content management. Its seamless interoperability with Exchange, Office Communications Server, and backend line-of-business (LOB) systems requires ever-increasing resilience and redundancy in the event of failure. Downtime that results in SharePoint 2010 being unavailable is unacceptable.

While redundancy is often focused on having redundant servers, the disk subsystem is perhaps the most critical component of the design to protect. The disk subsystem comprises the smallest unit of representation when it comes to hosting the data that end users access.

RAID

The first step in designing a fault-tolerant storage architecture is proper disk planning. Proper disk planning from a fault-tolerant–based design should include determining the appropriate Redundant Arrays of Independent Disks (RAID) architecture for the solution.

RAID can be implemented for both performance and fault tolerance. With RAID, you can choose to assemble disks to provide fault tolerance, performance, or both, depending on the RAID level that you configure. A variety of RAID types exist, both proprietary and common. However, the most common RAID types implemented with SharePoint 2010 are RAID 1, RAID 0+1, and RAID 5.

This section provides an overview of the various RAID options, and the solutions that they provide.

RAID 0

RAID 0 is referred to ask *disk striping.* In a RAID 0 set, two or more disks appear to the operating system as a single disk. In RAID 0, data is striped across each disk during read/write operations, which can potentially increase disk access speeds two times or better.

RAID 0 provides the fastest read and write performance. However, it does not offer any fault tolerance, so if a single disk in a RAID 0 array is lost, all data is lost and must be recovered from backup.

RAID 0 requires at minimum two disks to implement. To determine the effective capacity of RAID 0 use the following formula:

$$S*N$$

where *S* represents the smallest disk in the array and *N* represents the number of mirrored sets.

Figure 17-5 illustrates a RAID 0 implementation.

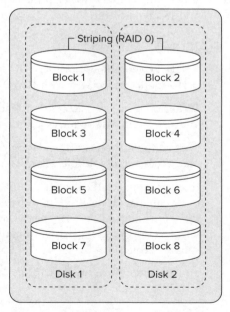

FIGURE 17-5: RAID 0 implementation

RAID 1

RAID 1 is the most common set used to support the operating system and data drives on front-end web, application, and database servers.

RAID 1 is referred to as *disk mirroring*. In a RAID 1 set, data is mirrored on two or more disks.

A RAID 1 configuration provides quick read. However, it also experiences relatively slow write performance and high availability in that a single disk can be lost without data loss. In a scenario where more than two disks exist in the RAID 1 configuration, the array can lose multiple disks, provided the mirrored pair is not lost. In a RAID 1 configuration, it is important to note that the amount of physical disk space required is two times the space required to store the data the array will host.

Figure 17-6 illustrates a RAID 1 implementation.

Partitions C and D are comprised of two disks in a RAID 1 array supporting the operating system and application data (for example, C:\Windows and D:\Program files). Partition E is comprised of the remaining four disks in a RAID 0+1 array supporting content (for example, E:\Inetpub). This example maximizes redundancy, performance, and storage utilization.

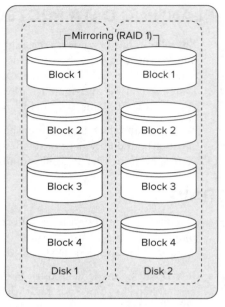

FIGURE 17-6: RAID 1 Implementation

RAID 1+0

RAID 1+0 combines both RAID 1 and RAID 0, providing the protection of RAID 1 and the performance associated with RAID 0.

Writes are generally slower, but reads provide similar performance. RAID 1+0 offers faster writes and reads, but also requires additional storage to create the mirrored stripe sets.

This configuration is often ideal for mission-critical database storage, because it offers both fast read access and fault tolerance. RAID 0+1 requires at minimum four disks to implement.

In contrast to RAID 5 (which is discussed shortly), RAID 1+0 does not require parity information to be calculated, resulting in more efficient writes. In the event that a disk fails in a RAID 1+0 array, there is no impact on write performance, because there is a member remaining that can still accept writes. However, reads are minimally affected, because only a single disk in the array is available to support requests.

To determine the effective capacity of a RAID 1+0 set, use the following formula:

$$S*N/M$$

where *S* represents the smallest disk in the array, *N* represents the number of disks in the array, and *M* represents the number of mirrored sets.

RAID 1+0 is suitable for supporting `tempdb`, Search Crawl, and other write-bound databases associated with SharePoint 2010.

Figure 17-7 illustrates a RAID 1+0 implementation.

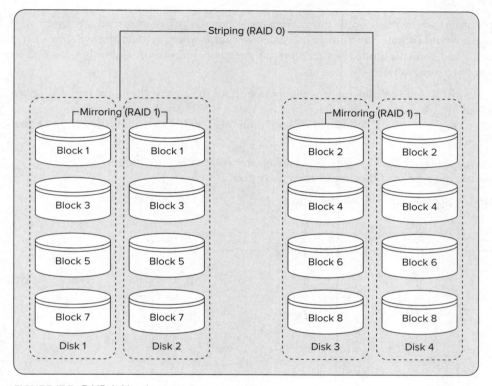

FIGURE 17-7: RAID 1+1 Implementation

RAID 5

RAID 5 is referred to as *disk striping with parity*, providing less performance than RAID 0 and limited fault tolerance in the event of failure of a single disk in the set without data loss.

In the event a single disk fails in a RAID 5 array, the array is in an exposed state, resulting in both performance degradation and higher latencies while the data is re-created on the surviving member through parity calculation.

Each write in a RAID 5 array requires up to four I/O operations per single I/O to be written. Depending on the size of the data set, data reconstruction in a RAID 5 array can require significant time to complete, and any additional failure during reconstruction will cause the array to fail.

RAID 5 operates much more slowly than RAID 0 because a parity bit must be calculated for all write operations. RAID 5 requires a minimum of three disks to implement.

To determine the effective capacity of a RAID 5 set, use the following formula:

$$S*(N-1)$$

where *S* represents the smallest disk in the array and *N* represents the number of disks in the array.

RAID 5 volumes are suitable for the following applications:

➤ Applications where reads occur much more often than writes, or that read randomly. An example would include a records-management scenario where artifacts have become official records, and access is limited to predominantly read operations, or read-only configurations in standby/recovery farms.

➤ In scenarios where fault tolerance is required without the cost of the additional disk space required for a RAID 1 volume. Keep in mind that a RAID 5 volume is significantly more efficient than a mirrored volume when larger numbers of disks are implemented to construct the volume.

➤ Recovery scenarios such as dedicated backup storage that require high write ratios to construct the data, and high read ratios thereafter.

Figure 17-8 illustrates a RAID 5 implementation.

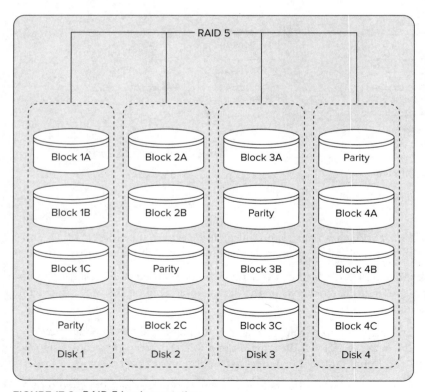

FIGURE 17-8: RAID 5 Implementation

Selecting a RAID type requires maintaining a balance between performance, capacity, I/O, protection, and rebuild performance. Table 17-2 compares the various RAID types on these considerations. In the table, stars represent how appropriate one or more RAID configurations are to varying characteristics, where five stars represent the most appropriate and one star represents least appropriate.

TABLE 17-2: RAID Performance Comparisons

TYPE	OVERALL PERFORMANCE	CAPACITY	REBUILD PERFORMANCE	DATA PROTECTION	I/O PERFORMANCE
RAID 0	****	*****	*	*	****
RAID 1	**	*	**	***	**
RAID 0+1	****	*	****	****	****
RAID 5	***	****	*	*	*

Choosing the Right RAID Architecture

Keep the following in mind when selecting a RAID architecture:

➤ RAID 0 provides the best storage capacity efficiency, because it does not require additional disks for redundancy. When implementing RAID 0, it is recommended that you use identical disks to provide 100 percent capacity efficiency.

➤ RAID 1 provides 50 percent capacity efficiency, because it requires half of the disks in the array to provide data mirroring.

➤ RAID 5 stores distributed parity bits. Its capacity can be defined using the equation provided previously in this chapter.

➤ RAID 0+1 provides 50 percent capacity efficiency, similar to RAID 1, because it is mirrored.

The type of RAID also depends on the type of data that the array will host. For example, with SharePoint 2010, tempdb remains the most important data set to maintain efficiency and acceptable performance. Good write latency is critical to ensuring the farm's overall performance. RAID 1+0 is the most effective solution overall for SharePoint 2010 to ensure an ideal configuration and maximize performance.

RAID 5 maximizes capacity. However, this comes at the expense of poor overall performance, and its application should be limited. In many cases, more disks are required with RAID 5 to mirror the transaction performance of RAID 0+1 on fewer disks. However, when combined with smaller, high-performance disks (such as SAS), RAID 5 can provide adequate throughput to support less mission-critical data sets (such as temporary disk backup storage).

When considering a RAID type, you should understand the rebuild performance characteristics, as well as the overall performance provided by that type. Rebuild performance can have a significant effect on storage throughput. It is important to understand the impact that rebuild performance will have on your deployment, and ensure that any business continuity management requirements account for both the duration of a rebuild and its performance characteristics. As a best practice, rebuilds should be scheduled outside of core business hours to minimize the impact on end users.

Table 17-3 provides a guide to RAID applications with SharePoint 2010.

TABLE 17-3: RAID Applications with SharePoint 2010

TYPE	APPLICATION	
RAID 0	N/A	
RAID 1	Operating system and application data	
RAID 0+1	`Tempdb`, Search Crawl database, Social and Synchronization databases, Usage and Health Data Collection database, Secure Store Service database, Web Analytics Staging and Reporting databases, Search Property Store database, PerformancePoint Service, Word Automation Service	
RAID 5	Content Databases, Configuration database, Business Connectivity Service (BCS), Application Registry, Subscription Settings database, State Service, Search Administration and Search Crawl databases, Profile database, Managed Metadata	

Hardware and Software RAID

RAID implementations can occur at the hardware or software layer. When using hardware-based RAID solutions, a hardware RAID controller is used to configure the RAID level of attached disks. When using software RAID, the operating system manages the RAID configuration, in addition to data reads and writes.

Windows Server 2003 and Windows Server 2008 support the following software RAID types:

- ➤ *RAID 0* — Up to 32 disks striped
- ➤ *RAID 1* — Two disks mirrored
- ➤ *RAID 5* — Up to 32 disks striped with parity

WINDOWS SERVER 2008 STORAGE PERFORMANCE IMPROVEMENTS

In addition to providing software RAID types, Windows Server 2008 includes additional storage solution performance improvements to include the following:

- ➤ Improved storage performance through reduced process utilization
- ➤ Improved storage I/O process performance
- ➤ Improved performance where multiple paths exist between servers and storage
- ➤ Improved connection performance for iSCSI attached storage
- ➤ Improved support for optimization of the storage subsystem

Software RAID is supported only for dynamic disks. Though software RAID does not provide performance parity when compared to hardware-based RAID solutions, its ease of implementation and cost effectiveness are beneficial where constrained by budget. Software RAID benefits from the fact that it does not require specialized hardware beyond having available multiple disks. However, it is typically reserved for non–mission-critical applications that can support the increased CPU load. For small and medium-sized businesses, software-based RAID may be an ideal solution to avoid the costs of hardware RAID controllers.

The choice between software and hardware RAID hinges on budget, flexibility, and performance. Table 17-4 provides some guidelines on choosing between software and hardware RAID.

TABLE 17-4: Hardware and Software RAID Comparisons

TYPE	IMPLEMENTATION	ADVANTAGES	DISADVANTAGES
Software	RAID 5	No additional hardware costs	Requires system processing resources
Hardware	RAID 0, 1, 0+1	Does not compete for processor cycles, and provides the highest scalability and performance	Additional hardware costs
Hardware	RAID 5	High performance	Additional hardware costs
Hardware	RAID 1	High redundancy	Additional hardware costs
Hardware	RAID 10	High performance and redundancy	Additional hardware costs
Software	RAID 10	Good redundancy and low cost	Uses processing resources
Software	RAID 5	High performance read and low cost	Uses processing resources

SQL SERVER PLANNING

SQL Server is the foundational layer of SharePoint, and is most associated with the underlying disk subsystem. When planning your storage layer, it is equally important to understand how that storage will apply to each database server in the topology.

Proper SQL Server planning, as well as understanding the features it provides, will lead to an efficient and scalable solution providing the performance and capacity necessary to meet current and future demands.

Understanding SQL Server Features and Capabilities

SQL Server provides a number of features and capabilities that can be leveraged to support both performance and manageability. Using these features and capabilities can help provide insight into issues before they occur, and ensure optimal performance through the life cycle of the deployments.

Page Checksum/Page Level Restore

Page checksum was introduced in SQL Server 2005 to increase data protection by detecting disk I/O errors that are not reported by the operating system or underlying hardware. A checksum is calculated and verified in the following situations:

➤ When a page is written to disk from the buffer pool

➤ When a page is read from disk into the buffer pool, if the page has been previously written to disk with a checksum

In SQL Server, page checksum is enabled by default, and can be modified using the ALTER DATABASE [] SET PAGE_VERIFY Transact-SQL statement.

With page checksum enabled, when a checksum error is detected, SQL Server will respond with an 824 error, which will appear as follows:

```
SQL Server detected a logical consistency-based I/O error: torn page
(expected signature: 0x0; actual signature: 0x9dc8cfec). It occurred
during a read of page (1:152) in database ID 4 at offset 0x00000000130000
in file 'D:\Program Files\Microsoft SQL Server\MSSQL.1\MSSQL\DATA
\MSDBData.mdf'. Additional messages in the SQL Server error log or system
event log may provide more detail. This is a severe error condition that
threatens database integrity and must be corrected immediately. Complete
a full database consistency check (DBCC CHECKDB). This error can be
caused by many factors; for more information, see SQL Server Books Online.
```

Page level restore is not supported with SharePoint 2010. In order to resolve this issue, an administrator must recover the last known good backup of the affected database and restore it to the environment.

Instant File Initialization

Windows *instant file initialization* was introduced in SQL Server 2005. When used, it allows for fast execution of file operations such as database creation, log or data file additions, increasing a database size to include autogrow, and restoring databases or filegroups. With instant file initialization, used disk space is reclaimed without filling that space with zeros, which is the default SQL Server behavior. Instead, disk content is overwritten as new data is written to the files.

 Log files cannot be initialized instantaneously.

Database Snapshots

Database snapshots provide an addressable point-in-time view of a given database. These snapshots are suitable for both reporting and recovery purposes. SharePoint 2010 extends support for database snapshots to its new backup and recovery features such as Unattached Content Database Data Recovery and Windows PowerShell, where administrators can pass the -UseSnapshot parameter when performing many common operations without impacting the production system.

It is important to understand that, while database snapshots provide a variety of use case scenarios in production environments, they can impact both scale and performance unless properly planned.

As a point-in-time view of a database, database snapshots consume storage resources for their hosting. However, the space required is generally less than the source database, because a snapshot is based on sparse file technology provided by the NTFS filesystem. Snapshots are maintained at a 1:1 ratio to the data files the snapshot represents. As pages are updated in the source database, they are copied to the snapshot. Therefore, in the event that all pages in the source database are updated, the snapshot can mirror the size of the source database on which it was created.

Performance is another point of planning when considering an architecture that relies on database snapshots. As previously explained, each write on the source database results in a write to the snapshot. The impact is minimal where a small number of snapshots are maintained. However, where several snapshots exist for a single source database, those writes should be accounted for as the source database is updated.

Topology Planning for SQL Server

Determining the appropriate topology for your database server is an important step to ensure adequate overall system performance. As you begin to plan your hardware, you should understand that SharePoint 2010 is a 64-bit only application and requires 64-bit versions of SQL Server.

Single-Server Deployment

A *single-server deployment* configuration is recommended under the following circumstances:

➤ For small to moderate user volumes, and when the number of concurrent sessions is easily handled by the processing capability of the server

➤ For developers who must develop custom solutions that integrate with SharePoint 2010

➤ When evaluating SharePoint 2010

The single-server deployment configuration is the easiest to install and maintain. The default SQL Server installation options result in this deployment topology. During the evaluation, if you find that this deployment configuration meets the needs of your organization, you should continue with this deployment configuration, knowing that you can upgrade hardware or add additional server instances later if report demand increases. Figure 17-9 shows an example of a single-server deployment configuration.

User Requests

Web, Applications, and Database Server Roles

FIGURE 17-9: Single-server deployment configuration

If you are using a design that is based on a single SQL Server instance, you should consider the use of SQL Server connection aliases to allow seamless migration to a new database server topology (such as Failover Clustering or Database Mirroring).

Through the use of a *connection alias*, you can keep the application configuration the same. However, you must instruct the underlying operating system to look somewhere else for the database.

You can create an alias using one of two utilities:

➤ SQL Server Configuration Manager

➤ SQL Server Client Network Utility

 To learn more about configuring aliases, see http://msdn.microsoft.com/en-us/library/ms188635.aspx.

Standard Server Deployment

In a *standard server* deployment, two database servers serve SharePoint databases in either a Failover Clustering or Database Mirroring design. Figure 17-10 shows an example of a standard server deployment configuration.

The standard deployment configuration is recommended for moderate user volumes where demand for processing is evenly spaced throughout the day, and the number of concurrent sessions is easily handled by the processing capability of the servers.

In addition to greater resiliency, the standard deployment scenario can offer improved performance over the single-server deployment. For example, in a database mirroring design, the load can be distributed across the principal and mirroring server, therefore mitigating common strains to include processing resources such as CPU time, memory, and disk access when they are hosted on the same computer. Some SharePoint operations are resource-intensive, so running these on separate

User Requests

Clustered Web Servers

Application Server

Clustered or Mirrored SQL Servers

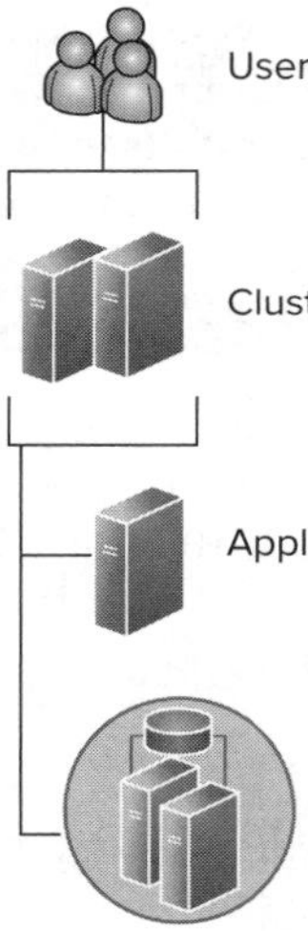

FIGURE 17-10: Standard server deployment configuration

servers can reduce the competition for processing resources. Additionally, the footprint of a SharePoint database might be small at first, but disk space requirements and I/O subsystem utilization can grow significantly at run time.

When you are deciding whether to choose a single-server deployment or a standard server deployment, consider the following points based on your hardware configuration:

➤ Processing resources

➤ Memory resources

➤ Disk space availability

> ➤ I/O capacity

> ➤ Redundancy

If you find that this deployment configuration meets the needs of your organization, you should continue with this deployment configuration, knowing that you can upgrade hardware or add additional server instances later if report demand increases.

Scale-Out Server Deployment

In a *scale-out server* deployment, multiple SQL Servers in a Failover Clustering or Database Mirroring configuration support SharePoint databases. Topologies include Active, Active, Passive (AAp) Failover Clustering topologies, or two distinct Database Mirroring pairs. Figure 17-11 shows an example of a scale-out server deployment configuration.

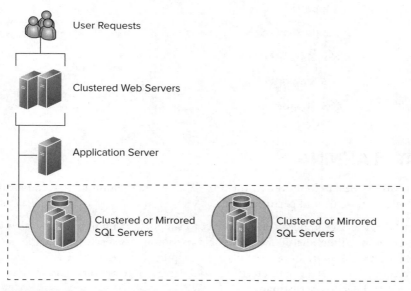

FIGURE 17-11: Scale-out server deployment configuration

A scale-out deployment enables workload distribution in high-volume environments. In a scale-out deployment, each back-end database server in the deployment is referred to as a *node*.

A scale-out server deployment configuration is recommended for the following circumstances:

> ➤ For high-volume user loads, where activity is measured in concurrent users, or in the complexity of operations that take a long time to process or render (such as high-capacity search scenarios)

> ➤ For high-availability scenarios, where it is important that the SharePoint environment does not encounter unplanned downtime or become unavailable

> ➤ When you want to improve the performance of scheduled operations or service applications

By hosting your SharePoint databases on an instance that is part of a failover cluster, you can enhance the fault tolerance of your environment. Failover clustering is also possible for standard deployments, but typically there is less need for failover clustering when the environment is not configured for high-availability scenarios (such as environments with scale-out deployments).

It is important to determine and document carefully your availability needs, and to test the solution to ensure that it provides the expected availability. Table 17-5 lists supported and non-supported high-availability configurations.

TABLE 17-5: Supported and Non-Supported High-Availability Configurations

CONFIGURATION	SUPPORTABILITY STATEMENT
Failover Clustering	Supported
Log Shipping	Supported
Database Mirroring	Supported
Transactional Replication	Not Supported
Merge Replication	Not Supported
Snapshot Replication	Not Supported

DATABASE LAYOUT PLANNING

SharePoint 2010 installs a variety of databases out of the box. With proper planning, you can meet current and future needs related to scale and performance.

Depending on both the SKU and service applications you elect to support, you will find a number of databases created as a result of installing SharePoint 2010 or provisioning its service applications — some service applications requiring more than one database to support their services. Understanding what each database purpose is, as well as its characteristics, will drive a SQL Server solution that supports both seamless scale and needed performance.

Configuration Database

The *configuration database* handles all administration of the deployment, directing requests to the appropriate database, and managing load-balancing for the back-end databases. When a front-end web server receives a request for a page in a particular site, it checks the configuration database to determine which content database holds the site's data.

You can run the configuration database on the same computer as a web server or on a remote computer running Microsoft SQL Server. The configuration database concepts are relatively unchanged in Microsoft SharePoint Server 2010.

In Microsoft Office SharePoint Server 2007 and Windows SharePoint Services 3.0, the `SiteMap` table was stored in the configuration database, which provided information about which content database contains data for a given site. When Windows SharePoint Services or Microsoft Office SharePoint Server 2007 received the URL of a request, settings in this database determined which content database contained data for the site.

In Microsoft SharePoint Server 2010, the `SiteMap` is serialized to disk to improve performance and reduce database callback operations that could result in contention when serving requests on large server farm deployments. As a result, the configuration database is safe to deploy on a RAID 5 array. Capacity planning should begin by sizing the configuration database to 2 GB, and allowing 40 MB growth for each 50,000 site collections created.

Central Administration Content Database

The *back-end content* database stores all site content, including site documents or files in document libraries, list data, and web part properties, as well as usernames and rights. All the data for the Central Administration website resides in one content database on only one computer. Similar to the configuration database, upon initial installation, light read volumes can be expected.

Usage and Health Data Collection Service

The *Usage and Health Data Collection Service* collects and logs SharePoint health indicators and usage metrics for analysis and reporting purposes.

The *logging database* is the Microsoft SQL Server, Microsoft SQL Server Data Engine (MSDE), or Microsoft Windows SQL Server Data Engine (WMSDE) database that stores health monitoring and usage data temporarily, and can be used for reporting and diagnostics.

Content Database

The back-end *content database* stores all site content, including site documents or files in document libraries, list data, and web part properties, as well as usernames and rights. All the data for a specific site resides in one content database on only one computer. SharePoint 2010 supports content databases up to 4 TB in size for traditional workloads, and exceeding 4 TB for document archive and/or records management scenarios. The minimum performance requirements for content databases is 0.25 IOPs per gigabyte of content and for optimal performance, and 2 IOPs per gigabyte stored.

State Service

The *State Service* maintains temporary state information for InfoPath Forms Services.

The *state database* maintains temporary state information for InfoPath Forms Services.

Secure Store Service

The *Secure Store Service* replaces the Single Sign On Service in previous versions of the product.

This service provides storage and mapping of credentials, such as account names and passwords. Portal site-based applications can retrieve information from third-party applications and back-end systems such as Enterprise Resource Planning (ERP) and Customer Relations Management (CRM) systems.

The use of Secure Store functionality enables users to authenticate without asking the user multiple times for the credentials needed to authenticate in that system.

The store database provides storage and mapping of credentials such as account names and passwords.

Business Data Connectivity Service

The Business Database Connectivity Service provides a means for storing, securing, and administering external content types and related objects. A database stores external content types and related objects.

Managed Metadata Service

The *Managed Metadata Service* publishes a term store and, optionally, a set of content types.

The *term store database* stores metadata. The web front end public application programming interfaces (APIs) interact with the data layer to get or set data. The data layer talks to the term store directly if the shared service is local to the farm, or it talks to a back-end web service on an application server if the shared service is not local. The back-end web service then interacts with the data layer on the application server to get to the term store.

User Profile Service

The *User Profile Service* encompasses user profiles and My Sites.

The *user profile database* is a flexible database that stores and manages user and associated information. The database allows for a flexible schema that supports multiple data types. It can be queried and it can be updated. For example, a company can define the attributes of an employee record in the profile database. Then, for each record, an employee object will be created and saved. This information would then be usable in a number of ways, such as in web parts, in the web service, or to create rule-based groups or roles.

The *synchronization database* is used to store configuration and staging data for synchronization of profile data from external sources such as Active Directory.

The *social tagging database* stores social tagging records and their respective URLs, which are coupled with information from the profile and taxonomy databases at the front-end layer at execution/request. This database is used to store social tags and notes created by users.

Web Analytics Service

The *Web Analytics Service* provides rich analytics to provide insights into your web traffic, search, and SharePoint assets, enabling you to better understand your user and deployments. With SharePoint Web Analytics, you'll be able to tailor the system to meet the needs of your users, optimize how they use and discover information, and create targeted content for your sites.

The Web Analytics *staging database* is a working database that stores un-aggregated fact data, asset metadata, and queued batch data, and provides short-term retention of this content.

The Web Analytics *reporting database* stores aggregated standard report tables, fact data aggregated by site group, date, and asset metadata, in addition to diagnostics information.

Search Service

The *administration database* is what the Shared Services Provider database was in Microsoft Office SharePoint Server 2007. It is instantiated once per search application, aligning with the Administration component. The administration database hosts the Search application configuration and access control lists (ACLs) for the content crawl.

The *property database* stores crawled properties associated with the crawled data to include properties, history data, crawl queues, and so on.

The *crawl databases* host the crawled data and drive crawls. The crawl database is what the Search database was in Microsoft Office SharePoint Server 2007.

WINDOWS SERVER 2008 R2

Windows Server 2008 is the core prerequisite for SharePoint 2010, and provides new and improved storage management features and capabilities. Using these features and capabilities in Windows Server 2008, organizations can increase the reliability and flexibility of their server infrastructures.

Following is a breakdown of some of these features and capabilities:

➤ *Simplified Partition Creation* — Partition creation has been streamlined, resulting in being able to use a simple right-click to create basic, spanned, or striped partitions from the context menu.

➤ *Conversion* — Windows provides advanced scenario detection. For example, when adding more than four partitions, a prompt is displayed to provide options for converting the disk to dynamic or GUID partition table partitions.

➤ *Extend and Shrink* — Similar to the advanced disk management offered through many SANS, Windows Server 2008 R2 provides the capability to extend and shrink partitions through the user interface.

➤ *Removable Storage* — New removable storage features enable simple tracking of tapes and optical disks.

➤ *Share and Storage Management* — The new Provision Storage Wizard provides an intuitive user interface to assist in the process of creating volumes on existing disks, or optionally on a storage subsystem attached to your server(s). In scenarios where you are creating volumes on a separate storage subsystem, the Provision Storage Wizard will enable the creation of a *logical unit number* (*LUN*) to host the new volume, or optionally creating only the LUN.

➤ *Storage Explorer* — The new Storage Explorer enables a simple view in managing FC and iSCSI fabrics available in the SAN. With Storage Explorer, you can view and manage the FC and iSCSI fabrics that are available in your SAN, including detailed information about servers connected to the SAN, and components in the fabrics to include host bus adapters, switchers, initiators, and targets.

➤ *Storage Manager for SANs* — The new Storage Manager for SANs helps to create and manage LUNs on both FC and iSCSI subsystems that support Virtual Disk Service (VDS) in the SAN.

To learn more about Storage and Print Solutions in Windows Server 2008 R2, see www.microsoft.com/windowsserver2008/en/us/storage-print.aspx.

SUMMARY

The storage architecture you elect will be driven by two dominant factors: business requirements and budget. These factors combined will drive the overall architecture you elect to support the solution. From this point, fault tolerance, performance, and the remaining requirements must be tailored to meet your needs.

It is equally important to understand that there is no one document that will provide the information necessary to plan and develop end-to-end storage solutions because of the dynamics of business requirements, as well as changes in hardware and software. You should understand the fundamentals included in this chapter, and use those as starting points in your planning.

In Chapter 18, you learn how develop, test, and deploy your solution.

18

Developing, Testing, and Deploying Your SharePoint 2010 Solution

By Vesa Juvonen

The planning of the development, testing, and deployment models has a large impact on the overall cost of investment for a SharePoint project. SharePoint development, testing, and deployment can be completed in many ways, depending on the size of your project and deployment.

It's important to realize that projects require various roles and processes to ensure that they are successful. It's not just planning the architecture of the infrastructure or customizations, but the development, testing, and deployment processes, project management, and resource planning that will affect the outcome of your project.

DECIDING ON WHAT ARCHITECTURAL APPROACH TO USE

One of the key considerations for a SharePoint project is the development model and the architectural approach for the customizations. This will not only have an impact on the development time, but also on activities conducted during the maintenance phase of the project. Let's take a look at some of the different models available for SharePoint development.

Custom Component Development Architectures

During the planning of the SharePoint solution development, special attention should be given to the architecture planning of the customizations. Architecture defines the way the different components work, such as how web parts are developed, and how the overall code and Visual Studio project structure will be created and developed.

Lack of architectural and design planning can severely decrease the reusability of code inside of your project. Unfortunately, relatively often, code architecture in SharePoint projects is often an afterthought. The lack of proper design manifests itself as issues in testing, such as difficulty in the creation of unit tests against your code.

As a rule of thumb, similar to any development work, code should be structured into different layers to provide flexibility and promote reusability of the code. By layering the code efficiently, unit tests can also be created efficiently, which can be performed automatically as part of the development.

You have numerous approaches to planning code architecture. The decision on the correct approach should be based partly on the skill of your development team. The development skills at your disposal help guide your decision-making as to whether advanced architectural patterns should be used, as opposed to simpler patterns.

Another key aspect to consider relates to the maintainability and future upgradeability of your code base. Will your maintenance developers be the original developers, or will they make up a slightly less skilled team? Will new developers be able to understand your code base when you or your original team is no longer on the project? These factors contribute to the long-term success of your code architecture, performance of your SharePoint environments, and, ultimately, the end-user experience.

Designing Reusable Frameworks in SharePoint

Reusable frameworks for SharePoint provide a cost-efficient way to reuse code for multiple projects without requiring recoding for each project. Common patterns and code classes will emerge during the creation of your initial release. These features can benefit your current and future SharePoint projects. Where possible, these should be included in separate framework-type code projects from the start.

A good example of a reusable framework is Microsoft's patterns and practices guidance package for SharePoint 2010. This package contains a lot of reusable generic code, which would be beneficial for multiple projects. Commonly, this type of code can either be copied to the project, or used directly from its own packages.

The usage also depends on the skill level of the developers involved in the project. Writing generic reusable code could be difficult for less-experienced developers, and could increase the overall work required for the project. However, reusable frameworks can be created relatively easily by an experienced team of developers, and the code can be used for multiple projects.

Following are some examples of common features included in reusable SharePoint frameworks:

- Logging
- Configuration management
- Caching
- Service locator model
- Generic list management
- Content type management
- Site provisioning management

The packaging and dependency planning of this type of framework-level code is examined in more detail later in this chapter.

Third-Party Component Considerations

One way to decrease the amount of custom code required for your SharePoint-based solutions is to use third-party components. Great components are available that can help fulfill your project objectives without implementing customizations. Aim to utilize your development resources and focus your development effort on activities that are not available out of the box, or where third-party solutions are not available. Remember, your goal is to deliver business value, not to develop features that can already be met by affordable third-party solutions.

Another reason to prefer third-party solutions is that the developers of these solutions provide continual support and enhancements over time to their products. They worry about the testing and development resources to maintain these products. This helps your development team focus on delivering business-specific customizations and value.

Key considerations with third-party components include ensuring that your project will have sufficient legal rights to the usage and source code to avoid any additional costs throughout the project. This is especially true for community code projects made available on sites such as CodePlex. For these types of projects, review the license and ensure that source code is acquired to enable you to maintain and enhance if the third-party component vendor closes, or the community code project is no longer available. Your SharePoint deployment should not be dependent on custom code that cannot be supported, or for which your business is not correctly licensed.

 It's important that you ensure that third-party components do not impact your upgrade experience to future versions of SharePoint. Always attempt to ensure that the source code for the third-party components is available. This will enable you to make changes required to upgrade to the next version of SharePoint. If not available, this may affect your future upgrade project. When source code is not available, the decision to use components should be carefully analyzed, since it can have a long-term impact for the future of the deployment.

Settling in with a Chosen Development Methodology

Usually, SharePoint projects are based on agile development methodologies. Development occurs iteratively, and deliverables are divided into a smaller set of entities, which can then be delivered at different times. These methodologies are popular because they provide visible progress on the project. By splitting projects into smaller iterations, you can track the individual tasks more easily, and follow up on the overall progress of your project.

Numerous adaptations of methodologies can be used as the base guide for your project. When choosing a methodology, ensure that it is familiar and suitable for the project team that will be using it. If the team is not familiar with the methodology, this may cause additional complexity and delay while the team learns to use the methodology.

One of most well-known methodologies or models for iterative projects is Scrum.

Scrum can be a useful model for development, but requires adequate resources to be able to use effectively. The core plank of Scrum is to develop in iterations and have regular follow-up meetings on progress and next tasks. If the development team does not have good development leadership, or individual team members cannot plan their work adequately, this strict methodology can cause additional resource requirements and confusion for the project team members.

Regardless of the methodology employed, each member should always have clear responsibilities, estimate accurately, and report risks and issues early to the development lead and project manager. Development teams must be able to break their work into tasks that can be managed against a project schedule. Methodologies can help projects move forward, as long as project members realize that methodology is not the objective of the project, and they concentrate on the deliverables. Unfortunately, for some projects, intense focus is placed on following a methodology rigidly, which can be a detriment to the project delivery and real business value.

Lastly, using a methodology provides an industry-proven process and team structure, with clear guidelines, responsibilities, and activities. This is highly beneficial to managing scope, avoiding cost, and schedule overruns.

The following sections cover key considerations for application life cycle management with SharePoint 2010.

APPLICATION LIFE CYCLE MANAGEMENT IN SHAREPOINT 2010

One of the most important processes to be planned as part of your SharePoint deployment is the application life cycle management (ALM) process, and defining the model of handling solution development. The ALM process includes the different tools and practices to be followed within the particular project.

Tools for Development

SharePoint solution development requires Microsoft Visual Studio. Other valuable extensions are available to further enhance the development experience. SharePoint 2010 development can be performed using previous Visual Studio versions, but the recommended version of Visual Studio is 2010, which introduces new SharePoint tools.

SharePoint tools in Visual Studio 2010 make it easy to develop simple web parts and Features, but they require minor modifications, especially for larger projects to be able to use them efficiently with large teams. Luckily, Visual Studio 2010 supports having SharePoint development extensions added, which provide additional support and functionalities to make large project development easier.

Source Control

One of the most important systems for your team-based development is *source control*. Source code and related assets are the most important deliverables from developers, and should be considered as critical assets and secured using a source control system.

Source control systems help to integrate the developed solutions. They enable development teams to work on different parts of the same system without overwriting other team members' changes. They protect against conflicts and additional work when code is checked in. They maintain code versions and can be set up to ensure that each check-in results in a successful build.

Even if you have only a small amount of development to complete, using a source control system is definitely recommended. This provides a single secure place for all your code that has been developed, and one place to manage. From a disaster recovery perspective, it is much easier to take backups from the single source control system, than it is to take backups from the individual development computers.

For larger projects, the most commonly used source control system in SharePoint development is Microsoft Team Foundation Server, which offers more than just source control. This does not mean that you are forced to invest in Team Foundation Server. Other viable options are available if you only want to invest in source control and not in the other great features Team Foundation Server provides.

Automated Builds

Automated builds are used to automate integration testing of the customizations using a daily schedule, or whenever a developer checks in code. The objective is to ensure that code created by your development team integrates without any issues. This prevents large integration phases where overlapping code requires fixing and rework, and enables you to take a build at any time to deploy to other environments (such as your test environment).

Quite often, automated builds are extended to include other activities, such as unit testing or automated functional testing. By scheduling these to be actioned automatically, you can save on overall costs concerning quality assurance (QA). It is possible to provide a new fully working version of the latest checked-in developer customizations in your test environment daily. When the customer or the tester arrives at work in the morning, results and indications of the expected test result will be available to analyze.

For example, let's say that you have already deployed a release of your solution to your customer (internal or external), and you would like to ensure that the following iterations or maintenance builds could be easily deployed or actually upgraded over the existing environment.

In this kind of scenario, you can use the model defined in Figure 18-1. Here, you test the upgrade actions that must be performed as part of your automated build. Combining virtualization techniques, you mimic your production environment against your daily build. In a best-case scenario, you would have a legacy copy of your customer content databases from the production environment to perform this daily test.

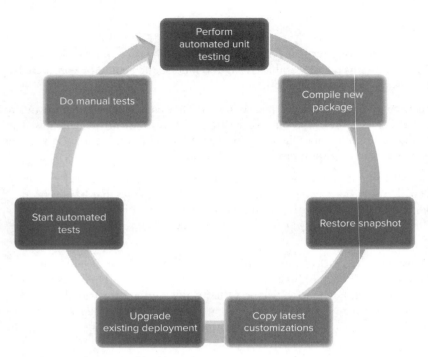

FIGURE 18-1: Automated build steps

Understandably, it is not always possible to have a copy of production data in your test environments. It is still possible to complete the following steps in Figure 18-1:

1. *Perform automated unit testing* — Before moving to the following steps, it's important to verify that the customizations actually work as expected. To verify business'logic handling of the solutions, you create unit tests, which are automatically executed as part of your automated build. This way, any business-level issue can be identified as early as possible in your development cycle without requiring manual testing.

2. *Compile new package* — The automated build compiles the code stored in your source control system (optimally based on labeled status) to enable you to use the latest stable build, rather than simply the latest source code version. This avoids code that is in flux and is labeled as not ready to be released. This requires minor tweaks to your automated build configuration files (MSBuild scripts). This helps ensure that only correct source code versions are used.

3. *Restore snapshot* — Because automated builds are executed on a daily basis, you must restore your test environment to a base configuration that mimics the state of your current production environment, ready for your new build. Depending on your virtualization platform, this could be difficult to establish. With Microsoft Hyper-V, you can perform this action easily (using Windows PowerShell, for example), so that it can be easily automated and included in the build process.

4. *Copy latest customizations* — After the testing environment has been restored to the point that matches the production environment (SharePoint and production customization version), you can start the server, and copy the latest solution packages (WSP) and any other customizations for deployment purposes.

5. *Upgrade existing deployment* — In this phase, you perform the upgrade of the environment with your latest build. Upgrade actions to perform depend on the project, solution artifacts, and your development model. However, upgrade solution commands are commonly performed from Windows PowerShell (as done during the production environment upgrade). If new site structures are required for the new customizations, you create the necessary scripts to make these structures available for testing purposes, and these scripts will be executed in this phase.

6. *Start automated tests* — In this phase, start any automated test scripts that verify the functional integrity of the code. Multiple different tools are available for recording this kind of web test. If you are using Visual Studio, you can integrate the tests and results directly with the source code projects.

 Visual Studio 2010 Team System provides project templates and test tools to create, automate, and execute tests against your test environment.

7. *Do manual tests* — All of the previous steps can be automated to be performed every night, or even multiple times each day. After automated testing has been performed, you can continue performing manual tests. In larger projects, dedicated test resources are responsible for reporting daily build results, and performing the manual actions required. If automated builds are performed during the night, the latest version of the package installed would be ready for the tester to continue testing the next morning.

Automated builds can provide much more than just integration testing of the customizations and code. You will notice that you can use a similar model before the initial version is available for re-creating the portal on a daily basis. As an example, this would mean that you could create Windows PowerShell scripts that would create the initial hierarchy for the future intranet. Once developers update the web templates with latest changes, you would be able to test the latest features on a daily basis. However, it is important to realize that the primary purpose for this kind of daily build environment is not to create content, because all content would be deleted or re-created every day.

The overall life-cycle models are examined in more detail later in this chapter. However, if you have requirements in your projects to provide a more long-term testing environment for your customer, then a target server for your daily builds would not be it. Good practices for these kinds of requirements would be to have a separate weekly release cycle for the environment, which can then be used for functional testing by your customer.

Testing and Quality Assurance

Testing practicalities depend on the project size and objectives. Unfortunately, projects quite often do not always concentrate on these topics enough during the development phase. A key indicator symptomatic of not understanding the value of testing is the time your project has reserved for it. This is a classic mistake in research and development (as well as in customer-oriented projects) that often delays the deployment to your production environments.

Unit Testing

Unit testing is used to ensure that individual units of source code work as expected. Unit testing can be performed either manually, or using automation by writing code-based tests to verify the code works properly.

When it comes to unit testing, one of the challenges in SharePoint development is the nature of SharePoint code and how developers implement logic in the user interface (UI) classes (such as a web part or custom control). This makes it difficult to test business logic residing in the UI class, and this makes it even more difficult to ensure that your automated unit tests cover the majority of your code base.

Developers should attempt to create unit tests for Features that follow common .NET patterns. For example, using the well-known model-view-controller (MVC) pattern will make it easier to test logic of your UI classes, and rendering different HTML values because output can be tested.

 The RTM version of Visual Studio doesn't support test projects being targeted to .NET version 3.5, which means that this default model in Visual Studio for unit testing cannot be used for SharePoint 2010 projects. However, this was changed in Service Pack 1, which added unit testing support for other .NET Framework versions.

Test Case Planning

Test cases should be documented based on the original business requirements to verify the Features of the individual elements and customizations. Test case documentation should be written at a level such that people who are not technical or part of the implementation phase can perform the testing by following the documented test cases.

Where possible, some of the test cases can be recorded as web tests using Visual Studio Team System. These can be automatically executed as part of your daily build. This way, you can decrease the amount of overall resources required for actual testing.

Test cases should always be created for your development customizations. At the highest priority, they should concentrate on verifying the customizations, not out-of-the-box Features, which have already been tested and are supported by Microsoft. If customizations include highly customized master pages, it is good practice to verify the standard out-of-the-box Features, because heavily customized master pages may break out-of-the-box Features.

A common mistake with test case creation is that they are written based on already developed customizations. This results in a low-quality test case that tests the current outcome, not the original business requirement. You should test based on the original business requirement!

Each test case should have a high coverage of main and alternate outcomes of the individual Feature. Another common issue is overly automating the setting of properties (for example, web part properties) in your script. This may lead to false verification, because each test is only testing success cases, and it does not verify issues related to wrong property values.

You should consider the following when planning test cases:

➤ Missing configurations in SharePoint for checking error handling of the web part

➤ Invalid entries as configuration values for the web part with expected error handling

➤ Using a web part in alternative places, not only in the planned location

Each test case should include a clear definition of what is and is not tested. This helps a tester focus on the most relevant issues. For example, a separate test should be used to check UI consistency across a number of customizations, rather than in a specific test case that is focused on the Features provided by the customization. Each test case should have clear passing or failing criteria. This requires the expected outcome to be defined in detail.

Because many of the SharePoint customizations are based on some out-of-the-box Features or services, each test case should also include the prerequisites from an environment and resource point of view. For example, testing a custom search results web part requires the correct configuration in your testing environment.

Performance Testing

Performance testing can be considered from either the IT professional or development point of view. From the IT professional point of view, performance testing is used to ensure that the hardware is adequate for the planned usage, and to identify performance bottlenecks. From the development perspective, performance testing focuses on reducing the impact on server resources per page request, page payload size reduction for first and subsequent requests, and, lastly, efficiency of client-side code.

A common mistake made by many development teams is a failure to use .NET code-performance profiling tools to proactively analyze and optimize the efficiency of their code during the project development cycle, rather than reactively when an issue is reported by the IT professional team, or, even worse, in production.

Following are some other performance testing considerations:

➤ *Mature test environments* — To be able to get repeatable results, the environment should be stabilized and documented so that, in subsequent releases, a similar setup can be created. Ensure that the environment does not have any other load, so that results and metrics are comparable to previous test results.

➤ *Population of test data set and information* — Create scripts and tools to populate the required information, which mimics the production usage. There's no point testing intranet performance if it actually doesn't have any content or site structures.

➤ *Deciding adequate stress level for testing* — Plan your stress test usage models based on available capabilities of the tools you use, such as how many concurrent users access the site.

Performance testing activities depend on the life-cycle stage of your project and deployment. You can conduct performance testing in this environment before initial release or public release is done to your production environment. Notice also that, since you most likely cannot repeat performance tests in your production environment in later releases, it's beneficial to also conduct tests in alternative environments, which can be then used in future phases as your baseline test environment. This means that if, in following phases, performance will decrease 10 percent in your reference environment, it will do the same in production.

Test results with this kind of baseline testing are not precise, but it will provide you with a clear indication of the performance impact of the changes applied in a particular version.

Multiple simulated performance tests should be performed before the implementation phase of the project starts. Identify performance bottlenecks as early as possible to avoid development rework in later iterations. A good practice is to conduct performance testing as soon as you have a "Feature-ready release." Continue to repeat performance tests to demonstrate improvements against your initial performance benchmark. Continue repeating performance testing for maintenance releases done after the initial release of the customizations.

As an example, let's say a previous intranet project follows the release cycle defined in Figure 18-2. As you can see from Figure 18-2, there were five iterative releases during development, and after that, development was changed to quarterly release mode, with optional bug-fix releases between quarterly releases.

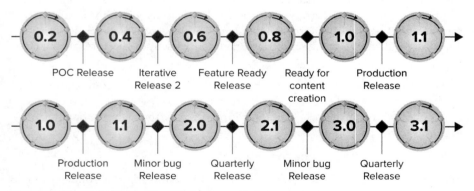

FIGURE 18-2: Global intranet project release cycle

Version 1.0 of the performance tests was created at the same time as the Feature-ready release, meaning release when all functionalities have at least high-level functionality available based on requirements, but when implementation has not yet been polished for actual production usage.

These tests were updated and performed three times before the actual production release to identify possible issues as early as possible, and to ensure that any fixes do not degrade performance. Each new major release provided updated performance tests. More importantly, the original performance tests used against Version 1.0 are performed to compare previous and current results.

By including performance tests in the portal life-cycle model in the maintenance phase, it becomes possible to test the implication of changes to your production environment (such as patches to an operating system, SQL Server, SharePoint cumulative updates, and service packs) and your customizations.

Functional Testing

Functional testing should be performed in an environment that simulates your production environment to ensure that your Features and customizations are working properly. Even though SharePoint 2010 can be deployed to a client operating system, do not use this as your testing platform because the behavior will differ from a server-side test environment.

For mid-size or large deployments, you should use a separate QA environment that mimics the production environment. It is important to realize that a testing environment should be based on multiple servers and not one server. For example, multiple Web Front Ends (WFEs) and load balancing cause a user's page request to behave differently than that of a single server.

Functional testing should be based on the test cases representing the business requirements to ensure Features are properly verified before moving to the next stage in the deployment process. If automated tests are used in the project, manual functional testing should concentrate on areas and Features that cannot be tested reliably using automation.

In SharePoint deployments, functional testing contains both solutions testing and UI styling verification. For example, issues related to UI rendering is a good example of a test that is quite often not precisely tested in projects.

User Acceptance Testing

User acceptance testing is the final verification of the version or deployment before it is deployed to the production environment. Quite often, business and key stakeholders are involved in the execution of the tests. This involves a combination of manual execution of "use cases" and test cases produced in previous steps of the project life cycle. User acceptance testing is a key milestone that helps the business and project stakeholders decide whether to move forward with your latest solution.

User acceptance testing should always be conducted for any solutions moving from pre-production to the production environment. It should also be conducted by the "customer" of the project, and not by the developers. It is important to document the findings to enable project stakeholders to decide on next actions. For example, these might include signoff or acceptance of your release, and possible remaining issues to be fixed.

From a project management point of view, always remember that a completely bug-free solution is rare. In most projects, the project and business teams have decided on the maximum number of bugs at each severity level. Ensure that you provide enough time to respond to issues that may be picked up in user acceptance testing. Therefore, do not schedule user acceptance testing too close to your release date. Ensure that you have a buffer.

Defect Tracking

Numerous methods exist to manage *defect tracking* and many different tools can be used. At a minimum, all relevant project team members should have access to enter and edit defects in one centralized location. In SharePoint projects, defects are usually tracked within SharePoint, or using Team Foundation Server.

SharePoint provides issue tracking lists that can be further customized based on project need. The challenge with using a SharePoint-based tracking list is that developers would have two different tools to use. Team Foundation Server is the preferred approach. It provides nice centralized task lists directly in Visual Studio for developers. All other project team members could use the Team Foundation Server web access to manage issues and bugs.

When testing is planned, it's also important to agree on the process of handling defects and how they should be documented. Following are some key considerations for creation of defects:

➤ *Priorities* — Each defect should be prioritized, so that bug fixing can start from the most-critical issues and move to less-important issues. Prioritization should be agreed on by team members for the project to avoid all defects being prioritized too high.

➤ *Descriptions* — Each defect should have a detailed description of the issue. There should always be some business requirement or specification pointer, which justifies why it is a defect. Defects shouldn't be used to sneak enhancements into your project scope. Only use defects for existing Features. The description should provide enough detail to reproduce the issue; otherwise, it will get lobbed back to the tester as "Unable to reproduce." If the issue cannot be reproduced, there's no way to ensure that it's fixed after code changes.

➤ *Screen shots* — Screen shots provide a simple and efficient way to provide more information on the encountered issues.

➤ *Time* — SharePoint has extensive logging, which provides additional information on an encountered error, or can even be used directly to solve the root cause of the defect. If there's no exact time on when the bug or issue was encountered, there's no way of utilizing this valuable information. Remember that your development team may work in different time zones.

Other Testing Considerations

Testing should be planned carefully to ensure that the required quality level is met. Testing should be a clear phase in the overall project plan, and not considered as a buffer for development.

Because testing is based on requirements of the project, test planning can be started at the same time as the planning of the technical architecture or customization architecture.

When testing is conducted, ensure that user accounts with different levels of permissions are used to identify any permission issues in the code or configuration. Ensure that your developers verify that their code works in their development environment using different users and permissions before checking in their code.

The next section concentrates more precisely on environmental flow, meaning how the developed solution will flow between environments from development to production.

SHAREPOINT ENVIRONMENTS AND DEPLOYMENT FLOW BETWEEN ENVIRONMENTS

The discussion in this section examines the environments required for SharePoint projects, and how your solutions flow between these environments.

Environments for Large Projects

In large projects, more environments are required than your production environment. The main reason for additional environments is to provide a reliable QA process to avoid downtime and lost business productivity in your production environment. Figure 18-3 shows the common stages most large projects will use to verify the quality of the solution.

FIGURE 18-3: Development cycle

Automated Build Environment

The *automated build environment* or *daily build environment* is used for daily automated integration testing. This environment is built automatically with the latest code from the source code system and, combined with virtual machine snapshots, can be used for daily testing and verification, depending on your environmental usage model.

The automated build environment is usually created from scratch on a daily or weekly basis using your customizations. Where your customizations include site definitions or web templates, these can be created relatively easily as large site hierarchies to mimic your future production environment. Therefore, you are able to smoke-test your project code and customizations before they are released to the next stage (for example, to your dedicated test environments).

Testing Environment

The *testing environment* is either the same environment as used for automated builds, or, in larger projects, it is a large, dedicated SharePoint testing farm where specific release builds can be tested. For example, the test environment can be used for weekly builds to enable business and other stakeholders to keep track of development progress.

Similar to the automated build environment, you can start by re-creating the site hierarchy on each release. After your initial production release, your test environment would be used to mimic the upgrade of the customizations already in production.

Although separate testing environments are typically used in larger projects, a dedicated testing environment is highly recommended for all projects that use third-party solutions or development customizations.

Quality Assurance (Pre-production) Environment

The *quality assurance (QA)* environment (more commonly known as the *User Acceptance Testing (UAT) environment* and the *pre-production environment*) should mimic the production environment from the point of view of a server layout and configuration, so that it can be used for UAT. The environment should follow the same guidance for accounts and network-level configuration. This way, you can use this environment to ensure that, if customizations work in this environment, they should be fine for production usage as well.

Identifying the Environments Your Developers Require

There are various adaptations of setting up team development environments for SharePoint 2010 development. However, this depends heavily on the project size and requirements. Development environments should be standardized between the developers to avoid any issues with different versions of SharePoint 2010 or with any other third-party extensions. Standardization also helps to avoid unexplained issues occurring on a developer's machine.

If virtualization is used, you can quite easily create new development environments for developers. These can be hosted on beefy servers, or, alternatively, depending on your virtualization software, hosted on your developer's machine. It is often more time-efficient to create a new environment (from an image), rather than trying to solve the issues caused by developer tinkering.

Generally, the setup of development environments should be automated as much as possible using scripting and other automation, so that new environments can be created as fast as possible.

It is strongly recommended not to share a single SharePoint environment between developers. SharePoint development involves IIS application pool recycles, repeated WSP builds, and code debugging against SharePoint. These cannot be isolated in a shared SharePoint instance. Overall developer productivity will suffer.

Physical Machine

SharePoint 2010 can be also installed on Windows 7 and Windows Vista (SP2) operating systems. This provides the capability to utilize the developer's computer for day-to-day work and SharePoint development. In this scenario, a local instance of SQL Server, SharePoint 2010, Visual Studio, and any other tools are installed on the physical computer. Performance of SharePoint is not degraded by using virtualization software, which will have positive impact on productivity.

 Setting up development using this model requires good hardware. See TechNet (`http://msdn.microsoft.com/en-us/library/ee554869(office.14).aspx`*) for Microsoft development recommendations.*

Figure 18-4 shows how SharePoint is installed on operating systems. Note the following in the figure:

➤ SharePoint is installed on the host operating system of the individual developers. These computers are in the corporate network, so that they can access different enterprise services (for example, Team Foundation Server) to centrally store the source code and other artifacts.

➤ A source code system (such as Team Foundation Server) is used as the centralized storage point for the implemented customizations. Team Foundation Server is considered to be the initial integration point where developers can retrieve the latest code and test their changes on their environment before checking in their customizations.

➤ Physical servers (or set of virtualization host servers) host testing environments and other services. Code must be tested in a production-like environment. Testing SharePoint 2010 on Windows 7 is not advisable because the production environment is based on multi-server Windows 2008 R2 deployments.

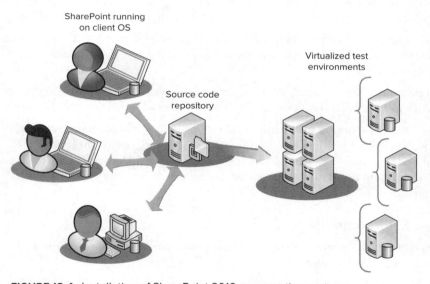

FIGURE 18-4: Installation of SharePoint 2010 on operating systems

From the developer's point of view, this is a relatively flexible model, because all other applications used in daily work (for example, Office client applications) can be easily accessed and used.

A key consideration is whether the development machine's main purpose is for development associated with a single project, or if it will be used across a number of clients or projects. If the physical machine is based on an image, and is solely for use on one project, the risk is reduced. If SharePoint is installed in the developer's client operating system, the risks increase. With constant development, the quality of a SharePoint 2010 instance degrades and becomes "fragmented." Even with a re-install, these problems may not be easy to eradicate (for example, Registry edit problems).

Following are some other challenges involved with the setup having SharePoint installed on primary operating system:

➤ Solving development machine issues can be extremely frustrating and time-consuming.

➤ You must still have additional server operating system environments for testing purposes, and for the centralized source control system.

➤ Scripting a physical client is not easy. It almost always requires manual intervention.

➤ It is difficult to provide common user accounts on each client development machine for verifying the end-user experience. Differentiating projects can be difficult, especially where developers require different levels of licensing for each project. Another issue relates to assembly references to code from other projects that are not available in a particular production environment.

➤ You do not have the capability to restore to a clean installation because no virtualization snapshot techniques can be used. After a few months of development, a number of solutions and configurations will have been applied to the environment. Restoring your environment to a previously known point is not possible without wasting significant time reinstalling.

➤ Depending on the network, there could be domain-level group polices where the developer's computer is installed, which could make it difficult to mimic the actual production environment situation.

➤ If the client's operating system is used, there are some unsupported features in SharePoint Server 2010. All foundation-level functionalities should be working as expected, however.

Installing on Windows 7 is a good option for learning and tinkering, but is not recommended as part of a large development effort. Installing on Windows 2008 is a better option if the physical machine is clean, dedicated, and not "fragmented" from previous projects. Unfortunately, as described earlier, both options do not result in maximum developer productivity and, as a result, they are not recommended.

Virtualized Dedicated Environments

This model is based on using virtualization software on the development computers to host an instance of the SharePoint and development environments.

This model has clear advantages when compared to a pure physical development environment. Development environment isolation avoids any issues with developing multiple projects at the same time. You can use a native server operating system during the development phase, which minimizes any issues caused by the operating system platform. This increases the overall knowledge of developers about the native operating systems used in SharePoint production environments. Developers can take advantage of virtualization snapshot techniques to experiment, and restore their environment back to its previous state, if required.

Figure 18-5 shows an example of a virtualized dedicated environment. Note the following in the figure:

➤ Each developer requires a powerful computer to host the virtualization environment.

➤ A SharePoint development environment hosted on the developer computer can be accessed either by using remote connections and a desktop, or by using Hyper-V. Virtual environments are either located directly in the corporate network to facilitate access to enterprise resources (such as Team Foundation Server), or environments have two network cards (one for the internal domain and environment, and another for accessing corporate resources).

➤ A centralized source code repository (such as Team Foundation Server) is used to store all developed source code.

➤ This includes an optional virtualization host for the testing environment, unless testing is conducted directly on the developer computers.

➤ This includes a virtualized environment for testing purposes.

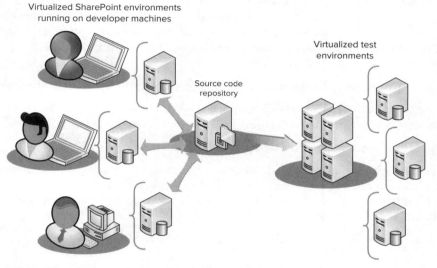

FIGURE 18-5: Virtualized dedicated environments

Dedicated computers require sufficient hardware to host the virtualized environments. Lack of sufficient hardware will impact the virtual SharePoint machine's performance, and may impact development productivity. If the virtualized development environment creation is automated, overall productivity will be better, because developers will be able to take new clean development environments when needed. An automated virtualized environment configuration can ensure that there's a new clean environment available (with the latest source code) within 15 minutes.

Numerous different virtualization techniques are available to choose from. Keep the following in mind:

➤ Because SharePoint 2010 is 64-bit only, it must support hosting 64-bit operating systems. This model requires a minimum of 8 GB of memory to ensure that both client and host 6perating systems are performing adequately. More memory equates to better productivity for each of your developers.

➤ Ensure that you provide hard disks that perform because these will host the virtual machines. One option with the Windows 7 and Window 2008 R2 is the "Boot from VHD" option, which enables the virtualization environment to be loaded as the primary operating system when the computer is started. With this option, the overall hardware requirements can be lower than mentioned previously. Nevertheless, the storage capacity must be sufficient to host multiple virtualization environments for different purposes.

One of the advantages of this kind of model is that individual developers don't need to have connectivity to the corporate network during development. This model enables easier and more flexible development, regardless of the developer location.

Centralized Virtualized Environments

A centralized virtualized environment is a development environment model where development environments are hosted on the centralized virtualization platform, and developers use remote connections to access these environments.

This model provides numerous advantages compared to environments hosted in the computers used by developers, since this model provides centralized management of the development environments. Individual computers used by the developers in their daily work do not require powerful hardware. These computers are only for hosting client-side applications (such as Office clients and other productivity applications).

Figure 18-6 shows an example of a centralized virtualized environment. Note the following in the figure:

➤ Individual developers don't have SharePoint installed on their local computers. They connect to the development environments using remote connections.

➤ Development environments are hosted in a centralized virtualization host.

➤ Each active developer has his or her own development environment, which can be accessed using a remote connection. The environment is located either directly in the corporate network, or it has two network cards for having an internal domain and still being able to connect to the corporate network.

➤ Source code and other artifacts are stored in a centralized source code repository.

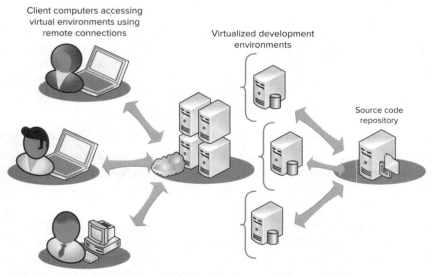

FIGURE 18-6: Centralized virtualized environments

Because virtualized environments are centrally managed, they can be more easily and efficiently utilized based on the current usage requirements. In times when they are not needed, this hardware can be dedicated to other environments. This results in cost savings based on the efficient utilization of your available hardware. Similar models can be used to suspend development environments while spinning up testing environments and performing overnight tests. Ensure that individual developers are not blocked because of a lack of access to their centrally hosted virtualized SharePoint environment.

Individual virtualized development environments should still have at least 4 GB of memory dedicated to them. However, overall memory can be more efficiently utilized by the physical virtualization host machine.

In large projects, centralized virtualization platforms nevertheless are often used to enable integration testing and QA environments.

Hosting development machines requires expensive hardware for the centralized virtualization hosts. In many projects, these environments have been purchased as part of the project set-up phase. After the primary development phase has ended, the same host can be used for hosting maintenance development environments, or, alternatively, for other projects.

Cloud Environments

In this model, development environments are placed and hosted in the cloud, and accessed from developer computers using remote connections. The biggest advantage of this model is that there's no requirement to invest in on-premise expensive hardware, but rather to rent and consume from cloud-based services for the duration of the project.

Depending on service provider, the costs may be based on usage (in other words, the actual time when the cloud services are accessed). This minimizes secondary costs, because you only pay for the time you use your environments. Using this model, you can spin-up your testing environments in the cloud whenever required.

From a cost-management perspective, the biggest advantage is quite simply that developers only need to have a computer with Internet access and be able to use remote connections to access the cloud-hosted development environments.

Figure 18-7 shows an example of a cloud environment. Note the following in the figure:

➤   Developers work from a computer with Internet access.

➤   Development environments are hosted in the cloud and are assigned to the same network segment as the cloud-located source code system.

➤   Source code systems (such as Team Foundation Server) are hosted in the cloud.

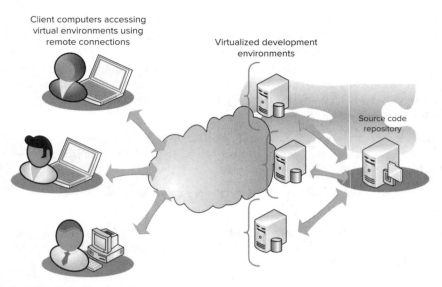

FIGURE 18-7: Cloud environments

Development environments set up based on this model are extremely interesting options because they provide the potential for endless hardware capacity for your project, and can be easily scaled up and out.

Identifying the Environments Your Testers Require

Efficient testing and QA require consistent and stable testing environments. Multiple testers can conduct testing in a single test farm because all are accessing the environment as users of the SharePoint 2010 system.

Testing is critical to the success of your project. Testers shouldn't have to worry about setting up environments or configuring preliminary settings as long as documentation and the configuration of environments is not part of the QA tasks to be taken.

All configurations required for the testing environment should be automated as much as possible. This way, the tester can concentrate on manual tests and verifying that your customizations work properly, rather than spending time on non-productive actions.

Ensure that testers perform tests on machines that reflect the operating system, Office System Suite, and browser version of the business. For example, different defects will be picked up on a "Windows Vista, Office 2007, Internet Explorer 8.0 browser" build as compared to a "Windows 7, Office 2010, and Internet Explorer 8.0/ 9.0/ Firefox 3.6 browser" build.

For more information on what setups SharePoint 2010 supports,
see `http://technet.microsoft.com/en-us/library/cc263526.aspx`.

Testers should be able to access the daily build environment to follow up on the progress of task and defect resolution, so that all code is immediately available for testing. This way, developers will be able to receive feedback on their enhancements and bug fixes. This enables issues to be resolved as soon as possible, before a build is available to a wider audience.

PLANNING PORTAL LIFE CYCLE AND MANAGEMENT

One of the most important (and, unfortunately, often overlooked) areas to consider in SharePoint deployments is detailed planning of the *portal life cycle model*. The portal life cycle model can be described as the process and flow from development to your production environment, and includes implementation and maintenance time. It also includes the planning of the processes for maintenance of the servers and software, not just the flow of the customizations.

Portal Life Cycle Models

This section examines several portal life cycle models, including the following:

➤   Direct release

➤   Phased release

➤   Rolling release

Direct Release

One of the models used to ensure flexible SharePoint usage is to use SharePoint Designer in the production environment to customize the portal behavior based on business requirements. The *direct release* model requires one client environment and your production environment. This approach carries a higher risk of causing issues to end users in your production environment because changes made may impact end-user productivity.

Even though SharePoint Designer provides the flexibility to customize your environment, keep in mind that it may still require some custom code or XML configurations. This would require separate environments to ensure that SharePoint Designer customizations don't break anything in already deployed customizations. It's also important to remember that there is no way of recording the SharePoint Designer customizations to enable you to apply them to multiple site collections. For example, if you have hundreds of different collaboration sites, this model is definitely not the most cost-efficient and is, therefore, not recommended.

Phased Release

The *phased release* model (shown in Figure 18-8) uses separate environments for different phases of the project, and incorporates clear decision points when moving forward. This model was commonly used in the SharePoint 2007 environments because, after the initial environments are built, there are not that many moving parts in the actual process.

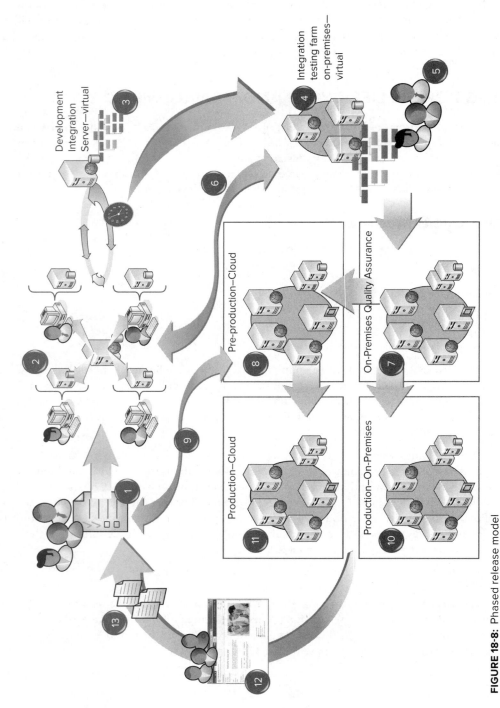

FIGURE 18-8: Phased release model

Figure 18-8 includes the following numbered tasks:

1. All requirements are transferred to tasks and assigned to project members.

2. Developers use their own standalone environments for development, and store all customizations in the source control system.

3. A separate environment is used for integration testing.

4. An optional build verification or test farm is commonly used in large projects. This farm has multiple servers, like in production and in pre-production farms.

5. Before builds are released to production, they are approved.

6. In this phase, it's important to test and report defects before moving forward.

7. and 8. A pre-production farm is used for final verification and to verify that the customizations will work in production environment configuration. As mentioned earlier in this chapter, it's highly recommended that the pre-production environment mimics the production environment (including, for example, patching and configuration levels).

9. All feedback and bugs are collected from the QA environment and reported back to development team.

10. and 11. The production environment is used for the actual production usage.

12. End users can access the production environment.

13. End users provide additional feedback for future development phases.

The biggest challenge in the phased release model is to keep the pre-production environment up to date with the production environment updates. This model requires following a process as strictly as possible, and all configurations are first tested in pre-production. One other challenge is that quite often a pre-production or QA farm does not mimic the production environment infrastructure. This makes it difficult to truly verify the deployment actions in detail, and, for example, to perform load testing.

> *If the pre-production environment is not using an infrastructure similar to the production environment, and you are required perform load testing, you must use the* base line *testing model. This means that when the initial deployment of the customizations is done, load testing is performed in the pre-production environment. In subsequent releases, all load testing results are compared to the initial test results from the pre-production environment. This way, you get an indication of the performance implications of your latest changes.*

Rolling Release

The *rolling release* model (shown in Figure 18-9) utilizes two primary environments in turn for production and QA environments. This model provides extreme flexibility and increases the overall quality of the released iterations. Basically, the development is phased similarly as the fully phased model, but the QA and production environments switch their roles during each release.

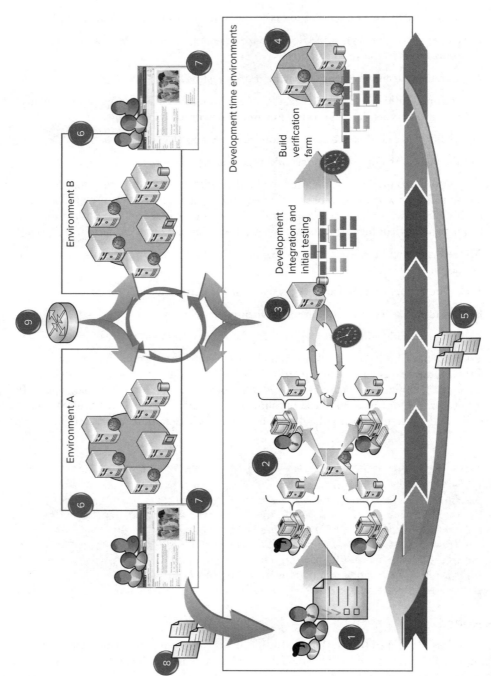

FIGURE 18-9: Rolling release model

Figure 18-9 includes the following numbered tasks:

1. All requirements are transferred to tasks and assigned to the actual project members.

2. Development is done by utilizing a standalone SharePoint deployment, and all customizations are stored in the source control system.

3. Integration and automated testing are happening in separate virtualized environments, so that testing does not interfere with actual development time activities.

4. Like in the phased model, depending on the project size, development style, and QA requirements, an additional build verification or test farm could be used for final acceptance testing before builds are transferred to the actual production environment. This environment is also used by the actual project testers to verify Features.

5. All issues and possible improvement ideas are reported back to the task log for prioritization and bug fixing.

6. The production environment consists of two dedicated SharePoint farms, which act as the pre-production (or QA) and production environments.

7. End users access the different available services.

8. End users report possible feedback and additional ideas for the project team.

9. The load balancer or DNS routes requests between multiple different environments.

Before customizations are deployed to the pre-production environment, content databases are copied from the production environment, so that initial deployment actions can be verified. Final acceptance testing (which optionally includes load testing) can be conducted in the pre-production environment, before the decision is made to move to production. For most flexible deployments, these environments should be virtualized, so that you can easily increase hardware if new customizations have some additional requirements.

The switch between the environments is done at the load-balancer or DNS level. Before it's done, content databases in the current production environment are set to read-only mode, which disables all editing options from the SharePoint 2010 UI (for example, Ribbon buttons are disabled by graying out). It's important to notice that the portal will behave otherwise as planned, but there's no way to add any new content. Afterward, the content databases of the currently used production environment are copied one more time to the pre-production environment. When all required databases are available, traffic is switched between the environments from the network load balancer, and the roles of the environments are switched.

The rolling release model decreases downtime required for the releases, and ensures that there's also a backup environment available if something critical happens on the farm (which is acting as the primary farm at the particular time). It's also important to notice that this not only improves the release model of the customizations, but also helps to minimize downtime during patching of the operating system and SharePoint 2010.

The rolling release model has obvious advantages with the SharePoint deployment. In many enterprise projects, there's a specific dedicated pre-production or QA environment, which mimics the production environment. Using the rolling release model, this environment and the investments done for the deployment are utilized more efficiently. In cases where the production environments are virtualized, you can more efficiently utilize the virtualization platform to provide flexibility between the environments, meaning that you can definitely scale down the hardware capacity of the current pre-production or QA environment, and scale up just before the traffic is switched again.

The rolling release model increases the availability of the services, because, when using this model, no service breaks are required during customization deployment, SharePoint patching, or even operating system patching. Depending on the virtualization platform architecture, the patching of the virtualized hosts may not even cause service downtime. Using Windows PowerShell, you could relatively easily automate the whole process of the getting databases between environments, and deploying customizations to a farm.

SHAREPOINT 2010 PATCHING CONSIDERATION WITH THE ROLLING RELEASE MODEL

Similar to SharePoint 2007, every time you deploy full trust customizations to a SharePoint 2010 farm, the IIS worker process is recycled. This will cause downtime for the service. Depending on the deployment, this can have an impact on the actual end users. If only sandboxed solutions are used, there's no downtime for the customization deployment.

SharePoint 2010 also supports phased patching of the actual SharePoint services. This means that you can take individual servers offline from the farm, and update the SharePoint services individually. SharePoint patches are backward-compatible, so that even though some of the servers are patched with newer versions in the farm, the primary version is still used. The actual upgrade to the latest version still requires downtime for the whole farm. This is because there might be database-level changes, which would not work with the previous version. So, patching has been improved, but an actual upgrade to latest version (for example Service Pack 1) still requires downtime.

Key Development Phases

This section examines several key development phases, including the following:

➤ Initial iterations

➤ Content creation starts

➤ Release models after production use starts

Initial Iterations

The development phase should be divided into a number of iterations or subphases, regardless of the development methodology used in the project. This way, you can more easily plan the tasks based on priorities, and follow up on development progress.

Most projects start with a proof of concept (POC) to ascertain the feasibility and suitability of using SharePoint 2010. When projects progress to the next stage, the POC is often used as a starting point and code for your project team. It's important to remember that the quality of most POCs is not adequate to directly continue to development. It's very important to start discussions with the customer to ensure that the development assumptions are correct, and that the implementation moves in the right direction.

Most project teams prefer detailed technical specifications to be in place before code is developed. This is a difficult challenge to tackle upfront in complex developments, and requires a waterfall approach to development. More often than not, especially if your customer is not familiar with SharePoint, the customer only knows what he or she wants when he or she sees it. Using an agile-based development methodology and philosophy helps to balance the amount of documentation required in the initial iteration.

Another important consideration is the design of your Visual Studio project and code structure. Visual Studio structure defines solution names, Features, and their behaviors. Take the time to design a proper Visual Studio structure, because this will save rework and development effort later in the project.

Assuming that your Visual Studio code and project structure are planned and available, the developer can start implementation. This means that each of the web part classes and all Feature definitions have been created based on the specification, but actual business code from the classes is missing. This way, you avoid issues in the structure deployment caused by changed Feature associations or new solution packages.

Figure 18-10 defines common development stages.

FIGURE 18-10: Common development stages

Content Creation Starts

One of the most important and critical milestones in a SharePoint project is when content creation starts. From this phase forward, daily or weekly builds cannot just re-create the site collection using scripts. You must start using an upgrade model to your environment, because you don't want to lose content that the content editors have already created.

An important consideration related to content creation is deciding on and finalizing the data structure (for example, site columns and content types) of your deployment. Although these can be changed after the initial release, their update requires additional work and potential content patching to ensure no content is lost.

Whenever content creation starts, the development model must be switched to a maintenance-and-upgrade model. For smaller projects with few customizations, this is not a difficult change. But if a solution consists of numerous site definitions or web templates, the change is much more dramatic, and must be carefully planned.

Release Models after Production Use Starts

When production use starts, you have additional considerations. All changes to your code base must be evaluated so that they don't cause any issues with the already deployed Features. Therefore, your production upgrade model should be carefully planned.

Similar to SharePoint 2007, downtime is required when new full trust solutions are deployed to SharePoint 2010. If you use the rolling release life-cycle model, a service break is not required. User (sandboxed) solutions can be updated without requiring a service break, as long as the interfaces and Features do not change too much.

The most important consideration when releasing new customizations is to ensure that a proper rollback strategy is available. SharePoint 2010 does not provide built-in roll-back functionality if your solution package deployment fails, or if you'd like to return the farm to a previous state. Depending on the issue encountered, either redeploying a previous version of the solution or restoring database backups are the only solutions to move forward.

Remember that if there's need to restore database backups, both configuration and content databases must be restored. This is because the solution store for full trust solutions is located in the configuration database. It's also important to synchronize the files in the filesystem, because a full trust solution is extracted to each of the servers in the farm. User (sandboxed) solutions are only stored in the content database, so their restoration is straightforward.

Because there are many considerations for the maintenance phase deployments, a detailed road map and process for the upgrades should be created. This is quite common for larger projects that release new versions of your customizations after the initial release.

Figure 18-11 shows a deployment plan where, after the initial release, deployments are done on a quarterly basis.

FIGURE 18-11: Deployment plan

Solution Package Design

Solution packages are used to deploy customizations to the SharePoint farms. You should always package your code and other customizations in solution packages, and use them to deploy your customizations. In SharePoint 2010, you have two different kinds of solution package types that can be used: fully trusted solutions and user (sandboxed) solutions. Each type has specific behaviors and implications.

Fully Trusted Solutions

As was the case in SharePoint 2007, SharePoint 2010 supports fully trusted solutions that can be deployed at the farm level to provide any customizations required for your projects.

Fully trusted solutions are deployed by adding them to the solution store located in the configuration database by either using the `stsadm` command-line tool or Windows PowerShell. When the solution is available, it can be deployed to your farm.

It is important to note that fully trusted solution customizations are deployed to the filesystem of each server, and can be considered to be deployed at the farm level, not simply for an individual web application. The web application choice in Central Administration only affects which `web.config` files are actually updated based on the configurations defined in the solution package. This also means that when the solution package contains Features, these Features are visible in multiple applications, which can lead to confusion.

The biggest advantage to using fully trusted solutions compared to deploying customizations manually is the automation of customization deployment. You can be sure that each server in your farm is a completely identical set of deployed customizations. Another advantage is that if you reinstall one of your servers or add a new server to your SharePoint farm, all customizations are automatically deployed, without any manual intervention.

One of the most important things to consider is that deployment or upgrade of a fully trusted solution requires downtime, as shown in Figure 18-12. This service break may not be long, but it can have an impact on users accessing the portal at the time the new package is deployed. This downtime is required to be able to refresh the assembly from the IIS worker process, and, in practice, requires either an IIS reset or application pool recycle.

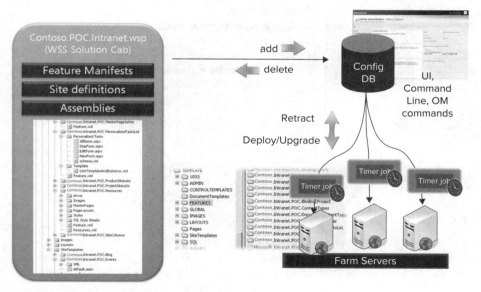

FIGURE 18-12: Deployment/upgrade of fully trusted solution

User (Sandboxed) Solutions

Sandboxed solutions are a new option available in SharePoint 2010 to deploy customizations at site-collection scope, and to safely execute customizations in a dedicated worker process. This enables a greater degree of flexibility when deploying small customizations, and does not require an administrator to perform deployment on the server side.

Sandboxed solutions are deployed to a sandbox solution gallery located in each site collection, and their usage can be monitored and controlled using an out-of-the-box monitoring system.

As shown in Figure 18-13, SharePoint 2010 imposes limitations on the types of solutions that can be created. This is to avoid code causing issues in the farm. Common usage scenarios include simple web parts and Feature-based deployment of artifacts (such as master pages and page layouts). Sandboxed solutions are great way to provide either department-level customizations, or customizations to cloud-based environments such as Microsoft Online.

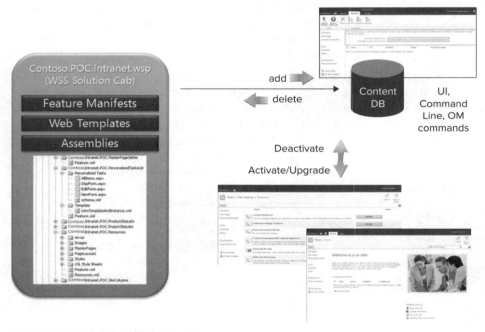

FIGURE 18-13: User (sandboxed) solutions

Design Practices

Because all SharePoint customizations are deployed using solution packages, planning the deployment architecture is extremely important. A well-planned deployment architecture provides flexibility for testing, and reduces the impact on the costs of subsequent maintenance phases.

SharePoint 2010 supports solution dependencies. This enables you to define dependencies between two different solutions, so that solutions are deployed to the farm or as sandboxed solutions in the correct order. This is great because it provides a mechanism to ensure additional checks where you might have multiple solution packages deployed and they must be deployed in the correct order.

One of the key considerations for the deployment architecture is the granularity of your customizations in each of the solution packages. Creating too many solution packages will create additional complexity for the overall solution. This has a direct impact on the activities required in the maintenance phase. On the other hand, having all your customizations in a single solution package can also cause difficulties in testing individual Features of a large solution package. This may also force you to do more regression testing than would be required if you split out your Features in multiple solution packages.

Having your customizations divided into solution packages based on their usage and functionalities will provide flexibility for testing and development.

Figure 18-14 shows a commonly used model, where Features are divided based on their usage. As you can see, all commonly used Features are placed in a common or shared solution package, and each key Feature area has a dedicated package. This way, individual Features (such as search or My Site) can be developed and tested without affecting other customizations.

One challenge with solution packages relates to shared resources between multiple packages — for example, third-party assemblies, utility classes, common base classes, or business logic layers. It is important to remember that if two different solution packages deploy the same resource, and the second package is retracted from the SharePoint farm, the shared resources are retracted. SharePoint doesn't track dependencies on individual artifacts and solutions.

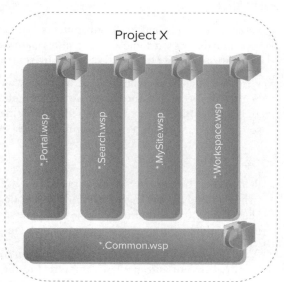

FIGURE 18-14: Design practices

This can be mitigated by using common or shared resources in a specific solution package. This way, all shared resources (such as third-party assemblies) are deployed centrally for the different services in the SharePoint farm.

Solution and Feature Upgrade

SharePoint 2010 provides new features for solution and Feature upgrade models that should be utilized in customization projects. These make the versioning of the customizations easier, and remove the complexity required to modify existing sites.

The solution package manifest now supports applying assembly redirections to the `web.config` file of the web applications. This helps to make the required changes to the applications, if assembly versioning is used as the versioning model for code.

From a versioning standpoint, the biggest change is the support for Feature framework versioning. This provides a solution to update existing sites. This can be used not only for updating customizations, but also to manipulate content. In previous versions of SharePoint, these maintenance builds were much more difficult to design because no common model existed for changing the existing structures (because there were no commonly used upgrade patterns — rather, each development project required its own versioning techniques for the existing sites when newer versions of customizations were deployed).

From a development perspective, you should start using the versioning option as soon as content creation starts, and you are not able to re-create the sites. After this key milestone, all new versions of the Features must be specifically planned, especially if any changes are required to existing sites.

Patching

Patching your production environments can be complicated. From a code perspective, this is primarily limited to how you deploy bug fixes to existing customizations, and how new customizations are deployed to your environment.

From a content and farm perspective, after your initial code release and when production use begins, users create content, set up and complete workflows, customize and configure sites, lists, and items, filling in metadata based on existing content types, creating their own content types, and so forth. Your production environment takes on a life of its own.

Code

Patching of the code in SharePoint is relatively easy, and can be done by updating the solution package (which already exists in the farm). From a code perspective, the only major thing to remember in SharePoint 2010 is that if you have newer versions of Features developed, you must remember to increase the Feature version and provide the required definitions for the Feature upgrade actions.

When new versions of the Feature are deployed as part of a new solution package version, the Features are not automatically upgraded to the newest version. The Feature framework follows the same patching model as other SharePoint patching, in that you can add newer versions of the definitions, but the upgrade doesn't have to be applied immediately.

The upgrade of Feature definitions is performed either by using the PSConfig tool or by using SharePoint APIs, which provide more granular options for the upgrade. Running PSConfig results in downtime for the whole farm, so upgrading using that method is not always the best option. The SharePoint API can be used to upgrade individual Features in a site collection or in the whole farm, and this approach doesn't require any downtime.

Content

Patching SharePoint content means patching or changing already provisioned sites in a production environment. Changing content types of individual list items can be a complex task, and requires detailed planning. A *content type* defines the data structure of individual data object in SharePoint 2010 that is stored in a SharePoint content database. Modification to existing content types should be carefully considered. SharePoint 2010 supports adding new fields to existing content types as part of the Feature framework upgrade functionality. But if you must change content types of existing items, this must be developed as custom code.

Complicated scenarios exist in which code and content updates need to be deployed to your production environment at the same time. For example, an upgraded site definition may now include a new site collection scoped feature. For new sites, this isn't a problem, because the updated site definition will activate the Feature automatically. However, if the business requires the Feature in existing sites, this will require code to activate the Feature based on a specific site definition. These types of updates require careful planning to coordinate content or code changes across your farm.

Another example that may require an update to a content type is a base business document type, specifically developed for a business, which is already in use in all sites in production. If the update requires new fields, and moving content between fields, this requires code to update each item that uses the outdated field.

In these scenarios, in SharePoint 2007, IT professionals would request a custom `stsadm` extension or custom Feature to perform these operations. In SharePoint 2010, a number of methods exist to perform these types of updates.

The recommended option is to start utilizing the new Feature upgrade options, which will also provide support for Feature versioning for existing sites. This functionality can be used to modify site structures and content in structured ways without any custom methodology, which would cause project-specific processes to be created. A Feature framework versioning model can be also extended by using custom code to fulfill additional capabilities.

Other content considerations may also include the existence of different lists and web parts on sites. These can be relatively easily modified using the new Feature framework upgrade functionality, which provides the capability to execute any custom code as part of the Feature upgrade. This custom code can be then developed to do required changes for the existing structures based on new requirements.

The following section concentrates more on practical considerations for your development team planning, which is as important as defining a clear portal life cycle model for deployment.

HANDLING DEVELOPMENT TEAMS

Like each SharePoint deployment, development teams are unique and have their own way of working. Nevertheless for successful projects, it's vital to set up the development team properly to ensure that you have right capabilities in place as required for particular project.

Large Project Considerations

Large SharePoint projects have challenges similar to any large project where many people are working on the same goals. For example, these challenges may include unclear (undefined) responsibilities, tasks, schedules, roles, and so on. Challenges can be addressed by proper planning of not just the project deliverables, but also the development process.

Large Project Life Cycle Models

Especially with large projects, it's important to have clear responsibilities and development processes defined for the different Features that are developed. The most common way to handle large development projects in SharePoint is to divide the Features into multiple code projects and solution packages. That way, each Feature project will consume common and shared services from one common framework. This means that, from a solution perspective, the design would be similar to the one shown in Figure 18-15.

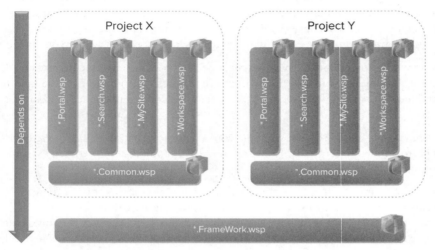

FIGURE 18-15: Large project life cycle models

Figure 18-15 demonstrates how code and Features could be efficiently divided between multiple different Visual Studio projects and solution packages. Framework.wsp contains abstract code, which can be utilized in any SharePoint deployment. Good examples for this kind of code would be logging, caching, and configuration services. Copying this kind of general code to each Visual Studio project or code structure is waste of resources, because it could be deployed and versioned as an individual package, and then used by different projects.

In the example shown in Figure 18-15, individual projects (Project X and Project Y) are large projects that provide different Features. Having a general common solution package or code layer, you can easily share project-dependent Features between different individual Features. A good example of this kind of functionality would be custom master pages, which are used in different site definitions or web templates. This way, you could easily maintain and update UI-dependent functionality without, for example, being forced to do changes on the news Feature or solution package.

Individual Features in projects are divided into individual Visual Studio projects and solution packages to be able to maintain and upgrade them individually. This way, these Features (such as News in Project Y) could be individually tested and verified, even if other functionality is not available.

Customization architecture and deployment architecture have a direct impact on the overall maintenance costs and processes. Therefore, your model should be carefully planned based on your requirements. The example in Figure 18-15 is suitable for independent software vendors (ISVs) that develop many services for multiple customers. By separating framework layer code at the deployment level, each project can take advantage of any new base services introduced. Possible fixes can be performed to multiple projects by updating an individual package. As a result, individual project developers can concentrate on solving business logic requirements.

Figure 18-16 demonstrates the flow of development in larger projects, where the framework-level code is separated into its own layer.

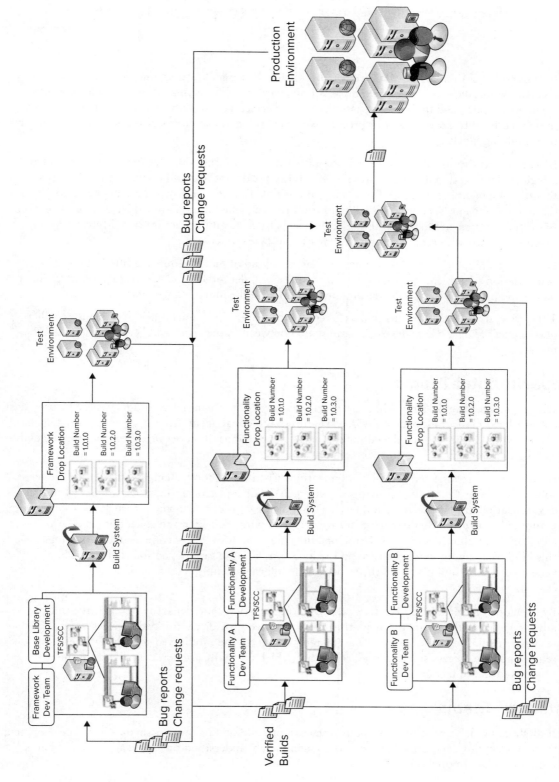

FIGURE 18-16: Development teams to specific versions

In this model, development teams are responsible for their own Features, and dependencies are created for specific versions. For example, a framework-level development team will have its own versioning model, and the team releases tested and verified versions on a weekly or monthly basis. Individual Feature development or projects will reference and use these stable and tested versions as their building blocks.

Feature teams can use any suitable version of the framework that matches their requirements and schedule. This kind of approach provides flexibility for the individual Feature teams when planning their development iterations and road map. If multiple Features or projects are deployed to the same target environment (such as a SharePoint farm), projects must use the same platform-level version. But if the Features are deployed to multiple targets (such as an intranet farm and Internet farm), Features can use different versions of the platform-level services.

From a road map–level planning point of view, this kind of model requires a little bit more coordination to implement. But in the long term, it will definitely produce a return on investment by increasing productivity and decreasing time required in the maintenance model.

This model doesn't require tens of developers on the team. This model is also suitable for smaller development teams, where developers are shared between framework- and Feature-orientated projects.

Departmental Teams

One of the growing development models is the departmental team-based model, where IT provides a centralized platform for the individual Features, and departments are responsible for (or in charge of) individual Features introduced for end users. These kinds of models are great and really flexible, as long as the platform and environment are carefully managed.

If departments require only small customizations (such as branding changes), sandboxed solutions in SharePoint 2010 provide an extremely flexible platform to introduce changes and customization at the site-collection level. This must be considered during information architecture planning by ensuring that departments are provided with their own site collection where they can deploy sandboxed solutions. Using one site collection for all departments and providing this kind of flexibility could be risky in the long run, because sandboxed solutions must be versioned and maintained carefully, especially if solutions contain actual code-based customizations.

By providing a centralized IT-driven platform, organizations and departments can take full advantage of the flexibility of the platform. IT may also provide centralized services to be available to departmental releases, such as fully trusted proxies for the sandboxed solutions if there are requirements to access some secured resources (which normally are not available from the sandboxed solution code).

Offshore Teams

If offshore models are utilized properly, they can provide significant cost savings in the development stage. Often, however, organizations do not completely understand the implications and what is required to use an offshore team.

For example, what methodology is suitable, what level of technical specifications are required, what onshore and offshore resources are required, what subtle cultural issues must be understood, QA, onsite development leadership, offsite project management, and planning and guidance for the customizations to be implemented all must be considered.

Efficiently utilizing offshore development teams and enabling individual Features to be developed unfortunately tends to require a waterfall-based approach, where a great deal of upfront planning, thinking, designing, and documenting is required. There must be little to no ambiguity in any documentation. Your user experience and portal brand design must be completed earlier on in the process to enable offshore developers to avoid delays and ambiguity during the development.

For example, this means good documentation of any platform-level services and details concerning individual styling of the customizations (such as web parts). If roles and responsibilities are defined properly, and there's constant follow-up on the customizations, offshore development can be extremely cost-efficient. It requires extremely good project management and QA on the onshore end to ensure that Features are working as specified in the documentation.

Other considerations for offshore development are the customization ownership and how the source code is secured. If development occurs both onshore and offshore, access to the same centralized source code system must be provided. Figure 18-17 shows one model of having development synchronized between onshore and offshore teams. Note the following in reference to the figure:

➤ The onshore development team uses remote connections to access centrally deployed development environments.

➤ A centralized virtualization host is used for development and QA environments.

➤ Individual development environments are included.

➤ A source code system (such as Team Foundation Server) is included.

➤ A virtual private network (VPN) or other remote connection port provides access to corporate resources from external networks.

➤ Offshore developers have their own development environments connecting to Team Foundation Server from Visual Studio.

Optionally, you could also provide individual development environments for the offshore team, which would also be hosted in the centralized virtualization host. This could be possible, as long as the offshore team could access the corporate network.

In this kind of model, the integration point of the onshore and offshore customization is the source code system from where actual builds can be then created.

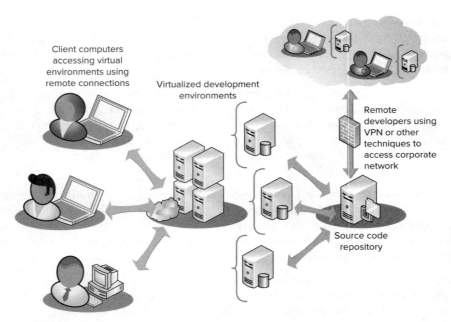

FIGURE 18-17: Offshore team model

SUMMARY

Many considerations that (unfortunately) are quite often overlooked in large SharePoint projects can help your project teams be more successful during the development, testing, and deployment phases of your project. This chapter discussed many of these considerations, and especially focused on a detailed look at what is required in large projects.

What does a large project really mean? When should you follow this guidance? The answers to these questions are based on many factors, such as the size of your SharePoint farms; the degree of customization; the priority of your project to the business; the quality you require of the development, testing, and deployment deliverables; and your future road map. Many of the concepts discussed in this chapter apply to projects of all sizes, and should be followed to improve the maturity and discipline of your development, testing, and deployment teams.

Future maintenance requirements should weigh heavily on your architecture patterns and key design decisions. Ensure key development through deployment processes are set up and followed. Consider that, after your initial version has been deployed, it is so much more expensive to fix than if you get these right in your initial version.

Unfortunately, there is no silver bullet to enable you to select the correct model for each project. Even though you may not plan processes and architecture in detail, it's important to make an informed choice, rather than making a decision with no understanding of the impact.

Chapter 19 examines the authentication and authorization model for SharePoint 2010.

19

Designing Your Authentication and Authorization Model

By Chris Gideon

Most consumers have experienced the need for identification when making a purchase with a credit card. When it's time to pay, the cardholder is asked to provide some trusted form of identification. The consumer may have several forms of identification, such as loyalty, library, or frequent flier program cards. Though these cards do prove identity for each of those respective systems, they are typically not accepted. The reason is that the authority used to issue those alternate forms of identification is not trusted by the merchant or bank. For most banking or credit card transactions in the United States, the trusted authority is the federal or state government. A driver's license or passport issued from the government is the preferred form of identification.

This experience may vary somewhat, depending on the cardholder's nationality, or if the purchase is made in another country. A key attribute of the identification in the process is the photo of the consumer. The determination of credit availability is a separate process once identity is confirmed.

This example is analogous to the authentication process experienced by users of information systems today. The user may have many usernames and passwords for several different systems in his or her company's enterprise network. The problem expands when partnering with other companies and additional systems are brought into play.

An information technology architect spends a great deal of time defining which systems must integrate, and what degree of trust must be established between disparate systems. In this context, "trust" is the degree to which data or security information can be exchanged. These decisions, combined with the lack of a central authority, or a single set of protocols for authentication, set the stage for user frustration.

Although many companies produce Single Sign-On (SSO) solutions, the problem of defining identity is larger than just authentication. In the eyes of the system, a user is often made up of various attributes and identifiers, each coming from a variety of sources. For example, a Human Resources system might be the authoritative source for an employee ID number, whereas a PBX or Voice over Internet Protocol (VoIP) system might be authoritative for phone number. A sales team may include members of an "opportunity" in a customer relationship management (CRM) system.

In SharePoint Server 2010, Microsoft took two big steps toward addressing these problems.

The first was to include a lite version of Microsoft Forefront Identity Manager (FIM) 2010. FIM, in conjunction with Business Connectivity Services (BCS), allows profile information to be imported from several different systems. To a limited extent, it was possible in previous versions of SharePoint to import from systems other than Microsoft Active Directory Domain Services (ADDS). However, there remained a tight coupling between authentication and the user profile. Although the implementation of FIM in SharePoint 2010 does not address as many directory services as the full version of the product, it does lay the foundation for more.

The second step was the implementation of the Windows Identity Framework (WIF) to provide support for claims-based security. WIF is an extension of the .NET Framework for Windows Communication Foundation (WCF) and ASP.NET applications. It provides classes and tools for authentication and authorization development. WIF enables SharePoint to become a claims-based application, thus shifting the responsibility of identity management out of the SharePoint platform to dedicated systems. In addition, WIF presents information from other systems to SharePoint in a validated form, thereby decreasing the number of places a user needs to make changes.

This chapter provides an explanation of the authentication changes in SharePoint Server 2010, and the impact these changes have on an architecture.

CLAIMS IN SHAREPOINT SERVER 2010

One of the most difficult things about discussing claims-based authentication is the vocabulary. While discussing this topic, you may feel the need for a fast Internet connection or a dictionary just to keep the terminology straight. To get this necessary evil out of the way a few definitions must be understood:

➤ According to Microsoft, a *claim* is "a statement that one subject makes about itself or another subject." The *subject* in the example at the beginning of this chapter would be the cardholder. Several things could qualify as a *statement* about the cardholder — the photo, cardholder's name, and account number are a few examples.

➤ The government in the earlier example (federal or state) is the *Identity Provider (IdP)*, or an entity that can authenticate the cardholder. The IdP maintains a store of the attributes that make up the cardholder identity, as well as the protocols used to authenticate the cardholder. An IdP that can create a security token is an *Issuer*.

➤ The merchant or *Relying Party (RP)* trusts the IdP as the authority for identity. The RP verifies identity through a *security token* (or driver's license, in the earlier example) that is formatted and signed in some manner by the IdP.

➤ The system used by the Issuer to create and sign the security token is the *Security Token Service (STS)*, which is usually a collection of web services. The RP will also have an STS to consume the security token (which, in the example, is the role played by the cashier).

➤ The RP, in turn, usually has a *policy* that informs the cardholder up front about the accepted forms of identification. The Issuer will have a policy that informs the cardholder of the process, and requirements for acquiring a security token.

Now, let's examine SharePoint as a claims-based application. SharePoint allows identity providers to plug in through the notion of a *claims provider*. A claims provider issues and packages claims into security tokens. These security tokens are consumed by a SharePoint STS (SPSTS). Three types of claims providers come out of the box:

➤ Trusted STS (or trusted provider) claims

➤ Active Directory (Windows) claims

➤ Forms-based authentication claims

Claims providers also provide claims *augmentation* and *picking*. Augmentation is the process of providing additional claims to the token during sign in. Picking is the process of displaying claims in the People Picker. Each of these functions is explained in the context of the claims provider type.

WIF provides the classes used to build the SharePoint STS, process claims, and much more through a series of libraries. In addition, it provides a few other critical pieces: `WSFederationAuthenticationModule` and `SessionAuthenticationModule`. The SharePoint versions of these modules are `SPFederationAuthenticationModule` and `SPSessionAuthenticationModule`. Both of these modules sit in front of SharePoint in the ASP.NET integrated pipeline. The modules are added to the `web.config` when a web application is defined as claims-based during creation. This can be seen in Listing 19-1:

LISTING 19-1: HttpModules section of web.config

```
<httpModules>
        <add name="FederatedAuthentication"
          type="Microsoft.SharePoint.IdentityModel
          .SPFederationAuthenticationModule, Microsoft.SharePoint
          .IdentityModel, Version=14.0.0.0, Culture=neutral,
          PublicKeyToken=71e9bce111e9429c" />
        <add name="SessionAuthentication"
          type="Microsoft.SharePoint.IdentityModel.SPSessionAuthenticationModule,
            Microsoft.SharePoint.IdentityModel, Version=14.0.0.0,
            Culture=neutral, PublicKeyToken=71e9bce111e9429c" />
        <add name="SPWindowsClaimsAuthentication"
           type="Microsoft.SharePoint.IdentityModel
           .SPWindowsClaimsAuthenticationHttpModule,
           Microsoft.SharePoint.IdentityModel, Version=14.0.0.0,
           Culture=neutral, PublicKeyToken=71e9bce111e9429c" />
        </httpModules>
```

The `SPFederationAuthenticationModule` (SPFAM) is used to redirect unauthenticated requests to the IdPs that SharePoint trusts. SPFAM calls several classes to validate and process the token. SPFAM is responsible for building `IClaimsPrincipal`, which is an extension of `IPrincipal`. `IClaimsPrincipal` contains a collection of identities that are based on `IClaimsIdentity`. These interfaces make claims available to SharePoint in the managed pipeline. The instances created exist in `HttpContext.Current.User`.

The `SPSessionAuthenticationModule` (SPSAM) is used to avoid going through the authentication process and rebuilding `IClaimsPrincipal` on each request. It does this by creating a session token and writing it to a persistent cookie. On subsequent requests, the SPSAM authenticates the cookie containing the session token, and rebuilds `IClaimsPrincipal`. It is the SPSAM that checks the expiration settings on the session cookie.

A third `HTTPModule` unique to SharePoint is the `SPWindowsClaimsAuthenticationHttpModule`. This module is used to perform Windows authentication when using Windows Claims.

To put the claims process into perspective, let's examine each of the types of claim providers individually.

Trusted Provider Claims

When using *trusted provider claims*, SharePoint acts as a Relying Party (RP) to different Identity Providers (IdPs). The IdPs that the SPSTS trusts are set up through Windows PowerShell via the SharePoint Object Model. The standards used for trusts are based on the `WS-Trust` version 1.4 and `WS-Federation` 1.1. `WS-Trust` and `WS-Federation` provide more than just the establishment of trust between STS. These standards also define the STS schema, the protocols for requesting and issuing security tokens, authorization, and cross-security realm access.

A *realm* is defined by `WS-Federation` as a single unit of security. The `WS-Federation` and `WS-Trust` standards also define two types of client profiles, *passive* and *active*. `WS-Federation` is primarily focused on the passive client, usually a web browser. `WS-Trust` is focused on the active client. In the case of SharePoint, the passive client is the web browser. SharePoint's service applications are an active client. Active and passive clients really come down to the capability to form Simple Object Access Protocol (SOAP) requests. A web browser is, therefore, the classic example of a passive client, while a web service that is designed to send specific SOAP messages is an active client. The users that come into SharePoint using the passive profile are subjects that make claims about various attributes.

The following steps further illustrate the sequence of events. The web application in this instance is configured for Trusted Provider claims.

1. Client (web browser) request (`GET`) to SharePoint Site as anonymous.

2. Server sends a `302 redirect` to `/`.

3. Client sends a `GET` for `/`.

4. Server sends a `302 redirect` to `/_layouts/Authenticate.aspx`.

5. Client sends a `GET` to `/_layouts/Authenticate.aspx`.

6. Server redirects to `/_login/default.aspx`.

7. Client sends a GET to `/_login/default.aspx`.

8. Server sends 200 OK with form.

9. Client chooses provider and posts to `/_login/default.aspx`.

10. Server sends a 302 redirect to `/_trust/default.aspx`.

11. Client sends a GET to `/_trust/default.aspx`.

12. Client redirected to trusted IdP STS.

13. Client sends a CONNECT to IdP STS.

14. IdP STS sends a response.

15. Client sends a GET for `/`.

16. Server sends a 302 redirect to `/_layouts/Authenticate.aspx`.

17. Client sends a GET to `/_layouts/Authenticate.aspx`.

18. Server redirects to `/_login/default.aspx`.

19. Client sends a GET to `/_login/default.aspx`.

20. Server sends 200 OK with form.

21. Client chooses provider and posts to `/_login/default.aspx`.

22. Server sends a 302 redirect to `/_trust/default.aspx`.

23. Client sends a GET to `/_trust/default.aspx`.

24. Client redirected to trusted IdP STS.10.

25. Client authenticates with IdP STS.

26. IdP STS sends client token.

27. Client sends a POST with token to `/_trust/default.aspx`.

28. Server sends 302 redirect to `/_layouts/Authenticate.aspx` and a cookie.

29. Client sends GET request with cookie to `/_layouts/Authenticate.aspx`.

30. Server sends 302 redirect to `/`.

31. Client sends GET request with cookie to `/`.

32. Server sends 302 redirect to home page specified.

33. Client sends get to home page with cookie.

Figure 19-1 shows this process.

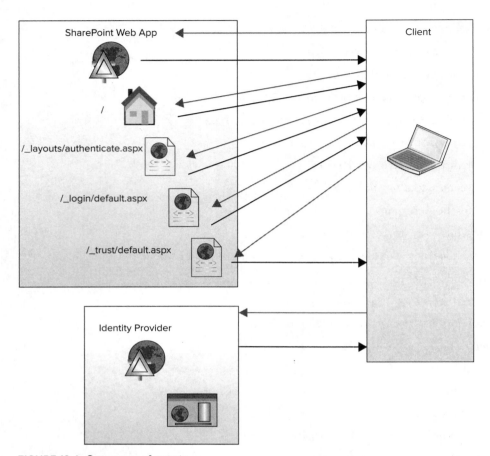

FIGURE 19-1: Sequence of events

When the users make their first request to a SharePoint site (web application) configured for trusted provider claims, the SPFAM is listening for the `AuthenticateRequest` event to fire, as is the SPSAM in case cookies are present. SPFAM and SPSAM will ignore the initial request, and it will be redirected to `/_layouts/Authenticate.aspx`.

`Authenticate.ASPX` has two methods in the page: `SPUtility.EnsureAuthentication()` and `SPUtility.Redirect()`. The `SPUtility.EnsureAuthentication` method does exactly what its name implies — it checks to see if the request has been authenticated, and that there is a `HttpContext.User`, which is a property present in the `IPrincipal` interface. The `SPUtility` `.Redirect()` method handles the redirection based on the URL, `SPRedirectFlags`, and context on the supplied parameters. On the first request, the user has not been authenticated so it is redirected to a sign-in page.

The default sign-in page is `/_login/default.aspx`. The registration can be found in the `web` `.config` file for the web application under `system.web` in the `authentication mode` element, as shown here:

```
<authentication mode="Forms">
    <forms loginUrl="/_login/default.aspx" />
</authentication>
```

The sign-in page provides users with a choice of claims providers for login. This page is very simple and can be customized. The user passes a return URL of /_layouts/Authenticate.aspx in the get request to /_login/default.aspx, which results in a 200 OK server response. Once the client chooses the claims provider in the list, a post to /_login/default.aspx is sent with the same return URL.

At this point, the PostAuthenticateRequest event should have fired in the pipeline, causing SPFAM to construct IClaimsPrincipal. Next, an AuthorizeRequest event fires and produces a 401 server response code (that will never be seen by the client), which fires the EndRequest event. On the EndRequest event, SPFAM checks the microsoft.identityModel section of the web .config file — specifically, the wsFederation passiveRedirectEnabled section, as shown here:

```
<microsoft.identityModel>
    <service saveBootstrapTokens="true">
        <issuerTokenResolver
          type="Microsoft.SharePoint.IdentityModel
          .SPIssuerTokenResolver" />
        <issuerNameRegistry
          type="Microsoft.SharePoint.IdentityModel
          .SPPassiveIssuerNameRegistry" />
        <securityTokenHandlers>
            <remove type=
              "Microsoft.IdentityModel.Tokens.Saml11
              .Saml11SecurityTokenHandler,
              Microsoft.IdentityModel, Version=3.5.0.0,
              Culture=neutral, PublicKeyToken=31bf3856ad364e35" />
            <remove type=
              "Microsoft.SharePoint.IdentityModel
              .SPSaml11SecurityTokenHandler,
              Microsoft.SharePoint.IdentityModel,
              Version=14.0.0.0, Culture=neutral,
              PublicKeyToken=71e9bce111e9429c" />
            <add type=
              "Microsoft.SharePoint.IdentityModel
              .SPSaml11SecurityTokenHandler,
              Microsoft.SharePoint.IdentityModel,
              Version=14.0.0.0, Culture=neutral,
              PublicKeyToken=71e9bce111e9429c" />
        </securityTokenHandlers>
        <federatedAuthentication>
            <wsFederation passiveRedirectEnabled="false"
              issuer="https://none" realm="https://none" />
            <cookieHandler mode="Custom" path="/">
                <customCookieHandler type=
                  "Microsoft.SharePoint.IdentityModel
                  .SPChunkedCookieHandler" />
            </cookieHandler>
        </federatedAuthentication>
    </service>
</microsoft.identityModel>
```

In the case of trusted provider claims, `wsFederation passiveRedirectEnabled` should be set to `true` and have the trusted provider-listed STS in the URL of the issuer. The realm should be set to a Uniform Resource Name (URN) for SharePoint. SPFAM will send a `302` redirect server code to another sign-in page, the `/_trust/default.aspx`. The client then does a `get` request for the `/_trust/default.aspx`, passing in the name of the trusted provider and the return URL of `/_layouts/Authenticate.aspx`. The `/_trust/default.aspx` will send the user to the URL of the trusted IdP STS specified in the `web.config` file.

The IdP STS will authenticate the user in the established authentication protocol defined by the IdP STS. The result is a login page on the IdP STS, in which the user will provide a username and password. Upon successful authentication, the user is returned to SharePoint with a security token in a predefined format. The security token is in a form of XML called Security Assertion Markup Language (SAML), specifically the 1.1 format. Security tokens are signed cryptographically using the IdP STS signing certificate, and contain the claims that were agreed to in the establishment of the trust. The signing process ensures the SPSTS of the integrity of the security token.

A claim is associated with a user or principal. The claims contained in a token are of a specific claim type. There are several pre-defined claim types in the Windows Identity Framework (WIF), more specifically in the `System.IdentityModel.Claims`. The schemas for the attributes are referenced in the token. The claims for a user are bundled together into a `ClaimSet`. The claims accepted by SharePoint and issued by the IdP's STS are predefined when establishing a trusted provider in SharePoint. For example, a common attribute, `EmailAddress`, is defined as a `claimType` by a URI, `http://schemas.xmlsoap.org/ws/2005/05/identity/claims/emailaddress`. These claim types and their mapping become the defining factor in the identification of a user from a trusted IdP STS. The definition of the claims that will be sent and accepted constitute the policy between Security Token Service (STS).

SPFAM and SPSAM process the returning user and take action at the `AuthenticateRequest` event. SPFAM extracts the security token from the trusted IdP STS, and a `SecurityTokenReceived` event is raised. `SecurityTokenHandlers` are used to handle the nuances of receiving the token. A few predefined `SecurityTokenHandlers` respond to the event: `X509SecurityTokenHandler`, `SPSaml11SecurityTokenHandler`, and `SPChunkedCookieHandler`. These are registered in the `web.config` file under the `Microsoft.identityModel` section.

```
<securityTokenHandlers>
        <clear />
        <add type="Microsoft.IdentityModel.Tokens.X509SecurityTokenHandler,
          Microsoft.IdentityModel,
          Version=3.5.0.0,
          Culture=neutral,
          PublicKeyToken=31bf3856ad364e35" />
        <add type=
          "Microsoft.SharePoint.IdentityModel.SPSaml11SecurityTokenHandler,
          Microsoft.SharePoint.IdentityModel,
          Version=14.0.0.0, Culture=neutral,
          PublicKeyToken=71e9bce111e9429c">
          <samlSecurityTokenRequirement>
            <nameClaimType value=
              "http://schemas.microsoft.com/sharepoint/2009/08
              /claims/userid" />
```

```
        </samlSecurityTokenRequirement>
      </add>
      <add type="Microsoft.SharePoint.IdentityModel.SPTokenCache,
        Microsoft.SharePoint.IdentityModel,
        Version=14.0.0.0, Culture=neutral,
        PublicKeyToken=71e9bce111e9429c" />
    </securityTokenHandlers>
```

Depending on the token type, the correct `SecurityTokenHandler` will fire. In the case of a trusted claims provider, `SPSaml11SecurityTokenHandler` validates the security token by decrypting and checking the signature, expiration date, copies, trusted provider, and the intended audience. If successful, it returns `ClaimsIdentityCollection`, which contain the claims from the token.

Next, `ClaimsIdentityCollection` is passed to a `ClaimsAuthenticationManager` class by way of the `Authenticate` method with the URL of the request. SharePoint accepts the claims sent from the IdP STS, and uses only those accounted for in the mappings established with that IdP STS. SharePoint disregards any additional claims for which there are no authoritative mappings. The `ClaimsAuthenticationManager` processes the accepted claims and the `SecurityTokenValidate` event is raised.

SPFAM creates a session token and writes it to a persistent cookie. This is done in part through a `SessionSecurityTokenHandler` class. The `SecurityTokenValidated` event is raised. The `HttpContext.Current.User` is set to `IClaimsPrincipal`, which is constructed from `SessionSecurityToken`. The persistent cookie created will be handled by `SPChunkedCookieHandler`. This is registered in the `web.config` file.

```
    <cookieHandler mode="Custom" path="/">
            <customCookieHandler type="Microsoft.SharePoint.IdentityModel
              .SPChunkedCookieHandler,
              Microsoft.SharePoint.IdentityModel,
              Version=14.0.0.0, Culture=neutral,
              PublicKeyToken=71e9bce111e9429c" />
            </cookieHandler>
```

The `SignedIn` event is raised and the user is then redirected to `/_layouts/Authenticate.aspx` via `SPUtility.Redirect`. The user performs a `get` on `/_login/default.aspx`, which redirects the client to the SPSTS. The SPSTS receives the token and checks to see if there are any registered claims providers to augment the token. If found, those additional claims are packaged into a security token formatted to SAML and issued by the SPSTS.

The resulting SPSTS token is then tied to a `SPUser` object. The server issues a `FedAuth` cookie to the client. The client is directed to the actual SharePoint site where the user posts the `FedAuth` cookie containing the SPSTS `SPUser` token. This SPSTS security token is used in all communication within the SharePoint farm. `SPUser` token has a default lifetime of 24 hours.

To recap the process, a user is redirected via a series of controls and `HttpModules` to the IdP STS. The IdP STS is responsible for authenticating the user and returning a signed token, which the user will post to SharePoint. That token will be validated and a new SharePoint STS token will be created and sent to the user in the form of a `FedAuth` cookie. The user will post cookie to the web application. The cookie will be persisted and submitted on each subsequent request.

Example of Trusted Provider Claims

To put trusted provider claims into perspective, it's necessary to set one up. The most straightforward example of an IdP STS is found in Active Directory Federation Services (ADFS) 2.0. ADFS is an enterprise claims provider that supports `WS-Federation` and SAML. It is not needed by SharePoint 2010 to use claims. It does, however, provide a dedicated claims system that can be used to broker SSO with other systems. This makes it a good choice for connecting to SharePoint for trusted provider claims.

ADFS is available as a download at `www.microsoft.com`. The instructions for installing ADFS are very well-documented and will not be repeated in this chapter. Once you have ADFS installed, follow these steps to configure ADFS to issue claims to SharePoint:

1. Log in to the ADFS server and launch the ADFS 2.0 Management console by clicking Start ➪ Administrative Tools ➪ AD FS 2.0 Management.

2. Click to expand the `Trust Relationships` node, and then click Relying Party trusts.

3. Click "Add Relying Party trust" to start the Add Relying Party trust wizard.

4. Click Start. This begins the wizard.

5. Select the option to "Enter data about the relying party manually," and then click the Next button.

6. Enter a Display name **SharePoint Claims** and click Next.

7. Select the option to use the AD FS 2.0 profile and click Next.

8. Click Next.

9. Check the box to "Enable support for the WS-Federation Passive protocol." For the WS-Federation Passive protocol URL, enter **https://wrox.com/_trust/**. `wrox.com` is the address of SharePoint web application that will be created later. The _trust was explained earlier in this chapter. After entering the URL click Next.

10. For the relying party trust identifier, you must enter the realm **urn:wrox:sharepoint**. This realm is passed by SharePoint to ADFS when users sign into the web application. The realm is associated on a web-application basis. ADFS uses the realm to map the sign-in request to the correct relying party trust. After ADFS authenticates the user, the WS-Federation Passive protocol URL is the redirection URL back to SharePoint. Later, SharePoint will be configured to use the realm `urn:wrox:sharepoint`. Also, add **https://wrox.com/_trust/**. Then click the Next button.

11. Click Next to permit all users to access SharePoint as a Relying Party.

12. Click Next.

13. Click Close.

14. The Edit Claims for SharePoint Claims will open.

15. Click the Add Rule button.

16. The default value for the claim rule template is "send LDAP attributes as claims." Because Active Directory (AD) is the attribute store used by ADFS in this example, accept the default and click Next.

17. In the claim rule name, type **AD Claims**.

18. In the Attribute store drop-down menu, choose Active Directory.

19. In the LDAP Attribute column, select "E-Mail-Addresses" for the outgoing Name claim, "Token-Groups – Unqualified Names" for the Role claim, and "E-Mail-Addresses" for the outgoing E-mail Address claim. Click Finish.

20. Click OK.

21. Expand the Service and click Certificates.

22. Click the Token-signing certificate.

23. Click View Certificate in the right pane.

24. Click the Details tab.

25. Click "Copy to File." This launches the Certificate Export wizard.

26. Click Next.

27. Accept the default by clicking Next.

28. Click Next to accept the default file format.

29. Choose a location to save the file and name it **ADFSSign.cer**.

30. Click Finish and copy the file to the SharePoint server.

To create a SharePoint web application, follow these steps:

1. Launch Central Administration. In the Application Management section, click "Manage web applications."

2. In the Ribbon, click New.

3. In the Create New Web Application page, in the Authentication section, click Claims Based Authentication.

4. Click "Create a new IIS website," and then type **Wrox** for the name of the website. It is assumed that the necessary hosts file entry or DNS record is in place to test.

5. In the Port box, type **443**.

6. In the Security Configuration section under Allow Anonymous, leave No checked.

7. In the Security Configuration section under Use Secure Sockets Layer (SSL), click Yes. It is assumed that you will have access to an SSL certificate and understand the necessary configuration.

8. In the Claims Authentication Types section, select Enable Windows Authentication and choose NTLM from the drop-down menu.

9. In the Sign In Page URL section, leave the default sign-in page.

10. In the Public URL section, type **Wrox.com**.

11. Click "Create a new application pool" and name it **TPClaims**.

12. Click Predefined to use a predefined security account.

13. Provide the correct Database Name and Authentication information.

14. Click OK.

15. Once the web application has been created, use Internet Information Server (IIS) Manager to edit the bindings and assign the appropriate SSL certificate to the site.

To set up SharePoint with the correct certificates, follow these steps:

1. Locate the `ADFSSign.cer` file copied from ADFS and double-click it. The Certificate properties window should open.

2. Click the Certification Path tab.

3. Click any parent certificates to the ADFS Signing Certificate and use the Export Certificate wizard as described earlier to save the certificates to SharePoint server. This step is critical to verification of the certificate chain. If you do not obtain and register the certificate, it will keep you from signing in later.

4. Copy all the relevant certificates to the `c:\` drive on the SharePoint server for ease of use in the following steps.

5. Click Start ➪ All Programs.

6. Click Microsoft SharePoint 2010 Products.

7. Click SharePoint 2010 Management Shell.

8. Type the following at the prompt and press Enter when finished:

```
$cert = New-Object
System.Security.Cryptography.X509Certificates.X509Certificate2
  ("c:\ADFSSign.cer")
```

9. Next, add it to the store through the following command.

```
New-SPTrustedRootAuthority -Name "ADFS Signing Cert" -Certificate $cert
```

10. Create the claim mappings with the following:

```
$map = New-SPClaimTypeMapping -IncomingClaimType
  "http://schemas.xmlsoap.org/ws/2005/05/identity/claims/emailaddress" -
  IncomingClaimTypeDisplayName "EmailAddress" -
  SameAsIncoming
$map2 = New-SPClaimTypeMapping -IncomingClaimType
  "http://schemas.microsoft.com/ws/2008/06/identity/claims/role" -
  IncomingClaimTypeDisplayName "Role" -SameAsIncoming
```

11. Create a variable for the realm:

```
$realm = "urn:wrox:sharepoint"
```

12. Create a variable for the sign-in URL:

```
$signinurl = "https://GideonADFS/adfs/ls"
```

13. Create the trusted provider:

```
$ap = New-SPTrustedIdentityTokenIssuer -Name
"ADFSTPClaims" -Description "ADFS Trusted Provider" -Realm
$realm -ImportTrustCertificate $cert
-ClaimsMappings $map,$map2 -SignInUrl
$signinurl -IdentifierClaim $map.InputClaimType
```

To configure SharePoint Web Application for Trusted Provider Claims, follow these steps:

1. In Central Administration, click Manage Web Applications.

2. Click the wrox web application and click Authentication Providers in the Ribbon.

3. Click the default zone.

4. Scroll down to the Authentication Types section and check the Trusted Provider Identity Provider check box.

5. Ensure that ADFSTPClaims is checked and click OK.

6. Create a site collection for the site.

After creating the site and visiting it, add a user from your environment by adding the user's e-mail address to the members group. This will be your first exposure to changes in the People Picker.

When you add a user and click the Check Names button, you will see the user underlined as though it has been validated. Unfortunately, this is not the case. Out of the box, the trusted claims provider does not return a list of trusted users, and does not provide a method to validate the user through a search. This means that when a user enters any value, the People Picker accepts the value. These failed attempts are written to the UserInfo table in the content database. This is because of the lack of an industry standard that defines claim resolution, search, or listings of claim values. To address the issue of name validation, a custom claims provider can be written and deployed. Through this claims provider, the developer can write his or her own protocol for validating input in People Picker.

Upon visiting the site, you will notice that you go through the redirection flow explained previously. In addition, the user will have his or her e-mail address as the display name. When users are later added to a site, they will appear in an encoded format (for example, i:0#.t|cgideon@wrox.com). Table 19-1 describes the encoding that a claim takes.

TABLE 19-1: Claim Encodings

CHARACTER	VALUE
i	This signifies an Identity claim.
:	This is used to separate the string.
0	This is reserved for future claims development.
#	This is dependent on the claim type.
.	This represents the start of the claim value.
w	This is an out-of-the-box Windows claim.
m	This is an out-of-the-box Membership claim.
r	This is an out-of-the-box Role claim.
t	This is an out-of-the-box trusted STS claim.

The display of a username can be changed by creating a custom claims provider. However, this involves the creation of a non-industry standard-based approach to resolving, listing, and searching claims from an STS.

If the need for a claim provider to correct this default behavior arises, Microsoft has provided examples in the "Implementing Claims-Based Authentication with SharePoint Server 2010" whitepaper available for download at `http://www`
`.microsoft.com/download/en/details.aspx?id=27569.`

Advantages of Trusted Provider Claims

Setting up trusted provider claims is certainly no easy task. However, it does offer some advantages.

The use of trusted provider claims frees the deployment from Windows authentication. This is a big advantage when considering Internet or extranet sites. The management of users from several partners from an ADDS perspective is a daunting one. The domain administrator and business users must constantly create, delete, or modify accounts in AD. Groups must be created to maintain the proper permissions of these external collaborators. In some environments, this might even include a separate forest for external users, which would create a need to maintain more domain controllers.

There is also the concern with setting up the trusts in the correct direction to ensure tight security. The use of trusted provider claims certainly eases this burden through its capability to federate with partners. This is made even easier if using ADFS to manage the trusts with each partner IP STS.

The use of claims in SharePoint 2010 is about more than federation. A claims infrastructure provides users with the capability to make security decisions based on information already available. An example might be setting the members of a site based on an opportunity ID in a CRM system. The use of an attribute in AD for defining access to a site becomes a possibility. This gives users the opportunity to have more logical choices for securing information.

The option to augment a user's token with additional claims provides even more capabilities. An example might be adding the audiences or distribution list membership to a user that could be used to make an authorization. However, some of the more intriguing advantages occur with the notion of outgoing claims.

Outgoing Claims

When a user signs into SharePoint via the web browser, and must access a service application within the farm, the SPSTS token is sent between servers. Even if the user authenticated with a protocol known for failing to cross the server barrier (sometimes referred to as a *double hop*), the user will still get to the application server with the right credentials. This is partly because of an "act as" token (also known as a *bootstrap token*).

With SharePoint, this "act as" token is requested for the user coming into SharePoint by the Web Front End (WFE) server from the SPSTS. The requested token will be to a specific service application on an application server. Another example of the "act as" token in action is in services farm deployment. Each farm is set up to establish a trust between the respective SPSTS. All inter-farm communication will utilize an "act as" token.

When a service application must connect to other claims-protected resources, a claims provider may have to be registered and utilized. The service application must know up front in its request which claims provider to use, and what claims to send.

This means that there must be a trust established between the destination claims-based application, the IP STS, and SharePoint. If these things are set up, it would be possible to make a request for a token to access the destination system. An example of this type of transaction might be to pull information back from the Service Access Point (SAP) to display to a user in a SharePoint web part. This would give the user the capability to front-end some aspects of the presentation of the SAP through SharePoint using claims for security.

But what happens when the destination application is not claims-aware? For example, SQL Server is not claims aware. The Claims to Windows Token Service is used to bridge this gap for Windows authentication–protected resources.

Claims to Windows Token Service (C2WTS)

The *Claims to Windows Token Service* (C2WTS) is a Windows service shipped as part of Windows Identity Foundation (WIF). The C2WTS takes a specific claim type, User Principal Name (UPN), from a SAML token and performs a protocol transition to a Windows token.

This is done by performing a Kerberos Services for User (S4U) UPN logon. When the C2WTS sees the SAML token, it checks for two things: the claim provider and a UPN. If the claim type is found to be of type Windows Claims, it will perform the S4U UPN logon and return with a Kerberos ticket for the user. This ticket will be sent to the back-end resource.

The C2WTS is a Windows service and must be started on all the servers using the feature. The account used for the C2WTS performs some high-privilege operations and, therefore, requires a high level of local permissions. Specifically, the C2WTS account must have permission to "act as part of the operating system."

To reduce the risk of running with such a high privilege, the C2WTS can be configured to restrict the list of callers to a specific set of users and/or groups in the C2WTS configuration file. The attribute in the file is called the `allowedCallers` element, and is present in the `Microsoft` `.IdentityModel` section. The name of the file is `c2wtshost.exe.config`, located in a folder inside the `C:\Program Files\Windows Identity Foundation\v3.5` folder on default installations.

In order for the C2WTS to get a Kerberos ticket to the back-end resource, the correct Service Principal Names (SPN) must be registered in advance. There are two types of delegation using Kerberos: basic and constrained.

Basic delegation allows the credentials of a user to be delegated or proxied to another security principal from the authenticated process on the box to any process or service off the box. In contrast, with a *constrained delegation,* a service or process delegates a user's credentials to a specific principal.

A basic delegation is limited to a single forest for the scope of the delegation. This means that the user's credentials can be delegated to any back-end resource or principal in the same forest.

A constrained delegation is limited to a single domain. In the case of the C2WTS, a constrained delegation must be created to the back-end resource. This means that the data contained in non-claims-aware back-end resources like SQL Server must exist in the same domain as SharePoint or the account chosen to run the C2WTS service account. The C2WTS service itself provided by the WIF is configured on a server-by-server basis. However, once the service is started through the SharePoint Central Administration service, all servers where C2WTS is started receive the same credentials. Thus, you cannot configure multiple instances of the C2WTS for each domain where a back-end data source exists.

In the case of a cross-forest deployment (where SharePoint is deployed in a resource forest, and users come from another forest), there are additional considerations. The act of performing an S4U UPN logon requires a two-way trust between the forests. This is necessary because of the constrained delegation that requires the account performing the delegation (C2WTS service account) must acquire tickets from the users' forest. The account performing the delegation (C2WTS service account) must have the permission to check the `token-groups-global-and-universal` (TGGAU) attribute. If the back-end resources being utilized are in the user accounts forest, as opposed to the SharePoint forest, the C2WTS will fail. This is because of the failure of Kerberos to delegate cross forest. Cross-forest authentication is possible, just not delegation of the user's credentials back over the trust.

Routing hints may be necessary in AD for the trust if you have overlapping tree names. Otherwise, the request for a ticket will be routed to the wrong forest during the referral process. This will lead to a `S_PRINICPAL_UNKNOWN` error being sent back. Windows 2000–based domain controllers do not support Kerberos S4U logons. This means that the C2WTS is restricted to Windows Server 2003 or higher domains.

The C2WTS is used by several services in SharePoint Server 2010. These include Excel Services, PerformancePoint Services, InfoPath Forms Services, and Visio Services.

Keep in mind that the C2WTS does not work for trusted provider claims. The C2WTS is only looking for UPN claims from the Windows claims provider. What then happens when trusted provider-based users must access resources such as Excel Services?

Secure Store Service

The service previously known as SSO in SharePoint Server 2007 is now called the Secure Store Service (SSS). The SSS acts as a credential store to keep usernames and passwords used in the connection to other back-end systems. It does this by associating the stored credentials to an identity or group of identities. For example, if access to a system is restricted to a specific account, all users can be configured to use those credentials to access the system.

SSS offers the trusted provider and Windows provider (in untrusted domains) the capability to access back-end resources for Excel Services, PerformancePoint Services, and Visio Services. In the case of data refresh, the PowerPivot service application can use credentials stored in SSS to refresh data from an external Analysis Services database. The benefit of this approach is the notion that many enterprises use a similar methodology today.

Disadvantages of Trusted Provider Claims

Although the inclusion of trusted provider claims opens the doors to many possibilities, it does come with a cost. Using trusted provider claims is likely to entail some form of development and customization to give users parity to the experience they had with Windows authentication.

The areas that will be most affected are People Picker, user profiles, search alerts, and audiences. User profiles must have their attributes populated programmatically, or manually tied to the user identity coming from trusted provider claims from a supported directory import. This may be mitigated by the method used to migrate users from Windows classic-mode authentication (discussed later in this chapter) to trusted provider users, because they had profiles to start with. Unless you are using a programmatic solution, each new trusted provider user must be manually mapped to their respective profiles. The profiles, of course, must first be created.

Search alerts are not available to trusted provider users. This is because of the lack of a notion of caching the SAML token and using it later for the query. This is unlikely to change in the future, because it is a fundamental architectural challenge.

User-based audiences are not supported out of the box. This means that options such as defining an audience by being a member of a group will not work. Instead, a property-based audience must be used. The user's profile must be pre-populated with correct attributes and values. Once completed, the property-based audience can be created and used.

SQL Reporting Services clients such as Report Builder, the Report Designer in Business Intelligence Development Studio (BIDS), and Management Studio do not work with trusted provider claims. These clients do not function on a web application that supports multiple authentication providers either. This leaves only one alternative: to create a new web application that is extended and mapped using only Windows claims as an authentication provider.

SharePoint Designer 2010 cannot discover Web Service Definition Language (WSDL) endpoints protected with claims. This creates difficulties when working with external content types.

The lack of support for ADFS-based trusted provider claims to use the C2WTS has frustrated many administrators. If ADFS has AD as an attribute store, and can provide a UPN for the user, it would seem natural to use the C2WTS. However, the C2WTS has been hard-coded to only accept Windows claims, as mentioned previously. The requirement of SSS is unacceptable for some companies. This is mainly because of regulatory requirements that require an audit trail from the initial user request from the browser to the data in SQL, something not provided with SSS. Another cause for dissatisfaction with this approach revolves around the personalization and securing of data through dashboards, because SSS provides a many-to-one mapping, as opposed to individual security.

Migrating to Trusted Provider Claims

If the advantages outweigh the disadvantages in a deployment, then the next natural step becomes migration. The first thing to understand about migration is that it is a one-way trip. Once the users have been migrated to trusted provider claims, the only supported method to go back to Windows claims is through a restore. There is not an out-of-the-box method to reverse the process. If you simply add support for trusted provider claims to an existing deployment, it will require a double-access control entry. There will be one for the Windows user and one for the trusted provider user.

The only way to migrate from Windows users to trusted provider users is through the `IMigrateUserCallback` interface, which was released as part of the August 2010 cumulative update. This means that there is no out-of-the-box method to convert on the upgrade or through a tool to perform this task. It must be written.

Windows Claims

When creating a new web application and choosing to use claims-based authentication, the default option is Windows Claims. The configuration options look nearly identical to those offered in classic mode. The options for NTLM, Negotiate (Kerberos), and Basic are apparent. This may lead one to the false impression that nothing has changed from classic mode.

Scrolling further down the dialog, an option for a sign-in page URL appears. Because claims are about redirecting the client to an authoritative source for authentication, the use of a sign-in page URL is very important. The value placed in this dialog is used by the client later when accessing any site secured with claims. In the case of Windows claims, the sign-in page will only be visible to a user if more than one authentication provider is chosen.

Once a web application has been configured to use Windows claims, the process will be similar to trusted provider claims. The difference is that after SPFAM has fired, it directs the user to the sign-in page. As mentioned previously, if using the default sign-in page, this will be the `/_login/ default.aspx`. A control on this page redirects the client to the `/_windows/default.aspx`.

The actual authentication is done through `SPWindowsClaimsAuthenticationHttpModule`, which ensures that the client is sent a `401` server code instead of a `302` redirect message. The interception of the `302` message must occur, because Windows claims are implemented as forms for the authentication mode.

`SPWindowsClaimsAuthenticationHttpModule` gets a Windows identity from `HttpContext` using the selected authentication method (NTLM, Kerberos, or Basic). To the client, this will appear to be silent in the sense that the user will not be required to type a username and password if on the corporate network. In much the same manner as trusted provider claims, SPSAM creates a persistent session cookie for use on subsequent requests.

In the case of the Windows claims provider, the augmentation comes in the form of additional Windows Security groups. The Windows token obtained from authentication is forwarded to SPSTS, which, in turn, augments the token it generates with Windows Security groups as claims. If any additional claims providers are registered, they are given the opportunity to return additional claims to augment the SPSTS token. An example of augmentation might be the use of distribution lists or SharePoint audiences.

Windows claims use the SPSTS token for all activity within the farm. This means that an NTLM authentication will still support accessing a service application on an application server through the use of an "act as" token.

Advantages of Windows Claims

The primary advantage of Windows claims is the consistent SharePoint experience. To users, this will appear (for all intents and purposes) as if they were still using the same system from SharePoint Server 2007. The experience in People Picker will be the same as before. Windows claims supports listing, validating, and searching for principals. The treatment of a Windows claim allows developers to use `IClaimsPrincipal` and other advantages in developing web parts or services. The potential to augment claims gives a distinct advantage over the SharePoint Server 2007 system.

Migrating to Windows Claims

Migrating to Windows claims is not something that happens automatically during an upgrade. The conversion process is manual and should be an activity that is well planned.

To convert a web application to Windows claims from Windows classic, `SPWebApplication` provides a method called `MigrateUsers`. The steps are fairly simple.

For this example, assume that the domain name is `wrox`, the user is `cgideon`, and the SharePoint web application URL is `http://SPWrox`. The following would be executed in the SharePoint Management console:

```
$WebAppName = "http://SPWrox"
$account = "wrox\cgideon"
$wa = get-SPWebApplication $WebAppName

Set-SPwebApplication $wa -AuthenticationProvider
   (New-SPAuthenticationProvider) -Zone Default
```

A Migration prompt will occur. Click Yes to continue. Type the following from SharePoint Management console:

```
$wa = get-SPWebApplication $WebAppName
$account = (New-SPClaimsPrincipal -identity $account
   -identitytype 1).ToEncodedString()
$zp = $wa.ZonePolicies("Default")
```

```
$p = $zp.Add($account,"PSPolicy")
$fc=$wa.PolicyRoles.GetSpecialRole("FullControl")
$p.PolicyRoleBindings.Add($fc)
$wa.Update()
$wa = get-SPWebApplication $WebAppName
$wa.MigrateUsers($true)
```

This process is executed in a timer job that must be started manually. This process will take time, depending on the number of users and site collections to be converted in the web application. You may have to update the `portalsuperuseraccount` property and the `portalsuperreaderaccount` property of the web application to use the new claims-based account. This only occurs if the properties were configured before the migration of the web application.

The search crawl account will have to be updated to the new claims account as well. Otherwise, crawl of the web application will fail after migration. In some cases, alerts must be re-created.

As with trusted provider claims, there is no supported way to revert from Windows claims back to Windows classic mode (legacy version). Plan accordingly.

Forms-Based Authentication Claims

Forms-Based Authentication (FBA) has changed to a claims implementation in SharePoint 2010. It is not an optional change. It's required if you want to continue using FBA.

The good news is that most existing providers will work fine under the new system. FBA follows the same pattern of trusted provider claims through the pipeline, with a few exceptions. The first exception lies in the fact that most FBA systems don't a have a token. FBA claims overcome this problem by SPSTS acting as the token provider.

SPFAM and SPSAM follow the same steps as trusted provider claims in terms of redirecting to `/_layouts/Authenticate.aspx`. However, the next redirect will be to `/_forms/default.aspx`. This will redirect to the ASP.NET FBA sign-in page. The user context is passed back to `/_layouts/Authenticate.aspx`, and then `/_login/default.aspx` and `/_forms/default.aspx`. The acquired user context is then sent to SPSTS, which checks for registered claims providers. In this case, any roles from an ASP.NET Role Provider are augmented into the SPSTS token. As with trusted provider claims, an `IPrincipal` is constructed and a session cookie created.

To configure an FBA claims web application during the creation process, the Claims Authentication Types section must have the Enable Forms Based Authentication (FBA) option selected. The membership provider name and a role manager name must be entered. As a result of the changes to FBA, a minimum of three `web.config` files must be updated. The Central Administration, SPSTS, and the web application using FBA will need updating in order to manage sites protected with FBA.

Advantages and Disadvantages of Using FBA Claims

If you already have FBA deployed, you are in a position to take advantage of claims upon upgrade. This process handles the migration logic for you with tools built in. The potential uses for claims are immediately recognized with this type of claim. The complexity is reduced from that of trusted provider claims. There are out-of-the-box options for FBA (such as the LDAP provider).

However, for search to crawl, an FBA site still requires a zone to be configured with Windows. User profile mappings and creation will still have the same requirements as trusted provider claims. People Picker integration will require additional work if features such as listing, resolving, or searching are required. Outgoing claims to services such as SQL will require additional work to convert to an outbound claim.

The claims produced by FBA are only valid in the SharePoint farm by default. The C2WTS does not permit FBA claims, so access to Excel Services, PerformancePoint, Visio Services, and InfoPath Forms Services will require SSS.

Migrating to FBA Claims

Migrating to FBA claims is done through `SPWebApplication MigrateUsers` via Windows PowerShell for migrating permissions. This should be done after the `web.config` files have been modified. To migrate the web application itself, use the following Windows PowerShell code:

```
$w = Get-SPWebApplication "http://<server>/"
$w.UseClaimsAuthentication = 1
$w.Update()

$w.ProvisionGlobally()
```

To migrate permissions, use the following:

```
$w = Get-SPWebApplication "http://<server>/"
$w.MigrateUsers(True)
```

This process is a multi-threaded operation that proceeds quickly. The move to FBA claims is one-way, and users cannot be migrated out of the box to Windows claims or trusted provider claims. Any conversion to FBA claims as part of an upgrade should be thoroughly tested prior to upgrading.

CLASSIC-MODE AUTHENTICATION IN SHAREPOINT 2010

The inclusion of claims into SharePoint Server 2010 does not mean the old methods of authentication are gone. Windows authentication methods such as NTLM and Kerberos are still available. When first creating a new web application through Central Administration, two options are presented: claims-based authentication or classic-mode authentication.

Classic-mode authentication is a backward-compatible mode of Windows authentication in which all users are from an AD Domain Services domain. The option to use or not use claims is always a per-web-application decision. Classic-mode authentication provides for Windows authentication only in the form of NTLM, Kerberos, anonymous, basic, and digest. It does not provide support for FBA, nor does classic-mode authentication provide support for Windows certificate authentication (such as smart cards).

Following is an example request process when the web application is configured as classic mode with NTLM as the authentication protocol:

1. The first request from the client is sent anonymously. This results in IIS sending back a `WWW-Authenticate: NTLM` header.

2. Internet Explorer (IE) calls `AcquireCredentialsHandle` and passes the appropriate Security Support Provider (SSP) — in this case, `NTLM`. Depending on the zone configured within IE and the options configured, a username and password prompt may appear. IE then calls `InitializeSecurityContext`, which constructs a Windows token containing the Domain Name and Machine name. The request is sent to IIS.

3. The request comes into IIS and an authorization token containing an NTLM challenge is sent to the client in a `401` response.

4. IE parses the server response and `InitializeSecurityContext` is called again. The resulting authorization token containing `NTLMChallengeResponse` is sent to IIS.

5. IIS passes the authentication request to the Local Security Authority Subsystem Service (LSASS). LSASS, in turn, utilizes the pre-established Secure Channel to the domain controller (DC) for the domain in which SharePoint resides. The DC is sent the username and challenge sent to the client, as well as the response received from the client. The DC takes the username, retrieves the password hash used in the challenge, and compares it to the challenge response. If they are identical, authentication is successful.

6. At this point, the user is represented by a Windows token in IIS, which is passed into SharePoint.

The use of the NTLM protocol provides some inherent challenges. The most notable is the inability to delegate credentials across process boundaries, application domains, or off the box to a back-end system. Some examples of this behavior can be seen when leaving SharePoint to delegate credentials to Excel Services, SQL Reporting Services, or authenticated RSS feeds.

NTLM is also very chatty, and can have an impact on ADDS infrastructure. This is especially true in environments with multiple forests. Users coming in from forests outside of the SharePoint forest must authenticate over the trust. The trust between forests has inherent bottlenecks that slow down the process.

However, NTLM does provide a method to use Windows authentication with clients not in a domain. This need may arise when working with contractors or partners who have machines that are not part of the domain. An extranet scenario is the prime example of such an activity.

Although easy to configure, NTLM is also considered a weak choice for security in some circles. Additional steps may be necessary (such as SSL to encrypt the traffic).

Excel Services, PerformancePoint Services, Visio Services, and PowerPivot for SharePoint 2010 all must use the SSS to authenticate to back-end resources. SSS maintains a shared low-privilege account utilized for the connections. This may create compliance issues for clients that require an audit trail for back-end resources, because the same account will be used for all users.

Using Windows authentication all the way to the back-end resource requires Kerberos. Kerberos uses a much different means of authenticating users by placing the burden on the client. Following is an example authentication process using Kerberos in classic mode:

1. The first request from the client is sent anonymously. This results in IIS sending back a `WWW-Authenticate: Negotiate` header.

2. IE calls `AcquireCredentialsHandle` and passes the appropriate SSP — in this case, `Negotiate`.

3. At this point, the client checks in the ticket cache to check for a Kerberos Ticket Granting Ticket (TGT). If present, the client performs a DNS lookup on the server address and makes a `KRB_TGS_REQ` (Kerberos Ticket-Granting Service Request) to the Key Distribution Center (KDC) running on the DC. The KDC searches ADDS for a Service Principal Name (SPN) of type `HTTP` for the address of the SharePoint server on the domain account running the application pool. If found, the server replies with a `KRB_TGS_REP` (Kerberos Ticket-Granting Service Reply) to the client. This ticket is stored in the ticket cache on the client. The client then sends the SharePoint server a `KRB_AP_REQ` (Kerberos Application Request) in the header of the request.

4. IIS decrypts the ticket via a call to LSASS. IIS then sends the client a `KRB_AP_REP` (Kerberos Application Reply). In this reply is a time stamp.

5. At this point, the user is represented by a Windows token in IIS, which is passed into SharePoint.

6. The client having received the `KRB_AP_REP` examines the time stamp.

Kerberos supports mutual authentication between the client and the server, making it an inherently more secure choice than NTLM. Kerberos is a time-sensitive protocol with the default for most domains being 5 minutes for the allowed clock skew, or difference between times on the client and server. Proper SPNs must be set up for each service for which Kerberos authentication is desired. Therefore, each back-end resource to which credentials are delegated requires SPNs.

The downside of Kerberos revolves around the fact that clients must contact the KDC running on a DC. This may not be possible in scenarios such as extranets or Internet-based collaboration environments (where it would be a bad practice to place a DC here).

Another concern with Kerberos is the failure to fall back to NTLM. If the server sends back the `Negotiate` header and no SPNs are registered, the client will immediately fall back to NTLM. However, if the `Negotiate` header is sent and SPNs are configured, the client will try Kerberos first. If Kerberos fails (typically because of a bad SPN registration, a duplicate SPN, or inaccessible KDC), then the behavior on the client will not fall back to NTLM. This results in access being denied on the client.

Disadvantages of Classic-mode Authentication

There are a few things to consider with regard to remaining with the status quo of classic mode. In a combined intranet and extranet design, a common approach is to create multiple zones. Each zone is configured with a different authentication provider. The intranet web application is configured to use Kerberos, whereas the extranet is configured for NTLM. This creates a different URL for each environment. It also restricts each zone to a single authentication provider.

Claims-based web applications can have more than one authentication provider, thus decreasing complexity and opening up to more than just Windows authentication. A claims-based web application also provides for more types of security principals (such as a distribution list, or attributes from a directory service). In short, ease of configuration is sacrificed for greater flexibility.

PLANNING FOR CLAIMS

The claims implementation in SharePoint 2010 clearly illustrates the need for careful planning and design. Understanding a company's overall identity strategy is the first step in planning a claims implementation. Several questions should be posed, including the following:

➤ Is there already an identity road map for the organization?

➤ Will claims be used?

➤ What will be the source of the claims?

➤ What claim types will be used?

➤ Where will the claims be sourced?

➤ Which users will be able to use claims?

➤ Will federation be used between partners?

➤ Which line of business (LOB) applications support claims, and will they be integrated with SharePoint?

Each of these questions requires careful consideration. Designing an enterprise claims infrastructure is beyond the scope of this chapter. However, the importance of each question should be addressed.

Claims-Based Identity

The removal of a specific protocol for authentication changes the view of identity. No longer are users defined by their AD `samAccountName` or Security ID (SID), but by the entirety of their identity.

This decoupling of identity from authentication gives developers writing the next generation of applications the opportunity to spend time on other features. Authentication is simply handled, and new options are available to applications. The capability to determine the office location of a user or the user's title for use in an authorization decision was simply not possible using Kerberos or other protocols.

Attribute Stores

Having a strategy to define the composition of identity is critical. The attributes chosen in the definition of identity must also consider the source. Consider the following attributes:

➤ First Name

➤ Last Name

➤ Phone Number

➤ Employee ID

➤ Manager

➤ Office Location

➤ Job title

➤ Email Address

If you have chosen AD for the attribute store, then chances are the information for these attributes is populated. But how fresh are the values in these attributes? Do these attributes get pushed into AD from another system, or are they manually entered?

In environments lacking a Identity Management system such as FIM, chances are that this information is entered manually. In some cases, this information is likely copied and pasted from different systems into AD. Perhaps the Job Title is maintained in the Human Resources system. The Human Resources system is kept up to date by that set of information. The information is moved by some process into AD. The frequency of the push or pull into each source or target becomes the controlling factor for freshness.

If you plan on using attributes through claims, then the freshness of identity data changes from a minor nuisance to a potential security breach. The need to know the authoritative source for an attribute becomes paramount. Choosing the location and type of attribute store for your claims to source must also be considered for securing the information itself. Some attributes carry very real privacy concerns, and exposing some of these attributes to others could result in legal problems. Therefore, the source for this information must be secured.

The attribute store must also be scalable and redundant for the increased load from SharePoint. Most applications are scaled for their current workload. Introducing SharePoint with claims could be enough to topple an old system that can barely keep up with the current workload. For example, if an old LDAP directory is used as an attribute store, will it handle the constant queries for claims authentication? Or, will the Excel spreadsheet that is maintained by a law firm acting as the authoritative store for employment be capable of scaling? The answer in some cases will be "no."

In some environments, the need for more than one attribute store will arise. This will necessitate the use of a broker- or proxy-like ADFS to reduce the number of claim providers trusting SharePoint. This is especially true of attribute stores that do not provide the necessary frame to trust SharePoint directly. For example, systems that only use SAML 2.0 may need to proxy through ADFS to provide claims to those users. This must be factored into the design.

Defining federation relationships with partners will also be of critical importance in planning. The attribute stores used by the partners will need to be configured for trust.

Building a picture of the components of identity and taking action through products like FIM will go a long way in helping establish a claims infrastructure. These factors will introduce the least-common denominator for what can be a claim.

Claim Types and Flow

Eventually, a picture of the most important points of identity will begin to emerge, and with it, the attributes that will become a claims surface. These claims must be further broken down into types. In the earlier example of ADFS trusting SharePoint, the type of claims to use had to be known. Email Address was used as the primary identifier. The attributes you choose to map into claims must be accompanied by a URI to define the schema. You should choose some of the more common attributes such as Email-Address, given name, name, UPN, common name, group, role, and surname. These are predefined and make the mapping easier. If the attributes must be mapped into others, then the flow of claims changes.

The claim type chosen may need to be calculated or transformed from some other type. Complex business rules will require a dedicated product such as ADFS to formulate the flow of claims. ADFS provides a rules-based engine to help make this process easier. This type of work can front-end the effort for SharePoint to reduce user confusion during the implementation.

How Many Claims Do I Need?

The subject of how many claims you need is always a topic of conversation. Some companies want to send everything they could ever want as a claim. But will they spend the effort to develop a custom claims provider to use those claims?

If the development effort is completed, then the next problem will be the volume of claims returned in the People Picker. Remember, each claim mapped will be returned when searching for a principal. This should emphasize the need to keep the number to a more manageable level. Find the core claims for permission, and execute on them. An example of a high number of claims would be 40 or 50 — especially if these claims must come from an identity broker such as ADFS from multiple attribute stores. This introduces latency at the time of claims retrieval.

When Do I Need to Write a Custom Claims Provider?

Whenever you need to augment a claim, a custom claim provider may be necessary. For example, you might have a user who logs in through Windows claims, but you would like to augment his or her token with information from CRM. This will require a claims provider. If you want to control the way that names are displayed in People Picker, you will need a custom claims provider. The most important factors for developing a claims provider are performance and security.

Creating a custom AD claims provider will require knowledge of the best methods for interacting with the directory. For example, if your claims provider pulls back information on an attribute that is mapped to a claim, it should be cached in a secure fashion. The attributes chosen should be from the list of indexed attributes to avoid slow and expensive queries.

Be careful not to choose attributes for claims that would require repeated lookups to the directory. It's one thing for AD to provide logins and group memberships, but another to constantly return a user's job title. Monitor the DCs in your environment to determine the impact of long-running queries, because they consume more memory.

Keep Global Catalog (GC) representation from each forest in close physical proximity to SharePoint to limit the impact of network latency. AD site topologies should be examined to ensure that the physical location of GC/DCs will result in their usage. The DC Locator process is working off of subnet and site configuration, so ensure that these are correct.

Using audience information or user profiles also requires the use of a custom claims provider. These two areas of the product require thorough testing to ensure scalability. Frequent requests to the claims provider increases the pressure on the User Profile Application (UPA). This may require you to revisit your storage architecture for UPA.

SUMMARY

The implementation of claims in SharePoint 2010 has separated identity from authentication. This will likely increase the number of discussions on identity in the enterprise. The demand from collaborators to move to a form of role-based security will put force behind existing efforts. This will be seen at an even faster pace in environments that may be considering a hybrid cloud model.

Trusted provider claims require the most planning. Spend the time to predetermine the claims needed up front to avoid building the wrong identity. Once SharePoint is built with a claims identity, it will be very difficult to change. This will entail a great deal of work to compile use cases for claims.

Forms-Based Authentication (FBA) claims provide new methods to extend the experience to users. The trade-off lies in the development required to write claims providers. Back-end systems will prove to be the most challenging, because a claims provider or SSS will be needed.

Windows claims are the easiest to deploy. This type of claims authentication will have the least impact on the user experience. The desire to extend the claims available in Active Directory requires the development of a custom claims provider. Custom claims providers must be carefully developed using all the same best practices already documented for Active Directory applications. Otherwise, the performance could be impacted in both Active Directory and SharePoint.

Classic-mode authentication provides time to move to the new system. Though not representing a leap forward in technology, it creates a Windows plan. Once the implications of claims are fully understood, this option will be chosen less and less.

Chapter 20 discusses how to define your SharePoint 2010 governance model and approach.

20

Defining Your Governance Model and Approach

By Simon Walker

Before you skip over this chapter, take a moment to remember where the real power of SharePoint 2010 lies. It provides a framework of capability that is almost unsurpassed, and a range of flexibility that is as wide as it is deep. This is the power of SharePoint, and also its biggest issue in relation to governance.

Let's say that you have read through this book and adopted all of the learning it has provided. You now have architected the perfect solution — it scales easily, it is well-managed, and the business recognizes the value it brings to the organization. Well done! But you skipped this chapter because governance just isn't for you — it is someone else's problem.

Roll the clock forward 12 months, and there you are, head in hands, wondering why your perfect SharePoint deployment is performing poorly, the end users are complaining about the capability to find information and navigate it, you have hundreds of sites but no way to tell what they do and how secure they are, there is no consistency in the use of metadata or look and feel, and your organization has relegated SharePoint 2010 to a non-enterprise toolset that is poorly adopted, and represents a risk rather than a benefit.

What happened? You didn't think about governing your SharePoint 2010 solution, and it is now out of control. In a SharePoint 2010 deployment, *governance is your best friend*. It will help you to control the platform over time, and ensure that it delivers full benefit to your business without introducing unnecessary risk.

Done correctly, governance will enable end users to act with confidence, and will help with your adoption. In fact, governance can even be popular (really!) because it provides clear guidance and rules. There is a balance to be struck, but, generally, people like to understand what the rules are. It makes their lives easier than guessing.

If you got this far, you're committed now, so why not read on and make your life easier in the long run?

UNDERSTANDING GOVERNANCE

Governance has become a difficult term to define. Over the past few years, it has become a buzzword that can apply in all sorts of ways to IS/IT, projects, business, and government. Given that is has become so ubiquitous, it is no surprise, perhaps, that it is not well understood in relation to SharePoint 2010. This, coupled with the fact that differing views exist about how governance relates to Information Architecture (IA), Information Management (IM), and corporate governance, the subject becomes too broad to address in a meaningful manner, and is not addressed appropriately.

So, before going any further, let's define a governance mission statement:

"SharePoint governance exists to ensure that expectations are met, consistency and performance is maintained, resources are managed, and risks are avoided and mitigated."

With that definition of what you are trying to achieve, it is a lot easier to talk about what governance is in practical terms. With effective governance, you can do the following:

➤ Manage the expectations of what SharePoint is being used for

➤ Ensure that a consistent experience and set of uses are applied

➤ Protect the performance and availability of SharePoint

➤ Ensure that the resources you have available (technology and people) are effectively managed, and you get the best value

➤ Protect yourself from inappropriate use that will introduce risk for all of the other users of SharePoint

➤ Avoid risks entirely, or at least mitigate their impact should they occur

➤ Ensure that the same approach is used to solve business and technical problems

➤ Understand the impact of change

➤ Be able to define what is "good" and what is "bad," and deal with it accordingly

Why Do I Need Governance?

Governance is essential for a deployment of almost any scale, because without it, SharePoint could introduce risk into the business. Following are some examples of situations that can occur without governance:

➤ Inappropriate usage

➤ Information chaos

➤ Poor user experience

➤ Infrastructure and configuration issues

➤ SharePoint instability

➤ Poor business alignment

➤ Reduced adoption

➤ End-user confusion

There is a simple analogy to help make this clearer. If you were to build the best car in the world, would you be comfortable with handing it over to someone with no guidance? Probably not. SharePoint without governance is worse than this. Not only are you handing over the keys to your shiny new car without instruction, you're letting it onto a road with no rules — no speed limits, road signs, correct sides of the road. How long do you think your new toy will last?

Governance is not an option with SharePoint deployments — it is an absolute necessity.

How Much Governance Is Good?

The most challenging aspect of governance is finding the right balance to get to "good" — a knife-edge position where there is the flexibility to free the power of SharePoint without tying it down to a level that will repress the success of the platform.

Governance has two key components. The first is the *strength* of the governance (that is, loose to strict governance). The optimum position will be driven by alignment with your business. The second is the *cost* of deploying, maintaining, and managing a governance model over time — the stricter the model, the higher the cost to enforce and maintain.

As the level of governance increases, the costs to manage, enforce, and work within the governance framework increase on all levels. From an IS/IT perspective, potentially more resources are required for enforcement, larger control structures must be in place with higher levels of senior stakeholder representation, and the level of customization and automation will be higher.

In reality, every organization will have an optimum point of governance that strikes the right balance between control, risk reduction, and associated cost. Following are some considerations that will drive this balance:

➤ *Corporate governance* — The level of corporate governance that is preexisting will set the tone for the level of SharePoint governance. It will also influence the structure of control and reporting, because SharePoint governance may sit within a wider governance structure such as IM governance.

➤ *Criticality* — The criticality of the SharePoint solution will affect the level of governance required. What problems does a failed SharePoint deployment create for the business? What types of information will SharePoint manage? Will you be using Features such as Records Management, and, if so, what types of records will be managed? Is SharePoint externally facing, and what is the impact of a lack of governance? Are there reputational issues at stake?

➤ *Risk* — The level of risk that is tolerable will influence the level of governance. The less governance, the higher the risk of problems will be. However, if the organization can accept the risks, then this may be a valid approach.

➤ *Scale* — Typically, larger deployments will drive higher levels of governance to protect the platform.

➤ *Range of capabilities* — The wider the range of capabilities offered, the more difficult it becomes to control how SharePoint will be used. Therefore, governance requires more effort to ensure that the right capabilities are used in the right places, and in accordance with your defined best practices.

➤ *Industry sector* — Different sectors tend to drive toward different requirements for governance. For example, a defense business is likely to require higher levels of governance than an events-management company.

➤ *Governmental/legal/industry compliance levels* — These vary from business to business, contract to contract. The higher the level of compliance required, typically the higher the levels of governance required.

➤ *Organizational structure* — A tightly controlled and centralized organization will typically be simpler to implement SharePoint governance in than a geographically spread federated business model. The levels of effort associated with governance (particularly around communication, audit, and enforcement) will increase with the complexity of the organizational structure.

➤ *Culture* — This has a big impact on the level of governance that is appropriate. Sometimes it is necessary to push against the culture to implement a good level of governance. Culture has an influence, but should not be an excuse for a lack of governance.

➤ *Maturity* — All organizations go through a life cycle with their SharePoint deployments. The lower the level of maturity around SharePoint, the harder governance will be to implement. A mature SharePoint user will recognize the pitfalls, and, therefore, governance will be simpler to implement and enforce.

If you are in an organization that is highly regulated, it stands to reason that your SharePoint 2010 deployment will be highly governed to ensure compliance and avoid risk. If you are in a small organization with limited use cases for SharePoint 2010, your governance effort can be scaled down. There is a level of governance below which you should not drop (which is discussed later in this chapter).

Table 20-1 provides a high-level matrix with some indicators for the level of governance for various scenarios. It is a generalization that is not capable of dealing with all of the details, but clarifies the fact that "good" governance will vary.

TABLE 20-1: Indicators for Governance Level in Various Scenarios

SCOPE OF SHAREPOINT DEPLOYMENT (AUDIENCE, USE CASES, COMPLEXITY)	ORGANIZATION SIZE		
	SMALL (LESS THAN 500 USERS)	MEDIUM (500 TO 5,000 USERS)	LARGE (MORE THAN 5,000 USERS)
Limited	Manual controls	Key governance processes are automated	Majority of governance processes automated
	Limited end-user representation	Strong end-user engagement in governance	Strong end-user engagement, which is likely to be reporting to wider organizational governance structure
	Small set of governance rules	Small set of governance rules	Small set of governance rules
Average	Request process automated in some instances — change itself is probably manual	Key governance processes are fully automated	Full automation of governance processes wherever feasible
	End-user engagement for governance deeper, but no senior stakeholder representation	End-user engagement will be significant — senior stakeholders may be required	End-user engagement will have senior stakeholders represented
	Broad set of governance rules that are enforced through ad-hoc manual audit	Broad set of governance rules with scheduled audits and reviews	Reports to wider governance framework in the organization
			Broad rule set with automated audit probably in place
Wide	Automation likely in some key areas of governance	Majority of governance processes are automated	Fully automated governance

continues

TABLE 20-1 *(continued)*

SCOPE OF SHAREPOINT DEPLOYMENT (AUDIENCE, USE CASES, COMPLEXITY)	ORGANIZATION SIZE		
	SMALL (LESS THAN 500 USERS)	**MEDIUM (500 TO 5,000 USERS)**	**LARGE (MORE THAN 5,000 USERS)**
	Senior stakeholders will form part of end-user representation	Dedicated resource for SharePoint governance with strong end-user engagement and senior stakeholder representation	Governance board reporting or engagement with C-level executive
	Broad rule set with automated audit controls and reports are likely	Broad rule set with audit automation	Broad rule set that is detailed and prescriptive, with full audit automation

Regardless of your situation, some things should always be done:

➤   You should *always* have a governance model in place — even if it is very simple.

➤   If you don't have a governance site somewhere in your SharePoint environment, then perhaps you should think again — no, really, think again.

➤   The end users will be impacted by your governance decisions. If you do not involve them from the outset, then don't expect them to play nicely.

➤   If you have no way of checking compliance with your governance, then you do not have good governance.

➤   If you have no authority to enforce your governance, then you have a "gummy shark" — they don't last long in the wild.

➤   Review your governance model, principles, and rules regularly — things change fast in the world of SharePoint.

➤   Ensure that you understand the scope of your governance, which is discussed next.

Where to Start

You're reading this, so you're already off to a great start, or perhaps you're trying to figure out where you went wrong. As with so many things in life, the starting point should be to define your scope — in particular, your scope is driven by your IA (see Chapter 14).

The scope of your governance model and approach should cover the following subjects:

➤ *Capabilities* — You should clearly define the capabilities you are planning to govern. Let's be clear here — if you are excluding capabilities that you have delivered in your SharePoint project, you are in trouble. You shouldn't pick and choose which bits you govern. By explicitly defining the capabilities, you effectively state that *all* other scenarios are ungoverned and, therefore, not allowed. (You have your first governing principle!)

➤ *Alignment* — Your scope should explain how you align with both the SharePoint solution and any other governance, change, or steering boards that may exist (for SharePoint or other technologies).

➤ *Authority* — You will define what authority the governance process has, and why it is appropriate and required. This generally needs some effort to define and get documented — without authority, it is impossible to govern, but internal politics will often come into play. There is no easy way to deal with this. Drive the importance of governance home, be patient with those who make the decisions, and work through the issues one at a time — just make sure you don't end up with a "gummy shark."

➤ *Sponsorship* — Who will be your governance sponsor? Let's keep this simple — go as high as you can in your organization. If you're uncomfortable with this, ask yourself why — what have you got to hide? The more senior your sponsor, the easier governance becomes, and, perhaps just as importantly, the more likely that SharePoint will become a success.

➤ *Area* — What areas will your governance model address? Perhaps, in your organization, security or IM is handled by another team, and, therefore, you can exclude this from the scope of your governance, except for those technology-specific rules that impact SharePoint. If there are SharePoint-specific rules, you should clarify if you own them or the other team does. (Can you see the politics yet?)

➤ *Audience and communication* — Who is your audience for your governance model, and how will you communicate with them? In some scenarios, the governance model and responsible team are tasked with communicating with all end users. In other instances, you may have nominated leads within the business with which to liaise. If you're not clear on this, you risk either a lack of communication, or perhaps bypassing someone in your organization who will be held responsible. Either way, if you get it wrong, it is painful and time-consuming to make it right.

➤ *Out of scope* — You should explicitly state what is out of the scope of your governance model. For example, in a mid-size environment, the governance model may take responsibility for change management or approvals. In larger organizations, there will often be a dedicated change board, and, therefore, you must align, but change management itself is largely out of your scope. (You won't avoid it completely in this scenario, by the way.)

Once you have your scope and it has been agreed on, everything gets that little bit easier to define moving forward. You'll rarely regret the time you put into this later on down the line.

UNDERSTANDING GOVERNANCE MODELS

You understand the need for governance, you have a good definition of your scope, and you have a feel for what is "good" in your own organization and circumstances. Now comes the time to put together a model of some description and flesh out the details. There is a *lot* of opinion on governance and associated models. Whichever approach you take, it should make absolute sense to you at a fundamental level. If you don't understand your own model, you should do the following:

➤ Take the time to work through your understanding of how this applies to you and your organization.

➤ Maybe change the approach to something more suitable if it feels wrong — one size does not fit all.

➤ Ask others about it — sometimes a second opinion can be really helpful.

➤ Collar the authors of this book — we all have an opinion!

For the purposes of this chapter, the objective is to keep this pretty practical and understandable. So, to achieve that goal, let's do the following:

➤ Define a high-level model for capturing governance "rules"

➤ Discuss a supporting structure for managing, reporting, and maintaining the model

➤ Define the roles that are associated with SharePoint governance and their relationship to the model.

You will undoubtedly have different roles, requirements, business drivers, and so on, that may require an amount of refinement or restructuring here, but at least you will have a way of building that up if you continue reading this chapter.

Governance Model Inputs

A SharePoint governance model must have a clear and well-defined structure with clear inputs and outputs. The model can then be maintained by a governance structure (that is, the resources, teams, and functions that maintain the model), which is discussed shortly.

Figure 20-1 shows a block diagram of the elements of a high-level SharePoint governance model.

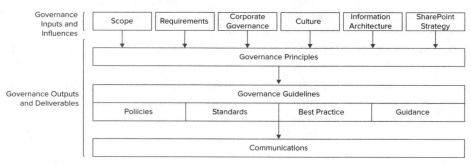

FIGURE 20-1: Governance overview

Figure 20-1 illustrates a model that has a series of governance principles that are driven by a range of inputs. Each of these inputs influences the overall governance landscape:

➤ *Scope* will define for which areas you must define governance. If your scope of deployment is limited to a document-management solution, your governance guidelines should reflect this.

➤ *Requirements* may be generated by the organization specifically against governance. A well-designed solution will always have some requirements specifically relating to governance. If you don't have any of these, then capture requirements from key stakeholders in this area.

➤ *Corporate governance* varies widely across organizations — generally influenced by the type of industry. If you have strong corporate governance (you should have at least some, right?), the SharePoint governance model must comply with it, and not step outside of its boundaries.

➤ *Culture* has a massive impact on the governance for a SharePoint solution. In fact, this input has the heaviest influence of all areas. You may find that you need a light-touch governance that delivers a high level of freedom to the users of your SharePoint solution. Alternatively, it may be necessary to introduce very strict governance to match the culture of your business. Often, SharePoint is part of wider program of change that is trying to drive cultural change — therefore, you must respond to these goals.

➤ Your *Information Architecture* (*IA*) will clearly have a significant influence on your governance. Specific guidelines will often be driven directly from an IA.

➤ Your overall *SharePoint strategy* will also have an impact on the governance that you deploy. For example, if there are future plans on your strategy, you may need to govern the use of certain aspects of SharePoint to ensure that alignment is maintained with the strategic road map.

All of these influences will drive your decisions concerning governance. Assessing and analyzing these inputs will allow a set of governance principles to be established.

Moving Forward with the Model

Governance principles define the very high-level policies within which all detailed guidelines will operate. They will be owned by senior stakeholders (normally represented by a Governance Board), and they are generally business-oriented and not technology-specific. The section, "Understanding Governance Principles," later in this chapter discusses governance principles in more detail, and provides a starter set.

Governance guidelines are the specific policies, standards, best practices, and guidance that you will issue through your communications. The section, "Governance Guidelines," later in this chapter discusses governance guidelines in more detail.

Once governance principles and governance guidelines are established, they must be communicated to the relevant parties — after all, there is little point having a wealth of governance that no one knows about. You should ensure that your communications plan aligns with your final governance structure, and you should try (where possible) not to overburden SharePoint users with information.

Those who are familiar with SharePoint may recognize that SharePoint itself may well be able to help with this communications process. If your IA does not have some sort of Governance site, perhaps it should. SharePoint is an effective mechanism for this. Placed prominently and made accessible, a Governance site can really help to drive awareness. A lack of a Governance site (and a Help site as an aside) indicates that the IA needs a little more work. (You may be worried that you missed this — don't worry, because you really won't be alone.)

UNDERSTANDING GOVERNANCE PRINCIPLES

It is worth spending some time working with your stakeholders to develop the overarching governance principles within which SharePoint will operate. Without strong and clearly defined principles, it is considerably more difficult to enforce your governance, because they are owned by senior business stakeholders, and, therefore, carry a high level of authority.

Your own principles will vary in response to requirements. However, here are a few ideas to get you going:

➤ All users of SharePoint *must* comply with the general policies and requirements pertaining to corporate and systems governance, usage policies, privacy, copyright, records retention, and confidentiality.

➤ Established security policies and principles apply fully to the SharePoint environment.

➤ Navigational techniques, language, processes, branding, and so on, must be standardized across the SharePoint environment to provide a consistent user experience.

➤ Functionality should be used for the purpose for which it was designed.

➤ The priority order for implementing functionality into the SharePoint environment should be as follows:

1. Out-of-the-box

2. Configuration

3. Third-party add-on

4. Future release of SharePoint

5. Customization (that is, development)

➤ All content must have a clearly identifiable owner.

➤ All content should be stored once, and once only.

➤ Content owners are ultimately accountable for content management, but *all* users are responsible.

➤ Copyrighted material will not be added without the proper authorizations.

➤ All governance guides, policies, and standards must have a defined owner.

➤ There should be only one solution for a given use case — this includes the use of third-party tools.

➤ Customizations/developments implemented into the SharePoint platform are available for all to re-use.

➤ Any solution should be assessed to ensure that its level of criticality to the business does not exceed the SharePoint solutions capability and availability.

➤ All users of SharePoint should be familiar and comply with the governance principles and applicable governance guidelines.

➤ Governance rules and principles can be changed, or exceptions raised, but the correct change control process must be followed, and appropriate authority gained and recorded.

All of the principles are pretty obvious — but it is surprising how often the basics are forgotten when working in a SharePoint environment. It should be clear to the experienced SharePoint architect that it won't always be possible to comply with the principles — there are always exceptions. That's fine — don't get hung up too much on this because, after all, they are principles rather than rules!

UNDERSTANDING GOVERNANCE GUIDELINES

Governance guidelines are the specific policies, standards, best practices, and guidance that you define. The range of content will vary from relatively technical rules (perhaps around how new content sources are governed into the SharePoint environment) through to business-oriented rules (the tone that should be used on content, for example).

You will often find that your governance is captured in other documentation (for example, development standards). Rather than creating duplication, refer to these documents in your guidelines. It may be helpful to do a document map that graphically displays all of the relevant documents and their relationships.

It is important to categorize the data in a meaningful manner to be able to manage the guidelines effectively. The following metadata is recommended:

➤ *Description* — This is a short description of the governance guideline.

➤ *Owner* — This is the defined owner (which may be an individual or team) of the guideline. This is mandatory, because all aspects of governance should always have a defined owner.

➤ *Maintenance schedule* — Governance guidelines should be regularly reviewed.

➤ *Type* — This is a marker to indicate whether the data is a policy, guidance, best practice, and so on.

The following sections discuss some of the elements you should consider in your governance guidelines. Governance of any solution covers a wide range of factors, and, therefore, it is helpful to provide some sort of grouping to aid the discussion.

You have a number of approaches to categorizing your governance rules — largely dependent upon the scale and maturity of your SharePoint deployment. However, following is a simple method of categorization:

➤ Design

➤ Development

➤ Deployment/operations

➤ User

This breakdown is simple to understand. Figure 20-2 illustrates the approach.

Design	Development	Deployment/ Operations	User
• IA • IM/IRM • Taxonomy • Branding • Search • Design Policies • Features • Third-party Tools • Communication Plan	• Tools • Environments • Site Defs and Templates • Development Plan • Development Standards • Source Control • Testing • Release Management	• Infrastructure Architecture • Security • Backup and Recovery • DR/BC • Monitoring • Change Management • Op Management • Life Cycle Management • Support	• Education and Training • Site Provisioning • Cost Allocation • SLA • Acceptable Use Policies

FIGURE 20-2: Governance areas

Design

Design relates to the guidelines provided to those stakeholders who will implement functionality (new or existing) into the platform. Without effective governance of the design process, SharePoint will slowly (or rapidly perhaps!) diverge from your original goals, and chaos will ultimately reign. Your governance guidelines should address the following:

➤ Compliance with your defined IA

➤ Compliance with IM strategy and policies

➤ Alignment with the organization's taxonomy

➤ Branding and style guidelines

➤ Conforming to any defined acceptable use policies

➤ Use/re-use of existing features that are available (including third-party components)

➤ Processes to support the design process, particularly around change management and gate reviews that may be necessary to maintain quality

Development

Sooner or later, you will undertake some form of "development" of your SharePoint solution. Whether this is customizing some cascading style sheet (CSS) to enable your "Chuck Norris" theme (by the way, Chuck Norris doesn't do CSS — he just stares at SharePoint until it rebrands itself through fear), or some form of in-depth enterprise n-tier customization involving lots of people with sandals, it's going to happen sooner or later.

At this point, as a SharePoint architect, you will begin to see your SharePoint environment start to morph into something that adds even better value to your organization. But, without governance, you run the risk of creating an unmanageable environment that will drive spiraling maintenance costs.

There is a temptation to think that because SharePoint is an "Office" product that the levels of control, standards, and process can be relaxed when developing SharePoint solutions. This is incorrect — SharePoint is a shared platform that will become critical to your business, and without effective control, you will introduce significant performance, reliability, and security problems.

Following are areas that need consideration for development governance:

➤ Coding standards to define best practice, common patterns, naming conventions, security constraints, and so on

➤ Leveraging sandboxed solutions

➤ Source code control to ensure that customizations are properly managed into the SharePoint environment

➤ Development and testing environments

➤ Build processes and solution packaging standards

➤ Testing standards and processes

➤ Reviews and gates to prove that developments comply at the earliest stages

➤ Available and approved toolsets (for example, use of SharePoint Designer)

Deployment/Operations

If there is a need to govern development, there is an equal need to govern the deployment and operational aspects of a SharePoint environment. This area is primarily responsible for ensuring that the overall platform is managed in alignment with the requirements of the organization. A helpful way to assess this area is to think about your SharePoint deployment in relation to CIA — Confidentiality, Integrity, and Availability.

Following are areas of SharePoint related to *confidentiality* that need consideration:

➤ *Active Directory (AD)* — The use of individual named users in SharePoint groups is regarded as poor practice. To avoid this, there are significant dependencies on AD in a SharePoint environment.

➤ *Groups* — Usually, the out-of-the-box, SharePoint groups are usable, but under certain configurations, it may be necessary to move away from these to take into account specialized permissions. At a minimum, your governance guidelines should provide standards and guidance for this area.

➤ *Roles* — The roles and associated permissions are another area where the out-of-the-box configuration will often suffice. However, your governance should also define what is acceptable to ensure that the environment has some level of standardization.

➤ *Managed accounts/service accounts* — Your use of service accounts and their associated permissions is critical to the security of your environment. Building SharePoint to a least-privilege configuration requires attention to detail. Your governance should explicitly state that service accounts with domain admin rights or equivalent are *not* acceptable.

➤ *App pool accounts/design* — The use of application pools and associated accounts needs consideration. Different approaches can be taken, with a trade-off between memory requirements, performance, security, process isolation, and so on. For example, in highly secure environments, there are likely to be separate application pools and accounts for each web application at the expense of memory.

➤ *Audit* — Standards and rules determine how security will be audited, and, from a governance perspective, what is required to prove alignment. This may be as simple as exception management, or as complex as full audits of permissions, access, and audit trails.

➤ *Exception/incident management* — There should be some defined governance rules for what will happen in the event of a security issue. If there is a compliancy issue, what will be the management process? For example, access may be removed immediately for all users while the issue is remediated, or a simple process to re-baseline the configuration may be carried out with little or no disruption to the end users.

Following are areas of SharePoint related to *integrity* that need consideration:

➤ *Recycle Bin settings* — The Recycle Bin is your friend. Use it wisely!

➤ *Granular backup and recovery* — You should provide the capability to recover individual items for the users. The frequency of the need to recover files in this manner has reduced compared to previous versions of SharePoint, but the issue still remains and should be addressed.

➤ *SQL configuration* — This covers a wide range of issues, but, from a governance perspective, there should be some clarity about database configuration and placement, log file configuration, recovery modes, database encryption, and so on.

➤ *Role-Based Security (RBS) configuration (if used)* — This entails detailing the policy for the use of RBS, including which databases this will apply to within SharePoint, and any related configuration items.

➤ *Database mirroring (where appropriate)* — This entails defining where (if anywhere) database mirroring will be used, and the level of configuration required — for example, if database mirroring is used should a witness server be deployed?

➤ *Storage configuration (including snapshots, replication, backup integration)* — Storage and SharePoint now share a closely coupled relationship in many SharePoint deployments. Increasingly, the underlying hardware capabilities can be leveraged to deliver better levels of data and integrity. Governance should define the use of these capabilities, particularly in the areas of snapshots and replication.

Following are areas of SharePoint related to *availability* that need consideration:

➤ *Web Front-Ends (WFEs)* — Governance should ensure that there is resilience in the WFE configuration.

➤ *Service applications* — With the advent of SharePoint 2010, there are significant capabilities to deliver better availability of key service applications (including search services, which were a particular challenge in SharePoint 2007). Governance should provide the basic requirements in this area, around which services are regarded as critical.

➤ *Clustering* — This may be used to deliver a "high availability" configuration to the business. Governance should outline the basic standards and requirements in this area to ensure that it is used consistently.

Note that defining governance in these areas does not mean detailing the operational processes, configuration, and general operation. Governance will define the standards and rules within which the deployment and operational activities must operate.

This area of governance also covers areas such as the following:

➤ *Budgeting* — This ensures that adequate budget is available both to manage the environment, and to deliver any road map that has been defined.

➤ *Chargeback/cost management* — These include mechanisms for chargeback or some level of cost allocation.

➤ *Site life cycle management* — This is an important aspect of any SharePoint environment. Some kind of governance mechanism is required in almost all instances to ensure that sites are provisioned appropriately, and that they are monitored and decommissioned at the end of their useful lives. If you don't have a process for this, you're probably not in a good place!

➤ *Release management* — The mechanisms required to release functionality to the Production environment is critical. Governance should define the levels of control, gate processes, and types of change permitted.

➤ *Monitoring/performance management* — This will define the baseline monitoring and performance requirements that will support effective governance.

➤ *Capacity management* — The governance of this will define the baseline metrics, growth profile, and constraints associated with capacity. For example, governance may define that content databases should be restricted to a certain size, and, therefore, utilization must be managed and capacity must be planned.

User

Perhaps the most important aspects of any governance guidelines are those that relate to a user. There is a desire to lock down features that are not appropriate, and this is a good approach where it is simple to achieve. Frequently, this approach is not possible, and, therefore, sooner or later you must trust your users to do the right thing (gulp!).

Time and again, SharePoint administrators have bemoaned their roles in life, and how the users are wrecking their fantastic environment. In these circumstances, it is interesting to see how rarely clear guidelines have been made available for the users. So, how is a user supposed to know which features are usable and which are not? Users generally appreciate clear guidelines — it makes their lives simpler. Of course, you will get the SharePoint "fans" who want to tweak outside of the box, and these will generally need some effort to control. But, as a rule, most people like defined boundaries because it makes life simpler.

User governance covers a wide range of areas, including the following:

➤ *Available features and capabilities* — It should be clear to end users what features are accessible to them, and how they should be used. As part of your governance guidance, you could even choose to identify best practice examples that exist in your SharePoint environment. Training is clearly related to this subject, but having governance rules that are well-publicized is just as important.

➤ *End-user customizations permitted* — Even at the end-user level, SharePoint is a toolset that has a range of available customizations, and, therefore, it is important to govern what is permitted. For example, custom lists may be permitted, but may also require certain site columns to be added to meet IM requirements.

➤ *End-user customizations* not *permitted* — This is even more important than what is permitted. You will never keep up with all of the available features, techniques, and work-arounds that SharePoint will have. (All users can be "experts" with Google at their side!) Therefore, you should be explicit about what is absolutely not permitted, and the consequences of breaking these rules. For example, you may not allow the removal of certain content types in a library, or prevent the use JavaScript or JQuery. You can't necessarily control these at the technical level, but you can offer a carrot (demonstrating best practice) and a stick (removing the offending customization)!

➤ *Language, content, and tone* — This is quite often overlooked, but it is common to see confusion around what is acceptable for a SharePoint site. Given a capability that is being portrayed as a social networking tool can create data that may be deemed inappropriate. At a minimum, a lack of clarity prevents adoption; at worst, content may be authored that carries legal implications for the organization. Ensure that your governance reminds people of their responsibilities. For example, if you wouldn't want to see what you are writing as headlines in a newspaper, then you should consider whether it is appropriate. Your governance may also call out the consequences of inappropriate language, content, and tone.

➤ *Style and branding* — You may have covered this by preventing any updates of style and branding but it is ultimately difficult to enforce this. By communicating clearly the rules and the degrees of freedom available, you will prevent your branding from degrading, and not waste users' time focusing on unnecessary look-and-feel issues that they cannot control (however much they would like to!). You will always get significant push-back on this type of governance. Your site design will never please everyone, and suppressing users' "freedom of expression" is not always popular! Hold your ground — it will save a lot of pain later.

➤ *Responsibilities (particularly site owners, contributors, editors, and so on)* — Any user interacting with SharePoint has some level of responsibility. SharePoint is somewhat unusual in that it devolves capability to the user, but with this comes responsibility. You should clearly define what you expect from the various roles that interact with SharePoint. Even "readers" have a responsibility to maintain the confidentiality of the information that they see.

➤ *Education and training (mandated and optional)* — Your governance is not responsible for defining the training program of your SharePoint deployment. However, it should define the minimum level of training, and what is regarded as optional, to ensure that you obtain a minimum level of skill base within the user community.

➤ *Support* — Clarity should be provided around what support the users can get, as well as when and how quickly they should get a response. Equally, it should be clear when users will *not* receive support — perhaps because they have broken governance rules, or have undertaken configuration/customization that is explicitly the responsibility of the user. Of course, you're a good SharePoint architect, so you'll still help them — but you'll make it known that you don't need to, so, you get a rare thank you!

➤ *Information Management* — There may be a well-formed and mature IM strategy within which SharePoint operates. This is a great position to be in, and if you can get there, it will really help. However, in the real world, relatively few organizations have reached this level of maturity. This doesn't mean that you should ignore it. Your governance guidelines can establish a basic framework covering base metadata requirements, protection of intellectual property, copyright protection and infringement, document distribution, and so on.

➤ *Acceptable use* — In some respects, your governance guidelines are an acceptable use policy. However, you may have other policies that impact your SharePoint governance. At a minimum you should be clear in your governance guidelines which policies apply.

Communications

How you communicate your governance will always be a challenge. Some of your audience will welcome the guidance — but, typically, they are the silent majority. A very vocal minority will challenge your governance, and look for ways around it to push the boundaries. Before you go all vigilante on them, bear in mind that these people are typically SharePoint fans, and are frustrated at not having all the power of the platform at their fingertips. Alternatively, they are SharePoint "newbies" who are desperately trying to learn the tool, and are butting against your pesky governance. Maybe you have a few people who are generally just mischief makers.

So, the first communication problem you must address is to let people know why you need governance, and how it will help rather than hinder them. At the same time, you should communicate your governance principles. Following are the key points you must get across:

➤ All the established industry practices recognize the need for good governance.

➤ Governance is about protecting the service for your users — if chaos worked why not allow it? The reality is that controls are needed to give the best service to the silent majority.

➤ Defining and providing rules and guidance drives best practice into your deployment. This maximizes the impact and your return on investment.

➤ Knowing what you are allowed to do up front (and indeed what you are not) will save a lot of time and frustration, and, therefore, it is in people's best interest.

➤ SharePoint is more than a straight "Office" product. It is incredibly powerful, but with this comes responsibility for all.

➤ If SharePoint isn't doing something you need now, then it may be coming down the line. Or, alternatively, if you have good business justification, then a change process should be in place to request that the capability is added to the road map. If it can be done safely and demonstrate good business value, then why not do it?

What about your detractors? Embrace them, but ensure that they put forward good business reasons that can be justified prior to updating your governance and/or SharePoint capability. It is amazing how many times you will be faced with a "must-have" feature that can be achieved easily with existing capabilities (or, in some cases, has no business justification!). Don't ignore the difficult minority — they will go underground and create a SharePoint "black market," which will only spell bad news. Treat everyone even-handedly, and your governance processes will force good practice and behaviors.

Once you have your basic message out there, you need a way to communicate some of the details. You can take a number of approaches:

➤ *Provide governance guidebooks* — Typically, split your governance into the respective areas already discussed. You will need to ensure that you provide an overview of the area (that is, design, development, and so on), and that the rules are clear and unambiguous.

➤ *Distribute summary leaflets* — These should serve as quick-reference guides with key governance guidance.

➤ *Run training sessions* — This can include classroom training or computer-based training.

➤ *Build a governance center* — This could be a SharePoint site dedicated to both communicating the governance guidelines, and providing governance capabilities (for example, site provisioning).

➤ *Regular announcements and updates* — Communicate updates regularly to the general community.

➤ *Publish best practices* — Publicize examples of best practices to the community so that others can review what has been done.

➤ *Build a governance community* — Establish a community (using SharePoint!) that will collaborate on governance issues. Nominate and award active participants with some kind of recognition to encourage involvement.

You may adopt one, all, or, indeed, none of these suggestions. In all cases, however, ensure that you have a plan associated and resourced correctly.

Governance Structure

You now should have some idea of the scope of your governance, some overriding principles, the start of a set of detailed rules and guidelines, and, finally, some ideas about how you might communicate that out to your community. All of that is a bit of a waste if you don't have a way of managing, developing, and refining your governance model over time, so let's take a look at some guidance in this area.

There are different ways of designing a governance structure with a multitude of ideas about how to achieve this. Your own governance structure will be influenced by the following:

➤ Existing boards, committees, and panels

➤ The scale of your SharePoint implementation

> ➤ The maturity of your organization when it comes to governance

> ➤ Your personal preference (that is, it must be something you understand)

What is the difference between a board, committee, and panel? In reality, they are interchangeable. For the purposes of this discussion, a board is authorized to make and execute decisions, a committee makes recommendations, and a panel provides input, but no specific recommendation.

For purposes of this discussion, let's say that you would like a structure that can cover most situations, is easily understood, and can be easily modified to suit your own specific scenario. Figure 20-3 illustrates such a model.

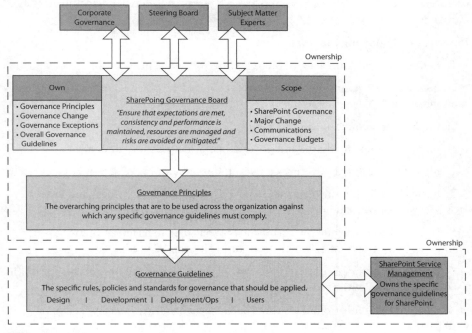

FIGURE 20-3: Governance structure

Figure 20-3 shows the following key elements:

> ➤ *Corporate Governance* — This includes any existing rule sets, boards, committees, and so on, that already exist that you must comply with.

> ➤ *Steering Board* — This board owns the overall solution, service, strategy, and road map. The Steering Board will define many of the key inputs for the scope of the governance model.

➤ *Subject Matter Experts* — This includes key resources that can provide expert input into the governance of SharePoint.

➤ *SharePoint Governance Board* — This board owns the governance aspects of SharePoint. Note that this is a board and, therefore, has authority to effectively make and execute decisions delegated by the Steering Board. This board owns the governance principles, is responsible for defining them, and will be held accountable for their application.

➤ *SharePoint Service Management* — This could be split across a range of people responsible for different aspects of the service (for example, development, design, business change, and so on), or an individual who ultimately owns the entire stack. The preference generally is to nominate a single owner for all aspects who reports to the Steering Board — this is the simplest and most accountable approach.

The SharePoint Governance Board has specific responsibility relating to governance. This is an important aspect of this model — governance needs a clear and strong focus unencumbered by the wider aspects of SharePoint deployment.

The SharePoint Governance Board should have an agreed "Terms of Reference" document that includes the following:

➤ *Key Objectives* — Following are some examples:

➤ To define and maintain a set of SharePoint governance principles

➤ To own and be responsible for key assets required for the effective governance of SharePoint

➤ To implement a communications plan

➤ To manage change to SharePoint governance principles and guidelines

➤ To identify SharePoint governance risks and issues, and take action appropriately

➤ To be accountable to the Steering Board on progress, risks, issues, and levels of governance compliance

➤ *Authority* — This should include the specific areas that the Governance Board is accountable for, and the extent to which their authority can be used.

➤ *Scope* — This should be a definition of the scope of the Governance Board's responsibilities (which will clearly align with the scope of SharePoint governance as a whole).

➤ *Owned Assets* — This is a list of assets that the Governance Board is responsible or accountable for.

➤ *Membership* — This defines who will be a member of the Governance Board.

➤ *Stakeholders* — This is a definition as to who the stakeholders are for the Governance Board, and how they will be managed and informed.

➤ *Measures* — These include some measures that the Governance Board will use to track progress. These would typically be measures around governance exceptions, rates of change to governance guidelines, and the level of compliance.

➤ *Schedule* — This is the frequency and duration of when the Governance Board will meet.

➤ *Agenda* — This is an outline agenda that will typically be used. This could include the following:

➤ Minutes and actions from last meeting

➤ Major governance change reviews

➤ Governance principles and guidelines reviews (noting that each principle and guideline should have an associated review schedule)

➤ Asset review (ensuring that all key owned assets are current and effective)

➤ Risks and issues review

However you create, capture, and present your principles and guidelines, this model will provide an effective mechanism that will mature your governance over time. Recognize that this is a journey, and it will take time to reach an optimum position. Don't lose heart, keep focused on maintaining an effective structure, and it will soon pay dividends.

UNDERSTANDING ROLES

This section discusses the roles that relate to the governance of SharePoint. These will be broken down into the Business, IS/IT, and governance-specific roles. There is no attempt to map these roles onto specific teams and individuals, because this will vary from site to site.

Business Roles

Business roles include the following:

➤ Site owners

➤ Content owners

➤ Power users

Site Owners

Site owners are perhaps the most important business role in relation to governance. They are the primary custodians of your governance guidelines, and without their support, it will be very difficult to reach a compliant position.

Following are the responsibilities for a site owner when it comes to governance:

➤ Understanding the governance guidelines and principles — particularly user guidelines

➤ Taking responsibility for compliance — typically, being held accountable for any compliance issues

➤ Ensuring that their site members use the site appropriately

➤ Ensuring that sites are active and delivering value to the business

Content Owners

Often, the person who owns the content of a site is distinguished from a site owner. A *content owner* is responsible for the IM aspects of SharePoint content, and specifically the following:

➤ Ensuring that all data complies with base metadata

➤ Ensuring that data on a site carries no copyright or intellectual property infringements

➤ Data is secured appropriately and in compliance with any current security policies

➤ Managing the life cycle of data appropriately (and, where relevant, ensuring records are declared where needed, and data is removed as it expires)

➤ Complying with any defined guidelines surrounding language, tone, and agreed terminology

➤ Holding legal responsibility for information for which they are owners

Power Users

Power users are those users who undertake some form of basic configuration and/or customization. They carry some extra responsibilities, including the following:

➤ An understanding of the relevant development guidelines

➤ A clear understanding of features that can and cannot be used

➤ Ongoing compliance with branding and style guidelines

IS/IT Roles

More roles in IS/IT get involved in SharePoint than you can shake the proverbial stick at! This is partly because SharePoint is a breadth product, and, therefore, touches on many areas. Let's focus on the roles that are impacted the most by governance, which include the following:

➤ Business analyst

➤ SharePoint architect

➤ SharePoint administrator

➤ Developer

➤ Support

Business Analyst

The *business analyst* is responsible for understanding the business needs, requirements, and benefits associated with any given use case for SharePoint. The analyst will ultimately define the new scenarios and use cases that the business needs to pass onto a SharePoint architect, or, perhaps, straight to a development team.

In relation to governance, therefore, a business analyst must do the following:

➤ Recognize the constraints that the governance guidelines create, including what features are available, what capacity constraints may exist, and so on

➤ Work within the constraints of the IA and any associated governance guidelines

➤ Comply with the overall governance guidelines — primarily in the design area

➤ Build use cases and designs that do not conflict with established governance

➤ Justify and manage the update appropriately (in the event that a new requirement forces a governance update)

➤ Own some of the user governance rules

SharePoint Architect

Of course, *SharePoint architects* comprise the most hard-working role, but what relevance does governance have? Surely SharePoint architects don't have to think about it and abide by it, right? The conscientious SharePoint architect will have the following responsibilities:

➤ Architect the overall governance framework in conjunction with the stakeholders within the business. The business analyst, in particular, is a key role to collaborate with.

➤ Define the mechanism by which your governance framework will be stored and maintained. Will you have a spreadsheet, a SharePoint site dedicated to governance, a set of Word documents, or tablets of stone? Choose wisely — if you can use SharePoint, and if you're really clever, you could use your Governance site to illustrate some of the power of SharePoint in communicating complex issues to a wide audience in a simple and engaging way.

➤ Be responsible for a percentage of the governance rules themselves. It is highly likely you will identify and author many of these, and, therefore, by default, you will become the owner.

➤ Assist in building an effective communications plan. (Indeed, it may be your entire responsibility.)

➤ Attend meetings of Governance Boards in an advisory capacity, or perhaps serve as the overall custodian of SharePoint governance within your organization.

SharePoint Administrator

SharePoint administrators have a difficult job. They spend their lives trying to hold onto jelly if there is no governance — good fun at first, but gets a bit messy later. Governance impacts a SharePoint administrator in the following areas:

➤ Awareness of the governance principles and rules is very important. Clearly, there should be a deep understanding of the deployment/operations area, and compliance is a must.

➤ Ownership of some rules is likely.

➤ Translation of the governance rules into supporting toolsets and their configuration — particularly around non-functional areas such as backups, anti-virus, security, monitoring, and capacity management.

Developer

The *developer* role will be significantly impacted by SharePoint governance. Without a clear understanding of the majority of the rules, it would be easy to develop functionality that does not comply. Lead developers or perhaps development managers/directors are likely to own the development rules.

Following are specific governance responsibilities for developers:

➤ Ownership and maintenance of individual rules, or, more often than not, the majority of the development governance rules

➤ Liaison with the SharePoint architect — particularly if they carry the overall responsibility for day-to-day governance

➤ Integration of governance into development processes

➤ Awareness and understanding of the majority of the governance rule set

Support

The *support* team can have a very positive impact on deploying good governance. While the business analysts are most likely to own the user rules, there is an argument that support will see the impact of governance on the users, as well as the impact of a lack of governance, and have a vested interest. In any case, user rules will need to be derived from a wide range of stakeholders.

Governance-Specific Roles

Following are some specific roles associated with governance:

➤ Governance Board member

➤ Governance Board chairperson

➤ Governance auditor

Governance Board Member

As a member of the Governance Board, it is important to note that this carries the responsibility of being the "ambassador" for governance into the business. Therefore, this role requires well-connected business stakeholders. If the majority of Board members are from IS/IT, then it's unlikely to gain any real traction. As a Board member, there are some specific responsibilities, including the following:

➤ Attend SharePoint Governance Board meetings

➤ Undertake any activities and actions required by the Governance Board

➤ Take ownership of specific governance principles or guidelines

➤ Regularly review any owned assets, and report progress and updates to the Board

➤ Take ownership of any defined communication activities out to the respective business area

➤ Act as a focal point for queries about governance in their business area

Governance Board Chairperson

The Governance Board chairperson carries all of the responsibility of a Governance Board member, with the following additional areas:

➤ Overall responsibility for SharePoint governance in the organization

➤ Reporting to any other steering groups or boards (for example, Information Strategy Boards, SharePoint Steering Groups, and so on)

➤ Resolving and adjudicating escalated issues surrounding governance exceptions or conflicts

➤ Chairing SharePoint Governance Board meetings

Governance Auditor

The Governance auditor role may be supplied by IS/IT, may come from an internal audit operation, or may come from any other appropriate aspect of the business. Some form of audit is necessary, though in some circumstances, the Governance Board itself could fulfill some of this role.

From an audit point of view, responsibilities include the following:

➤ Conduct regular audit reviews as scheduled and instructed by the Governance Board.

➤ Agree on appropriate measures to track the following:

  ➤ Compliance (sometimes a survey is enough)

  ➤ Governance coverage

  ➤ Exceptions and incidents

➤ Reporting back to the Board and other stakeholders on audits, and identifying actions associated with any findings.

BEST PRACTICES

Best practices entail ensuring that your SharePoint governance is in alignment with the scale, criticality, and scope of your SharePoint solution. Following are elements that are indicators of best practice:

➤ A documented governance framework with clear scope and terms of reference (an absolute necessity).

➤ A consistent approach to the recording, maintenance, ownership, and management of governance.

➤ An established and agreed-upon set of overarching governance principles with business signoff.

➤ An effective communication vehicle for your governance framework. A Governance site with a prominent place in your navigation hierarchy is a good indicator of a strong governance approach.

➤ A well-maintained set of guidelines with a clear maintenance schedule and ownership.

➤ Automate where possible. Site provisioning, changes to search configurations, and quotas are all good candidates for automation. Even if full automation isn't possible, a simple request list built within SharePoint is feasible with simple alerting to notify support of requests.

➤ Regular audits or, at a minimum, scheduled Governance Board meetings must be held to progress the subject over time.

SUMMARY

This chapter explained why governance is important to a SharePoint deployment, and presented a model that you can implement. It can be adjusted to suit your own requirements.

It is important to remember that there are many ways of achieving good governance, and, so, if you vary this model — or even do something entirely different — the key requirement is that you *do something.*

If you ignore governance, then the best advice to a SharePoint architect is to get out early — sooner or later, the platform will struggle, and you are likely to be held responsible. The truth is that governance isn't difficult, and it doesn't have to be onerous. Put the time in, and it will give you a far better SharePoint solution.

Chapter 21 covers business continuity management for SharePoint 2010, providing guidance for defining your business continuity requirements, and using them to design your backup and recovery, availability, and disaster-recovery strategies.

21

Defining Your Business Continuity Management Plan

By Chris Whitehead

SharePoint is fast becoming a key application within many organizations, whether used as the platform for a company's Internet presence, or as a departmental collaboration solution. More often than not, these types of usage scenarios would automatically deem an application as business-critical. Indeed, e-mail is a communication and collaboration tool that is often considered business-critical for most organizations with an IT function.

On an all-too-often basis, a business impact analysis is not performed for SharePoint within an organization. This is reflected by the lack of a suitable business continuity management plan, and associated service level agreements (SLAs) for the service. If you do not know the business importance of a service, or the costs associated with outage and data loss, you cannot effectively define SLAs for that service. These SLAs will not only define the agreements for recovery objectives and service availability, they will often help determine what backup, recovery, and availability solutions are required to meet them. Moreover, they are likely to feed into other key design aspects for a SharePoint deployment, ranging from storage planning, to governance guidance for the creation and deployment of customizations.

One approach would be to back up everything as often as possible, while providing multiple redundancy solutions for hardware and software. Unfortunately, because of cost and complexity, this is simply not possible for most organizations. The challenge for any architect is to understand all the options available for backup, recovery, and availability, and then provide the best solution for meeting SLAs, while weighing the cost and complexity of the solution.

SharePoint has always provided some interesting challenges in this area. SharePoint 2010 is no exception. However, it does provide another leap forward with the inclusion of new features such as native support for SQL Server database mirroring, unattached content database data recovery, and configuration-only backups. In fact, new features were even added in Service Pack 1, with the much sought addition of a Site Recycle Bin. This chapter explores both these new and proven methods for SharePoint business continuity management.

Of course, before you can choose the tools and techniques to use, you must determine and define your SharePoint business continuity requirements.

DEFINING YOUR BUSINESS CONTINUITY REQUIREMENTS

To define your SharePoint business continuity requirements, you must first analyze the potential business-impact scenarios and threats. Once complete, you will be in a position to determine your SLAs. This is likely to be a balancing act of cost versus business risk. Let's take a look at the information that you need to complete this process.

Analyzing Business-Impact Scenarios and Threats

When analyzing business-impact scenarios and threats, you should focus on understanding which could impact the continuity of your SharePoint environment, as well as the data and services built upon it. Defining your SLAs for each scenario should be left for later.

Impact scenarios and threats could range from loss of a single file, to an entire data center failure. Following is a list of potential business-impact scenarios and threats for any SharePoint deployment. Some may not be relevant to you, and you will likely find scenarios and threats that apply to your own specific environments.

➤ Loss of data (including specific scenarios for SharePoint objects such as individual items and their versions, lists and document libraries, and sites and site collections)

➤ Slow recovery of data

➤ Service outage caused by failure of individual hardware components (such as servers, storage, networking, and their sub-components)

➤ Failure or partial failure of the entire data center

➤ Failure of external services provided by third parties, such as Internet service providers (ISPs)

➤ Service outage caused by software failures or human error

You should always consider software and hardware on which SharePoint has dependencies. For example, lack of redundancy for Active Directory would be classed as a risk to SharePoint. Operating level agreements (OLAs), which are SLAs between functional IT groups and services, should be put in place where necessary.

Determining Your SLAs

When deciding on your SharePoint business continuity requirements, you will need to work with the business owners and key stakeholders to come up with realistic numbers for SLAs. They may initially provide unrealistically high numbers without thinking through the reasons and consequences of doing so. More often than not, these numbers will be accompanied by an unwillingness to provide the necessary infrastructure and resources to meet the SLAs. This is where negotiation starts, during which you will need to discuss the following:

➤ What the environment is going to be used for

➤ What data and services need protecting and the priority for each

➤ What the business impact is if the data and services are unavailable or unrecoverable, including the following:

    ➤ Measurement of cost or lost opportunity/revenue over time

    ➤ Possible legal implications that need discussing

➤ Any existing SLAs and the reason for choosing the proposed SLAs

➤ Potential chargeback levels for different SLAs

➤ Penalties for failing to meet SLAs

➤ How to report on adherence to SLAs

➤ What infrastructure and resources are needed to meet these SLAs

The last point is your biggest bargaining chip when negotiating SLAs. Business owners are likely to think in terms of costs, and will start to compromise in order to bring costs down. As such, you should be prepared to provide estimates of costs, and justify them accordingly.

At the end of the discussion, you should end up with SLAs around which you can design your business continuity plan. You will be in a position to choose the tools and techniques required to meet these SLAs, and should have the financial backing for the infrastructure and resources needed to put them in place and support them.

First, of course, you must understand which SLAs will need defining for any SharePoint business continuity plan.

 For further information about defining SLAs, see the "Service Level Management" section within the "Microsoft Operations Framework" at `http://technet.microsoft.com/en-gb/library/cc543312.aspx.`

Backup and Recovery SLAs

Backup and recovery SLAs usually identify the data and services to be backed up and recovered, and the recovery time objective, recovery point objective, and recovery level objective for each. Other information included in backup and recovery SLAs may include information on backup windows.

Determining Your Recovery Time Objectives

A *recovery time objective (RTO)* is the maximum allowed time for a recovery procedure to take place. In other words, it is the maximum amount of downtime allowed by the business for the data or service before normal operations must be resumed. For example, the RTO for an outage that can be resolved by restoring a backup includes the following:

➤ The lead time between the outage being recorded and recovery being initiated

➤ The time necessary to locate the backup media

➤ The time necessary to restore the backup

➤ The time necessary to perform any post-restoration procedures in order to resume operation of the failed system

You may wish to define different RTOs for differing items or times. For example, the RTO for the recovery of a single item may be different from that of the whole farm, and the RTO for each may be different on weekends.

Additionally, although much more complicated to restore, you may actually define a shorter RTO for the entire farm than an individual item. This is likely because a full farm outage will incur a much larger business impact. Additionally, individual items will likely have end-user content recovery mechanisms in place, such as versioning and the SharePoint Recycle Bin.

Determining Your Recovery Point Objectives

A *recovery point objective (RPO)* is the maximum allowed time between the last available backup and any point in time that a failure could occur. In other words, it is the point to which data must be restorable, and represents the maximum amount of acceptable data loss. This is also known as *freshness of backup*, or the latency between a production data set and its redundant or replicated copy.

For example, you might establish that no more than two hours of data can be lost if a system fails. For this example, taking daily full backups and transaction log backups or log shipping at least every two hours would be a feasible solution.

 You do not need to measure RPO as an amount of time. Instead, you might measure it as a number of transactions or changes to the system.

Determining Your Recovery Level Objectives

A *recovery level objective (RLO)* defines the granularity with which you must be able to recover data. In SharePoint, this can mean the entire farm, a web application and associated databases, site collection, site, list or library, or individual item.

For example, you may have an RLO that individual items must be restorable, and associated RTO and RPO for individual items. Built-in features such as versioning may be used in this example to give an RLO of major versions only, or, alternatively, major and minor versions.

> *A useful workbook to help you plan your backup and recovery SLAs and strategy for SharePoint 2010 is available from* www.microsoft.com/downloads/en/details.aspx?FamilyID=a4e1a142-0797-4675-922d-6cc5cdb623f1&displaylang=en.

Availability SLAs

One of the most common measures of availability for a system or component is as a percentage of available uptime. This is often measured by and called the *number of nines*. For example, a system with a 99.999 percentage of uptime is said to have "five nines of availability."

In general, the number of nines is not often used by engineers when modeling and measuring availability. More often, engineers speak of downtime per year. The number of nines is typically reserved for high-level discussion of availability SLAs, or in marketing documents. Table 21-1 correlates the number of nines to time equivalents.

TABLE 21-1: The Number of Nines to Time Equivalents

UPTIME PERCENTAGE	DOWNTIME PER DAY	DOWNTIME PER MONTH	DOWNTIME PER YEAR
95	72.00 minutes	36 hours	18.26 days
99	14.40 minutes	7 hours	3.65 days
99.9	86.40 seconds	43 minutes	8.77 hours
99.99	8.62 seconds	4 minutes	52.60 minutes
99.999	0.86 seconds	26 seconds	5.26 minutes

Notice how an availability SLA of five nines equates to a mere 5.26 minutes of downtime per year. As such, when discussing availability SLAs, you should think carefully about what the implications of designing for more than two nines will mean for costs.

Additionally, when calculating availability SLAs, consider that most organizations specifically exempt or add hours for planned maintenance activities. This is likely to be particularly relevant for SharePoint, where planned downtime is likely to be required for maintenance that cannot be avoided (such as patches).

Also, note that *uptime* and *availability* are not synonymous. A system can be up, but not available. For example, this may be the case if a partial network outage occurs and a web application is inaccessible to some hosts.

Disaster Recovery SLAs

For each component within a farm that is covered by a disaster recovery plan, an SLA may identify the RPOs and RTO. Different RTOs are often set for different circumstances. For example, in the event of a natural disaster, it is likely you will want (and indeed need) to define longer RTOs than those for a simple disk failure.

Balancing Costs versus Business Risk

The need to balance costs versus business risk was briefly discussed earlier in this chapter. In reality, availability SLAs that require many nines, as well as backup and recovery SLAs requiring low RTOs, RPOs, and granular RLOs, will require very expensive and complex solutions to meet them.

The answer is to ensure that the costs of the backup, recovery, and availability solutions are balanced against the risks to the business, and to the costs of outage or data loss. To achieve this, you need accurate cost estimates for outage or data loss from the business, and stakeholders will need to know the costs of various solutions from you or those responsible for providing them.

At this point, you will know what services and data you need to protect, what the SLAs are for each, and should have agreed on a budget with the business to choose the best backup, recovery, and availability solutions to help you achieve them. One final point to remember, though, is that business continuity management is an ongoing process, and you will likely need to adjust your SLAs and solutions at a later date as business requirements change.

The next section focuses on designing your backup and recovery strategy, and covers each data component within a farm, as well as some of the tools available for backing up and restoring each.

DESIGNING YOUR BACKUP AND RECOVERY STRATEGY

Once you have defined your SharePoint business continuity requirements, you can start designing an effective backup and recovery strategy. The requirements are likely to affect the following:

➤ Which tools you use, based on capability of the tools versus requirements

➤ Which strategy you choose for each requirement

➤ The location of backups and environments

For example, if you know you must meet a specific RTO and RPO for individual items, you can plan to use the Recycle Bin and versioning to protect this content. This planning will be based on the SLAs, and will extend to the amount of space allocated and the length of time items are held for. If the SLAs do not include items deleted from the Recycle Bin, it may include negotiating departmental charges for recovering items using an alternative solution. Of course, you will need to design and plan for these alternative solutions. However, if the business has not defined the need for item-level recovery, then there is no need to design and support solutions that enable it.

The majority of recoveries for a SharePoint environment are likely to be content recovery for end users at the site, list, or item level. However, you must design a backup and recovery strategy that covers all eventualities and all data components that make up a SharePoint environment. This incorporates everything ranging from the full farm, to service applications, individual items, and customizations. The following sections detail each of these data components, and some of the tools available for backing up and restoring each.

Farm

Full farm backups can be performed in SharePoint 2010 by using Central Administration or the SharePoint 2010 Management Shell. A farm backup includes backing up all the components that make up a SharePoint farm, with the exception of some customizations, configuration settings, and physical server backups for bare-metal recovery.

➤ You can choose from two options when you perform a farm backup:

➤ If you choose *content and configuration data* (the default), the entire server farm is backed up, including settings from the configuration database.

➤ If you choose *configuration only*, some of the configuration database settings for the farm are backed up without content.

> *Backing up a farm backs up the configuration database and the Central Administration content databases, but you cannot restore these by using SharePoint 2010 tools. This is because restoring these databases in SharePoint 2010 is still unsupported.*

➤ Web applications, associated content databases and various settings

➤ Service applications, associated databases, and various settings.

When a farm backup is initiated, a SQL Server database backup is started for content and service application databases. The search index files are backed up and synchronized with the search database backups. Configuration settings for the farm are written to XML files that are included in the backup.

> *For detailed steps on how to perform a farm backup and restore of a full farm or components by using either Central Administration or the SharePoint 2010 Management Shell, see* http://technet.microsoft.com/en-us/library/ee428316.aspx *and* http://technet.microsoft.com/en-us/library/ee428314.aspx, *respectively.*

Configuration-only Backup and Restore

A *configuration-only backup* extracts and backs up the configuration settings for the farm from a configuration database. A configuration backup can be restored to the same or any other server farm. For example, you might want to perform configuration-only restores in test, development, or standby environments. Additionally, if you are using SQL Server to back up the databases for a farm, you will want to back up the configuration separately.

In order to restore configuration settings, a new or alternate farm (configuration database) must already be provisioned. Upon restore, the settings contained within the backup will overwrite any settings in the new or alternate farm. If any settings present in the farm are not contained in the configuration backup, they will not be changed.

A configuration-only backup and restore can only be performed by using built-in tools. This includes Central Administration and the SharePoint 2010 Management Shell for both procedures. When using the SharePoint 2010 Management Shell, you can perform a configuration-only backup by using the `Backup-SPFarm` cmdlet with the `-ConfigurationOnly` parameter.

You can also perform a configuration-only backup of the current farm or a configuration database that comprises another farm by using the `Backup-SPConfigurationDatabase` cmdlet, as shown here:

```
Backup-SPConfigurationDatabase -DatabaseName SharePoint_Config -
DatabaseServer SqlServer1 -Directory \\server\share\Backup
```

A configuration-only restore can be performed by using the `Restore-SPFarm` cmdlet with the `-ConfigurationOnly` parameter.

> *For detailed steps on how to perform a configuration-only backup and restore, see* http://technet.microsoft.com/en-us/library/ee428320.aspx *and* http://technet.microsoft.com/en-us/library/ee428326.aspx, *respectively.*

Considerations for Using Farm Backups

There is no built-in scheduling for farm backups. If you wish to schedule full farm or configuration-only backups, you must create a backup script in Windows PowerShell, and then schedule the script to run as a Windows task.

Additionally, since all user data is stored in SQL Server databases, unless a remote BLOB storage solution is used, it is likely that most organizations will prefer to use existing backup and recovery strategies for their SharePoint data where possible. In most cases, this will mean backup and recovery by using SQL Server tools or third-party solutions. This is a perfectly acceptable approach for content databases and most service applications, and is discussed in more depth later in this chapter.

If this approach is adopted, you can still take full farm backups when needed, or take configuration-only backups by using Central Administration or Windows PowerShell to protect farm settings.

What's Backed Up?

In addition to web applications, service applications, and the settings and databases associated with them, a full farm backup will include the following settings and features of a server farm:

➤ Antivirus settings

➤ Information Rights Management (IRM) settings

➤ Outbound e-mail settings (only restored when performing an overwrite)

➤ Customizations deployed as trusted solutions

➤ Diagnostic logging settings (everything except for the trace log location)

➤ Managed account automatic password change settings

➤ InfoPath Forms Services settings and exempt user agents

➤ Active Directory account creation mode settings

➤ Quota templates

➤ Managed paths for host-named site collections

➤ Sandboxed user code service settings

Features at the web application level are backed up and restored as part of the default backup and restore behavior. Configuration-only backups take farm-scoped Features, as long as they are activated. Upon restore, the Features will be installed, and an attempt will be made to force-activate them.

> *Web application and service application settings are not included in a configuration-only backup. Only the items described previously will be included. You can back up settings for web applications and service applications as part of a full back up, or use Windows PowerShell cmdlets to manually document and copy these settings. For more information, refer to "Document farm configuration settings (SharePoint Server 2010)" at* `http://technet.microsoft.com/en-us/library/ff645391.aspx`.

What's Not Backed Up?

The following settings and features are not included in a full farm backup or configuration-only backup of a server farm:

➤ Direct changes to `web.config` files that are not made through the SharePoint API

➤ Customizations that are not deployed as part of a trusted solution

➤ Application pool account passwords

➤ HTTP compression settings

➤ Time-out settings

➤ Custom Internet Server Application Programming Interface (ISAPI) filters

➤ Computer domain membership

➤ Internet Protocol security (IPsec) settings

➤ Network Load Balancing (NLB) settings

➤ Secure Sockets Layer (SSL) certificates

➤ Dedicated IP address settings

➤ Certificates used to form trust relationships

These are settings that are stored on SharePoint servers. As such, you must plan to document these settings and features, and, where necessary, back them up manually.

Web Applications

As with farm backups, web applications can be backed up or restored by using Central Administration or the SharePoint 2010 Management Shell. You cannot back up a complete web application by using SQL Server tools. However, you can use SQL Server tools to back up the content databases individually. When you choose to back up a web application, all content databases associated with that web application and the following settings will be included in the backup:

➤ Application pool name and application pool account

➤ Service accounts

➤ Internet Information Services (IIS) binding information, such as the protocol type, host header, and port number

➤ General web application settings, such as alerts and managed paths

➤ Changes to the `web.config` file that have been made through the SharePoint API

➤ Authentication settings

 These settings are only included in a backup if made by using the SharePoint API. Changes made manually through IIS, for example, will not be included in the backup.

If you choose to use SQL Server tools or a third-party product to back up your content databases, and you perform configuration-only backups, the previously described settings will not be backed up. In order to back up these settings separately, you must either manually back them up by using other methods, or you could periodically perform a full farm backup without the content databases attached. This would allow you to back up the farm settings and the web application settings, in addition to any service applications that you select, but not duplicate content database backups. Alternatively, you could employ a scripted deployment strategy and create scripts containing these settings based on your design documentation.

Service Applications

Service applications can consist of both service settings and one or more databases, or just service settings. Central Administration and the SharePoint 2010 Management Shell are the only tools that you can use to back up and restore both the service settings and the databases. However, you can use other tools to back up and restore the databases for most service applications, and then manually reprovision the service application.

If you select the Shared Services node when using SharePoint to perform a backup, all of the shared service applications and proxies in the farm are backed up at once. For each service application, a database backup is started if the service application has an associated database, followed by a backup of the service configuration.

However, if you select individual service applications, the related proxies are not backed up. To back up both the service application and the proxy, you must perform two backups — first of the service application, and then of the proxy.

In the event a specific service application fails, it is likely that you will want to restore that service application only and not the complete farm. It is important to remember that some service applications provide data to other services and sites. As a result, users might experience some service interruption until the recovery process is finished. This could have significant impact on your ability to meet SLAs, and should be a key consideration when planning your backup and recovery strategy for your service applications.

In addition, if you are sharing service applications across farms, be aware that trust certificates that have been exchanged are not included in farm backups. You must back up your certificate store separately. When you restore a farm that shares a service application, you must import and redeploy the certificates, and then re-establish any inter-farm trusts. This process is likely to have an impact on your RTO for these service applications and services that depend on them.

Search Service Application

The *search service application* is a special case. You cannot use SQL Server tools to back up the search service application because of its distributed architecture and associated dependencies between the various search databases and index files. When a backup is started by using SharePoint, index merges are prevented, and crawling is paused when necessary to enable consistent backups. A restore will place all components and data back in the correct location, and resume search activities.

In past versions of SharePoint, if no SLAs were defined for the search service, one approach used by many was to perform a full crawl in the event of a failure. This approach is perfectly feasible; indeed it could be faster and simpler in some environments. But you should carefully consider the time it takes to perform a full crawl and the impact it will have on your users and farm before adopting this approach. Additionally, this approach will require that you document and the reconfigure all search settings such as content sources, crawl rules, and managed properties.

Content Databases

The SharePoint backup tools provide a good solution for farm settings and service applications. However, content databases are usually the most important item when discussing backup and recovery. For most organizations, making use of existing backup and recovery strategies and tools is the desired (and often the best) approach for content databases. They often account for the majority of the storage required for backups. As such, it is usually a sensible approach to separate backing them up from other services and settings.

In fact, this is a very common strategy. Provided you have a complete content database backup, you can restore a copy elsewhere, and then use granular backup and recovery procedures to extract content from within the content database and restore it to its original location.

If you have an RPO of 24 hours for all content in the farm, then you should ensure that backups are made of your content databases at least every 24 hours. You may choose to take weekly full backups and daily differential backups, depending on the size of your databases, your data churn, and the number of databases you must back up. If you have a much shorter RPO, or a very short RTO, you may need to adopt a strategy of transaction log backups on a frequent basis. This will allow you to recover to a much more recent point in time.

> *If you are designing an environment with a large number of high-churn databases that have very short RPOs and RTOs, you may need to choose different tools, or augment existing tools, to protect your farm. Products such as System Center Data Protection Manager provide continuous protection of SharePoint by using the efficient Volume Shadow Copy Service (VSS) technology to perform incremental backups allowing for very short RPOs and RTOs.*

Another consideration is that you can attach different SLAs to different content databases and the content that resides within them. For example, a recommended approach would be to separate business-critical site collections into their own content databases, and then design appropriate backup and recovery strategies for each. Content databases that host My Site data may not be a high priority; as such, they may have an RTO of 24 hours instead of 1 hour, as defined for a content database hosting a corporate intranet.

Post-Restore Steps

If you adopt a strategy of using tools outside of SharePoint to back up and restore content databases, you must consider the post-restore steps that may be required to ensure that all sites are accessible. If you restore a content database that contains a deleted site collection, the information about that site collection will not be present in the farm configuration database upon restore.

In SharePoint 2007, you had to detach and reattach content databases after a restore to refresh the sitemap table in the configuration database. This table contains a mapping of site URLs to content databases. When a request is received for a URL, the database containing the site is looked up and the content is fetched.

In SharePoint 2010, you can refresh the sitemap table by using the traditional method through the `Dismount-SPContentDatabase` and `Mount-SPContentDatabase` cmdlets. Or, you can update the sitemap without needing to detach and reattach a content database from the farm at all. This has the benefit of allowing the database to remain online once restored.

The following example shows how to refresh the configuration database with the site information from a database named WSS_Content:

```
$database = Get-SPContentDatabase -Identity WSS_Content
$database.RefreshSitesInConfigurationDatabase()
```

Content Stored in Remote BLOB Stores

Remote BLOB Storage (RBS) is designed to move the storage of BLOBs from database servers to commodity storage solutions. RBS saves significant space, conserves expensive server resources, and provides a standardized model for applications to access BLOB data. RBS is supported in SharePoint 2010 for content databases in SQL Server 2008. As such, the data stored outside of SharePoint content databases must be considered in any backup and recovery plan.

Fortunately, content in remote BLOB storage is backed up and restored transparently along with other content (such as traditional content databases), as long as the RBS provider in use has this capability. The SharePoint 2010 backup and restore tools and SQL Server 2008 can back up and restore content that is stored in remote BLOB stores when you use the SQL FILESTREAM provider. Third-party RBS providers will likely require additional consideration.

You can use granular tools in the same way as usual to back up/export or restore/import content when using RBS. For example, during restore or import, content will be placed inside the database if you are restoring or importing it to a database without RBS enabled. However, when performing a full database restore, if a content database is set to use the SQL FILESTREAM RBS provider, the RBS provider must be installed both on the database server that is being backed up, and on the database server that is being recovered to.

Granular Backup and Recovery

A SharePoint environment is likely to have an RLO defined that requires backup and recovery of content within a content database. This granularity includes the following:

➤ Site collections

➤ Sites

➤ Lists and libraries

➤ Individual items and their versions

End-user features such as the Recycle Bin and versioning help address the need for frequent item-level restores, but only provide a certain level of protection. If this functionality satisfies the defined SLAs, then there is no need to come up with a backup and recovery strategy for granular items. However, it is highly likely that additional protection will be required where content is deleted from the Recycle Bin.

 Much has been written regarding how to design and configure the Recycle Bin and versioning to support SLAs. For additional information, see the article "Plan to protect content by using recycle bins and versioning (SharePoint Server 2010)" at http://technet.microsoft.com/en-us/library/cc263011.aspx.

Recovering content from within a content database has always been a fairly strenuous task — often with the requirement for a secondary "recovery" farm that is used as a staging area for a restored copy of the database, while the offending site is extracted, before being manually restored back to its original location. SharePoint 2010 offers a number of enhancements and new features that make this task a lot easier and much better for system performance.

Site Collections

Site collections are the top-level logical container for content within SharePoint. As such, you may decide to attach SLAs at the site-collection level, and plan a strategy for site collection backup and recovery. Using this approach was examined earlier in this chapter during the discussion of content databases.

SharePoint has long provided the capability to perform site collection backup and recovery. In SharePoint 2010, you can use the `Backup-SPSite` and `Restore-SPSite` cmdlets to achieve this. Now, in SharePoint 2010, you can also use Central Administration to back up a site collection, as shown in Figure 21-1, although it cannot be used for restoring a site collection.

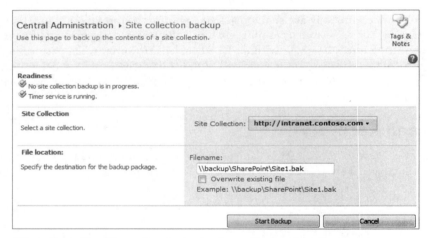

FIGURE 21-1: The "Site collection backup" page in Central Administration

An important point to remember before you start planning for multiple site collection backups is that a content database can contain many site collections. Performing an I/O-intensive operation on a site collection will affect all site collections that share the same content database.

As such, the use of site collection backups alone is not regarded as a very good backup strategy. In general, site collection backups should only be used to back up a site collection from a restored copy of a content database, and restore that site collection back to its original or a new location.

For both performance reasons and backup and recovery, when a site collection becomes large, it should be moved to its own content database. The upper limit for using site collection backup in SharePoint 2010 is 100 GB. However, moving a site collection to its own content database before it reaches less than half this size would be a sensible design decision.

When restoring a site collection, if it is 1 GB or larger in size, you can use the `GradualDelete` parameter for better performance during the restore process. When you use this parameter, the site collection that is overwritten is marked as deleted, which immediately prevents any additional access to its content. The data in the marked site collection is then deleted gradually over time by a timer job, instead of all at the same time, which reduces the impact on server performance.

> *For detailed steps on how to perform site collection backup and restore, see* http://technet.microsoft.com/en-us/library/ee748617.aspx *and* http://technet.microsoft.com/en-us/library/ee748655.aspx, *respectively.*

Sites, Lists, and Libraries

Previous versions of SharePoint provided the capability to export sites by using `stsadm` and the `Export` and `Import` operations. SharePoint 2010 now has PowerShell equivalents: `Export-SPWeb` and `Import-SPWeb`. These cmdlets still serve the purpose of being content migration tools, as opposed to full-fidelity backup tools. However, they do need to be considered as part of any backup and recovery strategy for recovering sites and lower-level content. Indeed, unless you choose to use third-party solutions, using export and import provides the only mechanism for extracting site-level content or below from a content database.

> *Using the export operation saves data, but it is not the same as using the backup operation. You cannot save workflows, alerts, Features, solutions, or the Recycle Bin state by using the export operation.*

It is important that you plan for this when designing your granular backup and recovery strategy. You will need to factor in the time and resources needed to perform these export and import operations. You may find that the manual process is too time-consuming or error-prone, and opt to use a third-party solution for your granular backup and recovery needs.

SharePoint 2010 provides some enhancements to export and import capabilities. You can now use Central Administration to export content, although you must use PowerShell to import the content. You can also export and import content down to the list or library level by using built-in tools, whereas previously you could only use built-in tools at the site level.

The second of these enhancements makes quite a significant difference to the time required for recovery when you just need to recover a list or library. It also makes it possible to easily design for an RLO at the list or library level without the need for third-party solutions when an item is no longer protected by the Recycle Bin. Figure 21-2 shows the Site Or List Export page in Central Administration.

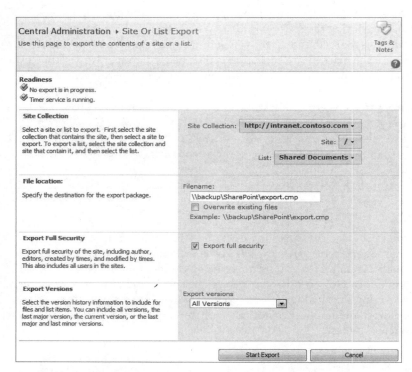

FIGURE 21-2: The Site Or List Export page in Central Administration

For detailed steps on how to perform an export and import of content, see http://technet.microsoft.com/en-us/library/ee428301.aspx *and* http://technet.microsoft.com/en-us/library/ee428322.aspx, *respectively.*

The Site Recycle Bin

SharePoint 2010 with Service Pack 1 adds new functionality that allows deleted sites and site collections to be stored in the Recycle Bin. In prior versions, if a site was accidentally deleted, a database restore was required to a "recovery farm," and then the site or site collection had to be backed up or exported, and restored or imported again. This approach was time-consuming and resource-intensive.

With Service Pack 1 for SharePoint 2010, a deleted site is stored in the second-stage Recycle Bin, and a deleted site collection is retained in the content database as an `SPDeletedSite` object.

Sites and site collections are subject to the standard web application settings for the Recycle Bin. By default, content is deleted from the Recycle Bin after 30 days. Sites will also be subject to the percent of live site quota for second-stage deleted items setting, which is set to 50 percent by default.

A site can be restored by a site collection administrator from the "Deleted from end user Recycle Bin" view of the site collection Recycle Bin. Restoring a site collection requires access to the SharePoint 2010 Management Shell and use of the `Get-SPDeletedSite` and `Restore-SPDeletedSite` cmdlets.

For example, you can use the following commands to get a list of deleted site collections and restore a specific site collection. The `SiteId` is obtained by first running the `Get-SPDeletedSite` cmdlet:

```
Get-SPDeletedSite
Get-SPDeletedSite | Where {$_.SiteId -eq "e4e57440-2933-42b7-a0f9-
    346a79c84865"} | Restore-SPDeletedSite
```

If a site has since been created using the same URL as the original site, the restore will fail. The existing site must be moved or deleted first.

 You can permanently remove a site collection from the Recycle Bin by using the `Remove-SPDeletedSite` *cmdlet. For more information on restoring a deleted site or site collection from the Recycle Bin, see "Restore a deleted site (SharePoint Server 2010)" and "Restore a deleted site collection (SharePoint Server 2010)" at* http://technet.microsoft.com/en-us/library/hh272540 .aspx *and* http://technet.microsoft.com/en-us/library/hh272537.aspx, *respectively.*

Unattached Content Database Data Recovery

The granular backup and recovery strategy for the content discussed previously has always required a secondary "recovery" farm or web application that is used as a staging area for backing up and extracting content from restored databases. The content would then be restored or imported back to its original location by the SharePoint administrator.

In previous versions of SharePoint, this approach was cumbersome because it required the ongoing maintenance, support, and licensing of a secondary environment. Any customizations or SharePoint updates applied to the production environment would also need to be applied to the recovery farm. Failure to do this would lead to database attach errors after restoring a copy of a database, or sites that would fail to export because of missing dependencies.

Possibly the biggest enhancement to granular backup and recovery in SharePoint 2010 is the new unattached content database data recovery feature. It allows you to connect to a content database that is not attached to a SharePoint web application, and select objects down to the list or library level for backup or export. These objects can then be restored or imported using standard approaches already discussed. Figure 21-3 shows the Unattached Content Database Data Recovery page.

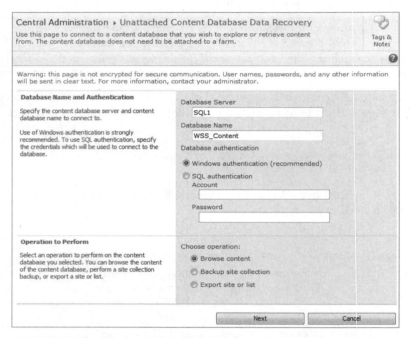

FIGURE 21-3: The Unattached Content Database Data Recovery page in Central Administration

You can also use Windows PowerShell to connect to an unattached content database by using the `ConnectAsUnattachedDatabase` parameter of the `Get-SPContentDatabase` cmdlet. You can then use the `Backup-SPSite` or `Export-SPWeb` cmdlets to retrieve content from the database.

 If you try to connect to a database at a different version level than the current farm, you will get a "Compatibility range mismatch" error. The farm and the database must be upgraded to the same version and build level in order to use the feature. This scenario is only likely to occur if you need to recover content from a database backup that is older than the installation of a recent SharePoint update.

This feature alone decreases the administrative burden when supporting granular backup and recovery SLAs in SharePoint 2010. Content can now be restored much easier and faster without the need for a recovery environment.

Database Snapshots

With SharePoint 2010, if you are using SQL Server Enterprise Edition, the granular backup system can optionally use SQL Server database snapshots to ensure that data remains consistent while the backup or export is in progress. Database snapshots are read-only, static views of a database. Each database snapshot is transactionally consistent with the source database as of the moment when the snapshot was created.

When a backup or export is requested, a SQL Server database snapshot of the appropriate content database is taken, SharePoint 2010 uses it to create the backup or export package, and then the snapshot is deleted. This functionality is unlikely to provide much benefit when recovering content from a restored copy of a content database. But if you need to back up or export content from a live database, it offers the benefit of consistency while the content remains unaffected by the backup or export process.

In order to use a snapshot during content export or backup, you must use the `UseSqlSnapshot` parameter with either the `Backup-SPSite` or `Export-SPWeb` cmdlets.

 Using database snapshots outside of the built-in SharePoint tools is also a valid backup and recovery strategy. For more information, see "Back up databases to snapshots (SharePoint Server 2010)" at `http://technet.microsoft.com/ en-us/library/ee748594.aspx.`

Individual Items

If you are not using third-party products, the backup and recovery strategy adopted for individual items in SharePoint has always been one of having to restore a copy of a content database, and then exporting the lowest-level object before importing it into a test site for download. You must then manually download the item from the test site and upload it back to the production site. As already discussed, in previous versions of SharePoint, this would have been a site; in SharePoint 2010, it is a list or document library. Additionally, the unattached content database data recovery feature in SharePoint 2010 makes this approach a whole lot easier and faster.

This strategy is often suitable for most organizations, since versioning and the Recycle Bin provide the first line of defense against accidentally deleted or overwritten items. However, this approach is both time-consuming and error-prone. If you have very tight RTOs for individual items, then you may need to look into third-party solutions for item-level recovery. These solutions automate much of this process, automatically restoring individual items back to their original location in a very short time, and without any manual steps.

Alternatively, you could use the SharePoint content migration API and the unattached content database data recovery feature to write your own solution that works at a lower level than lists or libraries.

Customizations

The way in which customizations are created and deployed has a significant impact on the tools and strategies that can be used to back up and recover them.

Customizations deployed in sandboxed solutions, or those that contain authored site elements (such as master pages, layout pages, cascading style sheets, and forms), are contained within content databases, and will be covered by your backup strategy for content databases.

Customizations deployed as trusted solutions offer the best method to package and deploy all other customizations, while also providing the easiest approach for backup and recovery. Since they are stored in the farm configuration database, the solutions are backed up in a farm backup or configuration-only backup. You simply restore and redeploy each solution when required. Solution packages are even deployed automatically to new servers, or servers that are rebuilt after a disaster.

Customizations that are not packaged as solution packages will have a more complex backup and recovery process. For example, changes to `web.config` files without using the SharePoint APIs, or manually copying feature files, will prevent SharePoint backup tools from "knowing" about the customizations. Where possible, you should consult the development team or customization vendor to determine if they can package the customizations in solution packages. If that is not possible, for each of these customizations, you must identify the files and settings that need backing up, and use manual procedures or other tools such as Windows Backup.

Common customizations that may be deployed to SharePoint servers without the use of solution packages can include the following:

➤ Web parts, site, or list definitions, custom columns, new content types, custom fields, custom actions, coded workflows, or workflow activities and conditions

➤ Third-party solutions and their associated binary files and Registry keys, such as IFilters

➤ Changes to standard XML files

➤ Custom site definitions

➤ Changes to the `web.config` files

 As part of your development backup procedures, you should ensure that you keep separate copies of your solution packages outside of SharePoint in case the farm configuration database fails and you do not have configuration backups.

Choosing Backup and Recovery Tools

Thus far, you have learned about some of the out-of-the-box backup and recovery tools. In order to choose the right tools for backup and recovery, you must determine whether you can meet the defined SLAs within your budget for providing business continuity.

It is not uncommon to use more than one tool when protecting an environment, especially when some tools better meet your needs, or they are already in use within the organization.

Following are some key factors to consider when choosing tools:

➤ Speed of backup and recovery

➤ Space required/backup type supported (full, differential, or incremental)

➤ Support for encryption, compression, and other common features of backup and recovery tools

➤ Completeness of recovery

➤ Granularity offered

➤ Complexity of managing the tool

➤ Familiarity with the tool

➤ Cost to license and support the tool

Designing your availability strategy is another key component of defining any SharePoint business continuity management plan. The next section provides guidance for redundancy of SharePoint across the application and data tiers.

DESIGNING YOUR AVAILABILITY STRATEGY

Planning for and ensuring that an IT service can continue to operate correctly after failure of an individual component is something that IT professionals deal with routinely. Common techniques for providing hardware fault tolerance of individual components include redundant hard drive disk arrays, redundant power supplies, and multiple network interface cards (NICs).

Regardless of this, protecting every component within a server is neither practical nor cost-effective. Multiple servers are often used to ensure both scalability and redundancy of server roles for any IT service. SharePoint is no exception. Where possible, you should plan for hardware fault tolerance, in addition to increased redundancy of server roles.

Figure 21-4 shows a server farm configured for a minimum level of redundancy at every tier. The focus of this section will be redundancy of server roles.

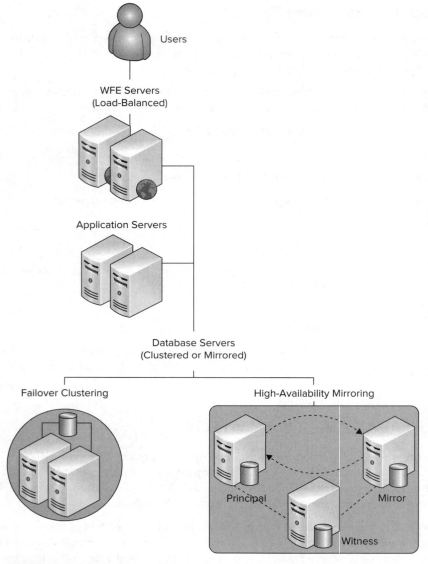

FIGURE 21-4: A typical server farm configured for redundancy at each tier

SQL Server Redundancy

Given the reliance on databases, SQL Server redundancy is extremely important for any SharePoint farm. Failover clustering and high-availability database mirroring can be used to ensure the availability of your databases in the event of a failure.

Failover Clustering

Failover clustering is one of the most common methods for providing redundancy for all databases at the instance level in SQL Server.

A failover cluster is a combination of one or more nodes (servers), and two or more shared disks. The failover cluster instance appears on the network as a single computer, but has functionality that provides failover from one node to another if the current node becomes unavailable. A basic failover cluster will consist of two nodes configured in an active/passive cluster configuration, where the *passive* node will remain redundant until the *active* node in the cluster fails.

A SQL Server failover cluster is seen as a single database service by SharePoint. Therefore, failover is automatic and transparent to SharePoint when it occurs. Failover clustering is the recommended approach for providing basic automated redundancy of the database role in a SharePoint farm.

For more information about failover clustering, refer to "Getting Started with SQL Server 2008 R2 Failover Clustering" at http://go.microsoft .com/fwlink/?LinkID=102837&clcid=0x409.

Database Mirroring

Database mirroring can be used to provide database redundancy on a per-database basis. It works by sending transactions from a principal database and server to a mirror database and server. A number of modes are available with database mirroring, but to provide redundancy with automatic failover, you must use high-availability mirroring, also known as *high-safety mode with automatic failover*.

High-availability database mirroring involves three server instances: a principal, a mirror, and a witness. To ensure consistency between principal server and mirror server, transactions are not committed on the principal server until they have been committed on the mirror server. The witness server enables automatic failover from the principal server to the mirror server (typically in a matter of seconds).

In previous versions of SharePoint, fully automatic failover was not easily possible because SharePoint was not mirroring-aware. It was necessary to manually update the name of the database server in SharePoint, or "trick" SharePoint through the use of SQL Server aliasing or some other method. Either approach required an IISReset on every server in the farm in order to refresh connection information on those servers.

SharePoint 2010 is mirroring-aware, allowing you to configure the mirror database server location for each database. Setting a mirror database location adds a parameter to the connection that SharePoint uses to connect to SQL Server. If the principal server becomes unavailable, the witness server automatically swaps the roles of the principal and mirror databases, and SharePoint automatically attempts to contact the server that is specified as the mirror location.

You can use Central Administration or Windows PowerShell to configure a mirror database server location. At the bottom of Figure 21-5, you can see the Failover Database Server option given when creating or editing the settings for a content database or service application database in Central Administration.

Central Administration ▸ Add Content Database

Use this page to create a new content database or to add an existing content database to this web application. Learn about changing settings for a content database.

Tags & Notes

Warning: this page is not encrypted for secure communication. User names, passwords, and any other information will be sent in clear text. For more information, contact your administrator.

Web Application

Select a web application.

Web Application: **http://intranet.contoso.com/** ▾

Database Name and Authentication

Use of the default database server and database name is recommended for most cases. Refer to the administrator's guide for advanced scenarios where specifying database information is required.

Use of Windows authentication is strongly recommended. To use SQL authentication, specify the credentials which will be used to connect to the database.

Database Server
SQL1

Database Name
WSS_Content

Database authentication
◉ Windows authentication (recommended)
◯ SQL authentication
Account

Password

Failover Server

You can choose to associate a database with a specific failover server that is used in conjuction with SQL Server database mirroring.

Failover Database Server
SQL2

FIGURE 21-5: The Failover Database Server option in Central Administration

You cannot use Central Administration to configure a failover server for the Central Administration content database or the configuration database. You must use Windows PowerShell to do this by using the following commands:

```
$db = Get-SPDatabase | where {$_.Name -match "DatabaseName"}
$db.AddFailoverServiceInstance("MirrorServerName")
$db.Update()
```

You can use the following commands to find out which databases have not been set up with a failover server:

```
$dbs = Get-SPDatabase
foreach ($db in $dbs) {if (!$db.FailoverServiceInstance) {$db.Name}}
```

 For information on configuring database mirroring (including requirements for database mirroring), see "Configure availability by using SQL Server database mirroring (SharePoint Server 2010)" at http://technet.microsoft.com/ en-us/library/dd207314.aspx.

Database mirroring provides a good alternative to failover clustering. It provides the same automatic failover, but also protects against failed storage and allows for the use of less-expensive direct-attached storage (DAS). However, this is at double the storage requirement, as well as some performance overhead, requiring additional memory and processor resources for each mirrored database.

When choosing the approach for your environment, you should take these points into consideration while also considering the SLAs that you need to meet. If you are planning to use RBS, you should also consider that you cannot mirror databases that have been configured to use the SQL Server FILESTREAM RBS provider.

SharePoint Server Redundancy

SharePoint servers that serve content to end users are typically labeled as Web Front End (WFE) servers. These servers have the Microsoft SharePoint Foundation Web Application role configured. To provide redundancy for WFE servers, you need more than one server hosting this role, and these servers require load-balancing technology in order to balance the load between them and provide redundancy should a server fail. You can implement load balancing by using software such as the Network Load Balancing (NLB) component of Windows Server, or by using a dedicated hardware device.

Software load balancing is cost-effective, because it is generally provided by a service running on the load-balanced servers themselves. In some cases (for example, with NLB), this has a result of consuming additional hardware resources.

Hardware load balancing is provided by a dedicated hardware device, which is generally running a proprietary operating system. The device does not consume additional resources on the load-balanced servers, because it acts independently. Hardware devices generally provide a richer feature set and greater scalability than software load balancers do.

SharePoint servers that hold roles such as search are typically labeled as application servers. These servers do not require load-balancing technology, since SharePoint provides load-balancing internally for service applications. In reality, servers labeled as either WFE servers or application servers may hold many different roles. For example, it is common for the search query role to be configured on WFE servers.

Redundancy Strategies for Service Applications

The redundancy strategy you choose for protecting service applications that run in a farm varies, depending on if the service application stores data in a database.

Service Applications that Store Data Outside of a Database

Protecting service applications that store data outside a database is as simple as provisioning the service application on multiple application servers to provide redundancy within the environment. This keeps the service application running, but does not guarantee against data loss. If an application server fails, the active connections for that application server will be lost, and users will lose some data. This is unavoidable.

The following service applications store data outside a database:

➤ Access Services

➤ Excel Services Application

Service Applications that Store Data in Databases

Protecting service applications that store data in databases requires that you provision the service application on multiple application servers, and that you configure SQL Server failover clustering or database mirroring.

The following service applications store data in databases:

➤ Search service application (Search Administration, Crawl, and Property databases)

 The Search service application is a special case for redundancy within a farm. For more information, see Chapter 27.

➤ User Profile service (Profiles, Social, and Synchronization databases)

➤ Business Data Connectivity service application

➤ Application Registry service application

➤ Usage and Health Data Collection service application

 Mirroring the Usage and Health Data Collection service application Logging database is not recommended because of high throughput.

➤ Managed Metadata service application

➤ Secure Store service application

➤ State service application

➤ Web Analytics service application (Reporting and Staging databases)

➤ Word Automation Services service application

➤ Microsoft SharePoint Foundation Subscription Settings Service

➤ PerformancePoint Services

 Mirroring some service application databases is only supported when using synchronous mirroring. Additionally, at release, mirroring was not supported at all for some databases. For the latest guidance, see "Plan for availability (SharePoint Server 2010)" at http://technet.microsoft.com/en-us/library/cc748824.aspx.

Redundancy for Closely Located Data Centers

It is common for large organizations to have multiple data centers, some of which are located close to one another with high-bandwidth, low-latency links. The purpose of having multiple local data centers is to provide redundancy and automatic failover in the event of a fault in one of them. Although this design does not provide a means for disaster recovery in the event of a local or regional disaster, it does provide a suitable redundancy solution for most applications that can be spanned across two or more data centers.

A SharePoint farm can be designed to span two or more closely located data centers, provided there is less than 1 millisecond (ms) latency between SQL Server and the WFE servers in one direction, and at least 1 gigabit per second (Gbps) bandwidth. These are tough requirements to meet, but certainly achievable for data centers located a small distance apart. It is not supported to design such a farm if you cannot meet these requirements.

The farm is designed in the same way as usual for providing redundancy, but redundant servers are located in each data center, and a load-balancing device directs traffic between both, as shown in Figure 21-6.

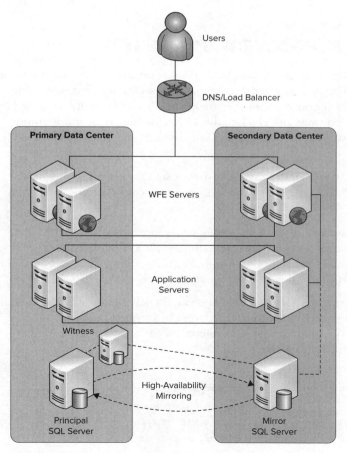

FIGURE 21-6: Redundancy for closely located data centers

SQL Server code-named "Denali" introduces a new feature called AlwaysOn Availability Groups for enhancing the availability of databases. The feature looks similar to database mirroring, but it is actually a combination of both database mirroring and clustering. Each availability group contains a set of databases known as availability databases *that fail over together. An availability group can have multiple failover targets (or secondary replicas), and you can configure secondary replicas to support read-only access to secondary databases. This is a vast improvement on current versions of SQL Server, and looks promising for high availability and disaster recovery in SharePoint. Importantly, this feature is supported for use with SharePoint versions from SharePoint 2010 Service Pack 1.*

An availability strategy covers the planning and design for providing redundancy of components within a SharePoint farm. However, when that data center hosting the servers in the farm fails, a disaster recovery strategy is required. The next section covers the considerations for designing a SharePoint disaster recovery strategy.

DESIGNING YOUR DISASTER RECOVERY STRATEGY

Disaster recovery means different things to different people, depending on the service or data. In the context of this chapter, you should think of a disaster recovery strategy as the plan for recovering from failure of a data center that hosts your SharePoint environment. This will usually be caused by a local disaster that cannot be recovered from quickly. Equally, failure of your farm configuration database while the data center is still active could be deemed as a disaster, and be classed as a trigger for initiating your disaster recovery plan.

A SharePoint disaster recovery strategy will almost always involve a standby farm running in a different location. A *standby farm* is often referred to as a *hot*, *warm*, or *cold standby*, depending on the time to get it up and running.

A hot standby farm can resume services within seconds or minutes, whereas a cold standby farm will take hours or even days to resume services. As with everything in the realm of business continuity management, you should base your solution on your SLAs. Providing a hot standby solution when the business does not ask for it does not make sense.

A hot standby farm would usually cost a lot more to design and run than a cold standby farm. As a rule of thumb, the shorter the interval between failure and recovery of services, the more complex and expensive the solution is likely to be. Additionally, the amount of data you are replicating between farms will have a large bearing on cost also.

No matter which disaster recovery solution you decide to implement for your environment, you are likely to incur some data loss, however small.

Designing for disaster recovery in SharePoint requires knowledge of the solutions that can be used, tied together with an understanding of how those solutions are supported for use with SharePoint. There are a number of supportability considerations when using solutions such as log shipping or database mirroring in a disaster recovery scenario. This section explains the various solutions available, and the supportability considerations for each.

It is important to note that your SharePoint disaster recovery strategy must be coordinated with the disaster recovery strategy for other services on which SharePoint depends (such as Active Directory). You shouldn't assume that a viable plan is in place for such services.

Cold Standby Farm

A *cold standby farm* disaster recovery strategy typically ships backups for bare-metal recovery to local and regional locations. You can recover in the event of a disaster by setting up a new farm in a new location and restoring your backups. Having arrangements in place for short-term equipment hire and hosting is usually the best approach to take.

This approach involves the following steps:

1. Install and configure SharePoint 2010 (preferably by using a scripted deployment)

2. Restore customizations

3. Restore a farm backup

This approach is often the cheapest option to maintain operationally, but with the disadvantage of additional costs associated with recovery from every disaster. It is also the slowest option for recovery, and relies on backups being fully restorable. If costs are an issue, and SharePoint is not a business-critical service, this is likely to be the best approach to take.

Warm Standby Farm

A *warm standby farm* disaster recovery strategy typically ships virtual server images to local and regional farms. Virtual images of servers in your farm are taken frequently and, when required, can be brought online to recover your farm in the secondary location.

This approach requires knowledge of virtualization options for a SharePoint farm, as well as performance and supportability implications. For example, taking a snapshot of a SharePoint server in an active farm is currently unsupported. For more information, see Chapter 23.

This approach offers a balance between the cold and hot standby farm options. It is relatively inexpensive to perform recovery, but does have relatively complex recovery procedures and operational costs. The trade-off is that you can perform a full farm recovery in a matter of minutes or hours if required.

This approach is likely to be the most suitable for most organizations that have secondary data centers, but do not need near-instant disaster recovery for their SharePoint environment. If you need near-instant disaster recovery, a hot standby farm is the approach to take.

Hot Standby Farm

A *hot standby farm* disaster recovery strategy typically involves maintaining a duplicate passive farm in another data center ready to be brought online in the event of a disaster. All settings, customizations, and updates are applied in both farms. Content databases and some service application databases are asynchronously mirrored or log-shipped to the secondary farm.

Upon failure, databases are bought online in the secondary farm, and DNS records are updated to resolve traffic to the servers in the secondary farm. Figure 21-7 shows a typical hot standby farm disaster recovery strategy for SharePoint before failover.

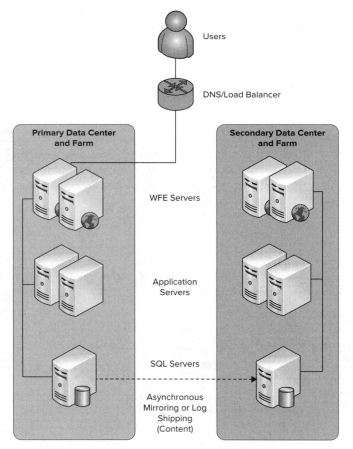

FIGURE 21-7: A typical hot standby farm disaster recovery strategy before failover

Asynchronously mirroring or log-shipping a configuration database, Central Administration content database, and some service application databases is not supported. You should maintain a separate configuration and Central Administration content database in your hot standby farm. Considerations for service applications are discussed later in this section.

If you choose to use log shipping, this strategy can be repeated across many data centers. Unfortunately, database mirroring only allows you to copy databases to a single mirror server. In larger organizations, making use of storage area network (SAN) replication is a viable alternative to log shipping or database mirroring. You should consult with your SAN vendor to determine if SAN replication is supported and feasible for your environment.

This approach offers superior speed to recovery, although this comes at a high cost and the additional complexity involved in configuring and maintaining both farms. If your disaster recovery SLAs require a very short RTO, this is the approach you should adopt.

 You will need to refresh the sitemap in the configuration database for the secondary farm when it is brought online. Information on how to achieve this was covered in the discussion, "Content Databases," in the "Designing Your Backup and Recovery Strategy" section earlier in this chapter.

When providing a hot standby farm disaster recovery solution, you must consider the various service applications configured in your primary farm. Where possible, services that can be run cross-farm should exist in a separate services farm that is accessible from both the primary and secondary data centers.

Service applications that cannot be run cross-farm, or that you do not wish to run cross-farm, will require a redundancy strategy that depends on your SLAs for the service applications. This will also depend on whether the databases associated with the service applications can be asynchronously mirrored or log-shipped.

For example, search requires complete synchronization between its databases and index. Because of this requirement, you cannot replicate search between farms by using an asynchronous replication mechanism. To provide up-to-date search on a failover farm, you must configure search separately on the secondary farm. This often presents a problem if you want search online quickly after a disaster, because you cannot crawl content databases while they are mirrored. A solution to this is to use SQL Server snapshots to periodically snapshot the content database, and then crawl the snapshot. Alternatively, you can log-ship in stand-by mode and crawl the read-only copy.

The profile database (which is part of the User Profile service application) is another example of a database that cannot be mirrored or log-shipped in this scenario. To provide redundancy for the User Profile service application, you must configure the service application in the secondary farm, and use the User Profile Replication Engine that is included in the SharePoint Administration Toolkit.

Rather than list each service application here, as well as the supportability implications and requirements for each, see "Planning for hot standby data centers" at http://technet.microsoft.com/en-us/library/ff628971.aspx#Section3 *for the latest guidance.*

DOCUMENTATION

Documentation to support any business continuity plan is as important as the solution itself. If you do not document the processes, policies, and procedures, your solution might fail to meet the SLAs that you have agreed to with the business. Worse still, your system might fail completely, or you could lose data.

Include time to develop this documentation within any SharePoint design and deployment process. The documentation should cover operational procedures, as well as the design of the solution. You should regularly review and maintain any documentation to ensure that it is accurate and up-to-date.

An effective business continuity plan should fully document every aspect of the plan. Some of the items that you may want to incorporate into your plan include the following:

➤ An explanation of when to use the plan

➤ A history of any updates

➤ Permissions required to execute the plan

➤ A list of key contacts

➤ A step-by-step execution plan for your environment

➤ The location of all installation files and customizations

➤ Installation and configuration instructions

➤ Testing instructions, including stability tests, performance tests, and security tests

➤ Comments from previous disasters and restorations

Your SharePoint environment and business continuity plan is only as good as the testing that is performed against it, so factor in time for full tests. Before you put a SharePoint environment into production, test it against a number of simulated situations, such as the following:

➤ Failure of hardware components

➤ Data corruption

➤ Loss of a server

➤ Network outage

➤ Loss of data center

Any issues arising from these tests should be addressed and documented. You should test regularly and after each major change to the environment.

BEST PRACTICES

Microsoft has documented a number of performance, quality assurance, and procedural best practices for SharePoint backup and recovery at `http://technet.microsoft.com/en-us/library/gg266381.aspx`. It is strongly recommended that you review these best practices and adopt them in your business continuity plan.

SUMMARY

This chapter covered business continuity management for SharePoint 2010, providing guidance for defining your business continuity requirements, and using them to design your backup and recovery, availability, and disaster recovery strategies.

Whether SharePoint is the primary collaboration tool in an organization, or it provides a company's Internet presence, a well-designed business continuity plan is critical for ensuring that you can provide availability for the service and fast recovery in the event of data loss or a disaster. It is important to remember that if you do not know the business importance of a service, or the costs associated with outage and data loss, you cannot effectively define SLAs for that service. These SLAs will not only define the agreements for recovery objectives and service availability, they will often help determine what backup, recovery, and availability solutions are required to meet them.

Once you know your business continuity requirements, you can plan, design, and execute a business continuity plan that works best for your environment using some of the tools and techniques discussed in this chapter.

Chapter 22 explores how to design for cloud-based solutions and multi-tenancy services.

22

Designing for Cloud-Based Solutions and Multi-Tenancy Services

By Bill Baer

This chapter describes the most common of cloud-based and on-premise hosted solution deployments available with SharePoint 2010, including implementation, features, and capabilities designed to support data partitioning, or to begin using SharePoint in the cloud with SharePoint Online.

CLOUD-BASED SOLUTIONS

In today's business climate, collaboration is essential. Most organizations require their employees to store and collaborate on shared information, while individuals still must maintain secure, private storage. Individuals also want personalized information (that is, what is relevant for them in their context or role). Key requirements for collaboration include a simple publish capability, integrated data storage, an easy-to-understand taxonomy, options for personalization, and search criteria that spans job function, business area, and multiple data stores — all available from home or work via a secure connection.

Office 365 offers organizations a flexible, web-based solution of tools and services to help users manage information and collaborate effectively with others. SharePoint Online is the premier hosted SharePoint solution provided by Microsoft as a component of the Office 365 suite. The SharePoint Online service provides users the capability to easily create and manage custom team and project-focused sites for collaboration and personal productivity, with limited dependency on lengthy management processes. Presence awareness helps teams improve overall communication. Users get the authority, flexibility, and customization they need to create smart places for collaboration as needed.

Getting to Know SharePoint Online

SharePoint Online is available in two unique offerings (Standard and Dedicated) tailored to an individual organization's size, requirements, and objectives — each provided at a per-user monthly fee. The SharePoint Online offerings can be differentiated at a high level based on capabilities, flexibility, and pricing.

SharePoint Online provides a rich feature set and collection of capabilities to both serve as an organization's primary collaborative platform, or to augment an organization's existing on-premise deployment to support lightweight extranet or external sharing scenarios, or to enable collaboration outside of an organization's firewall.

SharePoint Online delivers SharePoint as a cloud service through Microsoft data centers across the globe, enabling people to share ideas and expertise, build custom sites and solutions, and quickly locate information to respond to changing business needs — without the need to deploy SharePoint in their own data centers. In addition to the services and solutions provided by SharePoint, SharePoint Online provides high availability, comprehensive security, and simplified management, so organizations can be confident in choosing it for a collaboration platform.

SharePoint Online is designed to support some of the most complex user distribution patterns, whether users are centrally located or geographically dispersed. Without the need to purchase and deploy servers, organizations can quickly deploy SharePoint to remote offices, or support growth as the result of acquisitions. This flexibility enables users to quickly benefit from SharePoint with minimal cost and delay.

Security Features

SharePoint Online provides business-class reliability and flexibility through a set of features that ensure a secure collaborative environment. SharePoint Online provides the following set of common features:

➤ *Secure access* — SharePoint Online is provided through 128-bit Secure Sockets Layer (SSL) or Transport Layer Security (TLS) encryption.

➤ *Intrusion* — SharePoint Online is continuously monitored for unusual or suspicious activity.

➤ *Audit* — Microsoft regularly assesses the SharePoint Online infrastructure to ensure compliance policies and antivirus signatures are available. Configuration settings and security updates include the following:

  ➤ Achieved ISO 27001 certification

  ➤ Completed Statement on Audit Status (SAS) 70 Type I and II audits

  ➤ Added controls that assist customers in complying with Health Insurance Portability and Accountability Act (HIPAA) and Family Educational Rights and Privacy Act (FERPA)

  ➤ Achieved the European Union (EU) Safe Harbor seal

Identity Features

SharePoint Online provides multiple methods for the management and consumption of identity — whether a small to medium business without an existing identity infrastructure, or a larger organization using Active Directory Domain Services (ADDS).

Organizations with an existing identity infrastructure such as ADDS can implement a Single Sign-On (SSO) approach to authentication by configuring Active Directory Federation Services (ADFS) to federate with the Microsoft Online Services Federation gateway. Users whose identities are derived from the federated domain will be able to use their existing credentials to automatically authenticate to the service.

Microsoft Online Services provides the Directory Synchronization Tool to facilitate directory synchronization. The Directory Synchronization Tool provides one-way directory synchronization of all user accounts and mail-enabled contacts and groups from your local ADDS directory service to Microsoft Online Services. The Directory Synchronization Tool should be installed on a Windows Server 2003 or Windows Server 2008 computer joined to the ADDS Forest to be synchronized and capable of reaching all domain controllers for each domain in your forest.

Administration Model

Microsoft Online Services provides a delegated and granular administration model through role-based access. User accounts can be assigned either global or password administrator rights that provide either full access to all settings of the service, or the capability to read company and user information, reset user passwords, and manage support requests.

The administration of SharePoint Online occurs through a web portal where the SharePoint Online administrator creates and manages site collections, as shown in Figure 22-1.

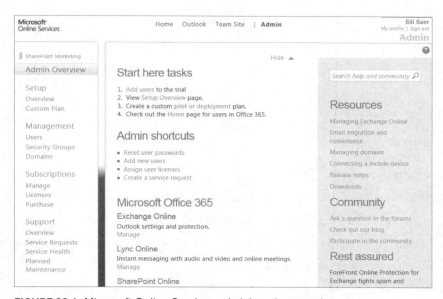

FIGURE 22-1: Microsoft Online Services administration portal

The SharePoint Online administrative web portal is independent from the overall Microsoft Online Services administration portal. As shown in Figure 22-2, the SharePoint Online administrative web portal enables an administrator to manage site collections, configure Send To connections, configure InfoPath Forms Services and a web service proxy, manage user profiles, and manage the Term Store used by the service's site collections.

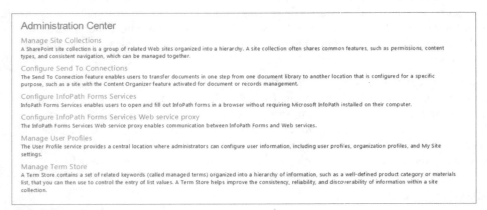

FIGURE 22-2: SharePoint Online Administration Center

Managing Site Collections

As shown in Figure 22-3, site collection management enables an administrator to create, manage, configure, and delete site collections provisioned on the service.

FIGURE 22-3: Site collection management

Creating Site Collections

To create a new site collection, administrators should follow these steps:

1. On the Administration Center page, click Manage Site Collections.

2. In the Site Collections Ribbon group, click New, as shown in Figure 22-4.

3. In the Title box, enter a title for the site collection.

4. For the Web Site Address, choose a domain name, URL path, and enter a URL name for the site collection.

5. In the Template list, select a template for the site collection.

6. In the Administrator box, enter the username for the site collection administrator.

7. In the Quota box, enter the amount of storage to allocate to this site collection.

8. Click Create.

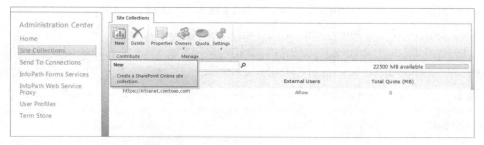

FIGURE 22-4: New site collection

 The first time you create a site collection, the access type is set to intranet by default.

Once the new site collection has been created, the new site collection URL is presented in the user interface. You can select the new site collection URL to navigate to its home page. If you are not the site collection administrator, you are redirected to the sign-in page that requests site collection administrator credentials.

Updating Site Collection Administrators

Site collection administrators are users with administrative permissions to manage a site collection, including management of its content, permissions, and so on. To update the site collection administrator for a site collection, follow these steps:

1. On the Administration Center page, click Manage Site Collections.

2. Select the checkbox next to the site collection for which you want to change the primary administrator, and then click Set Administrator in the Manage Ribbon group.

3. In the Set Administrator dialog box, change the administrator name in the box and then click the Check Names button to verify that the username is valid.

4. Click OK.

 To perform bulk operations, select all the site collections to update and follow the steps outlined here.

Updating Storage Quotas

Storage quotas are defined in two distinct tiers — total storage quota and allocated storage quota. *Total storage quota* refers to the amount of available storage space purchased for Microsoft Online Services. Total storage quota can be reviewed through the Microsoft Online Services administration portal. *Allocated storage quota* refers to the total amount of storage space allocated to one or more site collections. The minimum storage that can be allocated to a site collection is 50 MB.

To update the storage quota information for a site collection, follow these steps:

1. On the Administration Center page, click Manage Site Collections.

2. Select the checkbox next to the site collection for which you want to change the storage quota, and then click Set Quota in the Manage Ribbon group.

3. In the Set Quota dialog box, change the allocated quota and warning storage limit for the selected site collection. To receive an e-mail message when the storage reaches the warning storage limit, keep the checkbox selected.

> *The* warning storage limit *notifies site collection users when the storage in use approaches the warning threshold of the storage limit for one or more site collections.*

4. Click OK.

Converting Site Collection Access Type

SharePoint Online site collections are created in the initial state limited to intranet access for individuals in your organization. Site collections can be converted to enable external sharing, which enables users outside of your organization to participate in collaboration.

To convert the access type of a site collection, follow these steps:

1. On the Administration Center home page, click Manage Site Collections.

2. Select the checkbox next to the site collection for which you want to change the access type, and then click Set Access Type in the Manage Ribbon group.

3. In the Set Access Type dialog box, select Extranet.

4. Click OK.

Once a site collection has been converted to an extranet site collection, you can invite individuals outside of your organization to collaborate, and grant them permissions appropriately. (Figure 22-3 shows an extranet-enabled site collection.)

Extranet site collections can also be converted to intranet site collections, which prevents previously invited external users from collaborating on its content. Extranet site collections are suitable for supporting temporary external sharing on a project, or as a solution to augment an on-premise solution.

Inviting External Users

Extranet-enabled site collections allow an organization to invite external users to participate in collaboration on the content of one or more site collections. On site collections configured to enable external access, you can invite users outside of your organization to participate in collaboration, and grant them permissions appropriately.

To invite external users to an extranet-enabled site collection, follow these steps:

1. On the home page for the site collection, click Site Actions, and then click Site Settings from the list of available options.

2. Under "Users and Permissions," click "Collaboration permissions." The Change Collaboration Permissions dialog box appears.

In the event that the operations described here are performed against a site collection configured for intranet access, or if the site collection has not been converted to allow extranet access, the Change Collaboration Permissions dialog will display a notification prompting you to convert the site collection for extranet access.

3. In the Users box, enter the e-mail addresses for the external users you want to add.

When adding more than one user, separate the e-mail addresses with a semicolon.

4. In the Give Permission area, perform one of the following available options:

    a. Assign users to a SharePoint group by clicking "Add users to a SharePoint group," and then select an existing group from the list of available groups.

    b. Assign permissions individually by clicking "Grant users permission directly," and then select a permission level from the list of available permissions.

Groups simplify the administration and management of user permissions.

If you would like to send an e-mail message to the new users, in the "Send e-mail" section, select the "Send welcome e-mail" checkbox.

5. Click OK.

Managing Send To Connections

Send To connections are used to specify a connection path for sending documents to a repository or a records center, as shown in Figure 22-5. The Send To connection specifies the web application from which documents will be sent, the repository or records center to which documents will be sent, and the aspects of how the documents are sent. For example, an administrator can specify that documents can be sent from one document library to another location that is configured for a specific purpose, such as a site with the Content Organizer feature activated for document or records management.

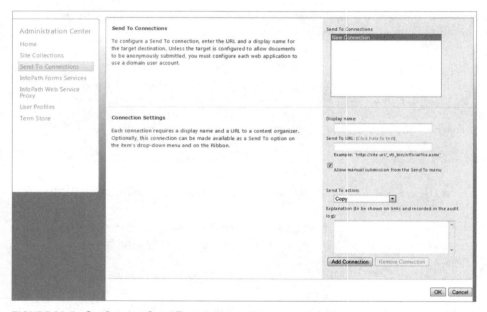

FIGURE 22-5: Configuring Send To connections

To configure a new Send To connection, follow these steps.

1. On the Administration Center home page, click Send To Connections.

2. On the Send To Connections dialog, click New Connection.

3. Under Connection Settings, specify the name to describe the new connection, and the URL to which content should be sent.

4. Select the checkbox labeled "Allow manual submission" from the Send To menu to allow users to manually submit content to the configured location.

5. Select an action to apply to this Send To connection from the list of available Send To actions:

   ➤ *Copy* — Creates a copy of the document and sends the copy to the destination repository.

➤ *Move* — Deletes the document from its current location and moves the document to the destination repository. Users will no longer be able to access the document from its original location.

➤ *Move and Leave a Link* — Deletes the document from its current location, moves it to the destination repository, and leaves a link at the current location indicating that the document has been moved. When a user clicks this link, a page appears that displays the URL of the document and the document's metadata.

6. In the Explanation dialog box, specify the information to be added to the audit log when the user sends a document by using this connection. If you selected "Move and Leave a Link" in the previous step, the page that appears when the user clicks the link will also display the explanation.

7. Click Add Connection to create the connection.

8. Click OK when you are finished configuring connections.

Managing InfoPath Forms Services

InfoPath Forms Services provides the capability to deploy your organization's forms to SharePoint Server, and to enable users to fill out these forms by using a web browser without the necessity of InfoPath being installed on the client.

Figure 22-6 shows how to configure InfoPath Forms Services, which can be done using the following steps:

1. On the Administration Center home page, click InfoPath Forms Services.

2. Select the "Allow users to browser-enable form templates" checkbox to allow users to publish browser-enabled form templates.

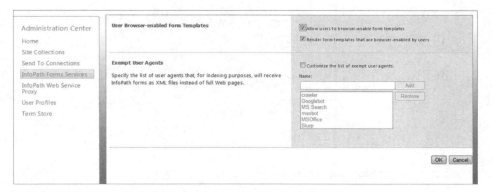

FIGURE 22-6: Configuring InfoPath Forms Services

 Clearing this checkbox disables browser-enabled form templates across all site collections.

3. Select the "Render form templates that are browser-enabled by users" checkbox to allow browser-enabled form templates that users publish to be rendered in a web browser.

4. Click OK when you are finished configuring InfoPath Forms Services.

 When deselecting this option, users can still publish browser-compatible form templates to form libraries, but these form templates cannot be filled out by using a web browser.

5. Click Add to add user agents or Remove or to remove user agents. Adding user agents can ease the indexing process in that when InfoPath encounters a user agent that has been specified, it returns an XML file instead of the entire web page.

Managing the InfoPath Web Service Proxy

The InfoPath Forms Services web service proxy specifies whether or not to use the proxy for data connections between InfoPath forms and web services. To use a proxy, this setting must be enabled, and a data connection must be defined in a universal data connection (UDC) file.

Figure 22-7 shows how to configure the InfoPath Web Service Proxy, which can be done by following these steps.

1. On the Administration Center home page, click InfoPath Web Service Proxy.

2. Select the checkbox labeled Enable to enable InfoPath Forms Services Web service proxy.

FIGURE 22-7: Configuring the InfoPath Web service proxy

Managing User Profiles

The User Profile Service application stores information about users in a central location. The User Profile Service is used to drive social computing features such as My Sites, and enable features such as social tagging and newsfeeds.

To provision My Sites, the User Profile Service must be configured.

For information on configuring the features associated with the User Profile Service (as shown in Figure 22-8), refer to the User Profile Service documentation at `http://technet.microsoft.com/ en-us/library/ee721050.aspx`.

FIGURE 22-8: Configuring the User Profile Service

Managing the Term Store

The Term Store provides a way to manage terms or phrases that can be associated with an item in SharePoint. A *term set* is a collection of related terms. Terms are defined in two distinct tiers:

➤ *Local term sets* — These are created within the context of one or more site collections. For example, when you add a column to a list in a document library and create a new term set to bind the column to, the new term set is local to the site collection that hosts that document library.

➤ *Global term sets* — These are created outside of the context of a site collection and are applicable to all site collections. Global term sets support delegated management. For example, if a term set is isolated to legal terms, an individual in the Legal department (or someone who acts in that capacity) can be assigned to manage that term set.

To begin using the Term Store , go to the Administration Center home page and click Term Store, as shown in Figure 22-9.

FIGURE 22-9: Configuring the Term Store

For information on planning, managing, and administering terms, see the "Managed Metadata Overview" at `http://technet.microsoft.com/en-us/library/ee424402.aspx`.

To learn more about Office 365 and SharePoint Online, go to `www.microsoft.com/en-us/office365/online-software.aspx`.

SHAREPOINT ON PREMISE

"On premise" can be loosely defined as the installation and operation of SharePoint on server machines that are under the direct control of the organization consuming their services within the boundaries of their facilities. This section discusses the value of dedicated versus hosted implementations of SharePoint 2010, as related to an on-premise deployment.

Dedicated Versus Hosted

An important first step as you begin planning your architecture is determining whether to use a dedicated SharePoint 2010 server farm environment versus a hosted SharePoint 2010 server farm environment. Although both server farm environments will be based on the on-premise model, both benefits and drawbacks exist as to how those deployments will be configured and maintained.

Dedicated environments are suitable for many organizations that either do not have to adhere to strict regulatory requirements or are comfortable with ad-hoc collaboration, and that have administrators who are both familiar with the SharePoint platform and have the resources to manage it end to end. Though these conditions lend themselves to a dedicated environment, they do not preclude a hosted environment.

Hosted environments are beneficial in scenarios where an organization requires usage and data isolation supporting industry or internal regulations that cannot be or are difficult to enforce in a dedicated environment. A hosted environment enables the isolation of business groups, product groups, or like data into a logically separated group of site collections within a server farm or web application.

The isolation of site collections is useful where the co-mingling of data is not desired. It provides the added benefit of enabling the IT professional responsible for the server farm environment to delegate common administrative tasks to the individual(s) responsible for managing a particular business unit, product, or data.

Let's take a look at the various hosting features available in SharePoint 2010 to support this model, and describe scenarios where these capabilities offer added value.

Hosting Features

SharePoint 2010 natively provides a hosting feature set that can be used in the enterprise for non-traditional hosting purposes.

The traditional (and most accurate) definition of *multi-tenancy* is a single instance of software that services multiple organizations or clients, virtually partitioning its data and configuration, and that allows clients to work within a customized application instance. New features and capabilities delivered by SharePoint Server 2010 contribute to supporting true multi-tenant architectures that are useful not only to hosting providers, but also equally to the enterprise.

When carefully planned and applied within the enterprise, multi-tenancy is one of many solutions that contribute to reduced cost, complexity, and overall management.

Figure 22-10 shows an example of a tenant model, where an airport is an example of multi-tenancy. Note the following:

➤ The airport provides the facilities to support operations and services such as concourses and terminals.

➤ Gates are rented by each airline from the airport authority, and some airlines may rent an entire terminal building in their "hub" airport.

➤ Private companies contracted by one or more airlines at an airport provide food and beverage services to the airlines in addition to aircraft maintenance.

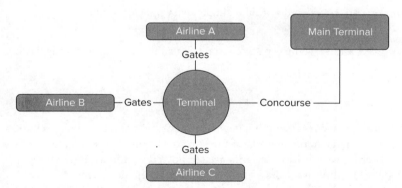

FIGURE 22-10: Tenant model example

In short, the airport authority provides the foundation to support the overall operations, and airlines are tenants of the airport authority.

Similarly, in SharePoint Server 2010, the organization provides the basic services required to support one or more solutions through SharePoint Server 2010. The IT professional creates tenants, and then delegates administrative control and routine operations to a tenant administrator, who consumes services from the core offering provided by the organization.

In SharePoint 2010, multi-tenancy is offered through several key contributing solutions:

➤ Site subscriptions

➤ Tenant administration

➤ Feature packs

➤ Partitioning

Site Subscriptions

Site subscriptions are the core of the hosting feature set in SharePoint 2010. Site collections are grouped together by their subscription ID, which forms the basis of the tenant. The subscription ID is used to map features, settings, and service partitions to tenants. In other words, site subscriptions can be loosely described as a collection of sites that subscribe to a set of service partitions, settings, and individual features. Site subscriptions are also known as *tenants*.

You can approach site subscriptions as a loose association of content. In the object model, site subscriptions are represented through `Microsoft.SharePoint.SPSiteSubscription`.

The limitations and constraints of this are as follows:

➤ Site collections grouped within a site subscription cannot span farms.

➤ Site subscriptions with site collections that span web applications cannot be managed through the Tenant Administration template. (More information about this is described next, in the section, "Tenant Administration.")

➤ Multiple site subscriptions are supported within a single web application and content database.

➤ Services can be partitioned and served to specific tenants to enable granular data isolation.

➤ Tenants can consume non-partitioned services.

Tenant Administration

The management of site subscriptions occurs through a new administration site template, Tenant Administration, which is used to manage many aspects of the site collections that consume services from their assigned subscription. Multiple tenants are supported within a single server farm environment, which enables IT administrators to centrally manage the deployment of both features and capabilities. In addition, the IT administrator can delegate specific administrative control of site collections contained within a tenant to the respective owner or business administrator.

For example, in a hosting scenario, the organization hosting the server farm environment manages farm-level settings and configurations. The consumer (or tenant) can manage the site collections, and, specifically, delegated features and capabilities (such as services). Figure 22-11 shows the Tenant Administration user interface.

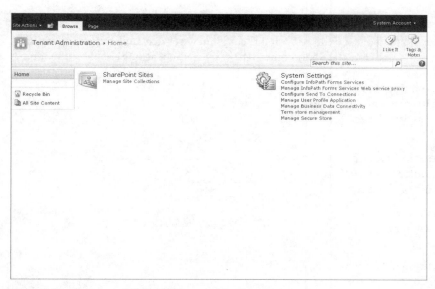

FIGURE 22-11: Tenant Administration user interface

To create a new site subscription object in SharePoint Server 2010, an administrator must create a `SPSiteSubscription` object, and then create and add an `SPSite` object to `SPSiteSubscription`.

To create a new `SPSiteSubscription` object, follow these steps:

1. Open the Microsoft SharePoint 2010 Management Shell by clicking Start ➪ All Programs ➪ Microsoft SharePoint 2010 ➪ Microsoft SharePoint 2010 Management Shell.

2. Within the Management Shell, at the command prompt, enter the following Windows PowerShell commands:

```
$subscription=New-SPSiteSubscription

$site=New-SPSite -Url http://contoso.com/sites
  /TenantAdministration -Template TenantAdmin#0
  -OwnerEmail someone@example.com
  -OwnerAlias Domain\Username
  -SiteSubscription $subscription
Set-SPSiteAdministration -Identity http://<server>/sites
  /TenantAdministration
  -AdministrationSiteType TenantAdministration
```

Feature Packs

Feature packs are a method that allows the developer to group a collection of individual features (site- or web-scoped) into a larger overall package. Feature packs are used to provide functionality or capabilities to individual site subscriptions in a multi-tenant model, enabling or preventing access to certain functionality or solutions on a tenant-by-tenant basis.

Partitioning

Data, usage, and operational isolation are provided through new service application capabilities. The capability to partition many of the SharePoint 2010 service applications enables individual and unique tenants to consume the service application, while maintaining logical separation from other tenants also consuming from the partitioned service application.

To create a new partitioned service application in SharePoint Server 2010, an administrator must follow these steps:

1. Create a partitioned Service Application using the `-partitionmode` flag.

2. Create a partitioned Service Application proxy using the `-partitionmode` flag.

Figure 22-12 shows the relationships between these concepts in a hosting model.

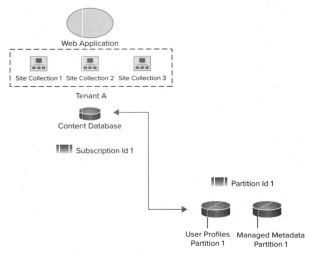

FIGURE 22-12: Subscription to partition ID mapping

SharePoint 2010 uses the Subscription ID for the site subscription to map to the Partition ID, which represents the subset of data exposed to the tenant.

The following sections describe the process for partitioning the most common service applications in a shared hosting on-premise environment.

For additional information on hosting features (including the steps for partitioning service applications not included in this chapter), refer to the "SharePoint 2010 for Hosters Guide" at `http://go.microsoft.com/fwlink/?LinkId=190783`.

Business Data Connectivity

Through a set of services and features, the Business Data Connectivity Service (BDC) in SharePoint Server 2010 provides a method to connect sources of external data and define external content types based on that data. A partitioned BDC Service can be used in scenarios where the isolation of external data connectivity is required, such as a Human Resources department that uses external data from systems such as Siebel to augment data contained in Active Directory. An organization can provide a secure collaborative environment through a partitioned BDC Service, and isolation of the Human Resources content through site subscriptions.

To learn more about the BDC Service, see Chapter 8.

Partitioning the BDC Service can be accomplished through the use of the `-PartitionMode` parameter when the service is provisioned.

To create a partitioned BDC Service application, follow these steps:

1. On the Start menu, click All Programs.

2. Click Microsoft SharePoint 2010 Products.

3. Click SharePoint 2010 Management Shell.

4. At the command prompt (PS>), enter the following:

```
$service=New-SPBusinessDataCatalogServiceApplication
  -PartitionMode
  -Name "Business Data Connectivity Service Application"
  -ApplicationPool "Business Data Connectivity Service Application Pool"
  -DatabaseName "Business_Data_Connectivity"
Get-SPServiceInstance | where-object{$_.TypeName
  -eq "Business Data Connectivity Service"} | Start-SPServiceInstance
```

Managed Metadata Service

The Managed Metadata Service in SharePoint Server 2010 is used to store a hierarchical collection of centrally managed terms defined by an organization (known as a *Term Store,* which was discussed earlier in this chapter). Terms included in the Term Store can be used as attributes for items in SharePoint Server 2010, such as documents.

Industries such as pharmaceuticals, legal, and banking and finance are commonly required to adhere to specific guidelines and regulations as related to their respective products. Combining site subscriptions and partitioning can help ensure that data integrity and isolation meet these requirements.

 To learn more about the Managed Metadata Service, see Chapter 8.

Partitioning the Managed Metadata Service can be accomplished through the use of the `-PartitionMode` parameter when the service is provisioned.

To create a partitioned Managed Metadata Service application, follow these steps:

1. On the Start menu, click All Programs.

2. Click Microsoft SharePoint 2010 Products.

3. Click SharePoint 2010 Management Shell.

4. At the command prompt (PS>), enter the following:

```
$service=New-SPMetadataServiceApplication
  -PartitionMode
  -Name "Managed Metadata Service Application"
  -ApplicationPool "Managed Metadata Service Application Pool"
```

```
   - DatabaseName "Managed_Metadata"
$proxy=New-SPMetadataServiceApplicationProxy
   -PartitionMode
   -Name "Managed Metadata Service Application Proxy"
   -ServiceApplication $service
   -DefaultProxyGroup
Get-SPServiceInstance | where($_.GetType().Name
   -eq MetadataWebServiceInstance | Start-SPServiceInstance
```

Secure Store Service

The Secure Store Service (SSS) is used to map user and group credentials to the credentials of external data sources.

 To learn more about the SSS, see Chapter 8.

Partitioning the SSS can be accomplished through the use of the -PartitionMode parameter when the service is provisioned.

To create a partitioned SSS application, follow these steps:

1. On the Start menu, click All Programs.

2. Click Microsoft SharePoint 2010 Products.

3. Click SharePoint 2010 Management Shell.

4. At the command prompt (PS>), enter the following:

```
$service=New-SPSecureStoreServiceApplication
   -PartitionMode
   -Name "Secure Store Service Application"
   -ApplicationPool "Secure Store Service Application Pool"
   -DatabaseName "Secure_Store_Service"
   -auditingEnabled:$true
   -auditlogmaxsize 30 -Sharing:$false
$proxy = New-SPSecureStoreServiceApplicationProxy
   -Name "Secure Store Service Application Proxy"
   -ServiceApplication $service
   -DefaultProxyGroup
Get-SPServiceInstance | where-object{$_.TypeName
   -eq "Secure Store Service"} | Start-SPServiceInstance
```

User Profile

The User Profile Service application stores information about users in a central location. The User Profile Service is used to drive social computing features such as My Sites, and enable features such as social tagging and newsfeeds.

To learn more about the User Profile Service, see Chapter 8.

Partitioning the User Profile Service can be accomplished through the use of the `-PartitionMode` parameter when the service is provisioned.

To create a partitioned User Profile Service application, follow these steps:

1. On the Start menu, click All Programs.

2. Click Microsoft SharePoint 2010 Products.

3. Click SharePoint 2010 Management Shell.

4. At the command prompt (PS>), enter the following:

```
$service = New-SPProfileServiceApplication
  -PartitionMode
  -Name "User Profile Service Service Application"
  -ApplicationPool "User Profile Service Application Pool"
  -ProfileDBName "Profile"
  -SocialDBName "Social"
  -ProfileSyncDBName "Synchronization"
New-SPProfileServiceApplicationProxy
  -PartitionMode -Name "User Profile Service Service Application Proxy"
  -ServiceApplication $service -DefaultProxyGroup
Get-SPServiceInstance | where-object {$_.TypeName
  -eq "User Profile Service"} | Start-SPServiceInstance
```

 *The default schema for the User Profile Service for the farm account should be configured as database owner (*dbo*). This can be accomplished using the following Transact-SQL statement on the* Profile *database:*

```
ALTER USER [<Farm Service Account>] WITH DEFAULT_SCHEMA=dbo
GO

Restart-Service SPTimerV4
$service = Get-SPServiceApplication | where-object
  {$_.Name -eq "User Profile Service Service Application"}
Get-SPServiceInstance | where-object
  {$_.TypeName -eq "User Profile Service"} | % {
    $_.Status = [Microsoft.SharePoint.Administration
      .SPObjectStatus] ::Provisioning
    $_.IsProvisioned = $false
    $_.UserProfileApplicationGuid = $service.Id
    $_.Update()
    $service.SetSynchronizationMachine($_.Server.Address,
      $_.Id, <Farm Account>, <Farm Account Password>)
    Start-SPServiceInstance $_
}

IISRESET
```

SUMMARY

Multi-tenancy in SharePoint Server 2010 is a method by which both traditional hosts and enterprises can gain value in both operation and data isolation. Properly planned and implemented, this can help reduce operating expenditures, and reduce the administrative burden on the IT professional.

For organizations seeking to expedite their deployment of SharePoint 2010, or for those with limited IT professional staffing and budget, SharePoint Online provides a rich feature set and collection of capabilities both to serve as an organization's primary collaborative platform, or to augment an organization's existing on-premise deployment to support lightweight extranet or external sharing scenarios, or optionally enable collaboration outside of that organization's firewall.

Chapter 23 describes the decision process and strategies for deploying SharePoint 2010 in a virtualized environment. These lessons supplement the many aspects of multi-tenancy that are core to delivering a SharePoint service that can both expand and contract dynamically when responding to changing business needs.

23

Designing Virtualized Deployments

By Brian Wilson

Modern organizations are increasingly using virtualization technologies and strategies to get better value from existing hardware investments.

In purely physical environments, the underlying hardware and infrastructure of your SharePoint environment predominantly does not change after your team has architected, implemented, and configured your SharePoint farm. Virtualization changes everything!

Large organizations tend to have a dedicated virtualization platform team that is responsible for a number of the organization's critical server applications. This team can have a subtle (but profound) impact on the performance of your farm. Their responsibilities involve managing, optimizing, and maintaining the virtualization infrastructure. These responsibilities include tasks such as moving virtual machines (VMs) between physical virtualization servers to increase the density of VMs hosted on the available virtualization servers.

Additionally, competing business solutions and priorities may result in the need to increase the density of the VMs on a single physical host. This has the net effect of increasing the contention for resources between VMs in your SharePoint farm, and VMs running other business solutions.

In the real world, it is not possible for the virtualization team to understand the intricacies, underlying design decisions, and future plans for each VM and virtual topology of machines hosted on physical servers under their control. For example, they may pick up a server role in your environment that has low usage, and increase the density of VMs on the physical virtualization server. Your SharePoint team may later release a new solution that takes advantage of the server role. When performance issues occur, the virtualization team may not have alternative physical hosts to decrease the VM density on physical servers that host your server role.

As a result, the SharePoint architect must have a good understanding of the underlying virtualization technology to protect your farm, to diagnose performance problems, to design for high availability, to design for disaster recovery, and to maintain, optimize, and ensure the continued performance of your SharePoint 2010 farm.

This chapter provides an overview of virtualization technologies, describes the difference between physical and virtual hardware, and takes a look at the options available for hosting VMs on-premise or in the cloud. The virtualization suitability of key SharePoint 2010 roles is discussed. The chapter provides a recommended deployment approach, followed by an example deployment scenario.

UNDERSTANDING VIRTUALIZATION

In short, *virtualization* is execution of software in an environment separated from the underlying hardware resources.

SharePoint 2010 environments benefit greatly from using virtualization technologies. Benefits include the following:

➤ *Reduce costs* — Costs can be reduced because fewer physical servers are required in a virtualized environment. Costs of energy, rack space, and upfront costs required to set up your SharePoint farm can be reduced. Virtualization technology enables your organization to get better usage from the hardware supporting your SharePoint environment.

➤ *Increased flexibility* — Virtualization technologies encourage better topology design decisions in that dedicated server roles can be supported without requiring new hardware. As your farm grows, virtual servers can be moved between physical hardware for the best fit in your environment. This results in increased operational agility in your data center.

➤ *Better infrastructure strategy* — Virtualization supports a truly dynamic data center, and enables your infrastructure team to manage physical hardware and VMs without impacting users in your environment. It enables you to grow your SharePoint 2010 environment because server roles that are not required early on can be easily added later. Virtualization provides the best SharePoint vNext strategy as your team is able to easily replicate your production environment to test upgrades. Once your upgrade is complete, the legacy VMs can be switched off, and the new SharePoint 2010 environment can be hosted on the same physical machines.

Physical machines result in higher costs to your organization that can be reduced by using a virtualization platform to host your SharePoint 2010 environments.

Microsoft Support for Virtualization

Microsoft has made an official statement of support for virtualization of SharePoint 2010 and related technologies on the Microsoft TechNet site.

See `http://technet.microsoft.com/en-us/library/ff607936.aspx` *for more information.*

The support statement makes it clear that any SharePoint 2010 environment hosted on a virtualization product that has been validated in the Microsoft's Server Virtualization Validation Program (SVVP) will continue to be supported by Microsoft.

 For more information on the list of validated virtualization products, see www `.windowsservercatalog.com/svvp.aspx.`

However, there are caveats that you must be aware of. Microsoft, and the SharePoint product group, does not test third-party virtualization products. It is the vendor's responsibility. Also, when using non-Microsoft virtualization products, those products may require issues to be reproduced independently from the third-party virtualization software. This policy is articulated in the Knowledge Base support article at `http://support.microsoft.com/kb/897615`. This will require you to demonstrate that the issue in your instance of SharePoint 2010 is not related to virtualization software.

For environments that use Microsoft Hyper-V, this is not the case, because Microsoft fully supports its own products (including SharePoint 2010) on the Hyper-V platform. In this case, you will receive full support from Microsoft, regardless of whether it is a Hyper-V issue or an issue with SharePoint 2010.

Another thing to be aware of is that Microsoft offers no support for environments that have been snapshotted. This is because snapshots can produce inconsistencies when rolling back to a previous snapshot on one of the servers in the farm (which may result in data corruption).

Types of Virtualization

As shown in Figure 23-1, a wide array of virtualization technologies is available for organizations to implement. With all these choices, SharePoint architects may find it challenging to understand which technologies should be used in SharePoint 2010 environments. This makes it difficult to recommend the appropriate virtualization solution.

From a SharePoint perspective, in the only areas of interest are server virtualization and virtualization management technologies because these are critical to hosting and support of the SharePoint 2010 environment.

Server Virtualization

As shown in Figure 23-2, with conventional computing, each physical server runs with a single operating system, which is tightly bound to the hardware. Server (hardware) virtualization breaks the tight dependency between the hardware and the operating system, and allows multiple operating systems to run on the same hardware.

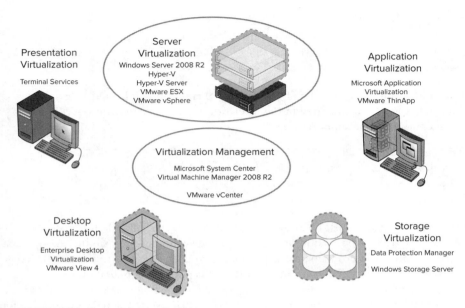

FIGURE 23-1: Types of virtualization

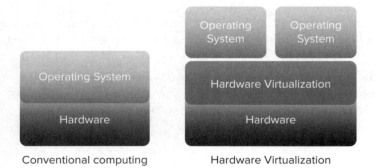

Conventional computing   Hardware Virtualization

FIGURE 23-2: Server (hardware) virtualization

The most important performance choice to make when virtualizing your SharePoint 2010 farm is whether to use a "hosted" or "bare metal" hypervisor virtualization technology to host your SharePoint farm.

➤ *"Bare metal" hypervisors* — These hypervisors are software systems (such as Windows Server 2008 R2 with Hyper-V and VMWARE ESX or V-Sphere Server) that execute directly on the host's hardware as a hardware control and guest operating system monitor. The guest operating system that hosts SharePoint software executes directly above the hypervisor.

➤ *"Hosted" hypervisors* — These hypervisors are software applications running within a conventional operating system environment, typically as a service. Examples include Microsoft Virtual Server 2005 R2 and VMWare Server. The guest operating system that hosts SharePoint software executes above the operating system, which then executes on the hardware. This results in three layers between hardware and SharePoint.

Only use "bare metal" hypervisors. *Do not use hosted hypervisors to host SharePoint 2010 VMs.* "Bare metal" technologies have fewer software layers between hardware and the guest operating system. They also perform better than "hosted" implementations, and, thus, will provide greater performance for your SharePoint 2010 farm.

Differences Between Physical and Virtual Hardware

There are subtle differences between the performance of physical and virtual hardware. This affects the performance of each virtual server in your SharePoint 2010 farm.

Table 23-1 lists the differences between physical and virtual hardware, and provides recommendations to improve the performance of your virtualization platform hosting your SharePoint 2010 environment.

TABLE 23-1: Differences between Physical and Virtual Hardware Performance

HARDWARE	PHYSICAL	VIRTUAL
CPU	A higher number of processors and multi-core processors is preferred.	Be sure you understand the difference between a virtual or logical processor versus a physical processor.
		A *physical processor* consists of a number of cores (for example, a quad-core processor equals four core processors).
		The number of virtual processors can be calculated as the number of core processors multiplied by the number physical CPUs on your physical machine. Therefore, a dual quad-core machine will provide eight virtual processors.
	Deciding between faster versus efficient processors requires understanding the hidden power consumption cost of the faster processor.	Be aware of the virtual processor limit for different guest virtual operating systems, and plan accordingly.
	Performance is governed by processor efficiency, power draw, and heat output.	Beware of "CPU bound" issues. Specifically, be aware that the capability of physical processors to process information for virtual devices will determine the maximum throughput of such a virtual device. (For example, virtual NICs use a physical CPU and NIC.)

continues

TABLE 23-1 *(continued)*

HARDWARE	PHYSICAL	VIRTUAL
	Beware of built-in processor software (such as performance throttling for thermal thresholds). This may cause unexpected performance issues during times of peak load.	
Memory	Ensure that there is sufficient memory installed on each server.	Non-uniform memory access (NUMA) may cause performance issues in your virtualization environment when memory access times to "non-local memory" take longer to complete.
	Be aware of page/swap files (disk bound) when the server is forced to use slower-performing disks as RAM.	There is a physical memory overhead to using virtual memory. Set aside enough physical memory when planning virtual host memory settings.
Disk	The disk type (for example, storage area network, or SAN), disk speed (for example, 15,000 RPM), RAID configuration, type of disk controller (for example, SCSI), and physical network (for example, SAN) all affect disk performance and throughput.	The choice of virtual disk type greatly affects the speed of the virtual disk. Virtualization technologies provide *fixed-size disks*, *dynamically expanding disks*, and *pass-through disks*. The fixed-size and pass-through disk choices are preferred over dynamically expanding disks.
	Use SCSI controllers rather than IDE controllers.	Beware of underlying disk read/write contention between different VMs to their virtual hard disks on the same underlying physical disks. Place virtual disks on a different physical disk infrastructure.
Network	Physical network interface cards (NICs), switches, and available network bandwidth affect the performance of your farm communication, as well as communication to end users of your portal environment.	Virtual network performance differs greatly based on the type of virtual network driver you use. Synthetic drivers are preferred over emulated network drivers. Synthetic drivers are more efficient, and use a dedicated VMBus to communicate to the virtual NIC. This results in lower CPU and network latency.
	Dedicate physical NICs to internal farm communication and end-user responses.	Physical NIC saturation often occurs in production environments. This produces longer response times between servers, and longer page response times for end users.
	Use Gigabit Ethernet adapters and switches.	In some cases, the bottleneck is caused by physical CPU contention. In other cases, it is caused I/O performance.

The key thing to keep in mind when planning your VM virtual hardware configurations is that you should not isolate each virtual SharePoint machine from the physical hosting environment. In some organizations, it may be that you have no access to your virtualization environment, and no control over which physical hosts are used to host your VMs. Building in a "virtualization buffer" to each VM specification you request will help to protect the performance of your SharePoint 2010 environment.

ON-PREMISE VM TECHNOLOGIES

The virtualization community has strong opinions on which virtualization technologies are the best, and which technology is actually enterprise-ready. There is a lot of religious zeal and debate focusing on the selection of the most appropriate virtualization technology for your organization.

From a SharePoint perspective, weighing all the factors, it doesn't really matter too much because the mainstream virtualization software vendors all provide mature solutions to the market. Additionally, your organization will most likely have already chosen a virtualization technology, installed the supporting software, and set up and trained a dedicated team to manage your physical and virtual infrastructure.

Therefore, unless there is a specific issue with your organization's chosen virtualization technology in the support of a SharePoint 2010 farm, you should probably avoid recommending an alternate virtualization technology, because this will require first-time setup of the hosting and supporting software technologies, ironing out of many non-technology issues (such as the training of personnel), and significant additional costs to your SharePoint project.

This section examines two mainstream solutions from Microsoft and VMWare. Although products from other vendors are not included in this discussion, you should remember that there are many other great vendors of virtualization technologies that have been validated by the Microsoft SVVP.

Microsoft Hyper-V 2008 R2

Microsoft provides a number of hosting and supporting virtualization technologies. The latest server virtualization solution to be made available is Microsoft Windows 2008 R2 Hyper-V. Supporting solutions required to use Hyper-V in an enterprise environment are Microsoft Virtual Machine Manager (VMM) 2008 R2 and the Microsoft System Center Suite.

Table 23-2 provides highlights of Microsoft Windows Hyper-V 2008 R2 and Microsoft VMM 2008 R2 products.

TABLE 23-2 Microsoft Hyper-V Software Ecosystem Highlights

HIGHLIGHT	DETAILS
Failover clustering	Failover clustering enables you to create and manage failover clusters. A *failover cluster* is a group of physical hosts that work together to increase the availability of VMs in your environment. The clustered physical hosts are connected by physical cables and software. If a physical host fails, another clustered server will begin to provide service. The end result is minimum disruption to end users because they can continue to use your SharePoint 2010 environment.
Live migration	Live migration provides the capability to move a VM from one node in a Microsoft Windows Server 2008 R2 failover cluster to another node without a perceived interruption in service by applications/clients connecting to the VM.
Cluster Shared Volumes (CSV)	CSV is a new failover clustering feature, which enables all nodes to concurrently access VM files on a single shared logical unit number (LUN). While it delivers functionality similar to a clustered file system, CSV is a Hyper-V-optimized solution. The capability to support multiple VMs per LUN greatly simplifies the creation and ongoing management of a SAN, and also allows VMs to be migrated on and off of hosts via live migration.
Quick Storage Migration (QSM)	QSM enables migration of a VM's storage both within the same host, and across hosts while the VM is running with minimum downtime.
Hot add/remove storage	This allows the addition and removal of new virtual hard disks (VHDs) and iSCSI pass-through disks running on virtual infrastructure.
Improved performance of virtual disks	The performance of both dynamic and difference disks is now at almost parity with fixed disks.
Memory management	Hyper-V Dynamic Memory is a memory-management enhancement for Hyper-V designed for production use that enables customers to achieve higher consolidation/VM density ratios by making better use of available physical host memory.
Improved network performance	Network performance has been improved to provide increased network throughput while decreasing CPU load.
Increased processor support	Hyper-V provides a greater support for the total number of physical, logical, and virtual processors in each physical host. This increases the density of VMs that can be hosted on a single physical host.

The technologies shown in Table 23-2 greatly simplify the deployment and management of the VMs hosting your SharePoint 2010 farm. A key highlight is the capability to ensure high availability. If a physical host keels over, live migration and failover clustering will ensure that your end user service is not interrupted.

Architecting virtualized SharePoint farms requires understanding not only the physical software and hardware requirements, but also the maximum supported virtual hardware configurations of Windows 2008 R2 Hyper-V, as shown in Table 23-3.

TABLE 23-3 Windows 2008 R2 Hyper-V Maximum Supported Configurations

RESOURCE	FEATURE	MICROSOFT WINDOWS 2008 HYPER-V R2
CPU	Physical processor support	Up to 8 physical processors
	Logical processor support	Up to 64
	Processors per guest	4 (depending on the chosen guest operating system)
Memory	Memory per host	32 GB (Standard license)
		2 TB (Enterprise/ data center license)
	Memory per guest	Approximately 31 GB (with Standard license)
		1 TB (Enterprise/data center license)
Networking	Networking	10 GB Ethernet adapters
		Unlimited virtual switches
		Unlimited VMs per switch
	Networking per guest	8 × synthetic
		4 × emulated
Disk	Disk — direct attached storage (DAS)	SATA, eSATA, PATA, SAS, SCSI, USB, Firewire
	Disk — SAN	iSCSI, Fiber Channel, SAS
	Disk — VHDs	Dynamically Expanding: up to 2 TB
		Fixed (up to 2 TB)
		Pass-through (no size limitation)
	Disk (virtual storage controllers)	4 × IDE
		4 × SCSI
		64 disks per controller
		256 disks per guest
		512 TB per VM

Microsoft is making giant strides in Hyper-V and its supporting technologies. It is continually breaking new boundaries of what hardware Hyper-V supports. For the latest information, see `http://technet.microsoft.com/en-us/library/ee405267(WS.10).aspx`.

VMWare ESX Server and V-Sphere

VMWare provides a number of hosting and supporting virtualization technologies. The latest server virtualization solution available is VMWare V-Sphere. However, many organizations currently use ESX Server. VMWare also provides vCenter to support VMWare production environments.

Table 23-4 provides highlights of the VMWare ecosystem of virtualization products.

TABLE 23-4: VMWare Ecosystem Highlights

HIGHLIGHT	DETAILS	
VMWare vMotion	vMotion enables the migration of VMs running any operating system across any type of hardware and storage supported by VMware ESX.	
VMWare Storage vMotion	Storage vMotion provides the capability to move a live VM from one storage device to another. It enables live migration of VM disk files between and across shared storage locations.	
VMWare Fault Tolerance	VMWare Fault Tolerance is a high-availability solution that provides continuous availability for VMs in the event of server failures. It does this by creating a live shadow instance of a VM that is in virtual lockstep with the primary instance. This allows instantaneous failover between two instances in the event of hardware failure.	
VMWare Hot Add	This capability enables the adding of CPU and memory to be added to running VMs without disruption. Additionally, NICs can be added or removed without disruption.	
VMware High Availability (HA)	VMWare HA is a business continuity solution. It monitors VMs to detect operating system and hardware failures. When a failure occurs, it restarts the VMs on other physical servers in a VMWare "resource pool" without manual intervention.	
VMware Distributed Resource Scheduling (DRS)	VMWare DRS continuously monitors utilization across a VMware resource pool, and intelligently allocates available resources among VMs.	
VMWare Backup Manager	VMWare Backup Manager manages the backup and recovery of your VMs.	

As you can see, VMWare provides a number of solutions to support a SharePoint 2010 farm. Some are similar to Hyper-V, while others are completely different. Be sure you understand the impact to your virtualized SharePoint 2010 farm.

Table 23-5 shows the maximum supported configurations for VMs hosted on VMWare ESX Server 3.5 or V-Sphere.

TABLE 23-5: VMware ESX Server 3.6 and vSphere Maximum Supported Configurations

RESOURCE	FEATURE	ESX SERVER 3.5	V-SPHERE
CPU	Physical processor support	32 core processors	64 core processors
	Logical processor support	192 virtual CPUs	512 virtual CPUs
	Processors per guest	4	8 (depending on the guest operating system)
Memory	Memory per host	256 GB	1 TB
	Memory per guest	64 GB (Enterprise/data center operating system license required)	256 GB (Enterprise/data center operating system license required)
Networking	Networking	32 × 1 GB	32 × 1 GB, 4 × 10 GB supported
		127 virtual switches	248 virtual switches
		4096 VLANS (port groups)	512 VLANS per virtual switch (port groups)
	Networking per guest	4 NICS per VM	10 NICS per VM
Disk	Disk — SAN	NFS, iSCSI, Fibre Channel	NFS, iSCSI, Fibre Channel
		VMFS-3 - 64 TB	VMFS-3 - 64 TB
			VMDirectPath
	Disk — Virtual Hard Disks	2TB virtual	2TB virtual
		Unlimited RAW (subject to operating system)	Unlimited RAW (subject to operating system)
	Disk (virtual storage controllers)	4 SCSI controllers	4 SCSI controllers

continues

TABLE 23-5 *(continued)*

RESOURCE	FEATURE	ESX SERVER 3.5	V-SPHERE
		15 devices per SCSI controller	15 devices per SCSI controller
		1 IDE controller	1 IDE controller
		4 IDE devices	4 IDE devices

> *Both Hyper-V and VMWare have guest operating system licensing implications. The licensing option you choose may limit your maximum virtual hardware configuration in either VMWare or Hyper-V. For example, if you choose the standard Windows license, the maximum physical memory supported is 32 GB. In Hyper-V, the licensing option also dictates if the guest operating systems licensing is covered by the host, or must be purchased separately.*

Decision Criterion for Selecting an On-Premise VM Technology

VMWare is a "pure play" virtualization vendor focused on providing a robust, mature, and proven toolset. The company has many years of experience in the field of virtualization, and many large organizations have been using its technology successfully for a long period of time.

Microsoft has caught up, and Microsoft Windows 2008 R2 Hyper-V and System Center Virtual Machine Manager (SCVMM) 2008 R2 are enterprise-ready. Windows 2008 has been completely redesigned to incorporate the hypervisor and Hyper-V technology. The Microsoft Office and SharePoint engineering product groups use Hyper-V in all stages of the development and testing life cycle.

From a SharePoint perspective, both do the job well:

➤ They both support the physical hardware requirements of SQL Server and SharePoint 2010.

➤ They both provide dynamic data center management software.

➤ They both provide VM and underlying storage migration capabilities that do not result in downtime to end users of your portal environment.

➤ They both provide enterprise-class availability solutions to ensure that your SharePoint 2010 farm is not impacted by physical hardware failures.

➤ Finally, both virtualization vendors have taken time to seriously optimize the performance of their competitive offerings, including many improvements to CPU, memory, network and disk management, and throughput.

Whatever virtualization technology you use, be sure to think about the effect of the shared underlying CPU, memory, network, and disk infrastructure on your SharePoint farm. Failure to do this will result in unexplained poor performance of your SharePoint 2010 farm, and frustrated end users of your SharePoint service. The resulting perception is a poorly designed and implemented solution by your SharePoint team, while the independent virtualization team gets off unscathed.

CLOUD-BASED VM HOSTING TECHNOLOGIES

Cloud-based hosting technologies enable your organization to host a SharePoint 2010 farm off-premise in an environment that your customers or employees can connect to via private or public networks. If the right hosting technology and partner is selected, this provides a lower-cost alternative to hosting on-premise.

There are many providers offering a bewildering array of options to the SharePoint architect. The most basic option of hosting VMs is through cloud-based services, such as Amazon EC2 and Windows Azure Virtual Machine Role.

The next level up includes fully hosted, managed SharePoint 2010 instances that are completely integrated into a customer's private business network and Active Directory (AD) infrastructure. These fully hosted options can scale at extremely low cost from one user to hundreds of thousands of users. Examples of these include Microsoft's current business productivity online suite (BPOS) and Microsoft's new Office 365 standard and dedicated offerings.

Additionally, there are a number of world-renowned Microsoft Certified Gold Partner hosting providers, such as `fpweb.net`. Chapter 22 discusses dedicated environments and multi-tenant options. This section is focuses only on machine virtualization options.

Windows Azure, SQL Azure, and VM Role

As of this writing, Microsoft has indicated that it does not support hosting SharePoint 2010 in Windows and SQL Azure cloud infrastructure. It fully supports shared and dedicated SharePoint 2010 environments hosted by Microsoft Online Office 365.

Microsoft does enable and support customers who are leveraging their cloud infrastructure in customer environments. For example, Windows Azure blob storage offers the capability to host large amounts of content in the cloud at very low cost. (See `www.microsoft.com/windowsazure/free-trial/sharepoint-integration/` for more information.) It is also possible to consume data from Azure web services.

> *For more information on what Microsoft provides, see* `www.microsoft.com/windowsazure/compute/default.aspx`.

It must be said that, while the VM role is new to Windows Azure, Microsoft has made significant investments in its cloud infrastructure, and is continually innovating and transforming the services it provides. While Office 365 provides the fully hosted option at great prices, let's hope Microsoft provides your organization with the "in-between" option — that is, a SharePoint 2010 infrastructure managed by your IT department, but hosted in Microsoft's Azure cloud.

Amazon Elastic Compute Cloud (EC2)

Amazon's Elastic Compute Cloud (EC2) provides a number of services in its cloud, including the following:

➤ *Rapid scalability* — Amazon promises rapid scalability and great flexibility in choice of VM instance types, operating systems, and software packages.

➤ *Persistent Storage* — Amazon provides cloud-based "off instance" persistent storage that is highly available using the Amazon Elastic Block Store.

➤ *Virtual Private Cloud* — Amazon provides a virtual private cloud to enable a bridge between your organization's existing IT network and the VM running in the cloud.

➤ *EC Compute Units* — EC Compute units are Amazon's way of "commodifying" processor performance speed. For example, 1 EC Compute unit equates to 1 virtual core and 1 physical core running at 2.6 GHz, while 20 EC Compute units equates to 8 virtual cores and 8 physical cores running at 2.4 GHz.

➤ *Virtual Machine* — Amazon's VMs use Citrix Zen virtualization technologies under the hood. Amazon provides a number of instance size options, from small to very large virtual instances containing 20 EC Compute units, 8 virtual cores, 15 GB of memory, and 1,690 GB of local instance storage on a 64-bit platform.

➤ *Virtual Machine Import* — This provides the capability to import VMs from your existing environment. This would enable you to set up your VMs on-premise and migrate them to the cloud when ready.

 More information can be found on the Amazon web services website at http://aws.amazon.com/ec2/.

A key stumbling block for most organizations is the lack of SharePoint 2010–specific information from the vendor. As of this writing, Amazon has not targeted SharePoint 2010 platform hosting as an area it is prepared to support, and no case studies on its website could be found detailing successful production deployments of medium- to large-scale SharePoint 2010 farms.

Another stumbling block is the cost of prototyping a SharePoint 2010 infrastructure in the EC2 cloud to ascertain what is feasible.

A final consideration is the support perspective. Microsoft will not support issues related to Amazon's cloud infrastructure. Microsoft has stated in Knowledge Base articles and support statements that it may require your organization to reproduce the issue in a physical environment. Therefore, if an issue occurs, how will your organization be able to reproduce it?

While this is not meant to dampen anyone's enthusiasm, hosting VMs in the cloud presents a number of known and unknown challenges for your SharePoint project. As VM hosting vendors currently stand today, given the cost and complexity, licensing, integration challenges (for example, how to crawl your Active Directory from cloud-hosted service), and troubleshooting helplessness, there are more cons than pros. This definitely requires the specialized support of the VM hosting vendor before we can all put our heads in the clouds!

UNDERSTANDING THE SHAREPOINT 2010 ROLES YOU CAN VIRTUALIZE

Although it is possible and supported to virtualize all roles in your SharePoint 2010 environment, this virtualization can differ with each deployment of SharePoint 2010. The virtualization for server roles in your SharePoint 2010 farm depends on the following factors related to your organization and SharePoint 2010 environment:

➤ *Scale of deployment* — The scale and size of your deployment and the number of physical machines or VMs affects what server roles can be virtualized.

➤ *Chosen topology* — SharePoint 2010 enables servers to operate multiple service applications on single or multiple machines. Your chosen topology will affect what server roles can be virtualized.

➤ *Usage scenarios* — Your usage scenarios will create more or less load on specific roles in your farm. Greater load requires greater performance of specific server roles in your SharePoint 2010 farm.

➤ *Underlying hardware and infrastructure* — The underlying hardware and infrastructure may result in unexpected performance issues, and this cannot be ignored in virtualized environments.

➤ *Virtualization platform* — Although each virtualization platform provides similar features, under the hood they operate differently. Ensure that you understand the common issues, as well as software and hardware constraints of the underlying virtualization platform.

➤ *Third-party software* — Third-party software installed will increase utilization of various resources required of your VMs. The servers that host the third-party software will require sufficient resources to perform their operations.

➤ *Level and types of customizations* — Customizations place additional requirements on the server resources to complete their operations in a timely manner. The amount and type of customization may influence your decision to virtualize server roles that host these customizations.

These factors should be taken into consideration when reviewing recommendations presented here. A SharePoint 2010 farm consists of a number of server roles that work together to provide a number of services to end users of your portal environment. As shown in Table 23-6, there are a number of areas to consider for each server role in your SharePoint 2010 farm.

TABLE 23-6: SharePoint 2010 Server Virtualization Role Recommendations

SERVER ROLE	VIRTUALIZATION RECOMMENDATION	CONSIDERATIONS AND REQUIREMENTS
Web	Ideal	The Web role manages the presentation layer of SharePoint 2010. It is generally more memory-intensive, depending on the number of web applications hosted in your environment.
		Other factors include dynamic compression technologies and Secure Sockets Layer (SSL) scenarios that are not terminated ahead of the web server. These may result in increased processor demands.
		From a storage perspective, the Web role is not I/O intensive. However, if your web role server hosts the Query role, and you have a large corpus of data, this can result in high disk usage when master merges and propagation occur to the Query role.
		Usage of a health service application stores usage information in blobs before they get picked up by the timer service and processed to the usage database.
		If you are using software-based load balancing (such as network load balancing), be sure to split your Web Front Ends (WFEs) over two or more physical hosts.
		Using virtualization technologies, it is easy to add additional WFE servers, and SharePoint 2010 fully supports provisioning additional WFE servers.
Query	Ideal	The Query role is responsible for maintaining a copy of the index, processing queries, and returning query result sets to the Web role.
		The Query role is an I/O read- and memory-intensive role. The Query role is CPU-intensive when combined with the Web role.
		Avoid storage contention by separating index and query component disks. Do not place these disks on the same LUN.
		SharePoint 2010 makes it easy to distribute the Query role over a number of VMs. Be sure to split these VMs into two or more hosts to protect against a failure of a physical host.
		Virtualization makes it easy to hot-add storage to support query index partition growth.

SERVER ROLE	VIRTUALIZATION RECOMMENDATION	CONSIDERATIONS AND REQUIREMENTS
Index (Crawl)	Ideal	The Index role is responsible for crawl and processing content sources, as well as maintaining its portion of the index.
		The Index role is CPU-, memory-, I/O-, and network-intensive.
		It is I/O-intensive because it writes to the crawl and property database, and maintains and continually updates a portion of the index (a query partition) on its file system.
		It's memory-, network-, and CPU-intensive in that it propagates its query partition to servers running the Query role.
		A self-crawl topology (as used in SharePoint 2007) can be used to reduce the impact of crawling activities, by enabling the Web role on the index server. *It is important that you do not add these to the network load balancer (NLB) because that would result in network traffic.*
		Ensure that you use physical or pass-through disks to optimize performance.
		It is now possible to scale out the Index (Crawl) role to multiple servers in SharePoint 2010. Additional CPU, memory, and disk space can be added as needed to VMs as your environment grows.
Application	Ideal	SharePoint 2010 supports a number of Application roles that run in the background to service requirements from the Web server role. Examples of these include Excel Calculation Services (ECS), Central Administration, web analytics, and user profiles.
		SharePoint 2010 supports and encourages a scaled-out environment. Virtualized application servers can be added to support service applications.
Database	Difficult decision	SQL Server 2005/2008 is used by SharePoint 2010 to manage complex data operations and a high number of transactions. The Database role is extremely CPU-, memory-, storage I/O-, and network-intensive.
		Microsoft fully supports virtualizing SQL Server 2005/2008.

continues

TABLE 23-6 *(continued)*

SERVER ROLE	VIRTUALIZATION RECOMMENDATION	CONSIDERATIONS AND REQUIREMENTS
		A key factor to consider is whether your organization decides to scale up versus scale out. SharePoint 2010 uses a number of application and content databases. Your organization has two options: either scale up your hardware supporting the single SQL instance, or scale out your databases over a number of SQL instances.
		In the scale-up scenario, it doesn't make sense to virtualize because you are trying to squeeze every last ounce of performance from your database layer. In the scale-out scenario, depending on the size and current performance of your farm, it may be reasonable to virtualize your SQL environment.
		A second important factor to consider is the licensing cost of multiple SQL instances. In this case, it may be more cost-effective to fully utilize the maximum performance and hardware of a single physical SQL instance, rather than multiple virtual SQL instances.
		Other key considerations include designing for high availability and redundancy. Ensure that you distribute your SQL cluster across two or more physical hosts.
		Do not virtualize half of your SQL cluster. For example, do not virtualize your passive node unless you can guarantee parity between the resources of the powerful physical (active) node and the virtual (passive) node. In the event of failure, the virtual (passive) node may not be able to cope, and your SharePoint 2010 solution will suffer or fail.

A key factor to consider across all server roles in your farm is that virtualization encourages further scale-out of your SharePoint 2010 farm more than in a physical-only environment. This implies additional operating system licensing costs for your environment.

It is critical to ensure that each server role meets the spirit of the hardware requirements detailed by Microsoft. For example, your VMs may be configured to meet or exceed the minimum requirements for the each server role in your SharePoint 2010 farm, but be hosted on physical hosts that are overburdened with other critical business applications. This could very likely cause unexpected failures or, as mentioned previously, poor unexplained performance because of bottlenecks and contention at the underlying shared hardware layers.

To safeguard against this, ensure that physical hosts and infrastructure are dedicated to your SharePoint 2010 farm. If this is not possible, ensure that Service Level Agreements (SLAs) are in place to guarantee minimum performance levels.

LOOKING AT A RECOMMENDED DEPLOYMENT APPROACH

This section concentrates on the steps you should undertake when architecting a virtualized SharePoint 2010 environment. As shown in Figure 23-3, there are four key steps in setting up a virtualized SharePoint 2010 environment:

1. Discover
2. Design
3. Deploy
4. Manage

FIGURE 23-3: Recommended deployment approach

Discover

The first step in designing your virtualized SharePoint 2010 farm is to understand where your organization is today before recommending and implementing virtualization for your SharePoint 2010 project. Discovery considerations include the following:

➤ *Where is your organization today?* — Has a virtualization platform (including the supporting technologies) been deployed in your environment? Will your project be the first major project to implement virtualization? The strategy of your IT department will also play a part in defining whether physical or VMs must be used, and the underlying virtualization technology.

➤ *What is your SharePoint project budget?* — There are a number of upfront *capital expenditure (CAPEX)* costs associated with implementing an enterprise virtualization platform. It requires "beefy" physical hardware, enterprise storage, and a network infrastructure to host your SharePoint 2010 farm, as well as the physical hardware to support the virtualization platform management software. Continuing *operational expenditure (OPEX)* costs include licensing for physical hosts and guest operating systems, and setting up and training a dedicated team to manage this virtual infrastructure.

➤ *IT maturity* — Be wary of being the first customer of a new virtualization team or infrastructure. The virtualization team will have a number of complex hardware and software issues to sort out. Additionally, *do not*, under any circumstances, deploy SharePoint 2010 to a virtual environment that has not deployed the enterprise virtualization software management tools, because this may affect the backup and availability of your SharePoint 2010 environment.

Virtualization technology adds an additional dependency and risk to manage in your SharePoint project. Ensure that you put SLAs in place to resolve issues in an environment that is outside of your SharePoint team's control.

Design

The next step is to architect and design your virtual SharePoint 2010 farm. This book provides a number of chapters that discuss detailed design considerations and recommendations based on aspects common to all SharePoint projects, and aspects specific to the scope of your SharePoint project.

 Microsoft also provides very strong technical advice and guidance in the architecture and design of physical and virtual SharePoint 2010 farms. Microsoft has set up a SharePoint 2010 virtualization resource center on Microsoft TechNet at `http://technet.microsoft.com/en-us/sharepoint/ff602849` `.aspx`. *Microsoft also provides an "Installation and Deployment" resource center at* `http://technet.microsoft.com/en-GB/sharepoint/ee518643.aspx`.

The SharePoint 2010 topology you design should take into account the unique constraints imposed by your budget, existing hardware, virtualization platform, and team. Other factors include the following:

➤ *Optimal hardware price point* — The higher the hardware specification, the greater the cost of your physical host servers. Examples of specifications that will increase your hardware cost include the form factor (chassis) of your rack server, the number of processor sockets, number of cores supported per processor, number of memory slots, and size and cost of each memory module.

➤ *Existing virtualization platform capacity* — Your virtualization team may provision some of your VMs on existing space capacity. Even though your VMs may be brand new, they will contend for resources with a number of other VMs.

➤ *Microsoft licensing costs* — The licensing decisions you make will dictate whether you implement Windows 2008 R2 Standard, Enterprise, or Data Center edition. This influences what features you can implement. For example, Windows 2008 R2 Standard license does not enable you to use failover cluster nodes, and limits your physical machine to 32 GB RAM and 4 X64 processor sockets. Other factors include the cost of licensing per processor.

You should also consider factors that affect the sizing of VMs, planning for virtualization high availability and failover, and the availability, capacity, and performance of the underlying physical, storage, and network infrastructure.

The remainder of this section provides specific guidance for you to use when designing your virtual SharePoint 2010 environment. As shown in Table 23-7, some of these steps are required, regardless of whether the environment is physical or virtual.

TABLE 23-7: Key Steps to Design a Virtualized SharePoint 2010 Environment

STEP	CONSIDERATIONS AND REQUIREMENTS
Plan your information and solution architecture	The logical topology requires a detailed information-and-solution architecture to derive the SharePoint 2010 features of your SharePoint 2010 environment.
	Refer to Chapters 11, 12, and 13 for detailed guidance on getting started with your project, and designing your SharePoint 2010 information-and-solution architecture.
Plan logical and physical topology	The logical and physical topology describes the layout of various components of your SharePoint 2010 farm (for example, which servers will host and operate service applications).
	Refer to Chapter 9 for detailed guidance on SharePoint 2010 platform architectures.
	Refer to Chapter 14 for detailed guidance on designing the logical and physical topology of your SharePoint 2010 farm.
	Microsoft provides detailed logical architecture planning guidance at `http://technet.microsoft.com/en-gb/library/ff829836.aspx`, as well as example server farms and topologies at `http://technet .microsoft.com/en-gb/library/cc263157.aspx`.
Estimate capacity and performance	Refer to Chapter 14 for detailed guidance on estimating the capacity and performance requirements of your SharePoint 2010 farm. This is critical to deciding on the minimum infrastructure that is required to meet your capacity and performance requirements.
	Microsoft provides detailed performance and capacity management guidance at `http://technet.microsoft.com/en-gb/library/cc262971.aspx`.
Decide which servers to virtualize	Using the logical and physical topology, decide which server roles can be virtualized. Base this on the server role recommendations in this chapter, testing and prototyping in your environment, and Microsoft virtualization recommendations at `http://technet.microsoft.com/en-gb/library/ ff607811.aspx`.
Plan your VM hardware	Plan the virtual hardware required for each server role that you decide to virtualize.
	Factor in the minimum hardware requirements of SharePoint 2010 (`http:// technet.microsoft.com/en-gb/library/cc262485.aspx`) and your minimum performance and capacity requirements.
	Balance your VM design against the cost and hardware specifications of the physical hosts required.

continues

TABLE 23-7 *(continued)*

STEP	CONSIDERATIONS AND REQUIREMENTS
Plan physical virtualization server topology	Plan which physical hosts will host each VM of your SharePoint 2010 farm.
	Ensure that either your team or the virtualization team reserve a percentage of the physical machine's CPU resources.
	Ensure that your underlying network and disk infrastructure is optimal. For example, a common read/write performance issue is the storing of multiple VM disks on the same LUN.
	Although most virtualized technologies provide "baked in" high-availability and failover solutions, insist on and ensure that key server roles are split across multiple physical hosts. This spreads the load on the underlying network and disk infrastructure across physical hardware, and ensures that your environment will continue to provide service to end users of your farm in the event of physical host hardware and/or virtualization live migration failure.
	Plan VM affinity settings. These govern which physical host VMs will fail over to in the event of a physical host hardware failure.
Plan business continuity	From a SharePoint perspective, refer to Chapter 21 for detailed guidance on planning business continuity of your SharePoint 2010 farm.
	From a virtualization perspective, virtualization technology provides features that enable live migration or vMotion of VMs to passive nodes in the event of failure of a physical virtualization server.
	Each virtualization vendor has specific guidance on enabling these features. If enabled, correctly configured, and enough capacity is available, it will appear to the SharePoint farm as if nothing happened!

Deploy

Once you have designed your physical and virtual SharePoint 2010 farm, the next stage is to set up, configure, and deploy these VMs on the underlying virtualization platform infrastructure. As with any large-scale project, there are a number of steps that precede the deployment of the VMs to your production virtualization environment:

1.   *Pilot/proof of concept* — Regardless of whether virtualization technologies are new or mature in your organization, both scenarios will benefit from a proof-of-concept virtual SharePoint 2010 environment. This environment is typically a temporary environment that can be used to design, test, and recommend the most appropriate design for your organization. This environment also enables your SharePoint architect to test the effects of specific vendor technologies (such as live migration or failover clustering). The end result is a design

that proves the various technologies work together, and helps both the virtualization and SharePoint teams cross-pollinate infrastructure knowledge.

2. *Virtualization platform preparation* — The next stage is procuring any additional hardware, and installing and configuring the hardware and supporting virtualization management software. Then, install, prepare, place, and configure the VMs on your virtualization platform.

3. *SharePoint installation and configuration* — Once the virtualization team hands over the VMs, the SharePoint team can begin the installation of software required to operate SharePoint 2010.

4. *Production performance testing and baselining* — A critical activity to perform is the performance testing of the base installation of your virtual SharePoint environment. This enables you to optimize the environment and create a performance baseline that can be referred to when end-user customizations are deployed.

5. *Transition to production* — Be sure that both the SharePoint and virtualization teams have clear responsibilities to ensure smooth running of your SharePoint farm. Put the appropriate governance rules in place, with appropriate escalation paths to resolve issues and disputes.

In the real world, especially in large SharePoint 2010 projects, factor in time and sufficient manpower to enable both your virtualization and SharePoint teams to work together in the preparation of various environments that are required. These environments include the development environments, test and user acceptance testing environments, pre-production, and production environments. This will not happen overnight.

Manage

Many large organizations use a dedicated team to manage their virtualized infrastructure. Because SharePoint 2010 infrastructure can scale out over many servers, having a close working relationship with the virtualization team can greatly reduce the time it takes to optimize the performance of your SharePoint 2010 environment. Following are key areas to optimize:

➤ *Physical host machine management* — Each physical host machine contains a number of VMs that demand resources. It is imperative that the combined demand of all VMs on each physical server is understood. For each physical machine, average and peak load usage of each physical resource must be understood to avoid hardware bottlenecks.

➤ *VM management* — Each VM should be monitored and managed using the virtualization vendor's supporting software. Additionally, Microsoft System Center Operations Manager (SCOM) provides a management pack to monitor all SharePoint 2010 products. This includes monitoring all events, collecting performance counters in a central location, and raising alerts for operator intervention to proactively prevent issues before they occur. This two-layered approach enables your virtualization team to manage the "box" and your SharePoint team to manage the "application."

➤ *Physical and virtual resource management* — Each VM can be optimized to improve its performance and protect the intensity of its resource usage.

➤ *Underlying storage infrastructure* — VMs support a number of disk types, including fixed-sized, dynamic disks, and pass-through disks. A number of factors contribute to the increased performance of your VMs. These include factors such as the chosen storage solution, connectivity to storage, and specific intentional placement of virtual disks in your storage solution.

➤ *Network infrastructure* — Managing your physical and virtual network infrastructure in your SharePoint 2010 environment is quite a challenge to maintain. The behavior of your network will change based on a number of factors, including average and peak load conditions, the placement of VMs, "business-induced" (for example, leadership communication) load conditions, and a number of other factors.

It is important that your organization either embeds dedicated SharePoint infrastructure skills in the virtualization team, or dedicated virtualization skills in the SharePoint team. Failure to do so may result in little or no communication and indecisiveness on the most appropriate physical and virtual hardware optimization strategies. In some cases, this results in no one taking full responsibility for the continued performance of your SharePoint 2010 infrastructure.

AN EXAMPLE DEPLOYMENT SCENARIO

This section discusses a sample large SharePoint 2010 production environment. The example scenario is intended to draw out principles and guidelines, and should not be interpreted as presenting hard-and-fast rules.

> *Microsoft provides a number of deployment models for virtualized SharePoint 2010 farms. These include models spanning evaluation and pilot environments, to full-scale production environments. These models are available to view and download at* www.microsoft.com/downloads/details.aspx?FamilyID=87f00 c5d-1f62-4d3f-ac92-b91eb70d317e.

This section makes the following assumptions about your organization's virtualization environment:

➤ The supporting virtualization platform hardware and software has already been installed, and is available to support your SharePoint 2010 deployment.

➤ The supporting technologies (such as AD, application monitoring, and Forefront for SharePoint Antivirus software) are available (and are correctly sized) to support your SharePoint 2010 environment.

➤ Your virtualization team will exploit high-availability virtualization technologies to protect your SharePoint 2010 VMs against hardware failure in your primary data center.

➤ Large organizations almost always standardize virtualization hardware specifications because this reduces procurement and support costs. Therefore, in the models presented here, one "low" hardware specification is used, consisting of dual quad-core processors

(8 logical processors) and 32 GB RAM. It is conceivable that your organization has much larger virtualization server specification. However, this will be at much greater cost to your organization.

➤ This section does not provide for disaster recovery scenarios outside of your primary data center (for example, business continuity scenarios where your primary data center is not available, and your organization must failover to a secondary business continuity failover data center).

A final and important assumption is that SharePoint 2010 is not the first and only customer of your virtualization environment. To support organizations getting the best value from their virtualization infrastructure, non-SharePoint 2010 VMs should be hosted on physical hosts that have free capacity. This enables you to plan for redundancy across multiple physical hosts, regardless of the farm size.

As shown in Figure 23-4, the large farm topology described in this section is based on large physical farm topologies recommended by Microsoft as part of its deployment topology models. Microsoft's physical model is a good reference point to gauge what you may need for your virtualized SharePoint 2010 farm.

The following virtualization characteristics are shown in Figure 23-4:

➤ *Web role* — The Web role VMs are load-balanced and made highly available by distributing these VMs over four physical virtualization hosts.

➤ *Query role* — The Query role VMs are hosted on each Web server role and made highly available by distributing this role over four physical virtualization hosts. SharePoint 2010 makes it easy to ensure that each index partition is highly available.

➤ *Crawl role* — The Crawl application role VMs are provided with 16 GB RAM and four virtual processors. More than one physical virtualization server is used to host this role. SharePoint 2010 makes it easy to scale out Crawl role VMs as more processing capacity is required.

➤ *Central Administration roles* — The Central Administration role is hosted on two application servers to ensure that the farm can be administered in the event of a physical virtualization server failure.

➤ *Application role* — Six VMs are provided with different starting point virtual processor and memory configurations. Figure 23-4 does not explicitly specify the exact service applications on each VM. The reason for this is that each organization's requirements will dictate the service applications required, and this will determine the computing resources required to run these service applications on each application role VM.

➤ *Database role* — Two physical database clusters support search and content database loads of the farm. While it is possible to virtualize this layer (and Microsoft does encourage and support the virtualization of SQL Server), large farm scenarios will benefit most from a physical instance of SQL Server.

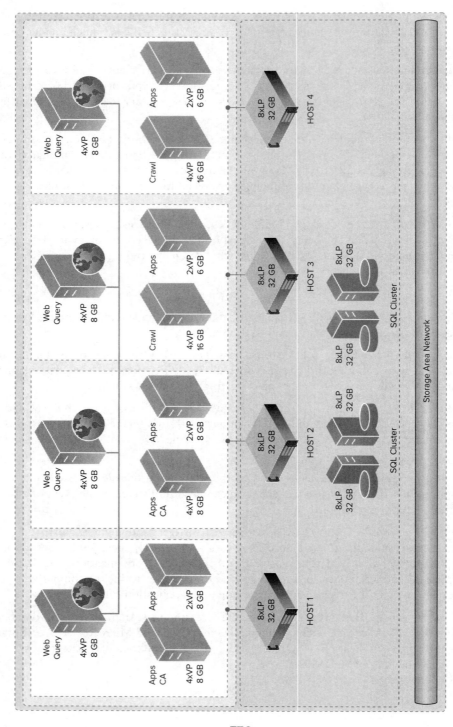

FIGURE 23-4 Large virtualized SharePoint 2010 farm example

Microsoft recommends a 1:1 ratio between logical and virtual processors. In this example, there is a slight over-commitment in an 8:10 ratio between logical and virtual processors. This is difficult to get perfect at the design stage because it depends on the production environment.

 For more information on capacity planning regarding SharePoint 2010, see `http://technet.microsoft.com/en-us/library/ff758645.aspx.`

BEST PRACTICES

The following are best practices to follow when designing virtualized SharePoint 2010 deployments:

➤ *Don't let governance slip in your virtualized SharePoint environment* — Apply the same rigor and change control processes to your virtual farm as you would a physical farm. Review and ensure that change control processes are in place and followed to protect your virtual SharePoint farm.

➤ *Beware of over-subscribing host servers* — It is easy to underestimate how load will increase over time on each of your guest machines, and cumulatively on each of your host servers. This problem is often caused by squeezing virtual servers in to temporarily meet short-term business objectives when no budget is available to purchase hardware. This is dangerous, not only for SharePoint 2010, but for all the VMs running in your SharePoint 2010 farm.

➤ *Host is a single point of failure* — If your host server dies, all VMs will fail as well. To overcome this, load-balance SharePoint 2010 server roles across physical virtualization servers. Use built-in failover clustering features and shared cluster storage volumes to ensure efficient and automatic failover of VMs between physical host servers.

➤ *Understand your virtualization vendor feature set* — Don't let a failure be the first time you actually use features such as a live migration or vMotion. For example, a live migration or vMotion failure may occur if your underlying physical virtualization servers use different CPU processor families. Test these features in a multi-machine SharePoint 2010 pre-production environment before using them in your live production environment.

➤ *Sometimes more is less* — Microsoft recommends that you maintain a 1:1 mapping between logical processors to virtual processors. The reason is that the hypervisor must swap out context for each virtual processor that is allocated to a VM.

➤ *Do not use snapshots* — Microsoft does not support snapshotting of individual SharePoint servers because the state stored in a snapshot may be incompatible with the rest of the farm. (Think of the effect of snapshotted timer jobs or crawl index propagation running on a SharePoint server.)

➤ *CPU* — Use the latest CPU generations, with as many cores as you can afford. In Hyper-V and VMWare, consider reserving and allocating minimum CPU resources.

➤ *Memory* — Don't forget to factor in physical memory overhead when calculating how many VMs a physical host can support. At all costs, avoid situations where the physical virtualization server must swap to page file!

➤ *NUMA memory boundaries and VM performance* — Non Uniform Memory Access (NUMA) is a memory design that controls how multiple processors work with RAM on the virtualization server. Each processor has local memory assigned, and access is faster to local memory than foreign (non-local) memory. The virtualization implication to your SharePoint 2010 environment is that you can assign memory to a VM that causes the hypervisor (and the underlying physical processor) to address memory in non-local memory. This reduces the performance of the VM. NUMA memory boundaries are calculated by dividing total physical memory by the number of logical processors. For example, a 64 GB RAM virtualization server with dual-quad core (which equates to 8 logical processors) results in NUMA boundaries at 8 GB RAM.

➤ *Disk* — I/O requires the most amount of planning to ensure that high Input Output Operations Per Second (IOPS) are maintained by your underlying disk infrastructure. Fewer spindles in virtual environments compared to physical environments will result in lower IOPS.

➤ *Network* — Dedicate multiple physical and virtual NICS to specific traffic types in your farm.

➤ *Availability* — Planning for high availability in a virtualized environment requires more consideration than in a purely physical environment. Consider affinity settings for redundant roles that should never reside on the same physical host.

➤ *Management and support software* — Do not use virtualization technology in environments that have not deployed the appropriate management suites and monitoring agents.

SUMMARY

Virtualization enables your organization to reduce costs, consolidate equipment, and take greatest advantage of hardware resources. It provides increased flexibility to grow and scale out your SharePoint 2010 farm, and enables the long-term dream of a truly dynamic data center where compute resources of your organization are continually put to best use.

Microsoft fully supports virtualized SharePoint 2010 environments, and provides detailed guidance to help SharePoint architects make the right design decisions during the life cycle of a virtualized SharePoint 2010 deployment.

Chapter 24 discusses intranet and internet Web Content Management (WCM) features provided by SharePoint 2010, and how you can use them to develop public-facing or internal-facing publishing sites.

PART IV
Real-World Service Design Considerations

24

Intranet and Internet Publishing Services

By Hugo Esperanca

Intranet and Internet publishing services form the foundation and core of any portal solution. They provide a starting point for a business to promote itself, and to share and publish information.

A corporate intranet is the new shopping window of a company. It allows users to interact and find out more about the products and services that the company offers, and it's one of the main channels for converting users into customers.

SharePoint 2010 enables you to build rich and interactive intranet and Internet sites without the headache of having to build all the "plumbing" from scratch. It provides a mature set of Web Content Management (WCM) tools and templates that empowers business users to take ownership of their content without having to rely on technical resources.

This chapter provides an overview of the WCM tools provided by SharePoint 2010, and how you can use them to build intranet or Internet sites.

In this chapter, you learn about the following:

➤ What out-of-the-box publishing functionality is provided by SharePoint via its publishing Features.

➤ What options are available for branding intranet and Internet sites, and what tools are provided to support each option.

➤ What tools SharePoint provides to create, manage, and publish content.

➤ How to create multi-language sites.

➤ How to plan your site navigation.

➤ How to deploy a site to different environments.

SHAREPOINT 2010 PUBLISHING FEATURES

SharePoint 2010 is an excellent web publishing platform that facilitates and enables most of the activities identified in other chapters in this book. The core of this functionality is provided by two Features:

➤ SharePoint Server Publishing Infrastructure Feature

➤ SharePoint Server Publishing Feature

The SharePoint Server Publishing Infrastructure Feature

The SharePoint Server Publishing Infrastructure Feature provides publishing functionality at the site collection level. Figure 24-1 shows the main artifacts and Features that are made available when the SharePoint Publishing Infrastructure Feature is activated.

The SharePoint Server Publishing Feature

The SharePoint Server Publishing Feature provides publishing functionality at the site level. Figure 24-2 shows the main artifacts and Features made available when the SharePoint Server Publishing Feature is enabled.

SharePoint Publishing Sites

SharePoint Publishing sites are SharePoint sites where the Publishing Features have been activated. By default, SharePoint comes with two site templates, where the publishing Features have been preconfigured:

➤ *Publishing Portal* — This is often used for the Internet and top-level intranet sites where the Publishing Activities are normally delegated to a small group of business users.

➤ *Enterprise Wiki* — This is normally used in a highly collaborative environment where most users will have permissions to edit and publish content.

BRANDING PUBLISHING SITES

Branding is the process of creating a name, symbol, or design to create a corporate image to identify or differentiate an organization. It uses a combination of colors, slogans, symbols, logos, and fonts to create a corporate identity.

When thinking about branding a SharePoint site, you have two options:

➤ *Simple branding* — This uses out-of-the-box master pages, and makes extensive use of the Microsoft Office theme infrastructure that is now supported by SharePoint 2010. This is the cheaper and lower-risk option, and does not require any development effort.

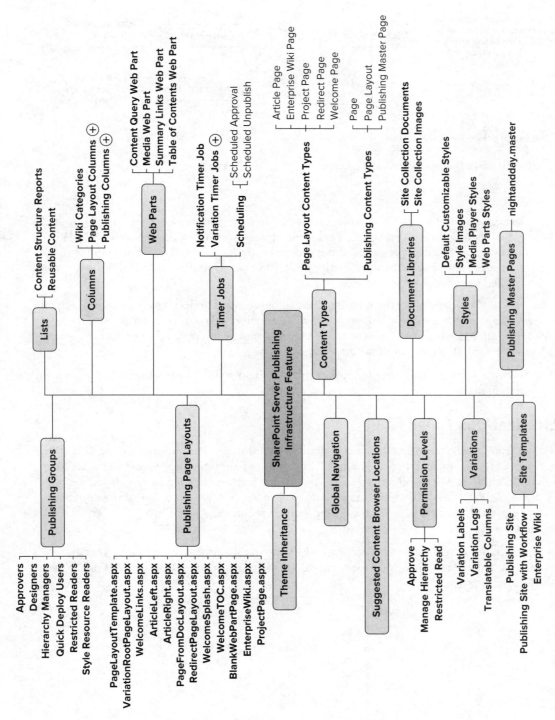

FIGURE 24-1: SharePoint Server Publishing Infrastructure Feature

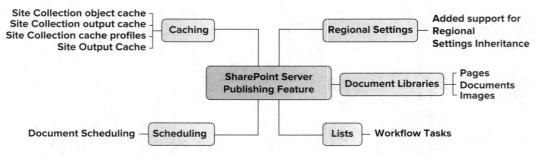

FIGURE 24-2: SharePoint Server Publishing Feature

> ➤ *Advanced branding* — This involves the creation of custom master pages, page layouts, and cascading style sheets (CSS). This is the most powerful option that will give you the biggest range of customizations. But it's also the higher risk, and is the most expensive of the options, because it involves development effort, and requires technical resources with detailed knowledge of SharePoint.

The one you use will depend on the requirements, resources, and budget available to you. Perhaps for internal sites, where the corporate branding rules are more relaxed, you can go with the first option. After all, Microsoft has invested much time and money to create a better user experience with SharePoint 2010, so why not take advantage of that?

This section takes you through the concepts required to help you understand what is involved with each of these options.

Simple Branding

Creating themes for SharePoint 2007 was a cumbersome process that required editing CSS style sheets and XML files located in the "12 hive," and required administrator access to the server. For SharePoint 2010, Microsoft adopted the same theme framework used by the Office client applications since Office 2007. This means that creating a new theme now is a simpler process that can be carried out by a non-technical user without requiring a single line of CSS code. And the new theme can be deployed via a browser.

For simpler branding requirements, users can select one of the out-of-the-box themes, and customize the colors and fonts using the new Site Theme page (Figure 24-3), which is accessible via the Site Settings page.

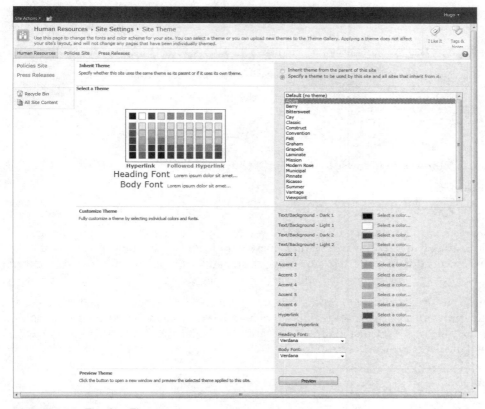

FIGURE 24-3: The Site Theme page

Creating a New Theme

Because SharePoint 2010 now uses the same framework theme as the Office client applications, users can create themes using PowerPoint, Excel, and Word. Microsoft has also created a standalone Theme Builder application that you can download from `http://connect.microsoft.com/themebuilder`.

When you use any of the tools to create a new theme, you get a `.thmx` file containing the 12 colors and the 2 fonts used by headings and body, as shown in Figure 24-3.

Deploying a New Theme

Themes live in a special document library called Theme Gallery within the SharePoint site. To deploy a new theme, you must place your newly created `.thmx` file in this Gallery. You have two ways to deploy a theme to the Theme Gallery:

➤ Manually via the SharePoint user interface (UI)

➤ Using the SharePoint Feature framework

Once the theme is in the Gallery, you can then use the Site Theme page to select it and customize it further if required.

You can deploy a new theme to a SharePoint site using the UI by simply following these steps:

1. Navigate to the Site Theme page (accessible via the Site Settings page).

2. Click the Theme Gallery link on top of the page.

3. Click the Documents tab.

4. Click Upload Document.

5. Click Browse and browse to the .thmx file that you want to upload.

6. Click OK.

7. Click Save.

Manual deployment is an acceptable solution when you only need to deploy the theme to a site collection that is already live. If you are creating a new SharePoint site that must be deployed to different environments (for example, test, acceptance test, and live), or if you must deploy the theme to more than one live site collection, you will be better off using the SharePoint Feature framework.

To deploy a theme using a SharePoint Feature, you must create a Feature that is scoped at the site level (as opposed to web) with an `elements.xml` file containing a `Module` element. Here is an example of the `elements.xml` file with the Collaborative Application Markup Language (CAML) required to deploy a theme called `MyNewTheme.thmx`:

```xml
<?xml version="1.0" encoding="utf-8" ?>
<Elements xmlns="http://schemas.microsoft.com/sharepoint/">
  <Module Name="CustomThemes" Url="_catalogs/theme" RootWebOnly="TRUE">
    <File Url="MyNewTheme.thmx" Type="GhostableInLibrary">
    </File>
  </Module>
</Elements>
```

 For detailed information on the SharePoint Feature framework, check out the MSDN documentation at http://msdn.microsoft.com/en-us/library/ms460318.aspx.

How Themes Work

It's very interesting to see how themes work behind the scenes. The new SharePoint 2010 theming engine generates styles dynamically when a new theme is activated, instead of layering them on top of the default styles like it used to do it with SharePoint 2007.

SharePoint 2010 stores all the default CSS files, used by each theme, under the SharePoint root folder, `{SharePoint root}\TEMPLATE\LAYOUTS\[language]\STYLES\Themable`. If you open one of the styles in that directory, you will notice most style declarations are preceded with a comment.

Here is an example extracted from `corev4.css`, one of the default style sheets provided with SharePoint 2010:

```
a.ms-toolbar:hover{
    text-decoration:underline;
    /* [ReplaceColor(themeColor:"Accent1",themeShade:"0.8")] */
    color:#005e9a;
}
```

Notice the `ReplaceColor` token inside of the comments. When you apply a theme to a site, SharePoint creates a copy of this CSS file and replaces the value of the CSS markup (immediately following the comment) with one of the 12 colors specified in the Site Theme page, as shown in Figure 24-3. SharePoint then appends a unique identifier to the end of the new CSS filename and copies the file to a hidden folder under the Theme Gallery.

The best way to understand this process is to look at the CSS link tag of a page without a theme applied (which is the default option when you create a new Publishing site):

```
<link rel="stylesheet" type="text/css"
    href="/_layouts/1033/styles/
    Themable/corev4.css?rev=iIikGkMuXBs8CWzKDAyjsQ%3D%3D"/>
```

Now, compare that with the CSS link tag of a page where a theme has been applied (in this case, the Azure theme):

```
<link rel="stylesheet" type="text/css"
    href="/sites/hr/_catalogs/theme/
    Themed/1386CE2C/corev4-8A0ABD2F.css?ctag=5"/>
```

As you can see, in this case, SharePoint created a new style sheet file called `corev4-8A0ABD2F.css` and saved it under `_catalogs/theme/Themed/1386CE2C/`.

If you open this file and compare it to the original un-themed file, you will see how SharePoint used the replacement technique, as shown in Figure 24-4.

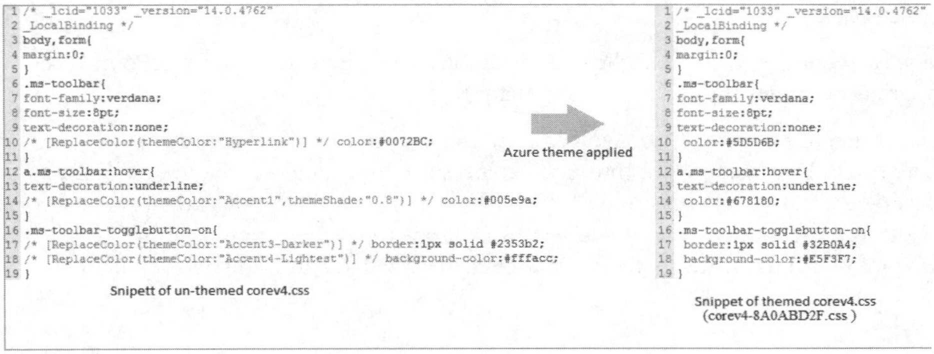

FIGURE 24-4: Comparing un-themed and themed corev4.css files

The SharePoint theming engine supports the following tokens:

➤ `ReplaceColor` — This replaces colors such as font colors and backgrounds with one of the 12 colors chosen on the Site Theme page.

➤ `ReplaceFont` — This replaces the fonts with one of the two fonts chosen on the Site Theme page.

➤ `RecolorImages` — This recolors images using one of three methods (blend, tint, and fill).

 For a detailed overview of the SharePoint 2010 theming engine, have a look at the blog post on the Microsoft SharePoint Designer Team blog at `http://blogs.msdn.com/b/sharepointdesigner/archive/2010/04/09/working-with-the-sharepoint-theming-engine.aspx`.

Custom Styles

There will be occasions when you must take your branding a step further and make some changes that are not supported by themes. In these situations, you might be tempted to tweak the out-of-the-box core styles. After all, the files are already there, so you would not need to worry with all the deployment stuff… right?

Wrong! Under no circumstances should you alter the out-of-the-box SharePoint styles. Imagine if Microsoft releases a service pack that changes some of those styles (for example, to fix bugs). You would find yourself in one of the following situations:

➤ If you made your changes using SharePoint Designer, your CSS files would be customized, and would be loaded from the content database instead of the filesystem, which means that you will never see the changes made by the service pack.

➤ In the worst-case scenario, if you made the changes directly on the filesystem, you would lose them altogether, because they will be overridden by the new CSS files deployed by the service pack.

The supported way to change (or tweak) the out-of-the-box styles provided by SharePoint is to create a CSS file that overrides the styles that you want to change.

To find out what styles you must override, you can use the developer tools that are part of Internet Explorer (press F12 inside of an Internet Explorer browser window). Figure 24-5 shows an example of using the developer tools to find the name of the class that applies the background style to the page status bar. In this case, if you want to change the background used by the status bar, you would need to create a CSS file that overrides the background style defined by the `s4-status-s1` class.

FIGURE 24-5: Internet Explorer developer tools

After creating your custom CSS file, you must deploy and register it with SharePoint. On a Publishing site, the recommended location to store CSS files and style images is in a special document library called the Style Library created by the Publishing Features on the root of a site collection.

The Style Library has two themable locations:

➤ `/Style Library/Themable` — This is for language-agnostic styles.

➤ `/Style Library/[language]/Themable` — This is for language-dependent styles.

Placing your styles in these locations (or any subfolder) makes them visible to the SharePoint theming engine, which enables you to use the tokens described earlier to make the colors and fonts configurable using the Site Theme page.

Images used by the CSS styles should also be saved to the Style Library in the `Images` folder.

It's a good practice to create a folder with the product or organization name to keep all your CSS styles and images clearly separated from the out-of-the-box ones.

After deploying your custom CSS styles to the Style Library, you must register them with SharePoint. You can do this in two ways:

➤ Register the style as an Alternate CSS style

➤ Register the style in the master page using the `CssRegistration` control

The first option is the easiest, has lower risk associated with it, and it does not require code. To do this, you can navigate to the Site Master Page Settings page (by following the Master Page link under the "Look and Feel" section of the Site Settings page), and provide the URL for where your CSS file is located under the Alternate CSS URL section, as shown in Figure 24-6.

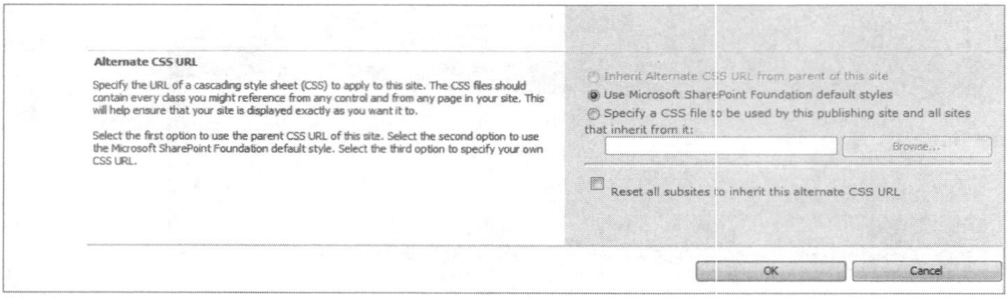

FIGURE 24-6 The Alternate CSS URL section of the Master Page settings page

SharePoint will ensure that the file indicated here will be the last CSS file loaded, which is how it enables you to override any of the out-of-the box styles.

Registering the style in the master page is a bit more complicated because it requires code changes to the master page used by the site collection. To implement this option, you must use the CssRegistration control (part of the Microsoft.SharePoint.WebControls namespace) inside the page header tag. For example, to register a CSS file called CustomStyles.css, you would add the following entry to the master page:

```
<SharePoint:CssRegistration runat="server"
    name="<%SPUrl:~sitecollection/Style Library/~language/Themable/
    CustomStyles.css %>" After="corev4.css"/>
```

The advantage of this option is that it will stop users from inadvertently changing the look and feel of your site by changing the settings on the Site Master Page Settings page. Another advantage is that it allows you to register more than one master page file.

> For those who are used the previous version of this control in SharePoint 2007, you will notice that there is new property called After that allows you to specify the name of the CSS file, after which the file being registered is rendered. In the example provided, you want the link to the CustomStyles.css to be rendered after the link to the corev4.css styles. This is a substantial improvement over the previous version, where the links were rendered in alphabetical order, which forced you to name the CSS files starting with z to ensure that they were rendered after all the other styles. That's why you see many custom CSS files created for SharePoint 2007 with names starting with z_ or z9_ and so on.

Advanced Branding

This section examines some advanced topics related to branding.

Master Pages

The new theming engine functionality in SharePoint 2010 is a big improvement over SharePoint 2007. Using the Microsoft Office tools that they are already familiar with, non-technical users can modify the colors and fonts of a site in minutes. However, for more-demanding use cases that require full control of the layout of pages and all of its content, you still need to use the master pages.

Master pages are a concept introduced in ASP.NET to help standardize the look and feel of a website. Master pages contain controls and styles that are shared across pages of a site, and normally contain the following artifacts:

➤ Global navigation elements (which normally includes the top navigation menu, breadcrumbs, footer menu, and so on)

➤ Branding artifacts (such as corporate logos and colors)

➤ Client-side scripts (that is, Java scripts) shared by all the pages

➤ Shared CSS files

➤ Shared web controls (such as search)

SharePoint stores all the master pages in a special hidden document library called Master Page Gallery. Whenever a new Publishing site is created, SharePoint automatically populates this Gallery with the following four master pages:

➤ `v4.master`

➤ `default.master`

➤ `minimal.master`

➤ `nightandday.master`

The `v4.master` is the main master page used by SharePoint for application pages and team sites. This is also the default master page used by SharePoint when it provisions an Enterprise Wiki Publishing site, as shown in Figure 24-7.

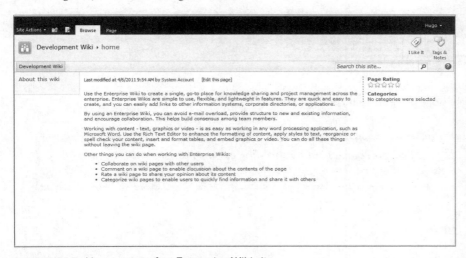

FIGURE 24-7: Home page of an Enterprise Wiki site

The `default.master` master page is primarily used for backward compatibility with SharePoint 2007. By default, when a site is upgraded from SharePoint 2007 to 2010, SharePoint will link the upgraded pages to `default.master` instead of the new `v4.master`. This ensures that the user experience and the look and feel of the upgraded site do not change.

The `minimal.master` is used by SharePoint for pages with a minimal amount of chrome and no global navigation. This master page is used by several of the standard site page templates, such as the Search Center.

For Publishing sites, SharePoint provisions an additional master page called `nightandday.master`. This master page was created specifically to support WCM functionality, and contains controls that are specific to WCM. This is the default master page used by Publishing portal sites, as shown in Figure 24-8.

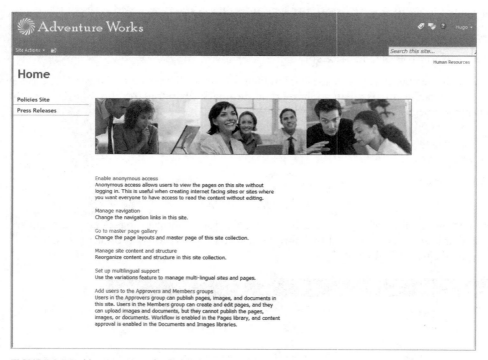

FIGURE 24-8: Home page of a Publishing portal site

 For details on all controls provided by this master page, see the MSDN page at `http://msdn.microsoft.com/en-us/library/ff625186.aspx`.

When choosing the master pages to be used on a Publishing site, you have the option to choose a different master page for content-managed pages and for application pages:

➤ *Site Master Page* — Used by all content-managed pages on the site.

➤ *System Master Page* — Used by application pages (that is, configuration and administration pages).

When the Publishing Features are activated, this configuration is available via a new link called *Master Page*, created in the Site Actions page, as shown in Figure 24-9.

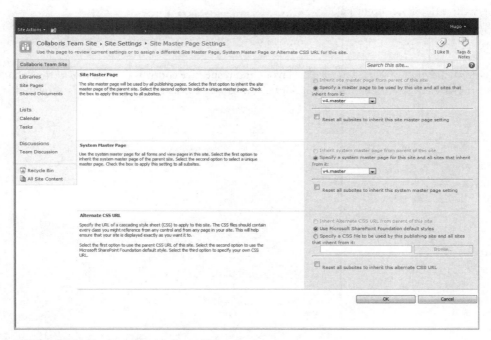

FIGURE 24-9: Master page configuration page

Page Layouts and Publishing Pages

A *page layout* is an ASP.NET page that is used by SharePoint to control what content is displayed, as well as how it is displayed. Think of a page layout as a page template that contains content placeholders that can be used when creating content-managed pages.

SharePoint stores page layouts in the Master Page Gallery of the top-level site in the site collection. When the SharePoint Server Publishing Infrastructure Feature is activated, a series of page layouts are automatically added to this Gallery. You can use any of these page layouts in your content-managed pages, or you can create your own layout using Visual Studio or SharePoint Designer.

Page layouts are always associated with a content type that defines the available metadata fields and their respective types. Given that most content-managed pages on a site share a core set of metadata fields (such as name, title, comments, and so on), they all tend to be associated with content types that derive from the System Page content type, which is provisioned when the SharePoint Server Publishing Infrastructure Feature is activated.

Page layouts use ASP.NET field controls to display content. These are controls that derive from the `BaseFieldControl` class that is part of the `Microsoft.SharePoint.WebControls` namespace. One of the main characteristics of these controls is that they contain a property that allows you to bind them with a field of the content type associated with the page layout.

The following code snippet shows an example of such controls where the `FieldValue` control is used to display the title of a content page:

```
<SharePointWebControls:FieldValue id="PageTitle"
    FieldName="Title" runat="server"/>
```

Figure 24-10 shows the `ArticleLeft.aspx` page layout and respective controls. This is one of the default page layouts provisioned when the SharePoint Server Publishing Infrastructure Feature is activated.

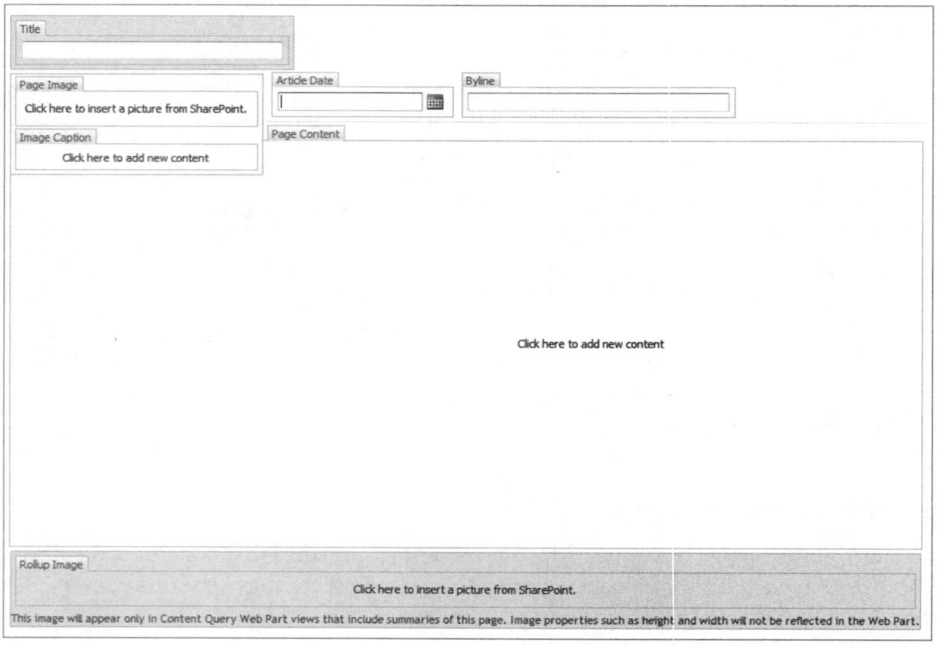

FIGURE 24-10: The ArticleLeft.aspx page layout

The content displayed by a WCM page layout is stored in a special document library called the Pages Library. At run time, SharePoint collates the master page, page layout, and page content into one web page, called a *publishing page*, as shown in Figure 24-11.

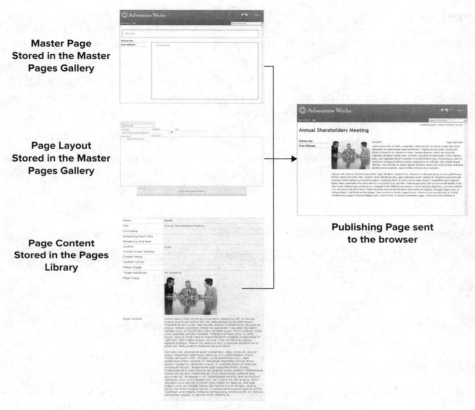

Master Page Stored in the Master Pages Gallery

Page Layout Stored in the Master Pages Gallery

Page Content Stored in the Pages Library

Publishing Page sent to the browser

FIGURE 24-11: The three layers that make up a publishing page

One of the main advantages of this layered approach is that it creates clear boundaries of ownership, where master pages and page layouts are created and owned by technical workers (that is, developers), and the page content itself owned by business users.

MANAGING PUBLISHING CONTENT

Content is the most important artifact on any website. People often say "Content is king!" and quite rightly. It's content that attracts people to a site, and it's content (or the lack of it) that drives them away.

The content-management features of SharePoint 2010 can be divided into the following categories:

➤ Records management

➤ Document management

➤ Web Content Management (WCM)

Records and document management are covered in detail in Chapter 32 and Chapter 7. Therefore, this section addresses some of the WCM capabilities of SharePoint 2010.

Content Creation

SharePoint includes several out-of-the-box controls that provide a rich environment for users to create content. These controls can be divided into two major groups:

➤ *Field controls* — These include simple ASP.NET server controls that can be placed directly on a page layout to create a rigid form containing content placeholders. Content authors can only create and edit content inside these placeholders.

➤ *Web parts* — These include standard ASP.NET web parts that can be added to web part zones.

As an architect, you are responsible for understanding the differences and tradeoffs between the two groups, and deciding which options you will make available on your site. Table 24-1 provides some details to help you make your decisions.

TABLE 24-1: Differences between Field Controls and Web Parts

	FIELD CONTROL	WEB PART
Type of control	Standard ASP.NET server control	Standard ASP.NET web part
Data Storage	Field in a list item in the pages list	Web part data associated with the page
Version history	Yes	No
Location	Fixed location in the page layout (not controlled by content author)	In a web part zone or inside a Rich HTML editor control in the page layout. Content author can choose which web part zone to use (if more than one is provided), as well as the location within the web part zone.
Personalization	No	Yes
Examples	Rich HTML field	Content Editor web part
	Image field	Table of Contents web part
	Summary links	
	Publishing start and end dates	

Reusable Content

In most websites, there is always some standardized common text that must be displayed in several locations. Following are some examples of such content:

➤ Copyright messages

➤ Product names and descriptions

- ➤ Company address
- ➤ Corporate slogans
- ➤ Department names
- ➤ Page footers and headers
- ➤ Reusable HTML snippets (such as content boxes)

To help you manage this type of content, the SharePoint Server Publishing Infrastructure Feature provisions a Reusable Content list at the root of the site collection. The main purpose of this list is to store in one central location text and HTML content that can be reused on any sites within the site collection. Content authors can access this shared content via the Ribbon's Reusable Content button on the Insert tab under the Editing Tools, as shown in Figure 24-12.

FIGURE 24-12: Accessing content via the Ribbon's Reusable Content button

When creating reusable content in this list, you have two options for how the content will be inserted on the destination page:

- ➤ *Keep content updated* — If you select this option, SharePoint actually inserts a link to the list item on the content page. This means that any changes made to the Reusable Content list item will automatically be seen by all content pages. This option also prevents content authors from changing the reusable content.
- ➤ *Do not keep content updated* — With this option, SharePoint inserts a copy of the reusable content in the content page. Content authors are free to change the content, and any changes made to the items on the Reusable Content list will not be reflected on the content pages.

 One of the not-so-obvious ways to use the Reusable Content list is to store HTML code snippets to render graphic elements. You can create a folder under this list called HTML Snippets *where you can store snippets to render graphic elements created by the design team (such content boxes, footer menus, and banners).*

Content Scheduling

You can specify when content stored in document libraries will be visible to users by enabling *item scheduling*. In addition to allowing users to create or upload documents to a document library, item scheduling allows users to schedule when to publish and unpublish the documents at a future time.

To enable content scheduling on a document library, you must ensure the following are set up:

➤ The SharePoint Server Publishing Feature is active on the site.

➤ The "Allow management of content types" setting is set in the Advanced Settings page (which is accessible from the Document Library Settings page).

➤ The Content Approval option and the "Create major and minor versions" option are set on the Versioning Settings page.

➤ The "Create major and minor versions" option is set under the "Document version history" section.

➤ The "Enable scheduling of items in this list" option is set in the Manage Item Scheduling page.

When you enable item scheduling on a document library via the Document Library Settings page, SharePoint adds two extra columns to the library called Scheduling Start Date and Scheduling End Date, as shown in Figure 24-13. Note that the columns are added to the library itself, and not to the content types used in the library. Content editors can then use those fields to specify when the content will be published and unpublished.

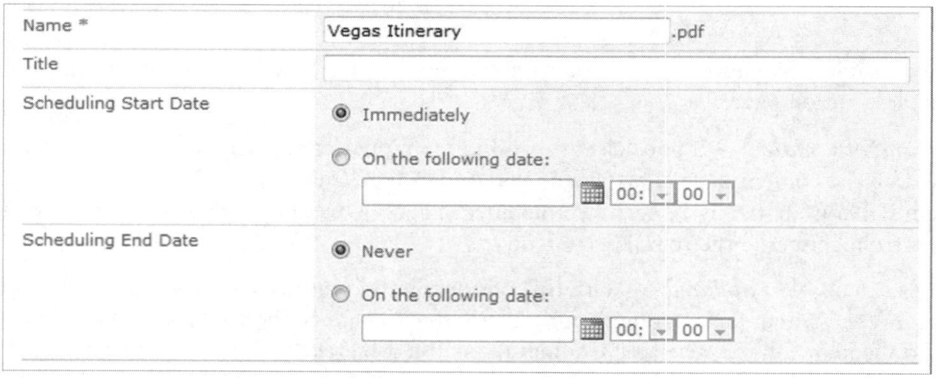

FIGURE 24-13: Content scheduling

When the content author sets the Scheduling Start Date to a value other than the "Immediately" option, and the current date and time has not reached the specified date and time, the document will be moved to a "Scheduled" state and left in a draft version. A SharePoint timer job runs every minute by default, and monitors all documents in a "Scheduled" state. When the current time and date matches the scheduled time and date, the timer job increases the version number to a major version, and changes the document status to "Published."

Multi-language Support

Occasionally, you will be required to provide support for users who speak different languages, and SharePoint 2010 provides multi-language support through the following key technologies:

➤ Language Packs

➤ Multi-lingual User Interface (MUI)

➤ Variations

The support for multiple languages has been substantially improved in SharePoint 2010. Unlike Variations, which is only available in Publishing sites, the new MUI Feature brings multi-language support to all versions of SharePoint (although is not a replacement for Variations). This section takes you through each of these technologies, and explains how you can use them to create multi-language sites.

Language Packs

Languages Packs provide the first layer of infrastructure required to support a specific language. When you install the Language Pack for a specific language, you are actually installing the files, templates, and resources that will be used by Variations and the MUI. The Language Packs also install the language-specific site templates that can be selected by users when creating new site collections through Central Administration.

Figure 24-14 shows the site templates that are made available in the Create Site Collection page in Central Administration after installing the Portuguese Language Pack.

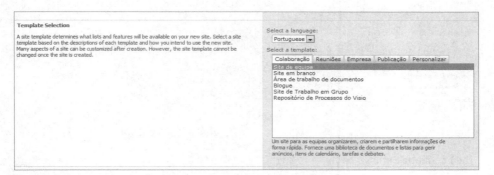

FIGURE 24-14: Create Site Collection page within Language Packs

 You can download Language Packs for SharePoint Server 2010 from Microsoft at http://go.microsoft.com/fwlink/?LinkID=192105&clcid=0x409.

The Multi-language User Interface (MUI)

The MUI is a new Feature introduced with SharePoint 2010 that uses the language-specific resource files (deployed by the Language Packs) to present some UI elements in different languages. The languages available to the MUI are dictated by the Language Packs that have been installed in the SharePoint farm. Some of the following elements are controlled by the MUI:

➤ Menus

➤ Actions

➤ Site title and description

➤ Managed Metadata Services

➤ Navigation

The MUI will use the resource files provisioned by the Language Packs as the source for the text that it displays. Because of this, the MUI will not translate site content. Support for content translation is still only provided by Variations.

The MUI can be enabled at a site level via the Language Settings page accessible from the Site Administration page. Figure 24-15 shows how you can add support for Portuguese by selecting the option from the "Alternate language(s)" section. In this example, only Portuguese is available as an alternate language because only the Portuguese Language Pack has been installed.

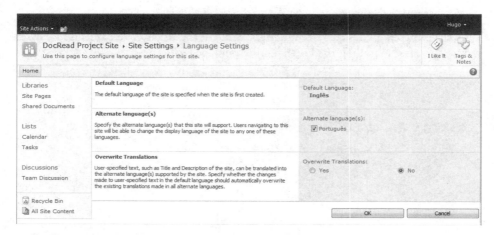

FIGURE 24-15: The Language Settings page

To enable the alternate language selected on the Language Settings page, you must select the language from the username menu, as shown in Figure 24-16.

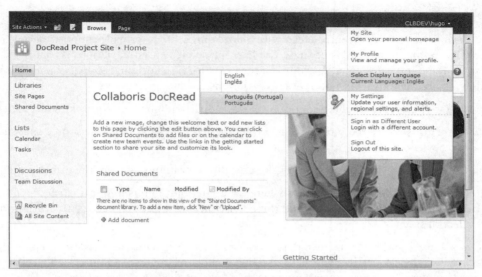

FIGURE 24-16: Choosing the language to be used by the MUI

Figure 24-17 shows the result of selecting Portuguese as the display language. The boxed areas in the figure show where the language has been translated.

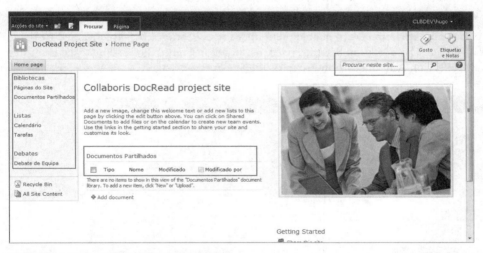

FIGURE 24-17: A site translated by the MUI

As you can see, only the static text that can be read from resource files has been translated. Any dynamic content or managed content created by a user has been left in its original language.

Variations

Site Variations is a Feature that was introduced with SharePoint 2007 to provide support for multi-language, multi-branding, or multi-device sites. The basic principle behind Variations is that when you select a source site, it creates copies of your site that vary from the original source in a number of ways. Following are the most common types of Variations:

➤ *Language* — This is where the Variation site uses a different language from the source site.

➤ *Device* — This is where the Variation site targets different devices from the source site (such as mobile devices).

➤ *Branding* — This is where the Variation site uses different branding from the original site.

Variations are available only on site collections where the SharePoint Publishing Infrastructure Feature has been enabled. You must understand three key concepts to properly configure Variations on your site collections:

➤ *Variation Labels* — This is the metadata associated with a specific site Variation. This metadata includes properties such as label name, template language, and locale. SharePoint will use this metadata to create and manage the copies of the original site (Variations).

➤ *Source Variation* — This is a property of the Variation Label that identifies a site as the source Variation. This information will be used by SharePoint to replicate the data from the source to the destination Variations. There can be only one Source Variation per site collection.

➤ *Label Hierarchy* — These are the connections between source and destination labels. There can be only one label hierarchy per site collection.

The first step to set up Variations is to enable them on a site collection (they are disabled by default). To do this, navigate to the Variation Settings page, as shown in Figure 24-18. This page is located under the Site Collection Administration group of the Site Settings page.

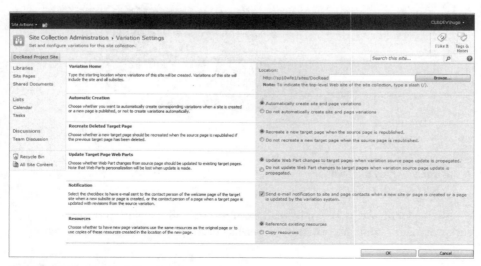

FIGURE 24-18: The Variation Settings page

The next step is to create a label for each Variation that you want to create. You can do this via the Create Variation Label page, which is accessible via the Variation Labels link in the Site Collection Administration page. Figure 24-19 shows an example of how you would configure a label for a Portuguese Variation of a site.

FIGURE 24-19: The Create Variation Label page

After creating the labels for your Variations, you must tell SharePoint to create the Variation sites. You can do this by selecting the Create Hierarchies link on top of the Variation Labels page, which is accessible from the Site Administration page. When you do this, SharePoint will schedule a timer job, which, by default, runs once per day, and will create a site inside of your site collection for each label. If you want to speed up the creation of the sites, you can go to Central Administration and manually run the job called Variations Create Hierarchies Job Definition.

Once Variations are set up on your site collection, any new pages created in the source Variation site will be duplicated in the linked Variation sites as a draft version. It will be the responsibility of the content editors on the destination site to manually merge the changes with the previous published version, and re-publish the content.

It's worth noting that when using Variations on multi-language sites, it's the responsibility of the content authors on the destination Variation site to manually perform the translation between the source and destination languages.

One of the improvements introduced with SharePoint 2010 is the addition of a new View Changes button, which allows content editors of the destination Variation site to easily view what content has changed between the current published version and the version recently propagated to the site. Figure 24-20 shows an example of a report that is displayed to the user when clicking this button.

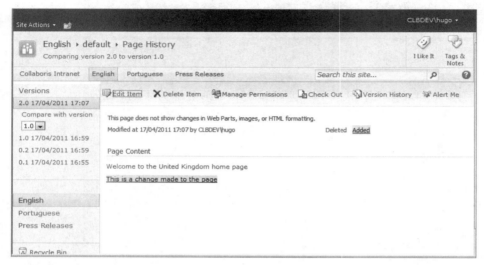

FIGURE 24-20: The View Changes report

For more information on Variations and on the improvements introduced by SharePoint 2010, check out the Microsoft Enterprise Content Management (ECM) Team blog at `http://blogs.msdn.com/b/ecm/archive/tags/variations/`.

PLANNING SITE NAVIGATION

A logical, intuitive, and consistent site hierarchy and navigation strategy are some of the most important characteristics of a successful site. According to researchers, the addictive nature of web browsing can leave site visitors with an attention span of nine seconds — the same as a goldfish (`http://news.bbc.co.uk/1/hi/1834682.stm`). This means that you have nine seconds to help users find what they want.

Following are some generic rules you should consider when planning your site navigation:

➤ *Keep navigation consistent* — Navigation elements should easily stand out from content, and be placed on the same location on every page. The colors and styles used should also be kept the same throughout the site.

➤ *Use standard locations* — Users come to expect the navigation elements to be positioned in certain locations on a page (such as on top of the page, or on the left of the main content area). So, placing your navigation controls on these locations will make navigation more intuitive for them.

➤ *Use standard names* — Use commonly used section names like "Products," "About us," "Contact us," and "Support." This will help users find what they want quickly.

➤ *Keep the number of clicks to a minimum* — Try to take users where they want to go quickly with a minimum number of choices and links.

➤ *Always show the current location* — Show users where they currently are in the site hierarchy, and always give them a way to go up.

Another important factor you should consider when planning your site navigation is to think about the requirements of the different user audiences. Corporate users connecting to an intranet site will have different requirements from customers connecting to an Internet site. Designing the navigation to meet the specific requirements of your site audiences will help users to easily find what they need, and, thus, become more efficient in completing their daily tasks.

Table 24-2 shows examples of some of the types of the audiences and use cases that should be considered when creating an intranet and an Internet site.

TABLE 24-2: Site Audiences and Use Cases

TYPE OF SITE	AUDIENCES	USE CASES
Intranet	Corporate Employees	Browse company news and press releases.
		Find contact information for a colleague or department.
		Find corporate policies and procedures.
Internet	Customers	Find information about products and services.
		Find contact information.
		Browse company news and press releases.
		Find support information for specific problems.

Navigation in SharePoint Sites

SharePoint provides an extensive out-of-the-box navigation infrastructure that can be easily customized and extended. This infrastructure uses the standard ASP.NET Site Map Provider Model to dynamically create navigation nodes based on the hierarchy and content of a site collection.

One of the main limitations of the SharePoint navigation infrastructure is its scope. Currently, the Site Map Provider is only capable of automatically displaying nodes for pages or sites under the current site collection. Links to sites or content outside the current site collection will have to be manually created.

Another important feature of the SharePoint navigation infrastructure is its capability to filter navigation nodes based on the user's permissions. This feature is known as *security trimming*, and it stops users from seeing links to pages that they do not have permission to access.

SharePoint navigation can be grouped into four major categories:

➤ *Global navigation (or top link bar navigation)* — This is used to navigate to sites below the current site.

➤ *Current navigation (or quick launch navigation)* — This is used to display links to content on the current site.

➤ *Breadcrumb navigation* — This is used to show the user's current location.

➤ *Custom navigation* — This is provided via a series of navigation web parts that can be placed directly on pages and configured by content authors.

➤ *Metadata navigation* — This allows users to filter library or list content based on column values.

SharePoint Foundation comes with a limited set of configuration options that allow administrators to manually add navigation links to the global and current navigation menus. These configuration options can be accessed via the "Quick launch" and the "Top link bar" links under the "Look and Feel" section of the Site Settings page.

A much richer set of configuration options is made available when the SharePoint Server Publishing Infrastructure Feature is activated on a site collection. Activating this Feature adds the following configuration links to the Site Settings page:

➤ *Site Collection Navigation (located under the Site Collection Administration section)* — This allows an administrator to configure site-wide navigation settings such as enabling or disabling navigation, security trimming, and audience targeting.

➤ *Navigation (located under the Look and Feel section)* — This allows an administrator to configure navigation hierarchy, navigation sorting, and to add or remove custom navigation nodes.

Global Navigation

Global navigation is normally placed at the top of every page and, by default, it automatically displays links to the home pages of all sites below the current site. Administrators can manually add or remove sites via the Navigation Settings page shown in Figure 24-21.

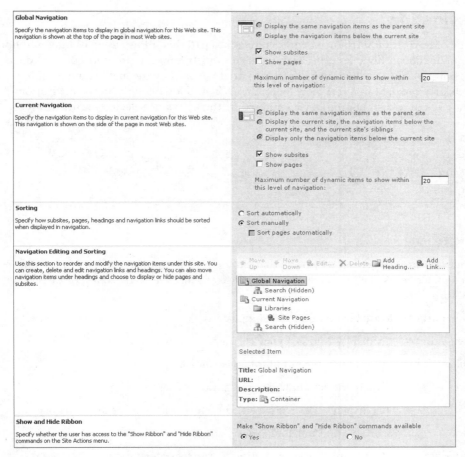

FIGURE 24-21: Navigation Settings page

By configuring the Global Navigation to display the same navigation items as the parent site, administrators can ensure that it's kept consistent across all sites within a site collection.

Current Navigation

The current navigation is used to display links to content on the current site such as document libraries, lists, and publishing pages. It's normally displayed on the left of the main content area.

Like global navigation, administrators can easily add or remove links to the current navigation via the Navigation Settings page.

Breadcrumb Navigation

Breadcrumb navigation is normally displayed at the top of the page. It displays a dynamically generated set of links used to remind the users of their current position in the site hierarchy. Breadcrumb navigation also allows users to navigate up in the site hierarchy.

Metadata Navigation

This is a new type of navigation introduced with SharePoint 2010 that allows users to filter and find content in lists and document libraries using metadata. Administrators can promote columns on a list or document library as key navigation fields, which are then used by the metadata navigation user controls to display the data in a tree view hierarchy. When following links in the navigation hierarchy, users are taken to a standard list view filtered by the key value selected in the hierarchy.

 For more information on metadata navigation, check out the TechNet page at http://technet.microsoft.com/en-us/library/ff608067 .aspx#bkmk_about_mdn.

Custom Navigation

SharePoint provides several navigation web parts that can be used by content creators to provide custom navigation experiences. These web parts can be inserted into web part zones, or directly into the Rich Text Editor.

The following web parts are available on non-Publishing sites:

- ➤ *Site Aggregator* — This displays sites of your choice.
- ➤ *Tag Cloud* — This displays the most popular tagged subjects.
- ➤ *Categories* — These display the site directory categories.
- ➤ *Site in Category* — This displays sites from a site directory within a specific category.

The following web parts are available on Publishing sites:

- ➤ *Table of Contents* — This displays the navigation hierarchy of a site.
- ➤ *Summary Links* — These allow content authors to create custom links that can be grouped.

DEPLOYING PUBLISHING SITES

The importance of planning your deployment from an early stage cannot be emphasized enough. There has always been much debate around the best way to deploy SharePoint applications. Some prefer the declarative approach that uses XML files, whereas others prefer the imperative approach that uses code.

Rather than going into that debate here, this section simply describes a time-proven mixed approach.

The Publishing Artifacts

When planning the deployment of a Publishing site, you must identify the different types of artifacts to deploy, and decide on a deployment strategy for each of them. As a starting point to simplify this task, artifacts should be organized into the following categories:

➤ *Infrastructure artifacts* — These normally store reference data used by web parts and custom controls. They are required for the correct functioning of the site. These normally include site columns, content types, and list definitions.

➤ *Content artifacts* — These normally include content pages, documents, list items, and images.

➤ *Branding artifacts* — These dictate the general look and feel of the site, which normally includes CSSs, style images, page layouts, and master pages.

➤ *Configuration artifacts* — These configure functionality such as permissions, navigation, and search.

It's important to have an approach to deploying the artifacts for each of these categories, and this approach should be adjusted and tuned based on the specific requirements of your project.

The Deployment Baseline

A *deployment baseline* is a clear definition of the artifacts that will be built and deployed when creating a site. These artifacts should be catalogued and grouped based on their purpose, functionalities, and on how you plan to deploy and maintain them once the application is live. This baseline will also help to clearly define the different areas of responsibility within the team.

For example, imagine that you are developing a new WCM application where the development team is responsible for the creation of all the technical artifacts (ASP, HTML, CSS, and so on), and the business team is responsible for the creation of content (pages and documents). In this scenario, it will make sense to create two separate packages: one for the technical artifacts, and the other for the content artifacts. These packages can then be maintained, managed, and version-controlled separately. To do a release, you would just need to release the package with the technical artifacts, followed by the content package. (You can also have more than one content package, but more on that later.)

In SharePoint development, the Features and Solution Framework gives you the right tools to define and create this deployment baseline, and it is worthwhile to familiarize yourself with it before developing any SharePoint application. Unfortunately, this framework also has a lot of limitations that are not immediately obvious when you start to use it, so be prepared to get your hands dirty and do some coding to overcome some of them.

 For more information about the Features and Solution Framework, check out the MSDN page at http://msdn.microsoft.com/en-us/library/aa543214 .aspx. *You should use the SharePoint Features and Solution Framework for the delivery of SharePoint applications. You should deploy most of the artifacts via Features that are activated via site definitions and deployed using Web Solution Packages (WSPs). One of the biggest advantages of using WSPs as a delivery mechanism is that SharePoint will automatically deploy the WSP contents to all Web Front-End (WFE) servers on the farm.*

The deployment artifacts should be identified early in the development life cycle, usually just after the initial requirements analysis. You might consider using Mind Maps during this stage, because they are very easy to produce, and can quickly give you a high-level overview of what needs to be deployed.

These documents are sometimes called "Deployment Artifacts Maps," and you should create two — one showing all the sites, pages, doc libraries, and lists (as shown in Figure 24-22), and another with all the UI controls. These are dynamic documents that will evolve during the project life cycle.

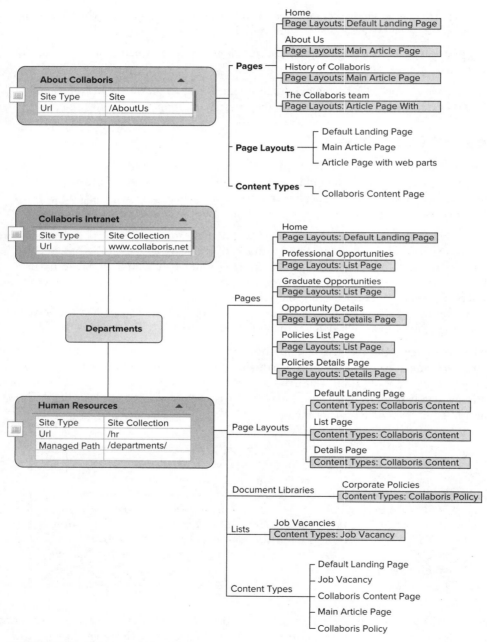

FIGURE 24-22 Deployment baseline

Deployment Strategy

The next step in planning the deployment of a Publishing site is to group the artifacts identified in the deployment baseline and define a deployment strategy for each group. Table 24-3 summarizes the default starting-point strategy you might apply to projects. This is just a rule of thumb, and it will always depend on the size and complexity of the site that you are trying to deploy.

TABLE 24-3: Deployment Strategy Deployment of a Publishing Site

ARTIFACT GROUP	DESCRIPTION	DEPLOYMENT STRATEGY
Infrastructure Artifacts	Site Columns	Deployed via Features and CAML scripts. Activated via site definitions (so that they are automatically activated when a site is created).
	Content Types	
	List Definitions	
	List Instances	
Branding Artifacts	Cascading Style Sheets	Deployed via Features and CAML scripts. Activated via site definitions (so that they are automatically activated when a site is created).
	Style images	
	Page layouts	
	Master pages	
Configuration Artifacts	Permissions groups	Deployed via Features, but using a mixture of CAML and custom code called from Feature receivers to overcome some of the CAML limitations. These features should also be automatically activated via a site definition so that the configuration is performed when the site is first provisioned.
	Permission levels	
	Navigation	
	Search scopes	
Default Content	Publishing pages	Deployed via Features with CAML scripts, and automatically activated by site definitions.
	List content	
	Document libraries	
Sample Content	Publishing pages	Deployed via Features with CAML scripts. These features should be manually activated when you want to populate the site with sample content.
	List content	
	Document libraries	
Test Content	Publishing pages	Deployed via Features with CAML scripts. These should be manually activated only during testing.
	List content	
	Document libraries	

SUMMARY

SharePoint 2010 is a flexible and mature Web Content Management (WCM) system that enables you to build functional and rich sites for your business and your customers.

This chapter provided an overview of the SharePoint WCM capabilities that allow you to build intranet and Internet sites without having to worry about the underlying plumbing infrastructure required by modern, interactive, and social-aware sites.

Chapter 25 describes the business collaboration features of SharePoint 2010 that provide teams the capability to interact with colleagues, customers, and suppliers.

25

Corporate Information Services

By Martin Kearn

The capability to store, collaborate on, and share documents and files has been at the heart of SharePoint products and technologies since its inception in 2001. The functionality has gone through several facelifts along the way, but the core principles of using SharePoint as a corporate information management system is really at the foundation of what SharePoint is all about.

This chapter examines some of the new functionality for SharePoint 2010 relating to corporate information services, as well as re-visiting some of the capabilities that have been around for several releases.

This chapter is organized as follows:

➤ *Designing corporate information services* — This discussion covers some high-level information and principles relating to how to design SharePoint-based corporate information services.

➤ *Working with documents* — This section provides some detailed information on key SharePoint features relating to document and information management.

➤ *Document management in the enterprise* — This section provides details on features, best practices, and techniques for information management in the enterprise.

➤ *Software boundaries* — This section discusses some important software limitations relating to large-scale information repositories.

DESIGNING CORPORATE INFORMATION SERVICES

As an architect, it is important to gauge exactly how much effort must go into the design of your corporate information services. SharePoint is a solid platform, and it is relatively simple for most business users to perform basic tasks — such as creating or uploading a document, and managing it. However, it is important to fully understand the needs of your users, and realize how much assistance and direction they will need when using SharePoint.

In some organizations, it may be appropriate to offer only minimal design and configuration, and then let users use SharePoint in the default configuration. However, in other organizations, this level of control is not practical, and the environment must be fine-tuned to suit the needs of the users.

Let's use Microsoft's own internal systems as an example. Microsoft has two main SharePoint-based collaboration systems. The first one is the place where users can go to create their own ad-hoc SharePoint sites. The environment is self-service oriented, and any user can create a site without approval. The sites created are chosen from the default SharePoint site templates, and they are largely unconfigured, apart from a small customization where users must state how business-critical the site is.

The second SharePoint environment is used for managing customer engagements. This environment has a little more "design" in that there are content types and document templates, as well as a more tailored default layout. These sites are created automatically whenever an engagement is set up, and is the official repository for customer documentation and deliverables.

Microsoft is an example of an organization where the corporate information services design is largely invisible to the user, and the underlying product is left open for users to simply use.

At the other end of the scale, some organizations have a need to provide a highly tailored and "locked down" SharePoint environment. This may include some or all of the following configurations:

➤ Disabling self-service site creation

➤ Providing customized site templates

➤ Preventing users from creating new lists and libraries

➤ Pre-configuring folder structures inside document libraries

➤ Providing content types and document templates

➤ Preventing users from adjusting the theme, master page, or web part layout, which includes adding new web parts

➤ Mandating document approval and other workflows

There can be many reasons for taking a more locked-down approach, but often it is because IT organizations perceive that SharePoint will be too complex for their users to understand without significant configuration, or they are worried about the environment "getting out of control."

Deviating from SharePoint's default configuration can be useful to gently introduce users to the SharePoint world, and to make SharePoint seem a bit more like the systems that they are used to.

It may also be useful if the data stored within SharePoint is very sensitive, or must conform to strict standards (for example, in terms of the way documents are written or regulatory compliance).

You have several factors to consider when judging how much to deviate from SharePoint's default configuration. Let's take a closer look at a few of them.

Familiarity of Users with Online Site-Based Collaboration Tools

Many of today's business people are highly familiar with using web-based collaboration tools because of the ever-increasing popularity of websites such as Facebook, MySpace, Yahoo Groups, blogs, and more. This is especially true with "Generation Z."

Conversely, if your organization has a history of using filesystems with mapped drives and the familiar tree view, the change to a web-based tool may have a huge usability impact. Users may find it difficult to navigate SharePoint because of the lack of over-arching tree view or structure. Users may also struggle to understand the concept of sites and how they relate to documents.

Budget Considerations

What financial resources do you have to be able to create and support any changes that are made to SharePoint's default configurations?

Though many configurations can be applied without having to write code, configuring SharePoint is often complex and costly, especially if you are trying to make configuration changes in a testable, repeatable manner.

Expected Longevity of the Deployment

For how long will the SharePoint environment be in use? Is this just a temporary system, or is it part of a wider business strategy?

It is also worth considering SharePoint's product road map. How far away is the next version of SharePoint, and will its default configuration include any of the customizations you are considering? How will the changes you are making upgrade to the next version? It is no secret that the simplest upgrade procedure is with a platform that has not been modified from the default configuration. Configuration often equates to complication when it comes to upgrading.

Security Requirements

How sensitive is the data that is stored in SharePoint?

If the data is very sensitive, then close attention must be paid to the security design of your corporate information services.

Generally speaking, it is possible to apply very tight security settings to SharePoint 2010 using configuration and no customization. This does not negate the importance of a solid design, strategy, and approach to consistent security and, more importantly, ongoing administration of your SharePoint 2010 sites.

Document Control

How much central control do you want to retain over the documents that are stored within SharePoint?

By default, users can upload any file (within the allowed file types list) to any document library where they have permissions. The base `Document` content type has only an optional `Title` field, so the users will not have to fill out a long, complex metadata form to upload their documents.

Although this approach requires the minimal amount of thinking from the user's point of view, it does not take advantage of SharePoint's many features for content types, metadata, and so on.

At the other end of the scale, many companies build rich sets of content types, each using specific document templates. The content types may include specific metadata properties, some of which may be mandatory for the user. This approach requires more upfront work on the part of the user when uploading content to SharePoint libraries, but results in content with better classification information. This makes the overall experience of finding and filtering content much better for the user.

It is important to judge which of these two approaches is most suitable for your user community. It is also important to note that different approaches may be relevant for different repositories. If you consider the Microsoft internal example outlined earlier in the chapter, the area where users can create ad-hoc sites is simple, out-of-the-box SharePoint, and the only default content types are those that come with SharePoint.

The second area that Microsoft users use to store content does have prescribed content types, mandatory metadata, and so on. This is because the content is generally more important because it relates to customer engagements.

Environments Conflicting with SharePoint

SharePoint provides lots of different services related to the storage and collaboration of documents. For many customers, SharePoint may "compete" with one or more existing systems, which are either being run in parallel to SharePoint, or as a legacy system from which the organization is migrating.

If this is the case in your organization, consider how SharePoint could be customized so that users who are familiar with competing systems will find the SharePoint interface and structure to be as intuitive as possible.

Next, let's explore some of the key features that users can enjoy when working with documents in SharePoint 2010.

WORKING WITH DOCUMENTS

This section examines some of the key features related to how users work with documents in SharePoint. All of these features are important considerations when designing your corporate information architecture.

Social Networking

One of the major new feature areas with SharePoint 2010 is the addition of social networking capabilities. There is a plethora of new capabilities in this area, which are covered in more detail in Chapter 28.

Three areas of social networking directly relate to corporate information services:

➤ Rating

➤ Tagging

➤ Note boards

Rating

Users now have the capability to rate documents in a document library. The feature works by allowing each user to provide a simple 1–5 rating for the document by using the familiar star-based rating system that is used in media players and other social tools.

Providing the item has at least one rating, the average will be shown via illuminated stars next to the document, as seen in Figure 25-1. The rating interface is rendered as a field, so it can be seen in any list views or list view web parts. The rating also shows up in Microsoft Office.

This feature is off by default, but it can be enabled on a per-library basis. The first design decision is whether or not to use ratings. Ratings are a powerful way of using the "wisdom of crowds" to highlight popular content. If used intelligently, ratings can be a key feed into systems that highlight popular content and introduce the social network to corporate information management.

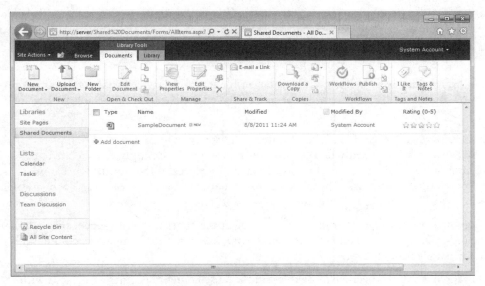

FIGURE 25-1: Ratings in a document library

However, the rating implementation in SharePoint 2010 is quite basic, and can lead to some undesirable scenarios. Some of these limitations include the following:

➤ *Lack of weighting* — The rating scores are not weighted by how many ratings have actually been given. This means that a document with two ratings of 4 stars each would be shown as the same as a document with 100 ratings of 4 stars each. This lack of weighting means that the rating system can easily be manipulated to show content as being more popular than it really is.

➤ *1–5 stars* — The rating system uses a score of 1–5 stars. There is no way to change this.

➤ *Design and presentation* — The ratings are shown as stars, and it is not possible to change the way ratings are presented.

➤ *Rate without reading* — The rating system will allow users to rate a document even if they have never opened it. This may be seen as unfair to the author of the document. However, this practice applies to all documents in the system, which means that everyone is subject to the same limitation.

➤ *Delayed presentation* — The back-end rating processing system is a timer job that processes ratings in batches. This means that ratings do not show up immediately after a user has rated a document. This often causes confusion for users.

➤ *Lack of identification* — The ratings are shown to end users in a rolled-up view, which prevents individual identification of specific ratings. This can be seen as both a limitation and a benefit.

The use and acceptance of ratings will really depend on the nature of your users. If your users are familiar with working in social networking systems, they will most likely be used to the rating concept, and understand the limitations of it. However, other types of users may find the rating system an overly open way for users to judge content without having to back up their judgments with comments or identification.

Tagging

The concept of *tagging* has been present on the Internet for several years in social networking sites such as Facebook and LinkedIn, and now has been introduced to SharePoint for the first time in the 2010 release.

The act of tagging in the context of SharePoint refers to a user applying a keyword to a piece of content. The keyword can typically be any word or phrase, and does not have to relate to a corporate metadata service (though it will resolve to managed terms, if they exist). Once a user has tagged a piece of content, the tag will appear in the user's newsfeed, and, therefore, be shown to any other users who are following the tagging user.

A benefit of tagging is that, when other users are looking at the content that is tagged, they will be able to see the tags that have been set, helping them form a fuller picture of what the community thinks about a given piece of content.

Tags also help search results to become more relevant, because content becomes associated with keywords that the end users have defined (normally making the relevance very high).

Any URL (including external URLs) can be tagged in SharePoint, as well as people, list items, and documents.

Tagging is very deeply integrated into SharePoint's user interface, and cannot easily be "turned off." Because of this, few design decisions can be made with regard to tagging, and it should be embraced as a core part of your corporate information services design.

Note Boards

As a complementary technology to tags, SharePoint 2010 also introduces the concept of a note board to sites, list items, documents, and people.

Conceptually, note boards are very similar to the wall feature in Facebook in that any user can add a public comment to the content, which will be shown both on the content itself and the user's newsfeed. Note boards are a very useful way of allowing users to comment and provide opinions on content within SharePoint.

Like tags, the note board concept is deeply integrated into SharePoint's interfaces and cannot easily be disabled.

Check-in/Check-out and Versioning

Check in/check-out and versioning have been primary features of SharePoint ever since it was invented in the late 1990s, and remain a core part of the way documents are managed in SharePoint 2010.

The act of checking out is a way of letting other users know that someone is editing a document, because they will see "checked out to Mr. X." In previous versions of SharePoint, a checked-out document was locked, and no one could edit the document until the user had checked it back in. Although this configuration is possible in SharePoint 2010, it is not the default option.

If a checked-out document is checked in by the user, a new version is created, and users can look at and restore old versions. The number of versions that are kept can be configured by administrators.

There are two numbering schemes to consider:

➤ *Major versions* — Major versions simply increment the version number. For example, the version number will go from 1, to 2, to 3 and so on.

➤ *Major and minor versions* — Minor versioning introduces major and minor versions, and uses a decimal point to differentiate. For example, 1.3, 1.4, and 1.5 are all minor versions, but 2.0 is a major version. Settings can define how minor and major versions are shown to users with differing rights. Minor versions are also known as *draft documents*.

The way version numbers increment and the format cannot be changed. This is seen as a limitation by some organizations that have more complex versioning schemes.

 Be sure to consider storage when enabling versioning. Each version of a document constitutes a completely separate BLOB object in the database. For example, if 10 versions of a 1 MB file are stored, then 10 MB of storage is required.

By default, new lists and libraries are not configured for versioning, and it is something that must be enabled on a library-by-library basis if required.

The act of enablement is relatively simple on a one-off basis. However, if your customer requires a company-wide policy that states all libraries (new and current) have versioning enabled, you would have to undertake some customization activity to achieve this, because SharePoint does not allow this sort of farm-wide configuration using out-of-the-box tools.

 Farm-wide configuration of versioning settings will require customization activity for your site templates, list definitions, or use of feature receivers.

If your users are using Office 2010, versioning may not be necessary because SharePoint 2010 supports co-authoring when used with Office 2010 on the client, thus removing the need to protect from save conflicts. You learn more about this later in this chapter.

 SharePoint 2010 supports co-authoring when used with Office 2010.

Document libraries can be configured to use workflows such as an approval process. Using this option ensures that draft documents must be approved before they become major versions. Major versions of documents are often exposed to more users than draft versions. Therefore, if you are using major and minor versioning, it makes sense to enable approval.

You have a number of key considerations to take into account when deciding how to design versioning, including the following:

➤ Is approval required?

➤ Do you have to mandate versioning as a farm-wide policy? Doing this will require customization.

➤ Is versioning required at all, especially in scenarios where users have Office 2010 installed?

➤ If versioning is required, how will it be configured, how many drafts will be kept, and how will the security be configured?

➤ Do not overlook the storage implications of maintaining versions.

Content Types

Content types are the most important aspect of any information services design, because they provide the building blocks that documents are created from. They define the data that is captured during document creation, what happens to the document after creation, and many other factors that affect the overall document life cycle.

Content types define many aspects of a document or list item, including the following:

➤ The underlying document file template that is used to create documents

➤ Workflows that are associated with any items created from the content type

➤ Custom document information panels that will appear in Office for a document created from the content type

➤ Information management policies that are applied to items created from the document type

➤ Metadata columns that are applied to the content type

All documents and list items are created based on a content type of some description. By default, it is likely to be one of the out-of-the-box content types such as `List item` or `Document` that define only basic information, such as a blank template and the `Title` metadata field.

One of the key design decisions that you must make as an architect is deciding whether you will use custom content types. If you choose to use custom content types, you must establish what types of content the organization uses, and how to use the various features of content types to the best effect.

This can be a time-consuming design process, but it is very important, and when completed effectively, it will provide a great baseline for other information management functions (such as search, record management, workflow, and many others).

Content Type Parentage

Content types support inheritance models, whereby every content type has a parent. If you work all the way up the chain, you'll find the out-of-the-box `Item` content type. The concept is that if a parent is changed in some way (such as additional metadata columns and so on), all child content types will pick up the change without administrator intervention.

When designing custom content types, it is best practice to establish a "base" content type that is the parent (or grandparent, great-grandparent, and so on) to all other custom content types. Typically, the base content type would not provide a template, but may provide metadata fields, information management policies, and even workflows that apply to all documents in the enterprise.

This approach is good practice even if the base content type does nothing. Having the base content type in place gives the customer flexibility in the future to add broad changes to all documents in the organization. If all content types had an out-of-the-box content type such as `Document` as the parent, these sorts of changes would involve modifying a content type that is owned by SharePoint. Although this is a supported activity, it is certainly not considered to be best practice.

If you are using a base content type, the next decision is which of the out-of-the-box content types to set as its parent. Common practice in this area is to use the top level `Document` content type as the parent.

The reason for this is that this content type does not provide anything other than a mandatory `Title` field (which is required for SharePoint to work properly). Therefore, by choosing `Document`, you'll minimize the dependencies.

The same conditions apply to the `Item` content type (`Document`'s parent). However, the Content Organizer Feature only works if documents are based on the `Document` content type (or a child of it). Later in this chapter, you learn more about the Content Organizer.

Content Type Hub

One of the issues with content types in SharePoint 2007 was that they were scoped at a site or site collection level. This meant that if a content type was configured in a specific site collection, there was no easy way to move it to a different site collection, other than via list and/or site templates.

The best-practice way to address this was to use XML features to add the content types and activate the feature on all site collections where the content was required. This approach worked well for new sites, but changing a content type after deployment was very difficult.

SharePoint 2010 introduced a new feature called the *content type hub* that addresses these issues. The content type hub is a site collection that houses enterprise-wide content types. The Managed Metadata Service (MMS) application then takes those content types and publishes them to any site collection that is consuming services from the MMS. This allows administrators to maintain a central library of content types that are consumed around the enterprise. Changes to the content types can be made locally in the content type hub, and replicated automatically by the MMS.

The really great thing about this feature is that the content type hub is just a regular site collection that can be created and managed like any other site collection, and the content types themselves are just normal content types. So, no special skills or knowledge are required to manage them. This allows the tasks of management to be assigned to non-administrative users, and leaves the task of replication to the MMS.

 Content types hubs are just regular SharePoint sites, and the content types contained within them are just regular content types. No special skills are required.

When designing content types, it is important to consider and plan how the content type hub will be used and where it will sit. Because the content type hub is just a regular site, it can reside anywhere in the farm.

The correct location of the content type hub will depend on who is responsible for managing content types, and how they intend to access the site. For example, if content type management is a role of the farm administrators, it could reside within the Central Administration web application. Otherwise, it may reside in the web application that is closest to the user that will manage and maintain the content types. However, typically, the Central Administration web application is a great place to store the content type hub.

As with SharePoint 2007, it is still best practice to add the content types to the content type hub via XML features, rather than manual configuration. This approach allows easy re-use across different environments.

Document Sets

One of the features new to SharePoint 2010 is *document sets*. Document sets are a collection of two or more document types that can be created and managed as a single file. The purpose of this feature is to address scenarios where teams are preparing a closely related group of documents. Examples of this include the following:

➤ A sales report that contains the main report, a Visio file for diagrams, and a presentation showing a summary of the report.

➤ An expense report that contains a spreadsheet detailing the expense claim, and scanned images of the receipts.

Document sets are enabled on a site collection by activating the Document Sets Feature, as shown in Figure 25-2. This will add a new content type to the site collection called `Document Set`. Any content types created with this as their parent will be document sets.

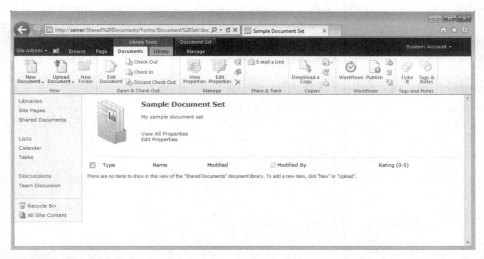

FIGURE 25-2: A document set

Document sets allow all of the capabilities of regular content types. However, any change to columns, workflow, information management policies, and so on, can be applied to all documents within the document set.

Document sets also have an additional interface called Document Set Settings, which is where the details of the document set are configured. This screen has several options:

➤ *Available Content Types* — This defines which content types are available for use within the document set. By default, this is just the default document content types, but you should consider adding your own in here.

➤ *Default Content* — This allows you to add default files that are included with the document set, and choose which content types they are based on. Typically, a blank version of the document templates will be added here.

➤ *Shared Columns* — This allows you to choose which columns from the document set are shared across all files. This means that if the column is changed once, it will apply to all files in the document set.

➤ *Welcome Page* — When users actually view a document set in the browser, they will receive a welcome page, which may include additional content that provides instructions on how to use the document set. This page can be customized in SharePoint Designer 2010.

If you plan to use document sets, it is imperative that you have a sound content types design first, because document sets will include several content types. It is also important to establish a base document set, just as you would with content types. This way, you can define a core range of settings that apply to any document sets that use the base as a parent. Even if the base document set contains no settings or content, it is still good practice to use a base document set so that broad changes can easily be applied in the future, if required.

Navigating Documents

The task of helping users navigate documents and files has been a key factor for many years. It is one of the more challenging areas of designing corporate information services for architects, because different users will think about documents in different ways, and it is important to accommodate all of the users who will be using your system.

Different Approaches to Locating Documents

Users within an organization may think about locating documents in many different ways. A corporate information services design that works well will understand and provide functionality for each of these approaches. Poorly designed systems will try to impose one or more of these approaches on users, thus alienating a portion of the user community.

Table 25-1 describes some of the typical user types that are commonly seen in organizations:

TABLE 25-1: Typical User Behaviors in Locating Documents in Organizations

USER TYPE	DESCRIPTION
Windows Explorer users	These users have been using IT systems for a long time, and have grown up with the all-familiar Windows Explorer tree view and mapped network drives. This group often likes to see documents organized into a structure of some kind that they can expand and collapse, just like they would with a network drive in Windows Explorer.
Facebook users	These users are typically from the younger generation, and their primary experience with IT systems is via the use of online social media sites such as Facebook. These users are used to simply placing documents in a flat location, and using metadata and tagging to help other users locate the files.
"Open in Office" users	These users will typically prefer to start creating or loading documents from the desktop application that corresponds with the document they are working on. For example, if a user wants to edit a Word document, he or she will first load Word, and then expect to navigate to the document via Word's File Open dialog.
Search users	These users will not generally navigate for documents, but will rely on Search to find what they are looking for. Typically, these users look to read content more than edit it, but this is still an important use case for document authoring, too.

SharePoint Tools for Finding Documents

Fortunately, SharePoint 2010 provides a lot of different ways to group and structure documents, which suits all of the approaches to locating documents outlined in this chapter.

SharePoint fully supports metadata and tagging. Users should be encouraged to provide metadata for all documents, and this can be enforced through the use of mandatory columns on content types. The provision of metadata is useful for lots of reasons, not the least of which is enabling metadata-driven navigation.

Within SharePoint, there are two ways to emulate the tree view approach that Windows Explorer users like to see. The traditional approach is to create a structure of folders and subfolders within a document library. Documents can then be physically placed in the folder that they are most closely related to. Although folders are a core and supported part of SharePoint, the use of folders should generally be discouraged for the following reasons:

➤ Files can only exist in a single folder, and one person's classification may not make sense to another person, thus creating a frustrating experience for one of the two people.

➤ Unlike Windows Explorer, it is not easy to physically move a document from one folder to another. It is possible via the Windows Explorer View, but a typical end user may not even realize this option exists, and may find using it a long-winded process.

➤ The navigation tools provided by SharePoint for navigating folder structures are quite basic, and a user who is used to Windows Explorer may find them fairly limited.

As an alternative to folder-driven navigation, SharePoint 2010 introduced *metadata-driven navigation*. As shown in Figure 25-3, metadata-driven navigation provides a tree-view style interface

FIGURE 25-3: Metadata-driven navigation tree

that will look very familiar to the Windows Explorer users. However, the critical difference is that documents are placed in the structure based on their metadata, not their physical location.

This introduces many benefits over folder-driven structures, including the following:

> ➤ Documents can reside in multiple logical locations. Therefore, different users can place them based on what makes sense to them, and others can place the same document in a different logical location.

> ➤ Because it is metadata that drives the structure, it can very easily be changed by simply changing the use of metadata in the documents.

> ➤ The metadata fields will map back to the MMS and can, therefore, be centrally managed terms, rather than any term that a user wishes to use. This enables companies to introduce consistent navigation structures.

If users have Office 2010, they will be able to use both metadata-driven and folder-driven structures to open documents. However, older versions of Office (including Office 2007) support only the folder-driven approach.

Workflow

SharePoint 2010 is built on top of the Windows Workflow Foundation (WF) and has a wide range of functionality related to workflow. This is discussed in detail in Chapter 31.

SharePoint includes several built-in workflows that are designed to facilitate common document-based workflow scenarios, including the following:

> ➤ *Disposition approval* — Manages document expiration and retention by allowing participants to decide whether to retain or delete expired documents.

> ➤ *Three state* — Manages a document between three different states that can be defined by administrators.

> ➤ *Collect feedback* — Routes a document for review. Reviewers can provide feedback, which is compiled and sent to the document owner when the workflow has completed.

> ➤ *Gather signatures* — Gathers signatures needed to complete a Microsoft Office document.

> ➤ *Approval* — Routes a document for approval. Approvers can approve or reject the document, reassign the approval task, or request changes to the document.

Each workflow can be configured on a content type or a library basis. However, it is best practice to try to map workflows to content types wherever possible. This way, the content is subject to the same workflow, no matter where it resides, whereas library-based workflow configurations will apply only to the items in the library where it was configured.

Offline

Users have several options for taking SharePoint content offline. The right option will depend on the use case and volume of data.

The simplest offline model is the use of Outlook 2010 to take specific lists offline in the same way that Outlook does with Exchange e-mail. Every list has a "Connect to Outlook" button in the List or Library tab. When users choose to connect a list or library to Outlook, the list will be downloaded as a new folder in Outlook, and be synchronized with the server when users perform a "Send and Receive" operation in Outlook. If the list contains Outlook-style content (such as Tasks, Contacts, and Events), the synchronization is two-way in that users can make changes in Outlook, and those changes are written back to SharePoint on the next synchronization.

In the case of documents, offline changes can be made to Office documents via SharePoint Drafts. This is a special folder in the user's My Documents that is used to store documents that are checked out. Items that are in SharePoint Drafts can be uploaded to SharePoint when the user is online. If a document library is offline in Outlook, and a user opens a document, Office will prompt the user to "edit offline," at which point it will copy the document from Outlook to SharePoint Drafts and allow the user to edit the document offline.

The final option for taking content offline is SharePoint Workspace, which is a separately installed Office application. SharePoint Workspace 2010 is seen as the premier offline application for SharePoint, and supports many more scenarios than Outlook or SharePoint Drafts.

When considering the offline strategy for SharePoint, it is important to think about the offline scenarios that your users may be facing. Here are some key considerations:

➤ Do users primarily read content offline? If so, then Outlook may be a good choice.

➤ Do users need to work offline most of the time and perform most of their editing offline? If so, then SharePoint Workspace is a good choice. However, this must be deployed on the user's desktop.

➤ How often are users actually offline? With the ever-increasing availability of mobile Internet, Wi-Fi hotspots, and technologies such as Direct Access or virtual private networks (VPNs), users are not fully offline as much as they used to be.

➤ What role will mobile devices play in the offline strategy?

Co-authoring in Office 2010

Users will always get a richer experience with the latest version of Office when using it against SharePoint, and Office and SharePoint 2010 are no exception. When combined, users will benefit from a plethora of rich integration features. The most impressive is probably co-authoring.

Using Office 2010, multiple users can simultaneously open and edit Office documents from SharePoint libraries. Although co-authoring is taking place, Office will lock out the section of the file that the user is actively using, and will ensure that no other user can edit that particular section at the same time. However, other users can edit other sections of the document, as well as add review comments.

As shown in Figure 25-4, the integration is so rich that users can even see where other users are in the document, and can communicate directly with them if they have Office Communicator or Lync installed.

This feature is enabled by default, and requires no administrative configuration to use.

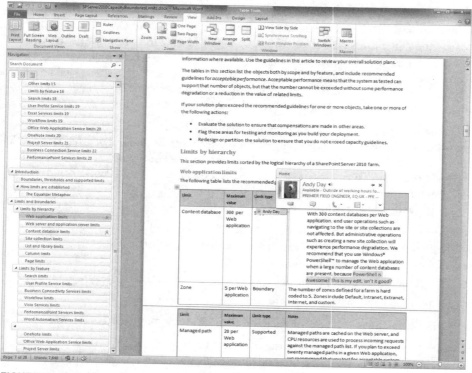

FIGURE 25-4: Seeing where other users are in a document

Though Office 2010 co-authoring is a great feature, it is only supported for Word 2010, PowerPoint 2010, or OneNote 2010. Excel 2010 is not supported.

Office Web Applications

Over recent years, a wide range of new hardware devices have become popular that do not necessarily have Office or Windows installed on them. To meet this trend, there has been an increasing need for web-based business productivity tools that allow users to perform basic authoring tasks directly through their browsers, without needing any client-side software installed (other than a browser).

Before SharePoint 2010, SharePoint really depended on and assumed there was a version of Microsoft Office installed on your user's desktop in order for the user to perform many of the document and content management tasks. However, in SharePoint 2010, you now have a web-based version of Office that can be used directly through the browser. This is called Office Web Applications (OWA).

In the past, the acronym OWA has referred to Outlook Web Access, which is a web-based companion to Outlook provided by Exchange server. In the 2010 product family, OWA now refers to the broader set of Office Web Applications, not just Outlook Web Access.

As shown in Figure 25-5, OWAs provide basic editing functionality for Word, Excel, PowerPoint, and OneNote files, which support the majority of a user's core authoring tasks.

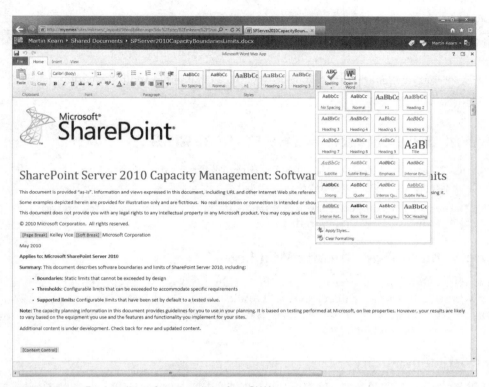

FIGURE 25-5: Basic editing functionality of an OWA

 OWAs are not a replacement for the full Office client. Instead they should be considered as a simple web companion.

Microsoft employees use both Office and OWA, and find that the two technologies complement each other very well. Office is used for day-to-day authoring, whereas the OWA is very useful if you want to read a document from a search result, or make a quick change to a document that is stored in a SharePoint site.

The OWA is a separate product that is built on top of SharePoint server, and must be installed and configured separately. When installed, the OWA will appear as service applications that can be grouped and accessed like any other service application.

As an architect, you should also consider the performance overhead of running OWAs, because they are a fairly resource-intensive service and, if used, must be factored into the overall server farm design. In some scenarios, it may be appropriate to have dedicated servers for running the OWA services.

When considering the use of OWA, the following factors should be taken into account:

➤   Do users need OWA?

➤   Do additional resources and/or servers need to be added to support OWA?

➤   Will users also have the full Office suite? If so, how will users understand when to use OWA versus when to use Office?

Let's now take a look at how SharePoint can help to manage documents and information in an enterprise-scale environment.

DOCUMENT MANAGEMENT IN THE ENTERPRISE

So far, this chapter has covered some of the end-user functionality that enables corporate information management in SharePoint 2010.

The rest of the chapter focuses on how SharePoint can help to manage content in an enterprise deployment, and introduces more administrative features.

Determining Where Documents Will Live

One of the key decisions architects need to make when planning corporate information services for SharePoint is working out where the documents will reside within the SharePoint system. SharePoint is a highly diverse technology, and has different types of repositories, nearly all of which provide the core capability of storing documents.

The Humble Document Library

The first fact to understand when planning corporate information services is that all SharePoint documents (that is, files) reside in a library of some sort. In SharePoint 2010, libraries come in various shapes and sizes, namely the following:

➤   Document library

➤   Forms library

➤   Picture library

➤   Slide library

➤   Asset library

➤   Data connection library

➤   Wiki page library

➤   Pages library

All libraries are just SharePoint lists with added functionality that relates to the type of file the library supports.

All libraries share the same core capabilities, just like any list within SharePoint. This was not the case in previous versions of SharePoint.

Libraries (just like any type of list) have the capability to contain folders. Contrary to popular belief, folders are used for more than simply organizing the documents stored within them. They can also be used to apply security information to the contents that may differ from the library itself. Folders can also be used to manage compliance information for the documents stored within.

Of course, folders are also used to organize content and provide the familiar "tree-view" interface that so many users still like to see.

However, in SharePoint 2010, the same "tree view" can be provided by creating virtual "folders" based on the metadata of the items within the library. This is part of the metadata-driven navigation functionality that is discussed later in this chapter.

Sites and Site Collection Structure

One of the other key factors for where documents will live inside SharePoint is your approach to site collections, and site structures within site collections.

Site collections are one of the primary administrative objects in SharePoint. As the name suggests, they are logical groupings of one or more sites. Site collections will always contain at least a root site, but may optionally contain up to 250,000 subsites that can be arranged in a hierarchical structure.

This leads to a key design decision about whether you want to encourage lots of site collections (arranged in a flat structure), or a fewer number of large site collections (with structures built inside them).

There is no best practice in this area, because it really depends on your users and how they will think about this kind of navigation mechanism. However, there has been a recent trend toward creating a larger number of top-level site collections that contain only a small number of subsites. This approach leads to a lot more flexibility with regard to what happens within the site collection, as well as how it is administered. However, the downside is that it becomes difficult to represent a logical structure with this approach.

This approach is also popular because a site collection cannot span databases. Therefore, having a larger number of smaller site collections helps with database sizing and capacity planning.

The site structure decision is key to helping users understand where documents live. This is because most sites in a site collection will have at least one document library, and the method by which users access the site is the first part of how they access the documents in the document library.

Information Management Policies

Information Management Policies (IMPs) are often overlooked when architects design corporate information services for SharePoint. They are often considered to purely relate to record management, and many organizations do not have record management on their radar for initial SharePoint adoption.

Although it is true that IMPs play a big part in record management, they apply much more broadly than just records, and should play a core part of your overall information management strategy.

IMPs can be created at a site collection level and can be applied to any list or library, thus managing the items stored within them. This is one of the biggest misconceptions around IMPs in SharePoint. Many people do not realize that they can apply IMPs to any list item or document, and that IMPs are not exclusively for items in a Record Center.

IMPs are managed at the site collection level in the Site Collection Policies gallery, which is accessible via Site Settings. However, your site must have the "In place record management" feature activated in order to see this option.

Generally speaking, IMPs should be created at the site collection level and then applied to your content types, which, in turn, will apply the policies to items created from the content types. It is possible to create policies directly at the list or library level, but it is better to use content types, because the policy will then apply wherever that content type is used, rather than being bound to a specific list or library.

IMPs define several different policies relating to how the files inheriting the policies are managed. These include the following:

➤ *Policy statement* — The policy statement is displayed to end users when they open items subject to this policy. The policy statement can explain which policies apply to the content, or indicate any special handling or information that users need to be aware of.

➤ *Retention* — This shows the schedule for how content is managed and disposed of by specifying a sequence of retention stages. If you specify multiple stages, each stage will occur one after the other in the order they appear on this page.

➤ *Auditing* — This specifies the events that should be audited for documents and items subject to this policy (as shown in Figure 25-6). These include the following:

➤ Opening or downloading documents, viewing items in lists, or viewing item properties

➤ Editing items

➤ Checking out or checking in items

➤ Moving or copying items to another location in the site

➤ Deleting or restoring items

➤ *Barcodes* — Assigns a barcode to each document or item. Optionally, Microsoft Office applications can require users to insert these barcodes into documents.

➤ *Labels* — You can add a label to a document to ensure that important information about the document is included when it is printed. To specify the label, type the text you want to use in the "Label format" box. You can use any combination of fixed text or document properties, except calculated or built-in properties such as `GUID` or `CreatedBy`.

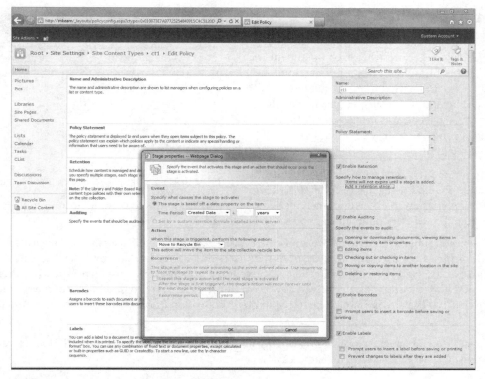

FIGURE 25-6: Defining Auditing policies in an IMP

As an architect, your first consideration should be whether or not you wish to manage documents and files in the general collaboration areas of SharePoint. Doing so will allow greater control over the information being produced. However, it may introduce additional burdens on the users as they provide the necessary information to comply with the policies.

> *Regardless of whether or not you use IMPs for general documents, you should consider a Record Center and SharePoint's wider record management capability, which is discussed in depth in Chapter 32.*

If you choose to use IMPs for general documents, you must decide on how polices are created and aligned with your content types. As discussed earlier in this chapter, having a sound content type design is critical, and will provide the building blocks for your IMP strategy.

It is also useful to note that you do not have to use all the features available in an IMP. For example, if you just wanted to add a retention policy, but did not require the other features available in IMPs, you simply leave the other features disabled.

Document IDs

SharePoint 2010 introduced a new feature called *Document ID*, which ensures that each document that is uploaded to SharePoint has a unique, human-readable ID. This can be used to easily reference the document. The advantage of this feature is that the document retains its ID if it is moved to a different location, and it can be referenced via its ID in a location-agnostic manner.

To get this functionality, the Document ID Service Feature must be enabled on each site collection. This

FIGURE 25-7: Using the Document ID Feature

will add a special column to every document called `Document ID`, and will contain a randomly generated unique ID for the document, as shown in Figure 25-7.

As an architect, you must decide on how useful this Feature will be to your users. The footprint is relatively low as far as the users are concerned in that users do not need to do anything. However, they will notice an ID field showing up in their document metadata. From a user's perspective, this Feature may add a lot of value for a relatively low cost. But from an overall design perspective, you must be sure that the Feature is enabled on every new site collection in order to ensure a consistent experience.

To achieve this, you may need to look at creating a Site Template Association Feature that activates the Document ID Service Feature upon site creation.

Managed Metadata Service Application

One of the major new feature sets in SharePoint 2010 is the Managed Metadata Service (MMS) application.

The MMS is an all-new service application that provides centrally managed, structured groups of terms available for use in metadata through the SharePoint infrastructure. This is coupled with an intuitive new user interface for tagging content and looking up terms from the MMS.

The MMS also provides content type replication, as discussed in the "Content Type Hub" section earlier in this chapter.

Understanding What a Term Is

A *term* is the most granular object in the MMS. It refers to a word or phrase that describes something, and might be used to tag documents, people, and other content.

Before SharePoint 2010, the concept of a term did not exist. This meant that the majority of metadata values were entered as free text, which could open up various issues, including the following:

➤ Misspellings and typographic errors.

➤ Varying use of terminology that means the same thing. For example, the words "car," "automobile," and "vehicle" all refer to the same thing.

➤ Users' not understanding what data was required for a given field. For example, a field entitled "document name" could refer to the filename of the document, the title of the document, or the type of document.

The difference between a term and normal free text is that a term is managed and can benefit from the following additional management features:

➤ A single official term can have multiple alternative labels. This will allow for synonyms, abbreviations, and other alternative ways of describing the same term.

➤ A description can help users identify whether or not they are referring to the right term.

➤ Language variations enable users to use terms in their native language, but still point to the same official term.

➤ The placement in a structure further provides context to the term. (See the "Understanding Term Sets" section later in chapter for more on this.)

The Act of Tagging

When users *tag* a piece of content, they associate that piece of content with a specific term from the MMS. This association can happen through various channels, such as the following:

➤ Completing a managed metadata field that has been defined as part of a content type or a list column

➤ Completing a user profile

➤ Tagging a page or other URL

When users perform the act of tagging, they will generally do so by simply typing into a text box. The MMS will then make some suggestions of terms that match the character the user has entered. The user can then choose a suggestion, or, if none applies and the term set is open, the user can enter a new term.

This interface is commonly used across all areas that use managed metadata within SharePoint, and is generally referred to as a *tagging application*. Figure 25-8 shows an example.

FIGURE 25-8: Tagging application

Understanding Term Sets

A *term set* is simply a structured hierarchy of terms that will typically relate to the same topic. Term sets can also be referred to as *taxonomy*.

The word "taxonomy" can mean different things to different people, so it is wise to avoid using it when describing managed metadata, or else ensure that you qualify it within the context of your discussion.

As well as simply providing a structure to store and organize terms, a term set has owners, contacts, and description, as well as a submission policy.

As an architect, your first job in designing an MMS is usually to understand what the customer's term sets are likely to be. This will entirely depend on the organization, and what members of the organization typically think about their content.

As an example, let's say that your two main term sets are as follows:

➤ *Product and Technologies* — Contains a structure hierarchy of all Microsoft products and technologies, listed by their formal name, with abbreviations and acronyms used as labels for each term.

➤ *Regions and Offices* — Contains all of Microsoft's physical offices, organized by country and region.

Other common term sets might include languages, document types, products or services, customers, and many more.

Where possible, it is best practice to create term sets around specific topics, rather than trying to use a single term set to represent the organization's entire terminology.

A *submission policy* is another important consideration for architects because this defines whether end users can submit terms to the term set (*open submission policy*), or whether they can only choose from predefined terms (*closed submission policy*). Some factors that may influence the policy here are as follows:

➤ How much do term set administrators understand about the real terminology used by the business? If the answer is "not sure" or "not a lot," then an open policy may work best because it allows the term set to organically grow (sometimes referred to as a *folksonomy*).

➤ Is there a dedicated term set administration process? If not, then it is important to consider how new terms are added if users cannot add them directly.

➤ How important is it that terms are authoritative? If the terms represent brand names or official product names, then a closed policy may work best to prevent users from adding incorrect terms that may confuse other users.

It is possible to add a "contact" to term sets. This is an e-mail address that users can use to send e-mail directly from within a tagging application, and suggest terms or provide feedback. This is a useful compromise between open and closed submission policies, because it gives users an alternative route to add terms.

Terms sets are grouped into *term groups*, which are the highest level in the MMS. Generally, you should try to stick with a single term group unless there is a good reason to have multiple ones. Reasons for multiple term groups might include the following:

➤ Securing terms so that they are available only to certain parts of the organization

➤ Separating terms groups so that different people or groups can manage them

The management of the MMS and its term sets happens through a Central Administration interface called the Term Store Management Tool, as shown in Figure 25-9.

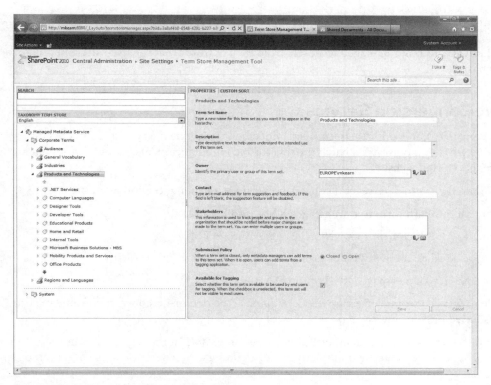

FIGURE 25-9: Term Store Management Tool

Enterprise Keywords

In addition to term sets, terms are also used in the *enterprise keyword* repository. An enterprise keyword is a feature that can be activated on any site collection that allows users to enter simple keywords as tags against any content where the feature is enabled.

Enterprise keywords can be used in addition to or instead of managed metadata fields. The act of tagging is exactly the same between the two. However, the difference is that enterprise keywords are not bound to any specific term set (or term set group), and allow users to enter anything they like (that is, the submission policy is open and cannot be closed).

If the term that the user enters matches existing managed terms, the interface will offer those terms as suggestions, but the users are under no obligation to use the suggestions.

MMS administrators can take keywords that are used in the keyword repository and do not match existing managed terms and move them into a term set, thus making them managed terms.

The first decision for architects is whether or not to allow the use of enterprise keywords. Enterprise keywords provide a very powerful facility, and can be used to very quickly gain an understanding of the organization's real terminology. However, the lack of control may worry administrators in certain organizations.

When starting out with MMS, many administrators will choose to only use enterprise keywords because this will give them the best indication of what the real terms are within the organization. They can then start to build managed term sets from the keywords that the users are entering on a day-to-day basis.

Document Conversion Services

With SharePoint 2010, it is possible to convert a document from one file type to another. This can be very useful if you must use a batch process for incoming documents for publication on an intranet site or external website.

By default, SharePoint provides several conversion services, including the following:

➤ From an InfoPath form to a web page (XML into HTML)

➤ From a Word document to a web page (`.docx` into HTML)

➤ From a Word document with macros to a web page (`.docm` into HTML)

➤ From XML to a web page (XML into HTML)

It is possible to write custom conversion services that use the document conversion framework to convert files based on your own criteria.

From an architect's perspective the important information to note in this section is that these services do exist, and they make a great platform for building any conversion application on top of.

Document Center Sites

A *Document Center* site is a special type of site collection that is designed to facilitate the storage of large volumes of documents. These sites are often used to store "official documents," and are more for final content than collaborative content.

A Document Center site is really just a standard site collection that is preconfigured with many of the features discussed in this chapter. The site also features some special web parts on the home page that lead users to common document-based activities (such as uploading a document and searching by Document ID). The site also features useful web parts that show the current use of the documents users have recently uploaded or modified, as well as the highest-rated documents.

If your organization has requirements focusing on an enterprise document repository, a Document Center site may be the right solution for them. However, it is important to consider whether requirements are best met by a Document Center or Record Center, because there is a lot of overlap.

Record Centers are discussed in detail in Chapter 32, and, if you are considering Document Center sites, ensure that you have read this chapter so that you can draw a well-balanced conclusion on which is the best fit.

The next section discusses some of the major software boundaries and imitations in SharePoint. These are very important because they may affect your design decisions in large-scale deployments.

SHAREPOINT SOFTWARE BOUNDARIES

Although SharePoint 2010 is certainly an enterprise-ready platform, boundaries exist for how far the platform will scale.

It is important that architects understand these boundaries because they can have a huge impact on how the platform is architected for corporation information services.

 A full list of published software boundaries is published online in a TechNet article called "SharePoint Server 2010 Capacity Management: Software Boundaries and Limits," which you can view at http://technet.microsoft .com/en-us/library/cc262787.aspx.

The key points that can sometimes trip up architects are as follows:

➤ *Content database size* — This is set at 200 GB per content database. This limitation applies especially when you consider that a single site collection can only be in a single database. Therefore, this effectively puts a limit of 200 GB on a site collection. (There are supported exceptions to this boundary for large sites like Record Centers and Document Centers. Refer to the online article referenced for more detail.)

➤ *File size* — This is set at 2 GB. Although, at first glance, this seems like a high limit, this does rule out SharePoint as a suitable storage repository for large files like some media files or CAD drawings.

➤ *Major versions* — This is set at 400,000. This boundary in itself is quite large. However, the architectural risk here is that this limit is much lower than recommended number of documents in a library (30 million). This means that if you have a library with major versioning enabled, you must work to the version retention boundary, not the overall number of documents boundary.

Most SharePoint deployments will never come anywhere close to the software boundaries, and if they do, the limitations can generally be worked around by altering the design. But the key point here is that these limitations are something you should know about before the system gets broadly adopted, not when it hits the limitation.

SUMMARY

This chapter has provided a broad summary of the features available to architects to help them manage, access, update, and derive value from documents stored in SharePoint 2010.

In this chapter, you have discovered some features that you may not have been familiar with, or are new to SharePoint 2010.

Content types are very important. Many of the corporate information management features are built on top of content types, and this is something that you should put a lot of thought into at the start of your SharePoint journey.

The MMS is a great new addition in SharePoint 2010, and provides a simple, powerful, but intuitive way for users to add metadata to content stored within SharePoint.

There are no "right" or "wrong" choices when it comes to corporate information services design. However, the key things to keep in mind are ensuring that you are making the right choice for your users, that you consider how they will use the technology, and how much of a jump you are asking them to make compared to their existing tools.

Chapter 26 examines some of the new business collaboration capabilities in SharePoint 2010.

26

Business Collaboration Services

By Bill Baer

Today's business environment has become increasingly competitive. Information workers must respond quicker and, in turn, collaborate more effectively to enhance the growth and performance of the enterprise. Information (and its ready access) plays an increasingly important role in the operations of today's business, and the role of the information worker has expanded in scope as a result.

By improving the efficiency of information workers, an enterprise can improve overall competitiveness, as well as streamline information searches, processing, analysis, and sharing.

In the context of this chapter, *business collaboration services* is defined as services that empower the information worker to more effectively collaborate on and share information across the enterprise. This chapter provides an overview of business collaboration features in SharePoint 2010.

INTRODUCING BUSINESS COLLABORATION FEATURES

Business collaboration features in SharePoint 2010 are designed to enable rapid collaboration through the packaging of the core capabilities within site templates, each designed to support a specific scenario (such as team-based collaboration, or simple informal information sharing). At the core of these capabilities are team and project sites, Document Workspace sites, Meeting Workspace sites, Blog sites, and Enterprise Wiki sites.

Team and Project Sites

As shown in Figure 26-1, team sites are the building blocks of collaboration in SharePoint 2010 products, designed specifically for team collaboration and the coordination of team activities with document collaboration and storage.

FIGURE 26-1: SharePoint 2010 team site

A typical scenario in which a team site is recommended is when an organization wants to separate business unit collaboration, and to provide a meaningful navigation and search experience. For example, a team site could be used in support of the Human Resources (HR) department, and another team site could be used in support of the Information Technology (IT) department. This design simplifies collaboration by providing ease of navigation and separation of duty, as well as enabling organizations to collaborate and conduct their business independently with minimal IT support. This is because the respective site collection administrators can administer and manage most aspects of the team site and its activities.

Document Workspace Sites

The Document Workspace site in SharePoint 2010 is designed to support the coordination of the development of one or more documents. Although it can be used independently, it is most commonly used to supplement existing team sites. Document Workspace sites provide unique out-of-the-box features and capabilities designed to help people stay informed about the status of documents supported by the sites, and provides tools to streamline the management of those documents.

In addition to management tools, as shown in Figure 26-2, Document Workspace sites provide additional value by supporting document collaboration and by providing solutions to publish announcements, assign tasks, share links, and receive alerts about the changing conditions of content stored in the workspace.

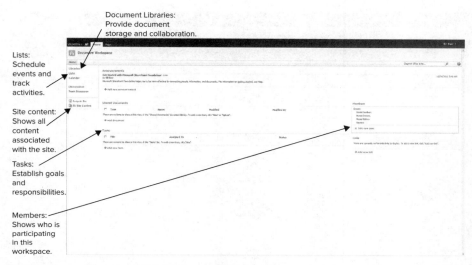

Document Libraries:
Provide document
storage and collaboration.

Lists:
Schedule
events and
track
activities.

Site content:
Shows all
content
associated
with the site.

Tasks:
Establish goals
and
responsibilities.

Members:
Shows who is
participating
in this
workspace.

FIGURE 26-2: SharePoint 2010 Document Workspace site

In most scenarios, Document Workspace sites are intended for short-term projects. However, they can be retained when required.

A typical scenario in which a Document Workspace site is recommended could be when a document already exists within an existing team site. For example, an organization may have an existing team site supported by its HR department that has started collaboration on new corporate HR policies in Shared Documents. To streamline and simplify the authoring and collaboration process, a new Document Workspace site could be created based on the policy document. The policy document then could provide the foundation for the Document Workspace, and authors and contributors could work in an environment where the recommended features and capabilities are readily accessible.

Document Workspace sites can be created based on an existing document, or created as an empty site for future documents and content.

To create a Document Workspace site based on an existing document, follow these steps:

1. Open the document library where the document is stored.

2. Select the name of the document, select Send To from the list of available options, and click Create Document Workspace, as shown in Figure 26-3.

3. Click OK.

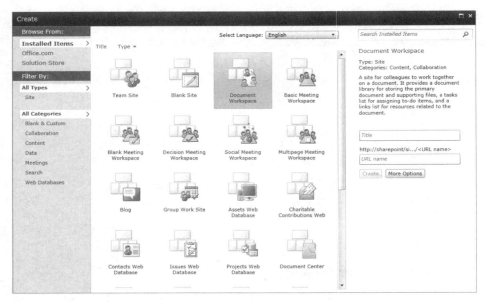

FIGURE 26-3: Create dialog

To create an empty Document Workspace site, follow these steps:

1. Click Site Actions, and then select New Site from the list of available options.

2. Select Document Workspace from the list of available options.

3. Enter the information about the Document Workspace site that you want to create, such as the title and the last part of the website address.

4. Click Create.

Meeting Workspace Sites

Similar to Document Workspace sites, SharePoint 2010 introduces (and extends) the concept of Meeting Workspace sites. These sites are designed to support the organization of meetings and recording of meeting results. Features associated with Meeting Workspace sites include preconfigured lists for managing the meeting agenda, attendees, and any documents associated with the meeting.

Meeting Workspace sites are offered in five out-of-the-box configurations associated with the following templates:

➤ Basic Meeting Workspace

➤ Blank Meeting Workspace

➤ Decision Meeting Workspace

➤ Social Meeting Workspace

➤ Multipage Meeting Workspace

As shown in Figure 26-4, the Basic Meeting Workspace template provides the essentials to support common, recurring meetings with a defined agenda and attendees, and revolves around a specific document or topic.

FIGURE 26-4: Basic Meeting Workspace template

As shown in Figure 26-5, the Blank Meeting Workspace template is an empty Meeting Workspace template that can be customized to support more fluid and dynamic meetings, or when the Basic Meeting Workspace template does not meet the needs of the meeting, and requires some degree of customization.

FIGURE 26-5: Blank Meeting Workspace template

As shown in Figure 26-6, the Decision Meeting Workspace template is designed to support meetings that have (or are anticipated to have) a specific outcome, and includes features to support tracking status and decision making. This template is not recommended for the support of recurring meetings, or when meetings do not have an actionable result.

FIGURE 26-6: Decision Meeting Workspace template

As shown in Figure 26-7, the Social Meeting Workspace template is designed to be used to plan social occasions (for example, a potluck or holiday party). It provides features to be used to manage attendees, provide directions, and upload images related to the event. The Social Meeting Workspace template is not designed to support recurring meetings, meetings with an actionable result, or most common business meetings.

FIGURE 26-7: Social Meeting Workspace template

As shown in Figure 26-8, the Multipage Meeting Workspace template is a combination of the Basic Meeting Workspace and Blank Meeting Workspace templates. It provides the predefined features of the Basic Meeting Workspace template, and includes additional blank pages that can be customized to support the meeting. The Multipage Meeting Workspace template is useful when meetings require supplemental content, such as a Wiki for brainstorming, or a collection of intellectual property generated throughout the course of the meeting.

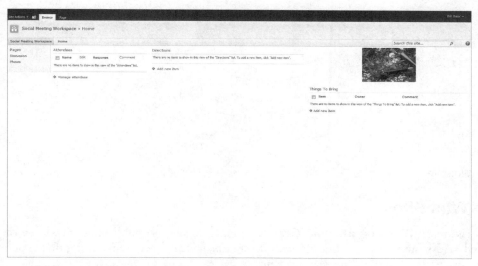

FIGURE 26-8: Multipage Meeting Workspace template

Blog Sites

Blog sites are designed to enable users to share thoughts and expertise using text, images, links, and other media through frequent short postings related to the users' interests or areas of expertise. Postings are stored in reverse chronological order, enabling viewers to quickly identify the most recent information. Blog sites serve as an active collaboration tool that can supplement team sites and other sites in SharePoint 2010.

As shown in Figure 26-9, organizations can use Blog sites to share corporate information both internally and externally, or to share thoughts on the business.

Categories:
Enable quick
filtering
of posts.

Archives:
Minimize
navigation
and enable
historical
views.

Subscription:
and
Syndication
Enables users
to stay up-to
date on
content.

Tools:
Provide access to
common blog
functions.

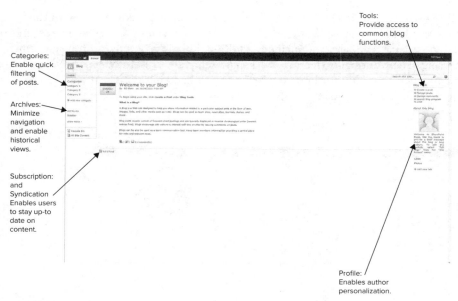

Profile:
Enables author
personalization.

FIGURE 26-9: Blog site

Enterprise Wiki Sites

As shown in Figure 26-10, Enterprise Wiki sites are designed to support publishing knowledge that is to be shared across the enterprise. Enterprise Wiki sites provide easy content editing that supports co-authoring, discussions, and project management.

The philosophy of wikis is to provide an information-sharing solution that can be easily updated, maintained, and corrected over time, thus allowing multiple users to participate in and co-author information that can be shared across the enterprise.

Ratings:
Help quickly identify
value and accuracy.

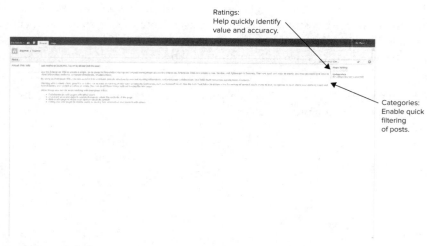

Categories:
Enable quick
filtering
of posts.

FIGURE 26-10: Enterprise Wiki site

Understanding your organization's business challenges will help define how the various business collaboration templates and definitions should be used to respond to those challenges, as well as promote efficient and effective collaboration and knowledge sharing.

KEY BUSINESS CHALLENGES

The primary business challenges associated with delivering a meaningful collaboration solution are based on the accessibility of its content, and how empowered the end users are to collaborate with minimal effort.

Understanding Your Requirements

Your organization's business requirements will define your site layout and provisioning scenarios, and will encompasses a number of technology considerations to include search and navigation. When planning your layout, you should understand the layout of your organization, and establish building blocks that map to that layout, and you could subsequently align your site strategy to that layout.

For example, if your organization encompasses large primary business units such as IT or HR, these organizations can be distributed in one of two ways. One way is through the isolation of those divisions into unique web applications (such as `http://itweb` or `http://hrweb`). Another way is to establish team sites to identify those organizations. For example, if you had a top-level website `http://intranet.contoso.com`, you could create `http://intranet.contoso.com/Sites/IT` and `http://intranet.contoso.com/Sites/HR` for those divisions.

The use of independent web applications provides the best possible logical separation of divisions, but it also lends itself to an increase in management overhead. Although it provides easily remembered URLs, it results in a more complex global search experience. This design is typically recommended for extremely large organizations whose concerns include the isolation of divisions to support security or other regulatory compliance.

Once a base hierarchy has been established, you can then consider how smaller independent entities of your divisions will be represented. If you are using a site collection–centric model (for example, `http://intranet.contoso.com/Sites/IT`), you should consider using sites to support those entities. For example, `http://intranet.contoso.com/Sites/IT/Exchange` could be used to provide a collaborative solution for the Microsoft Exchange support organization within IT.

Understanding Your Business Entities

Your organization's structure is useful for defining the appropriate information architecture suitable to support open collaboration. Understanding your business entities and their hierarchy is useful when planning the content structure and layout that will support enhanced content authoring, sharing, and discovery.

A common approach is to begin by identifying your top-level business units. In many organizations, these are IT, HR, Legal, and so on. In other organizations, these may be divisions responsible for the development of one or more products. Once identified, business units or divisions should then be considered for either site collections, or top-level site collections with separate web applications. This decision will be based on requirements and technology.

For example, though it may be preferred to leverage separate web applications to enable the broadest security boundary, your organization may not have the hardware required to support such a design, or the increased management complexity may preclude that choice. For smaller organizations whose business units such as IT are smaller, site collections are the preferred solutions (such as `http://intranet.contoso.com/Sites/IT`). For larger organizations whose IT unit may encompass thousands of employees, a web application–scoped approach is recommended (such as `http://itweb`).

Formal versus Ad-hoc (Unstructured) Sites

As you plan your business collaboration solution, you will need to decide whether formal versus ad-hoc sites are preferred in support of your goals.

Formal collaboration refers to a solution that is built according to predefined requirements, and adheres to an established hierarchy and set of processes. In a formal collaboration scenario, top-level sites are defined according to a model that represents the structure of your organization, and has a defined Term Store, navigation, and search configuration. Users are most productive when constrained to a formal collaboration solution because less time is spent looking for information and navigating the structure of the SharePoint environment. However, formal collaboration limits a user's creativity, and ability to work dynamically on projects or easily share ideas.

Ad-hoc (or *unstructured collaboration*) sites enable users to create content in SharePoint on demand to include sites and site collections. This is not generally tied to requirements or processes. Though an unstructured model empowers the end user and promotes open information sharing, brainstorming, and creativity, it lends itself to a complex structure that cannot be easily searched and navigated, and leads to information chaos where information is not easily discovered.

Developing a balance between structured and unstructured collaboration is essential to ensuring information is easily discovered, while promoting information sharing and empowering users of SharePoint. A common approach to achieving this balance is to define a structured collaboration layout that is designed around your organization's structure, such as predefined top-level sites that represent divisions or business units, followed by enabling capabilities such as self-service site creation to open the environment to ad-hoc collaboration.

Deciding on Site Self-Service Provisioning Options

SharePoint 2010 supports *self-service provisioning* of both site collections and sites when enabled by a farm or site collection administrator. Self-service provisioning enables users of a SharePoint 2010 deployment to rapidly provision and create new site collections that can be immediately used in support of ongoing collaboration. However, this can have a negative impact on governance and information architecture.

When considering the enabling of self-service provisioning of site collections on a web application (also known as *self-service site creation*), you should thoroughly consider the impact on your existing information architecture.

Although users are empowered to quickly create services that enable collaboration and information sharing, maintaining this information can become challenging, and search becomes the primary mechanism to find information within the organization.

For example, a well-defined information architecture implements a hierarchical approach to presenting information to potential consumers of it — such as ensuring divisions are represented by site collections, and business units within that division are represented as individual sites with the membership in their respective site collection. This approach enables users to identify and associate a URL with a respective division such as HR, and ensures permissions can be established appropriately both for contributors and consumers to and for that content.

Content accessibility and security should also be considered when planning for self-service provisioning. Because content is independently secured within a site collection, users both within and outside of the associated division, business unit, and/or other entity may not have the appropriate permission to access content which is required or needed to conduct their work.

Self-service provisioning can lead to fragmented collaboration, in that users create site collections to collaborate on documents with individuals, perhaps comprising a larger audience. It can also result in the isolation of stakeholders associated with the content.

To enable self-service site creation, follow these steps:

1. On the SharePoint 2010 Central Administration home page, select Application Management.

2. Click "Configure self-service Site creation" under Site Collections.

3. On the Self-Service Site Collection Management page, select the desired web application from the list of available web applications.

4. As shown in Figure 26-11, select the On checkbox to enable self-service site creation, and then select "Require secondary contact" to optionally require a secondary contact.

5. Click OK.

FIGURE 26-11: Self-service site creation settings

Deciding between Site Collections and Subsites

Site collections represent the top-level site element that can be created in a SharePoint environment, whereas sites are provisioned within site collections as subordinate objects. The decision to implement a site collection versus a site-scoped hierarchy should be based on how much sites have in common with one another, how they should be managed, and whether you would like a unified navigation and search experience.

Site collections are groups of sites that share a common owner and administrative configuration such as permissions. As mentioned, site collections represent the top-level sites that can be created in a SharePoint environment, and are commonly preceded by the /Sites managed path. Site collections help to avoid the complexity of managing multiple sites, because they provide a single element wherein content is organized and permissions are managed.

Site collections should be considered under the following conditions:

➤ Isolated permissions or security settings are required.

➤ Circumstances exist where content is often moved between content databases to support capacity-management scenarios.

➤ Simple backup and recovery solutions are required.

➤ Isolation of workflows is required.

➤ Independent quotas are required.

➤ Decentralized or delegated administration is preferred (such as access request approval).

➤ Life-cycle management processes are in place.

Sites should be considered under the following conditions:

➤ A unified navigation (including top navigation and breadcrumbs) is preferred.

➤ The sharing of content types is required, or pushdown is required.

➤ Reusable workflows are needed in support of collaboration.

➤ Security groups are commonly used to secure objects and access.

➤ Lookup fields across lists are required.

➤ Independent search scopes are desired to support content discovery.

➤ Feature sets are deployed to support a specific activity.

➤ Consistent theming or branding is preferred.

Sites are generally distributed across and created to adhere to a specific hierarchy based on the foundation element of a top-level site. Within the top-level site, there can be a number of subsites that contain other subsites. This structure comprises the site collection.

Site Life-Cycle Management

When not required for retention for regulatory compliance or legal needs, content should be periodically purged to support efficient utilization of storage resources, and to improve the relevancy of search results by expiring and removing content no longer required in support of business functions. SharePoint 2010 provides support for managing the life cycle of site collections, which can be interpreted in the same manner as a passport. For example, site collections are stamped with an issued date, and have a corresponding expiry date. Once the expiry date is reached, site collections that have not been renewed are deleted.

When planning your site life-cycle management strategy, you must plan how to handle sites that are inactive (that is, have not been renewed). The Feature in SharePoint 2010 that supports site life-cycle management is known as Site Use Confirmation and Deletion, which identifies sites that are no longer required, based on users either accepting the deletion of the site, or a failure to respond to renewal requests.

Site Use Confirmation and Deletion works by periodically sending an e-mail message to site collection administrators based on configurable intervals to either confirm usage of the site collection (which resets the expiry date), or by enabling users to delete the site collection if no longer required. In the event that users fail to respond to a configurable number of notifications, the site collection can be optionally deleted with no user action.

Planning the use of Site Use Confirmation and Deletion should include the following considerations:

➤ You should determine the expiration period in which site collections should be renewed. Keep in mind that, as recommended practice, structured collaboration should be configured to 180 days or more, and unstructured collaboration to 90 days or less. The default configuration is 90 days.

➤ The frequency of e-mail notifications to site collection administrators should be mapped to your users' characteristics. Frequent messages will drive responsiveness within an organization whose volume of work is conducted over e-mail, whereas infrequent notifications may go unnoticed or missed. E-mail notifications can be delivered daily, weekly, and monthly.

➤ You should decide on a site collection deletion strategy, specifically whether unused site collections should be deleted when an administrator does not respond to notifications. Automatic deletion should be carefully planned. For example, if the expiration is set to 30 days, and an individual is out of the office for 30 days or longer because of vacation or other commitment, there is a risk the site collection and its content will be inadvertently deleted. Best practice recommendations include ensuring that content database backups are regularly scheduled, as well as requiring that a secondary site collection administrator be specified for all site collections in the environment.

➤ You should decide on the number of notifications that should be sent prior to automatic deletion. The default configuration in SharePoint 2010 is 28 e-mail messages before the site collection is considered for automatic deletion. However, this can be increased or decreased as required.

To enable and configure Site Use Confirmation and Deletion, follow these steps:

1. On the SharePoint 2010 Central Administration home page, select Application Management.

2. As shown in Figure 26-12, traverse to "Confirmation and Automatic Deletion Settings" under Site Collections.

3. On the Site Use Confirmation and Deletion page select the desired web application from the list of available web applications.

4. Specify the values for "Send e-mail notification to owners of unused site collections," the schedule, and "Automatically delete the Site Collection if use is not confirmed" settings.

5. Click OK.

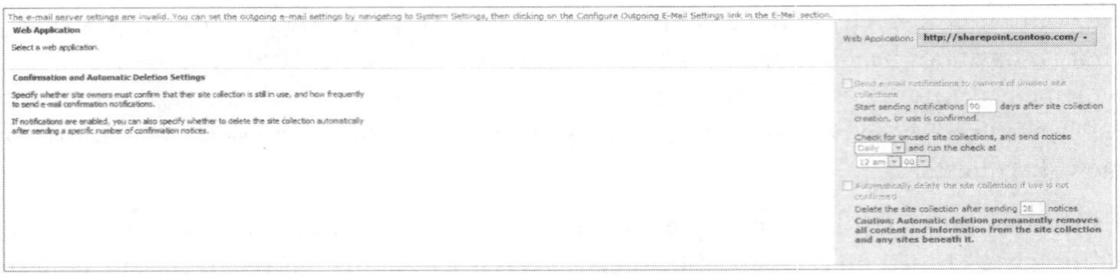

FIGURE 26-12: Site Use Confirmation and Deletion

COMMON BUSINESS SCENARIOS

Although SharePoint 2010 provides a number of capabilities to support of a meaningful collaboration experience, in some cases, users are not always online, but need access to information stored in SharePoint. SharePoint 2010 supports a number of methods that can be used in support of such scenarios.

Taking Sites and List Information Offline

SharePoint 2010 provides a number of solutions for taking sites and lists offline. These solutions enable users to select content that will be synchronized with their client machines.

SharePoint Workspace 2010

SharePoint Workspace 2010 is the evolution of Microsoft Office Groove, and includes new features that enable users to expand upon the traditional online-centric boundaries of SharePoint 2010 by allowing access to SharePoint content from anywhere.

SharePoint Workspace 2010 enables users to synchronize document libraries from SharePoint so that they can be accessed and viewed, and their content edited, at any time from a client machine, without requiring connectivity to the source SharePoint environment.

As mentioned, synchronized content can be accessed locally on a PC without connectivity to the source environment. It can also be edited locally on a PC without connectivity to the source environment, and automatically synchronized when the user is back online. Content may also be synchronized by sending on the delta between source and synchronized content.

Microsoft Outlook 2010

In addition to SharePoint Workspace 2010, users can also take content offline using Microsoft Outlook (for example, libraries, contact lists, and task lists). In many organizations, this is the preferred method for taking SharePoint content offline, because users of SharePoint will likely also be using Microsoft Outlook with Microsoft Exchange. The capability for users to take content offline with Microsoft Outlook enables them to become more efficient when they don't have access to SharePoint.

Synchronized content appears in Outlook under SharePoint Lists in the Navigation pane.

Content synchronized with Microsoft Outlook 2010 is unidirectional, meaning that content cannot be edited in Microsoft Outlook 2010 and synchronized back to the source environment.

Office Mobile 2010

Office Mobile 2010 on the Windows Phone provides access to powerful solutions that can be used in combination with SharePoint 2010, including SharePoint Workspace Mobile. With SharePoint Workspace Mobile, you can do the following:

➤ View document libraries and lists

➤ Access and open documents using Office Mobile, and synchronize them back to SharePoint

➤ Automatically synchronize offline content with SharePoint when changes are made to the source content

➤ View all content to include calendars and contacts

Geographically Distributed/Replicated Collaboration Sites

Keeping in mind that organizations today have a global presence, it is becoming increasingly important to ensure satellite, branch, regional, and global offices have the same information availability as the users in traditional corporate offices, and that information can be made accessible to suppliers and partners.

SharePoint 2010 does not provide an out-of-the-box solution to support content replication. However, several methods can be employed to make information available to users outside of the typical corporate office.

KEY ARCHITECTURAL CONSIDERATIONS

Several key architectural considerations should be evaluated when planning a collaborative solution, each with unique characteristics that may impact your previous design decisions. This section reviews some of these considerations.

Aggregating Content from Multiple Sites

In many SharePoint environments, related information is distributed across many site collections and sites. The capability to aggregate and surface this information under one structured location facilitates improved information discovery and, as a result, productivity. Information in SharePoint 2010 can be aggregated and surfaced using a number of out-of-the-box features and capabilities.

Prior to aggregating content, you should use the following guidelines to determine which technique is most appropriate to your scenario:

➤ *Scope* — Will content be aggregated from single or multiple sites? Will the query be isolated within a site hierarchy, or cross-site boundaries and hierarchies? Will site collections be spanned in the query scope?

➤ *Information* — What type of information will participate in the query or queries? What type of information will be targeted (for example, lists or other types of objects)?

➤ *Performance* — How much data will be in scope to be accessed and retrieved? Does the retrieved data need to be manipulated?

➤ *Readiness* — Does the retrieved data need to be updated in real time, or less frequently?

Once you have answered these questions and identified the scenarios, you can begin to understand the limitations that may be applicable. For example, SharePoint can use SQL to query a content database and retrieve data from within site collections. However, if the scope is intended to span site collections, SQL is no longer a viable option for the scenario. In this case, SharePoint 2010 Search may be the most suitable candidate, providing that users can accept the associated latency.

Several available and common aggregation techniques can be used in support of each of the aforementioned guidelines, including the following:

➤ Content Query web part

➤ Portal Site Map Provider

➤ Direct Cross-Site Collection Query

➤ Search

Content Query Web Part

The Content Query web part is the most common approach used to support data aggregation with SharePoint scoped at the site collection level, and can aggregate list data and content types within a site hierarchy (such as cross-list queries). The Content Query web part offers good performance characteristics for these types of queries, because it leverages the object cache and provides a high level of accuracy and real-time results, depending on the configuration of the object cache.

The Content Query web part is suitable for scenarios when querying list data along the site hierarchy, high performance and results accuracy are required, and a simple development experience is required.

 The Content Query web part supports only Extensible Stylesheet Language Transformations (XSLTs).

Portal Site Map Provider

Similar to the Content Query web part, the Portal Site Map Provider is also scoped at the site collection level. However, in addition to list data and content types, it also supports sites and webs (subordinate objects of sites) within a site hierarchy. Unlike the Content Query web part, the Portal Site Map Provider supports direct access to SharePoint data. Therefore, you can perform complex tasks such as the calculation of values.

The Portal Site Map Provider provides good performance characteristics with emphasis on query optimization because of its use of the object cache. However, it does not offer a high degree of accuracy because of results caching.

The Portal Site Map Provider is suitable for scenarios when querying list, site, or web data along the site hierarchy; high performance is required; results accuracy can be delayed; and when a more complex development experience is acceptable.

Direct Cross-Site Collection Query

Direct Cross-Site Collection Query is the most common approach when information must be aggregated across a server farm environment, but data aggregation is not required. Direct Cross-Site Collection Query is supported under the same scope as the Portal Site Map Provider. However, performance suffers, because it does not leverage the object cache.

Direct Cross-Site Collection Query is suitable for scenarios when target queries with high results accuracy are required that do not require traversing a site hierarchy, or require high performance.

Search

Search is the most effective method of data aggregation with SharePoint because of its simplicity and broad access. Search is capable of aggregating content across a server farm environment. Although Search does not provide direct access to the objects included in the aggregation scope (Search scope), it can aggregate along and across hierarchies, and query large data sets across a server farm, perform complex queries, and perform data searches as an efficient mechanism for aggregating different types of data across site collections with minimal overhead.

Search is suitable for scenarios when an out-of-the-box experience with minimal overhead is preferred, and information must be aggregated across a server farm.

 Results accuracy is directly attributed to the crawl schedule configured for the target content source.

Defining a Common User Experience

Defining a common user experience ensures that users of SharePoint 2010 are provided with consistent navigation, look, and feel.

Adhering to Compliance and Regulatory Requirements

Adhering to compliance and regulatory requirements is becoming increasingly important in a global business environment.

Electronic discovery (eDiscovery) is often defined as the process of locating and producing electronic information to support events associated with compliance and/or regulatory requirements, including audits or litigation.

SharePoint 2010 provides new features and capabilities such as auditing policies, expiration policies, and Search that should be considered when planning for these events.

eDiscovery commonly involves finding relevant documents, and restricting what users can do with the documents after they have been located.

In many cases, the initial response to an eDiscovery request is referred to as a *hold*. A hold is set of documents that may need to be produced in response to a request. SharePoint 2010 supports a hold at the site level through the Hold and eDiscovery Feature, and can be enabled and disabled by a site collection administrator or site owner.

 The Hold and eDiscovery Feature is enabled by default on a Records Center site.

The Hold and eDiscovery Feature enables users to create and manage holds, add existing items to a hold, use Search to discover content, and copy the content to an alternate location, in addition to locking down the content so that it cannot be further modified or deleted once a hold has been placed.

Using Search in the context of eDiscovery enables either the copying of content returned to a content organizer (which, in turn, routes the content to an alternate location based on content metadata), or allowing the content to remain in place and assigning a *lockdown policy*. A lockdown policy prevents content from being modified or deleted by users.

In the event that a compliance request is received, you can enable the Hold and eDiscovery Feature on each site collection where information relevant to the request may be stored, and further use Search to crawl sites where the Hold and eDiscovery Feature is enabled.

 When sending documents to a content organizer, the documents version history is erased.

To preserve important metadata associated with content, an auditing policy should be established on all site collections where the relevant information is stored. Auditing policies are a subset of information management policies in SharePoint 2010. The Auditing Policy Feature logs events and operations that are performed on documents and list items.

SharePoint 2010 supports configuring auditing to log events such as the following:

➤ Editing a document or item

➤ Viewing a document or item

➤ Checking a document in or out

➤ Changing the permissions for a document or item

➤ Deleting a document or item

Managing and Extending Metadata

In the context of SharePoint, *metadata* can mean "data about data," which is also known as *descriptive metadata*. Descriptive metadata is used to describe the contents and context of information or data, increasing the quality of the original information or data. Descriptive metadata helps to facilitate discovery of relevant information, and organize information by providing readily accessible identification.

With the proper implementation of metadata in a SharePoint environment, users can search and locate information by relevant criteria through Search and navigation, quickly identify resources, help distinguish dissimilar resources, and organize resources based on audience or topic.

In SharePoint 2010, metadata is provided through the Managed Metadata Service application. When provisioned in a SharePoint environment, the Managed Metadata Service application provides a Term Store and optional content types.

A *Term Store* contains terms that are reused across content stored in SharePoint. *Terms* are words or phrases that are associated with individual items within lists, libraries, and other content storage within a site. Terms are stored in *term sets,* which contain a set of related terms (for example, a term set called "document status" might include such terms as "pending," "in progress," "final," and so on). SharePoint 2010 provides two distinct term set configurations: a *local term set* and a *global term set.*

Local term sets are created within site collections, and, as such, are scoped to that site collection. Local term sets are useful when defining metadata that is specific to the content in that site collection, but may not be useful from a global perspective. For example, a local term set of "parts" might contain information such as "network card" or "monitor" that is relevant to an organization's IT department, but may not be useful enterprise-wide, such as in the HR department.

Global term sets are defined by a Term Store administrator outside of the context of a site collection. Global term sets commonly define industry or enterprise standard terms that are used throughout the organization. For example, a global term set of "regions and languages" might include all of the recognized regions and languages that the organization may do business in, such as the Asia and Pacific Area.

Term Stores are administered by Term Store administrators who manage the store and its associated terms. Term Store administrators can create and delete term groups, assign users to the Group Manager role, and modify Term Store languages. Term Store administrators should be designated by the organization as a representative of the legal and compliance organization who can identify the global terms most appropriate for organizational use, while ensuring that the terms meet any regulatory compliance.

Group Managers are specified by Term Store administrators, thus enabling the Term Store administrator to delegate access to certain administrative and management functions (such as importing term sets, assigning and removing users from the Contributors role, and all permissions associated with Contributors role). Group Managers should be business unit leaders (or a representative thereof) who have a fundamental understanding of business unit-wide terms that are used throughout the development of the product or function for which the unit is responsible.

Contributors are individuals specified by Group Managers who can create, rename, copy, reuse, move, and delete term sets. They can modify a term set's description, owner, contact, stakeholders, submission policy, and whether a term set is available for tagging. They can create, rename, copy, reuse, merge, deprecate, and delete terms, as well as modify a term's description, labels, default label, and whether or not the term is available for tagging. Contributors should be identified by the Group Manager as the individuals familiar with the business unit's process and unique terms used throughout the business unit. This should be a small body of individuals who meet regularly to review term submissions, and approve or deny them as required.

Users consume terms identified by the Term Store administrator, Group Manager, and Contributors. Users can validate values for managed metadata columns, and create new enterprise keywords if enabled by the Term Store administrator.

Figure 26-13 shows the administration of the Term Store as seen by the Term Store administrator, and also shows the terms and term sets hierarchy.

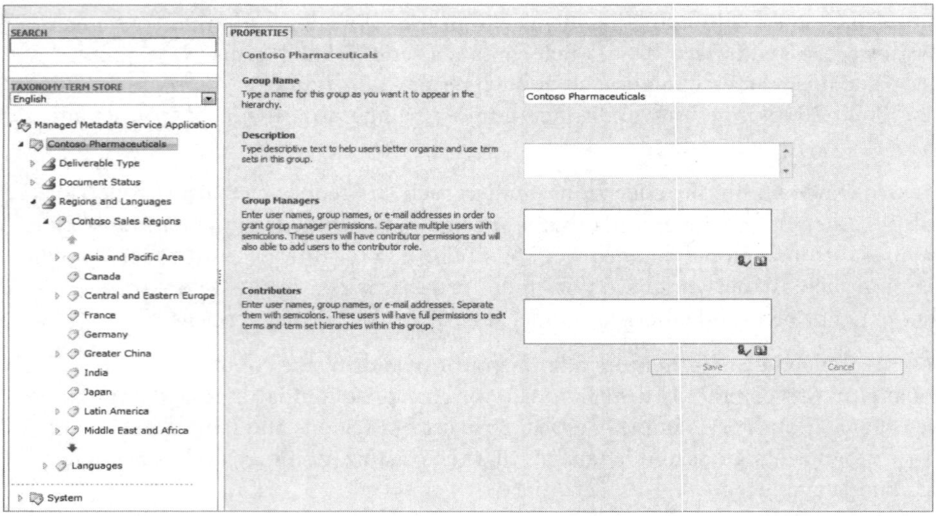

FIGURE 26-13: Term Store management

When planning metadata, you should identify individuals who fit within the description of the described roles, and who have insight into the business, can interface with or are members of a legal and compliance team, and who understand the fundamentals of metadata and its application to data, discovery, and compliance.

Deciding between Global and Local Navigation Elements

Users need the capability to move around within the system quickly and return to their original location with minimal effort. Site navigation provides the primary means for enabling users to browse the content and structure of a site. SharePoint 2010 provides a set of navigation features out-of-the-box that can be customized and extended to enable users to move around the content of a site.

The navigation experience should be aligned to the site collection or site hierarchy, and not planned independently. Once you have decided on the appropriate hierarchy for your site collections and sites, you can choose whether sites will inherit the navigation experience from the site collection they are subordinates of (including the top link bar and Quick Launch menu settings), or, optionally, you can plan to implement unique settings.

Inheriting Navigation

SharePoint 2010 supports the concept of *navigation inheritance* in that a site can inherit the navigation structure of the parent site collection. This enables site users to quickly identify their location within a site collection and navigate back to parent as needed.

When using links from the parent site collection or site, navigation links are drawn across the top link bar. In Figure 26-14, a `http://intranet.contoso.com/Sites/IT/SharePoint` site inherits links from its `http://intranet.contoso.com/Sites/IT` parent site collection.

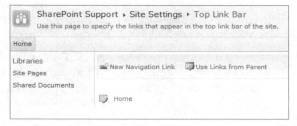

FIGURE 26-14: Top link bar

Such a design enables users to quickly identify where they are within a site collection or site. Site collections can also establish a connection to a top-level portal site. This enables users to navigate the entire structure of their organization, as shown in Figure 26-15. In Figure 26-16, a site collection at `http://intranet.contoso.com/Sites/IT` is connected to a parent portal site, `http://intranet.contoso.com`.

FIGURE 26-15: Inherited navigation

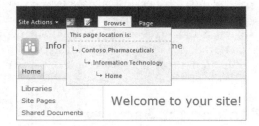

FIGURE 26-16: Portal site connection

A portal site connection can be used when you would like to link one site collection to another site collection, as shown in Figure 26-16. The connected portal site is included in the global breadcrumb navigation for the current site collection. When users of the connected site collection click the up folder, the configured portal site is listed as the parent of the site collection. This enables users to navigate to the portal site more easily.

To connect a site collection to a portal site, follow these steps:

1. Navigate to the site collection to be configured for a portal site connection.

2. On the Site Actions menu, click Site Settings.

3. On the Site Settings page, select Portal Site Connection under Site Collection Administration.

4. Select "Connect to portal Site" on the Portal Site Connection page.

5. Specify the name and URL for the portal site.

6. Click OK to commit the changes.

The navigation experience at the site collection level should be based on the unique purpose and structure of the site collection. The navigation experience can be implemented in one of two ways, either through a *granular* approach (under which lesser-used objects are also presented in the navigation experience), or through a *minimal* approach (under which navigation is related to top-level, common objects). There are trade-offs with these implementations.

Though a granular approach enables users to quickly discover a number of potential elements to work with, it often creates confusion caused by the number of available links. Conversely, the minimal approach enables a more appealing user experience that reduces confusion, but as a user navigates deeply within a site collection, it may be more difficult for users to return to their starting point.

Consider mapping navigation to how users are expected to interact with the site. For example, users might access a particular site to perform a specific task, such as to read announcements or access a specific document. In this scenario, a minimal navigation experience enables those users to quickly identify and work with the information they are seeking.

Planning for Performance

SharePoint 2010 performance is driven through the establishment of both the information architecture and database layer designed within the product's support boundaries. A properly planned and implemented information architecture ensures that content can be easily located, cataloged, and subsequently indexed for further discovery. Minimizing the effort required to locate content, in turn, minimizes the number of executed search queries and clicks issued by end users. As a result, the load across servers in the farm's topology is minimized.

Planning for Security

Controlling user access is a fundamental component of supporting an effective business collaboration strategy. Overly restrictive access controls can limit collaboration effectiveness, whereas open access controls can contribute to inadvertent information disclosure through the exposure of audience-specific content. SharePoint 2010 supports improved controls that enable a finer level of granularity and more authentication options than previous versions of SharePoint.

Planning for Storage

SharePoint 2010 implements a tiered approach to storage and capacity management. This hierarchy includes the content database, responsible for providing core storage for all subordinate objects, as well as web applications, site collections, sites, lists, and libraries, and the site collection responsible for hosting subordinate object content.

When planning storage, you should understand the relationships between each of these objects, as well as their impact on capacity and storage planning.

Content databases are the smallest unit of representation on the file system. SharePoint 2010 supports an individual content database size of up to 4 TB for core scenarios that include collaboration. Content databases can be more than 4 TB to an unlimited size (up to SQL Server's maximum capacity specification) for document archive and records management scenarios.

Site collection storage is limited by assigning a new or existing quota template to site collections either programmatically (as they are provisioned) or later through a manual process. Although, in theory, a site collection can be sized in parallel to its host content databases, many out-of-the-box tools used to manage those site collections may not function as intended (such as backup and restore).

As shown in Figure 26-17, the site collection quota will define how many site collections can be supported within a given content database before a new content database is required.

FIGURE 26-17: Storage planning

Two models can be used when planning the number of content databases that will be stored within a content database. These models can be referred to as the "airline booking" and "accounting" models.

Airline Booking Model

The airline booking model uses an open provisioning model in that the content database can receive more site collections than its size can support. This model uses the assumption that users will not consume the entirety of their assigned quotas, and typical life-cycle events (such as deleting content) will keep a content database within its limits.

An example of the airline booking model could be a content database whose limits are set to a maximum number of site collections of 10,000, with a site collection size of 10 GB. Using this model, if all users consumed the entirety of their quotas, the organization would exceed the maximum supported size of the content database.

Accounting Model

Conversely, the accounting model is more precise, and assumes that users will consume the entirety of their quotas. It takes into account the maximum number of site collections supported per content database, in addition to the maximum content database size.

For example, say that a content database supports 250,000 site collections per content database, and a content database size is supported up to 4 TB (4,096,000 MB). Using this model, and dividing the supported size by supported number of site collections, each site collection can support 17 MB of storage as an assigned quota.

Another approach to this model is where the site collections per content databases are limited, and the respective quota applied. For example, an organization may choose to establish a quota template of 5 GB. Using the "accounting" model on a 4 TB content database, this limits the number of site collections to 800.

The accounting model is least efficient in that it can be expected that users will not consume the entirety of their quotas. However, this model provides the best scenario when seeking to minimize management overhead and remain within product support boundaries.

Content Databases

In support of the airline booking and accounting models, SharePoint 2010 supports the configuration of the number of site collections that can be created within a content database. Once that limit is reached, site collections are created in the next available content database. If multiple content databases are associated with a web application, a round-robin load-balancing method is used when site collections are created, where the most available content database is used to provision the new site collection.

A content database can also be marked offline to prevent new site collections from being created within it. This enables an administrator to selectively mark content databases that should not be used when users are creating new site collections.

To configure site collection limits, follow these steps:

1. On the SharePoint 2010 Central Administration home page, select "Manage content databases" under Application Management.

2. On the Manage Content Databases page, select the web application from the list of available web applications, and then select the database to be configured under Content Databases.

3. To change the number of sites allowed for a content database, in the Database Capacity Settings section, enter a new warning and maximum number.

4. Click OK.

To configure the content database status, follow these steps:

1. On the SharePoint 2010 Central Administration home page, select "Manage content databases" under Application Management.

2. On the Manage Content Databases page, select the web application from the list of available web applications, and then select the database to be configured under Content Databases.

3. To change database status, in the Database Status box, select Ready or Offline.

4. Click OK.

Using Storage Metrics

SharePoint 2010 provides a set of features designed to help you collect, report, and analyze the usage and effectiveness of your SharePoint 2010 deployment. These features are provided through SharePoint 2010's Web Analytics capabilities, and supplemented with new storage metrics available in Service Pack 1.

Site Collection and Site Web Analytics Reports

Site collection Web Analytics reports and site Web Analytics reports are provided through SharePoint 2010's Web Analytics capabilities, and are designed to help administrators and owners analyze their site collection and site usage data. Web Analytics reports are divided across three categories: Traffic, Search, and Inventory. These are aggregated for entities including site collections and sites, and more broadly across web applications, service applications, and server farm environments.

Site collection and site Web Analytics reports require that the Web Analytics service application be provisioned on the server farm hosting those site collections and sites.

Out-of-the-box, when provisioned, Web Analytics provides data for a period of 30 days, but can be configured to provide data of up to 25 months, as shown in Figure 26-18.

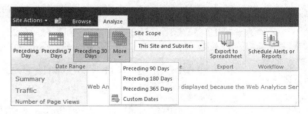

FIGURE 26-18: Web Analytics reports

Metrics are displayed in one of two ways: trend reports and rank reports. *Trend reports* show a particular metric's performance over 30 days, whereas *rank reports* show the top 2,000 results for a particular metric. In addition to the reports that are provided by default, administrators and owners can further analyze the data by applying filters such as string matches, usernames, queries, and so on.

Traffic Reports

Traffic reports capture user behavior related to clicks, frequency, popular pages, and other information about navigation, both to and from a site collection or site.

Available site collection Web Analytics traffic reports include the following:

➤ *Number of Page Views* — This shows the number of page views per day for the specified date range.

➤ *Number of Daily Unique Visitors* — This shows the number of unique visitors for the specified date range.

➤ *Number of Referrers* — This shows the amount of traffic from referrals.

➤ *Top Pages* — This shows the most popular pages based on page views for the specified date range.

➤ *Top Visitors* — This shows the top unique visitors to the site collection or site for the specified date range.

➤ *Top Referrers* — This shows the top web pages that refer traffic to the site collection or site.

➤ *Top Destinations* — This shows the external web pages that visitors most frequently navigate to from the site collection or site.

➤ *Top Browsers* — This shows the Internet browser types and versions most commonly used by visitors to the site collection or site.

Site Web Analytics traffic reports include the following:

➤ *Number of Page Views* — This shows the number of page views per day for the specified date range.

➤ *Number of Daily Unique Visitors* — This shows the number of unique visitors for the specified date range.

➤ *Number of Referrers* — This shows the amount of traffic from referrals.

➤ *Top Pages* — This shows the most popular pages based on page views for the specified date range.

➤ *Top Visitors* — This shows the top unique visitors to the site collection or site for the specified date range.

➤ *Top Referrers* — This shows the top web pages that refer traffic to the site collection or site.

➤ *Top Destinations* — This shows the external web pages that visitors most frequently navigate to from the site collection or site.

➤ *Top Browsers* — This shows the Internet browser types and versions most commonly used by visitors to the site collection or site.

Search Reports

Search reports capture user behavior information related to queries executed against the site collection or site. Site collection Web Analytics search reports include the following:

➤ *Number of Queries* — This shows the number of search queries performed for the specified date range.

➤ *Top Queries* — This shows the most popular search queries performed for the specified date range.

➤ *Failed Queries* — This shows the search queries that showed no search results, or received limited click-through.

➤ *Best Bet Usage* — This shows the number of click-throughs the Best Bet URLs received for the search keywords.

➤ *Best Bet Suggestions* — This shows the suggestions for Best Bet URLs for certain search keywords.

➤ *Best Bet Suggestions Action History* — This shows the actions that have been taken against the Best Bet Suggestions report for the site collection.

➤ *Search Keywords* — This shows the keywords used by the site collection.

 Search reports are not available at the site level.

Inventory Reports

Inventory reports are designed to help administrators and owners manage the site collection or site by providing graphical and textual insight into the site structure, storage, and version history.

Site collection Web Analytics inventory reports include the following:

➤ *Storage Usage* — This shows a trended daily snapshot of storage used for the site collection for the date range specified.

➤ *Number of Sites* — This shows a trended daily snapshot of the number of sites in the site collection for the specified date range.

➤ *Top Site Product Versions* — This shows the top site product versions based on the product version property of each site in the site collection for the specified date range.

➤ *Top Site Languages* — This shows the top site languages based on the number of sites created using each language for the specified date range.

Site Web Analytics inventory reports include the following:

➤ *Number of Sites* — This shows a trended daily snapshot of the number of sites in the site collection for the specified date range.

➤ *Top Site Product Versions* — This shows the top site product versions based on the product version property of each site in the site collection for the specified date range.

➤ *Top Site Languages* — This shows the top site languages based on the number of sites created using each language for the specified date range.

Storage Metrics

SharePoint 2010 removed Storage Space Allocation (`StorMan.aspx`), which, in previous versions of SharePoint, enabled granular management and insight into storage.

 For more information, see `http://support.microsoft.com/kb/982587/EN-US.`

For example, the page would show you the top 100 documents or document libraries in terms of size. With that information, end users could go to the page to clean up content from their site(s) by deleting the large content that they no longer needed.

In Service Pack 1, SharePoint 2010 brings back an improved `StorMan.aspx`, enabling users to better understand where their quota is going, and act on that information to reduce the size of their sites.

Storage metrics provide insight into how storage is being used across site collections and sites, thus enabling administrators and owners to quickly identify content that can be archived or removed in order to remain within their allocated quotas.

To begin using storage metrics, follow these steps:

1. On a site collection, select Site Actions, and then click Site Settings.

2. From Site Settings, select Storage Metrics under Site Collection Administration (Figure 26-19).

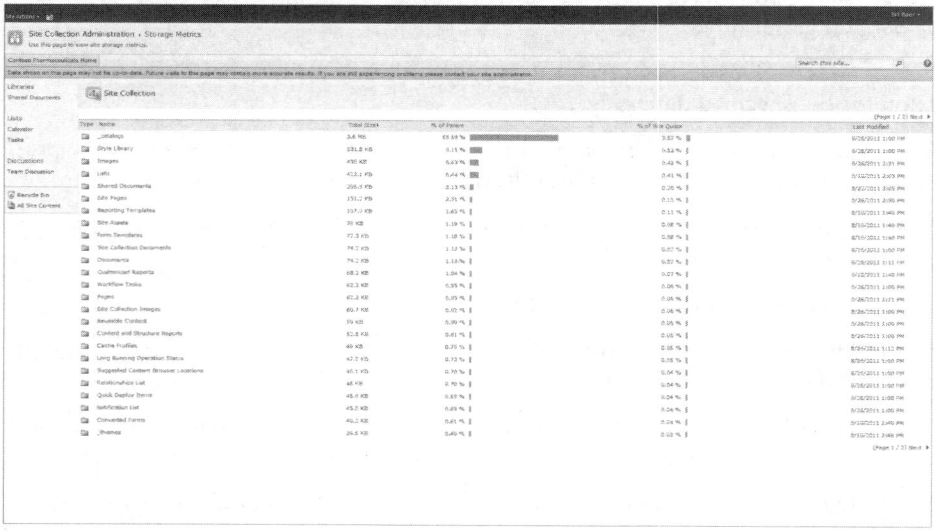

FIGURE 26-19: Storage metrics

SUMMARY

This chapter covered business collaboration services features available to you as you plan your information management strategy with SharePoint 2010. The foundation of business collaboration effectiveness begins with a well-thought-out information architecture aligned with an overarching governance plan, as well as proper end user education through both documentation and training. The successful implementation of business collaboration services within an enterprise drives efficiencies, and, as a result, improves overall productivity, while reducing management overhead and complexity.

Chapter 27 discusses the Enterprise Search Service, its characteristics, technology considerations, and how to effectively drive solutions that increase information discovery.

27

Enterprise Search Services

By Natalya Voskresenskaya

With the evolution of the SharePoint platform, and the ever-growing accumulation of data and information, the SharePoint search offering had to surpass the boundaries of SharePoint as an information container to make SharePoint the "go-to" search solution for all enterprise content, regardless of its format and location, by indexing enterprise data from multiple systems. This included shared data stored in SharePoint, file shares, and websites, as well as line-of-business (LOB) applications such as Customer Relationship Management (CRM) databases, Enterprise Resource Planning (ERP) solutions, and so on.

Microsoft recognized the need to offer a heavy-duty enterprise search platform, and in 2008 completed its acquisition of FAST Search and Transfer. The timely acquisition allowed Microsoft to integrate FAST Search into SharePoint 2010, and offer this search platform as a separate product that provides a superset of functionalities on top of the SharePoint Search offering.

Microsoft has released several search products to fit a wide spectrum of search requirements and possible budget restrictions. This chapter is largely concentrated on SharePoint 2010 Search and FAST Search for SharePoint 2010. The goal here is to help architects make educated decisions for selecting the right product based on the feature offerings, along with deployment guidance based on the real-world architect experiences and business scenarios.

GETTING TO KNOW SHAREPOINT 2010 SEARCH FEATURES

The SharePoint 2010 platform is more or less divided into two separate products: SharePoint Foundation Server and SharePoint Server 2010. (SharePoint Server 2010 provides a superset of capabilities on top of the SharePoint Foundation Server.) Though both products have search capabilities, the feature set for each is quite different.

Out-of-the-box, SharePoint Foundation 2010 search provides only basic SharePoint site search for sites within the same farm. This base search functionality can be extended by adding Search Server 2010 (either the Express or full version).

Table 27-1 shows a list of included features. Those who are familiar with the search included in SharePoint 2007 might deem these to be improvements.

TABLE 27-1: SharePoint 2010 Search Features/Improvements

QUERY IMPROVEMENTS AND END-USER EXPERIENCE FEATURES	SOCIALLY AWARE SEARCH (PEOPLE SEARCH)	CONNECTIVITY	SEARCH ADMINISTRATION
Support for searches with Boolean queries (such as AND, OR, and NOT).	Search by location, skills, projects, and expertise.	Connectors for Enterprise Search in Windows 7.	Windows PowerShell-scriptable deployments and operation.
Wildcard prefixes (important feature when searches must be performed only on partial string matching).	Higher ranking for people names and social tagging.	Refinement panels for users to refine search results.	GUI-based administration.
Query completion (suggestions while typing search queries). This feature enables the suggestion of previously executed queries, and aids in the process of forming a query.	Self-search and My Sites search.	Query federation.	Microsoft System Center Operations Management Pack.
Suggestions to a user after a query has been run (or "Related Searches"). This is based on the keyword synonyms that have been added to the site center.	Phonetic search, which is currently available only for the following languages: English, Spanish, French, German, Italian, Korean, Portuguese (Brazil), and Russian.	Out-of-the-box connectors that allow you to start indexing other content repositories outside of SharePoint, such as websites, SharePoint 2003/2007/2010 sites, and file shares.	Health monitoring.

QUERY IMPROVEMENTS AND END-USER EXPERIENCE FEATURES	SOCIALLY AWARE SEARCH (PEOPLE SEARCH)	CONNECTIVITY	SEARCH ADMINISTRATION
"Did you mean this?" suggestions for search query misspellings.		Integration with other LOB applications through Business Connectivity Services (BCS).	Windows PowerShell configuration cmdlets.
Ranking based on a search results history and rank profile.			Usage reporting.
Relevance based on inferred metadata.			Windows PowerShell support.
Relevancy tuning by document promotion and/ or site promotion.			
Best Bets.			
Shallow results refinement through the use of managed properties. They are called "shallow" because the exact number of managed properties will not be displayed if it is higher than 50.			
Click-through relevance.			

GETTING TO KNOW FAST SEARCH FOR SHAREPOINT FEATURES

As mentioned earlier in this chapter, FAST Search for SharePoint is a separate product that offers the superset of functionalities on top of the SharePoint search. FAST Search for SharePoint 2010 adds a whole new level of search capabilities that are a superset of what comes with the out-of-the-box SharePoint 2010 Search option. It is designed to be installed and operated on top of the SharePoint 2010 platform, and takes full advantage of the content and document management features of SharePoint.

The newly architected platform shares a common set of APIs with SharePoint 2010, and enables a richer end-user search experience by providing conversational search capabilities that allow end users to get to important information without executing search queries. It allows for the following:

➤ It increases the impact of knowledge and expertise search by leveraging social search features.

➤ Users can take advantage of extensible content processing to get the best of the enterprise data without compromising the security and data source structure.

➤ It empowers developers to build great search-driven applications and shape the end-user experience to maximize productivity.

➤ It enables IT professionals to deploy an industrial-strength scale and manageability enterprise search platform.

➤ Integration with System Center Operations Manager allows administrators to have a granular overview and monitoring of the performance of the system, and supports standard Windows monitoring services.

When FAST Search for SharePoint is deployed in addition to SharePoint 2010, it greatly enhances some of the core SharePoint search features, and adds some unique features that are available only through FAST. Following are significant enhancements provided by FAST Search to core SharePoint 2010 functionality:

➤ Updated, one-stop Search Center to find answers quickly

➤ Deep Refiners, allowing quick, visual exploration of results

➤ Added web parts for easy, out-of-the-box user experience customization

➤ Enterprise-class manageability, scalability, and performance of the system

FAST also provides a unique and powerful set of functionality all its own, including the following:

➤ Visual cues through presentation of visual Best Bets, document preview, and document thumbnails for rapid recognition of information

➤ Contextual search to meet the needs of diverse groups

➤ Customizable Relevance Ranking models

➤ Advanced content processing that allows complex Entity Extraction and content enhancements

➤ Easy-to-configure end-user experiences

➤ Advanced query capabilities that enable the creation of powerful applications

---

This chapter concentrates on SharePoint 2010 Search, and will only slightly mention FAST Search for SharePoint. If you would like to get more information on FAST Search, see Professional Microsoft Search: FAST Search, SharePoint Search, and Search Server *by Mark Bennett, Jeff Fried, Miles Kehoe, and Natalya Voskresenskaya (Indianapolis: Wiley, 2010).*

UNDERSTANDING THE SHAREPOINT 2010 SEARCH ARCHITECTURE

In the previous version of SharePoint, search was offered as a service within a Shared Service Provider (SSP), where services such as User Profiles, Excel, and Search were bundled together and could not be decoupled. Additionally, web applications were bound to a specific SSP, making it challenging to share these services across farms.

In the new SharePoint 2010 architecture, all services are offered à la carte, making it easy to share them across multiple farms and scale them. SharePoint 2010 Search is provided to web applications as a search application, with querying and indexing componentized to allow you to run multiple search service instances, or to have a completely dedicated search farm that provides a search service to other SharePoint farms in the environment. The advantage of having a separate search farm is that you can tune this farm to meet particular search needs without affecting other farms.

The SharePoint 2010 Search componentized architecture allows you to create greater redundancy within a single farm, and to scale in numerous directions. You can separately scale the components that make up the query and the crawling architecture based on volume of content, performance, redundancy, and the search availability needs of an organization. The web applications can be associated with one or another search service, depending on the search requirements of the specific web application.

With the new architecture of the application services and how they can provide search service as federated, there is a new notion of a services-only farm. A services farm can be set up and scaled depending on the load and needs of the particular service without affecting the content farm.

Administration

Every search application has one (and only one) *administration component*. It is responsible for the overall configuration of the search application, and can be run on any server in the farm. It is also the only element in the search topology that cannot be scaled out to multiple instances.

Crawler Component

The job of the *crawler component* is to orchestrate how disparate content sources are accessed, and how retrieved content is brought back into the search engine. Depending on where the information originally resides, the crawler component will use the appropriate connector to handle the specific source data.

The following content sources can be traversed by the SharePoint 2010 crawler using out-of-the-box connectors:

- ➤ SharePoint sites and people profiles
- ➤ Windows file shares
- ➤ Exchange public folders
- ➤ Databases through Java Database Connector (JDBC), such as SQL
- ➤ Non-SharePoint websites
- ➤ LOB applications through the content integration options available with SharePoint 2010

Crawler instances are entirely stateless, and do not depend on each other for the exchange of information. They depend on the crawl database to look up the data to be indexed, retrieve source data-utilizing protocol handlers, then record crawled items in the crawl search database. In this way, all configuration rules are applied through the crawl database residing in SQL Server, ensuring the true independence and redundancy of crawler instances, and further ensuring high availability and scalability.

A number of databases are associated with the crawler component, including the following:

➤ *Search Service application database* — This is a master database for the search application. In Microsoft Office SharePoint Server (MOSS) 2007, search was provided as a part of Shared Services. In SharePoint 2010, however, search is an entirely independent application, of which there can be multiple instances configured within the same farm. Each search application is associated with only one search application database. This database stores search application configuration information, crawler configuration data associated with the search application, and access control lists (ACLs) for crawled content.

➤ *Crawl database* — Although multiple crawlers can be configured within a single search application, each crawler component is associated with at least one crawl database. The crawl database stores detailed information about the content updates, crawler schedules, and timestamps for the last crawler run. Crawl databases can exist within a single SQL Server instance, or be distributed over multiple SQL Server instances for improved I/O performance. Similarly, crawlers associated with a given crawl database can be scattered across multiple index servers for high availability and load sharing.

➤ *Property database* — Even though it is considered part of the crawler component, the property database is also part of the query server. The crawler discovers metadata and records it into the property database. From there, it is later exposed to the end user at query time. The query server then gathers these properties and displays them within the search interface. These crawled properties are also used to calculate the relevancy of the results.

Administrators can control the behavior of the crawler by applying sets of rules that define how the crawler traverses content in disparate data repositories. The crawler search element can also be scaled to provide crawl distribution across the SharePoint farm with built-in load balancing by creating multiple crawler instances. Later, in the "Understanding Federation" section of this chapter, you learn about different models of search component distribution in greater detail.

Not all file types can be crawled by SharePoint 2010 out-of-the-box. There are iFilters that act as plug-ins for the Windows operating system. iFilters allow SharePoint to index file formats so that they are understood by the search engine and are searchable. Without an appropriate iFilter, SharePoint cannot understand the content and metadata of files and search within them. iFilters allow the index to understand the file's format, filter out embedded formatting, mine text from the file, and return it to the search engine.

iFilters are available for most major file types through a variety of vendors. In addition, there are usually several vendors offering iFilters for the same file type. Not all iFilters work the same, and depending on the amount of content being crawled that includes file types requiring an iFilter, crawl performance may be drastically different, depending on the installed iFilter. Slower iFilters result in slower crawl time, since SharePoint's index takes longer to understand the content of files.

Indexer

Content discovered and fetched by the crawler is passed to the indexing engine, where it is analyzed and later stored in a physical file. Based on the type of content delivered by the crawler, the *indexer* first checks to see if it is an update to what already exists in the index, or if it is new content to be added to the index. It optimizes the index file by removing noise words, managing word-breaking, identifying how and in which index partition to store this data, and finally propagates updates to an index (or index partitions) held by the query server.

Query and Index

When the query is submitted by the end user, the *query* component handles the query processing and serves the search result set to the Web Front End (WFE). It then forwards that request to the query components of all index partitions, and when results come back, the query processor combines all of them. It applies security trimming based on ACL items, detects and eliminates duplicates from the result set, and displays items or documents properties.

In the search application configuration, at least one server must be performing the query role. Additional servers may be added for redundancy and performance. This is discussed in more detail in the "Planning for Scale and Redundancy" section of this chapter.

When a query is executed, it is being passed to the query server, which is responsible for optimizing and serving query results to the end user from its own index partition or entire index. The *index* is being helped by this component either in its entirety, or only as a partition of the entire index, depending on the deployed topology of the search application. Multiple query servers can hold identical index partitions for failover purposes.

UNDERSTANDING CONTENT SOURCES

Content sources are the data repositories that can be crawled and indexed inside or outside of the SharePoint platform. The true enterprise search within SharePoint should never be scoped to SharePoint content only. Following are content sources that can be crawled out of the box:

➤ Websites (through a web connector using an HTTP protocol handler)

➤ Database (through BCS)

➤ Web services (BCS)

➤ Files within file shares

➤ SharePoint sites (for SharePoint 2010, 2007, 2003)

➤ Exchange public folders

Once the content source is identified, a number of questions must be answered in order to anticipate possible changes to the search topology to accommodate the proper volume, rate of indexing, query results serving, and security. The architecture of the search topology will largely be driven by the volume and location of content that is expected to be indexed, as well as the performance expectations.

Connectors

Connectors are the means for the crawler to connect to the content repository and fetch the content for indexing. Connectors are responsible for recognizing the type of content, content "metadata" or entities properties, its format, and the security for indexed entities. For example, the SharePoint connector has built-in intelligence to understand the content types, metadata, and types of items (such as a document with its metadata, or a list item and its ACL that is being passed to the indexer with the content entity itself).

The connector framework is an extensible framework that allows development of connectors for highly customized content repositories such as ERP, CRM, and document management systems.

Business Connectivity Services

Business Connectivity Services (BCS) is an evolved version of its predecessor from SharePoint 2007, Business Data Catalog (BDC). BCS supports connecting to databases, and the Windows Communication Foundation (WCF) or web services. You can create indexing connectors for database and web service external content types without writing any code. By creating a model file for the indexing connector, you can also expose external content types within the list, but there are performance limitations for that.

For example, you might use BCS to connect to a large database with the main reason of indexing the content. You would set up a BCS connector for that database external content type, with a read action that fetches the content into the indexer, but you would want to skip the step of creating a list view.

Microsoft SharePoint Designer 2010 provides an interface to create the model file for the indexing connector. In cases when the external content repository system is not directly supported by BCS, it is possible to expose that system's content for indexing through BCS by writing your own model file and connector.

If the external content types are of a static nature (in other words, they do not change often, and have a small set of known types), you can write web services or .NET connectivity assemblies in Visual Studio 2010 to expose the data from your external system.

In cases when the external content type in the system is dynamic, of a custom type, and of a massive volume, creating a custom connector is the best option to incorporate the data into your enterprise search platform.

FAST Search for SharePoint 2010 Connectors

Even though the crawler component is provided by SharePoint 2010 with FAST Search for SharePoint 2010 in the mix, you can use original connectors for FAST Search 2010. Out of the box, Fast Search for SharePoint 2010 has its own set of connectors that can be used on top of the SharePoint 2010 out-of-the-box set of connectors, including the following:

➤ *Enterprise crawler* — This is a highly configurable crawler that allows you to crawl HTTP websites, and provides about 200 configuration options. As an example, you would want to use this crawler if you are crawling sites that have "No Robots" directive. The out-of-the-box SharePoint website crawler would obey this rule and not index websites or portions of the websites that have this rule. Another example would center on the execution of Java scripts and following or not following some links for indexing.

➤ *JDBC connector* — This connector allows you to index JDBC databases. It would be rare that you would want to use this connector, because the SharePoint 2010 offers database indexing through BCS, and Microsoft is not planning on investing in this connector within the foreseeable future. But there is a set of features that offers more flexibility in configuration option than BCS does. As an example, this connector supports Transact-SQL (T-SQL) commands with the use of joins and push-based crawling, where the database can push an item into the indexer for immediate indexing. The JDBC connector is also useful in cases when the high-throughput performance is required. Table 27-2 provides some usage recommendations.

TABLE 27-2: JDBC and BCS Usage Recommendations

FEATURE	JDBC	BCS
Configuration	TSQL queries (data joining)	SharePoint Designer 2010 does not support SQL queries
Administration	Connector model file Stored procedures modification (if configured to use stored procedures)	Central Administration site
Indexing	Checksum-based change detection Timestamp-based change detection Detection based on update and delete flags	Crawling based on the change log

UNDERSTANDING FEDERATION

The concept of *federation* of search was introduced in SharePoint 2007. What this term really means is that the SharePoint search engine can pass queries to other search engines like Bing, Yahoo!, and any others that support OpenSearch format.

Federation is a powerful way of providing a unified search experience, while avoiding the cost of indexing content distributed across multiple repositories where search already exists, or when crawling of this content is not feasible to begin with. Federation enables the search engine to issue a query against multiple search engines, and renders result sets in a separate web part on a single results page. These searches can be executed against enterprise content repositories, portions of your Search Server index, and other search engines.

Out-of-the-box, SharePoint Server 2010 search provides federation of the following:

➤ SharePoint people search

➤ Related searches

➤ OpenSearch providers such as Bing and Yahoo!

➤   Windows 7 and Internet Explorer (IE) 8 searching SharePoint 2010

➤   Rich RSS feeds and federation generator

One of the points of an enterprise search is to create a central point of access to the data, and people do not want to search several different places to find information. Federating results saves time and frustration, and it makes people more productive, even though it has its pros and cons.

Table 27-3 summarizes and explains the advantages of indexing content versus federation of the search results, and Table 27-4 lists the advantages of using federation over indexing.

TABLE 27-3: Advantages of Indexing Content Versus Federation

INDEXING THE CONTENT	FEDERATION OF SEARCH RESULTS
An aggregated results set with a common relevance and ranking model	Provides a certain level of aggregation
Control over the scope of the searchable body of data	Depending on the provider, might be scoped by constructing more complex queries
Properties extraction for search results refinement	Custom code can provide refinement
Capability to control and expand the metadata extraction	Only through custom code
System performance and fault tolerance	No control over availability and performance of the search (depends on the provider)
Full control over document and items security and security trimming	Depends on the provider

 Federation is not an option, and indexing of content will be mandatory to enable search of the repositories where search is not available.

TABLE 27-4: Advantages of Using Federation Versus Indexing

INDEXING THE CONTENT	FEDERATING SEARCH RESULTS
Storage cost	Allows reduction of the storage cost by utilizing the index stored in a third-party system
Crawling is not feasible because of Geo-distribution, performance of crawling and indexing, or legal restrictions	Query results are served by third-party query services, bypassing the limitation or indexing of the content, and providing fresh results sets
Security-trimmed search results	Nothing built into OpenSearch

The OpenSearch format allows search engines to form a search results response in syndication formats (such as RSS and Atom) with the extra metadata needed to return search results. If the search engine that is desired to be used as a federated location does not support OpenSearch format, it is still possible to use it in the federation scenario through a custom connector.

KEY BUSINESS CHALLENGES WITH ENTERPRISE SEARCH

A primary business challenge many organizations face is understanding what enterprise search is, what it does, and the difference between enterprise search and Internet search (which most people are familiar with). Though enterprise search is not a new concept, the everyday usage of Internet search-based engines and the Internet search experience hinders the true meaning of enterprise search. The common phrase, "we just want Google search," is what most architects focused on building enterprise search platforms are facing when they start collecting the requirements for the platform.

Thus, the first step is to understand that, although Internet search engines have realized great maturity, the engine is tuned to be just for Internet World Wide Web purposes, and should not be used as a replacement for the enterprise search engine. This is because the Internet-based engines do not have a concept of a user — that is, a user within the context of the business purpose of the user, its role within the organization, and the security aspect of the content.

No two organizations are alike, even if the organizations are within the same vertical alignment and of the same size. Factors such as culture of the company, internal policies, and overall politics make each organization unique. The set of requirements that is collected within one organization will not fit another, even if (from a very high level) they seem identical.

Understanding the Need for Enterprise Search

The first and biggest challenge is for organizations to understand the need for enterprise search and the benefits of it. Common misconceptions are that "we are too small to need it" or "we don't have large volumes of content." You cannot be too small or too big, and do not have to have terabytes of content to need enterprise search.

Let's consider an anecdotal story of a manufacturing company where Research and Development (R&D) engineers came up with a product idea that should have started a whole line of new products. The main component of the new line was already patented by a competitor, but its patent was about to expire within two months. Engineers were busy at work developing prototypes and researching different angles, because there was not a single indicator that the competitor would ever renew this patent. The company had been investing a substantial amount of money into development, marketing research, and financial analysis.

One day before the patent expired, the competitor company renewed all patents that were in any way connected to the main component that was supposed to be the key component of the new product line. The company lost a lot of money, since they were unable to launch this new product line that they already invested in. It was obvious that information about the new product idea had leaked to the competitor. But how?

After thorough analysis, it became obvious that an Internet search in the form of Google Analytics was the traitor. The competitor had a process of monitoring keywords through this tool, keywords that were pertinent to its patents and main products. As a common procedure, the competitor company monitored a large volume of queries all containing sets of chosen keywords, and it noticed a spike of queries that all contained one of the monitored keywords. The analytics reports revealed where the volume of queries was coming from. The location was a suburban town where the only large settlement was of their competitor's corporate offices and R&D department.

The reason engineers were not using their internal systems resources for research was that they had too many siloed systems. Without involving the subject matter expert (SME) of a particular system, they would not be able to fully do the research for their new product line. Requests for the research within each siloed system would take too long, and in such mundane cases as the SME being out on vacation, would take weeks.

If the company had realized the importance of investing in implementation of the enterprise search system and the consequences of not having it, the story would be quite different. Unfortunately, companies nowadays are still in the process of understanding what enterprise search is, and the necessity of it.

Defining "Mature" Search Requirements

In a majority of cases, the implementation of enterprise search begins by taking baby steps and implementing the search tailored for a specific group of people/business unit/department. But it may also start because there is a clear need to have (or improve) search functionality for a specific LOB application. In any case, there must be a bigger picture from the very beginning, and the initial implementation must be done with that bigger picture in sight.

Although the technology *does* speak for itself, the real power is knowing how to couple the power of the search platform with an understanding of the business and the usage cases. The new paradigm demands understanding the business. Enterprise search is not one-size-fits-all. To derive the true return on investment, it is important to provide a measurable value of enterprise search to the organization. By assembling a team of business users and IT people who will influence, monitor, and tailor the search to the organization needs and processes, you will ensure that enterprise search evolves with the organization, and increases adoption by end users.

From the business value perspective, you can start simply, by answering the question, "What is the core business of the organization?" The value that search can provide will be realized. It's what drives and propels business. Tailoring a properly planned enterprise search solution creates opportunity and reveals what was once hidden. This is why assembling a search team can help leverage the value of the enterprise search capabilities.

As a true architect, you will not be designing a point solution by implementing enterprise search in an organization. It's taking all systems and search requirements of all other business units into account from the get-go that will ensure the success of the final state of the enterprise search platform. This will allow for the search platform evolution that will meet no boundaries that overlooked areas might produce and box in your platform.

Gathering Search Requirements

Search is not a "set it and forget it" technology. This is a misconception that often derives from experience with Internet search engines such as Bing, Google, and Yahoo!, where it seems effortless to maintain the good search experience. There is a lot of work going on behind the scenes in order to maintain the high level of expectations that users are used to.

The initial deployment is the first step on a long road to having effective enterprise search in place. Taking a phased approach when you initially deploy search for a limited group of people often helps. The phased approach also allows you to create a road map for the enterprise search development and penetration into other systems with solid milestones, which will justify the investment over time.

The initial phase for planning enterprise search (that is, getting the general overview of the organization's core business and systems that are involved in running it) helps to build the global picture of content sources and Information Architecture. Narrowing down to a group of people (preferably from different departments, but with a common search need) and identifying the *indexable and searchable entities* will provide the initial view into what a *master record* might look like.

Searchable Entity

In search scenarios, the *searchable* or *indexable entity* can come in many forms. From the technical perspective, it can be a database record, file on a file share, SharePoint list, site, page, library document, or a list item. The importance of the exercise of defining a searchable entity is not necessarily identifying it from a technology side, and should not necessarily matter if, on the search results page, this includes documents and list items. To identify the searchable entity, you must approach it from the business definition perspective.

As an example, from the technical perspective, in the case of an R&D systems search portal within a manufacturing company, you might just be indexing databases and, in some instances, documents attached to the database records. Treating rows as searchable entities would be right from the technical perspective. But this will provide no value from the perspective of the information type. In this example, most of the time you will find you are working with ingredients, formulae, formulations, testing, packaging, and regulations entities.

Master Record

Within the SharePoint index (as well as the search interface), every searchable and indexable record will have the same set of index metadata properties, or crawled properties, no matter where the entity came from. A *master record* is the indexable entity with all of the crawled properties with a managed metadata grouping layer on top of crawled properties. Having a clear master record will help you to understand that big-picture scenario of the search as it pertains to business function, as well as the enterprise search content.

Business Requirements

Remember that, even though it is not a true statement from the very beginning, search will eventually touch everything. As mentioned, there is no one-size-fits-all approach to requirements gathering. As a general guidance, create a search committee group. Assemble this group wisely. Members of the group should represent a nice balance between business and technical understanding of the technology.

If internal resources are not enough, find a vendor that is highly skilled and has a lot of experience in designing enterprise search systems. The right vendor can get you started on the right path, even if the initial engagement is not designed to satisfy the needs of the whole enterprise. The skilled vendor will ensure that you are self-sustainable in maintenance with a flexible implementation that eventually will span across all the systems in the organization.

Requirements gathering is not so much a question-and-answer process, but rather is more of an artful conversation. Following are some questions that you need answers to, and how you position conversations with your business folks will depend on the culture, internal politics, business, and current satisfaction and experience with search solutions (if they exist) for that particular individual.

➤ What disparate systems are users working with, and what are their current search solutions?

➤ How are people treating the information that they find, and what do they do with this information?

➤ Get some use cases. Use cases might clue you in on what other content repositories are important for users, and the types of searches they are looking for. It will also educate you on the refiners, metadata, and search results display properties that should be in place to improve the productivity of teams.

➤ Identify if manual steps are involved in the end-to-end information-finding process. For example, if a user searches for a chemical formulation by the formulation name, once found, discover if the user is calling the SME of the production system to find out if the formulation is being used currently in manufactured products.

➤ What business problem can search solve?

➤ Who are the primary users and what type of information are they interested in?

➤ Can your company afford not to have a search solution, and what are the risks associated with not finding information?

➤ What are the security requirements for the data?

➤ What is the desired search format? Should it include pre-filters? Is it an advanced search or a simple search box?

➤ Do multiple languages need to be supported?

Technical Requirements

The technical side of requirements gathering should not be overlooked, but is not always applicable to conversations with core business people. If you feel confident that the group is technical enough to answer technical questions, feel free to ask. Otherwise, you might confuse users and might receive false statements. You may get the following types of information by talking to either SMEs of those systems, or to the IT department:

➤ Repository or content sources of information

➤ Are APIs available?

➤ Are search connectors available?

> ➤ Document or records properties

> ➤ Security information

> ➤ Formats (that is, record, PDF, text, images, and so on) of information

> ➤ Available metadata and/or columns

> ➤ Required indexing and query performance information

Though business and technical requirements are essential to building any enterprise search engine, keep aligned to the long-term enterprise-wide objectives and corporate plans.

Advanced Business Scenarios

Although it may offer a search box from which people execute their queries and provide a list of results, enterprise search is not what it ought to be in some cases. A range of uses for the search may necessitate that you leverage its intelligence to serve as a building platform for specific purposes, such as Business Intelligence (BI), E-Discovery, or Operational BI.

The search and search analytics help to glean the information on how people are operating, what their current tasks are, and the information they are producing. By analyzing concepts from the content, you have the capability to build synergies between disparate groups of employees, and make recommendations for their next search relevance.

Search-Driven Applications

Developers and architects rarely look at search as a development platform. The current toolset and OpenSearch API allow developers to tap into the power of search, and leverage it in applications that are not any different than the applications as users currently know them. Instead, they are using the search technology for delivery of content that can come in any form: navigation, charts, dashboards, and matrices. SharePoint 2010 has made a big leap toward helping developers and power users to do more with search.

SharePoint 2010 allows you to greatly extend the user interface, and provides a customizable set of web parts that can be reused throughout the SharePoint farm (thus providing reusability). The addition of FAST Search for SharePoint into the environment will still allow for already developed web parts to function, because FAST provides a superset of functionality based on the same APIs as SharePoint 2010 Search.

SEARCH USER EXPERIENCE

The *Search Center* enhances the search experience for end users by providing a centralized and greatly customizable user interface to perform search queries and discover information. The availability of the Search Center template depends on the template originally chosen for the site collection site. It comes with a preset number of web parts, and can be customized through the web parts tool box by modifying its configuration settings or Extensible Stylesheet Language Transformation (XSLT).

The default homepage of the site allows you to search either an "All sites" scope so that users search across all content in the index, or navigate to the people search through tabular navigation above the search box. It provides links to the current user's search preferences and advanced search options.

Administrators can choose to add tabs to the available navigation options and associate them with custom scopes that users can use to query different subsets of the content index.

Crawled Properties and Managed Properties

Crawled properties are simply the metadata discovered and retrieved by the crawler, from defined content sources (such as SharePoint lists and libraries), and external sources. *Managed properties* are an additional layer that offers a powerful way to unify and standardize this metadata across the entire body of enterprise data, as well as define the weight of those properties in the search results.

By exposing managed properties to end users through the use of refiners, you can enable them to more easily understand and use this information without requiring any knowledge of the underlying information architecture.

Managed properties further improve the end-user experience by providing the capability to create complex, highly focused search queries on-the-fly without special knowledge of the search query language. These searches can also be scoped to a particular document or item property. For example, by selecting "Created By" managed property as the search criteria, and executing a query against a person's name, the user would receive a result set containing documents and/or items that were created by the person they searched for.

Managed properties can be created through the Search Server Administration (SSA) interface by mapping crawled properties to them. Single or multiple crawled properties can be mapped to a single managed property. This is specifically useful in cases where there is more than one metadata field that carries the same or a similar piece of information, and should be treated and searched as one entity.

Consider the following scenario. Within your SharePoint environment, you have multiple document libraries, each containing a "document purpose" field, which you use to describe the content of any given document. You also have other libraries in your installation that use an "author comments" field to store descriptions. Even further, you index external content repositories that define a "description" metadata field, also used to provide the same bit of data (the document description). Using managed properties, you can map all of these fields to a single property — "Document Description" — and expose it from within the search interface. This would enable end users to select "Document Description" and execute a single query against it, retrieving all documents where there is a match against their respective "description" field.

Advanced Search

The *Advanced Search page* allows users to construct advanced search queries. Queries can be fairly complex inclusion and exclusion rules for keywords, or searches by phrases. Users can also select property restrictions to limit the scope of a searchable body of the document, or an item to a specific metadata property that is discovered by the crawler and mapped to managed properties.

Managed properties can be created through the SSA interface, and multiple metadata properties can be mapped to one managed property. This is specifically useful in cases when more than one content type has a metadata field with different names, but logically all those fields carry the same information. Another case might be when multiple metadata fields should be searched as one content entity.

Consider the following example. One content type has a "description" field, and another content type has a field called "explanation." By mapping both of them to the newly created managed property "Description," and exposing this managed property from within the search interface, you can allow end users to select the "description" managed property and execute search query against it to retrieve both content types in the result set that have the desired keyword in the "Description" managed property.

To expose these managed properties in the property restrictions section of the advanced search box web part, you can modify the XSL from the web part tool box by clicking the "Edit this web part" web part menu option, or by selecting the Options Ribbon menu and going to Web Part Properties. The advanced search box tool box also allows you to control the search scopes and appearance of the advanced search options.

Search Results

When a user performs a search, the results are displayed on a search core results page that offers a very user-friendly, intuitive, and rich user interface with an easy-to-navigate layout.

On the left side of the page, users can drill down into the results by refining the result set, by clicking the value of a refiner fetched by search. Refiners allow end users to build complex queries on-the-fly, without knowledge of the search query language, and enable users to easily understand the structure of the information without any knowledge of custom metadata.

The right side of the results page presents federated search results web parts (such as people search and similar searches). The core results web part is located in the center of the page. The look and feel of the result items presentation is easily customizable through application of custom XSLT and configuration of the results properties.

If you do not have a Search Center site, use the following procedure to create a site collection based on the Search Center template:

1. In the Application Management section of the Central Administration site, click "Create site collections."

2. On the Create Site Collection page, provide the title and description for this site collection.

3. Type in the URL for this site.

4. In the Template Selection section, select the Enterprise tab and then select either the Enterprise Search Center or Basic Search Center template.

5. Select the username for the Primary Site Collection Administrator.

6. Click OK.

The Enterprise Search Center site template is not available on all site collections. To enable this site template, you should ensure that the "Server Enterprise Site Collection Features" through "Site collection feature administration" is enabled.

People Search

SharePoint Server 2010 provides an address book name lookup experience that enables users to search for all variations of common names, including nicknames. It includes better name matching through phonetic search that will return names that sound similar to what the user has typed in a query. Refiners built into the people search results page allow browsing and filtering out people by name, title, and other fields defined in the user profile.

 Only the Enterprise Search Center template includes people search.

The value of people search is in finding expertise and talents within the enterprise, and it increases as users add data to their profiles. The first thing that most people try to search for when presented with a people search option is for their own names. In people search, when users perform a search for themselves, the system treats it as a "self-search," and displays information as it pertains to the searches that led to the user. This information includes the number of times the My Site profile was viewed, and the keywords that other people used to get to this user's name.

The self-search feature is a good start for creating an incentive for people to populate their profiles by showing the number of searches that led to their profiles and associated search keywords. This can encourage users to add information to their profile pages to help people with common business interests, expertise, and responsibilities to find them. This increases productivity by helping to connect people who have common business interests and responsibilities.

Users can manually submit or automatically generate a list of colleagues mined from Microsoft Outlook as a way of rapidly inferring social relationships throughout the organization, which speeds the adoption and usefulness of people search results. SharePoint Server 2010 also infers expertise by automatically suggesting topics mined from the user's Outlook inbox and suggesting additions to their expertise profile in their My Site. This makes it easy to populate My Site profiles, and means that more people have well-populated profiles and get the benefits of this in both search and communities.

People search results can also include real-time presence through the IM client, Office Communication Server, Messenger, and Lync clients, making it easy to immediately connect with people once they are found through search. The more information that people share about their projects, responsibilities, and areas of expertise, the more relevant and focused a people search becomes.

Search User Interface

The importance of the search user interface is often neglected by architects, because, to them, the main beauty of the system lies in its inner workings, in the beauty of the overall architecture design, in the cleverness of the connectors, and in the overall index design. They often forget that too many good systems are hidden behind bad, non-intuitive user interfaces.

A good example is SharePoint itself as a public-facing site. Because of the seeming simplicity of the creation of new sites, content management, and all the heavy lifting that it does on the back end, since the very beginning, architects and solution designers have neglected the importance of a good user interface (UI). Thus, from the end-user perspective, the SharePoint platform has not been branded as a platform of choice when it comes to the public-facing site. However, in fact, SharePoint can be branded to look "nothing like SharePoint."

As an architect, you must remember that the user interacts with search through the UI, and the poor quality of that interaction may ultimately cause your search system to fail, no matter how technologically advanced it is, how many design considerations were put into the back end, and how resilient it is.

Search is an ever-evolving product, and is never at its end state. If it does not evolve, the engine becomes obsolete. The same is applicable to the UI.

Ensuring that search trends are monitored and the UI reflects the usage of the engine can be as simple as monitoring top ten keywords and making sure that Best Bets are provided for those, as well as synonyms. For example, at the end of the fiscal year you might spot that people are looking for benefits forms, because it's the time to switch a health provider. Ensure that people have the link to the benefits department forms library as their Best Bet. With FAST Search for SharePoint, you can even ensure that people from different regions in the company get their respective region form as a Best Bet through user context capability.

Even though this example can be applicable to the "relevancy improvement" topic rather than the UI, it is applicable to both. Usage of the Best Bets and synonyms affects the UI as well as relevancy. At the end of the day, it's all about intuitive and productive usage of the search results.

One thing that might help to identify the usability factor is doing user interaction testing while the project is still in beta. Involving user search interaction experts, user experience designers, and usability experts will help as well. But be sure that you do not over-engineer it. At the end of the day, they want it to be simple. And keeping it simple will allow changes in the core functionality to be easily reflected in the UI, and that the integration of the UI is seamless.

PLANNING FOR SCALE AND REDUNDANCY

Though all search components can be mirrored for redundancy, or moved from one server to another within the farm to provide the load spread, search administration is an exception. This is the only component that cannot be moved, and will reside on the server where the search application was created initially.

The volume of data (size) translated into number of items (sites, lists, items in document libraries, database records, files, and web pages) determines the storage and search architecture requirement, and plays a key role in determining architectural requirements for search.

Table 27-5 describes how the number of items you plan to crawl affects design decisions. Use this information to determine the initial architecture. As a starting point for hardware and architecture planning, you can use the metrics shown here.

TABLE 27-5: Items that Affect Design Decisions

NUMBER OF ITEMS TO BE INDEXED	SIZE OF THE FARM
0 to 10 million	Limited to a small-sized farm
10 to 20 million	Medium farm with shared resources
20 to 40 million	Medium farm dedicated to search application
40 to approximately 100 million	Large dedicated farm topologies

Crawl or content sources can be scheduled from the administrative interface, but the frequency of index updates in combination with index redundancy requirements and result set freshness will be the key factors influencing the search application architecture. When the content in crawled content sources is frequently updated, and the freshness of the search results is imperative to the business, multiple crawl servers and crawlers are needed to facilitate high crawl speed and indexing that will maximize freshness of query results.

After the first search server in the farm is provisioned, the topology of the search is simple, resulting in crawl and query components that reside on the same server. To scale out your search topology, you join additional SharePoint servers to the farm, and move search components to joined servers.

You can also add a mirror of the query component. When a mirror is added, it creates a replica of the query component.

OPTIMIZING SEARCH PERFORMANCE

To start optimizing performance, the most important things to understand are the components involved in it, and how the index is split into partitions and mirrors.

> *Index partitions* — The new search architecture has introduced a concept of index partitioning, where subsets of a full index are propagated to different query servers, thus spreading the load of queries across multiple query servers. In the multiple index partitions scenario, each partition must be associated with at least one query server. But multiple query servers can be associated with the same partition and hold a mirror of an index partition.

> *Query components* — This is the component that is responsible for satisfying query requests. As mentioned, the index partition cannot exist without having a query component associated with it. But multiple query components can be associated with the same partition.

> *Mirroring* — Mirroring is a way of providing redundancy for components. Mirrors are redundant copies of components. They can be either active or passive. Active mirrors address throughput. As requests are being sent, they will be sent to one of the active mirrors using a round-robin algorithm. Passive mirrors serve for availability in cases when no active components exist for a given partition.

SharePoint Server 2010 uses a hash of each document's ID to identify the partition that stores index entries for a document. At query time, each query server is contacted by the query object model so that results from all partitions are returned. For optimal performance, a query server should be allocated to no more than 10 million items. The sub-second query latency and high volume of queries to be executed concurrently are good indicators of a need for multiple query servers, and possibly multiple index partitions.

From the indexing perspective, the performance and results freshness depends on the crawl time. The time it takes to crawl items largely depends on the following factors: number of data sources, latency, size and type of files, and the query load while crawling is occurring.

It is important not to underestimate the role of SQL Server when scaling your SharePoint search application. Following are the two databases that play key roles in the topology planning:

➤ *Property database* — Each query component is associated with a property database, which is used for retrieving managed properties and ACLs for query component index partition.

➤ *Crawl database* — The crawl database contains crawled content, and should be located on a separate hard disk from the property database as a best practice to prevent I/O contention. If the crawling is in progress when end users are executing queries, or several crawler connections are concurrently established to the crawl database, it is best to deploy crawl databases to separate SQL servers.

Following are some general rules of thumb for scaling search components:

➤ If query throughput is low, add multiple query components with mirror index partitions.

➤ If SQL Server is memory/CPU bound, add additional SQL Server instances with additional crawl databases.

➤ When query availability is the key, deploy redundant query servers, and use clustered or mirrored database servers to host property databases.

➤ If you have multiple content locations for crawling, use multiple crawlers on redundant index servers, and add crawl databases.

➤ If query latency is caused by high peak query load, add query servers and index partitions. Each index partition can contain up to approximately 10 million items. The query throughput increases when you add index partition instances.

➤ If query latency is caused by database load, isolate the property database from crawl databases by moving it to a separate database server.

OPTIMIZING SEARCH RELEVANCY

The concept of *relevancy* is important to search because it is a direct result of a sorting order in which results that are most significant as answers to the executed query appear first in the result set. For example, when you search for a document and the query finds a match in the title of the document versus the body, the document with the matching title would be a better match. In SharePoint 2010 Search, there is a predefined ranking model that cannot be changed. But you can influence the relevancy of documents by defining keywords, Best Bets, synonyms, search scopes, managed properties, and sites promotion.

Initial relevance tuning provides a good start. But as part of ongoing operations, further adapting the out-of-the-box experience by analyzing user search behavior will drive higher end-user satisfaction and a higher productivity rate. The quality of a search-tuning cycle can make the search experience even better.

SharePoint 2010 comes with a number of reports that aid in search trends analysis. Site analytics reports identify popular queries — the queries that should work well, and can be good candidates for Best Bets keywords, or an indication of which queries need keyword management. Best Bets and synonyms can be created for queries that previously failed.

Failed queries occur when the queries return either zero search results, or when there was no click-through by end user from the search results returned. Failed queries can hint as to what content sources should be added to the crawl, or be an indicator that there are crawl issues. The first thing to check would be crawl sources and crawl logs to identify if documents that should match the query were actually crawled.

SUMMARY

Search is an important part of SharePoint 2010, and even more important for organizations because it spans the boundaries of SharePoint, and serves as a single entry point for all the enterprise data.

You can start small on your way to the fully scaled enterprise search engine, as long as you start with the grand vision in mind, and do not lose this vision throughout the process. Do not quickly sprint through development of search because this is prone to the tendency of over-engineering the search and over-complicating it, without getting real value out of it. Do not stop the development of the search capabilities, and continue to make steady progress with the evolution of your search engine.

A popular saying is, "Great search is not built; it is grown." Allow your search capability to evolve with the business, allow it to grow into the overall enterprise design, and allow your users to grow into search by proving its unparalleled capability to make them productive in what they need to accomplish.

Chapter 28 explores individual and social networking services.

28

Individual and Social Networking Features

By Matt Ranlett

SharePoint 2010 is more than an organization's content repository, capable of storing and versioning web pages and documents with ease. It is also an organization's social butterfly, finding common interests between various employees and stitching together the contents of the various repositories across organizational boundaries.

The social aspect of SharePoint is one of the feature areas that received the most attention and investment from Microsoft during the evolution from SharePoint 2007 to SharePoint 2010. The capabilities of prior versions have been significantly augmented in this latest offering, and include a number of personalization and organization capabilities.

This chapter will first focus on ensuring that a common social computing vocabulary is established with respect to SharePoint's functionalities. Once a firm understanding of the various capabilities has been imparted, the second portion of this chapter will focus on the incorporation of SharePoint's social networking capabilities in enterprise portal applications.

FIGURE 28-1: User-centric identities

A social computing application is inherently built around individual users. When considering a user-centric design approach, it is helpful to think of an individual's various identities. At every moment, each user thinks of himself or herself as having three concentric identities, as shown in Figure 28-1.

Note the following about each of these identities:

➤ *Myself* — From the core, the user's individual identity is of foremost importance. What is important to the user as an individual? What would the user like to share with others about himself or herself, and about their work?

➤ *My Team* — In one form or another each person is part of a team. The team might be a project team, an organizational department, an office location, or, most likely, all of the above. How can users easily find their teams and keep track of what happens without having to bookmark every important site?

➤ *My Company* — For employees in an organization, some important organizational messages should not be missed, and should be easy to find in the future.

SharePoint 2010 allows for a user-centric approach to content management and discovery through the social computing tools that are discussed in this chapter. However, right from the beginning, it is important to understand what SharePoint is *not*.

SharePoint is *not* a social networking tool. Installation of SharePoint does not bring Facebook into the organization, and employees should have no trouble delineating work-related activities in the corporate portal from personal activities that take place on social networking sites. The social computing tools available out-of-the-box with SharePoint 2010 are all focused on improving the user's experience when it comes to focusing on relevant content.

PERSONALIZATION

Among the social computing tools available within SharePoint 2010 are those that help the user to personalize the SharePoint browsing and interaction experience. This personalization toolkit includes a user's profile, My Site, and the capability to personalize the pages the user sees. These components build on one another to help each user have an individually relevant experience with his or her SharePoint portal.

User Profile Information

The core of any social application is the *user profile*. Referring back to Figure 28-1, the User Profile is SharePoint's answer to how the user can define himself or herself on the portal. Information inside of the User Profile is a combination of personal attributes that are pulled from various external application sources, and personal attributes that are manually maintained by the users themselves.

Out-of-the-box, a SharePoint 2010 User Profile will offer 75 distinct properties, including `LastName`, `FirstName`, `WorkEmail`, `SPS-Birthday`, `SPS-Interests`, and more.

 You can find a full listing of available default properties on TechNet under the SharePoint Server 2010 site and solution planning section at `http://technet.microsoft.com/en-us/library/ee721054.aspx#section2.`

Additional properties can also be created by system administrators should the default properties not fully meet the organization's needs. When creating properties, each property field offers independent configuration of a number of options, including the field-level privacy, the inclusion of the property in SharePoint's search index, and whether the property is synchronized from an external system or maintained manually by the user.

When connecting to an external system for User Profile data synchronization, it is important to understand that the default system for such connections is Microsoft's Active Directory (AD) or other Lightweight Directory Access Protocol (LDAP) directories (such as Novell's eDirectory and Sun's SunOne). Once the User Profile data from the AD/LDAP user directory has been imported, it is possible to import additional data from other systems, such as Human Resource (HR) systems and Customer Relationship Management (CRM) systems.

This technical consideration is significant when considering users who are not members of the organization. External users can be granted access to SharePoint without requiring their profiles to be included in automated profile synchronization. But those external users will not show up in SharePoint's People search, nor will they be eligible for My Sites. There are ways around this technical hurdle, but it is important to be aware of this when planning for User Profiles and profile synchronization.

Once a User Profile has been established, the foundation for SharePoint 2010's social computing capabilities has been laid. Now the users can begin to expose personal details, work on public and private documents, identify colleagues based on common interests and experiences, and improve the rest of their portal interactions based on their profile attributes.

My Site

If the User Profile is the foundation of SharePoint's social computing experiences, a user's My Site is the pinnacle of individualization. Again referring back to Figure 28-1, the user has now been defined in terms of his or her User Profile attributes. SharePoint's My Site is a way for that user to expose some or all of those details, personally manage content storage, individualize newsfeeds populated by ongoing portal activities, and more.

Activity Streams

The newsfeed is a stream of content interactions anywhere on the portal. When a colleague uploads or modifies a list item or document on the site, the newsfeed brings that activity to the user's My Site for easy discovery.

If the user does not have permission to view or interact with the content, SharePoint's native security trimming capabilities hide it from the user both on the source site, and in the user's newsfeed. It is important to note that this security trimming capability is provided by SharePoint's search indexer, which records user permissions as it crawls over the various content items. Users have the opportunity to customize the content of their newsfeeds by identifying colleagues, tags, and interests throughout the portal. You learn more about these concepts later in this chapter.

The power of an activity stream or newsfeed is that users are able to bridge site boundaries to see content updates in one location, rather than having to navigate from site to site the way SharePoint 2007 frequently made users do it. Time is saved, and users feel more connected to the rest of the portal activities because they have not been left out.

Public and Private File Sharing

Each My Site offers its user a pair of document libraries and a picture library on a My Content page. The document libraries are named as follows:

➤ *Personal Documents* — As expected, the Personal Documents library is viewable only by the individual user who is the owner of the site. This means that any documents placed in the Personal Documents library are secured and private to the site owner by default.

➤ *Shared Documents/Shared Pictures* — Again, as expected, the Shared Documents library and the Shared Pictures picture library are open to anyone who has been granted access to that user's My Site. This normally means that all domain users are able to view the contents of any My Site's Shared Documents and Shared Pictures.

This clearly defined split between public and private content in a user's My Site helps to drive users to the portal, especially those users who might otherwise be reluctant to tackle some of the technical challenges of using SharePoint over a less complex folder share on a file server.

Expertise

Each My Site offers its user a My Profile section. This is where the SharePoint User Profile is exposed. With its built-in status updates and micro-blogging, interactive organizational charts, colleague browser, and more, the My Profile section allows the users to advertise themselves to the rest of the organization.

It is also here that the users are able to advertise their interests and expertise through SharePoint's Ask Me About section. The Ask Me About section lets users capitalize on SharePoint's native tagging infrastructure. By associating a tag with Ask Me About, the user will show up on a Search page's People Matches during a search for one of those keywords. When viewing a user's profile, clicking an Ask Me About tag brings the user to SharePoint's Note Board functionality to ask a question that not only gets e-mailed to them, but is publically viewable in SharePoint from then on.

Search

This is the secret weapon of SharePoint when it comes to turning the portal into more than a file locker in the sky. By exposing the User Profile to search, SharePoint allows for a rich data-mining experience, which includes not only the content in the portal, but also the people responsible for the organization's knowledge capital.

Given the deep look at an individual's contribution to a social network, it is time to include groups of people and consider their relationships with each other.

COLLEAGUES, ORGANIZATIONS, AND MEMBERSHIPS

Moving out from the "Myself" circle from Figure 28-1, users will next consider themselves part of one or more teams. Part of these team interactions center on the people they work with, and the other part of these team interactions center on the content they work with on their various SharePoint portal sites.

The questions asked by employees in this context move from, "How do I advertise myself to the company?" to questions like, "How do I best work with my teammates in the office and around the globe?" Microsoft provides a number of integrated people and content organization tools inside of SharePoint that specifically target this segment of user needs.

Colleagues

Fundamentally, a workplace is comprised of people working together toward a common goal. It is in the context of a focused team like this where some of the strongest social capabilities of SharePoint 2010 come into play.

Users can leverage their My Sites and its activity feeds. SharePoint 2010 offers users the capability to identify certain people as colleagues worthy of closer attention. When a SharePoint 2010 portal user is identified as a colleague, that person is effectively being "followed" as one "follows" friends on Facebook or Twitter. Any public activity such as checking in documents (given the proper security permissions) or the change of a User Profile detail shows up as an entry in any of the My Site activity feeds of followers.

Consider for a moment how powerful and pervasive this simple concept is. Following "friends" is the foundation for most public social networks on the Internet, especially the world's most popular social sites (Facebook and Twitter). According to The Nielsen Company, global consumers spent more than five and a half hours on social networking sites like Facebook and Twitter in December 2009, which represents an 82 percent increase over the previous year.

 For more information, see the Nielsen blog post, "Lead by Facebook, Twitter, Global Time Spent on Social Media Sites up 82% Year over Year," at `http://blog.nielsen.com/nielsenwire/global/led-by-facebook-twitter-global-time-spent-on-social-media-sites-up-82-year-over-year/`.

Should this trend continue at this incredible growth rate, Nielsen will report social networks as consuming 10 hours 13 minutes per month in December 2010, and an astonishing 18 hours 42 minutes in December 2011 on average around the globe!

It is exactly this type of time-consuming trend that tends to frighten management teams who are worried about employees sacrificing productivity for the enterprise in order to "play" on Facebook. Fortunately, SharePoint 2010 builds in several automations that reduce the time-consuming maintenance aspects of interpersonal social networking.

Automatic Population of Colleagues

SharePoint 2010 takes advantage of its integration with AD to build out an understanding of each employee's place in the organization. By default, SharePoint adds the user's manager, reports, and peers as colleagues for each user. This is done initially at the time of full profile synchronization. But SharePoint keeps the colleagues list in synch with organizational change by scanning the AD for new people every time an incremental profile synchronization is run.

SharePoint Server Colleague Add-in for Outlook 2010

Outlook 2007 and Outlook 2010 each ship with an add-in called the Microsoft SharePoint Server Colleague Import add-in. Active by default, the SharePoint Server Colleague add-in scans through the user's Sent Items folder to look for names and keywords, along with the frequency of those names and keywords. The results of the scans are periodically updated and stored on each user's local computer.

 Colleague and keyword suggestions are stored by default at
`C:\Users\<loginname>\AppData\Local\Microsoft\Outlook\spscoll.dat.`

When a user visits his or her My Site, this list is accessed and is presented to the user as a set of suggested colleagues he or she may optionally want to add to My Site. Additionally, keyword suggestions loaded into the User Profile are proposed to the user as suggested keywords for the Ask Me About section of their My Site. The user can approve or reject contact names and keywords.

Although the scan is on by default, it is important to remember that each user must explicitly add anything discovered in the scan to SharePoint. However, if this feels too intrusive, it is easy to disable by using Microsoft's Active Directory Group Policy administrative capabilities. TechNet contains easy-to-follow instructions for group or individual disabling of this component in KB article 2020103.

Organizational Hierarchy Browser

Thanks to a person's profile page (`person.aspx`) in his or her My Site, it is easy to gain an understanding of that person's interests and expertise. However, before reaching out to that individual directly through the integrated presence capabilities such as instant messaging (IM) or e-mail, it is frequently helpful to understand exactly who that person is by virtue of the person's reporting relationships.

SharePoint offers two experiences to help with that understanding — an HTML page and an interactive Silverlight organizational browser. Both show the person's manager and peers. The Silverlight browser is interactive, smoothly scrolls through multiple levels of the organizational hierarchy, and shows direct reports as well as peers and managers.

The organizational hierarchy details (which are rendered by both the HTML page and Silverlight organizational hierarchy components) are created based on information imported during the profile synchronization process. Organizational hierarchy data is pulled from Active Directory, and reporting relationships are compiled based on names in the Manager field. Once the details have been imported automatically, and are stored in SharePoint's User Profile database, updates to the hierarchies continue to come from incremental profile synchronizations.

Site Memberships and Distribution Lists

In addition to understanding how a person fits into an organization, it is frequently helpful to understand how that person fits into SharePoint's system of portal and team sites. SharePoint 2010's My Profile page of a My Site offers a Memberships tab that lists the sites in which the user is in the default Members group. In addition to site memberships, SharePoint's MemberGroup concept also defines a distribution list (DL). Distribution lists that are configured and stored in Active Directory are imported along with other User Profile details during a profile synchronization. By default, the Memberships list is a simple, flat list of all available sites. But a user does have the option of grouping sites together, and even hiding membership from the general public in the same way User Profile details can be secured.

Presence

SharePoint offers integrations to Microsoft Office Communicator and Microsoft Lync as pieces of Microsoft's Unified Communications strategy. Microsoft Office Communications Server (OCS) 2007 and Microsoft Lync 2010 are Microsoft's offerings to organizations that want to fully deploy and manage their own instant messaging (IM) and online presence solutions. In addition to simple IM-style chat, OCS and Lync feature audio and video conferencing, IP telephony, web conferencing, and voicemail integration through Microsoft Exchange, as well as application and desktop sharing.

Microsoft's Unified Communications applications (OCS and Lync, as well as the free chat application Windows Live Messenger) offer a level of client integration into SharePoint that helps users understand the presence of their co-workers. The term "presence" can signify a number of different user experiences, some of them happening simultaneously.

Throughout this chapter, however, *presence* will be referred to only as the representation of a user's state in relation to his or her use of their computers. In other words, presence herein is considered the status of a user as the user interacts with a computer application that is designed to track the user's state. In this way, when a user logs in to the application, the user status can then be represented as being "online," and when the user leaves the application or shuts down the computer, the status can be represented as "offline."

When OCS, Lync, or Windows Live Messenger have been installed on the user's computer, and SharePoint is accessed through a compatible browser, an ActiveX control is launched automatically to render a presence as a green, red, or yellow button next to a SharePoint user's name. Hovering over that button pops out a context menu that reveals the selected user's availability and several communication options (including an OCS chat or e-mail, as shown in Figure 28-2).

FIGURE 28-2: Presence in SharePoint 2010

The power of presence is that any portal user is simply a click away. Whether engagement occurs via an e-mail, an ad-hoc IM chat, or a scheduled meeting, SharePoint's presence capabilities bring the office staff together more frequently and more efficiently. Furthermore, the presence capabilities outlined here not only work in SharePoint, but also in all other Microsoft Office applications, including Outlook, Word, and more. Users have the same integrated experience whether they start from Lync, Outlook, or SharePoint.

Presence is a powerful communications enabler, but the interactions through the presence icon tend to be one not preserved for the rest of the online community to participate in. This gap is where SharePoint offers several longer-lived and more widely accessible communications options, including blogs and wikis.

BLOGS AND WIKIS

As carried over from SharePoint 2007, blogs and wikis are easily visible social features of SharePoint 2010. The easiest way to think about these social aspects is that an entire SharePoint site can be built around the functionality of a blog or wiki. The hallmarks of these sites are the text-based solicitation of user feedback in the form of blog comments or wiki page edits.

Blogs

A *blog* is an application generally featuring owner-written content that is open for public comment. Although this is not a new concept to SharePoint, blogs can be incredibly useful to an individual or team attempting to communicate to an otherwise disconnected audience of readers. Since the 2007 versions of SharePoint, blogs have been used to replace e-mail distribution lists, as well as occasionally updated "interesting ideas" lists of links with a longer-lived and more functional medium. SharePoint 2010 refreshes the concept of corporate blogs with new features and a fresh look and feel.

While a blog is typically envisioned as the point of broadcast by an individual, it is becoming more and more frequent to see business teams using a blog as the focal point of their communications with each other and with the rest of the business. The easy-to-understand RSS capabilities, the bi-directional communication through blog comments, and easy-to-understand way to consume past activities on the web page have really begun to shine a light on this SharePoint site template.

Micro-blog

A *micro-blog* is a social networking phenomenon seen most apparently in Twitter, Yammer, and Facebook's activity streams.

When a user updates his or her status via the Web on the SharePoint 2010 My Site, it shows up in all of the activity streams of the user's followers. SharePoint's status updates and micro-blogging enable easy broadcasting of information to all of the user's followers in order to facilitate conversations, improve employee engagement, and encourage social collaboration. All of this happens behind the firewall in a secure environment without the risk of sensitive customer information (or perhaps even complaints *about* customers) falling into the wrong hands.

Users of Microsoft Lync 2010 actually have another micro-blog option. In addition to the native SharePoint status updates, when a user uses Lync to update his or her status, the presence pop-out menu will show that status in the portal, but will not keep a running history in activity feeds.

Wikis

Complementing blogs in the user-generated content category are *wikis*. Though wikis as a concept have been around since 1995, and available in SharePoint since 2007, the simple concept is deceptively difficult to employ in organizations that are used to working with documents as the primary means for disseminating information. Cemented in the public consciousness by Wikipedia, the hallmark features of wikis include simple data entry and ease of linking content inside of the wiki.

Wikis Everywhere

In SharePoint 2007, wikis were first introduced as a site template that featured a collection of text-based, cross-linked web pages in a page library. Users who have experienced the relative ease of editing a wiki page (complete with WYSIWYG editing and HTML-free page linking) frequently try to build team sites centered on wikis.

SharePoint 2010 turns the concept of a wiki on its head by offering the easy editing wiki functionality on every page, thanks to a new Rich Text Editor component built into SharePoint 2010 team site pages. Improving on the capabilities offered in previous versions, SharePoint 2010 makes the entry of text, images, lists, and functional web parts an effortless experience. This lends itself to an organic growth when combined with the traditional list and library-based information-management capabilities familiar to users of previous versions of SharePoint.

In a team collaboration environment, the easy text and image editing capabilities of team site pages in a "wikis everywhere" site dramatically eases the management and overhead required to maintain a site. Rather than focusing untrained users to think in terms of lists and web parts, web pages in the intranet become web pages again.

Despite this user-centric thinking, it is important to understand that there are actually different types of content pages, as well as how the ones that include the wiki editing fit into a SharePoint portal site.

Publishing Pages

Publishing pages exist only in sites that have the SharePoint Publishing infrastructure features installed. The chief difference between a publishing page and other page types is that a publishing page offers end users the capability to place specific content elements in specific layouts, much in the same way a magazine publisher would lay out magazine pages. The author or editor would select a page layout template with one or two columns, an image on the top left or bottom right, and perhaps some specific content rollups on the side or bottom of the page.

Once a layout has been selected and populated via the browser, it is easy to change to another layout without affecting the content. This is thanks to SharePoint's capability to keep content data separate from the page layout instructions.

Sites that leverage the Publishing infrastructure and publishing page layouts tend to be very concerned with consistency of look, often incorporate a strict content-approval scheme, and require significant pre-planning and development before being released by IT for content entry. Public (Internet) facing SharePoint sites almost always leverage this page type.

Web Part Pages

The focus of a web part page is the dynamic display of information in lists, charts, and other customizable functionality via SharePoint web parts. Although every SharePoint page has the native capability to host and display web parts, this web part page type eschews the strict formatting guidelines of publishing pages and the collaborative editing capabilities of wiki pages.

Wiki Pages

The Rich Text Editor wiki page is a default experience for almost all SharePoint 2010 template sites, excluding certain workspaces and enterprise site templates such as publishing sites. The focus of these team site wiki pages is easy manipulation of elements on the screen, complete with the capability to intermingle text, images, list data, and functional web parts in a single editor.

The experience feels a bit like editing a Word document with its Ribbon and its easy capability to manage different types of content. Wiki pages are intended for small team sites where the presentation of content is perhaps less important than the capability for the site to be flexible in the ways content can be presented.

Enterprise Wiki

In SharePoint 2007, the wiki site template was an excellent first attempt by Microsoft to introduce wikis to the masses. But it frequently fell flat because of the inherent limits of SharePoint 2007's site structure and scalability.

To remedy the frequently cited SharePoint 2007 wiki shortcomings, Microsoft introduced the Enterprise Wiki site template in SharePoint 2010. The Enterprise Wiki template uses a combination of publishing page layout template technology and wiki rich text editing in a high-capacity storage system. The result is a site that is perfectly suited for centralized Knowledge Management, and is ready to be turned into a "My Company" Wikipedia. (Contoso-pedia anybody?)

Blogs and wikis are fantastic tools that users tend to have no trouble understanding and interacting with. Unfortunately, not every community concept needs its own blog or wiki entry. To help with smaller concepts and categorizations, SharePoint 2010 incorporates functions that users are normally familiar with: tags, ratings, and comments/notes about content.

TAGGING, RATINGS, AND NOTES

Unlike blogs and wikis, tags and social feedback are totally new to the SharePoint 2010 experience. These new features take the social experience of SharePoint to a whole new level of user participation and interaction, allowing users to discover content and what other users think of that content.

Tags

The act of *tagging content* is the assignment of descriptor words or categories to that content. There are two types of tagging:

> *Social tagging* refers to content, and adds metadata to content to describe what it is, what it contains, or what it does.

> *Expertise tagging* is related to a person, and describes the person, (such as what she does, which projects she works on, or what skills she has).

Whereas social tagging of content enables users to organically flex and grow a portal's information architecture over time, expertise tagging helps build relationships and connections to other people in the organization.

One of the most compelling features of social tagging in SharePoint 2010 is that tags are given profile pages much in the same way people are. Clicking any tag (whether on a document or on a User Profile) brings the portal users to the profile page where they can see the sites where the tag has been applied, documents and content elements that have been associated with the tag, and people who are applying the tag. In essence, a tag profile page is an instant community with its own dynamic set of content and users!

Bookmarks

Internet users familiar with tools such as Delicious and Diig will recognize that *social bookmarking* is the practice of sharing bookmarks with a community of users to help build the knowledge and perspective of the community as a whole. Bookmarks in SharePoint 2010 replace the 2007 My Links feature, and allow a user to define how a link is shared and categorized.

SharePoint bookmarks even support the inclusion of non-SharePoint content! Through the use of web browser "bookmarklets" available on every user's My Profile page, SharePoint 2010 allows any piece of Internet content to be posted to that user's social bookmarks, and can be tagged at the moment of bookmarking.

Feedback and Rating

A popular social Internet activity is to rate and comment on the activities and contributions of other users. SharePoint incorporates the capability to rate content with a five-star metaphor, and to comment on that content much the same way a user can comment on a blog post. This rating system is most visible when viewing a list of documents in a document library as a column of five stars.

Note Board

Users of Facebook will recognize how easily they can communicate with each other via the Wall. SharePoint 2010 builds this concept of a communication accelerator into its *note board* application. Note boards are available for use on an individual user's profile page, a tag's profile page, and an organization's profile page.

The communication intent of the note board is different from e-mail, IM, and the preexisting discussion group's functionality. Note board comments are not generally intended for multiple users to respond back and forth as they might in a discussion group or in an e-mail distribution list. Instead, note boards are for quick casual comments that add color or context to the content in question.

Notes are a permanent addition to SharePoint, and remain discoverable on User Profile pages.

SharePoint 2010 offers some significant social components or building blocks for an enterprise architect to consider when constructing a larger enterprise solution. How should these building blocks be used to maximize value without distracting from general corporate business? The following sections step away from the technology enablers and focus on the more holistic business landscape.

KEY BUSINESS CHALLENGES

Deploying a new portal is not a small challenge. A lot must be considered, including hard costs such as software licenses and hardware platforms, ongoing costs such as new full-time equivalents (FTEs), training, and the effects of necessary organizational changes. All of this must be balanced against the return on investment (ROI) numbers, which are frequently difficult to predict with accuracy.

The remainder of this chapter focuses on how the social components of SharePoint 2010 may impact an organization in a positive or negative fashion.

Clarifying Business Requirements

When organizations start talking about new portals, the underlying reasons for the conversation tend to be centered on desires for increased employee engagement and better communication inside of a system, which is easier and cheaper to maintain compared to whatever solution exists now. When considering a SharePoint 2010 solution with all of these new social networking capabilities, the planning and deployment teams should give careful consideration to the social networking capabilities.

The social features may very well become an integral part of the glue that holds the portal together. They are almost certainly going to be a major part of why users keep returning to the portal.

Defining and Planning the List of User Profile Properties

SharePoint comes ready for users with hundreds of properties that may be selected for exposure on employee profile pages. A number of these properties may be auto-populated through integrations with AD or integrated HR systems such as PeopleSoft. It is up to the implementation team to choose from the pool of available attributes, as well as the subset of attributes for exposure on portal pages. In search terms, this is the difference between crawled properties and managed properties, or properties that are consumed by SharePoint's search indexer and the subset of those that are exposed to end users on profile pages.

In addition to metadata elements exposed during profile synchronizations, consider if any additional properties should be created and exposed for employees to manually populate. Though it may not specifically relate to business problems at hand, employee engagement could be increased by asking employees to expose silly trivia about themselves, such as their favorite movies or snack foods. It's impossible to guarantee that such activity will improve engagement and morale, but encouraging a little cognitive incongruence may bring levity and tighten relationships.

Storing Personally Identifiable Information

As user details are pulled from HR systems and user directories into the portal, it is important to remember that the underlying mechanisms of SharePoint actually create copies of this data in the various User Profile databases. Care should be taken with access to this information, because it is almost always a wealth of personally identifiable information (PII).

It would be a good policy to ensure that while users are storing their names and e-mail addresses, they are not storing their Social Security numbers or credit card numbers. User Profile data can be hidden from view on a field-by-field basis, but that security mechanism does not make this system an appropriate system for such sensitive personal data.

Another consideration for PII is that some global regions have different regulatory views on this type of data. For example, the U.S. has fairly relaxed government regulations about what is considered restricted PII. In the U.S., most PII is not protected, and that which is protected is covered under protective regulations such as the Health Insurance Portability and Accountability Act (HIPAA). On the other hand, European Union countries such as Germany are extremely rigid about PII, and refuse to allow any PII to cross the country's borders. This may have an impact on how your SharePoint environment is constructed.

Defining Clear Employee Code of Conduct

It can be tempting to consider a company SharePoint portal as just another social network. But users should be reminded that this particular social network is reserved for work-related activity, and should not be treated the same as Twitter or Facebook. SharePoint's social collaboration capabilities are a powerful tool, and should absolutely be used to keep co-workers informed of team activities and stream-of-consciousness thinking about project work. Depending on the organization, this may include turning to SharePoint's note boards and discussion groups for frank conversations about sensitive company information.

Phasing the Rollout of My Sites to Employees

Another key implementation decision is the schedule under which SharePoint's My Site functionality is released to the general employee base. Is it appropriate to release the functionality to all employees at the moment of the initial portal release? Should the release of social functions follow the initial portal release, perhaps in phase 2 or 3? Should all employees receive the functionality at the same time, or should there be a more gradual introduction of the capabilities?

These decisions will vary from organization to organization, and from implementation team to implementation team, based on organizational culture, change management, and IT capacity constraints.

It is sometimes the role of an architect to stretch an application's capabilities in order to provide the proper solution to business requirements. These advanced business scenarios require careful technology planning in order to properly customize application infrastructures and custom code without introducing otherwise avoidable risks. The following section examines a few commonly encountered advanced business scenarios.

ADVANCED BUSINESS SCENARIOS

Geography and corporate job descriptions can act together to isolate people and information in an organization. Fortunately, proper application of SharePoint 2010 can alleviate some of this isolation through native social computing capabilities. Of course, enhancing these social capabilities to meet the needs of a global marketplace may take some extra work, as described here.

Geographically Dispersed My Site Implementations

Building a SharePoint portal environment for an organization offers the opportunity to turn a single software application into the great equalizer. SharePoint's multi-lingual variations capabilities, content ratings, tagging infrastructure, and the rest of SharePoint's social capabilities can do an incredible job of bringing geographically distributed employees together.

However, if an organization is split geographically, such that it does not make sense for all of the data to live in a single SharePoint farm, it may make sense to consider dispersing the portal's My Site hosts. For example, if half of the employee base is in North America, and the other half is in Eurasia, it may make sense to have two My Site farms (two distinct farms with independent My Site hosts) to improve network and perceived application performance.

If distributing My Sites is the chosen option, be sure to pay attention to the following configuration elements:

➤ *Host farm infrastructure* — SharePoint service provider farms are not required to have identical hardware across all installations. If the employee base is concentrated in Eurasia, it may make sense to concentrate infrastructure investment on the most heavily taxed environment.

➤ *Fail-over replication* — What are the service-level agreements (SLAs) for My Sites? If a host farm goes down, can your users still access their personal content on the other region's farm, or on a standby disaster recovery (DR) farm? Consider content replication through tools such as Microsoft's SQL Mirroring or Synergy's Replicator to ensure data is always available. Allow your geographically distributed farms to provide DR resiliency for each other.

➤ *Time zones* — SharePoint content posts are generally recognized by the time zone the server is installed in. A single global web application instance will record all content entries in a single time zone. Consider distributing My Site host web applications to keep the logged time zone closer to the user's actual time zone.

➤ *Languages* — If your employee base is multi-lingual, consider allowing users to maintain their My Site in their own preferred language. Although SharePoint variations enable multi-lingual copies of the same content usually seen in web content management publishing sites, that is generally not appropriate for a My Site. On-demand machine translations such as those offered by the Microsoft Translator built into Internet Explorer (IE) 8 may be perfectly adequate for global consumers of localized My Site content where professional translators may be required for global HR content.

➤ *Consistent tagging* — Be sure to account for global distribution of content when planning for shared services such as the managed metadata service. Ensuring a consistent vocabulary throughout the organization is part of the process of increasing global employee engagement. Part of this consideration is whether or not to enable the multi-lingual tagging capabilities of the Managed Metadata Service (MMS).

Extending Activity Feeds for Custom Solutions

As an architect, a significant part of the job is to ensure that solutions fit together. This is a big reason why service-based architectures are so popular — SOA architectures promise easy integrations of new and existing applications to meet new demands. Do not forget the Activity Feed as an integration point for notifications of user actions when building custom components and workflows for SharePoint. SharePoint exposes several hooks to the Activity Feed process by using Activity Feed gatherers and ActivityEvent objects inside of the SharePoint API.

Using Role-Based My Site Dashboards

Microsoft released a set of application templates for SharePoint 2007 called the Fabulous 40. These application templates allowed for practically no-code installation of targeted functionality, and served as a model for additional application templates. In addition to the Fabulous 40 templates, Microsoft released seven role-based My Site templates. Unfortunately, none of these templates are being migrated by Microsoft from the SharePoint 2007 platform to the 2010 platform.

The fact that Microsoft is not planning to migrate the 2007 application and My Site templates does not mean that application templates or role-based My Site templates are invalid options. These customizations have simply been left up to the individual organizations and software vendors. Combining out-of-the-box solutions with SharePoint 2010's capability to save any site as a WSP package, software developers and architects can accelerate toward customized application templates.

These application templates are able to leverage new and previously existing functionality, such as the Business Connectivity Services and Content Query web parts to aggregate information onto dashboard pages. Vendors such as CorasWorks are already lining up SharePoint 2010 solutions to provide dynamic dashboards and content roll-ups. Don't be trapped into thinking that the only purpose for dashboard solutions is to surface financial analytics through traditional business intelligence (BI) tools.

Given the importance of the User Profile to the various constituent SharePoint 2010 social computing components and business scenarios described here, it is important to have a firm understanding of the SharePoint 2010 User Profile system and its data sources.

KEY ARCHITECTURAL CONSIDERATIONS

This section reviews the capability of SharePoint to import User Profile data from a variety of data sources, to customize the placement of data into User Profile properties, and the capability to exclude users from import through exclusion filters.

Identifying User Profile Import Sources

When planning for User Profile synchronizations, it is important to understand how SharePoint integrates with the various available data sources. Consider the following high-level overview:

➤ Identify and create connections to the appropriate user directory and line-of-business (LOB) systems

➤ Identify which properties should be imported into the User Profiles

➤ Identify which properties should be synched back to the source data sources in the event that they are updated in SharePoint

First, to initially create a User Profile, the user must exist in one of the supported user directories:

➤ Active Directory Domain Services (ADDS)

➤ Novell eDirectory v 8.7.3

➤ Sun Java System Directory Service 5.2

➤ IBM Tivoli version 5.2

Second, a properly configured farm account and synchronization service account must be created and applied to the SharePoint environment. In the event of multiple directories, multiple synchronization accounts should be created to maintain a least-privileged security environment, which is widely recognized as a best practice for production operating systems.

 To assist with this planning activity, Microsoft has created a pair of worksheets that can be freely downloaded. The Profile Synchronization Planning and Connection Planning worksheets are each available from `http://go.microsoft .com/fwlink/?LinkId=202832`.

Ensuring that Source User Profile Information Is Accurate

For many organizations, without systems like SharePoint to expose data in AD (or other user directory service), the data inside of the directory may become stale, disorganized, or otherwise suspect. Before importing data automatically via profile synchronization, it is important to ensure that the directory service contains accurate information. The effort to sanitize this data may require a project all to itself, but this important step prevents the cart-before-the-horse problem of doing an import and trying to clean up a mess later.

Identifying and Mapping Profile Import Properties to SharePoint User Profile Properties

Once a User Profile has been imported from the AD or other directory service, it is possible to augment that User Profile's data with details pulled from other LOB systems (for example, an HR system like PeopleSoft). The aforementioned Profile Synchronization Planning worksheet will help to identify User Profile properties, including those from business systems.

Combining Heterogeneous Data to Enrich the SharePoint User Profile

When importing data from business systems such as an HR application or a financial application, a wealth of data may be available. However, that data may not be present or consistent for all users. In a heterogeneous data environment such as this, SharePoint 2010 takes advantage of its built-in Business Data Connectivity (BDC) capabilities.

Once data elements from business systems have been identified, an External Content Type (ECT) in SharePoint is created to connect the business system to SharePoint as a data source. Once that connectivity has been established, a property map is defined to identify which external business system data elements flow into which User Profile properties.

To connect to external systems via the ECT connections during profile synchronization, the following methods and identifiers must be specified:

➤ *Read Item method* — The Read Item method (also known as the *Specific Finder method*) enables SharePoint to read all of the data elements or metadata properties of a single item in an external business system for import into an external content type.

➤ *Read List method* — The Read List method (also known as the *Finder method*) enables SharePoint to read all of the available data elements and expose them inside of SharePoint as a list of ECTs. Typically, this method does not return all of the data elements, just the important ones for individual item identification.

➤ *Item identifier* — The item identifier is a data element or set of data elements that acts as a primary key uniquely identifying each record. For example, in a personnel database, an item identifier may be the employee ID number, Social Security number, or e-mail address. Each one of those values could be input into the Read Item method to retrieve the single matching record.

➤ *Comparison filter* — The comparison filter is used if there is a one-to-many relationship between the SharePoint User Profile record and the ECT item instances. For example, a financial system may include a set of allowed charge codes to which the user is legitimately allowed to bill job costs. If that user is able to bill to several charge codes, the comparison filter may be used to find only those legitimate charge codes valid for the selected user.

Once the ECT has been defined inside of SharePoint's Business Connectivity Services (BCS) using the appropriate BDC objects and methods, the ECT is connected to the User Profile store for the purposes of augmenting existing User Profile data with business systems' data. SharePoint's Central Administration web application and SharePoint Designer 2010 make this entire set of activities a series of point-and-click operations with no developer intervention required.

Planning for Exclusion Filters

The default import process may import user accounts that are not desired (such as those accounts that have been disabled). In SharePoint 2007, a complex LDAP query was required to exclude such accounts.

In SharePoint 2010, the same challenge remains, but a brand new administrative configuration screen makes the process much simpler to understand. In the new configuration screen, each User Profile attribute is available for consideration as to whether or not the user should be imported during synchronization. This enables connections to the various source systems that are much easier to read and understand.

Figure 28-3 shows the web interface to exclude users and groups based on individual profile property values.

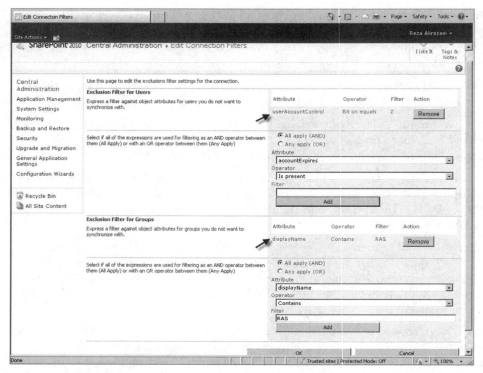

FIGURE 28-3: Web interface to exclude users

Planning for User Profile and My Site Storage Requirements

The spectrum of SharePoint capacity management and sizing considerations is vast, far too large for this chapter. Microsoft has done an excellent job of organizing SharePoint's sizing information on TechNet at `http://technet.microsoft.com/en-us/library/ff758647.aspx`.

Specifically calling out SharePoint's User Profile data storage requirements and My Site storage requirements can be a bit tricky. Several white papers have been written specifically about social environment capacity modeling, including the following:

➤ *Social environment technical case study* — `http://technet.microsoft.com/en-us/library/ff758654.aspx`

➤ `MySitesSocialComputingCapacityPlanningDoc.docx` — `http://www.microsoft.com/downloads/en/details.aspx?FamilyID=fd1eac86-ad47-4865-9378-80040d08ac55&displaylang=en`

➤ *Planning and Deploying SharePoint Server 2010 User Profiles for My Site Web Sites* — `http://www.microsoft.com/downloads/en/details.aspx?FamilyID=cd93bc74-d923-4dc9-b112-715d5ddb64fd&displaylang=en`

Table 28-1 shows the sizing-level guidance that Microsoft has provided for User Profiles:

TABLE 28-1: Sizing Level Guidance for User Profiles

SERVICE	SIZING GUIDANCE
User Profile	1 MB/User Profile
User Profile synch	630 KB/User Profile
User Profile social tagging	0.009 MB/social entry

Governing SharePoint My Sites in terms of data sizes can be a fairly simple affair if fully thought out ahead of time. It is possible to set a size quota on My Sites at the web application level, and any new My Site will have this sizing quota applied as the site is created. This sizing limit, combined with the capability for SharePoint to auto-provision new site collections into any number of databases that have been pre-created by a DBA, will help ensure that individual content databases don't grow too large, while the entire My Site environment remains easy to back up and restore.

Enriching People Search

SharePoint 2010 makes it easy to add User Profile properties to a user's My Profile page, but makes it less than an intuitive process to search on those custom properties. To extend SharePoint's People search to enable custom profile properties to function as search refiners, several non-obvious steps are required to ensure the functionality is available.

Assuming that the profile property has been created and added to the MMS, create a new Managed Property and map it to the `Crawled` (User Profile) Property inside of the search configuration screens in Central Administration. In these configuration screens, also set the property mapping to include the `ContentsHidden` property.

The result of this configuration of the new User Profile property as Managed Metadata is that the property is now searchable and usable as a refiner, but is the values themselves are not displayed inside of the People search results. Without the display of the new custom value in the search results, the ranking of returned people may seem suspect to users. To modify the presentation of the data to include the new field, adjust the XSLT of the People Search Results web part on the Search Results page.

 Refer to Steve McDonnell's website `SharePointSteve.com` *for more explicit details on how to make custom User Profile properties searchable in SharePoint 2010. You can find this information at* `www.sharepointsteve.com/2010/10/ making-custom-user-profile-properties-searchable-in-sharepoint-2010/.`

Using Multiple Farms

The majority of SharePoint 2010's social functionality is provided by the User Profile service application, a back-end component that manages User Profiles, synchronization to back-end data sources, audiences, activity feeds, My Sites, and social tags and notes. The service application stores all of its data in a trio of databases — the profile database, the synchronization database, and the social tagging database.

All of this data is used in My Sites, team sites, and any other site that leverages this information to provide a personalized portal experience. In addition to the User Profile service application, the MMS and the Search Service application round out the social functionality from the perspective of shared services.

The beauty of the SharePoint service application approach is that one service application can provide its services to multiple SharePoint farms. This means that even in an environment where the collaboration farm is physically distinct from the communications farm, both farms can still offer users a seamless social experience. User Profile details and activity stream information can flow between farms. People search will be experienced in an identical fashion because both farms offer up the same data to the search indexer.

However, it is important to note that, though multiple farms are supported by Microsoft, this does not mean that it is possible to use this in wide area network (WAN) environments. The User Profile service application requires direct database access and is not supported across WAN links.

 Instead, Microsoft recommends use of the User Profile Replication Engine. For more information, refer to the TechNet article at `http://technet.microsoft .com/en-us/library/cc560988.aspx`.

Assuming that the review of features allows for a match of functionality to requirement, the next step is to put together a project to implement these capabilities.

RECOMMENDED APPROACH

Given a good understanding of requirements and capabilities, it's time to focus on the project approach to enabling social computing in SharePoint 2010 deployment initiatives.

Focusing on Business Drivers and Requirements

SharePoint is truly a Swiss Army Knife, a tool that can be used to solve a myriad of business problems. It is an architect's job to ensure that the solution fits the problem, not too large or too small. Listen to the complaints of users and of IT to ensure that SharePoint is actually a fit for the organization, and that the components selected for implementation make sense given the business drivers and overall requirements. For example, if the main problem is one of external non-employee collaboration, PerformancePoint-style business intelligence (BI) may not be an immediate target for development and deployment.

When considering the social computing aspects of SharePoint, listen for the following types of requirements from users and IT:

➤ Users need to follow or contribute to content across numerous sites, and that effort has become too burdensome, thanks to the scale of the intranet environment. This is a classic activity feed target, as well as a search target, a tag profile page target, and a content query web part target. Weigh your options and choose the one (or ones) that best fits the corporate culture.

➤ Users have a difficult time identifying authoritative sources of information in the organization. More than just having trouble finding the right HR forms on the HR site, or marketing-approved logos in the Marketing site, users need ways to find the right person or expert to ask questions of. This is a classic combination of deep User Profiles/My Sites with its dynamic organizational chart and rich PII, as well as a strong case for integrated Microsoft Lync for presence and its casual IM-style communications. Bringing these concepts together allows a site reader to understand who created content, where they fit into the organization, and the capability to reach out and communicate with that content creator in the event of unanswered questions.

➤ Users want to create a site that lets them keep team members updated via regular communications. Blogs and wikis are great communications tools. Do not be afraid to look past the obvious personal blog to find enterprising ways to fit social site templates into your enterprise.

Considering a Phased Approach to Social Networking

SharePoint 2010 is generally a big change for an organization, and adoption of all features will not happen overnight, even if the audience is highly technically savvy. Although the social networking features seem comprehensive and exciting to a technology architect, these same features may seem overwhelming to a user whose main use of intranets before now started and ended with online file storage. Rather than attempting to introduce a user to all of the available functionality at once, it makes sense to slowly add capabilities in a "crawl-walk-run" approach.

Consider focusing on the immediate business problem at hand, and introducing the appropriate social features based on the user-centric thinking introduced in Figure 28-1.

For example, if the business problems fall into the "My Team" collaboration area, consider making heavy use of blogs and wikis with an emphasis on tagging content. Once users are comfortable with tagging content, consider the introduction of My Sites and the associated capability to enrich the portal's social connectivity via each user's Tags and Notes page in their My Site profile.

If, on the other hand, the business problem falls into the "My Company" communication area, SharePoint's activity feeds may be the perfect solution to keeping users alert to important content changes despite the sprawl of a large corporate portal. This, combined with a focus on search, will ensure that content remains discoverable. Future phases of this project may be to bring users closer together with dynamic team sites constructed around SharePoint 2010's native wikis-everywhere editing experience.

Designing, Planning, and Deploying My Sites

My Sites are fundamental building blocks in SharePoint's social experience, but that does not mean that every user needs a My Site, nor that the default My Site experience is appropriate. For example, is the organizational hierarchy an appropriate mechanism for users to discover human points of contact, or should the Silverlight organization hierarchy browser be suppressed?

When considering the design of My Sites, it is important to know the development targets.

First and foremost, the default master page for My Sites can be updated to reflect corporate branding and themes.

Second, it is possible to use the feature-stapling capabilities to attach logic to My Sites. Briefly, *feature stapling* allows for customized logic to be run every time a site of a specific template is created. This has the benefit of being disconnected from the template itself, allowing for easier revisions of this custom logic.

Common targets for feature stapling include automatically adjusting the site's master page, editing navigation elements, modifying lists and list items, installation of web parts to pages, and so on. For example, a custom feature stapled to the My Site template may update the master page and place a new tab in the My Profile page to display that user's vacation time on a calendar as stored in the organization's time-tracking system.

Once the My Site template and any custom logic or functionality has been decided upon, it is time to define the rollout plan. Do all users get their My Sites at once? Do all users even qualify for a My Site? What is the data size (site) quota that will be applied to all My Sites? Are the data storage tiers of the SharePoint farm prepared for the potential flood of new data?

After a thorough planning and testing period, turn on the SharePoint My Sites, turn the project's internal marketing team loose on the employees, and sit back to enjoy the buzz and accolades!

Overcoming Cultural Challenges

Regardless of how intuitive and simple a portal function seems to be to the portal deployment project team, ensure that end-user training is readily available. Frequently, SharePoint feels to end users like such a large change that users shy away from clicking around and trying things out. This can mean that users may otherwise remain oblivious to exciting new functionality.

A great way to expose new functionality is to create (or purchase) a series of short videos explaining how to accomplish specific targeted tasks. This way, a user who can't recall the difference between columns in a list or library versus a social tag can watch a short 3- to 5-minute video, rather than attempt to navigate a gigantic training document.

An important aspect of user adoption is getting users to try things without them feeling like they are going to be judged based on the quality of the output. Try creating a sandboxed environment for users to try out new functionality without feeling like changes there will be permanent reflections of their skills or capabilities. Focus on breaking down barriers to entry, and give people reasons to visit the portal frequently.

Implementing Improvements and New Features Regularly

Now that the scenario and the scope of functionality for the initial release have been determined, be sure to plan ahead for future phases. Taking an iterative approach for releasing functionality is a good way to show progress to the business, and allows for quick feedback on work that is being done.

Always be sure to start small and add additional features as needed. SharePoint is a forgiving platform, and the chances of making irreversible mistakes are very small. Likewise, the chances of a waterfall design approach to portal releases being completely successful are also small. The objective is to be comfortable with a "Launch and Learn" approach, as opposed to a "Launch and Cheer" approach.

Learn from mistakes and missteps. Survey the users frequently to understand what works and what is confusing or irrelevant to the portal experience. Iterate designs and new functionalities to prevent the portal from becoming stale. If users are enjoying activity streams, consider how they can be made more powerful. Bring like-minded people together through tags and content rollups. Use content ratings to identify strong content, and to revise the content that is not up to the company's (or the team's) quality standards.

When considering new functionality for SharePoint, be sure to investigate capabilities that come out-of-the-box, such as the Publishing framework and its ultra-powerful content query web part. Be sure to investigate the power of SharePoint Designer and customized workflows, as well as advanced design interfaces (including InfoPath-based list forms and dataview web parts). Finally, be sure to investigate the SharePoint marketplace. Hundreds of vendors are making SharePoint solutions, some of which fit naturally into and extend SharePoint's social computing experiences. Custom-coded solutions will also extend the capabilities of the SharePoint platform.

Promoting, Animating, and Incentivizing

As a technology architect, it may be tempting to focus on the technology side of a SharePoint portal rollout. However, like any social computing initiative, SharePoint 2010 is ultimately about the people who use it.

A complete project involves the users from the beginning, and doesn't end at the deployment of the technology. There must be ongoing training and internal engagement initiatives that continually direct users back to the portal. Work with the corporate marketing or communications teams to send periodic e-mails announcing new functionality. Highlight clever team site innovations such as calendar mashups or graphical user interfaces (GUIs). Invite users to participate in online opinion polls and contests. Regardless of the functionality a SharePoint 2010 portal exposes to users, it will fall flat if no one visits.

Defining Clear Goals and Metrics

In a chapter focusing on social networking features, it may be odd to see a section that calls out goals and metrics. However, not knowing the destination is the surest way to get lost.

When planning a social experience, it may not be immediately apparent how to calculate ROI numbers in a concrete fashion. Instead, focus on the softer benefits, such as an increase in employee engagement, and how that improvement in morale translates into impacts in the business. Over the long term, watch for trends in spaces such as employee retention and job satisfaction surveys.

Now it's time to review a few generally accepted good practices.

GOOD PRACTICES

When considering a social networking solution, be sure to keep the following good practices in mind:

➤ *Build for your users* — Before releasing anything, put the functionality before a steering committee or focus group to ensure that the users want what has been built. Identify any missing or wish-list functionality, and prioritize it on the backlog of tasks for the next phase of portal development.

➤ *Leverage SharePoint's social networking to reach everyone* — Know your audience, and where they live and work. Do not design a solution that only meets the needs of the few. Instead, emphasize the social networking capabilities to turn the portal into a truly democratic experience with open tagging and ratings, blog comments, and wiki participation.

➤ *Marketing never ends* — From before the launch of the portal to ongoing efforts to entice and involve users, never stop marketing the portal to the user base. This begins with messaging about the portal, extends to the name of the portal and its branding, and continues with the 360-degree feedback loop from users back to the portal development team.

SUMMARY

In recent years, an increasingly powerful paradigm shift in the software industry has been occurring as a reaction to end-user behavior patterns that have driven numerous studies and articles. Computer systems that used to focus on the input and reporting of data are now being designed to take human social behavior into account. This trend has been especially prevalent on the public Internet, giving rise to massive online communities such as MySpace and Facebook, as well as countless providers of blogs and wikis.

There are many names for the constituents of this software category, including social software, social computing, social media, social networking, and more. The goal of these social systems is to allow users to interact and share data with each other in order to facilitate human-to-human interactions, thereby enhancing the quality and availability of knowledge inside of the enterprise.

Contributing this paradigm shift toward socially connected online experiences on the Web are a host of online communication tools, including instant messaging (IM), text chat, forums, blogs, wikis, social networks, social bookmarks, and other social software design tools. Though these tools have been around on the Internet for years, they have recently begun to push their way into corporations in a phenomenon known as Enterprise 2.0, assisted by software applications such as SharePoint. When properly leveraged, tools such as SharePoint assist information workers in deepening their understanding of institutional knowledge through the discovery of otherwise hard-to-find information and relationships.

Although social software is a broad category, it is easiest to understand as an application that links a user's activity to his or her User Profile. This central User Profile is what provides the community of users a way to understand who they are collaborating and communicating with, and where their interests and activities align. This can most readily be seen within online social networks such as Facebook, where users contribute content that is then modified or commented on by other users. In this case, the User Profile functions as a conversation starter.

Another example is in the collaborative editing of documents, when one user makes a change that other users participating in the editorial process can quickly see and review. This interaction allows for a quick collaboration of ideas and thoughts without generating an overwhelming amount of content to keep track of. Though not typically considered a social activity by itself, editing and reviewing documents can certainly be considered a social process, especially when versioning and editorial handoffs occur and are tracked online.

This chapter has covered the following major social computing components of SharePoint 2010:

➤ Personalization and My Sites through extensive use of the User Profile information

➤ Colleagues, organizations, and memberships

➤ Blogs and wikis

➤ Tagging, ratings, and notes

Given an understanding of SharePoint's social capabilities, you then learned about key business challenges and advanced business scenarios. Finally, this chapter covered key architectural considerations and project approach recommendations, along with some generally accepted good practices.

Chapter 29 examines line-of-business services in SharePoint 2010.

29

Business Connectivity Services

By Reza Alirezaei

As much as SharePoint architects love to think of SharePoint as the only platform on top of which their applications can be built, in reality, SharePoint is not — and it won't be — the only option!

In today's world, enterprises operate in a hybrid model, where different platforms are used to implement business processes that they need to carry on with their business. Business processes often use different protocols and data that may span multiple structured or unstructured systems. The challenging part is always the increasing demand to integrate and share information between those systems.

This chapter gives you an architectural overview of Business Connectivity Services (BCS) in SharePoint 2010 and Microsoft Office 2010. It also covers how to use this technology to address integration challenges, and think of it as a data access layer to design and build robust and flexible applications.

INTRODUCING BUSINESS CONNECTIVITY SERVICES

As part of its composites workload, SharePoint 2010 includes a comprehensive set of presentation features, a connectivity framework, and tooling experience that provide an easy way to integrate SharePoint with various back-end systems across your organization. SharePoint 2010 brings all this new functionality under the umbrella of an enabling technology, called Business Connectivity Services (BCS).

If you have ever designed a solution based on Business Data Catalog (BDC) in Microsoft Office SharePoint Server (MOSS) 2007, then presumably you are familiar with the concept. BCS is the evolution of BDC, and the concept still remains the same — to separate the data source from the business logic and user interface. However, with SharePoint 2010, Microsoft took things to the next level by picking up where BDC left off.

BCS is all about the integration with the back-end systems. To achieve true integration, Microsoft focused the BCS enhancements on the following key areas:

➤ Presentation layer

➤ Connectivity framework

➤ Life cycle management

Presentation Layer

The Presentation layer of BCS has been improved in SharePoint 2010. SharePoint 2010 uses the notions of an external content type (a special type of content type) and an external list (a special type of list) to present back-end data onto SharePoint pages. Perhaps the biggest improvement in this area is that now there is a client aspect to BCS. Office 2010 includes these new client-side features, which allow users to connect from server or client (from within Office client applications) directly to external data.

The client aspect of BCS is an important concept. It opens the way for architects to think about "client" and design solutions that are capable of interacting with the Office client user interface, while consuming data from back-end systems. This helps users to work with their familiar user interface of the Office client applications, while data can be intelligently cached locally or completely taken offline.

Connectivity Framework

The connectivity framework in BCS is yet another part that received special attention in SharePoint 2010. Improvements in the connectivity framework fall under the following areas:

➤ *Symmetrical server and client run times* — This means that whatever object model call can be made on the server, it can be made on the client as well.

➤ *Improved stereotyped operations* — BCS in SharePoint 2010 has read and write capabilities in a supported way. This allows BCS solutions to perform full CRUD (create, read, update, and delete) operations against back-end systems.

For the list of all supported stereotyped operations in BCS, see the official documentation at http://msdn.microsoft.com/en-us/library/ee557363.aspx.

➤ *Batch and bulk APIs* — Another improvement is the batch and bulk operation support. For example, you can read multiple rows of data from a back-end system by a single call, which further reduces round trips to the back-end systems, traffic, and latency. Also, using the bulk APIs, you can ask BCS to return the results from the back-end system in chunks, rather than a large data set.

> ➤ *Extensibility* — The connectivity framework follows a pluggable model that can be extended by developers via custom external connectors. This makes literally any data source types accessible to BCS-based solutions.

> ➤ *Binary Large Object (BLOB) data support* — BCS now supports reading and indexing BLOBs of data from the back-end system. If the back-end system supports streaming, you can stream BLOB data through the BCS, and just react to a different MIME type.

> ➤ *Security* — Like many features in SharePoint 2010, connectivity BCS is a claims-aware technology. BCS also integrates with Secure Store Service (SSS) to cover the Single Sign-On (SSO) experience. It also offers its own security layer on the top of the security for the external systems.

Life Cycle Management

The BCS life cycle management has been improved, too. BCS solutions can be created using Visual Studio 2010 or SharePoint Designer 2010. The choice is between creating solutions declaratively, or by writing code. BCS-enabled solutions can be deployed using Web Site Project (WSP) packages on the server, or via a Visual Studio Tools for Office (VSTO) package to a rich Office client such as SharePoint Workspace, Outlook, and Word.

BCS Features by SharePoint Editions

As an architect, it's imperative to know the architectural trade-offs and the feature sets each edition of SharePoint offers to implement your BCS solutions. Table 29-1 compares specific components and features of BCS in different editions of SharePoint 2010.

TABLE 29-1: BCS Features by Editions

FEATURE	SHAREPOINT FOUNDATION	SHAREPOINT STANDARD	SHAREPOINT ENTERPRISE
Connectors (database, Windows Communication Foundation, .NET)	Yes	Yes	Yes
External lists	Yes	Yes	Yes
External data columns	Yes	Yes	Yes
Service applications	Yes	Yes	Yes
Multi-tenancy support	Yes	Yes	Yes
Administration object model	Yes	Yes	Yes
Runtime object model	Yes	Yes	Yes
Secure Store Services integration	No	Yes	Yes
Out-of-the-box web parts	No	No	Yes

continues

TABLE 29-1 *(continued)*

FEATURE	SHAREPOINT FOUNDATION	SHAREPOINT STANDARD	SHAREPOINT ENTERPRISE
Packaging and deployment	No	No	Yes
Rich client extensions	No	No	Yes
Support for InfoPath forms	No	No	Yes

Terms and Concepts

BCS uses various terms and concepts that can be quite confusing if you are new to this technology. In the interest of clarity, some of these terms are defined up front in this section, and then referenced later on throughout this chapter.

External System (or External Data Source)

Any supported source of data can be accessed via BCS. Obviously, this data repository resides outside of SharePoint. Examples of external systems are a web service, a database, a line-of-business (LOB) system, Web 2.0 service, or even a .NET object that contains data.

External Content Type (ECT)

An *external content type (ECT)*, formerly known as a BDC entity, defines the schema and data access capabilities of an external data source and its behavior. ECTs are often referred to as building blocks of BCS.

 Conceptually, you can think of an ECT as an entity. An entity is abstraction of something real, like a customer, sales order, and so on. An entity is an entity whether used in BCS, C# class, Entity Framework, or database schema. Each entity has a name, attributes, an identifier, associations, and methods for CRUD operations. Each entity can have multiple instances, like rows in a database table, SharePoint list items, or instances of an object.

BDC Model

The *BDC model* is an XML representation of one or more external content types, along with resources such as localized strings, metadata, permissions, and connectivity information. Figure 29-1 shows a sample BDC model around the `AdventureWorksLT2008R2` database.

 You can download this sample from `http://msdn.microsoft.com/en-us/library/ee559296.aspx`, *and the actual database at* `http://msftdbprodsamples.codeplex.com/releases/view/55926`.

```xml
<?xml version="1.0" encoding="utf-16" standalone="yes"?>
<Model xmlns:xsi="http://www.w3.org/2001/XMLSchema-instance"
    xsi:schemaLocation="http://schemas.microsoft.com/windows/2007/BusinessDataCatalog BDCMetadata.xsd"
    Name="AdventureWorksModel" IsCached="false" xmlns="http://schemas.microsoft.com/windows/2007/BusinessDataCatalog">
  <LobSystems>
    <LobSystem Type="Database" Name="AdventureWorks">
      <Properties>
        <Property Name="WildcardCharacter" Type="System.String">%</Property>
      </Properties>
      <LobSystemInstances>
        <LobSystemInstance Name="AdventureWorks">
          <Properties>
            <Property Name="AuthenticationMode" Type="System.String">PassThrough</Property>
            <Property Name="DatabaseAccessProvider" Type="System.String">SqlServer</Property>
            <Property Name="RdbConnection Data Source" Type="System.String">DEMO\POWERPIVOT</Property>
            <Property Name="RdbConnection Initial Catalog" Type="System.String">AdventureWorksLT2008R2</Property>
            <Property Name="RdbConnection Integrated Security" Type="System.String">SSPI</Property>
            <Property Name="RdbConnection Pooling" Type="System.String">True</Property>
            <Property Name="ShowInSearchUI" Type="System.String"></Property>
          </Properties>
        </LobSystemInstance>
      </LobSystemInstances>
      <Entities>
        <Entity Namespace="AdventureWorks" Version="1.3.0.0" EstimatedInstanceCount="10000" Name="Customer" DefaultDisplayName="Customer">...</Entity>
        <Entity Namespace="AdventureWorks" Version="1.0.0.0" EstimatedInstanceCount="10000" Name="SalesOrder" DefaultDisplayName="SalesOrder">
          <Identifiers>
            <Identifier TypeName="System.Int32" Name="SalesOrderID" />
          </Identifiers>
          <Methods>
            <Method Name="Delete" DefaultDisplayName="SalesOrder Dele">...</Method>
            <Method Name="Create" DefaultDisplayName="SalesOrder Crea">...</Method>
            <Method Name="Read Item" DefaultDisplayName="SalesOrder Read">...</Method>
            <Method Name="Bulk Read Item" DefaultDisplayName="SalesOrder Bulk">...</Method>
            <Method Name="Read List" DefaultDisplayName="SalesOrder Read">...</Method>
            <Method Name="Update" DefaultDisplayName="SalesOrder Upda">...</Method>
            <Method IsStatic="false" Name="Customers Sales" DefaultDisplayName="Customers Sales">...</Method>
            <Method IsStatic="false" Name="Bulk Customers " DefaultDisplayName="Customers Sales">...</Method>
          </Methods>
          <AssociationGroups>
            <AssociationGroup Name="SalesOrder-Cust">...</AssociationGroup>
          </AssociationGroups>
        </Entity>
      </Entities>
    </LobSystem>
  </LobSystems>
</Model>
```

FIGURE 29-1: Sample BDC model

External List

External lists enable users to present LOB data as if they are native SharePoint lists. It's important to note that in external lists, the data does not actually reside within SharePoint. Instead, it is pulled directly from the back-end system each time the list is accessed.

 End users can use external lists to interact with the back-end data, but that's not the only option. Developers can use the BDC runtime APIs to build solutions that interact with the back-end data.

BCS Architecture

Solutions based on BCS often involve multiple components that follow a multi-tiered architecture. Those solutions can be implemented using thin-server-based model, or rich-client-based model, or a mixture of both models, depending on your business needs.

BCS has two core components:

➤ BDC Service

➤ BDC runtime

The BDC is not the same as Business Data Catalog (also referred to as the BDC) in Microsoft Office SharePoint Server 2007. In this chapter, BDC always refers to the Business Data Connectivity Service, which is a form of a service application in SharePoint 2010.

Figure 29-2 shows some other components that comprise BCS.

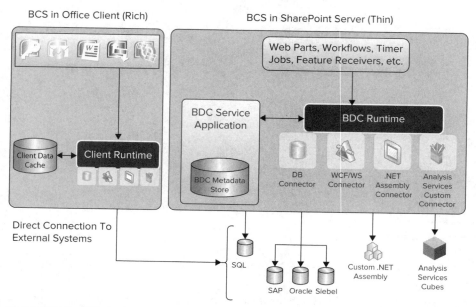

FIGURE 29-2: BDC Architecture

Starting with the right-hand part of Figure 29-2, there are SharePoint Server thin clients that call into the BDC runtime, requesting LOB data. SharePoint Server thin clients can be in the form of web parts, workflows, timer jobs, or other SharePoint-type applications.

Once BDC runtime takes the request, it performs three actions:

➤ It extracts the connection information necessary to connect to, authenticate, and return the requested data from the back-end system.

➤ It stores the connection information in a SQL database called the *BCS metadata store*.

➤ It also stores data schema in the BCS metadata store database (which is used to describe the types of returned data) and methods (which define how to operate on that data, such as how to perform CRUD operations).

BDC runtime uses various out-of-the-box connectors to actually connect to and pull back the information from the back-end systems. For example, BDC runtime passes the service URL to the Windows Communication Foundation (WCF) connector, which generates a proxy (based on the

Web Services Description Language, or WSDL) to connect to a back-end service, and perform a stereotyped operation such as CRUD.

Moving to the left side of Figure 29-2, you see BCS rich clients for Microsoft Office. When you install Office 2010 Professional Plus edition, it installs the BCS client run time. The client run time allows the same functionality described for the server to occur within Office client applications.

Symmetrical server and client run times in BCS allow architects to design applications that can be deployed to the server, or alternatively, within the Office clients.

 BDC client run time is not available in Silverlight or JavaScript applications. It's only available for Office Client applications, as well as full .NET applications.

The only difference is that the client run time doesn't use the metadata store database or the server-side connectors. Instead, it directly connects to the back-end systems (using different connectors) and uses a SQL Compact Edition (SQL CE) database to store the BCS metadata. This feature enables Office clients to work offline, and then later, when connected, sync any changes with the back-end systems.

Interaction with LOB Data

Through BCS, LOB data can surface both on the server and in the client. On the server, external data can be in the form of following options:

- ECT picker
- ECT instance picker
- External data column
- External lists
- Web parts
- SharePoint Designer XSLT List View (XLV) web part
- SharePoint Designer XSLT List Form (XLF) web part
- Chart web part
- InfoPath
- Workflow
- Search

On the client, external data can be in the form of following options:

- SharePoint Workspace
- Word, Excel, InfoPath, Access, and Outlook (which can be extended to include the Tasks pane)

➤ Full .NET applications (not including Silverlight or JavaScript)

➤ External data picker

Client-side Caching

As previously discussed, the symmetrical nature of BDC runtime offers the same features to both client and server applications. For the client applications, however, there is this notion of *offline mode*, where the data can be taken offline and the client uses cache to interact with data locally (read and write).

Offline mode and caching data locally helps BCS-based solutions in two ways:

➤ It allows users to be occasionally connected.

➤ It reduces the round trips to the back-end systems.

For example, if you sync an external list to Outlook, the cache comes into play and you can control the refresh interval using a cache subscription. This is a very important concept. Think about a SharePoint deployment, which provides access to various back-end systems through your corporate intranet. Although users in the field may have access to the corporate intranet remotely, it would be much better if they always have the information they need close at hand, even when they are offline.

Server-side Caching

Considering the new large list support in SharePoint 2010 (which is simply retrieving the data in the current page) and the introduction of external lists, you might imagine that there is a way to cache BCS external data on SharePoint servers. Unfortunately, caching external data is not available, and BCS only caches the model (specified by the IsCached property), as shown in the following code snippet:

```
<Model xmlns:xsi="http://www.w3.org/2001/XMLSchema-instance"
    xsi:schemaLocation="http://schemas.microsoft.com/windows/2007/
        BusinessDataCatalog BDCMetadata.xsd"
      Name="AdventureWorksModel" IsCached="true" xmlns=
          "http://schemas.microsoft.com/windows/2007/BusinessDataCatalog">
```

WHY YOU SHOULD CARE ABOUT BCS

At first glance, BCS may look just like another entity-modeling technology out there for you to use. Many architects who transition to SharePoint from ASP.NET are often inclined to use ADO.NET Entity Framework (or new Entity Framework 4.1) to design their data-oriented SharePoint solutions. Their argument is that ADO.NET has been well-proven over the years as an architecture, and seems to be a more mature technology, so why should they use BCS and introduce a whole new level of complexity to their solutions? Many developers build standalone ASP.NET applications and deploy them to the LAYOUTS folder in SharePoint (to make them look like SharePoint pages), or custom SharePoint web parts that directly interact with external systems.

What may appear to be simple CRUD operations require a lot of thought to see which solution is a good fit. Before jumping on whether or not such plain ol' ASP.NET solutions are the "right" solutions to handle your integration requirements, as an architect, you should be able to examine the data types and the relationships in the external system to understand what out-of-the-box BCS features will satisfy your requirements, and where you will need to use custom code.

If you need to write custom code, find out which solution can help you write less code, justifying the purpose of using SharePoint and making your application's maintenance much easier. Never put technology ahead of the business requirements. Let the business requirement drive technology, not the other way around!

Think of BCS in the following contexts:

- ➤ BCS is a SharePoint-centric solution. Remember, you chose SharePoint as your target platform for a reason.

- ➤ Once the BCS layer has a place in your architecture, you can create a presenter class that allows you to put whatever user interface (UI) you want on top of the BCS API. This makes your architecture extremely powerful and flexible.

- ➤ You get several presentation features (web parts, ASPX pages, external list columns, and field controls), security, throttling, and configuration right out of the box in BCS.

- ➤ End users can use external lists and InfoPath forms to interact with the back-end data using no-code solutions. Using Office integration, they can take the back-end data offline and sync the data.

- ➤ From the development perspective, BCS provides the unifying API that developers can use to connect up to external systems using the same paradigm in SharePoint and Office applications.

- ➤ BCS offers integration with User Profile and Search.

- ➤ Change in the external system is very easy to maintain in BCS solutions because of entity modeling.

In some scenarios BCS can be used as a layer on top of Entity Framework. For example, to support .NET 4, you can use Entity Framework inside of a WCF service, and then call the WCF service from BCS.

MOLDING YOUR BCS SOLUTIONS

In the world of BCS, everything starts with modeling. This is a process to define and analyze the data requirements of your BCS solution, and model the entities, relationships, and storage and retrieval operations, as well as the business problems your BCS solutions help to resolve. The outcome of this process is something referred to as the BDC model.

Like any other living solution, BCS modeling is often progressive. It must change in response to changing business requirements.

Although each application merits different business requirements that may dictate different modeling approaches, typically you can take three common approaches to building your BDC model:

➤ Build a declarative model with no custom coding

➤ Build a declarative model and offload the business logic and complex operations to web services or stored procedures

➤ Build a custom .NET assembly connector (requires custom coding), and then build your model around the connector

Modeling Entities

Each ECT (entity) is defined in one `<Entity>` node of the parent `<Entities>` node, as shown in Figure 29-3.

```
<Entities>
  <Entity Namespace="AdventureWorks" Version="1.3.0.0" EstimatedInstanceCount="10000" Name="Customer" DefaultDisplayName="Customer">
    <Identifiers>
      <Identifier TypeName="System.Int32" Name="CustomerID" />
    </Identifiers>
    <Methods>...</Methods>
  </Entity>
  <Entity Namespace="AdventureWorks" Version="1.0.0.0" EstimatedInstanceCount="10000" Name="SalesOrder" DefaultDisplayName="SalesOrder">
    <Identifiers>
      <Identifier TypeName="System.Int32" Name="SalesOrderID" />
    </Identifiers>
    <Methods>...</Methods>
    <AssociationGroups>...</AssociationGroups>
  </Entity>
</Entities>
```

FIGURE 29-3: Sample entities

As mentioned earlier, each entity is an abstraction of something real, like `Customer` or `SalesOrder`, and its behavior is defined in various methods.

> For more information on BDC model schema, see the official documentation at http://msdn.microsoft.com/en-us/library/ee556387.aspx.

Modeling Associations

Modeling associations is an important step in your overall BCS modeling. Associations in a BDC model tie external content types together, and help navigation between them. Think of associations like a foreign key in a database schema. An association defines a relationship between two entities by mapping a field in one entity to an identifier in another entity.

For example, suppose you create an ECT named `Customer`, with an identifier of `CustomerID`. You also create an ECT named `SalesOrderHeader`, which includes a `CustomerID` field. You create a foreign key association from the `SalesOrderHeader` ECT to the `Customer` ECT, as shown in Figure 29-4.

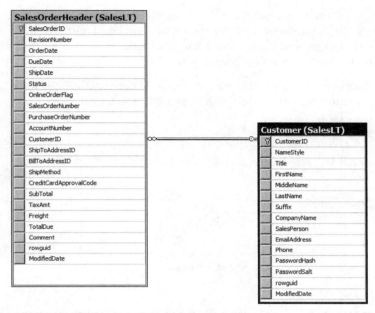

FIGURE 29-4: Customer and SalesOrderHeader tables

Just like the CRUD operations, associations are defined in the BDC model as methods, as shown in Figure 29-5.

```
<Method IsStatic="false" Name="Customers Sales Orders" DefaultDisplayName="Customers Sales Orders">
  <Properties>
    <Property Name="BackEndObject" Type="System.String">SalesOrderHeader</Property>
    <Property Name="BackEndObjectType" Type="System.String">SqlServerTable</Property>
    <Property Name="RdbCommandText" Type="System.String">SELECT [SalesOrderID] , [RevisionNumber] , [OrderDate] , [DueDate] , [ShipDate] , [Status] ,
[OnlineOrderFlag] , [SalesOrderNumber] , [PurchaseOrderNumber] , [AccountNumber] , [CustomerID], [BillToAddressID] , [ShipToAddressID], [SubTotal] ,
[TaxAmt] , [Freight] , [TotalDue] , [Comment] , [rowguid] , [ModifiedDate] FROM [SalesLT].[SalesOrderHeader] WHERE [CustomerID] = @CustomerID
</Property>
    <Property Name="RdbCommandType" Type="System.Data.CommandType, System.Data, Version=2.0.0.0, Culture=neutral, PublicKeyToken=b77a5c561934e089">Text</Property>
    <Property Name="Schema" Type="System.String">Sales</Property>
  </Properties>
  <Parameters>
    <Parameter Direction="In" Name="@CustomerID">
      <TypeDescriptor TypeName="System.Int32" IdentifierName="CustomerID" IdentifierEntityName="Customer" IdentifierEntityNamespace="AdventureWorks"
              ForeignIdentifierAssociationName="Customers Sales Orders" Name="CustomerID" />
    </Parameter>
    <Parameter Direction="Return" Name="Customers Sales Orders">
      <TypeDescriptor TypeName="System.Data.IDataReader, System.Data, Version=2.0.0.0, Culture=neutral, PublicKeyToken=b77a5c561934e089" IsCollection="true" Name="Read Item">
        <TypeDescriptors>
          <TypeDescriptor TypeName="System.Data.IDataRecord, System.Data, Version=2.0.0.0, Culture=neutral, PublicKeyToken=b77a5c561934e089" Name="Read ItemElement">
            <TypeDescriptors>
              <TypeDescriptor TypeName="System.Int32" ReadOnly="true" IdentifierName="SalesOrderID" Name="SalesOrderID" />
              <TypeDescriptor TypeName="System.Byte" Name="RevisionNumber">...</TypeDescriptor>
              <TypeDescriptor TypeName="System.DateTime" Name="OrderDate">...</TypeDescriptor>
              <TypeDescriptor TypeName="System.DateTime" Name="DueDate">...</TypeDescriptor>
              <TypeDescriptor TypeName="System.Nullable" Name="ShipDate">...</TypeDescriptor>
              <TypeDescriptor TypeName="System.Byte" Name="Status">...</TypeDescriptor>
              <TypeDescriptor TypeName="System.Boolean" Name="OnlineOrderFlag">...</TypeDescriptor>
              <TypeDescriptor TypeName="System.String" ReadOnly="true" Name="SalesOrderNumbe">...</TypeDescriptor>
              <TypeDescriptor TypeName="System.String" Name="PurchaseOrderNu">...</TypeDescriptor>
              <TypeDescriptor TypeName="System.String" Name="AccountNumber">...</TypeDescriptor>
              <TypeDescriptor TypeName="System.Int32" IdentifierName="CustomerID" IdentifierEntityName="Customer" IdentifierEntityNamespace="AdventureWorks" ForeignIdentifierAss
              <TypeDescriptor TypeName="System.Int32" Name="BillToAddressID">...</TypeDescriptor>
              <TypeDescriptor TypeName="System.Int32" Name="ShipToAddressID">...</TypeDescriptor>
              <TypeDescriptor TypeName="System.Decimal" Name="SubTotal">...</TypeDescriptor>
              <TypeDescriptor TypeName="System.Decimal" Name="TaxAmt">...</TypeDescriptor>
              <TypeDescriptor TypeName="System.Decimal" Name="Freight">...</TypeDescriptor>
              <TypeDescriptor TypeName="System.Nullable" ReadOnly="true" Name="TotalDue">...</TypeDescriptor>
              <TypeDescriptor TypeName="System.String" Name="Comment">...</TypeDescriptor>
              <TypeDescriptor TypeName="System.Guid" Name="rowguid">...</TypeDescriptor>
              <TypeDescriptor TypeName="System.DateTime" Name="ModifiedDate">...</TypeDescriptor>
              <TypeDescriptor TypeName="System.Nullable`1[[System.Int32, mscorlib, Version=2.0.0.0, Culture=neutral, PublicKeyToken=b77a5c561934e089]]" Name="TerritoryID" />
            </TypeDescriptors>
          </TypeDescriptor>
        </TypeDescriptors>
      </TypeDescriptor>
    </Parameter>
  </Parameters>
  <MethodInstances>...</MethodInstances>
</Method>
```

FIGURE 29-5: Sample associations

Each association includes an input parameter (`Direction="In"`), which is an identifier on the destination ECT, and one or more return parameters (`Direction="Return"`). In Figure 29-5, `CustomerID` is the input parameter, and `SalesOrderID` and a few other fields (`RevisionNumber`, `OrderDate`, `DueDate`, and so on) are choices for return parameters.

An association method also includes `AssociationNavigator` methods. In these methods, you should specify the source and destination entities participating in an association, as shown in Figure 29-6.

```
<Method IsStatic="false" Name="Customers Sales Orders" DefaultDisplayName="Customers Sales Orders">
    <Properties>...</Properties>
    <Parameters>...</Parameters>
    <MethodInstances>
        <Association Type="AssociationNavigator" ReturnParameterName="Customers Sales Orders" Name="Customers Sales Orders"
                    DefaultDisplayName="Customers Sales Orders">
        <SourceEntity Namespace="AdventureWorks" Name="Customer" />
        <DestinationEntity Namespace="AdventureWorks" Name="SalesOrder" />
        </Association>
    </MethodInstances>
</Method>
```

FIGURE 29-6: AssociationNavigator between Customers and Sales Orders

The actual T-SQL command that makes up the association is defined as a property of the method as follows:

```
<Property Name="RdbCommandText" Type="System.String">SELECT [SalesOrderID] ,
    [RevisionNumber] , [OrderDate] , [DueDate] , [ShipDate], [rowguid] ,
    [ModifiedDate] FROM [SalesLT].[SalesOrderHeader] WHERE [CustomerID] =
    @CustomerID
</Property>
```

Enforcing Referential Integrity

This is going to be shortest section of this chapter. Associations in a BDC model do not enforce referential integrity found in regular SharePoint lists in SharePoint 2010. It's totally up to the underlying data source to enforce referential integrity, such as cascade delete and restrict delete functionality.

Authoring Tools

To build a BDC model, two tools are available to you: SharePoint Designer and Visual Studio. Use SharePoint Designer for simple declarative models, and use Visual Studio for more advanced models, which often require custom coding.

The next few sections examine these tools in more detail.

BUILDING BCS SOLUTIONS USING SHAREPOINT DESIGNER

Creating ECTs in SharePoint Designer is a fairly simple process. Open a site in SharePoint Designer and, from the Site Objects pane in the left navigation, click the External Content Types link. By clicking the External Content Type icon in the Ribbon, you can create an ECT.

Figure 29-7 shows all the elements you need to create a new ECT, including ECT information, permissions, external lists, fields, and operations.

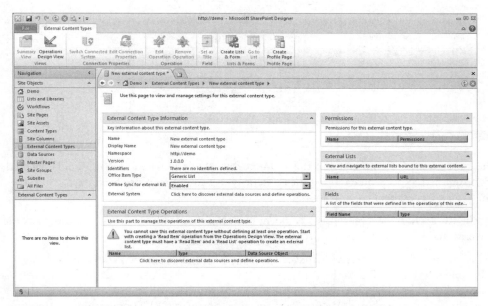

FIGURE 29-7: External Content Type landing page in SharePoint Designer

After you specify the general information about the ECT (such as Name, Office Item Type, and "Offline Sync for external list"), you must allow SharePoint Designer to discover your external system by clicking the link that says, "Click here to discover external data source and define operations." Define the connection to `AdventureWorksLT2008R2` database. Once the connection is available, right-click the `Customer` table. Note how SharePoint Designer allows you to select from several CRUD operations, as well as allowing you to create associations.

Selecting "Create All Operations"

Selecting this option opens a wizard that allows you to define parameters and filters that apply to some of the CRUD operations. For the sake of simplicity, accept the wizard default values and click the Finish button. Figure 29-8 shows the External Content Types landing page after the operation wizard has completed.

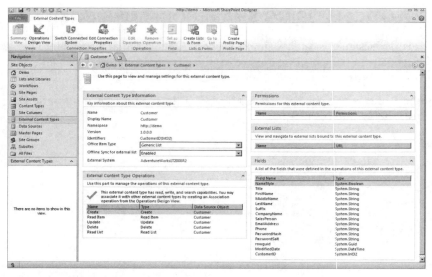

FIGURE 29-8: Configured ECT

You have the `Customer` ECT connected to the `AdventureWorksLT2008R2` database, fields selected, and operations defined. Now, you can save the content type and put it to use by clicking the Save button in the Quick Access menu.

After saving the ECT, click the Create Lists & Form button in the Ribbon. Enter **Customers** as the name for the external list, and select the Create InfoPath Form check box.

Once the list is created, in the External List section of the External Content Types landing page, you should be able to see the URL to the list (`/Lists/Customers/Read List.aspx`). If you browse to the URL, you should be able to see the list and all the customers pulling in from the back-end database. You should also be able to use InfoPath forms to perform CRUD operations against the back-end `Customer` table in the database, as shown in Figure 29-9.

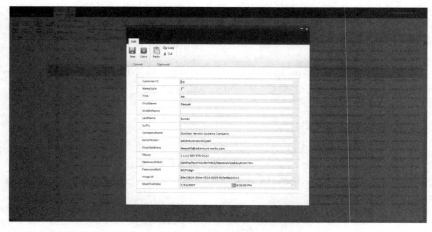

FIGURE 29-9: InfoPath Forms in the Customers external list

External Columns

Having an external list that shows all your customer information is good. But what if you wanted to use just one field in the Customer table in another list? That's where external columns in list schema come in handy.

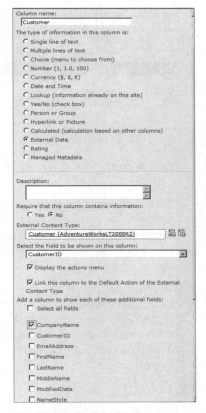

In your site, suppose you maintain a document library called Proposals that should be linked to CustomerID, as well as showing the customer's company name. You can do this in two ways:

➤ Create a Lookup column that points to the Customers external list.

➤ Create an External Data column that points to the Customer ECT.

Figure 29-10 shows the latter option.

Now, if you upload a new proposal to the document library, you can associate it with a customer, and have the customer's company name shown next to the uploaded proposal, as shown in Figure 29-11.

FIGURE 29-10: Customer external column

FIGURE 29-11: Customer external column in Proposals document library

Taking LOB Data Offline

One of the major improvements for BCS in SharePoint 2010 is the capability to take the external lists offline into Office client applications such as Outlook and SharePoint Workspace. The tight integration between Office and SharePoint enables information workers to update the external data offline, and synchronize it back to the external system later when they're online. This new feature is available in the Lists tab in the Ribbon, "Connect to Outlook" or "Sync to SharePoint Workspace," as shown in Figure 29-12.

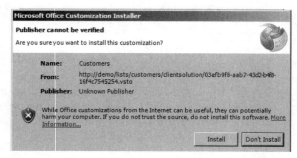

FIGURE 29-12: External list offline options

SharePoint will generate a VSTO package at run time, then prompt you to push it to your computer and make SharePoint Workspace aware of the external list, as shown in Figure 29-13.

Once the package is installed, you should be able to see your external list (Figure 29-14) and perform offline search and CRUD operations. Whenever you come back online, SharePoint Workspace will take care of the synchronization for you.

Microsoft Office Customization Installer

Publisher cannot be verified

Are you sure you want to install this customization?

Name: Customers

From: http://demo/lists/customers/clientsolution/03efb9f8-aab7-43d2-b4f8-16f4c7545254.vsto

Publisher: Unknown Publisher

While Office customizations from the Internet can be useful, they can potentially harm your computer. If you do not trust the source, do not install this software. More Information...

[Install] [Don't Install]

FIGURE 29-13: VSTO package for SharePoint Workspace

Demo - Customers - Microsoft SharePoint Workspace

CustomerID	NameStyle	Title	FirstName	MiddleName	LastName	Suffix	CompanyName	SalesPerson	EmailAddress
11	False	Ms.	Katherine		Harding		Sharp Bikes	adventure-works\josé1	katherine0@adventure-works.com
12	False	Mr.	Johnny	A.	Caprio	Jr.	Bikes and Motorbikes	adventure-works\garrett1	johnny0@adventure-works.com
16	False	Mr.	Christopher	R.	Beck	Jr.	Bulk Discount Store	adventure-works\jae0	christopher1@adventure-works...
18	False	Mr.	David	J.	Liu		Catalog Store	adventure-works\micha...	david20@adventure-works.com
19	False	Mr.	John	A.	Beaver		Center Cyde Shop	adventure-works\pamela0	john8@adventure-works.com
20	False	Ms.	Jean	P.	Handley		Central Discount Store	adventure-works\david8	jean1@adventure-works.com
21	False		Jinghao		Liu		Chic Department Stores	adventure-works\jillian0	jinghao1@adventure-works.com
22	False	Ms.	Linda	E.	Burnett		Travel Systems	adventure-works\jillian0	linda4@adventure-works.com
23	False	Mr.	Kerim		Hanif		Bike World	adventure-works\shu0	kerim0@adventure-works.com
24	False	Mr.	Kevin		Liu		Eastside Department Store	adventure-works\linda3	kevin5@adventure-works.com
25	False	Mr.	Donald	L.	Blanton		Coalition Bike Company	adventure-works\shu0	donald0@adventure-works.com
28	False	Ms.	Jackie	E.	Blackwell		Commuter Bicycle Store	adventure-works\jose1	jackie0@adventure-works.com
29	False	Mr.	Bryan		Hamilton		Cross-Country Riding Su...	adventure-works\josé1	bryan2@adventure-works.com
30	False	Mr.	Todd	R.	Logan		Cyde Merchants	adventure-works\garrett1	todd0@adventure-works.com
34	False	Ms.	Barbara	J.	German		Cycles Wholesaler & Mfg.	adventure-works\jae0	barbara4@adventure-works.com
37	False	Mr.	Jim		Geist		Two Bike Shops	adventure-works\pamela0	jim1@adventure-works.com
38	False	Ms.	Betty	M.	Haines		Finer Mart	adventure-works\david8	betty0@adventure-works.com
39	False	Ms.	Sharon	J.	Looney		Fitness Hotel	adventure-works\jillian0	sharon2@adventure-works.com
40	False	Mr.	Darren		Gehring		Journey Sporting Goods	adventure-works\shu0	darren0@adventure-works.com
41	False	Ms.	Erin	M.	Hagens		Distant Inn	adventure-works\shu0	erin1@adventure-works.com
42	False	Mr.	Jeremy		Los		Healthy Activity Store	adventure-works\linda3	jeremy0@adventure-works.com

Last synchronized 6/12/2011 11:17:39 PM

FIGURE 29-14: Customers external list in SharePoint Workspace

To make Outlook understand the `Customers` external list, you must perform an extra step. If you have closed SharePoint Designer, open it again, and open the SharePoint site in which you created the `Customers` external list. Click the External Content Types section in the navigation pane and then click the `Customer` type. In the External Content Type Information section of this page, there is a drop-down for specifying the Office Item Type. Click this drop-down to show the following options:

➤ Generic List

➤ Appointment

➤ Contact

➤ Task

➤ Post

These options allow you to control how the external list is displayed and synchronized with Office client applications. For example, selecting the Contact option lets users take the external list offline into Outlook, representing the list items as individual contacts. Similar to the Contact option, if your external list data can be mapped to Outlook calendar items, you can take it offline as appointments in Outlook.

Understanding the Limitations

BCS-enabled solutions created using SharePoint Designer are great to get started, but they lend themselves to several limitations. The most obvious issue with SharePoint Designer models is that you can't control the implementation, and you are pretty limited to what SharePoint Designer offers. There are also some limitations with regard to folders and attachments.

If there is a situation in which SharePoint Designer's limitations tie your hands, don't worry because there is an exit door — exporting your model! Within SharePoint Designer, you can export the `.bdcm` file (the BDC model) and manually edit the XML file to further extend it, as shown in Figure 29-15. Another option would be to author your model in Visual Studio from the beginning, and skip the entire process just discussed.

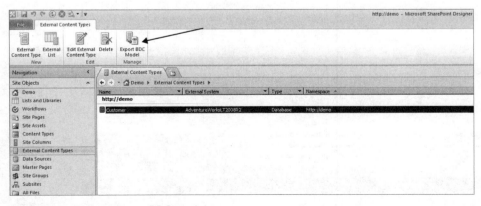

FIGURE 29-15: Exporting a BDC model

Unfortunately, after exporting and editing a .bdcm *file, you can't reuse it in SharePoint Designer again (that is, import it back). So, the general recommendation is to use SharePoint Designer to complete your model as far as you can, before exporting it for further manual changes.*

BUILDING BCS SOLUTIONS USING VISUAL STUDIO

As you just saw, you can author your BDC model using SharePoint Designer. This authoring tool helps knowledge workers to put together solutions that connect to external systems and surface data in a read/write fashion. If you really want to take your BCS solutions to the next level, you need a more powerful authoring tool.

Visual Studio 2010 provides yet another authoring tool for developers to implement solutions that perform complex operations not possible when using SharePoint Designer 2010. In this section, you create a simple BCS ECT and deploy it to a SharePoint site as a WSP package.

Getting Started

To create a BCS model using Visual Studio, choose the Business Data Connectivity Model project template, as shown in Figure 29-16. This project template contains all the assets a BCS model requires, as well as required C# or VB.NET classes that you need to implement your model and its behavior.

FIGURE 29-16: Business Data Connectivity Model project template

For security reasons, BCS projects can't be deployed as sandboxed solutions. If you want to access external data from a sandboxed application, you have two options: a full-trust proxy or through an external list.

Once the project is created, you can start working on your model that represents the back-end system. As shown in Figure 29-17, within the Visual Studio IDE, four main areas help you further extend your BDC model:

➤ *Designer surface (1)* — Used for adding or modifying entities.

➤ *Method details (2)* — Used for adding or editing methods in each entity.

➤ *BDC Explorer (3)* — Represents the BDC model in a tree view structure with copy/cut/paste functionality on some of the elements that make up the model.

➤ *Properties dialog (4)* — Allows editing various elements of the BDC model in the same familiar way you use it in other Visual Studio projects.

Any changes you make in the model through one of the four panes shown in Figure 29-17 changes the XML file in the `BdcModel1.bdcm` file (representing the BDC model). Obviously, at any time, you can edit the model, in which case your changes would be reflected back to the visual elements in the model.

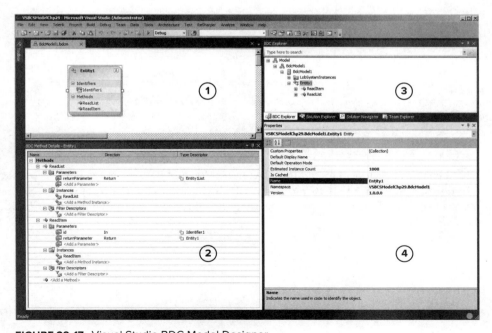

FIGURE 29-17: Visual Studio BDC Model Designer

Visual Studio creates an out-of-the-box entity called Entity1 to provide the bare minimum that you require to create an external list based on this entity. This entity contains code-behind as well. To view the code-behind, right-click the entity and select View Code (or press F7). The code-behind contains all the methods for retrieving, updating, and deleting data implemented as static methods. By default it comes with two methods:

➤ ReadItem — This is the specific finder method that allows a single instance of the entity to be returned.

➤ ReadList — This is the specific finder method that returns a number of instances of the entity.

You can see the generated code in the following code snippet:

```
public static Entity1 ReadItem(string id)
  {
      Entity1 entity1 = new Entity1();
      entity1.Identifier1 = id;
      entity1.Message = "Hello World";
      return entity1;
  }
public static IEnumerable<Entity1> ReadList()
  {
      Entity1[] entityList = new Entity1[1];
      Entity1 entity1 = new Entity1();
      entity1.Identifier1 = "0";
      entity1.Message = "Hello World";
      entityList[0] = entity1;
      return entityList;
  }
```

 If you want to rename or delete any methods in the code-behind, think about changing the XML in the BDC model file as well.

Visual Studio 2010 enables developers to add the BDC model file and BDC resource file as separate project items. To do so, right-click the BDC model for which you want to add a resource file. Select Add ➪ New Item. Then select Business Data Connectivity Resource Item as shown in Figure 29-18, and click Add.

FIGURE 29-18: Selecting Business Data Connectivity Resource Item

You'll learn more about resources later in this chapter.

Deploying Your BCS Solutions

Deploying BCS solutions in Visual Studio is no different than any other SharePoint project template. Because a BCS solution created in Visual Studio often contains code, you must ensure that you deploy everything along with your model. The right way is always to create a SharePoint solution file (*.WSP).

Before creating any package, you must do two things:

1. Ensure that the model contains no errors. From the BDC Explorer, right-click the model and select Validate. This action validates the XML in the model, and ensures that the model contains no errors.

2. Go back to Solution Explorer, click the project, and set the Site URL in the Properties pane to the target SharePoint site.

Once these steps are completed, you can deploy your model. In the context menu of the project or the solution, click Deploy. In the Visual Studio Output, you will see several steps taking place, including packaging, deployment, activating the feature, and so on. Open the target site. Create an external list based on the model you just deployed. Figure 29-19 shows this external list.

FIGURE 29-19: Hello World ECT created in Visual Studio

In the main menu under List Tools ➪ Items, you may find that only the View Item option is enabled. Guess why? Yes, it is because the default entity only has a `Finder` method to view the entire list, and a `Specific Finder` method to view a specific item.

BCS Extensibility Points

Though BCS ships with various out-of-the-box connectors (Database, WCF, and so on) that will allow you to connect to and retrieve information outside of SharePoint easily and securely, there are some scenarios where those connectors simply can't do the job for you.

The good news is that BCS ships with highly valuable extensibility mechanisms and follows a pluggable model. This allows you to plug your own connectors into the BDC runtime and literally reach out to any type of external systems. Typical scenarios in which you should consider creating your own connectors include the following:

➤ No out-of-the-box connector to access the external system

➤ Data aggregation from multiple external systems

➤ Data type or schema conversion to be compatible with BCS

You can create custom connectors in two ways:

➤ *Create a .NET assembly connector and build a declarative model around it* — A .NET assembly connector is a DLL that is deployed to BCS. This connector broker calls to the external system and maps everything back to your declarative model. This approach is good for static external systems that barely change.

➤ *Create a custom connector and build a programmatic model around it* — A custom connector is a DLL that implements an `ISystemUtility` interface at a minimum. SharePoint Designer doesn't support building declarative models around such connectors, so you must use Visual Studio to author your model. This approach is good for external systems that frequently change.

 For a breakdown of differences between using a .NET assembly connector and a custom connector, see the official MSDN documentation at `http://msdn` `.microsoft.com/en-us/library/ee554911(office.14).aspx`.

Although you don't have to use Entity Framework with BCS, you probably will if you write a .NET assembly connector or custom connector that accesses a database.

ADMINISTRATING THE BCS SERVICE APPLICATION

Typically, administrating your BCS solutions involves working with several service applications within the Central Administration site. BCS is administered primarily by using the Secure Store Service (which is covered later) and the Business Data Connectivity Service (BDCS).

Like all the other service applications, there can be multiple instances of the BDCS in one farm, or one instance can be shared across multiple farms. Each instance can have a unique set of administrators if necessary.

Implementing a solution based on BCS is a collaborative effort between administrators, developers, and often information workers.

At a high level, the BDCS provides administration at three levels — BDC models, external systems, and External Content Types, as shown in Figure 29-20.

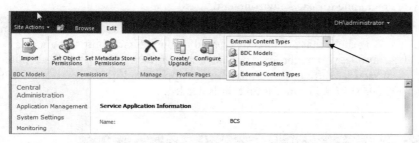

FIGURE 29-20: BCS service application

The BDC Models administration page provides a set of operations such as importing/exporting models into the service application, setting permissions on the models, and viewing the ECTs that a model contains, as shown in Figure 29-21.

FIGURE 29-21: BDC Model administration page

Similar to BDC models, you can import resource files into BDCS. A resource file contains localized strings, properties, and permissions for one or more ECTs in a model. Although you can have your resources combined in your model, the best practice is to separate out the BDC model XML file and resources in two different files. The model will be merged with the resources file when it's imported.

When resources are combined with the BDC models, making any change to the resources results in updating the entire model, which further forces you to import your model again, and perform a regression testing on your entire BCS application. Separating the BDC model from resources offers the following two advantages:

➤ Support for localization.

➤ Support for environment-dependent settings such as connecting string, URL, and so on. For example, on developer machines, the rdbConnectionString property contains a connecting string to a development SQL Server database, which is not the same production SQL Server database. This is the best way to handle development-to-QA-to-production farms because you create one for each environment.

The External Systems administration page may contain one or more instances of an external system for any external system, including those that are directly created through SharePoint Designer, as shown in Figure 29-22. For example, you might have two instances of the AdventureWorksLT2008R2 external system with different security settings or permissions to support multiple ways to connect to this database. In real life, a single system instance is all that is needed.

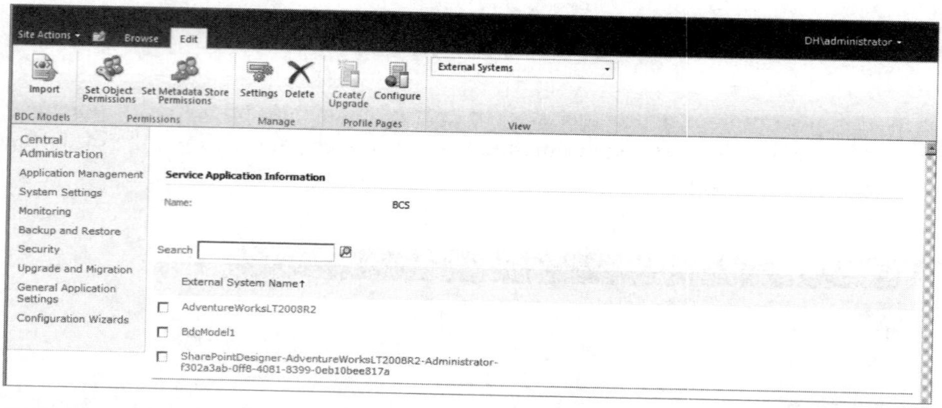

FIGURE 29-22: External Systems administration page

Finally, the External Content Types administration page (Figure 29-23) allows administrators of that service application to modify permissions of each ECT, or add more features (such as actions and profile pages).

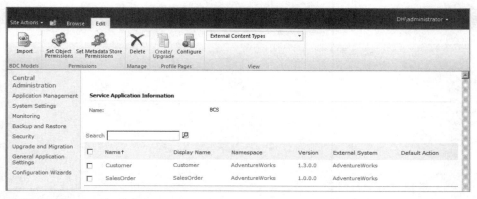

FIGURE 29-23: ECT administration page

Upgrading BDC to BCS

You can certainly upgrade BDC application definition files in SharePoint 2007 to the BDC model in SharePoint 2010. You have several factors to consider, however, such as upgrading the application definition file itself, SSO service, profile pages, and the application security.

All these factors are well-covered in a TechNet article at `http://technet` `.microsoft.com/en-us/library/ff607947.aspx.`

Two common issues may arise as part of the upgrade process:

➤ Once the upgrade is completed, MOSS 2007 BDC application definition files cannot be directly imported into the BCS service application anymore. This is because of the architectural changes in the technology, and the schema changes in BDC models.

➤ Another very common upgrade issue is BDC columns in SharePoint 2007. If you are doing a database-attach upgrade, the BDC columns become all blank in SharePoint 2010. If you have large document libraries with BDC metadata against a lot of documents, you may want to consider developing a tool (or using a third-party tool) that runs after the blank column creation to convert them to external data-based columns in BCS.

If you are doing a version-to-version upgrade from SharePoint Server 2007 to SharePoint Server 2010, the Application Registry Service (shown in Figure 29-24) will be used to store MOSS 2007 Business Data Catalog application definition files. As mentioned previously, BDCS replaces this service in SharePoint 2010. However, the object model of the BDCS is not backward-compatible with the object model that the Business Data Catalog uses. So, if you have custom code carried over from MOSS 2007 that relies on the object model or metadata schema of the Business Data Catalog, and it should continue to work in SharePoint Server 2010, this service should be kept started. Otherwise, you can turn it off to improve performance.

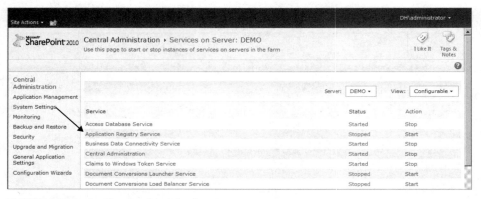

FIGURE 29-24: Application Registry Service

Overall, the BDC-to-BCS upgrade seems to be a hit-and-miss process to see whether everything will work in SharePoint 2010 without needing reconfiguration. If you are planning an upgrade, it's highly recommended to plan BCS requirements thoroughly before the actual SharePoint 2010 upgrade happens.

Filtering and Throttling

When accessing an external list, the throttling settings for the BDC runtime apply, which differ from throttling settings that apply to ordinary SharePoint lists. If you try to browse to an external list that exceeds the default BCS throttling limit (2,000 rows by default), you will receive a throttling exception.

Simply put, it is a preventive feature that administrators can use to control both the load that BDC operations put on SharePoint, as well as the external systems.

You can use two solutions to avoid throttling exceptions:

➤ Use the Windows PowerShell `Set-SPBusinessDataCatalogThrottleConfig` cmdlet to modify the BCS default throttling configurations. For more information, see the official documentation at `http://technet.microsoft.com/en-us/library/ff607630.aspx`.

➤ Use filters to constrain the result set returned from the external system. For the type of filters supported by BDCS, see the official MSDN documentation at `http://msdn.microsoft.com/en-us/library/ee556392.aspx`.

Searching External Systems

Search in SharePoint Server 2010 relies on BCS connectors to crawl external content (external to SharePoint, that is). As shown in Figure 29-25, you can create content sources that point to a BCS model, which allows searching and returning results from any external systems.

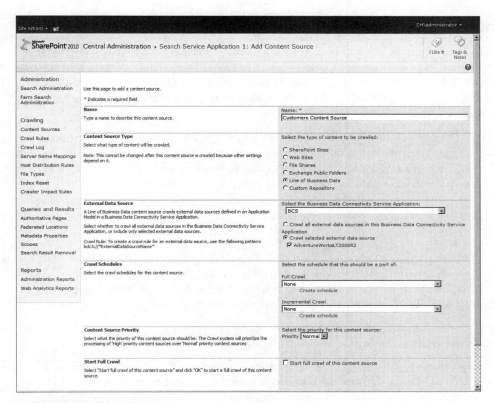

FIGURE 29-25: BCS in Search

There are several improvements in the way BCS crawls and indexes the external systems. However, two investment areas should be highlighted here:

➤ *Security Trimmed Search Results* — In the real world, the external data may be subject to some access restrictions. For example, not every user may have access to the Customer table, or some users might only have access to some customer records in that table, and not all. If BCS enables crawling and indexing the back-end data, it must ensure that returned result is properly security-trimmed so that users see only the information they are authorized to see. In SharePoint 2010, developers can implement the GetSecurityDescriptor method on each entity, which allows Search to perform a security-trimmed indexing operation against that entity, and caches the result. This allows SharePoint to render search results in a secure way where users only see the content they are authorized see.

➤ *BLOB Search Results* — Because BCS supports reading and streaming BLOBs of data from the external system, it also offers crawling and indexing of them. Suppose you have a BDC model that represents a flat file system that includes Word documents. Through BCS, you can make Search find, crawl, and index those files, and have them shown (with the link to the external system) in Search results.

Troubleshooting BCS Applications

Many times, when you get an error in BCS, it's a very generic message without any other information such as, "Cannot connect to the LobSystem (External System)." Ensure that the Unified Logging Service (ULS) logs are set to log verbosely to get as much as information as you can. After troubleshooting, ensure that you reduce the verbose logging to avoid unnecessary logging, which may reduce performance.

Another tool that can be helpful is the SQL Profiler on the SQL server side, or a similar profiling tool in other external systems. You should also check the Windows event log on the SQL box. For example, if you are using Kerberos and it is not working for some reason, the event log of SQL and Internet Information Services (IIS) should confirm if it is a Kerberos issue.

SECURITY

Understanding the security requirements of your BCS solutions is a must in the early stage of your design — especially for those solutions that involve the use of runtime APIs or external lists. Meeting those requirements can be done in several ways, depending on the level of protection desired. At a high level, BCS supports three different authentication models:

> *Delegation* — This model uses the security context of the logged-on user to authenticate to an external system. This model is called `PassThrough` in the BDC model.

> *Impersonation* — This model uses the security context of a fixed account to authenticate to an external system. This model is called `Credential` (Basic authentication), `WindowsCredentials` (Windows authentication), or `DigestCredentials` (Digest authentication) in the BDC model.

> *Trusted Subsystem Model* — This model uses the security context of the IIS application pool (servicing the request) to authenticate to an external system. This model is called `PassThrough` in the BDC model.

Authentication Modes

To support the three authentication models just described, BCS ships with different authentication modes that may vary, depending on the type of back-end external system. For example, when connecting to a back-end database, you have four different authentication modes to choose from, as shown in Figure 29-26.

User's Identity (the first option shown in Figure 29-26) is the authentication mode that follows the delegation model. As its name implies, it delegates the identity of the user all the way to the back-end system. Unless your external system supports anonymous access, this option only makes sense when you have implemented Kerberos, which natively supports delegation of user identities.

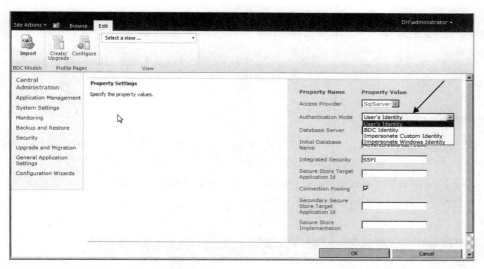

FIGURE 29-26: BCS authentication modes

BDC Identity (the second option) is an authentication mode that's carried over from MOSS 2007. It follows the trusted subsystem model in which the security context of the current process is used to authenticate to the external system. For example, when browsing an external list, the web application's application pool identity (W3wp.exe) will be used to authenticate to the external system. In a workflow that calls into BDC runtime, the application pool identity, timer service identity (OWSTimer.exe), or the user code proxy service identity (SPUCWorkerProcessProxy.exe) will be used to authenticate to the external system, depending on the state of the workflow and how it is being initiated.

 Because of security risks, BDC Identity authentication is disabled by default. Additionally, this option is not available in hosting environments like Office 365. When using this kind of authentication, you may need to be cautious because malicious code in the model can execute in an elevated context with unrestricted access to the SharePoint object model.

Typically, using BDC Identity is not recommended unless one or more of the following scenarios exist:

➤ You use SharePoint Foundation 2010, which does not support Secure Store Service (SSS).

➤ You do not want to include an additional credential mapping layer in your solution.

➤ You have evaluated the risk and still decided to use this authentication mode.

As an alternative to User's Identity and BDC Identity, there exist the impersonation modes. Impersonation modes use Secure Store Service (SSS) to map user identities to other external credentials that the back-end system understands.

For more information on available authentication modes per external system type, see the official documentation at `http://msdn.microsoft.com/en-us/library/ms566523.aspx`.

Secure Store Service

The SSO service in the last release of SharePoint was shipped with some limitations with non-Windows identity providers and anonymous users, which convinced a lot of organizations to put it aside.

In SharePoint Server 2010, this service was replaced with a brand new service application, the Secure Store Service (SSS), as shown in Figure 29-27.

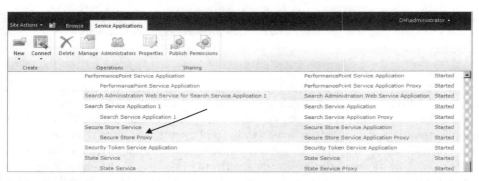

FIGURE 29-27: Secure Store Service

SSO was never really a true single sign-on service, and now the new name for the service accurately explains what the service is meant to be — a secure store for credentials. If you must use it as a true single sign-on service, then you could write your own code to wrap the SSS and provide that additional functionality.

SSS offers two obvious advantages over its predecessor (SSO in SharePoint 2007):

➤ It's claims-aware.

➤ It works with all types of authentication providers and identities, and is not just limited to Windows identities, as was the case with on the SSO service.

In a nutshell, this service application provides access to external systems under the security context of a predefined set of credentials stored in the service application's database.

 When you think about it, SSS is just yet another implementation of the trusted model, but in a safer way. That's because SSS does not use the application pool identity to authenticate and access the external system.

SSS plays an important role in BCS solutions, because it provides the following additional options for authenticating to external systems:

➤ Impersonate Custom Identity

➤ Impersonate Windows Identity

In addition to reducing licensing costs, SSS offers several advantages over the User's Identity authentication mode. When you map all your user identities to a single set of credentials, you gain a large performance improvement from connection pooling because all the connections are pooled for a single logon. It also makes the account management easier in the external system, and provides less complexity when dealing with various users and roles. The disadvantages of using SSS is the lack of per-user authorization in the external system, as well as the inability to audit and trace in the back-end system.

User Security Context

One of the things you may want to consider when designing your BCS solution is the user security context. In some scenarios the current user security context is not available. Without a valid security context, User's Identity authentication mode will not work, and you will get Access Denied errors when BCS tries to authenticate to the external system and delegate the user's identity.

For example, in workflows, the current user identity is not available. A workflow may run under the security context of several processes, depending on how it is being triggered and its state (initiation, hydrating, dehydrating, and so on). These processes are the application pool identity (W3wp.exe), timer service (OWSTimer.exe), or even perhaps user code proxy service (SPUCWorkerProcessProxy.exe) if the workflow is initiated by an action that is triggered by sandboxed code.

To resolve issues of this kind, you have two options:

➤ *Use SSS* — If there is no valid security context, the SSS mapping will not work either. So, first you must find all different processes under which your application may run, and then map their identities (instead of user identities) to a single account to impersonate to the external system. This way, all users will use the same account to access the external system.

➤ *Use BDC Identity Authentication mode* — Once you have evaluated all the risks associated with this authentication mode, you can use BDC Identity Authentication mode. This approach does not require the use of SSS, but the external system must allow all process identities under which your application may run to successfully authenticate.

Authorization

After the authentication is successfully completed, users are subject to another access-control check — *authorization*. This is the process to verify if the current user has the proper permissions to access the BCS model and its entities. If not, an error message will be thrown, as shown in Figure 29-28.

FIGURE 29-28: Common Access Denied error

The BCS service application administrator sets up the right permissions at three levels, as shown in Figure 29-29.

➤ External System

➤ BDC Model

➤ Each External Content Type

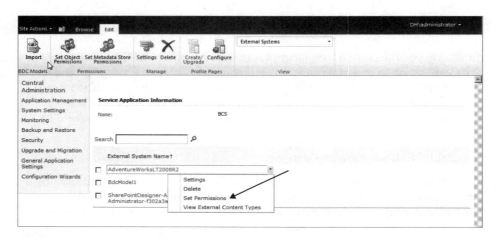

FIGURE 29-29: Setting permissions on an external system

Table 29-2 compares different permissions by different roles in your application.

TABLE 29-2: BCS Object Permissions

PERMISSION	ADMINISTRATOR	DESIGNER	END USER
Edit	Yes	Yes	No
Execute	Yes	Yes	Yes
Set Permissions	Yes	No	No
Selectable in Clients	Yes	Yes	No

SUMMARY

Business Connectivity Services provides a set of features that SharePoint 2010 and Office 2010 client applications utilize to access external systems. This chapter provided an overview of BCS, including modeling, building, and administration. With BCS, the possibilities are endless. So, as you continue learning about BCS, you'll find yourself wanting to go deeper and deeper into this robust technology.

Chapter 30 examines business intelligence services in SharePoint 2010.

30

Business Intelligence Services

By Reza Alirezaei

If you have ever done a Business Intelligence (BI) project before, chances are that at some point in your career, you have turned a paper-based report into a digitized format. Regardless of the technology you used to deliver your first project, the joy of eliminating an inefficient manual process stayed with you for a long time, if not forever. Well, that's what this chapter is all about!

This chapter is about how to design solutions that help organizations to harness and distribute information in a more intelligent way. It also covers key BI capabilities provided with SharePoint 2010 that help you design such solutions.

UNDERSTANDING BUSINESS INTELLIGENCE

For a long time, a big hurdle in IT was the fact that looking at historical or real-time data and making sense of it was just something restricted to a special group of people with specific talents and knowledge of specialized tools.

It's crystal clear that part the problem lies in the tools, hardware, and methodologies used to work with information. Regardless of the root cause, with all the advancements in the IT industry, this has caused a good deal of trouble for organizations, such as inaccurate statistics and bad decisions being made (which sometimes come with additional costs and lifelong consequences).

Ask any executive why he or she needs BI and the answer will most likely always boil down to one sentence: "*Because I need to make better operational and tactical decisions.*" Executives need BI, not just to show them the answer they were looking for or the problem, but to help them ask the right questions, and to help them get the insights they need to do their jobs.

The BI offering in SharePoint 2010 comes in three models:

➤ *Organizational model* — This is a set of tools and features that help people align strategies with overall company goals and objectives. Typically, this is done with IT involvement.

➤ *Self-service model* — This model is used to extend the reach of BI solutions to broader sets of users. The idea of making BI available to the masses is that everyone has access to the information they require to reduce the overload on IT.

➤ *Community model* — This is where SharePoint's innate collaboration features and BI come together to help not only the individuals find information they require, but teams and groups make better decisions when they come together and collaborate.

UNDERSTANDING INFORMATION STORAGE AND RETRIEVAL

One major improvement in SharePoint 2010 (when compared to prior versions) is the new features to work with internal and external information. In retrospect, this improvement is most likely because of the limitations in the earlier versions of the product.

In SharePoint 2007, SharePoint lists could store information in pretty much the same structured way a database does — in rows and columns. However, performing simple data retrieval operations was not necessarily easy because the only option was to use the server-side object model. This could potentially involve the use of SharePoint's weakly-typed object model and Collaborative Application Markup Language (CAML) language, which was a little bit challenging for most developers. Additionally, if you wanted to work with external data, you were on your own to handle security and CRUD (Create/Read/Update/Delete), unless you wanted to use Business Data Catalog (BDC) in a read-only manner. As you can tell, there were not so many options available.

In SharePoint 2010, lists are shipped with a lot more improved behaviors, and include capabilities that were traditionally exclusive to a database. Let's not forget that creating and managing those lists are a lot easier now, and they require no specialized skills in designing, implementing, and maintaining custom data models. External lists (a new notion in SharePoint 2010) are capable of surfacing external data from almost any line-of-business (LOB) applications.

SharePoint 2010 ships with a lot stronger server-side and client-side APIs that enable developers to interact with the underlying data a lot easier. The successor of BDC, Business Connectivity Services (BCS), supports full CRUD operations through both its server-side and client-side object models. More BI features are baked into the product, which makes data retrieval quite easy in SharePoint 2010. Figure 30-1 shows the data retrieval options in SharePoint 2010.

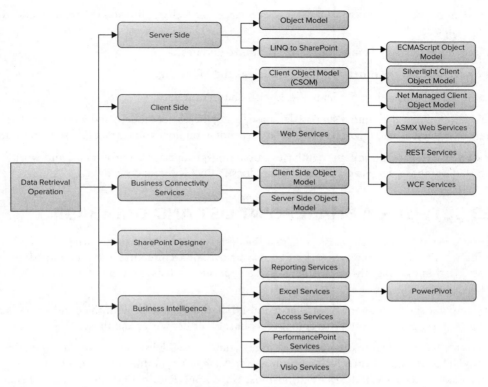

FIGURE 30-1: Data retrieval options in SharePoint 2010

Of course, more choices always come with tradeoffs and restrictions that must be understood up front. Understanding these factors can help a SharePoint architect design more robust applications on top of this great platform.

 No matter what data retrieval option you choose, never directly query SharePoint content databases. Content databases are not designed to be directly accessed and queried by custom solutions.

Aside from the denormalized nature of out-of-the-box SharePoint databases (to improve database access times), a number of other reasons exist why you should avoid directly retrieving data from SharePoint configuration and content databases:

➤ A direct call into the SharePoint configuration and content databases is not supported by Microsoft.

➤ You can cause deadlocks and performance issues.

➤ There can be multiple content databases per SharePoint web application that can be added at later time.

➤ Underlying database schema can change in future updates.

Instead, take advantage of the other approaches, such as the following:

➤ Use the SharePoint object model to work with SharePoint data.

➤ Extract SharePoint data into a staging database (using the object model), and work with that database instead. There might be some delay, depending on how you extract and stage the data.

➤ Back up and restore SharePoint databases into a non-production environment, and work with that database. However, this approach doesn't give you real-time data.

AFFINITIES BETWEEN A SHAREPOINT LIST AND DATABASE

A natural question that arises in the early stages of the design process is where to store the data. This surprisingly simple question reveals a lot about your overall architecture and data modeling. Basically, this question has only three possible answers: SharePoint lists, external databases, or a set of business services.

Before diving into a discussion about BI in SharePoint 2010, first let's start with the core concepts of data modeling. A good place to start is to compare a SharePoint list with a database.

You should be familiar with databases, and most likely you've designed some sort of data model at some point in your professional career. Essentially, a *database* is a container for a bunch of other objects (such as tables, security, indexes, relationships, and so on). Figure 30-2 shows some of the core concepts in a database, like tables, relationships, and columns.

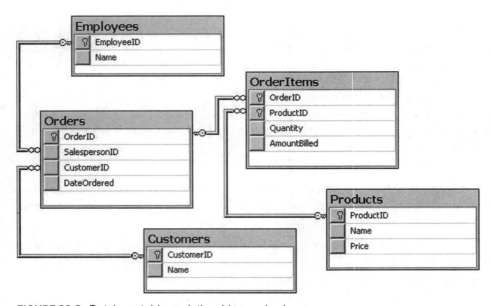

FIGURE 30-2: Database tables, relationships, and columns

Many of the database concepts have a similar notion in SharePoint. For example, in SharePoint, one could argue that a database is equivalent to a *site*. In a database, a table contains *entities*. The attributes of such entities are defined by database columns, and an instance of an entity is a database row. Similarly, a SharePoint list contains entities, and these entities are defined by list columns, and an instance of an entity is a list item.

Database tables can have *primary keys*. Although there really is no equivalent notion of a primary key in SharePoint lists, SharePoint creates an *ID* for every item it adds to a list, and it treats that column as a primary key under the covers. *Foreign keys* relate entities in a database, and, in the case of SharePoint, a similar concept is a *lookup column*.

There is a loose mapping between database *triggers* and *event receivers* in SharePoint. Triggers fire when something happens, like when you create, update, and delete objects. Think about event receivers that fire when list items are changed.

Some concepts in SharePoint really don't have a direct equivalent in a database. These concepts include content types, site columns, workflow, and the capability to associate these items to each other in a reusable way.

STRUCTURED VERSUS UNSTRUCTURED DATA

An important characteristic of any information management system is the capability to keep the information retrievable in its various forms and kept in any data sources. As an information management system, SharePoint Server 2010 enables users to find unstructured information (such as sites, documents, and videos) and structured information.

However, there is a general misconception that SharePoint is a humongous repository for unstructured data (such as sites, documents, and videos), and structured data (such as reports, spreadsheets, and analytical systems that are exclusive to databases or other systems). In reality, these two worlds are changing fast.

Nowadays, databases handle more aspects of unstructured data (that is, storing Binary Large Objects, or BLOBs), and SharePoint can contain more and more structured information. For example, you can use external lists to surface a database table onto SharePoint pages. Another example would be storing data in a highly structured way in Excel files and exposing it, in a true service model, to the consumers of the service in the current farm or in another farm.

One primary distinction between SharePoint lists and databases is that SharePoint lists enable a great experience in the browser, and databases can handle advanced data models that carry complex relationships with high availability.

Table 30-1 highlights the primary differences between databases and a SharePoint list. In particular, it shows the main cases that will drive you one way or another.

TABLE 30-1: Database Versus SharePoint List

SCENARIO	SHAREPOINT LIST	DATABASE
1:1 relationships	Straightforward	Straightforward
1:m relationships	Straightforward	Straightforward
m:m relationships	Straightforward	Complex
Relationships between non-integer primary keys	Not supported	Moderate
Events on add/update/delete	Straightforward	Limited support
Alerts	Straightforward	Not supported
RSS feeds	Straightforward	Not supported
Workflow	Straightforward	Not supported
Transactions	Not supported	Moderate
Aggregate calculations	Straightforward	Moderate
Right outer joins/cross joins	Not supported	Moderate
Distinct queries	Not supported	Straightforward
Item-level security	Moderate	Not supported
Field-level security	Not supported	Not supported
Storing BLOB data	Straightforward	Straightforward
Nested queries	Not supported	Straightforward
Complex BI features	Limited support	Straightforward
Simple user input validation	Straightforward	Not supported
Complex user input validation	Moderate	Not supported
Compatibility with sandboxed solutions	Straightforward	Moderate

GETTING STARTED WITH BUSINESS INTELLIGENCE

So far, you have seen some concepts and comparisons between traditional data modeling using databases and SharePoint lists. Now, let's examine some BI terms and concepts. When it comes to BI, sometimes there are terminologies with blurry lines between them, which makes them a bit difficult to understand. Let's have a look at few of them here.

Report

A *report* is a formal document (with or without visual elements) that presents focused information to a specific audience for a variety of reasons.

Dashboard

Conceptually, a *dashboard* is a report that contains real-time information used for evaluating performance, and for ensuring that operational goals are met.

Key Performance Indicator (KPI)

Goals of the business are typically defined by one of the company executives. In PerformancePoint, a primary metric used to implement and measure this success is something referred to as a *key performance indicator* (*KPI*) or a *status indicator*. Once a KPI is defined and implemented, it can be used to monitor the organization's progress in a specific area, such as sales average and expectations earned from Internet sales. Figure 30-3 shows a sample KPI.

Key Performance Indicators			✿ ▾
Indicator	Goal	Value	Status
Sales Expectations	75%	50%	◑
Sales Average	$500,000.00	$403,337.55	◑

FIGURE 30-3: A sample KPI

Scorecard

A *scorecard* stays at a higher level than a dashboard, and is more focused on monitoring the performance associated with organizational strategic objectives. So, the key difference here is short-term goals (operational) verses long-run success (strategy).

In reality, though, the distinction between a scorecard and a dashboard is absolutely unnecessary, because both are used to accomplish one thing — ensuring that executives are on the right track to make the right decision and reach established goals in the future.

In the context of BI in SharePoint, both dashboards and scorecards are built using PerformancePoint. A PerformancePoint dashboard is simply an .ASPX page that renders a bunch of heads-up displays, including a scorecard. That's it!

Figure 30-4 shows a sample dashboard that contains a scorecard on the left, with KPIs and a gauge on the right side.

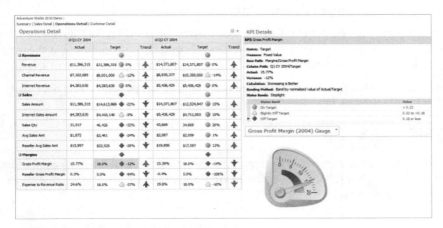

FIGURE 30-4: A sample dashboard with a scorecard

Data Source

A *data source* is a stored set of information about the physical storage of data used in reports, dashboards, and so on. The physical storage can be a database, a SharePoint list, or any other data object that contains the actual data.

Online Analytical Processing (OLAP)

Picture this. You are tasked to analyze Internet sales information of your company over the past ten years. You will be more interested in sums of sales per product, per country, and quarterly than in an analysis of the individual sales. Aggregating data at this level, although possible with most relational database management system (RDBMS) engines, isn't the most optimized process at all.

Online Analytical Processing (OLAP) is a technology that tends to remove any granularity in the underlying data, and focuses more on efficient data retrieval and facilitation of data navigation.

Data Warehouse

Typically, OLAP's information comes from a database, referred to as *data warehouse*. Compared to a relational database, a data warehouse requires much tighter design work up front for supporting analysis and data aggregation (such as summed totals and counts).

Cube

Because the storage unit used in OLAP is multidimensional, it's called a *cube* instead of table. The interesting aspect of OLAP is its capability to store aggregated data hierarchically, and give users the capability to drill down or up the aggregates by dimensional traits. In a cube, *dimensions* are a set of attributes representing an area of interest. For example, if you are looking at general sales figures, you would be interested in geography, time, and product sales.

Dimensions give contextual information to the numerical figures, or *measures*, on which you are aggregating. For example, OLAP calls the Internet sales amount, Internet gross profit, and Internet gross profit margin a measure. Because the measures are always pre-aggregated and anticipated by the cube, OLAP makes navigation through the data almost instantaneous.

If you wanted to look at a particular region that had a good quarter for sales, OLAP's navigational feature allows you to expand the quarterly view to see each month or day of the quarter. At the same time, you can also drill down into the region itself to find the cities with a major increase in sales.

Now, at this point, let's begin to focus on each BI service offering. Let's start with Excel Services!

USING EXCEL SERVICES

Excel is a popular analytical tool for viewing and changing corporate data, and it's been around for a long time. As far as it relates to SharePoint 2010, this technology comes in two flavors: the client application and the server component.

The client application is called Microsoft Office Excel 2010, and it's the same familiar tool that you may have been using for a long time. The server component is a service application called Excel Services. Excel Services has also been around since Microsoft Office SharePoint Server 2007, but it has been enhanced in SharePoint Server 2010.

Configuring Excel Services makes all this functionality available to the farm as a service application, which means that it can be scaled out independently to many individual application servers.

Whereas the client application gives end users the capability to create workbooks that retrieve and manipulate data from local or remote data sources, the service application allows the Excel workbooks to reside on the server. Thus, they can be shared across your organization.

An Excel workbook doesn't become available in Excel Services "automagically." The process of making an Excel workbook available in Excel Services in referred to as *publishing the workbook*, which is performed from within Microsoft Office Excel 2010. Figure 30-5 shows a published Excel workbook that's accessed through a browser.

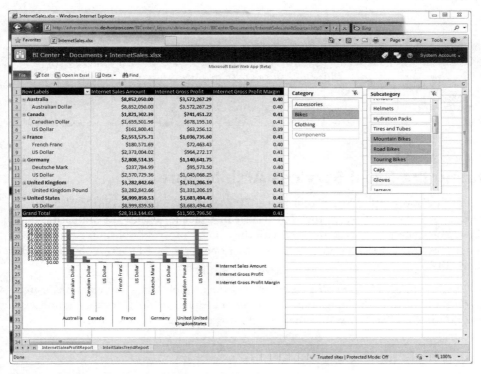

FIGURE 30-5: Browser view of an Excel workbook

Figure 30-6 shows the same workbook rendered in a mobile Safari browser on an iPhone.

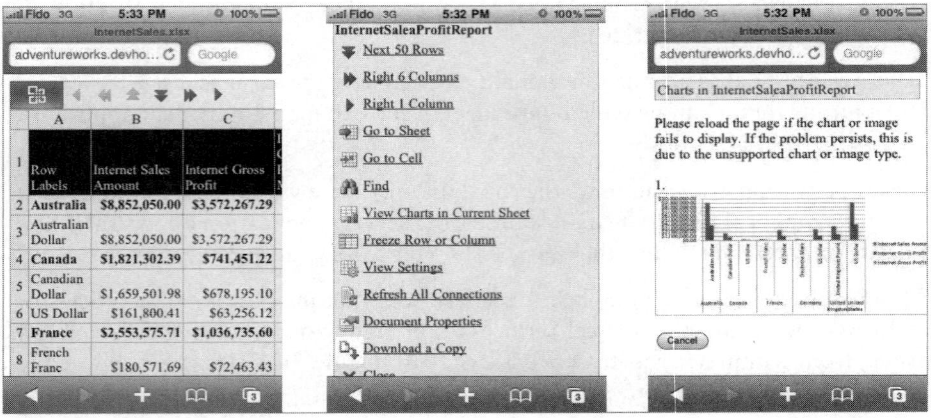

FIGURE 30-6: Mobile view of an Excel workbook

> *Publishing any BI assets (such as reports, Excel workbooks, or Visio diagrams) to SharePoint lets you take advantage of security operations, workflows, backup and recovery, trusted location, a familiar interface for storing and using BI data, and many other document management features in the product.*

Understanding the Excel Services Architecture

Excel Services in Microsoft Office SharePoint Server 2007 exposed only the ASMX Web Service interface. SharePoint Server 2010 keeps the Web Service interface for backward compatibility, but also adds two new access points to interact with the content of workbooks. One is the new representational state transfer (REST) API, and the other one is the ECMAScript object model, as shown in Figure 30-7.

The REST API makes it possible to expose Excel objects via a simple URL. For example, using REST APIs, you could retrieve the image representation of a chart within a workbook, and display it in a Content Editor Web Part (CEWP). When the chart is updated, so is the image.

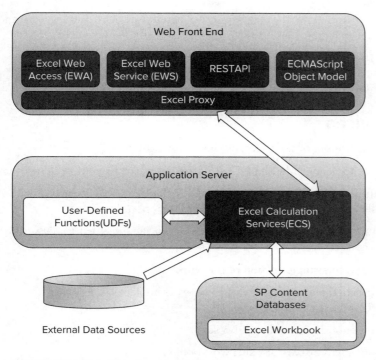

FIGURE 30-7: Excel Services architecture

Here is another example of exposing a specific range in a workbook published to Excel Services:

```
http://server/_vti_bin/ExcelRest.aspx/Shared%20Documents/
    InternetSales.xlsx/Model/Ranges('Sheet!A1')
```

 For the complete list of sample URIs for the REST service commands in Excel Services, see http://msdn.microsoft.com/en-us/library/ee556820.aspx.

The ECMAScript object model makes it possible to build custom scripts in more restricted environments like Office 365 where you must use the data from your Excel workbooks to customize your UI.

Following are a few more components in Figure 30-5 that deserve more attention:

➤ *Web front-end server* — On the Web Front-End (WFE) servers, the Excel Web Access Web Part (EWA) is the SharePoint web part that converts the results returned by the ECS to HTML, and sends it to the user's browser. EWA also makes it possible for users to interact with the returned result. It goes two ways: from ECS and to ECS.

➤ *Application server* — On the application server, the Excel Calculation Server (ECS) is responsible for loading and calculating the spreadsheets in a given workbook. It also runs in intervals for refreshing external data, executing server-based user-defined functions, and maintaining system state.

➤ *Database server* — Finally, on the database server, Excel Services uses SharePoint content databases for storing workbooks and content, which makes them like any other unstructured data stored in SharePoint (such as documents, sites, and so on).

When to Use Excel Services

Consider Excel Services when one or more of the following scenarios exist:

➤ The content of Excel workbooks must be shared with other users across your organization.

➤ An Excel workbook contains a model (such as a mortgage calculator) that must be consumed with other users or applications across your organization.

➤ The underlying intellectual property of the model or content of the Excel workbooks must be protected from unauthorized eyes.

➤ Everyone should have access to a single version of the workbooks.

➤ Business requirements dictate the interaction with Excel workbooks via a browser to increase the overall reach and use case scenarios.

➤ Users must collaborate on published Excel workbooks.

➤ Content owners must publish all or part of Excel workbooks.

➤ Content owners must control the granularity of data exposed in the workbooks (using EWA), in particular, which parts of workbooks are available and who has access to them.

Excel Services Is Not Just a Pretty Face

There is a general misconception that Excel Services is all about providing a web-based user interface for visualization consumption. Well, that's not necessarily true!

As previously mentioned, data analysts can generate models in Excel that can be widely consumed across your organization. The popular mortgage calculator (`http://msdn.microsoft.com/en-us/library/aa973804%28v=office.12%29.aspx`) is a great example of this use case.

In such scenarios, Excel Services can host the workbook on the server, perform the complex calculation on the server side, and provide raw data to other visualization tools or custom applications. For example, you can create a web part for entering and validating data, which uses Excel Services to perform complex calculations. This way, you can send the data that a user enters in the web part to the Excel workbook. Finally, you show the returned result from Excel Services in your web part.

USING POWERPIVOT FOR EXCEL

PowerPivot ships with several client- and server-side components that integrate with Excel and SharePoint. Together, the client application and server components provide an end-to-end solution that enables data analysis for users on their workstations, as well as on SharePoint sites.

Understanding the PowerPivot for Excel Architecture

The PowerPivot client application can be installed using an add-in called the PowerPivot for Excel Add-in. You can download and install it from `www.microsoft.com/downloads/en/details` `.aspx?FamilyID=e081c894-e4ab-42df-8c87-4b99c1f3c49b&displaylang=en`.

The add-in installs a separate tab in Excel called PowerPivot, and the Analysis Services VertiPaq engine, which runs in-process in Excel. To consume various data sources in Microsoft Office Excel 2010, the client application uses the Analysis Services object model (AMO and ADOMD.NET), which, in turn, use the Analysis Services OLE DB provider. Figure 30-8 shows the different components that make up PowerPivot data access from within Excel.

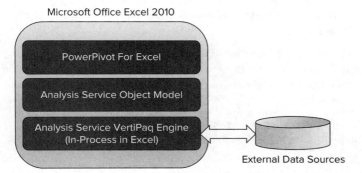

FIGURE 30-8: PowerPivot data access from within Excel

It's important to understand that PowerPivot workbooks are not separate workbooks or file extensions. They are just Excel workbook files that contain PowerPivot data.

When to Use PowerPivot for Excel

Consider using PowerPivot for Excel when you must combine Excel 2010 rich out-of-the-box functionality with the PowerPivot in-memory engine to let users work with really large data sets offline.

When using the PowerPivot client application in Excel, extremely large-scale data sets can be imported from multiple heterogeneous data sources at one time, all within the same Excel workbook files. You can also merge data sources and build sophisticated relationships, and treat the data as if it were all coming from a single data source.

 A 1 million row limit in Excel does not apply to the data sets imported into a PowerPivot workbook. However, the overall workbook size cannot exceed 2 GB. Additionally, if you have a requirement for large PowerPivot workbooks, consider using the 64-bit edition of Microsoft Office Excel 2010.

When you view and manipulate millions of rows of data into a single Excel workbook for ad-hoc reporting, obviously performance is king. To gain better performance and a more responsive user interface, PowerPivot uses the local VertiPaq engine to manage the compression and faster processing of the data. It also uses extensive caching.

USING POWERPIVOT FOR SHAREPOINT

If you publish a PowerPivot workbook to SharePoint, you must have already installed PowerPivot server components. Otherwise, users won't be able to view and interact with the workbook from a SharePoint site. But why?

Although PowerPivot data is visually rendered in an Excel workbook, internally the data is multidimensional and must be kept somewhere other than the workbook itself. Who wants to store millions of rows of data in the workbook?

When you work with PowerPivot data offline, the local VertiPaq engine manages the load, compression, and caching of the data. When you publish the workbook to SharePoint, there should be another mechanism to extract the data from the workbook, and load it in server memory for fast data analysis.

In a SharePoint farm, such a mechanism is implemented by server components (referred to as *PowerPivot Service*) that are made available by SQL Server Analysis Services R2, which also must be installed in the farm.

All server-side components are fully integrated with SharePoint, which means the farm administrators can use the Central Administration site to configure and manage the PowerPivot service application in the farm. The server components are as follows:

➤ A SharePoint service application

➤ A management dashboard

➤ Document library templates

➤ Application pages residing in the Layouts library

➤ A set of reports for using and managing the PowerPivot Service application

On-demand Server-Side Query Processing

PowerPivot server-side components are also tightly coupled with Excel Services. When a user clicks on a PowerPivot workbook, Excel Services receives the request, and processes the Excel workbook. But it doesn't do anything about the PowerPivot data. Instead, Excel Services detects the PowerPivot data and automatically forwards processing requests to an Analysis Services server operating in VertiPaq mode, as shown in Figure 30-9.

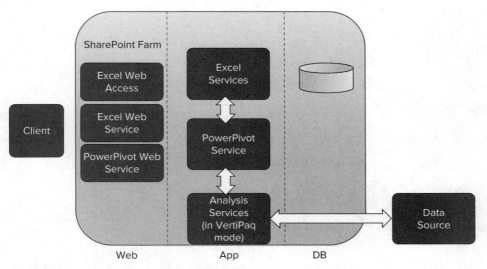

FIGURE 30-9: PowerPivot for SharePoint architecture

 Don't worry about the fact that PowerPivot data is loaded in the server memory. PowerPivot data is unloaded when it becomes inactive, or if the farm requires the allocated resources.

If you deploy SQL Server 2008 R2 Reporting Services and PowerPivot for SharePoint in the same SharePoint Server 2010 farm, you will get even more functionality:

➤ Reporting Services report data can be imported and consumed in a PowerPivot workbook as a data feed, as shown in Figure 30-10. This is ideal when data analysts do not have access to the back-end data sources.

➤ PowerPivot data can be consumed in a Reporting Services report as data sources. This is ideal when you must leverage Reporting Services' rich data visualization features, rendering formats (such as PDF), and subscription and delivery options. This requires the Analysis Services object model to be available on the machine used for authoring the reports.

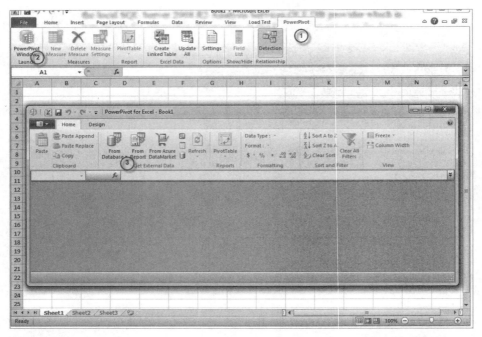

FIGURE 30-10: Consuming Reporting Services report data in a PowerPivot workbook

 A point of interest is that all BI services in SharePoint 2010 can work cohesively. For example, a PowerPivot workbook can consume a Reporting Services report's data source, or a PerformancePoint KPI can use Excel and Excel Services as data sources. This lets you combine multiple services in your solutions to take advantage of the unique feature each service has to offer.

When to Use PowerPivot for SharePoint

Consider using PowerPivot for SharePoint when you must use Excel Services, but you have a requirement to make really large amounts of BI data available to other people in your organization. For more information on when to use Excel Services, refer to "When to Use Excel Services" earlier in this chapter.

USING PERFORMANCEPOINT SERVICES

Many features in the SharePoint ecosystem help users build dashboard-style applications. However, such dashboards may not necessarily be powerful enough to convey the message top executives expect to see. That's where PerformancePoint Services can help.

PerformancePoint Services is a set of components to help users monitor and analyze their business. The outputs are dashboards, scorecards, and KPIs.

PerformancePoint Services starts with its authoring tool — the PerformancePoint Dashboard Designer. The Dashboard Designer is used for managing, arranging, and formatting the items on a PerformancePoint dashboard. The Designer is a Click-Once application that communicates with SharePoint using the web services and client object model. Figure 30-11 shows PerformancePoint Dashboard Designer.

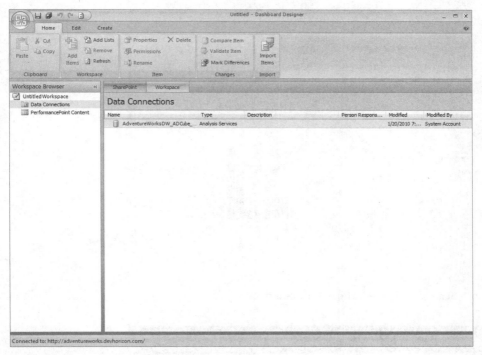

FIGURE 30-11: PerformancePoint Dashboard Designer

Once the workspace is created, PerformancePoint uses it as a container in which to store other content. In a workspace, you can bring together data from multiple data sources (including Analysis Services, SQL Server, SharePoint lists, and Excel Services), create PerformancePoint KPIs, scorecards, analytic charts and grids, reports, filters, and dashboards. Each of these components is unique to PerformancePoint Services, and provides functionality that interacts with a server component that handles the hard parts (like data connectivity and security). Once a workspace is ready, you can publish it to a SharePoint site.

 It's important to note that when you publish a workspace to SharePoint, all PerformancePoint assets are stored in SharePoint lists, and exposed via PerformancePoint web parts. Another point of interest is that the PerformancePoint web parts are built on a SharePoint connection framework, which means that they have the capability to send data or receive data from other web parts on the page.

The output of PerformancePoint is reports that can help with the tracking and monitoring of a business, such as those shown in Figure 30-12 and Figure 30-13.

FIGURE 30-12: A Sample PerformancePoint Dashboard

FIGURE 30-13: Another sample PerformancePoint Dashboard

Decomposition Tree

The Visualization Decomposition Tree is a new report type that ships with SharePoint Server 2010 and PerformancePoint Services.

Advantages of using this tool are that it keeps the report sorted and it buckets off insignificant contributors to the bottom of the hierarchy. It also provides an interactive style to navigating a dashboard while showing multidimensional data sets. Essentially, it makes it much easier for users to make sense of this high-level data, and provides more clarity for the underlying details and data behind those values. Figure 30-14 shows a sample Decomposition Tree.

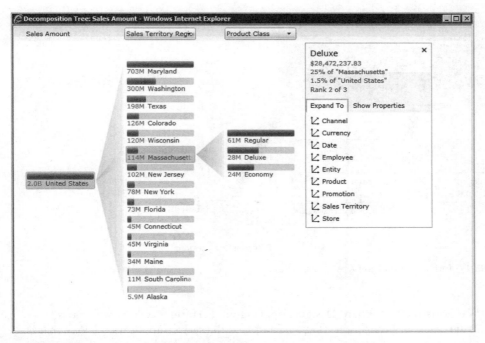

FIGURE 30-14: Visualization Decomposition Tree

Of course, if you want to analyze negativity, you can always flip the default sorting style using the drop-down menu on the top of each level.

Decomposition Tree is a Silverlight application and requires the Microsoft Silverlight 3 framework to be installed on the client machine.

Understanding the PerformancePoint Services Architecture

The PerformancePoint Services architecture is in three tiers of a SharePoint Server farm topology: Database Server, Application Server, and Web Front-End (WFE), as shown in Figure 30-15.

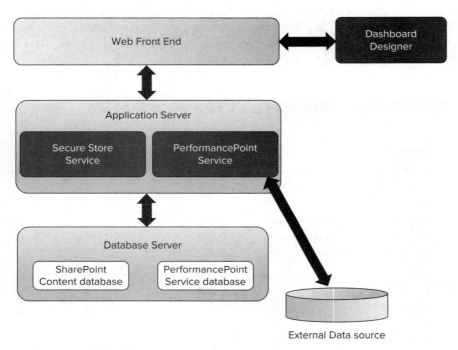

FIGURE 30-15: PerformancePoint Services architecture

The WFE server hosts the Dashboard Designer application, PerformancePoint web parts, PerformancePoint Web Services (in the ISAPI folder), and the service application proxy that is required to communicate to the PerformancePoint Services service application.

 Like all other service application proxies, the PerformancePoint proxy is natively claims-aware. This helps create a distributed architecture for PerformancePoint Services in the farms with no Kerberos implementation.

In the middle tier are two service applications that make the integration happen:

➤ Secure Store Service (SSS)

➤ PerformancePoint Services

In the database layer, most of configurations required for PerformancePoint service applications are stored in PerformancePoint service database.

The Unattended Service Account

One requirement to start PerformancePoint Services is to set up a special account in your SharePoint farm called the *unattended service* account.

Authentication in PerformancePoint Services 2010 is mostly implemented per data source. However, you can also set up an ad-hoc authentication scheme through the unattended service account and SSS, and use that account in your data sources. This is done directly in the PerformancePoint Services service application settings, as shown in Figure 30-16.

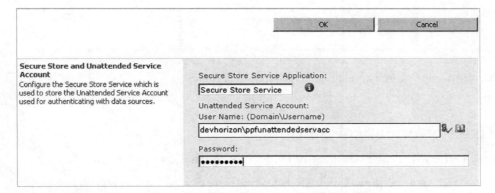

FIGURE 30-16: Configuring the PerformancePoint Services unattended account in SSS

In this case, the password is stored in SSS, and the actual username is stored in the PerformancePoint Services database. If you look at a PerformancePoint target application in SSS, you will find that it contains only the password field, and not the username.

When you set up the unattended service account, you can use it for authentication when creating PerformancePoint assets in Dashboard Designer, as shown in Figure 30-17.

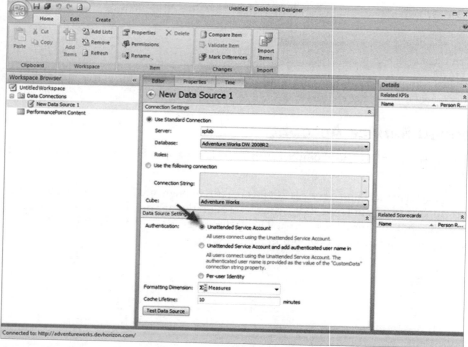

FIGURE 30-17: Unattended service account as an Authentication option

When to Use PerformancePoint

Consider using PerformancePoint when one or more of the following scenarios exist:

➤ Decision makers need the capability to gauge the state of a business at a glance to make agile decisions to keep the business moving forward.

➤ Decision makers must quickly and visually break down higher-level data values to understand the underlying details and driving forces behind such values.

USING REPORTING SERVICES

For a long time, reporting was a challenging IT task that involved report developers who had fairly good knowledge of the back-end data sources, and spent a lot of hours of coding and making reports look nice and professional. In the past few years, things have changed as many reporting platforms have been introduced to the IT market. One of these platforms is SQL Server Reporting Services.

SQL Server Reporting Services is a set of tools and services to help you build sophisticated reports that can render in various formats, as well as a programming feature that enables you to customize them.

From the perspective of SharePoint 2010, SQL Reporting Services reports can be exposed using a specific Report Services web part, or they can be delivered to users using various subscription and delivery options.

Figure 30-18 shows a sample Reporting Services report that is published to SharePoint.

Sales Summary

Sales Manager	Sales Person	2001	2002	2003	2004	AU	CA	DE	FR	GB	US	Total
Jiang, Stephen		8,036,509	20,330,657	22,930,001	10,931,024		9,535,866				52,692,326	62,228,191
Alberts, Amy	Pak, Joe		2,522,836	4,172,459	1,808,043					8,503,339		8,503,339
	Varkey Chudukatil, Ranjit		848,333	2,286,700	1,374,856				4,509,889			4,509,889
	Valdez, Rachel			978,435	848,632			1,827,067				1,827,067
			2,371,169	7,437,594	4,031,531			1,827,067	4,509,889	8,503,339		14,840,294
Abbas, Syed				701,487	720,324	1,421,811						1,421,811
Total		8,036,509	23,701,827	31,069,082	15,682,879	1,421,811	9,535,866	1,827,067	4,509,889	8,503,339	52,692,326	78,490,297

Category	Subcategory	Product	2001	2002	2003	2004	AU	CA	DE	FR	GB	US	Total
Accessories			20,175	90,777	282,583	157,178	18,599	87,599	33,380	46,688	67,989	296,459	550,713
							3%	18%	6%	6%	12%	54%	
Bikes			7,366,627	19,396,685	24,625,343	13,091,732	1,186,388	7,939,099	1,408,235	3,477,639	6,617,236	44,051,791	64,680,388
							2%	12%	2%	5%	10%	68%	
Clothing			34,232	473,341	843,545	377,599	33,683	235,000	71,183	125,403	246,448	1,017,000	1,728,717
							2%	14%	4%	7%	14%	59%	
Components			615,475	3,541,023	5,317,611	2,056,370	183,142	1,274,168	314,269	860,160	1,571,665	7,327,076	11,530,479
							2%	11%	3%	7%	14%	64%	
Total			8,036,509	23,701,827	31,069,082	15,682,879	1,421,811	9,535,866	1,827,067	4,509,889	8,503,339	52,692,326	78,490,297
							2%	12%	2%	6%	11%	67%	

FIGURE 30-18: Reporting Services report

Choosing a Report Authoring Tool

Just like PerformancePoint Services, everything starts with report authoring. Unlike PerformancePoint, however, two authoring tools are available in Reporting Services: Report Builder 3.0 and Business Intelligence Development Studio (BIDS) 2008 R2.

BIDS 2008 R2 is a lightweight version of Microsoft Visual Studio 2008 that enables you to build reports and deploy them to a SharePoint site. BIDS 2008 R2 supports two main operations:

➤ Building and previewing the Reporting Services report files (`*.rdl` files)

➤ Deploying a report to a SharePoint site (which also includes publishing it to SharePoint)

Although BIDS is the preferred tool for report developers, Report Builder 3.0 is yet another tool that is more geared toward the information worker. You can download and install this free tool from `www.microsoft.com/downloads/en/details.aspx?FamilyID=d3173a87-7c0d-40cc-a408-3d1a43ae4e33&displaylang=en`.

Report Builder is also a Click-Once application that is very similar in concept to PerformancePoint Dashboard Designer, and has all of the same features of BIDS.

Understanding the Reporting Services Architecture

Reporting Services 2008 R2 integration with SharePoint 2010 can be done in two modes:

➤ Local mode

➤ Connected mode

In local mode, there is no Report Server, and everything is installed on the WFE server where SharePoint is supposed to be installed. Local mode is made possible through the installation of the Reporting Services Add-in for SharePoint. The architecture of the local mode integration is pretty straightforward, as shown in Figure 30-19.

Local mode has three major components in the WFE:

➤ *Report Viewer web part* — This is an Ajax-enabled web part for rendering a Reporting Services report onto a SharePoint page.

➤ *Reporting Services proxy* — This is a Simple Object Access Protocol (SOAP) endpoint that sets up the connection between both products (not used in local mode).

➤ *Report Management UI* — This installs all the Central Administration pages for managing Reporting Services.

Additionally, the Reporting Services Add-in delivers the following new capabilities:

➤ Access Services reporting

➤ Reporting Services content types

➤ SharePoint list query support

➤ Ribbon user experience

➤ Unified Logging Service (ULS) logging

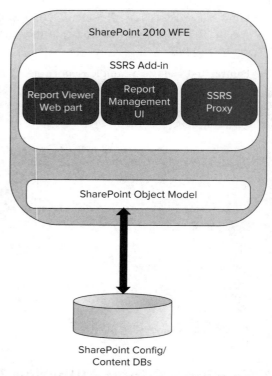

FIGURE 30-19: Local mode architecture

In connected mode, Reporting Services integrates with SharePoint at its full capacity. To make this integration possible, three additional components are installed on the Report Server, as shown in Figure 30-20:

➤ Security execution component

➤ Data management component

➤ SharePoint object model

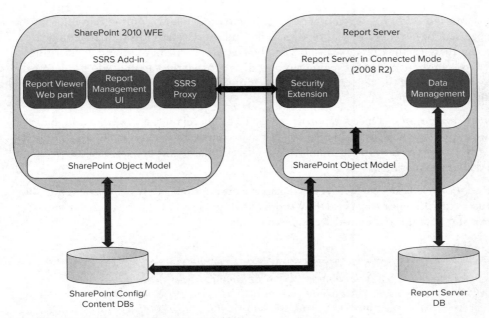

FIGURE 30-20: Connected mode architecture

The security extension component uses the SharePoint permissions security model to authorize access to Report Server operations (such as report processing, snapshots, subscriptions, and so on). The data management component is responsible for Report Server native tasks, and is the only component in the integration that has access to the Report Server database. The SharePoint object model is simply what makes Reporting Services capable of communicating with SharePoint.

Other Reporting Services Offerings

Although embedding reports onto SharePoint pages and on-demand report execution is a primary reason people use Reporting Services, that's not everything this great platform is capable of. A number of improvements and additions to Reporting Services integration with SharePoint can make it an appealing BI solution:

➤ *Parameterized reports* — Report authors can preconfigure parameters used in the reports before or after the reports are published to SharePoint, as well as allow end users to override them when viewing the reports.

➤ *Caching* — When users don't need to execute the reports in an on-demand manner, reports can be served from a server cache. Once a report is cached, it is, in fact, stored in the Report Server temporary database as an intermediate format image until the cache is invalidated. At this point, if any user requests the same report, the report server retrieves the image from the Report Server temporary database and translates it into a rendering format.

➤ *Snapshots and history* — As another alternative to on-demand report execution, snapshots can be used for faster delivery of reports to the end users. Snapshots fundamentally are different than caching. First, snapshots can be placed into history without overwriting previous snapshots. Second, caching a report does provide the capability to produce a persistent copy of the report from a specific point in time, because cached reports are not persisted into history.

➤ *Delivery extension* — Once a report is published to SharePoint, it can be executed in the browser, or it can be delivered using out-of-the-box delivery extensions. Out-of-the-box delivery extensions are e-mail, Windows file shares, SharePoint document libraries, and null delivery extensions.

➤ *Subscriptions* — Using the delivery extensions, subscriptions allow delivering reports to end users in different formats (PDF, Word, HTML, and so on). There are two types of subscriptions: static and data-driven subscriptions.

> *If you are interested in learning more about the Reporting Services with SharePoint, see the book* Professional Microsoft SharePoint 2007 Reporting with SQL Server 2008 Reporting Services *by Coskun Cavusoglu, Jacob J. Sanford, and Reza Alirezaei (Indianapolis: Wiley, 2009). Although this book is written for Microsoft Office SharePoint Server 2007, most of the information is still very applicable.*

When to Use Reporting Services

Consider Reporting Services when you must deliver reports on demand or at regular intervals using Reporting Service rich delivery formats and subscriptions features. Reporting Services is also the preferred BI tool when report requirements are well-defined, or when users are not very familiar with the underlying data sources used in the reports.

USING VISIO SERVICES

As the saying goes, a picture is worth a thousand words. Figure 30-21 shows a Visio diagram with data-driven shapes representing a network health status structure on an IT network.

If you have requirements for diagrams like the one shown in Figure 30-21, then Visio Services can help. Visio Services is a brand new service on the Microsoft SharePoint Server 2010 platform that makes it possible for users to create and share Visio diagrams in the browser. In other words, users can view the Visio diagrams in their browsers without having Microsoft Office Visio 2010 installed on their machines.

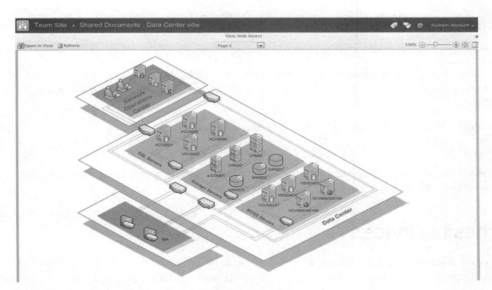

FIGURE 30-21: An example of a published Visio diagram

Capabilities of Visio Services

From a visualization perspective Visio Services can be used to render visual diagrams and structures that are bound directly to BI data, which puts information in context and makes it more meaningful.

From a rendering perspective, the resulting diagrams have full-fidelity rendering in modern browsers like Internet Explorer (IE), Firefox, or Safari. They can also be rendered using Silverlight or, optionally, .PNG files for a down-level experience.

Visio web diagrams can be connected to various data sources, and they can be updated and refreshed automatically when changes occur to the underlying data sources. This functionality on its own is compelling, and is especially more so when combined with other BI features available to users when creating dashboards and custom solutions.

From a developer point of view, the Visio Services mash-up API and web part connection support in the Visio Services web part are nice extensibility points. Most customizations in Visio Services can be implemented via JavaScript or .ASPX pages. Some of the typical scenarios for customizations include responding to user interactions on diagrams, sharing data with other web parts, annotating diagrams, and scrapping diagrams.

When to Use Visio Services

Consider Visio Services when one or more of the following scenarios exist:

➤ You must share Visio diagrams with other users across your organization, so that they can view and collaborate without having to install Microsoft Office Visio 2010 on their machines.

➤ You must render visual diagrams that are bound to BI data.

➤ You must build dashboards and use Visio diagrams that participate in mash-up scenarios.

➤ You must render visual diagrams that are updated and refreshed on-the-fly when changes occur to the underlying data sources.

USING ACCESS SERVICES

Access Services is a service application that allows Access 2010 databases to be hosted and shared in SharePoint. In nutshell, you create an Access database on your computer and, like all other BI tools, you publish it to SharePoint. Once the database is published, it lives in its database format, in SharePoint. Tables become SharePoint lists, reports become reports, forms become forms, and macros are converted to workflows.

Access Services uses Reporting Services 2008 R2 as its reporting engine. This means that a prerequisite for running Access Services reports in SharePoint is the installation of Microsoft SQL Server 2008 R2 Reporting Services Add-in, and setting up the integration in the local mode (at a minimum). Once you have installed the Reporting Services Add-in, you create a new Access Services service application in your farm.

 It's important to note that Access Services does require both the enterprise version of SharePoint 2010 and Microsoft Access 2010 on the desktop of users who will build Access databases that will be published to SharePoint.

Two types of clients might benefit from Access Services. One is small companies who use Access for its easy-to-use nature. The other one is big companies that let various departments be self-sufficient by using Access as a rapid development tool for smaller projects.

Consider Access Services when one or more of the following scenarios exist:

➤ You must perform complex queries such as joins, filtering, aggregates, and master-child and parent-child relationships between SharePoint lists that typically require custom coding.

➤ You must use the Access 2010 client as a flexible report designer tool to create and publish reports (.rdl files) to SharePoint.

Access Services 2010 offers a caching layer that addresses the limitations of the maximum number of list items that a query can return at one time (list view threshold). In another words, it overrides a web application's default list view threshold.

OTHER SOLUTIONS TO RETRIEVE DATA

Although this chapter is about BI, as a SharePoint architect it is crucially important to consider all your options, and design your solutions accordingly. Remember, it's all about empowering the end users with what the platform has to offer at its best, with or without BI.

Table 30-2 shows a quick comparison of the various options to consider when proposing data-retrieval solutions.

TABLE 30-2: No-code Solutions to Retrieve Information

SOLUTION	DESCRIPTION	ADVANTAGES	DISADVANTAGES
Rollup web parts	Content Query web part	Uses out-of-the-box caching to query SharePoint lists and libraries in the same site collection.	Only available in Publishing sites.
		Easy to use for end users.	Does not support non-SharePoint data sources such as databases and web services.
		Highly powerful and customizable using XSLT.	Can't be used for cross-site collection queries
SharePoint Designer web parts	XSLT List View (XLV) web part	All web parts support SharePoint lists and document libraries as a data source.	Only DFWP supports non-SharePoint data sources such as database and Web service.
	XSLT List Form (XLF) web part		
	Data Form Web Part (DFWP)		Only XLV and XLF support external lists.

continues

TABLE 30-2 *(continued)*

SOLUTION	DESCRIPTION	ADVANTAGES	DISADVANTAGES
	Data View Web Part (DVWP)		
	List Form Web Part (LFWP)		Only XLV supports customization in the browser. The rest must be customized in SharePoint Designer.
	List View Web Part (LVWP)		
InfoPath Form web part	Used to host InfoPath-based list forms	Can query SharePoint lists, document libraries, databases, and web services.	Requires InfoPath 2010 for customization.
		Powerful and customizable.	Only can be used as list forms or hosted in a SharePoint form library. Form library is a specialized document library.
Office client applications	Microsoft Outlook, SharePoint Workspace 2010	Supports SharePoint lists, document libraries, and external lists.	Difficult to customize.
		Allows end users to synchronize SharePoint data to an extent with their local computers.	

SECURITY

In SharePoint Server 2010, some important developments are centered on authentication and authorization, which affects all the services running on the top of the new platform. The BI services have similarities and differences in how to configure security, as shown in Figure 30-22.

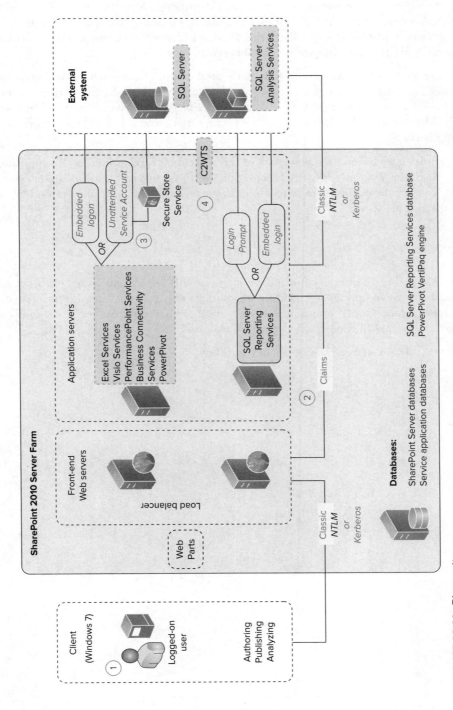

FIGURE 30-22: BI security

Everything starts with a user presenting a Windows identity to a SharePoint site, a process that is also known as *authentication*. SharePoint uses this identity to authorize access to various resources. Next, the Security Token Service translates the Windows identity to claims identity, which can freely hop across all different tiers within the SharePoint farm.

The SSS unattended service account is a frequently used method for removing the double-hop problem while authenticating to external sources of data. SSS is the enhanced version of the Single Sign-On (SSO) service in Microsoft Office SharePoint Server 2007. Alternatively, all BI assets can use an embedded logon in their data sources, or prompt users to enter their login information such as Reporting Services.

When the identity goes beyond the boundary of the SharePoint farm, some service applications require the use of the Windows Identity Foundation (WIF) Claims to Windows Token Service (C2WTS) to convert the claims identity to a Windows identity so it can be understood by other products such as SQL Server.

SUMMARY

When you put together all different Business Intelligence (BI) services presented in this chapter, you have a powerful array of options for building BI solutions that will solve critical business needs. Extending the reach of your BI solutions is a key feature of SharePoint Server 2010, and is aligned with Microsoft's slogan "Business Intelligence for masses."

Chapter 31 takes a look at Forms Services and workflow.

31

Forms Services and Workflow

By Martin Kearn

Electronic forms and workflows have been part of business software solutions for a very long time. Most user interaction with business software systems involves the completion of an electronic form, and most electronic forms depend on a workflow or process behind it.

For the first few releases of SharePoint Products and Technologies (the 2001 and 2003 versions), SharePoint never formally competed in this area. However, many users opted to build *forms* using the standard SharePoint list capabilities, and *workflows* were often implemented using a series of custom-code event handlers and other mechanisms.

In the 2007 release, SharePoint added workflow functionality, built on top of .NET's Windows Workflow Foundation (WF). SharePoint also introduced a feature called InfoPath Forms Services (or Forms Services). Forms Services is a server-side, browser-accessible companion to the already established InfoPath forms software. The main value proposition of Forms Services is that users do not need a local installation of InfoPath in order to complete InfoPath forms. It all happens via a browser.

These two technologies instantly combined to help users fill the gap around low-cost forms and workflow solutions based on SharePoint.

In SharePoint 2010, both Forms Services and workflow have been updated to make business solutions even easier to build. SharePoint 2010 reduces the need for custom code, and enhances the tools that are used to design and develop these applications.

This chapter will provide you with an overview of both the Forms Services and workflow capabilities within SharePoint.

WHAT IS A FORM?

For the purpose of this chapter, the term *form* refers to an electronic form that has been designed using Microsoft InfoPath Designer 2010. InfoPath forms provide a rich interface to help users enter data that conforms to a specific data schema defined by the designer.

Microsoft provides two client-based InfoPath technologies for interacting with forms:

> ➤ *InfoPath Filler 2010 (InfoPath Filler)* — Used by end users to complete the form or "fill it in."

> ➤ *InfoPath Designer 2010 (InfoPath Designer)* — Used by designers to build the form.

In addition to this, SharePoint's Forms Services can be used to render a form, such as an HTML rendering in the browser. This removes the need for any client software.

The data entered into the form is stored as an XML file and can be passed to one of many types of back-end systems, including the following:

> ➤ E-mail

> ➤ Web services

> ➤ Custom hosting environments (such as an ASP.NET page or a hosting application)

> ➤ SharePoint

In the case of SharePoint, the XML files are stored in a SharePoint library, and can be loaded for viewing or editing using the browser or client applications.

In addition to viewing and editing the form, users can use forms in SharePoint to trigger and subject the forms to a workflow. The key point is that the form is actually just a file, and, therefore, inherits the entire core SharePoint functionality around managing files (such as versions, check-in, metadata, Recycle Bin, and information-management policies).

WHAT IS A WORKFLOW?

For the purposes of this chapter, the term *workflow* is used to describe a business process that has been configured or developed for execution within the context of a SharePoint 2010 application. SharePoint workflows are groups of defined activities such as "send an e-mail" and "collect data from user." These activities are linked together using rules that govern the logic and flow of the workflow.

Workflows can be configured and developed using a range of different tools, including the following:

> ➤ *Visual Studio 2010 (Visual Studio)* — Used by developers to create advanced workflows that require custom code. Workflows can be imported from SharePoint Designer or created from scratch.

> ➤ *SharePoint Designer 2010 (SharePoint Designer)* — Used to create and deploy "no-code" workflows using built-in activities and conditions. Workflows can be modified from out-of-the-box workflows, imported from Visio, or created from scratch.

> ➤ *Visio 2010 (Visio)* — Used by business analysts and requirement owners to draw the workflow using the tools and techniques they are already familiar with.

The usage scenario of each tool is covered in detail later in this chapter.

USING FORMS AND WORKFLOW TOGETHER

Within SharePoint 2010, Forms Services and workflow are two separate technologies. However, experience shows that if a solution makes use of one of these technologies, the other one will invariably also be involved, or, at the very least, should be considered.

Forms are commonly used as the front end for workflow-driven applications. They are the part of the application that end users see and interact with. The *business logic* aspect is the part that acts on the entered data and routes through to the next workflow participant. The workflow can also update and manipulate the data, if appropriate.

Users can interact with a workflow in many ways in SharePoint. However, one of the most common is via a form. For example, all of the workflows that SharePoint provides out of the box use forms for the data capture and interactions.

A good example of a business solution that uses forms and workflow is the `Holiday Request` solution. Figure 31-1 shows the `Holiday Request` workflow at a high level.

For this solution, a user completes a holiday request form with details of a holiday he or she would like to take (such as a start date and end date). The user submits the form to his or her manager for approval or rejection. If approved, the holiday request is typically logged into a system that keeps a record of the holiday so that the employee or manager can refer to it at a later date. If rejected, the original requestor is normally notified of the rejection via e-mail.

The next section discusses how to determine whether InfoPath is the right technology choice for your form, as well as exploring other options.

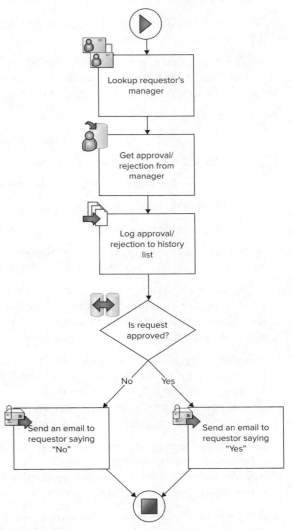

FIGURE 31-1: Holiday Request workflow diagram

DETERMINING IF INFOPATH IS THE RIGHT CHOICE

InfoPath has a lot to offer for SharePoint-based business solutions. However, a common mistake is to use InfoPath when it is not the right technology for the solution, or to use InfoPath excessively in a solution when other, more suitable alternatives are available.

This section outlines where InfoPath is the right choice and where alternatives should be considered.

InfoPath has some great capabilities for designing rich, powerful forms very quickly. The majority of InfoPath capabilities are accessible through a simple interface that can be used by those without significant technical knowledge and/or development experience.

The sweet spot for InfoPath are forms that meet the following requirements:

➤ Forms capturing information that is relevant and easily understood by a human

➤ Forms that use common data types, such as text, date, number, and so on

➤ Forms that will benefit from rich conditional formatting

➤ Forms that must be designed rapidly

➤ Forms that must be designed by a non-technical user

➤ Forms that must access data from external sources, such as line of business (LOB) databases (for example, SQL Server), SharePoint, or web services

A key factor for deciding on whether a solution fits with InfoPath is whether the customer has an existing strategy centering on forms and customizations in general. Does the customer have an overall strategy that is based on using Microsoft technology and, specifically, SharePoint? If so, then this adds weight to the choice of using InfoPath, rather than another form of technology.

What are the customer's preferences for use of custom code? Many customers prefer to avoid custom code for various reasons. If this is the case with your customer, again, this adds weight to the choice of using InfoPath, rather than a custom ASP.NET or web part–based solution. If your customer is okay with using custom code, then check his or her long-term plans for hosting. If the user intends to host some or all the SharePoint estate in "the cloud," custom code is often a blocker.

If InfoPath is seen by the customer as a strategic technology choice across many business solutions, it is worthwhile investing some time in core design principles that use InfoPath. This may include deployment methodologies, repeatable form sections, data schema standardization, data connections, and presentational aspects, to name just a few.

Although InfoPath is great in most scenarios, technical limitations exist when compared to other more developer-oriented technologies such as ASP.NET. The main limitations with InfoPath are covered in detail throughout this chapter, but can be summarized as follows:

➤ Deployment to different site collections, web applications, or farms is quite complex. Use of Features and administrator-approved forms (both covered later in this chapter) help in this area, but deployment is a key design area.

➤ InfoPath forms can become slow to use and difficult to develop if large amounts of conditional formatting and logic are included. These issues can be overcome by clever form design, but it is easier for an inexperienced form designer to make mistakes in this area.

➤ InfoPath does not have the level of flexibility that pure development technologies such as ASP.NET have. This flexibility of ASP.NET is balanced by the fact that ASP.NET generally requires a lot more work to produce the same results as InfoPath.

➤ Although InfoPath does allow custom code, the development environment must be Visual Studio Tools for Office (VSTO), which is not as rich or powerful as Visual Studio. In the previous version of InfoPath, full Visual Studio could be used. But in Visual Studio 2010, this support has been removed. This limitation has broad implications, which include packaging, deployment, and source control.

These limitations can be overcome with enough effort. However, in some cases, InfoPath is simply not the right technology choice for a solution. Table 31-1 describes the alternative choices and scenarios where those choices may be more suitable.

TABLE 31-1: Alternatives to InfoPath

ALTERNATIVE	DESCRIPTION	ADVANTAGES OVER INFOPATH	DISADVANTAGES COMPARED TO INFOPATH	IDEAL USAGE	WHEN NOT TO USE
SharePoint list forms	Use custom SharePoint lists with the standard `.ASPX` list forms. When users add a new list item, they will provide data for each field via the standard `.ASPX` form and save it.	Very quick to design.	No control over how the form is presented to users.	When very simple information is required.	Presentation is important.
		Can be upgraded to InfoPath at a later date.	SharePoint "chrome" is enforced, which may not be appropriate.	When time and resources are limited.	You have the time and resources to do something better.

continues

TABLE 31-1 *(continued)*

ALTERNATIVE	DESCRIPTION	ADVANTAGES OVER INFOPATH	DISADVANTAGES COMPARED TO INFOPATH	IDEAL USAGE	WHEN NOT TO USE
		No technical skills required.	No capability to pull in data from external data connections (apart from Business Connectivity Services lists).		
Custom SharePoint web parts	Use a custom web part to present an interface to users to add list items programmatically.	Interface is custom code, so it can be developed to meet exact requirements.	Custom code is required, which means it is difficult to change the solution without a developer.	When you need complete control over the user interface and you need to do things that you cannot do in InfoPath.	You want to avoid custom code.
			Custom code is required for functionality that is provided "for free" with InfoPath (for example, data validation, conditional formatting, mapping controls to a data source).		You have complex forms with different views, and so on.

ALTERNATIVE	DESCRIPTION	ADVANTAGES OVER INFOPATH	DISADVANTAGES COMPARED TO INFOPATH	IDEAL USAGE	WHEN NOT TO USE
			Web parts are only part of a page, and screen real estate may be limited.		
Custom SharePoint application pages (ASP. NET pages)	Use a SharePoint application page that may contain one or more web parts or server controls that enable the submission of data. Use code to create a list item from submitted data.	Interface is custom code, so can be developed to meet exact requirements.	Custom code is required, which means it is difficult to change the solution without a developer.	When you need complete control over the user interface and you need to do things that you cannot do in InfoPath.	You want to avoid custom code.
		Full pages, so more room than web parts.	Custom code is required for functionality that is provided "for free" with InfoPath.		You have complex forms with different views and so on.
Word 2010 and Content Controls	Use a Word 2010 template that makes use of Word's content control to bind sections of the Word document to SharePoint columns. When the document is saved to a SharePoint library, the list item columns (metadata) can be updated.	Requires very minimal technical skill.	Requires Word 2007 or 2010 installed to view the form.	When your form has a lot of explanatory text.	Users do not have Word 2007 or 2010.

continues

TABLE 31-1 *(continued)*

ALTERNATIVE	DESCRIPTION	ADVANTAGES OVER INFOPATH	DISADVANTAGES COMPARED TO INFOPATH	IDEAL USAGE	WHEN NOT TO USE
		Enabled use of all Word functionality.	No capability to pull in data from external data connections.		You want conditional formatting, views, and so on.
			No conditional formatting/views.		
			Cannot submit data to systems like web services and so on.		

Now let's look at using browser-based forms, which enable users to interact with InfoPath forms without needing InfoPath installed locally.

UNDERSTANDING BROWSER-BASED FORMS

One of the benefits of using SharePoint to host InfoPath form templates is that SharePoint has the capability to render forms to users via a browser by using the Forms Services technology. By using Form Services, users will not need any InfoPath software installed on their machines to use InfoPath forms. In many cases, users will not even be aware that they are using an InfoPath form. This technology was introduced in SharePoint 2007, and is largely unchanged in SharePoint 2010.

Web browser forms are normal InfoPath forms that have been created with the form type set to "Web browser" in InfoPath Designer. Nothing specific needs to be enabled on the server to allow Web browser forms, other than the enterprise client access license.

When using Web browser forms, any options that cannot be rendered in a browser will be hidden. Following are some of the key features that are not compatible with web browser forms:

➤ The `Vertical Label`, `Ink Picture`, `Signature Line`, `Scrolling Region`, `Horizontal Region`, `Repeating Recursive Region`, `Horizontal Recursive Region`, `Horizontal Repeating Table`, `Master/Detail`, `Repeating Choice Group` controls

➤ Submitting data directly to a database

➤ Restricted security level

➤ Dialog boxes for data validation

➤ Custom code used to save forms or merge data

➤ User roles

➤ Spell-check

➤ Undo/redo

For the full list, see `http://office.microsoft.com/en-gb/infopath-help/`
`infopath-2010-features-unavailable-in-web-browser-forms-HA101732796`
`.aspx.`

If a form is designed as a web browser form, it can still be opened in a full InfoPath client if one is available.

It should be noted that use of web browser forms is available only to users who have the Enterprise Client Access License (eCAL) for SharePoint. Users of SharePoint Foundation or SharePoint Server with the standard license cannot use Forms Services.

Another form type is *InfoPath filler form*, which enables the full set of InfoPath functionality, but also requires an InfoPath client application to be installed on the client's machine in order to open and work with the form. Two InfoPath client applications are available:

➤ *InfoPath Designer 2010* — This is the full version of InfoPath that can be used to fill out forms, as well as design and publish form templates. It is included in Office Professional Plus 2010. This can also be used to edit InfoPath 2007 format forms. This includes web browser forms and full client-side forms.

➤ *InfoPath Filler 2010* — This version of InfoPath can be used only to fill out forms. This cannot be used to design form templates. This is included in Office Professional Plus 2010, and is actually the same executable as InfoPath Designer 2010, but with a restricted user interface.

In most cases, it cannot be guaranteed that all users of a form will have InfoPath software installed locally. For this reason, it is good practice to try to design forms as web browser forms, even if you intend to use them in an InfoPath client.

Ensure that you have established whether users will have an InfoPath client-side application installed before starting work on your form. If they do not, then you must use web browser forms.

The next section looks into the underlying files that comprise an InfoPath form. It is important to understand this information when considering deployment options.

UNDERSTANDING INFOPATH XSN AND XML FILES

An *InfoPath form template* is a collection of several files that are packaged into a cabinet (.cab) file with an .xsn extension. Each file has a distinct purpose, ranging from defining the data structure of the form, to how the form will be rendered according to the rules and logic.

The .xsn file is often referred to as the *form template*, and it is what you will create when designing your form in InfoPath Designer 2010. Think of an .xsn file in a similar way as a document template file (.dotx) in Word 2010.

The supporting files contained within the .xsn file are referred to as the *InfoPath source files*.

When the end user accesses the form, the .xsn file is processed by InfoPath Filler or the InfoPath Forms Service to build and render the form's user interface. The output of a completed form is an XML file that contains the entered data and a reference to the .xsn file it was based on. The .xsn file retains all presentational information, rules, and logic.

From a user's point of view, this process is largely transparent. But it is important for architects to recognize that there is a connection between the XML file that a user creates and the .xsn template it was created from. If, for some reason, users cannot access the referenced .xsn file, the XML file will not be able to open, and the form will be shown as corrupted.

Now let's look at how InfoPath Form can be used in SharePoint 2010.

USING INFOPATH FORMS IN SHAREPOINT

InfoPath forms can be used in SharePoint sites in many different ways. The most suitable method of surfacing your form will depend entirely on what your form does, and how users will interact with it.

This section describes the main types of form usage.

Standard InfoPath Forms

Standard InfoPath forms are forms that have been published to a form library in a site collection. Users will go directly to the form library, click New, fill out the form, and save/submit the form. These actions will output an XML document that will be sent to the SharePoint library.

Typically, certain fields from the form's data schema will be promoted to SharePoint columns, so that the users can see data from within the form through the standard SharePoint views. This is called *property promotion*.

Standard forms are designed using InfoPath Designer, and can be either web browser forms or InfoPath Filler forms.

Standard forms can use the entire range of InfoPath functionality, limited only by the form compatibility type (that is, web browser or InfoPath Filler forms).

List Forms

In SharePoint 2010, it is possible to use any SharePoint list and upgrade the associated forms to be InfoPath forms. (These are .ASPX pages by default.) This enables all of the capabilities of InfoPath for adding formatting, rules, logic, calculations, and so on.

To use customized InfoPath forms, you can simply navigate to a list, go to the List section in the Ribbon, and click Customize Form. This opens InfoPath Designer, which allows you to start editing the form to meet your requirements. It is also possible to customize list forms with InfoPath using SharePoint Designer.

Although this capability may seem very powerful, it is limited. The main limitation is that it is very difficult to redeploy customized list forms to different server farms, web applications, or even site collections.

This is because when a list form is customized in InfoPath, several changes are made to the list and content type. Also, several new hidden files are created in the list. Many of these changes use hard-coded, absolute URLs, which is why it is so difficult to redeploy customized list forms. From an architectural perspective, it is a recommended practice to ensure that the components of a solution can be deployed in a consistent manner. This allows for the solution to be deployed to test and staging environments, as well as to the final production servers.

The recommended way to redeploy a customized list form is to save the entire list as a template (.stp file) and redeploy that. This approach mandates that .stp files are used for creating lists, rather than list definitions, which has its own limitations that include the following:

➤ Not all features of a list can be created in an .stp file.

➤ .stp files cannot easily be redeployed once they are deployed to an operational environment. This is because an .stp file is essentially a script that replays the differences between a list definition and a configured list.

➤ .stp files are difficult to manage in terms of source control.

Although the capability to customize list forms in InfoPath is a great feature to use on an ad-hoc basis, architects should probably avoid building a solution around this capability because of the deployment restrictions. A better approach would be to use centrally deployed standard InfoPath forms.

Workflow Forms

Forms are a key part of any SharePoint workflow because they commonly provide the main interface with which the user has to interact. All of the workflows that ship as part of SharePoint use InfoPath forms for various purposes.

The forms used in a workflow can be seen by opening a workflow in SharePoint Designer and looking at the Forms section, as shown in the lower right of Figure 31-2.

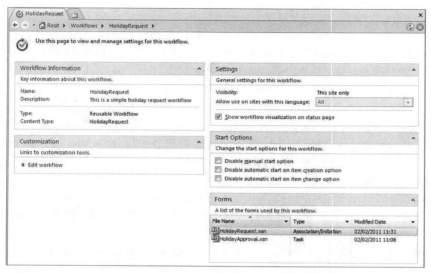

FIGURE 31-2: Workflow settings in SharePoint Designer

When a user accesses the form associated with a workflow, the form is rendered in an InfoPath Form web part that is hosted within an .ASPX page.

Workflows use three different types of forms for configuring, initiating, and providing data to a workflow. These form types apply regardless of whether the forms themselves are the default .ASPX forms, or have been upgraded to InfoPath forms.

Workflow Association Form

The *association form* is used for initially configuring a workflow instance on a particular list, site, or content type. Association forms often capture key configuration data about the workflow behavior and its participants. Association forms are generally used only by administrators.

Using the Holiday Request example introduced earlier in this chapter, the association form would be set up by administrators and may not include a lot of default data other than e-mail alias of the Human Resources team that must be informed of the approved holiday.

Workflow Initiation Form

The *initiation form* is used by users when they start (or initiate) a workflow. Initiation forms can be used to provide additional information on top of the default parameters defined by administrators in the association form. The association and initiation forms are often the same form, but could be different in scenarios where unique data is required to initiate the workflow, and the use of default values (from an association form) is not suitable.

Using the Holiday Request example, the initiation form would typically be the form that user fills out to initially request a holiday.

Workflow Task Form

The *workflow task form* is used to collect data from users by assigning workflow tasks to the user. When the user opens the task, he or she will be shown the task form, which may have any number of fields, conditional formatting, and all the other InfoPath functions.

 Workflow tasks are a core part of SharePoint workflow, and are explained in detail later in this chapter in the section, "Workflow Tasks."

In the `Holiday Request` example, the workflow task form would be used to assign a task to the user's manager, asking the manager to approve or reject the holiday request.

Business Connectivity Services External Content Type Forms

SharePoint's *Business Connectivity Services (BCS)* can enable rich read/write connections from SharePoint to external systems, including LOB databases (such as SQL Server) and web services.

An entity in the external LOB system is represented in SharePoint as an *External Content Type (ECT)*, which appears to users in the same way as a list does.

By default, ECTs use `.ASPX` forms to allow for reading and updating of fields. However, using SharePoint Designer or Visual Studio, it is possible to transition these forms to use InfoPath forms rather than the default `.ASPX` forms. This means that the forms can use the full suite of InfoPath capabilities.

Conceptually, ECT forms are very similar to list forms.

InfoPath Form Web Part

Unless configured otherwise, when loading an InfoPath web browser form, the form takes over the entire browser screen, including the Ribbon and other SharePoint content. This can be confusing for users because they may perceive a change in their systems and may be unsure of how to get back to where they were.

To address this issue, SharePoint provides the InfoPath Form web part, which provides a range of options for rendering a form inside a web part that can be placed in any SharePoint web part page. This is a change from SharePoint 2007, where form designers had to use the `XmlFormView` control and write code in Visual Studio to render their forms. The InfoPath Form web part does not require any code, and is configured via a task pane in the same way as any other web part.

This approach is suitable for very simple forms that quickly collect small amounts of information from the user. Examples include creating a new support ticket or providing feedback on an intranet page.

The form is contained within a web part inside a SharePoint page. The SharePoint page contains its own navigation and user interface. As such, if the form has a complex user interface of its own (that is, it includes multiple views, or enough content to span over more than a single page), it may not be suitable for use within a form web part. Doing so may cause multiple scroll bars or confusing navigation conflicts between the form itself and SharePoint.

SharePoint Workspace 2010

SharePoint Workspace 2010 is client software that enables users to take the lists in a SharePoint site offline. SharePoint Workspace also enables users to use InfoPath forms while they are offline; this includes updating existing forms or adding entirely new forms.

SharePoint Workspace 2010 also allows users to make offline changes and additions that are synchronized to the server when the user is online again.

SharePoint Workspace 2010 can only take list forms and workflow forms offline for editing and additions. Forms that require a connection to the .xsn template file (such as standard InfoPath forms) are not supported in SharePoint Workspace because the required .xsn file will not usually be available offline, at least not at the same URL. These forms will appear in SharePoint Workspace as simple XML files.

 To edit (that is, fill out) forms via SharePoint Workspace 2010, an InfoPath application like InfoPath Filler 2010 or InfoPath Designer 2010 is required to edit or add forms offline.

The next section discusses how data can be integrated into InfoPath forms.

WORKING WITH DATA IN INFOPATH

InfoPath provides many features that enable development of feature-rich forms. This section provides an overview of some of the key features that relate to SharePoint.

It is worth noting that InfoPath is a standalone product and can be used without SharePoint. This might be useful if your customer has an InfoPath client deployed and no SharePoint presence. In this scenario, your users will still be able to use forms via the InfoPath clients.

However, SharePoint provides the InfoPath Forms Services component that enables web browser forms. Therefore, to use this outside of SharePoint will mandate that users have an InfoPath client application installed.

Property Promotion

If you are publishing a form to a list in SharePoint, you can configure the fields in the form to map to list columns (metadata fields) in the list to which the forms are submitted, as shown in Figure 31-3. This is called *property promotion*.

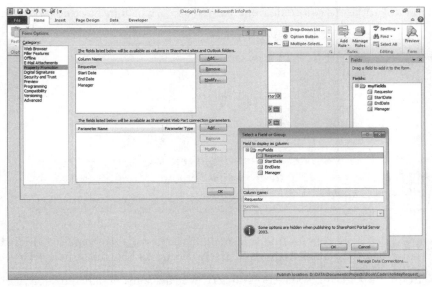

FIGURE 31-3: Property promotion in InfoPath Designer 2010

Property promotion creates a new column in the list to which the form is published (or binds to an existing column). When users submit the form, the values of the promoted properties are synchronized to the list item columns, and are visible in the SharePoint list without users having to open the form.

The benefit of property promotion is that the promoted columns are the same as any other list item's columns. This means that they can be used in different ways within SharePoint, including search, workflows, web parts, list views, and so on.

When configuring property promotion, you have the option to let InfoPath create new columns or bind to existing ones. Although the easiest route is to let InfoPath create new columns, this can cause issues if ever you want to reuse the form elsewhere, or reuse those columns for other documents.

The best practice in this area is to create your columns via a Feature in SharePoint prior to publishing your form, and then use those columns in the form publication wizard. It is important that the columns are created via a Feature, because that way they will retain their GUIDs when used in other lists, whereas columns created through the user interface will have unique GUIDs.

 Be sure to bind to existing columns that you have created via a Feature, rather than letting InfoPath create its own columns.

Data Connections

While InfoPath is good at letting users enter data, it is also good at showing data within the form through a range of rich user-interface controls.

The data that is used in InfoPath forms can come from many sources, which include the following:

➤ Simple Object Access Protocol (SOAP) Web Services

➤ Representational State Transfer (REST) Web Services

➤ SharePoint lists

➤ Database

➤ XML file

 When using InfoPath with SharePoint for workflow purposes, it is often best to use SharePoint lists as the data source for the form.

In terms of deployment, lists that store data for InfoPath should be deployed as custom lists, ideally by using a List Instance Feature. The location of the list will largely depend on how the form is deployed.

SharePoint offers a Feature called a Data Connection Library, which is a list designed to store data connection files for use in Office applications such as InfoPath and Excel Services. The advantage of using a Data Connection Library is that the details of the system to which the form connects are not hard-coded into the form. If the connection details change, only the data connection must be updated. This avoids needing to update and redeploy the form.

 Use of Data Connection Libraries means that data connection details are not stored in the form itself.

Save and Submit

When users have completed their forms, they will need to save and submit the forms somewhere so that they can be stored and possibly used in a workflow. You should keep a few options in mind in terms of how much control you give users in this area. For example, whether the Save or Submit buttons are made available determines how much control is given to the user over where the competed form is stored.

The simplest approach is to use the InfoPath toolbar on your forms and allow users to use the Save and "Save as" buttons to save their forms. This method is very similar to saving other Office documents in applications such as Word, Excel, and so on. However, this approach has two key drawbacks:

➤ Users can often become confused by this, because they may not realize that the form is a "document," or may not know where or how to save the file. This is especially true for web browser forms. In the context of a forms and workflow application, this is critical because workflows will normally depend on forms being placed in specific locations with specific filenames in order to initiate.

➤ As a designer, you have no control over where the forms get saved, or what filenames are used. This makes it difficult to use the forms in automated processes such as workflows.

A better approach is to hide the Save buttons and only allow users to submit the form either via your own button on the form itself, or via the InfoPath toolbar. Submitting a form means the XML file is sent to a data system. When using InfoPath forms for workflow, the XML file is sent to the SharePoint forms library so that it can be subjected to the workflow. The options are as follows:

➤ *Email* — The form can be sent either as an embedded e-mail or an attachment to an e-mail. E-mail fields can be set from data within the form.

➤ *SharePoint Document Library* — The form will be saved as an XML file in a SharePoint document library. If property promotion is configured, properties will be synchronized with SharePoint library columns.

➤ *Web Service* — The XML is submitted according to the specifications of the web service. For web services that expose the type System Dataset, InfoPath will track changes as the user edits the data. The web service can then do whatever the business logic dictates with the XML.

➤ *Hosting Environment* — This provides a way of submitting the XML data to a hosting environment, such as an ASP.NET page.

➤ *Web Server (HTTP)* — The XML is submitted to an HTTP web services and an HTTP `Post` command is used to submit the data in the form to that URL.

➤ *Data Connection* — You can also submit to a data connection in a SharePoint Data Connection Library.

Generally speaking, if the form is hosted as part of a SharePoint solution, it makes sense to submit the form to a SharePoint document library so that you can take advantage of property promotion and ideally use the form data in a workflow. If you are going to use a SharePoint document library, it is best practice to use a Data Connection Library, rather than hard-coding the data connection details into the form.

In the context of saving and submitting forms, the terms "library" and "list" mean the same thing. InfoPath forms can be published to either libraries or lists. However, there is a specific type of library called a *form library* designed to store forms. This is typically where InfoPath forms get stored.

The next section examines the options for deploying InfoPath. This is one of the most complex areas of InfoPath, and well-considered planning is essential.

INFOPATH DEPLOYMENT

You can have the best form in the world, but that is of little use if you cannot get it out of your development environment and users cannot access it.

In the context of SharePoint, deployment of InfoPath forms can prove problematic. It is well worth fully understanding the deployment process before you make other decisions about your form approach and design.

The term *deployment* is used to describe taking a form that has been developed in one environment and making it available for use in another environment.

In some areas deployment is not initially a requirement, such as scenarios where business users are designing very lightweight forms within the context of a specific site — for example, modifying a SharePoint list form. However, experience has shown that these sorts of forms can very quickly grow into something that other parts of the organization would like to use, and sooner or later, you may need to deploy it elsewhere.

To get a form from InfoPath Designer to SharePoint, it must be published. This is a process that is undertaken in InfoPath Designer, and it prepares the .xsn file, which is what actually gets deployed.

Several options for publishing exist, but the main option of interest in this discussion is SharePoint Server. When choosing to publish to SharePoint Server, you have several sub-options, as described in the following sections.

Deploying to a Form Library

If you choose to use a *form library*, the .xsn file is published to a specified library on a SharePoint site (or InfoPath will create a new one). The form will then be configured to be the default document for that library.

This process requires that the InfoPath Designer application has direct access to the SharePoint server to which the form is being published, and will only enable use of the form in the specified site/library.

This option is suitable for one-off forms that do not have to go through a testing process before being made available. Typically, business users would use this option.

If the form must be redeployed to another library (even in the same site), it must be specifically published to that library. The issue with this approach is that if the form is updated, it must be republished to all libraries separately.

Deploying to a Content Type

Deploying to a content type is a slightly more advanced option than deploying to a form library. However, this approach still has limitations.

Choosing this option creates a new content type in the specified site (or updates an existing one). The content type will be available for use on any list or library within the site.

The content type will be configured with the form .xsn file as the "document template." When choosing this option, you will be asked to which location the .xsn file should be loaded. Typically, this should be in a hidden library called FormServerTemplates, but it can be anywhere on the site. (The .xsn file must be in the same site collection as the content type.)

Once the form is published, you can then manually or programmatically assign the content type to any lists in which you want the form to be used.

However, this approach has two main issues:

➤ The form is deployed only within the context of the site collection. If you wish to use it on another site collection, web application, or farm, it must be specifically redeployed to that site collection. This poses the same issues as deploying to a Form Library.

➤ Unlike deploying to a Form Library, you must manually associate the content type with any lists or library that must use it.

It is worth noting that with the increasing trend toward hosted/cloud computing, deploying to a content type and/or form library may be the only options available. Most standard online hosting providers (Microsoft's Office 365 included) will allow access only to site collection-scoped areas of SharePoint. Therefore, the farm-wide options discussed in the following section may not be possible.

Administrator-Approved Form Templates

When architecting and designing SharePoint-based solutions, the principles of component reuse still hold, whereas the previous deployment mechanisms provided for limited reuse. Using administrator-approved form templates allows the InfoPath form to be reused throughout the entire SharePoint farm.

All the site collections in all web applications will potentially make use of the form that is deployed in a single location. This also provides for easier operational maintenance, because the form can be updated to provide additional functionality or address bugs, and it must be deployed only to a single location. In contrast, the other mechanisms would require an exhaustive process of finding where the form is used and repeatedly redeploying it.

This option is the only realistic option if your form's reach is (or will eventually be) broader than a single site collection, or if your form has custom code behind it.

 If your form has code behind it, then administrator-approved is the only option for SharePoint deployment.

This option will prepare the .xsn file to be uploaded to Central Administration and made available throughout the farm through activation of Features. Choosing this option prompts you to generate a copy of the .xsn file on a filesystem, which you can then pass to an administrator. From there, the administrator can upload the .xsn file to the SharePoint farm's Form Templates Library via Central Administration.

Once the form has been uploaded to Central Administration, administrators can use the "Activate to a site collection" option. This process will create a content type in the chosen site collection with the centrally located .xsn file as the document template.

This can be a fairly laborious process because the form must be manually "activated" to each site collection, and then the content type must be manually associated with the relevant lists and libraries. However, the main advantage of this approach is that there is only a single .xsn file, which can be centrally managed. Additionally, because a Feature is used, the activation and de-activation can be controlled through the site settings page or other associated Features.

Microsoft provides a number of Windows PowerShell commands to automate the process of verifying, uploading, and activating administrator-approved .xsn files. Following are the Windows PowerShell cmdlets that must be used:

➤ `Test-SPInfoPathFormTemplate` — This verifies that the form is browser-enabled.

➤ `Install-SPInfoPathFormTemplate` — This uploads the .xsn file to Central Administration.

➤ `Enable-SPInfoPathFormTemplate` — This activates the .xsn file to the specified site collection.

When architecting or designing a system, it is good practice to consider the operational elements of the system. On this basis, use of Windows PowerShell is recommended because it provides the operational staff with a simple and repeatable mechanism for activating the form in multiple environments. In addition, the use of Windows PowerShell is best practice in this area because it can easily be repeated on different environments (such as development to test to live), and used to activate the form to a large range of sites simultaneously.

If the form uses a data connection and is published to Central Administration as an administrator-approved form, it is best practice to also publish the data connection file itself (.udcx) to the Central Administration Data Connection Library.

To do this, the data connection must be converted to a data connection file (.udcx). This can be done using the Data Connection section in InfoPath Designer 2010. You have two choices:

➤   Site Relative

➤   Centrally Managed

If you want to deploy the data connection centrally, you must choose Centrally Managed here.

When choosing the Centrally Managed option, you will be prompted for a local SharePoint site that contains a Data Connection Library to save the new .udcx file to. This is used for development purposes only. When the form is deployed to a separate server environment, both the form and the .udcx file must be deployed to Central Administration. No action is necessary in the form itself to enable this functionality. The fact that you selected Centrally Managed when creating the .udcx file means that the form will automatically know where to find the file in the new environment.

> *Data connections that are published to Central Administration are available only to forms that are also published to Central Administration. It is recommended that Windows PowerShell be used for deployment to enable better consistency.*

Deploying with Features (XsnFeatureReceiver)

A class in the `Microsoft.Office.InfoPath.Server.Administration` namespace called `XsnFeatureReceiver` can assist with deployment of InfoPath forms via code or Features. *Features* are small collections of functionality that can be activated or deactivated against a site or site collection. Features are the best-practice method of packaging and deploying most SharePoint customizations.

When activated or deactivated, `XsnFeatureReceiver` Features can copy a specified .xsn file to a URL defined in the Feature's elements file (typically `FormServerTemplates`). This is effectively the same as publishing the form to a forms library from InfoPath Designer. However, because it is a Feature, it can be controlled more centrally and consistently (including deployment/retraction) via Windows PowerShell or Feature receivers.

To use this approach, your .xsn file must be published to a network location and then copied into your Feature's folder.

This approach is great if you are deploying your form only to a very small handful of sites. However, it is only suitable for site-specific deployment. Therefore, it has all the drawbacks of deploying to a form library or deploying to a content type.

 This approach cannot be used to deploy forms to Central Administration, which means that it is limited in how useful it is in an enterprise scenario.

Now let's take a look at workflow in SharePoint, and how forms and workflow can be used together to develop powerful business applications.

WORKFLOW IN SHAREPOINT 2010

Workflow was first introduced in SharePoint in the 2007 suite of products, and is a SharePoint Foundation feature that builds on top of the WF technology in the .NET Framework.

SharePoint workflow has always been all about connecting people with documents and list items. It does this by following a defined logical route that can change based on input from users, or changes in the data (typically list item columns) associated with the workflow.

SharePoint workflows make extensive use of SharePoint tasks to inform users of actions they need to take, such as to review a document, or to provide a specific piece of information about a given stage in the workflow (for example, whether the `Holiday Request` is approved). Completion of tasks with optional inclusion of additional data is generally what will move a workflow on to the next stage.

SharePoint workflows also make extensive use of InfoPath forms to provide the primary user interface for initiating the workflow, completing tasks (custom forms for tasks), or checking status of the workflow.

It is worth spending a little time understanding some of the things you can do with your workflows, specifically capabilities that are new to SharePoint 2010.

Site-Based Workflow

One of the biggest drawbacks to SharePoint 2007's workflow implementation was the fact that a workflow had to be bound to a list item. In many cases, this meant that workflow designers created dummy lists just to have somewhere to house the workflow, even if it did not make sense as a document/list item-based process.

In SharePoint 2010, workflows can now be bound to a site as well as a list item. This opens up a lot of opportunity around *site-based workflow*. Typical examples include a site disposition workflow, or perhaps a workflow that is initiated on site creation and guides the owner through common administrative tasks.

Visualization

As mentioned previously, Visio 2010 can be used to draw workflows that can then be exported to the SharePoint Designer for implementation. If a workflow has been drawn in Visio 2010, the diagram can be used within SharePoint to visualize the workflow. This tool shows users at which stage of the workflow they are. By default, the diagram is shown in the workflow properties screen.

This is made possible by the introduction of *Visio Services* to SharePoint 2010. Visio Services enable Visio diagrams to be rendered and viewed in a web browser.

All of the workflows that ship with SharePoint have Visio diagrams associated with them, so have a look at a default workflow to see this feature in action.

Figure 31-4 shows the simple `Holiday Request` workflow visualization as seen via the Workflow Information.

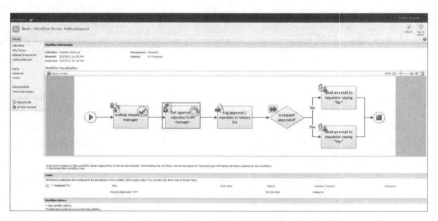

FIGURE 31-4: Workflow settings in SharePoint with Visio station

Customize Default Workflows

It is now possible to customize the workflows that are provided with SharePoint. This is very useful in scenarios where the default workflows do most of what you need, but a few activities must be added to meet your specific requirements.

In SharePoint 2007, the entire workflow had to be rebuilt in order to enable this.

New Activities and Events

In SharePoint 2010, a significant number of additional activities and events have been added to the base workflow foundation.

The new activities are too numerous to list. However, following are some of the more useful ones:

> `CoerceActivity` — This includes a range of activities that will help to cast user input to a specific type, such as `DateTime`, `String`, `Int`, and so on.

> ➤ `HTLookupActivity` — This includes activities that will look up values from the workflow's properties `HashTable`.

> ➤ `ImpersonationSequenceActivity` — This allows developers to run a workflow instance in the context of a specific user.

> ➤ `SubmitFileActivity` — This submits a file to a document library.

SharePoint 2010 also enables developers to write event receivers that can respond to any of the following events within the workflow:

> ➤ `WorkflowStarting`

> ➤ `WorkflowStarted`

> ➤ `WorkflowCompleted`

> ➤ `WorkflowLoading`

> ➤ `WorkflowUnloading`

> ➤ `WorkflowPostponed`

Event receivers are useful if secondary workflows must be called from within a primary workflow. Using events means that workflows can become much more modular in design.

Pluggable Workflow Services

Pluggable workflow services enable developers to integrate SharePoint workflows into other non-SharePoint workflows that may run on different platforms. Within the Microsoft software stack, BizTalk is a great example of such a system.

This capability means that workflows can both submit and, more importantly, respond to events outside the workflow. A typical example of where this capability might be useful is in the `Holiday Request` workflow discussed numerous times throughout this chapter. Most companies keep track of an employee's holidays in a Human Resources system of some sort. Using pluggable workflow services, the SharePoint-based workflow could pass data into an additional workflow in the Human Resources system, and then listen for a response back to say that the holiday has been processed correctly. At this point, the SharePoint workflow would finalize and mark itself as completed.

Reusable Workflow

SharePoint 2010 introduces the concept of *reusable workflows*, which are simply sequential workflows that are bound to a content type rather than list or library.

This means that the workflow can be used wherever the content type is available. This is only really a minor improvement over publishing workflows to a list, because the workflow is still bound to the scope of the site collection that contains the content type where it was published.

Reusable workflows mean that a workflow can be re-used within the context of a site collection. However, deployment across site collections, web applications, or farms is still tricky with SharePoint Designer 2010.

Deploying re-usable workflows to a small selection of specific sites is possible by exporting and explicitly importing the workflow on certain sites. However, this approach is not practical for large numbers of sites, and also has the disadvantage of each individual site maintaining its own copy of the workflow. Therefore, updates will be difficult.

> *Reusable workflows are only reusable within the context of a site collection by default. Even with reusable workflows, it is still problematic to deploy declarative workflows to different site collections, web applications, or farms.*

The next section provides an introduction to workflow tasks, which are one of the main methods for getting information from users, and assigning actions to users.

WORKFLOW TASKS

Tasks are a core part of SharePoint workflow. They are commonly used to determine the direction of the workflow, and collect data from users.

For example, in the `Holiday Request` workflow, the activity that involves the holiday request being accepted or rejected by the user's manager would typically be created as a workflow task. When the manager responds, the task will capture the acceptance/rejection decision, as well as any other data (such as reasoning if the request is rejected) and mark itself as completed. The workflow service will listen for the task to become complete, at which point it will proceed to the next stage of the workflow.

The path that the workflow takes may depend on the data that was collected as part of the workflow task. In the `Holiday Request` example, if the task were accepted, the employee may get an e-mail saying that it was accepted, and the workflow would proceed to updating the Human Resources system. Alternatively, if the task were rejected, the employee may get a rejection e-mail that includes the additional captured reasoning data, and the workflow may complete at this point.

> *This is a point where the decision around sequential or state machine workflows is relevant. See Chapter 32 for more information on these two types of workflow.*

Tasks used in workflows are based on a hidden content type within SharePoint called *workflow tasks*. By default, tasks used in workflows are stored in a list called Workflow Tasks. If the defaults are accepted when associating (setting up) workflows, all workflows in a site collection will use the same workflow tasks list to store tasks. For high-volume sites, this list could get very large, very quickly.

Although the support for large lists has been improved in SharePoint 2010, it is still best practice to minimize list sizes where possible. On this basis, it is recommended that each workflow be configured with its own dedicated Workflow Tasks list.

The next section examines the workflow history list, which is the primary audit trail for workflow activity.

WORKFLOW HISTORY

When associating (setting up) a workflow, the administrator will be asked for a *workflow history list*. This is a special type of SharePoint list that is used to store data about the workflow, and the route that a workflow has taken.

It is part of the workflow design process to establish when and how the workflow history list is used. The workflow history list is intended as a human-readable audit of what has occurred during the workflow, and is especially important if data collected in the workflow is needed for compliance or record management.

Typically, workflows will log to the history list at each activity point at the start and end of the workflow. However, remember that the workflow is intended to be read by humans, so it is important to ensure that any history list submissions are readable and relevant to any users who might be looking at the history.

The act of writing to the workflow history list is a built-in SharePoint activity that is available in both SharePoint Designer and Visual Studio workflows. The activity allows you to pull in data from the workflow itself, and gives you a good level of control on how the history list entry is displayed and laid out.

In the example of the `Holiday Request` workflow, the history list would be used extensively throughout the process. One of the key entries would be the acceptance or rejection of the holiday request by the employee's manager. The workflow history list would typically capture data such as who accepted/rejected the request, what date and time, and any reasoning that was given in the case of a rejection.

 It is worth noting that workflow histories automatically get removed from the SharePoint user interface 60 days after the workflow ends. If you need easy access to the history of a closed workflow, you should store the data elsewhere as part of the workflow itself.

Now let's look at the differences between Sequential and State Machine workflows, and best practices for deciding which one to use.

SEQUENTIAL WORKFLOW VERSUS STATE MACHINE WORKFLOW

SharePoint workflows are available in two main styles:

➤ Sequential workflow

➤ State Machine workflow

Sequential Workflow

Sequential workflows are perhaps the easiest to understand, because they are what someone may intuitively understand workflows to be. Sequential workflows have a starting point and an ending point, with various defined sequential paths between the two. Each path through the workflow is constituted from a series of workflow activities (things like "send an e-mail," "collect data from user," "update list item," "run some code," and so on). The outcome of an activity will determine the next path the workflow takes toward the end point.

The main point to remember with Sequential workflow is that the paths are predefined and sequential — that is, the workflow will follow a defined set of activities until it reaches an end point. Sequential workflow does not necessarily mean linear. The use of conditional logic, branching, and so on, means that there can be multiple paths through a sequential workflow, and the outcome of activities can change the path. However, the key point is that the paths are always predefined by the workflow designer.

A typical example of a Sequential workflow is the `Holiday Request` example. The starting point is that a user requests a holiday, and the ending point is that the holiday is approved or rejected and logged in the system. There may be several predefined paths and sets of activities between the start and end points.

State Machine Workflow

A *State Machine workflow* does not follow a predefined path, but simply moves between a set of states. These workflows are event-driven in that the outcome of a given event may change the state of the workflow. Although State Machine workflows do have a starting and ending state, the path between these two cannot be predetermined, and is driven by the workflow itself. State Machine workflows are generally very well-suited to long-running workflows where the process may stay in a particular state for a long period of time.

A State Machine workflow is ideal if the process must go backward and forward between states, rather than following a sequential path. A great example of a State Machine workflow is a support call that may get logged with your IT support organization. The call may have several states, and may transition between them several times before the call reaches the closed state.

For example, the end user may log the call, whereby at this point it may be in the "unassigned" state. A support engineer may pick up the call from the queue and assign it to himself, at which point the state becomes "with support worker." The support worker may contact the end user and request some data, where the state may change again to "awaiting data from end user." The end user may supply this data and the state would change back to "with support worker." The process may go on and on with the states constantly changing until the call gets closed off.

This kind of process is very difficult to implement as a Sequential workflow because the path between the start and end of the workflow is undetermined and, therefore, cannot be predefined as part of a sequential set of activities.

Another example of where a State Machine workflow may be more suitable is the `Holiday Request` workflow used throughout this chapter. In the scenario of a request being rejected, a Sequential workflow would typically end, and then the user would have to start a completely new workflow to re-request the holiday. A State Machine workflow would simply change the state to "rejected" and allow the user to update the request and re-submit, at which point the state would change to "awaiting approval." Using a State Machine workflow in this scenario avoids having to create multiple workflows for the same holiday request.

Choosing the Correct Type of Workflow

Choosing the type of workflow is probably the most important and impactful design decision you will make as part of your workflow design. It is also important to get this right, because it is very difficult to change the approach when the workflow is already developed. One main factor is that State Machine workflows can only be built using Visual Studio 2010. This introduces an increased level of complexity, and the need for custom code. SharePoint Designer 2010 supports only Sequential workflows.

 State Machine workflows can be developed only in Visual Studio. SharePoint Designer 2010 supports only Sequential workflows.

Within the context of SharePoint, the vast majority of workflows are implemented as Sequential workflows. However, this is not necessarily best practice. If you really look at your requirements, you may find that State Machine workflow is a better choice, and offers you much more flexibility than the Sequential workflow.

You have many factors to consider when choosing which type of workflow to use. Sequential workflows are generally easier to understand, and enable use of tools like SharePoint Designer and Visio 2010. However, State Machine workflows are generally more flexible because they enable the process to move backward and forward, whereas Sequential workflows are typically a single direction.

Although the right choice will depend on your requirements, the resources available to you, and the business process you are trying to map, the adage of "keep it simple" applies in this scenario. Generally, this will mean using Sequential workflows purely for the simplicity of development. (SharePoint Designer and Visio support only Sequential workflows.) However, it should be a carefully considered decision, and both Sequential and State Machine workflows should be fully evaluated before a decision is made.

There are several different tools that can be used to design, create, and develop SharePoint workflows. The next section provides an overview of the different workflow tools available.

WORKFLOW TOOLS

SharePoint offers a variety of tools that can be used in the creation of workflows. Unlike previous versions of SharePoint, three different tools are offered:

> *Visio Premium 2010* — It is now possible to draw the process flow, activities, and conditions of a SharePoint workflow in Visio. The Visio file can then be exported to SharePoint Designer 2010 to be fully implemented and deployed. Visio cannot generate complete, functional workflows. However, it is an invaluable tool that enables business analysts to visualize the workflow and give the designer/developer a head start in delivery.

➤ *SharePoint Designer 2010* — SharePoint Designer 2010 can be used to create simple, site collection–scoped, no-code workflows that use activities that ship with the product. It is also possible to build custom activities that can be used in SharePoint Designer.

➤ *Visual Studio 2010* — Visual Studio 2010 is used to write more advanced workflows that involve custom code. This is the choice for workflows that span beyond the realms of a specific site collection, and are widely accessible throughout the farm.

Visio 2010

Let's start the discussion with Visio, because this is the newest addition to the workflow-creation toolset.

Users have been drawing business processes in Visio long before WF was invented. Therefore, it makes perfect sense that users can now use Visio to visualize a SharePoint workflow and have their output used as a starting point for a fully operational workflow.

The user experience is almost the same as any other Visio diagram; the only difference is that the user must start the drawing from the Microsoft SharePoint Workflow template (New ➪ Flowchart ➪ Microsoft SharePoint Workflow) and use the SharePoint Workflow stencils when drawing the process.

> *The Microsoft SharePoint Workflow template is available only in Visio Premium 2010.*

A diagram in Visio must be augmented with additional information before it can be turned into an actual SharePoint workflow. To address this, it is possible to export the Visio diagram (Process ➪ Export) as a Visio Workflow Interchange file (.vwi), which can be imported into SharePoint Designer 2010 and further updated.

> *The .vwi file is a ZIP file with a different file extension that contains all of the files that SharePoint Designer needs to load the workflow. The .vwi file also includes a .vds file, which contains the Visio drawing.*

What is really awesome about this integration with SharePoint Designer is that it is two-way. This means that designers can export back to Visio for the drawers to make changes to the process, and then "round-trip" back to SharePoint Designer for further updates.

Another key feature of Visio integration is that if a Visio workflow diagram is available, it can be shown via the browser as part of the workflow status pages. This enables users to visually track what stage the workflow is in at any given time. This integration uses a SharePoint feature called Visio Service, which enables Visio diagrams to be shown via a browser without requiring any locally installed Visio software.

SharePoint Designer 2010

SharePoint Designer 2010 is the tool of choice to undertake no-code customization across the whole range of SharePoint capabilities, including designing, deploying, and configuring workflows.

SharePoint Designer enables designers to design a workflow using all of the activities that are installed on the SharePoint server to which they are attached (including custom activities). These workflows are essentially a set of rules that declare to SharePoint how the workflow should proceed. They are known as *declarative workflows*.

As mentioned earlier, it is possible to take .vwi files generated by Visio 2010 and import them into SharePoint Designer for further updates, deployment, or even export back to Visio. This enables a great round-trip between workflow designers and business analysts, which has not been possible before.

In SharePoint 2007, declarative workflows (the term used to describe no-code workflows in SharePoint) were bound to a specific list/library in a specific site on a specific SharePoint server. The URLs of the list and site were hard-coded into the workflow. This meant that although it was easy to deploy declarative workflows to a single site, it was more difficult to move them or deploy to other sites.

Despite the deployment limitations, SharePoint Designer 2010 is a very powerful tool that enables development and deployment of complex workflows without writing any code. However, it should be noted that "no code" does not necessarily mean "no technical skills." Generally speaking, designers will require some training or prior experience and a certain level of technical knowledge to get the most out of SharePoint Designer.

Visual Studio 2010

Visual Studio 2010 offers the ultimate level of control and customization over SharePoint workflows. Visual Studio introduces custom code that enables a range of workflow activities that can have code added to them, or make use of simple "code block" activities.

In SharePoint 2007, the Visual Studio 2008 workflow integration was functional, but sometimes difficult to use unless you were very familiar with SharePoint workflows, and knew the inner workings of the platform. In Visual Studio 2010, the workflow tools for SharePoint have been rewritten and workflow is a "first-class citizen" at the heart of Visual Studio. This means that workflow is a normal SharePoint project item and can be easily added to a solution, packaged, and deployed as part of a .wsp file, just like every other item in a SharePoint Visual Studio solution.

Reusable workflows that have been built in SharePoint Designer 2010 can be exported as a .wsp file and imported into Visual Studio 2010 for further customization. An example of this approach might be a final step of a Holiday Request workflow that needs to update a Human Resources system. This final activity may require custom code, and is, therefore, suited to Visual Studio. However, in many cases, this could also be implemented as custom activity developed in Visual Studio and used in SharePoint Designer.

 Note that once a workflow has been imported from SharePoint Designer to Visual Studio, it then must remain as a Visual Studio workflow. The integration is not two-way in the same way that it is between Visio and SharePoint Designer.

Now that you've seen the various tools for creating workflow, you are probably wondering whether to configure or develop. The next section guides you through some of the key factors when making this decision.

DEVELOPING, CONFIGURING, OR REUSING WORKFLOWS

One of the primary design decisions facing architects is whether to start a workflow in Visual Studio or SharePoint Designer. The direction you take here could have a huge impact on the time to develop the workflow, its supportability, and the flexibility of your workflow in the face of changing or evolving requirements.

As with most design decisions, the adage of "keep it simple" applies in this scenario. A good default starting point is always to use SharePoint Designer and look for reasons that force you down a Visual Studio (and, therefore, custom code) route.

The new reusable workflow feature means that you can build a workflow in SharePoint Designer and deploy it to any content type that you want, because declarative workflows are no longer bound to a specific list/library. However, remember that the content type is scoped only at a site collection level, so these workflows are not globally reusable.

Another key consideration is the fact that a designer working with SharePoint Designer can work with custom activities. This is a good approach to take if a large proportion of your requirements can be achieved with SharePoint Designer, but there is a small section that does not map to an out-of-the-box activity or set of activities. In this scenario, it makes sense to develop a single activity that can be used inside your otherwise no-code workflow. This way, the codebase is very distinct and small, and the majority of the workflow can still benefit from all of the flexibility of SharePoint Designer.

 Consider developing custom activities that can be used in declarative SharePoint Designer workflows.

It is also worth remembering that if a workflow is built as "reusable," it can be exported as a .wsp file and imported into Visual Studio at a later date if necessary.

It is possible to reuse an existing workflow in SharePoint Designer 2010. This is a new feature in SharePoint 2010 and is great if one of the workflows that ship with SharePoint provides the majority of the capabilities you need, but you just want to add one or two activities to them.

Although you should also start your design with SharePoint Designer as either a new workflow or configuration of an existing workflow, sometimes it is clear that Visual Studio will be required. Here are some of the key factors that may influence your decision to design in Visual Studio from the start:

➤ Your workflow will require a considerable amount of custom code, and it is not practical to implement the custom code entirely as custom activities.

➤ Your workflow is expected to be deployed many times to multiple farms as part of a wider solution or set of features.

➤ Your workflow is part of a wider customer solution that already has significant custom code investment, and is currently developed with Visual Studio.

➤ You are using a State Machine workflow. SharePoint Designer supports only Sequential workflows.

SUMMARY

This chapter has discussed some key design decisions related to using SharePoint workflow and InfoPath Forms Services to build business applications.

You have learned that these two technologies are very closely related, and when you are considering use of either InfoPath or SharePoint workflow, you should make sure you consider how the other one will play a part in your solution.

You have learned that SharePoint 2010 makes some major improvements in this area compared to SharePoint 2007. The range of tools provided can be used by anyone from non-technical business users to full-on developers. If the solution is planned and coordinated in the right way, it can be very quick and easy to create great solutions using these tools.

One of the key takeaways for this chapter is that if you use these tools in the right way, you can quickly build very powerful business applications. However, there are limitations, and you will never have the flexibility of a completely custom-made solution.

The trick as an architect is getting the right balance between making use of the out-of-the-box tools and customizing where necessary. Be aware of the limitations of the technology stack before you commit to building your solution on it. If you do choose to use InfoPath and SharePoint workflow for your solution, make the most of what the technology offers you.

In Chapter 32, you'll look at the record management features of SharePoint, and how to design highly scalable, enterprise-ready record management systems in SharePoint.

32

Records Management Services

By Nigel Bridport

Records management is an activity that is discussed by many organizations, but is not necessarily implemented by them. However, it is something that can be vitally important, especially if organizations find themselves under some form of lawsuit or litigation action. For example, organizations might be required to produce a document or e-mail that contains crucial evidence. Not being able to do so could adversely affect the outcome of the action.

In practical terms, *records management* is simply the act of managing information for as long as necessary throughout the life cycle of the content, from creation to eventual deletion.

Organizations will typically have their own view on what records management means to them, and will have a process that does not typically fit in with the myriad of currently existing legal requirements and standards (such as the ISO 15489, the United States DoD 5015.2, and the European MoReq). However, if the organization is affected by such a legal requirement, it must modify its processes to ensure that the detail therein is met. A non-conformant system is of little (or even no) use as in a legal case. The information is not considered authoritative or authentic.

This chapter helps you to understand what must be considered within an organization when thinking about the implementation of a records management system. In particular, this chapter explains how, when using Microsoft SharePoint Server 2010, the product can be used to fit in with the defined business processes.

UNDERSTANDING RECORDS MANAGEMENT

If you have no previous experience with records management, there may be a number of terms and processes with which you will not be familiar. This section helps you to understand what is meant by some of the basic records management terminology.

Understanding a Record

The first point to understand is what is meant by the term "record." Understanding what a record is is useful when considering what an organization should keep, manage, and, perhaps at a later date, be able to retrieve or ensure its eventual deletion.

It is necessary to balance a number of factors before making decisions regarding what is and is not a record. Some organizations would consider anything that is created on their infrastructure, in an electronic form, should be kept and maintained as a record within the records system — from a quickly created shopping list in Notepad to formal Human Resources documentation. However, organizations must also consider the volume of data that will be flowing around the system, and the storage requirements to manage that effectively.

Conversely, some organizations only want to consider formal documents that are passed to external agencies as a record.

So, the question that must be addressed is if your organization were taken to court over a decision that had been made, would you have all the necessary evidence to support the organization? If it does, then it is in a good position to defend itself. If not, the organization may well be subject to further legal action without the capability to defend its position in an adequate manner.

A typical business definition of a record is information that is considered important, and that is managed by a formal process. It can take a physical form (such as a paper letter) or an electronic form.

There are also a couple of types records to consider, including the following:

➤ *Ephemeral records* — These are records that have a very short life cycle (typically just days), but they may still need to be managed appropriately. A good example of this type of record would be a meeting invite. This is an electronic item that is potentially valid only for a few days, and, therefore, must be maintained in the system only until the meeting has taken place.

➤ *Vital records* — As the name implies, these records may be vital to the organization (such as a product design document), and, therefore, must be maintained differently. It usually has a much longer period of retention that can last many years after completion or delivery of the product.

Understanding Record Management

Organizations that have employed a *records management* process for many years have a large physical investment in files stored in onsite filing cabinets, and large off-site secure information storage repositories. A strict information and records management process is implemented and maintained by a team of *records managers*.

It can be difficult for the user community to discover what files are in the records system, and this may lead to duplication of files because of information coming from different sources, and the need to place the information in different parts of the system. In this scenario, records management could be thought of as a filing system, with business processes being used to manage that information.

Electronic records management systems include functionality and features used to help identify information as a record in association with methods to manage those records throughout their information life cycles. Following are the typical functions of the records management system:

➤ Identifying and creating the record

➤ Managing eDiscovery (the process of identifying data associated with a particular litigation case or query) or holds (the process of pausing any other business processes on identified items)

➤ Auditing of the actions conducted that affect the item (for example, noting who has viewed a particular record)

➤ Managing the expiration and disposal of items (that is, only managing items for as long as needed, and then controlling how that information is removed from the system)

All of these considerations must be addressed within the system to be able to adequately manage the records that are contained within it.

For a record to be valid, it must be possible for the records management system to prove that the item has been appropriately managed, and has not been changed or inappropriately deleted from the system when it was accepted.

Figure 32-1 shows a typical process for a records management system displaying the declaration of information, its management by the system as a record, and eventual disposal.

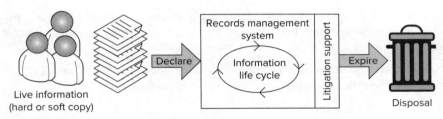

FIGURE 32-1: Records management system

Understanding the Roles That Are Involved

Within a records management system are several roles to consider. Some of the roles can be shared by the same person or a group of people, but the main participants are those shown in Table 32-1.

TABLE 32-1: Records Management Roles

ROLE	DESCRIPTION
Records managers or compliance officers	This can be one or two roles, depending on the structure of the organization.
	This role is responsible for the structure and management of the overall records management system. These people should be able to define the policies and procedures that the organization must follow to effectively deliver a records management capability. These are also the principal roles involved in the eDiscovery and hold procedures.
	These people should know what information is available to the organization, what sort of information must be discovered, and the information on which to potentially place a hold.

continues

TABLE 32-1 *(continued)*

ROLE	DESCRIPTION
Content managers	These people provide a link between the records managers and the user community. This role must lead by example by ensuring information goes to where it is intended, and encouraging the rest of the user community to do likewise.
Information workers	This role includes everyone who will be using the system to manage their records. They will be creating content in either hard or soft copy.
	These are the people who must use the records management system. Without their effective participation, the records management system will soon fail.

Now that you understand the necessary basic terminology used, let's explore how to use some of the foundations for records management.

USING A FILE PLAN

A *file plan* is a tool that details the organization data that must be stored and managed as a record. It defines the categories of information that are being used, along with the appropriate properties that the information must carry, and enables the consistent management of information.

Using a known and appropriate organizational structure of data provides an effective means to manage records. This makes the system simpler to interact with and understand.

A good file plan should aim to do the following:

➤ Create logical groups of information where data needs to be under the same level of business control.

➤ Structure information that makes sense to the organization. This is a really important point. A file plan differs between most organizations because it must reflect the way the organization works, thereby simplifying the choices that the records managers must make about where an item should be managed.

Having an overly complicated file plan will probably result in an unmanageable system with the users not being sure where certain information should be routed. Conversely, a too simplistic structure will not provide the organization with the capability to implement the processes defined by the records managers.

Following are the positive effects of having a well-defined file plan:

➤ An improvement in the access of the stored information

➤ The data being considered authentic, and, therefore, capable of being used for an external audit, an information request, or in response to a legal action

➤ A reduction in the overall cost of information handling by ensuring that data is expired appropriately

➤ A single location where an organization can identify what the current business policy is with regard to the retention of content

The Traditional File Plan

In the world of records management, a *traditional file plan* is typically a hierarchical structure of terms by which documentation can be stored, later retrieved from, and appropriately disposed of. It can be thought of simply as a structure of nested folders. Each level in the tree may have permissions set such that only a defined audience can access the information.

The traditional file plan is designed for the following:

➤ Defining what sort of information is to be kept and where

➤ Defining what the organization needs to keep as a record

➤ The relevant information policy for items that are kept

➤ The structure that must be built

This is a living system and, as such, it must reflect the business policy at any point in time. So, if a policy changes for some reason, that change must be applied to the file plan.

Microsoft TechNet (`http://technet.microsoft.com/en-us/library/cc261708 .aspx`*) provides a file plan worksheet that is good to use as a starting point. The worksheet can be adapted to fit your own requirements.*

For the most effective file plan, you should provide the following information:

➤ *Kind of record* — This relates to what the content is expected to be. A good example of this is "Training Manual."

➤ *Category* — This relates to the area to which the document belongs. Using the previous example ("Training Manual"), it could be "Learning Materials."

➤ *Description* — This describes what the record type is expected to be. An example might be, "Documents that provide instructions that relate to training activities."

➤ *Media* — This describes what form the record would take. This is where you can tell the organization that the item is a physical piece of paper, an electronic document, a web page, and so on.

➤ *Retention period* — This defines how long the organization must maintain the record. It could be days (for ephemeral records) or years (for formal or vital records). This must fit in with the business, financial, and legal responsibilities of the organization.

➤ *Disposition* — This describes what can be done to the record once the retention period lapses. Some items (such as personal information, for example, which could be related to a Data Protection Act) may have to be destroyed, and so cannot be archived. It is here that information is noted about what can and cannot be done to the record.

➤ *Contact* — This is the person who is responsible for the content. If a policy states that someone must review the "Training Material" after one year, for example, then the contact from this column would be the person responsible for managing that part of the process.

Using this list, you could create a file plan for a project team that generates project design documentation, as shown in the sample file plan in Table 32-2.

TABLE 32-2: A Sample File Plan

KIND OF RECORD	CATEGORY	DESCRIPTION	MEDIA	RETENTION PERIOD	DISPOSITION	CONTACT
High-level designs	Project Designs	High-level architectural information	Electronic document	10 years	Archive	John Doe
Low-level designs	Project Designs	Detailed application design	Electronic document	10 years	Archive	Jane Doe
Meeting minutes	Minutes	Minutes of meetings discussing the project designs	Electronic document	7 years	Archive	John Q. Public
E-mails	E-mail	E-mail threads relevant to the project	Electronic e-mail	10 years	Destroy	Jane Q. Public

In the example shown in Table 32-2, you can start to see how business requirements cross over. The organization must manage meeting minutes consistently, regardless of from where they have been generated.

Records Retention and Expiration

Record retention and record expiration are two important components of the file plan, and it is necessary to understand the difference between them. They control how long information must be managed, and how that information can be handled after that period of time has elapsed.

Record retention is concerned with keeping a record for as long as necessary — and no longer. For example, project documentation may have a retention schedule of seven years. This means that, once a document for a project has been formally declared as a record, a timer starts, and that item must be managed and remain unchanged for a period of seven years.

Record expiration refers to what happens to a record when the appropriate retention schedule for the item completes. There are a number of factors to take into consideration — some operational, and some legal. Legal documents may need to comply with laws of countries in which your organization operates. When your records come to the expiry stage, they may need to be completely removed from the system and "Destruction Certificates" generated, whereas other information may be fit for archiving.

File Plan Methodologies

There is no single piece of advice to give concerning what methodology should be used to define an organization's file plan. This is different for each organization, and must fit the business goals for records management.

Top-Down Classification

Top-down classification entails the key business stakeholders working with the records managers and deciding on how information should be categorized and organized. They would take a view of the information that is generated, and then how that is best managed. The focus for this method is to build a system that is determined by the needs of the organization.

A typical file plan structure for this approach is many layers deep, because the organization requires a rigid structure for the information to sit in, which then introduces a problem of complexity. When a user generates a piece of information and knows that the information must be stored as a record, the user may be expected to know where in the file plan to drop the item. If the hierarchy is deep and complex, and not intuitive to the user, users are less likely to follow the process fully. This could either result in the information being placed into the incorrect location, or worse, not being declared at all.

Bottom-Up Classification

Unsurprisingly, *bottom-up classification* is where the user community has a key role in determining how information should be managed. The focus for this method is to build a system that is determined by the needs of the user.

The benefit of this approach is that the records system that is delivered is one the user community would want to actively engage with, because it was built with their needs in mind. Enabling the user community to easily interact with the records management solution helps to ensure that it is adopted, because the users see and understand the value, and there is little impact on the users' time to actually follow the process.

However, if the structure is too simplistic, the organization will not be able to employ the necessary business processes defined, or the level of control necessary for the records.

The Content Life-cycle Approach

Organizations typically generate a large amount of electronic information, ranging from quick informal notes to the storage of personal data of their employees. Any of these artifacts could be considered to be a business asset, so these should therefore be managed appropriately in a particular stage of its life cycle. Information generated today may be particularly important, but in five years' time, less so. This demonstrates information flowing through its life.

Many different ideas exist about how many stages there are in the life cycle of a piece of content. However, Figure 32-2 shows the main stages that can be considered.

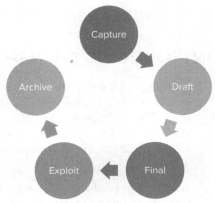

FIGURE 32-2: Typical content life cycle

The following stages are to be considered:

➤ *Capture* — This stage is concerned with the initial creation of the document, and the setting of metadata.

➤ *Draft* — This stage is concerned with the item going through a process before it is deemed a major version, or a version for release. There could be multiple review cycles, co-authoring of content, and so on.

➤ *Final* — When the content has been created, reviewed, and has been approved, it can then be considered to be in this stage. If the item is thought of as a record, it should then be placed in an appropriate location where it can be managed. This process is concerned with the audit of the item, and ensuring that it is authentic (that is, what has happened to the item since it was declared).

➤ *Exploit* — This stage is where the information that has been produced by the information workers is considered final and authoritative. It can now be discovered by others in the organization and reused by them. This ensures that people do not have to reinvent information, and also can help to ensure that a best practice is used by all.

➤ *Archive* — This stage is about what to do with the information once the organization decides that it is not necessary to keep. Typically, the information could just be copied off the records management system and into cheaper storage (such as tape backup or slower disks). This stage can also mean that the information must be destroyed, and a "Destruction Certificate" obtained for items such as personal data. The end result is that the information is removed from the records management system. This ensures that the records management data is as lean as possible, and that any eDiscovery processes that it executes do not retrieve unnecessary data.

Using a life-cycle approach to a document can help to create trigger points to define when an item should be submitted into the management of the file plan, and transition through the different stages.

At this point, you should understand the major principles of the records management process and what is required to be understood before attempting to build an appropriate system to deliver the business requirements. The following section discusses how those processes can then be implemented using Microsoft SharePoint Server 2010.

INTRODUCING SHAREPOINT RECORDS MANAGEMENT FEATURES

Microsoft Office SharePoint Server 2007 (MOSS) introduced a new type of site template called the Records Center. This was Microsoft's first attempt to deliver a system capable of being classified as a record management application. Previous to MOSS, any Electronic and Document Records Management System (EDRMS), using Microsoft SharePoint Portal Server 2003 or other version, would usually require a third-party application to deliver the records portion of the solution.

MOSS helped to simplify the infrastructure by potentially removing the need for a separate records management product, which would typically add further complexity and management overhead. The fewer products in the mix, the simpler the necessary management tasks become, because you are able to consolidate services such as backup and restore, and have no need to use separate management applications.

In MOSS, the records capability was available only through the Records Center, which was delivered as a separate site where all records would be expected to be stored and managed — in effect, a separate archive. There could be many Record Centers in a SharePoint farm because they were defined as a site template. However, it was only possible to define one Records Center as an external connection for the entire farm.

The result was that you could display only one destination in the context menu for documents that enabled users to submit information as a record. This in itself introduced some issues, typically for large organizations. Although the Records Center could be considered as a special site because it was not used as a typical collaboration area (with perhaps a high number of collaboration-type actions), it still had to obey a number of the SharePoint software boundaries and considerations.

The most important consideration was the size of the content database to meet a defined Service Level Agreement (SLA) for backup and restore times. Without custom code, it was difficult to circumvent these restrictions.

 Custom code would typically be of the form of either using a custom router implementing the `iRouter` *interface (*http://msdn.microsoft.com/en-us/library/ms563528.aspx*) to control how the routing table operates, or replacement of the* `OfficialFile.ASMX`, *which is the MOSS records management web service interface. Either of these approaches could be used to move information into different locations, sites, or even farms. This relates to MOSS, but the same code can also be implemented in SharePoint 2010, although the interface has been deprecated and replaced with* `iCustomRouter`, *which is the preferred method.*

With SharePoint 2010, the repository approach still remains. However, it has been enhanced with a common customer requirement to be able to manage records "in-place." This enables teams to manage records in the same document repository as active collaboration items.

Using this method to manage records means that when an item is declared as such, the item does not move from its current location, but can now be managed differently by SharePoint 2010. This operates by applying a core service of SharePoint, namely, Information Management policies.

For example, the document may inherit a different retention period as a record when it is declared, than that it may have been using as a work-in-progress item. This is performed by the definitions for the content type. A content type is the method SharePoint uses to describe information, its metadata, and how it is to be managed.

Looking at the content type information policies, you are able to specify different retention policies for an item, depending on if it is a collaboration item, or declared as a record. Figure 32-3 shows where the two policies are defined within the information policy of the item.

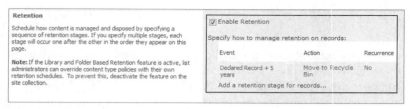

FIGURE 32-3: Retention policy for non-records and records

With the two methods now available, you can also deliver a system that blends both approaches. For example, an organization could use a "manage in-place" approach for the lifetime of the Collaboration site (such as that formed for the duration of a project). Participants could then declare records as needed in-place, and all of the information is co-located and easily discovered by the users of the site. When the project is then delivered and completed, the declared records could be sent off to the archive and the project site removed, thus ensuring that there is no further management overhead of maintaining a site that is no longer in use just because it contains a record.

There would obviously be a management overhead using a blended scenario, because there would be a need for someone to go through the now-defunct sites and submit the necessary information into the Record Center. This is an area that can be further automated via the use of the extended SharePoint 2010 workflow capabilities to ease this overhead.

New and Improved Features of SharePoint 2010

SharePoint 2010 has further enhanced the functionality made available in MOSS to support the new ways of working with records management. Some of these features are an evolution of already delivered functionality, and some are completely new to the product set (in response to common customer requests). Following are the main new and improved functions:

➤ Content Organizer

➤ Document identification

➤ Multi-stage policy improvements

➤ Widely accessible eDiscovery and legal holds

➤ Enhanced Records Center site template

➤ Location-based expiration schedules

➤ Component features of the Records Center that can be enabled on other site types

These new and improved features make SharePoint 2010 a flexible platform upon which a business or organization can build a records management solution that will fit its needs, as well as meet its legal and statutory obligations.

 Refer to http://technet.microsoft.com/en-us/library/cc261982.aspx *for further understanding of how Microsoft approaches records management with the SharePoint 2010 product.*

Let's take a closer look at these new and improved features.

Content Organizer

Users do not typically know (or even care) where content should be managed within the records management system. They want to follow good business practice, and know that the content they develop must be placed into a controlled process. But they do not want to be forced to make choices about how or where that happens.

To help with this business problem, MOSS introduced a new list within the Records Center called the *routing table*. This was the interception point for a records manager to control and direct information flowing into the Records Center to an appropriate document library. Out of the box, this was as granular as it got without customization of the solution (directing content types to a document library).

SharePoint 2010 has taken that concept to the next level with the introduction of a new site-level Feature called the *Content Organizer*. It retains all the functionality of the routing table, but has a number of enhancements in response to common customer feedback. Record managers still must define a set of rules that the system will follow, but many new controls can be used when defining those rules that make for a much more flexible solution.

There are two facets to configuring the Content Organizer:

➤ *Settings*, which relate to the instance of the Content Organizer

➤ *Rules*, which define what data should go where

Table 32-3 describes some of the main new features of the Content Organizer.

TABLE 32-3 Content Organizer Features

FEATURE	DESCRIPTION
Route directly to libraries, folders, other sites, or other records management systems	Anything external to the site collection must be managed through the web application external connections before it is a selectable option when creating rules. Using this feature extends the reach and scale of any solution based upon it. For example, you are able to identify incoming information, and then move that to a different farm to be managed.
Folder partitioning	This is a useful feature to automatically segment the incoming information into respective subfolders within the library. There is now the option to automatically create a folder when the library has reached a defined number of items (for example, 2,000). When the next item enters the system, the Content Organizer will create a new subfolder and attach a date/time stamp to the folder name. This ensures that the system stays within expected guidelines for view rendering. Similarly, in a Content Organizer rule, there is an option to automatically create a folder, but base it on a property called content type. For this option to be available, the content type that is being routed on must have at least one variable mandatory piece of metadata. If this is not apparent, the option to create new folders will be grayed out and not selectable.

continues

TABLE 32-3 *(continued)*

Conditions in the routing rules	With SharePoint 2010, you route on the content type, as well as one or more of the properties that exist for that type.
	There are many operators for defining the metadata rules that provide the records managers with many options for identifying incoming information, and then moving those items into the appropriate location. This means that you can have many rules operating on the same content type to ensure that the system is delivering the greatest benefit to a business process.
Managing duplicate content	SharePoint 2010 can automatically append a random character code at the end of a filename to make it unique within the store. However, SharePoint 2010 has also enabled the use of SharePoint document versioning. So, documents can be tied to a single entry, and you could view the copies through the records version history. The Document filename is not modified as before with a random character code.
	However, this option must be approached with caution. It is controlled as a Content Organizer site setting, so it used throughout the site, and matches incoming documents by the items' filenames only. For example, two different departments may have their own HR Policy document and call the document `HRPolicy.docx`. If each department submits the document into the Record Center, and the Content Organizer routes them both to the same library, they will only appear as a single entity, with the most recently submitted item being most visible. Care must be taken to ensure that these documents do not enter the same library, or that document versioning is enabled to keep all versions.
A "drop off" library	This library is automatically created when the Content Organizer Feature is activated, and it receives any items that are uploaded to the Records Center. It is from here that the Content Organizer rules will process content via a timer job.
	Each Content Organizer gets its own timer job created. Because it is just a document library, there are other spin-off benefits (such as running workflows on draft items, perhaps to collect some further data before routing to its intended final destination). If an item does not match any of the rules currently defined, it will remain in the "drop off " library waiting for a records manager, or even a rule manager (this can be a delegated role in the Content Organizer settings) to identify where the item should sit in the file plan.

All of this routing and folder creation can be handled automatically without further user intervention. After a document is uploaded and the required metadata applied, the upload form displays a permalink URL to the location to which it has been routed so that the user knows where to find it in the future.

There is one action of the Content Organizer to be aware of that is not commonly understood or described. If you submit a Document Set or employ an `ICustomRouter` to change the routing experience, the behavior of the Content Organizer is slightly different. Instead of the submitted item being immediately actioned from the "drop off" library (which is the normal mode of operation), a Document Set (or document that meets a rule that employs a custom router) will sit in the folder for, by default, up to a day. This is because SharePoint does not know what the Document Set contains, and, hence, what it needs to unpack or, in the case of a custom router, does not know what that process load will be.

Each of these actions could potentially be a long-running operation. To ensure that there is no blocking of the Content Organizer, these types are only processed when the web application's "Content Organizer Processing" job runs from the timer service. If this is a common scenario for you, you may want to consider managing the schedule of the timer job to run more frequently to deliver an acceptable experience.

> *The Content Organizer operates on content types that derive from the "Document" content type only.*

Document Identification

When an item enters the SharePoint Records Center, it is automatically assigned a document identifier. This is enacted by the Document ID Service site collection Feature.

When the Feature is enabled, a new column is automatically created called `Document ID`, which carries the assigned ID for the document. Through the site collection settings, the document ID prefix can be controlled to be a string of your choice. The document ID is formed with this string prefix, which then has a sequential number attached to the end to make the item unique within the site collection.

Following are some considerations about the document ID Service and its interaction with a records management system:

➤ If the item entering the records management site was delivered by a "Move" or "Move and Leave a Link" operation (this is where the item is moved to the repository and replaced with a shortcut), and it already has an ID, that ID will be retained. SharePoint assumes that the item identification is still valid.

➤ If the item entering the records management site has been placed there via a "Copy" operation, then it is assumed to be a new document, and, therefore, assigned a new ID.

Is the organization happy with this behavior? If so, then just use the functionality as it comes. If not, you could just use this feature in the Records Center, or even create your own document ID provider.

> *A sample custom* `Document ID` *Provider is available from MSDN at* `http://msdn.microsoft.com/en-us/library/ff521589.aspx`.

As mentioned previously, a permalink URL is created for an item entering the Records Center, and the document ID forms part of the link. What this results in is that no matter where the document moves to within the SharePoint farm, this link will always work to reference the document. You do not need to keep updating documentation with URLs to ensure that they are currently valid and correct.

There is also a "Find by Document ID" web part that is placed onto the Records Center homepage by default. This web part will take the supplied document ID and form a URL of the form `http://<site_collection>/_layouts/DocIdRedir.aspx?ID=<supplied_id>`.

You must be careful when configuring this service for each site collection. Uniqueness of the assignment of an ID is only valid for each site collection. So, if you use the same prefix for two or more site collections using the document ID Feature, it is highly likely that you will end up with more than one item sharing the same identification.

Figure 32-4 shows the Site Collection Administration settings for the relevant site, which enable you to define the correct settings for your environment.

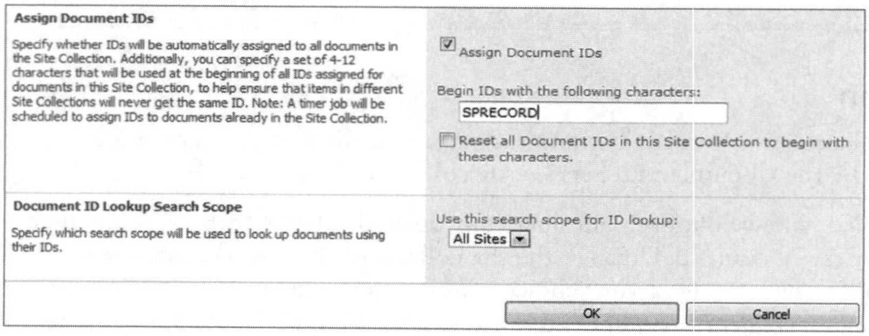

FIGURE 32-4: Document ID Feature setting

Multi-Stage Policies

It is now possible to specify a number of steps to run through when a policy-retention schedule becomes active. Previously, without customization of the actions used, it was only possible to perform a single operation when a policy forced the expiration of a record. You could create a multi-stage policy by custom coding a workflow in MOSS, but this would have been difficult to manage, and not necessarily the best approach in large systems with lots of workflows.

With SharePoint 2010, it is now possible to specify a number of actions to run against an item. This is particularly useful if you consider the example scenario where an item requires some sort of check annually to review feedback received, but the item should be deleted after seven years. Using multiple stages in the retention for the item, the system can automatically prompt a records manager to review the item annually, and then perform the expiration as expected.

Figure 32-5 shows an example of a multi-level retention policy.

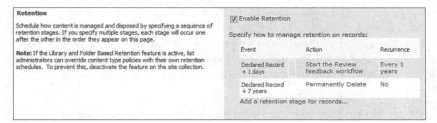

FIGURE 32-5: Multi-stage policy retention

Widely Accessible eDiscovery and Holds

eDiscovery describes the process whereby records managers are able to find, analyze, and identify content that relates to a litigation case or question from the organization. This process ties in very tightly with the hold functionality that is delivered by SharePoint 2010.

MOSS delivered some eDiscovery and hold functionality, but this was limited to the Records Center only. SharePoint 2010 has taken that functionality and expanded it across the whole SharePoint estate.

The first point to note is that the eDiscovery process is described by the Electronic Discovery Reference Model (EDRM). This is not to be confused with EDRMS, which is the Electronic Document Record Management System. SharePoint fits into several parts of the overall scheme, namely:

➤ Information management

➤ Identification

➤ Preservation

➤ Collection

SharePoint 2010 enables a user with appropriate permissions (usually the records manager) to search across the whole SharePoint corpus of information, which includes the collaboration and records areas. Information that is then discovered and deemed relevant to a litigation case can be placed into a legal hold.

An improvement to SharePoint 2010 over previous versions is the capability to search across more than just a single site collection, and being able to search many sites with identified items that have been placed in the hold. Through the new Compliance Details page for items, it is also possible to manually place items into a hold. Figure 32-6 shows a Compliance Details page.

FIGURE 32-6: Document Compliance Details page

Once the hold is activated on an item, it is no longer available to the user community for edits or deletion, and all retention policies relating to the item are frozen. For example, if a particular record is just about to expire, but is identified by the eDiscovery phase as relevant to a piece of litigation and, therefore, placed in a hold, then that item will not be expired. Rather, it will be held within the system. When the hold is removed from the item, it can continue its previous information life cycle, and expire as defined by the information policy.

The process of identifying the information is performed through the site setting, "Discover and hold content," which renders the page referenced by the URL `http://<site_collection>/_layouts/searchAndAddToHold.aspx`. This page enables you to specify keyword terms to search for, and preview the results before adding them to a hold. When the identified information is selected, records managers would have the option to be able to take a copy of that information into another separate repository, or keep it in place. Either way, the content on hold cannot be tampered with.

There may be good reasons to decide to send the document out of the current record locations and into a separately managed system, especially if the discovered data is widely dispersed throughout your infrastructure. In this case, it would be prudent to take a copy of the data and have that separate in case of server troubles later on. This would also ensure that, if data is discovered in the Collaboration areas, users can continue working on the content. However, if all of the discovered data is already in the Records Center, there is little point to increasing your burden. In that case, you should manage it in-place.

Enhanced Records Center Site Template

The Records Center site definition has been updated for SharePoint 2010 to include a number of functional changes. The look and feel between the two is quite different.

To show the differences between the default Records Center from MOSS and SharePoint 2010, Figure 32-7 displays an out-of-the-box MOSS Records Center, and Figure 32-8 shows the updated SharePoint 2010 version. You can see that there is a lot more on the page in the SharePoint 2010 layout, and that is just for the standard user view.

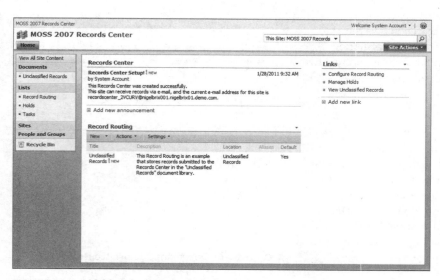

FIGURE 32-7: MOSS default Records Center

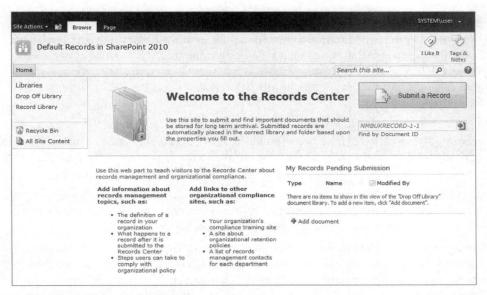

FIGURE 32-8: SharePoint 2010 default Records Center

There is also a Records Manager view that, once selected (as shown in Figure 32-9), displays the commonly expected Records Manager tasks.

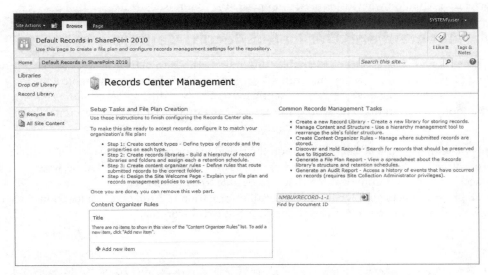

FIGURE 32-9: Records Manager view of the Records Center in SharePoint 2010

The SharePoint 2010 standard user page promotes tools (such as the "Submit a Record" web part) to help users engage with the record store more easily.

Location-Based Expiration Schedules

This functionality enables the configuration of retention policies at the library or folder level. This will overwrite the policy setting from the content type being submitted. This can be a very useful feature for providing consistent management of items where there is a requirement to employ a business process that takes priority over other locally based policies.

Component Features

Most of the features discussed so far have been developed as a SharePoint Feature, which means that they can be typically used throughout the SharePoint installation, and not just in the Records Center or for in-place management. The following Features can be enabled on other site types:

➤ *Content Organizer* — When activated in a Collaboration site, this Feature can help to apply record management processes (such as routing content to the correct location and automatically creating subfolders), to a work in progress environment.

➤ *Multi-stage retention* — This feature can be used in a Collaboration space. For example, the first stage could be to prune versions of a document to ensure that only a set number are stored, and then another stage could be used to ensure that when a major version of a document is more than a year old, it is automatically sent to the Records Center. There is a great deal of scope here to automatically apply or introduce a business process.

➤ *Document ID* — Again, this is something that can be used throughout the SharePoint estate, not just in the records management area.

➤ *Location-based expiration schedules* — This feature can help to deliver a consistent policy to information based on where it resides, as opposed to what it is.

In-Place Management and Dedicated Record Centers

As previously mentioned, SharePoint 2010 enables different methods to deliver records management capabilities, and has added to the functions available in MOSS. One of the most notable additions is the capability to manage items where they currently exist. This is called *in-place management*, and means that both collaboration and work-in-progress items sit alongside formally controlled records.

This can benefit a team because all the information they produce (or may need) is stored in a single logical location. When dedicated Record Centers are used, information is then spread between a number of places, and it can become more difficult to be able to gather all relevant information in just one view. Some customers go to great effort to pull information in from external locations in a single view. Using in-place management can circumvent this extra workload.

 Wherever the record exists within SharePoint, however, it is still the responsibility of the records managers to define and manage the information policies used.

In-place management is controlled by a SharePoint feature that must be activated on each site collection before use. With this feature activated, and the appropriate site record declaration settings made, the functionality is available to use in a site. However, there is still one further configuration to make before using the functionality.

Each document library where you want to use in-place management requires configuration of "Record Declaration settings." When this is completed, you will see the "Declare Record" option available in the Ribbon interface, as shown in Figure 32-10.

FIGURE 32-10: Declare Record option on the ribbon

When an item is selected and declared as a record, the options available to the information workers change. They can no longer edit the document, and the document icon will change to reflect the fact that it is now a record, as shown in Figure 32-11.

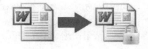

FIGURE 32-11: Icon change when declared as record

The Dedicated Record Centers site template provided by SharePoint 2010 enhances capabilities made available by MOSS with the addition of a number of features to make the solution more functional to a records manager.

Record Centers can still address a number of customer scenarios — specifically, where there is a need to apply a different set of permissions to content that is considered a record, or to be able to centrally manage all of the business records.

The Content Organizer is used to configure a set of rules to enable the automatic routing of content based on a number of different parameters (such as the content type and associated properties).

The SharePoint File Plan

As you have learned, a SharePoint 2010 classification scheme (or file plan) is typically constructed by the configuration of libraries and folders. It is used to categorize a record, and then apply the business-appropriate security, retention, and disposition requirements.

Let's take the categorization of project information as an example. You can start to build up a file plan as shown earlier in Table 32-2. In this scenario, all projects generate different forms of information (such as designs and e-mail threads that need to be controlled and kept). You could implement such a file plan inside a SharePoint Records Library, as shown in Figure 32-12.

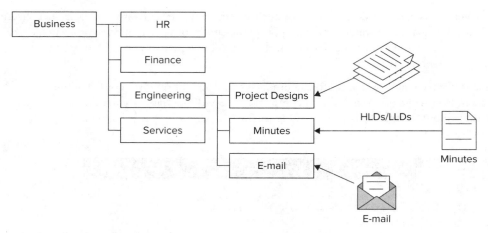

FIGURE 32-12: A typical file plan hierarchy

Each team in Figure 32-12 could have the same or different applied retention policies. To define the policy, you use a configuration setting for the retention source for the library. This setting will decide how to employ a retention schedule within the Records Center. The choices are either "content types" or "Library and Folders" as the source for the retention schedule.

Your business may have a corporate policy that must be applied across the entire estate that controls how certain documents are managed, regardless of the part of the organization from which they originate. In this scenario, you could be considering "content types" as the source of retention, which is the default setting in SharePoint.

However, if the different parts of the organization manage their own information and, therefore, have different policy settings for the same information, then you may find it more appropriate to use the "Library and Folders" as the source of retention. With this option, you can ensure that a consistent policy is employed across all of the information that is stored within the Records Center, regardless of the source of the information. This is because when the option is set, you are notified with a message that says, "When library and folder based retention schedules are used, all content type retention schedules are ignored. You may be overwriting policies defined by your site administrator."

Retention and Disposition

With the library and folder hierarchy built out, the retention and expiration policies from the file plan can then be applied, either to the content types, or to the library, folder, or site. This is performed by setting relevant information policies components.

Security and Permissions

SharePoint 2010 provides records managers with a simple mechanism to ensure that a part of the file plan (in essence, a SharePoint library or folder) is correctly secured with the correct set of user permissions. This ensures that the user community may only access the parts of the file plan that they should have access to.

It is probably not appropriate for the whole community to have complete and unfettered access to all of the business records because they may well contain business-sensitive or personal data. Setting appropriate security on the libraries and folders ensures that this level of access is managed and honored by other areas of the product (such as Search).

Obviously, it is much more difficult to achieve this goal if you are using manage-in-place functionality, because the security access settings do not change for items there. Users are simply prohibited from editing or deleting the item.

Retention

SharePoint 2010 provides records managers with the capability to define either simple or more complex retention schedules as part of an information policy. Information policies can be set on content types (such as a document), library, or folder, and can have a number of steps relevant to where the item sits.

A hold on an item that is part way through a retention policy has the effect of stopping the timer. Once the hold has been released from the content, the timer will continue as before.

Expiration

When the item stored in SharePoint 2010 passes its retention schedule, it is possible to start an action or series of actions to manage it out. By default, the item would be moved to the Recycle Bin. This then means that the item will be under the management of the Recycle Bin schedules.

However, it is possible to perform other operations (again, using the out-of-the-box functionality) such as permanently deleting the item (skipping the Recycle Bin) and starting a workflow. Other options are available at the expiration stage that may be more suited to a collaboration area, such as "Delete previous drafts."

Auditing

A common task for a records manager to perform is to audit information that the system is managing. This is initially delivered by SharePoint 2010 through the use of Audit Reporting, and is typically available directly from the Records Center management page.

This functionality is applied through an information policy to a content type directly. However, it is also possible to enable the audit of information directly on a list, library, site collection, and so on. This is particularly useful for a list that is receiving content from different sources, where the content itself does not have a consistent audit policy. By applying the audit policy directly to the list, you can ensure that all necessary actions are being captured in the SharePoint audit logs.

When enabled, the delivered reports will provide the following capabilities:

➤ Information regarding the viewing, modification, and deletion of items being managed

➤ The intended expiration and disposition of items within the store

➤ Changing of any policies

➤ Setting the current audit and security configurations

➤ Running a custom report based on parameters that you define

Record Workflows/Actions

With SharePoint 2010, it is possible to run a specific workflow or action on an item when the retention schedule has completed, or (in the case of a multi-stage retention policy) when a particular stage occurs. Options are delivered by the product by default or, if necessary, you are able to create your own SharePoint workflow and build that into the policy.

Out of the Box

Table 32-4 describes workflow actions delivered by SharePoint 2010 out of the box.

TABLE 32-4: Out-of-the-Box Workflow Actions

ACTION	DESCRIPTION
Move to Recycle Bin	When this policy runs, it will move the item out of the records area and into the site's Recycle Bin. This means that the item will then follow the policy defined for the Recycle Bin and users/records managers with appropriate permissions can still retrieve it if necessary. In some circumstances, though, this may be against data-protection policies, such as a piece of personal data that may only be stored for a period of time, and then must be completely removed from the system.
Permanently Delete	This could be the default action to take on the expiration of content from the record area. It does not fall foul of personal data protection. It ensures that the system is kept as lean as possible, and that you are not backing up unnecessary data or content. Information is purged from the system, though not any backups of that information. In some cases, when content is expired, it is expected that no instance of that content can then be retrieved, and this typically includes any instance of that data that you may have in any backup. In this scenario, you would require some other process to step through all of your backup data as well.
Transfer to another location	This is a useful option if you want to try to make use of other areas of the installation. For example, some organizations make use of cheaper storage via the Remote BLOB Storage (RBS). Using this option, it is possible to engage a multi-stage retention policy such that when content is more than a year old, it could be moved to another repository, freeing up space on your main repository. Similarly, an organization may want to keep its records in different places, dependent on the originating source or department. For this, the Content Organizer could be used initially, but if all content needs to be initially co-located and then only moved after a period of time, then this would be a good option to consider.
Start a workflow	See the following section, "Custom Workflows," for a discussion of this.

ACTION	DESCRIPTION
Skip to next stage	This can be used to run another retention action on an item. Perhaps a retention action states that an item must be moved to the Recycle Bin after seven years. It is possible to add a "Skip to next stage" retention operation based on some other criteria that would also enforce that action. Perhaps an item must be moved to another location one year after being declared as a record, or three years from initial creation. Using this action, that can be achieved.
Delete previous drafts	If a retention policy is set such that all content in the system more than six months old must be declared as a record, then this action could be used to ensure that only the major version of an item is kept, and that the previous minor versions of the document are not. This then starts to ensure that the content database is trimmed.
Delete all previous versions	As the name implies, this can be used to delete previous major versions of the item. However, if the customer requirement is to only store and manage as a record the latest version of a document, and the records system is using SharePoint versioning, then this option could be used to achieve that goal.

Custom Workflows

It is possible to write your own specific business process workflow and have that used in the retention policy if needed. The workflow should be written in either Microsoft SharePoint Designer, or Microsoft Visual Studio (for the more complex business processes). Once the workflow has been deployed, it should be associated with the relevant item. With the workflow attached, the option will be enabled such that it can be selected from the Actions drop-down menu.

If the library uses Content Types as its source of retention policies, then you are able to select any of the workflows connected with the acceptable content types into the library. However, if you are using location-based retention policies, you must instead attach the custom workflows to the library.

Reporting

Reporting relevant to records management has been improved in SharePoint 2010 over and above that delivered by MOSS. SharePoint 2010 offers the delivery of a number of different levels of reports available to the system managers, including the following:

➤ *Audit reports* — Using the information policy for the relevant item (that is, content type, folder, library, site collection, and so on) it is possible to switch on the audit of operations performed within that scope. This will display the audit actions configured to be reported on.

➤ *File Plan reports* — This report can display to records managers the current state of their section of the file plan. Information returned in this report includes the number of items at each stage of the file plan, as well as the retention policy in force throughout the libraries and folders.

Metadata Discovery in Records Management

Metadata navigation is available throughout SharePoint now, and enabled by activation of the "Metadata Navigation and Filtering" feature. By default, this is already activated in the Records Center and available for use.

This function can be particularly useful in the records management space, and is sometimes referred to as *virtual folders*. In essence, it enables the viewing of content based on some metadata value sitting on the items, instead of the hierarchical structure views that you may have implemented. For example, if you had a library with a deep folder structure, but you just wanted to see the items that had a particular metadata setting, this functionality will give you a flat view over the entire library of items with the metadata that you have selected.

Figure 32-13 shows a view of a library based on the selection of a record's "Products" value.

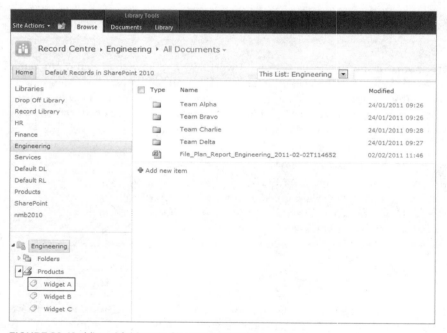

FIGURE 32-13: Virtual folders in SharePoint 2010 views

So far, you have learned about how SharePoint 2010 is able to meet some of the technical records management challenges of organizations. Let's now discuss some of the key business decision points that require addressing.

KEY BUSINESS CHALLENGES

You have a number of challenges to overcome when planning and implementing a records management system within an organization — ranging from the legal implications of what needs to be managed, to actually getting the user population to adopt the system effectively.

Understanding Regulatory Compliance Requirements

This can be a difficult piece of exploratory work, and provides the foundation for the file plan upon which the records management system depends. For a record to be compliant, it must adhere to the rules and laws as relevant to the organization as a whole.

Does your organization need to be able to apply acts such as Freedom of Information Act 2000, Data Protection Act 1998, and so on? These legally enforced Acts then have an influence over your legal compliance, and, therefore, directly affect the policies and procedures that must be adopted in the file plan.

When responding to these requirements, the organization will have to prove that the records it maintains are authentic, accurate, comprehensive, and secure.

Understanding the Expectations of eDiscovery

eDiscovery is intended to discover all information held by an organization that is relevant to a query. This not only includes all of the data in the running system (that is, in the Capture, Draft, Final, and Exploit stages), but also data stored on backups from the past, in the Archive state.

Following are the requirements for the eDiscovery process:

➤ Must show that an organization has the policies and practices in place to demonstrate the right actions are being performed, and there is a trail to prove that

➤ Must preserve current and historical data from being inappropriately removed from the system

➤ Must provide description by category and location of data in control of the organization relevant to a case

➤ Must produce the discovered data in the originally held form (if relevant)

Defining Records Management Policies

The challenge here is how an organization can ensure that, when a policy has been defined, it can be enforced and adopted by all departments.

When defining what records management policies to adopt, an organization needs to do the following:

➤ Ensure that the policy is relevant to all.

➤ Ensure that the policy is not over-complicated, causing the end users to have to perform lots of extra actions.

➤ Ensure that the policies meet the legal and regulatory requirements imposed.

If these points can be successfully addressed, there is a high likelihood that the system will be successful.

Selecting Analysis and Migration Tools

Lots of tools and options are currently available to help with the analysis and migration of information into a records management system of all types. Sometimes it is most appropriate for an organization to code its own tools because they provide the best way to understand the structure of its data, and how it would like that reflected in any new system.

When performing the analysis of data, the organization must be able to define all content sources of information, to understand what needs to be maintained, and to understand what can be removed. Keeping data unnecessarily increases exposure to having to provide information. If the business policy is to keep information for five years only and then destroy it, if a legal action is raised requesting information after that period has expired, the business can show its policy and state that it no longer has the data. That should be satisfactory, as long as it does not fall foul of any other legal or regulatory requirements.

Balancing Metadata Requirements with the End-User Experience

This area is typically problematic for organizations. A difficult compromise to reach may be balancing what an organization needs to be able to appropriately manage content with the organization not wanting to overburden users with extensive sets of metadata.

A records manager may "need" many properties set by the user so that the records manager can manage the items in the most correct and controlled fashion. However, users do not typically want to have to specify a large number of properties on their records. They just want to submit and forget it in terms of management. They typically consider records management an overhead, and do not see the benefit to the organization.

By overburdening users with lots of properties to fill in, you are running the risk of the user community not adopting record submission, and thereby resulting in the loss of valuable and potentially legally required information. Conversely, if appropriate metadata is missing from an item, it cannot necessarily be managed correctly by the records managers. The problem is that you then must be conservative in your retention schedules, which could result in keeping records for longer than they should be kept.

Deciding on an Appropriate Approach

The organization must be able to define an approach that will deliver a system that meets the requirement of the legal acts to which it is subjected. The approach must be one that will deliver enough capability for the records managers to maintain the system correctly, but also not be so complicated that the user population will not make use of it.

This last point is critical. Many systems fail, although they are technically very well-architected and built. But the users cannot understand how to correctly interact with it, and so the system becomes expensive to run for the small percentage of records that it holds. This delivers very little benefit to the organization.

Now let's take a look at what needs to be considered when deploying the necessary architecture.

KEY SHAREPOINT ARCHITECTURAL CONSIDERATIONS

This section looks at the main architectural components that must be considered when deploying a records management system based on the SharePoint 2010 product set.

Planning for the Record Storage

In a simple records management deployment, all records would typically be configured to deliver to a record library or document library. Use of the Content Organizer Feature can help to ensure that you are working within the best practices of SharePoint 2010, such as having only 5,000 items per folder in a library. But there are also times when you have a large number of records to manage that typically push your implementation over the recommended best practices boundaries for SharePoint content databases (such as size).

Document/Record Library Considerations

Records management can live outside some of the normal scaling implications of a Collaboration area in SharePoint because of the nature of user interaction with it. However, you should still carefully consider how you are going to structure the data, and the number of libraries that you intend to use.

Following are some factors to consider:

➤ For view rendering, ensure that no view will have more than 5,000 items to display.

➤ A library can contain a maximum of 30 million items.

➤ A library can have no more than 400,000 major versions.

Working with these figures gives you a good idea of how many libraries you need to consider. Perhaps you can use a library per department, or per content type, and so on. The choice you make can be based on organizational structure, or on technical detail. But whichever approach you take, you must ensure that you have a system that can take the current information and allow for expansion.

Remember that a record library is a document library with extra features already enabled and configured for use, and is appropriate for the storage of records. For example, the option to "Automatically declare items as records when they are added to this list" is selected for a record library by default, but not for a document library.

Using External Storage

As you are aware (and has already been mentioned), a number of software boundaries should be considered when thinking about using SharePoint 2010 for records management functions. Probably one of the most important areas to consider is the size to which your content databases are likely to grow, and the "live" nature of the records that are being managed.

SQL data storage is expensive and at a premium for large SharePoint deployments. A large amount of cheaper (although, perhaps, slower) storage is available outside of the SQL space that could be potentially used within an organization.

This cheaper storage could be exploited in SharePoint 2010 via the Remote BLOB Storage (RBS) provider. This provides a mechanism by which the actual content of the information being stored is managed outside of SQL in a different storage mechanism (such as Windows NTFS), while the metadata for the item is still stored within the appropriate tables inside of SharePoint. The end users are not aware of anything different, however. They do not know (or even should care) that the actual content is stored outside of SharePoint. They can still interact with the information just as if it were stored inside of SharePoint.

However, there are trade-offs to consider. The first major one would be the extra management tasks that would be necessary to ensure that the metadata stored in SQL ties up with the content stored outside of SharePoint. You would need to ensure that the two different areas are in sync when performing backups and restores, which is not a normal consideration for a SharePoint implementation. However, this could help your implementation when you have large amounts of data to manage, and you want to make use of cheaper disks (which, in turn, keeps your SharePoint databases trim).

Designing for eDiscovery

eDiscovery is about the organization being able to find and identify information, and then how to protect it.

The choice to make when running through the process and applying holds is what you are going to do with the identified data. Will you move a copy out to a new repository, or will you hold the items in place? You have already learned in this chapter about the pros and cons of each approach.

To ensure that a record is authentic, you should be sure that it carries around audit information. When you have identified where information exists across the organization (that is, in Record Centers and Collaboration sites), each collection should have the appropriate audit settings enabled.

Now that you understand what to consider when using SharePoint 2010 to deliver a records management system, let's look at some common scenarios and approaches.

COMMON BUSINESS SCENARIOS

Many scenarios exist where records management can be employed, and you have some considerations to make before you are able to effectively employ an appropriate solution. The first consideration is whether to use just the Records Center, in-place management, or perhaps a blend of the two. Table 32-5 provides some guidance.

TABLE 32-5: Record Management Considerations

CONSIDERATION	RECORDS CENTER	IN-PLACE
Hiding records from users	When an item enters the Records Center, a different set of security permissions are applied. Therefore, it is possible to hide away records from the user community.	You cannot change the permission of an item automatically without custom code, so you are not able to hide away content from the previous set of users.

CONSIDERATION	RECORDS CENTER	IN-PLACE
Centralizing information into a single location for a collaboration team	This is quite difficult without custom code. It is possible to use the "Move and leave a link" metaphor, which leaves a link in the library to an item in the external repository. But a local search of content would be affected because the content would not be included in the library.	This is the main driving factor for in-place management. Even though the item is declared to be a record and under a different information policy, the permissions do not change, and the item does not move out of its current location.
Centralizing information into a single location for the records management team	This is the best solution if the main business driving factor is to enable a records management team to be able to conduct their business in the most simple fashion. All records are typically stored in a single location, though spread over many libraries. Therefore, it is easy for the records management team to place consistent policies on the content that they are managing.	This scenario is a lot more difficult for a records manager to manage and to discover information because records could be spread anywhere where the in-place functionality has been activated.
Cluttering a Collaboration site with records	This is the best option for this consideration. Information is moved out from the Collaboration site, but still managed by the organization.	This does not help. When declared as a record, the item still remains in place, although it would be possible to manage the library views, or to remove the display of records and only display Collaboration items. However, this requires configuration of the library.
Managing a record-retention policy	This is the easiest solution. Information policies (including retention) are managed centrally by an identified team, and documented in the file plan. It is simple to employ a business-wide policy to items from different teams/departments, who may be using different local policies.	This is more difficult to manage. A retention policy may be applied to the content type, but it could be overwritten by the site administrator with a local library/folder policy.
Auditing activity performed on a record	This is centrally managed and at the control of the records managers.	This is controlled by the policy enforced on the current site. So, there may be no audit of the actions on a record without business policy enforcing the Collaboration site team owners to activate it.

In-Place Records Management Scenarios

In-place records management most commonly occurs in organizations where the Collaboration or work-in-progress sites have a long life span. Team sites could potentially be provisioned on a business structure as opposed to project duration.

In this scenario, you may expect the team site to be around for a long time. Therefore, here it may be more appropriate to enable the team to manage their records in a single location, along with their collaboration assets.

Dedicated Record Centers

Dedicated Record Centers can typically be used in a scenario where corporate records must be under the tight management of the records managers. This could be where the records managers want to ensure that they now control who can access the information, and also where a policy change can be effected instantly, and with confidence.

Also, being able to remove records from Collaboration sites can be seen as a good approach by site owners. Some users see records as an archive of data and, therefore, when they have declared an item to be a record, they want it taken away and managed by someone else.

Using In-Place and Dedicated Stores

Sometimes, it is appropriate to use a blend of the two previous approaches to deliver a capable system. Perhaps a team wants to be able to manage all of their information (that is, collaboration documents and records) in a single location for ease and speed of work. Then, when the team has completed their work, all of the defined material could be sent off to the Records Center for management by the company records managers, and the project site removed.

Legal Hold and eDiscovery

Some organizations maintain a large amount of backup data of content that has been archived off of their systems over the years. Therefore, these backups contain data that may be subject to a legal hold, and would need to be discovered in the first instance.

This is tightly integrated with the retention and expiration of content because you would not want to overly expose the organization in a legal action by supplying information not relevant to the case. So, you must ensure that the hold and eDiscovery phases bring back only that necessary relevant data.

You have now learned about the various options available to you, the processes that you need to discover, and the technical support from the SharePoint products. Let's take a look at what the recommended approach should be.

RECOMMENDED APPROACH

This section provides some advice and guidance that could be used in the development of a records management system within a business.

Business Analysis and Design

Before attempting to build any part of the records management system, it is important to follow a number of steps and procedures. Some of the typical steps are as noted in the following sections.

Gather Business Requirements

This is a discovery phase, and concerned with reaching out to all parts of the organization that are expected to play a part in consuming the records management system functionality being developed. You should be trying to gain knowledge about what sort of content they typically produce.

After this data has been gathered, you then need to apply the appropriate standards and policies.

Analyze Your Source Data

This phase is concerned with identifying which information used by the business should be considered a record. Using the output from the previous phase is essential in making these decisions.

The output from this phase is a classification of data that can be used in the file plan to ensure like information is managed consistently, and knowing what information must be managed as a record.

Define the Classification Structure

Using the information gathered so far, it is now time to define the structure of the records management system. This is an essential step for the successful creation of a file plan.

Typically, you should have the broadest terms or categories defined for the organization, and now you must drill down each of those branches to determine what further segmentation and control is needed over your data. This information should have been collected during the "Analyze" phase.

Care should be taken to ensure that a pragmatic approach is being used. You do not want to end up with a structure so deep that it is impossible for a user to navigate, but one that delivers all of the business requirements for control. Similarly, the structure cannot be too flat (which a user may like best), because this will not deliver the appropriate level of control.

Additionally, for each of the classifications that are defined, you must identify a key contact user. This user will be responsible for any records management actions or functions that are performed on the classification.

The aim here is to allocate appropriate rules to the data entering the records management system that are inherited by records as they are classified.

Define Metadata Definitions

Consistent metadata is a key component for any successful exploitation of information. The records management system should ensure that when records are being declared, the user is impacted as little as possible, while ensuring that enough metadata sits with the record to make it useful and authoritative content.

This is especially important when a records management system is receiving information from a number of different departments or sources that each has its own implementation of a metadata standard, where each is different from one another.

SharePoint 2010 can help with this task through the use of the Managed Metadata Service where a taxonomy can be centrally defined and shared.

Define Retention and Expiration Schedules

This action takes input from the "Gather Business Requirements" phase. For all of the classifications noted thus far, each must have an identified retention period and expiration process. In defining the classification scheme, certain information would have been noted as being legally admissible, and, therefore, it must be kept for the time period noted by the affecting policy. Also, the organization must decide what to do with the information once that retention period has elapsed. Certain information (such as personal data) cannot necessarily be kept after the expiration period because of laws such as the personal data acts referenced earlier in this chapter.

At the end of this stage, all the information necessary to generate the file plan should have been collected.

Develop a File Plan Schema

With the categories defined for the information that must be managed, you can then develop the schema for the file plan. The initial step is to place the categories into a hierarchy, and also show how information is going to be displayed within the category or folder.

For example, it may be appropriate to store information month by month so that a user can see all records for a particular category that were submitted in, say, "November." Or, if the category is concerned with the interworking with external agencies, it may be more appropriate to store by external company name.

When all of these decisions have been made, it all must be written down in a file plan document and placed under document control. This can then be used as a reference guide to understand what a business policy is regarding the management of particular information, and can be used by the records management implementers to build out the system.

Define an Implementation Plan

This plan is concerned with how the records management system will be deployed, managed, maintained, and communicated to users, as well as to train users.

The implementation plan can be used to show how the records management system is constructed and managed, and is a formal record of the decisions and steps already taken (using the previous phases already described).

The implementation plan should contain the following:

➤ *Business requirements* — This includes a list of the parts of the business that were consulted, and the decision points made. This may also include a list of the regulatory and compliance requirements that the records must meet.

➤ *Business process* — This is concerned with the documenting of a business process for items that are to be considered a record. It should show at what point an item is considered to be a record.

➤ *Supporting information* — For each of the records, this documents what information must be supplied to the records management system so that it can be considered an authoritative and authentic record.

➤ *Record policies* — This is a set of record policies and guidelines that are regularly reviewed to ensure that they are current for the business. This also covers procedures necessary to secure the information (that is, who needs access to what, and with what access permissions).

➤ *Responsibilities* — This is an allocation of tasks to named users or roles such that if an external inquiry were made, an identified person can be found.

➤ *Timetable* — This should be developed after consultation with the user groups. This is a timetable of events when specific groups will be expected to use the records management system. It is necessary to ensure that when groups work closely with each other, or groups are dispersed, they use the records management system and can still work without an interruption of service.

➤ *Training* — A new system that users are expected to work with requires some form of user awareness/training. Without the users knowing how they are expected to use the system, you will experience poor adoption rates.

Then, depending on business requirements, there may be the need to go back periodically to check records management system usage. At this point, you may be able to see that particular groups that have been moved onto the records management system are not declaring records. This can then be used to discuss with the group why there is little or no adoption, and adjust policies appropriately.

Determining Required Technology Enablers

To deliver a successful electronic records management system, a number of tools must be available to address more than just the storage of information. You have already learned that consistent metadata is needed and available for consumption, as is a method of applying information management policies. But there is also the eDiscovery process that relies on a search architecture to support this effort.

In SharePoint 2010, some tools delivered by the product that are not necessarily considered part of records management must be made available.

For the search piece, SharePoint assumes that you want to use the search components as delivered.

When looking into consistent metadata, the product enables the organization to deliver this function via the Managed Metadata service. Also, by making use of this service application, content type syndication can be consumed. This can result in a centrally managed and consistent delivery of content types to the different parts of the participating organization.

Planning and Configuring Records Management Repositories

In a SharePoint 2010 farm, it is possible to have many Record Repositories. This is the same as in MOSS, but a difference with SharePoint 2010 is that you are able to specify a number of different end-points per web application.

The issue with configuring a number of repositories is that you are then forcing the users to make choices as to where they must submit information, and the users may not know.

SharePoint 2010 does enable the Content Organizer, however, and using this means that you can get SharePoint to automatically route to other external locations (effectively enabling a hub-and-spoke design to a SharePoint deployment). This can then be used to help with any scaling or organizational issues.

Migrating Data

The migration of data is only valid for new records management systems that are intended to replace a current business system. Currently, many electronic records management systems are based on NTFS folder hierarchies to deliver functionality. Moving these into a SharePoint 2010 environment requires some effort and planning, as already discussed.

Each scenario must be considered carefully, and then judgments must be made as to what needs to be brought into the new system, what can be archived, and what needs to come with the items (such as metadata and supporting material). Also, is there a need for the records management system to store only certain document types? If so, are there any file conversions that must take place as part of the migration scenario?

An example here is that some organizations only want to store information in a text form, so some proprietary document formats are not relevant for the store. In this scenario, the documents must be converted before being placed into the SharePoint 2010 store. The Document Conversions Load Balancer service could be of use here.

Cleansing Your Source Data

It cannot be emphasized enough — cleansing data information before migration can save time and money. There is little or no point migrating information into a new system to overload it with invalid or out-of-date data. This just increases the migration time, backup and restore times, and necessary space for management. SharePoint 2010 uses SQL as its storage mechanism, and that storage can be relatively expensive to use and manage. So, not submitting information that can be archived will save space, time, and money.

Also, the application that currently houses your current records may not have the features and functions of new systems. Each system typically has a large percentage of duplicate information stored. This arises as users who have information, who know it should be maintained as a record, who cannot always find if it has already been declared or not, and, to be on the safe side, declare it again.

Using SharePoint, information can be de-duplicated by using the library features such as version control. Alternatively, it is possible to scan source documents via configuration of the SharePoint 2010 Search service application. The benefit of doing some work with this is that duplicates can be identified, and the Search service could discover what information can be removed prior to migration.

Migrating Data

There are lots of options for migrating data into SharePoint 2010. They range for the simple drag and drop of documentation into the appropriate location, to third-party tools that can be tailored to meet all of your migration needs, or even creating your own.

Following are some of the commonly used third parties (in no particular order):

➤ *AvePoint* — DocAve SharePoint Migrator
   (www.avepoint.com/sharepoint-to-sharepoint-migration-docave/)

➤ *Metalogix* — Migration Manager for SharePoint
   (www.metalogix.com/Products/Migration-Manager-for-SharePoint.aspx)

➤ *Quest* — Migration Manager
   (www.quest.com/Migration-Manager-for-SharePoint/)

➤ *Tzunami* — Tzunami Deployer for SharePoint 2010 Migration
   (www.tzunami.com/products/Pages/TDSharePoint2010Migration.aspx)

However data is expected to get into the records management system, it must be controlled and managed.

Validating Data

Once data has been migrated into the records management system, it is a good idea to run a few tests to ensure that it is functioning as expected. A good approach is to run an inquiry against the store and see what the results are. Then, compare that with what you know they should be. This would be fairly easy if you already have the results of a search against your old system, and compare that with the new.

BEST PRACTICES

In terms of "best practices" for records management, there are not many. This is because records management is different for most organizations, so a best practice for one organization may not hold true for another. However, the following provide some pointers of useful advice:

➤ *Use folders, inherit metadata* — This is a new function that can be used throughout the SharePoint deployment, but is particularly useful for a Records Center deployment. One task is to ensure that it is easy and simple for a user to submit data. One area where that effort can be simplified is in the completion of metadata. If the organization can apply metadata that should be added to record content as it comes into the store, then you do not need the user to add it, but rather you can automatically add it through a folder. Each folder in the hierarchy could have a different set of metadata values.

➤ *Test the system* — This is something that should be frequently performed, and is good advice for any part of the system such as backing up and restoring. You should try to run test cases on the data to ensure that your process for discovery and then hold works appropriately. Hopefully, your system will not be subjected to a legal incident. But if it is, you must know it is going to work as expected, thereby giving the business confidence that it is able to protect itself.

SUMMARY

Using SharePoint 2010 records management as delivered by default in the product is a major step up in functionality over what was previously available from Microsoft. Once you have identified the main driving factors behind why the organization needs to perform records management, you should quickly see whether SharePoint is appropriate. However, do not forget that many add-ons and additions to the product from third-party companies add further specific capability to the product to meet particular legal acts and standards (which can be the sticking point for an organization when deciding to use the product).

Also, do not be afraid to write custom code solutions on top of the delivered functionality. For example, it is a simple task to change the routing available in the Content Organizer and it is not a huge development task.

There are many benefits to derive from using SharePoint for records management that the product has inherited from other parts of the solution (for example, workflows on document libraries, versioning, content types, and so on). Having all of your system on a single platform results in simplified architecture, and simpler management.

INDEX

F

J

M

U

X

Z

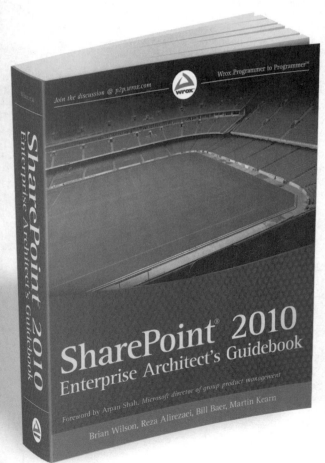